MW01009460

Bayesian Reasoning and Machine Learning

Extracting value from vast amounts of data presents a major challenge to all those working in computer science and related fields. Machine learning technology is already used to help with this task in a wide range of industrial applications, including search engines, DNA sequencing, stock market analysis and robot locomotion. As its usage becomes more widespread, the skills taught in this book will be invaluable to students.

Designed for final-year undergraduate and graduate students, this gentle introduction is ideally suited to readers without a solid background in linear algebra and calculus. It covers basic probabilistic reasoning to advanced techniques in machine learning, and crucially enables students to construct their own models for real-world problems by teaching them what lies behind the methods. A central conceptual theme is the use of Bayesian modelling to describe and build inference algorithms. Numerous examples and exercises are included in the text. Comprehensive resources for students and instructors are available online.

Bayesian Reasoning and Machine Learning

David Barber
University College London

CAMBRIDGE
UNIVERSITY PRESS

University Printing House, Cambridge CB2 8BS, United Kingdom

Published in the United States of America by Cambridge University Press, New York

Cambridge University Press is part of the University of Cambridge.

It furthers the University's mission by disseminating knowledge in the pursuit of education, learning and research at the highest international levels of excellence.

www.cambridge.org
Information on this title: www.cambridge.org/9780521518147

First published 2012
5th printing 2014

Printed in the United Kingdom by Bell and Bain Ltd, Glasgow

A catalogue record for this publication is available from the British Library

Library of Congress Cataloguing in Publication data
Barber, David, 1968–
Bayesian reasoning and machine learning / David Barber.
p. cm.
Includes bibliographical references and index.
ISBN 978-0-521-51814-7
1. Machine learning. 2. Bayesian statistical decision theory. I. Title.
QA267.B347 2012
006.3′1 – dc23 2011035553

ISBN 978-0-521-51814-7 Hardback

Additional resources for this publication at www.cambridge.org/brml and at www.cs.ucl.ac.uk/staff/D.Barber/brml

CONTENTS

II Learning in probabilistic models

Colour plate section between pp. 360 and 361

PREFACE

The data explosion

We live in a world that is rich in data, ever increasing in scale. This data comes from many different sources in science (bioinformatics, astronomy, physics, environmental monitoring) and commerce (customer databases, financial transactions, engine monitoring, speech recognition, surveillance, search). Possessing the knowledge as to how to process and extract value from such data is therefore a key and increasingly important skill. Our society also expects ultimately to be able to engage with computers in a natural manner so that computers can 'talk' to humans, 'understand' what they say and 'comprehend' the visual world around them. These are difficult large-scale information processing tasks and represent grand challenges for computer science and related fields. Similarly, there is a desire to control increasingly complex systems, possibly containing many interacting parts, such as in robotics and autonomous navigation. Successfully mastering such systems requires an understanding of the processes underlying their behaviour. Processing and making sense of such large amounts of data from complex systems is therefore a pressing modern-day concern and will likely remain so for the foreseeable future.

Machine learning

Machine learning is the study of data-driven methods capable of mimicking, understanding and aiding human and biological information processing tasks. In this pursuit, many related issues arise such as how to compress data, interpret and process it. Often these methods are not necessarily directed to mimicking directly human processing but rather to enhancing it, such as in predicting the stock market or retrieving information rapidly. In this probability theory is key since inevitably our limited data and understanding of the problem forces us to address uncertainty. In the broadest sense, machine learning and related fields aim to 'learn something useful' about the environment within which the agent operates. Machine learning is also closely allied with artificial intelligence, with machine learning placing more emphasis on using data to drive and adapt the model.

In the early stages of machine learning and related areas, similar techniques were discovered in relatively isolated research communities. This book presents a unified treatment via graphical models, a marriage between graph and probability theory, facilitating the transference of machine learning concepts between different branches of the mathematical and computational sciences.

Whom this book is for

The book is designed to appeal to students with only a modest mathematical background in undergraduate calculus and linear algebra. No formal computer science or statistical background is required to follow the book, although a basic familiarity with probability, calculus and linear algebra would be useful. The book should appeal to students from a variety of backgrounds, including computer science, engineering, applied statistics, physics and bioinformatics that wish to gain an entry to probabilistic approaches in machine learning. In order to engage with students, the book introduces fundamental concepts in inference using only minimal reference to algebra and calculus. More mathematical techniques are postponed until as and when required, always with the concept as primary and the mathematics secondary.

The concepts and algorithms are described with the aid of many worked examples. The exercises and demonstrations, together with an accompanying MATLAB toolbox, enable the reader to experiment and more deeply understand the material. The ultimate aim of the book is to enable the reader to construct novel algorithms. The book therefore places an emphasis on skill learning, rather than being a collection of recipes. This is a key aspect since modern applications are often so specialised as to require novel methods. The approach taken throughout is to describe the problem as a graphical model, which is then translated into a mathematical framework, ultimately leading to an algorithmic implementation in the BRMLTOOLBOX.

The book is primarily aimed at final year undergraduates and graduates without significant experience in mathematics. On completion, the reader should have a good understanding of the techniques, practicalities and philosophies of probabilistic aspects of machine learning and be well equipped to understand more advanced research level material.

The structure of the book

The book begins with the basic concepts of graphical models and inference. For the independent reader Chapters 1, 2, 3, 4, 5, 9, 10, 13, 14, 15, 16, 17, 21 and 23 would form a good introduction to probabilistic reasoning, modelling and machine learning. The material in Chapters 19, 24, 25 and 28 is more advanced, with the remaining material being of more specialised interest. Note that in each chapter the level of material is of varying difficulty, typically with the more challenging material placed towards the end of each chapter. As an introduction to the area of probabilistic modelling, a course can be constructed from the material as indicated in the chart.

The material from Parts I and II has been successfully used for courses on graphical models. I have also taught an introduction to probabilistic machine learning using material largely from Part III, as indicated. These two courses can be taught separately and a useful approach would be to teach first the graphical models course, followed by a separate probabilistic machine learning course.

A short course on approximate inference can be constructed from introductory material in Part I and the more advanced material in Part V, as indicated. The exact inference methods in Part I can be covered relatively quickly with the material in Part V considered in more depth.

A timeseries course can be made by using primarily the material in Part IV, possibly combined with material from Part I for students that are unfamiliar with probabilistic modelling approaches. Some of this material, particularly in Chapter 25, is more advanced and can be deferred until the end of the course, or considered for a more advanced course.

The references are generally to works at a level consistent with the book material and which are in the most part readily available.

Part	Chapter	Graphical models course	Probabilistic machine learning course	Approximate inference short course	Timeseries short course	Probabilistic modelling course
Part I: Inference in probabilistic models	1: Probabilistic reasoning	●	○	○	○	●
	2: Basic graph concepts	●	○	●	○	●
	3: Belief networks	●	●	●	●	●
	4: Graphical models	●	○	●	●	○
	5: Efficient inference in trees	●	○	●	●	○
	6: The junction tree algorithm	●	○	●	○	○
	7: Making decisions	●	○	○	●	○
Part II: Learning in probabilistic models	8: Statistics for machine learning	●	○	○	○	●
	9: Learning as inference	●	○	○	○	●
	10: Naive Bayes	●	●	○	○	○
	11: Learning with hidden variables	●	●	○	○	●
	12: Bayesian model selection	●	○	○	○	●
Part III: Machine learning	13: Machine learning concepts	○	●	○	○	○
	14: Nearest neighbour classification	○	○	○	○	○
	15: Unsupervised linear dimension reduction	○	●	○	○	○
	16: Supervised linear dimension reduction	○	●	○	○	○
	17: Linear models	○	●	○	○	○
	18: Bayesian linear models	○	○	○	○	●
	19: Gaussian processes	○	●	○	○	○
	20: Mixture models	○	●	○	○	●
	21: Latent linear models	○	○	○	○	●
	22: Latent ability models	○	○	○	○	●
Part IV: Dynamical models	23: Discrete-state Markov models	○	●	○	●	○
	24: Continuous-state Markov models	○	○	○	●	●
	25: Switching linear dynamical systems	○	○	○	●	○
	26: Distributed computation	○	●	○	●	○
Part V: Approximate inference	27: Sampling	○	○	●	○	○
	28: Deterministic approximate inference	○	○	●	○	○

Accompanying code

The BRMLtoolbox is provided to help readers see how mathematical models translate into actual MATLAB code. There is a large number of demos that a lecturer may wish to use or adapt to help illustrate the material. In addition many of the exercises make use of the code, helping the reader gain confidence in the concepts and their application. Along with complete routines for many machine learning methods, the philosophy is to provide low-level routines whose composition intuitively follows the mathematical description of the algorithm. In this way students may easily match the mathematics with the corresponding algorithmic implementation.

Website

The BRMLtoolbox along with an electronic version of the book is available from

`www.cs.ucl.ac.uk/staff/D.Barber/brml`

Instructors seeking solutions to the exercises can find information at www.cambridge.org/brml, along with additional teaching materials.

Other books in this area

The literature on machine learning is vast with much relevant literature also contained in statistics, engineering and other physical sciences. A small list of more specialised books that may be referred to for deeper treatments of specific topics is:

- Graphical models
  - *Graphical Models* by S. Lauritzen, Oxford University Press, 1996.
  - *Bayesian Networks and Decision Graphs* by F. Jensen and T. D. Nielsen, Springer-Verlag, 2007.
  - *Probabilistic Networks and Expert Systems* by R. G. Cowell, A. P. Dawid, S. L. Lauritzen and D. J. Spiegelhalter, Springer-Verlag, 1999.
  - *Probabilistic Reasoning in Intelligent Systems* by J. Pearl, Morgan Kaufmann, 1988.
  - *Graphical Models in Applied Multivariate Statistics* by J. Whittaker, Wiley, 1990.
  - *Probabilistic Graphical Models: Principles and Techniques* by D. Koller and N. Friedman, MIT Press, 2009.
- Machine learning and information processing
  - *Information Theory, Inference and Learning Algorithms* by D. J. C. MacKay, Cambridge University Press, 2003.
  - *Pattern Recognition and Machine Learning* by C. M. Bishop, Springer-Verlag, 2006.
  - *An Introduction to Support Vector Machines*, N. Cristianini and J. Shawe-Taylor, Cambridge University Press, 2000.
  - *Gaussian Processes for Machine Learning* by C. E. Rasmussen and C. K. I. Williams, MIT Press, 2006.

Acknowledgements

Many people have helped this book along the way either in terms of reading, feedback, general insights, allowing me to present their work, or just plain motivation. Amongst these I would like to thank Dan Cornford, Massimiliano Pontil, Mark Herbster, John Shawe-Taylor, Vladimir Kolmogorov, Yuri Boykov, Tom Minka, Simon Prince, Silvia Chiappa, Bertrand Mesot, Robert Cowell, Ali Taylan Cemgil, David Blei, Jeff Bilmes, David Cohn, David Page, Peter Sollich, Chris Williams, Marc Toussaint, Amos Storkey, Zakria Hussain, Le Chen, Serafín Moral, Milan Studený, Luc De Raedt, Tristan Fletcher, Chris Vryonides, Tom Furmston, Ed Challis and Chris Bracegirdle. I would also like to thank the many students that have helped improve the material during lectures over the years. I'm particularly grateful to Taylan Cemgil for allowing his GraphLayout package to be bundled with the BRMLTOOLBOX.

The staff at Cambridge University Press have been a delight to work with and I would especially like to thank Heather Bergman for her initial endeavours and the wonderful Diana Gillooly for her continued enthusiasm.

A heartfelt thankyou to my parents and sister – I hope this small token will make them proud. I'm also fortunate to be able to acknowledge the support and generosity of friends throughout. Finally, I'd like to thank Silvia who made it all worthwhile.

NOTATION

$\mathcal{V}$	A calligraphic symbol typically denotes a set of random variables	*page* 3
$\text{dom}(x)$	Domain of a variable	3
$x = \mathsf{x}$	The variable x is in the state x	3
$p(x = \mathsf{tr})$	Probability of event/variable x being in the state true	3
$p(x = \mathsf{fa})$	Probability of event/variable x being in the state false	3
$p(x, y)$	Probability of x and y	4
$p(x \cap y)$	Probability of x and y	4
$p(x \cup y)$	Probability of x or y	4
$p(x\|y)$	The probability of x conditioned on y	4
$\mathcal{X} \perp\!\!\!\perp \mathcal{Y} \| \mathcal{Z}$	Variables $\mathcal{X}$ are independent of variables $\mathcal{Y}$ conditioned on variables $\mathcal{Z}$	7
$\mathcal{X} \top\!\!\!\top \mathcal{Y} \| \mathcal{Z}$	Variables $\mathcal{X}$ are dependent on variables $\mathcal{Y}$ conditioned on variables $\mathcal{Z}$	7
$\int_x f(x)$	For continuous variables this is shorthand for $\int_x f(x)dx$ and for discrete variables means summation over the states of x, $\sum_x f(x)$	14
$\mathbb{I}[S]$	Indicator : has value 1 if the statement S is true, 0 otherwise	16
$\text{pa}(x)$	The parents of node x	24
$\text{ch}(x)$	The children of node x	24
$\text{ne}(x)$	Neighbours of node x	24
$\dim(x)$	For a discrete variable x, this denotes the number of states x can take	34
$\langle f(x) \rangle_{p(x)}$	The average of the function $f(x)$ with respect to the distribution $p(x)$	170
$\delta(a, b)$	Delta function. For discrete a, b, this is the Kronecker delta, $\delta_{a,b}$ and for continuous a, b the Dirac delta function $\delta(a - b)$	172
$\dim(\mathbf{x})$	The dimension of the vector/matrix $\mathbf{x}$	183
$\sharp(x = s, y = t)$	The number of times x is in state s and y in state t simultaneously	207
$\sharp_y^x$	The number of times variable x is in state y	293
$\mathcal{D}$	Dataset	303
n	Data index	303
N	Number of dataset training points	303
$\mathbf{S}$	Sample Covariance matrix	331
$\sigma(x)$	The logistic sigmoid $1/(1 + \exp(-x))$	371
$\text{erf}(x)$	The (Gaussian) error function	372
$x_{a:b}$	$x_a, x_{a+1}, \ldots, x_b$	372
$i \sim j$	The set of unique neighbouring edges on a graph	624
$\mathbf{I}_m$	The $m \times m$ identity matrix	644

BRMLTOOLBOX

The BRMLTOOLBOX is a lightweight set of routines that enables the reader to experiment with concepts in graph theory, probability theory and machine learning. The code contains basic routines for manipulating discrete variable distributions, along with more limited support for continuous variables. In addition there are many hard-coded standard machine learning algorithms. The website contains also a complete list of all the teaching demos and related exercise material.

BRMLTOOLKIT

Graph theory

`ancestors`	- Return the ancestors of nodes x in DAG A
`ancestralorder`	- Return the ancestral order or the DAG A (oldest first)
`descendents`	- Return the descendents of nodes x in DAG A
`children`	- Return the children of variable x given adjacency matrix A
`edges`	- Return edge list from adjacency matrix A
`elimtri`	- Return a variable elimination sequence for a triangulated graph
`connectedComponents`	- Find the connected components of an adjacency matrix
`istree`	- Check if graph is singly connected
`neigh`	- Find the neighbours of vertex v on a graph with adjacency matrix G
`noselfpath`	- Return a path excluding self-transitions
`parents`	- Return the parents of variable x given adjacency matrix A
`spantree`	- Find a spanning tree from an edge list
`triangulate`	- Triangulate adjacency matrix A
`triangulatePorder`	- Triangulate adjacency matrix A according to a partial ordering

Potential manipulation

`condpot`	- Return a potential conditioned on another variable
`changevar`	- Change variable names in a potential
`dag`	- Return the adjacency matrix (zeros on diagonal) for a belief network
`deltapot`	- A delta function potential
`disptable`	- Print the table of a potential
`divpots`	- Divide potential pota by potb
`drawFG`	- Draw the factor graph A
`drawID`	- Plot an influence diagram
`drawJTree`	- Plot a junction tree
`drawNet`	- Plot network
`evalpot`	- Evaluate the table of a potential when variables are set
`exppot`	- Exponential of a potential
`eyepot`	- Return a unit potential
`grouppot`	- Form a potential based on grouping variables together
`groupstate`	- Find the state of the group variables corresponding to a given ungrouped state
`logpot`	- Logarithm of the potential
`markov`	- Return a symmetric adjacency matrix of Markov network in pot
`maxpot`	- Maximise a potential over variables
`maxsumpot`	- Maximise or sum a potential over variables
`multpots`	- Multiply potentials into a single potential

numstates	- Number of states of the variables in a potential
orderpot	- Return potential with variables reordered according to order
orderpotfields	- Order the fields of the potential, creating blank entries where necessary
potsample	- Draw sample from a single potential
potscontainingonly	- Returns those potential numbers that contain only the required variables
potvariables	- Returns information about all variables in a set of potentials
setevpot	- Sets variables in a potential into evidential states
setpot	- Sets potential variables to specified states
setstate	- Set a potential's specified joint state to a specified value
squeezepots	- Eliminate redundant potentials (those contained wholly within another)
sumpot	- Sum potential pot over variables
sumpotID	- Return the summed probability and utility tables from an ID
sumpots	- Sum a set of potentials
table	- Return the potential table
ungrouppot	- Form a potential based on ungrouping variables
uniquepots	- Eliminate redundant potentials (those contained wholly within another)
whichpot	- Returns potentials that contain a set of variables

Routines also extend the toolbox to deal with Gaussian potentials: `multpotsGaussianMoment.m`, `sumpotGaussianCanonical.m`, `sumpotGaussianMoment.m`, `multpotsGaussianCanonical.m` See `demoSumprodGaussCanon.m`, `demoSumprodGaussCanonLDS.m`, `demoSumprodGaussMoment.m`

Inference

absorb	- Update potentials in absorption message passing on a junction tree
absorption	- Perform full round of absorption on a junction tree
absorptionID	- Perform full round of absorption on an influence diagram
ancestralsample	- Ancestral sampling from a belief network
binaryMRFmap	- Get the MAP assignment for a binary MRF with positive W
bucketelim	- Bucket elimination on a set of potentials
condindep	- Conditional independence check using graph of variable interactions
condindepEmp	- Compute the empirical log Bayes factor and MI for independence/dependence
condindepPot	- Numerical conditional independence measure
condMI	- Conditional mutual information I(x,y|z) of a potential
FactorConnectingVariable	- Factor nodes connecting to a set of variables
FactorGraph	- Returns a factor graph adjacency matrix based on potentials
IDvars	- Probability and decision variables from a partial order
jtassignpot	- Assign potentials to cliques in a junction tree
jtree	- Setup a junction tree based on a set of potentials
jtreeID	- Setup a junction tree based on an influence diagram
LoopyBP	- Loopy belief propagation using sum-product algorithm
MaxFlow	- Ford Fulkerson max-flow min-cut algorithm (breadth first search)
maxNpot	- Find the N most probable values and states in a potential
maxNprodFG	- N-max-product algorithm on a factor graph (returns the Nmax most probable states)
maxprodFG	- Max-product algorithm on a factor graph
MDPemDeterministicPolicy	- Solve MDP using EM with deterministic policy
MDPsolve	- Solve a Markov decision process
MesstoFact	- Returns the message numbers that connect into factor potential
metropolis	- Metropolis sample
mostprobablepath	- Find the most probable path in a Markov chain
mostprobablepathmult	- Find the all source all sink most probable paths in a Markov chain
sumprodFG	- Sum-product algorithm on a factor graph represented by A

Specific models

ARlds	- Learn AR coefficients using a linear dynamical system
ARtrain	- Fit auto-regressive (AR) coefficients of order L to v.
BayesLinReg	- Bayesian linear regression training using basis functions phi(x)
BayesLogRegressionRVM	- Bayesian logistic regression with the relevance vector machine
CanonVar	- Canonical variates (no post rotation of variates)

cca	- Canonical correlation analysis
covfnGE	- Gamma exponential covariance function
FA	- Factor analysis
GMMem	- Fit a mixture of Gaussian to the data X using EM
GPclass	- Gaussian process binary classification
GPreg	- Gaussian process regression
HebbML	- Learn a sequence for a Hopfield network
HMMbackward	- HMM backward pass
HMMbackwardSAR	- Backward pass (beta method) for the switching Auto-regressive HMM
HMMem	- EM algorithm for HMM
HMMforward	- HMM forward pass
HMMforwardSAR	- Switching auto-regressive HMM with switches updated only every Tskip timesteps
HMMgamma	- HMM posterior smoothing using the Rauch–Tung–Striebel correction method
yHMMsmooth	- Smoothing for a hidden Markov model (HMM)
HMMsmoothSAR	- Switching auto-regressive HMM smoothing
HMMviterbi	- Viterbi most likely joint hidden state of HMM
kernel	- A kernel evaluated at two points
Kmeans	- K-means clustering algorithm
LDSbackward	- Full backward pass for a latent linear dynamical system (RTS correction method)
LDSbackwardUpdate	- Single backward update for a latent linear dynamical system (RTS smoothing update)
LDSforward	- Full forward pass for a latent linear dynamical system (Kalman filter)
LDSforwardUpdate	- Single forward update for a latent linear dynamical system (Kalman filter)
LDSsmooth	- Linear dynamical system: filtering and smoothing
LDSsubspace	- Subspace method for identifying linear dynamical system
LogReg	- Learning logistic linear regression using gradient ascent
MIXprodBern	- EM training of a mixture of a product of Bernoulli distributions
mixMarkov	- EM training for a mixture of Markov models
NaiveBayesDirichletTest	- Naive Bayes prediction having used a Dirichlet prior for training
NaiveBayesDirichletTrain	- Naive Bayes training using a Dirichlet prior
NaiveBayesTest	- Test Naive Bayes Bernoulli distribution after max likelihood training
NaiveBayesTrain	- Train Naive Bayes Bernoulli distribution using max likelihood
nearNeigh	- Nearest neighbour classification
pca	- Principal components analysis
plsa	- Probabilistic latent semantic analysis
plsaCond	- Conditional PLSA (probabilistic latent semantic analysis)
rbf	- Radial basis function output
SARlearn	- EM training of a switching AR model
SLDSbackward	- Backward pass using a mixture of Gaussians
SLDSforward	- Switching latent linear dynamical system Gaussian sum forward pass
SLDSmargGauss	- Compute the single Gaussian from a weighted SLDS mixture
softloss	- Soft loss function
svdm	- Singular value decomposition with missing values
SVMtrain	- Train a support vector machine

General

argmax	- Performs argmax returning the index and value
assign	- Assigns values to variables
betaXbiggerY	- $p(x>y)$ for $x\sim$Beta(a,b), $y\sim$Beta(c,d)
bar3zcolor	- Plot a 3D bar plot of the matrix Z
avsigmaGauss	- Average of a logistic sigmoid under a Gaussian
cap	- Cap x at absolute value c
chi2test	- Inverse of the chi square cumulative density
count	- For a data matrix (each column is a datapoint), return the state counts
condexp	- Compute normalised p proportional to exp(logp)
condp	- Make a conditional distribution from the matrix
dirrnd	- Samples from a Dirichlet distribution
field2cell	- Place the field of a structure in a cell
GaussCond	- Return the mean and covariance of a conditioned Gaussian

hinton	- Plot a Hinton diagram
ind2subv	- Subscript vector from linear index
ismember_sorted	- True for member of sorted set
lengthcell	- Length of each cell entry
logdet	- Log determinant of a positive definite matrix computed in a numerically stable manner
logeps	- log(x+eps)
logGaussGamma	- Unnormalised log of the Gauss-Gamma distribution
logsumexp	- Compute log(sum(exp(a).*b)) valid for large a
logZdirichlet	- Log normalisation constant of a Dirichlet distribution with parameter u
majority	- Return majority values in each column on a matrix
maxarray	- Maximise a multi-dimensional array over a set of dimensions
maxNarray	- Find the highest values and states of an array over a set of dimensions
mix2mix	- Fit a mixture of Gaussians with another mixture of Gaussians
mvrandn	- Samples from a multivariate Normal (Gaussian) distribution
mygamrnd	- Gamma random variate generator
mynanmean	- Mean of values that are not nan
mynansum	- Sum of values that are not nan
mynchoosek	- Binomial coefficient v choose k
myones	- Same as ones(x), but if x is a scalar, interprets as ones([x 1])
myrand	- Same as rand(x) but if x is a scalar interprets as rand([x 1])
myzeros	- Same as zeros(x) but if x is a scalar interprets as zeros([x 1])
normp	- Make a normalised distribution from an array
randgen	- Generates discrete random variables given the pdf
replace	- Replace instances of a value with another value
sigma	- 1./(1+exp(-x))
sigmoid	- 1./(1+exp(-beta*x))
sqdist	- Square distance between vectors in x and y
subv2ind	- Linear index from subscript vector.
sumlog	- sum(log(x)) with a cutoff at 10e-200

Miscellaneous

compat	- Compatibility of object F being in position h for image v on grid Gx,Gy
logp	- The logarithm of a specific non-Gaussian distribution
placeobject	- Place the object F at position h in grid Gx,Gy
plotCov	- Return points for plotting an ellipse of a covariance
pointsCov	- Unit variance contours of a 2D Gaussian with mean m and covariance S
setup	- Run me at initialisation – checks for bugs in matlab and initialises path
validgridposition	- Returns 1 if point is on a defined grid

Part I

Inference in probabilistic models

Probabilistic models explicitly take into account uncertainty and deal with our imperfect knowledge of the world. Such models are of fundamental significance in Machine Learning since our understanding of the world will always be limited by our observations and understanding. We will focus initially on using probabilistic models as a kind of expert system.

In Part I, we assume that the model is fully specified. That is, given a model of the environment, how can we use it to answer questions of interest? We will relate the complexity of inferring quantities of interest to the structure of the graph describing the model. In addition, we will describe operations in terms of manipulations on the corresponding graphs. As we will see, provided the graphs are simple tree-like structures, most quantities of interest can be computed efficiently.

Part I deals with manipulating mainly discrete variable distributions and forms the background to all the later material in the book.

1 Probabilistic reasoning

We have intuition about how uncertainty works in simple cases. To reach sensible conclusions in complicated situations, however – where there may be many (possibly) related events and many possible outcomes – we need a formal 'calculus' that extends our intuitive notions. The concepts, mathematical language and rules of probability give us the formal framework we need. In this chapter we review basic concepts in probability – in particular, conditional probability and Bayes' rule, the workhorses of machine learning. Another strength of the language of probability is that it structures problems in a form consistent for computer implementation. We also introduce basic features of the BRMLtoolbox that support manipulating probability distributions.

1.1 Probability refresher

Variables, states and notational shortcuts

Variables will be denoted using either upper case X or lower case x and a set of variables will typically be denoted by a calligraphic symbol, for example $\mathcal{V} = \{a, B, c\}$.

The *domain* of a variable x is written $\text{dom}(x)$, and denotes the states x can take. States will typically be represented using sans-serif font. For example, for a coin c, $\text{dom}(c) = \{\mathsf{heads}, \mathsf{tails}\}$ and $p(c = \mathsf{heads})$ represents the probability that variable c is in state heads. The meaning of $p(\mathsf{state})$ will often be clear, without specific reference to a variable. For example, if we are discussing an experiment about a coin c, the meaning of $p(\mathsf{heads})$ is clear from the context, being shorthand for $p(c = \mathsf{heads})$. When summing over a variable $\sum_x f(x)$, the interpretation is that all states of x are included, i.e. $\sum_x f(x) \equiv \sum_{\mathsf{s} \in \text{dom}(x)} f(x = \mathsf{s})$. Given a variable, x, its domain $\text{dom}(x)$ and a full specification of the probability values for each of the variable states, $p(x)$, we have a *distribution* for x. Sometimes we will not fully specify the distribution, only certain properties, such as for variables x, y, $p(x, y) = p(x)p(y)$ for some unspecified $p(x)$ and $p(y)$. When clarity on this is required we will say distributions with structure $p(x)p(y)$, or a distribution class $p(x)p(y)$.

For our purposes, *events* are expressions about random variables, such as *Two heads in six coin tosses*. Two events are *mutually exclusive* if they cannot both be true. For example the events *The coin is heads* and *The coin is tails* are mutually exclusive. One can think of defining a new variable named by the event so, for example, $p(\textit{The coin is tails})$ can be interpreted as $p(\textit{The coin is tails} = \mathsf{true})$. We use the shorthand $p(x = \mathsf{tr})$ for the probability of event/variable x being in the state true and $p(x = \mathsf{fa})$ for the probability of variable x being in the state false.

Definition 1.1 Rules of probability for discrete variables The probability $p(x = \mathsf{x})$ of variable x being in state x is represented by a value between 0 and 1. $p(x = \mathsf{x}) = 1$ means that we are certain x

is in state x. Conversely, $p(x = \mathrm{x}) = 0$ means that we are certain x is not in state x. Values between 0 and 1 represent the degree of certainty of state occupancy.

The summation of the probability over all the states is 1:

$$\sum_{\mathrm{x}\in\mathrm{dom}(x)} p(x = \mathrm{x}) = 1. \tag{1.1.1}$$

This is called the normalisation condition. We will usually more conveniently write $\sum_x p(x) = 1$.

Two variables x and y can interact through

$$p(x = \mathrm{a} \text{ or } y = \mathrm{b}) = p(x = \mathrm{a}) + p(y = \mathrm{b}) - p(x = \mathrm{a} \text{ and } y = \mathrm{b}). \tag{1.1.2}$$

Or, more generally, we can write

$$p(x \text{ or } y) = p(x) + p(y) - p(x \text{ and } y). \tag{1.1.3}$$

We will use the shorthand $p(x, y)$ for $p(x \text{ and } y)$. Note that $p(y, x) = p(x, y)$ and $p(x \text{ or } y) = p(y \text{ or } x)$.

Definition 1.2 **Set notation** An alternative notation in terms of set theory is to write

$$p(x \text{ or } y) \equiv p(x \cup y), \qquad p(x, y) \equiv p(x \cap y). \tag{1.1.4}$$

Definition 1.3 **Marginals** Given a *joint distribution* $p(x, y)$ the distribution of a single variable is given by

$$p(x) = \sum_y p(x, y). \tag{1.1.5}$$

Here $p(x)$ is termed a *marginal* of the joint probability distribution $p(x, y)$. The process of computing a marginal from a joint distribution is called *marginalisation*. More generally, one has

$$p(x_1, \ldots, x_{i-1}, x_{i+1}, \ldots, x_n) = \sum_{x_i} p(x_1, \ldots, x_n). \tag{1.1.6}$$

Definition 1.4 **Conditional probability/Bayes' rule** The probability of event x conditioned on knowing event y (or more shortly, the probability of x given y) is defined as

$$p(x|y) \equiv \frac{p(x, y)}{p(y)}. \tag{1.1.7}$$

If $p(y) = 0$ then $p(x|y)$ is not defined. From this definition and $p(x, y) = p(y, x)$ we immediately arrive at Bayes' rule

$$p(x|y) = \frac{p(y|x)p(x)}{p(y)}. \tag{1.1.8}$$

Since Bayes' rule trivially follows from the definition of conditional probability, we will sometimes be loose in our language and use the terms Bayes' rule and conditional probability as synonymous.

As we shall see throughout this book, Bayes' rule plays a central role in probabilistic reasoning since it helps us 'invert' probabilistic relationships, translating between $p(y|x)$ and $p(x|y)$.

Definition 1.5 **Probability density functions** For a continuous variable x, the probability density $f(x)$ is defined such that

$$f(x) \geq 0, \qquad \int_{-\infty}^{\infty} f(x)dx = 1, \tag{1.1.9}$$

and the probability that x falls in an interval $[a, b]$ is given by

$$p(a \leq x \leq b) = \int_a^b f(x)dx. \tag{1.1.10}$$

As shorthand we will sometimes write $\int_x f(x)$, particularly when we want an expression to be valid for either continuous or discrete variables. The multivariate case is analogous with integration over all real space, and the probability that x belongs to a region of the space defined accordingly. Unlike probabilities, probability densities can take positive values greater than 1.

Formally speaking, for a continuous variable, one should not speak of the probability that $x = 0.2$ since the probability of a single value is always zero. However, we shall often write $p(x)$ for continuous variables, thus not distinguishing between probabilities and probability density function values. Whilst this may appear strange, the nervous reader may simply replace our $p(x)$ notation for $\int_{x\in\Delta} f(x)dx$, where Δ is a small region centred on x. This is well defined in a probabilistic sense and, in the limit Δ being very small, this would give approximately $\Delta f(x)$. If we consistently use the same Δ for all occurrences of pdfs, then we will simply have a common prefactor Δ in all expressions. Our strategy is to simply ignore these values (since in the end only relative probabilities will be relevant) and write $p(x)$. In this way, all the standard rules of probability carry over, including Bayes' rule.

Remark 1.1 (Subjective probability) Probability is a contentious topic and we do not wish to get bogged down by the debate here, apart from pointing out that it is not necessarily the rules of probability that are contentious, rather what interpretation we should place on them. In some cases potential repetitions of an experiment can be envisaged so that the 'long run' (or frequentist) definition of probability in which probabilities are defined with respect to a potentially infinite repetition of experiments makes sense. For example, in coin tossing, the probability of heads might be interpreted as 'If I were to repeat the experiment of flipping a coin (at "random"), the limit of the number of heads that occurred over the number of tosses is defined as the probability of a head occurring.'

Here's a problem that is typical of the kind of scenario one might face in a machine learning situation. A film enthusiast joins a new online film service. Based on expressing a few films a user likes and dislikes, the online company tries to estimate the probability that the user will like each of the 10 000 films in their database. If we were to define probability as a limiting case of infinite repetitions of the same experiment, this wouldn't make much sense in this case since we can't repeat the experiment. However, if we assume that the user behaves in a manner consistent with other users, we should be able to exploit the large amount of data from other users' ratings to make a reasonable 'guess' as to what this consumer likes. This *degree of belief* or *Bayesian* subjective interpretation of probability sidesteps non-repeatability issues – it's just a framework for manipulating real values consistent with our intuition about probability [158].

1.1.1 Interpreting conditional probability

Conditional probability matches our intuitive understanding of uncertainty. For example, imagine a circular dart board, split into 20 equal sections, labelled from 1 to 20. Randy, a dart thrower, hits any one of the 20 sections uniformly at random. Hence the probability that a dart thrown by Randy occurs in any one of the 20 regions is $p(\textit{region } i) = 1/20$. A friend of Randy tells him that he hasn't hit the 20 region. What is the probability that Randy has hit the 5 region? Conditioned on this information, only regions 1 to 19 remain possible and, since there is no preference for Randy to hit any of these regions, the probability is $1/19$. The conditioning means that certain states are now inaccessible, and the original probability is subsequently distributed over the remaining accessible states. From the rules of probability:

$$p(\textit{region } 5|\textit{not region } 20) = \frac{p(\textit{region } 5, \textit{not region } 20)}{p(\textit{not region } 20)} = \frac{p(\textit{region } 5)}{p(\textit{not region } 20)} = \frac{1/20}{19/20} = \frac{1}{19}$$

giving the intuitive result. An important point to clarify is that $p(A = \mathsf{a}|B = \mathsf{b})$ should not be interpreted as 'Given the event $B = \mathsf{b}$ has occurred, $p(A = \mathsf{a}|B = \mathsf{b})$ is the probability of the event $A = \mathsf{a}$ occurring'. In most contexts, no such explicit temporal causality is implied[1] and the correct interpretation should be '$p(A = \mathsf{a}|B = \mathsf{b})$ is the probability of A being in state a under the constraint that B is in state b'.

The relation between the conditional $p(A = \mathsf{a}|B = \mathsf{b})$ and the joint $p(A = \mathsf{a}, B = \mathsf{b})$ is just a normalisation constant since $p(A = \mathsf{a}, B = \mathsf{b})$ is not a distribution in A – in other words, $\sum_{\mathsf{a}} p(A = \mathsf{a}, B = \mathsf{b}) \neq 1$. To make it a distribution we need to divide: $p(A = \mathsf{a}, B = \mathsf{b}) / \sum_{\mathsf{a}} p(A = \mathsf{a}, B = \mathsf{b})$ which, when summed over a does sum to 1. Indeed, this is just the definition of $p(A = \mathsf{a}|B = \mathsf{b})$.

Definition 1.6 Independence Variables x and y are independent if knowing the state (or value in the continuous case) of one variable gives no extra information about the other variable. Mathematically, this is expressed by

$$p(x, y) = p(x)p(y). \tag{1.1.11}$$

Provided that $p(x) \neq 0$ and $p(y) \neq 0$ independence of x and y is equivalent to

$$p(x|y) = p(x) \Leftrightarrow p(y|x) = p(y). \tag{1.1.12}$$

If $p(x|y) = p(x)$ for all states of x and y, then the variables x and y are said to be independent. If

$$p(x, y) = kf(x)g(y) \tag{1.1.13}$$

for some constant k, and positive functions $f(\cdot)$ and $g(\cdot)$ then x and y are independent and we write $x \perp\!\!\!\perp y$.

Example 1.1 Independence

Let x denote the day of the week in which females are born, and y denote the day in which males are born, with dom $(x) =$ dom $(y) = \{1, \ldots, 7\}$. It is reasonable to expect that x is independent of y. We randomly select a woman from the phone book, Alice, and find out that she was born on a Tuesday. We also select a male at random, Bob. Before phoning Bob and asking him, what does knowing Alice's birthday add to which day we think Bob is born on? Under the independence assumption, the answer is nothing. Note that this doesn't mean that the distribution of Bob's birthday is necessarily uniform – it just means that knowing when Alice was born doesn't provide any extra information than we already knew about Bob's birthday, $p(y|x) = p(y)$. Indeed, the distribution of birthdays $p(y)$ and $p(x)$ are non-uniform (statistically fewer babies are born on weekends), though there is nothing to suggest that x are y are dependent.

Deterministic dependencies

Sometimes the concept of independence is perhaps a little strange. Consider the following: variables x and y are both binary (their domains consist of two states). We define the distribution such that x

[1] We will discuss issues related to causality further in Section 3.4.

and y are always both in a certain joint state:

$$p(x = \mathsf{a}, y = 1) = 1, \quad p(x = \mathsf{a}, y = 2) = 0, \quad p(x = \mathsf{b}, y = 2) = 0, \quad p(x = \mathsf{b}, y = 1) = 0.$$

Are x and y dependent? The reader may show that $p(x = \mathsf{a}) = 1$, $p(x = \mathsf{b}) = 0$ and $p(y = 1) = 1$, $p(y = 2) = 0$. Hence $p(x)p(y) = p(x, y)$ for all states of x and y, and x and y are therefore independent. This may seem strange – we know for sure the relation between x and y, namely that they are always in the same joint state, yet they are independent. Since the distribution is trivially concentrated in a single joint state, knowing the state of x tells you nothing that you didn't anyway know about the state of y, and vice versa. This potential confusion comes from using the term 'independent' which may suggest that there is no relation between objects discussed. The best way to think about statistical independence is to ask whether or not knowing the state of variable y tells you something more than you knew before about variable x, where 'knew before' means working with the joint distribution of $p(x, y)$ to figure out what we can know about x, namely $p(x)$.

Definition 1.7 Conditional independence

$$\mathcal{X} \perp\!\!\!\perp \mathcal{Y} \mid \mathcal{Z} \tag{1.1.14}$$

denotes that the two sets of variables $\mathcal{X}$ and $\mathcal{Y}$ are independent of each other provided we know the state of the set of variables $\mathcal{Z}$. For conditional independence, $\mathcal{X}$ and $\mathcal{Y}$ must be independent given *all* states of $\mathcal{Z}$. Formally, this means that

$$p(\mathcal{X}, \mathcal{Y} \mid \mathcal{Z}) = p(\mathcal{X} \mid \mathcal{Z}) p(\mathcal{Y} \mid \mathcal{Z}) \tag{1.1.15}$$

for all states of $\mathcal{X}, \mathcal{Y}, \mathcal{Z}$. In case the conditioning set is empty we may also write $\mathcal{X} \perp\!\!\!\perp \mathcal{Y}$ for $\mathcal{X} \perp\!\!\!\perp \mathcal{Y} \mid \emptyset$, in which case $\mathcal{X}$ is (unconditionally) independent of $\mathcal{Y}$.

If $\mathcal{X}$ and $\mathcal{Y}$ are not conditionally independent, they are conditionally dependent. This is written

$$\mathcal{X} \top\!\!\!\top \mathcal{Y} \mid \mathcal{Z} \tag{1.1.16}$$

Similarly $\mathcal{X} \top\!\!\!\top \mathcal{Y} \mid \emptyset$ can be written as $\mathcal{X} \top\!\!\!\top \mathcal{Y}$.

Intuitively, if x is conditionally independent of y given z, this means that, given z, y contains no additional information about x. Similarly, given z, knowing x does not tell me anything more about y. Note that $\mathcal{X} \perp\!\!\!\perp \mathcal{Y} \mid \mathcal{Z} \Rightarrow \mathcal{X}' \perp\!\!\!\perp \mathcal{Y}' \mid \mathcal{Z}$ for $\mathcal{X}' \subseteq \mathcal{X}$ and $\mathcal{Y}' \subseteq \mathcal{Y}$.

Remark 1.2 (Independence implications) It's tempting to think that if a is independent of b and b is independent of c then a must be independent of c:

$$\{a \perp\!\!\!\perp b, b \perp\!\!\!\perp c\} \Rightarrow a \perp\!\!\!\perp c. \tag{1.1.17}$$

However, this does not follow. Consider for example a distribution of the form

$$p(a, b, c) = p(b)p(a, c). \tag{1.1.18}$$

From this

$$p(a, b) = \sum_c p(a, b, c) = p(b) \sum_c p(a, c). \tag{1.1.19}$$

Hence $p(a, b)$ is a function of b multiplied by a function of a so that a and b are independent. Similarly, one can show that b and c are independent. However, a is not necessarily independent of c since the distribution $p(a, c)$ can be set arbitrarily.

Similarly, it's tempting to think that if a and b are dependent, and b and c are dependent, then a and c must be dependent:

$$\{a \top\!\!\!\top b, b \top\!\!\!\top c\} \Rightarrow a \top\!\!\!\top c. \tag{1.1.20}$$

However, this also does not follow. We give an explicit numerical example in Exercise 3.17.

Finally, note that conditional independence $x \perp\!\!\!\perp y|\, z$ does not imply marginal independence $x \perp\!\!\!\perp y$.

1.1.2 Probability tables

Based on the populations 60 776 238, 5 116 900 and 2 980 700 of England (E), Scotland (S) and Wales (W), the a priori probability that a randomly selected person from the combined three countries would live in England, Scotland or Wales, is approximately 0.88, 0.08 and 0.04 respectively. We can write this as a vector (or probability table):

$$\begin{pmatrix} p(Cnt = \mathsf{E}) \\ p(Cnt = \mathsf{S}) \\ p(Cnt = \mathsf{W}) \end{pmatrix} = \begin{pmatrix} 0.88 \\ 0.08 \\ 0.04 \end{pmatrix} \tag{1.1.21}$$

whose component values sum to 1. The ordering of the components in this vector is arbitrary, as long as it is consistently applied.

For the sake of simplicity, we assume that only three Mother Tongue languages exist: English (Eng), Scottish (Scot) and Welsh (Wel), with conditional probabilities given the country of residence, England (E), Scotland (S) and Wales (W). We write a (fictitious) conditional probability table

$$\begin{array}{lll} p(MT = \mathsf{Eng}|Cnt = \mathsf{E}) = 0.95 & p(MT = \mathsf{Eng}|Cnt = \mathsf{S}) = 0.7 & p(MT = \mathsf{Eng}|Cnt = \mathsf{W}) = 0.6 \\ p(MT = \mathsf{Scot}|Cnt = \mathsf{E}) = 0.04 & p(MT = \mathsf{Scot}|Cnt = \mathsf{S}) = 0.3 & p(MT = \mathsf{Scot}|Cnt = \mathsf{W}) = 0.0 \\ p(MT = \mathsf{Wel}|Cnt = \mathsf{E}) = 0.01 & p(MT = \mathsf{Wel}|Cnt = \mathsf{S}) = 0.0 & p(MT = \mathsf{Wel}|Cnt = \mathsf{W}) = 0.4. \end{array} \tag{1.1.22}$$

From this we can form a joint distribution $p(Cnt, MT) = p(MT|Cnt)p(Cnt)$. This could be written as a 3×3 matrix with columns indexed by country and rows indexed by Mother Tongue:

$$\begin{pmatrix} 0.95 \times 0.88 & 0.7 \times 0.08 & 0.6 \times 0.04 \\ 0.04 \times 0.88 & 0.3 \times 0.08 & 0.0 \times 0.04 \\ 0.01 \times 0.88 & 0.0 \times 0.08 & 0.4 \times 0.04 \end{pmatrix} = \begin{pmatrix} 0.836 & 0.056 & 0.024 \\ 0.0352 & 0.024 & 0 \\ 0.0088 & 0 & 0.016 \end{pmatrix}. \tag{1.1.23}$$

The joint distribution contains all the information about the model of this environment. By summing the columns of this table, we have the marginal $p(Cnt)$. Summing the rows gives the marginal $p(MT)$. Similarly, one could easily infer $p(Cnt|MT) \propto p(MT|Cnt)p(Cnt)$ from this joint distribution by dividing an entry of Equation (1.1.23) by its row sum.

For joint distributions over a larger number of variables, $x_i, i = 1, \ldots, D$, with each variable x_i taking K_i states, the table describing the joint distribution is an array with $\prod_{i=1}^{D} K_i$ entries. Explicitly storing tables therefore requires space exponential in the number of variables, which rapidly becomes impractical for a large number of variables. We discuss how to deal with this issue in Chapter 3 and Chapter 4.

A probability distribution assigns a value to each of the joint states of the variables. For this reason, $p(T, J, R, S)$ is considered equivalent to $p(J, S, R, T)$ (or any such reordering of the variables), since in each case the joint setting of the variables is simply a different index to the same probability. This situation is more clear in the set-theoretic notation $p(J \cap S \cap T \cap R)$. We abbreviate this set-theoretic notation by using the commas – however, one should be careful not to confuse the use of this indexing type notation with functions $f(x, y)$ which are in general dependent on the variable order. Whilst the variables to the left of the conditioning bar may be written in any order, and equally those to the right of the conditioning bar may be written in any order, moving variables across the bar is not generally equivalent, so that $p(x_1|x_2) \neq p(x_2|x_1)$.

1.2 Probabilistic reasoning

The central paradigm of probabilistic reasoning is to identify all relevant variables $x_1, \ldots, x_N$ in the environment, and make a probabilistic model $p(x_1, \ldots, x_N)$ of their interaction. Reasoning (inference) is then performed by introducing *evidence* that sets variables in known states, and subsequently computing probabilities of interest, conditioned on this evidence. The rules of probability, combined with Bayes' rule make for a complete reasoning system, one which includes traditional deductive logic as a special case [158]. In the examples below, the number of variables in the environment is very small. In Chapter 3 we will discuss reasoning in networks containing many variables, for which the graphical notations of Chapter 2 will play a central role.

Example 1.2 Hamburgers

Consider the following fictitious scientific information: Doctors find that people with Kreuzfeld-Jacob disease (KJ) almost invariably ate hamburgers, thus $p(\textit{Hamburger Eater}|\textit{KJ}) = 0.9$. The probability of an individual having *KJ* is currently rather low, about one in 100 000.

1. Assuming eating lots of hamburgers is rather widespread, say $p(\textit{Hamburger Eater}) = 0.5$, what is the probability that a hamburger eater will have Kreuzfeld-Jacob disease?
   This may be computed as

$$p(\textit{KJ}\,|\textit{Hamburger Eater}) = \frac{p(\textit{Hamburger Eater}, \textit{KJ})}{p(\textit{Hamburger Eater})} = \frac{p(\textit{Hamburger Eater}|\textit{KJ})p(\textit{KJ})}{p(\textit{Hamburger Eater})} \tag{1.2.1}$$

$$= \frac{\frac{9}{10} \times \frac{1}{100\,000}}{\frac{1}{2}} = 1.8 \times 10^{-5}. \tag{1.2.2}$$

2. If the fraction of people eating hamburgers was rather small, $p(\textit{Hamburger Eater}) = 0.001$, what is the probability that a regular hamburger eater will have Kreuzfeld-Jacob disease? Repeating the above calculation, this is given by

$$\frac{\frac{9}{10} \times \frac{1}{100\,000}}{\frac{1}{1000}} \approx 1/100. \tag{1.2.3}$$

   This is much higher than in scenario (1) since here we can be more sure that eating hamburgers is related to the illness.

Example 1.3 Inspector Clouseau

Inspector Clouseau arrives at the scene of a crime. The victim lies dead in the room alongside the possible murder weapon, a knife. The Butler (B) and Maid (M) are the inspector's main suspects and the inspector has a prior belief of 0.6 that the Butler is the murderer, and a prior belief of 0.2 that the Maid is the murderer. These beliefs are independent in the sense that $p(B, M) = p(B)p(M)$. (It is possible that both the Butler and the Maid murdered the victim or neither.) The inspector's *prior* criminal knowledge can be formulated mathematically as follows:

$$\text{dom}(B) = \text{dom}(M) = \{\text{murderer, not murderer}\}, \text{dom}(K) = \{\text{knife used, knife not used}\} \tag{1.2.4}$$

$$p(B = \text{murderer}) = 0.6, \qquad p(M = \text{murderer}) = 0.2 \tag{1.2.5}$$

$$\begin{array}{lll} p(\text{knife used}|B = \text{not murderer}, & M = \text{not murderer}) & = 0.3 \\ p(\text{knife used}|B = \text{not murderer}, & M = \text{murderer}) & = 0.2 \\ p(\text{knife used}|B = \text{murderer}, & M = \text{not murderer}) & = 0.6 \\ p(\text{knife used}|B = \text{murderer}, & M = \text{murderer}) & = 0.1. \end{array} \tag{1.2.6}$$

In addition $p(K, B, M) = p(K|B, M)p(B)p(M)$. Assuming that the knife is the murder weapon, what is the probability that the Butler is the murderer? (Remember that it might be that neither is the murderer.) Using b for the two states of B and m for the two states of M,

$$\begin{aligned} p(B|K) &= \sum_m p(B, m|K) = \sum_m \frac{p(B, m, K)}{p(K)} = \frac{\sum_m p(K|B, m)p(B, m)}{\sum_{m,b} p(K|b, m)p(b, m)} \\ &= \frac{p(B)\sum_m p(K|B, m)p(m)}{\sum_b p(b)\sum_m p(K|b, m)p(m)}. \end{aligned} \tag{1.2.7}$$

where we used the fact that in our model $p(B, M) = p(B)p(M)$. Plugging in the values we have (see also `demoClouseau.m`)

$$p(B = \text{murderer}|\text{knife used}) = \frac{\frac{6}{10}\left(\frac{2}{10} \times \frac{1}{10} + \frac{8}{10} \times \frac{6}{10}\right)}{\frac{6}{10}\left(\frac{2}{10} \times \frac{1}{10} + \frac{8}{10} \times \frac{6}{10}\right) + \frac{4}{10}\left(\frac{2}{10} \times \frac{2}{10} + \frac{8}{10} \times \frac{3}{10}\right)} = \frac{300}{412} \approx 0.73. \tag{1.2.8}$$

Hence knowing that the knife was the murder weapon strengthens our belief that the butler did it.

Remark 1.3 The role of $p(\text{knife used})$ in the Inspector Clouseau example can cause some confusion. In the above,

$$p(\text{knife used}) = \sum_b p(b) \sum_m p(\text{knife used}|b, m)p(m) \tag{1.2.9}$$

is computed to be 0.456. But surely, $p(\text{knife used}) = 1$, since this is given in the question! Note that the quantity $p(\text{knife used})$ relates to the *prior* probability the model assigns to the knife being used (in the absence of any other information). If we know that the knife is used, then the *posterior*

$$p(\text{knife used}|\text{knife used}) = \frac{p(\text{knife used, knife used})}{p(\text{knife used})} = \frac{p(\text{knife used})}{p(\text{knife used})} = 1 \tag{1.2.10}$$

which, naturally, must be the case.

Example 1.4 Who's in the bathroom?

Consider a household of three people, Alice, Bob and Cecil. Cecil wants to go to the bathroom but finds it occupied. He then goes to Alice's room and sees she is there. Since Cecil knows that only either Alice or Bob can be in the bathroom, from this he infers that Bob must be in the bathroom.

To arrive at the same conclusion in a mathematical framework, we define the following events

$$A = \text{Alice is in her bedroom}, \qquad B = \text{Bob is in his bedroom}, \qquad O = \text{Bathroom occupied}. \tag{1.2.11}$$

We can encode the information that if either Alice or Bob are not in their bedrooms, then they must be in the bathroom (they might both be in the bathroom) as

$$p(O = \mathsf{tr}|A = \mathsf{fa}, B) = 1, \qquad p(O = \mathsf{tr}|A, B = \mathsf{fa}) = 1. \tag{1.2.12}$$

The first term expresses that the bathroom is occupied if Alice is not in her bedroom, wherever Bob is. Similarly, the second term expresses bathroom occupancy as long as Bob is not in his bedroom. Then

$$\begin{aligned} p(B = \mathsf{fa}|O = \mathsf{tr}, A = \mathsf{tr}) &= \frac{p(B = \mathsf{fa}, O = \mathsf{tr}, A = \mathsf{tr})}{p(O = \mathsf{tr}, A = \mathsf{tr})} \\ &= \frac{p(O = \mathsf{tr}|A = \mathsf{tr}, B = \mathsf{fa})p(A = \mathsf{tr}, B = \mathsf{fa})}{p(O = \mathsf{tr}, A = \mathsf{tr})} \end{aligned} \tag{1.2.13}$$

where

$$\begin{aligned} p(O = \mathsf{tr}, A = \mathsf{tr}) = p(O = \mathsf{tr}|A = \mathsf{tr}, B = \mathsf{fa})p(A = \mathsf{tr}, B = \mathsf{fa}) \\ + p(O = \mathsf{tr}|A = \mathsf{tr}, B = \mathsf{tr})p(A = \mathsf{tr}, B = \mathsf{tr}). \end{aligned} \tag{1.2.14}$$

Using the fact $p(O = \mathsf{tr}|A = \mathsf{tr}, B = \mathsf{fa}) = 1$ and $p(O = \mathsf{tr}|A = \mathsf{tr}, B = \mathsf{tr}) = 0$, which encodes that if Alice is in her room and Bob is not, the bathroom must be occupied, and similarly, if both Alice and Bob are in their rooms, the bathroom cannot be occupied,

$$p(B = \mathsf{fa}|O = \mathsf{tr}, A = \mathsf{tr}) = \frac{p(A = \mathsf{tr}, B = \mathsf{fa})}{p(A = \mathsf{tr}, B = \mathsf{fa})} = 1. \tag{1.2.15}$$

This example is interesting since we are not required to make a full probabilistic model in this case thanks to the limiting nature of the probabilities (we don't need to specify $p(A, B)$). The situation is common in limiting situations of probabilities being either 0 or 1, corresponding to traditional logic systems.

Example 1.5 Aristotle: Resolution

We can represent the statement 'All apples are fruit' by $p(F = \mathsf{tr}|A = \mathsf{tr}) = 1$. Similarly, 'All fruits grow on trees' may be represented by $p(T = \mathsf{tr}|F = \mathsf{tr}) = 1$. Additionally we assume that whether or not something grows on a tree depends only on whether or not it is a fruit, $p(T|A, F) = P(T|F)$. From this we can compute

$$\begin{aligned} p(T = \mathsf{tr}|A = \mathsf{tr}) &= \sum_F p(T = \mathsf{tr}|F, A = \mathsf{tr})p(F|A = \mathsf{tr}) = \sum_F p(T = \mathsf{tr}|F)p(F|A = \mathsf{tr}) \\ &= p(T = \mathsf{tr}|F = \mathsf{fa})\underbrace{p(F = \mathsf{fa}|A = \mathsf{tr})}_{=0} + \underbrace{p(T = \mathsf{tr}|F = \mathsf{tr})}_{=1}\underbrace{p(F = \mathsf{tr}|A = \mathsf{tr})}_{=1} = 1. \end{aligned} \tag{1.2.16}$$

In other words we have deduced that 'All apples grow on trees' is a true statement, based on the information presented. (This kind of reasoning is called resolution and is a form of transitivity: from the statements $A \Rightarrow F$ and $F \Rightarrow T$ we can infer $A \Rightarrow T$.)

Example 1.6 Aristotle: Inverse Modus Ponens

According to Logic, from the statement: 'If A is true then B is true', one may deduce that 'If B is false then A is false'. To see how this fits in with a probabilistic reasoning system we can first express the statement: 'If A is true then B is true' as $p(B = \text{tr}|A = \text{tr}) = 1$. Then we may infer

$$
\begin{aligned}
p(A = \text{fa}|B = \text{fa}) &= 1 - p(A = \text{tr}|B = \text{fa}) \\
&= 1 - \frac{p(B = \text{fa}|A = \text{tr})p(A = \text{tr})}{p(B = \text{fa}|A = \text{tr})p(A = \text{tr}) + p(B = \text{fa}|A = \text{fa})p(A = \text{fa})} = 1.
\end{aligned}
\tag{1.2.17}
$$

This follows since $p(B = \text{fa}|A = \text{tr}) = 1 - p(B = \text{tr}|A = \text{tr}) = 1 - 1 = 0$, annihilating the second term.

Both the above examples are intuitive expressions of deductive logic. The standard rules of Aristotelian logic are therefore seen to be limiting cases of probabilistic reasoning.

Example 1.7 Soft XOR gate

A standard XOR logic gate is given by the table on the right. If we observe that the output of the XOR gate is 0, what can we say about A and B? In this case, either A and B were both 0, or A and B were both 1. This means we don't know which state A was in – it could equally likely have been 1 or 0.

A	B	A xor B
0	0	0
0	1	1
1	0	1
1	1	0

Consider a 'soft' version of the XOR gate given on the right, with additionally $A \perp\!\!\!\perp B$ and $p(A = 1) = 0.65$, $p(B = 1) = 0.77$. What is $p(A = 1|C = 0)$?

A	B	$p(C = 1\|A, B)$
0	0	0.1
0	1	0.99
1	0	0.8
1	1	0.25

$$
\begin{aligned}
p(A = 1, C = 0) &= \sum_B p(A = 1, B, C = 0) = \sum_B p(C = 0|A = 1, B)p(A = 1)p(B) \\
&= p(A = 1)\,(p(C = 0|A = 1, B = 0)p(B = 0) \\
&\quad + p(C = 0|A = 1, B = 1)p(B = 1)) \\
&= 0.65 \times (0.2 \times 0.23 + 0.75 \times 0.77) = 0.405\,275.
\end{aligned}
\tag{1.2.18}
$$

$$
\begin{aligned}
p(A = 0, C = 0) &= \sum_B p(A = 0, B, C = 0) = \sum_B p(C = 0|A = 0, B)p(A = 0)p(B) \\
&= p(A = 0)(p(C = 0|A = 0, B = 0)p(B = 0) \\
&\quad + p(C = 0|A = 0, B = 1)p(B = 1)) \\
&= 0.35 \times (0.9 \times 0.23 + 0.01 \times 0.77) = 0.075\,145.
\end{aligned}
$$

Then

$$
p(A = 1|C = 0) = \frac{p(A = 1, C = 0)}{p(A = 1, C = 0) + p(A = 0, C = 0)} = \frac{0.405\,275}{0.405\,275 + 0.075\,145} = 0.8436.
\tag{1.2.19}
$$

Example 1.8 Larry

Larry is typically late for school. If Larry is late, we denote this with $L = \text{late}$, otherwise, $L = \text{not late}$. When his mother asks whether or not he was late for school he never admits to being late. The response Larry gives R_L is represented as follows

$$p(R_L = \text{not late}|L = \text{not late}) = 1, \qquad p(R_L = \text{late}|L = \text{late}) = 0. \tag{1.2.20}$$

The remaining two values are determined by normalisation and are

$$p(R_L = \text{late}|L = \text{not late}) = 0, \qquad p(R_L = \text{not late}|L = \text{late}) = 1. \tag{1.2.21}$$

Given that $R_L = \text{not late}$, what is the probability that Larry was late, i.e. $p(L = \text{late}|R_L = \text{not late})$?

Using Bayes' we have

$$\begin{aligned} p(L = \text{late}|R_L = \text{not late}) &= \frac{p(L = \text{late}, R_L = \text{not late})}{p(R_L = \text{not late})} \\ &= \frac{p(L = \text{late}, R_L = \text{not late})}{p(L = \text{late}, R_L = \text{not late}) + p(L = \text{not late}, R_L = \text{not late})}. \end{aligned} \tag{1.2.22}$$

In the above

$$p(L = \text{late}, R_L = \text{not late}) = \underbrace{p(R_L = \text{not late}|L = \text{late})}_{=1} p(L = \text{late}) \tag{1.2.23}$$

and

$$p(L = \text{not late}, R_L = \text{not late}) = \underbrace{p(R_L = \text{not late}|L = \text{not late})}_{=1} p(L = \text{not late}). \tag{1.2.24}$$

Hence

$$p(L = \text{late}|R_L = \text{not late}) = \frac{p(L = \text{late})}{p(L = \text{late}) + p(L = \text{not late})} = p(L = \text{late}). \tag{1.2.25}$$

Where we used normalisation in the last step, $p(L = \text{late}) + p(L = \text{not late}) = 1$. This result is intuitive – Larry's mother knows that he never admits to being late, so her belief about whether or not he really was late is unchanged, regardless of what Larry actually says.

Example 1.9 Larry and Sue

Continuing the example above, Larry's sister Sue always tells the truth to her mother as to whether or not Larry was late for school.

$$p(R_S = \text{not late}|L = \text{not late}) = 1, \qquad p(R_S = \text{late}|L = \text{late}) = 1. \tag{1.2.26}$$

The remaining two values are determined by normalisation and are

$$p(R_S = \text{late}|L = \text{not late}) = 0, \qquad p(R_S = \text{not late}|L = \text{late}) = 0. \tag{1.2.27}$$

We also assume $p(R_S, R_L|L) = p(R_S|L)p(R_L|L)$. We can then write

$$p(R_L, R_S, L) = p(R_L|L)p(R_S|L)p(L). \tag{1.2.28}$$

Given that $R_S =$ late and $R_L =$ not late, what is the probability that Larry was late?

Using Bayes' rule, we have

$$p(L = \text{late}|R_L = \text{not late}, R_S = \text{late}) = \frac{1}{Z} p(R_S = \text{late}|L = \text{late}) p(R_L = \text{not late}|L = \text{late}) p(L = \text{late}) \quad (1.2.29)$$

where the normalisation Z is given by

$$p(R_S = \text{late}|L = \text{late}) p(R_L = \text{not late}|L = \text{late}) p(L = \text{late}) + p(R_S = \text{late}|L = \text{not late}) p(R_L = \text{not late}|L = \text{not late}) \times p(L = \text{not late}). \quad (1.2.30)$$

Hence

$$p(L = \text{late}|R_L = \text{not late}, R_S = \text{late}) = \frac{1 \times 1 \times p(L = \text{late})}{1 \times 1 \times p(L = \text{late}) + 0 \times 1 \times p(L = \text{not late})} = 1. \quad (1.2.31)$$

This result is also intuitive – since Larry's mother knows that Sue always tells the truth, no matter what Larry says, she knows he was late.

Example 1.10 Luke

Luke has been told he's lucky and has won a prize in the lottery. There are five prizes available of value £10, £100, £1000, £10 000, £1 000 000. The prior probabilities of winning these five prizes are p_1, p_2, p_3, p_4, p_5, with p_0 being the prior probability of winning no prize. Luke asks eagerly 'Did I win £1 000 000?!'. 'I'm afraid not sir', is the response of the lottery phone operator. 'Did I win £10 000?!' asks Luke. 'Again, I'm afraid not sir'. What is the probability that Luke has won £1000?

Note first that $p_0 + p_1 + p_2 + p_3 + p_4 + p_5 = 1$. We denote $W = 1$ for the first prize of £10, and $W = 2, \ldots, 5$ for the remaining prizes and $W = 0$ for no prize. We need to compute

$$p(W = 3|W \neq 5, W \neq 4, W \neq 0) = \frac{p(W = 3, W \neq 5, W \neq 4, W \neq 0)}{p(W \neq 5, W \neq 4, W \neq 0)} = \frac{p(W = 3)}{p(W = 1 \text{ or } W = 2 \text{ or } W = 3)} = \frac{p_3}{p_1 + p_2 + p_3} \quad (1.2.32)$$

where the term in the denominator is computed using the fact that the events W are mutually exclusive (one can only win one prize). This result makes intuitive sense: once we have removed the impossible states of W, the probability that Luke wins the prize is proportional to the prior probability of that prize, with the normalisation being simply the total set of possible probability remaining.

1.3 Prior, likelihood and posterior

Much of science deals with problems of the form: tell me something about the variable θ given that I have observed data $\mathcal{D}$ and have some knowledge of the underlying data generating mechanism.

Our interest is then the quantity

$$p(\theta|\mathcal{D}) = \frac{p(\mathcal{D}|\theta)p(\theta)}{p(\mathcal{D})} = \frac{p(\mathcal{D}|\theta)p(\theta)}{\int_\theta p(\mathcal{D}|\theta)p(\theta)}. \tag{1.3.1}$$

This shows how from a forward or *generative model* $p(\mathcal{D}|\theta)$ of the dataset, and coupled with a *prior* belief $p(\theta)$ about which variable values are appropriate, we can infer the *posterior* distribution $p(\theta|\mathcal{D})$ of the variable in light of the observed data. The *most probable a posteriori* (*MAP*) setting is that which maximises the posterior, $\theta_* = \arg\max_\theta p(\theta|\mathcal{D})$. For a 'flat prior', $p(\theta)$ being a constant, not changing with θ, the MAP solution is equivalent to the *maximum likelihood*, namely that θ that maximises the likelihood $p(\mathcal{D}|\theta)$ of the model generating the observed data. We will return to a discussion of summaries of the posterior and parameter learning in Chapter 9.

This use of a generative model sits well with physical models of the world which typically postulate how to generate observed phenomena, assuming we know the model. For example, one might postulate how to generate a timeseries of displacements for a swinging pendulum but with unknown mass, length and damping constant. Using this generative model, and given only the displacements, we could infer the unknown physical properties of the pendulum.

Example 1.11 Pendulum

As a prelude to scientific inference and the use of continuous variables, we consider an idealised pendulum for which x_t is the angular displacement of the pendulum at time t. Assuming that the measurements are independent, given the knowledge of the parameter of the problem, θ, we have that the likelihood of a sequence of observations $x_1, \ldots, x_T$ is given by

$$p(x_1, \ldots, x_T|\theta) = \prod_{t=1}^{T} p(x_t|\theta). \tag{1.3.2}$$

If the model is correct and our measurement of the displacements x is perfect, then the physical model is

$$x_t = \sin(\theta t) \tag{1.3.3}$$

where θ represents the unknown physical constants of the pendulum ($\sqrt{g/L}$, where g is the gravitational attraction and L the length of the pendulum). If, however, we assume that we have a rather poor instrument to measure the displacements, with a known variance of σ^2 (see Chapter 8), then

$$x_t = \sin(\theta t) + \epsilon_t \tag{1.3.4}$$

where ϵ_t is zero mean Gaussian noise with variance σ^2. We can also consider a set of possible parameters θ and place a prior $p(\theta)$ over them, expressing our prior belief (before seeing the measurements) in the appropriateness of the different values of θ. The posterior distribution is then given by

$$p(\theta|x_1, \ldots, x_T) \propto p(\theta) \prod_{t=1}^{T} \frac{1}{\sqrt{2\pi\sigma^2}} e^{-\frac{1}{2\sigma^2}(x_t - \sin(\theta t))^2}. \tag{1.3.5}$$

Despite noisy measurements, the posterior over the assumed possible values for θ becomes strongly peaked for a large number of measurements, see Fig. 1.1.

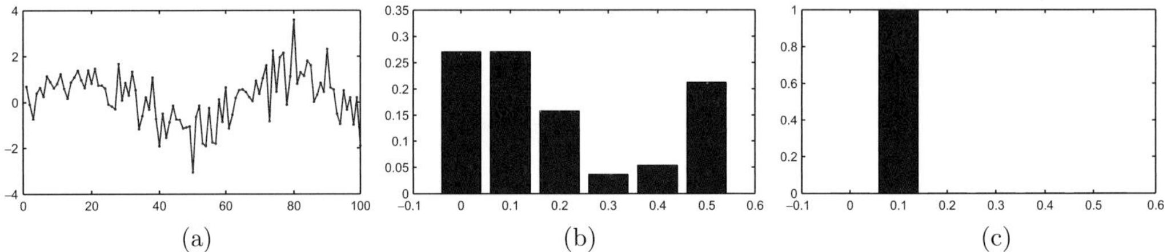

Figure 1.1 (**a**) Noisy observations of displacements $x_1, \ldots, x_{100}$ for a pendulum. (**b**) The prior belief on 5 possible values of θ. (**c**) The posterior belief on θ.

1.3.1 Two dice: what were the individual scores?

Two fair dice are rolled. Someone tells you that the sum of the two scores is 9. What is the posterior distribution of the dice scores[2]?

The score of die a is denoted s_a with $\text{dom}(s_a) = \{1, 2, 3, 4, 5, 6\}$ and similarly for s_b. The three variables involved are then s_a, s_b and the total score, $t = s_a + s_b$. A model of these three variables naturally takes the form

$$p(t, s_a, s_b) = \underbrace{p(t|s_a, s_b)}_{\text{likelihood}} \underbrace{p(s_a, s_b)}_{\text{prior}}. \tag{1.3.6}$$

The prior $p(s_a, s_b)$ is the joint probability of score s_a and score s_b without knowing anything else. Assuming no dependency in the rolling mechanism,

$$p(s_a, s_b) = p(s_a)p(s_b). \tag{1.3.7}$$

Since the dice are fair both $p(s_a)$ and $p(s_b)$ are uniform distributions, $p(s_a) = p(s_b) = 1/6$.

$p(s_a)p(s_b)$:

	$s_a = 1$	$s_a = 2$	$s_a = 3$	$s_a = 4$	$s_a = 5$	$s_a = 6$
$s_b = 1$	1/36	1/36	1/36	1/36	1/36	1/36
$s_b = 2$	1/36	1/36	1/36	1/36	1/36	1/36
$s_b = 3$	1/36	1/36	1/36	1/36	1/36	1/36
$s_b = 4$	1/36	1/36	1/36	1/36	1/36	1/36
$s_b = 5$	1/36	1/36	1/36	1/36	1/36	1/36
$s_b = 6$	1/36	1/36	1/36	1/36	1/36	1/36

Here the likelihood term is

$$p(t|s_a, s_b) = \mathbb{I}[t = s_a + s_b] \tag{1.3.8}$$

which states that the total score is given by $s_a + s_b$. Here $\mathbb{I}[A]$ is the *indicator function* defined as $\mathbb{I}[A] = 1$ if the statement A is true and 0 otherwise.

$p(t = 9|s_a, s_b)$:

	$s_a = 1$	$s_a = 2$	$s_a = 3$	$s_a = 4$	$s_a = 5$	$s_a = 6$
$s_b = 1$	0	0	0	0	0	0
$s_b = 2$	0	0	0	0	0	0
$s_b = 3$	0	0	0	0	0	1
$s_b = 4$	0	0	0	0	1	0
$s_b = 5$	0	0	0	1	0	0
$s_b = 6$	0	0	1	0	0	0

Hence, our complete model is

$$p(t, s_a, s_b) = p(t|s_a, s_b)p(s_a)p(s_b) \tag{1.3.9}$$

where the terms on the right are explicitly defined.

$p(t = 9|s_a, s_b)p(s_a)p(s_b)$:

	$s_a = 1$	$s_a = 2$	$s_a = 3$	$s_a = 4$	$s_a = 5$	$s_a = 6$
$s_b = 1$	0	0	0	0	0	0
$s_b = 2$	0	0	0	0	0	0
$s_b = 3$	0	0	0	0	0	1/36
$s_b = 4$	0	0	0	0	1/36	0
$s_b = 5$	0	0	0	1/36	0	0
$s_b = 6$	0	0	1/36	0	0	0

[2] This example is due to Taylan Cemgil.

The posterior is then given by,

$$p(s_a, s_b|t=9) = \frac{p(t=9|s_a, s_b)p(s_a)p(s_b)}{p(t=9)} \tag{1.3.10}$$

where

$$p(t=9) = \sum_{s_a,s_b} p(t=9|s_a, s_b)p(s_a)p(s_b). \tag{1.3.11}$$

$p(s_a, s_b|t=9)$:

	$s_a = 1$	$s_a = 2$	$s_a = 3$	$s_a = 4$	$s_a = 5$	$s_a = 6$
$s_b = 1$	0	0	0	0	0	0
$s_b = 2$	0	0	0	0	0	0
$s_b = 3$	0	0	0	0	0	1/4
$s_b = 4$	0	0	0	0	1/4	0
$s_b = 5$	0	0	0	1/4	0	0
$s_b = 6$	0	0	1/4	0	0	0

The term $p(t=9) = \sum_{s_a,s_b} p(t=9|s_a, s_b)p(s_a)p(s_b) = 4 \times 1/36 = 1/9$. Hence the posterior is given by equal mass in only four non-zero elements, as shown.

1.4 Summary

- The standard rules of probability are a consistent, logical way to reason with uncertainty.
- Bayes' rule mathematically encodes the process of inference.

A useful introduction to probability is given in [292]. The interpretation of probability is contentious and we refer the reader to [158, 197, 193] for detailed discussions. The website `understandinguncertainty.org` contains entertaining discussions on reasoning with uncertainty.

1.5 Code

The BRMLtoolbox code accompanying this book is intended to give the reader some insight into representing discrete probability tables and performing simple inference. We provide here only the briefest of descriptions of the code and the reader is encouraged to experiment with the demos to understand better the routines and their purposes.

1.5.1 Basic probability code

At the simplest level, we only need two basic routines. One for multiplying probability tables together (called potentials in the code), and one for summing a probability table. Potentials are represented using a structure. For example, in the code corresponding to the Inspector Clouseau example `demoClouseau.m`, we define a probability table as

```
>> pot(1)
ans =
     variables: [1 3 2]
         table: [2x2x2 double]
```

This says that the potential depends on the variables 1, 3, 2 and the entries are stored in the array given by the table field. The size of the array informs how many states each variable takes in the order given by `variables`. The order in which the variables are defined in a potential is irrelevant provided that one indexes the array consistently. A routine that can help with setting table entries is `setstate.m`. For example,

```
>> pot(1) = setstate(pot(1),[2 1 3],[2 1 1],0.3)
```

means that for potential 1, the table entry for variable 2 being in state 2, variable 1 being in state 1 and variable 3 being in state 1 should be set to value 0.3.

The philosophy of the code is to keep the information required to perform computations to a minimum. Additional information about the labels of variables and their domains can be useful to interpret results, but is not actually required to carry out computations. One may also specify the name and domain of each variable, for example

```
>>variable(3)
ans =
    domain: {'murderer'  'not murderer'}
      name: 'butler'
```

The variable name and domain information in the Clouseau example is stored in the structure `variable`, which can be helpful to display the potential table:

```
>> disptable(pot(1),variable);
knife  =  used      maid  =  murderer      butler  =  murderer      0.100000
knife  =  not used  maid  =  murderer      butler  =  murderer      0.900000
knife  =  used      maid  =  not murderer  butler  =  murderer      0.600000
knife  =  not used  maid  =  not murderer  butler  =  murderer      0.400000
knife  =  used      maid  =  murderer      butler  =  not murderer  0.200000
knife  =  not used  maid  =  murderer      butler  =  not murderer  0.800000
knife  =  used      maid  =  not murderer  butler  =  not murderer  0.300000
knife  =  not used  maid  =  not murderer  butler  =  not murderer  0.700000
```

Multiplying potentials

In order to multiply potentials, (as for arrays) the tables of each potential must be dimensionally consistent – that is the number of states of variable i must be the same for all potentials. This can be checked using `potvariables.m`. This consistency is also required for other basic operations such as summing potentials.

`multpots.m`: Multiplying two or more potentials
`divpots.m`: Dividing a potential by another

Summing a potential

`sumpot.m`: Sum (marginalise) a potential over a set of variables
`sumpots.m`: Sum a set of potentials together

Making a conditional potential

`condpot.m`: Make a potential conditioned on variables

Setting a potential

`setpot.m`: Set variables in a potential to given states
`setevpot.m`: Set variables in a potential to given states and return also an identity potential on the given states

The philosophy of BRMLToolbox is that all information about variables is local and is read off from a potential. Using `setevpot.m` enables one to set variables in a state whilst maintaining information about the number of states of a variable.

Maximising a potential

`maxpot.m`: Maximise a potential over a set of variables

See also `maxNarray.m` and `maxNpot.m` which return the N-highest values and associated states.

Other potential utilities

`setstate.m`: Set a potential state to a given value
`table.m`: Return a table from a potential
`whichpot.m`: Return potentials which contain a set of variables
`potvariables.m`: Variables and their number of states in a set of potentials
`orderpotfields.m`: Order the fields of a potential structure
`uniquepots.m`: Merge redundant potentials by multiplication and return only unique ones
`numstates.m`: Number of states of a variable in a domain
`squeezepots.m`: Find unique potentials and rename the variables 1,2,...
`normpot.m`: Normalise a potential to form a distribution

1.5.2 General utilities

`condp.m`: Return a table $p(x|y)$ from $p(x, y)$
`condexp.m`: Form a conditional distribution from a log value
`logsumexp.m`: Compute the log of a sum of exponentials in a numerically precise way
`normp.m`: Return a normalised table from an unnormalised table
`assign.m`: Assign values to multiple variables
`maxarray.m`: Maximise a multi-dimensional array over a subset

1.5.3 An example

The following code highlights the use of the above routines in solving the Inspector Clouseau, Example 1.3, and the reader is invited to examine the code to become familiar with how to numerically represent probability tables

`demoClouseau.m`: Solving the Inspector Clouseau example

1.6 Exercises

1.1 Prove

$$p(x, y|z) = p(x|z)p(y|x, z) \tag{1.6.1}$$

and also

$$p(x|y, z) = \frac{p(y|x, z)p(x|z)}{p(y|z)}. \tag{1.6.2}$$

1.2 Prove the *Bonferroni inequality*

$$p(a, b) \geq p(a) + p(b) - 1. \tag{1.6.3}$$

1.3 (Adapted from [181]) There are two boxes. Box 1 contains three red and five white balls and box 2 contains two red and five white balls. A box is chosen at random $p(box = 1) = p(box = 2) = 0.5$ and a ball chosen at random from this box turns out to be red. What is the posterior probability that the red ball came from box 1?

1.4 (Adapted from [181]) Two balls are placed in a box as follows: A fair coin is tossed and a white ball is placed in the box if a head occurs, otherwise a red ball is placed in the box. The coin is tossed again and a red ball is placed in the box if a tail occurs, otherwise a white ball is placed in the box. Balls are drawn from the box three times in succession (always with replacing the drawn ball back in the box). It is found that on all three occasions a red ball is drawn. What is the probability that both balls in the box are red?

1.5 (From David Spiegelhalter `understandinguncertainty.org`) A secret government agency has developed a scanner which determines whether a person is a terrorist. The scanner is fairly reliable; 95% of all scanned terrorists are identified as terrorists, and 95% of all upstanding citizens are identified as such. An informant tells the agency that exactly one passenger of 100 aboard an aeroplane in which you are seated is a terrorist. The agency decides to scan each passenger and the shifty-looking man sitting next to you is the first to test positive. What are the chances that this man is a terrorist?

1.6 Consider three variable distributions which admit the factorisation

$$p(a, b, c) = p(a|b)p(b|c)p(c) \tag{1.6.4}$$

where all variables are binary. How many parameters are needed to specify distributions of this form?

1.7 Repeat the Inspector Clouseau scenario, Example 1.3, but with the restriction that either the Maid or the Butler is the murderer, but not both. Explicitly, the probability of the Maid being the murderer and not the Butler is 0.04, the probability of the Butler being the murderer and not the Maid is 0.64. Modify `demoClouseau.m` to implement this.

1.8 Prove

$$p(a, (b \text{ or } c)) = p(a, b) + p(a, c) - p(a, b, c). \tag{1.6.5}$$

1.9 Prove

$$p(x|z) = \sum_y p(x|y, z)p(y|z) = \sum_{y,w} p(x|w, y, z)p(w|y, z)p(y|z). \tag{1.6.6}$$

1.10 As a young man Mr Gott visits Berlin in 1969. He's surprised that he cannot cross into East Berlin since there is a wall separating the two halves of the city. He's told that the wall was erected eight years previously. He reasons that: The wall will have a finite lifespan; his ignorance means that he arrives uniformly at random at some time in the lifespan of the wall. Since only 5% of the time one would arrive in the first or last 2.5% of the lifespan of the wall he asserts that with 95% confidence the wall will survive between $8/0.975 \approx 8.2$ and $8/0.025 = 320$ years. In 1989 the now Professor Gott is pleased to find that his prediction was correct and promotes his prediction method in prestigious journals. This 'delta-t' method is widely adopted and used to form predictions in a range of scenarios about which researchers are 'totally ignorant'. Would you 'buy' a prediction from Professor Gott? Explain carefully your reasoning.

1.11 Implement the soft XOR gate, Example 1.7 using BRMLToolbox. You may find `condpot.m` of use.

1.12 Implement the hamburgers, Example 1.2 (both scenarios) using BRMLToolbox. To do so you will need to define the joint distribution $p(hamburgers, KJ)$ in which $\text{dom}(hamburgers) = \text{dom}(KJ) = \{\text{tr}, \text{fa}\}$.

1.13 Implement the two-dice example, Section 1.3.1 using BRMLToolbox.

1.14 A redistribution lottery involves picking the correct four numbers from 1 to 9 (without replacement, so 3,4,4,1 for example is not possible). The order of the picked numbers is irrelevant. Every week a million people play this game, each paying £1 to enter, with the numbers 3,5,7,9 being the most popular (1 in every 100 people chooses these numbers). Given that the million pounds prize money is split equally between winners, and that any four (different) numbers come up at random, what is the expected amount of money each of the players choosing 3,5,7,9 will win each week? The least popular set of numbers is 1,2,3,4 with only 1 in 10 000 people choosing this. How much do they profit each week, on average? Do you think there is any 'skill' involved in playing this lottery?

1.15 In a test of 'psychometry' the car keys and wristwatches of five people are given to a medium. The medium then attempts to match the wristwatch with the car key of each person. What is the expected number of correct matches that the medium will make (by chance)? What is the probability that the medium will obtain at least one correct match?

1.16 1. Show that for any function f

$$\sum_x p(x|y)f(y) = f(y). \tag{1.6.7}$$

2. Explain why, in general,

$$\sum_x p(x|y)f(x,y) \neq \sum_x f(x,y). \tag{1.6.8}$$

1.17 (Inspired by `singingbanana.com`). Seven friends decide to order pizzas by telephone from Pizza4U based on a flyer pushed through their letterbox. Pizza4U has only four kinds of pizza, and each person chooses a pizza independently. Bob phones Pizza4U and places the combined pizza order, simply stating how many pizzas of each kind are required. Unfortunately, the precise order is lost, so the chef makes seven randomly chosen pizzas and then passes them to the delivery boy.

1. How many different combined orders are possible?
2. What is the probability that the delivery boy has the right order?

1.18 Sally is new to the area and listens to some friends discussing about another female friend. Sally knows that they are talking about either Alice or Bella but doesn't know which. From previous conversations Sally knows some independent pieces of information: She's 90% sure that Alice has a white car, but doesn't know if Bella's car is white or black. Similarly, she's 90% sure that Bella likes sushi, but doesn't know if Alice likes sushi. Sally hears from the conversation that the person being discussed hates sushi and drives a white car. What is the probability that the friends are talking about Alice?

1.19 The weather in London can be summarised as: if it rains one day there's a 70% chance it will rain the following day; if it's sunny one day there's a 40% chance it will be sunny the following day.

1. Assuming that the prior probability it rained yesterday is 0.5, what is the probability that it was raining yesterday given that it's sunny today?
2. If the weather follows the same pattern as above, day after day, what is the probability that it will rain on any day (based on an effectively infinite number of days of observing the weather)?
3. Use the result from part 2 above as a new prior probability of rain yesterday and recompute the probability that it was raining yesterday given that it's sunny today.

2 Basic graph concepts

Often we have good reason to believe that one event affects another, or conversely that some events are independent. Incorporating such knowledge can produce models that are better specified and computationally more efficient. Graphs describe how objects are linked and provide a convenient picture for describing related objects. We will ultimately introduce a graph structure among the variables of a probabilistic model to produce a 'graphical model' that captures relations among the variables as well as their uncertainties. In this chapter, we introduce the required basic concepts from graph theory.

2.1 Graphs

Definition 2.1 Graph A *graph* G consists of nodes (also called vertices) and edges (also called links) between the nodes. Edges may be directed (they have an arrow in a single direction) or undirected. Edges can also have associated weights. A graph with all edges directed is called a *directed graph*, and one with all edges undirected is called an *undirected graph*.

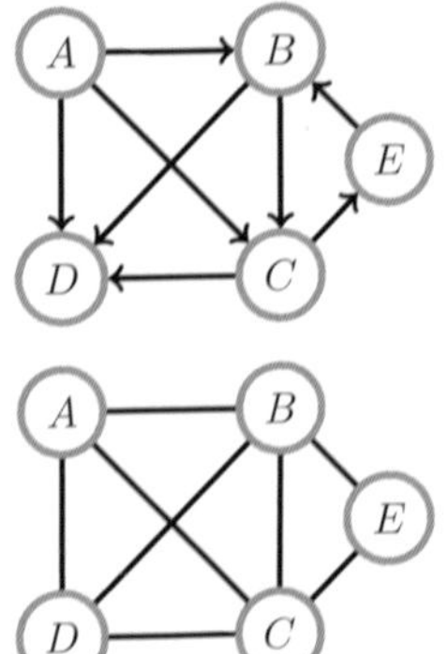

A directed graph G consists of directed edges between nodes.

An undirected graph G consists of undirected edges between nodes.

Graphs with edge weights are often used to model networks and flows along 'pipes', or distances between cities, where each node represents a city. We will also make use of these concepts in Chapter 5 and Chapter 28. Our main use of graphs though will be to endow them with a probabilistic interpretation and we develop a connection between directed graphs and probability in Chapter 3. Undirected graphs also play a central role in modelling and reasoning with uncertainty. Essentially, two variables will be independent if they are not linked by a path on the graph. We will discuss this in more detail when we consider Markov networks in Chapter 4.

Definition 2.2 Path, ancestors, descendants A *path* $A \mapsto B$ from node A to node B is a sequence of nodes that connects A to B. That is, a path is of the form $A_0, A_1, \ldots, A_{n-1}, A_n$, with $A_0 = A$ and $A_n = B$ and each edge (A_{k-1}, A_k), $k = 1, \ldots, n$ being in the graph. A directed path is a sequence of nodes which when we follow the direction of the arrows leads us from A to B. In directed graphs, the nodes A such that $A \mapsto B$ and $B \not\mapsto A$ are the *ancestors* of B. The nodes B such that $A \mapsto B$ and $B \not\mapsto A$ are the *descendants* of A.

Definition 2.3 Cycle, loop and chord A *cycle* is a directed path that starts and returns to the same node $a \to b \to \ldots \to z \to a$. A *loop* is a path containing more than two nodes, irrespective of edge direction, that starts and returns to the same node. For example in Fig. 2.2(b) $1-2-4-3-1$ forms a loop, but the graph is *acyclic* (contains no cycles). A *chord* is an edge that connects two non-adjacent nodes in a loop – for example, the $2-3$ edge is a chord in the $1-2-4-3-1$ loop of Fig. 2.2(a).

Definition 2.4 Directed Acyclic Graph (DAG) A DAG is a graph G with directed edges (arrows on each link) between the nodes such that by following a path of nodes from one node to another along the direction of each edge no path will revisit a node. In a DAG the ancestors of B are those nodes which have a directed path ending at B. Conversely, the descendants of A are those nodes which have a directed path starting at A.

Definition 2.5 Relationships in a DAG

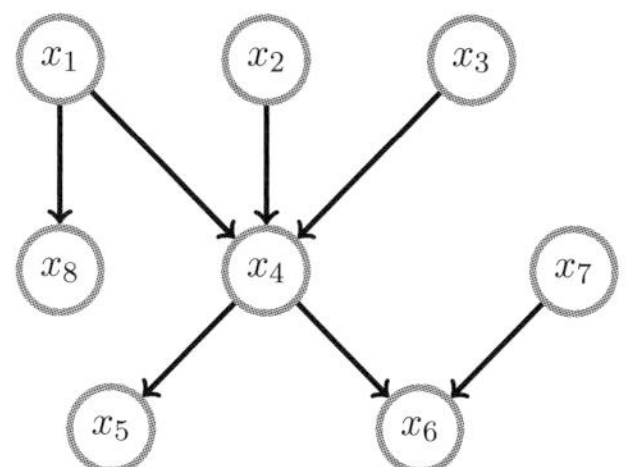

The *parents* of x_4 are $\text{pa}(x_4) = \{x_1, x_2, x_3\}$. The *children* of x_4 are $\text{ch}(x_4) = \{x_5, x_6\}$. The *family* of a node is itself and its parents. The *Markov blanket* of a node is its parents, children and the parents of its children. In this case, the Markov blanket of x_4 is $x_1, x_2, x_3, x_5, x_6, x_7$.

Directed acyclic graphs will play a central role in modelling environments with many variables, in particular they are used for the belief networks that we describe in the following chapter. One can view the directed links on a graph as 'direct dependencies' between parent and child variables. Naively, the acyclic condition prevents circular reasoning. These connections are discussed in detail in Chapter 3.

Definition 2.6 Neighbour For an undirected graph G the neighbours of x, $\text{ne}(x)$ are those nodes directly connected to x.

Definition 2.7 Clique

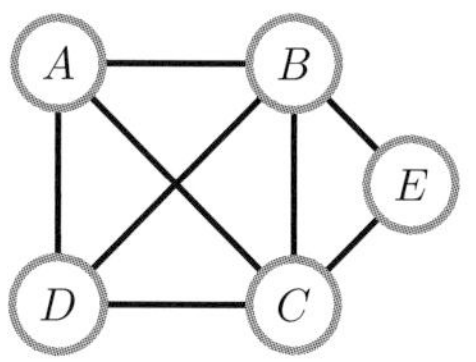

Given an undirected graph, a clique is a fully connected subset of nodes. All the members of the clique are neighbours; for a maximal clique there is no larger clique that contains the clique. For example this graph has two maximal cliques, $\mathcal{C}_1 = \{A, B, C, D\}$ and $\mathcal{C}_2 = \{B, C, E\}$. Whilst A, B, C are fully connected, this is a non-maximal clique since there is a larger fully connected set, A, B, C, D that contains this. A non-maximal clique is sometimes called a *cliquo*.

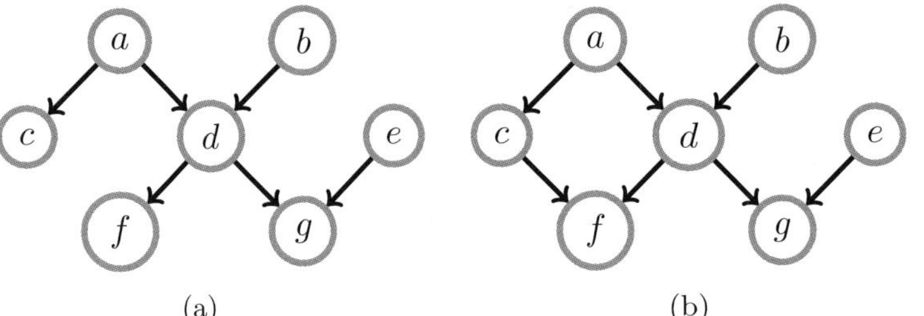

Figure 2.1 (**a**) Singly connected graph. (**b**) Multiply connected graph.

Cliques play a central role in both modelling and inference. In modelling they will describe variables that are all dependent on each other, see Chapter 4. In inference they describe sets of variables with no simpler structure describing the relationship between them and hence for which no simpler efficient inference procedure is likely to exist. We will discuss this issue in detail in Chapter 5 and Chapter 6.

Definition 2.8 Connected graph An undirected graph is *connected* if there is a path between every pair of nodes (i.e. there are no isolated islands). For a graph which is not connected, the connected components are those subgraphs which are connected.

Definition 2.9 Singly-connected graph A graph is *singly connected* if there is only one path from any node A to any other node B. Otherwise the graph is *multiply connected* (see Fig. 2.1). This definition applies regardless of whether or not the edges in the graph are directed. An alternative name for a singly connected graph is a *tree*. A multiply connected graph is also called *loopy*.

Definition 2.10 Spanning tree

A spanning tree of an undirected graph G is a singly connected subset of the existing edges such that the resulting singly connected graph covers all nodes of G. On the right is a graph and an associated spanning tree. A maximum weight spanning tree is a spanning tree such that the sum of all weights on the edges of the tree is at least as large as any other spanning tree of G.

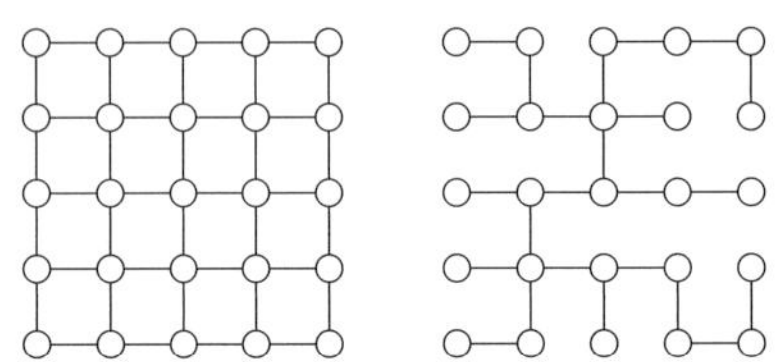

Procedure 2.1 (Finding a maximal weight spanning tree) An algorithm to find a spanning tree with maximal weight is as follows: Start by picking the edge with the largest weight and add this to the edge set. Then pick the next candidate edge which has the largest weight and add this to the edge set – if this results in an edge set with cycles, then reject the candidate edge and propose the next largest edge weight. Note that there may be more than one maximal weight spanning tree.

2.2 Numerically encoding graphs

Our ultimate goal is to make computational implementations of inference. Therefore, if we want to incorporate graph structure into our models, we need to express graphs in a way that a computer can understand and manipulate. There are several equivalent possibilities.

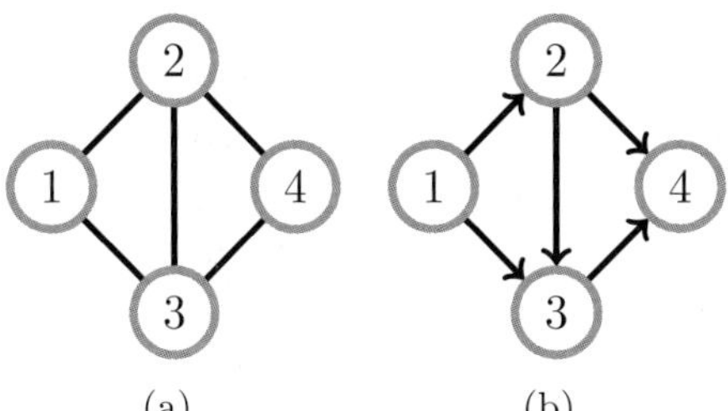

Figure 2.2 (**a**) An undirected graph can be represented as a symmetric adjacency matrix. (**b**) A directed graph with nodes labelled in ancestral order corresponds to a triangular adjacency matrix.

2.2.1 Edge list

As the name suggests, an *edge list* simply lists which node-node pairs are in the graph. For Fig. 2.2(a), an edge list is $L = \{(1,2), (2,1), (1,3), (3,1), (2,3), (3,2), (2,4), (4,2), (3,4), (4,3)\}$. Undirected edges are listed twice, once for each direction.

2.2.2 Adjacency matrix

An alternative is to use an *adjacency matrix*

$$\mathbf{A} = \begin{pmatrix} 0 & 1 & 1 & 0 \\ 1 & 0 & 1 & 1 \\ 1 & 1 & 0 & 1 \\ 0 & 1 & 1 & 0 \end{pmatrix} \tag{2.2.1}$$

where $A_{ij} = 1$ if there is an edge from node i to node j in the graph, and 0 otherwise. Some authors include self-connections and place 1's on the diagonal in this definition. An undirected graph has a symmetric adjacency matrix.

Provided that the nodes are labelled in *ancestral order* (parents always come before children) a directed graph Fig. 2.2(b) can be represented as a triangular adjacency matrix:

$$\mathbf{T} = \begin{pmatrix} 0 & 1 & 1 & 0 \\ 0 & 0 & 1 & 1 \\ 0 & 0 & 0 & 1 \\ 0 & 0 & 0 & 0 \end{pmatrix}. \tag{2.2.2}$$

Adjacency matrix powers

Adjacency matrices may seem wasteful since many of the entries are zero. However, they have a useful property that more than redeems them. For an $N \times N$ adjacency matrix $\mathbf{A}$, powers of the adjacency matrix $\left[\mathbf{A}^k\right]_{ij}$ specify how many paths there are from node i to node j in k edge hops. If we include 1's on the diagonal of $\mathbf{A}$ then $\left[\mathbf{A}^{N-1}\right]_{ij}$ is non-zero when there is a path connecting i to j in the graph. If $\mathbf{A}$ corresponds to a DAG the non-zero entries of the jth row of $\left[\mathbf{A}^{N-1}\right]$ correspond to the descendants of node j.

2.2.3 Clique matrix

For an undirected graph with N nodes and maximal cliques $\mathcal{C}_1, \ldots, \mathcal{C}_K$ a clique matrix is an $N \times K$ matrix in which each column c_k has zeros except for ones on entries describing the clique. For example

$$\mathbf{C} = \begin{pmatrix} 1 & 0 \\ 1 & 1 \\ 1 & 1 \\ 0 & 1 \end{pmatrix} \tag{2.2.3}$$

is a clique matrix for Fig. 2.2(a). A cliquo matrix relaxes the constraint that cliques are required to be maximal. A cliquo matrix containing only two-node cliques is called an *incidence matrix*. For example

$$\mathbf{C}_{inc} = \begin{pmatrix} 1 & 1 & 0 & 0 & 0 \\ 1 & 0 & 1 & 1 & 0 \\ 0 & 1 & 1 & 0 & 1 \\ 0 & 0 & 0 & 1 & 1 \end{pmatrix} \tag{2.2.4}$$

is an incidence matrix for Fig. 2.2(a). It is straightforward to show that $\mathbf{C}_{inc}\mathbf{C}_{inc}^{\mathsf{T}}$ is equal to the adjacency matrix except that the diagonals now contain the *degree* of each node (the number of edges it touches). Similarly, for any cliquo matrix the diagonal entry of $[\mathbf{C}\mathbf{C}^{\mathsf{T}}]_{ii}$ expresses the number of cliquos (columns) that node i occurs in. Off-diagonal elements $[\mathbf{C}\mathbf{C}^{\mathsf{T}}]_{ij}$ contain the number of cliquos that nodes i and j jointly inhabit.

Remark 2.1 (Graph confusions) Graphs are widely used, but differ markedly in what they represent. Two potential pitfalls are described below.

State-transition diagrams Such representations are used in Markov chains and finite state automata. Each state is a node and a directed edge between node i and node j (with an associated weight p_{ij}) represents that a transition from state i to state j can occur with probability p_{ij}. From the graphical models perspective we use a directed graph $x(t) \rightarrow x(t+1)$ to represent this Markov chain. The state-transition diagram provides a more detailed graphical description of the conditional probability table $p(x(t+1)|x(t))$.

Neural networks Neural networks also have nodes and edges. In general, however, neural networks are graphical representations of *functions*, whereas graphical models are representations of distributions.

2.3 Summary

- A graph is made of nodes and edges, which we will use to represent variables and relations between them.
- A DAG is an acyclic graph and will be useful for representing 'causal' relationships between variables.
- Neighbouring nodes on an undirected graph will represent dependent variables.
- A graph is singly connected if there is only one path from any node to any other – otherwise the graph is multiply connected.

- A clique is group of nodes all of which are connected to each other.
- The adjacency matrix is a machine-readable description of a graph. Powers of the adjacency matrix give information on the paths between nodes.

Good references for graphs, associated theories and their uses are [86, 121].

2.4 Code

2.4.1 Utility routines

`drawNet.m`: Draw a graph based on an adjacency matrix
`ancestors.m`: Find the ancestors of a node in a DAG
`edges.m`: Edge list from an adjacency matrix
`ancestralorder.m`: Ancestral order from a DAG
`connectedComponents.m`: Connected components
`parents.m`: Parents of a node given an adjacency matrix
`children.m`: Children of a node given an adjacency matrix
`neigh.m`: Neighbours of a node given an adjacency matrix

A connected graph is a tree if the number of edges plus 1 is equal to the number of nodes. However, for a disconnected graph this is not the case. The code `istree.m` below deals with the disconnected case. The routine is based on the observation that any singly connected graph must always possess a simplical node (a leaf node) which can be eliminated to reveal a smaller singly connected graph.

`istree.m`: If graph is singly connected return 1 and elimination sequence
`spantree.m`: Return a spanning tree from an ordered edge list
`singleparenttree.m`: Find a directed tree with at most one parent from an undirected tree

Additional routines for basic graph manipulations are given at the end of Chapter 6.

2.5 Exercises

2.1 Consider an adjacency matrix $\mathbf{A}$ with elements $[\mathbf{A}]_{ij} = 1$ if one can reach state i from state j in one timestep, and 0 otherwise. Show that the matrix $\left[\mathbf{A}^k\right]_{ij}$ represents the number of paths that lead from state j to i in k timesteps. Hence derive an algorithm that will find the minimum number of steps to get from state j to state i.

2.2 For an $N \times N$ symmetric adjacency matrix $\mathbf{A}$, describe an algorithm to find the connected components. You may wish to examine `connectedComponents.m`.

2.3 Show that for a connected graph that is singly connected, the number of edges E must be equal to the number of nodes minus 1, $E = V - 1$. Give an example graph with $E = V - 1$ that is not singly connected. Hence the condition $E = V - 1$ is a necessary but not sufficient condition for a graph to be singly connected.

2.4 Describe a procedure to determine if a graph is singly connected.

2.5 Describe a procedure to determine all the ancestors of a set of nodes in a DAG.

2.6 `WikiAdjSmall.mat` contains a random selection of 1000 Wiki authors, with a link between two authors if they 'know' each other (see `snap.stanford.edu/data/wiki-Vote.html`). Plot a histogram of the separation (the length of the path between two users on the graph corresponding to the adjacency matrix) between all users based on separations from 1 to 20. That is the bin $n(s)$ in the histogram contains the number of pairs with separation s.

2.7 The file `cliques.mat` contains a list of 100 non-maximal cliques defined on a graph of 10 nodes. Your task is to return a set of unique maximal cliques, eliminating cliques that are wholly contained within another. Once you have found a clique, you can represent it in binary form as, for example

$$(1110011110)$$

which says that this clique contains variables $1, 2, 3, 6, 7, 8, 9$, reading from left to right. Converting this binary representation to decimal (with the rightmost bit being the units and the leftmost 2^9) this corresponds to the number 926. Using this decimal representation, write the list of unique cliques, ordered from lowest decimal representation to highest. Describe fully the stages of the algorithm you use to find these unique cliques. Hint: you may find examining `uniquepots.m` useful.

2.8 Explain how to construct a graph with N nodes, where N is even, that contains at least $(N/2)^2$ maximal cliques.

2.9 Let N be divisible by 3. Construct a graph with N nodes by partitioning the nodes into $N/3$ subsets, each subset containing 3 nodes. Then connect all nodes, provided they are not in the same subset. Show that such a graph has $3^{N/3}$ maximal cliques. This shows that a graph can have an exponentially large number of maximal cliques [217].

3 Belief networks

We can now make a first connection between probability and graph theory. A belief network introduces structure into a probabilistic model by using graphs to represent independence assumptions among the variables. Probability operations such as marginalising and conditioning then correspond to simple operations on the graph, and details about the model can be 'read' from the graph. There is also a benefit in terms of computational efficiency. Belief networks cannot capture all possible relations among variables. However, they are natural for representing 'causal' relations, and they are a part of the family of graphical models we study further in Chapter 4.

3.1 The benefits of structure

It's tempting to think of feeding a mass of undigested data and probability distributions into a computer and getting back good predictions and useful insights in extremely complex environments. However, unfortunately, such a naive approach is likely to fail. The possible ways variables can interact is extremely large, so that without some sensible assumptions we are unlikely to make a useful model. Independently specifying all the entries of a table $p(x_1, \ldots, x_N)$ over binary variables x_i takes $O(2^N)$ space, which is impractical for more than a handful of variables. This is clearly infeasible in many machine learning and related application areas where we need to deal with distributions on potentially hundreds if not millions of variables. Structure is also important for computational tractability of inferring quantities of interest. Given a distribution on N binary variables, $p(x_1, \ldots, x_N)$, computing a marginal such as $p(x_1)$ requires summing over the 2^{N-1} states of the other variables. Even on the most optimistically fast supercomputer this would take far too long, even for an $N = 100$ variable system.

The only way to deal with such large distributions is to constrain the nature of the variable interactions in some manner, both to render specification and ultimately inference in such systems tractable. The key idea is to specify which variables are independent of others, leading to a structured factorisation of the joint probability distribution. For a distribution on a chain, $p(x_1, \ldots, x_{100}) = \prod_{i=1}^{99} \phi(x_i, x_{i+1})$, computing a marginal $p(x_1)$ can be computed in the blink of an eye on modern computers. Belief networks are a convenient framework for representing such independence assumptions. We will discuss belief networks more formally in Section 3.3, first discussing their natural role as 'causal' models.

Belief networks (also called Bayes' networks or Bayesian belief networks) are a way to depict the independence assumptions made in a distribution [161, 182]. Their application domain is widespread, ranging from troubleshooting [53] and expert reasoning under uncertainty to machine learning.

Before we more formally define a Belief Network (BN), an example will help motivate the development.[1]

3.1.1 Modelling independencies

One morning Tracey leaves her house and realises that her grass is wet. Is it due to overnight rain or did she forget to turn off the sprinkler last night? Next she notices that the grass of her neighbour, Jack, is also wet. This *explains away* to some extent the possibility that her sprinkler was left on, and she concludes therefore that it has probably been raining.

We can model the above situation by first defining the variables we wish to include in our model. In the above situation, the natural variables are

$R \in \{0, 1\}$ $R = 1$ means that it has been raining, and 0 otherwise
$S \in \{0, 1\}$ $S = 1$ means that Tracey has forgotten to turn off the sprinkler, and 0 otherwise
$J \in \{0, 1\}$ $J = 1$ means that Jack's grass is wet, and 0 otherwise
$T \in \{0, 1\}$ $T = 1$ means that Tracey's grass is wet, and 0 otherwise.

A model of Tracey's world then corresponds to a probability distribution on the joint set of the variables of interest $p(T, J, R, S)$ (the order of the variables is irrelevant).

Since each of the variables in this example can take one of two states, it would appear that we naively have to specify the values for each of the $2^4 = 16$ states, e.g. $p(T = 1, J = 0, R = 1, S = 1) = 0.7$ etc. However, since there are normalisation conditions for probabilities, we do not need to specify all the state probabilities. To see how many states need to be specified, consider the following decomposition. Without loss of generality and repeatedly using the definition of conditional probability, we may write

$$p(T, J, R, S) = p(T|J, R, S)p(J, R, S) \tag{3.1.1}$$
$$= p(T|J, R, S)p(J|R, S)p(R, S) \tag{3.1.2}$$
$$= p(T|J, R, S)p(J|R, S)p(R|S)p(S). \tag{3.1.3}$$

That is, we may write the joint distribution as a product of conditional distributions. The first term $p(T|J, R, S)$ requires us to specify $2^3 = 8$ values – we need $p(T = 1|J, R, S)$ for the 8 joint states of J, R, S. The other value $p(T = 0|J, R, S)$ is given by normalisation: $p(T = 0|J, R, S) = 1 - p(T = 1|J, R, S)$. Similarly, we need $4 + 2 + 1$ values for the other factors, making a total of 15 values in all. In general, for a distribution on n binary variables, we need to specify $2^n - 1$ values in the range $[0, 1]$. The important point here is that the number of values that need to be specified in general scales exponentially with the number of variables in the model – this is impractical in general and motivates simplifications.

Conditional independence

The modeller often knows constraints on the system. For example, in the scenario above, we may assume that Tracey's grass is wet depends only directly on whether or not is has been raining and whether or not her sprinkler was on. That is, we make a *conditional independence* assumption

$$p(T|J, R, S) = p(T|R, S) \tag{3.1.4}$$

[1] The scenario is adapted from [236].

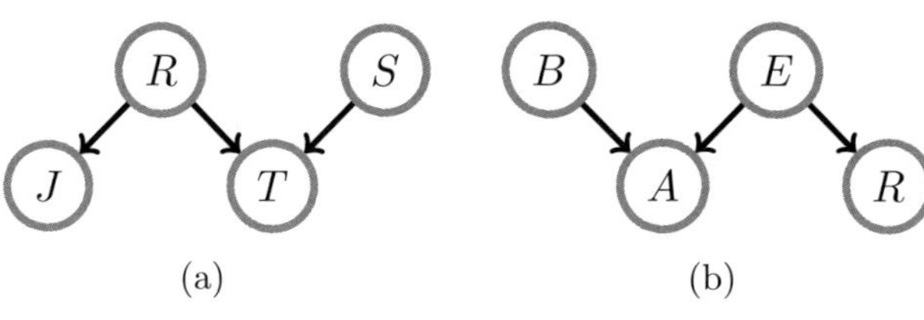

Figure 3.1 (**a**) Belief network structure for the 'wet grass' example. Each node in the graph represents a variable in the joint distribution, and the variables which feed in (the parents) to another variable represent which variables are to the right of the conditioning bar. (**b**) Belief network for the Burglar model.

Similarly, we assume that Jack's grass is wet is influenced only directly by whether or not it has been raining, and write

$$p(J|R, S) = p(J|R). \tag{3.1.5}$$

Furthermore, we assume the rain is not directly influenced by the sprinkler,

$$p(R|S) = p(R) \tag{3.1.6}$$

which means that our model equation now becomes

$$p(T, J, R, S) = p(T|R, S)p(J|R)p(R)p(S). \tag{3.1.7}$$

We can represent these conditional independencies graphically, as in Fig. 3.1(a). This reduces the number of values that we need to specify to $4 + 2 + 1 + 1 = 8$, a saving over the previous 15 values in the case where no conditional independencies had been assumed.

To complete the model, we need to numerically specify the values of each Conditional Probability Table (CPT). Let the prior probabilities for R and S be $p(R = 1) = 0.2$ and $p(S = 1) = 0.1$. We set the remaining probabilities to $p(J = 1|R = 1) = 1$, $p(J = 1|R = 0) = 0.2$ (sometimes Jack's grass is wet due to unknown effects, other than rain), $p(T = 1|R = 1, S = 0) = 1$, $p(T = 1|R = 1, S = 1) = 1$, $p(T = 1|R = 0, S = 1) = 0.9$ (there's a small chance that even though the sprinkler was left on, it didn't wet the grass noticeably), $p(T = 1|R = 0, S = 0) = 0$.

Inference

Now that we've made a model of an environment, we can perform inference. Let's calculate the probability that the sprinkler was on overnight, given that Tracey's grass is wet: $p(S = 1|T = 1)$. To do this we use:

$$p(S = 1|T = 1) = \frac{p(S = 1, T = 1)}{p(T = 1)} = \frac{\sum_{J,R} p(T = 1, J, R, S = 1)}{\sum_{J,R,S} p(T = 1, J, R, S)} \tag{3.1.8}$$

$$= \frac{\sum_{J,R} p(J|R)p(T = 1|R, S = 1)p(R)p(S = 1)}{\sum_{J,R,S} p(J|R)p(T = 1|R, S)p(R)p(S)} \tag{3.1.9}$$

$$= \frac{\sum_{R} p(T = 1|R, S = 1)p(R)p(S = 1)}{\sum_{R,S} p(T = 1|R, S)p(R)p(S)} \tag{3.1.10}$$

$$= \frac{0.9 \times 0.8 \times 0.1 + 1 \times 0.2 \times 0.1}{0.9 \times 0.8 \times 0.1 + 1 \times 0.2 \times 0.1 + 0 \times 0.8 \times 0.9 + 1 \times 0.2 \times 0.9} = 0.3382 \tag{3.1.11}$$

so the (posterior) belief that the sprinkler is on increases above the prior probability 0.1, due to the evidence that the grass is wet. Note that in Equation (3.1.9), the summation over J in the numerator is unity since, for any function $f(R)$, a summation of the form $\sum_J p(J|R)f(R)$ equals $f(R)$. This follows from the definition that a distribution $p(J|R)$ must sum to one, and the fact that $f(R)$ does not depend on J. A similar effect occurs for the summation over J in the denominator.

Let us now calculate the probability that Tracey's sprinkler was on overnight, given that her grass is wet and that Jack's grass is also wet, $p(S = 1|T = 1, J = 1)$. We use conditional probability again:

$$p(S = 1|T = 1, J = 1) = \frac{p(S = 1, T = 1, J = 1)}{p(T = 1, J = 1)} \tag{3.1.12}$$

$$= \frac{\sum_R p(T = 1, J = 1, R, S = 1)}{\sum_{R,S} p(T = 1, J = 1, R, S)} \tag{3.1.13}$$

$$= \frac{\sum_R p(J = 1|R)p(T = 1|R, S = 1)p(R)p(S = 1)}{\sum_{R,S} p(J = 1|R)p(T = 1|R, S)p(R)p(S)} \tag{3.1.14}$$

$$= \frac{0.0344}{0.2144} = 0.1604. \tag{3.1.15}$$

The probability that the sprinkler is on, given the extra evidence that Jack's grass is wet, is *lower* than the probability that the grass is wet given only that Tracey's grass is wet. This occurs since the fact that Jack's grass is also wet increases the chance that the rain has played a role in making Tracey's grass wet.

Naturally, we don't wish to carry out such inference calculations by hand all the time. General purpose algorithms exist for this, such as the junction tree algorithm, Chapter 6.

Example 3.1 Was it the burglar?

Here's another example using binary variables, adapted from [236]. Sally comes home to find that the burglar alarm is sounding ($A = 1$). Has she been burgled ($B = 1$), or was the alarm triggered by an earthquake ($E = 1$)? She turns the car radio on for news of earthquakes and finds that the radio broadcasts an earthquake alert ($R = 1$).

Using Bayes' rule, we can write, without loss of generality,

$$p(B, E, A, R) = p(A|B, E, R)p(B, E, R). \tag{3.1.16}$$

We can repeat this for $p(B, E, R)$, and continue

$$p(B, E, A, R) = p(A|B, E, R)p(R|B, E)p(E|B)p(B). \tag{3.1.17}$$

However, the alarm is surely not directly influenced by any report on the radio – that is, $p(A|B, E, R) = p(A|B, E)$. Similarly, we can make other conditional independence assumptions such that

$$p(B, E, A, R) = p(A|B, E)p(R|E)p(E)p(B) \tag{3.1.18}$$

as depicted in Fig. 3.1(b).

Specifying conditional probability tables

Alarm = 1	Burglar	Earthquake
0.9999	1	1
0.99	1	0
0.99	0	1
0.0001	0	0

Radio = 1	Earthquake
1	1
0	0

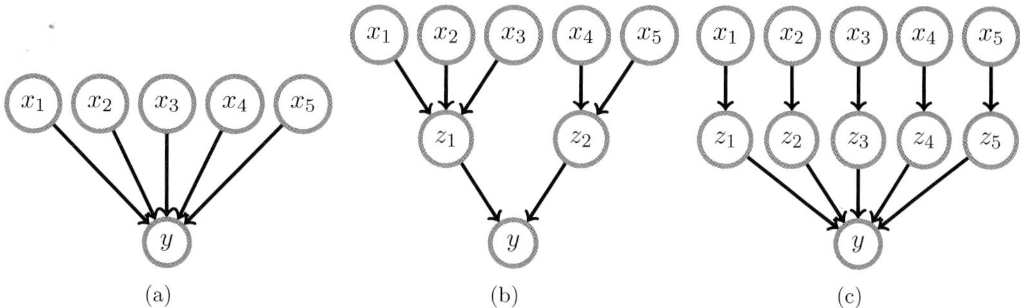

Figure 3.2 (**a**) If all variables are binary $2^5 = 32$ states are required to specify $p(y|x_1, \ldots, x_5)$. (**b**) Here only 16 states are required. (**c**) Noisy logic gates.

The remaining tables are $p(B = 1) = 0.01$ and $p(E = 1) = 0.000\,001$. The tables and graphical structure fully specify the distribution. Now consider what happens as we observe evidence.

Initial evidence: the alarm is sounding

$$p(B = 1|A = 1) = \frac{\sum_{E,R} p(B = 1, E, A = 1, R)}{\sum_{B,E,R} p(B, E, A = 1, R)} \tag{3.1.19}$$

$$= \frac{\sum_{E,R} p(A = 1|B = 1, E)p(B = 1)p(E)p(R|E)}{\sum_{B,E,R} p(A = 1|B, E)p(B)p(E)p(R|E)} \approx 0.99. \tag{3.1.20}$$

Additional evidence: the radio broadcasts an earthquake warning: A similar calculation gives $p(B = 1|A = 1, R = 1) \approx 0.01$. Thus, initially, because the alarm sounds, Sally thinks that she's been burgled. However, this probability drops dramatically when she hears that there has been an earthquake. That is, the earthquake 'explains away' to an extent the fact that the alarm is ringing. See `demoBurglar.m`.

Remark 3.1 (Causal intuitions) Belief networks as we've defined them are ways to express independence statements. Nevertheless, in expressing these independencies it can be useful (though also potentially misleading) to think of 'what causes what'. In Example 3.1 we chose the ordering of the variables as (reading from right to left) B, E, R, A in Equation (3.1.17) since B and E can be considered root 'causes' and A and R as 'effects'.

3.1.2 Reducing the burden of specification

Consider a discrete variable y with many discrete parental variables $x_1, \ldots, x_n$, Fig. 3.2(a). Formally, the structure of the graph implies nothing about the form of the parameterisation of the table $p(y|x_1, \ldots, x_n)$. If each parent x_i has $\dim(x_i)$ states, and there is no constraint on the table, then the table $p(y|x_1, \ldots, x_n)$ contains $(\dim(y) - 1) \prod_i \dim(x_i)$ entries. If stored explicitly for each state, this would require potentially huge storage. An alternative is to constrain the table to have a simpler parametric form. For example, one might write a decomposition in which only a limited number of parental interactions are required (this is called *divorcing parents* in [161]). For example, in Fig. 3.2(b), we have

$$p(y|x_1, \ldots, x_5) = \sum_{z_1,z_2} p(y|z_1, z_2)p(z_1|x_1, x_2, x_3)p(z_2|x_4, x_5). \tag{3.1.21}$$

Assuming all variables are binary, the number of states requiring specification is $2^3 + 2^2 + 2^2 = 16$, compared to the $2^5 = 32$ states in the unconstrained case.

Logic gates

Another technique to constrain tables uses simple classes of conditional tables. For example, in Fig. 3.2(c), one could use a logical OR gate on binary z_i, say

$$p(y|z_1, \ldots, z_5) = \begin{cases} 1 & \text{if at least one of the } z_i \text{ is in state 1} \\ 0 & \text{otherwise.} \end{cases} \tag{3.1.22}$$

We can then make a table $p(y|x_1, \ldots, x_5)$ by including the additional terms $p(z_i = 1|x_i)$. When each x_i is binary there are in total only $2 + 2 + 2 + 2 + 2 = 10$ quantities required for specifying $p(y|x)$. In this case, Fig. 3.2(c) can be used to represent any *noisy logic gate*, such as the *noisy OR* or *noisy AND*, where the number of parameters required to specify the noisy gate is linear in the number of parents.

The noisy-OR is particularly common in disease–symptom networks in which many diseases x can give rise to the same symptom y – provided that at least one of the diseases is present, the probability that the symptom will be present is high.

3.2 Uncertain and unreliable evidence

In the following we make a distinction between evidence that is uncertain, and evidence that is unreliable.

3.2.1 Uncertain evidence

In soft or *uncertain evidence*, the evidence variable is in more than one state, with the strength of our belief about each state being given by probabilities. For example, if x has the states dom $(x) = \{\text{red, blue, green}\}$ the vector $(0.6, 0.1, 0.3)$ represents the belief in the respective states. In contrast, for *hard-evidence* we are certain that a variable is in a particular state. In this case, all the probability mass is in one of the vector components, for example $(0, 0, 1)$.

Performing inference with soft-evidence is straightforward and can be achieved using Bayes' rule. For example, for a model $p(x, y)$, consider that we have some soft-evidence $\tilde{y}$ about the variable y, and wish to know what effect this has on the variable x – that is we wish to compute $p(x|\tilde{y})$. From Bayes' rule, and the assumption $p(x|y, \tilde{y}) = p(x|y)$, we have

$$p(x|\tilde{y}) = \sum_y p(x, y|\tilde{y}) = \sum_y p(x|y, \tilde{y})p(y|\tilde{y}) = \sum_y p(x|y)p(y|\tilde{y}) \tag{3.2.1}$$

where $p(y = \text{i}|\tilde{y})$ represents the probability that y is in state i under the soft-evidence. This is a generalisation of hard-evidence in which the vector $p(y|\tilde{y})$ has all zero component values, except for all but a single component. This procedure in which we first define the model conditioned on the evidence, and then average over the distribution of the evidence is also known as Jeffrey's rule.

In the BN we use a dashed circle to represent that a variable is in a soft-evidence state.

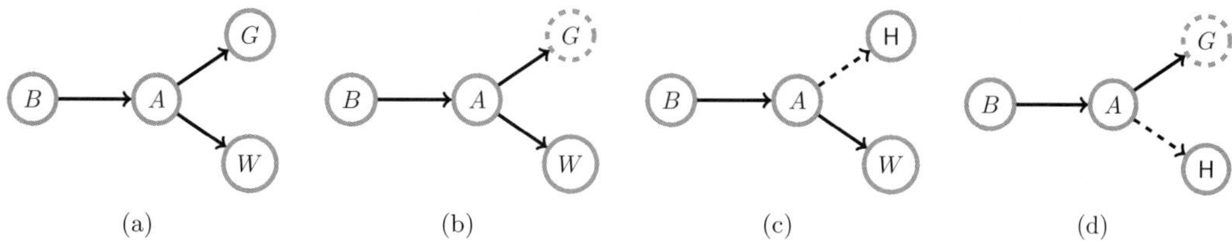

Figure 3.3 (**a**) Mr Holmes' burglary worries as given in [236]: (B)urglar, (A)larm, (W)atson, Mrs (G)ibbon. (**b**) Mrs Gibbon's uncertain evidence represented by a dashed circle. (**c**) Virtual evidence or the replacement of unreliable evidence can be represented by a dashed line. (**d**) Mrs Gibbon is uncertain in her evidence. Holmes also replaces the unreliable Watson with his own interpretation.

Example 3.2 Soft-evidence

Revisiting the burglar scenario, Example 3.1, imagine that we are only 70 per cent sure we heard the burglar alarm sounding. For this binary variable case we represent this soft-evidence for the states $(1, 0)$ as $\tilde{A} = (0.7, 0.3)$. What is the probability of a burglary under this soft-evidence?

$$p(B = 1|\tilde{A}) = \sum_{A} p(B = 1|A)p(A|\tilde{A}) = p(B = 1|A = 1) \times 0.7 + p(B = 1|A = 0) \times 0.3. \tag{3.2.2}$$

The probabilities $p(B = 1|A = 1) \approx 0.99$ and $p(B = 1|A = 0) \approx 0.0001$ are calculated using Bayes' rule as before to give

$$p(B = 1|\tilde{A}) \approx 0.6930. \tag{3.2.3}$$

This is lower than 0.99, the probability of having been burgled when we are sure we heard the alarm.

Holmes, Watson and Mrs Gibbon

An entertaining example of uncertain evidence is given by Pearl [236] that we adapt for our purposes here. The environment contains four variables:

$B \in \{\text{tr}, \text{fa}\}$	$B = \text{tr}$ means that Holmes' house has been burgled
$A \in \{\text{tr}, \text{fa}\}$	$A = \text{tr}$ means that Holmes' house alarm went off
$W \in \{\text{tr}, \text{fa}\}$	$W = \text{tr}$ means that Watson heard the alarm
$G \in \{\text{tr}, \text{fa}\}$	$G = \text{tr}$ means that Mrs Gibbon heard the alarm.

The BN below for this scenario is depicted in Fig. 3.3(a)

$$p(B, A, G, W) = p(A|B)p(B)p(W|A)p(G|A). \tag{3.2.4}$$

Watson states that he heard the alarm is sounding. Mrs Gibbon is a little deaf and cannot be sure herself that she heard the alarm, being 80 per cent sure she heard it. This can be dealt with using the soft-evidence technique, Fig. 3.3(b). From Jeffrey's rule, one uses the original model

Equation (3.2.4) to first compute the model conditioned on the evidence

$$p(B = \text{tr}|W = \text{tr}, G) = \frac{p(B = \text{tr}, W = \text{tr}, G)}{p(W = \text{tr}, G)}$$
$$= \frac{\sum_A p(G|A)p(W = \text{tr}|A)p(A|B = \text{tr})p(B = \text{tr})}{\sum_{B,A} p(G|A)p(W = \text{tr}|A)p(A|B)p(B)} \quad (3.2.5)$$

and then uses the soft-evidence

$$p(G|\tilde{G}) = \begin{cases} 0.8 & G = \text{tr} \\ 0.2 & G = \text{fa} \end{cases} \quad (3.2.6)$$

to compute

$$p(B = \text{tr}|W = \text{tr}, \tilde{G}) = p(B = \text{tr}|W = \text{tr}, G = \text{tr})p(G = \text{tr}|\tilde{G}) + p(B = \text{tr}|W = \text{tr}, G = \text{fa})p(G = \text{fa}|\tilde{G}). \quad (3.2.7)$$

A full calculation requires us to numerically specify all the terms in Equation (3.2.4); see for example Exercise 3.8.

3.2.2 Unreliable evidence

Holmes telephones Mrs Gibbon and realises that he doesn't trust her evidence (he suspects that she's been drinking) and he believes that, based on his interpretation of Mrs Gibbon's evidence, there is an 80 per cent chance that the alarm sounded. Note that this is not the same as Mrs Gibbon being 80 per cent sure herself that she heard the alarm – this would be soft-evidence whose effect on our calculations would also contain the term $p(G|A)$, as in Equation (3.2.5). Holmes rather wishes to discard all of this and simply replace it with his own interpretation of events. Mr Holmes can achieve this by replacing the term $p(G|A)$ by a so-called *virtual evidence* term

$$p(G|A) \rightarrow p(\mathsf{H}|A), \qquad \text{where} \quad p(\mathsf{H}|A) = \begin{cases} 0.8 & A = \text{tr} \\ 0.2 & A = \text{fa} \end{cases}. \quad (3.2.8)$$

Here the state H is arbitrary and fixed. This is used to modify the joint distribution to

$$p(B, A, \mathsf{H}, W) = p(A|B)p(B)p(W|A)p(\mathsf{H}|A), \quad (3.2.9)$$

see Fig. 3.3(c). When we then compute $p(B = \text{tr}|W = \text{tr}, \mathsf{H})$ the effect of Mr Holmes' judgement will count for a factor of four times more in favour of the alarm sounding than not. The values of the table entries are irrelevant up to normalisation since any constants can be absorbed into the proportionality constant. Note also that $p(\mathsf{H}|A)$ is not a distribution in A, and hence no normalisation is required. This form of evidence is also called *likelihood evidence*.

Uncertain and unreliable evidence

To demonstrate how to combine such effects as unreliable and uncertain evidence, consider the situation in which Mrs Gibbon is uncertain in her evidence, and Mr Holmes feels that Watson's evidence is unreliable and wishes to replaces it with his own interpretation, see Fig. 3.3(d). To account for this we first deal with the unreliable evidence

$$p(B, A, W, G) \rightarrow p(B, A, \mathsf{H}, G) = p(B)p(A|B)p(G|A)p(\mathsf{H}|A). \quad (3.2.10)$$

Using this modified model, we can now use Jeffrey's rule to compute the model conditioned on the evidence

$$p(B, A|\mathsf{H}, G) = \frac{p(B)p(A|B)p(G|A)p(\mathsf{H}|A)}{\sum_{A,B} p(B)p(A|B)p(G|A)p(\mathsf{H}|A)}. \tag{3.2.11}$$

We now include the uncertain evidence $\tilde{G}$ to form the final model

$$p(B, A|\mathsf{H}, \tilde{G}) = \sum_{G} p(B, A|\mathsf{H}, G)p(G|\tilde{G}) \tag{3.2.12}$$

from which we may compute the marginal $p(B|\mathsf{H}, \tilde{G})$

$$p(B|\mathsf{H}, \tilde{G}) = \sum_{A} p(B, A|\mathsf{H}, \tilde{G}). \tag{3.2.13}$$

3.3 Belief networks

Definition 3.1 Belief network A belief network is a distribution of the form

$$p(x_1, \ldots, x_D) = \prod_{i=1}^{D} p(x_i|\text{pa}(x_i)) \tag{3.3.1}$$

where pa (x_i) represent the *parental* variables of variable x_i. Represented as a directed graph, with an arrow pointing from a parent variable to child variable, a belief network corresponds to a Directed Acyclic Graph (DAG), with the ith node in the graph corresponding to the factor $p(x_i|\text{pa}(x_i))$.

Remark 3.2 (Graphs and distributions) A somewhat subtle point is whether or not a belief network corresponds to a specific instance of a distribution (as given in Definition 3.1) requiring also the numerical specification of the conditional probability tables, or whether or not it refers to any distribution which is consistent with the specified structure. In this one can potentially distinguish between a belief network distribution (containing a numerical specification) and a belief network graph (which contains no numerical specification). Normally this issue will not arise much throughout the book, but is potentially important in clarifying the scope of independence/dependence statements.

In the Wet Grass and Burglar examples, we had a choice as to how we recursively used Bayes' rule. In a general four-variable case we could choose the factorisation,

$$p(x_1, x_2, x_3, x_4) = p(x_1|x_2, x_3, x_4)p(x_2|x_3, x_4)p(x_3|x_4)p(x_4). \tag{3.3.2}$$

An equally valid choice is (see Fig. 3.4)

$$p(x_1, x_2, x_3, x_4) = p(x_3|x_4, x_1, x_2)p(x_4|x_1, x_2)p(x_1|x_2)p(x_2). \tag{3.3.3}$$

In general, two different graphs may represent the same independence assumptions, as we will discuss further in Section 3.3.1. If one wishes to make independence assumptions, then the choice of factorisation becomes significant.

The observation that any distribution may be written in the *cascade* form, Fig. 3.4, gives an algorithm for constructing a BN on variables $x_1, \ldots, x_n$: write down the n-node cascade graph; label the nodes with the variables in any order; now each successive independence statement corresponds

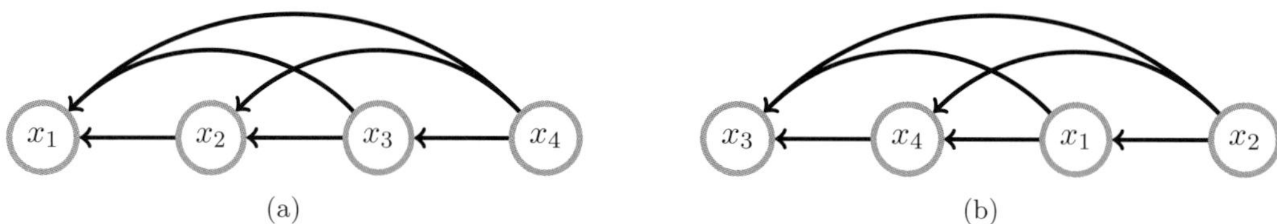

Figure 3.4 Two BNs for a four-variable distribution. Both graphs (a) and (b) represent the *same* distribution $p(x_1, x_2, x_3, x_4)$. Strictly speaking they represent the same (lack of) independence assumptions – the graphs say nothing about the content of the tables. The extension of this 'cascade' to many variables is clear and always results in a directed acyclic graph.

to deleting one of the edges. More formally, this corresponds to an ordering of the variables which, without loss of generality, we may write as $x_1, \ldots, x_n$. Then, from Bayes' rule, we have

$$p(x_1, \ldots, x_n) = p(x_1|x_2, \ldots, x_n)p(x_2, \ldots, x_n) \tag{3.3.4}$$

$$= p(x_1|x_2, \ldots, x_n)p(x_2|x_3, \ldots, x_n)p(x_3, \ldots, x_n) \tag{3.3.5}$$

$$= p(x_n)\prod_{i=1}^{n-1} p(x_i|x_{i+1}, \ldots, x_n). \tag{3.3.6}$$

The representation of any BN is therefore a *directed acyclic graph*.

Every probability distribution can be written as a BN, even though it may correspond to a fully connected 'cascade' DAG. The particular role of a BN is that the structure of the DAG corresponds to a set of conditional independence assumptions, namely which ancestral parental variables are sufficient to specify each conditional probability table. Note that this does not mean that non-parental variables have no influence. For example, for distribution $p(x_1|x_2)p(x_2|x_3)p(x_3)$ with DAG $x_1 \leftarrow x_2 \leftarrow x_3$, this does not imply $p(x_2|x_1, x_3) = p(x_2|x_3)$. The DAG specifies conditional independence statements of variables on their ancestors – namely which ancestors are direct 'causes' for the variable. The 'effects', given by the descendants of the variable, will generally be dependent on the variable. See also Remark 3.3.

Remark 3.3 (Dependencies and the Markov blanket) Consider a distribution on a set of variables $\mathcal{X}$. For a variable $x_i \in \mathcal{X}$ and corresponding belief network represented by a DAG G, let $MB(x_i)$ be the variables in the Markov blanket of x_i. Then for any other variable y that is also not in the Markov blanket of x_i ($y \in \mathcal{X} \backslash \{x_i \cup MB(x_i)\}$), then $x_i \perp\!\!\!\perp y | MB(x_i)$. That is, the Markov blanket of x_i carries all information about x_i. As an example, for Fig. 3.2(b), $MB(z_1) = \{x_1, x_2, x_3, y, z_2\}$ and $z_1 \perp\!\!\!\perp x_4 | MB(z_1)$.

The DAG corresponds to a statement of conditional independencies in the model. To complete the specification of the BN we need to define all elements of the conditional probability tables $p(x_i|\text{pa}(x_i))$. Once the graphical structure is defined, the entries of the Conditional Probability Tables (CPTs) $p(x_i|\text{pa}(x_i))$ can be expressed. For every possible state of the parental variables $\text{pa}(x_i)$, a value for each of the states of x_i needs to be specified (except one, since this is determined by normalisation). For a large number of parents, writing out a table of values is intractable, and the tables are usually parameterised in a low-dimensional manner. This will be a central topic of our discussion on the application of BNs in machine learning.

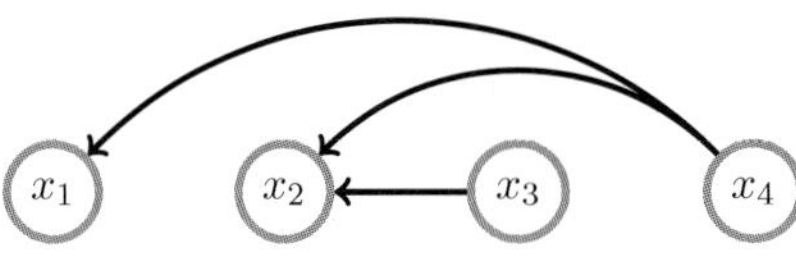

Figure 3.5 $p(x_1, x_2, x_3, x_4) = p(x_1|x_4)p(x_2|x_3, x_4)p(x_3)p(x_4)$.

3.3.1 Conditional independence

Whilst a BN corresponds to a set of conditional independence assumptions, it is not always immediately clear from the DAG whether a set of variables is conditionally independent of a set of other variables (see Definition 1.7). For example, in Fig. 3.5 are x_1 and x_2 independent, given the state of x_4? The answer is yes, since we have

$$p(x_1, x_2|x_4) = \frac{1}{p(x_4)} \sum_{x_3} p(x_1, x_2, x_3, x_4) = \frac{1}{p(x_4)} \sum_{x_3} p(x_1|x_4)p(x_2|x_3, x_4)p(x_3)p(x_4) \tag{3.3.7}$$

$$= p(x_1|x_4) \sum_{x_3} p(x_2|x_3, x_4)p(x_3). \tag{3.3.8}$$

Now

$$p(x_2|x_4) = \frac{1}{p(x_4)} \sum_{x_1, x_3} p(x_1, x_2, x_3, x_4) = \frac{1}{p(x_4)} \sum_{x_1, x_3} p(x_1|x_4)p(x_2|x_3, x_4)p(x_3)p(x_4) \tag{3.3.9}$$

$$= \sum_{x_3} p(x_2|x_3, x_4)p(x_3). \tag{3.3.10}$$

Combining the two results above we have

$$p(x_1, x_2|x_4) = p(x_1|x_4)p(x_2|x_4) \tag{3.3.11}$$

so that x_1 and x_2 are indeed independent conditioned on x_4.

We would like to have a general algorithm that will allow us to avoid doing such tedious manipulations by reading the result directly from the graph. To help develop intuition towards constructing such an algorithm, consider the three-variable distribution $p(x_1, x_2, x_3)$. We may write this in any of the six ways

$$p(x_1, x_2, x_3) = p(x_{i_1}|x_{i_2}, x_{i_3})p(x_{i_2}|x_{i_3})p(x_{i_3}) \tag{3.3.12}$$

where (i_1, i_2, i_3) is any of the six permutations of $(1, 2, 3)$. Whilst each factorisation produces a different DAG, all represent the same distribution, namely one that makes no independence statements. If the DAGs are of the cascade form, no independence assumptions have been made. The minimal independence assumptions then correspond to dropping a single link in the cascade graph. This gives rise to the four DAGs in Fig. 3.6. Are any of these graphs equivalent, in the sense that they represent the same distribution? Applying Bayes' rule gives:

$$\underbrace{p(x_2|x_3)p(x_3|x_1)p(x_1)}_{graph(c)} = p(x_2, x_3)p(x_3, x_1)/p(x_3) = p(x_1|x_3)p(x_2, x_3) \tag{3.3.13}$$

$$= \underbrace{p(x_1|x_3)p(x_3|x_2)p(x_2)}_{graph(d)} = \underbrace{p(x_1|x_3)p(x_2|x_3)p(x_3)}_{graph(b)} \tag{3.3.14}$$

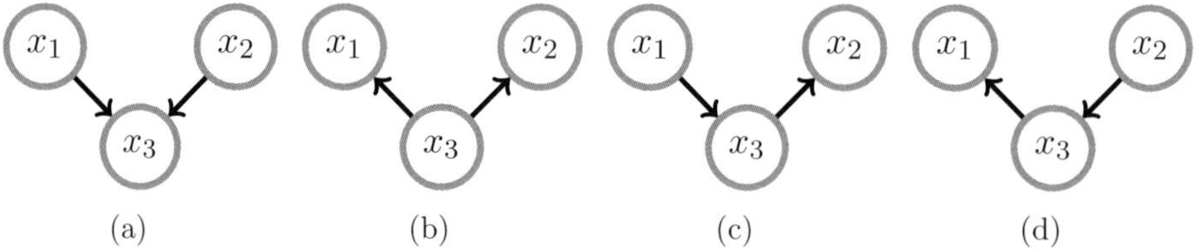

Figure 3.6 By dropping say the connection between variables x_1 and x_2, we reduce the six possible BN graphs amongst three variables to four. (The six fully connected 'cascade' graphs correspond to (a) with $x_1 \to x_2$, (a) with $x_2 \to x_1$, (b) with $x_1 \to x_2$, (b) with $x_2 \to x_1$, (c) with $x_1 \to x_3$ and (d) with $x_2 \to x_1$. Any other graphs would be cyclic and therefore not distributions.)

so that DAGs (b), (c) and (d) represent the same conditional independence (CI) assumptions – given the state of variable x_3, variables x_1 and x_2 are independent, $x_1 \perp\!\!\!\perp x_2 | x_3$.

However, graph (a) represents something fundamentally different, namely: $p(x_1, x_2) = p(x_1)p(x_2)$. There is no way to transform the distribution $p(x_3|x_1, x_2)p(x_1)p(x_2)$ into any of the others.

Remark 3.4 (Graphical dependence) Belief network (graphs) are good for encoding conditional independence but are not well suited for encoding dependence. For example, consider the graph $a \to b$. This may appear to encode the relation that a and b are dependent. However, a specific numerical instance of a belief network distribution could be such that $p(b|a) = p(b)$, for which $a \perp\!\!\!\perp b$. The lesson is that even when the DAG appears to show 'graphical' dependence, there can be instances of the distributions for which dependence does not follow. The same caveat holds for Markov networks, Section 4.2. We discuss this issue in more depth in Section 3.3.5.

3.3.2 The impact of collisions

Definition 3.2 Given a path $\mathcal{P}$, a collider is a node c on $\mathcal{P}$ with neighbours a and b on $\mathcal{P}$ such that $a \to c \leftarrow b$. Note that a collider is path specific, see Fig. 3.8.

In a general BN, how can we check if $x \perp\!\!\!\perp y | z$? In Fig. 3.7(a), x and y are independent when conditioned on z since

$$p(x, y|z) = p(x|z)p(y|z). \tag{3.3.15}$$

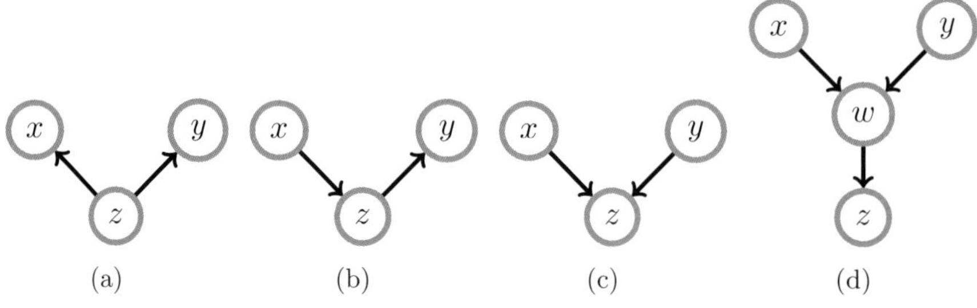

Figure 3.7 In graphs (a) and (b), variable z is not a collider. **(c)** Variable z is a collider. Graphs (a) and (b) represent conditional independence $x \perp\!\!\!\perp y | z$. In graphs (c) and (d), x and y are 'graphically' conditionally dependent given variable z.

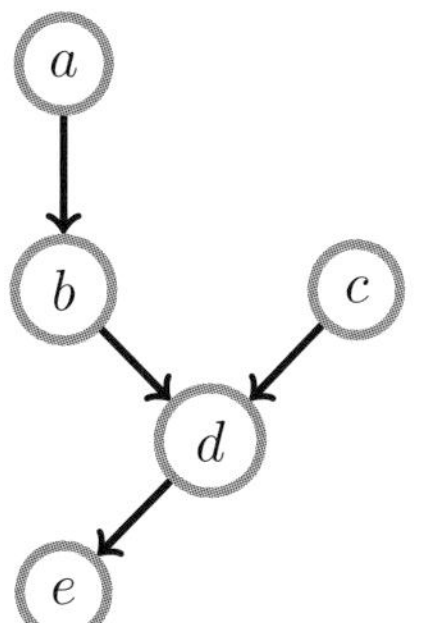

(**a**) The variable d is a collider along the path $a - b - d - c$, but not along the path $a - b - d - e$. Is $a \perp\!\!\!\perp e \,|\, b$? Variables a and e are *not* d-connected since there are no colliders on the only path between a and e, and since there is a non-collider b which is in the conditioning set. Hence a and e are d-separated by b, $\Rightarrow a \perp\!\!\!\perp e \,|\, b$.

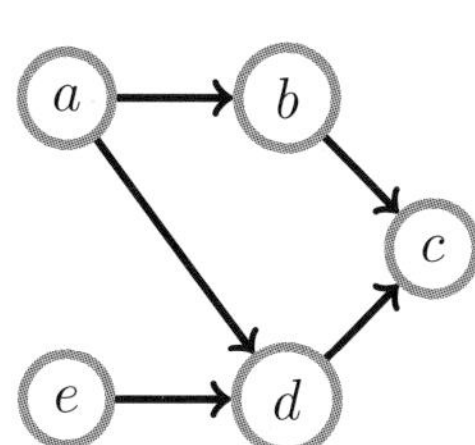

(**b**) The variable d is a collider along the path $a - d - e$, but not along the path $a - b - c - d - e$. Is $a \perp\!\!\!\perp e \,|\, c$? There are two paths between a and e, namely $a - d - e$ and $a - b - c - d - e$. The path $a - d - e$ is not blocked since although d is a collider on this path and d is not in the conditioning set, we have a descendant of the collider d in the conditioning set, namely c. For the path $a - b - c - d - e$, the node c is a collider on this path and c is in the conditioning set. For this path d is not a collider. Hence this path is not blocked and a and e are (graphically) dependent given c.

Figure 3.8 Collider examples for d-separation and d-connection.

Similarly, for Fig. 3.7(b), x and y are independent conditioned on z.

$$p(x, y|z) \propto p(z|x)p(x)p(y|z) \tag{3.3.16}$$

which is a function of x multiplied by a function of y. In Fig. 3.7(c), however, x and y are graphically dependent since $p(x, y|z) \propto p(z|x, y)p(x)p(y)$; in this situation, variable z is called a *collider* – the arrows of its neighbours are pointing towards it. What about Fig. 3.7(d)? In (d), when we condition on z, x and y will be graphically dependent, since

$$p(x, y|z) = \frac{p(x, y, z)}{p(z)} = \frac{1}{p(z)} \sum_w p(z|w)p(w|x, y)p(x)p(y) \neq p(x|z)p(y|z) \tag{3.3.17}$$

– intuitively, variable w becomes dependent on the value of z, and since x and y are conditionally dependent on w, they are also conditionally dependent on z.

If there is a non-collider z which is conditioned along the path between x and y (as in Fig. 3.7(a,b)), then this path cannot induce dependence between x and y. Similarly, if there is a path between x and y which contains a collider, provided that this collider is not in the conditioning set (and neither are any of its descendants) then this path does not make x and y dependent. If there is a path between x and y which contains no colliders and no conditioning variables, then this path 'd-connects' x and y. Note that a collider is defined *relative to a path*. In Fig. 3.8(a), the variable d is a collider along the path $a - b - d - c$, but not along the path $a - b - d - e$ (since, relative to this path, the two arrows do not point inwards to d).

Consider the BN: $A \to B \leftarrow C$. Here A and C are (unconditionally) independent. However, conditioning of B makes them 'graphically' dependent. Intuitively, whilst we believe the root causes are independent, given the value of the observation, this tells us something about the state of *both* the causes, coupling them and making them (generally) dependent. In Definition 3.3 below we describe the effect that conditioning/marginalisation has on the graph of the remaining variables.

Definition 3.3 Some properties of belief networks It is useful to understand what effect conditioning or marginalising a variable has on a belief network. We state here how these operations effect the remaining variables in the graph and use this intuition to develop a more complete description in Section 3.3.4.

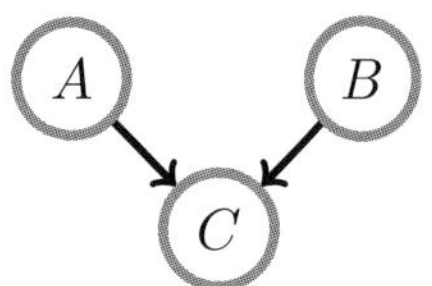

$$p(A, B, C) = p(C|A, B)p(A)p(B) \tag{3.3.18}$$

From a 'causal' perspective, this models the 'causes' A and B as a priori independent, both determining the effect C.

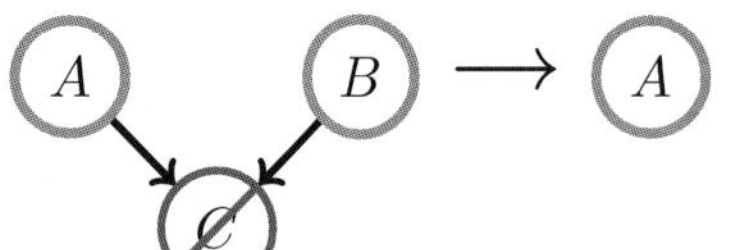

Marginalising over C makes A and B independent. A and B are (unconditionally) independent: $p(A, B) = p(A)p(B)$. In the absence of any information about the effect C, we retain this belief.

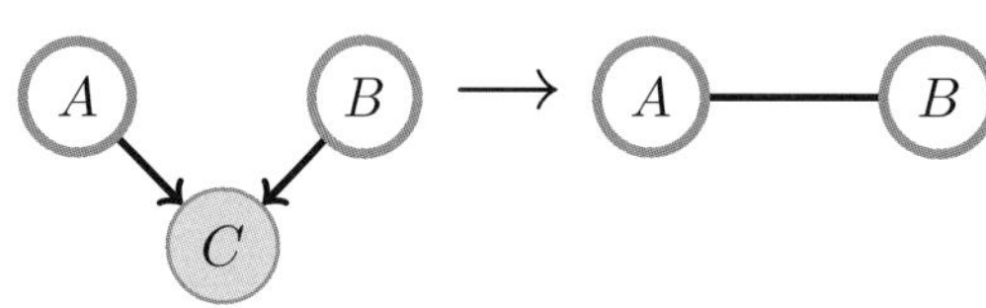

Conditioning on C makes A and B (graphically) dependent – in general $p(A, B|C) \neq p(A|C)p(B|C)$. Although the causes are a priori independent, knowing the effect C in general tells us something about how the causes colluded to bring about the effect observed.

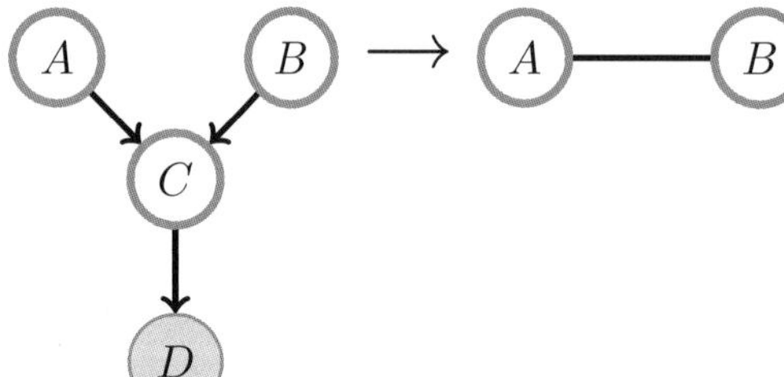

Conditioning on D, a descendent of a collider C, makes A and B (graphically) dependent – in general $p(A, B|D) \neq p(A|D)p(B|D)$.

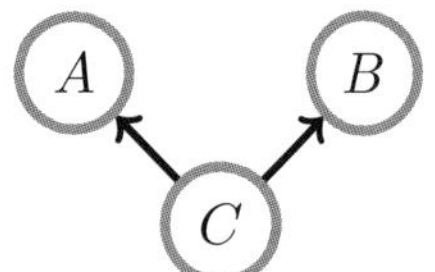

$$p(A, B, C) = p(A|C)p(B|C)p(C) \tag{3.3.19}$$

Here there is a 'cause' C and independent 'effects' A and B.

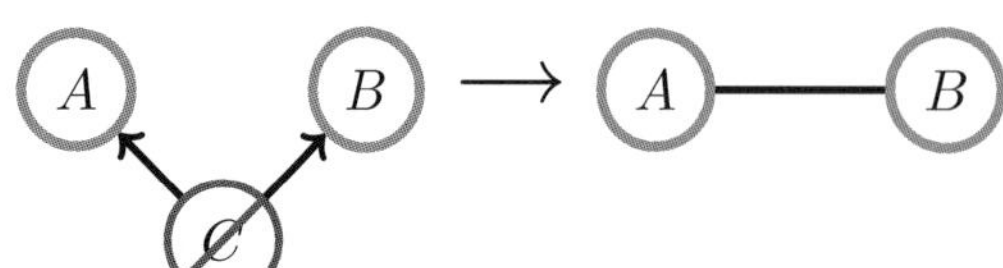

Marginalising over C makes A and B (graphically) dependent. In general, $p(A, B) \neq p(A)p(B)$. Although we don't know the 'cause', the 'effects' will nevertheless be dependent.

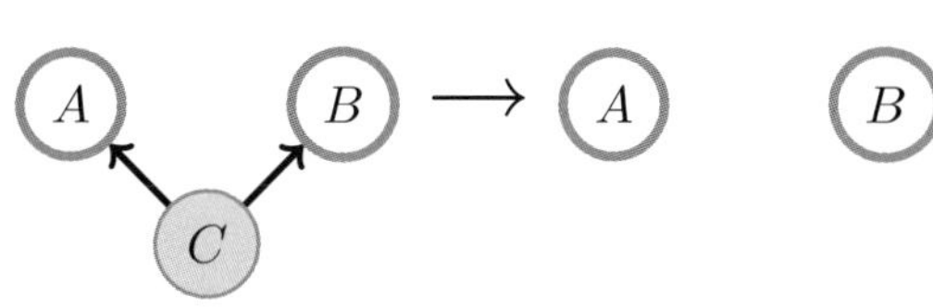

Conditioning on C makes A and B independent: $p(A, B|C) = p(A|C)p(B|C)$. If you know the 'cause' C, you know everything about how each effect occurs, independent of the other effect. This is also true for reversing the arrow from A to C – in this case A would 'cause' C and then C 'cause' B. Conditioning on C blocks the ability of A to influence B.

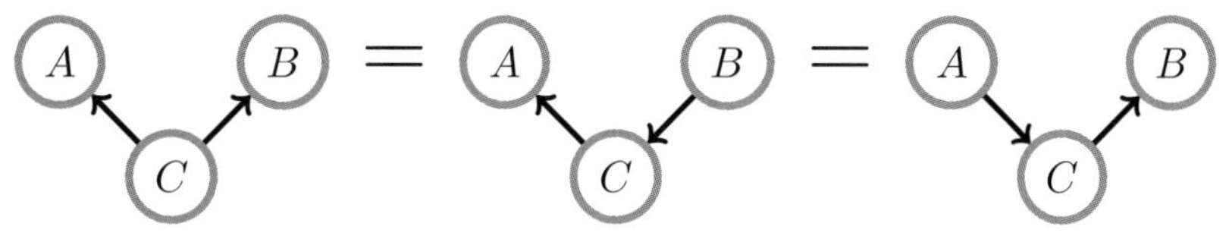

These graphs all express the same conditional independence assumptions.

3.3.3 Graphical path manipulations for independence

Intuitively, we now have all the tools we need to understand when x is independent of y conditioned on z. Examining the rules in Definition 3.3, we need to look at each path between x and y. Colouring x as dark grey, y as mid grey and the conditioning node z as light grey, we need to examine each path between x and y and adjust the edges, following the intuitive rules in Fig. 3.9.

3.3.4 d-separation

The above description is intuitive. A more formal treatment that is amenable to computational implementation is straightforward to obtain from these intuitions. First we define the DAG concepts of d-separation and d-connection that are central to determining conditional independence in any BN with structure given by the DAG [304].

Definition 3.4 d-connection, d-separation If G is a directed graph in which $\mathcal{X}$, $\mathcal{Y}$ and $\mathcal{Z}$ are disjoint sets of vertices, then $\mathcal{X}$ and $\mathcal{Y}$ are d-connected by $\mathcal{Z}$ in G if and only if there exists an undirected path U between some vertex in $\mathcal{X}$ and some vertex in $\mathcal{Y}$ such that for every collider C on U, either C or a descendant of C is in $\mathcal{Z}$, and no non-collider on U is in $\mathcal{Z}$.

$\mathcal{X}$ and $\mathcal{Y}$ are d-separated by $\mathcal{Z}$ in G if and only if they are not d-connected by $\mathcal{Z}$ in G.

One may also phrase this as follows. For every variable $x \in \mathcal{X}$ and $y \in \mathcal{Y}$, check every path U between x and y. A path U is said to be *blocked* if there is a node w on U such that either

1. w is a collider and neither w nor any of its descendants is in $\mathcal{Z}$, or
2. w is not a collider on U and w is in $\mathcal{Z}$.

If all such paths are blocked then $\mathcal{X}$ and $\mathcal{Y}$ are d-separated by $\mathcal{Z}$. If the variable sets $\mathcal{X}$ and $\mathcal{Y}$ are d-separated by $\mathcal{Z}$, they are independent conditional on $\mathcal{Z}$ in all probability distributions such a graph can represent.

If z is a collider (bottom path) keep undirected links between the neighbours of the collider.

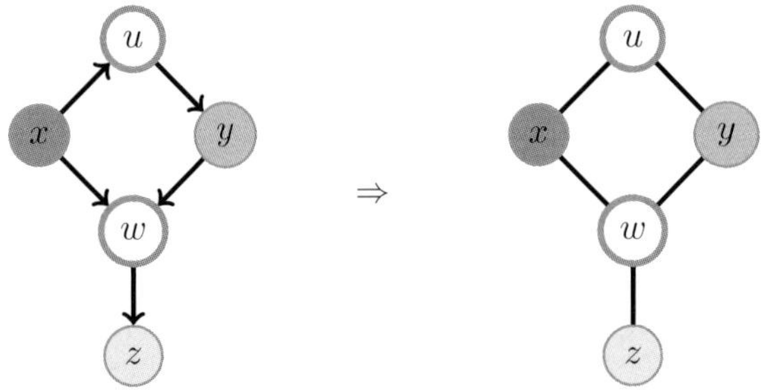

If z is a descendant of a collider, this could induce dependence so we retain the links (making them undirected).

If there is a collider not in the conditioning set (upper path) we cut the links to the collider variable. In this case the upper path between x and y is 'blocked'.

If there is a non-collider which is in the conditioning set (bottom path), we cut the link between the neighbours of this non-collider which cannot induce dependence between x and y. The bottom path is 'blocked'.

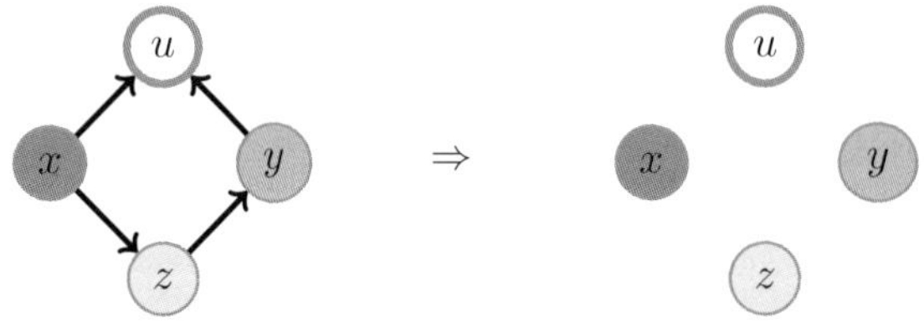

In this case, neither path contributes to dependence and hence $x \perp\!\!\!\perp y | z$. Both paths are 'blocked'.

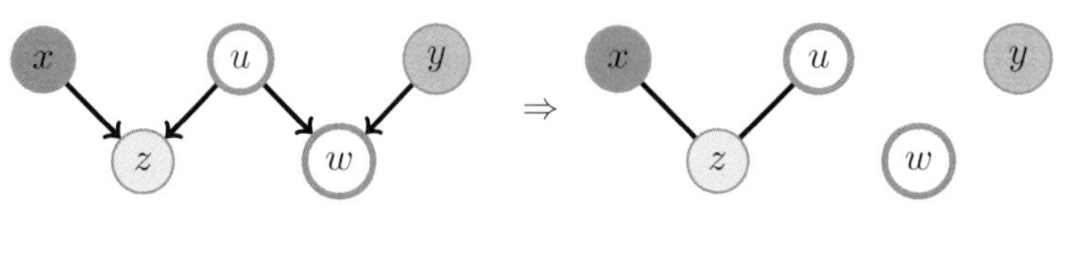

Whilst z is a collider in the conditioning set, w is a collider that is not in the conditioning set. This means that there is no path between x and y, and hence x and y are independent given z.

Figure 3.9 Graphical manipulations to determine independence $x \perp\!\!\!\perp y | z$. After these manipulations, if there is no undirected path between x and y, then x and y are independent, conditioned on z. Note that the graphical rules here differ from those in Definition 3.3 which considered the effect on the graph having eliminated a variable (via conditioning or marginalisation). Here we consider rules for determining independence based on a graphical representation in which the variables remain in the graph.

Remark 3.5 (Bayes ball) The Bayes ball algorithm [258] provides a linear time complexity algorithm which given a set of nodes $\mathcal{X}$ and $\mathcal{Z}$ determines the set of nodes $\mathcal{Y}$ such that $\mathcal{X} \perp\!\!\!\perp \mathcal{Y} | \mathcal{Z}$. $\mathcal{Y}$ is called the set of irrelevant nodes for $\mathcal{X}$ given $\mathcal{Z}$.

3.3.5 Graphical and distributional in/dependence

We have shown

> $\mathcal{X}$ and $\mathcal{Y}$ d-separated by $\mathcal{Z} \Rightarrow \mathcal{X} \perp\!\!\!\perp \mathcal{Y} | \mathcal{Z}$ in *all* distributions consistent with the belief network structure.

In other words, if one takes any instance of a distribution P which factorises according to the belief network structure and then writes down a list $\mathcal{L}_P$ of all the conditional independence statements that can be obtained from P, if $\mathcal{X}$ and $\mathcal{Y}$ are d-separated by $\mathcal{Z}$ then this list must contain the statement $\mathcal{X} \perp\!\!\!\perp \mathcal{Y} | \mathcal{Z}$. Note that the list $\mathcal{L}_P$ could contain more statements than those obtained from the graph. For example for the belief network graph

$$p(a, b, c) = p(c|a, b)p(a)p(b) \tag{3.3.20}$$

which is representable by the DAG $a \rightarrow c \leftarrow b$, then $a \perp\!\!\!\perp b$ is the only graphical independence statement we can make. Consider a distribution consistent with Equation (3.3.20), for example, on binary variables $\text{dom}(a) = \text{dom}(b) = \text{dom}(c) = \{0, 1\}$

$$p_{[1]}(c = 1|a, b) = (a - b)^2, \quad p_{[1]}(a = 1) = 0.3, \quad p_{[1]}(b = 1) = 0.4 \tag{3.3.21}$$

then numerically we must have $a \perp\!\!\!\perp b$ for this distribution $p_{[1]}$. Indeed the list $\mathcal{L}_{[1]}$ contains only the statement $a \perp\!\!\!\perp b$. On the other hand, we can also consider the distribution

$$p_{[2]}(c = 1|a, b) = 0.5, \quad p_{[2]}(a = 1) = 0.3, \quad p_{[2]}(b = 1) = 0.4 \tag{3.3.22}$$

from which $\mathcal{L}_{[2]} = \{a \perp\!\!\!\perp b, a \perp\!\!\!\perp c, b \perp\!\!\!\perp c\}$. In this case $\mathcal{L}_{[2]}$ contains more statements than $a \perp\!\!\!\perp b$.

An interesting question is whether or not d-connection similarly implies dependence? That is, do *all* distributions P consistent with the belief network possess the dependencies implied by the graph? If we consider the belief network structure Equation (3.3.20) above, a and b are d-connected by c, so that graphically a and b are dependent, conditioned on c. For the specific instance $p_{[1]}$ we have numerically $a \top\!\!\!\top b | c$ so that the list of dependence statements for $p_{[1]}$ contains the graphical dependence statement. Now consider $p_{[2]}$. The list of dependence statements for $p_{[2]}$ is empty. Hence the graphical dependence statements are not necessarily found in all distributions consistent with the belief network. Hence

> $\mathcal{X}$ and $\mathcal{Y}$ d-connected by $\mathcal{Z} \not\Rightarrow \mathcal{X} \top\!\!\!\top \mathcal{Y} | \mathcal{Z}$ in *all* distributions consistent with the belief network structure.

See also Exercise 3.17. This shows that belief networks are powerful in ensuring that distributions necessarily obey the independence assumptions we expect from the graph. However, belief networks are not suitable for ensuring that distributions obey desired dependency statements.

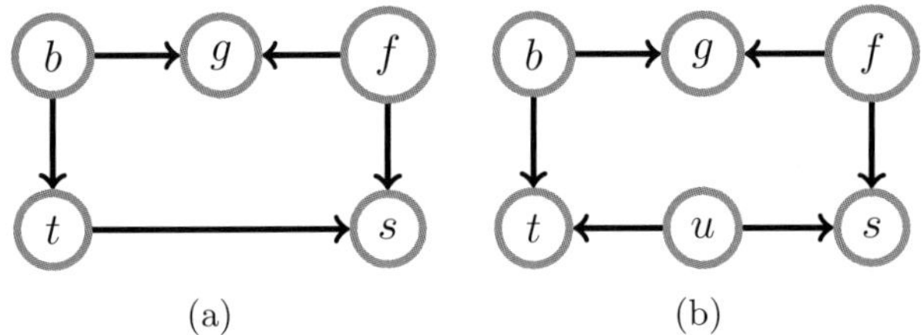

Figure 3.10 (**a**) t and f are d-connected by g. (**b**) b and f are d-separated by u.

Example 3.3

Consider the graph in Fig. 3.10(a).

1. Are the variables t and f unconditionally independent, i.e. $t \perp\!\!\!\perp f \mid \emptyset$? Here there are two colliders, namely g and s – however, these are not in the conditioning set (which is empty), and hence t and f are d-separated and therefore unconditionally independent.
2. What about $t \perp\!\!\!\perp f \mid g$? There is a path between t and f for which all colliders are in the conditioning set. Hence t and f are d-connected by g, and therefore t and f are graphically dependent conditioned on g.

Example 3.4

Is $\{b, f\} \perp\!\!\!\perp u \mid \emptyset$ in Fig. 3.10(b)? Since the conditioning set is empty and every path from either b or f to u contains a collider, 'b and f' are unconditionally independent of u.

3.3.6 Markov equivalence in belief networks

We have invested a lot of effort in learning how to read conditional independence relations from a DAG. Happily, we can determine whether two DAGs represent the same set of conditional independence statements (even when we don't know what they are) by using a relatively simple rule.

Definition 3.5 **Markov equivalence** Two graphs are Markov equivalent if they both represent the same set of conditional independence statements. This definition holds for both directed and undirected graphs.

Example 3.5

Consider the belief network with edges $A \to C \leftarrow B$, from which the set of conditional statements is $A \perp\!\!\!\perp B \mid \emptyset$. For another belief network with edges $A \to C \leftarrow B$ and $A \to B$, the set of conditional independence statements is empty. In this case, the two belief networks are not Markov equivalent.

Procedure 3.1 (Determining Markov equivalence) Define an *immorality* in a DAG as a configuration of three nodes, A, B, C such that C is a child of both A and B, with A and B not directly connected. Define the *skeleton* of a graph by removing the directions on the arrows. Two DAGs represent the

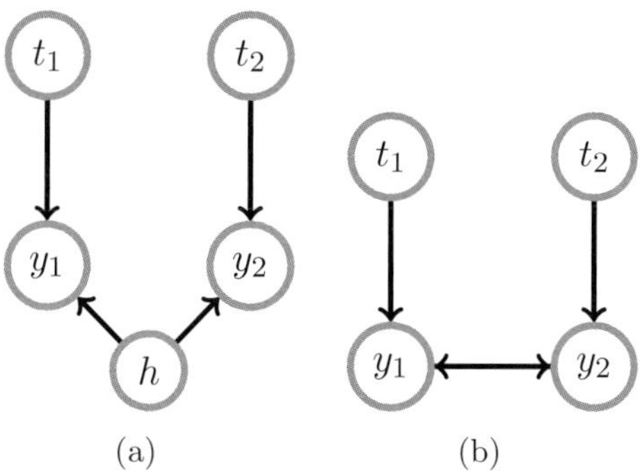

Figure 3.11 (**a**) Two treatments t_1, t_2 and corresponding outcomes y_1, y_2. The health of a patient is represented by h. This DAG embodies the conditional independence statements $t_1 \perp\!\!\!\perp t_2, y_2 | \emptyset$, $t_2 \perp\!\!\!\perp t_1, y_1 | \emptyset$, namely that the treatments have no effect on each other. (**b**) One could represent the effect of marginalising over h using a bi-directional edge.

same set of independence assumptions (they are *Markov equivalent*) if and only if they have the same skeleton and the same set of immoralities [78].

Using Procedure 3.1 we see that in Fig. 3.6, BNs (b,c,d) have the same skeleton with no immoralities and are therefore equivalent. However BN (a) has an immorality and is therefore not equivalent to BNs (b,c,d).

3.3.7 Belief networks have limited expressibility

Belief networks fit well with our intuitive notion of modelling 'causal' independencies. However, formally speaking they cannot necessarily graphically represent all the independence properties of a given distribution.

Consider the DAG in Fig. 3.11(a) (from [249]). This DAG could be used to represent two successive experiments where t_1 and t_2 are two treatments and y_1 and y_2 represent two outcomes of interest; h is the underlying health status of the patient; the first treatment has no effect on the second outcome hence there is no edge from y_1 to y_2. Now consider the implied independencies in the marginal distribution $p(t_1, t_2, y_1, y_2)$, obtained by marginalising the full distribution over h. There is no DAG containing only the vertices t_1, y_1, t_2, y_2 which represents the independence relations and does not also imply some other independence relation that is not implied by Fig. 3.11(a). Consequently, any DAG on vertices t_1, y_1, t_2, y_2 alone will either fail to represent an independence relation of $p(t_1, t_2, y_1, y_2)$, or will impose some additional independence restriction that is not implied by the DAG. In the above example

$$p(t_1, t_2, y_1, y_2) = p(t_1)p(t_2)\sum_h p(y_1|t_1, h)p(y_2|t_2, h)p(h) \tag{3.3.23}$$

cannot in general be expressed as a product of functions defined on a limited set of the variables. However, it is the case that the conditional independence conditions $t_1 \perp\!\!\!\perp (t_2, y_2)$, $t_2 \perp\!\!\!\perp (t_1, y_1)$ hold in $p(t_1, t_2, y_1, y_2)$ – they are there, encoded in the form of the conditional probability tables. It is just that we cannot 'see' this independence since it is not present in the structure of the marginalised graph (though one can naturally infer this in the larger graph $p(t_1, t_2, y_1, y_2, h)$). For example, for the BN with link from y_2 to y_1, we have $t_1 \perp\!\!\!\perp t_2 | y_2$, which is not true for the distribution in (3.3.23). Similarly, for the BN with link from y_1 to y_2, the implied statement $t_1 \perp\!\!\!\perp t_2 | y_1$ is also not true for (3.3.23).

This example demonstrates that BNs cannot express all the conditional independence statements that could be made on that set of variables (the set of conditional independence statements can be increased by considering additional variables however). This situation is rather general in the sense that any graphical model has limited expressibility in terms of independence statements [281]. It is worth bearing in mind that BNs may not always be the most appropriate framework to express one's independence assumptions and intuitions.

A natural consideration is to use a bi-directional arrow when a variable is marginalised. For Fig. 3.11(a), one could depict the marginal distribution using a bi-directional edge, Fig. 3.11(b). For a discussion of extensions of BNs using bi-directional edges see [249].

3.4 Causality

Causality is a contentious topic and the purpose of this section is to make the reader aware of some pitfalls that can occur and which may give rise to erroneous inferences. The reader is referred to [237] and [78] for further details.

The word 'causal' is contentious particularly in cases where the model of the data contains no explicit temporal information, so that formally only correlations or dependencies can be inferred. For a distribution $p(a, b)$, we could write this as either (i) $p(a|b)p(b)$ or (ii) $p(b|a)p(a)$. In (i) we might think that b 'causes' a, and in (ii) a 'causes' b. Clearly, this is not very meaningful since they both represent exactly the same distribution, see Fig. 3.12. Formally BNs only make independence statements, not causal ones. Nevertheless, in constructing BNs, it can be helpful to think about dependencies in terms of causation since our intuitive understanding is usually framed in how one variable 'influences' another. First we discuss a classic conundrum that highlights potential pitfalls that can arise.

3.4.1 Simpson's paradox

Simpson's 'paradox' is a cautionary tale in causal reasoning in BNs. Consider a medical trial in which patient treatment and outcome are recovered. Two trials were conducted, one with 40 females and one with 40 males. The data is summarised in Table 3.1. The question is: Does the drug cause increased recovery? According to the table for males, the answer is no, since more males recovered when they were not given the drug than when they were. Similarly, more females recovered when not given the drug than recovered when given the drug. The conclusion appears that the drug cannot be beneficial since it aids neither subpopulation.

However, ignoring the gender information, and collating both the male and female data into one combined table, we find that more people recovered when given the drug than when not. Hence, even though the drug doesn't seem to work for either males or females, it does seem to work overall! Should we therefore recommend the drug or not?

Figure 3.12 Both (a) and (b) represent the same distribution $p(a, b) = p(a|b)p(b) = p(b|a)p(a)$. **(c)** The graph represents $p(rain, grasswet) = p(grasswet|rain)p(rain)$. **(d)** We could equally have written $p(rain|grasswet)p(grasswet)$, although this appears to be causally non-sensical.

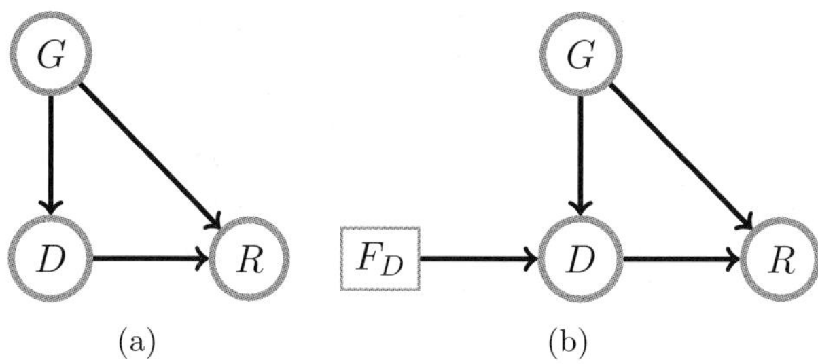

Figure 3.13 (**a**) A DAG for the relation between Gender (G), Drug (D) and Recovery (R), see Table 3.1. (**b**) Influence diagram. No decision variable is required for G since G has no parents.

Resolution of the paradox

The 'paradox' occurs because we are asking a *causal* (interventional) question – If we give someone the drug, what happens? – but we are performing an observational calculation. Pearl [237] would remind us that there is a difference between 'given that we see' (observational evidence) and 'given that we do' (interventional evidence). We want to model a causal experiment in which we first intervene, setting the drug state, and then observe what effect this has on recovery.

A model of the Gender, Drug and Recovery data (which makes no conditional independence assumptions) is, Fig. 3.13(a),

$$p(G, D, R) = p(R|G, D)p(D|G)p(G). \tag{3.4.1}$$

In a causal interpretation, however, if we intervene and give the drug, then the term $p(D|G)$ in Equation (3.4.1) should play no role in the experiment – we decide to give the drug or not independent of gender. The term $p(D|G)$ therefore needs to be replaced by a term that reflects the set-up of the experiment. We use the idea of an atomic intervention, in which a single variable is set in a particular state. In our atomic causal intervention, where we set D, we deal with the modified distribution

$$\tilde{p}(G, R|D) = p(R|G, D)p(G) \tag{3.4.2}$$

where the terms on the right-hand side of this equation are taken from the original BN of the data. To denote an intervention we use $||$:

$$p(R||G, D) \equiv \tilde{p}(R|G, D) = \frac{p(R|G, D)p(G)}{\sum_R p(R|G, D)p(G)} = p(R|G, D). \tag{3.4.3}$$

Table 3.1 Table for Simpson's Paradox (from [237])

	Recovered	Not recovered	Rec. rate
Males			
Given drug	18	12	60%
Not given drug	7	3	70%
Females			
Given drug	2	8	20%
Not given drug	9	21	30%
Combined			
Given drug	20	20	50%
Not given drug	16	24	40%

(One can also consider here G as being interventional – in this case it doesn't matter since the fact that the variable G has no parents means that for any distribution conditional on G, the prior factor $p(G)$ will not be present.) Using Equation (3.4.3), for the males given the drug 60% recover, versus 70% recovery when not given the drug. For the females given the drug 20% recover, versus 30% recovery when not given the drug.

Similarly,

$$p(R||D) \equiv \tilde{p}(R|D) = \frac{\sum_G p(R|G, D)p(G)}{\sum_{R,G} p(R|G, D)p(G)} = \sum_G p(R|G, D)p(G). \tag{3.4.4}$$

Using the post intervention distribution, Equation (3.4.4), we have

$$p(\text{recovery}|\text{drug}) = 0.6 \times 0.5 + 0.2 \times 0.5 = 0.4 \tag{3.4.5}$$
$$p(\text{recovery}|\text{no drug}) = 0.7 \times 0.5 + 0.3 \times 0.5 = 0.5. \tag{3.4.6}$$

Hence we infer that the drug is overall not helpful, as we intuitively expect, and is consistent with the results from both subpopulations.

Summarising the above argument, $p(G, D, R) = p(R|G, D)p(G)p(D)$ means that we choose either a Male or Female patient and give them the drug or not independent of their gender, hence the absence of the term $p(D|G)$ from the joint distribution. One way to think about such models is to consider how to draw a sample from the joint distribution of the random variables – in most cases this should clarify the role of causality in the experiment.

In contrast to the interventional calculation, the observational calculation makes no conditional independence assumptions. This means that, for example, the term $p(D|G)$ plays a role in the calculation (the reader might wish to verify that the result given in the combined data in Table 3.1 is equivalent to inferring with the full distribution Equation (3.4.1)).

3.4.2 The do-calculus

In making causal inferences we've seen above that we must adjust the model to reflect any causal experimental conditions. In setting any variable into a particular state we need to surgically remove all parental links of that variable. Pearl calls this the *do operator*, and contrasts an observational ('see') inference $p(x|y)$ with a causal ('make' or 'do') inference $p(x|do(y))$.

Definition 3.6 Pearl's do operator Inferring the effect of setting variables $X_{c_1}, \ldots, X_{c_K}, c_k \in \mathcal{C}$, in states $\mathrm{x}_{c_1}, \ldots, \mathrm{x}_{c_K}$, is equivalent to standard evidential inference in the *post intervention distribution*:

$$p(X|do(X_{c_1} = \mathrm{x}_{c_1}), \ldots, do(X_{c_K} = \mathrm{x}_{c_K})) = \frac{p(X_1, \ldots, X_n|\mathrm{x}_{c_1}, \ldots, \mathrm{x}_{c_K})}{\prod_{i=1}^K p(X_{c_i}|\mathrm{pa}(X_{c_i}))} = \prod_{j \notin \mathcal{C}} p(X_j|\mathrm{pa}(X_j)) \tag{3.4.7}$$

where any parental states $\mathrm{pa}(X_j)$ of X_j are set in their evidential states. An alternative notation is $p(X||\mathrm{x}_{c_1}, \ldots, \mathrm{x}_{c_K})$.

In words, for those variables for which we causally intervene and set in a particular state, the corresponding terms $p(X_{c_i}|\mathrm{pa}(X_{c_i}))$ are removed from the original belief network. For variables which are evidential but non-causal, the corresponding factors are not removed from the distribution. The interpretation is that the post intervention distribution corresponds to an experiment in which the causal variables are first set and non-causal variables are subsequently observed.

3.4.3 Influence diagrams and the do-calculus

Another way to represent intervention is to modify the basic BN by appending a parental decision variable F_X to any variable X on which an intervention can be made, giving rise to a so-called influence diagram [78]. For example, for the Simpson's paradox example, we may use, Fig. 3.13(b),[2]

$$\tilde{p}(D, G, R, F_D) = p(D|F_D, G)p(G)p(R|G, D)p(F_D) \tag{3.4.8}$$

where

$$p(D|F_D = \emptyset, G) \equiv p(D|\mathrm{pa}\,(D)), \quad p(D|F_D = \mathrm{d}, G) = 1 \text{ for } D = \mathrm{d} \text{ and } 0 \text{ otherwise.}$$

Hence, if the decision variable F_D is set to the empty state, the variable D is determined by the standard observational term $p(D|\mathrm{pa}\,(D))$. If the decision variable is set to a state of D, then the variable puts all its probability in that single state of $D = \mathrm{d}$. This has the effect of replacing the conditional probability term by a unit factor and any instances of D set to the variable in its interventional state.[3] A potential advantage of this influence diagram approach over the do-calculus is that conditional independence statements can be derived using standard techniques for the augmented BN. Additionally, for learning, standard techniques apply in which the decision variables are set to the condition under which each data sample was collected (a causal or non-causal sample).

Remark 3.6 (Learning the edge directions) In the absence of data from causal experiments, one should be justifiably sceptical about learning 'causal' networks. Nevertheless, one might prefer a certain direction of a link based on assumptions of the 'simplicity' of the CPTs. This preference may come from a physical intuition that whilst root causes may be uncertain, the relationship from cause to effect is clear. In this sense a measure of the complexity of a CPT is required, such as entropy. Such heuristics can be numerically encoded and the edge directions learned in an otherwise Markov equivalent graph.

3.5 Summary

- We can reason with certain or uncertain evidence using repeated application of Bayes' rule.
- A belief network represents a factorisation of a distribution into conditional probabilities of variables dependent on parental variables.
- Belief networks correspond to directed acyclic graphs.
- Variables are conditionally independent $x \perp\!\!\!\perp y|z$ if $p(x, y|z) = p(x|z)p(y|z)$; the absence of a link in a belief network corresponds to a conditional independence statement.
- If in the graph representing the belief network, two variables are independent, then they are independent in any distribution consistent with the belief network structure.
- Belief networks are natural for representing 'causal' influences.
- Causal questions must be addressed by an appropriate causal model.

2 Here the influence diagram is a distribution over variables including decision variables, in contrast to the application of IDs in Chapter 7.

3 More general cases can be considered in which the variables are placed in a distribution of states [78].

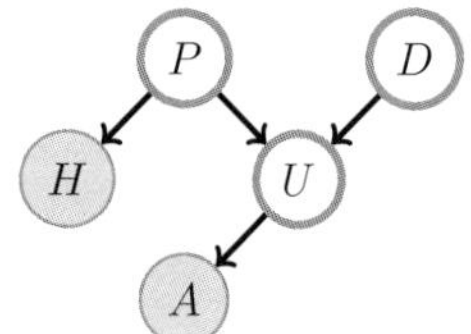

Figure 3.14 Party animal. Here all variables are binary. P = Been to party, H = Got a headache, D = Demotivated at work, U = Underperform at work, A = Boss angry. Shaded variables are observed in the true state.

3.6 Code

3.6.1 Naive inference demo

`demoBurglar.m`: Was it the burglar demo
`demoChestClinic.m`: Naive inference on chest clinic. See Exercise 3.4.

3.6.2 Conditional independence demo

The following demo determines whether $\mathcal{X} \perp\!\!\!\perp \mathcal{Y} | \mathcal{Z}$ for the Chest Clinic network, Fig. 3.15, and checks the result numerically.[4] The independence test is based on the Markov method of Section 4.2.4. This is an alternative to the d-separation method and also more general in that it deals also with conditional independence in Markov Networks as well as belief networks. Running the demo code below, it may happen that the numerical dependence is very small – that is

$$p(\mathcal{X}, \mathcal{Y}|\mathcal{Z}) \approx p(\mathcal{X}|\mathcal{Z})p(\mathcal{Y}|\mathcal{Z}) \tag{3.6.1}$$

even though $\mathcal{X} \top\!\!\!\top \mathcal{Y} | \mathcal{Z}$. This highlights the difference between 'structural' and 'numerical' independence.

`condindepPot.m`: Numerical measure of conditional independence
`demoCondindep.m`: Demo of conditional independence (using Markov method)

3.6.3 Utility routines

`dag.m`: Find the DAG structure for a belief network

3.7 Exercises

3.1 (Party animal) The party animal problem corresponds to the network in Fig. 3.14. The boss is angry and the worker has a headache – what is the probability the worker has been to a party? To complete the specifications, the probabilities are given as follows:

$$\begin{array}{lll} p(U = \text{tr}|P = \text{tr}, D = \text{tr}) = 0.999 & p(U = \text{tr}|P = \text{fa}, D = \text{tr}) = 0.9 & p(H = \text{tr}|P = \text{tr}) = 0.9 \\ p(U = \text{tr}|P = \text{tr}, D = \text{fa}) = 0.9 & p(U = \text{tr}|P = \text{fa}, D = \text{fa}) = 0.01 & p(H = \text{tr}|P = \text{fa}) = 0.2 \\ p(A = \text{tr}|U = \text{tr}) = 0.95 & p(A = \text{tr}|U = \text{fa}) = 0.5 & p(P = \text{tr}) = 0.2,\ p(D = \text{tr}) = 0.4 \end{array}$$

3.2 Consider the distribution $p(a, b, c) = p(c|a, b)p(a)p(b)$. (i) Is $a \perp\!\!\!\perp b | \emptyset$? (ii) Is $a \perp\!\!\!\perp b | c$?

[4] The code for graphical conditional independence is given in Chapter 4.

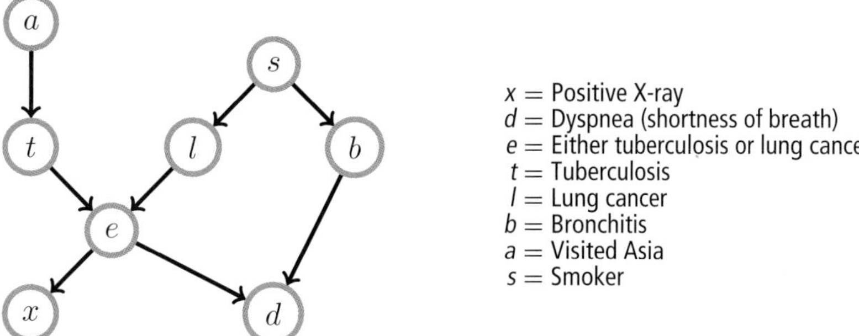

Figure 3.15 Belief network structure for the Chest Clinic example.

3.3 The Chest Clinic network [184] concerns the diagnosis of lung disease (tuberculosis, lung cancer, or both, or neither), see Fig. 3.15. In this model a visit to Asia is assumed to increase the probability of tuberculosis. State if the following conditional independence relationships are true or false

1. tuberculosis $\perp\!\!\!\perp$ smoking| shortness of breath
2. lung cancer $\perp\!\!\!\perp$ bronchitis| smoking
3. visit to Asia $\perp\!\!\!\perp$ smoking| lung cancer
4. visit to Asia $\perp\!\!\!\perp$ smoking| lung cancer, shortness of breath

3.4 Consider the Chest Clinic belief network in Fig. 3.15 [184]. Calculate by hand the values for $p(d)$, $p(d|s = \text{tr})$, $p(d|s = \text{fa})$. The table values are:

$$
\begin{array}{llll}
p(a = \text{tr}) & = 0.01 & p(s = \text{tr}) & = 0.5 \\
p(t = \text{tr}|a = \text{tr}) & = 0.05 & p(t = \text{tr}|a = \text{fa}) & = 0.01 \\
p(l = \text{tr}|s = \text{tr}) & = 0.1 & p(l = \text{tr}|s = \text{fa}) & = 0.01 \\
p(b = \text{tr}|s = \text{tr}) & = 0.6 & p(b = \text{tr}|s = \text{fa}) & = 0.3 \\
p(x = \text{tr}|e = \text{tr}) & = 0.98 & p(x = \text{tr}|e = \text{fa}) & = 0.05 \\
p(d = \text{tr}|e = \text{tr}, b = \text{tr}) & = 0.9 & p(d = \text{tr}|e = \text{tr}, b = \text{fa}) & = 0.7 \\
p(d = \text{tr}|e = \text{fa}, b = \text{tr}) & = 0.8 & p(d = \text{tr}|e = \text{fa}, b = \text{fa}) & = 0.1
\end{array}
$$

$p(e = \text{tr}|t, l) = 0$ only if both t and l are fa, 1 otherwise.

3.5 If we interpret the Chest Clinic network Exercise 3.4 causally, how can we help a doctor answer the question 'If I could cure my patients of bronchitis, how would this affect my patients' chance of being short of breath?'. How does this compare with $p(d = \text{tr}|b = \text{fa})$ in a non-causal interpretation, and what does this mean?

3.6 ([140]) The network in Fig. 3.16 concerns the probability of a car starting, with

$$
\begin{array}{ll}
p(b = \text{bad}) = 0.02 & p(f = \text{empty}) = 0.05 \\
p(g = \text{empty}|b = \text{good}, f = \text{not empty}) = 0.04 & p(g = \text{empty}|b = \text{good}, f = \text{empty}) = 0.97 \\
p(g = \text{empty}|b = \text{bad}, f = \text{not empty}) = 0.1 & p(g = \text{empty}|b = \text{bad}, f = \text{empty}) = 0.99 \\
p(t = \text{fa}|b = \text{good}) = 0.03 & p(t = \text{fa}|b = \text{bad}) = 0.98 \\
p(s = \text{fa}|t = \text{tr}, f = \text{not empty}) = 0.01 & p(s = \text{fa}|t = \text{tr}, f = \text{empty}) = 0.92 \\
p(s = \text{fa}|t = \text{fa}, f = \text{not empty}) = 1.0 & p(s = \text{fa}|t = \text{fa}, f = \text{empty}) = 0.99
\end{array}
$$

Calculate $P(f = \text{empty}|s = no)$, the probability of the fuel tank being empty conditioned on the observation that the car does not start.

3.7 There is a synergistic relationship between Asbestos (A) exposure, Smoking (S) and Cancer (C). A model describing this relationship is given by

$$p(A, S, C) = p(C|A, S)p(A)p(S). \tag{3.7.1}$$

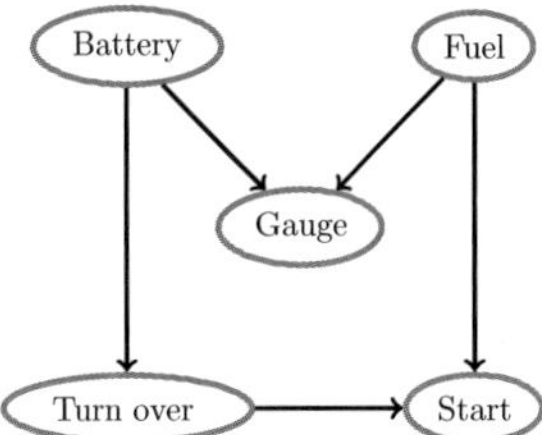

Figure 3.16 Belief network of car starting, see Exercise 3.6.

1. Is $A \perp\!\!\!\perp S \mid \emptyset$?
2. Is $A \perp\!\!\!\perp S \mid C$?
3. How could you adjust the model to account for the fact that people who work in the building industry have a higher likelihood to also be smokers and also a higher likelihood to be exposed to asbestos?

3.8 Consider the belief network on the right which represents Mr Holmes' burglary worries as given in Fig. 3.3(a): (B)urglar, (A)larm, (W)atson, Mrs (G)ibbon.

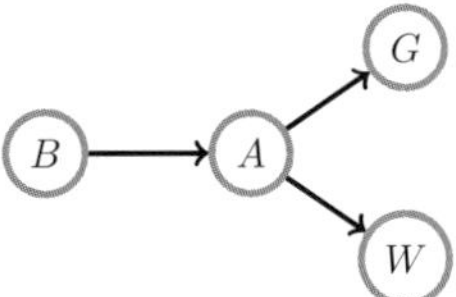

All variables are binary with states $\{\text{tr}, \text{fa}\}$. The table entries are

$$\begin{aligned} &p(B = \text{tr}) &&= 0.01 && && \\ &p(A = \text{tr}|B = \text{tr}) &&= 0.99 &\quad &p(A = \text{tr}|B = \text{fa}) &&= 0.05 \\ &p(W = \text{tr}|A = \text{tr}) &&= 0.9 &\quad &p(W = \text{tr}|A = \text{fa}) &&= 0.5 \\ &p(G = \text{tr}|A = \text{tr}) &&= 0.7 &\quad &p(G = \text{tr}|A = \text{fa}) &&= 0.2 \end{aligned} \tag{3.7.2}$$

1. Compute 'by hand' (i.e. show your working):
   (a) $p(B = \text{tr}|W = \text{tr})$
   (b) $p(B = \text{tr}|W = \text{tr}, G = \text{fa})$
2. Consider the same situation as above, except that now the evidence is uncertain. Mrs Gibbon thinks that the state is $G = \text{fa}$ with probability 0.9. Similarly, Dr Watson believes in the state $W = \text{fa}$ with value 0.7. Compute 'by hand' the posteriors under these uncertain (soft) evidences:
   (a) $p(B = \text{tr}|\tilde{W})$
   (b) $p(B = \text{tr}|\tilde{W}, \tilde{G})$

3.9 A doctor gives a patient a (D)rug (drug or no drug) dependent on their (A)ge (old or young) and (G)ender (male or female). Whether or not the patient (R)ecovers (recovers or doesn't recover) depends on all D, A, G. In addition $A \perp\!\!\!\perp G \mid \emptyset$.

1. Write down the belief network for the above situation.
2. Explain how to compute $p(\text{recover}|\text{drug})$.
3. Explain how to compute $p(\text{recover}|do(\text{drug}), \text{young})$.

3.10 Implement the Wet Grass scenario in Section 3.1.1 using the BRMLTOOLBOX.

3.11 (LA Burglar) Consider the Burglar scenario, Example 3.1. We now wish to model the fact that in Los Angeles the probability of being burgled increases if there is an earthquake. Explain how to include this effect in the model.

3.12 Given two belief networks represented as DAGs with associated adjacency matrices **A** and **B**, write a MATLAB function `MarkovEquiv(A,B).m` that returns 1 if **A** and **B** are Markov equivalent, and zero otherwise.

3.13 The adjacency matrices of two belief networks are given below (see `ABmatrices.mat`). State if they are Markov equivalent.

$$\mathbf{A} = \begin{pmatrix} 0 & 0 & 1 & 1 & 0 & 1 & 0 & 0 & 0 \\ 0 & 0 & 1 & 0 & 1 & 0 & 0 & 0 & 0 \\ 0 & 0 & 0 & 0 & 0 & 0 & 1 & 0 & 0 \\ 0 & 0 & 0 & 0 & 0 & 0 & 0 & 1 & 1 \\ 0 & 0 & 1 & 0 & 0 & 0 & 1 & 0 & 0 \\ 0 & 0 & 0 & 1 & 0 & 0 & 0 & 1 & 0 \\ 0 & 0 & 0 & 0 & 0 & 0 & 0 & 0 & 1 \\ 0 & 0 & 0 & 0 & 0 & 0 & 0 & 0 & 0 \\ 0 & 0 & 0 & 0 & 0 & 0 & 0 & 0 & 0 \end{pmatrix}, \quad \mathbf{B} = \begin{pmatrix} 0 & 0 & 1 & 1 & 0 & 0 & 0 & 0 & 0 \\ 0 & 0 & 1 & 0 & 0 & 0 & 0 & 0 & 0 \\ 0 & 0 & 0 & 0 & 0 & 0 & 1 & 0 & 0 \\ 0 & 0 & 0 & 0 & 0 & 0 & 0 & 1 & 1 \\ 0 & 1 & 1 & 0 & 0 & 0 & 1 & 0 & 0 \\ 1 & 0 & 0 & 1 & 0 & 0 & 0 & 1 & 0 \\ 0 & 0 & 0 & 0 & 0 & 0 & 0 & 0 & 1 \\ 0 & 0 & 0 & 0 & 0 & 0 & 0 & 0 & 0 \\ 0 & 0 & 0 & 0 & 0 & 0 & 0 & 0 & 0 \end{pmatrix}. \tag{3.7.3}$$

3.14 There are three computers indexed by $i \in \{1, 2, 3\}$. Computer i can send a message in one timestep to computer j if $C_{ij} = 1$, otherwise $C_{ij} = 0$. There is a fault in the network and the task is to find out some information about the communication matrix $\mathbf{C}$ ($\mathbf{C}$ is not necessarily symmetric). To do this, Thomas, the engineer, will run some tests that reveal whether or not computer i can send a message to computer j in t timesteps, $t \in \{1, 2\}$. This is expressed as $C_{ij}(t)$, with $C_{ij}(1) \equiv C_{ij}$. For example, he might know that $C_{13}(2) = 1$, meaning that according to his test, a message sent from computer 1 will arrive at computer 3 in at most two timesteps. Note that this message could go via different routes – it might go directly from 1 to 3 in one timestep, or indirectly from 1 to 2 and then from 2 to 3, or both. You may assume $C_{ii} = 1$. A priori Thomas thinks there is a 10% probability that $C_{ij} = 1$, $i \neq j$, and assumes that each such connection is independent of the rest. Given the test information $\mathcal{C} = \{C_{12}(2) = 1, C_{23}(2) = 0\}$, compute the a posteriori probability vector

$$[p(C_{12} = 1|\mathcal{C}), p(C_{13} = 1|\mathcal{C}), p(C_{23} = 1|\mathcal{C}), p(C_{32} = 1|\mathcal{C}), p(C_{21} = 1|\mathcal{C}), p(C_{31} = 1|\mathcal{C})]. \tag{3.7.4}$$

3.15 A belief network models the relation between the variables oil, inf, eh, bp, rt which stand for the price of oil, inflation rate, economy health, British Petroleum Stock price, retailer stock price. Each variable takes the states low, high, except for bp which has states low, high, normal. The belief network model for these variables has tables

$p(eh$=low$)=0.2$	
$p(bp$=low$\|oil$=low$)=0.9$	$p(bp$=normal$\|oil$=low$)=0.1$
$p(bp$=low$\|oil$=high$)=0.1$	$p(bp$=normal$\|oil$=high$)=0.4$
$p(oil$=low$\|eh$=low$)=0.9$	$p(oil$=low$\|eh$=high$)=0.05$
$p(rt$=low$\|inf$=low,eh=low$)=0.9$	$p(rt$=low$\|inf$=low,eh=high$)=0.1$
$p(rt$=low$\|inf$=high,eh=low$)=0.1$	$p(rt$=low$\|inf$=high,eh=high$)=0.01$
$p(inf$=low$\|oil$=low,eh=low$)=0.9$	$p(inf$=low$\|oil$=low,eh=high$)=0.1$
$p(inf$=low$\|oil$=high,eh=low$)=0.1$	$p(inf$=low$\|oil$=high,eh=high$)=0.01$

1. Draw a belief network for this distribution.
2. Given that the BP stock price is normal and the retailer stock price is high, what is the probability that inflation is high?

3.16 There is a set of C potentials with potential c defined on a subset of variables $\mathcal{X}_c$. If $\mathcal{X}_c \subseteq \mathcal{X}_d$ we can merge (multiply) potentials c and d since the variables in potential c are contained within potential d. With reference to suitable graph structures, describe an efficient algorithm to merge a set of potentials so that for the new set of potentials no potential is contained within the other.

3.17 This exercise explores the distinction between d-connection and dependence. Consider the distribution class

$$p(a, b, c) = p(c|b)p(b|a)p(a) \tag{3.7.5}$$

for which a is d-connected to c. One might expect that this means that a and c are dependent, $a \top\!\!\!\top c$. Our interest is to show that there are non-trivial distributions for which $a \perp\!\!\!\perp c$.

1. Consider dom $(a) =$ dom $(c) = \{1, 2\}$ and dom $(b) = \{1, 2, 3\}$. For

$$p(a) = \begin{pmatrix} 3/5 \\ 2/5 \end{pmatrix}, \quad p(b|a) = \begin{pmatrix} 1/4 & 15/40 \\ 1/12 & 1/8 \\ 2/3 & 1/2 \end{pmatrix}, \quad p(c|b) = \begin{pmatrix} 1/3 & 1/2 & 15/40 \\ 2/3 & 1/2 & 5/8 \end{pmatrix} \tag{3.7.6}$$

   show that $a \perp\!\!\!\perp c$.

2. Consider

$$p(a, b, c) = \frac{1}{Z}\phi(a, b)\psi(b, c) \tag{3.7.7}$$

   for positive function ϕ, ψ and $Z = \sum_{a,b,c} \phi(a, b)\psi(b, c)$. Defining matrices $\mathbf{M}$ and $\mathbf{N}$ with elements

$$M_{ij} = \phi(a = i, b = j), \qquad N_{kj} = \psi(b = j, c = k) \tag{3.7.8}$$

   show that the marginal distribution $p(a = i, c = k)$ is represented by the matrix elements

$$p(a = i, c = k) = \frac{1}{Z}\left[\mathbf{M}\mathbf{N}^{\mathsf{T}}\right]_{ik}. \tag{3.7.9}$$

3. Show that if

$$\mathbf{M}\mathbf{N}^{\mathsf{T}} = \mathbf{m}_0\mathbf{n}_0^{\mathsf{T}}. \tag{3.7.10}$$

   for some vectors $\mathbf{m}_0$ and $\mathbf{n}_0$, then $a \perp\!\!\!\perp c$.

4. Writing

$$\mathbf{M} = [\mathbf{m}_1 \quad \mathbf{m}_2 \quad \mathbf{m}_3], \qquad \mathbf{N} = [\mathbf{n}_1 \quad \mathbf{n}_2 \quad \mathbf{n}_3] \tag{3.7.11}$$

   for two-dimensional vectors $\mathbf{m}_i, \mathbf{n}_i, i = 1, \ldots, 3$, show that

$$\mathbf{M}\mathbf{N}^{\mathsf{T}} = \mathbf{m}_1\mathbf{n}_1^{\mathsf{T}} + \mathbf{m}_2\mathbf{n}_2^{\mathsf{T}} + \mathbf{m}_3\mathbf{n}_3^{\mathsf{T}}. \tag{3.7.12}$$

5. Show that by setting

$$\mathbf{m}_2 = \lambda\mathbf{m}_1, \quad \mathbf{n}_3 = \gamma\left(\mathbf{n}_1 + \lambda\mathbf{n}_2\right) \tag{3.7.13}$$

   for scalar λ, γ then $\mathbf{M}\mathbf{N}^{\mathsf{T}}$ can be written as $\mathbf{m}_0\mathbf{n}_0^{\mathsf{T}}$ where

$$\mathbf{m}_0 \equiv \mathbf{m}_1 + \gamma\mathbf{m}_3, \qquad \mathbf{n}_0 \equiv \mathbf{n}_1 + \lambda\mathbf{n}_2. \tag{3.7.14}$$

6. Hence construct example tables $p(a)$, $p(b|a)$, $p(c|b)$ for which $a \perp\!\!\!\perp c$. Verify your examples explicitly using BRMLTOOLBOX.

3.18 Alice and Bob share a bank account which contains an a priori unknown total amount of money T. Whenever Alice goes to the cash machine, the available amount for withdrawal A for Alice is always 10% of the total T. Similarly, when Bob goes to the cash machine the available amount for withdrawal B for Bob is 10% of the total T. Whatever the amount in the bank, Alice and Bob check their available amounts for withdrawal independently. Draw a belief network that expresses this situation and show that $A \top\!\!\!\top B$.

3.19 Assume that the day of the week that females are born on, x, is independent of the day of the week, y, on which males are born. Assume, however, that the old rhyme is true and that personality is dependent on the day of the week you're born on. If a represents the female personality type and b the male personality type, then $a \top\!\top x$ and $b \top\!\top y$, but $a \perp\!\!\!\perp b$. Whether or not a male and a female are married, m, depends strongly on their personality types, $m \top\!\top \{a, b\}$, but is independent of x and y if we know a and b. Draw a belief network that can represent this setting. What can we say about the (graphical) dependency between the days of the week that John and Jane are born on, given that they are not married?

4 Graphical models

In Chapter 3 we saw how belief networks are used to represent statements about independence of variables in a probabilistic model. Belief networks are simply one way to unite probability and graphical representation. Many others exist, all under the general heading of 'graphical models'. Each has specific strengths and weaknesses. Broadly, graphical models fall into two classes: those useful for modelling, such as belief networks, and those useful for inference. This chapter will survey the most popular models from each class.

4.1 Graphical models

Graphical Models (GMs) are depictions of independence/dependence relationships for distributions. Each class of GM is a particular union of graph and probability constructs and details the form of independence assumptions represented. Graphical models are useful since they provide a framework for studying a wide class of probabilistic models and associated algorithms. In particular they help to clarify modelling assumptions and provide a unified framework under which inference algorithms in different communities can be related.

It needs to be emphasised that all forms of GM have a limited ability to graphically express conditional (in)dependence statements [281]. As we've seen, belief networks are useful for modelling ancestral conditional independence. In this chapter we'll introduce other types of GM that are more suited to representing different assumptions. Here we'll focus on Markov networks, chain graphs (which marry belief and Markov networks) and factor graphs. There are many more inhabitants of the zoo of graphical models, see [73, 314].

The general viewpoint we adopt is to describe the problem environment using a probabilistic model, after which reasoning corresponds to performing probabilistic inference. This is therefore a two-part process:

Modelling After identifying all potentially relevant variables of a problem environment, our task is to describe how these variables can interact. This is achieved using structural assumptions as to the form of the joint probability distribution of all the variables, typically corresponding to assumptions of independence of variables. Each class of graphical model corresponds to a factorisation property of the joint distribution.

Inference Once the basic assumptions as to how variables interact with each other is formed (i.e. the probabilistic model is constructed) all questions of interest are answered by performing inference on the distribution. This can be a computationally non-trivial step so that coupling GMs with accurate inference algorithms is central to successful graphical modelling.

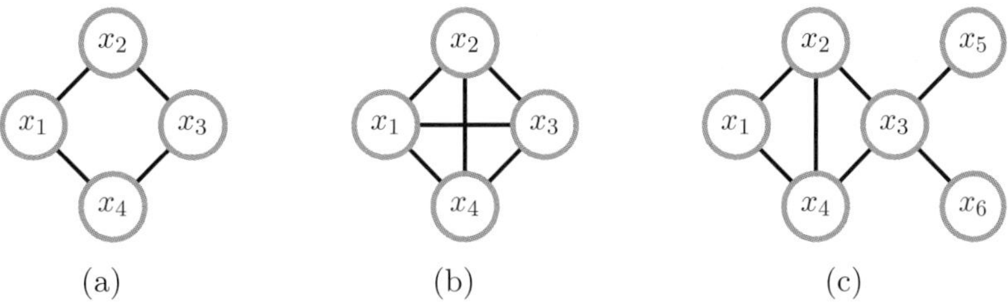

Figure 4.1 **(a)** $\phi(x_1, x_2)\phi(x_2, x_3)\phi(x_3, x_4)\phi(x_4, x_1)/Z_a$. **(b)** $\phi(x_1, x_2, x_3, x_4)/Z_b$. **(c)** $\phi(x_1, x_2, x_4)\phi(x_2, x_3, x_4) \times \phi(x_3, x_5)\phi(x_3, x_6)/Z_c$.

Whilst not a strict separation, GMs tend to fall into two broad classes – those useful in modelling, and those useful in representing inference algorithms. For modelling, belief networks, Markov networks, chain graphs and influence diagrams are some of the most popular. For inference one typically 'compiles' a model into a suitable GM for which an algorithm can be readily applied. Such inference GMs include factor graphs and junction trees.

4.2 Markov networks

Belief networks correspond to a special kind of factorisation of the joint probability distribution in which each of the factors is itself a distribution. An alternative factorisation is, for example

$$p(a, b, c) = \frac{1}{Z}\phi(a, b)\phi(b, c) \tag{4.2.1}$$

where $\phi(a, b)$ and $\phi(b, c)$ are *potentials* (see below) and Z is a constant which ensures normalisation, called the *partition function*

$$Z = \sum_{a,b,c} \phi(a, b)\phi(b, c). \tag{4.2.2}$$

Definition 4.1 **Potential** A potential $\phi(x)$ is a non-negative function of the variable x, $\phi(x) \geq 0$. A joint potential $\phi(x_1, \ldots, x_n)$ is a non-negative function of the set of variables. A distribution is a special case of a potential satisfying normalisation, $\sum_x \phi(x) = 1$. This holds similarly for continuous variables, with summation replaced by integration.

We will typically use the convention that the ordering of the variables in the potential is not relevant (as for a distribution) – the joint variables simply index an element of the potential table. Markov Networks (MNs) are defined as products of potentials defined on maximal cliques of an undirected graph – see below and Fig. 4.1.

Definition 4.2 **Markov network** For a set of variables $\mathcal{X} = \{x_1, \ldots, x_n\}$ a Markov network is defined as a product of potentials on subsets of the variables $\mathcal{X}_c \subseteq \mathcal{X}$:

$$p(x_1, \ldots, x_n) = \frac{1}{Z}\prod_{c=1}^{C} \phi_c(\mathcal{X}_c). \tag{4.2.3}$$

The constant Z ensures the distribution is normalised. Graphically this is represented by an undirected graph G with $\mathcal{X}_c$, $c = 1, \ldots, C$ being the maximal cliques of G. For the case in which clique potentials are strictly positive, this is called a *Gibbs distribution*.

Definition 4.3 Pairwise Markov network In the special case that the graph contains cliques of only size 2, the distribution is called a *pairwise Markov Network*, with potentials defined on each link between two variables.

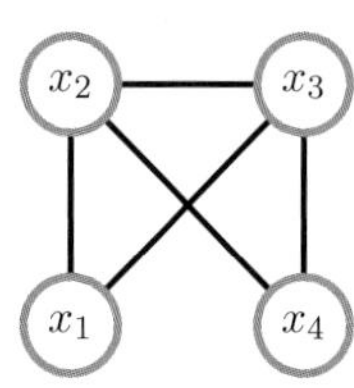

Whilst a Markov network is formally defined on maximal cliques, in practice authors often use the term to refer to non-maximal cliques. For example, in the graph on the right, the maximal cliques are x_1, x_2, x_3 and x_2, x_3, x_4, so that the graph describes a distribution $p(x_1, x_2, x_3, x_4) = \phi(x_1, x_2, x_3)\phi(x_2, x_3, x_4)/Z$. In a pairwise network though the potentials are assumed to be over two cliques, giving $p(x_1, x_2, x_3, x_4) = \phi(x_1, x_2)\phi(x_1, x_3)\phi(x_2, x_3)\phi(x_2, x_4)\phi(x_3, x_4)/Z$.

Example 4.1 Boltzmann machine

A Boltzmann machine is an MN on binary variables $\text{dom}(x_i) = \{0, 1\}$ of the form

$$p(\mathbf{x}) = \frac{1}{Z(\mathbf{w}, b)} e^{\sum_{i<j} w_{ij} x_i x_j + \sum_i b_i x_i} \tag{4.2.4}$$

where the interactions w_{ij} are the 'weights' and the b_i the 'biases'. This model has been studied in the machine learning community as a basic model of distributed memory and computation [2]. The graphical model of the BM is an undirected graph with a link between nodes i and j for $w_{ij} \neq 0$. Consequently, for all but specially constrained $\mathbf{W}$, the graph is multiply connected and inference will be typically intractable.

Definition 4.4 Properties of Markov networks

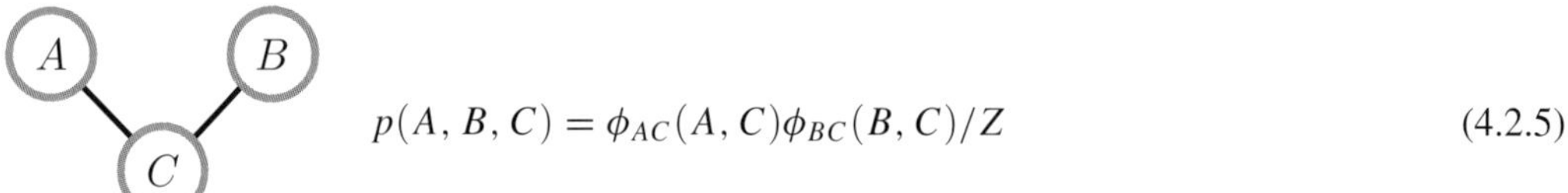

$$p(A, B, C) = \phi_{AC}(A, C)\phi_{BC}(B, C)/Z \tag{4.2.5}$$

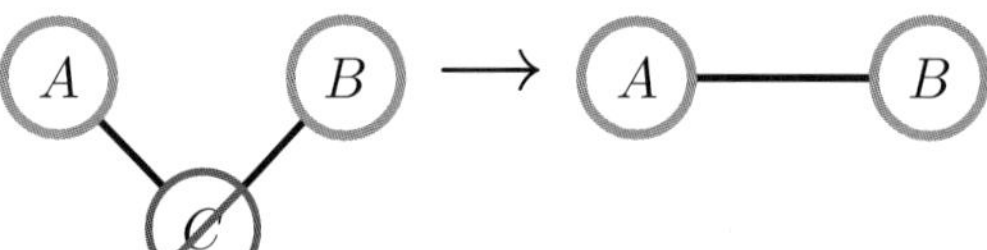

Marginalising over C makes A and B (graphically) dependent. In general $p(A, B) \neq p(A)p(B)$.

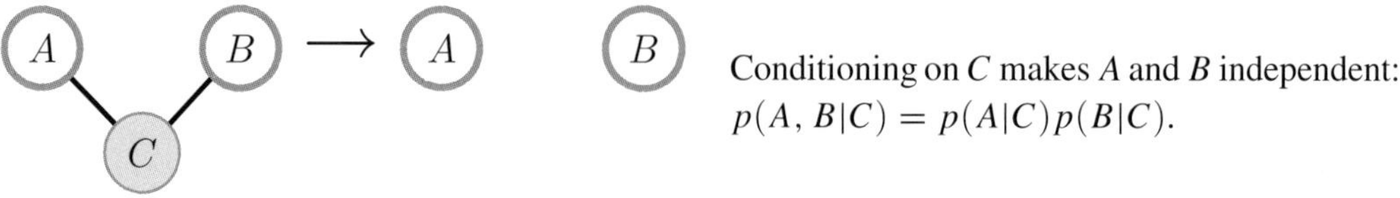

Conditioning on C makes A and B independent: $p(A, B|C) = p(A|C)p(B|C)$.

4.2.1 Markov properties

We consider here informally the properties of Markov networks and the reader is referred to [182] for detailed proofs. Consider the MN in Fig. 4.2(a) in which we use the shorthand $p(1) \equiv p(x_1)$,

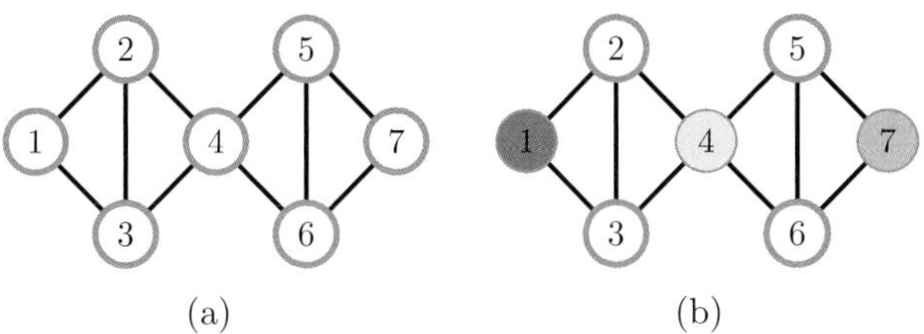

Figure 4.2 **(a)** $\phi(1, 2, 3)\phi(2, 3, 4)\phi(4, 5, 6)\phi(5, 6, 7)$. **(b)** By the global Markov property, since every path from 1 to 7 passes through 4, then $1 \perp\!\!\!\perp 7 | 4$.

$\phi(1, 2, 3) \equiv \phi(x_1, x_2, x_3)$ etc. We will use this undirected graph to demonstrate conditional independence properties. Note that throughout we will be often dividing by potentials and, in order to ensure this is well defined, we assume the potentials are positive. For positive potentials the following local, pairwise and global Markov properties are all equivalent.

Definition 4.5 **Separation** A subset $\mathcal{S}$ separates a subset $\mathcal{A}$ from a subset $\mathcal{B}$ (for disjoint $\mathcal{A}$ and $\mathcal{B}$) if every path from any member of $\mathcal{A}$ to any member of $\mathcal{B}$ passes through $\mathcal{S}$. If there is no path from a member of $\mathcal{A}$ to a member of $\mathcal{B}$ then $\mathcal{A}$ is separated from $\mathcal{B}$. If $\mathcal{S} = \emptyset$ then provided no path exists from $\mathcal{A}$ to $\mathcal{B}$, $\mathcal{A}$ and $\mathcal{B}$ are separated.

Definition 4.6 **Global Markov property** For disjoint sets of variables, $(\mathcal{A}, \mathcal{B}, \mathcal{S})$ where $\mathcal{S}$ separates $\mathcal{A}$ from $\mathcal{B}$ in G, then $\mathcal{A} \perp\!\!\!\perp \mathcal{B} | \mathcal{S}$.

As an example of the global Markov property, consider

$$p(1, 7|4) \propto \sum_{2,3,5,6} p(1, 2, 3, 4, 5, 6, 7) \tag{4.2.6}$$

$$= \sum_{2,3,5,6} \phi(1, 2, 3)\phi(2, 3, 4)\phi(4, 5, 6)\phi(5, 6, 7) \tag{4.2.7}$$

$$= \left\{ \sum_{2,3} \phi(1, 2, 3)\phi(2, 3, 4) \right\} \left\{ \sum_{5,6} \phi(4, 5, 6)\phi(5, 6, 7) \right\}. \tag{4.2.8}$$

This implies that $p(1, 7|4) = p(1|4)p(7|4)$. This can be inferred since all paths from 1 to 7 pass through 4, see Fig. 4.2(a).

Procedure 4.1 (An algorithm for independence) The separation property implies a simple algorithm for deciding $\mathcal{A} \perp\!\!\!\perp \mathcal{B} | \mathcal{S}$. We simply remove all links that neighbour the set of variables $\mathcal{S}$. If there is no path from any member of $\mathcal{A}$ to any member of $\mathcal{B}$, then $\mathcal{A} \perp\!\!\!\perp \mathcal{B} | \mathcal{S}$ is true – see also Section 4.2.4.

For positive potentials, the so-called local Markov property holds

$$p(x|\mathcal{X} \backslash x) = p(x|\text{ne}(x)). \tag{4.2.9}$$

That is, when conditioned on its neighbours, x is independent of the remaining variables of the graph. In addition, the so-called pairwise Markov property holds that for any non-adjacent vertices x and y

$$x \perp\!\!\!\perp y | \mathcal{X} \backslash \{x, y\}. \tag{4.2.10}$$

4.2.2 Markov random fields

A Markov Random Field (MRF) is a set of conditional distributions, one for each indexed 'location'.

Definition 4.7 Markov random field A MRF is defined by a set of distributions $p(x_i|\text{ne}(x_i))$ where $i \in \{1, \dots, n\}$ indexes the distributions and $\text{ne}(x_i)$ are the neighbours of variable x_i, namely that subset of the variables $x_1, \dots, x_n$ that the distribution of variable x_i depends on. The term Markov indicates that this is a proper subset of the variables.

A distribution is an MRF with respect to an undirected graph G if

$$p(x_i|x_{\setminus i}) = p(x_i|\text{ne}(x_i)) \tag{4.2.11}$$

where $\text{ne}(x_i)$ are the neighbouring variables of variable x_i, according to the undirected graph G. The notation $x_{\setminus i}$ is shorthand for the set of all variables $\mathcal{X}$ excluding variable x_i, namely $\mathcal{X} \setminus x_i$ in set notation.

4.2.3 Hammersley–Clifford theorem

An undirected graph G specifies a set of independence statements. An interesting challenge is to find the most general functional form of a distribution that satisfies these independence statements. A trivial example is the graph $x_1 - x_2 - x_3$, from which we have $x_1 \perp\!\!\!\perp x_3 | x_2$. From this requirement we must have

$$p(x_1|x_2, x_3) = p(x_1|x_2). \tag{4.2.12}$$

Hence

$$p(x_1, x_2, x_3) = p(x_1|x_2, x_3)p(x_2, x_3) = p(x_1|x_2)p(x_2, x_3) = \phi_{12}(x_1, x_2)\phi_{23}(x_2, x_3) \tag{4.2.13}$$

where the ϕ are potentials.

More generally, for any decomposable graph G, see Definition 6.9, we can start at the edge and work inwards to reveal that the functional form must be a product of potentials on the cliques of G. For example, for Fig. 4.2(a), we can start with the variable x_1 and the corresponding local Markov statement $x_1 \perp\!\!\!\perp x_4, x_5, x_6, x_6 | x_2, x_3$ to write

$$p(x_1, \dots, x_7) = p(x_1|x_2, x_3)p(x_2, x_3, x_4, x_5, x_6, x_7). \tag{4.2.14}$$

Now we consider x_1 eliminated and move to the neighbours of x_1, namely x_2, x_3. The graph specifies that x_1, x_2, x_3 are independent of x_5, x_6, x_7 given x_4:

$$p(x_1, x_2, x_3|x_4, x_5, x_6, x_7) = p(x_1, x_2, x_3|x_4). \tag{4.2.15}$$

By summing both sides above over x_1 we have that $p(x_2, x_3|x_4, x_5, x_6, x_7) = p(x_2, x_3|x_4)$. Hence

$$p(x_2, x_3, x_4, x_5, x_6, x_7) = p(x_2, x_3|x_4, x_5, x_6, x_7)p(x_4, x_5, x_6, x_7) = p(x_2, x_3|x_4)p(x_4, x_5, x_6, x_7) \tag{4.2.16}$$

and

$$p(x_1, \dots, x_7) = p(x_1|x_2, x_3)p(x_2, x_3|x_4)p(x_4, x_5, x_6, x_7). \tag{4.2.17}$$

Having eliminated x_2, x_3, we now move to their neighbour(s) on the remaining graph, namely x_4. Continuing in this way, we necessarily end up with a distribution of the form

$$p(x_1, \dots, x_7) = p(x_1|x_2, x_3)p(x_2, x_3|x_4)p(x_4|x_5, x_6)p(x_5, x_6|x_7)p(x_7). \tag{4.2.18}$$

The pattern here is clear and shows that the Markov conditions mean that the distribution is expressible as a product of potentials defined on the cliques of the graph. That is $G \Rightarrow F$ where F is a factorisation into clique potentials on G. The converse is easily shown, namely that given a factorisation into clique potentials, the Markov conditions on G are implied. Hence $G \Leftrightarrow F$. It is clear that for any decomposable G, this always holds since we can always work inwards from the edges of the graph.

The Hammersley–Clifford theorem is a stronger result and shows that this factorisation property holds for any undirected graph, provided that the potentials are positive. For a formal proof, the reader is referred to [182, 36, 219]. An informal argument can be made by considering a specific example, and we take the 4-cycle $x_1 - x_2 - x_3 - x_4 - x_1$ from Fig. 4.1(a). The theorem states that for positive potentials ϕ, the Markov conditions implied by the graph mean that the distribution must be of the form

$$p(x_1, x_2, x_3, x_4) = \phi_{12}(x_1, x_2)\phi_{23}(x_2, x_3)\phi_{34}(x_3, x_4)\phi_{41}(x_4, x_1). \tag{4.2.19}$$

One may readily verify that for any distribution of this form $x_1 \perp\!\!\!\perp x_3 | x_2, x_4$. Consider including an additional term that links x_1 to a variable not a member of the cliques that x_1 inhabits. That is we include a term $\phi_{13}(x_1, x_3)$. Our aim is to show that a distribution of the form

$$p(x_1, x_2, x_3, x_4) = \phi_{12}(x_1, x_2)\phi_{23}(x_2, x_3)\phi_{34}(x_3, x_4)\phi_{41}(x_4, x_1)\phi_{13}(x_1, x_3) \tag{4.2.20}$$

cannot satisfy the Markov property $x_1 \perp\!\!\!\perp x_3 | x_2, x_4$. To do so we examine

$$p(x_1|x_2, x_3, x_4) = \frac{\phi_{12}(x_1, x_2)\phi_{23}(x_2, x_3)\phi_{34}(x_3, x_4)\phi_{41}(x_4, x_1)\phi_{13}(x_1, x_3)}{\sum_{x_1} \phi_{12}(x_1, x_2)\phi_{23}(x_2, x_3)\phi_{34}(x_3, x_4)\phi_{41}(x_4, x_1)\phi_{13}(x_1, x_3)} \tag{4.2.21}$$

$$= \frac{\phi_{12}(x_1, x_2)\phi_{41}(x_4, x_1)\phi_{13}(x_1, x_3)}{\sum_{x_1} \phi_{12}(x_1, x_2)\phi_{41}(x_4, x_1)\phi_{13}(x_1, x_3)}. \tag{4.2.22}$$

If we assume that the potential ϕ_{13} is weakly dependent on x_1 and x_3,

$$\phi_{13}(x_1, x_3) = 1 + \epsilon\psi(x_1, x_3) \tag{4.2.23}$$

where $\epsilon \ll 1$, then $p(x_1|x_2, x_3, x_4)$ is given by

$$\frac{\phi_{12}(x_1, x_2)\phi_{41}(x_4, x_1)}{\sum_{x_1} \phi_{12}(x_1, x_2)\phi_{41}(x_4, x_1)} (1 + \epsilon\psi(x_1, x_3)) \left(1 + \epsilon \frac{\sum_{x_1} \phi_{12}(x_1, x_2)\phi_{41}(x_4, x_1)\psi(x_1, x_3)}{\sum_{x_1} \phi_{12}(x_1, x_2)\phi_{41}(x_4, x_1)}\right)^{-1}. \tag{4.2.24}$$

By expanding $(1 + \epsilon f)^{-1} = 1 - \epsilon f + O\left(\epsilon^2\right)$ and retaining only terms that are first order in ϵ, we obtain

$$\begin{aligned} p(x_1|x_2, x_3, x_4) &= \frac{\phi_{12}(x_1, x_2)\phi_{41}(x_4, x_1)}{\sum_{x_1} \phi_{12}(x_1, x_2)\phi_{41}(x_4, x_1)} \\ &\times \left(1 + \epsilon\left[\psi(x_1, x_3) - \frac{\sum_{x_1} \phi_{12}(x_1, x_2)\phi_{41}(x_4, x_1)\psi(x_1, x_3)}{\sum_{x_1} \phi_{12}(x_1, x_2)\phi_{41}(x_4, x_1)}\right]\right) + O\left(\epsilon^2\right). \end{aligned} \tag{4.2.25}$$

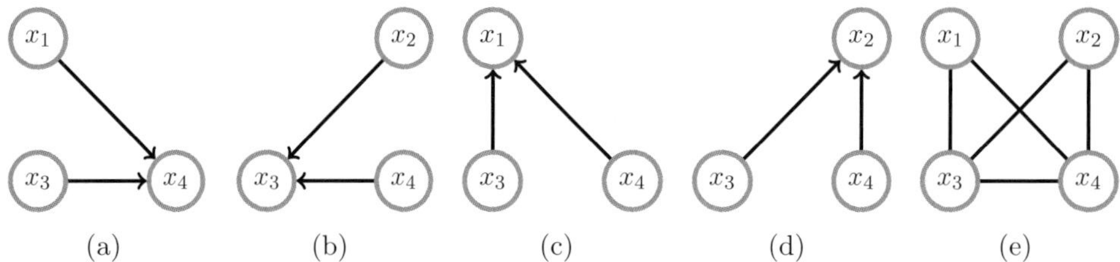

Figure 4.3 (**a–d**) Local conditional distributions. Note that no distribution is implied for the parents of each variable. That is, in (a) we are given the conditional $p(x_4|x_1, x_3)$ – one should not read from the graph that we imply x_1 and x_3 are marginally independent. (**e**) The Markov network consistent with the local distributions. If the local distributions are positive, by the Hammersley–Clifford theorem, the only joint distribution that can be consistent with the local distributions must be a Gibbs distribution with structure given by (e).

The first factor above is independent of x_3, as required by the Markov condition. However, for $\epsilon \neq 0$, the second term varies as a function of x_3. The reason for this is that one can always find a function $\psi(x_1, x_3)$ for which

$$\psi(x_1, x_3) \neq \frac{\sum_{x_1} \phi_{12}(x_1, x_2)\phi_{41}(x_4, x_1)\psi(x_1, x_3)}{\sum_{x_1} \phi_{12}(x_1, x_2)\phi_{41}(x_4, x_1)} \tag{4.2.26}$$

since the term $\psi(x_1, x_3)$ on the left is functionally dependent on x_1 whereas the term on the right is not a function of x_1. Hence, the only way we can ensure the Markov condition holds is if $\epsilon = 0$, namely that there is no connection between x_1 and x_3.

One can generalise this argument to show that if the graph of potentials in the distribution contains a link which is not present in G, then there is some distribution for which a corresponding Markov condition cannot hold. Informally, therefore, $G \Rightarrow F$. The converse $F \Rightarrow G$ is trivial.

The Hammersley–Clifford theorem also helps resolve questions as to when a set of positive local conditional distributions $p(x_i|\text{pa}(x_i))$ could ever form a consistent joint distribution $p(x_1, \ldots, x_n)$. Each local conditional distribution $p(x_i|\text{pa}(x_i))$ corresponds to a factor on the set of variables $\{x_i, \text{pa}(x_i)\}$, so we must include such a term in the joint distribution. The MN can form a joint distribution consistent with the local conditional distributions if and only if $p(x_1, \ldots, x_n)$ factorises according to

$$p(x_1, \ldots, x_n) = \frac{1}{Z} \exp\left(-\sum_c V_c(\mathcal{X}_c)\right) \tag{4.2.27}$$

where the sum is over all cliques and $V_c(\mathcal{X}_c)$ is a real function defined over the variables in the clique indexed by c. Equation (4.2.27) is equivalent to $\prod_c \phi(\mathcal{X}_c)$, namely an MN on positive clique potentials. The graph over which the cliques are defined is an undirected graph constructed by taking each local conditional distribution $p(x_i|\text{pa}(x_i))$ and drawing a clique on $\{x_i, \text{pa}(x_i)\}$. This is then repeated over all the local conditional distributions, see Fig. 4.3. Note that the Hammersley–Clifford theorem does not mean that, given a set of conditional distributions, we can always form a consistent joint distribution from them – rather it states what the functional form of a joint distribution has to be for the conditionals to be consistent with the joint, see Exercise 4.8.

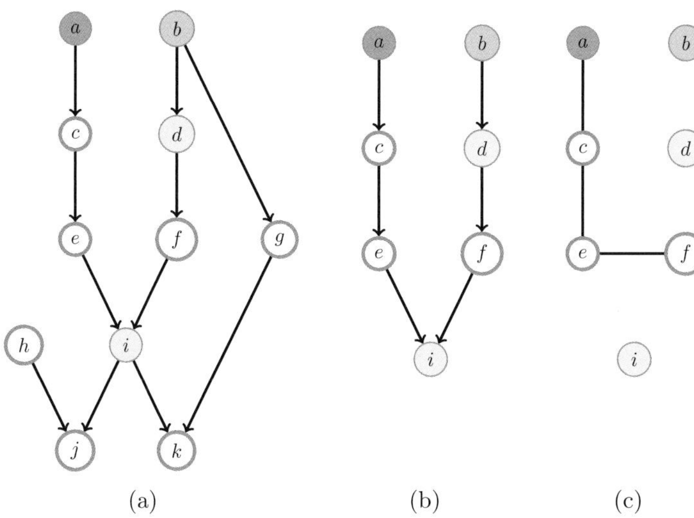

Figure 4.4 (**a**) Belief network for which we are interested in checking conditional independence $a \perp\!\!\!\perp b | \{d, i\}$. (**b**) Ancestral graph. (**c**) Ancestral moralised and separated graph for $a \perp\!\!\!\perp b | \{d, i\}$. There is no path from node a to node b so a and b are independent given d, i.

4.2.4 Conditional independence using Markov networks

For $\mathcal{X}$, $\mathcal{Y}$, $\mathcal{Z}$ each being collections of variables, in Section 3.3.4 we discussed an algorithm to determine if $\mathcal{X} \perp\!\!\!\perp \mathcal{Y} | \mathcal{Z}$ for belief networks. An alternative and more general method (since it handles directed and undirected graphs) uses the procedure below (see [78, 183]). See Fig. 4.4 for an example.

Procedure 4.2 (Ascertaining independence in Markov and belief networks) For Markov networks only the final separation criterion needs to be applied:

Ancestral Graph Remove from the DAG any node which is not in $\mathcal{X} \cup \mathcal{Y} \cup \mathcal{Z}$ and not an ancestor of a node in this set, together with any edges in or out of such nodes.

Ancestral Graph Identify the ancestors $\mathcal{A}$ of the nodes $\mathcal{X} \cup \mathcal{Y} \cup \mathcal{Z}$. Retain the nodes $\mathcal{X} \cup \mathcal{Y} \cup \mathcal{Z}$ but remove all other nodes which are not in $\mathcal{A}$, together with any edges in or out of such nodes.

Moralisation Add a link between any two remaining nodes which have a common child, but are not already connected by an arrow. Then remove remaining arrowheads.

Separation Remove links neighbouring $\mathcal{Z}$. In the undirected graph so constructed, look for a path which joins a node in $\mathcal{X}$ to one in $\mathcal{Y}$. If there is no such path deduce that $\mathcal{X} \perp\!\!\!\perp \mathcal{Y} | \mathcal{Z}$.

Note that the ancestral step in Procedure 4.2 for belief networks is intuitive since, given a set of nodes $\mathcal{X}$ and their ancestors $\mathcal{A}$, the remaining nodes $\mathcal{D}$ form a contribution to the distribution of the form $p(\mathcal{D}|\mathcal{X}, \mathcal{A})p(\mathcal{X}, \mathcal{A})$, so that summing over $\mathcal{D}$ simply has the effect of removing these variables from the DAG.

4.2.5 Lattice models

Undirected models have a long history in different branches of science, especially statistical mechanics on lattices and more recently as models in visual processing in which the models encourage neighbouring variables to be in the same states [36, 37, 116].

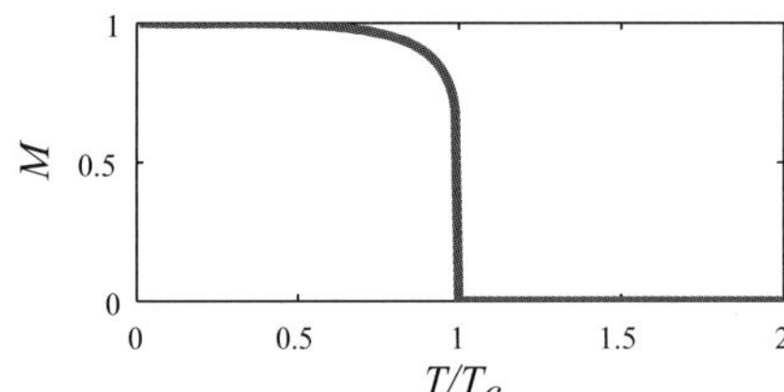

Figure 4.5 Onsagar magnetisation. As the temperature T decreases towards the critical temperature T_c a phase transition occurs in which a large fraction of the variables become aligned in the same state.

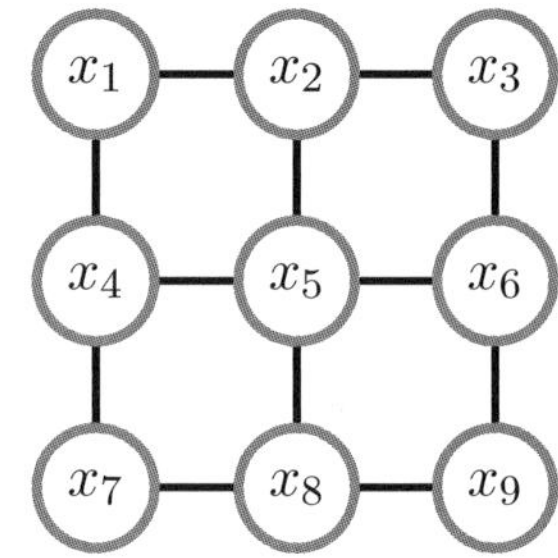

Consider a model in which our desire is that states of the binary valued variables $x_1, \ldots, x_9$, arranged on a lattice (right) should prefer their neighbouring variables to be in the same state

$$p(x_1, \ldots, x_9) = \frac{1}{Z} \prod_{i \sim j} \phi_{ij}(x_i, x_j) \tag{4.2.28}$$

where $i \sim j$ denotes the set of indices where i and j are neighbours in the undirected graph.

The Ising model

A set of potentials for Equation (4.2.28) that encourages neighbouring variables to have the same state is

$$\phi_{ij}(x_i, x_j) = e^{-\frac{1}{2T}(x_i - x_j)^2}, x_i \in \{-1, +1\}. \tag{4.2.29}$$

This corresponds to a well-known model of the physics of magnetic systems, called the *Ising model* which consists of 'mini-magnets' which prefer to be aligned in the same state, depending on the temperature T. For high T the variables behave independently so that no global magnetisation appears. For low T, there is a strong preference for neighbouring mini-magnets to become aligned, generating a strong macro-magnet. Remarkably, one can show that, in a very large two-dimensional lattice, below the so-called Curie temperature, $T_c \approx 2.269$ (for ± 1 variables), the system admits a phase change in that a large fraction of the variables become aligned – above T_c, on average, the variables are unaligned. This is depicted in Fig. 4.5 where $M = \left|\sum_{i=1}^{N} x_i\right| / N$ is the average alignment of the variables. That this phase change happens for non-zero temperature has driven considerable research in this and related areas [41]. Global coherence effects such as this that arise from weak local constraints are present in systems that admit *emergent behaviour*. Similar local constraints are popular in image restoration algorithms to clean up noise, under the assumption that noise will not show any local spatial coherence, whilst 'signal' will.

Example 4.2 Cleaning up images

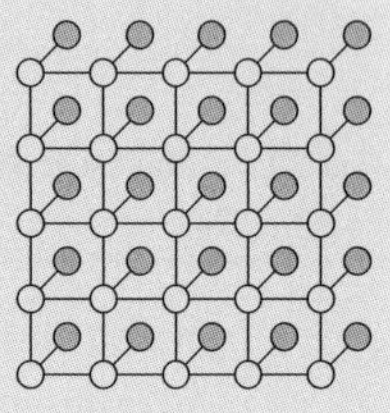

Consider a binary image defined on a set of pixels $x_i \in \{-1, +1\}, i = 1, \ldots, D$. We observe a noise-corrupted version y_i of each pixel x_i, in which the state of $y_i \in \{-1, +1\}$ is opposite to x_i with some probability. Here the filled nodes indicate observed noisy pixels and the unshaded nodes the latent clean pixels. Our interest is to 'clean up' the observed dirty image $\mathcal{Y}$, and find the most likely joint clean image $\mathcal{X}$.

A model for this situation is

$$p(\mathcal{X}, \mathcal{Y}) = \frac{1}{Z}\left[\prod_{i=1}^{D} \phi(x_i, y_i)\right]\left[\prod_{i\sim j} \psi(x_i, x_j)\right], \quad \phi(x_i, y_i) = e^{\beta x_i y_i}, \quad \psi(x_i, x_j) = e^{\alpha x_i x_j} \tag{4.2.30}$$

here $i \sim j$ indicates the set of latent variables that are neighbours. The potential ϕ encourages the noisy and clean pixel to be in the same state. Similarly, the potential $\psi(x_i, x_j)$ encourages neighbouring pixels to be in the same state. To find the most likely clean image, we need to compute

$$\underset{\mathcal{X}}{\text{argmax}}\ p(\mathcal{X}|\mathcal{Y}) = \underset{\mathcal{X}}{\text{argmax}}\ p(\mathcal{X}, \mathcal{Y}). \tag{4.2.31}$$

This is a computationally difficult task but can be approximated using iterative methods, see Section 28.9.

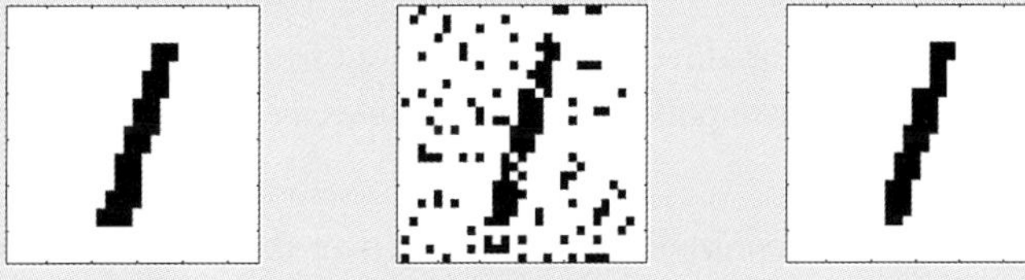

On the left is the clean image, from which a noisy corrupted image $\mathcal{Y}$ is formed (middle). The most likely restored image is given on the right. See `demoMRFclean.m`. Note that the parameter β is straightforward to set, given knowledge of the corruption probability $p_{corrupt}$, since $p(y_i \neq x_i|x_i) = \sigma(2\beta)$, so that $\beta = \frac{1}{2}\sigma^{-1}(p_{corrupt})$. Setting α is more complex since relating $p(x_i = x_j)$ to α is not straightforward, see Section 28.4.1. In the demonstration we set $\alpha = 10$, $p_{corrupt} = 0.15$.

4.3 Chain graphical models

Chain Graphs (CGs) contain both directed and undirected links. To develop the intuition, consider Fig. 4.6(a). The only terms that we can unambiguously specify from this depiction are $p(a)$ and $p(b)$ since there is no mixed interaction of directed and undirected edges at the a and b vertices. By probability, therefore, we must have

$$p(a, b, c, d) = p(a)p(b)p(c, d|a, b). \tag{4.3.1}$$

Looking at the graph, we might expect the interpretation to be

$$p(c, d|a, b) = \phi(c, d)p(c|a)p(d|b). \tag{4.3.2}$$

However, to ensure normalisation, and also to retain generality, we interpret this as

$$p(c, d|a, b) = \phi(c, d)p(c|a)p(d|b)\phi(a, b), \text{ with } \phi(a, b) \equiv \left(\sum_{c,d} \phi(c, d)p(c|a)p(d|b)\right)^{-1}. \tag{4.3.3}$$

This leads to the interpretation of a CG as a DAG over the chain components see below.

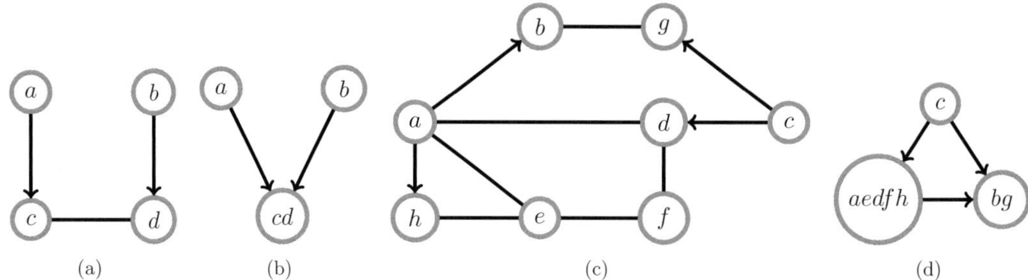

Figure 4.6 Chain graphs. The chain components are identified by deleting the directed edges and identifying the remaining connected components. (**a**) Chain components are (a), (b), (c, d), which can be written as a BN on the cluster variables in (b). (**c**) Chain components are (a, e, d, f, h), (b, g), (c), which has the cluster BN representation (d).

Definition 4.8 Chain component The chain components of a graph G are obtained by:

1. Forming a graph G' with directed edges removed from G.
2. Then each connected component in G' constitutes a chain component.

Each chain component represents a distribution over the variables of the component, conditioned on the parental components. The conditional distribution is itself a product over the cliques of the undirected component and moralised parental components, including also a factor to ensure normalisation over the chain component.

Definition 4.9 Chain graph distribution The distribution associated with a chain graph G is found by first identifying the chain components, τ. Then

$$p(x) = \prod_{\tau} p\left(\mathcal{X}_\tau | \text{pa}\left(\mathcal{X}_\tau\right)\right) \tag{4.3.4}$$

and

$$p\left(\mathcal{X}_\tau | \text{pa}\left(\mathcal{X}_\tau\right)\right) \propto \prod_{c \in \mathcal{C}_\tau} \phi\left(\mathcal{X}_{\mathcal{C}_\tau}\right) \tag{4.3.5}$$

where $\mathcal{C}_\tau$ denotes the union of the cliques in component τ together with the moralised parental components of τ, with ϕ being the associated functions defined on each clique. The proportionality factor is determined implicitly by the constraint that the distribution sums to 1.

BNs are CGs in which the connected components are singletons. MNs are CGs in which the chain components are simply the connected components of the undirected graph. Chain graphs can be useful since they are more expressive of CI statements than either belief networks or Markov networks alone. The reader is referred to [182] and [106] for further details.

Example 4.3 Chain graphs are more expressive than belief or Markov networks

Consider the chain graph in Fig. 4.7(a), which has chain component decomposition

$$p(a, b, c, d, e, f) = p(a)p(b)p(c, d, e, f|a, b) \tag{4.3.6}$$

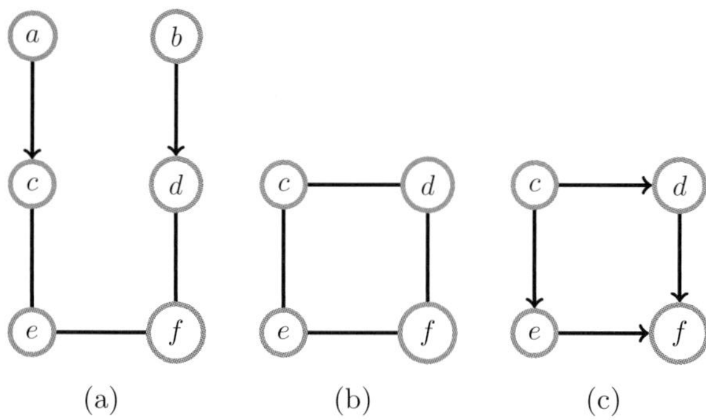

Figure 4.7 The CG (a) expresses $a \perp\!\!\!\perp b | \emptyset$ and $d \perp\!\!\!\perp e | (c, f)$. No directed graph could express both these conditions since the marginal distribution $p(c, d, e, f)$ is an undirected 4-cycle, (b). Any DAG on a 4-cycle must contain a collider, as in (c) and therefore express a different set of CI statements than (b). Similarly, no connected Markov network can express unconditional independence and hence (a) expresses CI statements that no belief network or Markov network alone can express.

where

$$p(c, d, e, f | a, b) = \phi(a, c)\phi(c, e)\phi(e, f)\phi(d, f)\phi(d, b)\phi(a, b) \tag{4.3.7}$$

with the normalisation requirement

$$\phi(a, b) \equiv \left(\sum_{c,d,e,f} \phi(a, c)\phi(c, e)\phi(e, f)\phi(d, f)\phi(d, b) \right)^{-1}. \tag{4.3.8}$$

The marginal $p(c, d, e, f)$ is given by

$$\phi(c, e)\phi(e, f)\phi(d, f) \underbrace{\sum_{a,b} \phi(a, b)p(a)p(b)\phi(a, c)\phi(d, b)}_{\phi(c,d)}. \tag{4.3.9}$$

Since the marginal distribution of $p(c, d, e, f)$ is an undirected 4-cycle, no DAG can express the CI statements contained in the marginal $p(c, d, e, f)$. Similarly no undirected distribution on the same skeleton as Fig. 4.7(a) could express that a and b are independent (unconditionally), i.e. $p(a, b) = p(a)p(b)$.

4.4 Factor graphs

Factor Graphs (FGs) are mainly used as part of inference algorithms.[1]

Definition 4.10 Factor graph Given a function

$$f(x_1, \ldots, x_n) = \prod_i \psi_i(\mathcal{X}_i), \tag{4.4.1}$$

the FG has a node (represented by a square) for each factor ψ_i, and a variable node (represented by a circle) for each variable x_j. For each $x_j \in \mathcal{X}_i$ an undirected link is made between factor ψ_i and variable x_j.

[1] Formally a FG is an alternative graphical depiction of a hypergraph [86] in which the vertices represent variables, and a hyperedge a factor as a function of the variables associated with the hyperedge. A FG is therefore a hypergraph with the additional interpretation that the graph represents a function defined as products over the associated hyperedges. Many thanks to Robert Cowell for this observation.

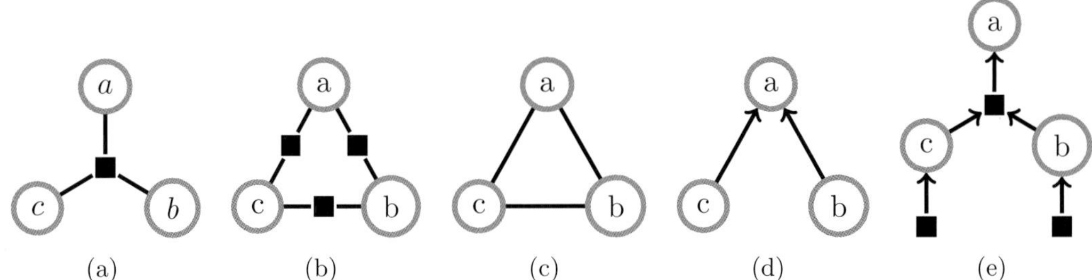

Figure 4.8 **(a)** $\phi(a, b, c)$. **(b)** $\phi(a, b)\phi(b, c)\phi(c, a)$. **(c)** $\phi(a, b, c)$. Both (a) and (b) have the same undirected graphical model, (c). **(d)** (a) is an undirected FG of (d). **(e)** Directed FG of the BN in (d). A directed factor represents a term $p(\text{children}|\text{parents})$. The advantage of (e) over (a) is that information regarding the marginal independence of variables b and c is clear from graph (e), whereas one could only ascertain this by examination of the numerical entries of the factors in graph (a).

When used to represent a distribution

$$p(x_1, \ldots, x_n) = \frac{1}{Z}\prod_i \psi_i(\mathcal{X}_i) \tag{4.4.2}$$

a normalisation constant $Z = \sum_{\mathcal{X}} \prod_i \psi_i(\mathcal{X}_i)$ is assumed.

For a factor $\psi_i(\mathcal{X}_i)$ which is a conditional distribution $p(x_i|\text{pa}(x_i))$, we may use directed links from the parents to the factor node, and a directed link from the factor node to the child x_i. This has the same structure as an (undirected) FG, but preserves the information that the factors are distributions.

Factor graphs are useful since they can preserve more information about the form of the distribution than either a belief network or a Markov network (or chain graph) can do alone. Consider the distribution

$$p(a, b, c) = \phi(a, b)\phi(a, c)\phi(b, c). \tag{4.4.3}$$

Represented as an MN, this must have a single clique, as given in Fig. 4.8(c). However, Fig. 4.8(c) could equally represent some unfactored clique potential $\phi(a, b, c)$ so that the factorised structure within the clique is lost. In this sense, the FG representation in Fig. 4.8(b) more precisely conveys the form of distribution equation (4.4.3). An unfactored clique potential $\phi(a, b, c)$ is represented by the FG Fig. 4.8(a). Hence different FGs can have the same MN since information regarding the structure of the clique potential is lost in the MN. Similarly, for a belief network, as in Fig. 4.8(d) one can represent this using a standard undirected FG, although more information about the independence is preserved by using a directed FG representation, as in Fig. 4.8(e). One can also consider partially directed FGs which contain both directed and undirected edges; this requires a specification of how the structure is normalised, one such being to use an approach analogous to the chain graph – see [103] for details.

4.4.1 Conditional independence in factor graphs

Conditional independence questions can be addressed using a rule which works with directed, undirected and partially directed FGs [103]. To determine whether two variables are independent given a set of conditioned variables, consider all paths connecting the two variables. If all paths

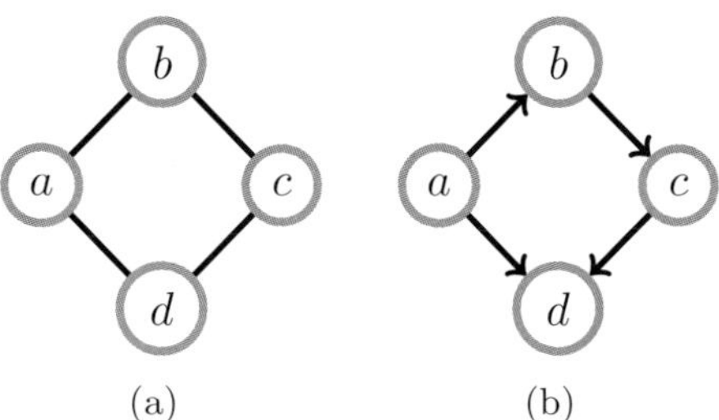

Figure 4.9 (**a**) An undirected model for which we wish to find a directed equivalent. (**b**) Every DAG with the same structure as the undirected model must have a situation where two arrows will point to a node, such as node *d* (otherwise one would have a cyclic graph). Summing over the states of variable *d* will leave a DAG on the variables *a*, *b*, *c* with no link between *a* and *c*. This cannot represent the undirected model since when one marginalises over *d* this adds a link between *a* and *c*.

are blocked, the variables are conditionally independent. A path is blocked if one or more of the following conditions is satisfied:

- One of the variables in the path is in the conditioning set.
- One of the variables or factors in the path has two incoming edges that are part of the path (variable or factor collider), and neither the variable or factor nor any of its descendants are in the conditioning set.

4.5 Expressiveness of graphical models

It is clear that directed distributions can be represented as undirected distributions since one can associate each (normalised) factor of the joint distribution with a potential. For example, the distribution $p(a|b)p(b|c)p(c)$ can be factored as $\phi(a, b)\phi(b, c)$, where $\phi(a, b) = p(a|b)$ and $\phi(b, c) = p(b|c)p(c)$, with $Z = 1$. Hence every belief network can be represented as some MN by simple identification of the factors in the distributions. However, in general, the associated undirected graph (which corresponds to the moralised directed graph) will contain additional links and independence information can be lost. For example, the MN of $p(c|a, b)p(a)p(b)$ is a single clique $\phi(a, b, c)$ from which one cannot graphically infer that $a \perp\!\!\!\perp b$.

The converse question is whether every undirected model can be represented by a BN with a readily derived link structure. Consider the example in Fig. 4.9. In this case, there is no directed model with the same link structure that can express the (in)dependencies in the undirected graph. Naturally, every probability distribution can be represented by some BN though it may not necessarily have a simple structure and be a 'fully connected' cascade style graph. In this sense the DAG cannot always graphically represent the independence properties that hold for the undirected distribution.

Definition 4.11 Independence maps A graph is an *independence map* (I-map) of a given distribution P if every conditional independence statement that one can derive from the graph G is true in the distribution P. That is

$$\mathcal{X} \perp\!\!\!\perp \mathcal{Y} | \mathcal{Z}_G \Rightarrow \mathcal{X} \perp\!\!\!\perp \mathcal{Y} | \mathcal{Z}_P \tag{4.5.1}$$

for all disjoint sets $\mathcal{X}$, $\mathcal{Y}$, $\mathcal{Z}$.

Similarly, a graph is a *dependence map* (D-map) of a given distribution P if every conditional independence statement that one can derive from P is true in the graph G. That is

$$\mathcal{X} \perp\!\!\!\perp \mathcal{Y} | \mathcal{Z}_G \Leftarrow \mathcal{X} \perp\!\!\!\perp \mathcal{Y} | \mathcal{Z}_P \tag{4.5.2}$$

for all disjoint sets $\mathcal{X}$, $\mathcal{Y}$, $\mathcal{Z}$.

A graph G which is both an I-map and a D-map for P is called a *perfect map* and

$$\mathcal{X} \perp\!\!\!\perp \mathcal{Y} | \mathcal{Z}_G \Leftrightarrow \mathcal{X} \perp\!\!\!\perp \mathcal{Y} | \mathcal{Z}_P \tag{4.5.3}$$

for all disjoint sets $\mathcal{X}$, $\mathcal{Y}$, $\mathcal{Z}$. In this case, the set of all conditional independence and dependence statements expressible in the graph G are consistent with P and vice versa.

Note that by contraposition, a dependence map is equivalent to

$$\mathcal{X} \top\!\!\!\top \mathcal{Y} | \mathcal{Z}_G \Rightarrow \mathcal{X} \top\!\!\!\top \mathcal{Y} | \mathcal{Z}_P \tag{4.5.4}$$

meaning that if $\mathcal{X}$ and $\mathcal{Y}$ are graphically dependent given $\mathcal{Z}$, then they are dependent in the distribution.

One way to think about this is to take a distribution P and write out a list $\mathcal{L}_P$ of all the independence statements. For a graph G, one writes a list of all the possible independence statements $\mathcal{L}_G$. Then:

$$\begin{array}{ll} \mathcal{L}_P \subseteq \mathcal{L}_G & \text{Dependence map (D-map)} \\ \mathcal{L}_P \supseteq \mathcal{L}_G & \text{Independence map (I-map)} \\ \mathcal{L}_P = \mathcal{L}_G & \text{Perfect map} \end{array} \tag{4.5.5}$$

In the above we assume the statement l is contained in $\mathcal{L}$ if it is consistent with (can be derived from) the independence statements in $\mathcal{L}$.

One can also discuss whether or not a distribution class has an associated map. That is whether or not all numerical instances of distributions consistent with the specified form obey the constraints required for the map. To do so we take any numerical instance of a distribution P_i consistent with a given class P and write out a list $\mathcal{L}_{P_i}$ of all the independence statements. One then takes the intersection $\mathcal{L}_P = \cap_i \mathcal{L}_{P_i}$ of all the lists from all possible distribution instances. This list is then used in Equation (4.5.5) to determine if there is an associated map. For example the distribution class

$$p(x, y, z) = p(z|x, y)p(x)p(y) \tag{4.5.6}$$

has a directed perfect map $x \rightarrow z \leftarrow y$. However, the undirected graph for the class Equation (4.5.6) is fully connected so that $\mathcal{L}_G$ is empty. For any distribution consistent with Equation (4.5.6) x and y are independent, a statement which is not contained in $\mathcal{L}_G$ – hence there is no undirected D-map and hence no perfect undirected map for the class represented in Equation (4.5.6).

Example 4.4

Consider the distribution (class) defined on variables t_1, t_2, y_1, y_2 [249]:

$$p(t_1, t_2, y_1, y_2) = p(t_1)p(t_2)\sum_h p(y_1|t_1, h)p(y_2|t_2, h)p(h). \tag{4.5.7}$$

In this case the list of all independence statements (for all distribution instances consistent with p) is

$$\mathcal{L}_P = \{t_1 \perp\!\!\!\perp (t_2, y_2),\ \ t_2 \perp\!\!\!\perp (t_1, y_1)\}. \tag{4.5.8}$$

Consider the graph of the BN

$$p(y_2|y_1, t_2)p(y_1|t_1)p(t_1)p(t_2). \tag{4.5.9}$$

For this we have

$$\mathcal{L}_G = \{t_2 \perp\!\!\!\perp (t_1, y_1)\}. \tag{4.5.10}$$

Hence $\mathcal{L}_G \subset \mathcal{L}_P$ so that the BN is an I-map for (4.5.7) since every independence statement in the BN is true for the distribution class in Equation (4.5.7). However, it is not a D-map since $\mathcal{L}_P \not\subseteq \mathcal{L}_G$. In this case no perfect map (a BN or an MN) can represent (4.5.7).

Remark 4.1 (Forcing dependencies?) Whilst graphical models as we have defined them ensure specified independencies, they seem to be inappropriate for ensuring specified dependencies. Consider the undirected graph $x - y - z$. Graphically this expresses that x and z are dependent. However, there are numerical instances of distributions for which this does not hold, for example

$$p_1(x, y, z) = \phi(x, y)\phi(y, z)/Z_1 \tag{4.5.11}$$

with $\phi(x, y) = \text{const}$. One might complain that this is a pathological case since any graphical representation of this particular instance contains no link between x and y. Maybe one should therefore 'force' potentials to be non-trivial functions of their arguments and thereby ensure dependency? Consider

$$\phi(x, y) = \frac{x}{y}, \qquad \phi(y, z) = yz. \tag{4.5.12}$$

In this case both potentials are non-trivial in the sense that they are truly functionally dependent on their arguments. Hence, the undirected network contains 'genuine' links $x - y$ and $y - z$. Nevertheless,

$$p_2(x, y, z) = \phi(x, y)\phi(y, z)/Z_2 \propto \frac{x}{y} yz = xz. \tag{4.5.13}$$

Hence $p_2(x, z) \propto xz \Rightarrow x \perp\!\!\!\perp z$. So 'forcing' local non-trivial functions does not guarantee dependence of path-connected variables. In this case, the algebraic cancellation is clear and the problem is again rather trivial since for p_2, $x \perp\!\!\!\perp y$ and $y \perp\!\!\!\perp z$, so one might assume that $x \perp\!\!\!\perp z$ (see however, Remark 1.2). However, there may be cases where such algebraic simplifications are highly non-trivial, though nevertheless true. See, for example, Exercise 3.17 in which we construct $p(x, y, z) \propto \phi(x, y)\phi(y, z)$ for which $x \top\!\!\!\top y$ and $y \top\!\!\!\top z$, yet $x \perp\!\!\!\perp z$.

4.6 Summary

- Graphical modelling is the discipline of representing probability models graphically.
- Belief networks intuitively describe which variables 'causally' influence others and are represented using directed graphs.
- A Markov network is represented by an undirected graph.
- Intuitively, linked variables in a Markov network are graphically dependent, describing local cliques of graphically dependent variables.
- Markov networks are historically important in physics and may be used to understand how global collaborative phenomena can emerge from only local dependencies.
- Graphical models are generally limited in their ability to represent all the possible logical consequences of a probabilistic model.
- Some special probabilistic models can be 'perfectly' mapped graphically.

- Factor graphs describe the factorisation of functions and are not necessarily related to probability distributions.

A detailed discussion of the axiomatic and logical basis of conditional independence is given in [47] and [280].

4.7 Code

`condindep.m`: Conditional independence test $p(X, Y|Z) = p(X|Z)p(Y|Z)$?

4.8 Exercises

4.1 1. Consider the pairwise Markov network,

$$p(x) = \phi(x_1, x_2)\phi(x_2, x_3)\phi(x_3, x_4)\phi(x_4, x_1). \tag{4.8.1}$$

Express in terms of ϕ the following:

$$p(x_1|x_2, x_4), \qquad p(x_2|x_1, x_3), \qquad p(x_3|x_2, x_4), \qquad p(x_4|x_1, x_3). \tag{4.8.2}$$

2. For a set of local distributions defined as

$$p_1(x_1|x_2, x_4), \qquad p_2(x_2|x_1, x_3), \qquad p_3(x_3|x_2, x_4), \qquad p_4(x_4|x_1, x_3) \tag{4.8.3}$$

is it always possible to find a joint distribution $p(x_1, x_2, x_3, x_4)$ consistent with these local conditional distributions?

4.2 Consider the Markov network

$$p(a, b, c) = \phi_{ab}(a, b)\phi_{bc}(b, c). \tag{4.8.4}$$

Nominally, by summing over b, the variables a and c are dependent. For binary b, explain a situation in which this is not the case, so that marginally, a and c are independent.

4.3 Show that for the Boltzmann machine defined on binary variables x_i with

$$p(\mathbf{x}) = \frac{1}{Z(\mathbf{W}, \mathbf{b})} \exp\left(\mathbf{x}^\mathsf{T}\mathbf{W}\mathbf{x} + \mathbf{x}^\mathsf{T}\mathbf{b}\right) \tag{4.8.5}$$

one may assume, without loss of generality, $\mathbf{W} = \mathbf{W}^\mathsf{T}$.

4.4 The *restricted Boltzmann machine* (or *Harmonium* [269]) is a constrained Boltzmann machine on a bipartite graph, consisting of a layer of visible variables $\mathbf{v} = (v_1, \ldots, v_V)$ and hidden variables $\mathbf{h} = (h_1, \ldots, h_H)$:

$$p(\mathbf{v}, \mathbf{h}) = \frac{1}{Z(\mathbf{W}, \mathbf{a}, \mathbf{b})} \exp\left(\mathbf{v}^\mathsf{T}\mathbf{W}\mathbf{h} + \mathbf{a}^\mathsf{T}\mathbf{v} + \mathbf{b}^\mathsf{T}\mathbf{h}\right) \tag{4.8.6}$$

All variables are binary taking states 0, 1.

1. Show that the distribution of hidden units conditional on the visible units factorises as

$$p(\mathbf{h}|\mathbf{v}) = \prod_i p(h_i|\mathbf{v}), \qquad \text{with } p(h_i = 1|\mathbf{v}) = \sigma\left(b_i + \sum_j W_{ji} v_j\right) \tag{4.8.7}$$

where $\sigma(x) = e^x/(1 + e^x)$.

2. By symmetry arguments, write down the form of the conditional $p(\mathbf{v}|\mathbf{h})$.
3. Is $p(\mathbf{h})$ factorised?
4. Can the partition function $Z(\mathbf{W}, \mathbf{a}, \mathbf{b})$ be computed efficiently for the RBM?

4.5 You are given that

$$x \perp\!\!\!\perp y | (z, u), \qquad u \perp\!\!\!\perp z | \emptyset. \tag{4.8.8}$$

Derive the most general form of probability distribution $p(x, y, z, u)$ consistent with these statements. Does this distribution have a simple graphical model?

4.6 The undirected graph represents a Markov network with nodes x_1, x_2, x_3, x_4, x_5, counting clockwise around the pentagon with potentials $\phi(x_i, x_j)$. Show that the joint distribution can be written as

$$p(x_1, x_2, x_3, x_4, x_5) = \frac{p(x_1, x_2, x_5)p(x_2, x_4, x_5)p(x_2, x_3, x_4)}{p(x_2, x_5)p(x_2, x_4)} \tag{4.8.9}$$

and express the marginal probability tables explicitly as functions of the potentials $\phi(x_i, x_j)$.

4.7 Consider the belief network on the right.

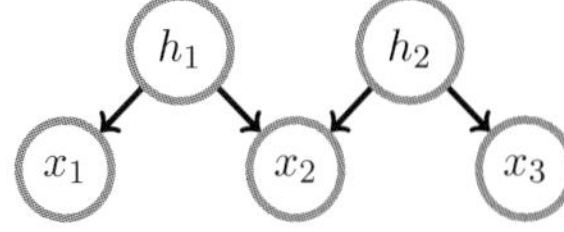

1. Write down a Markov network of $p(x_1, x_2, x_3)$.
2. Is your Markov network a perfect map of $p(x_1, x_2, x_3)$?

4.8 Two research labs work independently on the relationship between discrete variables x and y. Lab A proudly announces that they have ascertained distribution $p_A(x|y)$ from data. Lab B proudly announces that they have ascertained $p_B(y|x)$ from data.

1. Is it always possible to find a joint distribution $p(x, y)$ consistent with the results of both labs?
2. Is it possible to define consistent marginals $p(x)$ and $p(y)$, in the sense that $p(x) = \sum_y p_A(x|y)p(y)$ and $p(y) = \sum_x p_B(y|x)p(x)$? If so, explain how to find such marginals. If not, explain why not.

4.9 Research lab A states its findings about a set of variables $x_1, \ldots, x_n$ as a list L_A of conditional independence statements. Lab B similarly provides a list of conditional independence statements L_B.

1. Is it always possible to find a distribution which is consistent with L_A and L_B?
2. If the lists also contain dependence statements, how could one attempt to find a distribution that is consistent with both lists?

4.10 Consider the distribution

$$p(x, y, w, z) = p(z|w)p(w|x, y)p(x)p(y). \tag{4.8.10}$$

1. Write $p(x|z)$ using a formula involving (all or some of) $p(z|w)$, $p(w|x, y)$, $p(x)$, $p(y)$.
2. Write $p(y|z)$ using a formula involving (all or some of) $p(z|w)$, $p(w|x, y)$, $p(x)$, $p(y)$.
3. Using the above results, derive an explicit condition for $x \perp\!\!\!\perp y | z$ and explain if this is satisfied for this distribution.

4.11 Consider the distribution

$$p(t_1, t_2, y_1, y_2, h) = p(y_1|y_2, t_1, t_2, h)p(y_2|t_2, h)p(t_1)p(t_2)p(h). \tag{4.8.11}$$

1. Draw a belief network for this distribution.
2. Does the distribution

$$p(t_1, t_2, y_1, y_2) = \sum_h p(y_1|y_2, t_1, t_2, h)p(y_2|t_2, h)p(t_1)p(t_2)p(h) \tag{4.8.12}$$

have a perfect map belief network?
3. Show that for $p(t_1, t_2, y_1, y_2)$ as defined above $t_1 \perp\!\!\!\perp y_2|\emptyset$.

4.12 Consider the distribution

$$p(a, b, c, d) = \phi_{ab}(a, b)\phi_{bc}(b, c)\phi_{cd}(c, d)\phi_{da}(d, a) \tag{4.8.13}$$

where the ϕ are potentials.

1. Draw a Markov network for this distribution.
2. Explain if the distribution can be represented as a ('non-complete') belief network.
3. Derive explicitly if $a \perp\!\!\!\perp c|\emptyset$.

4.13 Show how for any singly connected Markov network, one may construct a Markov equivalent belief network.

4.14 Consider a pairwise binary Markov network defined on variables $s_i \in \{0, 1\}, i = 1, \ldots, N$, with $p(s) = \prod_{ij\in\mathcal{E}} \phi_{ij}(s_i, s_j)$, where $\mathcal{E}$ is a given edge set and the potentials ϕ_{ij} are arbitrary. Explain how to translate such a Markov network into a Boltzmann machine.

5 Efficient inference in trees

In previous chapters we discussed how to set up models. Inference then corresponds to operations such as summing over subsets of variables. In machine learning and related areas we will often deal with distributions containing hundreds of variables. In general inference it is computationally very expensive and it is useful to understand for which graphical structures this could be cheap in order that we may make models which we can subsequently compute with. In this chapter we discuss inference in a cheap case, namely trees, which has links to classical algorithms in many different fields from computer science (dynamic programming) to physics (transfer matrix methods).

5.1 Marginal inference

Given a distribution $p(x_1, \ldots, x_n)$, *inference* is the process of computing functions of the distribution. *Marginal inference* is concerned with the computation of the distribution of a subset of variables, possibly conditioned on another subset. For example, given a joint distribution $p(x_1, x_2, x_3, x_4, x_5)$ and evidence $x_1 = \text{tr}$, a marginal inference calculation is

$$p(x_5|x_1 = \text{tr}) \propto \sum_{x_2, x_3, x_4} p(x_1 = \text{tr}, x_2, x_3, x_4, x_5). \tag{5.1.1}$$

Marginal inference for discrete models involves summation and will be the focus of our development. In principle the algorithms carry over to continuous variable models although the lack of closure of most continuous distributions under marginalisation (the Gaussian being a notable exception) can make the direct transference of these algorithms to the continuous domain problematic. The focus here is on efficient inference algorithms for marginal inference in singly connected structures. An efficient algorithm for multiply connected graphs will be considered in Chapter 6.

5.1.1 Variable elimination in a Markov chain and message passing

A key concept in efficient inference is *message passing* in which information from the graph is summarised by local edge information. To develop this idea, consider the four-variable Markov chain (Markov chains are discussed in more depth in Section 23.1)

$$p(a, b, c, d) = p(a|b)p(b|c)p(c|d)p(d) \tag{5.1.2}$$

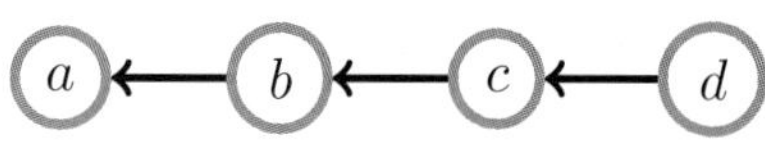

Figure 5.1 A Markov chain is of the form $p(x_T)\prod_{t=1}^{T-1} p(x_t|x_{t+1})$ for some assignment of the variables to labels x_t. Variable elimination can be carried out in time linear in the number of variables in the chain.

as given in Fig. 5.1, for which our task is to calculate the marginal $p(a)$. For simplicity, we assume that each of the variables has domain $\{0, 1\}$. Then

$$p(a=0) = \sum_{b\in\{0,1\},c\in\{0,1\},d\in\{0,1\}} p(a=0,b,c,d) = \sum_{b\in\{0,1\},c\in\{0,1\},d\in\{0,1\}} p(a=0|b)p(b|c)p(c|d)p(d). \tag{5.1.3}$$

We could carry out this computation by simply summing each of the probabilities for the $2\times 2\times 2 = 8$ states of the variables b, c and d. This would therefore require seven addition-of-two-numbers calls.

A more efficient approach is to push the summation over d as far to the right as possible:

$$p(a=0) = \sum_{b\in\{0,1\},c\in\{0,1\}} p(a=0|b)p(b|c) \underbrace{\sum_{d\in\{0,1\}} p(c|d)p(d)}_{\gamma_d(c)}. \tag{5.1.4}$$

where $\gamma_d(c)$ is a (two state) potential. Defining $\gamma_d(c)$ requires two addition-of-two-numbers calls, one call for each state of c. Similarly, we can distribute the summation over c as far to the right as possible:

$$p(a=0) = \sum_{b\in\{0,1\}} p(a=0|b) \underbrace{\sum_{c\in\{0,1\}} p(b|c)\gamma_d(c)}_{\gamma_c(b)}. \tag{5.1.5}$$

Then, finally,

$$p(a=0) = \sum_{b\in\{0,1\}} p(a=0|b)\gamma_c(b). \tag{5.1.6}$$

By distributing the summations we have made $3\times 2 = 6$ addition-of-two-numbers calls, compared to $2^3 - 1 = 7$ from the naive approach. Whilst this saving may not appear much, the important point is that the number of computations for a chain of length $T+1$ would be linear, $2T$, as opposed to exponential, $2^T - 1$ for the naive approach.

This procedure is called *variable elimination* since each time we sum over the states of a variable we eliminate it from the distribution. We can always perform variable elimination in a chain efficiently since there is a natural way to distribute the summations, working inwards from the edges. Note that in the above case, the potentials are in fact always distributions – we are just recursively computing the marginal distribution of the right leaf of the chain.

One can view the elimination of a variable as passing a *message* (information) to a neighbouring node on the graph. We can calculate a univariate-marginal of any tree (singly connected graph) by starting at a leaf of the tree, eliminating the variable there, and then working inwards, nibbling off each time a leaf of the remaining tree. Provided we perform elimination from the leaves inwards, then the structure of the remaining graph is simply a subtree of the original tree, albeit with the conditional probability table entries modified. This is guaranteed to enable us to calculate any marginal $p(x_i)$ using a number of summations which scales linearly with the number of variables in the tree.

Finding conditional marginals for a chain

Consider the following inference problem, Fig. 5.1: Given

$$p(a, b, c, d) = p(a|b)p(b|c)p(c|d)p(d), \tag{5.1.7}$$

find $p(d|\mathsf{a})$. This can be computed using

$$p(d|\mathsf{a}) \propto \sum_{b,c} p(\mathsf{a}, b, c, d) = \sum_{b,c} p(\mathsf{a}|b)p(b|c)p(c|d)p(d)$$
$$= \sum_{c} \underbrace{\sum_{b} p(\mathsf{a}|b)p(b|c)}_{\gamma_b(c)}\, p(c|d)p(d) \equiv \gamma_c(d). \tag{5.1.8}$$

The missing proportionality constant is found by repeating the computation for all states of variable d. Since we know that $p(d|\mathsf{a}) = k\gamma_c(d)$, where $\gamma_c(d)$ is the unnormalised result of the summation, we can use the fact that $\sum_d p(d|\mathsf{a}) = 1$ to infer that $k = 1/\sum_d \gamma_c(d)$.

In this example, the potential $\gamma_b(c)$ is not a distribution in c, nor is $\gamma_c(d)$. In general, one may view variable elimination as the passing of messages in the form of potentials from nodes to their neighbours. For belief networks variable elimination passes messages that are distributions when following the direction of the edge, and non-normalised potentials when passing messages against the direction of the edge.

Remark 5.1 (Variable elimination in trees as matrix multiplication) Variable elimination is related to the associativity of matrix multiplication. For Equation (5.1.2) above, we can define matrices

$$[\mathbf{M}_{ab}]_{i,j} = p(a = i|b = j), \quad [\mathbf{M}_{bc}]_{i,j} = p(b = i|c = j),$$
$$[\mathbf{M}_{cd}]_{i,j} = p(c = i|d = j), \quad [\mathbf{M}_d]_i = p(d = i), \quad [\mathbf{M}_a]_i = p(a = i). \tag{5.1.9}$$

Then the marginal $\mathbf{M}_a$ can be written

$$\mathbf{M}_a = \mathbf{M}_{ab}\mathbf{M}_{bc}\mathbf{M}_{cd}\mathbf{M}_d = \mathbf{M}_{ab}(\mathbf{M}_{bc}(\mathbf{M}_{cd}\mathbf{M}_d)) \tag{5.1.10}$$

since matrix multiplication is associative. This matrix formulation of calculating marginals is called the *transfer matrix* method, and is particularly popular in the physics literature [26].

Example 5.1 Where will the fly be?

You live in a house with three rooms, labelled 1, 2, 3. There is a door between rooms 1 and 2 and another between rooms 2 and 3. One cannot directly pass between rooms 1 and 3 in one timestep. An annoying fly is buzzing from one room to another and there is some smelly cheese in room 1 which seems to attract the fly more. Using x_t to indicate which room the fly is in at time t, with $\mathrm{dom}(x_t) = \{1, 2, 3\}$, the movement of the fly can be described by a transition

$$p(x_{t+1} = i|x_t = j) = M_{ij} \tag{5.1.11}$$

where M_{ij} is an element of the transition matrix

$$\mathbf{M} = \begin{pmatrix} 0.7 & 0.5 & 0 \\ 0.3 & 0.3 & 0.5 \\ 0 & 0.2 & 0.5 \end{pmatrix}. \tag{5.1.12}$$

The matrix $\mathbf{M}$ is called 'stochastic' meaning that, as required of a conditional probability table, its columns sum to 1, $\sum_{i=1}^{3} M_{ij} = 1$. Given that the fly is in room 1 at time $t = 1$, what is the probability of room occupancy at time $t = 5$? Assume a Markov chain which is defined by the joint distribution

$$p(x_1, \dots, x_T) = p(x_1) \prod_{t=1}^{T-1} p(x_{t+1}|x_t). \tag{5.1.13}$$

We are asked to compute $p(x_5|x_1 = 1)$ which is given by

$$\sum_{x_4,x_3,x_2} p(x_5|x_4)p(x_4|x_3)p(x_3|x_2)p(x_2|x_1 = 1). \tag{5.1.14}$$

Since the graph of the distribution is a Markov chain, we can easily distribute the summation over the terms. This is most easily done using the transfer matrix method, giving

$$p(x_5 = i|x_1 = 1) = [\mathbf{M}^4\mathbf{v}]_i \tag{5.1.15}$$

where $\mathbf{v}$ is a vector with components $(1, 0, 0)^\mathsf{T}$, reflecting the evidence that at time $t = 1$ the fly is in room 1. Computing this we have (to four decimal places of accuracy)

$$\mathbf{M}^4\mathbf{v} = \begin{pmatrix} 0.5746 \\ 0.3180 \\ 0.1074 \end{pmatrix}. \tag{5.1.16}$$

Similarly, at time $t = 6$, the occupancy probabilities are $(0.5612, 0.3215, 0.1173)$. The room occupancy probability is converging to a particular distribution – the *stationary* distribution of the Markov chain. One might ask where the fly is after an *infinite* number of timesteps. That is, we are interested in the large t behaviour of

$$p(x_{t+1}) = \sum_{x_t} p(x_{t+1}|x_t)p(x_t). \tag{5.1.17}$$

At convergence $p(x_{t+1}) = p(x_t)$. Writing $\mathbf{p}$ for the vector describing the stationary distribution, this means

$$\mathbf{p} = \mathbf{M}\mathbf{p}. \tag{5.1.18}$$

In other words, $\mathbf{p}$ is the eigenvector of $\mathbf{M}$ with eigenvalue 1 [134]. Computing this numerically, the stationary distribution is $(0.5435, 0.3261, 0.1304)$. Note that software packages usually return eigenvectors with $\sum_i e_i^2 = 1$ – the unit eigenvector therefore will usually require normalisation to make this a probability with $\sum_i e_i = 1$.

5.1.2 The sum-product algorithm on factor graphs

Both Markov and belief networks can be represented using factor graphs. For this reason it is convenient to derive a marginal inference algorithm for FGs since this then applies to both Markov

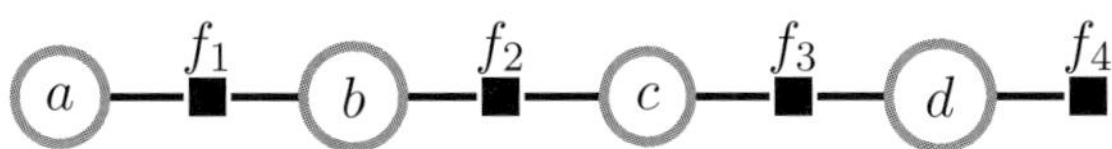

Figure 5.2 For singly connected structures without branches, simple messages from one variable to its neighbour may be defined to form an efficient marginal inference scheme.

and belief networks. This is termed the sum-product algorithm since to compute marginals we need to distribute the sum over variable states over the product of factors. In other texts, this is also referred to as *belief propagation*.

Non-branching graphs: variable-to-variable messages

Consider the distribution

$$p(a, b, c, d) = f_1(a, b) f_2(b, c) f_3(c, d) f_4(d) \tag{5.1.19}$$

which has the factor graph represented in Fig. 5.2. To compute the marginal $p(a, b, c)$, since the variable d only occurs locally, we use

$$\begin{aligned} p(a, b, c) &= \sum_d p(a, b, c, d) = \sum_d f_1(a, b) f_2(b, c) f_3(c, d) f_4(d) \\ &= f_1(a, b) f_2(b, c) \underbrace{\sum_d f_3(c, d) f_4(d)}_{\mu_{d\to c}(c)}. \end{aligned} \tag{5.1.20}$$

Here $\mu_{d\to c}(c)$ defines a message from node d to node c and is a function of the variable c. Similarly,

$$p(a, b) = \sum_c p(a, b, c) = f_1(a, b) \underbrace{\sum_c f_2(b, c) \mu_{d\to c}(c)}_{\mu_{c\to b}(b)}. \tag{5.1.21}$$

Hence

$$\mu_{c\to b}(b) = \sum_c f_2(b, c) \mu_{d\to c}(c). \tag{5.1.22}$$

It is clear how one can recurse this definition of messages so that for a chain of n variables the marginal of the first node can be computed in time linear in n. The term $\mu_{c\to b}(b)$ can be interpreted as carrying marginal information from the graph beyond c. For simple linear structures with no branching, messages from variables to variables are sufficient. However, as we will see below in more general structures with branching, it is useful to consider two types of messages, namely those from variables to factors and vice versa.

General singly connected factor graphs

The slightly more complex example,

$$p(a|b)p(b|c, d)p(c)p(d)p(e|d) \tag{5.1.23}$$

has the factor graph depicted in Fig. 5.3

$$f_1(a, b) f_2(b, c, d) f_3(c) f_4(d, e) f_5(d). \tag{5.1.24}$$

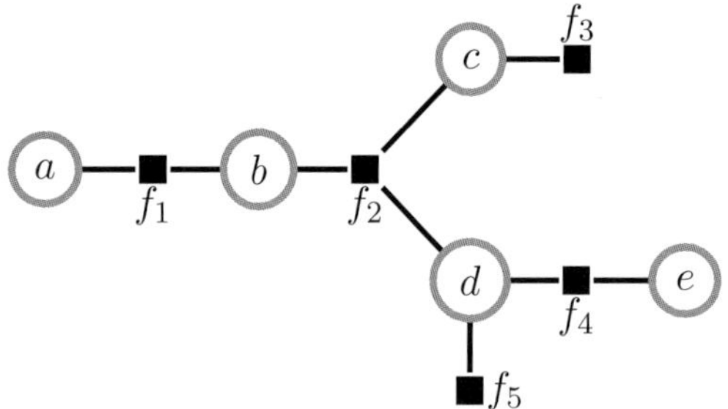

Figure 5.3 For a branching singly connected graph, it is useful to define messages from both factors to variables, and variables to factors.

The marginal $p(a, b)$ can be represented by an amputated graph with a message, since

$$p(a, b) = f_1(a, b) \underbrace{\sum_{c,d} f_2(b, c, d) f_3(c) f_5(d) \sum_e f_4(d, e)}_{\mu_{f_2 \to b}(b)} \tag{5.1.25}$$

where $\mu_{f_2 \to b}(b)$ is a message from a factor to a variable. This message can be constructed from messages arriving from the two branches through c and d, namely

$$\mu_{f_2 \to b}(b) = \sum_{c,d} f_2(b, c, d) \underbrace{f_3(c)}_{\mu_{c \to f_2}(c)} \underbrace{f_5(d) \sum_e f_4(d, e)}_{\mu_{d \to f_2}(d)}. \tag{5.1.26}$$

Similarly, we can interpret

$$\mu_{d \to f_2}(d) = \underbrace{f_5(d)}_{\mu_{f_5 \to d}(d)} \underbrace{\sum_e f_4(d, e)}_{\mu_{f_4 \to d}(d)}. \tag{5.1.27}$$

To complete the interpretation we identify $\mu_{c \to f_2}(c) \equiv \mu_{f_3 \to c}(c)$. In a non-branching link, one can more simply use a variable-to-variable message. To compute the marginal $p(a)$, we then have

$$p(a) = \underbrace{\sum_b f_1(a, b) \mu_{f_2 \to b}(b)}_{\mu_{f_1 \to a}(a)}. \tag{5.1.28}$$

For consistency of interpretation, one also can view the above as

$$\mu_{f_1 \to a}(a) = \sum_b f_1(a, b) \underbrace{\mu_{f_2 \to b}(b)}_{\mu_{b \to f_1}(b)}. \tag{5.1.29}$$

We can now see how a message from a factor to a node is formed from summing the product of incoming node-to-factor messages. Similarly, a message from a node to a factor is given by the product of incoming factor-to-node messages.

A convenience of this approach is that the messages can be reused to evaluate other marginal inferences. For example, it is clear that $p(b)$ is given by

$$p(b) = \underbrace{\sum_a f_1(a, b)}_{\mu_{f_1 \to b}(b)} \mu_{f_2 \to b}(b). \tag{5.1.30}$$

If we additionally desire $p(c)$, we need to define the message from f_2 to c,

$$\mu_{f_2 \to c}(c) = \sum_{b,d} f_2(b, c, d)\, \mu_{b \to f_2}(b)\, \mu_{d \to f_2}(d) \tag{5.1.31}$$

where $\mu_{b \to f_2}(b) \equiv \mu_{f_1 \to b}(b)$. This demonstrates the reuse of already computed message from d to f_2 to compute the marginal $p(c)$.

Definition 5.1 Message schedule A message schedule is a specified sequence of message updates. A valid schedule is that a message can be sent from a node only when that node has received all requisite messages from its neighbours. In general, there is more than one valid updating schedule.

Sum-product algorithm

The sum-product algorithm is described below in which messages are updated as a function of incoming messages. One then proceeds by computing the messages in a schedule that allows the computation of a new message based on previously computed messages, until all messages from all factors to variables and vice versa have been computed.

Procedure 5.1 (Sum-product messages on factor graphs) Given a distribution defined as a product on subsets of the variables, $p(\mathcal{X}) = \frac{1}{Z}\prod_f \phi_f(\mathcal{X}_f)$, provided the factor graph is singly connected we can carry out summation over the variables efficiently.

Initialisation Messages from leaf node factors are initialised to the factor. Messages from leaf variable nodes are set to unity.

Variable-to-factor message

$$\mu_{x \to f}(x) = \prod_{g \in \{\mathrm{ne}(x) \setminus f\}} \mu_{g \to x}(x)$$

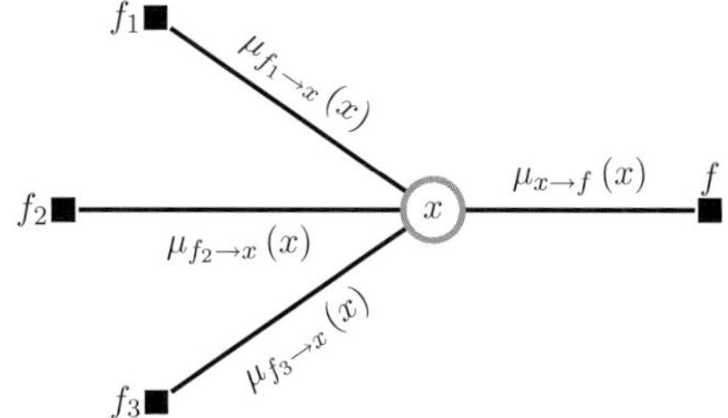

Factor-to-variable message

$$\mu_{f \to x}(x) = \sum_{\mathcal{X}_f \setminus x} \phi_f(\mathcal{X}_f) \prod_{y \in \{\mathrm{ne}(f) \setminus x\}} \mu_{y \to f}(y)$$

We write $\sum_{\mathcal{X}_f \setminus x}$ to denote summation over all states in the set of variables $\mathcal{X}_f \setminus x$.

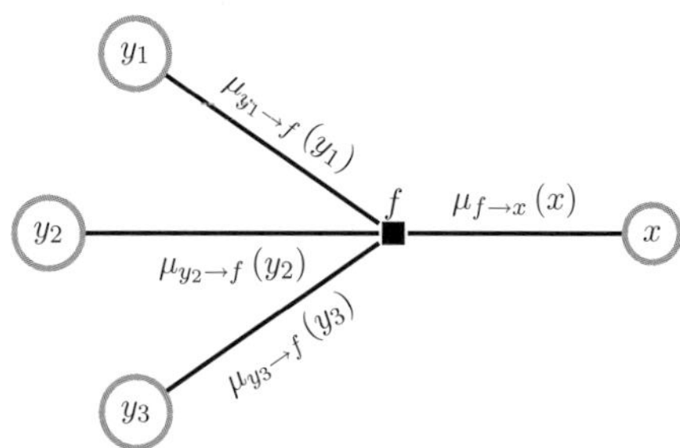

Marginal

$$p(x) \propto \prod_{f \in \text{ne}(x)} \mu_{f \to x}(x)$$

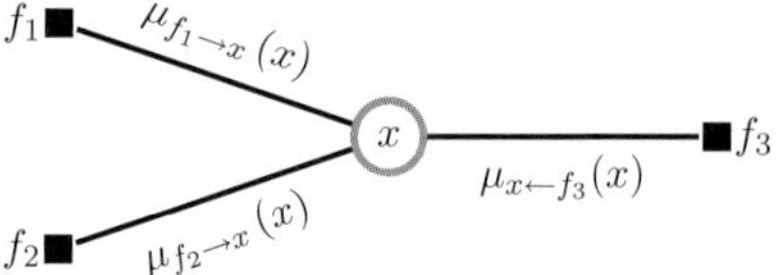

For marginal inference, the important information is the relative size of the message states so that we may renormalise messages as we wish. Since the marginal will be proportional to the incoming messages for that variable, the normalisation constant is trivially obtained using the fact that the marginal must sum to 1. However, if we wish to also compute any normalisation constant using these messages, we cannot normalise the messages since this global information will then be lost.

5.1.3 Dealing with evidence

For a distribution which splits into evidential and non-evidential variables, $\mathcal{X} = \mathcal{X}_e \cup \mathcal{X}_n$, the marginal of a non-evidential variable $p(x_i, \mathcal{X}_e)$ is given by summing over all the variables in $\mathcal{X}_n$ (except for x_i) with $\mathcal{X}_e$ set into their evidential states. There are two ways to reconcile this with the factor graph formalism. Either we can simply say that by setting the variables $\mathcal{X}_e$, we define a new factor graph on $\mathcal{X}_n$, and then pass messages on this new factor graph. Alternatively, we can define the potentials which contain the variables $\mathcal{X}_e$ by multiplying each potential that contains an evidential variable by a delta function (an indicator) that is zero unless the variable x_n is in the specified evidential state. When we then perform a factor-to-variable message, the sum of this modified potential over any of the evidential variable states will be zero except for that state which corresponds to the evidential setting. Another way to view this is that the sum in the factor-to-variable message is only over the non-evidential variables, with any evidential variables in the potential set into their evidential states.

5.1.4 Computing the marginal likelihood

For a distribution defined as products over potentials $\phi_f(\mathcal{X}_f)$

$$p(\mathcal{X}) = \frac{1}{Z} \prod_f \phi_f(\mathcal{X}_f) \tag{5.1.32}$$

the normalisation is given by

$$Z = \sum_{\mathcal{X}} \prod_f \phi_f(\mathcal{X}_f). \tag{5.1.33}$$

To compute this summation efficiently we take the product of all incoming messages to an arbitrarily chosen variable x and then sum over the states of that variable:

$$Z = \sum_x \prod_{f \in \text{ne}(x)} \mu_{f \to x}(x). \tag{5.1.34}$$

If the factor graph is derived from setting a subset of variables of a BN in evidential states then the summation over all non-evidential variables will yield the marginal on the visible (evidential) variables. For example

$$p(\mathsf{b}, \mathsf{d}) = \sum_{a,c} p(a|\mathsf{b}) p(\mathsf{b}|c) p(c|\mathsf{d}) p(\mathsf{d}). \tag{5.1.35}$$

This can be interpreted as requiring the sum over a product of suitably defined factors. Hence one can readily find the marginal likelihood of the evidential variables for singly connected BNs.

Log messages

For the above method to work, the absolute (not relative) values of the messages are required, which prohibits renormalisation at each stage of the message-passing procedure. However, without normalisation the numerical value of messages can become very small, particularly for large graphs, and numerical precision issues can occur. A remedy in this situation is to work with log messages,

$$\lambda = \log \mu. \tag{5.1.36}$$

For this, the variable-to-factor messages

$$\mu_{x\to f}(x) = \prod_{g\in\{\mathrm{ne}(x)\setminus f\}} \mu_{g\to x}(x) \tag{5.1.37}$$

become simply

$$\lambda_{x\to f}(x) = \sum_{g\in\{\mathrm{ne}(x)\setminus f\}} \lambda_{g\to x}(x). \tag{5.1.38}$$

More care is required for the factors to variable messages, which are defined by

$$\mu_{f\to x}(x) = \sum_{\mathcal{X}_f\setminus x} \phi_f(\mathcal{X}_f) \prod_{y\in\{\mathrm{ne}(f)\setminus x\}} \mu_{y\to f}(y). \tag{5.1.39}$$

Naively, one may write

$$\lambda_{f\to x}(x) = \log\left(\sum_{\mathcal{X}_f\setminus x} \phi_f(\mathcal{X}_f) \exp\left(\sum_{y\in\{\mathrm{ne}(f)\setminus x\}} \lambda_{y\to f}(y)\right)\right). \tag{5.1.40}$$

However, the exponentiation of the log messages will cause potential numerical precision problems. A solution to this numerical difficulty is obtained by finding the largest value of the incoming log messages,

$$\lambda^*_{y\to f} = \max_{y\in\{\mathrm{ne}(f)\setminus x\}} \lambda_{y\to f}(y). \tag{5.1.41}$$

Then

$$\lambda_{f\to x}(x) = \lambda^*_{y\to f} + \log\left(\sum_{\mathcal{X}_f\setminus x} \phi_f(\mathcal{X}_f) \exp\left(\sum_{y\in\{\mathrm{ne}(f)\setminus x\}} \lambda_{y\to f}(y) - \lambda^*_{y\to f}\right)\right). \tag{5.1.42}$$

By construction the terms $\exp\left(\sum_{y\in\{\mathrm{ne}(f)\setminus x\}} \lambda_{y\to f}(y) - \lambda^*_{y\to f}\right)$ will be ≤ 1, with at least one term being equal to 1. This ensures that the dominant numerical contributions to the summation are computed accurately.

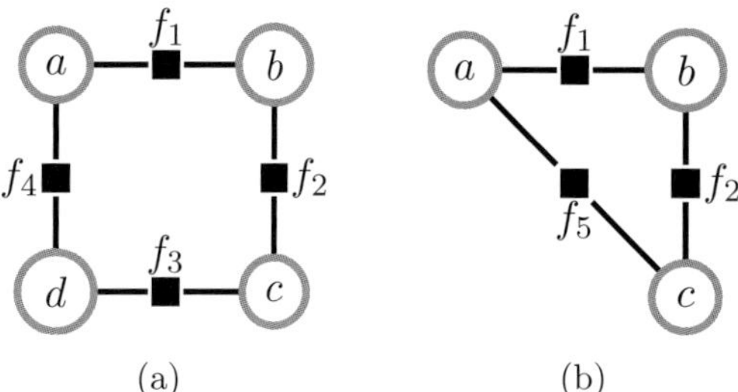

Figure 5.4 (**a**) Factor graph with a loop. (**b**) Eliminating the variable d adds an edge between a and c, demonstrating that, in general, one cannot perform marginal inference in loopy graphs by simply passing messages along existing edges in the original graph.

Log marginals are readily found using

$$\log p(x) = \sum_{f \in \text{ne}(x)} \lambda_{f \to x}(x). \tag{5.1.43}$$

5.1.5 The problem with loops

Loops cause a problem with variable elimination (or message-passing) techniques since once a variable is eliminated the structure of the 'amputated' graph in general changes. For example, consider the FG

$$p(a, b, c, d) = f_1(a, b)\, f_2(b, c)\, f_3(c, d)\, f_4(a, d) \tag{5.1.44}$$

depicted in Fig. 5.4(a). The marginal $p(a, b, c)$ is given by

$$p(a, b, c) = f_1(a, b)\, f_2(b, c) \underbrace{\sum_d f_3(c, d)\, f_4(a, d)}_{f_5(a,c)} \tag{5.1.45}$$

which adds a link ac in the amputated graph, see Fig. 5.4(b). This means that one cannot account for information from variable d by simply updating potentials on links in the original graph – one needs to account for the fact that the structure of the graph changes. The junction tree algorithm, Chapter 6, deals with this by combining variables to make a new singly connected graph for which the graph structure remains singly connected under variable elimination.

5.2 Other forms of inference

5.2.1 Max-product

A common interest is the most likely state of distribution. That is

$$\underset{x_1, x_2, \ldots, x_n}{\text{argmax}}\; p(x_1, x_2, \ldots, x_n). \tag{5.2.1}$$

To compute this efficiently for trees we exploit any factorisation structure of the distribution, analogous to the sum-product algorithm. That is, we aim to distribute the maximisation so that only local computations are required. To develop the algorithm, consider a function which can be represented as an undirected chain,

$$f(x_1, x_2, x_3, x_4) = \phi(x_1, x_2)\phi(x_2, x_3)\phi(x_3, x_4) \tag{5.2.2}$$

for which we wish to find the joint state $x_1^*, x_2^*, x_3^*, x_4^*$ which maximises f. Firstly, we calculate the maximum *value* of f. Since potentials are non-negative, we may write

$$\max_{\mathbf{x}} f(\mathbf{x}) = \max_{x_1,x_2,x_3,x_4} \phi(x_1,x_2)\phi(x_2,x_3)\phi(x_3,x_4) = \max_{x_1,x_2,x_3} \phi(x_1,x_2)\phi(x_2,x_3) \underbrace{\max_{x_4} \phi(x_3,x_4)}_{\gamma_4(x_3)}$$

$$= \max_{x_1,x_2} \phi(x_1,x_2) \underbrace{\max_{x_3} \phi(x_2,x_3)\gamma_4(x_3)}_{\gamma_3(x_2)} = \max_{x_1,x_2} \phi(x_1,x_2)\gamma_3(x_2) = \max_{x_1} \underbrace{\max_{x_2} \phi(x_1,x_2)\gamma_3(x_2)}_{\gamma_2(x_1)}.$$

The final equation corresponds to solving a single variable optimisation and determines both the optimal value of the function f and also the optimal state $x_1^* = \underset{x_1}{\text{argmax}}\, \gamma_2(x_1)$. Given x_1^*, the optimal x_2 is given by $x_2^* = \underset{x_2}{\text{argmax}}\, \phi(x_1^*, x_2)\gamma_3(x_2)$, and similarly $x_3^* = \underset{x_3}{\text{argmax}}\, \phi(x_2^*, x_3)\gamma_4(x_3)$, $x_4^* = \underset{x_4}{\text{argmax}}\, \phi(x_3^*, x_4)$. This procedure is called *backtracking*. Note that we could have equally started at the other end of the chain by defining messages γ that pass information from x_i to x_{i+1}. The chain structure of the function ensures that the maximal value (and its state) can be computed in time which scales *linearly* with the number of factors in the function. There is no requirement here that the function f corresponds to a probability distribution (though the factors must be non-negative).

Example 5.2

Consider a distribution defined over binary variables:

$$p(a, b, c) \equiv p(a|b)p(b|c)p(c) \tag{5.2.3}$$

with

$$p(a = \text{tr}|b = \text{tr}) = 0.3, \quad p(a = \text{tr}|b = \text{fa}) = 0.2, \quad p(b = \text{tr}|c = \text{tr}) = 0.75$$
$$p(b = \text{tr}|c = \text{fa}) = 0.1, \quad p(c = \text{tr}) = 0.4.$$

What is the most likely joint configuration, $\underset{a,b,c}{\text{argmax}}\, p(a, b, c)$?

Naively, we could evaluate $p(a, b, c)$ over all the eight joint states of a, b, c and select that state with highest probability. An alternative message passing approach is to define

$$\gamma_c(b) \equiv \max_c p(b|c)p(c). \tag{5.2.4}$$

For the state $b = \text{tr}$,

$$p(b = \text{tr}|c = \text{tr})p(c = \text{tr}) = 0.75 \times 0.4, \quad p(b = \text{tr}|c = \text{fa})p(c = \text{fa}) = 0.1 \times 0.6. \tag{5.2.5}$$

Hence, $\gamma_c(b = \text{tr}) = 0.75 \times 0.4 = 0.3$. Similarly, for $b = \text{fa}$,

$$p(b = \text{fa}|c = \text{tr})p(c = \text{tr}) = 0.25 \times 0.4, \quad p(b = \text{fa}|c = \text{fa})p(c = \text{fa}) = 0.9 \times 0.6. \tag{5.2.6}$$

Hence, $\gamma_c(b = \text{fa}) = 0.9 \times 0.6 = 0.54$.

We now consider

$$\gamma_b(a) \equiv \max_b p(a|b)\gamma_c(b). \tag{5.2.7}$$

For $a = \text{tr}$, the state $b = \text{tr}$ has value

$$p(a = \text{tr}|b = \text{tr})\gamma_c(b = \text{tr}) = 0.3 \times 0.3 = 0.09 \tag{5.2.8}$$

and state $b = \text{fa}$ has value

$$p(a = \text{tr}|b = \text{fa})\gamma_c(b = \text{fa}) = 0.2 \times 0.54 = 0.108. \tag{5.2.9}$$

Hence $\gamma_b(a = \text{tr}) = 0.108$. Similarly, for $a = \text{fa}$, the state $b = \text{tr}$ has value

$$p(a = \text{fa}|b = \text{tr})\gamma_c(b = \text{tr}) = 0.7 \times 0.3 = 0.21 \tag{5.2.10}$$

and state $b = \text{fa}$ has value

$$p(a = \text{fa}|b = \text{fa})\gamma_c(b = \text{fa}) = 0.8 \times 0.54 = 0.432 \tag{5.2.11}$$

giving $\gamma_b(a = \text{fa}) = 0.432$. Now we can compute the optimal state

$$a^* = \underset{a}{\text{argmax}}\ \gamma_b(a) = \text{fa}. \tag{5.2.12}$$

Given this optimal state, we can backtrack, giving

$$b^* = \underset{b}{\text{argmax}}\ p(a = \text{fa}|b)\gamma_c(b) = \text{fa}, \quad c^* = \underset{c}{\text{argmax}}\ p(b = \text{fa}|c)p(c) = \text{fa}. \tag{5.2.13}$$

Note that in the backtracking process, we already have all the information required from the computation of the messages γ.

If we want to find the most likely state for a variable in the centre of the chain we can therefore pass messages from one end to the other followed by backtracking. This is the approach for example taken by the Viterbi algorithm for HMMs, Section 23.2. Alternatively, we can send messages (carrying the result of maximisations) simultaneously from both ends of the chain and then read off the maximal state of the variable from the state which maximises the product of incoming messages. The first is a sequential procedure since we must have passed messages along the chain before we can backtrack. The second is a parallel procedure in which messages can be sent concurrently. The latter approach can be represented using a factor graph as described below.

Using a factor graph

One can also use the factor graph to compute the joint most probable state. Provided that a full schedule of message passing has occurred, the product of messages into a variable equals the maximum value of the joint function with respect to all other variables. One can then simply read off the most probable state by maximising this local potential.

Procedure 5.2 (Max-product messages on factor graphs) Given a distribution defined as a product on subsets of the variables, $p(\mathcal{X}) = \frac{1}{Z}\prod_f \phi_f(\mathcal{X}_f)$, provided the factor graph is singly connected we can carry out maximisation over the variables efficiently.

Initialisation Messages from leaf node factors are initialised to the factor. Messages from leaf variable nodes are set to unity.

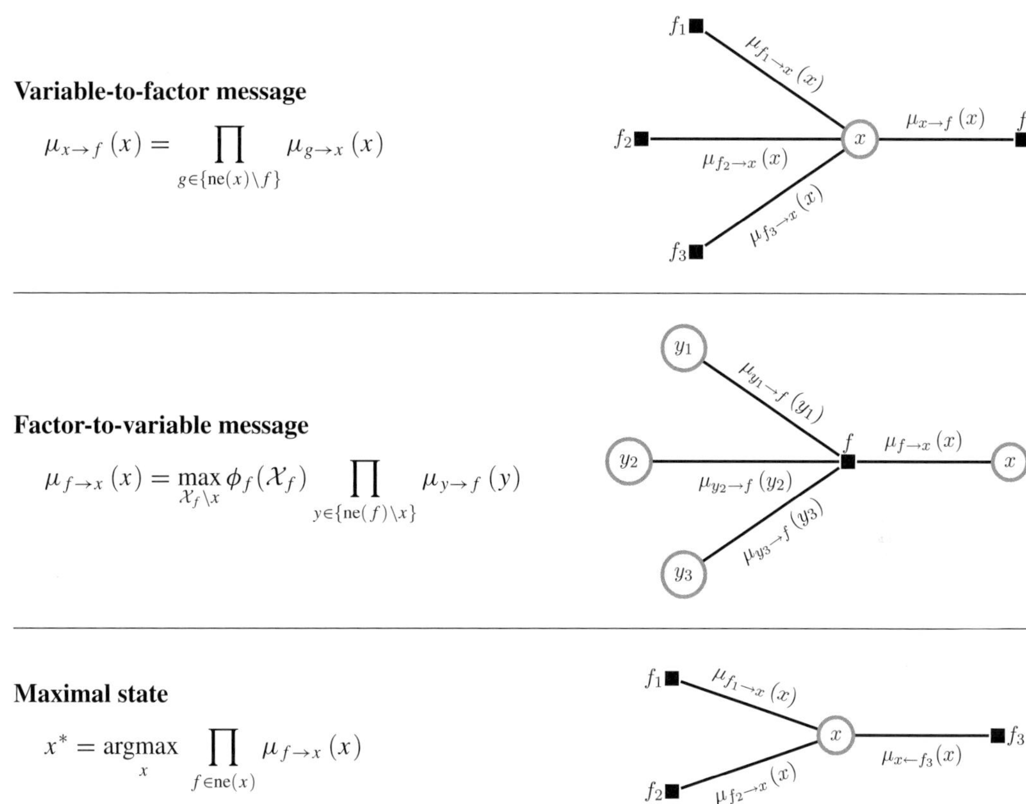

This algorithm is also called *belief revision*.

5.2.2 Finding the N most probable states

It is often of interest to calculate not just the most likely joint state, but the N most probable states, particularly in cases where the optimal state is only slightly more probable than other states. This is an interesting problem in itself and can be tackled with a variety of methods. A general technique is given by Nilson [226] which is based on the junction tree formalism, Chapter 6, and the construction of candidate lists, see for example [72].

For singly connected structures, several approaches have been developed [227, 319, 285, 272]. For the hidden Markov model, Section 23.2, a simple algorithm is the N-Viterbi approach which stores the N-most probable messages at each stage of the propagation. For more general singly connected graphs one can extend the max-product algorithm to an N-max-product algorithm by retaining at each stage the N most probable messages, see below.

N-max-product

The algorithm for N*-max-product* is a minor modification of the standard max-product algorithm. Computationally, a straightforward way to accomplish this is to introduce an additional variable for each message that is used to index the most likely messages. We will first develop this for message passing on an undirected graph. Consider the distribution

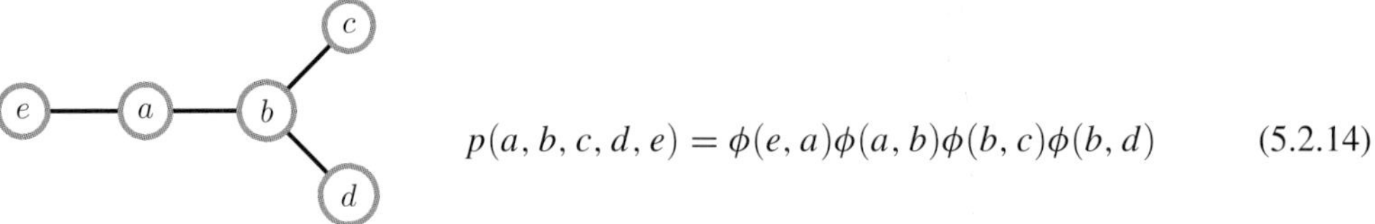

$$p(a, b, c, d, e) = \phi(e, a)\phi(a, b)\phi(b, c)\phi(b, d) \tag{5.2.14}$$

for which we wish to find the two most probable values. Using the notation

$$\overset{i}{\max_x} f(x) \tag{5.2.15}$$

for the ith highest value of $f(x)$, the maximisation over d can be expressed using the message

$$\gamma_d(b, 1) = \overset{1}{\max_d} \phi(b, d), \qquad \gamma_d(b, 2) = \overset{2}{\max_d} \phi(b, d). \tag{5.2.16}$$

Defining messages similarly, the two most likely values of $p(a, b, c, d, e)$ can be computed using

$$\overset{1:2}{\max_{a,b,c,d,e}} \phi(e, a)\phi(a, b)\phi(b, c)\phi(b, d) = \overset{1:2}{\max_{e,m_a}} \underbrace{\overset{1:2}{\max_{a,m_b}} \phi(e, a) \underbrace{\overset{1:2}{\max_{b,m_c,m_d}} \phi(a, b) \underbrace{\overset{1:2}{\max_c} \phi(b, c)}_{\gamma_c(b,m_c)} \underbrace{\overset{1:2}{\max_d} \phi(b, d)}_{\gamma_d(b,m_d)}}_{\gamma_b(a,m_b)}}_{\gamma_a(e,m_a)} \tag{5.2.17}$$

where m_a, m_b, m_c and m_d index the two highest values. At the final stage we now have a table with $\dim(e) \times 2$ entries, from which we compute the highest two joint states of e, m_a. Given these first most likely joint states, e^*, m_a^* one then backtracks to find the most likely state of a, m_b using $\arg\max^{1:2}_{a,m_b} \phi(e^*, a)\gamma_b(a, m_b)$. One continues backtracking, then finding the most likely state of b, m_c, m_d and finally c and d. One may then restart the backtracking using the second most likely state of e, m_a and continue to find the most likely states to have given rise to this, leading to the second most likely joint state.

The translation of this to the factor graph formalism is straightforward and contained in `maxNprodFG.m`. Essentially the only modification required is to define extended messages which contain the N-most likely messages computed at each stage. A variable-to-factor message consists of the product of extended messages. For a factor-to-variable message, all extended messages from the neighbours are multiplied together into a large table. The N-most probable messages are retained, defining a new extended message. The N-most probable states for each variable can then be read off by finding the variable state that maximises the product of incoming extended messages.

Branches are the bottleneck in the above computation. Consider a term as part of a larger system with

$$\phi(z, a)\phi(a, b)\phi(a, c). \tag{5.2.18}$$

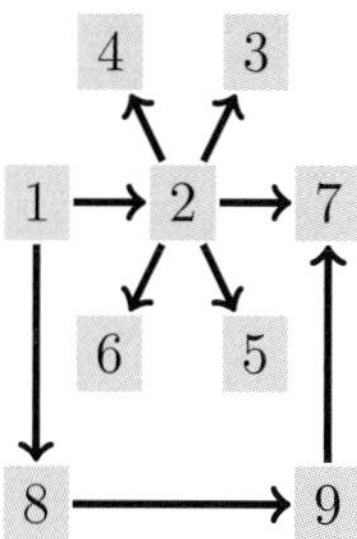

Figure 5.5 State-transition diagram (weights not shown). The shortest (unweighted) path from state 1 to state 7 is 1 – 2 – 7. Considered as a Markov chain (random walk), the most probable path from state 1 to state 7 is 1 – 8 – 9 – 7. The latter path is longer but more probable since for the path 1 – 2 – 7, the probability of exiting from state 2 into state 7 is 1/5 (assuming each transition is equally likely). See `demoMostProbablePath.m`.

We would like to pass a message along the branch from b to a and then from c to a and then from a to the rest of the graph. To compute the most likely value we can find this from

$$\max_a \phi(z,a) \left\{ \max_b \phi(a,b) \right\} \left\{ \max_c \phi(a,c) \right\} \tag{5.2.19}$$

which represents an efficient approach since the maximisation can be carried out over each branch separately. However, to find the second most likely value, we cannot write

$$\overset{2}{\max_a} \phi(z,a) \left\{ \max_b \phi(a,b) \right\} \left\{ \max_c \phi(a,c) \right\}. \tag{5.2.20}$$

For a fixed z, this would erroneously always force a to be in a different state than the state corresponding to the most likely value. Similarly, we cannot assume that the second most likely state corresponds to finding the second most likely state of each factor. Unlike the single most likely state case, therefore, we cannot distribute the maximisations over each branch but have to search over all branch contributions concurrently. This therefore corresponds to an exponentially complex search for the N-highest joint branch states. Whilst non-branching links are non-problematic, the degree D of a variable's node (in either the FG or undirected representation) contributes an additional exponential term N^D to the computational complexity.

5.2.3 Most probable path and shortest path

What is the most likely path from state a to state b for an N state Markov chain? Note that this is not necessarily the same as the shortest path, as explained in Fig. 5.5. If we consider a path of length T, this has probability

$$p(s_2|s_1 = \mathsf{a}) p(s_3|s_2) \dots p(s_T = \mathsf{b}|s_{T-1}). \tag{5.2.21}$$

Finding the most probable path can then be readily solved using the max-product (or max-sum algorithm for the log-transitions) on a simple serial factor graph. To deal with the issue that we don't know the optimal T, one approach is to redefine the probability transitions such that the desired state b is an *absorbing state* of the chain (that is, one can enter this state but not leave it). With this redefinition, the most probable joint state will correspond to the most probable state on the product of $N-1$ transitions. This approach is demonstrated in `demoMostProbablePath.m`, along with the more direct approaches described below.

An alternative, cleaner approach is as follows: for the Markov chain we can dispense with variable-to-factor and factor-to-variable messages and use only variable-to-variable messages. If we want to find the most likely set of states a, $s_2, \dots, s_{T-1}$, b to get us there, then this can be computed by defining the maximal path probability $E(\mathsf{a} \to \mathsf{b}, T)$ to get from a to b in T-timesteps:

$$E(\mathsf{a} \to \mathsf{b}, T) = \max_{s_2,\ldots,s_{T-1}} p(s_2|s_1 = \mathsf{a})p(s_3|s_2)p(s_4|s_3)\ldots p(s_T = \mathsf{b}|s_{T-1}) \tag{5.2.22}$$

$$= \max_{s_3,\ldots,s_{T-1}} \underbrace{\max_{s_2} p(s_2|s_1 = \mathsf{a})p(s_3|s_2)}_{\gamma_{2\to3}(s_3)} p(s_4|s_3)\ldots p(s_T = \mathsf{b}|s_{T-1}). \tag{5.2.23}$$

To compute this efficiently we define messages

$$\gamma_{t\to t+1}(s_{t+1}) = \max_{s_t} \gamma_{t-1\to t}(s_t)\, p(s_{t+1}|s_t), \quad t \geq 2, \quad \gamma_{1\to2}(s_2) = p(s_2|s_1 = \mathsf{a}) \tag{5.2.24}$$

until the point

$$E(\mathsf{a} \to \mathsf{b}, T) = \max_{s_{T-1}} \gamma_{T-2\to T-1}(s_{T-1})\, p(s_T = \mathsf{b}|s_{T-1}) = \gamma_{T-1\to T}(s_T = \mathsf{b}). \tag{5.2.25}$$

We can now proceed to find the maximal path probability for timestep $T + 1$. Since the messages up to time $T - 1$ will be the same as before, we need only compute one additional message, $\gamma_{T-1\to T}(s_T)$, from which

$$E(\mathsf{a} \to \mathsf{b}, T+1) = \max_{s_T} \gamma_{T-1\to T}(s_T)\, p(s_{T+1} = \mathsf{b}|s_T) = \gamma_{T\to T+1}(s_{T+1} = \mathsf{b}). \tag{5.2.26}$$

We can proceed in this manner until we reach $E(\mathsf{a} \to \mathsf{b}, N)$ where N is the number of nodes in the graph. We don't need to go beyond this number of steps since those that do must necessarily contain non-simple paths. (A *simple path* is one that does not include the same state more than once.) The optimal time t^* is then given by which of $E(\mathsf{a} \to \mathsf{b}, 2), \ldots, E(\mathsf{a} \to \mathsf{b}, N)$ is maximal. Given t^* one can begin to backtrack.[1] Since

$$E(\mathsf{a} \to \mathsf{b}, t^*) = \max_{s_{t^*-1}} \gamma_{t^*-2\to t^*-1}(s_{t^*-1})\, p(s_{t^*} = \mathsf{b}|s_{t^*-1}) \tag{5.2.27}$$

we know the optimal state

$$\mathsf{s}^*_{t^*-1} = \operatorname*{argmax}_{s_{t^*-1}} \gamma_{t^*-2\to t^*-1}(s_{t^*-1})\, p(s_{t^*} = \mathsf{b}|s_{t^*-1}). \tag{5.2.28}$$

We can then continue to backtrack:

$$\mathsf{s}^*_{t^*-2} = \operatorname*{argmax}_{s_{t^*-2}} \gamma_{t^*-3\to t^*-2}(s_{t^*-2})\, p(\mathsf{s}^*_{t^*-1}|s_{t^*-2}) \tag{5.2.29}$$

and so on. See `mostprobablepath.m`.

- In the above derivation we do not use any properties of probability, except that p must be non-negative (otherwise sign changes can flip a whole sequence 'probability' and the local message recursion no longer applies). One can consider the algorithm as finding the optimal 'product' path from a to b.
- It is straightforward to modify the algorithm to solve the (single-source, single-sink) *shortest weighted path* problem. One way to do this is to replace the Markov transition probabilities with $\exp(-u(s_t|s_{t-1}))$, where $u(s_t|s_{t-1})$ is the edge weight and is infinite if there is no edge from s_{t-1} to s_t. This approach is taken in `shortestpath.m` which is able to deal with either positive or negative edge weights. This method is therefore more general than the well-known Dijkstra's algorithm [121] which requires weights to be positive. If a negative edge cycle exists, the code

[1] An alternative to finding t^* is to define self-transitions with probability 1, and then use a fixed time $T = N$. Once the desired state b is reached, the self-transition then preserves the chain in state b for the remaining timesteps. This procedure is used in `mostprobablepathmult.m`.

returns the shortest weighted length N path, where N is the number of nodes in the graph. See `demoShortestPath.m`.

- The above algorithm is efficient for the single-source, single-sink scenario, since the messages contain only N states, meaning that the overall storage is $O(N^2)$.
- As it stands, the algorithm is numerically impractical since the messages are recursively multiplied by values usually less than 1 (at least for the case of probabilities). One will therefore quickly run into numerical underflow (or possibly overflow in the case of non-probabilities) with this method.

To fix the final point above, it is best to work by defining the logarithm of E. Since this is a monotonic transformation, the most probable path defined through $\log E$ is the same as that obtained from E. In this case

$$L(\mathsf{a} \to \mathsf{b}, T) = \max_{s_2,\ldots,s_{T-1}} \log\left[p(s_2|s_1 = \mathsf{a})p(s_3|s_2)p(s_4|s_3)\ldots p(s_T = b|s_{T-1})\right] \tag{5.2.30}$$

$$= \max_{s_2,\ldots,s_{T-1}} \left[\log p(s_2|s_1 = \mathsf{a}) + \sum_{t=2}^{T-1} \log p(s_t|s_{t-1}) + \log p(s_T = \mathsf{b}|s_{T-1})\right]. \tag{5.2.31}$$

We can therefore define new messages

$$\lambda_{t\to t+1}(s_{t+1}) = \max_{s_t}\left[\lambda_{t-1\to t}(s_t) + \log p(s_{t+1}|s_t)\right]. \tag{5.2.32}$$

One then proceeds as before by finding the most probable t^* defined on L, and backtracks.

> **Remark 5.2** A possible confusion is that optimal paths can be efficiently found 'when the graph is loopy'. Note that the graph in Fig. 5.5 is a state-transition diagram, not a graphical model. The graphical model corresponding to this simple Markov chain is the belief network $\prod_t p(s_t|s_{t-1})$, a linear serial structure. Hence the underlying graphical model is a simple chain, which explains why computation is efficient.

Most probable path (multiple-source, multiple-sink)

If we need the most probable path between all states a and b, one could re-run the above single-source, single-sink algorithm for all a and b. A computationally more efficient approach is to observe that one can define a message for each starting state a:

$$\gamma_{t\to t+1}(s_{t+1}|\mathsf{a}) = \max_{s_t} \gamma_{t-1\to t}(s_t|\mathsf{a})\, p(s_{t+1}|s_t) \tag{5.2.33}$$

and continue until we find the maximal path probability matrix for getting from any state a to any state b in T timesteps:

$$E(\mathsf{a} \to \mathsf{b}, T) = \max_{s_{T-1}} \gamma_{T-2\to T-1}(s_{T-1}|\mathsf{a})\, p(s_T = \mathsf{b}|s_{T-1}). \tag{5.2.34}$$

Since we know the message $\gamma_{T-2\to T-1}(s_{T-1}|\mathsf{a})$ for all states a, we can readily compute the most probable path from all starting states a to all states b after T steps. This requires passing an $N \times N$ matrix message γ. We can then proceed to the next timestep $T + 1$. Since the messages up to time $T - 1$ will be the same as before, we need only compute one additional message, $\gamma_{T-1\to T}(s_T)$, from which

$$E(\mathsf{a} \to \mathsf{b}, T+1) = \max_{s_T} \gamma_{T-1\to T}(s_T|\mathsf{a})\, p(s_{T+1} = \mathsf{b}|s_T). \tag{5.2.35}$$

In this way one can then efficiently compute the optimal path probabilities for all starting states a and end states b after t timesteps. To find the optimal corresponding path, backtracking proceeds as before, see `mostprobablepathmult.m` and `demoMostProbablePathMult.m`. One can also use the same algorithm to solve the multiple-source, multiple-sink shortest weighted path problem using exponentiated negative edge weights, as before. This is a variant of the Floyd–Warshall–Roy algorithm [121].

5.2.4 Mixed inference

An often encountered situation is to infer the most likely state of a joint marginal, possibly given some evidence. For example, given a distribution $p(x_1, \ldots, x_n)$, find

$$\operatorname*{argmax}_{x_1,x_2,\ldots,x_m} p(x_1, x_2, \ldots, x_m) = \operatorname*{argmax}_{x_1,x_2,\ldots,x_m} \sum_{x_{m+1},\ldots,x_n} p(x_1, \ldots, x_n). \tag{5.2.36}$$

In general, even for tree structured $p(x_1, \ldots, x_n)$, the optimal marginal state cannot be computed efficiently. One way to see this is that due to the summation the resulting joint marginal does not have a structured factored form as products of simpler functions of the marginal variables. Finding the most probable joint marginal then requires a search over all the joint marginal states – a task exponential in m. An approximate solution is provided by the EM algorithm (see Section 11.2 and Exercise 5.7).

5.3 Inference in multiply connected graphs

We briefly discuss here some relatively straightforward approaches to dealing with multiply connected graphs that are conceptually straightforward, or build on the repeated use of singly connected structures. We discuss a more general algorithm in Chapter 6.

5.3.1 Bucket elimination

We consider here a general conditional marginal variable elimination method that works for any distribution (including multiply connected graphs). Bucket elimination is presented in Algorithm 5.1 and can be considered a way to organise the distributed summation [83]. The algorithm is perhaps best explained by a simple example, as given below.

Example 5.3 Bucket elimination

Consider the problem of calculating the marginal $p(f)$ of

$$p(a, b, c, d, e, f, g) = p(f|d)p(g|d, e)p(c|a)p(d|a, b)p(a)p(b)p(e), \tag{5.3.1}$$

see Fig. 2.1a. Whilst this is singly-connected, this serves to explain the general procedure.

$$p(f) = \sum_{a,b,c,d,e,g} p(a, b, c, d, e, f, g) = \sum_{a,b,c,d,e,g} p(f|d)p(g|d, e)p(c|a)p(d|a, b)p(a)p(b)p(e). \tag{5.3.2}$$

Algorithm 5.1 Compute marginal $p(x_1|\text{evidence})$ from distribution $p(x) = \prod_f \phi_f(\{x\}_f)$. Assumes non-evidential variables are ordered $x_1, \ldots, x_n$.

---

procedure BUCKET ELIMINATION($p(x) = \prod_f \phi_f(\{x\}_f)$.)
 Initialise all bucket potentials to unity. ▷ Fill buckets
 while There are potentials left in the distribution **do**
  For each potential ϕ_f, find its highest variable x_j (according to the ordering).
  Multiply ϕ_f with the potential in bucket j and remove ϕ_f the distribution.
 end while
 for $i =$ bucket n to 1 **do** ▷ Empty buckets
  For bucket i sum over the states of variable x_i and call this potential γ_i
  Identify the highest variable x_h of potential γ_i
  Multiply the existing potential in bucket h by γ_i
 end for
 The marginal $p(x_1|\text{evidence})$ is proportional to γ_1.
 return $p(x_1|\text{evidence})$ ▷ The conditional marginal
end procedure

We can distribute the summation over the various terms as follows: e, b and c are end nodes, so that we can sum over their values:

$$p(f) = \sum_{d,a,g} p(f|d)p(a) \left(\sum_b p(d|a,b)p(b)\right) \left(\sum_c p(c|a)\right) \left(\sum_e p(g|d,e)p(e)\right). \tag{5.3.3}$$

For convenience, let's write the terms in the brackets as $\sum_b p(d|a,b)p(b) \equiv \gamma_b(a,d)$, $\sum_e p(g|d,e)p(e) \equiv \gamma_e(d,g)$. The term $\sum_c p(c|a)$ is equal to unity, and we therefore eliminate this node directly. Rearranging terms, we can write

$$p(f) = \sum_{d,a,g} p(f|d)p(a)\gamma_b(a,d)\,\gamma_e(d,g). \tag{5.3.4}$$

If we think of this graphically, the effect of summing over b, c, e is effectively to remove or 'eliminate' those variables. We can now carry on summing over a and g since these are end points of the new graph:

$$p(f) = \sum_d p(f|d) \left(\sum_a p(a)\gamma_b(a,d)\right) \left(\sum_g \gamma_e(d,g)\right). \tag{5.3.5}$$

Again, this defines new potentials $\gamma_a(d)$, $\gamma_g(d)$, so that the final answer can be found from

$$p(f) = \sum_d p(f|d)\gamma_a(d)\,\gamma_g(d). \tag{5.3.6}$$

We illustrate this in Fig. 5.6. Initially, we define an ordering of the variables, beginning with the one that we wish to find the marginal for – a suitable ordering is therefore, f, d, a, g, b, c, e. Then starting with the highest bucket e (according to our ordering f, d, a, g, b, c, e), we put all the potentials that mention e in the e bucket. Continuing with the next highest bucket, c, we put all the remaining potentials that mention c in this c bucket, etc. The result of this initialisation procedure is that terms

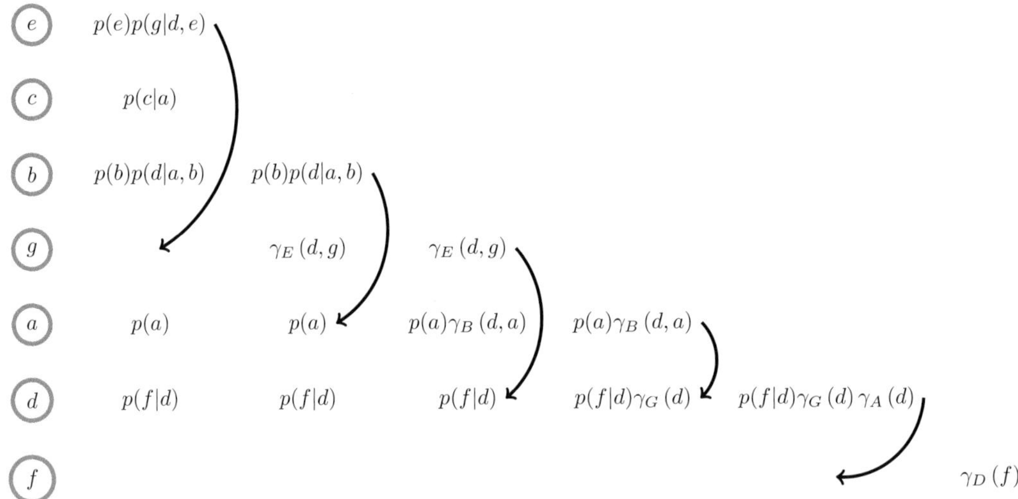

Figure 5.6 The bucket elimination algorithm applied to the graph Fig. 2.1. At each stage, at least one node is eliminated from the graph. The second stage of eliminating c is trivial since $\sum_c p(c|a) = 1$ and has therefore been skipped over since this bucket does not send any message.

(conditional distributions) in the DAG are distributed over the buckets, as shown in the left most column of Fig. 5.6. Eliminating then the highest bucket e, we pass a message to node g. Immediately, we can also eliminate bucket c since this sums to unity. In the next column, we have now two fewer buckets, and we eliminate the highest remaining bucket, this time b, passing a message to bucket a, and so on.

There are some important observations we can make about bucket elimination:

1. To compute say $p(x_2|\text{evidence})$ we need to re-order the variables (so that the required marginal variable is labelled x_1) and repeat bucket elimination. Hence each query (calculation of a marginal in this case) requires re-running the algorithm. It would be more efficient to reuse messages, rather than recalculating them each time.
2. In general, bucket elimination constructs multi-variable messages γ from bucket to bucket. The storage requirements of a multi-variable message are exponential in the number of variables of the message.
3. For trees we can always choose a variable ordering to render the computational complexity to be linear in the number of variables. Such an ordering is called perfect, Definition 6.9, and indeed it can be shown that a perfect ordering can always easily be found for singly connected graphs (see [92]). However, orderings exist for which bucket elimination will be extremely inefficient.

5.3.2 Loop-cut conditioning

For multiply connected distributions we run into some difficulty with the message passing routines such as the sum-product algorithm which are designed to work on singly connected graphs only. One way to solve the difficulties of multiply connected (loopy) graphs is to identify nodes that,

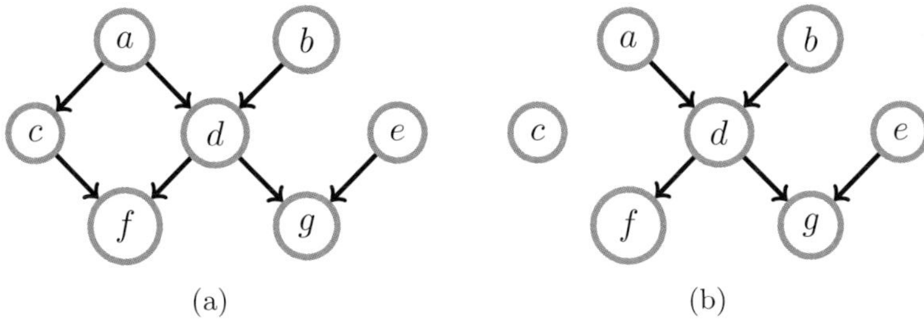

Figure 5.7 A multiply connected graph (a) reduced to a singly connected graph (b) by conditioning on the variable c.

when removed, would reveal a singly connected subgraph [236]. Consider the example of Fig. 5.7. Imagine that we wish to calculate a marginal, say $p(d)$. Then

$$p(d) = \sum_{c} \sum_{a,b,e,f,g} \underbrace{p(c|a)p(a)}_{p^*(a)} p(d|a,b)p(b) \underbrace{p(f|c,d)}_{p^*(f|d)} p(g|d,e) \tag{5.3.7}$$

where the p^* potentials are not necessarily distributions. For each state of c, the product of the new potentials on the variables a, b, e, f, g is singly connected, so that standard singly connected message passing can be used to perform inference. We will need to perform inference for each state of variable c, each state defining a new singly connected graph (with the same structure) but with modified potentials.

More generally, we can define a set of variables $\mathcal{C}$, called the *loop-cut set* and run singly connected inference for each joint state of the cut-set variables $\mathcal{C}$. This can also be used for finding the most likely state of a multiply connected joint distribution as well. Hence, for a computational price exponential in the loop-cut size, we can calculate the marginals (or the most likely state) for a multiply connected distribution. However, determining a small cut set is in general difficult, and there is no guarantee that this will anyway be small for a given graph. Whilst this method is able to handle loops in a general manner, it is not particularly elegant since the concept of messages now only applies conditioned on the cut-set variables, and how to re-use messages for inference of additional quantities of interest becomes unclear. We will discuss an alternative method for handling multiply connected distributions in Chapter 6.

5.4 Message passing for continuous distributions

For parametric continuous distributions $p(x|\theta_x)$, message passing corresponds to passing parameters θ of the distributions. For the sum-product algorithm, this requires that the operations of multiplication and integration over the variables are closed with respect to the family of distributions. This is the case, for example, for the Gaussian distribution – the marginal (integral) of a Gaussian is another Gaussian, and the product of two Gaussians is a Gaussian, see Section 8.4. This means that we can then implement the sum-product algorithm based on passing mean and covariance parameters. To implement this requires some tedious algebra to compute the appropriate message parameter updates. At this stage, the complexities from performing such calculations are a potential distraction, though the interested reader may refer to `demoSumprodGaussMoment.m`, `demoSumprodGaussCanon.m` and `demoSumprodGaussCanonLDS.m` and also Chapter 24 for examples of message passing with Gaussians. For more general exponential family distributions, message passing is essentially straightforward, though again the specifics of the updates may be tedious to work out. In cases where the operations of marginalisation and products are not closed within the family, the distributions need to be projected back to the chosen message family. Expectation propagation, Section 28.8, is relevant in this case.

5.5 Summary

- For a tree-structured factor graph, non-mixed inference is essentially linear in the number of nodes in the graph (provided the variables are discrete or the inference operations form a tractable closed family).
- Computation on trees can be achieved using local 'message-passing' algorithms, analogous to dynamic programming.
- The sum-product and max-product algorithms are particularly useful for computing marginal and most likely inferences respectively.
- Message passing also holds for continuous variables based on passing messages that update the parameters of the distribution.
- Shortest-path problems can be solved using such message-passing approaches.
- Inference in non-trees (multiply connected distributions) is more complex since there is a fill-in effect when variables are eliminated that adds additional links to the graph.
- Inference in multiply connected graphs can be achieved using techniques such as cut-set conditioning which, by conditioning on a subset of variables, reveal a singly connected structure. However, this is generally inefficient since the messages cannot be readily re-used.

A take-home message from this chapter is that (non-mixed) inference in singly connected structures is usually computationally tractable. Notable exceptions are when the message-passing operations are not closed within the message family, or representing messages explicitly requires an exponential amount of space. This happens for example when the distribution can contain both discrete and continuous variables, such as the switching linear dynamical system, which we discuss in Chapter 25.

Broadly speaking, inference in multiply connected structures is more complex and may be intractable. However, we do not want to give the impression that this is always the case. Notable exceptions are: finding the most likely state in an attractive pairwise MN, Section 28.9; finding the most likely state and marginals state in a binary planar MN with pure interactions, see for example [127, 260]. For N variables in the graph, a naive use of general purpose routines such as the junction tree algorithm for these inferences would result in an $O\left(2^N\right)$ computation, whereas clever algorithms are able to return the exact results in $O\left(N^3\right)$ operations. Of interest is *bond propagation* [191] which is an intuitive node elimination method to perform marginal inference in pure-interaction Ising models.

5.6 Code

The code below implements message passing on a tree-structured factor graph. The FG is stored as an adjacency matrix with the message between FG node i and FG node j given in $A_{i,j}$.

`FactorGraph.m`: Return a factor graph adjacency matrix and message numbers
`sumprodFG.m`: Sum-product algorithm on a factor graph

In general it is recommended to work in log-space in the Max-Product case, particularly for large graphs since the product of messages can become very small. The code provided does not work in log-space and as such may not work on large graphs; writing this using log-messages is straightforward but leads to less readable code. An implementation based on log-messages is left as an exercise for the interested reader.

`maxprodFG.m`: Max-product algorithm on a factor graph
`maxNprodFG.m`: N-Max-product algorithm on a factor graph

5.6.1 Factor graph examples

For the distribution from Fig. 5.3, the following code finds the marginals and most likely joint states. The number of states of each variable is chosen at random.

`demoSumprod.m`: Test the sum-product algorithm
`demoMaxprod.m`: Test the max-product algorithm
`demoMaxNprod.m`: Test the max-N-product algorithm

5.6.2 Most probable and shortest path

`mostprobablepath.m`: Most probable path
`demoMostProbablePath.m`: Most probable versus shortest path demo
`demoShortestPath.m`: The shortest path demo works for both positive and negative edge weights. If negative weight cycles exist, the code finds the best length N shortest path.
`mostprobablepathmult.m`: Most probable path – multi-source, multi-sink
`demoMostProbablePathMult.m`: Demo of most probable path – multi-source, multi-sink

5.6.3 Bucket elimination

The efficiency of bucket elimination depends critically on the elimination sequence chosen. In the demonstration below we find the marginal of a variable in the Chest Clinic exercise using a randomly chosen elimination order. The desired marginal variable is specified as the last to be eliminated. For comparison we use an elimination sequence based on decimating a triangulated graph of the model, as discussed in Section 6.5.1, again under the constraint that the last variable to be 'decimated' is the marginal variable of interest. For this smarter choice of elimination sequence, the complexity of computing this single marginal is roughly the same as that for the junction tree algorithm, using the same triangulation.

`bucketelim.m`: Bucket Elimination
`demoBucketElim.m`: Demo Bucket Elimination

5.6.4 Message passing on Gaussians

The following code hints at how message passing may be implemented for continuous distributions. The reader is referred to the BRMLtoolbox for further details and also Section 8.4 for the algebraic manipulations required to perform marginalisation and products of Gaussians. The same principle holds for any family of distributions which is closed under products and marginalisation, and the reader may wish to implement specific families following the method outlined for Gaussians.

`demoSumprodGaussMoment.m`: Sum-product message passing based on Gaussian Moment parameterisation

5.7 Exercises

5.1 Given a pairwise singly connected Markov network of the form

$$p(x) = \frac{1}{Z}\prod_{i\sim j}\phi(x_i, x_j) \tag{5.7.1}$$

explain how to efficiently compute the normalisation factor (also called the partition function) Z as a function of the potentials ϕ.

5.2 Consider a pairwise Markov network defined on binary variables:

$$p(x) = \phi(x_1, x_{100})\prod_{i=1}^{99}\phi(x_i, x_{i+1}). \tag{5.7.2}$$

Is it possible to compute $\underset{x_1,\dots,x_{100}}{\operatorname{argmax}}\ p(x)$ efficiently?

5.3 You are employed by a web start up company that designs virtual environments, in which players can move between rooms. The rooms which are accessible from another in one timestep is given by the 100×100 matrix $\mathbf{M}$, stored in `virtualworlds.mat`, where $M_{ij} = 1$ means that there is a door between rooms i and j ($M_{ij} = M_{ji}$); $M_{ij} = 0$ means that there is no door between rooms i and j; $M_{ii} = 1$ meaning that in one timestep, one can stay in the same room. You can visualise this matrix by typing `imagesc(M)`.

1. Write a list of rooms which cannot be reached from room 2 after 10 timesteps.
2. The manager complains that takes at least 13 timesteps to get from room 1 to room 100. Is this true?
3. Find the most likely path (sequence of rooms) to get from room 1 to room 100.
4. If a single player were to jump randomly from one room to another (or stay in the same room), with no preference between rooms, what is the probability at time $t \gg 1$ the player will be in room 1? Assume that effectively an infinite amount of time has passed and the player began in room 1 at $t = 1$.
5. If two players are jumping randomly between rooms (or staying in the same room), explain how to compute the probability that, after an infinite amount of time, at least one of them will be in room 1? Assume that both players begin in room 1.

5.4 Consider the hidden Markov model:

$$p(v_1, \dots, v_T, h_1, \dots, h_T) = p(h_1)p(v_1|h_1)\prod_{t=2}^{T}p(v_t|h_t)p(h_t|h_{t-1}) \tag{5.7.3}$$

in which $\text{dom}(h_t) = \{1, \dots, H\}$ and $\text{dom}(v_t) = \{1, \dots, V\}$ for all $t = 1, \dots, T$.

1. Draw a belief network representation of the above distribution.
2. Draw a factor graph representation of the above distribution.
3. Use the factor graph to derive a sum-product algorithm to compute marginals $p(h_t|v_1, \dots, v_T)$. Explain the sequence order of messages passed on your factor graph.
4. Explain how to compute $p(h_t, h_{t+1}|v_1, \dots, v_T)$.
5. Show that the belief network for $p(h_1, \dots h_T)$ is a simple linear chain, whilst $p(v_1, \dots v_T)$ is a fully connected cascade belief network.

5.5 For a singly connected Markov network, $p(x) = p(x_1, \dots, x_n)$, the computation of a marginal $p(x_i)$ can be carried out efficiently. Similarly, the most likely joint state $x^* = \arg\max_{x_1,\dots,x_n} p(x)$ can be computed efficiently. Explain when the most likely joint state of a marginal can be computed efficiently, i.e. under what circumstances could one efficiently (in $O(m)$ time) compute $\underset{x_1,x_2,\dots,x_m}{\operatorname{argmax}}\ p(x_1, \dots, x_m)$ for $m < n$?

5.6 Consider the Internet with webpages labelled $1, \ldots, N$. If webpage j has a link to webpage i, then we place an element of the matrix $L_{ij} = 1$, otherwise $L_{ij} = 0$. By considering a random jump from webpage j to webpage i to be given by the transition probability

$$M_{ij} = \frac{L_{ij}}{\sum_i L_{ij}} \tag{5.7.4}$$

what is the probability that after an infinite amount of random surfing, one ends up on webpage i? How could you relate this to the potential 'relevance' of a webpage in terms of a search engine?

5.7 A special time-homogeneous hidden Markov model is given by

$$p(x_1, \ldots, x_T, y_1, \ldots, y_T, h_1, \ldots, h_T) = p(x_1|h_1)p(y_1|h_1)p(h_1) \prod_{t=2}^{T} p(h_t|h_{t-1})p(x_t|h_t)p(y_t|h_t). \tag{5.7.5}$$

The variable x_t has four states, $\text{dom}(x_t) = \{\mathsf{A}, \mathsf{C}, \mathsf{G}, \mathsf{T}\}$ (numerically labelled as states 1, 2, 3, 4). The variable y_t has four states, $\text{dom}(y_t) = \{\mathsf{A}, \mathsf{C}, \mathsf{G}, \mathsf{T}\}$. The hidden or latent variable h_t has five states, $\text{dom}(h_t) = \{1, \ldots, 5\}$. The HMM models the following (fictitious) process:

In humans, Z-factor proteins are a sequence on states of the variables $x_1, x_2, \ldots, x_T$. In bananas Z-factor proteins are also present, but represented by a different sequence $y_1, y_2, \ldots, y_T$. Given a sequence $x_1, \ldots, x_T$ from a human, the task is to find the corresponding sequence $y_1, \ldots, y_T$ in the banana by first finding the most likely joint latent sequence, and then the most likely banana sequence given this optimal latent sequence. That is, we require

$$\underset{y_1,\ldots,y_T}{\text{argmax}}\ p(y_1, \ldots, y_T|h_1^*, \ldots, h_T^*) \tag{5.7.6}$$

where

$$h_1^*, \ldots, h_T^* = \underset{h_1,\ldots,h_T}{\text{argmax}}\ p(h_1, \ldots, h_T|x_1, \ldots, x_T). \tag{5.7.7}$$

The file `banana.mat` contains the emission distributions `pxgh` $(p(x|h))$, `pygh` $(p(y|h))$ and transition `phtghtm` $(p(h_t|h_{t-1}))$. The initial hidden distribution is given in `ph1` $(p(h_1))$. The observed x sequence is given in `x`.

1. Explain mathematically and in detail how to compute the optimal y-sequence, using the two-stage procedure as stated above.
2. Write a MATLAB routine that computes and displays the optimal y-sequence, given the observed x-sequence. Your routine must make use of the factor graph formalism.
3. Explain whether or not it is computationally tractable to compute

$$\underset{y_1,\ldots,y_T}{\text{argmax}}\ p(y_1, \ldots, y_T|x_1, \ldots, x_T). \tag{5.7.8}$$

4. Bonus question: By considering $y_1, \ldots, y_T$ as parameters, explain how the EM algorithm, Section 11.2, may be used to find $\underset{y_1,\ldots,y_T}{\text{argmax}}\ p(y_1, \ldots, y_T|x_1, \ldots, x_T)$. Implement this approach with a suitable initialisation for the optimal parameters $y_1, \ldots, y_T$.

6 The junction tree algorithm

When the distribution is multiply connected it would be useful to have a generic inference approach that is efficient in its reuse of messages. In this chapter we discuss an important structure, the junction tree, that by clustering variables enables one to perform message passing efficiently (although the structure on which the message passing occurs may consist of intractably large clusters). The most important thing is the junction tree itself, based on which different message-passing procedures can be considered. The junction tree helps forge links with the computational complexity of inference in fields from computer science to statistics and physics.

6.1 Clustering variables

In Chapter 5 we discussed efficient inference for singly connected graphs, for which variable elimination and message-passing schemes are appropriate. In the multiply connected case, however, one cannot in general perform inference by passing messages only along existing links in the graph. The idea behind the Junction Tree Algorithm (JTA) is to form a new representation of the graph in which variables are clustered together, resulting in a singly connected graph in the cluster variables (albeit on a different graph). The main focus of the development will be on marginal inference, though similar techniques apply to different inferences, such as finding the most probable state of the distribution.

At this stage it is important to point out that the JTA is not a magic method to deal with intractabilities resulting from multiply connected graphs; it is simply a way to perform correct inference on a multiply connected graph by transforming to a singly connected structure. Carrying out the inference on the resulting junction tree may still be computationally intractable. For example, the junction tree representation of a general two-dimensional Ising model is a single supernode containing all the variables. Inference in this case is exponentially complex in the number of variables. Nevertheless, even in cases where implementing the JTA may be intractable, the JTA provides useful insight into the representation of distributions that can form the basis for approximate inference. In this sense the JTA is key to understanding issues related to representations and complexity of inference and is central to the development of efficient inference algorithms.

6.1.1 Reparameterisation

Consider the chain

$$p(a, b, c, d) = p(a|b)p(b|c)p(c|d)p(d). \tag{6.1.1}$$

From the definition of conditional probability, we can reexpress this as

$$p(a,b,c,d) = \frac{p(a,b)}{p(b)}\frac{p(b,c)}{p(c)}\frac{p(c,d)}{p(d)}p(d) = \frac{p(a,b)p(b,c)p(c,d)}{p(b)p(c)}. \tag{6.1.2}$$

A useful insight is that the distribution can therefore be written as a product of marginal distributions, divided by a product of the intersection of the marginal distributions: Looking at the numerator $p(a,b)p(b,c)p(c,d)$ this cannot be a distribution over a, b, c, d since we are overcounting b and c, where this overcounting of b arises from the overlap between the sets $\{a,b\}$ and $\{b,c\}$, which have b as their intersection. Similarly, the overcounting of c arises from the overlap between the sets $\{b,c\}$ and $\{c,d\}$. Intuitively, we need to correct for this overcounting by dividing by the distribution on the intersections. Given the transformed representation as a product of marginals divided by a product of their intersection (the right equation in (6.1.2)), a marginal such as $p(a,b)$ can be read off directly from the factors in the new expression. The aim of the junction tree algorithm is to form just such a representation of the distribution which contains the marginals explicitly. We want to do this in a way that works for belief and Markov networks, and also deals with the multiply connected case. In order to do so, an appropriate way to parameterise the distribution is in terms of a clique graph, as described in the next section.

6.2 Clique graphs

Definition 6.1 **Clique graph** A clique graph consists of a set of potentials, $\phi_1(\mathcal{X}^1), \ldots, \phi_n(\mathcal{X}^n)$ each defined on a set of variables $\mathcal{X}^i$. For neighbouring cliques on the graph, defined on sets of variables $\mathcal{X}^i$ and $\mathcal{X}^j$, the intersection $\mathcal{X}^s = \mathcal{X}^i \cap \mathcal{X}^j$ is called the *separator* and has a corresponding potential $\phi_s(\mathcal{X}^s)$. A clique graph represents the function

$$\frac{\prod_c \phi_c(\mathcal{X}^c)}{\prod_s \phi_s(\mathcal{X}^s)}. \tag{6.2.1}$$

For notational simplicity we will usually drop the clique potential index c. Graphically clique potentials are represented by circles/ovals, and separator potentials by rectangles.

$\mathcal{X}^1$ — $\mathcal{X}^1 \cap \mathcal{X}^2$ — $\mathcal{X}^2$ The graph on the left represents $\phi(\mathcal{X}^1)\phi(\mathcal{X}^2)/\phi(\mathcal{X}^1 \cap \mathcal{X}^2)$.

Clique graphs translate Markov networks into structures convenient for carrying out inference. Consider the Markov network in Fig. 6.1(a)

$$p(a,b,c,d) = \frac{\phi(a,b,c)\phi(b,c,d)}{Z}. \tag{6.2.2}$$

An equivalent representation is given by the clique graph in Fig. 6.1(b), defined as the product of the numerator clique potentials, divided by the product of the separator potentials. In this case the separator potential may be set to the normalisation constant Z. By summing we have

$$Zp(a,b,c) = \phi(a,b,c)\sum_d \phi(b,c,d), \quad Zp(b,c,d) = \phi(b,c,d)\sum_a \phi(a,b,c). \tag{6.2.3}$$

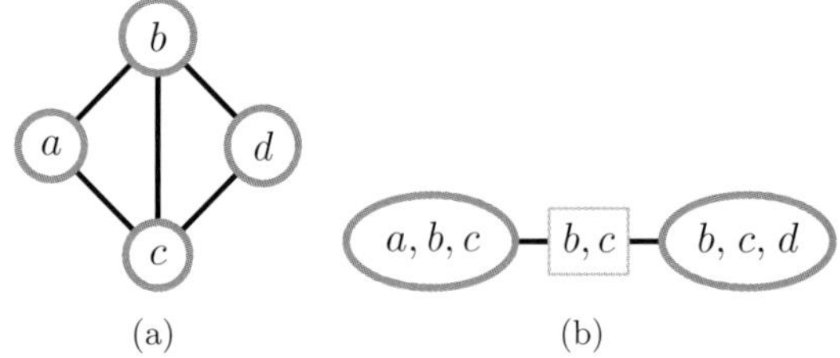

Figure 6.1 **(a)** Markov network $\phi(a, b, c)\phi(b, c, d)$. **(b)** Clique graph representation of (a).

Multiplying the two expressions, we have

$$
\begin{aligned}
Z^2 p(a, b, c)p(b, c, d) &= \left(\phi(a, b, c)\sum_d \phi(b, c, d)\right)\left(\phi(b, c, d)\sum_a \phi(a, b, c)\right) \\
&= Z^2 p(a, b, c, d) \sum_{a,d} p(a, b, c, d).
\end{aligned}
\tag{6.2.4}
$$

In other words

$$
p(a, b, c, d) = \frac{p(a, b, c)p(b, c, d)}{p(c, b)}. \tag{6.2.5}
$$

The important observation is that the distribution can be written in terms of its marginals on the variables in the original cliques and that, as a clique graph, it has the same structure as before. All that has changed is that the original clique potentials have been replaced by the marginals of the distribution and the separator by the marginal defined on the separator variables $\phi(a, b, c) \rightarrow p(a, b, c), \phi(b, c, d) \rightarrow p(b, c, d), Z \rightarrow p(c, b)$. The usefulness of this representation is that if we are interested in the marginal $p(a, b, c)$, this can be read off from the transformed clique potential. To make use of this representation, we require a systematic way of transforming the clique graph potentials so that at the end of the transformation the new potentials contain the marginals of the distribution.

> **Remark 6.1** Note that, whilst visually similar, a factor graph and a clique graph are different representations. In a clique graph the nodes contain sets of variables, which may share variables with other nodes.

6.2.1 Absorption

Consider neighbouring cliques $\mathcal{V}$ and $\mathcal{W}$, sharing the variables $\mathcal{S}$ in common. In this case, the distribution on the variables $\mathcal{X} = \mathcal{V} \cup \mathcal{W}$ is

$$
p(\mathcal{X}) = \frac{\phi(\mathcal{V})\phi(\mathcal{W})}{\phi(\mathcal{S})} \tag{6.2.6}
$$

$\phi(\mathcal{V})$ — $\phi(\mathcal{S})$ — $\phi(\mathcal{W})$

and our aim is to find a new representation

$$
p(\mathcal{X}) = \frac{\hat{\phi}(\mathcal{V})\hat{\phi}(\mathcal{W})}{\hat{\phi}(\mathcal{S})} \tag{6.2.7}
$$

$\hat{\phi}(\mathcal{V})$ — $\hat{\phi}(\mathcal{S})$ — $\hat{\phi}(\mathcal{W})$

in which the potentials are given by

$$\hat{\phi}(\mathcal{V}) = p(\mathcal{V}), \quad \hat{\phi}(\mathcal{W}) = p(\mathcal{W}), \quad \hat{\phi}(\mathcal{S}) = p(\mathcal{S}). \tag{6.2.8}$$

In the figures on the above right we denote also the potentials in the cliques to emphasise how the potentials update under absorption. In this example, we can explicitly work out the new potentials as function of the old potentials by computing the marginals as follows:

$$p(\mathcal{W}) = \sum_{\mathcal{V}\setminus\mathcal{S}} p(\mathcal{X}) = \sum_{\mathcal{V}\setminus\mathcal{S}} \frac{\phi(\mathcal{V})\phi(\mathcal{W})}{\phi(\mathcal{S})} = \phi(\mathcal{W})\frac{\sum_{\mathcal{V}\setminus\mathcal{S}}\phi(\mathcal{V})}{\phi(\mathcal{S})} \tag{6.2.9}$$

and

$$p(\mathcal{V}) = \sum_{\mathcal{W}\setminus\mathcal{S}} p(\mathcal{X}) = \sum_{\mathcal{W}\setminus\mathcal{S}} \frac{\phi(\mathcal{V})\phi(\mathcal{W})}{\phi(\mathcal{S})} = \phi(\mathcal{V})\frac{\sum_{\mathcal{W}\setminus\mathcal{S}}\phi(\mathcal{W})}{\phi(\mathcal{S})}. \tag{6.2.10}$$

There is a symmetry present in the two equations above – they are the same under interchanging $\mathcal{V}$ and $\mathcal{W}$. One way to describe these equations is through 'absorption'. We say that the cluster $\mathcal{W}$ 'absorbs' information from cluster $\mathcal{V}$ by the following updating procedure. First we define a new separator

$$\phi^*(\mathcal{S}) = \sum_{\mathcal{V}\setminus\mathcal{S}} \phi(\mathcal{V}) \tag{6.2.11}$$

and refine the $\mathcal{W}$ potential using

$$\phi^*(\mathcal{W}) = \phi(\mathcal{W})\frac{\phi^*(\mathcal{S})}{\phi(\mathcal{S})}. \tag{6.2.12}$$

The advantage of this interpretation is that the new representation is still a valid clique graph representation of the distribution since

$$\frac{\phi(\mathcal{V})\phi^*(\mathcal{W})}{\phi^*(\mathcal{S})} = \frac{\phi(\mathcal{V})\phi(\mathcal{W})\frac{\phi^*(\mathcal{S})}{\phi(\mathcal{S})}}{\phi^*(\mathcal{S})} = \frac{\phi(\mathcal{V})\phi(\mathcal{W})}{\phi(\mathcal{S})} = p(\mathcal{X}). \tag{6.2.13}$$

For this simple two clique graph, we see that after $\mathcal{W}$ absorbs information from $\mathcal{V}$ then $\phi^*(\mathcal{W}) = p(\mathcal{W})$, which can be verified by comparing the right of Equation (6.2.9) with Equation (6.2.12). With these new updated potentials, we now go back along the graph, from $\mathcal{W}$ to $\mathcal{V}$. After $\mathcal{V}$ absorbs information from $\mathcal{W}$ then $\phi^*(\mathcal{V})$ contains the marginal $p(\mathcal{V})$. After the separator $\mathcal{S}$ has participated in absorption along both directions, then the separator potential will contain $p(\mathcal{S})$ (this is not the case after only a single absorption). To see this, consider absorbing from $\mathcal{W}$ to $\mathcal{V}$ using the updated potentials $\phi^*(\mathcal{W})$ and $\phi^*(\mathcal{S})$

$$\phi^{**}(\mathcal{S}) = \sum_{\mathcal{W}\setminus\mathcal{S}} \phi^*(\mathcal{W}) = \sum_{\mathcal{W}\setminus\mathcal{S}} \frac{\phi(\mathcal{W})\phi^*(\mathcal{S})}{\phi(\mathcal{S})} = \sum_{\{\mathcal{W}\cup\mathcal{V}\}\setminus\mathcal{S}} \frac{\phi(\mathcal{W})\phi(\mathcal{V})}{\phi(\mathcal{S})} = p(\mathcal{S}). \tag{6.2.14}$$

Continuing, we have the new potential $\phi^*(\mathcal{V})$ given by

$$\phi^*(\mathcal{V}) = \frac{\phi(\mathcal{V})\phi^{**}(\mathcal{S})}{\phi^*(\mathcal{S})} = \frac{\phi(\mathcal{V})\sum_{\mathcal{W}\setminus\mathcal{S}}\phi(\mathcal{W})\phi^*(\mathcal{S})/\phi(\mathcal{S})}{\phi^*(\mathcal{S})} = \frac{\sum_{\mathcal{W}\setminus\mathcal{S}}\phi(\mathcal{V})\phi(\mathcal{W})}{\phi(\mathcal{S})} = p(\mathcal{V}). \tag{6.2.15}$$

Hence, in terms of Equation (6.2.7), the new representation is $\hat{\phi}(\mathcal{V}) = \phi^*(\mathcal{V})$, $\hat{\phi}(\mathcal{S}) = \phi^{**}(\mathcal{S})$, $\hat{\phi}(\mathcal{W}) = \phi^*(\mathcal{W})$.

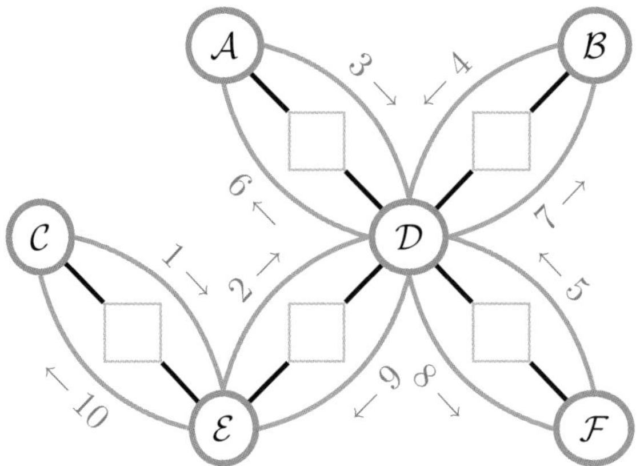

Figure 6.2 An example absorption schedule on a clique tree. Many valid schedules exist under the constraint that messages can only be passed to a neighbour when all other messages have been received.

Definition 6.2 Absorption

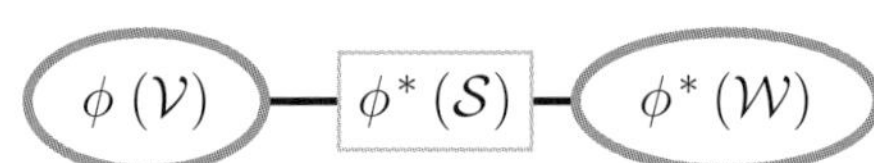

Let $\mathcal{V}$ and $\mathcal{W}$ be neighbours in a clique graph, let $\mathcal{S}$ be their separator, and let $\phi(\mathcal{V})$, $\phi(\mathcal{W})$ and $\phi(\mathcal{S})$ be their potentials. Absorption from $\mathcal{V}$ to $\mathcal{W}$ through $\mathcal{S}$ replaces the tables $\phi(\mathcal{S})$ and $\phi(\mathcal{W})$ with

$$\phi^*(\mathcal{S}) = \sum_{\mathcal{V}\setminus\mathcal{S}} \phi(\mathcal{V}), \qquad \phi^*(\mathcal{W}) = \phi(\mathcal{W})\frac{\phi^*(\mathcal{S})}{\phi(\mathcal{S})}. \tag{6.2.16}$$

We say that clique $\mathcal{W}$ absorbs information from clique $\mathcal{V}$. The potentials are written on the clique graph (left) to highlight the potential updating.

6.2.2 Absorption schedule on clique trees

Having defined the local message propagation approach, we need to define an update ordering for absorption. In general, a node $\mathcal{V}$ can send exactly one message to a neighbour $\mathcal{W}$, and it may only be sent when $\mathcal{V}$ has received a message from each of its other neighbours. We continue this sequence of absorptions until a message has been passed in both directions along every link. See, for example, Fig. 6.2. Note that there are many valid message passing schemes in this case.

Definition 6.3 Absorption schedule A clique can send a message to a neighbour, provided it has already received messages from all other neighbours.

6.3 Junction trees

There are a few stages we need to go through in order to transform a distribution into an appropriate structure for inference. Initially we explain how to do this for singly connected structures before moving on to the multiply connected case.

Consider the singly connected Markov network, Fig. 6.3(a)

$$p(x_1, x_2, x_3, x_4) = \phi(x_1, x_4)\phi(x_2, x_4)\phi(x_3, x_4). \tag{6.3.1}$$

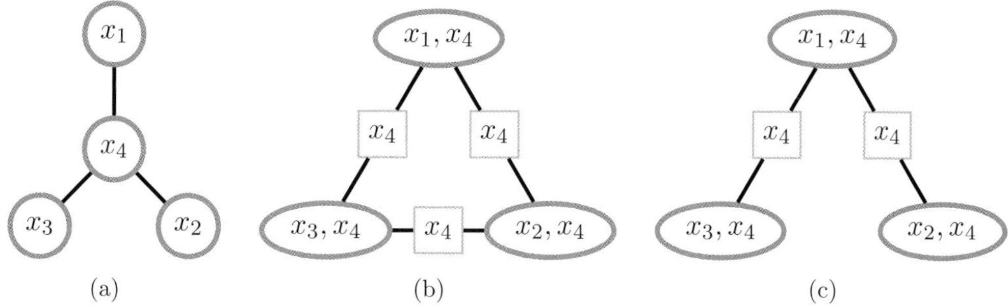

Figure 6.3 (**a**) Singly connected Markov network. (**b**) Clique graph. (**c**) Clique tree.

The clique graph of this singly connected Markov network is multiply connected, Fig. 6.3(b), where the separator potentials are all set to unity. Nevertheless, let's try to reexpress the Markov network in terms of marginals. First we have the relations

$$p(x_1, x_4) = \sum_{x_2,x_3} p(x_1, x_2, x_3, x_4) = \phi(x_1, x_4) \sum_{x_2} \phi(x_2, x_4) \sum_{x_3} \phi(x_3, x_4) \tag{6.3.2}$$

$$p(x_2, x_4) = \sum_{x_1,x_3} p(x_1, x_2, x_3, x_4) = \phi(x_2, x_4) \sum_{x_1} \phi(x_1, x_4) \sum_{x_3} \phi(x_3, x_4) \tag{6.3.3}$$

$$p(x_3, x_4) = \sum_{x_1,x_2} p(x_1, x_2, x_3, x_4) = \phi(x_3, x_4) \sum_{x_1} \phi(x_1, x_4) \sum_{x_2} \phi(x_2, x_4). \tag{6.3.4}$$

Taking the product of the three marginals, we have

$$p(x_1, x_4)p(x_2, x_4)p(x_3, x_4) = \phi(x_1, x_4)\phi(x_2, x_4)\phi(x_3, x_4) \times \underbrace{\left(\sum_{x_1} \phi(x_1, x_4) \sum_{x_2} \phi(x_2, x_4) \sum_{x_3} \phi(x_3, x_4)\right)^2}_{p(x_4)^2}. \tag{6.3.5}$$

This means that the Markov network can be expressed in terms of marginals as

$$p(x_1, x_2, x_3, x_4) = \frac{p(x_1, x_4)p(x_2, x_4)p(x_3, x_4)}{p(x_4)p(x_4)}. \tag{6.3.6}$$

Hence a valid clique graph is also given by the representation Fig. 6.3(c). Indeed, if a variable (here x_4) occurs on every separator in a clique graph loop, one can remove that variable from an arbitrarily chosen separator in the loop. If this leaves an empty separator, we may then simply remove. This shows that in such cases we can transform the clique graph into a clique tree (i.e. a singly connected clique graph). Provided that the original Markov network is singly connected, one can always form a clique tree in this manner.

6.3.1 The running intersection property

Sticking with the above example, consider the clique tree in Fig. 6.3

$$\frac{\phi(x_3, x_4)\phi(x_1, x_4)\phi(x_2, x_4)}{\phi_1(x_4)\phi_2(x_4)} \tag{6.3.7}$$

as a representation of the distribution (6.3.1) where we set $\phi_1(x_4) = \phi_2(x_4) = 1$ to make this match. Now perform absorption on this clique tree:

We absorb $(x_3, x_4) \rightsquigarrow (x_1, x_4)$. The new separator is

$$\phi_1^*(x_4) = \sum_{x_3} \phi(x_3, x_4) \tag{6.3.8}$$

and the new potential is

$$\phi^*(x_1, x_4) = \phi(x_1, x_4)\frac{\phi_1^*(x_4)}{\phi_1(x_4)} = \phi(x_1, x_4)\phi_1^*(x_4). \tag{6.3.9}$$

Now $(x_1, x_4) \rightsquigarrow (x_2, x_4)$. The new separator is

$$\phi_2^*(x_4) = \sum_{x_1} \phi^*(x_1, x_4) \tag{6.3.10}$$

and the new potential is

$$\phi^*(x_2, x_4) = \phi(x_2, x_4)\frac{\phi_2^*(x_4)}{\phi_2(x_4)} = \phi(x_2, x_4)\phi_2^*(x_4). \tag{6.3.11}$$

Since we've 'hit the buffers' in terms of message passing, the potential $\phi(x_2, x_4)$ cannot be updated further. Let's examine more carefully the value of this new potential,

$$\phi^*(x_2, x_4) = \phi(x_2, x_4)\phi_2^*(x_4) = \phi(x_2, x_4)\sum_{x_1} \phi^*(x_1, x_4) \tag{6.3.12}$$

$$= \phi(x_2, x_4)\sum_{x_1} \phi(x_1, x_4)\sum_{x_3} \phi(x_3, x_4) = \sum_{x_1, x_3} p(x_1, x_2, x_3, x_4) = p(x_2, x_4). \tag{6.3.13}$$

Hence the new potential $\phi^*(x_2, x_4)$ contains the marginal $p(x_2, x_4)$.

To complete a full round of message passing we need to have passed messages in a valid schedule along both directions of each separator. To do so, we continue as follows:

We absorb $(x_2, x_4) \rightsquigarrow (x_1, x_4)$. The new separator is

$$\phi_2^{**}(x_4) = \sum_{x_2} \phi^*(x_2, x_4) \tag{6.3.14}$$

and

$$\phi^{**}(x_1, x_4) = \phi^*(x_1, x_4)\frac{\phi_2^{**}(x_4)}{\phi_2^*(x_4)}. \tag{6.3.15}$$

Note that $\phi_2^{**}(x_4) = \sum_{x_2} \phi^*(x_2, x_4) = \sum_{x_2} p(x_2, x_4) = p(x_4)$ so that now, after absorbing through both directions, the separator contains the marginal $p(x_4)$. The reader may show that $\phi^{**}(x_1, x_4) = p(x_1, x_4)$.

Finally, we absorb $(x_1, x_4) \rightsquigarrow (x_3, x_4)$. The new separator is

$$\phi_1^{**}(x_4) = \sum_{x_1} \phi^{**}(x_1, x_4) = p(x_4) \tag{6.3.16}$$

and

$$\phi^*(x_3, x_4) = \phi(x_3, x_4)\frac{\phi_1^{**}(x_4)}{\phi_1^*(x_4)} = p(x_3, x_4). \tag{6.3.17}$$

Hence, after a full round of message passing, the new potentials all contain the correct marginals.

The new representation is *consistent* in the sense that for any (not necessarily neighbouring) cliques $\mathcal{V}$ and $\mathcal{W}$ with intersection $\mathcal{I}$, and corresponding potentials $\phi(\mathcal{V})$ and $\phi(\mathcal{W})$,

$$\sum_{\mathcal{V}\backslash\mathcal{I}} \phi(\mathcal{V}) = \sum_{\mathcal{W}\backslash\mathcal{I}} \phi(\mathcal{W}). \tag{6.3.18}$$

Note that bidirectional absorption following a valid schedule guarantees local consistency for neighbouring cliques, as in the example above, provided that we started with a clique tree which is a correct representation of the distribution.

To ensure global consistency, if a variable occurs in two cliques it must be present in all cliques on any path connecting these cliques. An extreme example would be if we removed the link between cliques (x_3, x_4) and (x_1, x_4). In this case this is still a clique tree; however global consistency could not be guaranteed since the information required to make clique (x_3, x_4) consistent with the rest of the graph cannot reach this clique.

Formally, the requirement for the propagation of local to global consistency is that the clique tree is a junction tree, as defined below.

Definition 6.4 Junction tree A clique tree is a junction tree if, for each pair of nodes, $\mathcal{V}$ and $\mathcal{W}$, all nodes on the path between $\mathcal{V}$ and $\mathcal{W}$ contain the intersection $\mathcal{V} \cap \mathcal{W}$. This is also called the *running intersection property*.

From this definition local consistency will be passed on to any neighbours and the distribution will be globally consistent. Proofs for these results are contained in [161].

Example 6.1 A consistent junction tree

To gain some intuition about the meaning of consistency, consider the junction tree in Fig. 6.4(d). After a full round of message passing on this tree, each link is consistent, and the product of the potentials divided by the product of the separator potentials is just the original distribution itself. Imagine that we are interested in calculating the marginal for the node abc. That requires summing over all the other variables, $defgh$. If we consider summing over h then, because the link is consistent,

$$\sum_h \phi^*(e, h) = \phi^*(e) \tag{6.3.19}$$

so that the ratio $\sum_h \frac{\phi^*(e,h)}{\phi^*(e)}$ is unity, and the effect of summing over node h is that the link between eh and dce can be removed, along with the separator. The same happens for the link between node eg and dce, and also for cf to abc. The only nodes remaining are now dce and abc and their separator c, which have so far been unaffected by the summations. We still need to sum out over d and e. Again, because the link is consistent,

$$\sum_{de} \phi^*(d, c, e) = \phi^*(c) \tag{6.3.20}$$

so that the ratio $\sum_{de} \frac{\phi^*(d,c,e)}{\phi^*(c)} = 1$. The result of the summation of all variables not in abc therefore produces unity for the cliques and their separators, and the summed potential representation reduces simply to the potential $\phi^*(a, b, c)$ which is the marginal $p(a, b, c)$. It is clear that a similar effect will happen for other nodes. We can then obtain the marginals for individual variables by simple brute force summation over the other variables in that potential, for example $p(f) = \sum_c \phi^*(c, f)$.

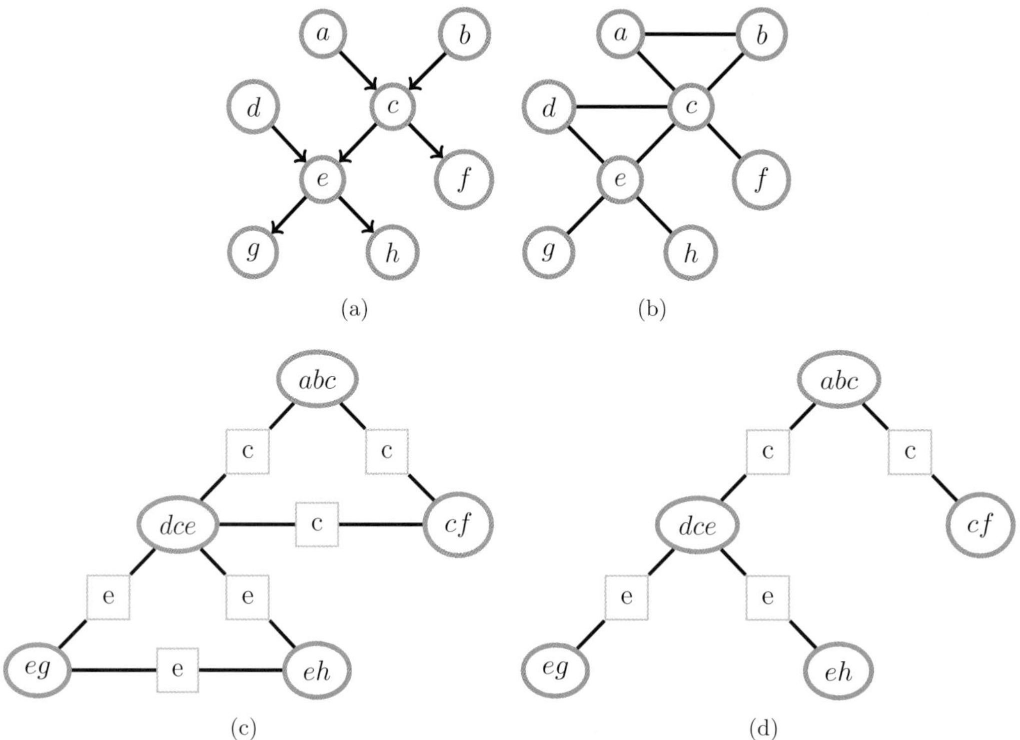

Figure 6.4 (**a**) Belief network. (**b**) Moralised version of (a). (**c**) Clique graph of (b). (**d**) A junction tree. This satisfies the running intersection property that for any two nodes which contain a variable in common, any clique on the path linking the two nodes also contains that variable.

6.4 Constructing a junction tree for singly connected distributions

6.4.1 Moralisation

For belief networks an initial step is required, which is not required in the case of undirected graphs.

Definition 6.5 **Moralisation** For each variable x add an undirected link between all parents of x and replace the directed link from x to its parents by undirected links. This creates a 'moralised' Markov network.

6.4.2 Forming the clique graph

The clique graph is formed by identifying the cliques in the Markov network and adding a link between cliques that have a non-empty intersection. Add a separator between the intersecting cliques.

6.4.3 Forming a junction tree from a clique graph

For a singly connected distribution, any maximal weight spanning tree of a clique graph is a junction tree.

Definition 6.6 Junction tree A junction tree is obtained by finding a maximal weight spanning tree of the clique graph. The weight of the tree is defined as the sum of all the separator weights of the tree, where the separator weight is the number of variables in the separator.

If the clique graph contains loops, then all separators on the loop contain the same variable. By continuing to remove loop links until a tree is revealed, we obtain a junction tree.

Example 6.2 Forming a junction tree

Consider the belief network in Fig. 6.4(a). The moralisation procedure gives Fig. 6.4(b). Identifying the cliques in this graph and linking them together gives the clique graph in Fig. 6.4(c). There are several possible junction trees one could obtain from this clique graph, and one is given in Fig. 6.4(d).

6.4.4 Assigning potentials to cliques

Definition 6.7 Clique potential assignment Given a junction tree and a function defined as the product of a set of potentials $\phi\left(\mathcal{X}^1\right), \ldots, \phi\left(\mathcal{X}^n\right)$, a valid clique potential assignment places potentials in JT cliques whose variables can contain them such that the product of the JT clique potentials, divided by the JT separator potentials, is equal to the function.

A simple way to achieve this assignment is to list all the potentials and order the JT cliques arbitrarily. Then, for each potential, search through the JT cliques until the first is encountered for which the potential variables are a subset of the JT clique variables. Subsequently the potential on each JT clique is taken as the product of all clique potentials assigned to the JT clique. Lastly, we assign all JT separators to unity. This approach is taken in `jtassignpot.m`. Note that in some instances it can be that a junction tree clique is assigned to unity.

Example 6.3

For the belief network of Fig. 6.4(a), we wish to assign its potentials to the junction tree Fig. 6.4(d). In this case the assignment is unique and is given by

$$\begin{aligned}
\phi(abc) &= p(a)p(b)p(c|a,b) \\
\phi(dce) &= p(d)p(e|d,c) \\
\phi(cf) &= p(f|c) \\
\phi(eg) &= p(g|e) \\
\phi(eh) &= p(h|e).
\end{aligned} \tag{6.4.1}$$

All separator potentials are initialised to unity.

6.5 Junction trees for multiply connected distributions

When the distribution contains loops, the construction outlined in Section 6.4 does not result in a junction tree. The reason is that, due to the loops, variable elimination changes the structure of the remaining graph. To see this, consider the following distribution,

$$p(a,b,c,d) = \phi(a,b)\phi(b,c)\phi(c,d)\phi(d,a) \tag{6.5.1}$$

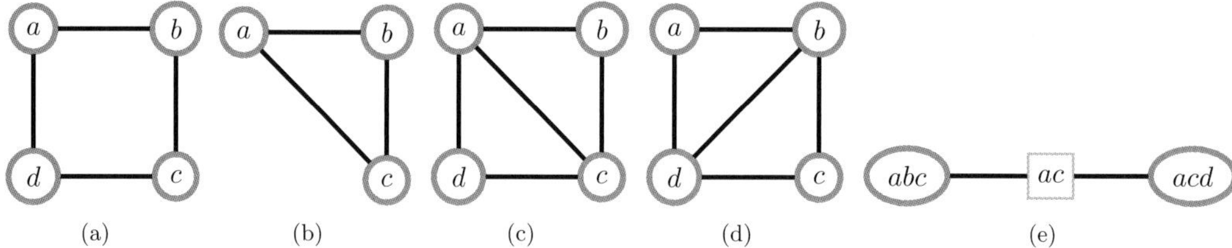

Figure 6.5 (**a**) An undirected graph with a loop. (**b**) Eliminating node *d* adds a link between *a* and *c* in the subgraph. (**c**) The induced representation for the graph in (a). (**d**) Equivalent induced representation. (**e**) Junction tree for (a).

as shown in Fig. 6.5(a). Let's first try to make a clique graph. We have a choice about which variable first to marginalise over. Let's choose d:

$$p(a, b, c) = \phi(a, b)\phi(b, c)\sum_{d}\phi(c, d)\phi(d, a). \tag{6.5.2}$$

The remaining subgraph therefore has an extra connection between a and c, see Fig. 6.5(b). We can express the joint in terms of the marginals using

$$p(a, b, c, d) = \frac{p(a, b, c)}{\sum_d \phi(c, d)\phi(d, a)}\phi(c, d)\phi(d, a). \tag{6.5.3}$$

To continue the transformation into marginal form, let's try to replace the numerator terms with probabilities. We can do this by considering

$$p(a, c, d) = \phi(c, d)\phi(d, a)\sum_{b}\phi(a, b)\phi(b, c). \tag{6.5.4}$$

Plugging this into the above equation, we have

$$p(a, b, c, d) = \frac{p(a, b, c)p(a, c, d)}{\sum_d \phi(c, d)\phi(d, a)\sum_b \phi(a, b)\phi(b, c)}. \tag{6.5.5}$$

We recognise that the denominator is simply $p(a, c)$, hence

$$p(a, b, c, d) = \frac{p(a, b, c)p(a, c, d)}{p(a, c)}. \tag{6.5.6}$$

This means that a valid clique graph for the distribution Fig. 6.5(a) must contain cliques larger than those in the original distribution. To form a JT based on products of cliques divided by products of separators, we could start from the *induced representation* Fig. 6.5(c). Alternatively, we could have marginalised over variables a and c, and ended up with the equivalent representation Fig. 6.5(d).

Generally, the result from variable elimination and re-representation in terms of the induced graph is that a link is added between any two variables on a loop (of length 4 or more) which does not have a chord. This is called *triangulation*. A Markov network on a triangulated graph can always be written in terms of the product of marginals divided by the product of separators. Armed with this new induced representation, we can form a junction tree.

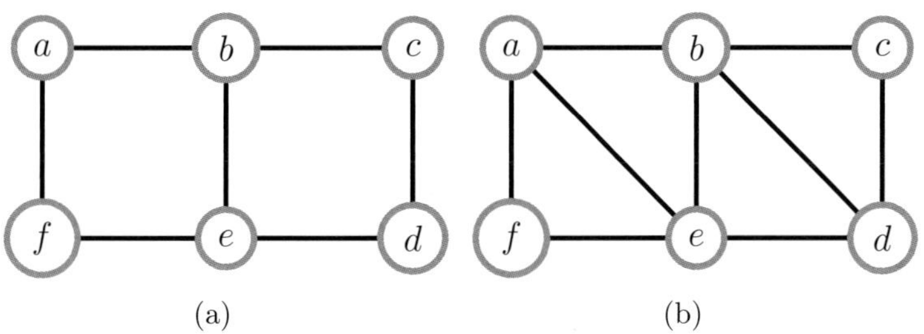

Figure 6.6 (**a**) Loopy 'ladder' Markov network. (**b**) Induced representation.

Example 6.4

A slightly more complex loopy distribution is depicted in Fig. 6.6(a),

$$p(a, b, c, d, e, f) = \phi(a, b)\phi(b, c)\phi(c, d)\phi(d, e)\phi(e, f)\phi(a, f)\phi(b, e). \tag{6.5.7}$$

There are different induced representations depending on which variables we decide to eliminate. The reader may convince herself that one such induced representation is given by Fig. 6.6(b).

Definition 6.8 Triangulated (decomposable) graph An undirected graph is triangulated if every loop of length 4 or more has a chord. An equivalent term is that the graph is *decomposable* or *chordal*. From this definition, one may show that an undirected graph is triangulated if and only if its clique graph has a junction tree.

6.5.1 Triangulation algorithms

When a variable is eliminated from a graph, links are added between all the neighbours of the eliminated variable. A triangulation algorithm is one that produces a graph for which there exists a variable elimination order that introduces no extra links in the graph.

For discrete variables the complexity of inference scales exponentially with clique sizes in the triangulated graph since absorption requires computing tables on the cliques. It is therefore of some interest to find a triangulated graph with small clique sizes. However, finding the triangulated graph with the smallest maximal clique is a computationally hard problem for a general graph, and heuristics are unavoidable. Below we describe two simple algorithms that are generically reasonable, although there may be cases where an alternative algorithm may be considerably more efficient [56, 28, 206].

Remark 6.2 ('Triangles') Note that a triangulated graph is not one in which 'squares in the original graph have triangles within them in the triangulated graph'. Whilst this is the case for Fig. 6.6(b), this is not true for Fig. 6.10(d). The term triangulation refers to the fact that *every* 'square' (i.e. loop of length 4) must have a 'triangle', with edges added until this criterion is satisfied. See also Fig. 6.7.

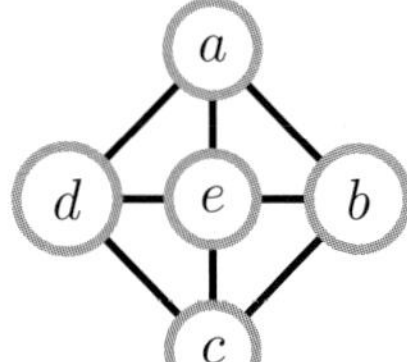

Figure 6.7 This graph is not triangulated, despite its 'triangular' appearance. The loop $a - b - c - d - a$ does not have a chord.

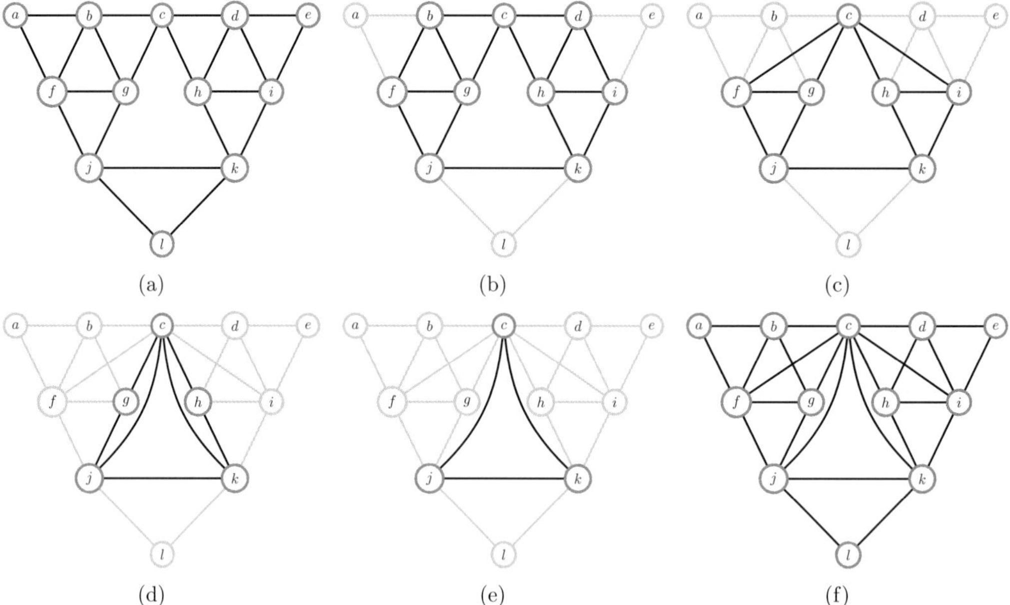

Figure 6.8 (**a**) Markov network for which we seek a triangulation via greedy variable elimination. We first eliminate the simplical nodes a, e, l. (**b**) We then eliminate variables b, d since these only add a single extra link to the induced graph. (**c**) There are no simplical nodes at this stage, and we choose to eliminate f and i, each elimination adding only a single link. (**d**) We eliminate g and h since this adds only single extra links. (**e**) The remaining variables $\{c, j, k\}$ may be eliminated in any order. (**f**) Final triangulation. The variable elimination (partial) order is $\{a, e, l\}, \{b, d\}, \{f, i\}, \{g, h\}, \{c, j, k\}$ where the brackets indicate that the order in which the variables inside the bracket are eliminated is irrelevant. Compared with the triangulation produced by the max-cardinality checking approach in Fig. 6.10(d), this triangulation is more parsimonious.

Greedy variable elimination

An intuitive way to think of triangulation is to first start with *simplical nodes*, namely those which when eliminated do not introduce any extra links in the remaining graph. Next consider a non-simplical node of the remaining graph that has the minimal number of neighbours. Then add a link between all neighbours of this node and then eliminate this node from the graph. Continue until all nodes have been eliminated. (This procedure corresponds to Rose Tarjan elimination [250] with a particular node elimination choice.) By labelling the nodes eliminated in sequence, we obtain a perfect ordering (see below). In the case that (discrete) variables have different numbers of states, a more refined version is to choose the non-simplical node i which, when eliminated, leaves the smallest clique table size (the product of the size of all the state dimensions of the neighbours of node i). See Fig. 6.8 for an example, and Fig. 6.9 for the resulting junction tree.

Procedure 6.1 (Variable elimination) In variable elimination, one simply picks any non-deleted node x in the graph, and then adds links to all the neighbours of x. Node x is then deleted. One repeats this until all nodes have been deleted [250].

Definition 6.9 **Perfect elimination order** Let the n variables in a Markov network be ordered from 1 to n. The ordering is perfect if, for each node i, the neighbours of i that are later in the ordering, and i itself, form a (maximal) clique. This means that when we eliminate the variables in sequence

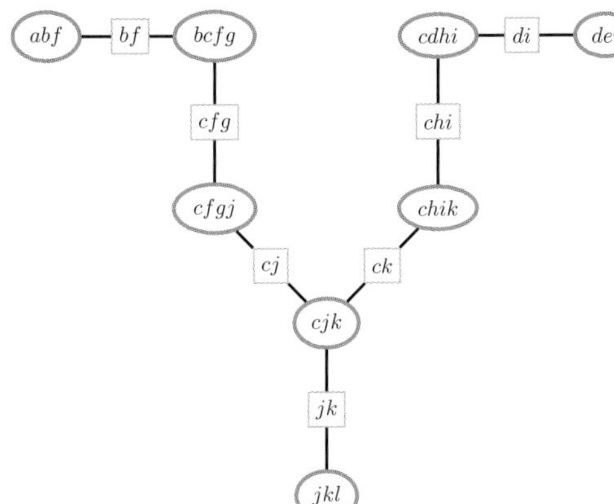

Figure 6.9 Junction tree formed from the triangulation Fig. 6.8(f). One may verify that this satisfies the running intersection property.

from 1 to n, no additional links are induced in the remaining marginal graph. A graph which admits a perfect elimination order is decomposable, and vice versa.

Whilst this variable elimination guarantees a triangulated graph, its efficiency depends heavily on the sequence of nodes chosen to be eliminated. Several heuristics for this have been proposed, including the one below, which corresponds to choosing x to be the node with the minimal number of neighbours.

Maximum cardinality checking

Algorithm 6.1 terminates with success if the graph is triangulated. Not only is this a sufficient condition for a graph to be triangulated, but it is also necessary [287]. It processes each node and the time to process a node is quadratic in the number of adjacent nodes. This triangulation checking algorithm also suggests a triangulation construction algorithm – we simply add a link between the two neighbours that caused the algorithm to FAIL, and then restart the algorithm. The algorithm is restarted from the beginning, not just continued from the current node. This is important since the new link may change the connectivity between previously labelled nodes. See Fig. 6.10 for an example.[1]

6.6 The junction tree algorithm

We now have all the steps required for inference in multiply connected graphs, given in the procedure below.

Procedure 6.2 (Junction three algorithm).

Moralisation Marry the parents. This is required only for directed distributions. Note that all the parents of a variable are married together – a common error is to marry only the 'neighbouring' parents.

[1] This example is due to David Page `www.cs.wisc.edu/~dpage/cs731`

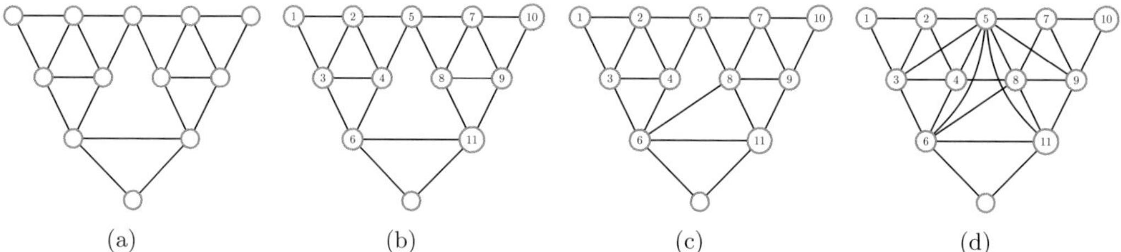

Figure 6.10 Starting with the Markov network in (a), the maximum cardinality check algorithm proceeds until (b), where an additional link is required, see (c). One continues until the fully triangulated graph (d) is found.

Algorithm 6.1 A check if a graph is decomposable (triangulated). The graph is triangulated if, after cycling through all the n nodes in the graph, the FAIL criterion is not encountered.

Choose any node in the graph and label it 1.
for $i = 2$ to n **do**
    Choose the node with the most labelled neighbours and label it i.
    If any two labelled neighbours of i are not adjacent to each other, FAIL.
end for

Where there is more than one node with the most labelled neighbours, the tie may be broken arbitrarily.

Triangulation Ensure that every loop of length 4 or more has a chord.

Junction tree Form a junction tree from cliques of the triangulated graph, removing any unnecessary links in a loop on the cluster graph. Algorithmically, this can be achieved by finding a tree with maximal spanning weight with weight w_{ij} given by the number of variables in the separator between cliques i and j. Alternatively, given a clique elimination order (with the lowest cliques eliminated first), one may connect each clique i to the single neighbouring clique $j > i$ with greatest edge weight w_{ij}.

Potential assignment Assign potentials to junction tree cliques and set the separator potentials to unity.

Message propagation Carry out absorption until updates have been passed along both directions of every link on the JT. The clique marginals can then be read off from the JT.

An example is given in Fig. 6.11.

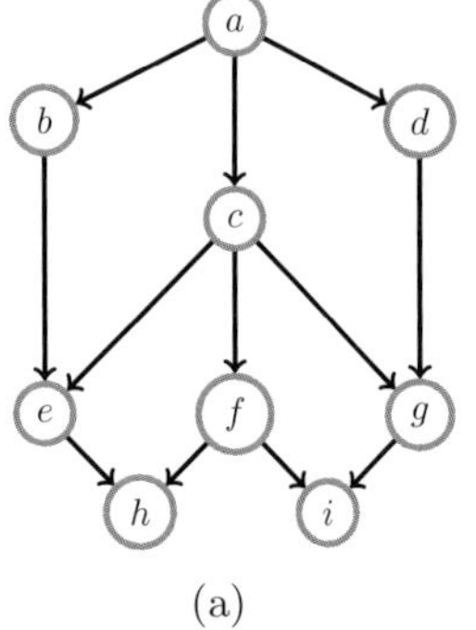

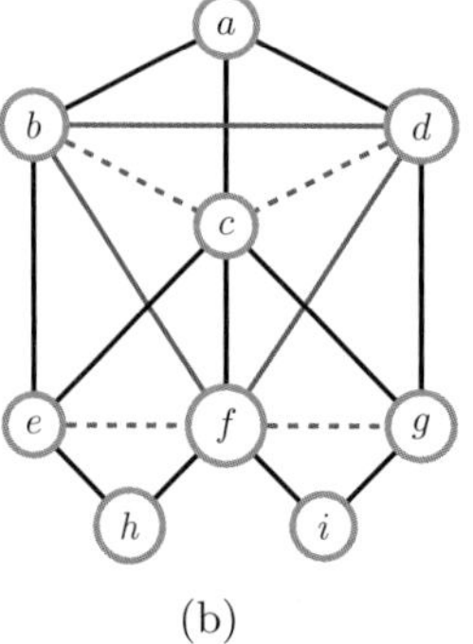

Figure 6.11 (**a**) Original loopy belief network. (**b**) The moralisation links (dashed) are between nodes e and f and between nodes f and g. The other additional links come from triangulation. The clique size of the resulting clique tree (not shown) is four.

6.6.1 Remarks on the JTA

- The algorithm provides an upper bound on the computation required to calculate marginals in the graph. There may exist more efficient algorithms in particular cases, although generally it is believed that there cannot be much more efficient approaches than the JTA since every other approach must perform a triangulation [160, 187]. One particular special case is that of marginal inference for a binary variable Markov network on a two-dimensional lattice containing only pure quadratic interactions. In this case the complexity of computing a marginal inference is $O(n^3)$ where n is the number of variables in the distribution. This is in contrast to the pessimistic exponential complexity suggested by the JTA.
- One might think that the only class of distributions for which essentially a linear time algorithm is available are singly connected distributions. However, there are decomposable graphs for which the cliques have limited size meaning that inference is tractable. For example an extended version of the 'ladder' in Fig. 6.6(a) has a simple induced decomposable representation Fig. 6.6(b), for which marginal inference would be linear in the number of rungs in the ladder. Effectively these structures are *hyper trees* in which the complexity is then related to the *tree width* of the graph [86].
- Ideally, we would like to find a triangulated graph which has minimal clique size. However, it can be shown to be a computationally hard problem to find the most efficient triangulation. In practice, most general purpose triangulation algorithms are chosen to provide reasonable, but clearly not always optimal, generic performance.
- Numerical over/under flow issues can occur under repeated multiplication of potentials. If we only care about marginals we can avoid numerical difficulties by normalising potentials at each step; these missing normalisation constants can always be found under the normalisation constraint. If required one can always store the values of these local renormalisations, should, for example, the global normalisation constant of a distribution be required, see Section 6.6.2.
- After clamping variables in evidential states, running the JTA returns the joint distribution on the non-evidential variables $\mathcal{X}_c$ in a clique with all the evidential variables clamped in their evidential states, $p(\mathcal{X}_c, \text{evidence})$. From this conditionals are straightforward to calculate.
- Representing the marginal distribution of a set of variables $\mathcal{X}$ which are not contained within a single clique is in general computationally difficult. Whilst the probability of any state of $p(\mathcal{X})$ may be computed efficiently, there is in general an exponential number of such states. A classical example in this regard is the HMM, Section 23.2 which has a singly connected joint distribution $p(\mathcal{V}, \mathcal{H})$. However the marginal distribution $p(\mathcal{V})$ is fully connected. This means that for example whilst the entropy of $p(\mathcal{V}, \mathcal{H})$ is straightforward to compute, the entropy of the marginal $p(\mathcal{V})$ is intractable.

6.6.2 Computing the normalisation constant of a distribution

For a Markov network

$$p(\mathcal{X}) = \frac{1}{Z}\prod_i \phi(\mathcal{X}_i) \tag{6.6.1}$$

how can we find Z efficiently? If we used the JTA on the unnormalised distribution $\prod_i \phi(\mathcal{X}_i)$, we would have the equivalent representation:

$$p(\mathcal{X}) = \frac{1}{Z}\frac{\prod_c \phi(\mathcal{X}_c)}{\prod_s \phi(\mathcal{X}_s)}. \tag{6.6.2}$$

where s and c are the separator and clique indices. Since the distribution must normalise, we can obtain Z from

$$Z = \sum_{\mathcal{X}} \frac{\prod_c \phi(\mathcal{X}_c)}{\prod_s \phi(\mathcal{X}_s)}. \tag{6.6.3}$$

For a consistent JT, summing first over the variables of a simplical JT clique (not including the separator variables), the marginal clique will cancel with the corresponding separator to give a unity term so that the clique and separator can be removed. This forms a new JT for which we then eliminate another simplical clique. Continuing in this manner we will be left with a single numerator potential so that

$$Z = \sum_{\mathcal{X}_c} \phi(\mathcal{X}_c). \tag{6.6.4}$$

This is true for any clique c, so it makes sense to choose one with a small number of states so that the resulting raw summation is efficient. Hence in order to compute the normalisation constant of a distribution one runs the JT algorithm on an unnormalised distribution and the global normalisation is then given by the local normalisation of any clique. Note that if the graph is disconnected (there are isolated cliques), the normalisation is the product of the connected component normalisation constants.

6.6.3 The marginal likelihood

Our interest here is the computation of $p(\mathcal{V})$ where $\mathcal{V} \subset \mathcal{X}$ is a subset of the full variable set $\mathcal{X}$. Naively, one could carry out this computation by summing over all the non-evidential variables (hidden variables $\mathcal{H} = \mathcal{X} \backslash \mathcal{V}$) explicitly. In cases where this is computationally impractical an alternative is to use

$$p(\mathcal{H}|\mathcal{V}) = \frac{p(\mathcal{V}, \mathcal{H})}{p(\mathcal{V})}. \tag{6.6.5}$$

One can view this as a product of clique potentials divided by the normalisation $p(\mathcal{V})$, for which the general method of Section 6.6.2 may be directly applied. See `demoJTree.m`.

6.6.4 Some small JTA examples

Example 6.5 A simple example of the JTA

Consider running the JTA on the simple graph

$$p(a, b, c) = p(a|b)p(b|c)p(c). \tag{6.6.6}$$

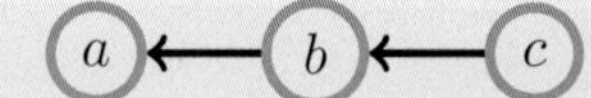

The moralisation and triangulation steps are trivial, and the JTA is given immediately by the figure on the right. A valid assignment is

$$\phi(a, b) = p(a|b), \phi(b) = 1, \phi(b, c) = p(b|c)p(c). \tag{6.6.7}$$

To find a marginal $p(b)$ we first run the JTA:

- Absorbing from ab through b, the new separator is $\phi^*(b) = \sum_a \phi(a, b) = \sum_a p(a|b) = 1$.

- The new potential on (b, c) is given by

$$\phi^*(b, c) = \frac{\phi(b, c)\phi^*(b)}{\phi(b)} = \frac{p(b|c)p(c) \times 1}{1}. \tag{6.6.8}$$

- Absorbing from bc through b, the new separator is

$$\phi^{**}(b) = \sum_c \phi^*(b, c) = \sum_c p(b|c)p(c). \tag{6.6.9}$$

- The new potential on (a, b) is given by

$$\phi^*(a, b) = \frac{\phi(a, b)\phi^{**}(b)}{\phi^*(b)} = \frac{p(a|b)\sum_c p(b|c)p(c)}{1}. \tag{6.6.10}$$

This is therefore indeed equal to the marginal since $\sum_c p(a, b, c) = p(a, b)$.

The new separator $\phi^{**}(b)$ contains the marginal $p(b)$ since

$$\phi^{**}(b) = \sum_c p(b|c)p(c) = \sum_c p(b, c) = p(b). \tag{6.6.11}$$

Example 6.6 Finding a conditional marginal

Continuing with the distribution in Example 6.5, we consider how to compute $p(b|a = 1, c = 1)$. First we clamp the evidential variables in their states. Then we claim that the effect of running the JTA is to produce on a set of clique variables $\mathcal{X}$ the marginals on the cliques $p(\mathcal{X}, \mathcal{V})$. We demonstrate this below:

- In general, the new separator is given by $\phi^*(b) = \sum_a \phi(a, b) = \sum_a p(a|b) = 1$. However, since a is clamped in state $a = 1$, then the summation is not carried out over a, and we have instead $\phi^*(b) = p(a = 1|b)$.
- The new potential on the (b, c) clique is given by

$$\phi^*(b, c) = \frac{\phi(b, c)\phi^*(b)}{\phi(b)} = \frac{p(b|c = 1)p(c = 1)p(a = 1|b)}{1}. \tag{6.6.12}$$

- The new separator is normally given by

$$\phi^{**}(b) = \sum_c \phi^*(b, c) = \sum_c p(b|c)p(c). \tag{6.6.13}$$

However, since c is clamped in state 1, we have instead

$$\phi^{**}(b) = p(b|c = 1)p(c = 1)p(a = 1|b). \tag{6.6.14}$$

- The new potential on (a, b) is given by

$$\phi^*(a, b) = \frac{\phi(a, b)\phi^{**}(b)}{\phi^*(b)} = \frac{p(a = 1|b)p(b|c = 1)p(c = 1)p(a = 1|b)}{p(a = 1|b)}$$
$$= p(a = 1|b)p(b|c = 1)p(c = 1). \tag{6.6.15}$$

The effect of clamping a set of variables $\mathcal{V}$ in their evidential states and running the JTA is that, for a clique i which contains the set of non-evidential variables $\mathcal{H}^i$, the consistent potential from the JTA

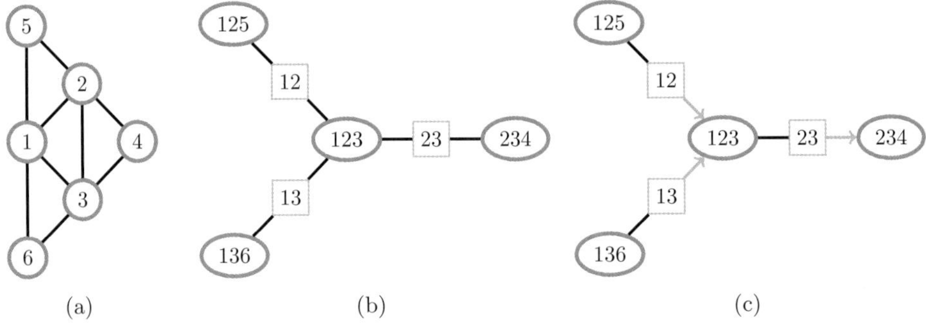

Figure 6.12 (**a**) Markov network. (**b**) Junction tree. Under absorption, once we have absorbed from 125 to 123 and 136 to 123, the result of these absorptions is stored in the new potential on 123. After this we can absorb from 123 to 234 by operating on the 123 potential and then sending this information to 234. (**c**) In Shafer–Shenoy updating, we send a message from a clique to a neighbouring clique based on the product of all incoming messages.

contains the marginal $p(\mathcal{H}^i, \mathcal{V})$. Finding a conditional marginal is then straightforward by ensuring normalisation.

Example 6.7 Finding the likelihood $p(a = 1, c = 1)$

One may also use the JTA to compute the marginal likelihood for variables not in the same clique since the effect of clamping the variables in their evidential states and running the JTA produces the joint marginals, such as $\phi^*(a, b) = p(a = 1, b, c = 1)$. Then calculating the likelihood is easy since we just sum out over the non-evidential variables of any converged potential: $p(a = 1, c = 1) = \sum_b \phi^*(a, b) = \sum_b p(a = 1, b, c = 1)$.

6.6.5 Shafer–Shenoy propagation

Consider the Markov network in Fig. 6.12(a) for which a junction tree is given in Fig. 6.12(b). We use the obvious notation shortcut of writing the variable indices alone. In the absorption procedure, we essentially store the result of message passing in the potentials and separators. An alternative message-passing scheme for the junction tree can be derived as follows: Consider computing the marginal on the variables 2, 3, 4, which involves summing over variables 1, 5, 6:

$$\phi(2, 3, 4) = \sum_{1,5,6} \phi(1, 2, 5)\phi(1, 3, 6)\phi(1, 2, 3)\phi(2, 3, 4) \tag{6.6.16}$$

$$= \underbrace{\sum_1 \underbrace{\sum_5 \phi(1, 2, 5)}_{\lambda_{125\to123}} \underbrace{\sum_6 \phi(1, 3, 6)}_{\lambda_{136\to123}} \phi(1, 2, 3)}_{\lambda_{123\to234}} \phi(2, 3, 4). \tag{6.6.17}$$

In general, for a clique i with potential $\phi(\mathcal{V}_i)$, and neighbouring clique j with potential $\phi(\mathcal{V}_j)$, provided we have received messages from the other neighbours of i, we can send a message

$$\lambda_{i\to j} = \sum_{\mathcal{V}_i \setminus \mathcal{V}_j} \phi(\mathcal{V}_i) \prod_{k \neq j} \lambda_{k\to i}. \tag{6.6.18}$$

Once a full round of message passing has been completed, the marginal of any clique is given by the product of incoming messages.

This message-passing scheme is called Shafer–Shenoy propagation and has the property that no division of potentials is required, unlike absorption. On the other hand, to compute a message we need to take the product of all incoming messages; in absorption this is not required since the effect of the message passing is stored in the clique potentials. The separators are not required in the Shafer–Shenoy approach and we use them here only to indicate which variables the messages depend on. Both absorption and Shafer–Shenoy propagation are valid message-passing schemes on the junction tree and the relative efficacy of the approaches depends on the topology of the junction tree [187].

6.7 Finding the most likely state

It is often of interest to compute the most likely joint state of a distribution:

$$\underset{x_1,\ldots,x_n}{\operatorname{argmax}}\ p(x_1,\ldots,x_n). \tag{6.7.1}$$

Since the development of the JTA is based around a variable elimination procedure and the max operator distributes over the distribution as well, eliminating a variable by maximising over that variable will have the same effect on the graph structure as summation did. This means that a junction tree is again an appropriate structure on which to perform max operations. Once a JT has been constructed, one then uses the max absorption procedure (see below), to perform maximisation over the variables. After a full round of absorption has been carried out, the cliques contain the distribution on the variables of the clique with all remaining variables set to their optimal states. The optimal local states can then be found by explicit optimisation of each clique potential separately.

Note that this procedure holds also for non-distributions – in this sense this is an example of a more general dynamic programming procedure applied in a case where the underlying graph is multiply connected. This demonstrates how to efficiently compute the optimum of a multiply connected function defined as the product on potentials.

Definition 6.10 Max absorption

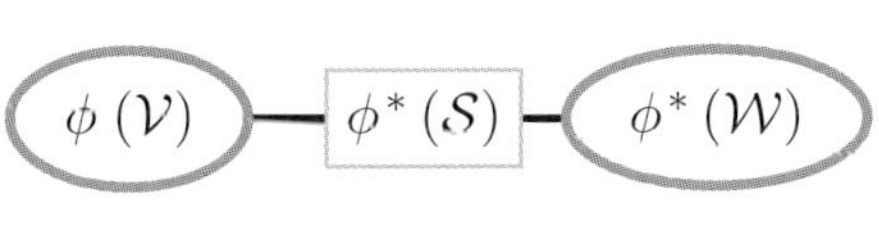

Let $\mathcal{V}$ and $\mathcal{W}$ be neighbours in a clique graph, let $\mathcal{S}$ be their separator, and let $\phi(\mathcal{V})$, $\phi(\mathcal{W})$ and $\phi(\mathcal{S})$ be their potentials. Absorption replaces the tables $\phi(\mathcal{S})$ and $\phi(\mathcal{W})$ with

$$\phi^*(\mathcal{S}) = \max_{\mathcal{V}\setminus\mathcal{S}} \phi(\mathcal{V}), \qquad \phi^*(\mathcal{W}) = \phi(\mathcal{W})\frac{\phi^*(\mathcal{S})}{\phi(\mathcal{S})}.$$

Once messages have been passed in both directions over all separators, according to a valid schedule, the most likely joint state can be read off from maximising the state of the clique potentials. This is implemented in `absorb.m` and `absorption.m` where a flag is used to switch between either sum or max absorption.

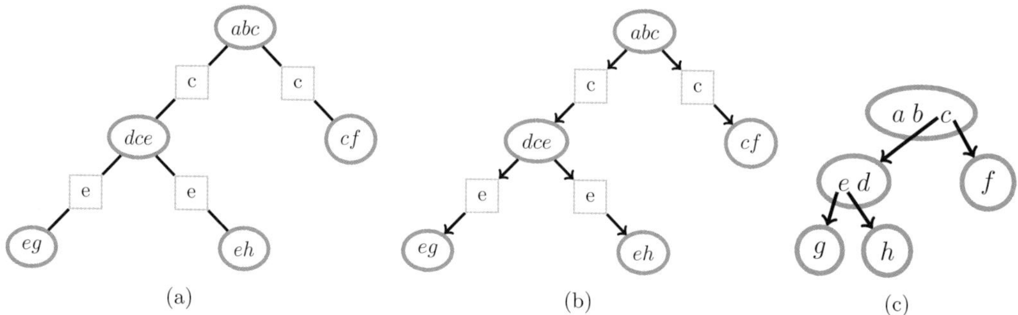

Figure 6.13 (**a**) Junction tree. (**b**) Directed junction tree in which all edges are consistently oriented away from the clique (abc). (**c**) A set chain formed from the junction tree by reabsorbing each separator into its child clique.

6.8 Reabsorption: converting a junction tree to a directed network

It is sometimes useful to be able to convert the JT back to a BN of a desired form. For example, if one wishes to draw samples from a Markov network, this can be achieved by ancestral sampling on an equivalent directed structure, see Section 27.2.2.

Definition 6.11 Reabsorption

$$\mathcal{V} \rightarrow \mathcal{S} \rightarrow \mathcal{W} \quad \Rightarrow \quad \mathcal{V} \rightarrow \mathcal{W}\backslash\mathcal{S}$$

Let $\mathcal{V}$ and $\mathcal{W}$ be neighbouring cliques in a directed JT in which each clique in the tree has at most one parent. Furthermore, let $\mathcal{S}$ be their separator, and $\phi(\mathcal{V})$, $\phi(\mathcal{W})$ and $\phi(\mathcal{S})$ be the potentials. Reabsorption into $\mathcal{W}$ removes the separator and forms a (set) conditional distribution

$$p(\mathcal{W}\backslash\mathcal{S}|\mathcal{V}) = \frac{\phi(\mathcal{W})}{\phi(\mathcal{S})}. \tag{6.8.1}$$

We say that clique $\mathcal{W}$ reabsorbs the separator $\mathcal{S}$.

Revisiting the example from Fig. 6.4, we have the JT given in Fig. 6.13(a). To find a valid directed representation we first orient the JT edges consistently away from a chosen root node (see `singleparenttree.m`), thereby forming a directed JT which has the property that each clique has at most one parent clique.

Consider Fig. 6.13(a) which represents

$$p(a, b, c, d, e, f, g, h) = \frac{p(e, g)p(d, c, e)p(a, b, c)p(c, f)p(e, h)}{p(e)p(c)p(c)p(e)}. \tag{6.8.2}$$

We now have many choices as to which clique re-absorbs a separator. One such choice would give

$$p(a, b, c, d, e, f, g, h) = p(g|e)p(d, e|c)p(a, b, c,)p(f|c)p(h|e). \tag{6.8.3}$$

This can be represented using a so-called *set chain* [184] in Fig. 6.13(c) (set chains generalise belief networks to a product of clusters of variables conditioned on parents). By writing each of the set

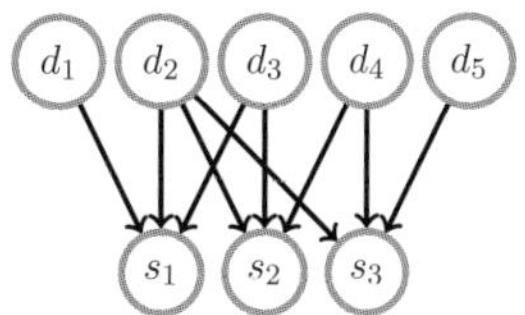

Figure 6.14 Five diseases giving rise to three symptoms. The triangulated graph contains a 5 clique of all the diseases.

conditional probabilities as local conditional BNs, one may also form a BN. For example, one such would be given from the decomposition

$$p(c|a, b)p(b|a)p(a)p(g|e)p(f|c)p(h|e)p(d|e, c)p(e|c). \tag{6.8.4}$$

6.9 The need for approximations

The JTA provides an upper bound on the complexity of (marginal/max) inference and attempts to exploit the structure of the graph to reduce computations. However, in a great deal of interesting applications the use of the JTA algorithm would result in clique-sizes in the triangulated graph that are prohibitively large. A classical situation in which this can arise are disease–symptom networks. For example, for the graph in Fig. 6.14, the triangulated graph of the diseases is fully connected, meaning that no simplification can occur in general. This situation is common in such bipartite networks, even when the children only have a small number of parents. Intuitively, as one eliminates each parent, links are added between other parents, mediated via the common children. Unless the graph is highly regular, analogous to a form of hidden Markov model, this fill-in effect rapidly results in large cliques and intractable computations.

Dealing with large cliques in the triangulated graph is an active research topic and we'll discuss strategies for approximate inference in Chapter 28.

6.9.1 Bounded width junction trees

In some applications we may be at liberty to choose the structure of the Markov network. For example, if we wish to fit a Markov network to data, we may wish to use as complex a Markov network as we can computationally afford. In such cases we desire that the clique sizes of the resulting triangulated Markov network are smaller than a specified 'tree width' (considering the corresponding junction tree as a hypertree). This results in a 'thin' junction tree. A simple way to do this is to start with a graph and include a randomly chosen edge provided that the size of all cliques in the resulting triangulated graph is below a specified maximal width. See `demoThinJT.m` and `makeThinJT.m` which assumes an initial graph G and a graph of candidate edges C, iteratively expanding G until a maximal tree width limit is reached. See also [10] for a discussion on learning an appropriate Markov structure based on data.

6.10 Summary

- The junction tree is a structure on clusters of variables such that, under inference operations such as marginalisation, the junction tree structure remains invariant. This resolves the fill-in issue when using message passing on a multiply connected graph.
- The key stages are moralisation, triangulation, potential assignment and message passing.

- There are different propagation algorithms, including absorption and Shafer–Shenoy. These are both valid message-passing algorithms on the junction tree and differ in their efficiency depending on the branch-structure of the junction tree.
- The junction tree algorithm does not make a difficult inference problem necessarily any easier. It is simply a way to organise the computations required to correctly carry out message passing. The computational complexity is dominated by the clique-size and there is no guarantee that one can find cliques with small sizes in general.
- The junction tree algorithm is clever, but not clairvoyant. It provides only an upper bound on the computational complexity of inference. It may be that there are problems which possess additional structure, not immediately apparent, that can be exploited to reduce the computational complexity of inference much below that suggested by the junction tree approach.

6.11 Code

`absorb.m`: Absorption update $\mathcal{V} \to \mathcal{S} \to \mathcal{W}$
`absorption.m`: Full absorption schedule over tree
`jtree.m`: Form a junction tree
`triangulate.m`: Triangulation based on simple node elimination

6.11.1 Utility routines

Knowing if an undirected graph is a tree, and returning a valid elimination sequence is useful. A connected graph is a tree if the number of edges plus 1 is equal to the number of nodes. However, for a possibly disconnected graph this is not the case. The code `istree.m` deals with the possibly disconnected case, returning a valid elimination sequence if the graph is singly connected. The routine is based on the observation that any singly connected graph must always possess a simplical node which can be eliminated to reveal a smaller singly connected graph.
`istree.m`: If graph is singly connected return 1 and elimination sequence
`elimtri.m`: Node elimination on a triangulated graph, with given end node
`demoJTree.m`: Chest clinic demo

6.12 Exercises

6.1 Show that the Markov network 1–2–3 (with 4 attached to 2) is not perfect elimination ordered and give a perfect elimination labelling for this graph.

6.2 Consider the following distribution:

$$p(x_1, x_2, x_3, x_4) = \phi(x_1, x_2)\phi(x_2, x_3)\phi(x_3, x_4). \tag{6.12.1}$$

1. Draw a clique graph that represents this distribution and indicate the separators on the graph.
2. Write down an alternative formula for the distribution $p(x_1, x_2, x_3, x_4)$ in terms of the marginal probabilities $p(x_1, x_2)$, $p(x_2, x_3)$, $p(x_3, x_4)$, $p(x_2)$, $p(x_3)$.

6.3 Consider the distribution

$$p(x_1, x_2, x_3, x_4) = \phi(x_1, x_2)\phi(x_2, x_3)\phi(x_3, x_4)\phi(x_4, x_1). \tag{6.12.2}$$

1. Write down a junction tree for the above distribution.
2. Carry out the absorption procedure and demonstrate that this gives the correct result for the marginal $p(x_1)$.

6.4 Consider the distribution

$$p(a, b, c, d, e, f, g, h, i) = p(a)p(b|a)p(c|a)p(d|a)p(e|b)p(f|c)p(g|d)p(h|e, f)p(i|f, g). \tag{6.12.3}$$

1. Draw the belief network for this distribution.
2. Draw the moralised graph.
3. Draw the triangulated graph. Your triangulated graph should contain cliques of the smallest size possible.
4. Draw a junction tree for the above graph and verify that it satisfies the running intersection property.
5. Describe a suitable initialisation of clique potentials.
6. Describe the absorption procedure and write down an appropriate message updating schedule.

6.5 This question concerns the distribution

$$p(a, b, c, d, e, f) = p(a)p(b|a)p(c|b)p(d|c)p(e|d)p(f|a, e). \tag{6.12.4}$$

1. Draw the belief network for this distribution.
2. Draw the moralised graph.
3. Draw the triangulated graph. Your triangulated graph should contain cliques of the smallest size possible.
4. Draw a junction tree for the above graph and verify that it satisfies the running intersection property.
5. Describe a suitable initialisation of clique potentials.
6. Describe the absorption procedure and an appropriate message updating schedule.
7. Show that the distribution can be expressed in the form

$$p(a|f)p(b|a, c)p(c|a, d)p(d|a, e)p(e|a, f)p(f). \tag{6.12.5}$$

6.6 For the undirected graph on the square lattice as shown, draw a triangulated graph with the smallest clique sizes possible.

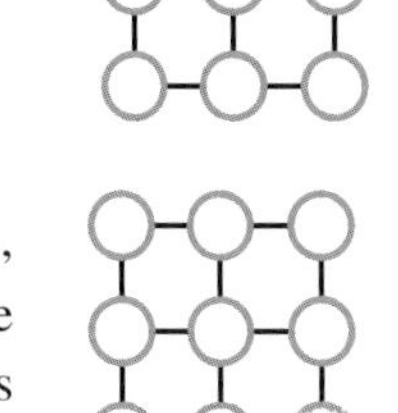

6.7 Consider a binary variable Markov random field $p(x) = Z^{-1} \prod_{i>j} \phi(x_i, x_j)$, defined on the $n \times n$ lattice with $\phi(x_i, x_j) = e^{\mathbb{I}[x_i = x_j]}$ for i a neighbour of j on the lattice and $i > j$. A naive way to perform inference is to first stack all the variables in the tth column and call this cluster variable X_t, as shown. The resulting graph is then singly connected. What is the complexity of computing the normalisation constant based on this cluster representation? Compute $\log Z$ for $n = 10$.

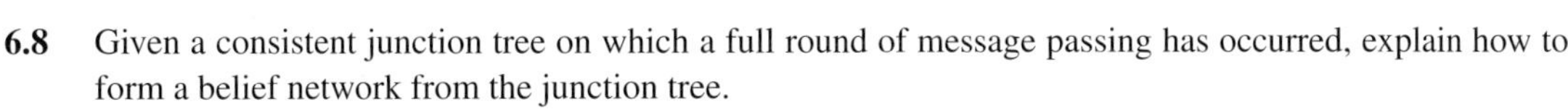

6.8 Given a consistent junction tree on which a full round of message passing has occurred, explain how to form a belief network from the junction tree.

6.9 The file `diseaseNet.mat` contains the potentials for a disease bi-partite belief network, with 20 diseases $d_1, \ldots, d_{20}$ and 40 symptoms, $s_1, \ldots, s_{40}$. The disease variables are numbered from 1 to 20 and the Symptoms from 21 to 60. Each disease and symptom is a binary variable, and each symptom connects to 3 parent diseases.

1. Using the BRMLToolbox, construct a junction tree for this distribution and use it to compute all the marginals of the symptoms, $p(s_i = 1)$.
2. Explain how to compute the marginals $p(s_i = 1)$ in a more efficient way than using the junction tree formalism. By implementing this method, compare it with the results from the junction tree algorithm.
3. Symptoms 1 to 5 are present (state 1), symptoms 6 to 10 not present (state 2) and the rest are not known. Compute the marginal $p(d_i = 1|s_{1:10})$ for all diseases.

6.10 Consider the distribution

$$p(y|x_1, \ldots, x_T)p(x_1)\prod_{t=2}^{T} p(x_t|x_{t-1})$$

where all variables are binary.

1. Draw a junction tree for this distribution and explain the computational complexity of computing $p(x_T)$, as suggested by the junction tree algorithm.
2. By using an approach different from the plain JTA above, explain how $p(x_T)$ can be computed in time that scales linearly with T.

6.11 Analogous to `jtpot=absorption(jtpot,jtsep,infostruct)`, write a routine `[jtpot jtmess]=ShaferShenoy(jtpot,infostruct)` that returns the clique marginals and messages for a junction tree under Shafer–Shenoy updating. Modify `demoJTree.m` to additionally output your results for marginals and conditional marginals alongside those obtained using absorption.

7 Making decisions

So far we've considered modelling and inference of distributions. In cases where we need to make decisions under uncertainty, we need to additionally express how useful making the right decision is. In this chapter we are particularly interested in the case when a sequence of decisions needs to be taken. The corresponding sequential decision theory problems can be solved using either a general decision tree approach or by exploiting structure in the problem based on extending the belief network framework and the corresponding inference routines. The framework is related to problems in control theory and reinforcement learning.

7.1 Expected utility

This chapter concerns situations in which decisions need to be taken under uncertainty. Consider the following scenario: you are asked if you wish to take a bet on the outcome of tossing a fair coin. If you bet and win, you gain £100. If you bet and lose, you lose £200. If you don't bet, the cost to you is zero. We can set this up using a two state variable x, with $\mathrm{dom}(x) = \{\mathsf{win}, \mathsf{lose}\}$, a decision variable d with $\mathrm{dom}(d) = \{\mathsf{bet}, \mathsf{no\ bet}\}$ and utilities as follows:

$$U(\mathsf{win}, \mathsf{bet}) = 100, \quad U(\mathsf{lose}, \mathsf{bet}) = -200, \quad U(\mathsf{win}, \mathsf{no\ bet}) = 0, \quad U(\mathsf{lose}, \mathsf{no\ bet}) = 0. \tag{7.1.1}$$

Since we don't know the state of x, in order to make a decision about whether or not to bet, arguably the best we can do is work out our expected winnings/losses under the situations of betting and not betting [257]. If we bet, we would expect to gain

$$U(\mathsf{bet}) = p(\mathsf{win}) \times U(\mathsf{win}, \mathsf{bet}) + p(\mathsf{lose}) \times U(\mathsf{lose}, \mathsf{bet}) = 0.5 \times 100 - 0.5 \times 200 = -50.$$

If we don't bet, the expected gain is zero, $U(\mathsf{no\ bet}) = 0$. Based on taking the decision which maximises expected utility, we would therefore be advised not to bet.

Definition 7.1 Subjective expected utility The utility of a decision is

$$U(d) = \langle U(d, x) \rangle_{p(x)} \tag{7.1.2}$$

where $p(x)$ is the distribution of the outcome x and d represents the decision.

7.1.1 Utility of money

You are a wealthy individual, with £1 000 000 in your bank account. You are asked if you would like to participate in a fair coin tossing bet in which, if you win, your bank account will become

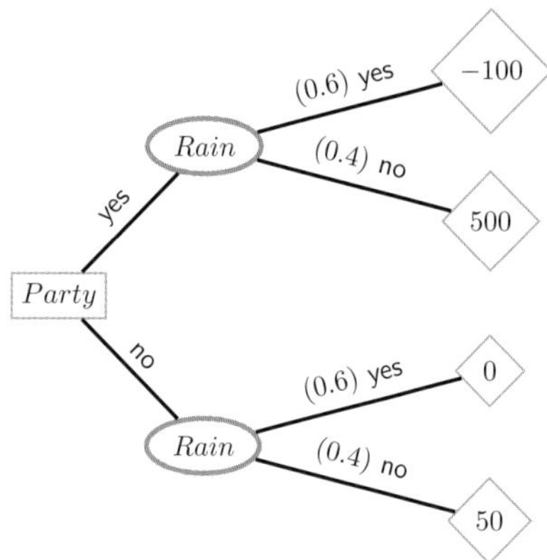

Figure 7.1 A decision tree containing chance nodes (denoted by ovals), decision nodes (denoted by rectangles) and utility nodes (denoted by diamonds). Note that a decision tree is not a graphical representation of a belief network with additional nodes. Rather, a decision tree is an explicit enumeration of the possible choices that can be made, beginning with the leftmost decision node, with probabilities on the links out of chance nodes.

£1 000 000 000. However, if you lose, your bank account will contain only £1000. Assuming the coin is fair, should you take the bet? If we take the bet our expected bank balance would be

$$U(\text{bet}) = 0.5 \times 1\,000\,000\,000 + 0.5 \times 1000 = 500\,000\,500.00. \tag{7.1.3}$$

If we don't bet, our bank balance will remain at £1 000 000. Based on expected utility, we are therefore advised to take the bet. (Note that if one considers instead the amount one will win or lose, one may show that the difference in expected utility between betting and not betting is the same, Exercise 7.7.)

Whilst the above makes mathematical sense, few people who are millionaires are likely to be willing to risk losing almost everything in order to become a billionaire. This means that the subjective utility of money is not simply the quantity of money. In order to better reflect the situation, the utility of money would need to be a non-linear function of money, growing slowly for large quantities of money and decreasing rapidly for small quantities of money, Exercise 7.2.

7.2 Decision trees

Decision Trees (DTs) are a way to graphically organise a sequential decision process. A decision tree contains decision nodes, each with branches for each of the alternative decisions. Chance nodes (random variables) also appear in the tree, with the utility of each branch computed at the leaf of each branch. The expected utility of any decision can then be computed on the basis of the weighted summation of all branches from the decision to all leaves from that branch.

Example 7.1 Party

Consider the decision problem as to whether or not to go ahead with a fund-raising garden party. If we go ahead with the party and it subsequently rains, then we will lose money (since very few people will show up); on the other hand, if we don't go ahead with the party and it doesn't rain we're free to go and do something else fun. To characterise this numerically, we use:

$$p(Rain = \text{rain}) = 0.6, \quad p(Rain = \text{no rain}) = 0.4. \tag{7.2.1}$$

The utility is defined as

$$U\,(\text{party, rain}) = -100,\; U\,(\text{party, no rain}) = 500,\; U\,(\text{no party, rain}) = 0,\; U\,(\text{no party, no rain}) = 50. \tag{7.2.2}$$

We represent this situation in Fig. 7.1. The question is, should we go ahead with the party? Since we don't know what will actually happen to the weather, we compute the expected utility of each decision:

$$U\,(\text{party}) = \sum_{Rain} U(\text{party}, Rain)p(Rain) = -100 \times 0.6 + 500 \times 0.4 = 140, \tag{7.2.3}$$

$$U\,(\text{no party}) = \sum_{Rain} U(\text{no party}, Rain)p(Rain) = 0 \times 0.6 + 50 \times 0.4 = 20. \tag{7.2.4}$$

Based on expected utility, we are therefore advised to go ahead with the party. The maximal expected utility is given by (see `demoDecParty.m`)

$$\max_{Party} \sum_{Rain} p(Rain)U(Party, Rain) = 140. \tag{7.2.5}$$

Example 7.2 Party–Friend

An extension of the Party problem is that if we decide not to go ahead with the party, we have the opportunity to visit a friend. However, we're not sure if this friend will be in. The question is should we still go ahead with the party?

We need to quantify all the uncertainties and utilities. If we go ahead with the party, the utilities are as before:

$$U_{party}\,(\text{party, rain}) = -100, \quad U_{party}\,(\text{party, no rain}) = 500 \tag{7.2.6}$$

with

$$p(Rain = \text{rain}) = 0.6, \quad p(Rain = \text{no rain}) = 0.4. \tag{7.2.7}$$

If we decide not to go ahead with the party, we will consider going to visit a friend. In making the decision not to go ahead with the party we have utilities

$$U_{party}\,(\text{no party, rain}) = 0, \quad U_{party}\,(\text{no party, no rain}) = 50. \tag{7.2.8}$$

The probability that the friend is in depends on the weather according to

$$p(Friend = \text{in}|\text{rain}) = 0.8, \quad p(Friend = \text{in}|\text{no rain}) = 0.1. \tag{7.2.9}$$

The other probabilities are determined by normalisation. We additionally have

$$U_{visit}\,(\text{friend in, visit}) = 200, \quad U_{visit}\,(\text{friend out, visit}) = -100 \tag{7.2.10}$$

with the remaining utilities zero. The two sets of utilities add up so that the overall utility of any decision sequence is $U_{party} + U_{visit}$. The decision tree for the Party–Friend problem is shown is Fig. 7.2. For each decision sequence the utility of that sequence is given at the corresponding leaf of the DT. Note that the leaves contain the total utility $U_{party} + U_{visit}$. Solving the DT corresponds to finding for each decision node the maximal expected utility possible (by optimising over future decisions). At any point in the tree choosing that action which leads to the child with highest expected utility will lead to the optimal strategy. Using this, we find that the optimal expected utility has value 140 and is given by going ahead with the party, see `demoDecPartyFriend.m`.

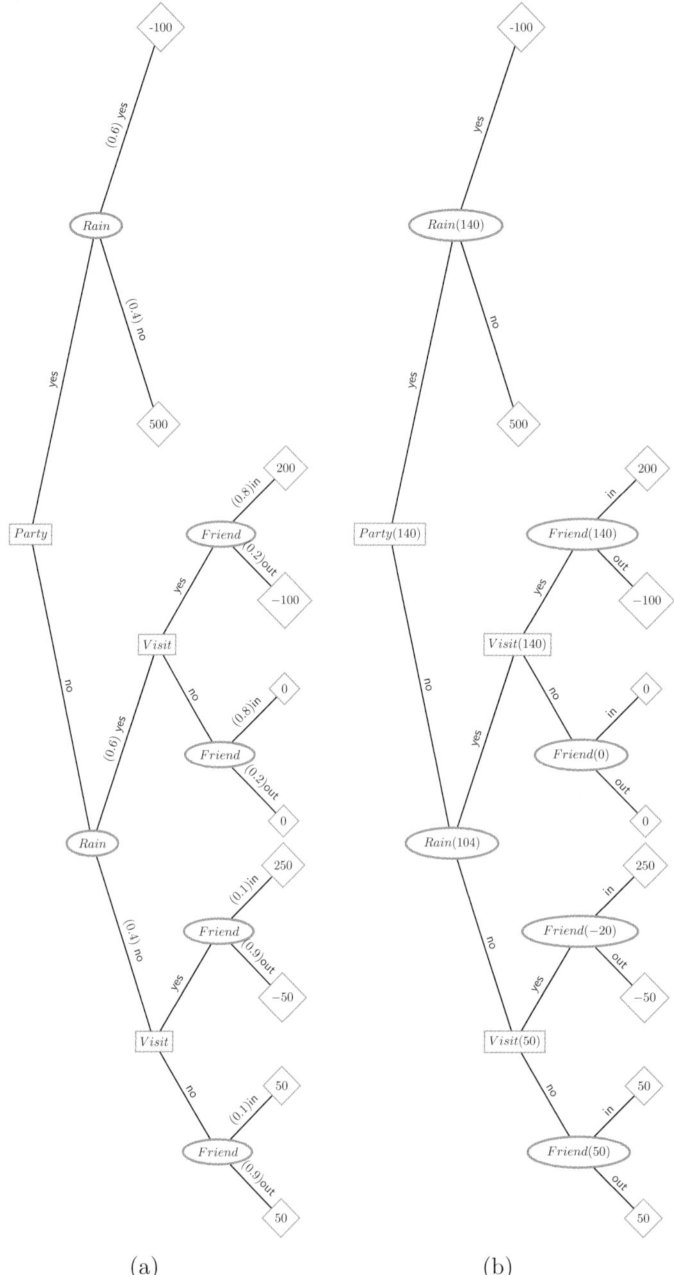

Figure 7.2 Solving a decision tree. (**a**) Decision Tree for the Party–Friend problem, Example 7.2. (**b**) Solving the DT corresponds to making the decision with the highest expected future utility. This can be achieved by starting at the leaves (utilities). For a chance parent node x, the utility of the parent is the expected utility of that variable. For example, at the top of the DT we have the *Rain* variable with the children -100 (probability 0.6) and 500 (probability 0.4). Hence the expected utility of the *Rain* node is $-100 \times 0.6 + 500 \times 0.4 = 140$. For a decision node, the value of the node is the optimum of its child values. One recurses thus backwards from the leaves to the root. For example, the value of the *Rain* chance node in the lower branch is given by $140 \times 0.6 + 50 \times 0.4 = 104$. The optimal decision sequence is then given at each decision node by finding which child node has the maximal value. Hence the overall best decision is to decide to go ahead with the party. If we decided not to do so, and it does not rain, then the best decision we could take would be to not visit the friend (which has an expected utility of 50). A more compact description of this problem is given by the influence diagram, Fig. 7.4. See also `demoDecPartyFriend.m`.

Mathematically, we can express the optimal expected utility for the Party–Friend example by summing over un-revealed variables and optimising over future decisions:

$$\max_{Party} \sum_{Rain} p(Rain) \max_{Visit} \sum_{Friend} p(Friend|Rain)$$
$$\times \left[U_{party}(Party, Rain) + U_{visit}(Visit, Friend)\mathbb{I}\left[Party = \text{no}\right]\right] \tag{7.2.11}$$

where the term $\mathbb{I}[Party = \text{no}]$ has the effect of curtailing the DT if the party goes ahead. To answer the question as to whether or not to go ahead with the party, we take that state of *Party* that corresponds to the maximal expected utility above. The way to read Equation (7.2.11) is to start from the last decision that needs to be taken, in this case *Visit*. When we are at the *Visit* stage we assume that we will have previously made a decision about *Party* and also will have observed whether or not it is raining. However, we don't know whether or not our friend will be in, so we compute the expected utility by averaging over this unknown. We then take the optimal decision by maximising over *Visit*. Subsequently we move to the next-to-last decision, assuming that what we will do in the future is optimal. Since in the future we will have taken a decision under the uncertain *Friend* variable, the current decision can then be taken under uncertainty about *Rain* and maximising this expected optimal utility over *Party*. Note that the sequence of maximisations and summations matters – changing the order will in general result in a different problem with a different expected utility.[1]

For the Party–Friend example the DT is asymmetric since if we decide to go ahead with the party we will not visit the friend, curtailing the further decisions present in the lower half of the tree. Whilst the DT approach is flexible and can handle decision problems with arbitrary structure, a drawback is that the same nodes are often repeated throughout the decision tree. For a longer sequence of decisions, the number of branches in the tree can grow exponentially with the number of decisions, making this representation impractical.

7.3 Extending Bayesian networks for decisions

An *influence diagram* is a Bayesian network with additional decision nodes and utility nodes [149, 161, 175]. The decision nodes have no associated distribution and the utility nodes are deterministic functions of their parents. The utility and decision nodes can be either continuous or discrete; for simplicity, in the examples here the decisions will be discrete.

A benefit of decision trees is that they are general and explicitly encode the utilities and probabilities associated with each decision and event. In addition, we can readily solve small decision problems using decision trees. However, when the sequence of decisions increases, the number of leaves in the decision tree grows and representing the tree can become an exponentially complex problem. In such cases it can be useful to use an Influence Diagram (ID). An ID states which information is required in order to make each decision, and the order in which these decisions are to be made. The details of the probabilities and utilities are not specified in the ID, and this can enable a more compact description of the decision problem.

7.3.1 Syntax of influence diagrams

Information links An *information link* from a random variable into a decision node

X - - - → D ← - - - d

indicates that the state of the variable X will be known before decision D is taken. Information links from another decision node d in to D similarly indicate that decision d is known before decision D is taken. We use a dashed link to denote that decision D is not functionally related to its parents.

[1] If one only had a sequence of summations, the order of the summations is irrelevant – likewise for the case of all maximisations. However, summation and maximisation operators do not in general commute.

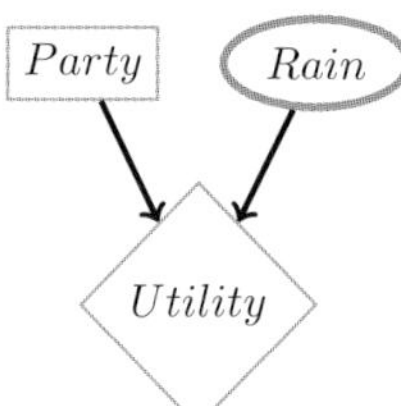

Figure 7.3 An influence diagram which contains random variables (denoted by ovals/circles), decision nodes (denoted by rectangles) and utility nodes (denoted by diamonds). Contrasted with Fig. 7.1 this is a more compact representation of the structure of the problem. The diagram represents the expression $p(rain)u(party, rain)$. In addition the diagram denotes an ordering of the variables by $party \prec rain$ (according to the convention given by Equation (7.3.1)).

Random variables Random variables may depend on the states of parental random variables (as in belief networks), but also decision node states:

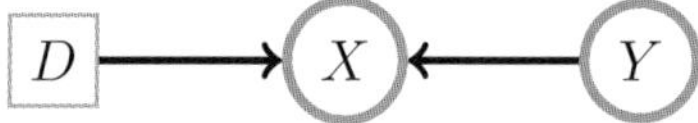

As decisions are taken, the states of some random variables will be revealed. To emphasise this we typically shade a node to denote that its state will be revealed during the sequential decision process.

Utilities A utility node is a deterministic function of its parents. The parents can be either random variables or decision nodes.

In the party example, the BN trivially consists of a single node, and the influence diagram is given in Fig. 7.3. The more complex Party–Friend problem is depicted in Fig. 7.4. The ID generally provides a more compact representation of the structure of problem than a DT, although details about the specific probabilities and utilities are not present in the ID.

Partial ordering

An ID defines a *partial ordering* of the nodes. We begin by writing those variables $\mathcal{X}_0$ whose states are known (evidential variables) before the first decision D_1. We then find that set of variables $\mathcal{X}_1$ whose states are revealed before the second decision D_2. Subsequently the set of variables $\mathcal{X}_t$ is

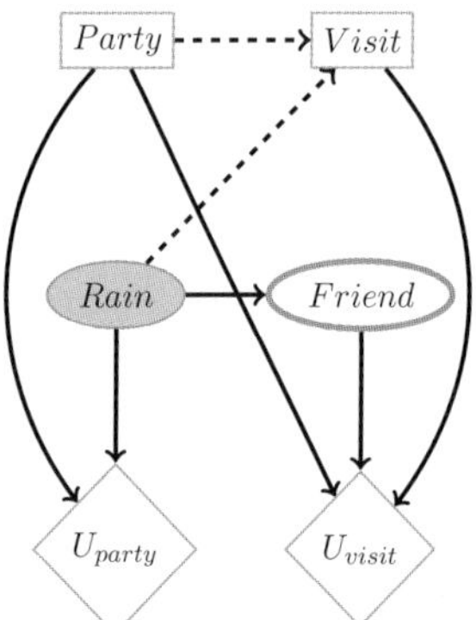

Figure 7.4 An influence diagram for the Party–Friend problem, Example 7.2. The partial ordering is $Party^* \prec Rain \prec Visit^* \prec Friend$. The dashed link from party to visit is not strictly necessary but retained in order to satisfy the convention that there is a directed path connecting all decision nodes.

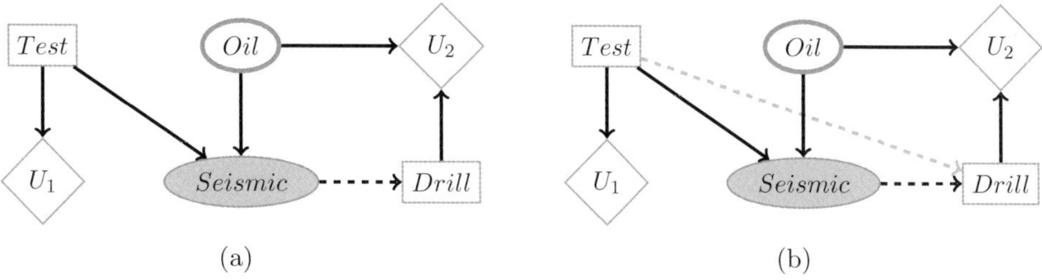

Figure 7.5 (**a**) The partial ordering is *Test** $\prec$ *Seismic* $\prec$ *Drill** $\prec$ *Oil*. The explicit information links from *Test* to *Seismic* and from *Seismic* to *Drill* are both fundamental in the sense that removing either results in a different partial ordering. The shaded node emphasises that the state of this variable will be revealed during the sequential decision process. Conversely, the non-shaded node will never be observed. (**b**) Based on the ID in (a), there is an implicit link from *Test* to *Drill* since the decision about *Test* is taken before *Seismic* is revealed.

revealed before decision D_{t+1}. The remaining fully unobserved variables are placed at the end of the ordering:

$$\mathcal{X}_0 \prec D_1 \prec \mathcal{X}_1 \prec D_2, \ldots, \prec \mathcal{X}_{n-1} \prec D_n \prec \mathcal{X}_n \tag{7.3.1}$$

with $\mathcal{X}_k$ being the variables revealed between decision D_k and D_{k+1}. The term 'partial' refers to the fact that there is no order implied amongst the variables within the set $\mathcal{X}_n$. For notational clarity, at points below we will indicate decision variables with * to reinforce that we maximise over these variables, and sum over the non-starred variables. Where the sets are empty we omit writing them. For example, in Fig. 7.5(a) the ordering is $Test^* \prec Seismic \prec Drill^* \prec Oil$.

The optimal first decision D_1 is determined by computing

$$U(D_1|\mathcal{X}_0) \equiv \sum_{\mathcal{X}_1} \max_{D_2} \ldots \sum_{\mathcal{X}_{n-1}} \max_{D_n} \sum_{\mathcal{X}_n} \prod_{i\in\mathcal{I}} p\left(x_i|\mathrm{pa}\left(x_i\right)\right) \sum_{j\in\mathcal{J}} U_j\left(\mathrm{pa}\left(u_j\right)\right) \tag{7.3.2}$$

for each state of the decision D_1, given $\mathcal{X}_0$. In Equation (7.3.2) above $\mathcal{I}$ denotes the set of indices for the random variables, and $\mathcal{J}$ the indices for the utility nodes. For each state of the conditioning variables, the optimal decision D_1 is found using

$$\operatorname*{argmax}_{D_1} U(D_1|\mathcal{X}_0). \tag{7.3.3}$$

Remark 7.1 (Reading off the partial ordering) Sometimes it can be tricky to read the partial ordering from the ID. A method is to identify the first decision D_1 and then any variables $\mathcal{X}_0$ that need to be observed to make that decision. Then identify the next decision D_2 and the variables $\mathcal{X}_1$ that are revealed after decision D_1 is taken and before decision D_2 is taken, etc. This gives the partial ordering $\mathcal{X}_0 \prec D_1 \prec \mathcal{X}_1 \prec D_2, \ldots$ Place any unrevealed variables at the end of the ordering.

Implicit and explicit information links

The information links are a potential source of confusion. An information link specifies explicitly which quantities are known before that decision is taken.[2] We also implicitly assume the *no forgetting principle* that all past decisions and revealed variables are available at the current decision (the

[2] Some authors prefer to write all information links where possible, and others prefer to leave them implicit. Here we largely take the implicit approach. For the purposes of computation, all that is required is a partial ordering; one can therefore view this as 'basic' and the information links as superficial (see [72]).

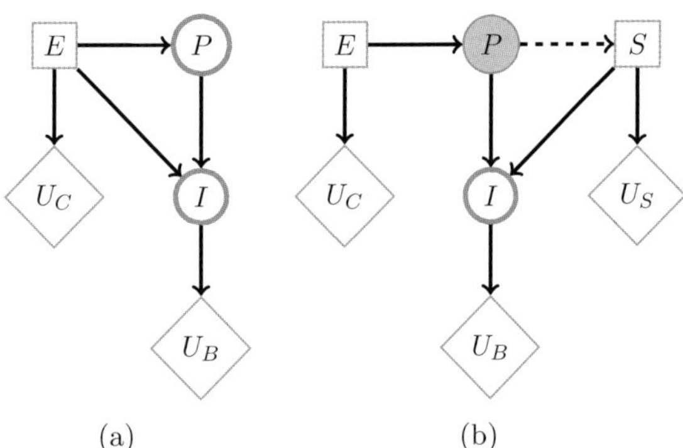

Figure 7.6 (**a**) Education E incurs some cost, but also gives a chance to win a prestigious science prize. Both of these affect our likely incomes, with corresponding long-term financial benefits. (**b**) The start-up scenario.

revealed variables are necessarily the parents of all past decision nodes). If we were to include all such information links, IDs would get potentially rather messy. In Fig. 7.5, both explicit and implicit information links are demonstrated. We call an information link *fundamental* if its removal would alter the partial ordering.

Causal consistency

For an influence diagram to be consistent a current decision cannot affect the past. This means that any random variable descendants of a decision D in the ID must come later in the partial ordering. Assuming the no-forgetting principle, this means that for any valid ID there must be a directed path connecting all decisions. This can be a useful check on the consistency of an ID.

Asymmetry

Influence diagrams are most convenient when the corresponding DT is symmetric. However, some forms of asymmetry are relatively straightforward to deal with in the ID framework. For our Party–Friend example, the DT is asymmetric. However, this is easily dealt with in the ID by using a link from *Party* to U_{visit} which removes the contribution from U_{visit} when the party goes ahead.

More complex issues arise when the set of variables that can be observed depends on the decision sequence taken. In this case the DT is asymmetric. In general, influence diagrams are not well suited to modelling such asymmetries, although some effects can be mediated either by careful use of additional variables, or extending the ID notation. See [72] and [161] for further details of these issues and possible resolutions.

Example 7.3 Should I do a PhD?

Consider a decision whether or not to do a PhD as part of our education (E). Taking a PhD incurs costs, U_C both in terms of fees, but also in terms of lost income. However, if we have a PhD, we are more likely to win a Nobel Prize (P), which would certainly be likely to boost our Income (I), subsequently benefitting our finances (U_B). This setup is depicted in Fig. 7.6(a). The ordering is (excluding empty sets)

$$E^* \prec \{I, P\} \tag{7.3.4}$$

and

$$\text{dom}(E) = (\text{do PhD, no PhD}), \quad \text{dom}(I) = (\text{low, average, high}), \quad \text{dom}(P) = (\text{prize, no prize}). \tag{7.3.5}$$

The probabilities are

$$p(\text{win Nobel prize}|\text{no PhD}) = 0.000\,000\,1 \quad p(\text{win Nobel prize}|\text{do PhD}) = 0.001 \tag{7.3.6}$$

$$\begin{array}{lll} p(\text{low}|\text{do PhD, no prize}) = 0.1 & p(\text{average}|\text{do PhD, no prize}) = 0.5 & p(\text{high}|\text{do PhD, no prize}) = 0.4 \\ p(\text{low}|\text{no PhD, no prize}) = 0.2 & p(\text{average}|\text{no PhD, no prize}) = 0.6 & p(\text{high}|\text{no PhD, no prize}) = 0.2 \\ p(\text{low}|\text{do PhD, prize}) = 0.01 & p(\text{average}|\text{do PhD, prize}) = 0.04 & p(\text{high}|\text{do PhD, prize}) = 0.95 \\ p(\text{low}|\text{no PhD, prize}) = 0.01 & p(\text{average}|\text{no PhD, prize}) = 0.04 & p(\text{high}|\text{no PhD, prize}) = 0.95. \end{array} \tag{7.3.7}$$

The utilities are

$$U_C(\text{do PhD}) = -50\,000, \quad U_C(\text{no PhD}) = 0, \tag{7.3.8}$$

$$U_B(\text{low}) = 100\,000, \quad U_B(\text{average}) = 200\,000, \quad U_B(\text{high}) = 500\,000. \tag{7.3.9}$$

The expected utility of Education is

$$U(E) = \sum_{I,P} p(I|E, P)p(P|E)\left[U_C(E) + U_B(I)\right] \tag{7.3.10}$$

so that $U(\text{do phd}) = 260\,174.000$, whilst not taking a PhD is $U(\text{no phd}) = 240\,000.0244$, making it on average beneficial to do a PhD. See `demoDecPhD.m`.

Example 7.4 PhDs and start-up companies

Influence diagrams are particularly useful when a sequence of decisions is taken. For example, in Fig. 7.6(b) we model a new situation in which someone has first decided whether or not to take a PhD. Ten years later in their career they decide whether or not to form a start-up company. This decision is based on whether or not they won the Nobel Prize. The start-up decision is modelled by S with $\text{dom}(S) = (\text{tr, fa})$. If we form a start-up, this will cost some money in terms of investment. However, the potential benefit in terms of our income could be high.

We model this with (the other required table entries being taken from Example 7.3):

$$\begin{array}{lll} p(\text{low}|\text{start up, no prize}) = 0.1 & p(\text{average}|\text{start up, no prize}) = 0.5 & p(\text{high}|\text{start up, no prize}) = 0.4 \\ p(\text{low}|\text{no start up, no prize}) = 0.2 & p(\text{average}|\text{no start up, no prize}) = 0.6 & p(\text{high}|\text{no start up, no prize}) = 0.2 \\ p(\text{low}|\text{start up, prize}) = 0.005 & p(\text{average}|\text{start up, prize}) = 0.005 & p(\text{high}|\text{start up, prize}) = 0.99 \\ p(\text{low}|\text{no start up, prize}) = 0.05 & p(\text{average}|\text{no start up, prize}) = 0.15 & p(\text{high}|\text{no start up, prize}) = 0.8 \end{array} \tag{7.3.11}$$

and

$$U_S(\text{start up}) = -200\,000, \qquad U_S(\text{no start up}) = 0. \tag{7.3.12}$$

Our interest is to advise whether or not it is desirable (in terms of expected utility) to take a PhD, now bearing in mind that later one may or may not win the Nobel Prize, and may or may not form a start-up company.

The ordering is (eliding empty sets)

$$E^* \prec P \prec S^* \prec I. \tag{7.3.13}$$

The expected optimal utility for any state of E is

$$U(E) = \sum_{P} \max_{S} \sum_{I} p(I|S, P)p(P|E) \left[U_S(S) + U_C(E) + U_B(I)\right] \tag{7.3.14}$$

where we assume that the optimal decisions are taken in the future. Computing the above, we find

$$U(\text{do PhD}) = 190\,195.00, \qquad U(\text{no PhD}) = 240\,000.02. \tag{7.3.15}$$

Hence, we are better off not doing a PhD. See `demoDecPhd.m`.

7.4 Solving influence diagrams

Solving an influence diagram means computing the optimal decision or sequence of decisions. The direct variable elimination approach is to take Equation (7.3.2) and perform the required sequence of summations and maximisations explicitly. Due to the causal consistency requirement the future cannot influence the past. To help matters with notation, we order the variables and decisions such that we may write the belief network of the influence diagram as

$$p(x_{1:T}, d_{1:T}) = \prod_{t=1}^{T} p(x_t|x_{1:t-1}, d_{1:t}). \tag{7.4.1}$$

For a general utility $u(x_{1:T}, d_{1:T})$, solving the ID the corresponds to carrying out the operations

$$\max_{d_1} \sum_{x_1} \dots \max_{d_T} \sum_{x_T} \prod_{t=1}^{T} p(x_t|x_{1:t-1}, d_{1:t}) u(x_{1:T}, d_{1:T}). \tag{7.4.2}$$

Let's look at eliminating first x_T and then d_T. Our aim is to write a new ID on the reduced variables $x_{1:T-1}, d_{1:T-1}$. Since x_T and d_T only appear in the final factor of the belief network, we can write

$$\max_{d_1} \sum_{x_1} \dots \max_{d_{T-1}} \sum_{x_{T-1}} \prod_{t=1}^{T-1} p(x_t|x_{1:t-1}, d_{1:t}) \max_{d_T} \sum_{x_T} p(x_T|x_{1:T-1}, d_{1:T}) u(x_{1:T}, d_{1:T}) \tag{7.4.3}$$

which is then a new ID

$$\max_{d_1} \sum_{x_1} \dots \max_{d_{T-1}} \sum_{x_{T-1}} \prod_{t=1}^{T-1} p(x_t|x_{1:t-1}, d_{1:t}) \tilde{u}(x_{1:T-1}, d_{1:T-1}) \tag{7.4.4}$$

with modified potential

$$\tilde{u}(x_{1:T-1}, d_{1:T-1}) \equiv \max_{d_T} \sum_{x_T} p(x_T|x_{1:T-1}, d_{1:T}) u(x_{1:T}, d_{1:T}). \tag{7.4.5}$$

This however doesn't exploit the fact that the utilities will typically have structure. Without loss of generality, we may also write the utility as one that is independent of x_T, d_T and one that depends on x_T, d_T:

$$u(x_{1:T}, d_{1:T}) = u_a(x_{1:T-1}, d_{1:T-1}) + u_b(x_{1:T}, d_{1:T}). \tag{7.4.6}$$

Then eliminating x_T, d_T updates the utility to

$$\tilde{u}(x_{1:T-1}, d_{1:T-1}) = u_a(x_{1:T-1}, d_{1:T-1}) + \max_{d_T} \sum_{x_T} p(x_T|x_{1:T-1}, d_{1:T}) u_b(x_{1:T}, d_{1:T}). \tag{7.4.7}$$

7.4.1 Messages on an ID

For an ID with two sets of variables $\mathcal{X}_1$, $\mathcal{X}_2$ and associated decision sets $\mathcal{D}_1$ and $\mathcal{D}_2$, we can write the belief network as

$$p(\mathcal{X}|\mathcal{D}) = p(\mathcal{X}_2|\mathcal{X}_1, \mathcal{D}_1, \mathcal{D}_2)p(\mathcal{X}_1|\mathcal{D}_1) \tag{7.4.8}$$

where $\mathcal{D}_1 \prec \mathcal{X}_1 \prec \mathcal{D}_2 \prec \mathcal{X}_2$, and corresponding utilities

$$u(\mathcal{X}, \mathcal{D}) = u(\mathcal{X}_1, \mathcal{D}) + u(\mathcal{X}_1, \mathcal{X}_2, \mathcal{D}). \tag{7.4.9}$$

The optimal utility is given by

$$u^{opt} = \max_{\mathcal{D}_1} \sum_{\mathcal{X}_1} \max_{\mathcal{D}_2} \sum_{\mathcal{X}_2} p(\mathcal{X}|\mathcal{D})u(\mathcal{X}, \mathcal{D}). \tag{7.4.10}$$

After eliminating $\mathcal{X}_2$ and $\mathcal{D}_2$, we obtain the ID

$$p(\mathcal{X}_1|\mathcal{D}_1)\left(u(\mathcal{X}_1, \mathcal{D}) + \max_{\mathcal{D}_2} \sum_{\mathcal{X}_2} u(\mathcal{X}_1, \mathcal{X}_{\in}, \mathcal{D})\right) \tag{7.4.11}$$

which we can express in terms of the original distribution $p(\mathcal{X}|\mathcal{D})$ as

$$\left(\sum_{(\mathcal{X},\mathcal{D})_2}^{*} p(\mathcal{X}|\mathcal{D})\right)\left(u(\mathcal{X}_1, \mathcal{D}) + \frac{1}{\sum^{*}_{(\mathcal{X},\mathcal{D})_2} p(\mathcal{X}|\mathcal{D})} \sum_{(\mathcal{X},\mathcal{D})_2}^{*} p(\mathcal{X}|\mathcal{D})u(\mathcal{X}_1, \mathcal{X}_2, \mathcal{D})\right) \tag{7.4.12}$$

where $\sum^{*}_{\mathcal{Y}}$ refers to summing first over the chance variables in $\mathcal{Y}$ and then maximising over the decision variables in $\mathcal{Y}$. These updates then define an ID on a reduced set of variables and can be viewed as messages. The potential usefulness of Equation (7.4.12) is that it may be applied to IDs that are causally consistent (future decisions cannot affect the past) but which are not expressed directly in a causal form.

7.4.2 Using a junction tree

In complex IDs computational efficiency in carrying out the series of summations and maximisations may be an issue and one therefore seeks to exploit structure in the ID. It is intuitive that some form of junction tree style algorithm is applicable. The treatment here is inspired by [159]; a related approach which deals with more general chain graphs is given in [72]. We can first represent an ID using decision potentials which consist of two parts, as defined below.

Definition 7.2 Decision potential A *decision potential* on a clique C contains two potentials: a *probability potential* ρ_C and a *utility potential* μ_C. The joint potentials for the junction tree are defined as

$$\rho = \prod_{C \in \mathcal{C}} \rho_C, \qquad \mu = \sum_{C \in \mathcal{C}} \mu_C \tag{7.4.13}$$

with the junction tree representing the term $\rho\mu$.

In this case there are constraints on the triangulation, imposed by the partial ordering which restricts the variables elimination sequence. This results in a so-called *strong junction tree*. The sequence of steps required to construct a JT for an ID is given by the following procedure:

Procedure 7.1 (Making a strong junction tree).

Remove Information Edges Parental links of decision nodes are removed.

Moralization Marry all parents of the remaining nodes.

Remove Utility Nodes Remove the utility nodes and their parental links.

Strong Triangulation Form a triangulation based on an elimination order which obeys the partial ordering of the variables.

Strong Junction Tree From the strongly triangulated graph, form a junction tree and orient the edges towards the strong root (the clique that appears last in the elimination sequence).

The cliques are then ordered according to the sequence in which they are eliminated. The separator probability cliques are initialised to the identity, with the separator utilities initialised to zero. The probability cliques are then initialised by placing conditional probability factors into the lowest available clique (that is the probability factors are placed in the cliques closest to the leaves of the tree, furthest from the root) that can contain them, and similarly for the utilities. Remaining probability cliques are set to the identity and utility cliques to zero.

Example 7.5 Junction tree

An example of a junction tree for an ID is given in Fig. 7.7(a). The moralisation and triangulation links are given in Fig. 7.7(b). The orientation of the edges follows the partial ordering with the leaf cliques being the first to disappear under the sequence of summations and maximisations.

A by-product of the above steps is that the cliques describe the fundamental dependencies on previous decisions and observations. In Fig. 7.7(a), for example, the information link from f to D_2 is not present in the moralised-triangulated graph Fig. 7.7(b), nor in the associated cliques of Fig. 7.7(c). This is because once e is revealed, the utility U_4 is independent of f, giving rise to the two-branch structure in Fig. 7.7(b). Nevertheless, the information link from f to D_2 is fundamental since it specifies that f will be revealed – removing this link would therefore change the partial ordering.

Absorption

By analogy with the definition of messages in Section 7.4.1, for two neighbouring cliques C_1 and C_2, where C_1 is closer to the strong root of the JT (the last clique defined through the elimination order), we define

$$\rho_S = \sum_{C_2 \backslash S}^{*} \rho_{C_2}, \qquad \mu_S = \sum_{C_2 \backslash S}^{*} \rho_{C_2}\mu_{C_2} \tag{7.4.14}$$

$$\rho_{C_1}^{new} = \rho_{C_1}\rho_S, \qquad \mu_{C_1}^{new} = \mu_{C_1} + \frac{\mu_S}{\rho_S}. \tag{7.4.15}$$

In the above $\sum_C^*$ is a 'generalised marginalisation' operation – it sums over those elements of clique C which are random variables and maximises over the decision variables in the clique. The order of this sequence of sums and maximisations follows the partial ordering defined by $\prec$.

Absorption is then carried out from the leaves inwards to the root of the strong JT. The optimal setting of a decision D_1 can then be computed from the root clique. Subsequently backtracking may be applied to infer the optimal decision trajectory. The optimal decision for D can be obtained by

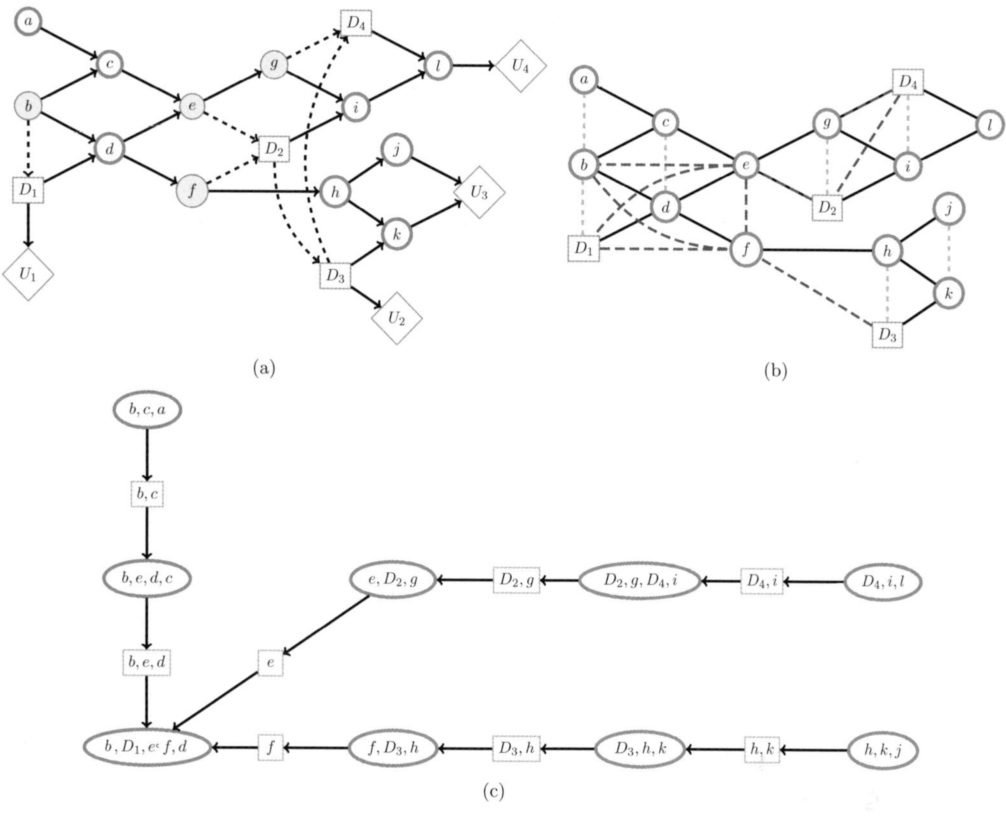

Figure 7.7 (**a**) Influence diagram, adapted from [159]. Causal consistency is satisfied since there is a directed path linking all decisions in sequence. The partial ordering is $b \prec D_1 \prec (e, f) \prec D_2 \prec (\cdot) \prec D_3 \prec g \prec D_4 \prec (a, c, d, h, i, j, k, l)$. (**b**) Moralised and strongly triangulated graph. Moralisation links are short dashes, strong triangulation links are long dashes. (**c**) Strong junction tree. Absorption passes information from the leaves of the tree towards the root.

working with the clique containing D which is closest to the strong root and setting any previously taken decisions and revealed observations into their evidential states. See `demoDecAsia.m` for an example.

Example 7.6 Absorption on a chain

For the ID of Fig. 7.8, the moralisation and triangulation steps are trivial and give the JT:

3: x_1, x_2, d_1 — x_2 — 2: x_2, x_3, d_2 — x_3 — 1: x_3, x_4, d_3

where the cliques are indexed according the elimination order. The probability and utility cliques are initialised to

$$\begin{aligned}
\rho_3(x_1, x_2, d_1) &= p(x_2|x_1, d_1) \quad & \mu_3(x_1, x_2, d_1) &= 0 \\
\rho_2(x_2, x_3, d_2) &= p(x_3|x_2, d_2) \quad & \mu_2(x_2, x_3, d_2) &= u(x_2) \\
\rho_1(x_3, x_4, d_3) &= p(x_4|x_3, d_3) \quad & \mu_1(x_3, x_4, d_3) &= u(x_3) + u(x_4)
\end{aligned} \tag{7.4.16}$$

with the separator cliques initialised to

$$\rho_{1-2}(x_3) = 1 \quad \mu_{1-2}(x_3) = 0$$
$$\rho_{2-3}(x_2) = 1 \quad \mu_{2-3}(x_2) = 0. \tag{7.4.17}$$

Updating the separator we have the new probability potential

$$\rho_{1-2}(x_3)^* = \max_{d_3} \sum_{x_4} \rho_1(x_3, x_4, d_3) = 1 \tag{7.4.18}$$

and utility potential

$$\mu_{1-2}(x_3)^* = \max_{d_3} \sum_{x_4} \rho_1(x_3, x_4, d_3)\,\mu_1(x_3, x_4, d_3) = \max_{d_3} \sum_{x_4} p(x_4|x_3, d_3)\,(u(x_3) + u(x_4)) \tag{7.4.19}$$

$$= \max_{d_3}\left(u(x_3) + \sum_{x_4} p(x_4|x_3, d_3)u(x_4)\right). \tag{7.4.20}$$

At the next step we update the probability potential

$$\rho_2(x_2, x_3, d_2)^* = \rho_2(x_2, x_3, d_2)\,\rho_{1-2}(x_3)^* = 1 \tag{7.4.21}$$

and utility potential

$$\mu_2(x_2, x_3, d_2)^* = \mu_2(x_2, x_3, d_2) + \frac{\mu_{1-2}(x_3)^*}{\rho_{1-2}(x_3)} = u(x_2) + \max_{d_3}\left(u(x_3) + \sum_{x_4} p(x_4|x_3, d_3)u(x_4)\right). \tag{7.4.22}$$

The next separator decision potential is

$$\rho_{2-3}(x_2)^* = \max_{d_2} \sum_{x_3} \rho_2(x_2, x_3, d_2)^* = 1 \tag{7.4.23}$$

$$\mu_{2-3}(x_2)^* = \max_{d_2} \sum_{x_3} \rho_2(x_2, x_3, d_2)\,\mu_2(x_2, x_3, d_2)^* \tag{7.4.24}$$

$$= \max_{d_2} \sum_{x_3} p(x_3|x_2, d_2)\left(u(x_2) + \max_{d_3}\left(u(x_3) + \sum_{x_4} p(x_4|x_3, d_3)u(x_4)\right)\right). \tag{7.4.25}$$

Finally we end up with the root decision potential

$$\rho_3(x_1, x_2, d_1)^* = \rho_3(x_1, x_2, d_1)\,\rho_{2-3}(x_2)^* = p(x_2|x_1, d_1) \tag{7.4.26}$$

and

$$\mu_3(x_1, x_2, d_1)^* = \mu_3(x_2, x_1, d_1) + \frac{\mu_{2-3}(x_2)^*}{\rho_{2-3}(x_2)^*} \tag{7.4.27}$$

$$= \max_{d_2} \sum_{x_3} p(x_3|x_2, d_2)\left(u(x_2) + \max_{d_3}\left(u(x_3) + \sum_{x_4} p(x_4|x_3, d_3)u(x_4)\right)\right). \tag{7.4.28}$$

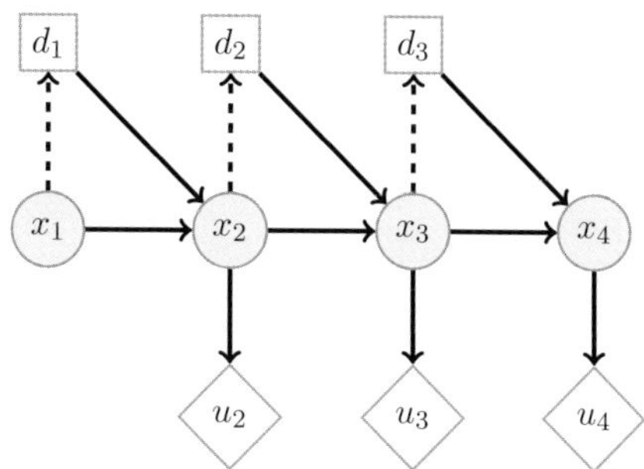

Figure 7.8 Markov decision process. These can be used to model planning problems of the form 'how do I get to where I want to be incurring the lowest total cost?'. They are readily solvable using a message-passing algorithm.

From the final decision potential we have the expression

$$\rho_3(x_1, x_2, d_1)^* \mu_3(x_1, x_2, d_1)^* \tag{7.4.29}$$

which is equivalent to that which would be obtained by simply distributing the summations and maximisations over the original ID. At least for this special case, we therefore have verified that the JT approach yields the correct root clique potentials.

7.5 Markov decision processes

Consider a Markov chain with transition probabilities $p(x_{t+1} = i|x_t = j)$. At each time t we consider an action (decision), which affects the state at time $t + 1$. We describe this by

$$p(x_{t+1} = i|x_t = j, d_t = k). \tag{7.5.1}$$

Associated with each state x_t is a utility $u(x_t)$, as depicted in Fig. 7.8. More generally one could consider utilities that depend on transitions and decisions, $u(x_{t+1} = i, x_t = j, d_t = k)$ and also time-dependent versions of all of these, $p_t(x_{t+1} = i|x_t = j, d_t = k)$, $u_t(x_{t+1} = i, x_t = j, d_t = k)$. We'll stick with the time-independent (stationary) case here since the generalisations are conceptually straightforward at the expense of notational complexity. Markov Decision Processes (MDPs) can be used to solve planning tasks such as how to get to a desired goal state as quickly as possible.

For positive utilities, the total utility of any state-decision path $x_{1:T}, d_{1:T}$ is defined as (assuming we know the initial state x_1)

$$U(x_{1:T}) \equiv \sum_{t=2}^{T} u(x_t) \tag{7.5.2}$$

and the probability with which this happens is given by

$$p(x_{2:T}|x_1, d_{1:T-1}) = \prod_{t=1}^{T-1} p(x_{t+1}|x_t, d_t). \tag{7.5.3}$$

At time $t = 1$ we want to make that decision d_1 that will lead to maximal expected total utility

$$U(d_1|x_1) \equiv \sum_{x_2} \max_{d_2} \sum_{x_3} \max_{d_3} \sum_{x_4} \dots \max_{d_{T-1}} \sum_{x_T} p(x_{2:T}|x_1, d_{1:T-1}) U(x_{1:T}). \tag{7.5.4}$$

Our task is to compute $U(d_1|x_1)$ for each state of d_1 and then choose that state with maximal expected total utility. To carry out the summations and maximisations efficiently, we could use the junction tree approach, as described in the previous section. However, in this case, the ID is sufficiently simple that a direct message-passing approach can be used to compute the expected utility.

7.5.1 Maximising expected utility by message passing

Consider the time-dependent decisions (non-stationary policy) MDP

$$\prod_{t=1}^{T-1} p(x_{t+1}|x_t, d_t) \sum_{t=2}^{T} u(x_t). \tag{7.5.5}$$

For the specific example in Fig. 7.8 the joint model of the BN and utility is

$$p(x_4|x_3, d_3)p(x_3|x_2, d_2)p(x_2|x_1, d_1)\left(u(x_2) + u(x_3) + u(x_4)\right). \tag{7.5.6}$$

To decide on how to take the first optimal decision, we need to compute

$$U(d_1|x_1) = \sum_{x_2} \max_{d_2} \sum_{x_3} \max_{d_3} \sum_{x_4} p(x_4|x_3, d_3)p(x_3|x_2, d_2)p(x_2|x_1, d_1)(u(x_2) + u(x_3) + u(x_4)). \tag{7.5.7}$$

Since only $u(x_4)$ depends on x_4 explicitly, we can write

$$U(d_1|x_1) = \sum_{x_2} \max_{d_2} \sum_{x_3} p(x_3|x_2, d_2)p(x_2|x_1, d_1)\left(u(x_2) + u(x_3) + \max_{d_3} \sum_{x_4} p(x_4|x_3, d_3)u(x_4)\right). \tag{7.5.8}$$

Defining a message and corresponding *value*

$$u_{3\leftarrow 4}(x_3) \equiv \max_{d_3} \sum_{x_4} p(x_4|x_3, d_3)u(x_4), \qquad v(x_3) \equiv u(x_3) + u_{3\leftarrow 4}(x_3) \tag{7.5.9}$$

we can write

$$U(d_1|x_1) = \sum_{x_2} \max_{d_2} \sum_{x_3} p(x_3|x_2, d_2)p(x_2|x_1, d_1)\left(u(x_2) + v(x_3)\right) \tag{7.5.10}$$

In a similar manner, only the last term depends on x_3 and hence

$$U(d_1|x_1) = \sum_{x_2} p(x_2|x_1, d_1)\left(u(x_2) + \max_{d_2} \sum_{x_3} p(x_3|x_2, d_2)v(x_3)\right). \tag{7.5.11}$$

Defining similarly the value

$$v(x_2) \equiv u(x_2) + \max_{d_2} \sum_{x_3} p(x_3|x_2, d_2)v(x_3) \tag{7.5.12}$$

then

$$U(d_1|x_1) = \sum_{x_2} p(x_2|x_1, d_1)v(x_2) \tag{7.5.13}$$

Given $U(d_1|x_1)$ above, we can then find the optimal decision d_1 by

$$d_1^*(x_1) = \underset{d_1}{\text{argmax}}\ U(d_1|x_1). \tag{7.5.14}$$

7.5.2 Bellman's equation

In a Markov decision process, as above, we can define utility messages recursively as

$$u_{t-1\leftarrow t}(x_{t-1}) \equiv \max_{d_{t-1}} \sum_{x_t} p(x_t|x_{t-1}, d_{t-1}) \left[u(x_t) + u_{t\leftarrow t+1}(x_t)\right]. \tag{7.5.15}$$

It is more common to define the *value* of being in state x_t as

$$v_t(x_t) \equiv u(x_t) + u_{t\leftarrow t+1}(x_t), \qquad v_T(x_T) = u(x_T) \tag{7.5.16}$$

and write then the equivalent recursion

$$v_{t-1}(x_{t-1}) = u(x_{t-1}) + \max_{d_{t-1}} \sum_{x_t} p(x_t|x_{t-1}, d_{t-1}) v_t(x_t). \tag{7.5.17}$$

The optimal decision d_t^* is then given by

$$d_t^*(x_t) = \underset{d_t}{\text{argmax}} \sum_{x_{t+1}} p(x_{t+1}|x_t, d_t) v_{t+1}(x_{t+1}). \tag{7.5.18}$$

Equation (7.5.17) is called Bellman's equation [30].[3]

7.6 Temporally unbounded MDPs

In the previous discussion about MDPs we assumed a given end time, T, from which one can propagate messages back from the end of the chain. The infinite T case would appear to be ill-defined since the sum of utilities

$$u(x_1) + u(x_2) + \cdots + u(x_T) \tag{7.6.1}$$

will in general be unbounded. There is a simple way to avoid this difficulty. If we let $u^* = \max_s u(s)$ be the largest value of the utility and consider the sum of modified utilities for a chosen *discount factor* $0 < \gamma < 1$

$$\sum_{t=1}^{T} \gamma^t u(x_t) \le u^* \sum_{t=1}^{T} \gamma^t = \gamma u^* \frac{1-\gamma^T}{1-\gamma} \tag{7.6.2}$$

where we used the result for a geometric series. In the limit $T \to \infty$ this means that the summed modified utility $\gamma^t u(x_t)$ is finite. The only modification required to our previous discussion is to include a factor γ in the message definition. Assuming that we are at convergence, we define a value

[3] The continuous-time analog has a long history in physics and is called the Hamilton-Jacobi equation.

$v(x_t = \mathsf{s})$ dependent only on the state s, and not the time. This means we replace the time-dependent Bellman's value recursion equation (7.5.17) with the time-independent equation

$$v(\mathsf{s}) \equiv u(\mathsf{s}) + \gamma \max_{\mathsf{d}} \sum_{\mathsf{s}'} p(x_t = \mathsf{s}'|x_{t-1} = \mathsf{s}, d_{t-1} = \mathsf{d}) v(\mathsf{s}'). \tag{7.6.3}$$

We then need to solve Equation (7.6.3) for the value $v(\mathsf{s})$ for all states s. The optimal decision *policy* when one is in state $x_t = \mathsf{s}$ is then given by

$$\mathsf{d}^*(\mathsf{s}) = \operatorname*{argmax}_{\mathsf{d}} \sum_{\mathsf{s}'} p(x_{t+1} = \mathsf{s}'|x_t = \mathsf{s}, d_t = \mathsf{d}) v(\mathsf{s}'). \tag{7.6.4}$$

For a deterministic transition p (i.e. for each decision d, only one state s′ is available), this means that the best decision is the one that takes us to the accessible state with highest value.

Equation (7.6.3) seems straightforward to solve. However, the max operation means that the equations are non-linear in the value v and no closed form solution is available. Two popular techniques for solving Equation (7.6.3), are Value and Policy iteration, which we describe below. When the number of states S is very large, approximate solutions are required. Sampling and state-dimension reduction techniques are described in [61].

7.6.1 Value iteration

A naive procedure is to iterate Equation (7.6.3) until convergence, assuming some initial guess for the values (say uniform). One can show that this value iteration procedure is guaranteed to converge to a unique optimum [35]. The convergence rate depends on γ – the smaller γ is, the faster is the convergence. An example of value iteration is given in Fig. 7.10.

7.6.2 Policy iteration

In policy iteration we first assume we know the optimal decision $\mathsf{d}^*(\mathsf{s})$ for any state s. We may use this in Equation (7.6.3) to give

$$v(\mathsf{s}) = u(\mathsf{s}) + \gamma \sum_{\mathsf{s}'} p(x_t = \mathsf{s}'|x_{t-1} = \mathsf{s}, \mathsf{d}^*(\mathsf{s})) v(\mathsf{s}'). \tag{7.6.5}$$

The maximisation over d has disappeared since we have assumed we already know the optimal decision for each state s. For fixed $\mathsf{d}^*(\mathsf{s})$, Equation (7.6.5) is now linear in the value. Defining the value $\mathbf{v}$ and utility $\mathbf{u}$ vectors and transition matrix $\mathbf{P}$,

$$[\mathbf{v}]_{\mathsf{s}} = v(\mathsf{s}), \qquad [\mathbf{u}]_{\mathsf{s}} = u(\mathsf{s}), \qquad [\mathbf{P}]_{\mathsf{s}',\mathsf{s}} = p(\mathsf{s}'|\mathsf{s}, \mathsf{d}^*(\mathsf{s})) \tag{7.6.6}$$

in matrix notation, Equation (7.6.5) becomes

$$\mathbf{v} = \mathbf{u} + \gamma \mathbf{P}^{\mathsf{T}} \mathbf{v} \Leftrightarrow \left(\mathbf{I} - \gamma \mathbf{P}^{\mathsf{T}}\right) \mathbf{v} = \mathbf{u} \Leftrightarrow \mathbf{v} = \left(\mathbf{I} - \gamma \mathbf{P}^{\mathsf{T}}\right)^{-1} \mathbf{u}. \tag{7.6.7}$$

These linear equations are readily solved with Gaussian elimination. Using this, the optimal policy is recomputed using Equation (7.6.4). The two steps of solving for the value, and recomputing the policy are iterated until convergence. The procedure may be initialised by guessing an initial $\mathsf{d}^*(\mathsf{s})$, then solve the linear equations (7.6.5) for the value, or alternatively guessing the initial values and solving for the initial policy.

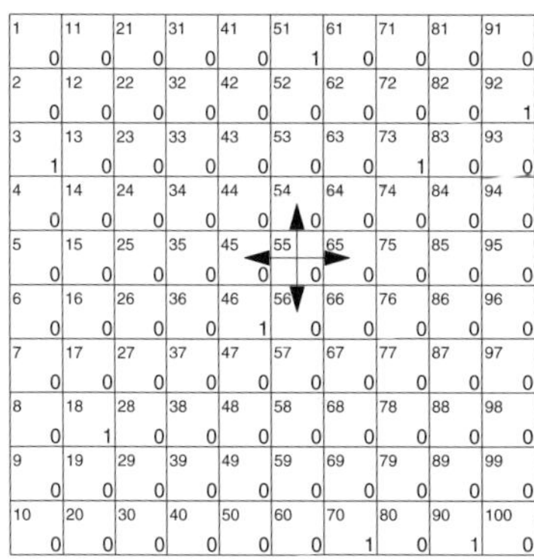

Figure 7.9 States defined on a two-dimensional grid. In each square the top left value is the state number, and the bottom right is the utility of being in that state. An 'agent' can move from a state to a neighbouring state, as indicated. The task is to solve this problem such that for any position (state) one knows how to move optimally to maximise the expected utility. This means that we need to move towards the goal states (states with non-zero utility). See `demoMDP`.

Example 7.7 A grid-world MDP

We define a set of states on a grid with corresponding utilities for each state as given in Fig. 7.9. The agent is able to deterministically move to a neighbouring grid state at each timestep. After initialising the value of each grid state to unity, the converged value for each state is given in Fig. 7.10. The optimal policy is then given by moving to the neighbouring grid state with highest value.

7.6.3 A curse of dimensionality

Consider the following Tower of Hanoi problem. There are 4 pegs a, b, c, d and 10 disks numbered from 1 to 10. You may move a single disk from one peg to another – however, you are not allowed to put a bigger numbered disk on top of a smaller numbered disk. Starting with all disks on peg a, how can you move them all to peg d in the minimal number of moves?

This would appear to be a straightforward Markov decision process in which the transitions are allowed disk moves. If we use x to represent the state of the disks on the four pegs, naively this has $4^{10} = 1\,048\,576$ states (some are equivalent up to permutation of the pegs, which reduces this by a factor of 2). This large number of states renders this naive approach computationally problematic.

Many interesting real-world problems suffer from this large number of states issue so that a naive approach to find the best decision is computationally infeasible. Finding efficient exact

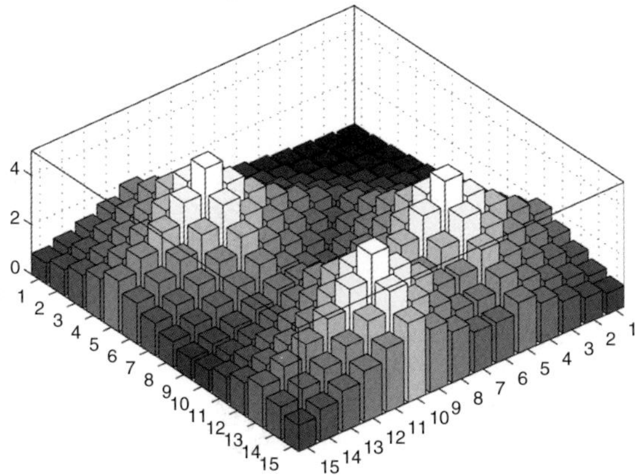

Figure 7.10 Value Iteration on a set of 225 states, corresponding to a 15×15 two-dimensional grid. Deterministic transitions are allowed to neighbours on the grid, {stay, left, right, up, down}. There are three goal states, each with utility 1 – all other states have utility 0. Plotted is the value $v(s)$ for $\gamma = 0.9$ after 30 updates of Value Iteration, where the states index a point on the $x - y$ grid. The optimal decision for any state on the grid is to go to the neighbouring state with highest value. See `demoMDP`.

and also approximate state representations is a key aspect to solving large-scale MDPs, see for example [208].

7.7 Variational inference and planning

For the finite-horizon stationary policy MDP, learning the optimal policy can be addressed by a variety of methods. Two popular approaches are policy gradients and EM style procedures – see for example [109] and Section 11.2.

For many MDPs of interest the optimal policy is deterministic [283], so that methods which explicitly seek for deterministic policies are of interest. For this reason and to remain close to our discussion on policy and value iteration, which involved deterministic policies, we focus on this case in our brief discussion here, referring the reader to other texts [81, 298, 107, 108] for the details on the non-deterministic case. For a time-independent deterministic policy $d(\mathsf{s})$ that maps a state s to a decision d (which we write as π for short), we have the expected utility

$$U(\pi) = \sum_{t=1}^{T} \sum_{x_t} u_t(x_t) \sum_{x_{1:t-1}} \prod_{\tau=1}^{t} p(x_\tau | x_{\tau-1}, d(x_{\tau-1})) \tag{7.7.1}$$

with the convention $p(x_1|x_0, d(x_0)) = p(x_1)$. Viewed as a factor graph, this is simply a set of chains, so that for any policy π, the expected utility can be computed easily. In principle one could then attempt to optimise U with respect to the policy directly. An alternative is to use an EM-style procedure [107]. To do this we define a (trans-dimensional) distribution

$$\hat{p}(x_{1:t}, t) = \frac{u_t(x_t)}{Z(\pi)} \prod_{\tau=1}^{t} p(x_\tau | x_{\tau-1}, d(x_{\tau-1})). \tag{7.7.2}$$

The normalisation constant $Z(\pi)$ of this distribution is

$$\sum_{t=1}^{T} \sum_{x_{1:t}} u_t(x_t) \prod_{\tau=1}^{t} p(x_\tau | x_{\tau-1}, d(x_{\tau-1})) = \sum_{t=1}^{T} \sum_{x_{1:t}} u_t(x_t) \prod_{\tau=1}^{t} p(x_\tau | x_{\tau-1}, d(x_{\tau-1})) = U(\pi). \tag{7.7.3}$$

If we now define a variational distribution $q(x_{1:t}, t)$, and consider

$$\mathrm{KL}(q(x_{1:t}, t) | \hat{p}(x_{1:t}, t)) \geq 0 \tag{7.7.4}$$

this gives the lower bound

$$\log U(\pi) \geq -H(q(x_{1:t}, t)) + \left\langle \log u_t(x_t) \prod_{\tau=1}^{t} p(x_\tau | x_{\tau-1}, d(x_{\tau-1})) \right\rangle_{q(x_{1:t}, t)} \tag{7.7.5}$$

where $H(q(x_{1:t}, t))$ is the entropy of the distribution $q(x_{1:t}, t)$. In terms of an EM algorithm, the M-step requires the dependency on π alone, which is

$$E(\pi) = \sum_{t=1}^{T} \sum_{\tau=1}^{t} \langle \log p(x_\tau | x_{\tau-1}, d(x_{\tau-1})) \rangle_{q(x_\tau, x_{\tau-1}, t)} \tag{7.7.6}$$

$$= \sum_{t=1}^{T} \sum_{\tau=1}^{t} q(x_\tau = \mathsf{s}', x_{\tau-1} = \mathsf{s}, t) \log p(x_\tau = \mathsf{s}' | x_{\tau-1} = \mathsf{s}, d(x_{\tau-1}) = \mathsf{d}). \tag{7.7.7}$$

For each given state s we now attempt to find the optimal decision d, which corresponds to maximising

$$\hat{E}(\mathsf{d}|\mathsf{s}) = \sum_{\mathsf{s}'} \left\{ \sum_{t=1}^{T} \sum_{\tau=1}^{t} q(x_\tau = \mathsf{s}', x_{\tau-1} = \mathsf{s}, t) \right\} \log p(\mathsf{s}'|\mathsf{s}, \mathsf{d}). \tag{7.7.8}$$

Defining

$$q(\mathsf{s}'|\mathsf{s}) \propto \sum_{t=1}^{T} \sum_{\tau=1}^{t} q(x_\tau = \mathsf{s}', x_{\tau-1} = \mathsf{s}, t) \tag{7.7.9}$$

we see that for given s, up to a constant, $\hat{E}(\mathsf{d}|\mathsf{s})$ is the Kullback–Leibler divergence between $q(\mathsf{s}'|\mathsf{s})$ and $p(\mathsf{s}'|\mathsf{s}, \mathsf{d})$ so that the optimal decision d is given by the index of the distribution $p(s'|\mathsf{s}, \mathsf{d})$ most closely aligned with $q(s'|\mathsf{s})$:

$$\mathsf{d}^*(\mathsf{s}) = \underset{\mathsf{d}}{\operatorname{argmin}} \operatorname{KL}(q(s'|\mathsf{s})|p(s'|\mathsf{s}, \mathsf{d})). \tag{7.7.10}$$

The E-step concerns the computation of the marginal distributions required in the M-step. The optimal q distribution is proportional to $\hat{p}$ evaluated at the previous decision function d:

$$q(x_{1:t}, t) \propto u_t(x_t) \prod_{\tau=1}^{t} p(x_\tau|x_{\tau-1}, d(x_{\tau-1})). \tag{7.7.11}$$

For a constant discount factor γ at each timestep and an otherwise time-independent utility[4]

$$u_t(x_t) = \gamma^t u(x_t) \tag{7.7.12}$$

using this

$$q(x_{1:t}, t) \propto \gamma^t u(x_t) \prod_{\tau=1}^{t} p(x_\tau|x_{\tau-1}, d(x_{\tau-1})). \tag{7.7.13}$$

For each t this is a simple Markov chain for which the pairwise transition marginals required for the M-step, Equation (7.7.9), are straightforward. This requires inference in a series of Markov models of different lengths. This can be done efficiently using a single forward and backward pass [298, 109].

EM and related methods follow closely the spirit of inference in graphical models, but can exhibit disappointingly slow convergence. More recently, an alternative method using Lagrange Duality shows very promising performance and the reader is referred to [110] for details. Note that this EM algorithm formally fails in the case of a deterministic environment (the transition $p(x_t|x_{t-1}, d_{t-1})$ is deterministic) – see Exercise 7.8 for an explanation and Exercise 7.9 for a possible resolution.

Remark 7.2 (Solving an MDP – easy or hard?) The discussion in Section 7.5.1 highlights that solving a linear-chain influence diagram (finding the optimal decision at each timestep) is straightforward, and can be achieved using a simple message-passing algorithm, scaling linearly with the length of the chain. In contrast, finding the optimal time-independent policy π typically is much more complex – hence the reason for many different algorithms that attempt to find optimal policies in areas such as time-independent control, reinforcement learning and games. Mathematically, the reason for this difference is that the constraint in the time-independent case

4 In the standard MDP framework it is more common to define $u_t(x_t) = \gamma^{t-1}u(x_t)$ so that for comparison with the standard Policy/Value routines one needs to divide the expected utility by γ.

Figure 7.11 Options pricing: An asset has market value £S at time $t = 1$. We assume that the asset will have market value either £S_u or £S_d at time T. The owner and 'options buyer' (client) agree that if the market value is greater than the 'strike price' £S_* at time T, the client has the right to purchase the asset for £S_*. The question is: how much should the owner of the asset charge the client for the privilege of having the right to purchase the asset?

that the policy must be the same over all timesteps, leads to a graphical structure that is no longer a chain, with all timepoints connected to a single π. In this case, in general, no simple linear time message-passing algorithm is available to optimise the resulting objective.

7.8 Financial matters

Utility and decision theory play a major role in finance, both in terms of setting prices based on expected future gains, but also in determining optimal investments. In the following sections we briefly outline two such basic applications.

7.8.1 Options pricing and expected utility

An owner has an asset currently priced by the market at £S. The owner wants to give us the opportunity to purchase this asset at time T for an agreed price of £S_*. At time T, if the market price goes 'up' beyond the strike price to £S_u we will decide to purchase the asset from the owner for £S_* and sell the asset at this increased value, see Fig. 7.11. If, however, the price remains 'down' below the strike price at £S_d, we will walk away, leaving the owner with the asset. The question is, how much should the owner charge, £C for this option of us being able to buy the asset for the agreed price at time T? To help answer this, we also need to know how much a risk-free investment would make over the same time period (i.e. how much we would get from putting money in a safe bank). We assume the interest rate R is known for the time period T, say 0.06. We call the two people the owner and the client (who may or may not buy the asset).

Two possibilities case

For simplicity, we assume the asset can take only the prices S_u or S_d at time T. We also assume we know the probabilities of these events (see below), namely ρ and $1 - \rho$. Let's work out the expected utilities for both parties:

Asset goes up:

$$U(\text{up, client}) = \underbrace{S_u - S_*}_{\text{immediate profit from selling}} - \underbrace{C}_{\text{option cost}} - \underbrace{CR}_{\text{lost interest on option cost}} \tag{7.8.1}$$

$$U(\text{up, owner}) = \underbrace{S_* - S}_{\text{immediate loss from sale}} + \underbrace{C}_{\text{option cost}} + \underbrace{CR}_{\text{gained interest on option cost}} - \underbrace{SR}_{\text{lost interest}}. \tag{7.8.2}$$

The final SR term above comes from entering into the option deal – otherwise the owner could have just sold the asset at time 1, and then put the resulting sum in the bank.

Asset goes down:

$$U(\text{down, client}) = -\underbrace{C}_{\text{option cost}} - \underbrace{CR}_{\text{lost interest on option cost}}. \tag{7.8.3}$$

The above follows since in this case the client doesn't act on his option to sell the asset.

$$U(\text{down, owner}) = \underbrace{S_d - S}_{\text{change in asset value}} + \underbrace{C}_{\text{option cost}} + \underbrace{CR}_{\text{gained interest on option cost}} - \underbrace{SR}_{\text{lost interest}}. \tag{7.8.4}$$

The expected utility for the client is

$$U(\text{client}) = \rho \times U(\text{up, client}) + (1-\rho) \times U(\text{down, client}) \tag{7.8.5}$$
$$= \rho\,(S_u - S_* - C - CR) + (1-\rho)\,(-C - CR) \tag{7.8.6}$$
$$= \rho\,(S_u - S_*) - C(1+R). \tag{7.8.7}$$

The expected utility for the owner is

$$U(\text{owner}) = \rho \times U(\text{up, owner}) + (1-\rho) \times U(\text{down, owner}) \tag{7.8.8}$$
$$= \rho\,(S_* - S + C + CR - SR) + (1-\rho)\,(S_d - S + C + CR - SR) \tag{7.8.9}$$
$$= \rho\,(S_* - S_d) + S_d - S + C(1+R) - SR. \tag{7.8.10}$$

It seems reasonable to assume that both the client and the owner should have the same expected benefit, $U(\text{client}) = U(\text{owner})$. Hence

$$\rho\,(S_u - S_*) - C(1+R) = \rho\,(S_* - S_d) + S_d - S + C(1+R) - SR. \tag{7.8.11}$$

Solving for C, we find

$$C = \frac{\rho\,(S_u - 2S_* + S_d) - S_d + S(1+R)}{2(1+R)}. \tag{7.8.12}$$

All the quantities required to price the option are assumed, except for ρ. One way to set this is described below.

Setting ρ

It seems reasonable to expect ρ to be set by some process which describes the true probability of the price increase. However, given a value for ρ and knowing the two possible prices S_u and S_d, the owner can compute the expected utility of just holding on to the asset. This is

$$\rho S_u + (1-\rho)S_d - S. \tag{7.8.13}$$

Alternatively, the owner could sell the asset for £S and put his money in the bank, collecting the interest RS at time T. In a fair market we must have that the expected reward for holding on to the asset is the same as the risk-free return on the asset:

$$\rho S_u + (1-\rho)S_d - S = RS \quad \Rightarrow \quad \rho = \frac{S(1+R) - S_d}{S_u - S_d}. \tag{7.8.14}$$

Using this value to price the option in Equation (7.8.12) ensures that the expected gain from offering the option and not offering the option is the same to the owner and, furthermore, that if the option is available, the expected reward for both parties is the same.

7.8.2 Binomial options pricing model

If we have more than two timepoints, we can readily extend the above. It's easiest to assume that at each time t we have two price change possibilities – either the price can go up by a factor $u > 1$ or down by a factor $d < 1$. For T timesteps, we then have a set of possible values the asset can take at time T. For some of them the client will sell the asset (when $S_T > S_*$) otherwise not. We need to work out the expected gains for both the owner and client as before, assuming first that we know ρ (which is the probability of the price increasing by a factor u in one timestep). For a sequence of n ups and $T - n$ downs, we have a price $S_T = Su^n d^{T-n}$. If this is greater than S_*, then the client will sell the asset and have utility

$$\mathbb{I}\left[Su^n d^{T-n} > S_*\right](Su^n d^{T-n} - S_* - C(1+R)). \tag{7.8.15}$$

The probability of n ups and $T - n$ downs is

$$\beta(T, n, \rho) \equiv \binom{T}{n} \rho^n (1-\rho)^{T-n} \tag{7.8.16}$$

where $\binom{T}{n}$ is the binomial coefficient. Hence the total expected utility for the client on the upside is

$$U(\text{client, up}) = \sum_{n=0}^{T} \beta(T, n, \rho)\mathbb{I}\left[Su^n d^{T-n} > S_*\right](Su^n d^{T-n} - S_* - C(1+R)). \tag{7.8.17}$$

Similarly,

$$U(\text{client, down}) = -C(1+R)\sum_{n=0}^{T} \beta(T, n, \rho)\mathbb{I}\left[Su^n d^{T-n} < S_*\right]. \tag{7.8.18}$$

The total expected utility for the client is then

$$U(\text{client}) = U(\text{client, up}) + U(\text{client, down}). \tag{7.8.19}$$

Similarly, for the owner

$$U(\text{owner, up}) = (S_* - S(1+R) + C(1+R))\sum_{n=0}^{T} \beta(T, n, \rho)\mathbb{I}\left[Su^n d^{T-n} > S_*\right] \tag{7.8.20}$$

and

$$U(\text{owner, down}) = -C(1+R)\sum_{n=0}^{T} \beta(T, n, \rho)\mathbb{I}\left[Su^n d^{T-n} < S_*\right] \times \left(Su^n d^{T-n} - S(1+R) + C(1+R)\right) \tag{7.8.21}$$

and

$$U(\text{owner}) = U(\text{owner, up}) + U(\text{owner, down}). \tag{7.8.22}$$

Setting

$$U(\text{client}) = U(\text{owner}) \tag{7.8.23}$$

results in a simple linear equation for C.

Setting ρ

To set ρ, we can use a similar logic as in the two timestep case. First we compute thc expected value of the asset at time T, which is

$$\sum_{n=0}^{T} \beta(T, n, \rho) S u^n d^{T-n} \tag{7.8.24}$$

and equate the expected gain equal to the gain from a risk-free investment in the asset:

$$\sum_{n=0}^{T} \beta(T, n, \rho) S u^n d^{T-n} - S = RS \quad \Rightarrow \quad \sum_{n=0}^{T} \beta(T, n, \rho) u^n d^{T-n} = R + 1. \tag{7.8.25}$$

Knowing u and d, we can solve the above for ρ, and then use this in the equation for C. We can learn u and d from past observed data (in the literature they are often related to the observed variance in the prices [74]).

The binomial options pricing approach is a relatively simplistic way to price options. The celebrated Black–Scholes method [45] is essentially a limiting case in which the number of timepoints becomes infinite [150].

7.8.3 Optimal investment

Another example of utility in finance, and which is related to Markov decision processes, is the issue of how best to invest your wealth in order to maximise some future criterion. We'll consider here a very simple setup, but one which can be readily extended to more complex scenarios. We assume that we have two assets, a and b, with prices at time t given by s_t^a, s_t^b. The prices are assumed to independently follow Markovian updating:

$$s_t^a = s_{t-1}^a(1 + \epsilon_t^a) \quad \Rightarrow \quad p(s_t^a | s_{t-1}^a, \epsilon_t^a) = \delta\left(s_t^a - (1 + \epsilon_t^a) s_{t-1}^a\right) \tag{7.8.26}$$

where $\delta(\cdot)$ is the Dirac delta function. The price increments follow a Markov transition

$$p(\epsilon_t^a, \epsilon_t^b | \epsilon_{t-1}^a, \epsilon_{t-1}^b) = p(\epsilon_t^a | \epsilon_{t-1}^a) p(\epsilon_t^b | \epsilon_{t-1}^b). \tag{7.8.27}$$

Using this one can model effects such as price increments being likely to stay the same (as in bank interest) or more variable (as in the stock market).

We have an investment decision $0 \leq d_t \leq 1$ that says what fraction of our current wealth w_t we buy of asset a at time t. We will invest the rest of our wealth in asset b. If asset a is priced at s_t^a and we decide to use a fraction d_t of our current wealth w_t to purchase a quantity q_t^a of asset a and quantity q_t^b of asset b, these are given by

$$q_t^a = \frac{d_t w_t}{s_t^a}, \qquad q_t^b = \frac{w_t(1 - d_t)}{s_t^b}. \tag{7.8.28}$$

At timestep $t + 1$, the prices of assets a and b will have changed to s_{t+1}^a, s_{t+1}^b, so that our new wealth will be

$$\begin{aligned} w_{t+1} &= q_t^a s_{t+1}^a + q_t^b s_{t+1}^b = \frac{d_t w_t s_{t+1}^a}{s_t^a} + \frac{w_t(1 - d_t) s_{t+1}^b}{s_t^b} \\ &= w_t\left(d_t(1 + \epsilon_{t+1}^a) + (1 - d_t)(1 + \epsilon_{t+1}^b)\right). \end{aligned} \tag{7.8.29}$$

This can be expressed as a transition

$$p(w_{t+1}|w_t, \epsilon^a_{t+1}, \epsilon^b_{t+1}, d_t) = \delta\left(w_{t+1} - w_t\left(d_t(1+\epsilon^a_{t+1}) + (1-d_t)(1+\epsilon^b_{t+1})\right)\right). \tag{7.8.30}$$

At an end time T we have a utility $u(w_T)$ that expresses our satisfaction with our wealth. Given that we start with a wealth w_1 and assume we know $\epsilon^a_1, \epsilon^b_1$, we want to find the best decision d_1 that will maximise our expected utility at time T. To do so, we also bear in mind that at any intermediate time $1 < t < T$ we can adjust the fraction d_t of wealth in asset a. The Markov chain is given by (see also Section 23.1)

$$p(\epsilon^a_{1:T}, \epsilon^b_{1:T}, w_{2:T}|\epsilon^a_1, \epsilon^b_1, w_1, d_{1:T-1}) = \prod_{t=2}^{T} p(\epsilon^a_t|\epsilon^a_{t-1})p(\epsilon^b_t|\epsilon^b_{t-1})p(w_t|w_{t-1}, \epsilon^a_t, \epsilon^b_t, d_{t-1}). \tag{7.8.31}$$

The expected utility of a decision d_1 is

$$U(d_1|\epsilon^a_1, \epsilon^b_1, w_1) = \sum_{\epsilon^a_2, \epsilon^b_2, w_2} \dots \max_{d_{T-2}} \sum_{\epsilon^a_{T-1}, \epsilon^b_{T-1}, w_{T-1}} \times \max_{d_{T-1}} \sum_{\epsilon^a_T, \epsilon^b_T, w_T} p(\epsilon^a_{1:T}, \epsilon^b_{1:T}, w_{2:T}|\epsilon^a_1, \epsilon^b_1, w_1, d_{1:T-1})u(w_T). \tag{7.8.32}$$

which, for the corresponding influence diagram, corresponds to the ordering

$$d_1 \prec \{\epsilon^a_2, \epsilon^b_2, w_2\} \prec d_2 \prec \dots \prec \{\epsilon^a_{T-1}, \epsilon^b_{T-1}, w_{T-1}\} \prec d_{T-1} \prec \{\epsilon^a_T, \epsilon^b_T, w_T\}. \tag{7.8.33}$$

To compute $U(d_1|\epsilon^a_1, \epsilon^b_1, w_1)$, we first can carry out the operations at T to give a message

$$\gamma_{T-1\leftarrow T}(\epsilon^a_{T-1}, \epsilon^b_{T-1}, w_{T-1}) \equiv \max_{d_{T-1}} \sum_{\epsilon^a_T, \epsilon^b_T, w_T} p(\epsilon^a_T|\epsilon^a_{T-1})p(\epsilon^b_T|\epsilon^b_{T-1})p(w_T|w_{T-1}, \epsilon^a_T, \epsilon^b_T, d_{T-1})u(w_T). \tag{7.8.34}$$

And, generally,

$$\gamma_{t-1\leftarrow t}(\epsilon^a_{t-1}, \epsilon^b_{t-1}, w_{t-1}) \equiv \max_{d_{t-1}} \sum_{\epsilon^a_t, \epsilon^b_t, w_t} p(\epsilon^a_t|\epsilon^a_{t-1})p(\epsilon^b_t|\epsilon^b_{t-1})p(w_t|w_{t-1}, \epsilon^a_t, \epsilon^b_t, d_{t-1})\gamma_{t\leftarrow t+1}(\epsilon^a_t, \epsilon^b_t, w_t) \tag{7.8.35}$$

so that

$$U(d_1|\epsilon^a_1, \epsilon^b_1, w_1) = \sum_{\epsilon^a_2, \epsilon^b_2} p(\epsilon^a_2|\epsilon^a_1)p(\epsilon^b_2|\epsilon^b_1)p(w_2|w_1, \epsilon^a_2, \epsilon^b_2, d_1)\gamma_{2\leftarrow 3}(\epsilon^a_2, \epsilon^b_2, w_2). \tag{7.8.36}$$

Note that this process is not equivalent to a 'myopic' strategy which would make an investment decision to maximise the expected next-period wealth.

For a continuous wealth w_t the above messages are difficult to represent. A simple strategy, therefore, is to discretise all wealth values and also the price changes $\epsilon^a_t, \epsilon^b_t$ and investment decisions d_t, see Exercise 7.13. In this case, one needs to approximate the delta function $\delta(x)$ by the distribution which is zero for every state except that discrete state which is closest to the real value x.

Example 7.8 Optimal investment

We demonstrate a simple optimal portfolio investment problem in Fig. 7.12, in which there is a safe bank asset and a risky 'stock market' asset. We start with a unit wealth and wish to obtain a wealth

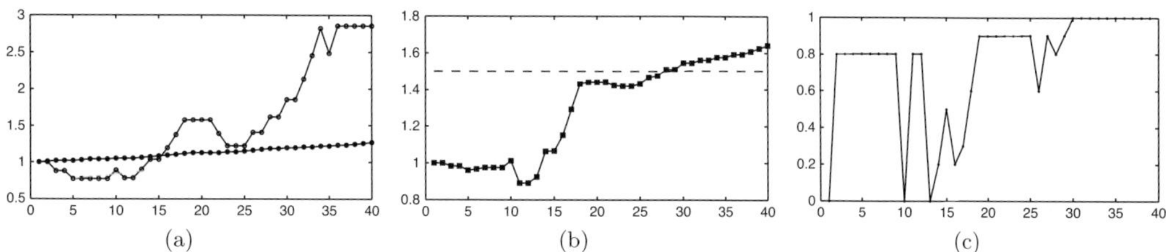

Figure 7.12 (**a**) Two assets through time – a risky asset whose value fluctuates wildly, and a stable asset that grows slowly. (**b**) The wealth of our portfolio over time, based on investing with the hope to achieve a wealth of 1.5 at $T = 40$. (**c**) The optimal investment decisions through time, with 1 corresponding to placing all wealth in the safe asset and 0 placing all the money on the risky asset.

of 1.5 at time $t = 40$. If we place all our money in the bank, we will not be able to reach this desired amount, so we must place some of our wealth at least in the risky asset. In the beginning the stock market does poorly, and our wealth is correspondingly poor. The stock market picks up sufficiently so that after around $t = 20$, we no longer need to take many risks and may place most of our money in the bank, confident that we will reach our investment objective.

7.9 Further topics

7.9.1 Partially observable MDPs

In a *POMDP* there are states that are not observed. This seemingly innocuous extension of the MDP case can lead however to computational difficulties. Let's consider the situation in Fig. 7.13, and attempt to compute the optimal expected utility based on the sequence of summations and maximisations. The sum over the hidden variables couples all the decisions and observations, meaning that we no longer have a simple chain structure for the remaining maximisations. For a POMDP of length t, this leads to an intractable problem with complexity exponential in t. An alternative view is to recognise that all past decisions and observations $v_{1:t}$, $d_{1:t-1}$, can be summarised

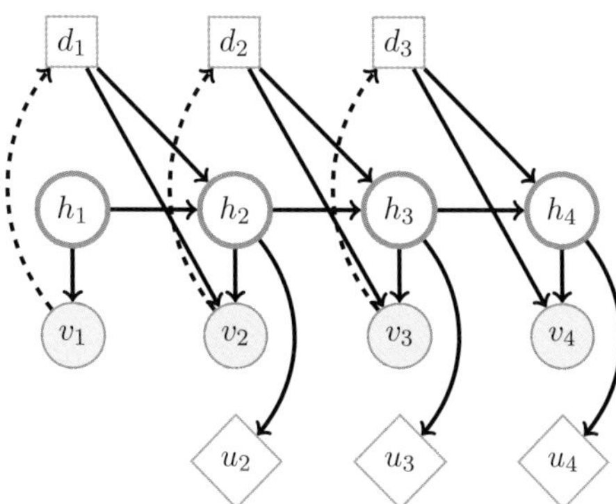

Figure 7.13 An example Partially Observable Markov Decision Process (POMDP). The 'hidden' variables h are never observed. In solving the influence diagram we are required to first sum over variables that are never observed; doing so will couple together all past observed variables and decisions; any decision at time t will then depend on all previous decisions. Note that the no-forgetting principle means that we do not need to explicitly write that each decision depends on all previous observations – this is implicitly assumed.

in terms of a belief in the current latent state, $p(h_t|v_{1:t}, d_{1:t-1})$. This suggests that instead of having an actual state, as in the MDP case, we need to use a *distribution* over states to represent our current knowledge. One can therefore write down an effective MDP albeit over belief distributions, as opposed to finite states. Approximate techniques are required to solve the resulting 'infinite' state MDPs, and the reader is referred to more specialised texts for a study of approximation procedures. See for example [161, 164].

7.9.2 Reinforcement learning

Reinforcement Learning (RL) deals mainly with time-independent Markov decision processes. The added twist is that the transition $p(\mathrm{s}'|\mathrm{s}, \mathrm{d})$ (and possibly the utility) is unknown. Initially an 'agent' begins to explore the set of states and utilities (rewards) associated with taking decisions. The set of accessible states and their rewards populates as the agent traverses its environment. Consider for example a maze problem with a given start and goal state, though with an unknown maze structure. The task is to get from the start to the goal in the minimum number of moves on the maze. Clearly there is a balance required between curiosity and acting to maximise the expected reward. If we are too curious (don't take optimal decisions given the currently available information about the maze structure) and continue exploring the possible maze routes, this may be bad. On the other hand, if we don't explore the possible maze states, we might never realise that there is a much more optimal short-cut to follow than that based on our current knowledge. This exploration–exploitation tradeoff is central to the difficulties of RL. See [283] for an extensive discussion of reinforcement learning.

From model-based to model-free learning

Consider an MDP with state transitions $p(x_{t+1}|x_t, d_t)$ and policy $p(d_t|x_t)$. For simplicity we consider utilities that depend only on the state x_t. The expected utility of taking decision d_t in state x_t, $U(x_t, d_t)$, can be derived using a similar argument as in Section 7.5.2, for a discount factor γ. As a shortcut, consider

$$U(x_t, d_t) = u(x_t) + \gamma \sum_{x_{t+1}} u(x_{t+1}) p(x_{t+1}|x_t, d_t) + \gamma^2 \max_{d_{t+1}} \sum_{x_{t+1}, x_{t+2}} u(x_{t+2}) p(x_{t+2}|x_{t+1}, d_{t+1}) p(d_{t+1}|x_{t+1}) p(x_{t+1}|x_t, d_t) + \cdots \tag{7.9.1}$$

Similarly,

$$U(x_{t+1}, d_{t+1}) = u(x_{t+1}) + \gamma \sum_{x_{t+2}} u(x_{t+2}) p(x_{t+2}|x_{t+1}, d_{t+1}) + \gamma^2 \max_{d_{t+2}} \sum_{x_{t+2}, x_{t+3}} u(x_{t+3}) p(x_{t+3}|x_{t+2}, d_{t+2}) p(d_{t+2}|x_{t+2}) \times p(x_{t+2}|x_{t+1}, d_{t+1}) + \cdots \tag{7.9.2}$$

From these we derive a Bellman recursion for the expected utility of taking decision d_t in state x_t:

$$U(x_t, d_t) = u(x_t) + \gamma \max_{d} \sum_{x_{t+1}} U(x_{t+1}, d) p(x_{t+1}|x_t, d_t). \tag{7.9.3}$$

If we know the model $p(x_{t+1}|x_t, d_t)$ we can solve Equation (7.9.3) for $U(x, d)$. Given this solution, when we are in state x, the optimal policy is to take the decision d that maximises $U(x, d)$: $d = \arg\max_d U(x, d)$. In the case that we do not wish to explicitly store or describe a model $p(x_{t+1}|x_t, d_t)$ we can use a sample from this transition to approximate Equation (7.9.3); if we are in state x_t and take decision d_t the environment returns for us a sample x_{t+1}. This gives the one-sample estimate to Equation (7.9.3):

$$\tilde{U}(x_t, d_t) = u(x_t) + \gamma \max_d \tilde{U}(x_{t+1}, d). \tag{7.9.4}$$

This gives a procedure called Q-learning for updating the approximation to U based on samples from the environment. This is a simple and powerful scheme and as such is one of the most popular model-free methods in reinforcement learning. A complicating factor is that if we select a decision based on $d = \arg\max_d \tilde{U}(x, d)$ this influences the sample that will be next drawn. Nevertheless, under certain conditions (essentially all decisions are repeatedly sampled for each state), this sample estimate $\tilde{U}(x, d)$ converges to the exact $U(x, d)$ in the limit $t \to \infty$ [311].

Bayesian reinforcement learning

For a given set of environment data $\mathcal{X}$ (observed transitions and utilities) one aspect of the RL problem can be considered as finding the policy that maximises expected reward, given only prior belief about the environment and observed decisions and states. If we assume we know the utility function but not the transition, we may write

$$U(\pi|\mathcal{X}) = \langle U(\pi|\theta)\rangle_{p(\theta|\mathcal{X})} \tag{7.9.5}$$

where θ represents the environment state transition,

$$\theta = p(x_{t+1}|x_t, d_t). \tag{7.9.6}$$

Given a set of observed states and decisions,

$$p(\theta|\mathcal{X}) \propto p(\mathcal{X}|\theta)p(\theta) \tag{7.9.7}$$

where $p(\theta)$ is a prior on the transition. Similar techniques to the EM-style training can be carried through in this case as well [81, 298, 108]. Rather than the policy being a function of the state and the environment θ, optimally one needs to consider a policy $p(d_t|x_t, b(\theta))$ as a function of the state and the belief in the environment, $b(\theta) \equiv p(\theta|\mathcal{X})$. This means that, for example, if the belief in the environment has high entropy, the agent can recognise this and explicitly carry out decisions/actions to explore the environment. A further complication in RL is that the data collected $\mathcal{X}$ depends on the policy π. If we write t for an 'episode' in which policy π_t is followed and data $\mathcal{X}_t$ collected, then the utility of the policy π given all the historical information is

$$U(\pi|\pi_{1:t}, \mathcal{X}_{1:t}) = \langle U(\pi|\theta)\rangle_{p(\theta|\mathcal{X}_{1:t}, \pi_{1:t})}. \tag{7.9.8}$$

Depending on the prior on the environment, and also on how long each episode is, we will have different posteriors for the environment parameters. If we then set

$$\pi_{t+1} = \underset{\pi}{\operatorname{argmax}}\, U(\pi|\pi_{1:t}, \mathcal{X}_{1:t}) \tag{7.9.9}$$

this affects the data we collect at the next episode $\mathcal{X}_{t+1}$. In this way, the trajectory of policies $\pi_1, \pi_2, \ldots$ can be very different depending on the episodes and priors.

7.10 Summary

- One way to take decisions is to take that decision that maximises the expected utility of the decision.
- Sequential decision problems can be modelled using decision trees. These are powerful but unwieldy in long decision sequences.
- Influence diagrams extend belief networks to the decision arena. Efficient inference approaches carry over to this case as well, including extensions using the strong junction tree formalism.
- The sequence in which information is revealed and decisions are taken is specified in the influence diagram. The optimal utility is not invariant to the corresponding partial-ordering.
- Markov decision processes correspond to a simple chain-like influence diagram, for which inference is straightforward, and corresponds to the classical Bellman equations.
- Reinforcement learning can be considered an extension of the Markov decision framework when the model of the environment in which the agent acts needs to be learned on the basis of experience.

In this chapter we discussed planning and control as an inference problem with particular attention to discrete variables. See Example 28.2 for an application of approximate inference to continuous control.

7.11 Code

7.11.1 Sum/Max under a partial order

`maxsumpot.m`: Generalised elimination operation according to a partial ordering
`sumpotID.m`: Sum/max an ID with probability and decision potentials
`demoDecParty.m`: Demo of summing/maxing an ID

7.11.2 Junction trees for influence diagrams

There is no need to specify the information links provided that a partial ordering is given. In the code `jtreeID.m` no check is made that the partial ordering is consistent with the influence diagram. In this case, the first step of the junction tree formulation in Section 7.4.2 is not required. Also the moralisation and removal of utility nodes is easily dealt with by defining utility potentials and including them in the moralisation process.

The strong triangulation is found by a simple variable elimination scheme which seeks to eliminate a variable with the least number of neighbours, provided that the variable may be eliminated according to the specified partial ordering. The junction tree is constructed based only on the elimination clique

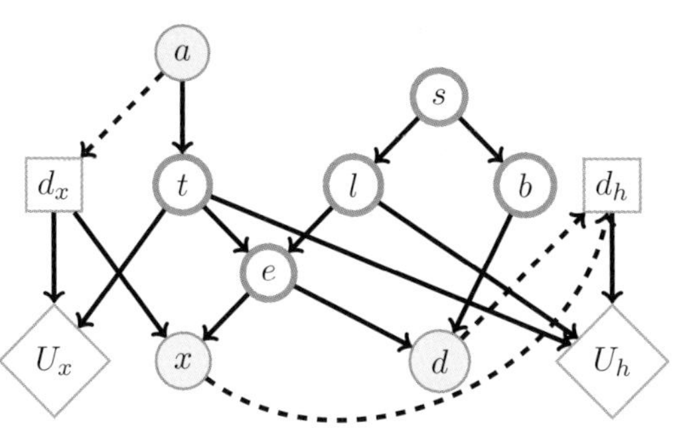

s = Smoking
x = Positive X-ray
d = Dyspnea (shortness of breath)
e = Either tuberculosis or lung cancer
t = Tuberculosis
l = Lung cancer
b = Bronchitis
a = Visited Asia
d_h = Hospitalise?
d_x = Take X-ray?

Figure 7.14 Influence diagram for the 'Chest Clinic' decision example.

sequence $\mathcal{C}_1, \ldots, \mathcal{C}_N$ obtained from the triangulation routine. The junction tree is then obtained by connecting a clique $\mathcal{C}_i$ to the first clique $j > i$ that is connected to this clique. Clique $\mathcal{C}_i$ is then eliminated from the graph. In this manner a junction tree of connected cliques is formed. We do not require the separators for the influence diagram absorption since these can be computed and discarded on the fly.

Note that the code only computes messages from the leaves to the root of the junction tree, which is sufficient for taking decisions at the root. If one desires an optimal decision at a non-root, one would need to absorb probabilities into a clique which contains the decision required. These extra forward probability absorptions are required because information about any unobserved variables can be affected by decisions and observations in the past. This extra forward probability schedule is not given in the code and left as an exercise for the interested reader.

`jtreeID.m`: Junction tree for an influence diagram
`absorptionID.m`: Absorption on an influence diagram
`triangulatePorder.m`: Triangulation based on a partial ordering
`demoDecPhD.m`: Demo for utility of Doing PhD and Startup

7.11.3 Party–Friend example

The code below implements the Party–Friend example in the text. To deal with the asymmetry the *Visit* utility is zero if *Party* is in state yes.
`demoDecPartyFriend.m`: Demo for Party–Friend

7.11.4 Chest Clinic with decisions

The table for the Chest Clinic decision network, Fig. 7.14 is taken from Exercise 3.4, see [131, 72]. There is a slight modification however to the $p(x|e)$ table. If an X-ray is taken, then information about x is available. However, if the decision is not to take an X-ray no information about x is available. This is a form of asymmetry. A straightforward approach in this case is to make d_x a parent of the x variable and set the distribution of x to be uninformative if $d_x = \text{fa}$.

$$\begin{array}{ll} p(a=\text{tr})=0.01 & p(s=\text{tr})=0.5 \\ p(t=\text{tr}|a=\text{tr})=0.05 & p(t=\text{tr}|a=\text{fa})=0.01 \\ p(l=\text{tr}|s=\text{tr})=0.1 & p(l=\text{tr}|s=\text{fa})=0.01 \\ p(b=\text{tr}|s=\text{tr})=0.6 & p(b=\text{tr}|s=\text{fa})=0.3 \\ p(x=\text{tr}|e=\text{tr},d_x=\text{tr})=0.98 & p(x=\text{tr}|e=\text{fa},d_x=\text{tr})=0.05 \\ p(x=\text{tr}|e=\text{tr},d_x=\text{fa})=0.5 & p(x=\text{tr}|e=\text{fa},d_x=\text{fa})=0.5 \\ p(d=\text{tr}|e=\text{tr},b=\text{tr})=0.9 & p(d=\text{tr}|e=\text{tr},b=\text{fa})=0.3 \\ p(d=\text{tr}|e=\text{fa},b=\text{tr})=0.2 & p(d=\text{tr}|e=\text{fa},b=\text{fa})=0.1 \end{array} \tag{7.11.1}$$

The two utilities are designed to reflect the costs and benefits of taking an X-ray and hospitalising a patient:

$$\begin{array}{lll|l} d_h=\text{tr} & t=\text{tr} & l=\text{tr} & 180 \\ d_h=\text{tr} & t=\text{tr} & l=\text{fa} & 120 \\ d_h=\text{tr} & t=\text{fa} & l=\text{tr} & 160 \\ d_h=\text{tr} & t=\text{fa} & l=\text{fa} & 15 \\ d_h=\text{fa} & t=\text{tr} & l=\text{tr} & 2 \\ d_h=\text{fa} & t=\text{tr} & l=\text{fa} & 4 \\ d_h=\text{fa} & t=\text{fa} & l=\text{tr} & 0 \\ d_h=\text{fa} & t=\text{fa} & l=\text{fa} & 40 \end{array} \tag{7.11.2}$$

$$\begin{array}{ll|l} d_x=\text{tr} & t=\text{tr} & 0 \\ d_x=\text{tr} & t=\text{fa} & 1 \\ d_x=\text{fa} & t=\text{tr} & 10 \\ d_x=\text{fa} & t=\text{fa} & 10 \end{array} \tag{7.11.3}$$

We assume that we know whether or not the patient has been to Asia, before deciding on taking an X-ray. The partial ordering is then

$$a \prec d_x \prec \{d, x\} \prec d_h \prec \{b, e, l, s, t\}. \tag{7.11.4}$$

The demo `demoDecAsia.m` produces the results:

```
utility table:
asia = yes takexray = yes  49.976202
asia = no  takexray = yes  46.989441
asia = yes takexray = no   48.433043
asia = no  takexray = no   47.460900
```

which shows that optimally one should take an X-ray only if the patient has been to Asia.

`demoDecAsia.m`: Junction Tree Influence Diagram demo

7.11.5 Markov decision processes

In `demoMDP.m` we consider a simple two-dimensional grid in which an 'agent' can move to a grid square either above, below, left, right of the current square, or stay in the current square. We defined goal states (grid squares) that have high utility, with others having zero utility.

`demoMDPclean.m`: Demo of value and policy iteration for a simple MDP
`MDPsolve.m`: MDP solver using value or policy iteration

Routines for efficient MDP variational solvers are available from the book website. There is also code for fast Lagrange duality techniques, which are beyond the scope of our discussion here.

7.12 Exercises

7.1 You play a game in which you have a probability p of winning. If you win the game you gain an amount £S and if you lose the game you lose an amount £S. Show that the expected gain from playing the game is £$(2p - 1)S$.

7.2 It is suggested that the utility of money is based, not on the amount, but rather how much we have relative to other people. Assume a distribution $p(i)$, $i = 1, \ldots, 10$ of incomes using a histogram with 10 bins, each bin representing an income range. Use a histogram to roughly reflect the distribution of incomes in society, namely that most incomes are around the average with few very wealthy and few extremely poor people. Now define the utility of an income x as the chance that income x will be higher than a randomly chosen income y (under the distribution you defined) and relate this to the cumulative distribution of p. Write a program to compute this probability and plot the resulting utility as a function of income. Now repeat the coin tossing bet of Section 7.1.1 so that if one wins the bet one's new income will be placed in the top histogram bin, whilst if one loses one's new income is in the lowest bin. Compare the optimal expected utility decisions under the situations in which one's original income is (i) average, and (ii) much higher than average.

7.3

Derive a partial ordering for the ID on the right, and explain how this ID differs from that of Fig. 7.5.

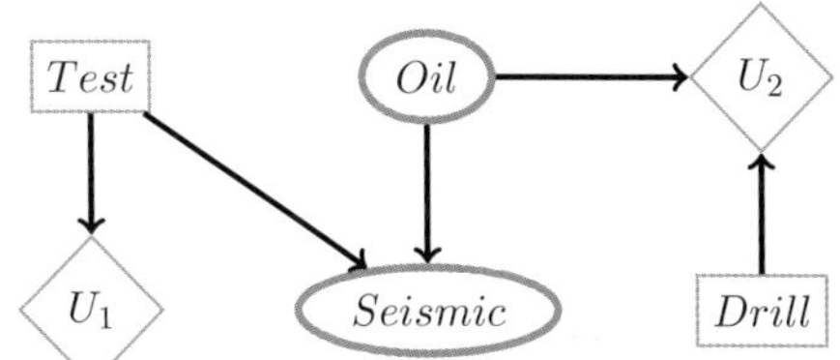

7.4 This question follows closely `demoMDP.m`, and represents a problem in which a pilot wishes to land an airplane. The matrix $U(x, y)$ in the file `airplane.mat` contains the utilities of being in position x, y and is a very crude model of a runway and taxiing area. The airspace is represented by an 18×15 grid ($Gx = 18$, $Gy = 15$ in the notation employed in `demoMDP.m`). The matrix $U(8, 4) = 2$ represents that position $(8, 4)$ is the desired parking bay of the airplane (the vertical height of the airplane is not taken in to account). The positive values in U represent runway and areas where the airplane is allowed. Zero utilities represent neutral positions. The negative values represent unfavourable positions for the airplane. By examining the matrix U you will see that the airplane should preferably not veer off the runway, and also should avoid two small villages close to the airport.

At each timestep the plane can perform one of the following actions stay up down left right:

For stay, the airplane stays in the same x, y position.
For up, the airplane moves to the $x, y + 1$ position.
For down, the airplane moves to the $x, y - 1$ position.
For left, the airplane moves to the $x - 1, y$ position.
For right, the airplane moves to the $x + 1, y$ position.

A move that takes the airplane out of the airspace is not allowed.

1. The airplane begins in at point $x = 1, y = 13$. Assuming that an action deterministically results in the intended grid move, find the optimal x_t, y_t sequence for times $t = 1, \ldots,$ for the position of the aircraft.
2. The pilot tells you that there is a fault with the airplane. When the pilot instructs the plane to go right, with probability 0.1 it actually goes up (provided this remains in the airspace). Assuming again that the airplane begins at point $x = 1, y = 13$, return the optimal x_t, y_t sequence for times $t = 1, \ldots,$ for the position of the aircraft.

7.5 The influence diagram depicted describes the first stage of a game. The decision variable $\text{dom}(d_1) = \{\text{play}, \text{not play}\}$ indicates the decision to either play the first stage or not. If you decide to play, there is a cost $c_1(\text{play}) = C_1$, but no cost otherwise, $c_1(\text{no play}) = 0$. The variable x_1 describes if you win or lose the game, $\text{dom}(x_1) = \{\text{win}, \text{lose}\}$, with probabilities:

$$p(x_1 = \text{win}|d_1 = \text{play}) = p_1, \quad p(x_1 = \text{win}|d_1 = \text{no play}) = 0. \tag{7.12.1}$$

The utility of winning/losing is

$$u_1(x_1 = \text{win}) = W_1, \quad u_1(x_1 = \text{lose}) = 0. \tag{7.12.2}$$

Show that the expected utility gain of playing this game is

$$U(d_1 = \text{play}) = p_1 W_1 - C_1. \tag{7.12.3}$$

7.6 Exercise 7.5 above describes the first stage of a new two-stage game. If you win the first stage $x_1 = \text{win}$, you have to make a decision d_2 as to whether or not play in the second stage $\text{dom}(d_2) = \{\text{play}, \text{not play}\}$. If you do not win the first stage, you cannot enter the second stage. If you decide to play the second stage, you win with probability p_2:

$$p(x_2 = \text{win}|x_1 = \text{win}, d_2 = \text{play}) = p_2. \tag{7.12.4}$$

If you decide not to play the second stage there is no chance to win:

$$p(x_2 = \text{win}|x_1 = \text{win}, d_2 = \text{not play}) = 0. \tag{7.12.5}$$

The cost of playing the second stage is

$$c_2(d_2 = \text{play}) = C_2, \qquad c_2(d_2 = \text{no play}) = 0 \tag{7.12.6}$$

and the utility of winning/losing the second stage is

$$u_2(x_2 = \text{win}) = W_2, \qquad u_2(x_2 = \text{lose}) = 0. \tag{7.12.7}$$

1. Draw an influence diagram that describes this two-stage game.
2. A gambler needs to decide if he should even enter the first stage of this two-stage game. Show that based on taking the optimal future decision d_2 the expected utility based on the first decision is:

$$U(d_1 = \text{play}) = \begin{cases} p_1(p_2 W_2 - C_2) + p_1 W_1 - C_1 & \text{if} \quad p_2 W_2 - C_2 \geq 0 \\ p_1 W_1 - C_1 & \text{if} \quad p_2 W_2 - C_2 \leq 0 \end{cases}. \tag{7.12.8}$$

7.7 You have £B in your bank account. You are asked if you would like to participate in a bet in which, if you win, your bank account will become £W. However, if you lose, your bank account will contain only £L. You win the bet with probability p_w.

1. Assuming that the utility is given by the number of pounds in your bank account, write down a formula for the expected utility of taking the bet, $U(\text{bet})$ and also the expected utility of not taking the bet, $U(\text{no bet})$.
2. The above situation can be formulated differently. If you win the bet you gain £$(W - B)$. If you lose the bet you lose £$(B - L)$. Compute the expected amount of money you gain if you bet $U_{gain}(\text{bet})$ and if you don't bet $U_{gain}(\text{no bet})$.
3. Show that $U(\text{bet}) - U(\text{no bet}) = U_{gain}(\text{bet}) - U_{gain}(\text{no bet})$.

7.8 Consider an objective

$$F(\theta) = \sum_x U(x)p(x|\theta) \tag{7.12.9}$$

for a positive function $U(x)$ and that our task is to maximise F with respect to θ. An Expectation-Maximisation style bounding approach (see Section 11.2) can be derived by defining the auxiliary distribution

$$\tilde{p}(x|\theta) = \frac{U(x)p(x|\theta)}{F(\theta)} \tag{7.12.10}$$

so that by considering $\mathrm{KL}(q(x)|\tilde{p}(x))$ for some variational distribution $q(x)$ we obtain the bound

$$\log F(\theta) \geq -\langle \log q(x)\rangle_{q(x)} + \langle \log U(x)\rangle_{q(x)} + \langle \log p(x|\theta)\rangle_{q(x)}. \tag{7.12.11}$$

The M-step states that the optimal q distribution is given by

$$q(x) = \tilde{p}(x|\theta_{old}). \tag{7.12.12}$$

At the E-step of the algorithm the new parameters θ_{new} are given by maximising the 'energy' term

$$\theta_{new} = \underset{\theta}{\operatorname{argmax}} \ \langle \log p(x|\theta)\rangle_{\tilde{p}(x|\theta_{old})}. \tag{7.12.13}$$

Show that for a deterministic distribution

$$p(x|\theta) = \delta(x, f(\theta)) \tag{7.12.14}$$

the E-step fails, giving $\theta_{new} = \theta_{old}$.

7.9 Consider an objective

$$F_\epsilon(\theta) = \sum_x U(x)p_\epsilon(x|\theta) \tag{7.12.15}$$

for a positive function $U(x)$ and

$$p_\epsilon(x|\theta) = (1-\epsilon)\delta(x, f(\theta)) + \epsilon n(x), \quad 0 \leq \epsilon \leq 1 \tag{7.12.16}$$

and an arbitrary distribution $n(x)$. Our task is to maximise F with respect to θ. As the previous exercise showed, if we attempt an EM algorithm in the limit of a deterministic model $\epsilon = 0$, then no-updating occurs and the EM algorithm fails to find θ that optimises $F_0(\theta)$.

1. Show that

$$F_\epsilon(\theta) = (1-\epsilon)F_0(\theta) + \epsilon \sum_x n(x)U(x) \tag{7.12.17}$$

and hence

$$F_\epsilon(\theta_{new}) - F_\epsilon(\theta_{old}) = (1-\epsilon)\left[F_0(\theta_{new}) - F_0(\theta_{old})\right]. \tag{7.12.18}$$

2. Show that if for $\epsilon > 0$ we can find a θ_{new} such that $F_\epsilon(\theta_{new}) > F_\epsilon(\theta_{old})$, then necessarily $F_0(\theta_{new}) > F_0(\theta_{old})$.
3. Using this result, derive an EM-style algorithm that guarantees to increase $F_\epsilon(\theta)$ (unless we are already at an optimum) for $\epsilon > 0$ and therefore guarantees to increase $F_0(\theta)$. Hint: use

$$\tilde{p}(x|\theta) = \frac{U(x)p_\epsilon(x|\theta)}{F_\epsilon(\theta)} \tag{7.12.19}$$

and consider $\mathrm{KL}(q(x)|\tilde{p}(x))$ for some variational distribution $q(x)$.

7.10 The file `IDjensen.mat` contains probability and utility tables for the influence diagram of Fig. 7.7(a). Using BRMLTOOLBOX, write a program that returns the maximal expected utility for this ID using a strong junction tree approach, and check the result by explicit summation and maximisation. Similarly, your program should output the maximal expected utility for both states of d_1, and check that the computation using the strong junction tree agrees with the result from explicit summation and maximisation.

7.11 For a POMDP, explain the structure of the strong junction tree, and relate this to the complexity of inference in the POMDP.

7.12

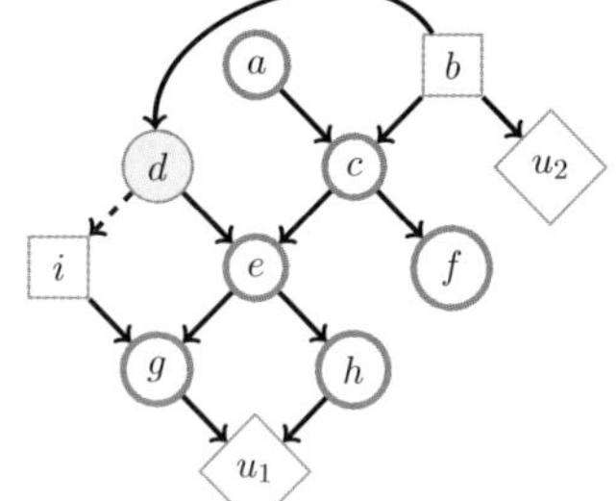

(i) Define a partial order for the ID depicted. (ii) Draw a (strong) junction tree for this ID.

7.13 `exerciseInvest.m` contains the parameters for a simple investment problem in which the prices of two assets, a and b, follow Markovian updating, as in Section 7.8.3. The transition matrices of these are given, as is the end time T and initial wealth w_1, and initial price movements ϵ_1^a, ϵ_1^b, wealth and investment states. Write a function of the form

[`d1val`] = `optdec(epsilonA1, epsilonB1, desired, T, w1, pars)`

where desired is the wealth level at time T. The end utility is defined by

$$u(w_T) = \begin{cases} 10000 & w_T \geq 1.5w_1 \\ 0 & w_T < 1.5w_1 \end{cases}. \tag{7.12.20}$$

Using your routine, compute the optimal expected utility and decision at time 1. Draw also an influence diagram that describes this Markov decision problem.

Part II

Learning in probabilistic models

In Part II we address how to learn a model from data. In particular we will discuss learning a model as a form of inference on an extended distribution, now taking into account the parameters of the model.

Learning a model or model parameters from data forces us to deal with uncertainty since with only limited data we can never be certain which is the 'correct' model. We also address how the structure of a model, not just its parameters, can in principle be learned.

In Part II we show how learning can be achieved under simplifying assumptions, such as maximum likelihood that set parameters by those that would most likely reproduce the observed data. We also discuss the problems that arise when, as is often the case, there is missing data.

Together with Part I, Part II prepares the basic material required to embark on understanding models in machine learning, having the tools required to learn models from data and subsequently query them to answer questions of interest.

8 Statistics for machine learning

In this chapter we discuss some classical distributions and their manipulations. In previous chapters we've assumed that we know the distributions and have concentrated on the inference problem. In machine learning we will typically not fully know the distributions and need to learn them from available data. This means we need familiarity with standard distributions, for which the data will later be used to set the parameters.

8.1 Representing data

The numeric encoding of data can have a significant effect on performance and an understanding of the options for representing data is therefore of considerable importance. We briefly outline three central encodings below.

8.1.1 Categorical

For categorical (or nominal) data, the observed value belongs to one of a number of classes, with no intrinsic ordering, and can be represented simply by an integer. An example of a categorical variable would be the description of the type of job that someone does, e.g. healthcare, education, financial services, transport, homeworker, unemployed, engineering etc. which could be represented by the values $1, 2, \ldots, 7$. Another way to transform such data into numerical values would be to use 1-of-m encoding. For example, if there are four kinds of jobs: soldier, sailor, tinker, spy, we could represent a soldier as $(1,0,0,0)$, a sailor as $(0,1,0,0)$, a tinker as $(0,0,1,0)$ and a spy as $(0,0,0,1)$. In this encoding the distance between the vectors representing two different professions is constant. Note that 1-of-m encoding induces dependencies in the profession attributes since if one of the attributes is 1, the others must be zero.

8.1.2 Ordinal

An ordinal variable consists of categories with an ordering or ranking of the categories, e.g. cold, cool, warm, hot. In this case, to preserve the ordering, we could use say -1 for cold, 0 for cool, $+1$ for warm and $+2$ for hot. This choice is somewhat arbitrary, and one should bear in mind that results may be dependent on the numerical coding used.

8.1.3 Numerical

Numerical data takes on values that are real numbers, e.g. a temperature measured by a thermometer, or the salary that someone earns.

8.2 Distributions

Distributions over discrete variables, Section 1.1 are the focus of much of the book up to this point. Here we discuss also distributions over continuous variables, for which the concepts of marginalisation and conditioning carry over from the discrete case, simply on replacing summation over the discrete states by integration over the continuous domain of the variable.

Definition 8.1 Probability density functions For a continuous variable x, the probability density $p(x)$ is defined such that

$$p(x) \geq 0, \qquad \int_{-\infty}^{\infty} p(x)dx = 1, \qquad p(a \leq x \leq b) = \int_{a}^{b} p(x)dx. \tag{8.2.1}$$

We will also refer to continuous probability densities as distributions.

Definition 8.2 Averages and expectation

$$\langle f(x) \rangle_{p(x)} \tag{8.2.2}$$

denotes the average or expectation of $f(x)$ with respect to the distribution $p(x)$. A common alternative notation is

$$\mathbb{E}(f(x)). \tag{8.2.3}$$

When the context is clear, one may drop the notational dependency on $p(x)$. The notation

$$\langle f(x)|y \rangle \tag{8.2.4}$$

is shorthand for the average of $f(x)$ conditioned on knowing the state of variable y, i.e. the average of $f(x)$ with respect to the distribution $p(x|y)$.

An advantage of the expectation notations is that they hold whether the distribution is over continuous or discrete variables. In the discrete case

$$\langle f(x) \rangle \equiv \sum_{\mathsf{x}} f(x = \mathsf{x}) p(x = \mathsf{x}) \tag{8.2.5}$$

and for continuous variables,

$$\langle f(x) \rangle \equiv \int_{-\infty}^{\infty} f(x)p(x)dx. \tag{8.2.6}$$

The reader might wonder what $\langle x \rangle$ means when x is discrete. For example, if $\text{dom}(x) = \{\mathsf{apple}, \mathsf{orange}, \mathsf{pear}\}$, with associated probabilities $p(x)$ for each of the states, what does $\langle x \rangle$ refer to? Clearly, $\langle f(x) \rangle$ makes sense if $f(x = \mathsf{x})$ maps the state x to a numerical value. For example $f(x = \mathsf{apple}) = 1$, $f(x = \mathsf{orange}) = 2$, $f(x = \mathsf{pear}) = 3$ for which $\langle f(x) \rangle$ is meaningful. Unless the states of the discrete variable are associated with a numerical value, then $\langle x \rangle$ has no meaning.

Result 8.1 (Change of variables) For a univariate continuous random variable x with distribution $p(x)$ the transformation $y = f(x)$, where $f(x)$ is a monotonic function, has distribution

$$p(y) = p(x) \left(\frac{df}{dx} \right)^{-1}, \quad x = f^{-1}(y). \tag{8.2.7}$$

For multivariate $\mathbf{x}$ and bijection $\mathbf{f}(\mathbf{x})$, then $\mathbf{y} = \mathbf{f}(\mathbf{x})$ has distribution

$$p(\mathbf{y}) = p(\mathbf{x} = \mathbf{f}^{-1}(\mathbf{y})) \left| \det \left(\frac{\partial \mathbf{f}}{\partial \mathbf{x}} \right) \right|^{-1} \tag{8.2.8}$$

where the Jacobian matrix has elements

$$\left[\frac{\partial \mathbf{f}}{\partial \mathbf{x}} \right]_{ij} = \frac{\partial f_i(\mathbf{x})}{\partial x_j}. \tag{8.2.9}$$

Sometimes one needs to consider transformations between different dimensions. For example, if $\mathbf{z}$ has lower dimension than $\mathbf{x}$, then one may introduce additional variables $\mathbf{z}'$ to define a new multivariate $\mathbf{y} = (\mathbf{z}, \mathbf{z}')$ with the same dimension as $\mathbf{x}$. Then one applies the above transformation to give the distribution on the joint variables $\mathbf{y}$, from which $p(\mathbf{z})$ can be obtained by marginalisation.

Definition 8.3 **Moments** The kth moment of a distribution is given by the average of x^k under the distribution:

$$\left\langle x^k \right\rangle_{p(x)}. \tag{8.2.10}$$

For $k = 1$, we have the mean, typically denoted by μ,

$$\mu \equiv \langle x \rangle. \tag{8.2.11}$$

Definition 8.4 **Cumulative distribution function** For a univariate distribution $p(x)$, the CDF is defined as

$$cdf(y) \equiv p(x \leq y) = \langle \mathbb{I}[x \leq y] \rangle_{p(x)}. \tag{8.2.12}$$

For an unbounded domain, $cdf(-\infty) = 0$ and $cdf(\infty) = 1$.

Definition 8.5 **Moment generating function** For a distribution $p(x)$, we define the moment generating function $g(t)$ as

$$g(t) = \langle e^{tx} \rangle_{p(x)}. \tag{8.2.13}$$

The usefulness of this is that by differentiating $g(t)$, we generate the moments,

$$\lim_{t \to 0} \frac{d^k}{dt^k} g(t) = \langle x^k \rangle_{p(x)}. \tag{8.2.14}$$

Definition 8.6 **Mode** The mode x_* of a distribution $p(x)$ is the state of x at which the distribution takes its highest value, $x_* = \arg\max_x p(x)$. A distribution could have more than one mode (be multi-modal). A widespread abuse of terminology is to refer to any isolated local maximum of $p(x)$ as a mode.

Definition 8.7 **Variance and correlation**

$$\sigma^2 \equiv \left\langle (x - \langle x \rangle)^2 \right\rangle_{p(x)}. \tag{8.2.15}$$

The variance measures the 'spread' of a distribution around the mean. The square root of the variance, σ is called the *standard deviation* and is a natural length scale suggesting how far typical values drawn from $p(x)$ might be from the mean. The notation $\text{var}(x)$ is also used to emphasise for which variable the variance is computed. The reader may show that an equivalent expression is

$$\sigma^2 \equiv \left\langle x^2 \right\rangle - \langle x \rangle^2. \tag{8.2.16}$$

For a multivariate distribution the matrix with elements

$$\Sigma_{ij} = \langle (x_i - \mu_i)(x_j - \mu_j) \rangle \tag{8.2.17}$$

where $\mu_i = \langle x_i \rangle$ is called the *covariance matrix*. The diagonal entries of the covariance matrix contain the variance of each variable. An equivalent expression is

$$\Sigma_{ij} = \langle x_i x_j \rangle - \langle x_i \rangle \langle x_j \rangle . \tag{8.2.18}$$

The *correlation matrix* has elements

$$\rho_{ij} = \left\langle \frac{(x_i - \mu_i)}{\sigma_i} \frac{(x_j - \mu_j)}{\sigma_j} \right\rangle \tag{8.2.19}$$

where σ_i is the deviation of variable x_i. The correlation is a normalised form of the covariance so that each element is bounded $-1 \leq \rho_{ij} \leq 1$. The reader will note a resemblance of the correlation coefficient and the scalar product, Equation (A.1.3). See also Exercise 8.40.

For independent variables x_i and x_j, $x_i \perp\!\!\!\perp x_j$ the covariance Σ_{ij} is zero. Similarly independent variables have zero correlation – they are 'uncorrelated'. Note however that the converse is not generally true – two variables can be uncorrelated but dependent. A special case is for when x_i and x_j are Gaussian distributed for which independence is equivalent to being uncorrelated, see Exercise 8.2.

Definition 8.8 Skewness and kurtosis The skewness is a measure of the asymmetry of a distribution:

$$\gamma_1 \equiv \frac{\left\langle (x - \langle x \rangle)^3 \right\rangle_{p(x)}}{\sigma^3} \tag{8.2.20}$$

where σ^2 is the variance of x with respect to $p(x)$. A positive skewness means the distribution has a heavy tail to the right. Similarly, a negative skewness means the distribution has a heavy tail to the left.

The kurtosis is a measure of how peaked around the mean a distribution is:

$$\gamma_2 \equiv \frac{\left\langle (x - \langle x \rangle)^4 \right\rangle_{p(x)}}{\sigma^4} - 3. \tag{8.2.21}$$

A distribution with positive kurtosis has more mass around its mean than would a Gaussian with the same mean and variance. These are also called *super Gaussian*. Similarly a negative kurtosis (*sub Gaussian*) distribution has less mass around its mean than the corresponding Gaussian. The kurtosis is defined such that a Gaussian has zero kurtosis (which accounts for the -3 term in the definition).

Definition 8.9 Delta function For continuous x, we define the Dirac delta function

$$\delta(x - x_0) \tag{8.2.22}$$

which is zero everywhere expect at x_0, where there is a spike; $\int_{-\infty}^{\infty} \delta(x - x_0)dx = 1$ and

$$\int_{-\infty}^{\infty} \delta(x - x_0) f(x) dx = f(x_0). \tag{8.2.23}$$

One can view the Dirac delta function as an infinitely narrow Gaussian: $\delta(x - x_0) = \lim_{\sigma \to 0} \mathcal{N}\left(x \middle| x_0, \sigma^2\right)$.

The Kronecker delta,

$$\delta_{x,x_0} \tag{8.2.24}$$

Figure 8.1 Empirical distribution over a discrete variable with four states. The empirical samples consist of n samples at each of states 1, 2, 4 and $2n$ samples at state 3 where $n > 0$. On normalising this gives a distribution with values 0.2, 0.2, 0.4, 0.2 over the four states.

is similarly zero everywhere, except for $\delta_{x_0,x_0} = 1$. The Kronecker delta is equivalent to $\delta_{x,x_0} = \mathbb{I}[x = x_0]$. We use the expression $\delta(x, x_0)$ to denote either the Dirac or Kronecker delta, depending on the context.

Definition 8.10 Empirical distribution For a set of datapoints $x^1, \ldots, x^N$, which are states of a random variable x, the empirical distribution has probability mass distributed evenly over the datapoints, and zero elsewhere.

For a discrete variable x the empirical distribution is, see Fig. 8.1,

$$p(x) = \frac{1}{N}\sum_{n=1}^{N}\mathbb{I}[x = x^n] \tag{8.2.25}$$

where N is the number of datapoints.

For a continuous distribution we have

$$p(x) = \frac{1}{N}\sum_{n=1}^{N}\delta(x - x^n) \tag{8.2.26}$$

where $\delta(x)$ is the Dirac Delta function.

The mean of the empirical distribution is given by the sample mean of the datapoints

$$\hat{\mu} = \frac{1}{N}\sum_{n=1}^{N} x^n. \tag{8.2.27}$$

Similarly, the variance of the empirical distribution is given by the sample variance

$$\hat{\sigma}^2 = \frac{1}{N}\sum_{n=1}^{N}(x^n - \hat{\mu})^2. \tag{8.2.28}$$

For vectors the sample mean vector has elements

$$\hat{\mu}_i = \frac{1}{N}\sum_{n=1}^{N} x_i^n \tag{8.2.29}$$

and sample covariance matrix has elements

$$\hat{\Sigma}_{ij} = \frac{1}{N}\sum_{n=1}^{N}(x_i^n - \hat{\mu}_i)\left(x_j^n - \hat{\mu}_j\right). \tag{8.2.30}$$

8.2.1 The Kullback–Leibler divergence KL$(q|p)$

The Kullback–Leibler divergence KL$(q|p)$ measures the 'difference' between distributions q and p [71].

Definition 8.11 **KL divergence** For two distributions $q(x)$ and $p(x)$

$$\mathrm{KL}(q|p) \equiv \langle \log q(x) - \log p(x) \rangle_{q(x)} \geq 0 \tag{8.2.31}$$

The KL divergence is ≥ 0

The KL divergence is widely used and it is therefore important to understand why the divergence is positive.

To see this, consider the following linear bound on the function $\log(x)$

$$\log(x) \leq x - 1 \tag{8.2.32}$$

as plotted in the figure on the right. Replacing x by $p(x)/q(x)$ in the above bound

$$\frac{p(x)}{q(x)} - 1 \geq \log \frac{p(x)}{q(x)}. \tag{8.2.33}$$

Since probabilities are non-negative, we can multiply both sides by $q(x)$ to obtain

$$p(x) - q(x) \geq q(x) \log p(x) - q(x) \log q(x). \tag{8.2.34}$$

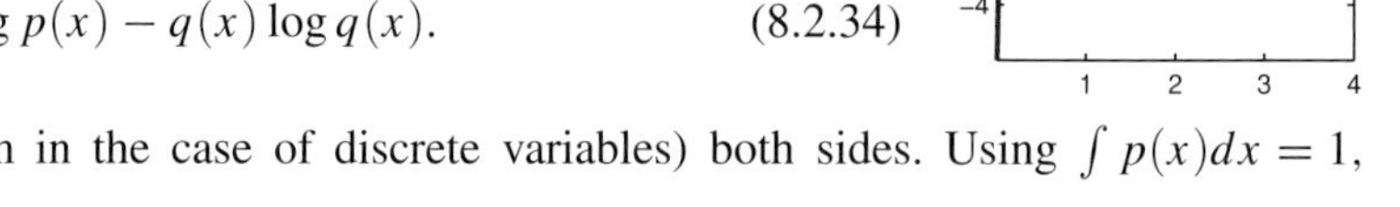

We now integrate (or sum in the case of discrete variables) both sides. Using $\int p(x)dx = 1$, $\int q(x)dx = 1$,

$$1 - 1 \geq \langle \log p(x) - \log q(x) \rangle_{q(x)}. \tag{8.2.35}$$

Rearranging gives

$$\langle \log q(x) - \log p(x) \rangle_{q(x)} \equiv \mathrm{KL}(q|p) \geq 0. \tag{8.2.36}$$

The KL divergence is zero if and only if the two distributions are exactly the same.

Definition 8.12 **α-divergence** For two distributions $q(x)$ and $p(x)$ and real α the α-divergence is defined as

$$D_\alpha(p|q) \equiv \frac{1 - \left\langle \frac{p^{\alpha-1}(x)}{q^{\alpha-1}(x)} \right\rangle_{p(x)}}{\alpha(1-\alpha)} \geq 0. \tag{8.2.37}$$

The Kullback-Leibler divergence $\mathrm{KL}(p|q)$ corresponds to $D_1(p|q)$ and $\mathrm{KL}(q|p) = D_0(p|q)$, which is readily verified using L'Hôpital's rule.

8.2.2 Entropy and information

For both discrete and continuous variables, the *entropy* is defined as

$$H(p) \equiv - \langle \log p(x) \rangle_{p(x)}. \tag{8.2.38}$$

For continuous variables, this is also called the *differential entropy*, see also Exercise 8.34. The entropy is a measure of the uncertainty in a distribution. One way to see this is that

$$H(p) = -\mathrm{KL}(p|u) + \mathrm{const.} \tag{8.2.39}$$

where u is a uniform distribution. Since $\mathrm{KL}(p|u) \geq 0$, the less like a uniform distribution p is, the smaller will be the entropy. Or, vice versa, the more similar p is to a uniform distribution, the greater will be the entropy. Since the uniform distribution contains the least information a priori about which state $p(x)$ is in, the entropy is therefore a measure of the a priori uncertainty in the state occupancy. For a discrete distribution we can permute the state labels without changing the entropy. For a discrete distribution the entropy is positive, whereas the differential entropy can be negative.

The mutual information is a measure of dependence between (sets of) variables $\mathcal{X}$ and $\mathcal{Y}$, conditioned on variables $\mathcal{Z}$.

Definition 8.13 Mutual information

$$\mathrm{MI}(\mathcal{X};\mathcal{Y}|\mathcal{Z}) \equiv \langle \mathrm{KL}(p(\mathcal{X},\mathcal{Y}|\mathcal{Z})|p(\mathcal{X}|\mathcal{Z})p(\mathcal{Y}|\mathcal{Z}))\rangle_{p(\mathcal{Z})} \geq 0. \tag{8.2.40}$$

If $\mathcal{X} \perp\!\!\!\perp \mathcal{Y}|\mathcal{Z}$ is true, then $\mathrm{MI}(\mathcal{X};\mathcal{Y}|\mathcal{Z})$ is zero, and vice versa. When $\mathcal{Z} = \emptyset$, the average over $p(\mathcal{Z})$ is absent and one writes $\mathrm{MI}(\mathcal{X};\mathcal{Y})$.

8.3 Classical distributions

Definition 8.14 Bernoulli distribution The Bernoulli distribution concerns a discrete binary variable x, with $\mathrm{dom}(x) = \{0, 1\}$. The states are not merely symbolic, but real values 0 and 1.

$$p(x = 1) = \theta. \tag{8.3.1}$$

From normalisation, it follows that $p(x = 0) = 1 - \theta$. From this

$$\langle x \rangle = 0 \times p(x = 0) + 1 \times p(x = 1) = \theta. \tag{8.3.2}$$

The variance is given by $\mathrm{var}(x) = \theta(1 - \theta)$.

Definition 8.15 Categorical distribution The categorical distribution generalises the Bernoulli distribution to more than two (symbolic) states. For a discrete variable x, with symbolic states $\mathrm{dom}(x) = \{1, \ldots, C\}$,

$$p(x = c) = \theta_c, \qquad \sum_c \theta_c = 1. \tag{8.3.3}$$

The Dirichlet is conjugate to the categorical distribution.

Definition 8.16 Binomial distribution The Binomial describes the distribution of a discrete two-state variable x, with $\mathrm{dom}(x) = \{1, 0\}$ where the states are symbolic. The probability that in n Bernoulli trials (independent samples), $x^1, \ldots, x^n$ there will be k 'success' states 1 observed is

$$p(y = k|\theta) = \binom{n}{k}\theta^k(1 - \theta)^{n-k}, \qquad y \equiv \sum_{i=1}^{n} \mathbb{I}\left[x^i = 1\right] \tag{8.3.4}$$

where $\binom{n}{k} \equiv n!/(k!(n-k)!)$ is the binomial coefficient. The mean and variance are

$$\langle y \rangle = n\theta, \qquad \mathrm{var}(y) = n\theta(1 - \theta). \tag{8.3.5}$$

The Beta distribution is the conjugate prior for the Binomial distribution.

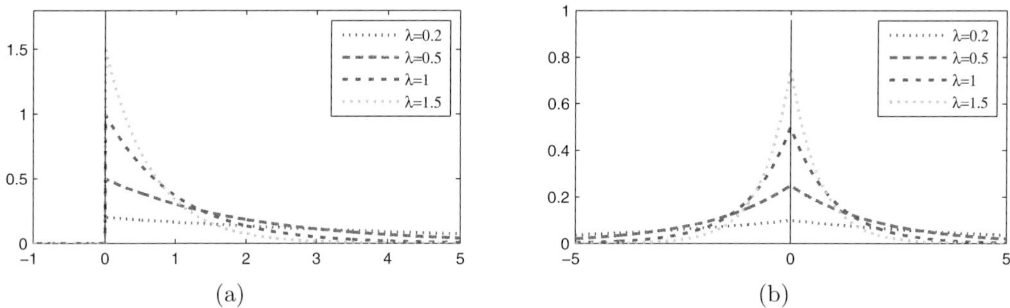

Figure 8.2 (**a**) Exponential distribution. (**b**) Laplace (double exponential) distribution.

Definition 8.17 **Multinomial distribution** Consider a multi-state variable x, with $\text{dom}(x) = \{1, \ldots, K\}$, with corresponding state probabilities $\theta_1, \ldots, \theta_K$. We then draw n samples from this distribution. The probability of observing the state 1 y_1 times, state 2 y_2 times, ..., state K y_K times in the n samples is

$$p(y_1, \ldots, y_K|\theta) = \frac{n!}{y_1! \ldots y_K!} \prod_{i=1}^{n} \theta_i^{y_i} \tag{8.3.6}$$

where $n = \sum_{i=1}^{n} y_i$.

$$\langle y_i \rangle = n\theta_i, \quad \text{var}(y_i) = n\theta_i (1 - \theta_i), \quad \langle y_i y_j \rangle - \langle y_i \rangle \langle y_j \rangle = -n\theta_i\theta_j \ (i \neq j). \tag{8.3.7}$$

The Dirichlet distribution is the conjugate prior for the multinomial distribution.

Definition 8.18 **Poisson distribution** The Poisson distribution can be used to model situations in which the expected number of events scales with the length of the interval within which the events can occur. If λ is the expected number of events per unit interval, then the distribution of the number of events x within an interval $t\lambda$ is

$$p(x = k|\lambda) = \frac{1}{k!} e^{-\lambda t} (\lambda t)^k, \qquad k = 0, 1, 2, \ldots \tag{8.3.8}$$

For a unit length interval ($t = 1$),

$$\langle x \rangle = \lambda, \quad \text{var}(x) = \lambda. \tag{8.3.9}$$

The Poisson distribution can be derived as a limiting case of a Binomial distribution in which the success probability scales as $\theta = \lambda/n$, in the limit $n \to \infty$.

Definition 8.19 **Uniform distribution** For a variable x, the distribution is uniform if $p(x) = \text{const.}$ over the domain of the variable.

Definition 8.20 **Exponential distribution** For $x \geq 0$, see Fig. 8.2(a),

$$p(x|\lambda) \equiv \lambda e^{-\lambda x}. \tag{8.3.10}$$

One can show that for rate λ

$$\langle x \rangle = \frac{1}{\lambda}, \qquad \text{var}(x) = \frac{1}{\lambda^2}. \tag{8.3.11}$$

The alternative parameterisation $b = 1/\lambda$ is called the scale.

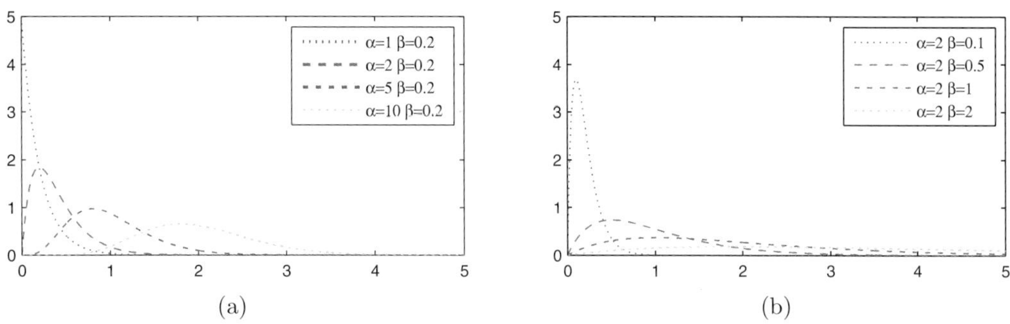

Figure 8.3 Gamma distribution. (**a**) varying α for fixed β. (**b**) varying β for fixed α.

Definition 8.21 Gamma distribution

$$Gam\left(x|\alpha,\beta\right) = \frac{1}{\beta\Gamma(\alpha)}\left(\frac{x}{\beta}\right)^{\alpha-1} e^{-\frac{x}{\beta}}, \qquad x \geq 0, \alpha > 0, \beta > 0 \tag{8.3.12}$$

α is called the shape parameter, β is the scale parameter and the Gamma function is defined as

$$\Gamma(a) = \int_0^\infty t^{a-1}e^{-t}dt. \tag{8.3.13}$$

The parameters are related to the mean and variance through

$$\alpha = \left(\frac{\mu}{s}\right)^2, \qquad \beta = \frac{s^2}{\mu} \tag{8.3.14}$$

where μ is the mean of the distribution and s is the standard deviation. The mode is given by $(\alpha - 1)\,\beta$, for $\alpha \geq 1$, see Fig. 8.3.

An alternative parameterisation uses the inverse scale

$$Gam^{is}\left(x|\alpha,\beta\right) = Gam\left(x|\alpha,1/\beta\right) \propto x^{\alpha-1}e^{-\beta x}. \tag{8.3.15}$$

Definition 8.22 Inverse Gamma distribution

$$InvGam\left(x|\alpha,\beta\right) = \frac{\beta^\alpha}{\Gamma\left(\alpha\right)}\frac{1}{x^{\alpha+1}}e^{-\beta/x}. \tag{8.3.16}$$

This has mean $\beta/(\alpha-1)$ for $\alpha > 1$ and variance $\frac{\beta^2}{(\alpha-1)^2(\alpha-2)}$ for $\alpha > 2$.

Definition 8.23 Beta distribution

$$p(x|\alpha,\beta) = B\left(x|\alpha,\beta\right) = \frac{1}{B(\alpha,\beta)}x^{\alpha-1}\left(1-x\right)^{\beta-1}, \quad 0 \leq x \leq 1 \tag{8.3.17}$$

where the Beta function is defined as

$$B(\alpha,\beta) = \frac{\Gamma(\alpha)\Gamma(\beta)}{\Gamma(\alpha+\beta)} \tag{8.3.18}$$

and $\Gamma(x)$ is the Gamma function. Note that the distribution can be flipped by interchanging x for $1-x$, which is equivalent to interchanging α and β. See Fig. 8.4.

The mean and variance are given by

$$\langle x\rangle = \frac{\alpha}{\alpha+\beta}, \qquad \mathrm{var}(x) = \frac{\alpha\beta}{\left(\alpha+\beta\right)^2\left(\alpha+\beta+1\right)}. \tag{8.3.19}$$

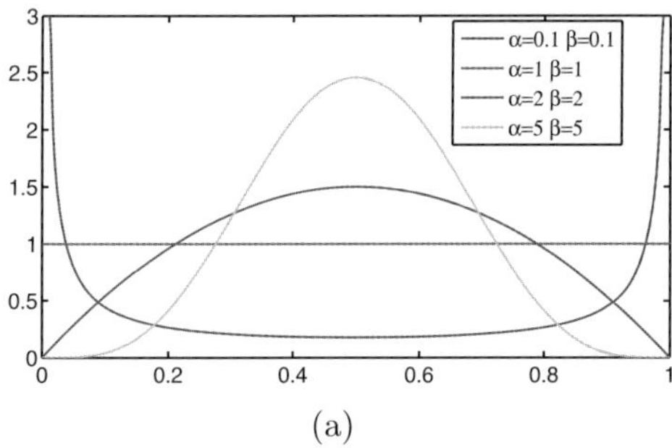

(a)

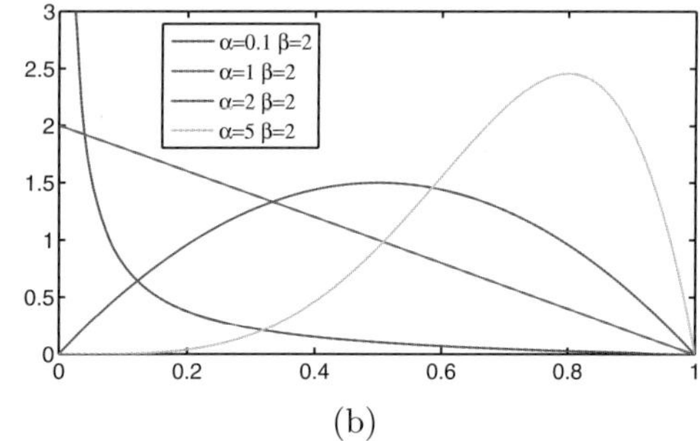

(b)

Figure 8.4 Beta distribution. The parameters α and β can also be written in terms of the mean and variance, leading to an alternative parameterisation, see Exercise 8.16.

Definition 8.24 Laplace distribution

$$p(x|\lambda) \equiv \lambda e^{-\frac{1}{b}|x-\mu|}. \tag{8.3.20}$$

For scale b

$$\langle x \rangle = \mu, \qquad \text{var}(x) = 2b^2. \tag{8.3.21}$$

The Laplace distribution is also known as the Double Exponential distribution. See Fig. 8.2(b).

Definition 8.25 Univariate Gaussian distribution

$$p(x|\mu, \sigma^2) = \mathcal{N}\left(x|\mu, \sigma^2\right) \equiv \frac{1}{\sqrt{2\pi\sigma^2}} e^{-\frac{1}{2\sigma^2}(x-\mu)^2} \tag{8.3.22}$$

where μ is the mean of the distribution, and σ^2 the variance. This is also called the *normal distribution*.

One can show that the parameters indeed correspond to

$$\mu = \langle x \rangle_{\mathcal{N}(x|\mu,\sigma^2)}, \qquad \sigma^2 = \left\langle (x-\mu)^2 \right\rangle_{\mathcal{N}(x|\mu,\sigma^2)}. \tag{8.3.23}$$

For $\mu = 0$ and $\sigma = 1$, the Gaussian is called the *standard normal distribution*. See Fig. 8.5 for a depiction of the univariate Gaussian and samples therefrom.

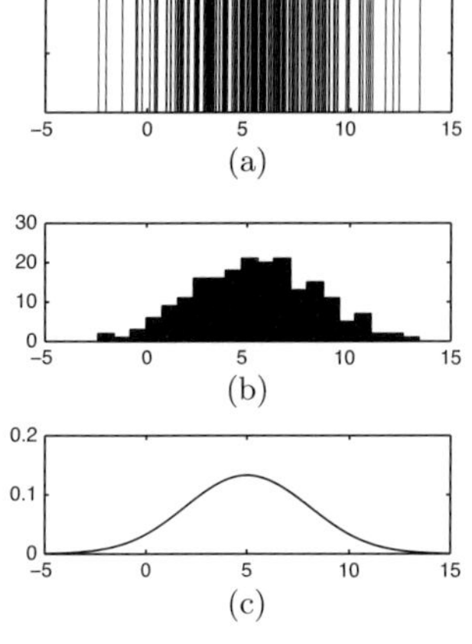

Figure 8.5 (**a**) 200 datapoints $x^1, \ldots, x^{200}$ drawn from a Gaussian distribution. Each vertical line denotes a datapoint at the corresponding x value on the horizontal axis. (**b**) Histogram using 10 equally spaced bins of the datapoints. (**c**) Gaussian distribution $\mathcal{N}(x|\mu = 5, \sigma = 3)$ from which the datapoints were drawn. In the limit of an infinite amount of data, and limitingly small bin size, the normalised histogram tends to the Gaussian probability density function.

Definition 8.26 Student's *t*-distribution

$$p(x|\mu, \lambda, \nu) = \text{Student}\left(x|\mu, \lambda, \nu\right) = \frac{\Gamma(\frac{\nu+1}{2})}{\Gamma(\frac{\nu}{2})}\left(\frac{\lambda}{\nu\pi}\right)^{\frac{1}{2}}\left[1 + \frac{\lambda\left(x-\mu\right)^2}{\nu}\right]^{-\frac{\nu+1}{2}} \tag{8.3.24}$$

where μ is the mean, ν the degrees of freedom and λ scales the distribution. The variance is given by

$$\text{var}(x) = \frac{\nu}{\lambda\left(\nu - 2\right)}, \quad \text{for } \nu > 2. \tag{8.3.25}$$

For $\nu \to \infty$ the distribution tends to a Gaussian with mean μ and variance $1/\lambda$. As ν decreases the tails of the distribution become fatter.

The t-distribution can be derived from a *scaled mixture*

$$p(x|\mu, a, b) = \int_{\tau=0}^{\infty} \mathcal{N}\left(x|\mu, \tau^{-1}\right) Gam^{is}\left(\tau|a, b\right) d\tau \tag{8.3.26}$$

$$= \int_{\tau=0}^{\infty} \left(\frac{\tau}{2\pi}\right)^{\frac{1}{2}} e^{-\frac{\tau}{2}(x-\mu)^2} b^a e^{-b\tau}\tau^{a-1}\frac{1}{\Gamma(a)} d\tau \tag{8.3.27}$$

$$= \frac{b^a}{\Gamma(a)}\frac{\Gamma(a+\frac{1}{2})}{\sqrt{2\pi}}\frac{1}{\left(b+\frac{1}{2}\left(x-\mu\right)^2\right)^{a+\frac{1}{2}}}. \tag{8.3.28}$$

This matches (8.3.24) on setting $\nu = 2a$ and $\lambda = a/b$.

Definition 8.27 Dirichlet distribution The Dirichlet distribution is a distribution on probability distributions, $\boldsymbol{\alpha} = (\alpha_1, \ldots, \alpha_Q)$, $\alpha_i \geq 0$, $\sum_i \alpha_i = 1$:

$$p(\boldsymbol{\alpha}) = \frac{1}{Z(\mathbf{u})}\delta\left(\sum_{i=1}^{Q}\alpha_i - 1\right)\prod_{q=1}^{Q}\alpha_q^{u_q-1}\mathbb{I}\left[\alpha_q \geq 0\right] \tag{8.3.29}$$

where

$$Z(\mathbf{u}) = \frac{\prod_{q=1}^{Q}\Gamma(u_q)}{\Gamma\left(\sum_{q=1}^{Q}u_q\right)}. \tag{8.3.30}$$

It is conventional to denote the distribution as

$$\text{Dirichlet}\left(\boldsymbol{\alpha}|\mathbf{u}\right). \tag{8.3.31}$$

The parameter $\mathbf{u}$ controls how strongly the mass of the distribution is pushed to the corners of the simplex. Setting $u_q = 1$ for all q corresponds to a uniform distribution, Fig. 8.6. In the binary case $Q = 2$, this is equivalent to a Beta distribution.

The product of two Dirichlet distributions is another Dirichlet distribution

$$\text{Dirichlet}\left(\boldsymbol{\theta}|\mathbf{u}_1\right)\text{Dirichlet}\left(\boldsymbol{\theta}|\mathbf{u}_2\right) = \text{Dirichlet}\left(\boldsymbol{\theta}|\mathbf{u}_1 + \mathbf{u}_2\right). \tag{8.3.32}$$

The marginal of a Dirichlet is also Dirichlet:

$$\int_{\theta_j}\text{Dirichlet}\left(\boldsymbol{\theta}|\mathbf{u}\right) = \text{Dirichlet}\left(\boldsymbol{\theta}_{\setminus j}|\mathbf{u}_{\setminus j}\right). \tag{8.3.33}$$

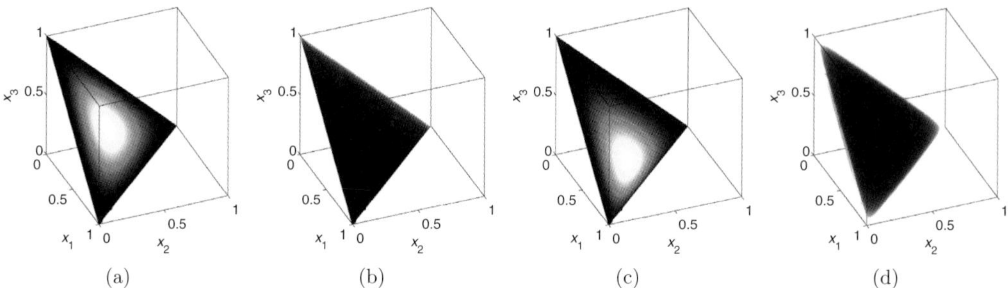

Figure 8.6 Dirichlet distribution with parameter (u_1, u_2, u_3) displayed on the simplex $x_1, x_2, x_3 \geq 0$, $x_1 + x_2 + x_3 = 1$. Black denotes low probability and white high probability. **(a)** (3, 3, 3). **(b)** (0.1, 1, 1). **(c)** (4, 3, 2). **(d)** (0.05, 0.05, 0.05).

The marginal of a single component θ_i is a Beta distribution:

$$p(\theta_i) = B\left(\theta_i | u_i, \sum_{j \neq i} u_j\right). \tag{8.3.34}$$

8.4 Multivariate Gaussian

The multivariate Gaussian plays a central role in data analysis and as such we discuss its properties in some detail.

Definition 8.28 Multivariate Gaussian distribution

$$p(\mathbf{x}|\boldsymbol{\mu}, \boldsymbol{\Sigma}) = \mathcal{N}(\mathbf{x}|\boldsymbol{\mu}, \boldsymbol{\Sigma}) \equiv \frac{1}{\sqrt{\det(2\pi\boldsymbol{\Sigma})}} e^{-\frac{1}{2}(\mathbf{x}-\boldsymbol{\mu})^{\mathsf{T}}\boldsymbol{\Sigma}^{-1}(\mathbf{x}-\boldsymbol{\mu})} \tag{8.4.1}$$

where $\boldsymbol{\mu}$ is the mean vector of the distribution, and $\boldsymbol{\Sigma}$ the covariance matrix. The inverse covariance $\boldsymbol{\Sigma}^{-1}$ is called the *precision*.

One may show

$$\boldsymbol{\mu} = \langle \mathbf{x} \rangle_{\mathcal{N}(\mathbf{x}|\boldsymbol{\mu},\boldsymbol{\Sigma})}, \qquad \boldsymbol{\Sigma} = \left\langle (\mathbf{x}-\boldsymbol{\mu})(\mathbf{x}-\boldsymbol{\mu})^{\mathsf{T}} \right\rangle_{\mathcal{N}(\mathbf{x}|\boldsymbol{\mu},\boldsymbol{\Sigma})}. \tag{8.4.2}$$

Note that $\det(\rho\mathbf{M}) = \rho^D \det(\mathbf{M})$, where $\mathbf{M}$ is a $D \times D$ matrix, which explains the dimension independent notation in the normalisation constant of Definition 8.28.

The *moment representation* uses $\boldsymbol{\mu}$ and $\boldsymbol{\Sigma}$ to parameterise the Gaussian. The alternative *canonical representation*

$$p(\mathbf{x}|\mathbf{b}, \mathbf{M}, c) = c e^{-\frac{1}{2}\mathbf{x}^{\mathsf{T}}\mathbf{M}\mathbf{x} + \mathbf{x}^{\mathsf{T}}\mathbf{b}} \tag{8.4.3}$$

is related to the moment representation via

$$\boldsymbol{\Sigma} = \mathbf{M}^{-1}, \qquad \boldsymbol{\mu} = \mathbf{M}^{-1}\mathbf{b}, \qquad \frac{1}{\sqrt{\det(2\pi\boldsymbol{\Sigma})}} = c e^{\frac{1}{2}\mathbf{b}^{\mathsf{T}}\mathbf{M}^{-1}\mathbf{b}}. \tag{8.4.4}$$

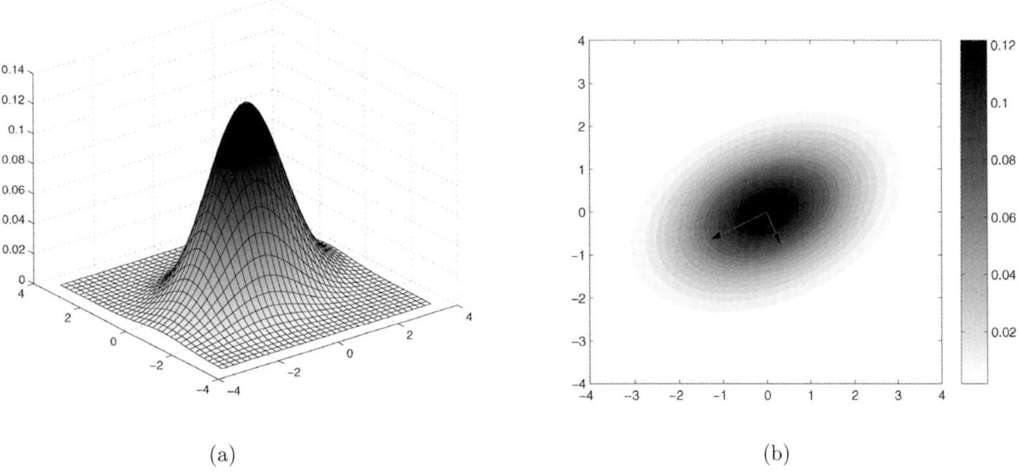

Figure 8.7 (**a**) Bivariate Gaussian with mean $(0, 0)$ and covariance $[1, 0.5; 0.5, 1.75]$. Plotted on the vertical axis is the probability density value $p(x)$. (**b**) Probability density contours for the same bivariate Gaussian. Plotted are the unit eigenvectors scaled by the square root of their eigenvalues, $\sqrt{\lambda_i}$.

The multivariate Gaussian is widely used and it is instructive to understand the geometric picture. This can be achieved by viewing the distribution in a different coordinate system. First we use the fact that every real symmetric matrix $D \times D$ has an eigendecomposition

$$\mathbf{\Sigma} = \mathbf{E}\mathbf{\Lambda}\mathbf{E}^{\mathsf{T}} \tag{8.4.5}$$

where $\mathbf{E}^{\mathsf{T}}\mathbf{E} = \mathbf{I}$ and $\mathbf{\Lambda} = \text{diag}(\lambda_1, \ldots, \lambda_D)$. In the case of a covariance matrix, all the eigenvalues λ_i are positive. This means that one can use the transformation

$$\mathbf{y} = \mathbf{\Lambda}^{-\frac{1}{2}}\mathbf{E}^{\mathsf{T}}(\mathbf{x} - \boldsymbol{\mu}) \tag{8.4.6}$$

so that

$$(\mathbf{x} - \boldsymbol{\mu})^{\mathsf{T}} \mathbf{\Sigma}^{-1} (\mathbf{x} - \boldsymbol{\mu}) = (\mathbf{x} - \boldsymbol{\mu})^{\mathsf{T}} \mathbf{E}\mathbf{\Lambda}^{-1}\mathbf{E}^{\mathsf{T}} (\mathbf{x} - \boldsymbol{\mu}) = \mathbf{y}^{\mathsf{T}}\mathbf{y}. \tag{8.4.7}$$

Under this transformation, the multivariate Gaussian reduces to a product of D univariate zero mean unit variance Gaussians (since the Jacobian of the transformation is a constant). This means that we can view a multivariate Gaussian as a shifted, scaled and rotated version of a 'standard' (zero mean, unit covariance) Gaussian in which the centre is given by the mean, the rotation by the eigenvectors, and the scaling by the square root of the eigenvalues, as depicted in Fig. 8.7(b). A Gaussian with covariance $\mathbf{\Sigma} = \rho\mathbf{I}$ for some scalar ρ is an example of an *isotropic* meaning 'same under rotation'. For any isotropic distribution, contours of equal probability are spherical around the origin.

Result 8.2 (Product of two Gaussians) The product of two Gaussians is another Gaussian, with a multiplicative factor, Exercise 8.35:

$$\mathcal{N}(\mathbf{x}|\boldsymbol{\mu}_1, \mathbf{\Sigma}_1)\,\mathcal{N}(\mathbf{x}|\boldsymbol{\mu}_2, \mathbf{\Sigma}_2) = \mathcal{N}(\mathbf{x}|\boldsymbol{\mu}, \mathbf{\Sigma})\,\frac{\exp\left(-\frac{1}{2}(\boldsymbol{\mu}_1 - \boldsymbol{\mu}_2)^{\mathsf{T}}\mathbf{S}^{-1}(\boldsymbol{\mu}_1 - \boldsymbol{\mu}_2)\right)}{\sqrt{\det(2\pi\mathbf{S})}} \tag{8.4.8}$$

where $\mathbf{S} \equiv \mathbf{\Sigma}_1 + \mathbf{\Sigma}_2$ and the mean and covariance are given by

$$\boldsymbol{\mu} = \mathbf{\Sigma}_1\mathbf{S}^{-1}\boldsymbol{\mu}_2 + \mathbf{\Sigma}_2\mathbf{S}^{-1}\boldsymbol{\mu}_1 \qquad \mathbf{\Sigma} = \mathbf{\Sigma}_1\mathbf{S}^{-1}\mathbf{\Sigma}_2. \tag{8.4.9}$$

8.4.1 Completing the square

A useful technique in manipulating Gaussians is completing the square. For example, the expression

$$\exp\left(-\frac{1}{2}\mathbf{x}^\mathsf{T}\mathbf{A}\mathbf{x} + \mathbf{b}^\mathsf{T}\mathbf{x}\right) \tag{8.4.10}$$

can be transformed as follows. First we complete the square:

$$\frac{1}{2}\mathbf{x}^\mathsf{T}\mathbf{A}\mathbf{x} - \mathbf{b}^\mathsf{T}\mathbf{x} = \frac{1}{2}\left(\mathbf{x} - \mathbf{A}^{-1}\mathbf{b}\right)^\mathsf{T}\mathbf{A}\left(\mathbf{x} - \mathbf{A}^{-1}\mathbf{b}\right) - \frac{1}{2}\mathbf{b}^\mathsf{T}\mathbf{A}^{-1}\mathbf{b}. \tag{8.4.11}$$

Hence

$$\exp\left(-\frac{1}{2}\mathbf{x}^\mathsf{T}\mathbf{A}\mathbf{x} - \mathbf{b}^\mathsf{T}\mathbf{x}\right) = \mathcal{N}\left(\mathbf{x}|\mathbf{A}^{-1}\mathbf{b}, \mathbf{A}^{-1}\right)\sqrt{\det\left(2\pi\mathbf{A}^{-1}\right)}\exp\left(\frac{1}{2}\mathbf{b}^\mathsf{T}\mathbf{A}^{-1}\mathbf{b}\right). \tag{8.4.12}$$

From this one can derive

$$\int \exp\left(-\frac{1}{2}\mathbf{x}^\mathsf{T}\mathbf{A}\mathbf{x} + \mathbf{b}^\mathsf{T}\mathbf{x}\right)d\mathbf{x} = \sqrt{\det\left(2\pi\mathbf{A}^{-1}\right)}\exp\left(\frac{1}{2}\mathbf{b}^\mathsf{T}\mathbf{A}^{-1}\mathbf{b}\right). \tag{8.4.13}$$

Result 8.3 (Linear transform of a Gaussian) Let $\mathbf{y}$ be linearly related to $\mathbf{x}$ through

$$\mathbf{y} = \mathbf{M}\mathbf{x} + \boldsymbol{\eta} \tag{8.4.14}$$

where $\mathbf{x} \perp\!\!\!\perp \boldsymbol{\eta}$, $\boldsymbol{\eta} \sim \mathcal{N}(\boldsymbol{\mu}, \mathbf{\Sigma})$, and $\mathbf{x} \sim \mathcal{N}(\boldsymbol{\mu}_x, \mathbf{\Sigma}_x)$. Then the marginal $p(\mathbf{y}) = \int_\mathbf{x} p(\mathbf{y}|\mathbf{x})p(\mathbf{x})$ is a Gaussian

$$p(\mathbf{y}) = \mathcal{N}\left(\mathbf{y}|\mathbf{M}\boldsymbol{\mu}_x + \boldsymbol{\mu}, \mathbf{M}\mathbf{\Sigma}_x\mathbf{M}^\mathsf{T} + \mathbf{\Sigma}\right). \tag{8.4.15}$$

Result 8.4 (Partitioned Gaussian) Consider a distribution $\mathcal{N}(\mathbf{z}|\boldsymbol{\mu}, \mathbf{\Sigma})$ defined jointly over two vectors $\mathbf{x}$ and $\mathbf{y}$ of potentially differing dimensions,

$$\mathbf{z} = \begin{pmatrix} \mathbf{x} \\ \mathbf{y} \end{pmatrix} \tag{8.4.16}$$

with corresponding mean and partitioned covariance

$$\boldsymbol{\mu} = \begin{pmatrix} \boldsymbol{\mu}_x \\ \boldsymbol{\mu}_y \end{pmatrix} \qquad \mathbf{\Sigma} = \begin{pmatrix} \mathbf{\Sigma}_{xx} & \mathbf{\Sigma}_{xy} \\ \mathbf{\Sigma}_{yx} & \mathbf{\Sigma}_{yy} \end{pmatrix} \tag{8.4.17}$$

where $\mathbf{\Sigma}_{yx} \equiv \mathbf{\Sigma}_{xy}^\mathsf{T}$. The marginal distribution is given by

$$p(\mathbf{x}) = \mathcal{N}(\mathbf{x}|\boldsymbol{\mu}_x, \mathbf{\Sigma}_{xx}) \tag{8.4.18}$$

and conditional

$$p(\mathbf{x}|\mathbf{y}) = \mathcal{N}\left(\mathbf{x}|\boldsymbol{\mu}_x + \mathbf{\Sigma}_{xy}\mathbf{\Sigma}_{yy}^{-1}\left(\mathbf{y} - \boldsymbol{\mu}_y\right), \mathbf{\Sigma}_{xx} - \mathbf{\Sigma}_{xy}\mathbf{\Sigma}_{yy}^{-1}\mathbf{\Sigma}_{yx}\right). \tag{8.4.19}$$

Result 8.5 (Gaussian average of a quadratic function)

$$\left\langle \mathbf{x}^{\mathsf{T}}\mathbf{A}\mathbf{x}\right\rangle_{\mathcal{N}(\mathbf{x}|\boldsymbol{\mu},\boldsymbol{\Sigma})} = \boldsymbol{\mu}^{\mathsf{T}}\mathbf{A}\boldsymbol{\mu} + \operatorname{trace}(\mathbf{A}\boldsymbol{\Sigma}). \tag{8.4.20}$$

8.4.2 Conditioning as system reversal

For a joint Gaussian distribution $p(\mathbf{x}, \mathbf{y})$, consider the conditional $p(\mathbf{x}|\mathbf{y})$. The formula for this Gaussian is given in Equation (8.4.19). An equivalent and useful way to write this result is to consider a 'reversed' linear system of the form

$$\mathbf{x} = \overleftarrow{\mathbf{A}}\,\mathbf{y} + \overleftarrow{\boldsymbol{\eta}}, \qquad \text{where} \quad \overleftarrow{\boldsymbol{\eta}} \sim \mathcal{N}\left(\overleftarrow{\boldsymbol{\eta}} \,\middle|\, \overleftarrow{\boldsymbol{\mu}}, \overleftarrow{\boldsymbol{\Sigma}}\right) \tag{8.4.21}$$

and show that the marginal over the 'reverse' noise $\overleftarrow{\boldsymbol{\eta}}$ is equivalent to conditioning. That is, for a Gaussian

$$p(\mathbf{x}|\mathbf{y}) = \int \delta\left(\mathbf{x} - \overleftarrow{\mathbf{A}}\,\mathbf{y} - \overleftarrow{\boldsymbol{\eta}}\right) p(\overleftarrow{\boldsymbol{\eta}}), \qquad p(\overleftarrow{\boldsymbol{\eta}}) = \mathcal{N}\left(\overleftarrow{\boldsymbol{\eta}} \,\middle|\, \overleftarrow{\boldsymbol{\mu}}, \overleftarrow{\boldsymbol{\Sigma}}\right) \tag{8.4.22}$$

for suitably defined $\overleftarrow{\mathbf{A}}$, $\overleftarrow{\boldsymbol{\mu}}$, $\overleftarrow{\boldsymbol{\Sigma}}$. To show this, we need to make the statistics of $\mathbf{x}$ under this linear system match those given by the conditioning operation, (8.4.19). The mean and covariance of the linear system equation (8.4.21) are given by

$$\boldsymbol{\mu}_x = \overleftarrow{\mathbf{A}}\mathbf{y} + \overleftarrow{\boldsymbol{\mu}}, \qquad \boldsymbol{\Sigma}_{xx} = \overleftarrow{\boldsymbol{\Sigma}}. \tag{8.4.23}$$

We can make these match Equation (8.4.19) by setting

$$\overleftarrow{\mathbf{A}} = \boldsymbol{\Sigma}_{xy}\boldsymbol{\Sigma}_{yy}^{-1}, \qquad \overleftarrow{\boldsymbol{\Sigma}} = \boldsymbol{\Sigma}_{xx} - \boldsymbol{\Sigma}_{xy}\boldsymbol{\Sigma}_{yy}^{-1}\boldsymbol{\Sigma}_{yx}, \qquad \overleftarrow{\boldsymbol{\mu}} = \boldsymbol{\mu}_x - \boldsymbol{\Sigma}_{xy}\boldsymbol{\Sigma}_{yy}^{-1}\boldsymbol{\mu}_y. \tag{8.4.24}$$

This means that we can write an explicit linear system of the form Equation (8.4.21) where the parameters are given in terms of the statistics of the original system. This is particularly useful in deriving results in inference with linear dynamical systems, Section 24.3.

8.4.3 Whitening and centring

For a set of data $\mathbf{x}^1, \ldots, \mathbf{x}^N$, with $\dim \mathbf{x}^n = D$, we can transform this data to $\mathbf{y}^1, \ldots, \mathbf{y}^N$ with zero mean using *centring*:

$$\mathbf{y}^n = \mathbf{x}^n - \mathbf{m} \tag{8.4.25}$$

where the mean $\mathbf{m}$ of the data is given by

$$\mathbf{m} = \frac{1}{N}\sum_{n=1}^{N} \mathbf{x}^n. \tag{8.4.26}$$

Furthermore, we can transform to values $\mathbf{z}^1, \ldots, \mathbf{z}^N$ that have zero mean and unit covariance using *whitening*

$$\mathbf{z}^n = \mathbf{S}^{-\frac{1}{2}}\left(\mathbf{x}^n - \mathbf{m}\right) \tag{8.4.27}$$

where the covariance $\mathbf{S}$ of the data is given by

$$\mathbf{S} = \frac{1}{N}\sum_{n=1}^{N}\left(\mathbf{x}^n - \mathbf{m}\right)\left(\mathbf{x}^n - \mathbf{m}\right)^{\mathsf{T}}. \tag{8.4.28}$$

An equivalent approach is to compute the SVD decomposition of the matrix of centered datapoints

$$\mathbf{U}\mathbf{S}\mathbf{V}^{\mathsf{T}} = \mathbf{Y}, \qquad \mathbf{Y} = \left[\mathbf{y}^1, \ldots, \mathbf{y}^N\right] \tag{8.4.29}$$

then for the $D \times N$ matrix

$$\mathbf{Z} = \sqrt{N}\text{diag}\left(1/S_{1,1}, \ldots, 1/S_{D,D}\right)\mathbf{U}^{\mathsf{T}}\mathbf{Y} \tag{8.4.30}$$

the columns of $\mathbf{Z} = \left(\mathbf{z}^1, \ldots, \mathbf{z}^N\right)$ have zero mean and unit covariance, see Exercise 8.32.

Result 8.6 (Entropy of a Gaussian) The differential entropy of a multivariate Gaussian $p(\mathbf{x}) = \mathcal{N}(\mathbf{x}|\boldsymbol{\mu}, \boldsymbol{\Sigma})$ is

$$H(\mathbf{x}) \equiv -\langle \log p(\mathbf{x}) \rangle_{p(\mathbf{x})} = \frac{1}{2}\log\det(2\pi\boldsymbol{\Sigma}) + \frac{D}{2} \tag{8.4.31}$$

where $D = \dim \mathbf{x}$. Note that the entropy is independent of the mean $\boldsymbol{\mu}$.

8.5 Exponential family

A theoretically convenient class of distributions are the exponential family, which contains many standard distributions, including the Gaussian, Gamma, Poisson, Dirichlet, Wishart, Multinomial.

Definition 8.29 Exponential family For a distribution on a (possibly multidimensional) variable x (continuous or discrete) an *exponential family* model is of the form

$$p(x|\boldsymbol{\theta}) = h(x)\exp\left(\sum_i \eta_i(\boldsymbol{\theta}) T_i(x) - \psi(\boldsymbol{\theta})\right), \tag{8.5.1}$$

where $\boldsymbol{\theta}$ are the parameters, $T_i(x)$ the test statistics and $\psi(\boldsymbol{\theta})$ is the log partition function that ensures normalisation

$$\psi(\boldsymbol{\theta}) = \log \int_x h(x)\exp\left(\sum_i \eta_i(\boldsymbol{\theta}) T_i(x)\right). \tag{8.5.2}$$

One can always transform the parameters to the form $\boldsymbol{\eta}(\boldsymbol{\theta}) = \boldsymbol{\theta}$ in which case the distribution is in *canonical form*:

$$p(x|\boldsymbol{\theta}) = h(x)\exp\left(\boldsymbol{\theta}^{\mathsf{T}}\mathbf{T}(x) - \psi(\boldsymbol{\theta})\right). \tag{8.5.3}$$

For example the univariate Gaussian can be written

$$\frac{1}{\sqrt{2\pi\sigma^2}}\exp\left(-\frac{1}{2\sigma^2}(x-\mu)^2\right) = \exp\left(-\frac{1}{2\sigma^2}x^2 + \frac{\mu}{\sigma^2}x - \frac{\mu^2}{2\sigma^2} - \frac{1}{2}\log\pi\sigma^2\right). \tag{8.5.4}$$

Defining $t_1(x) = x$, $t_2(x) = -x^2/2$ and $\theta_1 = \mu$, $\theta_2 = \sigma^2$, $h(x) = 1$, then

$$\eta_1(\boldsymbol{\theta}) = \frac{\theta_1}{\theta_2}, \qquad \eta_2(\boldsymbol{\theta}) = \frac{1}{\theta_2}, \qquad \psi(\boldsymbol{\theta}) = \frac{1}{2}\left(\frac{\theta_1^2}{\theta_2} + \log\pi\theta_2\right). \tag{8.5.5}$$

Note that the parameterisation is not necessarily unique – we can for example rescale the functions $T_i(x)$ and inversely scale η_i by the same amount to arrive at an equivalent representation.

8.5.1 Conjugate priors

For an exponential family likelihood

$$p(x|\boldsymbol{\theta}) = h(x)\exp\left(\boldsymbol{\theta}^{\mathsf{T}}\mathbf{T}(x) - \psi(\boldsymbol{\theta})\right) \tag{8.5.6}$$

and prior with hyperparameters $\boldsymbol{\alpha}$, γ,

$$p(\boldsymbol{\theta}|\boldsymbol{\alpha}, \gamma) \propto \exp\left(\boldsymbol{\theta}^{\mathsf{T}}\boldsymbol{\alpha} - \gamma\psi(\boldsymbol{\theta})\right) \tag{8.5.7}$$

the posterior is

$$p(\boldsymbol{\theta}|x, \boldsymbol{\alpha}, \gamma) \propto p(x|\boldsymbol{\theta})p(\boldsymbol{\theta}|\boldsymbol{\alpha}, \gamma) \propto \exp\left(\boldsymbol{\theta}^{\mathsf{T}}\left[\mathbf{T}(x) + \boldsymbol{\alpha}\right] - \left[\gamma + 1\right]\psi(\boldsymbol{\theta})\right) \tag{8.5.8}$$

$$= p(\boldsymbol{\theta}|\mathbf{T}(x) + \boldsymbol{\alpha}, 1 + \gamma) \tag{8.5.9}$$

so that the prior, Equation (8.5.7), is conjugate for the exponential family likelihood equation (8.5.6); that is, the posterior is of the same form as the prior, but with modified hyperparameters. Whilst the likelihood is in the exponential family, the conjugate prior is not necessarily in the exponential family.

8.6 Learning distributions

For a distribution $p(x|\theta)$, parameterised by θ, and data $\mathcal{X} = \left\{x^1, \ldots, x^N\right\}$, learning corresponds to inferring the θ that best explains the data $\mathcal{X}$. There are various criteria for defining this:

Bayesian methods In this one examines the posterior $p(\theta|\mathcal{X}) \propto p(\mathcal{X}|\theta)p(\theta)$. This gives rise to a distribution over θ. The Bayesian method itself says nothing about how to best summarise this posterior.

Maximum a posteriori This is a summarisation of the posterior, that is

$$\theta^{MAP} = \underset{\theta}{\operatorname{argmax}}\ p(\theta|\mathcal{X}). \tag{8.6.1}$$

Maximum likelihood Under a flat prior, $p(\theta) = \text{const.}$, the MAP solution is equivalent to setting θ to that value that maximises the likelihood of observing the data

$$\theta^{ML} = \underset{\theta}{\operatorname{argmax}}\ p(\mathcal{X}|\theta). \tag{8.6.2}$$

Moment matching Based on an empirical estimate of a moment (say the mean), θ is set such that the moment (or moments) of the distribution matches the empirical moment.

Pseudo likelihood For multivariate $\mathbf{x} = (x_1, \ldots, x_N)$, one sets the parameters based on

$$\theta = \underset{\theta}{\operatorname{argmax}} \sum_{n=1}^{N}\sum_{i=1}^{D} \log p(x_i^n|x_{\setminus i}^n, \theta). \tag{8.6.3}$$

The pseudo-likelihood method is sometimes used when the full likelihood $p(\mathbf{x}|\theta)$ is difficult to compute.

In seeking the 'best' single parameter θ, we are often required to carry out a numerical optimisation. This is not necessarily a trivial step, and considerable effort is often spent either in attempting to define models for which the resulting computational difficulties are minimal, or in finding good approximations that find useful optima of complex objective functions, see Section A.5.

In this book we focus on the Bayesian methods and maximum likelihood. We first reiterate some of the basic ground covered in Section 1.3, in which the Bayesian and maximum likelihood methods are related.

Definition 8.30 Prior, likelihood and posterior
For data $\mathcal{X}$ and variable θ, Bayes' rule tells us how to update our prior beliefs about the variable θ in light of the data to a posterior belief:

$$\underbrace{p(\theta|\mathcal{X})}_{\text{posterior}} = \frac{\overbrace{p(\mathcal{X}|\theta)}^{\text{likelihood}}\ \overbrace{p(\theta)}^{\text{prior}}}{\underbrace{p(\mathcal{X})}_{\text{evidence}}}. \tag{8.6.4}$$

The *evidence* is also called the *marginal likelihood*. Note that the term 'evidence' is (rather unfortunately) used for both the marginal likelihood of observations and the observations themselves.

The term 'likelihood' is used for the probability that a model generates observed data. More fully, if we condition on the model M, we have

$$p(\theta|\mathcal{X}, M) = \frac{p(\mathcal{X}|\theta, M)p(\theta|M)}{p(\mathcal{X}|M)}$$

where we see the role of the likelihood $p(\mathcal{X}|\theta, M)$ and *model likelihood* $p(\mathcal{X}|M)$.

The *most probable a posteriori* (*MAP*) setting is that which maximises the posterior,

$$\theta^{MAP} = \underset{\theta}{\operatorname{argmax}}\ p(\theta|\mathcal{X}, M). \tag{8.6.5}$$

For a 'flat prior', $p(\theta|M)$ being a constant, the MAP solution is equivalent to *maximum likelihood* namely that θ that maximises $p(\mathcal{X}|\theta, M)$,

$$\theta^{ML} = \underset{\theta}{\operatorname{argmax}}\ p(\mathcal{X}|\theta, M). \tag{8.6.6}$$

Definition 8.31 **Conjugacy** If the posterior is of the same parametric form as the prior, then we call the prior the conjugate distribution for the likelihood distribution. That is, for a prior on parameter θ, with hyperparameter α, $p(\theta|\alpha)$, the posterior given data $\mathcal{D}$ is the same form as the prior, but with updated hyperparameters, $p(\theta|\mathcal{D}, \alpha) = p(\theta|\alpha')$.

Definition 8.32 **Independent and identically distributed** For a variable x, and a set of i.i.d. observations, $x^1, \ldots, x^N$, conditioned on θ, we assume there is no dependence between the observations

$$p(x^1, \ldots, x^N|\theta) = \prod_{n=1}^{N} p(x^n|\theta). \tag{8.6.7}$$

For non-Bayesian methods which return a single value for θ, based on the data $\mathcal{X}$, it is interesting to know how 'good' the procedure is. Concepts that can help in this case are 'bias' and 'consistency'. The bias measures if the estimate of θ is correct 'on average'. The property of an estimator such that the parameter θ converges to the true model parameter θ^0 as the sequence of data increases is termed *consistency*.

Definition 8.33 Unbiased estimator Given data $\mathcal{X} = \{x^1, \ldots, x^N\}$, formed from i.i.d. samples of distribution $p(x|\theta)$ we can use the data $\mathcal{X}$ to estimate the parameter θ that was used to generate the data. The estimator is a function of the data, which we write $\hat{\theta}(\mathcal{X})$. For an *unbiased estimator*

$$\left\langle \hat{\theta}(\mathcal{X}) \right\rangle_{p(\mathcal{X}|\theta)} = \theta. \tag{8.6.8}$$

More generally, one can consider any function of the distribution $p(x)$, with scalar value θ, for example the mean $\theta = \langle x \rangle_{p(x)}$. Then $\hat{\theta}(\mathcal{X})$ is an unbiased estimator of θ with respect to the data distribution $\tilde{p}(\mathcal{X})$ if $\left\langle \hat{\theta}(\mathcal{X}) \right\rangle_{\tilde{p}(\mathcal{X})} = \theta$.

A classical example for estimator bias are those of the mean and variance. Let

$$\hat{\mu}(\mathcal{X}) = \frac{1}{N} \sum_{n=1}^{N} x^n. \tag{8.6.9}$$

This is an unbiased estimator of the mean $\langle x \rangle_{p(x)}$ since, for i.i.d. data

$$\langle \hat{\mu}(\mathcal{X}) \rangle_{p(\mathcal{X})} = \frac{1}{N} \sum_{n=1}^{N} \langle x^n \rangle_{p(x^n)} = \frac{1}{N} N \langle x \rangle_{p(x)} = \langle x \rangle_{p(x)}. \tag{8.6.10}$$

On the other hand, consider the estimator of the variance,

$$\hat{\sigma}^2(\mathcal{X}) = \frac{1}{N} \sum_{n=1}^{N} (x^n - \hat{\mu}(\mathcal{X}))^2. \tag{8.6.11}$$

This is biased since (omitting a few lines of algebra)

$$\left\langle \hat{\sigma}^2(\mathcal{X}) \right\rangle_{p(\mathcal{X})} = \frac{1}{N} \sum_{n=1}^{N} \left\langle (x^n - \hat{\mu}(\mathcal{X}))^2 \right\rangle = \frac{N-1}{N} \sigma^2. \tag{8.6.12}$$

8.7 Properties of maximum likelihood

A crude summary of the posterior is given by a distribution with all its mass in a single most likely state, $\delta\left(\theta, \theta^{MAP}\right)$, see Definition 8.30. In making such an approximation, potentially useful information concerning the reliability of the parameter estimate is lost. In contrast the full posterior reflects our beliefs about the range of possibilities and their associated credibilities.

The term 'maximum likelihood, refers to the parameter θ for which the observed data is most likely to be generated by the model. One can motivate MAP from a decision-theoretic perspective. If we assume a utility that is zero for all but the correct θ,

$$U(\theta_{true}, \theta) = \mathbb{I}\left[\theta_{true} = \theta\right] \tag{8.7.1}$$

then the expected utility of θ is

$$U(\theta) = \sum_{\theta_{true}} \mathbb{I}\left[\theta_{true} = \theta\right] p(\theta_{true}|\mathcal{X}) = p(\theta|\mathcal{X}). \tag{8.7.2}$$

This means that the maximum utility decision is to return that θ with the highest posterior value.

When a 'flat' prior $p(\theta) = \text{const.}$ is used the MAP parameter assignment is equivalent to the maximum likelihood setting

$$\theta^{ML} = \underset{\theta}{\text{argmax}}\ p(\mathcal{X}|\theta). \tag{8.7.3}$$

Since the logarithm is a strictly increasing function, then for a positive function $f(\theta)$

$$\theta_{opt} = \underset{\theta}{\text{argmax}}\ f(\theta) \Leftrightarrow \theta_{opt} = \underset{\theta}{\text{argmax}}\ \log f(\theta) \tag{8.7.4}$$

so that the MAP parameters can be found either by optimising the MAP objective or, equivalently, its logarithm,

$$\log p(\theta|\mathcal{X}) = \log p(\mathcal{X}|\theta) + \log p(\theta) - \log p(\mathcal{X}) \tag{8.7.5}$$

where the normalisation constant, $p(\mathcal{X})$, is not a function of θ. The log likelihood is convenient since, under the i.i.d. assumption, it is a summation of data terms,

$$\log p(\theta|\mathcal{X}) = \sum_n \log p(x^n|\theta) + \log p(\theta) - \log p(\mathcal{X}) \tag{8.7.6}$$

so that quantities such as derivatives of the log-likelihood w.r.t. θ are straightforward to compute.

8.7.1 Training assuming the correct model class

Consider a dataset $\mathcal{X} = \{x^n, n = 1, \ldots, N\}$ generated from an underlying parametric model $p(x|\theta^0)$. Our interest is to fit a model $p(x|\theta)$ of the same form as the correct underlying model $p(x|\theta^0)$ and examine if, in the limit of a large amount of data, the parameter θ learned by maximum likelihood matches the correct parameter θ^0. Our derivation below is non-rigorous, but highlights the essence of the argument.

Assuming the data is i.i.d., the scaled log likelihood is

$$L(\theta) \equiv \frac{1}{N} \log p(\mathcal{X}|\theta) = \frac{1}{N} \sum_{n=1}^{N} \log p(x^n|\theta). \tag{8.7.7}$$

In the limit $N \to \infty$, the sample average can be replaced by an average with respect to the distribution generating the data

$$L(\theta) \overset{N\to\infty}{=} \langle \log p(x|\theta) \rangle_{p(x|\theta^0)} = -\text{KL}\big(p(x|\theta^0)|p(x|\theta)\big) + \big\langle \log p(x|\theta^0) \big\rangle_{p(x|\theta^0)}. \tag{8.7.8}$$

Up to a negligible constant, this is the Kullback–Leibler divergence between two distributions in x, just with different parameter settings. The θ that maximises $L(\theta)$ is that which minimises the Kullback–Leibler divergence, namely $\theta = \theta^0$. In the limit of a large amount of data we can therefore, in principle, learn the correct parameters (assuming we know the correct model class). That is, maximum likelihood is a consistent estimator.

8.7.2 Training when the assumed model is incorrect

We write $q(x|\theta)$ for the assumed model, and $p(x|\phi)$ for the correct generating model. Repeating the above calculations in the case of the assumed model being correct, we have that, in the limit of a large amount of data, the scaled log likelihood is

$$L(\theta) = \langle \log q(x|\theta) \rangle_{p(x|\phi)} = -\text{KL}(p(x|\phi)|q(x|\theta)) + \langle \log p(x|\phi) \rangle_{p(x|\phi)}. \tag{8.7.9}$$

Since q and p are not of the same form, setting θ to ϕ does not necessarily minimise $\mathrm{KL}(p(x|\phi)|q(x|\theta))$, and therefore does not necessarily optimize $L(\theta)$.

8.7.3 Maximum likelihood and the empirical distribution

Given a dataset of discrete variables $\mathcal{X} = \{x^1, \ldots, x^N\}$ we define the empirical distribution as

$$q(x) = \frac{1}{N}\sum_{n=1}^{N} \mathbb{I}[x = x^n] \tag{8.7.10}$$

in the case that x is a vector of variables,

$$\mathbb{I}[x = x^n] = \prod_i \mathbb{I}[x_i = x_i^n]. \tag{8.7.11}$$

The Kullback–Leibler divergence between the empirical distribution $q(x)$ and a distribution $p(x)$ is

$$\mathrm{KL}(q|p) = \langle \log q(x)\rangle_{q(x)} - \langle \log p(x)\rangle_{q(x)}. \tag{8.7.12}$$

Our interest is the functional dependence of $\mathrm{KL}(q|p)$ on p. Since the entropic term $\langle \log q(x)\rangle_{q(x)}$ is independent of $p(x)$ we may consider this constant and focus on the second term alone. Hence

$$\mathrm{KL}(q|p) = -\langle \log p(x)\rangle_{q(x)} + \text{const.} = -\frac{1}{N}\sum_{n=1}^{N} \log p(x^n) + \text{const.} \tag{8.7.13}$$

We recognise $\sum_{n=1}^{N} \log p(x^n)$ as the log likelihood under the model $p(x)$, assuming that the data is i.i.d. This means that setting parameters by maximum likelihood is equivalent to setting parameters by minimising the Kullback–Leibler divergence between the empirical distribution and the parameterised distribution. In the case that $p(x)$ is unconstrained, the optimal choice is to set $p(x) = q(x)$, namely the maximum likelihood optimal distribution corresponds to the empirical distribution.

8.8 Learning a Gaussian

Given the importance of the Gaussian distribution, it is instructive to explicitly consider maximum likelihood and Bayesian methods for fitting a Gaussian to data.

8.8.1 Maximum likelihood training

Given a set of training data $\mathcal{X} = \{\mathbf{x}^1, \ldots, \mathbf{x}^N\}$, drawn from a Gaussian $\mathcal{N}(\mathbf{x}|\boldsymbol{\mu}, \boldsymbol{\Sigma})$ with unknown mean $\boldsymbol{\mu}$ and covariance $\boldsymbol{\Sigma}$, how can we find these parameters? Assuming the data are drawn i.i.d. the log likelihood is

$$L(\boldsymbol{\mu}, \boldsymbol{\Sigma}) \equiv \sum_{n=1}^{N} \log p(\mathbf{x}|\boldsymbol{\mu}, \boldsymbol{\Sigma}) = -\frac{1}{2}\sum_{n=1}^{N} (\mathbf{x}^n - \boldsymbol{\mu})^{\mathsf{T}} \boldsymbol{\Sigma}^{-1} (\mathbf{x}^n - \boldsymbol{\mu}) - \frac{N}{2}\log\det(2\pi\boldsymbol{\Sigma}). \tag{8.8.1}$$

Optimal μ

Taking the partial derivative with respect to the vector $\boldsymbol{\mu}$ we obtain the vector derivative

$$\nabla_{\mu} L(\boldsymbol{\mu}, \boldsymbol{\Sigma}) = \sum_{n=1}^{N} \boldsymbol{\Sigma}^{-1} (\mathbf{x}^n - \boldsymbol{\mu}). \tag{8.8.2}$$

Equating to zero gives that at the optimum of the log likelihood,

$$\sum_{n=1}^{N} \boldsymbol{\Sigma}^{-1} \mathbf{x}^n = N \boldsymbol{\mu} \boldsymbol{\Sigma}^{-1} \tag{8.8.3}$$

and therefore optimally $\boldsymbol{\mu}$ is given by the sample mean

$$\boldsymbol{\mu} = \frac{1}{N} \sum_{n=1}^{N} \mathbf{x}^n. \tag{8.8.4}$$

Optimal Σ

The derivative of L with respect to the matrix $\boldsymbol{\Sigma}$ requires more work. It is convenient to isolate the dependence on the covariance, and also parameterise using the inverse covariance, $\boldsymbol{\Sigma}^{-1}$,

$$L = -\frac{1}{2} \text{trace} \left(\boldsymbol{\Sigma}^{-1} \underbrace{\sum_{n=1}^{N} (\mathbf{x}^n - \boldsymbol{\mu}) (\mathbf{x}^n - \boldsymbol{\mu})^{\mathsf{T}}}_{\equiv \mathbf{M}} \right) + \frac{N}{2} \log \det \left(2\pi \boldsymbol{\Sigma}^{-1} \right). \tag{8.8.5}$$

Using $\mathbf{M} = \mathbf{M}^{\mathsf{T}}$, we obtain

$$\frac{\partial}{\partial \boldsymbol{\Sigma}^{-1}} L = -\frac{1}{2} \mathbf{M} + \frac{N}{2} \boldsymbol{\Sigma}. \tag{8.8.6}$$

Equating the derivative to the zero matrix and solving for $\boldsymbol{\Sigma}$ gives the sample covariance

$$\boldsymbol{\Sigma} = \frac{1}{N} \sum_{n=1}^{N} (\mathbf{x}^n - \boldsymbol{\mu}) (\mathbf{x}^n - \boldsymbol{\mu})^{\mathsf{T}}. \tag{8.8.7}$$

Equations (8.8.4) and (8.8.7) define the maximum likelihood solution mean and covariance for training data $\mathcal{X}$. Consistent with our previous results, in fact these equations simply set the parameters to their sample statistics of the empirical distribution. That is, the mean is set to the sample mean of the data and the covariance to the sample covariance.

8.8.2 Bayesian inference of the mean and variance

For simplicity we here deal only with the univariate case. Assuming i.i.d. data the likelihood is

$$p(\mathcal{X}|\mu, \sigma^2) = \frac{1}{(2\pi\sigma^2)^{N/2}} \exp \left(-\frac{1}{2\sigma^2} \sum_{n=1}^{N} (x^n - \mu)^2 \right). \tag{8.8.8}$$

For a Bayesian treatment, we require the posterior of the parameters

$$p(\mu, \sigma^2|\mathcal{X}) \propto p(\mathcal{X}|\mu, \sigma^2) p(\mu, \sigma^2) = p(\mathcal{X}|\mu, \sigma^2) p(\mu|\sigma^2) p(\sigma^2). \tag{8.8.9}$$

Our aim is to find conjugate priors for the mean and variance. A convenient choice for a prior on the mean μ is that it is a Gaussian centred on μ_0:

$$p(\mu|\mu_0, \sigma_0^2) = \frac{1}{\sqrt{2\pi\sigma_0^2}} \exp\left(-\frac{1}{2\sigma_0^2}(\mu_0 - \mu)^2\right). \tag{8.8.10}$$

The posterior is then

$$p(\mu, \sigma^2|\mathcal{X}) \propto \frac{1}{\sigma_0}\frac{1}{\sigma^N} \exp\left(-\frac{1}{2\sigma_0^2}(\mu_0 - \mu)^2 - \frac{1}{2\sigma^2}\sum_n (x^n - \mu)^2\right) p(\sigma^2). \tag{8.8.11}$$

It is convenient to write this in the form

$$p(\mu, \sigma^2|\mathcal{X}) = p(\mu|\sigma^2, \mathcal{X})p(\sigma^2|\mathcal{X}). \tag{8.8.12}$$

Since Equation (8.8.11) has quadratic contributions in μ in the exponent, the conditional posterior $p(\mu|\sigma^2, \mathcal{X})$ is Gaussian. To identify this Gaussian we multiply out the terms in the exponent to arrive at

$$\exp\left(-\frac{1}{2}\left(a\mu^2 - 2b\mu + c\right)\right) \tag{8.8.13}$$

with

$$a = \frac{1}{\sigma_0^2} + \frac{N}{\sigma^2}, \quad b = \frac{\mu_0}{\sigma_0^2} + \frac{\sum_n x^n}{\sigma^2}, \quad c = \frac{\mu_0^2}{\sigma_0^2} + \sum_n \frac{(x^n)^2}{\sigma^2}. \tag{8.8.14}$$

Using the identity

$$a\mu^2 - 2b\mu + c = a\left(\mu - \frac{b}{a}\right)^2 + \left(c - \frac{b^2}{a}\right) \tag{8.8.15}$$

we can write

$$p(\mu, \sigma^2|\mathcal{X}) \propto \underbrace{\sqrt{a}\exp\left(-\frac{1}{2}a\left(\mu - \frac{b}{a}\right)^2\right)}_{p(\mu|\mathcal{X},\sigma^2)} \underbrace{\frac{1}{\sqrt{a}}\exp\left(-\frac{1}{2}\left(c - \frac{b^2}{a}\right)\right)\frac{1}{\sigma_0}\frac{1}{\sigma^N}p(\sigma^2)}_{p(\sigma^2|\mathcal{X})}. \tag{8.8.16}$$

We encounter a difficulty in attempting to find a conjugate prior for σ^2 because the term b^2/a is not a simple expression of σ^2. For this reason we constrain

$$\sigma_0^2 \equiv \gamma\sigma^2 \tag{8.8.17}$$

for some fixed hyperparameter γ. Defining the constants

$$\tilde{a} = \frac{1}{\gamma} + N, \quad \tilde{b} = \frac{\mu_0}{\gamma} + \sum_n x^n, \quad \tilde{c} = \frac{\mu_0^2}{\gamma} + \sum_n (x^n)^2 \tag{8.8.18}$$

we have

$$c - \frac{b^2}{a} = \frac{1}{\sigma^2}\left(\tilde{c} - \frac{\tilde{b}^2}{\tilde{a}}\right). \tag{8.8.19}$$

Using this expression in Equation (8.8.16) we obtain

$$p(\sigma^2|\mathcal{X}) \propto \left(\sigma^2\right)^{-N/2} \exp\left(-\frac{1}{2\sigma^2}\left(\tilde{c} - \frac{\tilde{b}^2}{\tilde{a}}\right)\right)p(\sigma^2). \tag{8.8.20}$$

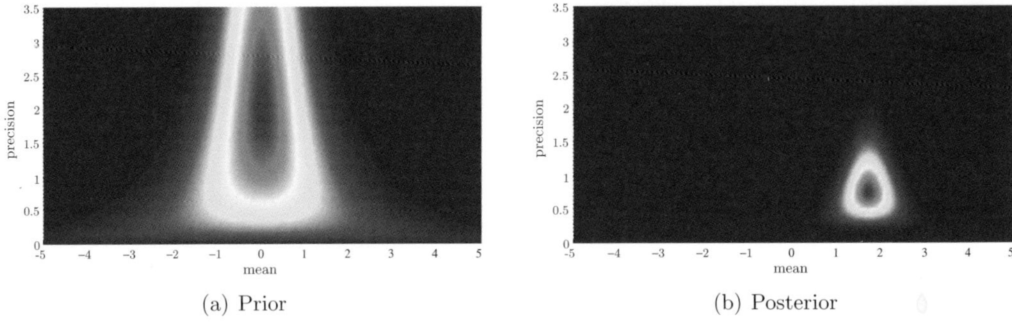

Figure 8.8 Bayesian approach to inferring the mean and precision (inverse variance) of a Gaussian based on $N = 10$ randomly drawn datapoints. (**a**) A Gauss-gamma prior with $\mu_0 = 0, \alpha = 2, \beta = 1, \gamma = 1$. (**b**) Gauss-gamma posterior conditional on the data. For comparison, the sample mean of the data is 1.87 and maximum likelihood optimal variance is 1.16 (computed using the N normalisation). The 10 datapoints were drawn from a Gaussian with mean 2 and variance 1. See `demoGaussBayes.m`.

An inverse Gamma distribution for the prior $p(\sigma^2)$ is therefore conjugate. For a Gauss-Inverse-Gamma prior:

$$p(\mu, \sigma^2) = \mathcal{N}\left(\mu|\mu_0, \gamma\sigma^2\right) InvGam\left(\sigma^2|\alpha, \beta\right) \tag{8.8.21}$$

the posterior is also *Gauss-Inverse-Gamma* with

$$p(\mu, \sigma^2|\mathcal{X}) = \mathcal{N}\left(\mu \left| \frac{\tilde{b}}{\tilde{a}}, \frac{\sigma^2}{\tilde{a}}\right.\right) InvGam\left(\sigma^2|\alpha + \frac{N}{2}, \beta + \frac{1}{2}\left(\tilde{c} - \frac{\tilde{b}^2}{\tilde{a}}\right)\right). \tag{8.8.22}$$

8.8.3 Gauss-gamma distribution

It is common to use a prior on the *precision*, defined as the inverse variance

$$\lambda \equiv \frac{1}{\sigma^2}. \tag{8.8.23}$$

If we then use a Gamma prior

$$p(\lambda|\alpha, \beta) = Gam\left(\lambda|\alpha, \beta\right) = \frac{1}{\beta^\alpha \Gamma(\alpha)} \lambda^{\alpha-1} e^{-\lambda/\beta}, \tag{8.8.24}$$

the posterior will be

$$p(\lambda|\mathcal{X}, \alpha, \beta) = Gam\left(\lambda|\alpha + N/2, \tilde{\beta}\right) \tag{8.8.25}$$

where

$$\frac{1}{\tilde{\beta}} = \frac{1}{\beta} + \frac{1}{2}\left(\tilde{c} - \frac{\tilde{b}^2}{\tilde{a}}\right). \tag{8.8.26}$$

The *Gauss-gamma* prior distribution

$$p(\mu, \lambda|\mu_0, \alpha, \beta, \gamma) = \mathcal{N}\left(\mu|\mu_0, \gamma\lambda^{-1}\right) Gam\left(\lambda|\alpha, \beta\right) \tag{8.8.27}$$

is therefore the conjugate prior for a Gaussian with unknown mean μ and precision λ. The posterior for this prior is a Gauss-gamma distribution with parameters

$$p(\mu, \lambda|\mathcal{X}, \mu_0, \alpha, \beta, \gamma) = \mathcal{N}\left(\mu \middle| \frac{\tilde{b}}{\tilde{a}}, \frac{1}{\tilde{a}\lambda}\right) Gam\left(\lambda|\alpha + N/2, \tilde{\beta}\right). \tag{8.8.28}$$

The marginal $p(\mu|\mathcal{X}, \mu_0, \alpha, \beta, \gamma)$ is a Student's t-distribution. An example of a Gauss-gamma prior/posterior is given in Fig. 8.8. The maximum likelihood solution is recovered in the limit of a 'flat' prior $\mu_0 = 0, \gamma \to \infty, \alpha = 1/2, \beta \to \infty$, see Exercise 8.23. The unbiased estimators for the mean and variance are given using the prior $\mu_0 = 0, \gamma \to \infty, \alpha = 1, \beta \to \infty$, Exercise 8.24.

For the multivariate case, the extension of these techniques uses a multivariate Gaussian distribution for the conjugate prior on the mean, and an Inverse Wishart distribution for the conjugate prior on the covariance [136].

8.9 Summary

- Classical univariate distributions include the exponential, Gamma, Beta, Gaussian and Poisson.
- A classical distribution of distributions is the Dirichlet distribution.
- Multivariate distributions are often difficult to deal with computationally. A special case is the multivariate Gaussian, for which marginals and normalisation constants can be computed in time cubic in the number of variables in the model.
- A useful measure of the difference between distributions is the Kullback–Leibler divergence.
- Bayes' rule rule enables us to achieve parameter learning by translating a priori parameter belief into a posterior parameter belief based on observed data.
- Bayes' rule rule itself says nothing about how best to summarise the posterior distribution.
- Conjugate distributions are such that the prior and posterior are from the same distribution, just with different parameters.
- Maximum likelihood corresponds to a simple summarisation of the posterior under a flat prior.
- Provided that we are using the correct model class, maximum likelihood will learn the optimal parameters in the limit of a large amount of data – otherwise there is no such guarantee.

8.10 Code

`demoGaussBayes.m`: Bayesian fitting of a univariate Gaussian
`logGaussGamma.m`: Plotting routine for a Gauss-Gamma distribution

8.11 Exercises

8.1 In a public lecture, the following phrase was uttered by a Professor of Experimental Psychology: 'In a recent data survey, 90% of people claim to have above average intelligence, which is clearly nonsense!' [Audience Laughs]. Is it theoretically possible for 90% of people to have above average intelligence? If so, give an example, otherwise explain why not. What about above median intelligence?

8.2 Consider the distribution defined on real variables x, y:

$$p(x, y) \propto (x^2 + y^2)^2 e^{-x^2-y^2}, \qquad \text{dom}(x) = \text{dom}(y) = \{-\infty \dots \infty\}. \tag{8.11.1}$$

Show that $\langle x \rangle = \langle y \rangle = 0$. Furthermore show that x and y are uncorrelated, $\langle xy \rangle = \langle x \rangle \langle y \rangle$. Whilst x and y are uncorrelated, show that they are nevertheless dependent.

8.3 For a variable x with $\text{dom}(x) = \{0, 1\}$, and $p(x = 1) = \theta$, show that in n independent draws $x_1, \dots, x_n$ from this distribution, the probability of observing k states 1 is the Binomial distribution

$$\binom{n}{k} \theta^k (1 - \theta)^{n-k}. \tag{8.11.2}$$

8.4 (Normalisation constant of a Gaussian) The normalisation constant of a Gaussian distribution is related to the integral

$$I = \int_{-\infty}^{\infty} e^{-\frac{1}{2}x^2} dx. \tag{8.11.3}$$

By considering

$$I^2 = \int_{-\infty}^{\infty} e^{-\frac{1}{2}x^2} dx \int_{-\infty}^{\infty} e^{-\frac{1}{2}y^2} dy = \int_{-\infty}^{\infty} \int_{-\infty}^{\infty} e^{-\frac{1}{2}(x^2+y^2)} dx dy \tag{8.11.4}$$

and transforming to polar coordinates,

$$x = \mathrm{r}\cos\theta, \quad y = \mathrm{r}\sin\theta, \quad dxdy \to \mathrm{r}d\mathrm{r}d\theta, \quad \mathrm{r} = 0, \dots, \infty, \quad \theta = 0, \dots, 2\pi$$

show that

1. $I = \sqrt{2\pi}$
2. $\int_{-\infty}^{\infty} e^{-\frac{1}{2\sigma^2}(x-\mu)^2} dx = \sqrt{2\pi\sigma^2}$.

8.5 For a univariate Gaussian distribution, show that

1. $\mu = \langle x \rangle_{\mathcal{N}(x|\mu,\sigma^2)}$
2. $\sigma^2 = \left\langle (x - \mu)^2 \right\rangle_{\mathcal{N}(x|\mu,\sigma^2)}$.

8.6 Using

$$\mathbf{x}^\mathsf{T}\mathbf{A}\mathbf{x} = \text{trace}\left(\mathbf{A}\mathbf{x}\mathbf{x}^\mathsf{T}\right) \tag{8.11.5}$$

derive Result 8.5.

8.7 Show that the marginal of a Dirichlet distribution is another Dirichlet distribution:

$$\int_{\theta_j} \text{Dirichlet}(\theta|\mathbf{u}) = \text{Dirichlet}\left(\theta_{\setminus j}|\mathbf{u}_{\setminus j}\right). \tag{8.11.6}$$

8.8 For a Beta distribution, show that

$$\left\langle x^k \right\rangle = \frac{B(\alpha + k, \beta)}{B(\alpha, \beta)} == \frac{(\alpha + k - 1)(\alpha + k - 2) \dots (\alpha)}{(\alpha + \beta + k - 1)(\alpha + \beta + k) \dots (\alpha + \beta)} \tag{8.11.7}$$

where we used $\Gamma(x + 1) = x\Gamma(x)$.

8.9 For the moment generating function $g(t) \equiv \langle e^{tx} \rangle_{p(x)}$, show that

$$\lim_{t \to 0} \frac{d^k}{dt^k} g(t) = \left\langle x^k \right\rangle_{p(x)}. \tag{8.11.8}$$

8.10 (Change of variables) Consider a one-dimensional continuous random variable x with corresponding $p(x)$. For a variable $y = f(x)$, where $f(x)$ is a monotonic function, show that the distribution of y is

$$p(y) = p(x)\left(\frac{df}{dx}\right)^{-1}, \quad x = f^{-1}(y). \tag{8.11.9}$$

More generally, for vector variables, and $\mathbf{y} = \mathbf{f}(\mathbf{x})$, we have:

$$p(\mathbf{y}) = p(\mathbf{x} = \mathbf{f}^{-1}(\mathbf{y}))\left|\det\left(\frac{\partial \mathbf{f}}{\partial \mathbf{x}}\right)\right|^{-1} \tag{8.11.10}$$

where the Jacobian matrix has elements

$$\left[\frac{\partial \mathbf{f}}{\partial \mathbf{x}}\right]_{ij} = \frac{\partial f_i(\mathbf{x})}{\partial x_j}. \tag{8.11.11}$$

8.11 (Normalisation of a multivariate Gaussian) Consider

$$I = \int_{-\infty}^{\infty} \exp\left(-\frac{1}{2}(\mathbf{x}-\boldsymbol{\mu})^{\mathsf{T}}\boldsymbol{\Sigma}^{-1}(\mathbf{x}-\boldsymbol{\mu})\right) d\mathbf{x}. \tag{8.11.12}$$

By using the transformation

$$\mathbf{z} = \boldsymbol{\Sigma}^{-\frac{1}{2}}(\mathbf{x}-\boldsymbol{\mu}) \tag{8.11.13}$$

show that

$$I = \sqrt{\det(2\pi\boldsymbol{\Sigma})}. \tag{8.11.14}$$

8.12 Consider the partitioned matrix

$$\mathbf{M} = \begin{pmatrix} \mathbf{A} & \mathbf{B} \\ \mathbf{C} & \mathbf{D} \end{pmatrix} \tag{8.11.15}$$

for which we wish to find the inverse $\mathbf{M}^{-1}$. We assume that $\mathbf{A}$ is $m \times m$ and invertible, and $\mathbf{D}$ is $n \times n$ and invertible. By definition, the partitioned inverse

$$\mathbf{M}^{-1} = \begin{pmatrix} \mathbf{P} & \mathbf{Q} \\ \mathbf{R} & \mathbf{S} \end{pmatrix} \tag{8.11.16}$$

must satisfy

$$\begin{pmatrix} \mathbf{A} & \mathbf{B} \\ \mathbf{C} & \mathbf{D} \end{pmatrix}\begin{pmatrix} \mathbf{P} & \mathbf{Q} \\ \mathbf{R} & \mathbf{S} \end{pmatrix} = \begin{pmatrix} \mathbf{I}_m & 0 \\ 0 & \mathbf{I}_n \end{pmatrix} \tag{8.11.17}$$

where $\mathbf{I}_m$ is the $m \times m$ identity matrix, and 0 the zero matrix of the same dimension as $\mathbf{D}$. Using the above, derive the results

$$\begin{array}{ll} \mathbf{P} = \left(\mathbf{A} - \mathbf{B}\mathbf{D}^{-1}\mathbf{C}\right)^{-1} & \mathbf{Q} = -\mathbf{A}^{-1}\mathbf{B}\left(\mathbf{D} - \mathbf{C}\mathbf{A}^{-1}\mathbf{B}\right)^{-1} \\ \mathbf{R} = -\mathbf{D}^{-1}\mathbf{C}\left(\mathbf{A} - \mathbf{B}\mathbf{D}^{-1}\mathbf{C}\right)^{-1} & \mathbf{S} = \left(\mathbf{D} - \mathbf{C}\mathbf{A}^{-1}\mathbf{B}\right)^{-1}. \end{array} \tag{8.11.18}$$

8.13 Show that for Gaussian distribution $p(x) = \mathcal{N}\left(x \mid \mu, \sigma^2\right)$ the skewness and kurtosis are both zero.

8.14 Consider a small interval of time δt and let the probability of an event occurring in this small interval be $\theta\delta t$. Derive a distribution that expresses the probability of at least one event in an interval from 0 to t.

8.15 Consider a vector variable $\mathbf{x} = (x_1, \ldots, x_n)^{\mathsf{T}}$ and set of functions defined on each component of x, $\phi_i(x_i)$. For example for $\mathbf{x} = (x_1, x_2)^{\mathsf{T}}$ we might have

$$\phi_1(x_1) = -|x_1|, \quad \phi_2(x_2) = -x_2^2. \tag{8.11.19}$$

Consider the distribution

$$p(\mathbf{x}|\boldsymbol{\theta}) = \frac{1}{Z}\exp\left(\boldsymbol{\theta}^{\mathsf{T}}\boldsymbol{\phi}(\mathbf{x})\right) \tag{8.11.20}$$

where $\phi(\mathbf{x})$ is a vector function with ith component $\phi_i(x_i)$, and $\boldsymbol{\theta}$ is a parameter vector. Each component is tractably integrable in the sense that

$$\int_{-\infty}^{\infty} \exp\left(\theta_i \phi_i(x_i)\right) dx_i \tag{8.11.21}$$

can be computed either analytically or to an acceptable numerical accuracy. Show that

1. $x_i \perp\!\!\!\perp x_j$.
2. The normalisation constant Z can be tractably computed.
3. Consider the transformation

$$\mathbf{x} = \mathbf{M}\mathbf{y} \tag{8.11.22}$$

for an invertible matrix $\mathbf{M}$. Show that the distribution $p(\mathbf{y}|\mathbf{M}, \boldsymbol{\theta})$ is tractable (its normalisation constant is known), and that, in general, $y_i \top\!\!\!\top y_j$. Explain the significance of this in deriving tractable multivariate distributions.

8.16 Show that we may reparameterise the Beta distribution, Definition 8.23 by writing the parameters α and β as functions of the mean m and variance s using

$$\alpha = \beta\gamma, \qquad \gamma \equiv m/(1-m), \tag{8.11.23}$$

$$\beta = \frac{1}{1+\gamma}\left(\frac{\gamma}{s(1+\gamma)^2} - 1\right). \tag{8.11.24}$$

8.17 Consider the function

$$f(\gamma+\alpha, \beta, \theta) \equiv \theta^{\gamma+\alpha-1}(1-\theta)^{\beta-1} \tag{8.11.25}$$

show that

$$\lim_{\gamma\to 0}\frac{\partial}{\partial\gamma} f(\gamma+\alpha,\beta,\theta) = \theta^{\alpha-1}(1-\theta)^{\beta-1}\log\theta \tag{8.11.26}$$

and hence that

$$\int \theta^{\alpha-1}(1-\theta)^{\beta-1}\log\theta d\theta = \lim_{\gamma\to 0}\frac{\partial}{\partial\gamma}\int f(\gamma+\alpha,\beta,\theta)d\theta = \frac{\partial}{\partial\alpha}\int f(\alpha,\beta,\theta)d\theta. \tag{8.11.27}$$

Using this result, show therefore that

$$\langle\log\theta\rangle_{B(\theta|\alpha,\beta)} = \frac{\partial}{\partial\alpha}\log B(\alpha,\beta) \tag{8.11.28}$$

where $B(\alpha, \beta)$ is the Beta function. Show additionally that

$$\langle\log(1-\theta)\rangle_{B(\theta|\alpha,\beta)} = \frac{\partial}{\partial\beta}\log B(\alpha,\beta). \tag{8.11.29}$$

Using the fact that

$$B(\alpha,\beta) = \frac{\Gamma(\alpha)\Gamma(\beta)}{\Gamma(\alpha+\beta)} \tag{8.11.30}$$

where $\Gamma(x)$ is the gamma function, relate the above averages to the *digamma function*, defined as

$$\psi(x) = \frac{d}{dx}\log\Gamma(x). \tag{8.11.31}$$

8.18 Using a similar 'generating function' approach as in Exercise 8.17, explain how to compute

$$\langle \log \theta_i \rangle_{\text{Dirichlet}(\boldsymbol{\theta}|\mathbf{u})}. \tag{8.11.32}$$

8.19 Consider the function

$$f(x) = \int_0^\infty \delta\left(\sum_{i=1}^n \theta_i - x\right) \prod_i \theta_i^{u_i - 1} d\theta_1 \dots d\theta_n. \tag{8.11.33}$$

Show that the Laplace transform $\tilde{f}(s) \equiv \int_0^\infty e^{-sx} f(x) dx$ is

$$\tilde{f}(s) = \prod_{i=1}^n \left\{ \int_0^\infty e^{-s\theta_i} \theta_i^{u_i - 1} d\theta_i \right\} = \frac{1}{s^{\sum_i u_i}} \prod_{i=1}^n \Gamma(u_i). \tag{8.11.34}$$

By using that the inverse Laplace transform of $1/s^{1+q}$ is $x^q / \Gamma(1+q)$, show that

$$f(x) = \frac{\prod_{i=1}^n \Gamma(u_i)}{\Gamma\left(\sum_i u_i\right)} x^{\sum_i u_i}. \tag{8.11.35}$$

Hence show that the normalisation constant of a Dirichlet distribution with parameters $\mathbf{u}$ is given by

$$\frac{\prod_{i=1}^n \Gamma(u_i)}{\Gamma\left(\sum_i u_i\right)}. \tag{8.11.36}$$

8.20 Derive the formula for the differential entropy of a multivariate Gaussian.

8.21 Show that for a gamma distribution $Gam(x|\alpha, \beta)$ the mode is given by

$$x^* = (\alpha - 1)\beta \tag{8.11.37}$$

provided that $\alpha \geq 1$.

8.22 Consider a distribution $p(x|\theta)$ and a distribution $p(x|\theta + \delta)$ for small δ.

1. Take the Taylor expansion of

$$\text{KL}(p(x|\theta)|p(x|\theta + \delta)) \tag{8.11.38}$$

for small δ and show that this is equal to

$$-\frac{\delta^2}{2} \left\langle \frac{\partial^2}{\partial \theta^2} \log p(x|\theta) \right\rangle_{p(x|\theta)}. \tag{8.11.39}$$

2. More generally for a distribution parameterised by a vector with elements $\theta_i + \delta_i$, show that a small change in the parameter results in

$$\sum_{i,j} \frac{\delta_i \delta_j}{2} F_{ij} \tag{8.11.40}$$

where the *Fisher Information* matrix is defined as

$$F_{ij} = -\left\langle \frac{\partial^2}{\partial \theta_i \partial \theta_j} \log p(x|\theta) \right\rangle_{p(x|\theta)}. \tag{8.11.41}$$

3. Show that the Fisher information matrix is positive semidefinite by expressing it equivalently as

$$F_{ij} = \left\langle \frac{\partial}{\partial \theta_i} \log p(x|\theta) \frac{\partial}{\partial \theta_j} \log p(x|\theta) \right\rangle_{p(x|\theta)}. \tag{8.11.42}$$

8.23 Consider the joint prior distribution

$$p(\mu, \lambda|\mu_0, \alpha, \beta, \gamma) = \mathcal{N}\left(\mu|\mu_0, \gamma\lambda^{-1}\right) Gam\left(\lambda|\alpha, \beta\right). \tag{8.11.43}$$

Show that for $\mu_0 = 0, \gamma \to \infty, \beta \to \infty$, then the prior distribution becomes 'flat' (independent of μ and λ) for $\alpha = 1/2$. Show that for these settings the mean and variance that jointly maximise the posterior equation (8.8.28) are given by the standard maximum likelihood settings

$$\mu_* = \frac{1}{N}\sum_n x^n, \qquad \sigma_*^2 = \frac{1}{N}\sum_n (x^n - \mu_*)^2. \tag{8.11.44}$$

8.24 Show that for Equation (8.8.28) in the limit $\mu_0 = 0, \gamma \to \infty, \alpha = 1, \beta \to \infty$, the jointly optimal mean and variance obtained from

$$\underset{\mu,\lambda}{\operatorname{argmax}}\ p(\mu, \lambda|\mathcal{X}, \mu_0, \alpha, \beta, \gamma) \tag{8.11.45}$$

are given by

$$\mu_* = \frac{1}{N}\sum_n x^n, \qquad \sigma_*^2 = \frac{1}{N+1}\sum_n (x^n - \mu_*)^2 \tag{8.11.46}$$

where $\sigma_*^2 = 1/\lambda_*$. Note that these correspond to the standard 'unbiased' estimators of the mean and variance.

8.25 For the Gauss-gamma posterior $p(\mu, \lambda|\mu_0, \alpha, \beta, \mathcal{X})$ given in Equation (8.8.28) compute the marginal posterior $p(\mu|\mu_0, \alpha, \beta, \mathcal{X})$. What is the mean of this distribution?

8.26 This exercise concerns the derivation of Equation (8.4.15).

1. By considering

$$p(\mathbf{y}) = \int p(\mathbf{y}|\mathbf{x})p(\mathbf{x})d\mathbf{x} \tag{8.11.47}$$

$$\propto \int \exp\left(-\frac{1}{2}\left(\mathbf{y} - \mathbf{M}\mathbf{x} - \boldsymbol{\mu}\right)^{\mathsf{T}} \boldsymbol{\Sigma}^{-1}\left(\mathbf{y} - \mathbf{M}\mathbf{x} - \boldsymbol{\mu}\right) - \frac{1}{2}\left(\mathbf{x} - \boldsymbol{\mu}_x\right)^{\mathsf{T}} \boldsymbol{\Sigma}_x^{-1}\left(\mathbf{x} - \boldsymbol{\mu}_x\right)\right)d\mathbf{x} \tag{8.11.48}$$

show that

$$p(\mathbf{y}) \propto \exp\left(-\frac{1}{2}\mathbf{y}^{\mathsf{T}}\boldsymbol{\Sigma}^{-1}\mathbf{y}\right)\int \exp\left(-\frac{1}{2}\mathbf{x}^{\mathsf{T}}\mathbf{A}\mathbf{x} + \mathbf{x}^{\mathsf{T}}\left(\mathbf{B}\mathbf{y} + \mathbf{c}\right)\right) \tag{8.11.49}$$

for suitably defined $\mathbf{A}, \mathbf{B}, \mathbf{c}$.

2. Using Equation (8.4.13), show that

$$p(\mathbf{y}) \propto \exp\left(-\frac{1}{2}\mathbf{y}^{\mathsf{T}}\boldsymbol{\Sigma}^{-1}\mathbf{y} - \frac{1}{2}\left(\mathbf{B}\mathbf{y} + \mathbf{c}\right)^{\mathsf{T}}\mathbf{A}^{-1}\left(\mathbf{B}\mathbf{y} + \mathbf{c}\right)\right).$$

3. This establishes that $p(\mathbf{y})$ is Gaussian. We now need to find the mean and covariance of this Gaussian. We can do this by the lengthy process of completing the square. Alternatively, we can appeal to

$$\langle \mathbf{y} \rangle = \mathbf{M}\langle \mathbf{x} \rangle + \langle \boldsymbol{\eta} \rangle = \mathbf{M}\boldsymbol{\mu}_x + \boldsymbol{\mu}.$$

By considering

$$\left\langle \left(\mathbf{y} - \langle \mathbf{y} \rangle\right)\left(\mathbf{y} - \langle \mathbf{y} \rangle\right)^{\mathsf{T}} \right\rangle = \left\langle \left(\mathbf{M}\mathbf{x} + \boldsymbol{\eta} - \mathbf{M}\boldsymbol{\mu}_x - \boldsymbol{\mu}\right)\left(\mathbf{M}\mathbf{x} + \boldsymbol{\eta} - \mathbf{M}\boldsymbol{\mu}_x - \boldsymbol{\mu}\right)^{\mathsf{T}} \right\rangle \tag{8.11.50}$$

and the independence of $\mathbf{x}$ and $\boldsymbol{\eta}$, derive the formula for the covariance of $p(\mathbf{y})$.

8.27 Consider the multivariate Gaussian distribution $p(\mathbf{x}) \sim \mathcal{N}(\mathbf{x}|\boldsymbol{\mu}, \boldsymbol{\Sigma})$ on the vector $\mathbf{x}$ with components $x_1, \ldots, x_n$:

$$p(\mathbf{x}) = \frac{1}{\sqrt{\det(2\pi\boldsymbol{\Sigma})}} e^{-\frac{1}{2}(\mathbf{x}-\boldsymbol{\mu})^\mathsf{T}\boldsymbol{\Sigma}^{-1}(\mathbf{x}-\boldsymbol{\mu})}. \tag{8.11.51}$$

Calculate $p(x_i|x_1, \ldots, x_{i-1}, x_{i+1}, \ldots, x_n)$. Hint: make use of Equation (8.4.19).

8.28 Observations $y_0, \ldots, y_{n-1}$ are noisy i.i.d. measurements of an underlying variable x with $p(x) \sim \mathcal{N}(x|0, \sigma_0^2)$ and $p(y_i|x) \sim \mathcal{N}(y_i|x, \sigma^2)$ for $i = 0, \ldots, n-1$. Show that $p(x|y_0, \ldots, y_{n-1})$ is Gaussian with mean

$$\mu = \frac{n\sigma_0^2}{n\sigma_0^2 + \sigma^2}\overline{y} \tag{8.11.52}$$

where $\overline{y} = (y_0 + y_1 + \cdots + y_{n-1})/n$ and variance σ_n^2 such that

$$\frac{1}{\sigma_n^2} = \frac{n}{\sigma^2} + \frac{1}{\sigma_0^2}. \tag{8.11.53}$$

8.29 Consider a set of data $\mathcal{X} = x^1, \ldots, x^N$ where each x^n is independently drawn from a Gaussian with known mean μ and unknown variance σ^2. Assume a gamma distribution prior on $\tau = 1/\sigma^2$,

$$p(\tau) = Gam^{is}(\tau|a, b). \tag{8.11.54}$$

1. Show that the posterior distribution is

$$p(\tau|\mathcal{X}) = Gam^{is}\left(\tau|a + \frac{N}{2}, b + \frac{1}{2}\sum_{n=1}^{N}(x^n - \mu)^2\right). \tag{8.11.55}$$

2. Show that the distribution for x is

$$p(x|\mathcal{X}) = \int p(x|\tau)p(\tau|\mathcal{X})d\tau = Student\left(x|\mu, \lambda = \frac{a'}{b'}, \nu = 2a'\right) \tag{8.11.56}$$

where $a' = \frac{1}{2}N$, $b' = b + \frac{1}{2}\sum_{n=1}^{N}(x^n - \mu)^2$.

8.30 The Poisson distribution is a discrete distribution on the non-negative integers, with

$$p(x) = \frac{e^{-\lambda}\lambda^x}{x!} \qquad x = 0,\ 1,\ 2, \ldots \tag{8.11.57}$$

You are given a sample of n observations $x_1, \ldots, x_n$ independently drawn from this distribution. Determine the maximum likelihood estimator of the Poisson parameter λ.

8.31 For a Gaussian mixture model

$$p(\mathbf{x}) = \sum_i p_i \mathcal{N}(\mathbf{x}|\boldsymbol{\mu}_i, \boldsymbol{\Sigma}_i), \qquad p_i > 0, \sum_i p_i = 1 \tag{8.11.58}$$

show that $p(\mathbf{x})$ has mean

$$\langle \mathbf{x} \rangle = \sum_i p_i \boldsymbol{\mu}_i \tag{8.11.59}$$

and covariance

$$\sum_i p_i \left(\boldsymbol{\Sigma}_i + \boldsymbol{\mu}_i\boldsymbol{\mu}_i^\mathsf{T}\right) - \sum_i p_i\boldsymbol{\mu}_i \sum_j p_j\boldsymbol{\mu}_j^\mathsf{T}. \tag{8.11.60}$$

8.32 Show that for the whitened data matrix, given in Equation (8.4.30), $\mathbf{Z}\mathbf{Z}^\mathsf{T} = N\mathbf{I}$.

8.33 Consider a uniform distribution $p_i = 1/N$ defined on states $i = 1, \ldots, N$. Show that the entropy of this distribution is

$$H = -\sum_{i=1}^{N} p_i \log p_i = \log N \tag{8.11.61}$$

and that therefore as the number of states N increases to infinity, the entropy diverges to infinity.

8.34 Consider a continuous distribution $p(x)$, $x \in [0, 1]$. We can form a discrete approximation with probabilities p_i to this continuous distribution by identifying a continuous value i/N for each state $i = 1, \ldots, N$. With this

$$p_i = \frac{p(i/N)}{\sum_i p(i/N)} \tag{8.11.62}$$

show that the entropy $H = -\sum_i p_i \log p_i$ is given by

$$H = -\frac{1}{\sum_i p(i/N)} \sum_i p(i/N) \log p(i/N) + \log \sum_i p(i/N). \tag{8.11.63}$$

Since for a continuous distribution

$$\int_0^1 p(x)dx = 1 \tag{8.11.64}$$

a discrete approximation of this integral into bins of size $1/N$ gives

$$\frac{1}{N} \sum_{i=1}^{N} p(i/N) = 1. \tag{8.11.65}$$

Hence show that for large N,

$$H \approx -\int_0^1 p(x) \log p(x)dx + \text{const.} \tag{8.11.66}$$

where the constant tends to infinity as $N \to \infty$. Note that this result says that as a continuous distribution has essentially an infinite number of states, the amount of uncertainty in the distribution is infinite (alternatively, we would need an infinite number of bits to specify a continuous value). This motivates the definition of the differential entropy, which neglects the infinite constant of the limiting case of the discrete entropy.

8.35 Consider two multivariate Gaussians $\mathcal{N}(\mathbf{x}|\boldsymbol{\mu}_1, \boldsymbol{\Sigma}_1)$ and $\mathcal{N}(\mathbf{x}|\boldsymbol{\mu}_2, \boldsymbol{\Sigma}_2)$.

1. Show that the log product of the two Gaussians is given by

$$-\frac{1}{2}\mathbf{x}^{\mathsf{T}}\left(\boldsymbol{\Sigma}_1^{-1} + \boldsymbol{\Sigma}_2^{-1}\right)\mathbf{x} + \mathbf{x}^{\mathsf{T}}\left(\boldsymbol{\Sigma}_1^{-1}\boldsymbol{\mu}_1 + \boldsymbol{\Sigma}_2^{-1}\boldsymbol{\mu}_2\right) - \frac{1}{2}\left(\boldsymbol{\mu}_1^{\mathsf{T}}\boldsymbol{\Sigma}_1^{-1}\boldsymbol{\mu}_1 + \boldsymbol{\mu}_2^{\mathsf{T}}\boldsymbol{\Sigma}_2^{-1}\boldsymbol{\mu}_2\right)$$
$$-\frac{1}{2}\log\det(2\pi\boldsymbol{\Sigma}_1)\det(2\pi\boldsymbol{\Sigma}_2).$$

2. Defining $\mathbf{A} = \boldsymbol{\Sigma}_1^{-1} + \boldsymbol{\Sigma}_2^{-1}$ and $\mathbf{b} = \boldsymbol{\Sigma}_1^{-1}\boldsymbol{\mu}_1 + \boldsymbol{\Sigma}_2^{-1}\boldsymbol{\mu}_2$ we can write the above as

$$-\frac{1}{2}\left(\mathbf{x} - \mathbf{A}^{-1}\mathbf{b}\right)^{\mathsf{T}}\mathbf{A}\left(\mathbf{x} - \mathbf{A}^{-1}\mathbf{b}\right) + \frac{1}{2}\mathbf{b}^{\mathsf{T}}\mathbf{A}^{-1}\mathbf{b} - \frac{1}{2}\left(\boldsymbol{\mu}_1^{\mathsf{T}}\boldsymbol{\Sigma}_1^{-1}\boldsymbol{\mu}_1 + \boldsymbol{\mu}_2^{\mathsf{T}}\boldsymbol{\Sigma}_2^{-1}\boldsymbol{\mu}_2\right)$$
$$-\frac{1}{2}\log\det(2\pi\boldsymbol{\Sigma}_1)\det(2\pi\boldsymbol{\Sigma}_2).$$

Writing $\boldsymbol{\Sigma} = \mathbf{A}^{-1}$ and $\boldsymbol{\mu} = \mathbf{A}^{-1}\mathbf{b}$ show that the product of two Gaussians is a Gaussian with covariance

$$\boldsymbol{\Sigma} = \boldsymbol{\Sigma}_1\left(\boldsymbol{\Sigma}_1 + \boldsymbol{\Sigma}_2\right)^{-1}\boldsymbol{\Sigma}_2 \tag{8.11.67}$$

mean

$$\boldsymbol{\mu} = \boldsymbol{\Sigma}_1 \left(\boldsymbol{\Sigma}_1 + \boldsymbol{\Sigma}_2\right)^{-1} \boldsymbol{\mu}_2 + \boldsymbol{\Sigma}_2 \left(\boldsymbol{\Sigma}_1 + \boldsymbol{\Sigma}_2\right)^{-1} \boldsymbol{\mu}_1 \tag{8.11.68}$$

and log prefactor

$$\frac{1}{2}\mathbf{b}^{\mathsf{T}}\mathbf{A}^{-1}\mathbf{b} - \frac{1}{2}\left(\boldsymbol{\mu}_1^{\mathsf{T}}\boldsymbol{\Sigma}_1^{-1}\boldsymbol{\mu}_1 + \boldsymbol{\mu}_2^{\mathsf{T}}\boldsymbol{\Sigma}_2^{-1}\boldsymbol{\mu}_2\right) - \frac{1}{2}\log\det\left(2\pi\boldsymbol{\Sigma}_1\right)\det\left(2\pi\boldsymbol{\Sigma}_2\right) + \frac{1}{2}\log\det\left(2\pi\boldsymbol{\Sigma}\right).$$

3. Show that this can be written as

$$\mathcal{N}\left(\mathbf{x}|\boldsymbol{\mu}_1, \boldsymbol{\Sigma}_1\right)\mathcal{N}\left(\mathbf{x}|\boldsymbol{\mu}_2, \boldsymbol{\Sigma}_2\right) = \mathcal{N}\left(\mathbf{x}|\boldsymbol{\mu}, \boldsymbol{\Sigma}\right)\frac{\exp\left(-\frac{1}{2}\left(\boldsymbol{\mu}_1 - \boldsymbol{\mu}_2\right)^{\mathsf{T}}\mathbf{S}^{-1}\left(\boldsymbol{\mu}_1 - \boldsymbol{\mu}_2\right)\right)}{\sqrt{\det\left(2\pi\mathbf{S}\right)}} \tag{8.11.69}$$

where $\mathbf{S} = \boldsymbol{\Sigma}_1 + \boldsymbol{\Sigma}_2$.

8.36 Show that

$$\frac{\partial}{\partial\theta}\left\langle \log p(x|\theta)\right\rangle_{p(x|\theta^0)} |_{\theta=\theta^0} = 0. \tag{8.11.70}$$

8.37 Using $\left\langle f^2(x)\right\rangle - \left\langle f(x)\right\rangle^2 \geq 0$, and a suitably chosen function $f(x)$, show that

$$\left\langle \frac{p(x)}{q(x)}\right\rangle_{p(x)} \geq 1 \tag{8.11.71}$$

for distributions $q(x)$ and $p(x)$. This is related to the $\alpha = 2$ divergence.

8.38 Show that for any α, $D_\alpha(p|p) = 0$ and that $D_\alpha(p|q) \geq 0$ for any distributions $p(x)$, $q(x)$.

8.39 Show that for two D-dimensional Gaussians,

$$2\mathrm{KL}(\mathcal{N}\left(\mathbf{x}|\boldsymbol{\mu}_1, \boldsymbol{\Sigma}_1\right)|\mathcal{N}\left(\mathbf{x}|\boldsymbol{\mu}_2, \boldsymbol{\Sigma}_2\right)) = \mathrm{trace}\left(\boldsymbol{\Sigma}_2^{-1}\boldsymbol{\Sigma}_1\right) + \left(\boldsymbol{\mu}_1 - \boldsymbol{\mu}_2\right)^{\mathsf{T}}\boldsymbol{\Sigma}_2^{-1}\left(\boldsymbol{\mu}_1 - \boldsymbol{\mu}_2\right) + \log\det\left(\boldsymbol{\Sigma}_2\boldsymbol{\Sigma}_1^{-1}\right) - D.$$

8.40 For data pairs (x^n, y^n), $n = 1, \ldots, N$, the correlation can be considered a measure of the extent to which a linear relationship holds between x and y. For simplicity, we consider that both x and y have zero mean, and wish to consider the validity of the linear relation

$$x = \alpha y. \tag{8.11.72}$$

A measure of the discrepancy of this linear assumption is given by

$$E(\alpha) \equiv \sum_{n=1}^{N}\left(x^n - \alpha y^n\right)^2. \tag{8.11.73}$$

1. Show that the α that minimises $E(\alpha)$ is given by

$$\alpha^* = \frac{c}{\sigma_y^2} \tag{8.11.74}$$

where

$$c = \frac{1}{N}\sum_n x^n y^n, \qquad \sigma_y^2 = \frac{1}{N}\sum_n \left(y^n\right)^2. \tag{8.11.75}$$

2. A measure of the 'linearity' between x and y is then

$$\frac{E(\alpha^*)}{E(0)} \tag{8.11.76}$$

which is 1 when there is no linear relation ($\alpha = 0$) and 0 when there is a perfect linear relation (since then $E(\alpha^*) = 0$). Show that the correlation coefficient, Definition 8.7, is given by

$$\rho = \sqrt{1 - \frac{E(\alpha^*)}{E(0)}}. \tag{8.11.77}$$

3. Defining the vectors $\mathbf{x} = (x^1, \ldots, x^N)^\mathsf{T}$, $\mathbf{y} = (y^1, \ldots, y^N)^\mathsf{T}$, show that the correlation coefficient is the cosine of the angle between $\mathbf{x}$ and $\mathbf{y}$,

$$\rho = \frac{\mathbf{x}^\mathsf{T}\mathbf{y}}{|\mathbf{x}||\mathbf{y}|} \tag{8.11.78}$$

and hence show that $-1 \le \rho \le 1$.

4. Show that for the more general relation

$$x = \alpha y + \gamma \tag{8.11.79}$$

for constant offset γ, setting γ to minimise

$$E(\alpha, \gamma) \equiv \sum_{n=1}^{N} (x^n - \alpha y^n - \gamma)^2 \tag{8.11.80}$$

has the effect of simply replacing x^n by $x^n - \bar{x}$ and y^n by $y^n - \bar{y}$, where $\bar{x}$ and $\bar{y}$ are the mean of the x and y data respectively.

8.41 For variables x, y, and $z = x + y$, show that the correlation coefficients are related by $\rho_{x,z} \ge \rho_{x,y}$. With reference to the correlation coefficient as the angle between two vectors, explain why $\rho_{x,z} \ge \rho_{x,y}$ is geometrically obvious.

8.42 Consider a 'Boltzman machine' distribution on binary variables $x_i \in \{0, 1\}$, $i = 1, \ldots, D$

$$p(\mathbf{x}|\mathbf{W}) = \frac{1}{Z_p(\mathbf{W})} \exp\left(\mathbf{x}^\mathsf{T}\mathbf{W}\mathbf{x}\right) \tag{8.11.81}$$

and that we wish to fit another distribution q of the same form to p

$$q(\mathbf{x}|\mathbf{U}) = \frac{1}{Z_q(\mathbf{U})} \exp\left(\mathbf{x}^\mathsf{T}\mathbf{U}\mathbf{x}\right). \tag{8.11.82}$$

1. Show that

$$\underset{\mathbf{U}}{\text{argmin}}\, \text{KL}(p|q) = \underset{\mathbf{U}}{\text{argmax}}\, \text{trace}\,(\mathbf{U}\mathbf{C}) - \log Z_q(\mathbf{U}), \qquad C_{ij} \equiv \left\langle x_i x_j \right\rangle_p. \tag{8.11.83}$$

2. Hence show that knowing the 'cross moment' matrix $\mathbf{C}$ of p is sufficient to fully specify p.
3. Generalise the above result to all models in the exponential family.

9 Learning as inference

In previous chapters we largely assumed that all distributions are fully specified for the inference tasks. In machine learning and related fields, however, the distributions need to be learned on the basis of data. Learning is then the problem of integrating data with domain knowledge of the model environment. In this chapter we discuss how learning can be phrased as an inference problem.

9.1 Learning as inference

9.1.1 Learning the bias of a coin

Consider data expressing the results of tossing a coin. We write $v^n = 1$ if on toss n the coin comes up heads, and $v^n = 0$ if it is tails. Our aim is to estimate the probability θ that the coin will be a head, $p(v^n = 1|\theta) = \theta$ – called the 'bias' of the coin. For a fair coin, $\theta = 0.5$. The variables in this environment are $v^1, \ldots, v^N$ and θ and we require a model of the probabilistic interaction of the variables, $p(v^1, \ldots, v^N, \theta)$. Assuming there is no dependence between the observed tosses, except through θ, we have the belief network

$$p(v^1, \ldots, v^N, \theta) = p(\theta) \prod_{n=1}^{N} p(v^n|\theta) \tag{9.1.1}$$

which is depicted in Fig. 9.1. The assumption that each observation is identically and independently distributed is called the i.i.d. assumption.

Learning refers to using the observations $v^1, \ldots, v^N$ to infer θ. In this context, our interest is

$$p(\theta|v^1, \ldots, v^N) = \frac{p(v^1, \ldots, v^N, \theta)}{p(v^1, \ldots, v^N)} = \frac{p(v^1, \ldots, v^N|\theta)p(\theta)}{p(v^1, \ldots, v^N)}. \tag{9.1.2}$$

We still need to fully specify the prior $p(\theta)$. To avoid complexities resulting from continuous variables, we'll consider a discrete θ with only three possible states, $\theta \in \{0.1, 0.5, 0.8\}$. Specifically, we assume

$$p(\theta = 0.1) = 0.15, \qquad p(\theta = 0.5) = 0.8, \qquad p(\theta = 0.8) = 0.05 \tag{9.1.3}$$

as shown in Fig. 9.2(a). This prior expresses that we have 80% belief that the coin is 'fair', 5% belief the coin is biased to land heads (with $\theta = 0.8$) and 15% belief the coin is biased to land tails

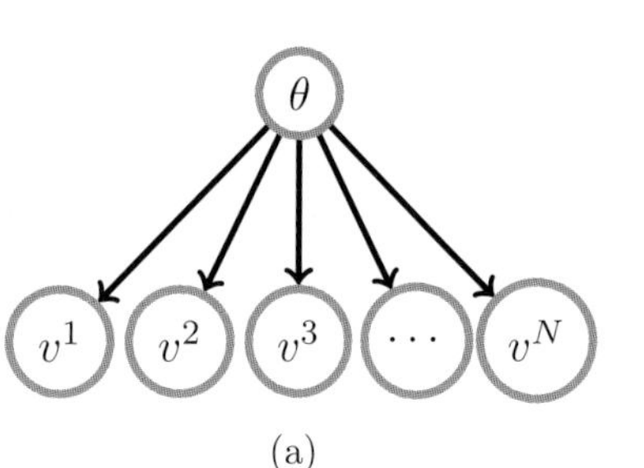

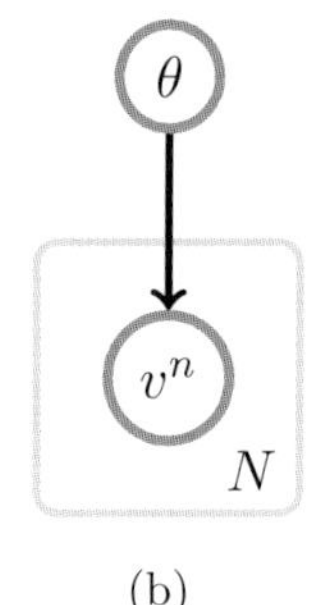

Figure 9.1 (**a**) Belief network for coin tossing model. (**b**) *Plate* notation equivalent of (a). A plate replicates the quantities inside the plate a number of times as specified in the plate.

(with $\theta = 0.1$). The distribution of θ given the data and our beliefs is

$$p(\theta|v^1, \ldots, v^N) \propto p(\theta) \prod_{n=1}^{N} p(v^n|\theta) = p(\theta) \prod_{n=1}^{N} \theta^{\mathbb{I}[v^n=1]} (1-\theta)^{\mathbb{I}[v^n=0]} \tag{9.1.4}$$

$$\propto p(\theta)\theta^{\sum_{n=1}^{N} \mathbb{I}[v^n=1]} (1-\theta)^{\sum_{n=1}^{N} \mathbb{I}[v^n=0]}. \tag{9.1.5}$$

In the above $\sum_{n=1}^{N} \mathbb{I}[v^n = 1]$ is the number of occurrences of heads, which we more conveniently denote as N_H. Likewise, $\sum_{n=1}^{N} \mathbb{I}[v^n = 0]$ is the number of tails, N_T. Hence

$$p(\theta|v^1, \ldots, v^N) \propto p(\theta)\theta^{N_H} (1-\theta)^{N_T}. \tag{9.1.6}$$

For an experiment with $N_H = 2$, $N_T = 8$, the posterior distribution is

$$p(\theta = 0.1|\mathcal{V}) = k \times 0.15 \times 0.1^2 \times 0.9^8 = k \times 6.46 \times 10^{-4} \tag{9.1.7}$$

$$p(\theta = 0.5|\mathcal{V}) = k \times 0.8 \times 0.5^2 \times 0.5^8 = k \times 7.81 \times 10^{-4} \tag{9.1.8}$$

$$p(\theta = 0.8|\mathcal{V}) = k \times 0.05 \times 0.8^2 \times 0.2^8 = k \times 8.19 \times 10^{-8} \tag{9.1.9}$$

where $\mathcal{V}$ is shorthand for $v^1, \ldots, v^N$. From the normalisation requirement we have $1/k = 6.46 \times 10^{-4} + 7.81 \times 10^{-4} + 8.19 \times 10^{-8} = 0.0014$, so that

$$p(\theta = 0.1|\mathcal{V}) = 0.4525, \qquad p(\theta = 0.5|\mathcal{V}) = 0.5475, \qquad p(\theta = 0.8|\mathcal{V}) = 0.0001 \tag{9.1.10}$$

as shown in Fig. 9.2(b). These are the 'posterior' parameter beliefs. In this case, if we were asked to choose a single a posteriori most likely value for θ, it would be $\theta = 0.5$, although our confidence in this is low since the posterior belief that $\theta = 0.1$ is also appreciable. This result is intuitive since, even though we observed more tails than heads, our prior belief was that it was more likely the coin is fair.

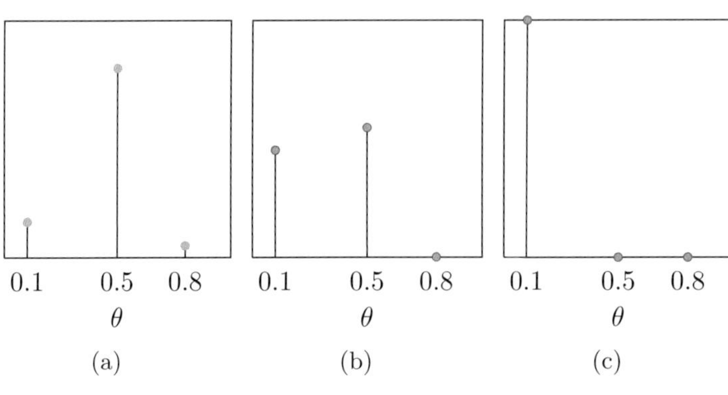

Figure 9.2 (**a**) Prior encoding our beliefs about the amount the coin is biased to heads. (**b**) Posterior having seen 2 heads and 8 tails. (**c**) Posterior having seen 20 heads and 80 tails.

Repeating the above with $N_H = 20$, $N_T = 80$, the posterior changes to

$$p(\theta = 0.1|\mathcal{V}) \approx 1 - 1.93 \times 10^{-6}, \qquad p(\theta = 0.5|\mathcal{V}) \approx 1.93 \times 10^{-6},$$
$$p(\theta = 0.8|\mathcal{V}) \approx 2.13 \times 10^{-35}. \tag{9.1.11}$$

Figure 9.2(c), so that the posterior belief in $\theta = 0.1$ dominates. This is reasonable since in this situation there are so many more tails than heads that this is unlikely to occur from a fair coin. Even though we a priori thought that the coin was fair, a posteriori we have enough evidence to change our minds.

9.1.2 Making decisions

In itself, the Bayesian posterior merely represents our beliefs and says nothing about how best to summarise these beliefs. In situations in which decisions need to be taken under uncertainty we need to additionally specify what the utility of any decision is, as in Chapter 7.

In the coin tossing scenario where θ is assumed to be either 0.1, 0.5 or 0.8, we set up a decision problem as follows: If we correctly state the bias of the coin we gain 10 points; being incorrect, however, loses 20 points. We can write this using

$$U(\theta, \theta^0) = 10\mathbb{I}\left[\theta = \theta^0\right] - 20\mathbb{I}\left[\theta \neq \theta^0\right] \tag{9.1.12}$$

where θ^0 is the true value for the bias. The expected utility of the decision that the coin is $\theta = 0.1$ is

$$U(\theta = 0.1) = U(\theta = 0.1, \theta^0 = 0.1)p(\theta^0 = 0.1|\mathcal{V})$$
$$+ U(\theta = 0.1, \theta^0 = 0.5)p(\theta^0 = 0.5|\mathcal{V}) + U(\theta = 0.1, \theta^0 = 0.8)p(\theta^0 = 0.8|\mathcal{V}). \tag{9.1.13}$$

Plugging in the numbers from Equation (9.1.10), we obtain

$$U(\theta = 0.1) = 10 \times 0.4525 - 20 \times 0.5475 - 20 \times 0.0001 = -6.4270. \tag{9.1.14}$$

Similarly

$$U(\theta = 0.5) = 10 \times 0.5475 - 20 \times 0.4525 - 20 \times 0.0001 = -3.5770 \tag{9.1.15}$$

and

$$U(\theta = 0.8) = 10 \times 0.0001 - 20 \times 0.4525 - 20 \times 0.5475 = -19.999. \tag{9.1.16}$$

The best (that with the highest utility) is to say that the coin is unbiased, $\theta = 0.5$.

Repeating the above calculations for $N_H = 20$, $N_T = 80$, we arrive at

$$U(\theta = 0.1) = 10 \times (1 - 1.93 \times 10^{-6}) - 20\left(1.93 \times 10^{-6} + 2.13 \times 10^{-35}\right) = 9.9999 \tag{9.1.17}$$
$$U(\theta = 0.5) = 10 \times 1.93 \times 10^{-6} - 20\left(1 - 1.93 \times 10^{-6} + 2.13 \times 10^{-35}\right) \approx -20.0 \tag{9.1.18}$$
$$U(\theta = 0.8) = 10 \times 2.13 \times 10^{-35} - 20\left(1 - 1.93 \times 10^{-6} + 1.93 \times 10^{-6}\right) \approx -20.0 \tag{9.1.19}$$

so that the best decision in this case is to choose $\theta = 0.1$.

As more information about the distribution $p(v, \theta)$ becomes available the posterior $p(\theta|\mathcal{V})$ becomes increasingly peaked, aiding our decision making process.

9.1.3 A continuum of parameters

In Section 9.1.1 we considered only three possible values for θ. Here we discuss a continuum of parameters.

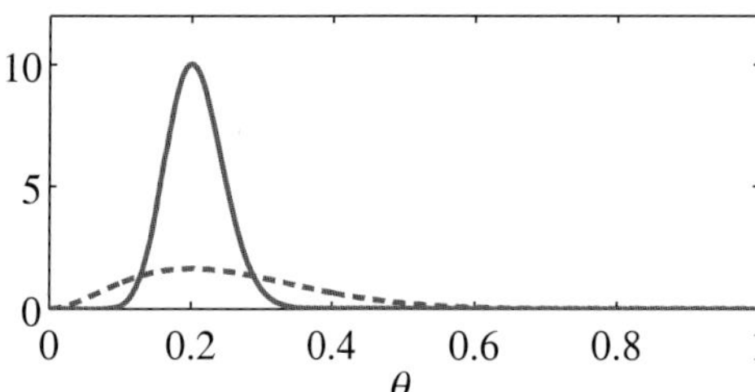

Figure 9.3 Posterior $p(\theta|\mathcal{V})$ assuming a flat prior on θ: (dashed) $N_H = 2$, $N_T = 8$ and (solid) $N_H = 20$, $N_T = 80$. In both cases, the most probable state of the posterior (maximum a posteriori) is 0.2, which makes intuitive sense, since the fraction of heads to tails in both cases is 0.2. Where there is more data, the posterior is more certain and sharpens around the most probable value.

Using a flat prior

We first examine the case of a 'flat' or *uniform* prior $p(\theta) = k$ for some constant k. For continuous variables, normalisation requires

$$\int p(\theta)d\theta = 1. \tag{9.1.20}$$

Since θ represents a probability we must have $0 \le \theta \le 1$,

$$\int_0^1 p(\theta)d\theta = k = 1. \tag{9.1.21}$$

Repeating the previous calculations with this flat continuous prior, we have

$$p(\theta|\mathcal{V}) = \frac{1}{c}\theta^{N_H}(1-\theta)^{N_T} \tag{9.1.22}$$

where c is a constant to be determined by normalisation,

$$c = \int_0^1 \theta^{N_H}(1-\theta)^{N_T}d\theta \equiv B(N_H+1, N_T+1) \tag{9.1.23}$$

where $B(\alpha, \beta)$ is the Beta function. See Fig. 9.3 for an example.

Using a conjugate prior

Determining the normalisation constant of a continuous distribution requires that the integral of the unnormalised posterior can be carried out. For the coin tossing case, it is clear that if the prior is of the form of a Beta distribution, then the posterior will be of the same parametric form. For prior

$$p(\theta) = \frac{1}{B(\alpha, \beta)}\theta^{\alpha-1}(1-\theta)^{\beta-1} \tag{9.1.24}$$

the posterior is

$$p(\theta|\mathcal{V}) \propto \theta^{\alpha-1}(1-\theta)^{\beta-1}\theta^{N_H}(1-\theta)^{N_T} \tag{9.1.25}$$

so that

$$p(\theta|\mathcal{V}) = B(\theta|\alpha+N_H, \beta+N_T). \tag{9.1.26}$$

The prior and posterior are of the same form (both Beta distributions) but simply with different parameters. Hence the Beta distribution is 'conjugate' to the Binomial distribution.

9.1.4 Decisions based on continuous intervals

To illustrate the use of continuous variables in decision making, we consider a simple decision problem. The result of a coin tossing experiment is $N_H = 2$ heads and $N_T = 8$ tails. You now need to make a decision: you win 10 dollars if you correctly guess which way the coin is biased – towards heads or tails. If your guess is incorrect, you lose a million dollars. What is your decision? (Assume an uninformative prior.)

We need two quantities, θ for our guess and θ^0 for the truth. Then the utility of saying heads is

$$U(\theta > 0.5, \theta^0 > 0.5)p(\theta^0 > 0.5|\mathcal{V}) + U(\theta > 0.5, \theta^0 < 0.5)p(\theta^0 < 0.5|\mathcal{V}). \tag{9.1.27}$$

In the above,

$$p(\theta^0 < 0.5|\mathcal{V}) = \int_0^{0.5} p(\theta^0|\mathcal{V})d\theta^0 \tag{9.1.28}$$

$$= \frac{1}{B(\alpha + N_H, \beta + N_T)} \int_0^{0.5} \theta^{\alpha+N_H-1} (1-\theta)^{\beta+N_T-1} \, d\theta \tag{9.1.29}$$

$$\equiv I_{0.5}(\alpha + N_H, \beta + N_T) \tag{9.1.30}$$

where $I_x(a, b)$ is the *regularised incomplete Beta function*. For the case of $N_H = 2$, $N_T = 8$, under a flat prior,

$$p(\theta^0 < 0.5|\mathcal{V}) = I_{0.5}(N_H + 1, N_T + 1) = 0.9673. \tag{9.1.31}$$

Since the events are exclusive, $p(\theta^0 \geq 0.5|\mathcal{V}) = 1 - 0.9673 = 0.0327$. Hence the expected utility of saying heads is more likely is

$$10 \times 0.0327 - 1\,000\,000 \times 0.9673 = -9.673 \times 10^5. \tag{9.1.32}$$

Similarly, the utility of saying tails is more likely can be computed to be

$$10 \times 0.9673 - 1\,000\,000 \times 0.0327 = -3.269 \times 10^4. \tag{9.1.33}$$

Since the expected utility of deciding 'tails' is highest, we are better off taking the decision that the coin is more likely to come up tails.

If we modify the above so that we lose 100 million dollars if we guess tails when in fact it is heads, the expected utility of saying tails would be -3.27×10^6. In this case, even though we are more confident that the coin is likely to come up tails, we would pay such a penalty of making a mistake in saying tails, that it is in fact better to say heads.

9.2 Bayesian methods and ML-II

Consider a parameterised distribution $p(v|\theta)$, for which we wish to the learn the optimal parameters θ given some data. The model $p(v|\theta)$ is depicted in Fig. 9.5(a), where a dot indicates that no distribution is present on that variable. For a single observed datapoint v, setting θ by maximum likelihood corresponds to finding the parameter θ that maximises $p(v|\theta)$.

In some cases we may have an idea about which parameters θ are more appropriate and can express this prior preference using a distribution $p(\theta)$. If the prior were fully specified, then there is nothing to 'learn' since $p(\theta|v)$ is now fully known. However, in many cases in practice, we are unsure of the exact parameter settings of the prior, and hence specify a parametersised prior using a distribution $p(\theta|\theta')$ with hyperparameter θ'. This is depicted in Fig. 9.5(b). Learning then

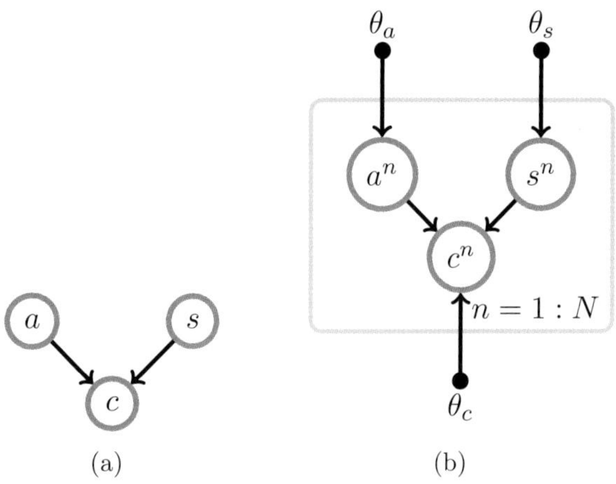

Figure 9.4 (**a**) A model for the relationship between lung Cancer, Asbestos exposure and Smoking. (**b**) Plate notation replicating the observed n datapoints with the CPTs tied across all datapoints.

corresponds to finding the optimal θ' that maximises the likelihood $p(v|\theta') = \int_\theta p(v|\theta)p(\theta|\theta')$. This is known as an ML-II procedure since it corresponds to maximum likelihood, but at the higher, hyperparameter level [33, 197]. By treating the parameters θ as variables, one can view this then as learning under hidden variables, for which the methods of Chapter 11 are applicable. We will encounter examples of this ML-II procedure later, for example in Section 18.1.2.

9.3 Maximum likelihood training of belief networks

Consider the following model of the relationship between exposure to asbestos (a), being a smoker (s) and the incidence of lung cancer (c)

$$p(a, s, c) = p(c|a, s)p(a)p(s) \tag{9.3.1}$$

which is depicted in Fig. 9.4(a). Each variable is binary, $\mathrm{dom}(a) = \{0, 1\}$, $\mathrm{dom}(s) = \{0, 1\}$, $\mathrm{dom}(c) = \{0, 1\}$. We assume that there is no direct relationship between smoking and exposure to asbestos. This is the kind of assumption that we may be able to elicit from medical experts. Furthermore, we assume that we have a list of patient records, Fig. 9.6, where each row represents a patient's data. To learn the table entries $p(c|a, s)$ we can do so by counting the number of times variable c is in state 1 for each of the four parental states of a and s:

$$\begin{aligned} &p(c = 1|a = 0, s = 0) = 0, && p(c = 1|a = 0, s = 1) = 0.5, \\ &p(c = 1|a = 1, s = 0) = 0.5, && p(c = 1|a = 1, s = 1) = 1. \end{aligned} \tag{9.3.2}$$

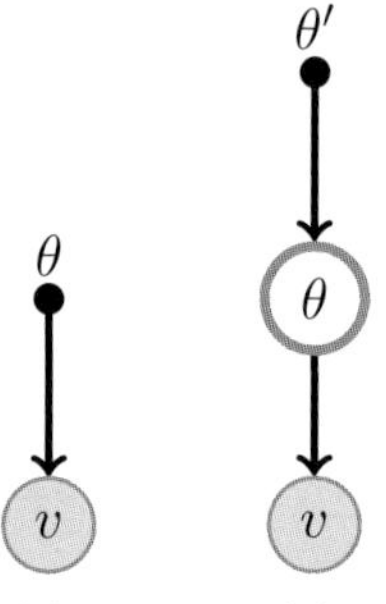

Figure 9.5 (**a**) Standard ML learning. The best parameter θ is found by maximising the probability that the model generates the observed data $\theta_{opt} = \arg\max_\theta p(v|\theta)$. (**b**) ML-II learning. In cases where we have a prior preference for the parameters θ, but with unspecified hyperparameter θ', we can find θ' by $\theta'_{opt} = \arg\max_{\theta'} p(v|\theta') = \arg\max_{\theta'} \langle p(v|\theta)\rangle_{p(\theta|\theta')}$.

a	s	c
1	1	1
1	0	0
0	1	1
0	1	0
1	1	1
0	0	0
1	0	1

Figure 9.6 A database containing information about the Asbestos exposure (1 signifies exposure), being a Smoker (1 signifies the individual is a smoker), and lung Cancer (1 signifies the individual has lung Cancer). Each row contains the information for each of the seven individuals in the database.

Similarly, based on counting, $p(a = 1) = 4/7$, and $p(s = 1) = 4/7$. These three CPTs then complete the full distribution specification.

Setting the CPT entries in this way by counting the relative number of occurrences corresponds mathematically to maximum likelihood learning under the i.i.d. assumption, as we show below.

Maximum likelihood corresponds to counting

For a BN there is a constraint on the form of $p(x)$, namely

$$p(x) = \prod_{i=1}^{K} p(x_i|\text{pa}\,(x_i)). \tag{9.3.3}$$

To compute the maximum likelihood setting of each term $p(x_i|\text{pa}\,(x_i))$, as shown in Section 8.7.3, we can equivalently minimise the Kullback–Leibler divergence between the empirical distribution $q(x)$ and $p(x)$. For the BN $p(x)$, and empirical distribution $q(x)$ we have

$$\text{KL}(q|p) = -\left\langle \sum_{i=1}^{K} \log p\,(x_i|\text{pa}\,(x_i)) \right\rangle_{q(x)} + \text{const.} = -\sum_{i=1}^{K} \langle \log p\,(x_i|\text{pa}\,(x_i)) \rangle_{q(x_i,\text{pa}(x_i))} + \text{const.} \tag{9.3.4}$$

This follows using the general result

$$\langle f(\mathcal{X}_i) \rangle_{q(\mathcal{X})} = \langle f(\mathcal{X}_i) \rangle_{q(\mathcal{X}_i)} \tag{9.3.5}$$

which says that if the function f only depends on a subset of the variables, we only need to know the marginal distribution of this subset of variables in order to carry out the average.

Since $q(x)$ is fixed, we can add on entropic terms in q and equivalently mimimise

$$\text{KL}(q|p) = \sum_{i=1}^{K} \left[\langle \log q(x_i|\text{pa}\,(x_i)) \rangle_{q(x_i,\text{pa}(x_i))} - \langle \log p\,(x_i|\text{pa}\,(x_i)) \rangle_{q(x_i,\text{pa}(x_i))} \right] \tag{9.3.6}$$

$$= \sum_{i=1}^{K} \langle \text{KL}(q(x_i|\text{pa}\,(x_i))|p(x_i|\text{pa}\,(x_i))) \rangle_{q(\text{pa}(x_i))}. \tag{9.3.7}$$

The final line is a positive weighted sum of individual Kullback–Leibler divergences. The minimal Kullback–Leibler setting, and that which corresponds to maximum likelihood, is therefore

$$p(x_i|\text{pa}\,(x_i)) = q(x_i|\text{pa}\,(x_i)). \tag{9.3.8}$$

In terms of the original data, this is

$$p(x_i = \mathsf{s}|\text{pa}\,(x_i) = \mathsf{t}) \propto \sum_{n=1}^{N} \mathbb{I}\left[x_i^n = \mathsf{s}, \text{pa}\,(x_i^n) = \mathsf{t}\right]. \tag{9.3.9}$$

This expression corresponds to the intuition that the table entry $p(x_i|\text{pa}(x_i))$ can be set by counting the number of times the state $\{x_i = \text{s}, \text{pa}(x_i) = \text{t}\}$ occurs in the dataset (where t is a vector of parental states). The table is then given by the relative number of counts of being in state s compared to the other states s′, for fixed joint parental state t.

An alternative method to derive this intuitive result is to use Lagrange multipliers, see Exercise 9.4. For readers less comfortable with the above Kullback–Leibler derivation, a more direct example is given below which makes use of the notation

$$\sharp(x_1 = s_1, x_2 = s_2, x_3 = s_3, \ldots) \tag{9.3.10}$$

to denote the number of times that states $x_1 = s_1, x_2 = s_2, x_3 = s_3, \ldots$ occur together in the training data. See also Section 10.1 for further examples.

Example 9.1

We wish to learn the table entries of the distribution $p(x_1, x_2, x_3) = p(x_1|x_2, x_3)p(x_2)p(x_3)$. We address here how to find the CPT entry $p(x_1 = 1|x_2 = 1, x_3 = 0)$ using maximum likelihood. For i.i.d. data, the contribution from $p(x_1|x_2, x_3)$ to the log likelihood is

$$\sum_n \log p(x_1^n|x_2^n, x_3^n).$$

The number of times $p(x_1 = 1|x_2 = 1, x_3 = 0)$ occurs in the log likelihood is $\sharp(x_1 = 1, x_2 = 1, x_3 = 0)$, the number of such occurrences in the training set. Since (by the normalisation constraint) $p(x_1 = 0|x_2 = 1, x_3 = 0) = 1 - p(x_1 = 1|x_2 = 1, x_3 = 0)$, the total contribution of $p(x_1 = 1|x_2 = 1, x_3 = 0)$ to the log likelihood is

$$\sharp(x_1 = 1, x_2 = 1, x_3 = 0) \log p(x_1 = 1|x_2 = 1, x_3 = 0) \\ + \sharp(x_1 = 0, x_2 = 1, x_3 = 0) \log(1 - p(x_1 = 1|x_2 = 1, x_3 = 0)). \tag{9.3.11}$$

Using $\theta \equiv p(x_1 = 1|x_2 = 1, x_3 = 0)$ we have

$$\sharp(x_1 = 1, x_2 = 1, x_3 = 0) \log \theta + \sharp(x_1 = 0, x_2 = 1, x_3 = 0) \log(1 - \theta). \tag{9.3.12}$$

Differentiating the above expression w.r.t. θ and equating to zero gives

$$\frac{\sharp(x_1 = 1, x_2 = 1, x_3 = 0)}{\theta} - \frac{\sharp(x_1 = 0, x_2 = 1, x_3 = 0)}{1 - \theta} = 0. \tag{9.3.13}$$

The solution for optimal θ is then

$$p(x_1 = 1|x_2 = 1, x_3 = 0) = \frac{\sharp(x_1 = 1, x_2 = 1, x_3 = 0)}{\sharp(x_1 = 1, x_2 = 1, x_3 = 0) + \sharp(x_1 = 0, x_2 = 1, x_3 = 0)}, \tag{9.3.14}$$

corresponding to the intuitive counting procedure.

Conditional probability functions

Consider a binary variable y with n binary parental variables, $\mathbf{x} = (x_1, \ldots, x_n)$, see Fig. 9.7. There are 2^n entries in the CPT of $p(y|x)$ so that it is infeasible to explicitly store these entries for even

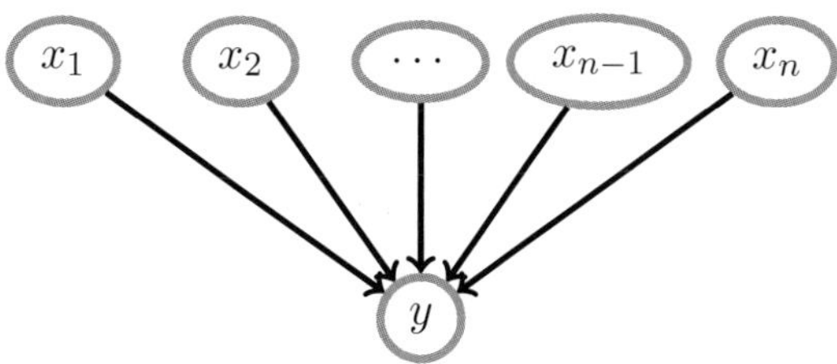

Figure 9.7 A variable y with a large number of parents $x_1, \ldots, x_n$ requires the specification of an exponentially large number of entries in the conditional probability $p(y|x_1, \ldots, x_n)$. One solution to this difficulty is to parameterise the conditional, $p(y|x_1, \ldots, x_n, \theta)$.

moderate values of n. To reduce the complexity of this CPT we may constrain the form of the table. For example, one could use a function

$$p(y = 1|\mathbf{x}, \mathbf{w}) = \frac{1}{1 + e^{-\mathbf{w}^\mathsf{T}\mathbf{x}}} \tag{9.3.15}$$

where we only need to specify the n-dimensional parameter vector $\mathbf{w}$.

In this case, rather than using maximum likelihood to learn the entries of the CPTs directly, we instead learn the value of the parameter $\mathbf{w}$. Since the number of parameters in $\mathbf{w}$ is small (n, compared with 2^n in the unconstrained case), we also have some hope that with a small number of training examples we can learn a reliable value for $\mathbf{w}$.

Example 9.2

Consider the following 3-variable model $p(x_1, x_2, x_3) = p(x_1|x_2, x_3)p(x_2)p(x_3)$, where $x_i \in \{0, 1\}, i = 1, 2, 3$. We assume that the CPT is parameterised using $\theta = (\theta_1, \theta_2)$ with

$$p(x_1 = 1|x_2, x_3, \theta) \equiv e^{-\theta_1^2 - \theta_2^2(x_2 - x_3)^2}. \tag{9.3.16}$$

One may verify that the above probability is always positive and lies between 0 and 1. Due to normalisation, we must have

$$p(x_1 = 0|x_2, x_3) = 1 - p(x_1 = 1|x_2, x_3). \tag{9.3.17}$$

For unrestricted $p(x_2)$ and $p(x_3)$, the maximum likelihood setting is $p(x_2 = 1) \propto \sharp\,(x_2 = 1)$, and $p(x_3 = 1) \propto \sharp\,(x_3 = 1)$. The contribution to the log likelihood from the term $p(x_1|x_2, x_3, \theta)$, assuming i.i.d. data, is

$$L(\theta_1, \theta_2) = \sum_{n=1}^{N} \mathbb{I}\left[x_1^n = 1\right]\left(-\theta_1^2 - \theta_2^2(x_2^n - x_3^n)^2\right) + \mathbb{I}\left[x_1^n = 0\right]\log\left(1 - e^{-\theta_1^2 - \theta_2^2(x_2^n - x_3^n)^2}\right). \tag{9.3.18}$$

This objective function needs to be optimised numerically to find the best θ_1 and θ_2. The gradient is

$$\frac{dL}{d\theta_1} = \sum_{n=1}^{N} -2\mathbb{I}\left[x_1^n = 1\right]\theta_1 + 2\mathbb{I}\left[x_1^n = 0\right]\frac{\theta_1 e^{-\theta_1^2 - \theta_2^2(x_2^n - x_3^n)^2}}{1 - e^{-\theta_1^2 - \theta_2^2(x_2^n - x_3^n)^2}}, \tag{9.3.19}$$

$$\frac{dL}{d\theta_2} = \sum_{n=1}^{N} -2\mathbb{I}\left[x_1^n = 1\right]\theta_2\left(x_2^n - x_3^n\right)^2 + 2\theta_2\mathbb{I}\left[x_1^n = 0\right]\frac{(x_2^n - x_3^n)^2 e^{-\theta_1^2 - \theta_2^2(x_2^n - x_3^n)^2}}{1 - e^{-\theta_1^2 - \theta_2^2(x_2^n - x_3^n)^2}}. \tag{9.3.20}$$

The gradient can be used as part of a standard optimisation procedure (such as conjugate gradients, see Appendix A) to find the maximum likelihood parameters θ_1, θ_2.

9.4 Bayesian belief network training

An alternative to maximum likelihood training of a BN is to use a Bayesian approach in which we maintain a distribution over parameters. We continue with the Asbestos, Smoking, Cancer scenario,

$$p(a, c, s) = p(c|a, s)p(a)p(s) \tag{9.4.1}$$

as represented in Fig. 9.4(a). So far we've only specified the independence structure, but not the entries of the tables $p(c|a, s)$, $p(a)$, $p(s)$. Given a set of visible observations, $\mathcal{V} = \{(a^n, s^n, c^n), n = 1, \ldots, N\}$, we would like to learn appropriate distributions for the table entries.

To begin we need a notation for the table entries. With all variables binary we have parameters such as

$$p(a = 1|\theta_a) = \theta_a, \quad p(c = 1|a = 0, s = 1, \theta_c) = \theta_c^{0,1} \tag{9.4.2}$$

and similarly for the remaining parameters $\theta_c^{1,1}, \theta_c^{0,0}, \theta_c^{1,0}$. For our example, the parameters are

$$\theta_a, \theta_s, \underbrace{\theta_c^{0,0}, \theta_c^{0,1}, \theta_c^{1,0}, \theta_c^{1,1}}_{\theta_c}. \tag{9.4.3}$$

In the following section, Section 9.4.1, we describe first useful independence assumptions on the general form of the prior variables, before making a specific numerical prior specification in Section 9.4.2.

9.4.1 Global and local parameter independence

In Bayesian learning of BNs, we need to specify a prior on the joint table entries. Since in general dealing with multi-dimensional continuous distributions is computationally problematic, it is useful to specify only uni-variate distributions in the prior. As we show below, this has a pleasing consequence that for i.i.d. data the posterior also factorises into uni-variate distributions.

Global parameter independence

A convenient assumption is that the prior factorises over parameters. For our Asbestos, Smoking, Cancer example, we assume

$$p(\theta_a, \theta_s, \theta_c) = p(\theta_a)p(\theta_s)p(\theta_c). \tag{9.4.4}$$

Assuming the data is i.i.d., we then have the joint model

$$p(\theta_a, \theta_s, \theta_c, \mathcal{V}) = p(\theta_a)p(\theta_s)p(\theta_c) \prod_n p(a^n|\theta_a)p(s^n|\theta_s)p(c^n|s^n, a^n, \theta_c) \tag{9.4.5}$$

the belief network for which is given in Fig. 9.8.

A convenience of the factorised prior for a BN is that the posterior also factorises, since

$$\begin{aligned} p(\theta_a, \theta_s, \theta_c|\mathcal{V}) &\propto p(\theta_a, \theta_s, \theta_c, \mathcal{V}) \\ &= \left\{p(\theta_a)\prod_n p(a^n|\theta_a)\right\}\left\{p(\theta_s)\prod_n p(s^n|\theta_s)\right\}\left\{p(\theta_c)\prod_n p(c^n|s^n, a^n, \theta_c)\right\} \\ &\propto p(\theta_a|\mathcal{V}_a)p(\theta_s|\mathcal{V}_s)p(\theta_c|\mathcal{V}_c) \end{aligned} \tag{9.4.6}$$

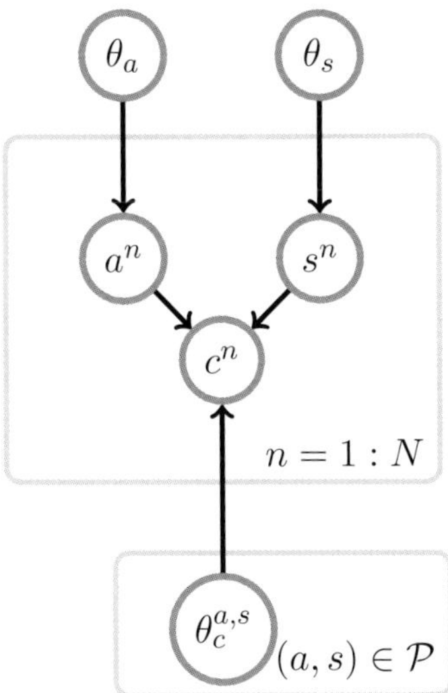

Figure 9.8 A Bayesian parameter model for the relationship between lung Cancer, Asbestos exposure and Smoking with factorised parameter priors. The global parameter independence assumption means that the prior over tables factorises into priors over each conditional probability table. The local independence assumption, which in this case comes into effect only for $p(c|a, s)$, means that $p(\theta_c)$ factorises in $\prod_{a,s\in\mathcal{P}} p(\theta_c^{a,s})$, where $\mathcal{P} = \{(0,0), (0,1), (1,0), (1,1)\}$.

so that one can consider each parameter posterior separately. In this case, 'learning' involves computing the posterior distributions $p(\theta_i|\mathcal{V}_i)$ where $\mathcal{V}_i$ is the set of training data restricted to the family of variable i.

The global independence assumption conveniently results in a posterior distribution that factorises over the conditional tables. However, the parameter θ_c is itself four dimensional. To simplify this we need to make a further assumption as to the structure of each local table.

Local parameter independence

If we further assume that the prior for the table factorises over all states a, c:

$$p(\theta_c) = p(\theta_c^{0,0})p(\theta_c^{1,0})p(\theta_c^{0,1})p(\theta_c^{1,1}) \tag{9.4.7}$$

then the posterior is given by

$$\begin{aligned} p(\theta_c|\mathcal{V}_c) &\propto p(\mathcal{V}_c|\theta_c)p(\theta_c^{0,0})p(\theta_c^{1,0})p(\theta_c^{0,1})p(\theta_c^{1,1}) \\ &= \underbrace{\left[\theta_c^{0,0}\right]^{\sharp(a=0,s=0,c=1)}\left[1-\theta_c^{0,0}\right]^{\sharp(a=0,s=0,c=0)} p(\theta_c^{0,0})}_{\propto p(\theta_c^{0,0}|\mathcal{V}_c)} \underbrace{\left[\theta_c^{0,1}\right]^{\sharp(a=0,s=1,c=1)}\left[1-\theta_c^{0,1}\right]^{\sharp(a=0,s=1,c=0)} p(\theta_c^{0,1})}_{\propto p(\theta_c^{0,1}|\mathcal{V}_c)} \\ &\times \underbrace{\left[\theta_c^{1,0}\right]^{\sharp(a=1,s=0,c=1)}\left[1-\theta_c^{1,0}\right]^{\sharp(a=1,s=0,c=0)} p(\theta_c^{1,0})}_{\propto p(\theta_c^{1,0}|\mathcal{V}_c)} \underbrace{\left[\theta_c^{1,1}\right]^{\sharp(a=1,s=1,c=1)}\left[1-\theta_c^{1,1}\right]^{\sharp(a=1,s=1,c=0)} p(\theta_c^{1,1})}_{\propto p(\theta_c^{1,1}|\mathcal{V}_c)} \end{aligned} \tag{9.4.8}$$

so that the posterior also factorises over the parental states of the local conditional table.

Posterior marginal table

A marginal probability table is given by, for example,

$$p(c=1|a=1, s=0, \mathcal{V}) = \int_{\theta_c} p(c=1|a=1, s=0, \theta_c^{1,0})p(\theta_c|\mathcal{V}_c). \tag{9.4.9}$$

The integral over all the other tables in Equation (9.4.9) is unity, and we are left with

$$p(c = 1|a = 1, s = 0, \mathcal{V}) = \int_{\theta_c^{1,0}} p(c = 1|a = 1, s = 0, \theta_c^{1,0}) p(\theta_c^{1,0}|\mathcal{V}_c) = \int_{\theta_c^{1,0}} \theta_c^{1,0} p(\theta_c^{1,0}|\mathcal{V}_c). \tag{9.4.10}$$

9.4.2 Learning binary variable tables using a Beta prior

We continue the example of Section 9.4.1 where all variables are binary, but using a continuous valued table prior. The simplest case is to start with $p(a|\theta_a)$ since this requires only a univariate prior distribution $p(\theta_a)$. The likelihood depends on the table variable via

$$p(a = 1|\theta_a) = \theta_a \tag{9.4.11}$$

so that the total likelihood term is

$$\theta_a^{\sharp(a=1)} (1 - \theta_a)^{\sharp(a=0)}. \tag{9.4.12}$$

The posterior is therefore

$$p(\theta_a|\mathcal{V}_a) \propto p(\theta_a) \theta_a^{\sharp(a=1)} (1 - \theta_a)^{\sharp(a=0)}. \tag{9.4.13}$$

This means that if the prior is also of the form $\theta_a^{\alpha} (1 - \theta_a)^{\beta}$ then conjugacy will hold, and the mathematics of integration will be straightforward. This suggests that the most convenient choice is a Beta distribution,

$$p(\theta_a) = B(\theta_a|\alpha_a, \beta_a) = \frac{1}{B(\alpha_a, \beta_a)} \theta_a^{\alpha_a - 1} (1 - \theta_a)^{\beta_a - 1}, \tag{9.4.14}$$

for which the posterior is also a Beta distribution:

$$p(\theta_a|\mathcal{V}_a) = B(\theta_a|\alpha_a + \sharp(a = 1), \beta_a + \sharp(a = 0)). \tag{9.4.15}$$

The marginal table is given by (following similar reasoning as for Equation (9.4.11))

$$p(a = 1|\mathcal{V}_a) = \int_{\theta_a} p(\theta_a|\mathcal{V}_a) \theta_a = \frac{\alpha_a + \sharp(a = 1)}{\alpha_a + \sharp(a = 1) + \beta_a + \sharp(a = 0)} \tag{9.4.16}$$

using the result for the mean of a Beta distribution, Definition 8.23.

The situation for the table $p(c|a, s)$ is slightly more complex since we need to specify a prior for each of the parental tables. As above, this is most convenient if we specify a Beta prior, one for each of the (four) parental states. Let's look at a specific table

$$p(c = 1|a = 1, s = 0). \tag{9.4.17}$$

Assuming the local independence property, we have $p(\theta_c^{1,0}|\mathcal{V}_c)$ given by

$$B\left(\theta_c^{1,0}|\alpha_c(a = 1, s = 0) + \sharp(c = 1, a = 1, s = 0), \beta_c(a = 1, s = 0) + \sharp(c = 0, a = 1, s = 0)\right). \tag{9.4.18}$$

As before, the marginal probability table is then given by

$$p(c = 1|a = 1, s = 0, \mathcal{V}_c) = \frac{\alpha_c(a = 1, s = 0) + \sharp(c = 1, a = 1, s = 0)}{\alpha_c(a = 1, s = 0) + \beta_c(a = 1, s = 0) + \sharp(a = 1, s = 0)} \tag{9.4.19}$$

since $\sharp(a = 1, s = 0) = \sharp(c = 0, a = 1, s = 0) + \sharp(c = 1, a = 1, s = 0)$.

The prior parameters $\alpha_c(a, s)$ are called *hyperparameters*. A complete ignorance prior would correspond to setting $\alpha = \beta = 1$, see Fig. 8.4.

It is instructive to examine this Bayesian solution under various conditions:

No data limit $N \to 0$ In the limit of no data, the marginal probability table corresponds to the prior, which is given in this case by

$$p(c = 1|a = 1, s = 0) = \frac{\alpha_c(a = 1, s = 0)}{\alpha_c(a = 1, s = 0) + \beta_c(a = 1, s = 0)}. \tag{9.4.20}$$

For a flat prior $\alpha = \beta = 1$ for all states a, c, this would give a prior probability of $p(c = 1|a = 1, s = 0) = 0.5$.

Infinite data limit $N \to \infty$ In this limit the marginal probability tables are dominated by the data counts, since these will typically grow in proportion to the size of the dataset. This means that in the infinite (or very large) data limit,

$$p(c = 1|a = 1, s = 0, \mathcal{V}) \to \frac{\sharp(c = 1, a = 1, s = 0)}{\sharp(c = 1, a = 1, s = 0) + \sharp(c = 0, a = 1, s = 0)} \tag{9.4.21}$$

which corresponds to the maximum likelihood solution.

This effect that the large data limit of a Bayesian procedure corresponds to the maximum likelihood solution is general unless the prior has a pathologically strong effect.

Zero hyperparameter limit When $\alpha_c = \beta_c = 0$, the marginal table equation (9.3.20) corresponds to the maximum likelihood setting for any amount of data. When $\alpha_c = \beta_c = 0$, the Beta distributrion places mass 0.5 at 0 and mass 0.5 at 1. Note that this equivalence of the maximum likelihood solution with the marginal table under zero hyperparameter values contrasts with the equivalence of the MAP table under uniform hyperparameter values.

Example 9.3 Asbestos–Smoking–Cancer

Consider the binary variable network

$$p(c, a, s) = p(c|a, s)p(a)p(s) \tag{9.4.22}$$

The data $\mathcal{V}$ is given in Fig. 9.6. Using a flat Beta prior $\alpha = \beta = 1$ for all conditional probability tables, the marginal posterior tables are given by

$$p(a = 1|\mathcal{V}) = \frac{1 + \sharp(a = 1)}{2 + N} = \frac{1 + 4}{2 + 7} = \frac{5}{9} \approx 0.556. \tag{9.4.23}$$

By comparison, the maximum likelihood setting is $4/7 = 0.571$. The Bayesian result is a little more cautious, which squares with our prior belief that any setting of the probability is equally likely, pulling the posterior towards 0.5.

Similarly,

$$p(s = 1|\mathcal{V}) = \frac{1 + \sharp(s = 1)}{2 + N} = \frac{1 + 4}{2 + 7} = \frac{5}{9} \approx 0.556 \tag{9.4.24}$$

and

$$p(c=1|a=1,s=1,\mathcal{V}) = \frac{1+\sharp(c=1,a=1,s=1)}{2+\sharp(c=1,a=1,s=1)+\sharp(c=0,a=1,s=1)} = \frac{1+2}{2+2} = \frac{3}{4} \tag{9.4.25}$$

$$p(c=1|a=1,s=0,\mathcal{V}) = \frac{1+\sharp(c=1,a=1,s=0)}{2+\sharp(c=1,a=1,s=0)+\sharp(c=0,a=1,s=0)} = \frac{1+1}{2+1} = \frac{2}{3} \tag{9.4.26}$$

$$p(c=1|a=0,s=1,\mathcal{V}) = \frac{1+\sharp(c=1,a=0,s=1)}{2+\sharp(c=1,a=0,s=1)+\sharp(c=0,a=0,s=1)} = \frac{1+1}{2+2} = \frac{1}{2} \tag{9.4.27}$$

$$p(c=1|a=0,s=0,\mathcal{V}) = \frac{1+\sharp(c=1,a=0,s=0)}{2+\sharp(c=1,a=0,s=0)+\sharp(c=0,a=0,s=0)} = \frac{1+0}{2+1} = \frac{1}{3}. \tag{9.4.28}$$

9.4.3 Learning multivariate discrete tables using a Dirichlet prior

The natural generalisation to our discussion of Bayesian learning of BNs is to consider variables that can take more than two states. In this case the natural conjugate prior is given by the Dirichlet distribution, which generalises the Beta distribution to more than two states. Again we assume throughout i.i.d. data and the local and global parameter prior independencies. Since under the global parameter independence assumption the posterior factorises over variables (as in Equation (9.4.6)), we can concentrate on the posterior of a single variable.

No parents

Let's consider a variable v with $\text{dom}(v) = \{1, \ldots, I\}$. If we denote the probability of v being in state i by θ_i, i.e. $p(v = i|\boldsymbol{\theta}) = \theta_i$, the contribution to the posterior from a datapoint v^n is

$$p(v^n|\boldsymbol{\theta}) = \prod_{i=1}^{I} \theta_i^{\mathbb{I}[v^n=i]}, \qquad \sum_{i=1}^{I} \theta_i = 1 \tag{9.4.29}$$

so that the posterior for $\boldsymbol{\theta}$ given a dataset $\mathcal{V} = \{v^1, \ldots, v^N\}$

$$p(\boldsymbol{\theta}|\mathcal{V}) \propto p(\boldsymbol{\theta}) \prod_{n=1}^{N} \prod_{i=1}^{I} \theta_i^{\mathbb{I}[v^n=i]} = p(\boldsymbol{\theta}) \prod_{i=1}^{I} \theta_i^{\sum_{n=1}^{N} \mathbb{I}[v^n=i]}. \tag{9.4.30}$$

It is convenient to use a Dirichlet prior distribution with hyperparameters $\mathbf{u}$

$$p(\boldsymbol{\theta}) = \text{Dirichlet}(\boldsymbol{\theta}|\mathbf{u}) \propto \prod_{i=1}^{I} \theta_i^{u_i-1}. \tag{9.4.31}$$

Using this prior the posterior becomes

$$p(\boldsymbol{\theta}|\mathcal{V}) \propto \prod_{i=1}^{I} \theta_i^{u_i-1} \prod_{i=1}^{I} \theta_i^{\sum_{n=1}^{N} \mathbb{I}[v^n=i]} = \prod_{i=1}^{I} \theta_i^{u_i-1+\sum_{n=1}^{N} \mathbb{I}[v^n=i]} \tag{9.4.32}$$

which means that the posterior is given by

$$p(\boldsymbol{\theta}|\mathcal{V}) = \text{Dirichlet}\,(\boldsymbol{\theta}|\mathbf{u}+\mathbf{c}) \tag{9.4.33}$$

where $\mathbf{c}$ is a count vector with components

$$c_i = \sum_{n=1}^{N} \mathbb{I}\left[v^n = i\right] \tag{9.4.34}$$

being the number of times state i was observed in the training data.

The marginal table is given by integrating

$$p(v=i|\mathcal{V}) = \int_{\boldsymbol{\theta}} p(v=i|\boldsymbol{\theta})p(\boldsymbol{\theta}|\mathcal{V}) = \int_{\theta_i} \theta_i p(\theta_i|\mathcal{V}). \tag{9.4.35}$$

The single-variable marginal distribution of a Dirichlet is a Beta distribution,

$$p(\theta_i|\mathcal{V}) = B\left(\theta_i|u_i+c_i, \sum_{j\neq i} u_j + c_j\right). \tag{9.4.36}$$

The marginal table is then given by the mean of the Beta distribution

$$p(v=i|\mathcal{V}) = \frac{u_i+c_i}{\sum_j u_j + c_j} \tag{9.4.37}$$

which generalises the binary state formula Equation (9.4.16).

Parents

To deal with the general case of a variable v with parents $\text{pa}\,(v)$ we denote the probability of v being in state i, conditioned on the parents being in state j as

$$p(v=i|\text{pa}\,(v)=j,\boldsymbol{\theta}) = \theta_i(v;j) \tag{9.4.38}$$

where $\sum_i \theta_i(v;j) = 1$. This forms the components of a vector $\boldsymbol{\theta}(v;j)$. Note that if v has K parents then the number of parental states S will be exponential in K.

Writing $\boldsymbol{\theta}(v) = [\boldsymbol{\theta}(v;1),\ldots,\boldsymbol{\theta}(v;S)]$, local (parental state) independence means

$$p(\boldsymbol{\theta}(v)) = \prod_j p(\boldsymbol{\theta}(v;j)). \tag{9.4.39}$$

and global independence means

$$p(\boldsymbol{\theta}) = \prod_v p(\boldsymbol{\theta}(v)) \tag{9.4.40}$$

where $\boldsymbol{\theta} = (\boldsymbol{\theta}(v), v=1,\ldots,V)$ represents the combined table of all the variables.

a	s	c
1	1	2
1	0	0
0	1	1
0	1	0
1	1	2
0	0	0
1	0	1

Figure 9.9 A database of patient records about Asbestos exposure (1 signifies exposure), being a Smoker (1 signifies the individual is a smoker), and lung Cancer (0 signifies no cancer, 1 signifies early stage cancer, 2 signifies late state cancer). Each row contains the information for each of the seven individuals in the database.

Parameter posterior

Thanks to the global parameter independence assumption the posterior factorises, with one posterior table per variable. Each posterior table for a variable v depends only on the data $\mathcal{D}(v)$ of the family of the variable. Assuming a Dirichlet distribution prior

$$p(\boldsymbol{\theta}(v;j)) = \text{Dirichlet}\left(\boldsymbol{\theta}(v;j)|\mathbf{u}(v;j)\right) \tag{9.4.41}$$

the posterior is also Dirichlet

$$p(\boldsymbol{\theta}(v)|\mathcal{D}(v)) = \prod_j \text{Dirichlet}\left(\boldsymbol{\theta}(v;j)|\mathbf{u}'(v;j)\right) \tag{9.4.42}$$

where the hyperparameter prior term is updated by the observed counts,

$$u'_i(v;j) \equiv u_i(v;j) + \sharp\left(v=i, \text{pa}\left(v\right)=j\right). \tag{9.4.43}$$

By analogy with the no-parents case, the marginal table is given by

$$p(v=i|\text{pa}\left(v\right)=j, \mathcal{D}(v)) \propto u'_i(v;j). \tag{9.4.44}$$

Example 9.4

Consider the $p(c|a,s)p(s)p(a)$ asbestos example with $\text{dom}\left(a\right) = \text{dom}\left(s\right) = \{0,1\}$, except now with the variable c taking three states, $\text{dom}\left(c\right) = \{0,1,2\}$, accounting for different kinds of cancer, see Fig. 9.9. The marginal table under a Dirichlet prior is then given by, for example

$$p(c=0|a=1,s=1,\mathcal{V}) = \frac{u_0(a=1,s=1) + \sharp\left(c=0,a=1,s=1\right)}{\sum_{i\in\{0,1,2\}} u_i(a=1,s=1) + \sharp\left(c=i,a=1,s=1\right)}. \tag{9.4.45}$$

Assuming a flat Dirichlet prior, which corresponds to setting all components of $\mathbf{u}$ to 1, this gives

$$p(c=0|a=1,s=1,\mathcal{V}) = \frac{1+0}{3+2} = \frac{1}{5} \tag{9.4.46}$$

$$p(c=1|a=1,s=1,\mathcal{V}) = \frac{1+0}{3+2} = \frac{1}{5} \tag{9.4.47}$$

$$p(c=2|a=1,s=1,\mathcal{V}) = \frac{1+2}{3+2} = \frac{3}{5} \tag{9.4.48}$$

and similarly for the other three tables $p(c|a=1,s=0)$, $p(c|a=0,s=1)$, $p(c|a=1,s=1)$.

Model likelihood

For a variable v, and i.i.d. data $\mathcal{D}(v) = \{(v^n|\text{pa}(v^n)), n = 1, \ldots, N\}$ for the family of this variable,

$$\prod_n p(v^n|\text{pa}(v^n)) = \int_{\boldsymbol{\theta}(v)} p(\boldsymbol{\theta}(v)) \prod_n p(v^n|\text{pa}(v^n), \boldsymbol{\theta}(v)) \tag{9.4.49}$$

$$= \int_{\boldsymbol{\theta}(v)} \left\{ \prod_j \frac{1}{Z(\mathbf{u}(v;j))} \prod_i \theta_i(v;j)^{u_i(v;j)-1} \right\} \prod_n \prod_j \prod_i \theta_i(v;j)^{\mathbb{I}[v^n=i,\text{pa}(v^n)=j]} \tag{9.4.50}$$

$$= \prod_j \frac{1}{Z(\mathbf{u}(v;j))} \int_{\boldsymbol{\theta}(v;j)} \prod_i \theta_i(v;j)^{u_i(v;j)-1+\sharp(v=i,\text{pa}(v)=j)} \tag{9.4.51}$$

$$= \prod_j \frac{Z(\mathbf{u}'(v;j))}{Z(\mathbf{u}(v;j))} \tag{9.4.52}$$

where $Z(\mathbf{u})$ is the normalisation constant of a Dirichlet distribution with hyperparameters $\mathbf{u}$; $\mathbf{u}'$ is as given in Equation (9.4.43).

For a belief network on variables $\mathbf{v} = (v_1, \ldots, v_D)$ the joint probability of all variables factorises into the local probabilities of each variable conditioned on its parents. The likelihood of a complete set of i.i.d. data $\mathcal{D} = \{\mathbf{v}^1, \ldots, \mathbf{v}^N\}$ is then given by:

$$p(\mathcal{D}) = \prod_k \prod_n p(v_k^n|\text{pa}(v_k^n)) = \prod_k \prod_j \frac{Z(\mathbf{u}'(v_k;j))}{Z(\mathbf{u}(v_k;j))} \tag{9.4.53}$$

where $\mathbf{u}'$ is given by Equation (9.4.43). Expression (9.4.53) can be written explicitly in terms of Gamma functions, see Exercise 9.9. In the above expression in general the number of parental states differs for each variable v_k, so that implicit in the above formula is that the state product over j goes from 1 to the number of parental states of variable v_k. Due to the local and global parameter independence assumptions, the logarithm of the model likelihood is a product of terms, one for each variable v_k and parental configuration j. This is called the *likelihood decomposable* property.

9.5 Structure learning

Up to this point we have assumed that we are given both the structure of the distribution and a dataset $\mathcal{D}$. A more complex task is when we need to learn the structure of the network as well. We'll consider the case in which the data is complete (i.e. there are no missing observations). Since for D variables, there is an exponentially large number (in D) of BN structures, it's clear that we cannot search over all possible structures. For this reason structure learning is a computationally challenging problem and we must rely on constraints and heuristics to help guide the search. Whilst in general structure learning is intractable, a celebrated tractable special case is when the network is constrained to have at most one parent, see Section 9.5.4.

For all but the sparsest networks, estimating the dependencies to any accuracy requires a large amount of data, making testing of dependencies difficult. Consider the following simple situation of two independent variables, $p(x, y) = p(x)p(y)$. Based on a finite sample from this joint distribution $\mathcal{D} = \{(x^n, y^n), n = 1, \ldots, N\}$, we want to try to understand if x is independent of y. One way to do this is to compute the empirical mutual information $I(x, y)$; if this is zero then, empirically, x and y are independent. However, for a finite amount of data, two variables will typically have non-zero

Algorithm 9.1 PC algorithm for skeleton learning.

Start with a complete undirected graph G on the set $\mathcal{V}$ of all vertices.
$i = 0$
repeat
    for $x \in \mathcal{V}$ **do**
        for $y \in Adj\{x\}$ **do**
            Determine if there is a subset $\mathcal{S}$ of size i of the neighbours of x (not including y) for which $x \perp\!\!\!\perp y | \mathcal{S}$. If this set exists remove the x–y link from the graph G and set $\mathcal{S}_{xy} = \mathcal{S}$.
        end for
    end for
    $i = i + 1$.
until all nodes have $\leq i$ neighbours.

---

mutual information, so that a threshold needs to be set to decide if the measured dependence is significant under the finite sample, see Section 9.5.2.

Other complexities arise from the concern that a Belief or Markov Network on the visible variables alone may not be a parsimonious way to represent the observed data if, for example, there may be latent variables which are driving the observed dependencies. We will not enter into such issues in our discussion here and limit the presentation to two central approaches, one which attempts to make a network structure consistent with local empirical dependencies (the PC algorithm), and one which builds a structure that is most probable for the global data (network scoring).

9.5.1 PC algorithm

The PC algorithm [274] first learns the skeleton of a graph, after which edges may be oriented to form a (partially oriented) DAG. The procedure to learn the skeleton is based on using the empirical data to test if two variables are independent. A variety of approaches can be used to ascertain independence, as described in Section 9.5.2.

The PC algorithm begins at the first round with a complete skeleton G and attempts to remove as many links as possible. At the first step we test all pairs $x \perp\!\!\!\perp y | \emptyset$. If an x and y pair are deemed independent then the link x–y is removed from the complete graph. One repeats this for all the pairwise links. In the second round, for the remaining graph, one examines each x–y link and conditions on a single neighbour z of x. If $x \perp\!\!\!\perp y | z$ then remove the link x–y. One repeats in this way through all the variables. At each round the number of neighbours in the conditioning set is increased by one. See Algorithm 9.1, Fig. 9.10 and `demoPCoracle.m`.[1] A refinement of this algorithm, known as NPC for necessary path PC [276] limit the number of independence checks to remove inconsistencies resulting from the empirical estimates of conditional mutual information.

Given a learned skeleton, a partial DAG can be constructed using Algorithm 9.2. Note that this is necessary since the undirected graph G is a skeleton – not a belief network of the independence assumptions discovered. For example, we may have a graph G with x–z–y in which the x–y link was removed on the basis $x \perp\!\!\!\perp y | \emptyset \rightarrow \mathcal{S}_{xy} = \emptyset$. As an MN the graph x–z–y (graphically) implies $x \top\!\!\!\top y$, although this is inconsistent with the discovery in the first round $x \perp\!\!\!\perp y$. This is the reason for the orientation part: for consistency, we must have $x \rightarrow z \leftarrow y$, for which $x \perp\!\!\!\perp y$ and $x \top\!\!\!\top y | z$, see Example 9.5. See also Fig. 9.11.

[1] This example appears in [161] and [223] – thanks also to Serafín Moral for his online notes.

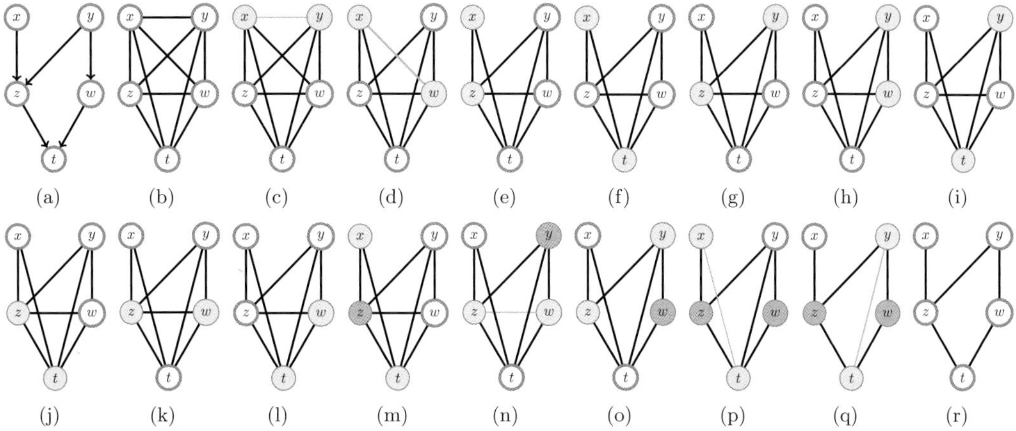

Figure 9.10 PC algorithm. (**a**) The BN from which data is assumed generated and against which conditional independence tests will be performed. (**b**) The initial skeleton is fully connected. (**c–l**) In the first round ($i = 0$) all the pairwise mutual informations $x \perp\!\!\!\perp y | \emptyset$ are checked, and the link between x and y removed if deemed independent (grey line). (**m–o**) $i = 1$. We now look at connected subsets on three variables x, y, z of the remaining graph, removing the link x–y if $x \perp\!\!\!\perp y | z$ is true. Not all steps are shown. (**p, q**) $i = 2$. We now examine all $x \perp\!\!\!\perp y | \{a, b\}$. The algorithm terminates after this round (when i gets incremented to 3) since there are no nodes with three or more neighbours. (**r**) Final skeleton. During this process the sets $S_{x,y} = \emptyset$, $S_{x,w} = \emptyset$, $S_{z,w} = y$, $S_{x,t} = \{z, w\}$, $S_{y,t} = \{z, w\}$ were found. See also `demoPCoracle.m`.

Example 9.5 Skeleton orienting

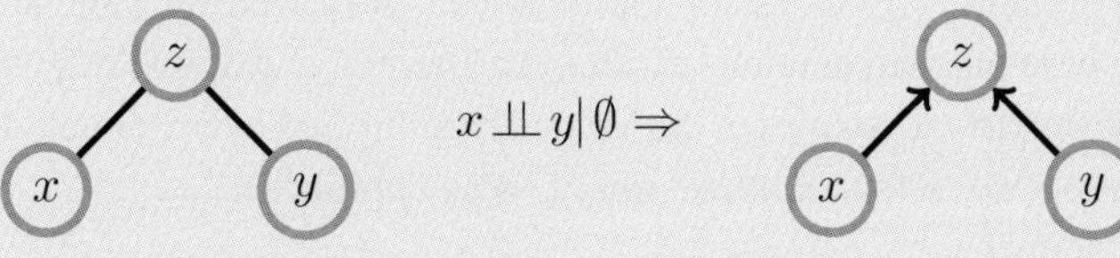

If x is (unconditionally) independent of y, it must be that z is a collider since otherwise marginalising over z would introduce a dependence between x and y.

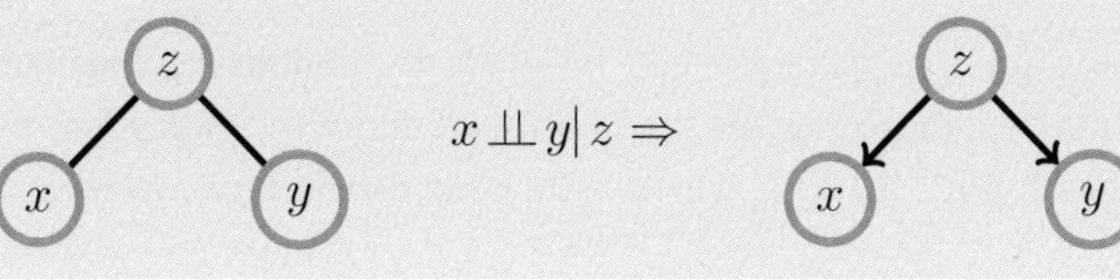

If x is independent of y conditioned on z, z must not be a collider. Any other orientation is appropriate.

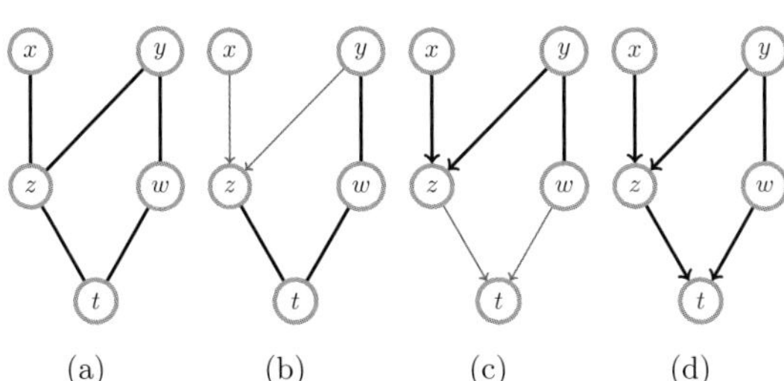

Figure 9.11 Skeleton orientation algorithm. (**a**) The skeleton along with $S_{x,y} = \emptyset$, $S_{x,w} = \emptyset$, $S_{z,w} = y$, $S_{x,t} = \{z, w\}$, $S_{y,t} = \{z, w\}$. (**b**) $z \notin S_{x,y}$, so form collider. (**c**) $t \notin S_{z,w}$, so form collider. (**d**) Final partially oriented DAG. The remaining edge may be oriented as desired, without violating the DAG condition. See also `demoPCoracle.m`.

Example 9.6

In Fig. 9.10 we describe the processes of the PC algorithm in learning the structure for a belief network on the variables x, y, z, w, t. In this case, rather than using data to assess independence, we assume that we have access to an 'oracle' that can correctly answer any independence question put to it. In practice, of course, we will not be so fortunate! Once the skeleton has been found, we then orient the skeleton, as in Fig. 9.11.

9.5.2 Empirical independence

Mutual information test

Given data we can obtain an estimate of the conditional mutual information by using the empirical distribution $p(x, y, z)$ estimated by simply counting occurrences in the data. In practice, however, we only have a finite amount of data to estimate the empirical distribution. This means that for data sampled from a distribution for which the variables truly are independent, the empirical mutual information will nevertheless typically be greater than zero. An issue therefore is what threshold to use for the empirical conditional mutual information to decide if this is sufficiently far from zero to be caused by dependence. A frequentist approach is to compute the distribution of the conditional mutual information and then see where the sample value is compared to the distribution. According to [178], under the null hypothesis that the variables are independent, $2N\text{MI}(x; y|z)$ is Chi-square distributed with $(X-1)(Y-1)Z$ degrees of freedom with $\dim(x) = X$, $\dim(y) = Y$, $\dim(z) = Z$. This can then be used to form a hypothesis test; if the sample value of the empirical mutual information is 'significantly' in the tails of the chi-square distribution, we deem that the variables are conditionally dependent. This classical approach can work well for large amounts of data, but is less effective in the case of small amounts of data. An alternative pragmatic approach is to estimate the threshold based on empirical samples of the MI under controlled independent/dependent conditions – see `demoCondindepEmp.m` for a comparison of these approaches.

Bayesian conditional independence test

A Bayesian approach to testing for independence can be made by comparing the likelihood of the data under the independence hypothesis, versus the likelihood under the dependent hypothesis. For the independence hypothesis, Fig. 9.12(a), we have a joint distribution over variables and parameters:

$$p(x, y, z, \theta|\mathcal{H}_{indep}) = p(x|z, \theta_{x|z})p(y|z, \theta_{y|z})p(z|\theta_z)p(\theta_{x|z})p(\theta_{y|z})p(\theta_z). \tag{9.5.1}$$

For categorical distributions, it is convenient to use a prior Dirichlet $(\theta|u)$ on the parameters θ, assuming also local as well as global parameter independence. For a set of assumed i.i.d. data $(\mathcal{X}, \mathcal{Y}, \mathcal{Z}) = (x^n, y^n, z^n)$, $n = 1, \ldots, N$, the likelihood is then given by integrating over the parameters θ:

$$p(\mathcal{X}, \mathcal{Y}, \mathcal{Z}|\mathcal{H}_{indep}) = \int_\theta \prod_n p(x^n, y^n, z^n, \theta|\mathcal{H}_{indep}).$$

Algorithm 9.2 Skeleton orientation algorithm (returns a DAG).

Unmarried collider: Examine all undirected links x–z–y. If $z \notin \mathcal{S}_{xy}$ set $x \to z \leftarrow y$.
repeat
  $x \to z$–$y \Rightarrow x \to z \to y$
  For x–y, if there is a directed path from x to y orient $x \to y$
  If for x–z–y there is a w such that $x \to w$, $y \to w$, z–w then orient $z \to w$
until No more edges can be oriented.
The remaining edges can be arbitrarily oriented provided that the graph remains a DAG and no additional colliders are introduced.

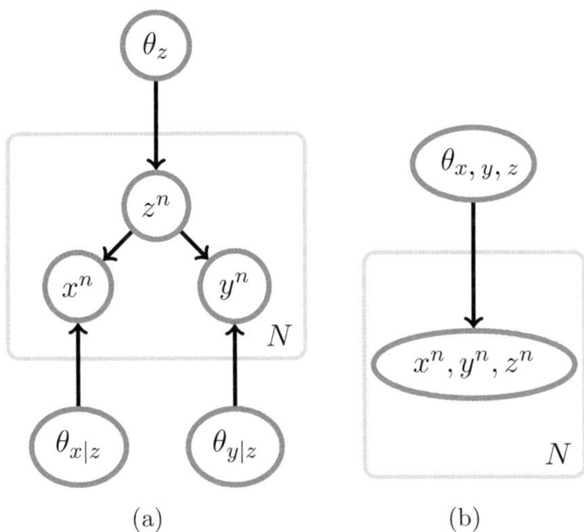

Figure 9.12 Bayesian conditional independence test using Dirichlet priors on the tables. (**a**) A model $\mathcal{H}_{indep}$ for conditional independence $x \perp\!\!\!\perp y \mid z$. (**b**) A model $\mathcal{H}_{dep}$ for conditional dependence $x \top\!\!\!\top y \mid z$. By computing the likelihood of the data under each model, a numerical score for the validity of the conditional independence assumption can be formed. See `demoCondindepEmp.m`.

Thanks to conjugacy, this is straightforward and gives the expression

$$p(\mathcal{X}, \mathcal{Y}, \mathcal{Z}|\mathcal{H}_{indep}) = \frac{Z(u_z + \sharp(z))}{Z(u_z)} \prod_z \frac{Z(u_{x|z} + \sharp(x, z))}{Z(u_{x|z})} \frac{Z(u_{y|z} + \sharp(y, z))}{Z(u_{y|z})} \tag{9.5.2}$$

where $u_{x|z}$ is a hyperparameter matrix of pseudo counts for each state of x given each state of z; $Z(v)$ is the normalisation constant of a Dirichlet distribution with vector parameter v.

For the dependent hypothesis, Fig. 9.12(b), we have

$$p(x, y, z, \theta|\mathcal{H}_{dep}) = p(x, y, z|\theta_{x,y,z})p(\theta_{x,y,z}). \tag{9.5.3}$$

The likelihood is then

$$p(\mathcal{X}, \mathcal{Y}, \mathcal{Z}|\mathcal{H}_{dep}) = \frac{Z(u_{x,y,z} + \sharp(x, y, z))}{Z(u_{x,y,z})}. \tag{9.5.4}$$

Assuming each hypothesis is equally likely, for a Bayes factor

$$\frac{p(\mathcal{X}, \mathcal{Y}, \mathcal{Z}|\mathcal{H}_{indep})}{p(\mathcal{X}, \mathcal{Y}, \mathcal{Z}|\mathcal{H}_{dep})} \tag{9.5.5}$$

greater than 1, we assume that conditional independence holds; otherwise we assume the variables are conditionally dependent. `demoCondindepEmp.m` suggests that the Bayesian hypothesis test tends

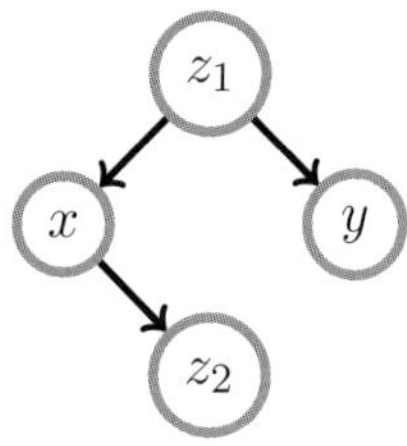

Figure 9.13 Conditional independence test of $x \perp\!\!\!\perp y \mid z_1, z_2$ with x, y, z_1, z_2 having 3, 2, 4, 2 states respectively. From the oracle belief network shown, in each experiment the tables are drawn at random and 20 examples are sampled to form a dataset. For each dataset a test is carried out to determine if x and y are independent conditioned on z_1, z_2 (the correct answer being that they are independent). Over 500 experiments, the Bayesian conditional independence test correctly states that the variables are conditionally independent 74% of the time, compared with only 50% accuracy using the chi-square mutual information test. See `demoCondindepEmp.m`.

to outperform the conditional mutual information approach, particularly in the small sample size case, see Fig. 9.13.

9.5.3 Network scoring

An alternative to local methods such as the PC algorithm is to evaluate the whole network structure on the set of variables $\mathbf{v}$. That is we wish to ascertain how well a belief network with a particular structure $p(\mathbf{v}) = \prod_k p(v_k|\text{pa}(v_k))$ fits the data. In a probabilistic context, given a model structure M, we wish to compute $p(M|\mathcal{D}) \propto p(\mathcal{D}|M)p(M)$. Some care is needed here since we have to first 'fit' each model with parameters θ, $p(\mathbf{v}|\theta, M)$ to the data $\mathcal{D}$. If we do this using maximum likelihood alone, with no constraints on θ, we will always end up favouring that model M with the most complex structure (assuming $p(M) = \text{const.}$). This can be remedied by using the Bayesian technique

$$p(\mathcal{D}|M) = \int_\theta p(\mathcal{D}|\theta, M)p(\theta|M). \tag{9.5.6}$$

In the case of directed networks, as we saw in Section 9.4, the assumptions of local and global parameter independence make the integrals tractable. For a discrete state network and Dirichlet priors, we have $p(\mathcal{D}|M)$ given explicitly by the *Bayesian Dirichlet score*, Equation (9.4.53). First we specify the hyperparameters $\mathbf{u}(v; j)$, and then search over structures M, to find the one with the best score $p(\mathcal{D}|M)$. The simplest setting for the hyperparameters is set them all to unity [69]. Another setting is the 'uninformative prior' [55]

$$u_i(v; j) = \frac{\alpha}{\dim(v)\dim(\text{pa}(v))} \tag{9.5.7}$$

where $\dim(x)$ is the number of states of the variable(s) x, giving rise to the *BDeu* score, for an 'equivalent sample size' parameter α. A discussion of these settings is given in [141] under the concept of likelihood equivalence, namely that two networks which are Markov equivalent should have the same score. How dense the resulting network is can be sensitive to α [278, 266, 277]. Including an explicit prior $p(M)$ on the networks to favour those with sparse connections is also a sensible idea, for which one considers the modified score $p(\mathcal{D}|M)p(M)$.

Searching over structures is a computationally demanding task. However, since the log-score decomposes into additive terms involving only the family of each variable v, we can compare two networks differing in a single edge efficiently since when we make an adjustment within a family, no other terms outside the family are affected. This means that, given a candidate family, we can find which parents in this family should connect to the child; this computation can be carried out for all families independently. To help find the best families, search heuristics based on local addition/removal/reversal of edges [69, 141] that increase the score are popular [141]. In

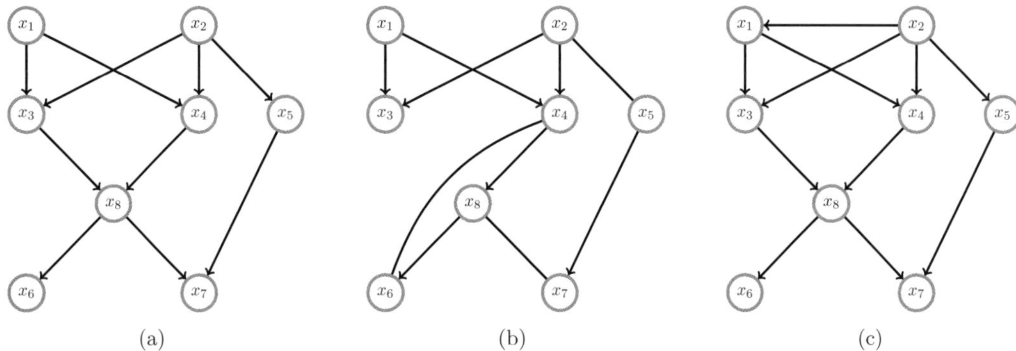

Figure 9.14 Learning the structure of a Bayesian network. (**a**) The correct structure in which all variables are binary. The ancestral order is $x_2, x_1, x_5, x_4, x_3, x_8, x_7, x_6$. The dataset is formed from 1000 samples from this network. (**b**) The learned structure based on the PC algorithm using the Bayesian empirical conditional independence test. Undirected edges may be oriented arbitrarily (provided the graph remains acyclic). (**c**) The learned structure based on the Bayes Dirichlet network scoring method. See `demoPCdata.m` and `demoBDscore.m`.

`learnBayesNet.m` we simplify the problem for demonstration purposes in which we assume we know the ancestral order of the variables, and also the maximal number of parents of each variable. In practice, it is unlikely that a large number of parents will influence a variable; even if this were the case, we would in general require an amount of data exponential in the number of parents to ascertain this. One could in principle approach this by assuming parametric forms for such large tables, although this is not common in practice.

Example 9.7 PC algorithm versus network scoring

In Fig. 9.14 we compare the PC algorithm with network scoring based (with Dirichlet hyperparameters set to unity) on 1000 samples from a known belief network. The PC algorithm conditional independence test is based on the Bayesian factor (9.5.5) in which Dirichlet priors with $u = 0.1$ were used throughout.

In the network scoring approach, in general there is no need to assume an ancestral ordering. However, here we assume that we know the correct ancestral ordering, and also limit the number of parents of each variable to be at most two. In this case, we can then easily search over all possible graph structures, choosing that with the highest posterior score. This proceeds by for example looking at the contribution of variable x_7 and its family. Since, according to the given ancestral ordering, $x_1, x_2, x_3, x_4, x_5, x_8$ are possible parents of x_7, in principle we need to search over all the 2^6 parental configurations for this family. However, since we assume that there are only maximally two parents, this reduces to $1 + \binom{6}{1} + \binom{6}{2} = 22$ parental configurations. We can perform this optimisation for the parental structure of variable x_7 independently of the parental structure of the other variables, thanks to the likelihood decomposable property of the network score. Similarly, we carry out this optimisation for the other variables separately, based on their possible parents according to the ancestral order.

In Fig. 9.14 the network scoring technique outperforms the PC algorithm. This is partly explained by the network scoring technique being provided with the correct ancestral order and the constraint that each variable has maximally two parents.

Figure 9.15 A Chow–Liu tree in which each variable x_i has at most one parent. The variables may be indexed such that $1 \leq i \leq D$.

9.5.4 Chow–Liu trees

Consider a multivariate distribution $p(x)$ that we wish to approximate with a distribution $q(x)$. Furthermore, we constrain the approximation $q(x)$ to be a belief network in which each node has at most one parent, see Fig. 9.15. First we assume that we have chosen a particular labelling of the D variables so that children have higher parent indices than their parents. The DAG single parent constraint then means

$$q(x) = \prod_{i=1}^{D} q(x_i|x_{pa(i)}), \qquad pa(i) < i, \quad \text{or } pa(i) = \emptyset \tag{9.5.8}$$

where $pa(i)$ is the single-parent index of node i. To find the best approximating distribution q in this constrained class, we may minimise the Kullback–Leibler divergence

$$\mathrm{KL}(p|q) = \langle \log p(x) \rangle_{p(x)} - \sum_{i=1}^{D} \left\langle \log q(x_i|x_{pa(i)}) \right\rangle_{p(x_i,x_{pa(i)})}. \tag{9.5.9}$$

Since $p(x)$ is fixed, the first term is constant. By adding a term $\left\langle \log p(x_i|x_{pa(i)}) \right\rangle_{p(x_i,x_{pa(i)})}$ that depends on $p(x)$ alone, we can write

$$\mathrm{KL}(p|q) = \text{const.} - \sum_{i=1}^{D} \left\langle \left\langle \log q(x_i|x_{pa(i)}) \right\rangle_{p(x_i|x_{pa(i)})} - \left\langle \log p(x_i|x_{pa(i)}) \right\rangle_{p(x_i|x_{pa(i)})} \right\rangle_{p(x_{pa(i)})}. \tag{9.5.10}$$

This enables us to recognise that, up to a negligible constant, the overall Kullback–Leibler divergence is a positive sum of individual Kullback–Leibler divergences so that the optimal setting is therefore

$$q(x_i|x_{pa(i)}) = p(x_i|x_{pa(i)}). \tag{9.5.11}$$

Plugging this solution into Equation (9.5.9) and using $\log p(x_i|x_{pa(i)}) = \log p(x_i, x_{pa(i)}) - \log p(x_{pa(i)})$ we obtain

$$\mathrm{KL}(p|q) = \text{const.} - \sum_{i=1}^{D} \left\langle \log p(x_i, x_{pa(i)}) \right\rangle_{p(x_i,x_{pa(i)})} + \sum_{i=1}^{D} \left\langle \log p(x_{pa(i)}) \right\rangle_{p(x_{pa(i)})}. \tag{9.5.12}$$

We still need to find the optimal parental structure $pa(i)$ that minimises the above expression. If we add and subtract an entropy term we can write

$$\begin{aligned}\mathrm{KL}(p|q) = &- \sum_{i=1}^{D} \left\langle \log p(x_i, x_{pa(i)}) \right\rangle_{p(x_i,x_{pa(i)})} + \sum_{i=1}^{D} \left\langle \log p(x_{pa(i)}) \right\rangle_{p(x_{pa(i)})} \\ &+ \sum_{i=1}^{D} \langle \log p(x_i) \rangle_{p(x_i)} - \sum_{i=1}^{D} \langle \log p(x_i) \rangle_{p(x_i)} + \text{const.}\end{aligned} \tag{9.5.13}$$

For two variables x_i and x_j and distribution $p(x_i, x_j)$, the *mutual information* (Definition 8.13) can be written as

$$\mathrm{MI}(x_i; x_j) = \left\langle \log \frac{p(x_i, x_j)}{p(x_i)p(x_j)} \right\rangle_{p(x_i, x_j)} \tag{9.5.14}$$

which can be seen as the Kullback–Leibler divergence $\mathrm{KL}(p(x_i, x_j)|p(x_i)p(x_j))$ and is therefore non-negative. Using this, Equation (9.5.13) is

$$\mathrm{KL}(p|q) = -\sum_{i=1}^{D} \mathrm{MI}\big(x_i; x_{pa(i)}\big) - \sum_{i=1}^{D} \langle \log p(x_i) \rangle_{p(x_i)} + \text{const.} \tag{9.5.15}$$

Since our task is to find the optimal parental indices $pa(i)$, and the entropic term $\sum_i \langle \log p(x_i) \rangle_{p(x_i)}$ of the fixed distribution $p(x)$ is independent of this mapping, finding the optimal mapping is equivalent to maximising the summed mutual informations

$$\sum_{i=1}^{D} \mathrm{MI}\big(x_i; x_{pa(i)}\big) \tag{9.5.16}$$

under the constraint that $pa(i) < i$. Since we also need to choose the optimal initial labelling of the variables as well, the problem is equivalent to computing all the pairwise mutual informations

$$w_{ij} = \mathrm{MI}(x_i; x_j) \tag{9.5.17}$$

and then finding a maximal spanning tree for the graph with edge weights w (see `spantree.m`) [64]. Once found, we need to identify a directed tree with at most one parent. This is achieved by choosing any node and then orienting edges consistently away from this node.

Maximum likelihood Chow–Liu trees

If $p(x)$ is the empirical distribution

$$p(x) = \frac{1}{N} \sum_{n=1}^{N} \delta\,(x, x^n) \tag{9.5.18}$$

then

$$\mathrm{KL}(p|q) = \text{const.} - \frac{1}{N} \sum_{n} \log q(x^n). \tag{9.5.19}$$

Hence the distribution q that minimises $\mathrm{KL}(p|q)$ is equivalent to that which maximises the likelihood of the data. This means that if we use the mutual information found from the empirical distribution, with

$$p(x_i = \mathsf{a}, x_j = \mathsf{b}) \propto \sharp\,(x_i = \mathsf{a}, x_j = \mathsf{b}) \tag{9.5.20}$$

then the Chow–Liu tree produced corresponds to the maximum likelihood solution amongst all single-parent trees. An outline of the procedure is given in Algorithm 9.3. An efficient algorithm for sparse data is also available [205].

Remark 9.1 (Learning tree structured belief networks) The Chow–Liu algorithm pertains to the discussion in Section 9.5 on learning the structure of belief networks from data. Under the special constraint that each variable has at most one parent, the Chow–Liu algorithm returns the maximum likelihood structure to fit the data.

Algorithm 9.3 Chow–Liu trees.

---

for $i = 1$ to D **do**
    for $j = 1$ to D **do**
        Compute the mutual information for the pair of variables x_i, x_j: $w_{ij} = \mathrm{MI}(x_i; x_j)$.
    end for
end for
For the undirected graph $\mathcal{G}$ with edge weights w, find a maximum weight undirected spanning tree $\mathcal{T}$.
Choose an arbitrary variable as the root node of the tree $\mathcal{T}$.
Form a directed tree by orienting all edges away from the root node.

9.6 Maximum likelihood for undirected models

Consider a Markov network $p(\mathcal{X})$ defined on (not necessarily maximal) cliques $\mathcal{X}_c \subseteq \mathcal{X}, c = 1, \ldots, C$ with clique parameters $\theta = (\theta_1, \ldots, \theta_C)$

$$p(\mathcal{X}|\theta) = \frac{1}{Z(\theta)} \prod_c \phi_c(\mathcal{X}_c|\theta_c) \tag{9.6.1}$$

The term

$$Z(\theta) = \sum_{\mathcal{X}} \prod_c \phi_c(\mathcal{X}_c|\theta_c) \tag{9.6.2}$$

ensures normalisation, with the notation $\sum_{\mathcal{X}}$ indicating a summation over all states of the set of variables $\mathcal{X}$. Given a set of data, $\{\mathcal{X}^n, n = 1, \ldots, N\}$, and assuming i.i.d. data, the log likelihood is

$$L(\theta) = \sum_n \log p(\mathcal{X}^n|\theta) = \sum_n \sum_c \log \phi_c(\mathcal{X}_c^n|\theta_c) - N \log Z(\theta). \tag{9.6.3}$$

Our interest is to find the parameters that maximise the log likelihood $L(\theta)$. In general learning the optimal parameters $\theta_c, c = 1, \ldots, C$ is awkward since they are coupled via $Z(\theta)$. Unlike the BN, the objective function does not split into a set of isolated parameter terms and in general we need to resort to numerical methods. In special cases, however, exact results still apply, in particular when the MN is decomposable and no constraints are placed on the form of the clique potentials, as we discuss in Section 9.6.3. More generally, however, gradient-based techniques may be used and also give insight into properties of the maximum likelihood solution.

9.6.1 The likelihood gradient

The gradient of the log likelihood with respect to a clique parameter θ_c is given by

$$\frac{\partial}{\partial \theta_c} L(\theta) = \sum_n \frac{\partial}{\partial \theta_c} \log \phi_c(\mathcal{X}_c^n|\theta_c) - N \left\langle \frac{\partial}{\partial \theta_c} \log \phi_c(\mathcal{X}_c|\theta_c) \right\rangle_{p(\mathcal{X}_c|\theta)}. \tag{9.6.4}$$

This is obtained by using the result

$$\frac{\partial}{\partial \theta_c} \log Z(\theta) = \frac{1}{Z(\theta)} \sum_{\mathcal{X}} \frac{\partial}{\partial \theta_c} \phi_c(\mathcal{X}_c|\theta_c) \prod_{c' \neq c} \phi_{c'}(\mathcal{X}_{c'}|\theta_{c'}) = \left\langle \frac{\partial}{\partial \theta_c} \log \phi_c(\mathcal{X}_c|\theta_c) \right\rangle_{p(\mathcal{X}_c|\theta)}. \tag{9.6.5}$$

The gradient can then be used as part of a standard numerical optimisation package.

Exponential form potentials

A common form of parameterisation is to use an exponential form

$$\phi_c(\mathcal{X}_c) = \exp\left(\boldsymbol{\theta}_c^{\mathsf{T}} \boldsymbol{\psi}_c(\mathcal{X}_c)\right) \tag{9.6.6}$$

where $\boldsymbol{\theta}_c$ are the vector parameters and $\boldsymbol{\psi}_c(\mathcal{X}_c)$ is a fixed 'feature function' defined on the variables of clique c. From Equation (9.6.4) to find the gradient, we need

$$\frac{\partial}{\partial \theta_c} \log \phi_c(\mathcal{X}_c|\theta_c) = \frac{\partial}{\partial \boldsymbol{\theta}_c} \boldsymbol{\theta}_c^{\mathsf{T}} \boldsymbol{\psi}_c(\mathcal{X}_c) = \boldsymbol{\psi}_c(\mathcal{X}_c). \tag{9.6.7}$$

Using this in Equation (9.6.4), we find that the $L(\theta)$ has a zero derivative when

$$\frac{1}{N} \sum_n \boldsymbol{\psi}_c(\mathcal{X}_c^n) = \langle \boldsymbol{\psi}_c(\mathcal{X}_c) \rangle_{p(\mathcal{X}_c)}. \tag{9.6.8}$$

Hence the maximum likelihood solution satisfies that the empirical average of a feature function matches the average of the feature function with respect to the model. By defining the empirical distribution on the clique variables $\mathcal{X}_c$ as

$$\epsilon(\mathcal{X}_c) \equiv \frac{1}{N} \sum_{n=1}^{N} \mathbb{I}\left[\mathcal{X}_c = \mathcal{X}_c^n\right] \tag{9.6.9}$$

we can write Equation (9.6.8) more compactly as

$$\langle \boldsymbol{\psi}_c(\mathcal{X}_c) \rangle_{\epsilon(\mathcal{X}_c)} = \langle \boldsymbol{\psi}_c(\mathcal{X}_c) \rangle_{p(\mathcal{X}_c)}. \tag{9.6.10}$$

An example of learning such an exponential form is given in Example 9.8. We return to learning the parameters of these models in Section 9.6.4.

Example 9.8 Boltzmann machine learning

We define the Boltzman Machine (BM) as

$$p(\mathbf{v}|\mathbf{W}) = \frac{1}{Z(\mathbf{W})} e^{\frac{1}{2}\mathbf{v}^{\mathsf{T}}\mathbf{W}\mathbf{v}}, \qquad Z(\mathbf{W}) = \sum_{\mathbf{v}} e^{\frac{1}{2}\mathbf{v}^{\mathsf{T}}\mathbf{W}\mathbf{v}} \tag{9.6.11}$$

for symmetric $\mathbf{W}$ and binary variables $\mathrm{dom}(v_i) = \{0, 1\}$. Given a set of training data, $\mathcal{D} = \left\{\mathbf{v}^1, \ldots, \mathbf{v}^N\right\}$, the log likelihood is

$$L(\mathbf{W}) = \frac{1}{2} \sum_{n=1}^{N} (\mathbf{v}^n)^{\mathsf{T}} \mathbf{W} \mathbf{v}^n - N \log Z(\mathbf{W}). \tag{9.6.12}$$

Differentiating w.r.t w_{ij}, $i \neq j$ and w_{ii} we have the gradients

$$\frac{\partial L}{\partial w_{ij}} = \sum_{n=1}^{N} \left(v_i^n v_j^n - \langle v_i v_j \rangle_{p(\mathbf{v}|\mathbf{W})}\right), \qquad \frac{\partial L}{\partial w_{ii}} = \frac{1}{2} \sum_{n=1}^{N} \left(v_i^n - \langle v_i \rangle_{p(\mathbf{v}|\mathbf{W})}\right). \tag{9.6.13}$$

A simple algorithm to optimise the weight matrix $\mathbf{W}$ is to use gradient ascent,

$$w_{ij}^{new} = w_{ij}^{old} + \eta_1 \frac{\partial L}{\partial w_{ij}}, \qquad w_{ii}^{new} = w_{ii}^{old} + \eta_2 \frac{\partial L}{\partial w_{ii}} \tag{9.6.14}$$

for learning rates $\eta_1, \eta_2 > 0$. The intuitive interpretation is that learning will stop (the gradient is zero) when the second-order statistics of the model $\langle v_i v_j \rangle_{p(\mathbf{v}|\mathbf{W})}$ match those of the empirical distribution, $\sum_n v_i^n v_j^n / N$. Boltzmann Machine learning however is difficult since $\langle v_i v_j \rangle_{p(\mathbf{v}|\mathbf{W})}$ is typically computationally intractable for an arbitrary interaction matrix $\mathbf{W}$ and therefore needs to be approximated. Indeed, one cannot compute the likelihood $L(\mathbf{W})$ exactly for a general matrix $\mathbf{W}$ so that monitoring performance is also difficult.

9.6.2 General tabular clique potentials

For unconstrained clique potentials we have a separate table for each of the states defined on the clique. In writing the log likelihood, it is convenient to use the identity

$$\phi_c(\mathcal{X}_c^n) = \prod_{\mathcal{Y}_c} \phi_c(\mathcal{Y}_c)^{\mathbb{I}[\mathcal{Y}_c = \mathcal{X}_c^n]} \tag{9.6.15}$$

where the product is over all states of potential c. This expression follows since the indicator is zero for all but the single observed state $\mathcal{X}_c^n$. The log likelihood is then

$$L(\theta) = \sum_c \sum_{\mathcal{Y}_c} \sum_n \mathbb{I}[\mathcal{Y}_c = \mathcal{X}_c^n] \log \phi_c(\mathcal{Y}_c) - N \log Z(\phi) \tag{9.6.16}$$

where

$$Z(\phi) = \sum_{\mathcal{Y}_c} \prod_c \phi_c(\mathcal{Y}_c). \tag{9.6.17}$$

Differentiating the log likelihood with respect to a specific table entry $\phi_c(\mathcal{Y}_c)$ we obtain

$$\frac{\partial}{\partial \phi_c(\mathcal{Y}_c)} L(\theta) = \sum_n \mathbb{I}[\mathcal{Y}_c = \mathcal{X}_c^n] \frac{1}{\phi_c(\mathcal{Y}_c)} - N \frac{p(\mathcal{Y}_c)}{\phi_c(\mathcal{Y}_c)}. \tag{9.6.18}$$

Equating to zero, and rewriting in terms of the variables $\mathcal{X}$, the maximum likelihood solution is obtained when

$$p(\mathcal{X}_c) = \epsilon(\mathcal{X}_c) \tag{9.6.19}$$

where the empirical distribution is defined in Equation (9.6.9). That is, the unconstrained optimal maximum likelihood solution is given by setting the clique potentials such that the marginal distribution on each clique $p(\mathcal{X}_c)$ matches the empirical distribution on each clique $\epsilon(\mathcal{X}_c)$. Note that this only describes the form that the optimal maximum likelihood solution should take, and doesn't give us a closed form expression for setting the tables. To find the optimal tables in this case would still require a numerical procedure, such as gradient based methods based on Equation (9.6.18), or the IPF method described below.

Iterative proportional fitting

According to the general result of Equation (9.6.19) the maximum likelihood solution is such that the clique marginals match the empirical marginals. Assuming that we can absorb the normalisation constant into an arbitrarily chosen clique, we can drop explicitly representing the normalisation constant. For a clique c, the requirement that the marginal of p matches the empirical marginal on the variables in the clique is

$$\phi(\mathcal{X}_c)\sum_{\mathcal{X}_{\backslash c}}\prod_{d\neq c}\phi(\mathcal{X}_d)=\epsilon(\mathcal{X}_c). \tag{9.6.20}$$

Given an initial setting for the potentials we can then update $\phi(\mathcal{X}_c)$ to satisfy the above marginal requirement,

$$\phi^{new}(\mathcal{X}_c)=\frac{\epsilon(\mathcal{X}_c)}{\sum_{\mathcal{X}_{\backslash c}}\prod_{d\neq c}\phi(\mathcal{X}_d)} \tag{9.6.21}$$

which is required for each of the states of $\mathcal{X}_c$. By multiplying and dividing the right-hand side by $\phi(\mathcal{X}_c)$ this is equivalent to ascertaining if

$$\phi^{new}(\mathcal{X}_c)=\frac{\phi(\mathcal{X}_c)\epsilon(\mathcal{X}_c)}{p(\mathcal{X}_c)}. \tag{9.6.22}$$

This is a so-called Iterative Proportional Fitting (IPF) update and corresponds to a coordinate-wise optimisation of the log likelihood in which the coordinate corresponds to $\phi_c(\mathcal{X}_c)$, with all other parameters fixed. In this case this conditional optimum is analytically given by the above setting. One proceeds by selecting another potential to update, and continues updating until some convergence criterion is met. Note that in general, with each update, the marginal $p(\mathcal{X}_c)$ needs to be recomputed; computing these marginals may be expensive unless the width of the junction tree formed from the graph is suitably limited.

9.6.3 Decomposable Markov networks

Whilst for general Markov networks we require numerical methods to find the maximum likelihood solution, there is an important special case for which we can find the optimal tables very easily. If the MN corresponding is decomposable, then we know (from the junction tree representation) that we can express the distribution in the form of a product of local marginals divided by the separator distributions

$$p(\mathcal{X})=\frac{\prod_c p(\mathcal{X}_c)}{\prod_s p(\mathcal{X}_s)}. \tag{9.6.23}$$

By reabsorbing the separators into the numerator terms, we can form a set chain distribution, Section 6.8

$$p(\mathcal{X})=\prod_c p(\mathcal{X}_c|\mathcal{X}_{\backslash c}). \tag{9.6.24}$$

Since this is directed, and provided no constraint is placed on the tables, the maximum likelihood solution to learning the tables is given by assigning each set chain factor $p(\mathcal{X}_c|\mathcal{X}_{\backslash c})$ based on counting the instances in the dataset [182], see `learnMarkovDecom.m`. The procedure is perhaps best explained by an example, as given below. See Algorithm 9.4 for a general description.

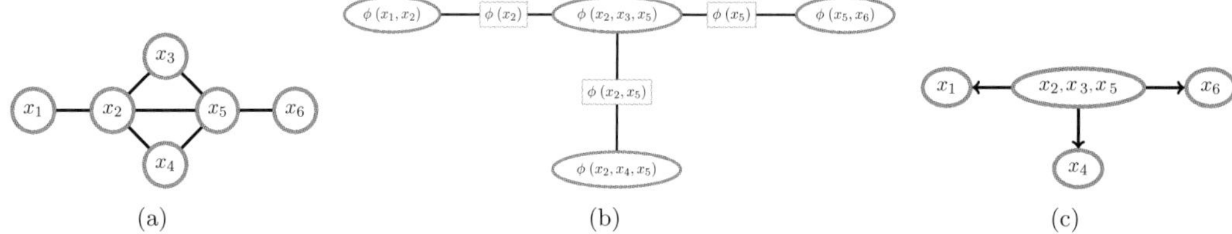

Figure 9.16 (**a**) A decomposable Markov network. (**b**) A junction tree for (a). (**c**) Set chain for (a) formed by choosing clique x_2, x_3, x_5 as root and orienting edges consistently away from the root. Each separator is absorbed into its child clique to form the set chain.

Algorithm 9.4 Learning of an unconstrained decomposable Markov network using maximum likelihood. We have a triangulated (decomposable) Markov network on cliques $\phi_c(\mathcal{X}_c)$, $c = 1, \ldots, C$ and the empirical marginal distributions on all cliques and separators, $\epsilon(\mathcal{X}_c)$, $\epsilon(\mathcal{X}_s)$.

1: Form a junction tree from the cliques.
2: Initialise each clique $\phi_c(\mathcal{X}_c)$ to $\epsilon(\mathcal{X}_c)$ and each separator $\phi_s(\mathcal{X}_s)$ to $\epsilon(\mathcal{X}_s)$.
3: Choose a root clique on the junction tree and orient edges consistently away from this root.
4: For this oriented junction tree, divide each clique by its parent separator.
5: Return the new potentials on each clique as the maximum likelihood solution.

Example 9.9

Given a dataset $\{\mathcal{X}^n, n = 1, \ldots, N\}$, with corresponding empirical distribution $\epsilon(\mathcal{X})$, we wish to fit by maximum likelihood an MN of the form

$$p(x_1, \ldots, x_6) = \frac{1}{Z}\phi(x_1, x_2)\phi(x_2, x_3, x_5)\phi(x_2, x_4, x_5)\phi(x_5, x_6) \tag{9.6.25}$$

where the potentials are unconstrained tables, see Fig. 9.16(a). Since the graph is decomposable, we know it admits a factorisation of clique potentials divided by the separators:

$$p(x_1, \ldots, x_6) = \frac{p(x_1, x_2)p(x_2, x_3, x_5)p(x_2, x_4, x_5)p(x_5, x_6)}{p(x_2)p(x_2, x_5)p(x_5)}. \tag{9.6.26}$$

We can convert this to a set chain by reabsorbing the denominators into numerator terms, see Section 6.8. For example, by choosing the clique x_2, x_3, x_5 as root, we can write

$$p(x_1, \ldots, x_6) = \underbrace{p(x_1|x_2)}_{\phi(x_1,x_2)}\underbrace{p(x_2, x_3, x_5)}_{\phi(x_2,x_3,x_5)}\underbrace{p(x_4|x_2, x_5)}_{\phi(x_2,x_4,x_5)}\underbrace{p(x_6|x_5)}_{\phi(x_5,x_6)} \tag{9.6.27}$$

where we identified the factors with clique potentials, and the normalisation constant Z is unity, see Fig. 9.16(b). The advantage is that in this representation, the clique potentials are independent since the distribution is a BN on cluster variables. The log likelihood for an i.i.d. dataset is

$$L = \sum_n \log p(x_1^n|x_2^n) + \log p(x_2^n, x_3^n, x_5^n) + \log p(x_4^n|x_2^n, x_5^n) + \log p(x_6^n|x_5^n) \tag{9.6.28}$$

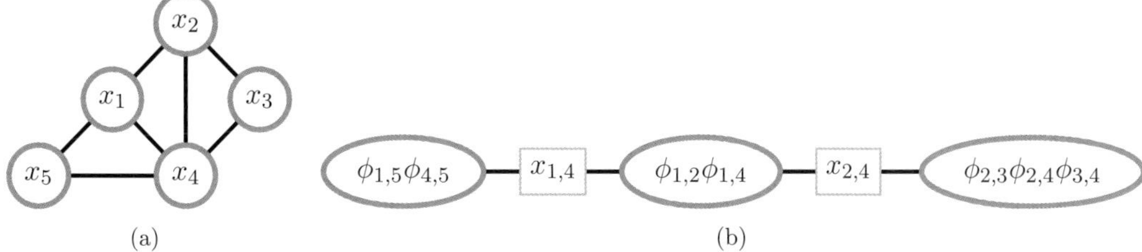

Figure 9.17 (**a**) Interpreted as a Markov network, the graph represents the distribution $\phi(x_1, x_4, x_5)\phi(x_1, x_2, x_4)\phi(x_2, x_4, x_3)$. As a pairwise MN, the graph represents $\phi(x_4, x_5)\phi(x_1, x_4)\phi(x_4, x_5)\phi(x_1, x_2)\phi(x_2, x_4)\phi(x_2, x_3)\phi(x_3, x_4)$. (**b**) A junction tree for the pairwise MN in (a). We have a choice where to place the pairwise cliques, and this is one valid choice, using the shorthand $\phi_{a,b} = \phi_{a,b}(x_a, x_b)$ and $x_{a,b} = \{x_a, x_b\}$.

where each of the terms is an independent parameter of the model. The maximum likelihood solution then corresponds (as for the BN case) to simply setting each factor to the empirical distribution

$$\phi(x_1, x_2) = \epsilon(x_1|x_2), \quad \phi(x_2, x_3, x_5) = \epsilon(x_2, x_3, x_5), \quad \phi(x_2, x_4, x_5) = \epsilon(x_4|x_2, x_5),$$
$$\phi(x_5, x_6) = \epsilon(x_6|x_5) \tag{9.6.29}$$

Constrained decomposable Markov networks

If there are no constraints on the forms of the maximal clique potentials of the Markov network, as we've seen, learning is straightforward. Here our interest is when the functional form of the maximal clique is constrained to be a product of potentials on smaller cliques:[2]

$$\phi_c(\mathcal{X}_c) = \prod_i \phi_c^i(\mathcal{X}_c^i) \tag{9.6.30}$$

with no constraint being placed on the non-maximal clique potentials $\phi_c^i(\mathcal{X}_c^i)$. In general, in this case one cannot write down directly the maximum likelihood solution for the non-maximal clique potentials $\phi_c^i(\mathcal{X}_c^i)$.

Consider the graph in Fig. 9.17 which we consider a pairwise MN. In this case, the clique potentials are constrained, so that we cannot simply write down the solution, as we did in the unconstrained decomposable case. Since the graph is decomposable, there are however, computational savings that can be made in this case [10]. For an empirical distribution ϵ, maximum likelihood requires that all the pairwise marginals of the MN match the corresponding marginals obtained from ϵ. As explained in Fig. 9.17 we have a choice as to which junction tree clique each potential is assigned to, with one valid choice being given in Fig. 9.17(b).

Let's consider updating the potentials within the 1, 2, 4 clique. Keeping the potentials of the other cliques $\phi_{4,5}\phi_{1,5}$ and $\phi_{2,3}\phi_{2,4}\phi_{3,4}$ fixed we can update the potentials $\phi_{1,2}$, $\phi_{1,4}$. Using a bar to denote

[2] A Boltzmann machine is of this form since any unconstrained binary pairwise potentials can be converted into a BM. For other cases in which the ϕ_c^i are constrained, then Iterative scaling may be used in place of IPF.

fixed potentials, the marginal requirement that the MN marginal $p(x_1, x_2, x_4)$ matches the empirical marginal $\epsilon(x_1, x_2)$ can be written in shorthand as

$$p_{1,2,4} = \epsilon_{1,2,4}. \tag{9.6.31}$$

We can express this requirement in terms of the pairs of variables x_1, x_2 and x_1, x_4 within the $\phi_{1,2}\phi_{1,4}$ clique as

$$p_{1,2} = \epsilon_{1,2}, \qquad p_{1,4} = \epsilon_{1,4}. \tag{9.6.32}$$

Taking the first marginal requirement, this means

$$p_{1,2} = \sum_{x_3,x_4,x_5} \bar{\phi}_{1,5}\bar{\phi}_{4,5}\phi_{1,4}\phi_{1,2}\bar{\phi}_{2,4}\bar{\phi}_{2,3}\bar{\phi}_{3,4} = \epsilon_{1,2} \tag{9.6.33}$$

which can be expressed as

$$\sum_{x_4} \underbrace{\left(\sum_{x_5} \bar{\phi}_{1,5}\bar{\phi}_{4,5}\right)}_{\gamma_{1,4}} \phi_{1,4}\phi_{1,2} \underbrace{\left(\sum_{x_3} \bar{\phi}_{2,4}\bar{\phi}_{2,3}\bar{\phi}_{3,4}\right)}_{\gamma_{2,4}} = \epsilon_{1,2}. \tag{9.6.34}$$

The 'messages' $\gamma_{1,4}$ and $\gamma_{1,2}$ are the boundary separator tables when we choose the central clique as root and carry out absorption towards the root. Given these fixed messages we can then perform IPF updates of the root clique using

$$\phi_{1,2}^{new} = \frac{\epsilon_{1,2}}{\sum_{x_4} \gamma_{1,4}\phi_{1,4}\gamma_{2,4}}. \tag{9.6.35}$$

After making this update, we can subsequently update $\phi_{1,4}$ similarly using the constraint

$$\sum_{x_2} \underbrace{\left(\sum_{x_5} \bar{\phi}_{1,5}\bar{\phi}_{4,5}\right)}_{\gamma_{1,4}} \phi_{1,4}\phi_{1,2} \underbrace{\left(\sum_{x_3} \bar{\phi}_{2,4}\bar{\phi}_{2,3}\bar{\phi}_{3,4}\right)}_{\gamma_{2,4}} = \epsilon_{1,4} \tag{9.6.36}$$

so that

$$\phi_{1,4}^{new} = \frac{\epsilon_{1,4}}{\sum_{x_2} \gamma_{1,4}\phi_{1,2}\gamma_{2,4}}. \tag{9.6.37}$$

We then iterate these updates until convergence within this 1, 2, 4 clique. Given converged updates for this clique, we can choose another clique as root, propagate towards the root and compute the separator cliques on the boundary of the root. Given these fixed boundary clique potentials we again perform IPF within the clique.

This 'efficient' IPF procedure is described more generally in Algorithm 9.5 for an empirical distribution ϵ. More generally, IPF minimises the Kullback–Leibler divergence between a given reference distribution ϵ and the Markov network. See `demoIPFeff.m` and `IPF.m`.

Algorithm 9.5 Efficient Iterative Proportional Fitting. Given a set of ϕ_i, $i = 1, \ldots, I$ and a corresponding set of reference (empirical) marginal distributions on the variables of each potential, ϵ_i, we aim to set all ϕ such that all marginals of the Markov network match the given empirical marginals.

Given a Markov network on potentials ϕ_i, $i = 1, \ldots, I$, triangulate the graph and form the cliques $\mathcal{C}_1, \ldots, \mathcal{C}_C$.
Assign potentials to cliques. Thus each clique has a set of associated potentials $\mathcal{F}_c$
Initialise all potentials (for example to unity).
repeat
    Choose a clique c as root.
    Propagate messages towards the root and compute the separators on the boundary of the root.
    repeat
        Choose a potential ϕ_i in clique c, $i \in \mathcal{F}_c$.
        Perform an IPF update for ϕ_i, given fixed boundary separators and other potentials in c.
    until Potentials in clique c converge.
until All Markov network marginals converge to the reference marginals.

Example 9.10 Learning with a structured Markov network

In this example we aim to fit a Markov network to data, constrained so that inference in the Markov network is computationally cheap by ensuring that the junction tree of the Markov network has limited clique sizes.

In Fig. 9.18 36 examples of $18 \times 14 = 252$ binary pixel handwritten twos are presented, forming the training set from which we wish to fit a Markov network. First all pairwise empirical entropies $H(x_i, x_j)$, $i, j = 1, \ldots, 252$ were computed and used to rank edges, with highest entropy edges ranked first. Edges were included in a graph G, highest ranked first, provided the triangulated G had all cliques less than size 15. This resulted in 238 unique cliques and an adjacency matrix for the triangulated G as presented in Fig. 9.18(a). In Fig. 9.18(b) the number of times that a pixel appears in the 238 cliques is shown, and indicates the degree of importance of each pixel in distinguishing between the 36 examples. Two models were then trained and used to compute the most likely reconstruction based on missing data $p(x_{missing}|x_{visible})$.

The first model was a Markov network on the maximal cliques of the graph, for which essentially no training is required, and the settings for each clique potential can be obtained as explained in Algorithm 9.4. The model makes 3.8 per cent errors in reconstruction of the missing pixels. Note that the unfortunate effect of reconstructing a white pixel surrounded by black pixels is an effect of the limited training data. With larger amounts of data the model would recognise that such effects do not occur.

In the second model, the same maximal cliques were used, but the maximal clique potentials restricted to be the product of all pairwise two-cliques within the maximal clique. This is equivalent to using a structured Boltzmann machine, and was trained using the efficient IPF approach of Algorithm 9.5. The corresponding reconstruction error is 20 per cent. This performance is worse than the first model since the Boltzmann machine is a more constrained Markov network and struggles to represent the data well. See `demoLearnThinMNDigit.m`.

Figure 9.18 Learning digits (from Simon Lucas' algoval system) using a Markov network. Top row: the 36 training examples. Each example is a binary image on 18×14 pixels. Second row: the training data with 50 per cent missing pixels (grey represents a missing pixel). Third row: Reconstructions from the missing data using a thin-junction-tree MN with maximum clique size 15. Bottom row: Reconstructions using a thin-junction-tree Boltzmann machine with maximum clique size 15, trained using efficient IPF.

9.6.4 Exponential form potentials

For exponential form potentials

$$\phi_c(\mathcal{X}_c) = \exp\left(\boldsymbol{\theta}_c^{\mathsf{T}} \boldsymbol{\psi}_c(\mathcal{X}_c)\right) \tag{9.6.38}$$

we saw in Section 9.6.1 how to compute the derivatives for use in standard numerical optimisation procedures. In the following section we outline another popular numerical technique.

Iterative scaling

We consider Markov networks of the exponential form

$$p(\mathcal{X}|\theta) = \frac{1}{Z(\theta)} \prod_c e^{\theta_c f_c(\mathcal{X}_c)} \tag{9.6.39}$$

where the 'feature functions' $f_c(\mathcal{X}_c) \geq 0$ and c ranges of the non-maximal cliques $\mathcal{X}_c \subset \mathcal{X}$ (Note that Equation (9.6.38) can be written in this form by having multiple potentials within the same clique.). The normalisation requirement is

$$Z(\theta) = \sum_{\mathcal{X}} \prod_c \exp\left(\theta_c f_c(\mathcal{X}_c)\right). \tag{9.6.40}$$

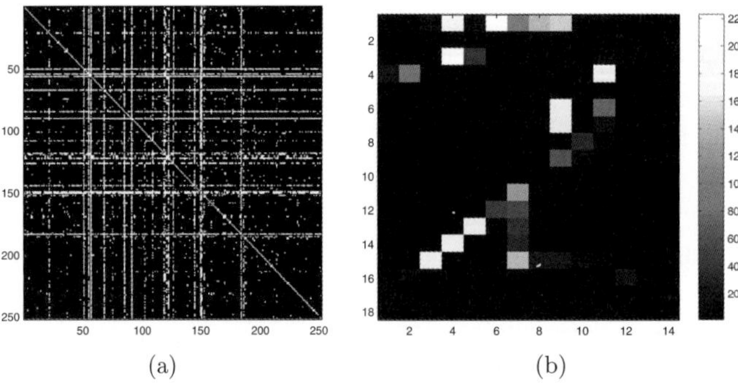

Figure 9.19 (**a**) Based on the pairwise empirical entropies $H(x_i, x_j)$ edges are ordered, high entropy edges first. Shown is the adjacency matrix of the resulting Markov network whose junction tree has cliques ≤ 15 in size (white represents an edge). (**b**) Indicated are the number of cliques that each pixel is a member of, indicating a degree of importance. Note that the lowest clique membership value is 1, so that each pixel is a member of at least one clique.

A maximum likelihood training algorithm for a Markov network, somewhat analogous to the EM approach of Section 11.2 can be derived as follows [32]. Consider the bound, for positive x:

$$\log x \leq x - 1 \Rightarrow -\log x \geq 1 - x. \tag{9.6.41}$$

Hence

$$-\log \frac{Z(\theta)}{Z(\theta^{old})} \geq 1 - \frac{Z(\theta)}{Z(\theta^{old})} \Rightarrow -\log Z(\theta) \geq -\log Z(\theta^{old}) + 1 - \frac{Z(\theta)}{Z(\theta^{old})}. \tag{9.6.42}$$

Then we can write a bound on the log likelihood

$$\frac{1}{N} L(\theta) \geq \frac{1}{N} \sum_{c,n} \theta_c f_c(\mathcal{X}_c^n) - \log Z(\theta^{old}) + 1 - \frac{Z(\theta)}{Z(\theta^{old})}. \tag{9.6.43}$$

As it stands, the bound (9.6.43) is in general not straightforward to optimise since the parameters of each potential are coupled through the $Z(\theta)$ term. For convenience it is useful to first reparameterise and write

$$\theta_c = \underbrace{\theta_c - \theta_c^{old}}_{\alpha_c} + \theta_c^{old}. \tag{9.6.44}$$

Then

$$Z(\theta) = \sum_{\mathcal{X}} \exp\left(\sum_c f_c(\mathcal{X}_c)\theta_c\right) = \sum_{\mathcal{X}} \exp\left(\sum_c f_c(\mathcal{X}_c)\theta_c^{old}\right) \exp\left(\sum_c f_c(\mathcal{X}_c)\alpha_c\right). \tag{9.6.45}$$

One can decouple this using an additional bound derived by first considering:

$$\exp\left(\sum_c \alpha_c f_c(\mathcal{X}_c)\right) = \exp\left(\sum_c p_c \left[\alpha_c \sum_d f_d(\mathcal{X}_d)\right]\right) \tag{9.6.46}$$

where

$$p_c \equiv \frac{f_c(\mathcal{X}_c)}{\sum_d f_d(\mathcal{X}_d)}. \tag{9.6.47}$$

Since $p_c \geq 0$ and $\sum_c p_c = 1$ we may apply Jensen's inequality to give

$$\exp\left(\sum_c \alpha_c f_c(\mathcal{X}_c)\right) \leq \sum_c p_c \exp\left(\sum_d f_d(\mathcal{X}_d)\alpha_c\right). \tag{9.6.48}$$

Hence

$$Z(\theta) \leq \sum_{\mathcal{X}} \exp\left(\sum_c f_c(\mathcal{X}_c)\theta_c^{old}\right) \sum_c p_c \exp\left(\alpha_c \sum_f f_d(\mathcal{X}_c)\right). \tag{9.6.49}$$

Plugging this bound into (9.6.43) we have

$$\frac{1}{N} L(\theta) \geq \sum_c \underbrace{\left\{ \frac{1}{N} \sum_n f_c(\mathcal{X}_c^n)\theta_c - \left\langle p_c \exp\left(\alpha_c \sum_d f_d(\mathcal{X}_c)\right)\right\rangle_{p(\mathcal{X}|\theta^{old})} \right\}}_{LB(\theta_c)} + 1 - \log Z(\theta^{old}). \tag{9.6.50}$$

The term in curly brackets contains the potential parameters θ_c in an uncoupled fashion. Differentiating with respect to θ_c the gradient of each lower bound is given by

$$\frac{\partial LB(\theta_c)}{\partial \theta_c} = \frac{1}{N}\sum_n f_c(\mathcal{X}_c^n) - \left\langle f_c(\mathcal{X}_c)\exp\left(\left(\theta_c - \theta_c^{old}\right)\sum_d f_d(\mathcal{X}_d)\right)\right\rangle_{p(\mathcal{X}|\theta^{old})}. \tag{9.6.51}$$

This can be used as part of a gradient-based optimisation procedure to learn the parameters θ_c. Intuitively, the parameters converge when the empirical average of the functions f match the average of the functions with respect to samples drawn from the distribution, in line with our general condition for maximum likelihood optimal solution.

In general, there would appear to be little advantage in using the above procedure over the general gradient approach in Section 9.6.1 [211]. However, in the special case that the functions sum to 1, $\sum_c f_c(\mathcal{X}_c) = 1$, the zero of the gradient (9.6.51) can be found analytically, giving the iterative scaling (IS) update

$$\theta_c = \theta_c^{old} + \log \frac{1}{N}\sum_n f_c(\mathcal{X}_c^n) - \log \left\langle f_c(\mathcal{X}_c)\right\rangle_{p(\mathcal{X}_c|\theta^{old})}. \tag{9.6.52}$$

The constraint that the features f_c need to be non-negative can be relaxed at the expense of additional variational parameters, see Exercise 9.12.

If the junction tree formed from this exponential form Markov network has limited tree width, computational savings can be made by performing IPF over the cliques of the junction tree and updating the parameters θ within each clique using IS [10]. This is a modified version of the constrained decomposable case. See also [290] for a unified treatment of propagation and scaling on junction trees.

9.6.5 Conditional random fields

For an input x and output y, a Conditional Random Field (CRF) is defined by a conditional distribution [282, 180]

$$p(y|x) = \frac{1}{Z(x)}\prod_k \phi_k(y, x) \tag{9.6.53}$$

for (positive) potentials $\phi_k(y, x)$. To make learning more straightforward, the potentials are usually defined as $\exp(\lambda_k f_k(y, x))$ for fixed functions $f(y, x)$ and parameters λ_k. In this case the distribution of the output conditioned on the input is

$$p(y|x, \lambda) = \frac{1}{Z(x, \lambda)}\prod_k \exp(\lambda_k f_k(y, x)). \tag{9.6.54}$$

CRFs can also be viewed simply as Markov networks with exponential form potentials, as in Section 9.6.4. Equation (9.6.54) is equivalent to Equation (9.6.39) where the parameters θ are here denoted by λ and the variables x are here denoted by y. In the CRF case the inputs x simply have the effect of determining the feature $f_k(y, x)$.

For an i.i.d. dataset of input–outputs, $\mathcal{D} = \{(x^n, y^n), n = 1, \ldots, N\}$, training based on conditional maximum likelihood requires the maximisation of

$$L(\lambda) \equiv \sum_{n=1}^N \log p(y^n|x^n, \lambda) = \sum_{n=1}^N \sum_k \lambda_k f_k(y^n, x^n) - \log Z(x^n, \lambda). \tag{9.6.55}$$

In general no closed form solution for the optimal λ exists and this needs to be determined numerically. The methods we've discussed, such as iterative scaling may be readily adapted to this optimisation problem, although in practice gradient based techniques are to be preferred [211]. For completeness we describe gradient based training. The gradient has components

$$\frac{\partial}{\partial \lambda_i} L = \sum_n \left(f_i(y^n, x^n) - \langle f_i(y, x^n) \rangle_{p(y|x^n,\lambda)} \right). \tag{9.6.56}$$

The terms $\langle f_i(y, x^n) \rangle_{p(y|x^n,\lambda)}$ can be problematic and their tractability depends on the structure of the potentials. For a multivariate y, provided the structure of the cliques defined on subsets of y is singly connected, then computing the average is generally tractable. More generally, provided the cliques of the resulting junction tree have limited width, then exact marginals are available. An example of this is given for a linear-chain CRF in Section 23.4.3 – see also Example 9.11 below.

Another quantity often useful for numerical optimisation is the Hessian which has components

$$\frac{\partial^2}{\partial \lambda_i \partial \lambda_j} L = \sum_n \left(\langle f_i(y, x^n) \rangle \langle f_j(y, x^n) \rangle - \langle f_i(y, x^n) f_j(y, x^n) \rangle \right) \tag{9.6.57}$$

where the averages above are with respect to $p(y|x^n, \lambda)$. This expression is a (negated) sum of covariance elements, and is therefore negative (semi) definite. Hence the function $L(\lambda)$ is concave and has only a single global optimum. In practice CRFs often have many thousands if not millions of parameters λ so that computing the Newton update associated with the inverse of the Hessian may be prohibitively expensive. In this case alternative optimisation methods such as conjugate gradients are preferable.

In practice regularisation terms are often added to prevent overfitting (see Section 13.2.2 for a discussion of regularisation). Using a term

$$-\sum_k c_k^2 \lambda_k^2 \tag{9.6.58}$$

for positive regularisation constants c_k^2 discourages the weights λ from being too large. This term is also negative definite and hence the overall objective function remains concave.

Once trained a CRF can be used for predicting the output distribution for a novel input x^*. The most likely output y^* is equivalently given by

$$y^* = \underset{y}{\text{argmax}} \log p(y|x^*) = \underset{y}{\text{argmax}} \sum_k \lambda_k f_k(y, x^*) - \log Z(x^*, \lambda). \tag{9.6.59}$$

Since the normalisation term is independent of y, finding the most likely output is equivalent to

$$y^* = \underset{y}{\text{argmax}} \sum_k \lambda_k f_k(y, x^*). \tag{9.6.60}$$

Natural language processing

In a natural language processing application, x_t might represent a word and y_t a corresponding linguistic tag ('noun','verb', etc.). A more suitable form in this case is to constrain the CRF to be of the form

$$\exp\left(\sum_k \mu_k g_k(y_t, y_{t-1}) + \sum_l \rho_l h_l(y_t, x_t) \right) \tag{9.6.61}$$

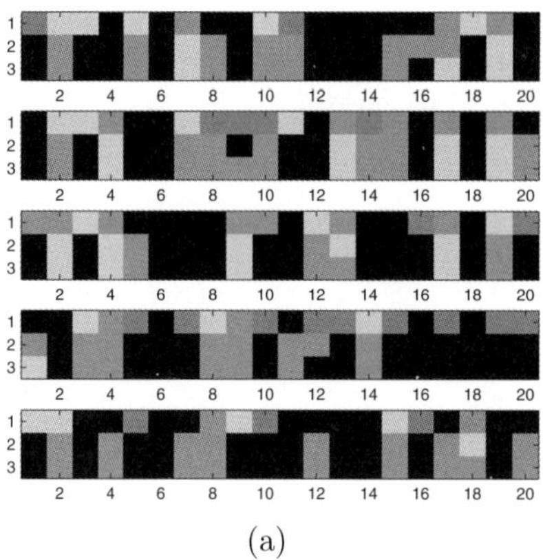

(a)

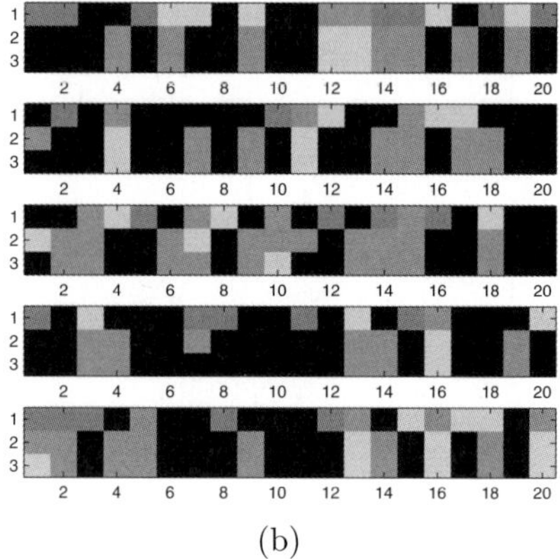

(b)

Figure 9.20 (**a**) Training results for a linear chain CRF. There are five training sequences, one per subpanel. In each subpanel the top row corresponds to the input sequence $x_{1:20}$, $x_t \in \{1, \ldots, 5\}$ (each state represented by a different shade). The middle row is the correct output sequence $y_{1:20}$, $y_t \in \{1, 2, 3\}$ (each state represented by a different shade). Together the input and output sequences make the training data $\mathcal{D}$. The bottom row contains the most likely output sequence given the trained CRF, $\arg\max_{y_{1:20}} p(y_{1:20}|x_{1:20}, \mathcal{D})$. (**b**) Five additional test input sequences (top), correct output sequence (middle) and predicted output sequence (bottom).

for binary functions g_k and h_l and parameters μ_k and ρ_l. The grammatical structure of tag–tag transitions is encoded in $g_k(y_t, y_{t-1})$ and linguistic tag information in $h_k(y_t, x_t)$, with the importance of these being determined by the corresponding parameters [180]. In this case inference of the marginals $\langle y_t y_{t-1} | x_{1:T} \rangle$ is straightforward since the factor graph corresponding to the inference problem is a linear chain.

Variants of the linear chain CRF are used heavily in natural language processing, including part-of-speech tagging and machine translation (in which the input sequence x represents a sentence say in English and the output sequence y the corresponding translation into French). See, for example, [229].

Example 9.11 Linear chain CRF

We consider a CRF with $X = 5$ input states and $Y = 3$ output states of the form

$$p(y_{1:T}|x_{1:T}) = \prod_{t=2}^{T} e^{\sum_k \mu_k g_k(y_t, y_{t-1}) + \sum_l \rho_l h_l(y_t, x_t)}. \tag{9.6.62}$$

Here the binary functions $g_k(y_t, y_{t-1}) = \mathbb{I}[y_t = a_k]\,\mathbb{I}[y_{t-1} = b_k]$, $k = 1, \ldots, 9$, $a_k \in \{1, 2, 3\}$, $b_k \in \{1, 2, 3\}$, simply index the transitions between two consecutive outputs. The binary functions $h_l(y_t, x_t) = \mathbb{I}[y_t = a_l]\,\mathbb{I}[x_t = c_l]$, $l = 1, \ldots, 15$, $a_l \in \{1, 2, 3\}$, $c_l \in \{1, 2, 3, 4, 5\}$, index the translation of the input to the output. There are therefore $9 + 15 = 24$ parameters in total. In Fig. 9.20 we plot the training and test results based on a small set of data. As we see, the model learns to predict the output well, both for the training and test data. The training of the CRF is obtained using 50 iterations of gradient ascent with a learning rate of 0.1. See `demoLinearCRF.m`.

9.6.6 Pseudo likelihood

Consider an MN on variables $\mathbf{x}$ with $\dim(\mathbf{x}) = D$ of the form

$$p(\mathbf{x}|\theta) = \frac{1}{Z}\prod_c \phi_c(\mathcal{X}_c|\theta_c). \tag{9.6.63}$$

For all but specially constrained ϕ_c, the partition function Z will be intractable and the likelihood of a set of i.i.d. data intractable as well. A surrogate is to use the *pseudo likelihood* of each variable conditioned on all other variables (which is equivalent to conditioning on only the variable's neighbours for an MN)

$$L'(\theta) = \sum_{n=1}^{N}\sum_{i=1}^{D} \log p(x_i^n|\mathbf{x}_{\setminus i}^n|\theta). \tag{9.6.64}$$

The terms $p(x_i^n|\mathbf{x}_{\setminus i}^n|\theta)$ are usually straightforward to work out since they require finding the normalisation of a univariate distribution only. In this case the gradient can be computed exactly, and learning of the parameters θ carried out. In general, the solution found does not correspond to the maximum likelihood solution. However, at least for some special cases, such as the Boltzmann machine, this forms a consistent estimator [152].

9.6.7 Learning the structure

Learning the structure of a Markov network can also be based on independence tests, as for belief networks in Section 9.5. A criterion for finding an MN on a set of nodes $\mathcal{X}$ is to use the fact that no edge exits between x and y if, conditioned on all other nodes, x and y are deemed independent. This is the pairwise Markov property described in Section 4.2.1. By checking $x \perp\!\!\!\perp y|\mathcal{X}\setminus\{x, y\}$ for every pair of variables x and y, this edge deletion approach in principle reveals the structure of the network [236]. For learning the structure from an oracle, this method is sound. However, a practical difficulty in the case where the independencies are determined from data is that checking if $x \perp\!\!\!\perp y|\mathcal{X}\setminus\{x, y\}$ requires in principle enormous amounts of data. The reason for this is that the conditioning selects only those parts of the dataset consistent with the conditioning. In practice this will result in very small numbers of remaining datapoints, and estimating independencies on this basis is unreliable.

The Markov boundary criterion [236] uses the local Markov property, Section 4.2.1, namely that conditioned on its neighbours, a variable is independent of all other variables in the graph. By starting with a variable x and an empty neighbourhood set, one can progressively include neighbours, testing if their inclusion renders the remaining non-neighbours independent of x. A difficulty with this is that, if one doesn't have the correct Markov boundary, then including a variable in the neighbourhood set may be deemed necessary. To see this, consider a network which corresponds to a linear chain and that x is at the edge of the chain. In this case, only the nearest neighbour of x is in the Markov boundary of x. However, if this nearest neighbour were not currently in the set, then any other non-nearest neighbour would be included, even though this is not strictly required. To counter this, the neighbourhood variables included in the neighbourhood of x may be later removed if they are deemed superfluous to the boundary [112].

In cases where specific constraints are imposed, such as learning structures whose resulting triangulation has a bounded tree-width, whilst still formally difficult, approximate procedures are available [275].

In terms of network scoring methods for undirected networks, computing a score is hampered by the fact that the parameters of each clique become coupled in the normalisation constant of the distribution. This issue can be addressed using hyper Markov priors [79].

9.7 Summary

- For discrete belief networks, it is particularly convenient to use a Dirichlet parameter prior since this is conjugate to the categorical distribution.
- Provided we assume local and global parameter independence, the posterior over belief network tables factorises.
- Learning the structure of a belief network is more complex. The PC algorithm uses local independence tests to decide if two variables should be linked. A global alternative is based on using a network scoring method such as the model likelihood of a network structure under a Dirichlet prior.
- Learning the maximum likelihood parameters of a decomposable Markov network is straightforward and can be achieved by counting.
- For non-decomposable Markov networks, no closed form solution exists. The maximum likelihood criterion is equivalent to ensuring that clique marginals match empirical marginals. The iterative proportional fitting algorithm is a technique to set the tables to ensure these marginals match.
- For Markov networks parameterised using feature functions, iterative scaling is a maximum likelihood technique that enables individual parameter updates to be made. Gradient-based approaches are also straightforward and popular in conditional random fields.

9.8 Code

`condindepEmp.m`: Bayes test and mutual information for empirical conditional independence
`condMI.m`: Conditional mutual information
`condMIemp.m`: Conditional mutual information of empirical distribution
`MIemp.m`: Mutual information of empirical distribution

9.8.1 PC algorithm using an oracle

This demo uses an oracle to determine $x \perp\!\!\!\perp y \mid z$, rather than using data to determine the empirical dependence. The oracle is itself a belief network. For the partial orientation only the first 'unmarried collider' rule is implemented.

`demoPCoracle.m`: Demo of PC algorithm with an oracle
`PCskeletonOracle.m`: PC algorithm using an oracle
`PCorient.m`: Orient a skeleton

9.8.2 Demo of empirical conditional independence

For half of the experiments, the data is drawn from a distribution for which $x \perp\!\!\!\perp y \mid z$ is true. For the other half of the experiments, the data is drawn from a random distribution for which $x \perp\!\!\!\perp y \mid z$

is false. We then measure the fraction of experiments for which the Bayes test correctly decides $x \perp\!\!\!\perp y | z$. We also measure the fraction of experiments for which the Mutual Information (MI) test correctly decides $x \perp\!\!\!\perp y | z$, based on setting the threshold equal to the median of all the empirical conditional mutual information values. A similar empirical threshold can also be obtained for the Bayes' factor (although this is not strictly kosher in the pure Bayesian spirit since one should in principle set the threshold to zero). The test based on the assumed chi-squared distributed MI is included for comparison, although it seems to be impractical in these small data cases.

`demoCondIndepEmp.m`: Demo of empirical conditional independence based on data

9.8.3 Bayes Dirichlet structure learning

It is interesting to compare the result of `demoPCdata.m` with `demoBDscore.m`.

`PCskeletonData.m`: PC algorithm using empirical conditional independence
`demoPCdata.m`: Demo of PC algorithm with data
`BDscore.m`: Bayes Dirichlet (BD) score for a node given parents
`learnBayesNet.m`: Given an ancestral order and maximal parents, learn the network
`demoBDscore.m`: Demo of structure learning

9.9 Exercises

9.1 (Printer Nightmare) Cheapco is, quite honestly, a pain in the neck. Not only did they buy a dodgy old laser printer from StopPress and use it mercilessly, but try to get away with using substandard components and materials. Unfortunately for StopPress, they have a contract to maintain Cheapco's old warhorse, and end up frequently sending the mechanic out to repair the printer. They decide to make a statistical model of Cheapco's printer, so that they will have a reasonable idea of the fault based only on the information that Cheapco's secretary tells them on the phone. In that way, StopPress hopes to be able to send out to Cheapco only a junior repair mechanic, having most likely diagnosed the fault over the phone.

Based on the manufacturer's information, StopPress has a good idea of the dependencies in the printer, and what is likely to directly affect other printer components. The belief network in Fig. 9.21 represents these assumptions. However, the specific way that Cheapco abuse their printer is a mystery, so that the exact probabilistic relationships between the faults and problems is idiosyncratic to Cheapco. StopPress has the following table of faults in which each column represents a visit.

fuse assembly malfunction	0	0	0	1	0	0	0	0	0	0	0	0	1	0	1
drum unit	0	0	0	0	1	0	0	1	0	0	1	1	0	0	0
toner out	1	1	0	0	0	1	0	1	0	0	0	1	0	0	0
poor paper quality	1	0	1	0	1	0	1	0	1	1	0	1	1	0	0
worn roller	0	0	0	0	0	0	1	0	0	0	0	0	0	1	1
burning smell	0	0	0	1	0	0	0	0	0	0	0	0	1	0	0
poor print quality	1	1	1	0	1	1	0	1	0	0	1	1	0	0	0
wrinkled pages	0	0	1	0	0	0	0	0	1	0	0	0	1	1	1
multiple pages fed	0	0	1	0	0	0	1	0	1	0	0	0	0	0	1
paper jam	0	0	1	1	0	0	1	1	1	1	0	0	0	1	0

1. The above table is contained in `printer.mat`. Learn all table entries on the basis of maximum likelihood.

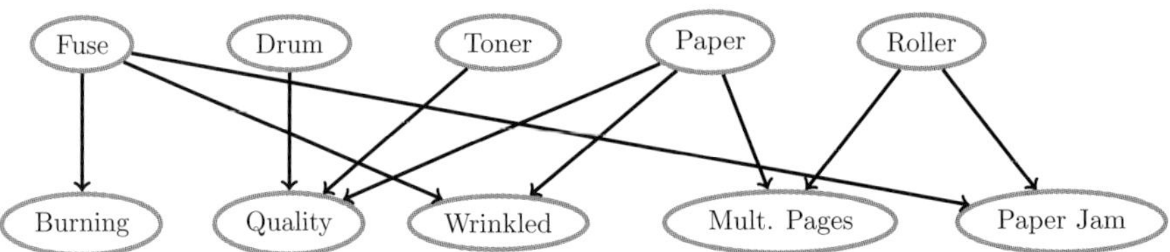

Figure 9.21 Printer Nightmare belief network. All variables are binary. The upper variables without parents are possible problems (diagnoses), and the lower variables consequences of problems (faults).

2. Program the belief network using the maximum likelihood tables and BRMLTOOLBOX. Compute the probability that there is a fuse assembly malfunction given that the secretary complains there is a burning smell and that the paper is jammed, and that there are no other problems.
3. Repeat the above calculation using a Bayesian method in which a flat Beta prior is used on all tables.
4. Given the above information from the secretary, what is the most likely joint diagnosis over the diagnostic variables – that is the joint most likely $p(Fuse, Drum, Toner, Paper, Roller|\text{evidence})$? Use the max-absorption method on the associated junction tree.
5. Compute the joint most likely state of the distribution

   $$p(Fuse, Drum, Toner, Paper, Roller|\text{burning smell, paper jammed}).$$

   Explain how to compute this efficiently using the max-absorption method.

9.2 Consider data $x^n, n = 1, \ldots, N$. Show that for a Gaussian distribution, the maximum likelihood estimator of the mean is $\hat{m} = \frac{1}{N}\sum_{n=1}^{N} x^n$ and variance is $\hat{\sigma}^2 = \frac{1}{N}\sum_{n=1}^{N}(x^n - \hat{m})^2$.

9.3 A training set consists of one-dimensional examples from two classes. The training examples from class 1 are

$$0.5, 0.1, 0.2, 0.4, 0.3, 0.2, 0.2, 0.1, 0.35, 0.25 \tag{9.9.1}$$

and from class 2 are

$$0.9, 0.8, 0.75, 1.0. \tag{9.9.2}$$

Fit a (one-dimensional) Gaussian using maximum likelihood to each of these two classes. Also estimate the class probabilities p_1 and p_2 using maximum likelihood. What is the probability that the test point $x = 0.6$ belongs to class 1?

9.4 For a set of N observations (training data), $\mathcal{X} = \{\mathbf{x}^1, \ldots, \mathbf{x}^N\}$, and independently gathered observations, the log likelihood for a belief network to generate $\mathcal{X}$ is

$$\log p(\mathcal{X}) = \sum_{n=1}^{N}\sum_{i=1}^{K} \log p\left(x_i^n|\text{pa}\left(x_i^n\right)\right). \tag{9.9.3}$$

We define the notation

$$\theta_s^i(t) = p(x_i = s|\text{pa}\left(x_i\right) = t) \tag{9.9.4}$$

representing the probability that variable x_i is in state s given the parents of variable x_i are in the vector of states $\mathbf{t}$. Using a Lagrangian

$$L \equiv \sum_{n=1}^{N}\sum_{i=1}^{K} \log p\left(x_i^n|\text{pa}\left(x_i^n\right)\right) + \sum_{i=1}^{K}\sum_{t^i} \lambda_{t^i}^i \left(1 - \sum_{s} \theta_s^i\left(t^i\right)\right). \tag{9.9.5}$$

Show that the maximum likelihood setting of $\theta_s^i(\mathbf{t})$ is

$$\theta_s^j(t^j) = \frac{\sum_{n=1}^{N} \mathbb{I}\left[x_j^n = s\right] \mathbb{I}\left[\text{pa}\left(x_j^n\right) = t^j\right]}{\sum_{n=1}^{N} \sum_s \mathbb{I}\left[x_j^n = s\right] \mathbb{I}\left[\text{pa}\left(x_j^n\right) = t^j\right]}. \tag{9.9.6}$$

9.5 (Conditional likelihood training) Consider a situation in which we partition observable variables into disjoint sets x and y and that we want to find the parameters that maximise the *conditional likelihood*,

$$CL(\theta) = \frac{1}{N} \sum_{n=1}^{N} \log p(y^n | x^n, \theta), \tag{9.9.7}$$

for a set of training data $\{(x^n, y^n), n = 1, \ldots, N\}$. All data is assumed generated from the same distribution $p(x, y|\theta^0) = p(y|x, \theta^0)p(x|\theta^0)$ for some unknown parameter θ^0. In the limit of a large amount of i.i.d. training data, does $CL(\theta)$ have an optimum at θ^0?

9.6 (Moment matching) One way to set parameters of a distribution is to match the moments of the distribution to the empirical moments. This sometimes corresponds to maximum likelihood (for the Gaussian distribution for example), though generally this is not consistent with maximum likelihood.

For data with mean m and variance s, show that to fit a Beta distribution $B(x|\alpha, \beta)$ by moment matching, we use

$$\alpha = \frac{m(m - m^2 - s)}{s}, \quad \beta = \alpha \frac{1 - m}{m}. \tag{9.9.8}$$

Does this correspond to maximum likelihood?

9.7 For i.i.d. data $0 \leq x^n \leq 1, n = 1, \ldots, N$, generated from a Beta distribution $B(x|a, b)$, show that the log likelihood is given by

$$L(a, b) \equiv (a - 1) \sum_{n=1}^{N} \log x^n + (b - 1) \sum_{n=1}^{N} \log(1 - x^n) - N \log B(a, b) \tag{9.9.9}$$

where $B(a, b)$ is the Beta function. Show that the derivatives are

$$\frac{\partial}{\partial a} L = \sum_{n=1}^{N} \log x^n - N\psi(a) - N\psi(a + b),$$

$$\frac{\partial}{\partial b} L = \sum_{n=1}^{N} \log(1 - x^n) - N\psi(b) - N\psi(a + b) \tag{9.9.10}$$

where $\psi(x) \equiv d \log \Gamma(x)/dx$ is the digamma function, and suggest a method to learn the parameters a, b.

9.8 Consider the Boltzmann machine as defined in Example 9.8. Write down the pseudo likelihood for a set of i.i.d. data $\mathbf{v}^1, \ldots, \mathbf{v}^N$ and derive the gradient of this with respect to w_{ij}, $i \neq j$.

9.9 Show that the model likelihood equation (9.4.53) can be written explicitly as

$$p(\mathcal{D}|M) = \prod_k \prod_j \frac{\Gamma\left(\sum_i u_i(v_k; j)\right)}{\Gamma\left(\sum_i u_i'(v_k; j)\right)} \prod_i \left[\frac{\Gamma\left(u_i'(v_k; j)\right)}{\Gamma\left(u_i(v_k; j)\right)}\right]. \tag{9.9.11}$$

9.10 Define the set $\mathcal{N}$ as consisting of eight node belief networks in which each node has at most two parents. For a given ancestral order a, the restricted set is written $\mathcal{N}_a$.

1. How many belief networks are in $\mathcal{N}_a$?
2. What is the computational time to find the optimal member of $\mathcal{N}_a$ using the Bayesian Dirichlet score, assuming that computing the BD score of any member of $\mathcal{N}_a$ takes 1 second and bearing in mind the decomposability of the BD score.
3. What is the time to find the optimal member of $\mathcal{N}$?

9.11 For the Markov network

$$p(x, y, z) = \frac{1}{Z}\phi_1(x, y)\phi_2(y, z) \tag{9.9.12}$$

derive an iterative scaling algorithm to learn the unconstrained tables $\phi_1(x, y)$ and $\phi_2(x, y)$ based on a set of i.i.d. data $\mathcal{X}, \mathcal{Y}, \mathcal{Z}$.

9.12 In Section 9.6.4 we considered maximum likelihood learning of a Markov network $p(\mathcal{X}) \propto \prod_c \phi_c(\mathcal{X}_c)$ with parameters θ_c and potentials of the form

$$\phi_c(\mathcal{X}_c) = \exp\left(\theta_c f_c(\mathcal{X}_c)\right) \tag{9.9.13}$$

with the constraint $f_c(\mathcal{X}_c) \geq 0$. Our interest here is to drop this positive constraint on $f_c(\mathcal{X}_c)$. By considering

$$\sum_c \theta_c f_c(\mathcal{X}_c) = \sum_c p_c \frac{\theta_c f_c(\mathcal{X}_c)}{p_c} \tag{9.9.14}$$

for auxiliary variables $p_c > 0$ such that $\sum_c p_c = 1$, explain how to derive a form of iterative scaling training algorithm for general f_c in which each parameter θ_c can be updated separately.

9.13 Write a MATLAB routine `A = ChowLiu(X)` where X is a $D \times N$ data matrix containing a multivariate datapoint on each column that returns a Chow–Liu maximum likelihood tree for X. The tree structure is to be returned in the sparse matrix A. You may find the routine `spantree.m` useful. The file `ChowLiuData.mat` contains a data matrix for 10 variables. Use your routine to find the maximum likelihood Chow–Liu tree, and draw a picture of the resulting DAG with edges oriented away from variable 1.

10 Naive Bayes

So far we've discussed methods in some generality without touching much on how we might use the methods in a practical setting. Here we discuss one of the simplest methods that is widely used in practice to classify data. This is a useful junction since it enables us to discuss the issues of parameter learning from data and also (constrained) structure learning.

10.1 Naive Bayes and conditional independence

We shall discuss machine learning concepts in some detail in Chapter 13. Here, we require only the intuitive concept of classification, which means giving a discrete label to an input. For example, one might wish to classify an input image into one of two classes – male or female. Naive Bayes (NB) is a popular classification method and aids our discussion of conditional independence, overfitting and Bayesian methods. In NB, we form a joint model a D-dimensional attribute (input) vector $\mathbf{x}$ and the corresponding class label c

$$p(\mathbf{x}, c) = p(c) \prod_{i=1}^{D} p(x_i|c) \tag{10.1.1}$$

whose belief network is depicted in Fig. 10.1(a). Coupled with a suitable choice for each conditional distribution $p(x_i|c)$, we can then use Bayes' rule to form a classifier for a novel input vector $\mathbf{x}^*$:

$$p(c|\mathbf{x}^*) = \frac{p(\mathbf{x}^*|c)p(c)}{p(\mathbf{x}^*)} = \frac{p(\mathbf{x}^*|c)p(c)}{\sum_c p(\mathbf{x}^*|c)p(c)}. \tag{10.1.2}$$

In practice it is common to consider only two classes dom $(c) = \{0, 1\}$. The theory we describe below is valid for any number of classes c, though our examples are restricted to the binary class

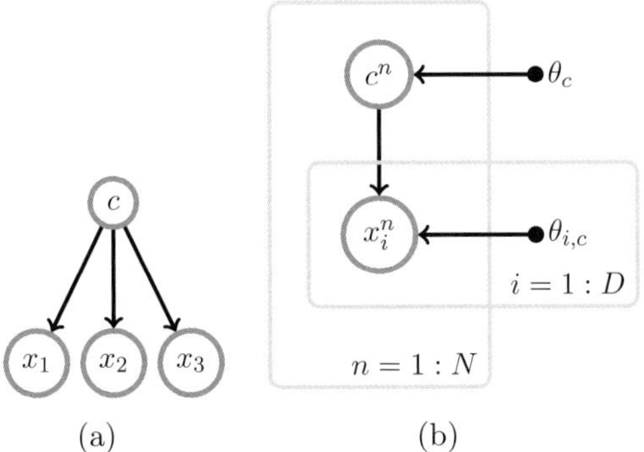

Figure 10.1 Naive Bayes classifier. (**a**) The central assumption is that given the class c, the attributes x_i are independent. (**b**) Assuming the data is i.i.d., maximum likelihood learns the optimal parameters θ_c of the distribution $p(c)$ and the parameters $\theta_{i,c}$ of the class-dependent attribute distributions $p(x_i|c)$.

case. Also, the attributes x_i are often taken to be binary, as we shall do initially below as well. The extension to more than two attribute states, or continuous attributes is straightforward.

Example 10.1

EZsurvey.org partitions radio station listeners into two groups – the 'young' and 'old'. They assume that, given the knowledge that a customer is either 'young' or 'old', this is sufficient to determine whether or not a customer will like a particular radio station, independent of their likes or dislikes for any other stations:

$$p(r_1, r_2, r_3, r_4|age) = p(r_1|age)p(r_2|age)p(r_3|age)p(r_4|age) \tag{10.1.3}$$

where each of the variables r_1, r_2, r_3, r_4 can take the states like or dislike, and the 'age' variable can take the value young or old. Thus the information about the age of the customer determines the individual radio station preferences without needing to know anything else. To complete the specification, given that a customer is young, she has a 95% chance to like Radio1, a 5% chance to like Radio2, a 2% chance to like Radio3 and a 20% chance to like Radio4. Similarly, an old listener has a 3% chance to like Radio1, an 82% chance to like Radio2, a 34% chance to like Radio3 and a 92% chance to like Radio4. They know that 90% of the listeners are old.

Given this model, and the fact that a new customer likes Radio1 and Radio3, but dislikes Radio2 and Radio4, what is the probability that the new customer is young? This is given by

$$\begin{aligned} &p(\text{young}|r_1 = \text{like}, r_2 = \text{dislike}, r_3 = \text{like}, r_4 = \text{dislike}) \\ &\qquad = \frac{p(r_1 = \text{like}, r_2 = \text{dislike}, r_3 = \text{like}, r_4 = \text{dislike}|\text{young})p(\text{young})}{\sum_{age} p(r_1 = \text{like}, r_2 = \text{dislike}, r_3 = \text{like}, r_4 = \text{dislike}|age)p(age)}. \end{aligned} \tag{10.1.4}$$

Using the naive Bayes structure, the numerator above is given by

$$p(r_1 = \text{like}|\text{young})p(r_2 = \text{dislike}|\text{young})p(r_3 = \text{like}|\text{young})p(r_4 = \text{dislike}|\text{young}) \times p(\text{young}). \tag{10.1.5}$$

Plugging in the values we obtain

$$0.95 \times 0.95 \times 0.02 \times 0.8 \times 0.1 = 0.0014.$$

The denominator is given by this value plus the corresponding term evaluated assuming the customer is old,

$$0.03 \times 0.18 \times 0.34 \times 0.08 \times 0.9 = 1.3219 \times 10^{-4}$$

which gives

$$p(\text{young}|r_1 = \text{like}, r_2 = \text{dislike}, r_3 = \text{like}, r_4 = \text{dislike}) = \frac{0.0014}{0.0014 + 1.3219 \times 10^{-4}} = 0.9161. \tag{10.1.6}$$

10.2 Estimation using maximum likelihood

Learning the table entries for NB is a straightforward application of the more general BN learning discussed in Section 9.3. For a fully observed dataset, maximum likelihood learning of the table entries corresponds to counting the number of occurrences in the training data, as we show below. This is a useful exercise to reinforce and make more concrete the general theory of Section 9.3.

10.2.1 Binary attributes

Consider a dataset $\{(\mathbf{x}^n, c^n), n = 1, \ldots, N\}$ of binary attributes, $x_i^n \in \{0, 1\}$, $i = 1, \ldots, D$ and associated class label c^n. The number of datapoints from class $c = 0$ is denoted n_0 and the number from class $c = 1$ is denoted n_1. For each attribute of the two classes, we need to estimate the values $p(x_i = 1|c) \equiv \theta_i^c$. The other probability, $p(x_i = 0|c)$ is given by the normalisation requirement, $p(x_i = 0|c) = 1 - p(x_i = 1|c) = 1 - \theta_i^c$.

Based on the NB conditional independence assumption the probability of observing a vector $\mathbf{x}$ can be compactly written[1]

$$p(\mathbf{x}|c) = \prod_{i=1}^{D} p(x_i|c) = \prod_{i=1}^{D} (\theta_i^c)^{x_i}(1 - \theta_i^c)^{1-x_i}. \tag{10.2.1}$$

In the above expression, x_i is either 0 or 1 and hence each i term contributes a factor θ_i^c if $x_i = 1$ or $1 - \theta_i^c$ if $x_i = 0$. Together with the assumption that the training data is i.i.d. generated, the log likelihood of the attributes and class labels is

$$L = \sum_n \log p(\mathbf{x}^n, c^n) = \sum_n \log p(c^n) \prod_i p(x_i^n|c^n) \tag{10.2.2}$$

$$= \left\{ \sum_{i,n} x_i^n \log \theta_i^{c^n} + (1 - x_i^n) \log(1 - \theta_i^{c^n}) \right\} + n_0 \log p(c = 0) + n_1 \log p(c = 1). \tag{10.2.3}$$

This can be written more explicitly in terms of the parameters as

$$L = \sum_{i,n} \{ \mathbb{I}[x_i^n = 1, c^n = 0] \log \theta_i^0 + \mathbb{I}[x_i^n = 0, c^n = 0] \log(1 - \theta_i^0) + \mathbb{I}[x_i^n = 1, c^n = 1] \log \theta_i^1$$

$$+ \mathbb{I}[x_i^n = 0, c^n = 1] \log(1 - \theta_i^1) \} + n_0 \log p(c = 0) + n_1 \log p(c = 1). \tag{10.2.4}$$

We can find the maximum likelihood optimal θ_i^c by differentiating w.r.t. θ_i^c and equating to zero, giving

$$\theta_i^c = p(x_i = 1|c) = \frac{\sum_n \mathbb{I}[x_i^n = 1, c^n = c]}{\sum_n \mathbb{I}[x_i^n = 0, c^n = c] + \mathbb{I}[x_i^n = 1, c^n = c]} \tag{10.2.5}$$

$$= \frac{\text{number of times } x_i = 1 \text{ for class c}}{\text{number of datapoints in class c}}. \tag{10.2.6}$$

Similarly, optimising Equation (10.2.3) with respect to $p(c)$ gives

$$p(c) = \frac{\text{number of times class c occurs}}{\text{total number of data points}}. \tag{10.2.7}$$

These results are consistent with our general theory in Section 9.3 that maximum likelihood corresponds to setting tables by counting.

[1] This makes use of the general notation that any quantity raised to the power 0 is 1, i.e. $x^0 \equiv 1$. Unfortunately, there is a potential general mathematical notational confusion with x^y meaning possibly x raised to the power y, or alternatively that y is simply indexing a set of x variables. This potential conflict will not hopefully arise too often, and can most often be resolved by reference to the meaning of the symbols involved.

Classification boundary

We classify a novel input $\mathbf{x}^*$ as class 1 if

$$p(c = 1|\mathbf{x}^*) > p(c = 0|\mathbf{x}^*). \tag{10.2.8}$$

Using Bayes' rule and writing the log of the above expression, this is equivalent to

$$\log p(\mathbf{x}^*|c = 1) + \log p(c = 1) - \log p(\mathbf{x}^*) > \log p(\mathbf{x}^*|c = 0) + \log p(c = 0) - \log p(\mathbf{x}^*). \tag{10.2.9}$$

From the definition of the classifier, this is equivalent to (the normalisation constant $-\log p(\mathbf{x}^*)$ can be dropped from both sides)

$$\sum_i \log p(x_i^*|c = 1) + \log p(c = 1) > \sum_i \log p(x_i^*|c = 0) + \log p(c = 0). \tag{10.2.10}$$

Using the binary encoding $x_i \in \{0, 1\}$, we therefore classify $\mathbf{x}^*$ as class 1 if

$$\sum_i \left\{x_i^* \log \theta_i^1 + (1 - x_i^*) \log(1 - \theta_i^1)\right\} + \log p(c = 1)$$
$$> \sum_i \left\{x_i^* \log \theta_i^0 + (1 - x_i^*) \log(1 - \theta_i^0)\right\} + \log p(c = 0). \tag{10.2.11}$$

This decision rule can be expressed in the form: classify $\mathbf{x}^*$ as class 1 if $\sum_i w_i x_i^* + a > 0$ for some suitable choice of weights w_i and constant a, see Exercise 10.4. The interpretation is that $\mathbf{w}$ specifies a hyperplane in the attribute space and $\mathbf{x}^*$ is classified as 1 if it lies on the positive side of the hyperplane.

Example 10.2 Are they Scottish?

Consider the following vector of binary attributes:

$$(\text{shortbread, lager, whiskey, porridge, football}) \tag{10.2.12}$$

A vector $\mathbf{x} = (1, 0, 1, 1, 0)^\mathsf{T}$ would describe that a person likes shortbread, does not like lager, drinks whiskey, eats porridge, and has not watched England play football. Together with each vector $\mathbf{x}$, there is a label nat describing the nationality of the person, dom $(nat) = \{\text{scottish, english}\}$, see Fig. 10.2.

We wish to classify the vector $\mathbf{x} = (1, 0, 1, 1, 0)^\mathsf{T}$ as either scottish or english. Using Bayes' rule:

$$p(\text{scottish}|\mathbf{x}) = \frac{p(\mathbf{x}|\text{scottish})\,p(\text{scottish})}{p(\mathbf{x})} = \frac{p(\mathbf{x}|\text{scottish})\,p(\text{scottish})}{p(\mathbf{x}|\text{scottish})\,p(\text{scottish}) + p(\mathbf{x}|\text{english})\,p(\text{english})}. \tag{10.2.13}$$

By maximum likelihood the 'prior' class probability $p(\text{scottish})$ is given by the fraction of people in the database that are Scottish, and similarly $p(\text{english})$ is given as the fraction of people in the database that are English. This gives $p(\text{scottish}) = 7/13$ and $p(\text{english}) = 6/13$.

For $p(\mathbf{x}|nat)$ under the naive Bayes assumption:

$$p(\mathbf{x}|nat) = p(x_1|nat)\,p(x_2|nat)\,p(x_3|nat)\,p(x_4|nat)\,p(x_5|nat) \tag{10.2.14}$$

0	1	1	1	0	0
0	0	1	1	1	0
1	1	0	0	0	0
1	1	0	0	0	1
1	0	1	0	1	0

(a)

1	1	1	1	1	1	1
0	1	1	1	1	0	0
0	0	1	0	0	1	1
1	0	1	1	1	1	0
1	1	0	0	1	0	0

(b)

Figure 10.2 (**a**) English tastes for 6 people over attributes (*shortbread, lager, whiskey, porridge, football*). Each column represents the tastes of an individual. (**b**) Scottish tastes for 7 people.

so that knowing whether not someone is Scottish, we don't need to know anything else to calculate the probability of their likes and dislikes. Based on the table in Fig. 10.2 and using maximum likelihood we have:

$$\begin{array}{ll} p(x_1 = 1|\text{english}) = 1/2 & p(x_1 = 1|\text{scottish}) = 1 \\ p(x_2 = 1|\text{english}) = 1/2 & p(x_2 = 1|\text{scottish}) = 4/7 \\ p(x_3 = 1|\text{english}) = 1/3 & p(x_3 = 1|\text{scottish}) = 3/7 \\ p(x_4 = 1|\text{english}) = 1/2 & p(x_4 = 1|\text{scottish}) = 5/7 \\ p(x_5 = 1|\text{english}) = 1/2 & p(x_5 = 1|\text{scottish}) = 3/7. \end{array} \tag{10.2.15}$$

For $\mathbf{x} = (1, 0, 1, 1, 0)^{\mathsf{T}}$, we get

$$p(\text{scottish}|\mathbf{x}) = \frac{1 \times \frac{3}{7} \times \frac{3}{7} \times \frac{5}{7} \times \frac{4}{7} \times \frac{7}{13}}{1 \times \frac{3}{7} \times \frac{3}{7} \times \frac{5}{7} \times \frac{4}{7} \times \frac{7}{13} + \frac{1}{2} \times \frac{1}{2} \times \frac{1}{3} \times \frac{1}{2} \times \frac{1}{2} \times \frac{6}{13}} = 0.8076. \tag{10.2.16}$$

Since this is greater than 0.5, we would classify this person as being Scottish.

Small data counts

In Example 10.2, consider trying to classify the vector $\mathbf{x} = (0, 1, 1, 1, 1)^{\mathsf{T}}$. In the training data, all Scottish people say they like shortbread. This means that for this particular $\mathbf{x}$, $p(\mathbf{x}, \text{scottish}) = 0$, and therefore that we make the extremely confident classification $p(\text{scottish}|\mathbf{x}) = 0$. This demonstrates a difficulty using maximum likelihood with sparse data. One way to ameliorate this is to smooth the probabilities, for example by adding a small number to the frequency counts of each attribute. This ensures that there are no zero probabilities in the model. An alternative is to use a Bayesian approach that discourages extreme probabilities, as discussed in Section 10.3.

Potential pitfalls with encoding

In many off-the-shelf packages implementing naive Bayes, binary attributes are assumed. In practice, however, the case of non-binary attributes often occurs. Consider the following attribute: age. In a survey, a person's age is marked down using the variable $a \in 1, 2, 3$; $a = 1$ means the person is between 0 and 10 years old, $a = 2$ means the person is between 10 and 20 years old, $a = 3$ means the person is older than 20. One way to transform the variable a into a binary representation would be to use three binary variables (a_1, a_2, a_3) with $(1, 0, 0)$, $(0, 1, 0)$, $(0, 0, 1)$ representing $a = 1, a = 2, a = 3$ respectively. This is called *1-of-M coding* since only 1 of the binary variables is active in encoding the M states. By construction, this means that the variables a_1, a_2, a_3 are dependent – for example, if we know that $a_1 = 1$, we know that $a_2 = 0$ and $a_3 = 0$. Regardless of any class conditioning, these variables will always be dependent, contrary to the assumption of naive Bayes. A correct approach is to use variables with more than two states, as explained in Section 10.2.2.

10.2.2 Multi-state variables

The extension of the above method to class variables c with more than two states is straightforward. We concentrate here therefore on extending the attribute variables to having more than two states. For a variable x_i with states, $\text{dom}(x_i) = \{1, \ldots, S\}$, the likelihood of observing a state $x_i = s$ is denoted

$$p(x_i = s|c) = \theta_s^i(c) \tag{10.2.17}$$

with $\sum_s p(x_i = s|c) = 1$. The class conditional likelihood of generating the i.i.d. data $\mathcal{D} = (\mathbf{x}^n, c^n), n = 1, \ldots, N$ is

$$\prod_{n=1}^{N} p(\mathbf{x}^n|c^n) = \prod_{n=1}^{N}\prod_{i=1}^{D}\prod_{s=1}^{S}\prod_{c=1}^{C} \theta_s^i(c)^{\mathbb{I}[x_i^n=s]\mathbb{I}[c^n=c]}. \tag{10.2.18}$$

The effect of the indicators is that only those terms $\theta_s^i(c)$ survive for which there are attributes i in state s for class c. This then gives the class conditional log-likelihood

$$L(\theta) = \sum_{n=1}^{N}\sum_{i=1}^{D}\sum_{s=1}^{S}\sum_{c=1}^{C} \mathbb{I}[x_i^n = s]\,\mathbb{I}[c^n = c] \log \theta_s^i(c). \tag{10.2.19}$$

We can optimise with respect to the parameters θ using a Lagrange multiplier (one for each of the attributes i and classes c) to ensure normalisation. This gives the Lagrangian

$$\mathcal{L}(\theta, \lambda) = \sum_{n=1}^{N}\sum_{i=1}^{D}\sum_{s=1}^{S}\sum_{c=1}^{C} \mathbb{I}[x_i^n = s]\,\mathbb{I}[c^n = c] \log \theta_s^i(c) + \sum_{c=1}^{C}\sum_{i=1}^{D} \lambda_i^c \left(1 - \sum_{s=1}^{S} \theta_s^i(c)\right). \tag{10.2.20}$$

To find the optimum of this function we may differentiate with respect to $\theta_s^i(c)$ and equate to zero. Solving the resulting equation we obtain

$$\sum_{n=1}^{N} \frac{\mathbb{I}[x_i^n = s]\,\mathbb{I}[c^n = c]}{\theta_s^i(c)} = \lambda_i^c. \tag{10.2.21}$$

Hence, by normalisation,

$$\theta_s^i(c) = p(x_i = s|c) = \frac{\sum_n \mathbb{I}[x_i^n = s]\,\mathbb{I}[c^n = c]}{\sum_{s',n'} \mathbb{I}\left[x_i^{n'} = s'\right]\mathbb{I}\left[c^{n'} = c\right]}. \tag{10.2.22}$$

The maximum likelihood setting for the parameter $p(x_i = s|c)$ equals the relative number of times that attribute i is in state s for class c.

10.2.3 Text classification

Consider a set of documents about politics, and another set about sport. Our interest is to make a method that can automatically classify a new document as pertaining to either sport or politics.

We search through both sets of documents to find say the 100 most commonly occurring words (not including so-called 'stop words' such as 'a' or 'the'). Each document is then represented by a 100-dimensional vector representing the number of times that each of the words occurs in that document – the so-called *bag of words* representation (this is a crude representation of the document since it discards word order). A naive Bayes model specifies a distribution of these number of occurrences $p(x_i|c)$, where x_i is the count of the number of times word i appears in documents of type c. One can achieve this using either a multistate representation (as discussed in Section 10.2.2) or using a continuous x_i to represent the relative frequency of word i in the document. In the latter case $p(x_i|c)$ could be conveniently modelled using for example a Beta distribution.

Despite the simplicity of naive Bayes, it can classify novel documents surprisingly well [137] (although naturally the real practical methods work with many more attributes and choose them wisely). Intuitively a potential justification for the conditional independence assumption is that if we know that a document is about politics, this is a good indication of the kinds of other words we will find in the document. Because naive Bayes is a reasonable classifier in this sense, and has minimal storage and fast training, it has been applied to time and storage critical applications, such as automatically classifying webpages into types [309], and spam filtering [8]. It also forms one of the simplest yet most commonly used basic machine learning classification routines.

10.3 Bayesian naive Bayes

As we saw in the previous section, naive Bayes can be a powerful method for classification, yet can be overly zealous in the case of small counts. If a single attribute i has no counts for class c then, irrespective of the other attributes, the classifier will say that $\mathbf{x}$ cannot be from class c. This happens because the product of 0 with anything else remains 0. To counter overconfidence effect, we can use a simple Bayesian method.

Given a dataset $\mathcal{D} = \{(\mathbf{x}^n, c^n), n = 1, \ldots, N\}$, we predict the class c of an input $\mathbf{x}$ using

$$p(c|\mathbf{x}, \mathcal{D}) \propto p(\mathbf{x}, \mathcal{D}, c)p(c|\mathcal{D}) \propto p(\mathbf{x}|\mathcal{D}, c)p(c|\mathcal{D}). \tag{10.3.1}$$

For convenience we will simply set $p(c|\mathcal{D})$ using maximum likelihood

$$p(c|\mathcal{D}) = \frac{1}{N}\sum_n \mathbb{I}[c^n = c]. \tag{10.3.2}$$

However, as we've seen, setting the parameters of $p(\mathbf{x}|\mathcal{D}, c)$ using maximum likelihood training can yield over-confident predictions in the case of sparse data. A Bayesian approach that addresses this difficulty uses priors on the probabilities $p(x_i = s|c) \equiv \theta^i_s(c)$ to discourage extreme values. The model is depicted in Fig. 10.3.

The prior

Writing $\boldsymbol{\theta}^i(c) = (\theta^i_1(c), \ldots, \theta^i_S(c))$ as the vector of probabilities and $\theta = \{\boldsymbol{\theta}^i(c), i = 1, \ldots, D, c = 1, \ldots, C\}$, we make the global factorisation assumption (see Section 9.4) and use a prior

$$p(\theta) = \prod_{i,c} p(\boldsymbol{\theta}^i(c)). \tag{10.3.3}$$

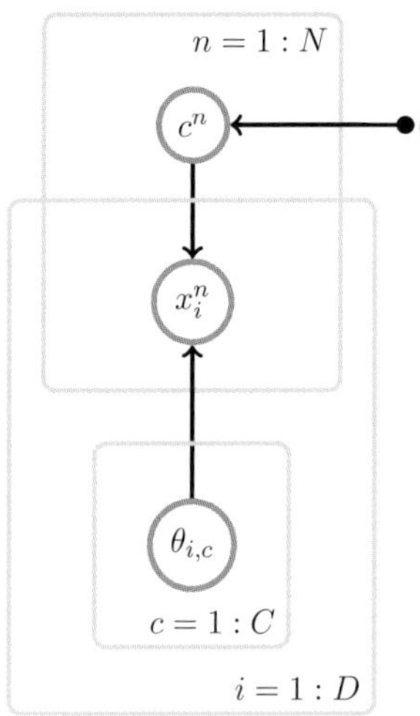

Figure 10.3 Bayesian naive Bayes with a factorised prior on the class conditional attribute probabilities $p(x_i = s|c)$. For simplicity we assume that the class probability $\theta_c \equiv p(c)$ is learned with maximum likelihood, so that no distribution is placed over this parameter.

We consider discrete x_i each of which take states from $1, \ldots, S$. In this case $p(x_i = s|c)$ corresponds to a categorical distribution, for which the conjugate prior is a Dirichlet distribution. Under the factorised prior assumption (10.3.3) we define a prior for each attribute i and class c,

$$p(\boldsymbol{\theta}^i(c)) = \text{Dirichlet}\left(\boldsymbol{\theta}^i(c)|\mathbf{u}^i(c)\right) \tag{10.3.4}$$

where $\mathbf{u}^i(c)$ is the hyperparameter vector of the Dirichlet distribution for table $p(x_i|c)$.

The posterior

Consistent with our general Bayesian BN training result in Section 9.4, the parameter posterior factorises

$$p(\theta(c^*)|\mathcal{D}) = \prod_i p(\boldsymbol{\theta}^i(c^*)|\mathcal{D}) \tag{10.3.5}$$

where

$$p(\boldsymbol{\theta}^i(c^*)|\mathcal{D}) \propto p(\boldsymbol{\theta}^i(c^*)) \prod_{n:c^n=c^*} p(x_i^n|\boldsymbol{\theta}^i(c^*)). \tag{10.3.6}$$

By conjugacy, the posterior for class c^* is a Dirichlet distribution,

$$p(\boldsymbol{\theta}^i(c^*)|\mathcal{D}) = \text{Dirichlet}\left(\boldsymbol{\theta}^i(c^*)|\hat{\mathbf{u}}^i(c^*)\right) \tag{10.3.7}$$

where the vector $\hat{\mathbf{u}}^i(c^*)$ has components

$$\left[\hat{\mathbf{u}}^i(c^*)\right]_s = u_s^i(c^*) + \sum_{n:c^n=c^*} \mathbb{I}\left[x_i^n = s\right]. \tag{10.3.8}$$

For Dirichlet hyperparameters $\mathbf{u}^i(c^*)$ the above equation updates the hyperparameter by the number of times variable i is in state s for class c^* data. A common default setting is to take all components of $\mathbf{u}$ to be 1.

Classification

The posterior class distribution for a novel input $\mathbf{x}^*$ is given by

$$p(c^*|\mathbf{x}^*, \mathcal{D}) \propto p(c^*, \mathbf{x}^*, \mathcal{D}) \propto p(c^*|\mathcal{D})p(\mathbf{x}^*|\mathcal{D}, c^*) = p(c^*|\mathcal{D}) \prod_i p(x_i^*|\mathcal{D}, c^*). \tag{10.3.9}$$

To compute $p(x_i^*|\mathcal{D}, c^*)$ we use

$$p(x_i^* = s|\mathcal{D}, c^*) = \int_{\boldsymbol{\theta}^i(c^*)} p(x_i^* = s, \boldsymbol{\theta}^i(c^*)|\mathcal{D}, c^*) = \int_{\boldsymbol{\theta}^i(c^*)} p(x_i^* = s|\boldsymbol{\theta}^i(c^*))p(\boldsymbol{\theta}^i(c^*)|\mathcal{D}) \tag{10.3.10}$$

$$= \int_{\boldsymbol{\theta}^i(c^*)} \theta_s^i(c^*)p(\boldsymbol{\theta}^i(c^*)|\mathcal{D}). \tag{10.3.11}$$

Using the general identity

$$\int \theta_s \text{Dirichlet}\left(\boldsymbol{\theta}|\mathbf{u}\right) d\boldsymbol{\theta} = \frac{1}{Z(\mathbf{u})} \int \prod_{s'} \theta_{s'}^{u_{s'}-1+\mathbb{I}[s'=s]} d\boldsymbol{\theta} = \frac{Z(\mathbf{u}')}{Z(\mathbf{u})} \tag{10.3.12}$$

where $Z(\mathbf{u})$ is the normalisation constant of the distribution Dirichlet $(\cdot|\mathbf{u})$ and

$$u'_s = \begin{cases} u_s & s \neq s' \\ u_s + 1 & s = s' \end{cases} \tag{10.3.13}$$

we obtain

$$p(c^*|\mathbf{x}^*, \mathcal{D}) \propto p(c^*|\mathcal{D}) \prod_i \frac{Z(\mathbf{u}^{*i}(c^*))}{Z(\hat{\mathbf{u}}^i(c^*))} \tag{10.3.14}$$

where

$$u_s^{*i}(c^*) = \hat{u}_s^i(c^*) + \mathbb{I}\left[x_i^* = s\right]. \tag{10.3.15}$$

Example 10.3 Bayesian naive Bayes

Repeating the previous analysis for the 'Are they Scottish?' data from Example 10.2, the probability under a uniform Dirichlet prior for all the tables, gives a value of 0.764 for the probability that $(1, 0, 1, 1, 0)$ is Scottish, compared with a value of 0.9076 under the standard naive Bayes assumption. See `demoNaiveBayes.m`.

10.4 Tree augmented naive Bayes

A natural extension of naive Bayes is to relax the assumption that the attributes are independent given the class:

$$p(\mathbf{x}|c) \neq \prod_{i=1}^{D} p(x_i|c). \tag{10.4.1}$$

The question then arises – which structure should we choose for $p(\mathbf{x}|c)$? As we saw in Section 9.5, learning a structure is computationally infeasible for all but very small numbers of attributes. A practical algorithm therefore requires a specific form of constraint on the structure. In

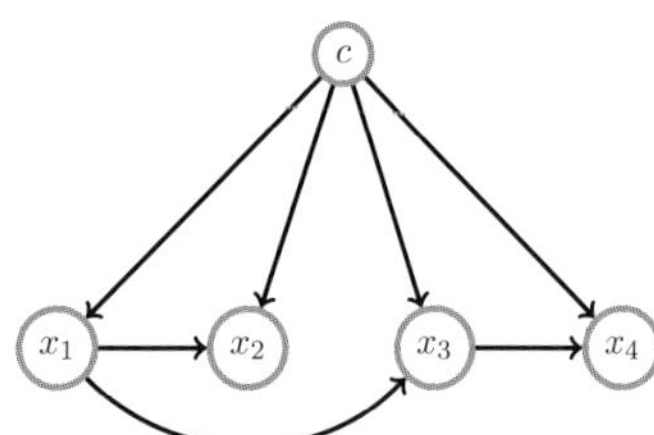

Figure 10.4 Tree Augmented Naive (TAN) Bayes. Each variable x_i has at most one parent. The maximum likelihood optimal TAN structure is computed using a modified Chow–Liu algorithm in which the conditional mutual information $\mathrm{MI}(x_i; x_j|c)$ is computed for all i, j. A maximum weight spanning tree is then found and turned into a directed graph by orienting the edges outwards from a chosen root node. The table entries can then be read off using the usual maximum likelihood counting argument.

Section 9.5.4 we saw that we can learn single-parent tree-structured networks efficiently. Below we extend this to learning class dependent tree networks for classification.

10.4.1 Learning tree augmented naive Bayes networks

For a distribution $p(x_1, \ldots, x_D|c)$ of the form of a tree structure with a single-parent constraint, see Fig. 10.4, we can readily find the class conditional maximum likelihood solution by computing the Chow–Liu tree for each class. One then adds links from the class node c to each variable and learns the class conditional probabilities from c to x, which can be read off for maximum likelihood using the usual counting argument. Note that this would generally result in a different Chow–Liu tree for each class.

Practitioners typically constrain the network to have the same structure for all classes. The maximum likelihood objective under the TAN constraint then corresponds to maximising the *conditional mutual information* [104]

$$\mathrm{MI}(x_i; x_j|c) = \langle \mathrm{KL}(p(x_i, x_j|c)|p(x_i|c)p(x_j|c)) \rangle_{p(c)} \tag{10.4.2}$$

see Exercise 10.7. Once the structure is learned one subsequently sets parameters by maximum likelihood counting. Techniques to prevent overfitting are discussed in [104] and can be addressed using Dirichlet priors, as for the simpler naive Bayes structure.

One can readily consider less restrictive structures than single-parent belief networks. However, finding optimal BN structures is generally computationally infeasible and heuristics are required to limit the search space.

10.5 Summary

- Naive Bayes is a simple class-conditional generative model of data that can be used to form a simple classifier.
- Bayesian training of the parameters is straightforward.
- An extension of the standard naive Bayes model is to consider attributes with at most a single-parent attribute (in addition to the class label). Finding the maximum likelihood optimal tree augmented structure is straightforward and corresponds to a maximum spanning tree problem with weights given by the class conditional mutual information.

10.6 Code

`NaiveBayesTrain.m`: Naive Bayes trained with maximum likelihood
`NaiveBayesTest.m`: Naive Bayes test

`NaiveBayesDirichletTrain.m`: Naive Bayes trained with Bayesian Dirichlet
`NaiveBayesDirichletTest.m`: Naive Bayes testing with Bayesian Dirichlet
`demoNaiveBayes.m`: Demo of naive Bayes

10.7 Exercises

10.1 A local supermarket specialising in breakfast cereals decides to analyse the buying patterns of its customers. They make a small survey asking six randomly chosen people their age (older or younger than 60 years) and which of the breakfast cereals (Cornflakes, Frosties, Sugar Puffs, Branflakes) they like. Each respondent provides a vector with entries 1 or 0 corresponding to whether they like or dislike the cereal. Thus a respondent with (1101) would like Cornflakes, Frosties and Branflakes, but not Sugar Puffs. The older than 60 years respondents provide the following data $(1000), (1001), (1111), (0001)$. The younger than 60 years old respondents responded $(0110), (1110)$. A novel customer comes into the supermarket and says she only likes Frosties and Sugar Puffs. Using naive Bayes trained with maximum likelihood, what is the probability that she is younger than 60?

10.2 A psychologist does a small survey on 'happiness'. Each respondent provides a vector with entries 1 or 0 corresponding to whether they answer 'yes' to a question or 'no', respectively. The question vector has attributes

$$\mathbf{x} = (\text{rich, married, healthy}). \tag{10.7.1}$$

Thus, a response $(1, 0, 1)$ would indicate that the respondent was 'rich', 'unmarried', 'healthy'. In addition, each respondent gives a value $c = 1$ if they are content with their lifestyle, and $c = 0$ if they are not. The following responses were obtained from people who claimed also to be 'content': $(1, 1, 1), (0, 0, 1), (1, 1, 0), (1, 0, 1)$ and for 'not content': $(0, 0, 0), (1, 0, 0), (0, 0, 1), (0, 1, 0), (0, 0, 0)$.

1. Using naive Bayes, what is the probability that a person who is 'not rich', 'married' and 'healthy' is 'content'?
2. What is the probability that a person who is 'not rich' and 'married' is 'content'? (That is, we do not know whether or not they are 'healthy'.)
3. Consider the following vector of attributes:

$$x_1 = 1 \text{ if customer is younger than 20; } x_1 = 0 \text{ otherwise} \tag{10.7.2}$$

$$x_2 = 1 \text{ if customer is between 20 and 30 years old; } x_2 = 0 \text{ otherwise} \tag{10.7.3}$$

$$x_3 = 1 \text{ if customer is older than 30; } x_3 = 0 \text{ otherwise} \tag{10.7.4}$$

$$x_4 = 1 \text{ if customer walks to work; } x_4 = 0 \text{ otherwise.} \tag{10.7.5}$$

Each vector of attributes has an associated class label 'rich' or 'poor'. Point out any potential difficulties with using your previously described approach to training using naive Bayes. Hence describe how to extend your previous naive Bayes method to deal with this dataset.

10.3 Whizzco decide to make a text classifier. To begin with they attempt to classify documents as either sport or politics. They decide to represent each document as a (row) vector of attributes describing the presence or absence of words.

$$\mathbf{x} = (\text{goal, football, golf, defence, offence, wicket, office, strategy.}) \tag{10.7.6}$$

Training data from sport documents and from politics documents is represented below in MATLAB using a matrix in which each row represents the eight attributes.

```
xP=[1 0 1 1 1 0 1 1;  % Politics     xS=[1 1 0 0 0 0 0 0; % Sport
    0 0 0 1 0 0 1 1;                     0 0 1 0 0 0 0 0;
    1 0 0 1 1 0 1 0;                     1 1 0 1 0 0 0 0;
    0 1 0 0 1 1 0 1;                     1 1 0 1 0 0 0 1;
    0 0 0 1 1 0 1 1;                     1 1 0 1 1 0 0 0;
    0 0 0 1 1 0 0 1]                     0 0 0 1 0 1 0 0;
                                         1 1 1 1 1 0 1 0].
```

Using a maximum likelihood naive Bayes classifier, what is the probability that the document $\mathbf{x} = (1, 0, 0, 1, 1, 1, 1, 0)$ is about politics?

10.4 A naive Bayes classifier for binary attributes $x_i \in \{0, 1\}$ is parameterised by $\theta_i^1 = p(x_i = 1|\text{class} = 1)$, $\theta_i^0 = p(x_i = 1|\text{class} = 0)$, and $p_1 = p(\text{class} = 1)$ and $p_0 = p(\text{class} = 0)$. Show that the decision to classify a datapoint $\mathbf{x}$ as class 1 holds if $\mathbf{w}^\mathsf{T}\mathbf{x} + b > 0$ for some $\mathbf{w}$ and b, and state explicitly $\mathbf{w}$ and b as a function of $\boldsymbol{\theta}^1, \boldsymbol{\theta}^0, p_1, p_0$.

10.5 This question concerns spam filtering. Each email is represented by a vector

$$x = (x_1, \ldots, x_D) \tag{10.7.7}$$

where $x_i \in \{0, 1\}$. Each entry of the vector indicates if a particular symbol or word appears in the email. The symbols/words are

$$\text{money, cash, !!!, viagra, } \ldots \text{, etc.} \tag{10.7.8}$$

so that for example $x_2 = 1$ if the word 'cash' appears in the email. The training dataset consists of a set of vectors along with the class label c, where $c = 1$ indicates the email is spam, and $c = 0$ not spam. Hence, the training set consists of a set of pairs (x^n, c^n), $n = 1, \ldots, N$. The naive Bayes model is given by

$$p(c, x) = p(c) \prod_{i=1}^{D} p(x_i|c). \tag{10.7.9}$$

1. Derive expressions for the parameters of this model in terms of the training data using maximum likelihood. Assume that the data is independent and identically distributed

   $$p(c^1, \ldots, c^N, x^1, \ldots, x^N) = \prod_{n=1}^{N} p(c^n, x^n). \tag{10.7.10}$$

   Explicitly, the parameters are

   $$p(c = 1), p(x_i = 1|c = 1), p(x_i = 1|c = 0), i = 1, \ldots, D. \tag{10.7.11}$$

2. Given a trained model $p(x, c)$, explain how to form a classifier $p(c|x)$.
3. If 'viagra' never appears in the spam training data, discuss what effect this will have on the classification for a new email that contains the word 'viagra'. Explain how you might counter this effect. Explain how a spammer might try to fool a naive Bayes spam filter.

10.6 For a distribution $p(x, c)$ and an approximation $q(x, c)$, show that when $p(x, c)$ corresponds to the empirical distribution, finding $q(x, c)$ that minimises the Kullback–Leibler divergence

$$\text{KL}(p(x, c)|q(x, c)) \tag{10.7.12}$$

corresponds to maximum likelihood training of $q(x, c)$ assuming i.i.d. data.

10.7 Consider a distribution $p(x, c)$ and a tree augmented approximation

$$q(x, c) = q(c) \prod_i q(x_i | x_{pa(i)}, c), \qquad pa(i) < i \quad \text{or } pa(i) = \emptyset. \tag{10.7.13}$$

Show that for the optimal $q(x, c)$ constrained as above, the solution $q(x, c)$ that minimises $\text{KL}(p(x, c)|q(x, c))$ when plugged back into the Kullback–Leibler expression gives, as a function of the parental structure,

$$\text{KL}(p(x, c)|q(x, c)) = -\sum_i \left\langle \log \frac{p(x_i, x_{pa(i)}|c)}{p(x_{pa(i)}|c)p(x_i|c)} \right\rangle_{p(x_i, x_{pa(i)}, c)} + \text{const.} \tag{10.7.14}$$

This shows that under the single-parent constraint and that each tree $q(x|c)$ has the same structure, minimising the Kullback–Leibler divergence is equivalent to maximising the sum of conditional mutual information terms. From Exercise 10.6, we know therefore that this also corresponds to the maximum likelihood setting for the parental structure. This can then be achieved by finding a maximal weight spanning tree, as in the case of the Chow-Liu tree.

11 Learning with hidden variables

In many models some variables are not directly observed, but are latent or 'hidden'. This can also occur when some data are not observed. In this chapter we discuss methods for learning in the presence of such missing information, and in particular develop the expectation maximisation algorithm and related variants.

11.1 Hidden variables and missing data

In practice data entries are often missing resulting in incomplete information to specify a likelihood. Observational variables may be split into *visible* (those for which we actually know the state) and *missing* (those whose states would nominally be known but are missing for a particular datapoint).

Another scenario in which not all variables in the model are observed are the so-called hidden or *latent variable models*. In this case there are variables which are essential for the model description but never observed. For example, the underlying physics of a model may contain latent processes which are essential to describe the model, but cannot be directly measured.

11.1.1 Why hidden/missing variables can complicate proceedings

In learning the parameters of models as previously described in Chapter 9, we assumed we have complete information to define all variables of the joint model of the data $p(x|\theta)$. Consider the Asbestos-Smoking-Cancer network of Section 9.3. Using the multivariate variable $x = (a, s, c)$, if patient n has a complete record, the likelihood of this record is

$$p(x^n|\theta) = p(a^n, s^n, c^n|\theta) = p(c^n|a^n, s^n, \theta_c)p(a^n|\theta_a)p(s^n|\theta_s) \tag{11.1.1}$$

which is factorised in terms of the table entry parameters. We exploited this property to show that table entries θ can be learned by considering only local information, both in the maximum likelihood and Bayesian frameworks.

Now consider the case that for some of the patients, only partial information is available. For example, for patient n with incomplete record $x^n = \{c = 1, s = 1\}$ it is known that the patient has cancer and is a smoker, but whether or not they had exposure to asbestos is unknown. Since we can only use the 'visible' available information it would seem reasonable (see Section 11.1.2) to assess parameters using the marginal likelihood

$$p(x^n|\theta) = \sum_a p(a, s^n, c^n|\theta) = \sum_a p(c^n|a, s^n, \theta_c)p(a|\theta_a)p(s^n|\theta_s). \tag{11.1.2}$$

Using the marginal likelihood, however, may result in computational difficulties since the likelihood Equation (11.1.2) cannot now be factorised into a product of the separate table parameters of the

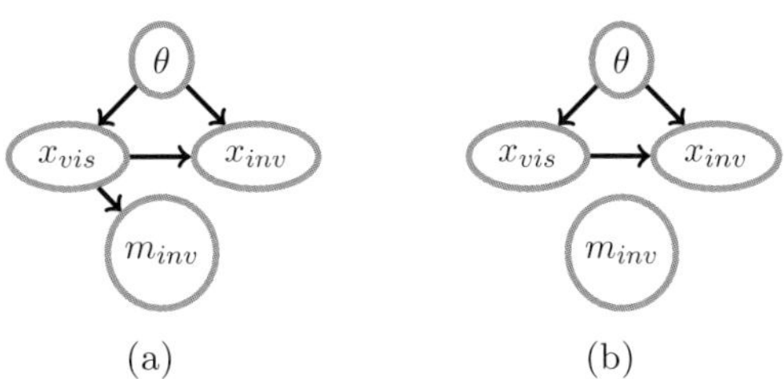

Figure 11.1 (**a**) Missing at random assumption. The mechanism that generates the missing data does not depend on either the parameter θ of the model, or on the value of the missing data. (**b**) Missing completely at random assumption. The mechanism generating the missing data is completely independent of the model. Note that in both cases the direction of the arrow between x_{vis} and x_{inv} is irrelevant.

form $f_s(\theta_s)f_a(\theta_a)f_c(\theta_c)$. In this case the maximisation of the likelihood is more complex since the parameters of different tables are coupled.

A similar complication holds for Bayesian learning. As we saw in Section 9.4.1, under a prior factorised over each CPT θ, the posterior is also factorised. However, the missing variable introduces dependencies in the posterior parameter distribution, making the posterior more complex. In both the maximum likelihood and Bayesian cases, one has a well defined likelihood function of the table parameters/posterior.

Note that missing data does not always make the parameter posterior non-factorised. For example, if the cancer state is unobserved above, because cancer is a collider with no descendants, the conditional distribution simply sums to 1, and one is left with a factor dependent on a and another on s.

11.1.2 The missing at random assumption

Under what circumstances is it valid to use the marginal likelihood to assess parameters? We partition the variables x into those that are 'visible', x_{vis} and 'invisible', x_{inv}, so that the set of all variables can be written $x = [x_{vis}, x_{inv}]$. For the visible variables we have an observed state $x_{vis} = \mathsf{v}$, whereas the state of the invisible variables is unknown. To complete the picture we also need to model the process that informs when data will be missing. We use an indicator $m_{inv} = 1$ to denote that the state of the invisible variables is unknown and require then a model $p(m_{inv}|x_{vis}, x_{inv}, \theta)$. Then for a datapoint which contains both visible and invisible information,

$$p(x_{vis} = \mathsf{v}, m_{inv} = 1|\theta) = \sum_{x_{inv}} p(x_{vis} = \mathsf{v}, x_{inv}, m_{inv} = 1|\theta) \tag{11.1.3}$$

$$= \sum_{x_{inv}} p(m_{inv} = 1|x_{vis} = \mathsf{v}, x_{inv}, \theta)p(x_{vis} = \mathsf{v}, x_{inv}|\theta). \tag{11.1.4}$$

If we assume that the mechanism which generates invisible data is independent of the parameter and the missing value x_{inv}

$$p(m_{inv} = 1|x_{vis} = \mathsf{v}, x_{inv}, \theta) = p(m_{inv} = 1|x_{vis} = \mathsf{v}) \tag{11.1.5}$$

then

$$p(x_{vis} = \mathsf{v}, m_{inv} = 1|\theta) = p(m_{inv} = 1|x_{vis} = \mathsf{v}) \sum_{x_{inv}} p(x_{vis} = \mathsf{v}, x_{inv}|\theta) \tag{11.1.6}$$

$$= p(m_{inv} = 1|x_{vis} = \mathsf{v})p(x_{vis} = \mathsf{v}|\theta). \tag{11.1.7}$$

Only the term $p(x_{vis} = \mathsf{v}|\theta)$ conveys information about the parameter θ of the model. Therefore, provided the mechanism by which the data is missing depends only on the visible states, we may simply use the marginal likelihood to assess parameters. This is called the *missing at random* (MAR) assumption, see Fig. 11.1.

Example 11.1 Not missing at random

EZsurvey.org stop men on the street and ask them their favourite colour. All men whose favourite colour is pink decline to respond to the question – for any other colour, all men respond to the question. Based on the data, EZsurvey.org produce a histogram of men's favourite colour, based on the likelihood of the visible data alone, confidently stating that none of them likes pink. For simplicity, we assume there are only three colours, blue, green and pink. EZsurvey.org attempts to find the histogram with probabilities $\theta_b, \theta_g, \theta_p$ with $\theta_b + \theta_g + \theta_p = 1$. Each respondent produces a visible response x with $\text{dom}(x) = \{\text{blue, green, pink}\}$, otherwise $m = 1$ if there is no response. Three men are asked their favourite colour, giving data

$$\{x^1, x^2, x^3\} = \{\text{blue, missing, green}\}. \tag{11.1.8}$$

Based on the likelihood of the visible data alone we have the log likelihood for i.i.d. data

$$L(\theta_b, \theta_g, \theta_p) = \log \theta_b + \log \theta_g + \lambda (1 - \theta_b - \theta_g - \theta_p) \tag{11.1.9}$$

where the last Lagrange term ensures normalisation. Maximising the expression we arrive at

$$\theta_b = \frac{1}{2}, \quad \theta_g = \frac{1}{2}, \quad \theta_p = 0. \tag{11.1.10}$$

Hence EZsurvey.org arrive at the erroneous conclusion that no men like pink, even though the reality is that some men like pink – they just don't want to say so. The unreasonable result that EZsurvey.org produce is due to not accounting correctly for the mechanism which produces the data. In this case the data is not MAR since whether or not the data is missing depends on the state of the missing variable.

The correct mechanism that generates the data (including the missing data) is

$$p(x^1 = \text{blue}|\theta)p(m^2 = 1|\theta)p(x^3 = \text{green}|\theta) = \theta_b\theta_p\theta_g = \theta_b (1 - \theta_b - \theta_g) \theta_g \tag{11.1.11}$$

where we used $p(m^2 = 1|\theta) = \theta_p$ since the probability that a datapoint is missing is the same as the probability that the favourite colour is pink. Maximising the likelihood, we arrive at

$$\theta_b = \frac{1}{3}, \quad \theta_g = \frac{1}{3}, \quad \theta_p = \frac{1}{3} \tag{11.1.12}$$

as we would expect. On the other hand if there is another visible variable, t, denoting the time of day, and the probability that men respond to the question depends only on the time t alone (for example the probability of having missing data is high during rush hour), then we may indeed treat the missing data as missing at random.

A stronger assumption than MAR is that the missing data mechanism is completely independent of all other model processes

$$p(m_{inv} = 1|x_{vis} = \text{v}, x_{inv}, \theta) = p(m_{inv} = 1) \tag{11.1.13}$$

which is called *missing completely at random*. This applies for example to latent variable models in which the variable state is always missing, independent of anything else.

11.1.3 Maximum likelihood

Throughout the remaining discussion we will assume any missing data is MAR or missing completely at random. We partition the variables into 'visible' variables v for which we know the states and 'hidden' variables h whose states will not be observed. For maximum likelihood we may then learn model parameters θ by optimising on the visible variables alone

$$p(v|\theta) = \sum_h p(v, h|\theta) \tag{11.1.14}$$

with respect to θ.

11.1.4 Identifiability issues

The marginal likelihood objective function depends on the parameters only through $p(v|\theta)$, so that equivalent parameter solutions may exist. For example, consider a latent variable model with distribution

$$p(x_1, x_2|\theta) = \theta_{x_1,x_2} \tag{11.1.15}$$

in which variable x_2 is never observed. This means that the marginal likelihood only depends on the entry $p(x_1|\theta) = \sum_{x_2} \theta_{x_1,x_2}$. Given a maximum likelihood solution θ^*, we can then always find an equivalent maximum likelihood solution θ' provided (see Exercise 11.9)

$$\sum_{x_2} \theta'_{x_1,x_2} = \sum_{x_2} \theta^*_{x_1,x_2}. \tag{11.1.16}$$

In other cases there is an inherent symmetry in the parameter space of the marginal likelihood. For example, consider the network over binary variables

$$p(c, a, s) = p(c|a, s)p(a)p(s). \tag{11.1.17}$$

We assume we know the table for $p(s)$ and that our aim is to learn the asbestos table $\hat{p}(a = 1)$ and cancer tables

$$\hat{p}(c = 1|a = 1, s = 1),\ \hat{p}(c = 1|a = 1, s = 0),\ \hat{p}(c = 1|a = 0, s = 1),\ \hat{p}(c = 1|a = 0, s = 0) \tag{11.1.18}$$

where we used a '^' to denote that these are parameter estimates.

We assume that we have missing data such that the states of variable a are never observed. In this case an equivalent solution (in the sense that it has the same marginal likelihood) is given by interchanging the states of a:

$$\hat{p}'(a = 0) = \hat{p}(a = 1) \tag{11.1.19}$$

and the four tables

$$\begin{aligned} &\hat{p}'(c = 1|a = 0, s = 1) = \hat{p}(c = 1|a = 1, s = 1), \quad \hat{p}'(c = 1|a = 0, s = 0) = \hat{p}(c = 1|a = 1, s = 0) \\ &\hat{p}'(c = 1|a = 1, s = 1) = \hat{p}(c = 1|a = 0, s = 1), \quad \hat{p}'(c = 1|a = 1, s = 0) = \hat{p}(c = 1|a = 0, s = 0). \end{aligned} \tag{11.1.20}$$

A similar situation occurs in a more general setting in which the state of a variable is consistently unobserved (mixture models are a case in point) yielding an inherent symmetry in the solution space. A well-known characteristic of maximum likelihood algorithms is that 'jostling' occurs in the initial stages of training in which these symmetric solutions compete.

11.2 Expectation maximisation

The Expectation maximisation (EM) algorithm is a convenient and general purpose iterative approach to maximising the likelihood under missing data/hidden variables [202]. It is generally straightforward to implement and can achieve large jumps in parameter space, particularly in the initial iterations.

11.2.1 Variational EM

The key feature of the EM algorithm is to form an alternative objective function for which the parameter coupling effect discussed in Section 11.1.1 is removed, meaning that individual parameter updates can be achieved, akin to the case of fully observed data. The way this works is to replace the marginal likelihood with a lower bound – it is this lower bound that has the useful decoupled form.

We first consider a single variable pair (v, h), where v stands for 'visible' and h for 'hidden'. The model of the data is then $p(v, h|\theta)$ and our interest is to set θ by maximising the marginal likelihood $p(v|\theta)$. To derive the bound on the marginal likelihood, consider the Kullback–Leibler divergence (which is always non-negative) between a 'variational' distribution $q(h|v)$ and the parametric model $p(h|v, \theta)$:

$$\mathrm{KL}(q(h|v)|p(h|v,\theta)) \equiv \langle \log q(h|v) - \log p(h|v,\theta)\rangle_{q(h|v)} \geq 0. \tag{11.2.1}$$

The term 'variational' refers to the fact that this distribution will be a parameter of an optimisation problem. Using $p(h|v, \theta) = p(h, v|\theta)/p(v|\theta)$ and the fact that $p(v|\theta)$ does not depend on h,

$$\mathrm{KL}(q(h|v)|p(h|v,\theta)) = \langle \log q(h|v)\rangle_{q(h|v)} - \langle \log p(h,v|\theta)\rangle_{q(h|v)} + \log p(v|\theta) \geq 0. \tag{11.2.2}$$

Rearranging, we obtain a bound on the marginal likelihood[1]

$$\log p(v|\theta) \geq \underbrace{-\langle \log q(h|v)\rangle_{q(h|v)}}_{\text{Entropy}} + \underbrace{\langle \log p(h,v|\theta)\rangle_{q(h|v)}}_{\text{Energy}}. \tag{11.2.3}$$

The energy term is also called the 'expected complete data log likelihood'. The bound is potentially useful since the θ dependent energy term is similar in form to the fully observed case, except that terms with missing data have their log likelihood weighted by a prefactor. Equation (11.2.3) is a marginal likelihood bound for a single training example. Under the i.i.d. assumption, the log likelihood of all training data $\mathcal{V} = \{v^1, \ldots, v^N\}$ is the sum of the individual log likelihoods:

$$\log p(\mathcal{V}|\theta) = \sum_{n=1}^{N} \log p(v^n|\theta). \tag{11.2.4}$$

Summing over the training data, we obtain a bound on the log (marginal) likelihood

$$\log p(\mathcal{V}|\theta) \geq \tilde{L}(\{q\},\theta) \equiv \underbrace{-\sum_{n=1}^{N} \langle \log q(h^n|v^n)\rangle_{q(h^n|v^n)}}_{\text{entropy}} + \underbrace{\sum_{n=1}^{N} \langle \log p(h^n, v^n|\theta)\rangle_{q(h^n|v^n)}}_{\text{energy}}. \tag{11.2.5}$$

[1] This is analogous to a standard partition function bound in statistical physics, from where the terminology 'energy' and 'entropy' hails.

Algorithm 11.1 Expectation maximisation. Compute maximum likelihood value for data with hidden variables. Input: a distribution $p(x|\theta)$ and dataset $\mathcal{V}$. Returns ML candidate θ.

$t = 0$ ▷ Iteration counter
Choose an initial setting for the parameters θ^0. ▷ Initialisation
while θ not converged (or likelihood not converged) **do**
    $t \leftarrow t + 1$
    for $n = 1$ to N **do** ▷ Run over all datapoints
        $q_t^n(h^n|v^n) = p(h^n|v^n, \theta^{t-1})$ ▷ E-step
    end for
    $\theta^t = \arg\max_\theta \sum_{n=1}^N \langle \log p(h^n, v^n|\theta) \rangle_{q_t^n(h^n|v^n)}$ ▷ M-step
end while
return θ^t ▷ The max likelihood parameter estimate

Note that the bound $\tilde{L}(\{q\}, \theta)$ is exact (that is, the right-hand side is equal to the log likelihood) when we set $q(h^n|v^n) = p(h^n|v^n, \theta), n = 1, \ldots, N$.

The bound depends both on θ and the set of variational distributions $\{q\}$. Our aim is then to try to optimise this bound w.r.t. θ and $\{q\}$; in doing so we will push up the lower bound, and hopefully increase thereby the likelihood itself. A simple iterative procedure to optimise the bound is to first fix θ and then optimise w.r.t. $\{q\}$, and then fix $\{q\}$ and optimise the bound w.r.t. θ. These are known as the 'E' and 'M' steps and are repeated until convergence:

E-step For fixed θ, find the distributions $q(h^n|v^n), n = 1, \ldots, N$ that maximise Equation (11.2.5).

M-step For fixed $q(h^n|v^n), n = 1, \ldots, N$, find the parameters θ that maximise Equation (11.2.5).

11.2.2 Classical EM

In the variational E-step above, the fully optimal setting is

$$q(h^n|v^n) = p(h^n|v^n, \theta). \tag{11.2.6}$$

Since q is fixed during the M-step, performing the M-step optimisation is equivalent to maximising the energy term alone, see Algorithm 11.1. From here onwards we shall use the term 'EM' to refer to the classical EM algorithm, unless otherwise stated. It is important to note that the EM algorithm cannot generally guarantee to find the fully optimal maximum likelihood solution and can get trapped in local optima, as discussed in Example 11.2.

Example 11.2 EM for a one-parameter model

We consider a model small enough that we can plot fully the evolution of the EM algorithm. The model is on a single visible variable v with $\text{dom}(v) = \mathbb{R}$ and single two-state hidden variable h with $\text{dom}(h) = \{1, 2\}$. We define a model $p(v, h|\theta) = p(v|h, \theta)p(h)$ with

$$p(v|h, \theta) = \frac{1}{\sqrt{\pi}} e^{-(v-\theta h)^2} \tag{11.2.7}$$

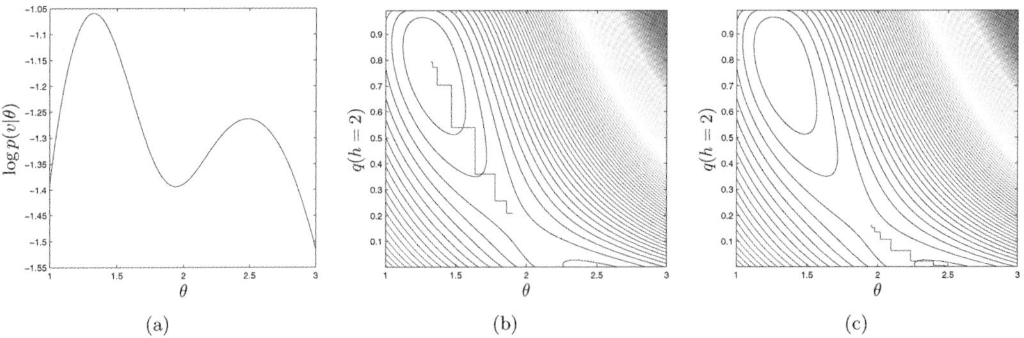

Figure 11.2 (**a**) The log likelihood for the model described in Example 11.2. (**b**) Contours of the lower bound $\tilde{L}(q(h=2),\theta)$. For an initial choice $\theta=1.9$, successive updates of the E (vertical) and M (horizontal) steps are plotted, with the algorithm converging to the global optimum maximum likelihood setting for θ. (**c**) Starting at $\theta=1.95$, the EM algorithm converges to a local optimum.

and $p(h=1)=p(h=2)=0.5$. For an observation $v=2.75$ our interest is to find the parameter θ that optimises the likelihood

$$p(v=2.75|\theta)=\sum_{h=1,2}p(v=2.75|h,\theta)p(h)=\frac{1}{2\sqrt{\pi}}\left(e^{-(2.75-\theta)^2}+e^{-(2.75-2\theta)^2}\right). \tag{11.2.8}$$

The log likelihood is plotted in Fig. 11.2(a) with optimum at $\theta=1.325$. If the state of h were given, the log likelihood would be a single bump, rather than the more complex double bump in the case of missing data. To use the EM approach to find the optimum θ, we need to work out the energy

$$\langle\log p(v,h|\theta)\rangle_{q(h|v)}=\langle\log p(v|h,\theta)\rangle_{q(h|v)}+\langle\log p(h)\rangle_{q(h|v)} \tag{11.2.9}$$

$$=-\left\langle(v-\theta h)^2\right\rangle_{q(h|v)}+\text{const.} \tag{11.2.10}$$

There are two h states of the q and distribution and normalisation requires $q(1)+q(2)=1$. Due to the normalisation, we can fully parameterise q using $q(2)$ alone. The EM procedure then iteratively optimises the lower bound

$$\log p(v=2.75|\theta)\geq\tilde{L}(q(2),\theta)$$
$$\equiv-q(1)\log q(1)-q(2)\log q(2)-\sum_{h=1,2}q(h)\left(2.75-\theta h\right)^2+\text{const.} \tag{11.2.11}$$

From an initial starting θ, the EM algorithm finds the q distribution that optimises $\tilde{L}(q(2),\theta)$ (E-step) and then updates θ (M-step). Depending on the initial θ, the solution found is either a global or local optimum of the likelihood, see Fig. 11.2.

The M-step is easy to work out analytically in this case with $\theta^{new}=v\,\langle h\rangle_{q(h)}/\left\langle h^2\right\rangle_{q(h)}$. Similarly, the E-step sets $q^{new}(h)=p(h|v,\theta)$ so that

$$q^{new}(h=2)=\frac{p(v=2.75|h=2,\theta)p(h=2)}{p(v=2.75)}=\frac{e^{-(2.75-2\theta)^2}}{e^{-(2.75-2\theta)^2}+e^{-(2.75-\theta)^2}} \tag{11.2.12}$$

where we used

$$p(v=2.75)=p(v=2.75|h=1,\theta)p(h=1)+p(v=2.75|h=2,\theta)p(h=2). \tag{11.2.13}$$

Example 11.3

Consider a simple model

$$p(x_1, x_2|\theta) \tag{11.2.14}$$

where dom (x_1) = dom $(x_2) = \{1, 2\}$. Assuming an unconstrained distribution

$$p(x_1, x_2|\theta) = \theta_{x_1,x_2}, \qquad \theta_{1,1} + \theta_{1,2} + \theta_{2,1} + \theta_{2,2} = 1 \tag{11.2.15}$$

our aim is to learn θ from the data $\mathbf{x}^1 = (1, 1)$, $\mathbf{x}^2 = (1, ?)$, $\mathbf{x}^3 = (?, 2)$. The energy term for the classical EM is

$$\log p(x_1 = 1, x_2 = 1|\theta) + \langle \log p(x_1 = 1, x_2|\theta)\rangle_{p(x_2|x_1=1,\theta^{old})} + \langle \log p(x_1, x_2 = 2|\theta)\rangle_{p(x_1|x_2=2,\theta^{old})}. \tag{11.2.16}$$

Writing out fully each of the above terms on a separate line gives the energy

$$\log \theta_{1,1} \tag{11.2.17}$$
$$+ p(x_2 = 1|x_1 = 1, \theta^{old}) \log \theta_{1,1} + p(x_2 = 2|x_1 = 1, \theta^{old}) \log \theta_{1,2} \tag{11.2.18}$$
$$+ p(x_1 = 1|x_2 = 2, \theta^{old}) \log \theta_{1,2} + p(x_1 = 2|x_2 = 2, \theta^{old}) \log \theta_{2,2}. \tag{11.2.19}$$

This expression resembles the standard log likelihood of fully observed data except that terms with missing data have their weighted log parameters. The parameters are conveniently decoupled in this bound (apart from the trivial normalisation constraint) so that finding the optimal parameters is straightforward. This is achieved by the M-step update which gives

$$\begin{array}{ll} \theta_{1,1} \propto 1 + p(x_2 = 1|x_1 = 1, \theta^{old}) & \theta_{1,2} \propto p(x_2 = 2|x_1 = 1, \theta^{old}) + p(x_1 = 1|x_2 = 2, \theta^{old}) \\ \theta_{2,1} = 0 & \theta_{2,2} \propto p(x_1 = 2|x_2 = 2, \theta^{old}) \end{array} \tag{11.2.20}$$

where $p(x_2|x_1, \theta^{old}) \propto \theta^{old}_{x_1,x_2}$ (E-step) etc. The E and M-steps are iterated till convergence.

The EM algorithm increases the likelihood

Whilst, by construction, the EM algorithm cannot decrease the lower bound on the likelihood, an important question is whether or not the log likelihood itself is necessarily increased by this procedure.

We use θ' for the new parameters, and θ for the previous parameters in two consecutive iterations. Using $q(h^n|v^n) = p(h^n|v^n, \theta)$ we see that as a function of the parameters, the lower bound for a single variable pair (v, h) depends on θ and θ':

$$LB(\theta'|\theta) \equiv -\langle \log p(h|v, \theta)\rangle_{p(h|v,\theta)} + \langle \log p(h, v|\theta')\rangle_{p(h|v,\theta)}. \tag{11.2.21}$$

From the definition of the lower bound, Equation (11.2.3), we have

$$\log p(v|\theta') = LB(\theta'|\theta) + KL(p(h|v, \theta)|p(h|v, \theta')). \tag{11.2.22}$$

That is, the Kullback–Leibler divergence is the difference between the lower bound and the true likelihood. We may then also write

$$\log p(v|\theta) = LB(\theta|\theta) + \underbrace{KL(p(h|v, \theta)|p(h|v, \theta))}_{0}. \tag{11.2.23}$$

s	c
1	1
0	0
1	1
1	0
1	1
0	0
0	1

Figure 11.3 A database containing information about being a Smoker (1 signifies the individual is a smoker), and lung Cancer (1 signifies the individual has lung Cancer). Each row contains the information for an individual, so that there are seven individuals in the database.

Hence

$$\log p(v|\theta') - \log p(v|\theta) = \underbrace{LB(\theta'|\theta) - LB(\theta|\theta)}_{\geq 0} + \underbrace{KL(p(h|v,\theta)|p(h|v,\theta'))}_{\geq 0}. \tag{11.2.24}$$

The first assertion is true since, by definition of the M-step, we search for a θ' which has a higher value for the bound than our starting value θ. The second assertion is true by the non-negative property of the Kullback–Leibler divergence.

For more than a single datapoint, we simply sum each individual bound for $\log p(v^n|\theta)$. Hence we reach the important conclusion that the EM algorithm increases, not only the lower bound on the marginal likelihood, but the marginal likelihood itself (more correctly, EM cannot decrease these quantities).

Shared parameters and tables

It is often the case in models that parameters are shared between components of the model. The application of EM to this shared parameter case is essentially straightforward. According to the energy term, we need to identify all those terms in which the shared parameter occurs. The objective for the shared parameter is then the sum over all energy terms containing the shared parameter.

11.2.3 Application to belief networks

Conceptually, the application of EM to training belief networks with missing data is straightforward. The battle is more notational than conceptual. We begin the development with an example, from which intuition about the general case can be gleaned.

Example 11.4

Consider the network

$$p(a, c, s) = p(c|a, s)p(a)p(s) \tag{11.2.25}$$

for which we have a set of data, but that the states of variable a are never observed, see Fig. 11.3. Our goal is to learn the CPTs $p(c|a, s)$ and $p(a)$ and $p(s)$. To apply EM, Algorithm 11.1 to this case, we first assume initial parameters $\theta_a^0, \theta_s^0, \theta_c^0$.

The first E-step, for iteration $t = 1$ then defines a set of distributions on the hidden variables (here the hidden variable is a). For notational convenience, we write $q_t^n(a)$ in place of $q_t^n(a|v^n)$.

Then

$$q_{t=1}^{n=1}(a) = p(a|c=1, s=1, \theta^0), \qquad q_{t=1}^{n=2}(a) = p(a|c=0, s=0, \theta^0) \tag{11.2.26}$$

and so on for the seven training examples, $n = 2, \ldots, 7$.

We now move to the first M-step. The energy term for any iteration t is:

$$E(\theta) = \sum_{n=1}^{7} \langle \log p(c^n|a^n, s^n) + \log p(a^n) + \log p(s^n) \rangle_{q_t^n(a)} \tag{11.2.27}$$

$$= \sum_{n=1}^{7} \left\{ \langle \log p(c^n|a^n, s^n) \rangle_{q_t^n(a)} + \langle \log p(a^n) \rangle_{q_t^n(a)} + \log p(s^n) \right\}. \tag{11.2.28}$$

The final term is the log likelihood of the variable s, and $p(s)$ appears explicitly only in this term. Hence, the usual maximum likelihood rule applies, and $p(s=1)$ is simply given by the relative number of times that $s=1$ occurs in the database, giving $p(s=1) = 4/7$, $p(s=0) = 3/7$.

The contribution of parameter $p(a=1)$ to the energy occurs in the terms

$$\sum_n \{ q_t^n(a=0) \log p(a=0) + q_t^n(a=1) \log p(a=1) \} \tag{11.2.29}$$

which, using the normalisation constraint is

$$\log p(a=0) \sum_n q_t^n(a=0) + \log(1 - p(a=0)) \sum_n q_t^n(a=1). \tag{11.2.30}$$

Differentiating with respect to $p(a=0)$ and solving for the zero derivative we get the M-step update for $p(a=0)$

$$p(a=0) = \frac{\sum_n q_t^n(a=0)}{\sum_n q_t^n(a=0) + \sum_n q_t^n(a=1)} = \frac{1}{N} \sum_n q_t^n(a=0). \tag{11.2.31}$$

That is, whereas in the standard maximum likelihood estimate, we would have the real counts of the data in the above formula, here they have been replaced with our guessed values $q_t^n(a=0)$ and $q_t^n(a=1)$.

A similar story holds for $p(c=1|a=0, s=1)$. Again we need to consider that normalisation means that $p(c=0|a=0, s=1)$ also contributes. The contribution of this term to the energy is from those data indices n for which $s=1$

$$\sum_{n:c^n=1, s^n=1} q_t^n(a=0) \log p(c=1|a=0, s=1)$$
$$+ \sum_{n:c^n=0, s^n=1} q_t^n(a=0) \log (1 - p(c=1|a=0, s=1)).$$

Optimising with respect to $p(c=1|a=0, s=1)$ gives

$$p(c=1|a=0, s=1) = \frac{\sum_n \mathbb{I}[c^n=1] \mathbb{I}[s^n=1] q_t^n(a=0)}{\sum_n \mathbb{I}[c^n=1] \mathbb{I}[s^n=1] q_t^n(a=0) + \sum_n \mathbb{I}[c^n=0] \mathbb{I}[s^n=1] q_t^n(a=0)}. \tag{11.2.32}$$

For comparison, the setting in the complete data case is

$$p(c=1|a=0, s=1) = \frac{\sum_n \mathbb{I}[c^n=1] \mathbb{I}[s^n=1] \mathbb{I}[a^n=0]}{\sum_n \mathbb{I}[c^n=1] \mathbb{I}[s^n=1] \mathbb{I}[a^n=0] + \sum_n \mathbb{I}[c^n=0] \mathbb{I}[s^n=1] \mathbb{I}[a^n=0]}. \tag{11.2.33}$$

There is an intuitive relationship between these updates: in the missing data case we replace the indicators by the assumed distributions q. Iterating the E and M steps, these parameters will converge to a local likelihood optimum.

11.2.4 General case

A belief network on a multivariate variable x takes the general form

$$p(x) = \prod_i p(x_i|\text{pa}(x_i)). \tag{11.2.34}$$

Some of the variables will be observed, and others hidden. We therefore partition the variable x into visible and hidden multivariate parts $x = (v, h)$. Given an i.i.d. dataset $\mathcal{V} = \{v^1, \ldots, v^N\}$ our interest is to learn the tables of $p(x)$ to maximise the likelihood on the visible data $\mathcal{V}$. For each datapoint index n, each multivariate variable $x^n = (v^n, h^n)$ decomposes into its visible and hidden parts; an upper variable index will typically the datapoint, and a lower index the variable number.

From Equation (11.2.5), the form of the energy term for belief networks is

$$\sum_n \langle \log p(x^n) \rangle_{q_t(h^n|v^n)} = \sum_n \sum_i \langle \log p(x_i^n|\text{pa}(x_i^n)) \rangle_{q_t(h^n|v^n)}. \tag{11.2.35}$$

Here t indexes the iteration count for the EM algorithm. It is useful to define the following notation:

$$q_t^n(x) = q_t(h^n|v^n)\delta(v, v^n). \tag{11.2.36}$$

This means that $q_t^n(x)$ sets the visible variables in the observed state, and defines a conditional distribution on the unobserved variables. We then define the mixture distribution

$$q_t(x) = \frac{1}{N} \sum_{n=1}^{N} q_t^n(x). \tag{11.2.37}$$

The energy term in the left-hand side of Equation (11.2.35) can be written more compactly using this notation as

$$\sum_n \langle \log p(x^n) \rangle_{q_t(h^n|v^n)} = N \langle \log p(x) \rangle_{q_t(x)}. \tag{11.2.38}$$

To see this consider the right-hand side of the above

$$N \langle \log p(x) \rangle_{q_t(x)} = N \sum_x [\log p(x)] \frac{1}{N} \sum_n q_t(h^n|v^n)\delta(v, v^n) = \sum_n \langle \log p(x^n) \rangle_{q_t(h^n|v^n)}. \tag{11.2.39}$$

Using this compact notation for the energy, and the structure of the belief network, we can decompose the energy as

$$\langle \log p(x) \rangle_{q_t(x)} = \sum_i \langle \log p(x_i|\text{pa}(x_i)) \rangle_{q_t(x)} = \sum_i \left\langle \langle \log p(x_i|\text{pa}(x_i)) \rangle_{q_t(x_i|\text{pa}(x_i))} \right\rangle_{q_t(\text{pa}(x_i))}. \tag{11.2.40}$$

Algorithm 11.2 EM for belief networks. Input: a BN DAG and dataset on the visible variables $\mathcal{V}$. Returns the maximum likelihood estimate of the tables $p(x_i|\mathrm{pa}(x_i))$, $i = 1, \ldots, K$.

$t = 1$ ▷ Iteration counter
Set $p_t(x_i|\mathrm{pa}(x_i))$ to initial values. ▷ Initialisation
while $p(x_i|\mathrm{pa}(x_i))$ not converged (or likelihood not converged) **do**
  $t \leftarrow t + 1$
  for $n = 1$ to N **do**
    $q_t^n(x) = p_t(h^n|v^n)\,\delta(v, v^n)$ ▷ E-step
  end for
  for $i = 1$ to K **do** ▷ Run over all variables
    $p_{t+1}(x_i|\mathrm{pa}(x_i)) = \frac{1}{N}\sum_{n=1}^{N} q_t^n(x_i|\mathrm{pa}(x_i))$ ▷ M-step
  end for
end while
return $p_t(x_i|\mathrm{pa}(x_i))$ ▷ The max likelihood parameter estimate

---

This means that maximising the energy is equivalent to minimising

$$\sum_i \left\langle \langle \log q_t(x_i|\mathrm{pa}(x_i)) \rangle_{q_t(x_i|\mathrm{pa}(x_i))} - \langle \log p(x_i|\mathrm{pa}(x_i)) \rangle_{q_t(x_i|\mathrm{pa}(x_i))} \right\rangle_{q_t(\mathrm{pa}(x_i))} \tag{11.2.41}$$

where we added the constant first term to make this into the form of a Kullback–Leibler divergence. Since this is a sum of independent Kullback–Leibler divergences, optimally the M-step is given by setting

$$p^{new}(x_i|\mathrm{pa}(x_i)) = q_t(x_i|\mathrm{pa}(x_i)). \tag{11.2.42}$$

In practice, storing the $q_t(x)$ over the states of all variables x is prohibitively expensive. Fortunately, since the M-step only requires the distribution on the family of each variable x_i, one only requires the local distributions $q_t^n(x_i, \mathrm{pa}(x_i))$. We may therefore dispense with the global $q_t(x)$ and equivalently use

$$p^{new}(x_i|\mathrm{pa}(x_i)) = \frac{\sum_n q_t^n(x_i, \mathrm{pa}(x_i))}{\sum_{n'} q_t^{n'}(\mathrm{pa}(x_i))}. \tag{11.2.43}$$

Using the EM algorithm, the optimal setting for the E-step is to use $q_t(h^n|v^n) = p^{old}(h^n|v^n)$. With this notation, the EM algorithm can be compactly stated as in Algorithm 11.2. See also `EMbeliefnet.m`. An illustration of the evolution of the log likelihood under EM iterations is given in Fig. 11.4. For

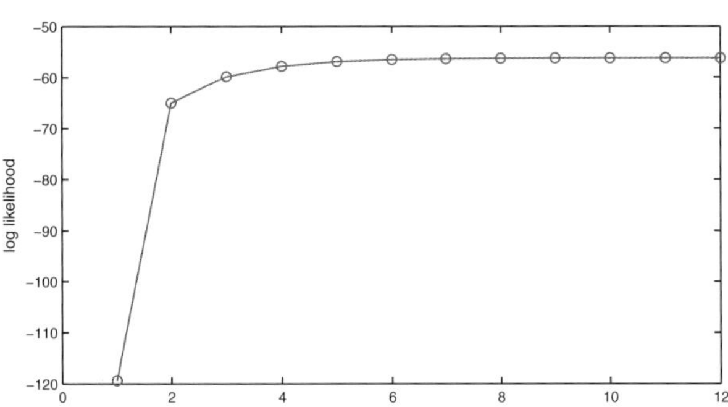

Figure 11.4 Evolution of the log likelihood versus iterations under the EM training procedure (from solving the Printer Nightmare with missing data, Exercise 11.1). Note how rapid progress is made at the beginning, but convergence can be slow.

readers less comfortable with the above KL-based derivation, we describe a more classical approach based on Lagrange multipliers for a specific case in Example 11.5.

Example 11.5 Another belief network example

Consider a five-variable distribution with discrete variables,

$$p(x_1, x_2, x_3, x_4, x_5) = p(x_1|x_2)p(x_2|x_3)p(x_3|x_4)p(x_4|x_5)p(x_5) \tag{11.2.44}$$

in which the variables x_2 and x_4 are consistently hidden in the training data, and training data for x_1, x_3, x_5 are always present. The distribution can be represented as a belief network

The M-step is given by maximising the energy. According to the general form for the energy, Equation (11.2.35), we need to consider a variational distribution $q(h|v)$ on the hidden variables $h = (x_2, x_4)$ conditioned on the visible variables $v = (x_1, x_3, x_5)$. Using n as the datapoint index and t as the EM iteration counter, we require variational distributions for each datapoint

$$q_t(x_2^n, x_4^n|x_1^n, x_3^n, x_5^n). \tag{11.2.45}$$

To keep the notation more compact, we drop here the iteration counter index and write the above as simply $q^n(x_2, x_4)$. In this case, the contributions to the energy have the form

$$\sum_n \langle \log p(x_1^n|x_2)p(x_2|x_3^n)p(x_3^n|x_4)p(x_4|x_5^n)p(x_5^n)\rangle_{q^n(x_2,x_4)} \tag{11.2.46}$$

which may be written as

$$\sum_n \langle \log p(x_1^n|x_2)\rangle_{q^n(x_2,x_4)} + \sum_n \langle \log p(x_2|x_3^n)\rangle_{q^n(x_2,x_4)}$$
$$+ \sum_n \langle \log p(x_3^n|x_4)\rangle_{q^n(x_2,x_4)} + \sum_n \langle \log p(x_4|x_5^n)\rangle_{q^n(x_2,x_4)} + \sum_n \log p(x_5^n). \tag{11.2.47}$$

A useful property can now be exploited, namely that each term depends on only those hidden variables in the family that that term represents. Thus we may write

$$\sum_n \langle \log p(x_1^n|x_2)\rangle_{q^n(x_2)} + \sum_n \langle \log p(x_2|x_3^n)\rangle_{q^n(x_2)}$$
$$+ \sum_n \langle \log p(x_3^n|x_4)\rangle_{q^n(x_4)} + \sum_n \langle \log p(x_4|x_5^n)\rangle_{q^n(x_4)} + \sum_n \log p(x_5^n). \tag{11.2.48}$$

The final term can be set using maximum likelihood. Let us consider therefore a more difficult table, $p(x_1|x_2)$. When will the table entry $p(x_1 = i|x_2 = j)$ occur in the energy? This happens whenever x_1^n is in state i. Since there is a summation over all the states of variables x_2 (due to the average), there is also a term with variable x_2 in state j. Hence the contribution to the energy from terms of the form $p(x_1 = i|x_2 = j)$ is

$$\sum_n \mathbb{I}[x_1^n = i]\, q^n(x_2 = j) \log p(x_1 = i|x_2 = j) \tag{11.2.49}$$

where the indicator function $\mathbb{I}[x_1^n = i]$ equals 1 if x_1^n is in state i and is zero otherwise. To ensure normalisation of the table, we add a Lagrange term:

$$\sum_n \mathbb{I}[x_1^n = i] q^n(x_2 = j) \log p(x_1 = i|x_2 = j) + \lambda \left\{1 - \sum_k p(x_1 = k|x_2 = j)\right\}. \quad (11.2.50)$$

Differentiating with respect to $p(x_1 = i|x_2 = j)$ and equating to zero we get

$$\sum_n \mathbb{I}[x_1^n = i] \frac{q^n(x_2 = j)}{p(x_1 = i|x_2 = j)} = \lambda \quad (11.2.51)$$

or

$$p(x_1 = i|x_2 = j) \propto \sum_n \mathbb{I}[x_1^n = i] q^n(x_2 = j). \quad (11.2.52)$$

Hence

$$p(x_1 = i|x_2 = j) = \frac{\sum_n \mathbb{I}[x_1^n = i] q^n(x_2 = j)}{\sum_{n,k} \mathbb{I}[x_1^n = k] q^n(x_2 = j)}. \quad (11.2.53)$$

From the E-step we have

$$q^n(x_2 = j) = p^{old}(x_2 = j|x_1^n, x_3^n, x_5^n). \quad (11.2.54)$$

This optimal distribution is easy to compute since this is the marginal on the family, given some evidential variables. Hence, the M-step update for the table is

$$p^{new}(x_1 = i|x_2 = j) = \frac{\sum_n \mathbb{I}[x_1^n = i] p^{old}(x_2 = j|x_1^n, x_3^n, x_5^n)}{\sum_{n,k} \mathbb{I}[x_1^n = k] p^{old}(x_2 = j|x_1^n, x_3^n, x_5^n)}. \quad (11.2.55)$$

If there were no hidden data, Equation (11.2.55) would read

$$p^{new}(x_1 = i|x_2 = j) \propto \sum_n \mathbb{I}[x_1^n = i] \mathbb{I}[x_2^n = j]. \quad (11.2.56)$$

All that we do, therefore, in the general EM case, is to replace those deterministic functions such as $\mathbb{I}[x_2^n = i]$ by their missing variable equivalents $p^{old}(x_2 = i|x_1^n, x_3^n, x_5^n)$.

11.2.5 Convergence

Convergence of EM can be slow, particularly when the number of missing observations is greater than the number of visible observations. In practice, one often combines the EM with gradient-based procedures to improve convergence, see Section 11.6. Note also that the log likelihood is typically a non-convex function of the parameters. This means that there may be multiple local optima and the solution found often depends on the initialisation.

11.2.6 Application to Markov networks

Whilst our examples have been for belief networks, we may also apply the EM application to learning the parameters of Markov networks that have missing data. For an MN defined over visible and hidden variables with separate parameters θ_c for each clique c

$$p(v, h|\theta) = \frac{1}{Z(\theta)} \prod_c \phi_c(h, v|\theta_c) \tag{11.2.57}$$

the EM variational bound is

$$\log p(v|\theta) \geq H(q) + \sum_c \langle \log \phi_c(h, v|\theta_c) \rangle_{q(h)} - \log Z(\theta) \tag{11.2.58}$$

where $H(p)$ is the entropy function of a distribution, $H(p) \equiv - \langle \log p(x) \rangle_{p(x)}$. Whilst the bound decouples the clique parameters in the second term, the parameters are nevertheless coupled in the normalisation

$$Z(\theta) = \sum_{v,h} \prod_{c=1}^{C} \phi_c(h, v|\theta_c), \qquad \theta = (\theta_1, \ldots, \theta_C). \tag{11.2.59}$$

Because of this we cannot directly optimise the above bound on a parameter by parameter basis. One approach is to use an additional bound $\log Z(\theta)$ from above, as for iterative scaling, Section 9.6.4 to decouple the clique parameters in Z; we leave the details as an exercise for the interested reader.

11.3 Extensions of EM

11.3.1 Partial M-step

It is not necessary to find the full optimum of the energy term at each iteration. As long as one finds a parameter θ' which has a higher energy than that of the current parameter θ, then the conditions required in Section 11.2.2 still hold, and the likelihood cannot decrease at each iteration.

11.3.2 Partial E-step

The E-step requires us to find the optimum of

$$\log p(\mathcal{V}|\theta) \geq - \sum_{n=1}^{N} \langle \log q(h^n|v^n) \rangle_{q(h^n|v^n)} + \sum_{n=1}^{N} \langle \log p(h^n, v^n|\theta) \rangle_{q(h^n|v^n)} \tag{11.3.1}$$

with respect to $q(h^n|v^n)$. The fully optimal setting is

$$q(h^n|v^n) = p(h^n|v^n). \tag{11.3.2}$$

For a guaranteed increase in likelihood at each iteration, from Section 11.2.2 we required that this fully optimal setting of q is used. Unfortunately, therefore, one cannot in general guarantee that a partial E-step (in which one would only partially optimsise the lower bound with respect to q for fixed θ) would always increase the likelihood. Of course, it *is* guaranteed to increase the lower bound on the likelihood, though not the likelihood itself. We discuss some partial E-step scenarios below.

Intractable energy

The EM algorithm assumes that we can calculate

$$\langle \log p(h, v|\theta) \rangle_{q(h|v)}. \tag{11.3.3}$$

However, there may be cases in which we cannot computationally carry out the averages with respect to the fully optimal form of q. In this case one may consider a restricted class $\mathcal{Q}$ of q-distributions for which the averages can be carried out. For example, one class for which the averages may become computationally tractable is the factorised distributions $q(h|v) = \prod_j q(h_j|v)$; another popular class are Gaussian q distributions. We can then find the best distribution in the class $\mathcal{Q}$ by using a numerical optimisation routine:

$$q^{opt} = \underset{q \in \mathcal{Q}}{\text{argmin}} \, \text{KL}(q(h)|p(h|v,\theta)). \tag{11.3.4}$$

Alternatively, one can assume a certain structured form for the q distribution, and learn the optimal factors of the distribution by free form functional calculus. This approach is taken for example in Section 28.4.2.

Viterbi training

An extreme case of a partial E-step is to restrict $q(h^n|v^n)$ to a delta function. In this case, the entropic term $\langle \log q(h^n|v^n) \rangle_{q(h^n|v^n)}$ is constant (zero for discrete h), so that the optimal delta function q is to set

$$q(h^n|v^n) = \delta\left(h^n, h_*^n\right) \tag{11.3.5}$$

where

$$h_*^n = \underset{h}{\text{argmax}} \; p(h, v^n|\theta). \tag{11.3.6}$$

When used in the energy, the average with respect to q is trivial and the energy becomes simply

$$\sum_{n=1}^{N} \log p(h_*^n, v^n|\theta). \tag{11.3.7}$$

The corresponding bound on the log-likelihood is then

$$\log p(\mathcal{V}|\theta) \geq H + \sum_{n=1}^{N} \log p(h_*^n, v^n|\theta) \tag{11.3.8}$$

where H is the entropy of the delta function (zero for discrete h).

As a partial justification for this technique, provided there is sufficient data, one might hope that the likelihood as a function of the parameter θ will be sharply peaked around the optimum value. This means that at convergence the approximation of the posterior $p(h|v, \theta^{opt})$ by a delta function will be reasonable, and an update of EM using Viterbi training will produce a new θ approximately the same as θ^{opt}. For any highly suboptimal θ, however, $p(h|v, \theta)$ may be far from a delta function, and therefore a Viterbi update is less reliable in terms of leading to an increase in the likelihood itself. This suggests that the initialisation of θ for Viterbi training is more critical than for the standard EM. Note that since Viterbi training corresponds to a partial E-step, EM training with this restricted class of q distribution is therefore only guaranteed to increase the lower bound on the log likelihood, not the likelihood itself.

This technique is popular in the speech recognition community for training HMMs, Section 23.2, from where the terminology Viterbi training arises.

Stochastic EM

Another approximate $q(h^n|v^n)$ distribution that is popular is to use an empirical distribution formed by samples from the fully optimal distribution $p(h^n|v^n, \theta)$. That is one draws samples (see Chapter 27 for a discussion on sampling) $h_1^n, \ldots, h_L^n$ from $p(h^n|v^n, \theta)$ and forms a q distribution

$$q(h^n|v^n) = \frac{1}{L}\sum_{l=1}^{L} \delta\left(h^n, h_l^n\right). \tag{11.3.9}$$

The energy then becomes proportional to

$$\sum_{n=1}^{N}\sum_{l=1}^{L} \log p(h_l^n, v^n|\theta) \tag{11.3.10}$$

so that, as in Viterbi training, the energy is always computationally tractable for this restricted q class. Provided that the samples from $p(h^n|v^n)$ are reliable, stochastic training will produce an energy function with (on average) the same characteristics as the true energy under the classical EM algorithm. This means that the solution obtained from stochastic EM should tend to that from classical EM as the number of samples increases.

11.4 A failure case for EM

Whilst the EM algorithm is very useful, there are some cases in which it does not work. Consider a likelihood of the form

$$p(v|\theta) = \int_h p\left(v|h, \theta\right) p(h), \qquad \text{with } p\left(v|h, \theta\right) = \delta\left(v, f(h|\theta)\right) p(h). \tag{11.4.1}$$

If we attempt an EM approach for this, this will fail (see also Exercise 7.8). To see why this happens, the M-step sets

$$\theta_{new} = \underset{\theta}{\operatorname{argmax}} \left\langle \log p(v, h|\theta)\right\rangle_{p(h|\theta_{old})} = \underset{\theta}{\operatorname{argmax}} \left\langle \log p(v|h, \theta)\right\rangle_{p(h|\theta_{old})} \tag{11.4.2}$$

where we used the fact that for this model $p(h)$ is independent of θ. In the case that $p\left(v|h, \theta\right) = \delta\left(v, f(h|\theta)\right)$ then

$$p(h|\theta_{old}) \propto \delta\left(v, f(h|\theta_{old})\right) p(h) \tag{11.4.3}$$

so that optimising the energy gives the update

$$\theta_{new} = \underset{\theta}{\operatorname{argmax}} \left\langle \log \delta\left(v, f(h|\theta)\right)\right\rangle_{p(h|\theta_{old})}. \tag{11.4.4}$$

Since $p(h|\theta_{old})$ is zero everywhere expect that h^* for which $v = f(h^*|\theta_{old})$, then the energy term becomes $\log \delta\left(f(h^*|\theta_{old}), f(h^*|\theta)\right)$. This is effectively negative infinity if $\theta \neq \theta_{old}$ and zero when $\theta = \theta_{old}$. Hence $\theta = \theta_{old}$ is optimal and the EM algorithm fails to produce a meaningful parameter update.[2] This situation occurs in practice, and has been noted in particular in the context of Independent Component Analysis [239]. Whilst using a delta-function for the output is clearly extreme,

[2] For discrete variables and the Kronecker delta, the energy attains the maximal value of zero when $\theta = \theta_{old}$. In the case of continuous variables, however, the log of the Dirac delta function is not well defined. Considering the delta function as the limit of a narrow width Gaussian, for any small but finite width, the energy is largest when $\theta = \theta_{old}$.

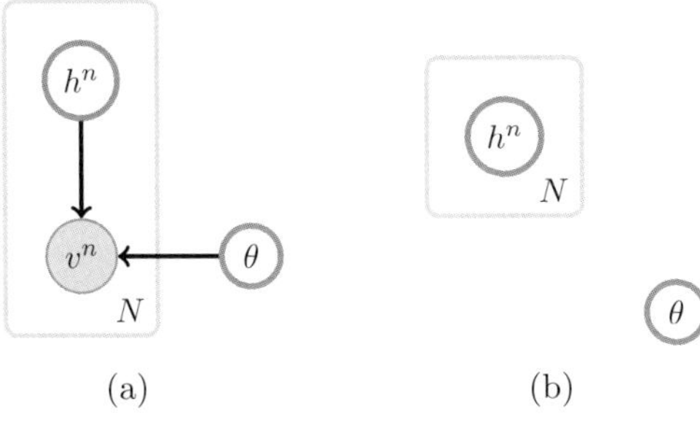

Figure 11.5 (**a**) Generic form of a model with hidden variables. (**b**) A factorised posterior approximation uses in variational Bayes.

a similar slowing down of parameter updates can occur when the term $p(v|h,\theta)$ becomes close to deterministic.

One can attempt to heal this behaviour by deriving an EM algorithm based on the distribution

$$p_\epsilon(v|h,\theta) = (1-\epsilon)\delta\left(v, f(h|\theta)\right) + \epsilon n(h), \quad 0 \le \epsilon \le 1 \tag{11.4.5}$$

where $n(h)$ is an arbitrary distribution on the hidden variable h. The original deterministic model corresponds to $p_0(v|h,\theta)$. Defining

$$p_\epsilon(v|\theta) = \int_h p_\epsilon(v|h,\theta)p(h), \qquad p_\epsilon(v|\theta) = (1-\epsilon)p_0(v|\theta) + \epsilon \left\langle n(h)\right\rangle_{p(h)}, \tag{11.4.6}$$

an EM algorithm for $p_\epsilon(v|\theta)$, $0 < \epsilon < 1$ satisfies

$$p_\epsilon(v|\theta_{new}) - p_\epsilon(v|\theta_{old}) = (1-\epsilon)\left(p_0(v|\theta_{new}) - p_0(v|\theta_{old})\right) > 0 \tag{11.4.7}$$

which implies

$$p_0(v|\theta_{new}) - p_0(v|\theta_{old}) > 0. \tag{11.4.8}$$

This means that the EM algorithm for the non-deterministic case $0 < \epsilon < 1$ is guaranteed to increase the likelihood under the deterministic model $p_0(v|\theta)$ at each iteration (unless we are at convergence). See [107] for an application of this 'antifreeze' technique to learning Markov Decision Processes with EM.

11.5 Variational Bayes

Variational Bayes (VB) is analogous to EM in that it helps us to deal with hidden variables; however it is a Bayesian method that returns a posterior distribution on parameters, rather than a single best θ as given by maximum likelihood. To keep the notation simple, we'll initially assume only a single datapoint with observation v. Our interest is then the parameter posterior

$$p(\theta|v) \propto p(v|\theta)p(\theta) \propto \sum_h p(v,h|\theta)p(\theta). \tag{11.5.1}$$

The VB approach assumes a factorised approximation of the joint hidden and parameter posterior, see Fig. 11.5:

$$p(h,\theta|v) \approx q(h)q(\theta). \tag{11.5.2}$$

Algorithm 11.3 Variational Bayes.

$t = 0$ ▷ Iteration counter
Choose an initial distribution $q_0(\theta)$. ▷ Initialisation
while θ not converged (or likelihood bound not converged) **do**
  $t \leftarrow t+1$
  $q_t(\mathcal{H}) = \arg\min_{q(\mathcal{H})} \mathrm{KL}(q(\mathcal{H})q_{t-1}(\theta)|p(\mathcal{H},\theta|\mathcal{V}))$ ▷ E-step
  $q_t(\theta) = \arg\min_{q(\theta)} \mathrm{KL}(q_t(\mathcal{H})q(\theta)|p(\mathcal{H},\theta|\mathcal{V}))$ ▷ M-step
end while
return $q_t(\theta)$ ▷ The posterior parameter approximation

The optimal settings for the factors $q(h)$ and $q(\theta)$ can be found by minimising the Kullback–Leibler divergence between $p(h,\theta|v)$ and $q(h)q(\theta)$ as discussed below.

A bound on the marginal likelihood

By minimising the KL divergence,

$$\mathrm{KL}(q(h)q(\theta)|p(h,\theta|v)) = \langle \log q(h)\rangle_{q(h)} + \langle \log q(\theta)\rangle_{q(\theta)} - \langle \log p(h,\theta|v)\rangle_{q(h)q(\theta)} \geq 0 \tag{11.5.3}$$

we arrive at the bound

$$\log p(v) \geq -\langle \log q(h)\rangle_{q(h)} - \langle \log q(\theta)\rangle_{q(\theta)} + \langle \log p(v,h,\theta)\rangle_{q(h)q(\theta)}. \tag{11.5.4}$$

Minimising the Kullback–Leibler divergence with respect to $q(\theta)$ and $q(h)$ is equivalent to obtaining the tightest lower bound on $\log p(v)$. A simple coordinate-wise procedure in which we first fix the $q(\theta)$ and solve for $q(h)$ and then vice versa is analogous to the E and M steps of the EM algorithm:

E-step

$$q^{new}(h) = \underset{q(h)}{\mathrm{argmin}}\ \mathrm{KL}\big(q(h)q^{old}(\theta)|p(h,\theta|v)\big). \tag{11.5.5}$$

M-step

$$q^{new}(\theta) = \underset{q(\theta)}{\mathrm{argmin}}\ \mathrm{KL}(q^{new}(h)q(\theta)|p(h,\theta|v)). \tag{11.5.6}$$

For a set of observations $\mathcal{V}$ and hidden variables $\mathcal{H}$, the procedure is described in Algorithm 11.3. For distributions $q(\mathcal{H})$ and $q(\theta)$ which are parameterised or otherwise constrained, the best distributions in the minimal KL sense are returned. In general, each iteration of VB is guaranteed to increase the bound on the marginal likelihood, but not the marginal likelihood itself. Like the EM algorithm, VB can (and often does) suffer from local maxima issues. This means that the converged solution can be dependent on the initialisation.

Unconstrained approximations

For fixed $q(\theta)$ the contribution to the KL divergence Equation (11.5.3) from $q(h)$ is

$$\langle \log q(h)\rangle_{q(h)} - \langle \log p(v,h,\theta)\rangle_{q(h)q(\theta)} = \mathrm{KL}(q(h)|\tilde{p}(h)) + \text{const.} \tag{11.5.7}$$

Algorithm 11.4 Variational Bayes (i.i.d. data).

$t = 0$ ▷ Iteration counter
Choose an initial distribution $q_0(\theta)$. ▷ Initialisation
while θ not converged (or likelihood bound not converged) **do**
  $t \leftarrow t+1$
  for $n = 1$ to N **do** ▷ Run over all datapoints
    $q_t^n(h^n) \propto \exp\left(\langle \log p(v^n, h^n|\theta)\rangle_{q_{t-1}(\theta)}\right)$ ▷ E-step
  end for
  $q_t(\theta) \propto p(\theta)\exp\left(\sum_n \langle \log p(v^n, h^n|\theta)\rangle_{q_t^n(h^n)}\right)$ ▷ M-step
end while
return $q_t^n(\theta)$ ▷ The posterior parameter approximation

---

where

$$\tilde{p}(h) \equiv \frac{1}{\tilde{Z}} \exp\left(\langle \log p(v, h, \theta)\rangle_{q(\theta)}\right) \tag{11.5.8}$$

and $\tilde{Z}$ is a normalising constant. Hence, for fixed $q(\theta)$, the E-step sets $q(h)$ to $\tilde{p}$,

$$q(h) \propto \exp \langle \log p(v, h, \theta)\rangle_{q(\theta)} \propto \exp \langle \log p(v, h|\theta)\rangle_{q(\theta)}. \tag{11.5.9}$$

Similarly, for fixed $q(h)$, the M-step sets

$$q(\theta) \propto \exp \langle \log p(v, h, \theta)\rangle_{q(h)} = p(\theta) \exp \langle \log p(v, h|\theta)\rangle_{q(h)}. \tag{11.5.10}$$

These E and M-step updates are iterated to convergence.

i.i.d. Data

Under the i.i.d. assumption, we obtain a bound on the marginal likelihood for the whole dataset $\mathcal{V} = \{v^1, \ldots, v^N\}$:

$$\log p(\mathcal{V}|\theta) \geq \sum_n \left\{- \langle \log q(h^n)\rangle_{q(h^n)} - \langle \log q(\theta)\rangle_{q(\theta)} + \langle \log p(v^n, h^n, \theta)\rangle_{q(h^n)q(\theta)}\right\}. \tag{11.5.11}$$

The bound holds for any $q(h^n)$ and $q(\theta)$ but is tightest for the converged estimates from the VB procedure. For an i.i.d. dataset, it is straightforward to show that without loss of generality we may assume

$$q(h^1, \ldots, h^N) = \prod_n q(h^n). \tag{11.5.12}$$

Under this we arrive at Algorithm 11.4.

11.5.1 EM is a special case of variational Bayes

If we wish to find a summary of the parameter posterior corresponding to only the most likely point θ_*, then we may use a restricted $q(\theta)$ of the form

$$q(\theta) = \delta(\theta, \theta_*) \tag{11.5.13}$$

where θ_* is the single optimal value of the parameter. If we plug this assumption into Equation (11.5.4) we obtain the bound

$$\log p(v|\theta_*) \geq -\langle \log q(h)\rangle_{q(h)} + \langle \log p(v, h, \theta_*)\rangle_{q(h)} + \text{const.} \tag{11.5.14}$$

The M-step is then given by

$$\theta_* = \underset{\theta}{\operatorname{argmax}} \left(\langle \log p(v, h|\theta)\rangle_{q(h)} + \log p(\theta) \right). \tag{11.5.15}$$

For a flat prior $p(\theta) = \text{const.}$, this is therefore equivalent to energy maximisation in the EM algorithm. Using this single optimal value in the VB E-step update for $q(h^n)$ we have

$$q_t^n(h) \propto p(v, h|\theta_*) \propto p(h|v, \theta_*) \tag{11.5.16}$$

which is the standard E-step of EM. Hence EM is a special case of VB under a flat prior $p(\theta) = \text{const.}$ and delta function approximation of the parameter posterior.

11.5.2 An example: VB for the Asbestos-Smoking-Cancer network

In Section 9.4 we showed how to apply Bayesian methods to train a belief network, giving rise to a posterior distribution over parameter. In our previous discussion, the data was fully observed. Here, however, we wish to revisit this case, now assuming however that some of the observations can be missing. This complicates the Bayesian analysis and motivates approximate methods such as VB.

Let's reconsider Bayesian learning in the binary variable asbestos-smoking-cancer network, as described in Section 9.4

$$p(a, c, s) = p(c|a, s)p(a)p(s) \tag{11.5.17}$$

in which we use a factorised parameter prior

$$p(\theta_c)p(\theta_a)p(\theta_s). \tag{11.5.18}$$

When all the data $\mathcal{V}$ is i.i.d. and observed, the parameter posterior factorises. However, as we discussed in Section 11.1.1 if the state of a (asbestos) is not observed, the parameter posterior no longer factorises:

$$p(\theta_a, \theta_s, \theta_c|\mathcal{V}) \propto p(\theta_a)p(\theta_s)p(\theta_c)p(\mathcal{V}|\theta_a, \theta_s, \theta_c) \tag{11.5.19}$$

$$\propto p(\theta_a)p(\theta_s)p(\theta_c)\prod_n p(v^n|\theta_a, \theta_s, \theta_c) \tag{11.5.20}$$

$$\propto p(\theta_a)p(\theta_s)p(\theta_c)\prod_n p(s^n|\theta_s)\sum_{a^n} p(c^n|s^n, a^n, \theta_c)p(a^n|\theta_a) \tag{11.5.21}$$

where the summation over a prevents the factorisation into a product of the individual table parameters. This means that it becomes more awkward to represent the posterior since we cannot exactly do this by using posterior distributions on each parameter table alone. This is a situation in which VB can be useful since it enables us to impose factorisations on the posterior. In VB we consider an approximation to the posterior over the parameters and latent variables $q(h)q(\theta)$. In this case $\theta = (\theta_a, \theta_s, \theta_c)$ and the latent variables are asbestos, a^n (one for each datapoint). For this example the

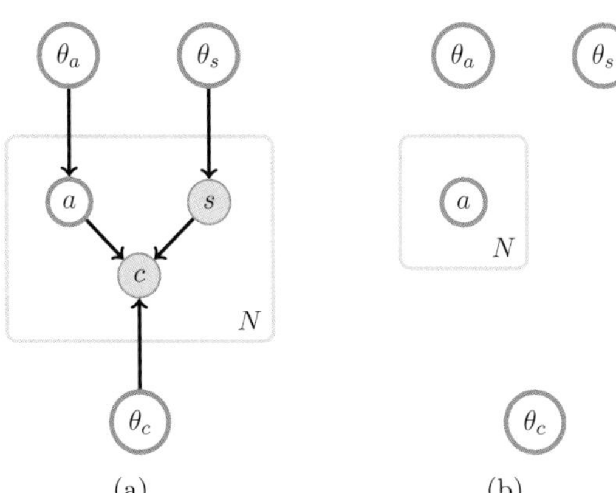

Figure 11.6 (**a**) A model for the relationship between lung Cancer, Asbestos exposure and Smoking with factorised parameter priors. Variables c and s are observed, but variable a is consistently missing. (**b**) A factorised parameter posterior approximation.

visible variables are smoking and cancer: $\mathcal{V} = \{s^n, c^n\}, n = 1, \ldots, N$. The exact joint distribution over all these variables is then

$$p(\theta_a, \theta_s, \theta_c, a^1, \ldots, a^N | \mathcal{V}) \propto \underbrace{p(\theta_a)p(\theta_s)p(\theta_c)}_{\text{prior}} \underbrace{\prod_n p(c^n | s^n, a^n, \theta_c) p(s^n | \theta_s) p(a^n | \theta_a)}_{\text{posterior}}. \tag{11.5.22}$$

In VB we make a factorised assumption, splitting the parameters and latent variables:

$$p(\theta, a^{1:N} | \mathcal{V}) \approx q(\theta) q(a^{1:N}). \tag{11.5.23}$$

From the general results in Equation (11.5.9), we have (ignoring terms that are independent of a in the exponent)

$$q(a^{1:N}) \propto \exp\left(\sum_n \langle \log p(c^n | s^n, a^n, \theta_c) \rangle_{q(\theta_c)} \right). \tag{11.5.24}$$

From this we see immediately that our approximation automatically factorises

$$q(a^{1:N}) = \prod_n q(a^n). \tag{11.5.25}$$

Similarly, from Equation (11.5.10) we have

$$q(\theta) \propto p(\theta) \exp\left(\sum_n \langle \log p(c^n | s^n, a^n, \theta_c) p(s^n | \theta_s) p(a^n | \theta_a) \rangle_{q(a^n)} \right) \tag{11.5.26}$$

$$= p(\theta) \exp\left(\sum_n \langle \log p(c^n | s^n, a^n, \theta_c) \rangle_{q(a^n)} \right) \left\{ \prod_n p(s^n | \theta_s) \right\} \exp\left(\sum_n \langle \log p(a^n | \theta_a) \rangle_{q(a^n)} \right). \tag{11.5.27}$$

Since the parameter prior is factorised, we can collect terms in θ_a, θ_s and θ_c and see that the VB assumption automatically results in a factorised parameter posterior approximation. Hence, our VB approximation is of the form, see Fig. 11.6,

$$p(\theta_a, \theta_s, \theta_c, a^1, \ldots, a^N | \mathcal{V}) \approx q(\theta_a) q(\theta_c) q(\theta_s) \prod_n q(a^n). \tag{11.5.28}$$

All that remains is to form E-step ($q(a^n)$ updates) and M-step ($q(\theta)$ updates), as described below.

M-step: $q(\theta)$ updates

From above we have

$$q(\theta_a) \propto p(\theta_a) \prod_n \exp \langle \log p(a^n|\theta_a) \rangle_{q(a^n)} \tag{11.5.29}$$

where

$$\langle \log p(a^n|\theta_a) \rangle_{q(a^n)} = q(a^n = 1) \log \theta_a + q(a^n = 0) \log (1 - \theta_a). \tag{11.5.30}$$

Hence

$$\exp \langle \log p(a^n|\theta_a) \rangle_{q(a^n)} = \theta_a^{q(a^n=1)} (1 - \theta_a)^{q(a^n=0)}. \tag{11.5.31}$$

It is convenient to use a Beta distribution prior,

$$p(\theta_a) = B(\theta_a|\alpha, \beta) \propto \theta_a^{\alpha-1} (1 - \theta_a)^{\beta-1} \tag{11.5.32}$$

since the posterior approximation is then also a Beta distribution:

$$q(\theta_a) = B\left(\theta_a|\alpha + \sum_n q(a^n = 1), \beta + \sum_n q(a^n = 0)\right). \tag{11.5.33}$$

A similar calculation gives

$$q(\theta_s) = B\left(\theta_s|\alpha + \sum_n \mathbb{I}[s^n = 1], \beta + \sum_n \mathbb{I}[s^n = 0]\right). \tag{11.5.34}$$

Finally, we have a table for each of the parental states of c. For example

$$q(\theta_c(a = 0, s = 1)) = B\left(\theta_c|\alpha + \sum_n \mathbb{I}[s^n = 1] q(a^n = 0), \beta + \sum_n \mathbb{I}[s^n = 0] q(a^n = 1)\right). \tag{11.5.35}$$

These are reminiscent of the standard Bayesian equations, Equation (9.4.15), except that the missing data counts have been replaced by q's.

E-step: $q(a^n)$ updates

From Equation (11.5.24), we have

$$q(a^n) \propto \exp\left(\langle \log p(c^n|s^n, a^n, \theta_c) \rangle_{q(\theta_c)} + \langle \log p(a^n|\theta_a) \rangle_{q(\theta_a)}\right). \tag{11.5.36}$$

For example, if we assume that for datapoint n, s is in state 1 and c in state 0, then

$$q(a^n = 1) \propto \exp \langle \log (1 - \theta_c(s = 1, a = 1)) \rangle_{q(\theta_c(s=1,a=1))} + \langle \log \theta_a \rangle_{q(\theta_a)} \tag{11.5.37}$$

and

$$q(a^n = 0) \propto \exp\left(\langle \log (1 - \theta_c(s = 1, a = 0)) \rangle_{q(\theta_c(s=1,a=1))} + \langle \log (1 - \theta_a) \rangle_{q(\theta_a)}\right). \tag{11.5.38}$$

These updates require the Beta distribution averages $\langle \log \theta \rangle_{B(\theta|\alpha,\beta)}$ and $\langle \log (1 - \theta) \rangle_{B(\theta|\alpha,\beta)}$; these are straightforward to compute, see Exercise 8.17.

The complete VB procedure is then given by iterating Equations (11.5.33)–(11.5.35) and (11.5.37)–(11.5.38) until convergence.

Given a converged factorised approximation, computing a marginal table such as $p(a = 1|\mathcal{V})$ is then straightforward under the approximation

$$p(a = 1|\mathcal{V}) \approx \int_{\theta_a} q(a = 1|\theta_a)q(\theta_a) = \frac{\alpha + \sum_n q(a^n = 1)}{\alpha + \sum_n q(a^n = 0) + \beta + \sum_n q(a^n = 1)}. \tag{11.5.39}$$

The application of VB to learning the tables in arbitrarily structured BNs is a straightforward extension of the technique outlined here. Under the factorised approximation, $q(h, \theta) = q(h)q(\theta)$, one will always obtain a simple updating equation analogous to the full data case, but with the missing data replaced by variational approximations. Nevertheless, if a variable has many missing parents, the number of states in the average with respect to the q distribution can become intractable, and further constraints on the form of the approximation, or additional bounds are required.

One may readily extend the above to the case of Dirichlet distributions on multinomial variables, see Exercise 11.5. Indeed, the extension to the exponential family is straightforward.

11.6 Optimising the likelihood by gradient methods

The EM algorithm typically works well when the amount of missing information is small compared to the complete information. In this case EM exhibits approximately the same convergence as Newton-based gradient method [255]. However, if the fraction of missing information approaches unity, EM can converge very slowly. In the case of continuous parameters θ, an alternative is to compute the gradient of the likelihood directly and use this as part of a standard continuous variable optimisation routine. The gradient is straightforward to compute using the following identity. Consider the log likelihood

$$L(\theta) = \log p(v|\theta). \tag{11.6.1}$$

The derivative can be written

$$\partial_\theta L(\theta) = \frac{1}{p(v|\theta)}\partial_\theta p(v|\theta) = \frac{1}{p(v|\theta)}\partial_\theta \int_h p(v, h|\theta). \tag{11.6.2}$$

At this point, we take the derivative inside the integral

$$\partial_\theta L(\theta) = \frac{1}{p(v|\theta)}\int_h \partial_\theta p(v, h|\theta) = \int_h p(h|v, \theta)\partial_\theta \log p(v, h|\theta) = \langle \partial_\theta \log p(v, h|\theta)\rangle_{p(h|v,\theta)} \tag{11.6.3}$$

where we used $\partial \log f(x) = (1/f(x))\partial f(x)$. The right-hand side is the average of the derivative of the log complete likelihood. This is closely related to the derivative of the energy term in the EM algorithm, though note that the average here is performed with respect to the current distribution parameters θ and not θ^{old} as in the EM case. Used in this way, computing the derivatives of latent variable models is relatively straightforward. These derivatives may then be used as part of a standard optimisation routine such as conjugate gradients [255].

11.6.1 Undirected models

Whilst Equation (11.6.3) represents the general case, it is not always possible to easily compute the required averages. Consider an undirected model which contains both hidden and visible variables

$$p(v, h|\theta) = \frac{1}{Z(\theta)}\exp\left(\phi(v, h|\theta)\right). \tag{11.6.4}$$

For i.i.d. data, the log likelihood on the visible variables is (assuming discrete v and h)

$$L(\theta) = \sum_n \left(\log \sum_h \exp \phi(v^n, h|\theta) - \log \sum_{h,v} \exp \phi(v, h|\theta) \right) \tag{11.6.5}$$

which has gradient

$$\frac{\partial}{\partial \theta} L = \sum_n \left(\underbrace{\left\langle \frac{\partial}{\partial \theta} \phi(v^n, h|\theta) \right\rangle_{p(h|v^n,\theta)}}_{\text{clamped average}} - \underbrace{\left\langle \frac{\partial}{\partial \theta} \phi(v, h|\theta) \right\rangle_{p(h,v|\theta)}}_{\text{free average}} \right). \tag{11.6.6}$$

For a Markov network that is intractable (the partition function Z cannot be computed efficiently), the gradient is particularly difficult to estimate since it is the difference of two averages, each of which needs to be estimated. Even getting the sign of the gradient correct can therefore be computationally difficult. For this reason learning in general unstructured Markov networks is particularly difficult (the unstructured Boltzmann machine with hidden units being a particular case in point).

11.7 Summary

- Provided the data is missing at random, we can safely learn parameters by maximising the likelihood of the observed data.
- Variational Expectation Maximisation is a general-purpose algorithm for maximum likelihood learning under missing information.
- The classical EM algorithm is a special case of V-EM and guarantees an improvement (non-decrease) in the likelihood at each iteration.
- Bayesian learning in the case of missing information is potentially problematic since the posterior is typically not factored according to the prior assumptions. In this case approximations are useful, such as variational Bayes, which assumes a factorisation between the parameters and the latent/missing variables.
- The gradient can be easily computed for latent variable models and may be used as part of an optimisation routine. This provides an alternative training approach in cases when EM is slow to converge.

11.8 Code

`demoEMchestclinic.m`: Demo of EM in learning the Chest Clinic tables

In the demo code we take the original Chest Clinic network [184] and draw data samples from this network. Our interest is then to see if we can use the EM algorithm to estimate the tables based on the data (with some parts of the data missing at random). We assume that we know the correct BN structure, only that the CPTs are unknown. We assume the logic gate table is known, so we do not need to learn this.

`EMbeliefnet.m`: EM training of a Belief Network

The code implements maximum likelihood learning of BN tables based on data with possibly missing values.

11.9 Exercises

11.1 (Printer nightmare continued) Continuing with the BN given in Fig. 9.21, the following table represents data gathered on the printer, where ? indicates that the entry is missing. Each column represents a datapoint. Use the EM algorithm to learn all CPTs of the network.

fuse assembly malfunction	?	?	?	1	0	0	?	0	?	0	0	?	1	?	1
drum unit	?	0	?	0	1	0	0	1	?	?	1	1	?	0	0
toner out	1	1	0	?	?	1	0	1	0	?	0	1	?	0	?
poor paper quality	1	0	1	0	1	?	1	0	1	1	?	1	1	?	0
worn roller	0	0	?	?	?	0	1	?	0	0	?	0	?	1	1
burning smell	0	?	?	1	0	0	0	0	0	?	0	?	1	0	?
poor print quality	1	1	1	0	1	1	0	1	0	0	1	1	?	?	0
wrinkled pages	0	0	1	0	0	0	?	0	1	?	0	0	1	1	1
multiple pages fed	0	?	1	0	?	0	1	0	1	?	0	0	?	0	1
paper jam	?	0	1	1	?	0	1	1	1	1	0	?	0	1	?

The table is contained in `EMprinter.mat`, using states `1`, `2`, `nan` in place of `0`, `1`, ? (since BRMLtoolbox requires states to be numbered 1, 2, ...). Given no wrinkled pages, no burning smell and poor print quality, what is the probability there is a drum unit problem?

11.2 Consider the following distribution over discrete variables,

$$p(x_1, x_2, x_3, x_4, x_5) = p(x_1|x_2, x_4)p(x_2|x_3)p(x_3|x_4)p(x_4|x_5)p(x_5), \tag{11.9.1}$$

in which the variables x_2 and x_4 are consistently hidden in the training data, and training data for x_1, x_3, x_5 are always present. Derive the EM update for the table $p(x_1|x_2)$.

11.3 Consider a simple two-variable BN

$$p(y, x) = p(y|x)p(x) \tag{11.9.2}$$

where both y and x are binary variables, $\text{dom}(x) = \{1, 2\}$, $\text{dom}(y) = \{1, 2\}$. You have a set of training data $\{(y^n, x^n), n = 1, \dots, N\}$, in which for some cases x^n may be missing. We are specifically interested in learning the table $p(x)$ from this data. A colleague suggests that one can set $p(x)$ by simply looking at datapoints where x is observed, and then setting $p(x = 1)$ to be the fraction of observed x that is in state 1. Explain how this suggested procedure relates to maximum likelihood and EM.

11.4 Assume that a sequence $v_1, \dots v_T, v_t \in \{1, \dots V\}$ is generated by a Markov chain. For a single chain of length T, we have

$$p(v_1, \dots, v_T) = p(v_1) \prod_{t=1}^{T-1} p(v_{t+1}|v_t). \tag{11.9.3}$$

For simplicity, we denote the sequence of visible variables as

$$\mathbf{v} = (v_1, \dots, v_T). \tag{11.9.4}$$

For a single Markov chain labelled by h,

$$p(\mathbf{v}|h) = p(v_1|h) \prod_{t=1}^{T-1} p(v_{t+1}|v_t, h). \tag{11.9.5}$$

In total there are a set of H such Markov chains ($h = 1, \ldots, H$). The distribution on the visible variables is therefore

$$p(\mathbf{v}) = \sum_{h=1}^{H} p(\mathbf{v}|h)p(h). \tag{11.9.6}$$

1. There is a set of training sequences, $\mathbf{v}^n$, $n = 1, \ldots, N$. Assuming that each sequence $\mathbf{v}^n$ is independently and identically drawn from a Markov chain mixture model with H components, derive the Expectation Maximisation algorithm for training this model.
2. The file `sequences.mat` contains a set of fictitious bio-sequence in a cell array `sequences{mu}(t)`. Thus `sequences{3}(:)` is the third sequence, `GTCTCCTGCCCTCTCTGAAC` which consists of 20 timesteps. There are 20 such sequences in total. Your task is to cluster these sequences into two clusters, assuming that each cluster is modelled by a Markov chain. State which of the sequences belong together by assigning a sequence $\mathbf{v}^n$ to that state for which $p(h|\mathbf{v}^n)$ is highest. You may wish to use `mixMarkov.m`.

11.5 Write a general purpose routine `VBbeliefnet(pot,x,pars)` along the lines of `EMbeliefnet.m` that performs variational Bayes under a Dirichlet prior, using a factorised parameter approximation. Assume both global and local parameter independence for the prior and the approximation q, Section 9.4.1.

11.6 Consider a three-'layered' Boltzmann machine which has the form

$$p(\mathbf{v}, \mathbf{h}_1, \mathbf{h}_2, \mathbf{h}_3|\theta) = \frac{1}{Z}\phi(\mathbf{v}, \mathbf{h}_1|\theta^1)\phi(\mathbf{h}_1, \mathbf{h}_2|\theta^2)\phi(\mathbf{h}_2, \mathbf{h}_3|\theta^3) \tag{11.9.7}$$

where $\dim \mathbf{v} = \dim \mathbf{h}_1 = \dim \mathbf{h}_2 = \dim \mathbf{h}_3 = V$

$$\phi(\mathbf{x}, \mathbf{y}|\theta) = \exp\left(\sum_{i,j=1}^{V} W_{ij}x_i y_j + A_{ij}x_i x_j + B_{ij}y_i y_j\right). \tag{11.9.8}$$

All variables are binary with states 0, 1 and the parameters for each layer l are $\theta^l = \left\{\mathbf{W}^l, \mathbf{A}^l, \mathbf{B}^l\right\}$.

1. In terms of fitting the model to visible data $\mathbf{v}^1, \ldots, \mathbf{v}^N$, is the three-layered model above any more powerful than fitting a two-layered model (the factor $\phi(\mathbf{h}_2, \mathbf{h}_3|\theta^3)$ is not present in the two-layer case)?
2. If we use a restricted potential

$$\phi(\mathbf{x}, \mathbf{y}|\theta) = \exp\left(\sum_{i,j} W_{ij}x_i y_j\right) \tag{11.9.9}$$

is the three-layered model more powerful in being able to fit the visible data than the two-layered model?

11.7 The *sigmoid belief network* is defined by the layered network

$$p(\mathbf{x}^L)\prod_{l=1}^{L} p(\mathbf{x}^{l-1}|\mathbf{x}^l) \tag{11.9.10}$$

where vector variables have binary components $\mathbf{x}^l \in \{0, 1\}^{w_l}$ and the width of layer l is given by w_l. In addition

$$p(\mathbf{x}^{l-1}|\mathbf{x}^l) = \prod_{i=1}^{w_l} p(x_i^{l-1}|\mathbf{x}^l) \tag{11.9.11}$$

and

$$p(x_i^{l-1} = 1|\mathbf{x}^l) = \sigma\left(\mathbf{w}_{i,l}^{\mathsf{T}}\mathbf{x}^l\right), \qquad \sigma(x) = 1/(1 + e^{-x}) \tag{11.9.12}$$

for a weight vector $\mathbf{w}_{i,l}$ describing the interaction from the parental layer. The top layer, $p(\mathbf{x}^L)$ describes a factorised distribution $p(x_1^L), \ldots, p(x_{w_L}^L)$.

1. Draw the belief network structure of this distribution.
2. For the layer $\mathbf{x}^0$, what is the computational complexity of computing the likelihood $p(\mathbf{x}^0)$, assuming that all layers have equal width w?
3. Assuming a fully factorised approximation for an equal width network,

$$p(\mathbf{x}^1, \ldots, \mathbf{x}^L|\mathbf{x}^0) \approx \prod_{l=1}^{L}\prod_{i=1}^{w} q(x_i^l) \tag{11.9.13}$$

write down the energy term of the variational EM procedure for a single data observation $\mathbf{x}^0$, and discuss the tractability of computing the energy.

11.8 Show how to find the components $0 \leq (\theta_b, \theta_g, \theta_p) \leq 1$ that maximise Equation (11.1.9).

11.9 A 2×2 probability table, $p(x_1 = i, x_2 = j) = \theta_{i,j}$, with $0 \leq \theta_{i,j} \leq 1$, $\sum_{i=1}^{2}\sum_{j=1}^{2}\theta_{i,j} = 1$ is learned using maximal marginal likelihood in which x_2 is never observed. Show that if

$$\theta = \begin{pmatrix} 0.3 & 0.3 \\ 0.2 & 0.2 \end{pmatrix} \tag{11.9.14}$$

is given as a maximal marginal likelihood solution, then

$$\theta = \begin{pmatrix} 0.2 & 0.4 \\ 0.4 & 0 \end{pmatrix} \tag{11.9.15}$$

has the same marginal likelihood score.

12 Bayesian model selection

So far we've mostly used Bayes' rule for inference at the parameter level. Applied at the model level, Bayes' rule gives a method for evaluating competing models. This provides an alternative to classical statistical hypothesis testing techniques.

12.1 Comparing models the Bayesian way

Given two models M_1 and M_2 with parameters θ_1, θ_2 and associated parameter priors,

$$p(x, \theta_1|M_1) = p(x|\theta_1, M_1)p(\theta_1|M_1), \qquad p(x, \theta_2|M_2) = p(x|\theta_2, M_2)p(\theta_2|M_2) \tag{12.1.1}$$

how can we compare the performance of the models in fitting a set of data $\mathcal{D} = \{x_1, \dots, x_N\}$? The application of Bayes' rule to models gives a framework for answering questions like this – a form of Bayesian hypothesis testing, applied at the model level. More generally, given an indexed set of models $M_1, \dots, M_m$, and associated prior beliefs in the appropriateness of each model $p(M_i)$, our interest is the model posterior probability

$$p(M_i|\mathcal{D}) = \frac{p(\mathcal{D}|M_i)p(M_i)}{p(\mathcal{D})} \tag{12.1.2}$$

where

$$p(\mathcal{D}) = \sum_{i=1}^{m} p(\mathcal{D}|M_i)p(M_i). \tag{12.1.3}$$

Model M_i is parameterised by θ_i, and the model likelihood is given by

$$p(\mathcal{D}|M_i) = \int p(\mathcal{D}|\theta_i, M_i)p(\theta_i|M_i)d\theta_i. \tag{12.1.4}$$

In discrete parameter spaces, the integral is replaced with summation. Note that the number of parameters $\dim(\theta_i)$ need not be the same for each model.

A point of caution here is that $p(M_i|\mathcal{D})$ only refers to the probability relative to the set of models specified $M_1, \dots, M_m$. This is not the *absolute* probability that model M fits 'well'. To compute such a quantity would require one to specify *all* possible models. Whilst interpreting the posterior $p(M_i|\mathcal{D})$ requires some care, comparing two competing model hypotheses M_i and M_j is straightforward and only requires the *Bayes' factor*

$$\underbrace{\frac{p(M_i|\mathcal{D})}{p(M_j|\mathcal{D})}}_{\text{Posterior Odds}} = \underbrace{\frac{p(\mathcal{D}|M_i)}{p(\mathcal{D}|M_j)}}_{\text{Bayes' Factor}} \underbrace{\frac{p(M_i)}{p(M_j)}}_{\text{Prior Odds}} \tag{12.1.5}$$

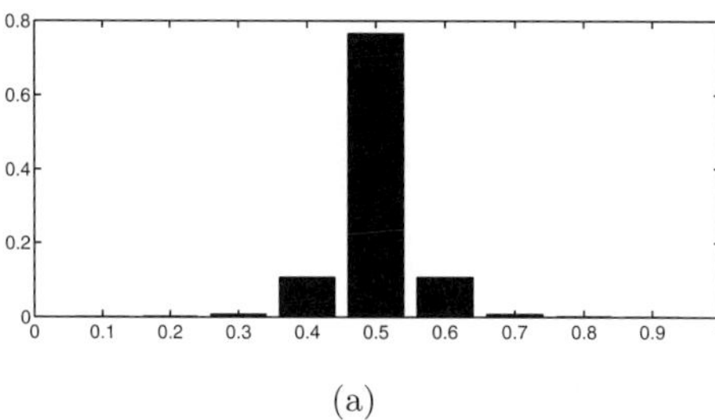

(a)

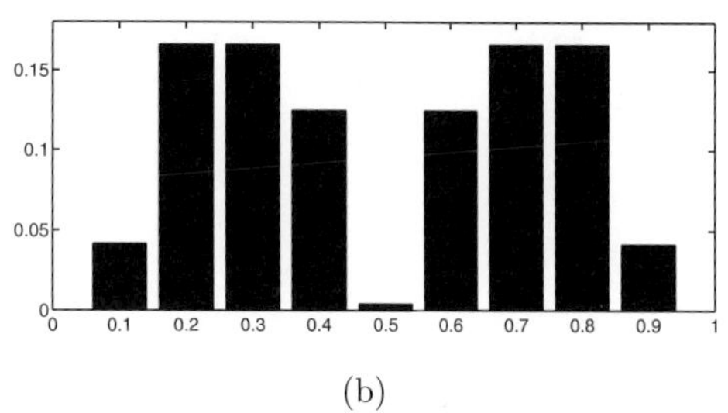

(b)

Figure 12.1 (**a**) Discrete prior $p(\theta|M_{fair})$ model of a 'fair' coin. A perfectly unbiased coin has $\theta = 0.5$, which would corresponds to a prior $\delta(\theta, 0.5)$ – however, we assume a more general form here to illustrate how richer prior assumptions can be used. (**b**) Prior $p(\theta|M_{biased})$ for a biased 'unfair' coin. In both cases we are making explicit choices here about what we consider to be 'fair' and 'unfair'.

which does not require integration/summation over all possible models. We also call the posterior odds the posterior Bayes' factor.

12.2 Illustrations: coin tossing

We'll consider two illustrations for testing whether a coin is biased or not. The first uses a discrete parameter space to keep the mathematics simple. In the second we use a continuous parameter space. In both cases we have a dataset $\mathcal{D}$ that consists of a sequence $x^1, \ldots, x^N$ of outcomes $\text{dom}(x^n) = \{\text{heads, tails}\}$.

12.2.1 A discrete parameter space

We consider two competing models, one corresponding to a fair coin, and the other a biased coin. The bias of the coin, namely the probability that the coin will land heads, is specified by θ, so that a truly fair coin has $\theta = 0.5$. For simplicity we assume $\text{dom}(\theta) = \{0.1, 0.2, \ldots, 0.9\}$. For the fair coin we use the distribution $p(\theta|M_{fair})$ in Fig. 12.1(a) and for the biased coin the distribution $p(\theta|M_{biased})$ in Fig. 12.1(b). Note that these priors essentially encode our subjective beliefs about what we mean for a coin to be biased, or not. We are free to choose any prior distributions we wish. A strength of the Bayesian framework is that in doing so, we spell out what we mean by (in this case) 'biased' or 'unbiased'. This is the 'subjective' beauty of the framework; if others disagree with the subjective choice of the prior, they are free to declare their own competing assumptions and carry through the corresponding analysis, adding to the possible models available.

For each model M, the likelihood for the model to generate the data $\mathcal{D}$, which contains N_H heads and N_T tails, is given by

$$p(\mathcal{D}|M) = \sum_\theta p(\mathcal{D}|\theta, M)p(\theta|M) = \sum_\theta \theta^{N_H} (1-\theta)^{N_T} p(\theta|M) \tag{12.2.1}$$

$$= 0.1^{N_H} (1-0.1)^{N_T} p(\theta = 0.1|M) + \cdots + 0.9^{N_H} (1-0.9)^{N_T} p(\theta = 0.9|M). \tag{12.2.2}$$

Assuming that $p(M_{fair}) = p(M_{biased})$ the posterior odds is given by the ratio of the two model likelihoods.

Example 12.1 Discrete parameter space

5 heads and 2 tails Using $N_H = 5$, $N_T = 2$ in Equation (12.2.2) we obtain $p(\mathcal{D}|M_{fair}) = 0.00786$ and $p(\mathcal{D}|M_{biased}) = 0.0072$. The posterior odds is

$$\frac{p(M_{fair}|\mathcal{D})}{p(M_{biased}|\mathcal{D})} = 1.09 \tag{12.2.3}$$

indicating that there is little to choose between the two models.

50 heads and 20 tails For this case, repeating the above calculation, we obtain $p(\mathcal{D}|M_{fair}) = 1.5 \times 10^{-20}$ and $p(\mathcal{D}|M_{biased}) = 1.4 \times 10^{-19}$. The posterior odds is

$$\frac{p(M_{fair}|\mathcal{D})}{p(M_{biased}|\mathcal{D})} = 0.109 \tag{12.2.4}$$

indicating that we have around 10 times the belief in the biased model as opposed to the fair model.

12.2.2 A continuous parameter space

Here we repeat the above calculation but for continuous parameter spaces. As for the discrete case, we are free to choose any prior we wish; below we consider some simple priors for which the integrations required are straightforward.

Fair coin

For the fair coin, a uni-modal prior is appropriate. We use Beta distribution

$$p(\theta) = B(\theta|a, b), \qquad B(\theta|a, b) \equiv \frac{1}{B(a, b)}\theta^{a-1}(1-\theta)^{b-1} \tag{12.2.5}$$

for convenience since this is conjugate to the binomial distribution and the required integrations are trivial. For the fair coin prior we chose $a = 50$, $b = 50$, as shown in Fig. 12.2(a). The likelihood is then given by

$$p(\mathcal{D}|M_{fair}) = \int_\theta p(\theta)\theta^{N_H}(1-\theta)^{N_T} = \frac{1}{B(a, b)}\int_\theta \theta^{a-1}(1-\theta)^{b-1}\theta^{N_H}(1-\theta)^{N_T} \tag{12.2.6}$$

$$= \frac{1}{B(a, b)}\int_\theta \theta^{N_H+a-1}(1-\theta)^{N_T+b-1} = \frac{B(N_H+a, N_T+b)}{B(a, b)}. \tag{12.2.7}$$

Biased coin

For the biased coin, we use a bimodal distribution formed, for convenience, as a mixture of two Beta distributions:

$$p(\theta|M_{biased}) = \frac{1}{2}\left[B(\theta|a_1, b_1) + B(\theta|a_2, b_2)\right] \tag{12.2.8}$$

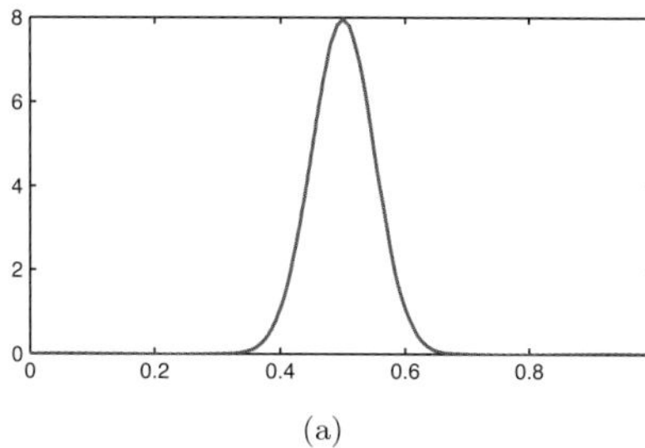

(a)

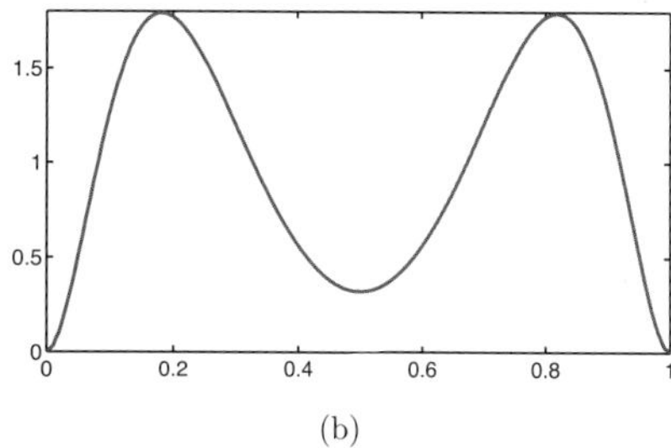

(b)

Figure 12.2 Probability density priors on the probability of a Head $p(\theta)$. (**a**) For a fair coin we choose $p(\theta|M_{fair}) = B(\theta|50, 50)$. (**b**) For a biased we choose $p(\theta|M_{biased}) = 0.5\,(B(\theta|3, 10) + B(\theta|10, 3))$. Note the different vertical scales in the two cases.

as shown in Fig. 12.2(b). The model likelihood $p(\mathcal{D}|M_{biased})$ is given by

$$p(\mathcal{D}|M_{fair}) = \int_{\theta} p(\theta|M_{biased})\theta^{N_H}(1-\theta)^{N_T}$$
$$= \frac{1}{2}\left\{\frac{B(N_H+a_1, N_T+b_1)}{B(a_1, b_1)} + \frac{B(N_H+a_2, N_T+b_2)}{B(a_2, b_2)}\right\}. \tag{12.2.9}$$

Assuming no prior preference for either a fair or biased coin $p(M) = \text{const.}$, and repeating the above scenario in the discrete parameter case:

Example 12.2 Continuous parameter space

5 heads and 2 tails Here $p(\mathcal{D}|M_{fair}) = 0.0079$ and $p(\mathcal{D}|M_{biased}) = 0.006\,22$. The posterior odds is

$$\frac{p(M_{fair}|\mathcal{D})}{p(M_{biased}|\mathcal{D})} = 1.27 \tag{12.2.10}$$

indicating that there is little to choose between the two models.

50 heads and 20 tails Here $p(\mathcal{D}|M_{fair}) = 9.4 \times 10^{-21}$ and $p(\mathcal{D}|M_{biased}) = 1.09 \times 10^{-19}$. The posterior odds is

$$\frac{p(M_{fair}|\mathcal{D})}{p(M_{biased}|\mathcal{D})} = 0.087 \tag{12.2.11}$$

indicating that we have around 11 times the belief in the biased model as opposed to the fair model.

12.3 Occam's razor and Bayesian complexity penalisation

We return to the dice scenario of Section 1.3.1. There we assumed there are two dice whose scores s_1 and s_2 are not known. Only the sum of the two scores $t = s_1 + s_2$ is known. We then computed the posterior joint score distribution $p(s_1, s_2|t = 9)$ for the two dice. We repeat the calculation here but now for multiple dice and with the twist that we don't know how many dice there are,[1] only that the sum of the scores is 9. That is, we know $\sum_{i=1}^{n} s_i = 9$ but are not told the number of dice

[1] This description of Occam's razor is due to Taylan Cemgil.

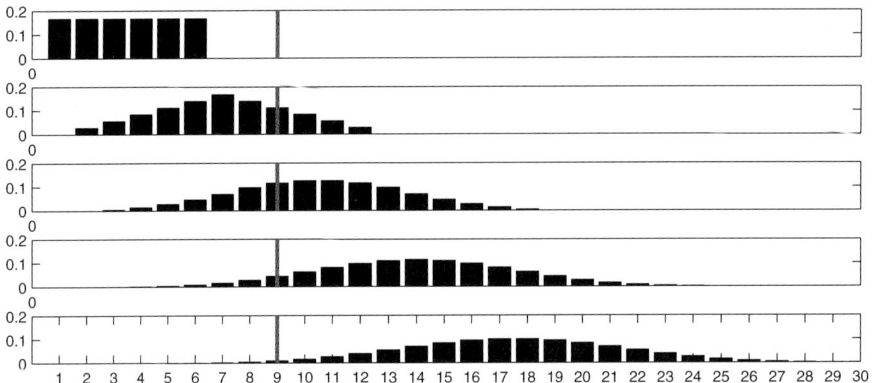

Figure 12.3 The likelihood of the total dice score, $p(t|n)$ for $n = 1$ (top) to $n = 5$ (bottom) die. Plotted along the horizontal axis is the total score t. The vertical line marks the comparison for $p(t = 9|n)$ for the different number of die. The more complex models, which can reach more states, have lower likelihood, due to normalisation over t.

involved n. Assuming a priori that any number n is equally likely, what is the posterior distribution over n?

From Bayes' rule, we need to compute the posterior distribution over models

$$p(n|t) = \frac{p(t|n)p(n)}{p(t)}. \tag{12.3.1}$$

In the above the likelihood term is given by

$$\begin{aligned} p(t|n) &= \sum_{s_1,\ldots,s_n} p(t, s_1, \ldots, s_n|n) = \sum_{s_1,\ldots,s_n} p(t|s_1, \ldots, s_n) \prod_i p(s_i) \\ &= \sum_{s_1,\ldots,s_n} \mathbb{I}\left[t = \sum_{i=1}^{n} s_i\right] \prod_i p(s_i) \end{aligned} \tag{12.3.2}$$

where $p(s_i) = 1/6$ for all scores s_i. By enumerating all 6^n states, we can explicitly compute $p(t|n)$, as displayed in Fig. 12.3. The important observation is that as the models explaining the data become more 'complex' (n increases), more states become accessible. Assuming $p(n) = \text{const.}$, the posterior $p(n|t = 9)$ is plotted in Fig. 12.4. A posteriori, there are only three plausible models, namely $n = 2, 3, 4$ since the rest are either too complex, or impossible. This demonstrates the *Occam's razor* effect of Bayesian model inference which penalises models which are over complex.

12.4 A continuous example: curve fitting

Consider an additive set of periodic functions

$$y_0(x) \equiv w_0 + w_1 \cos(x) + w_2 \cos(2x) + \cdots + w_K \cos(Kx). \tag{12.4.1}$$

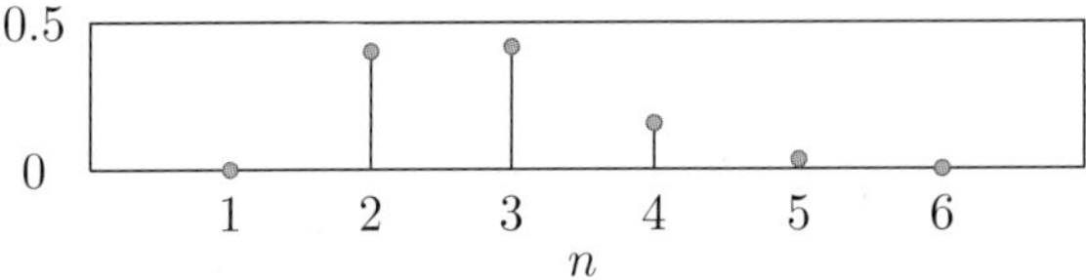

Figure 12.4 The posterior distribution $p(n|t = 9)$ of the number of dice given the observed summed score of 9.

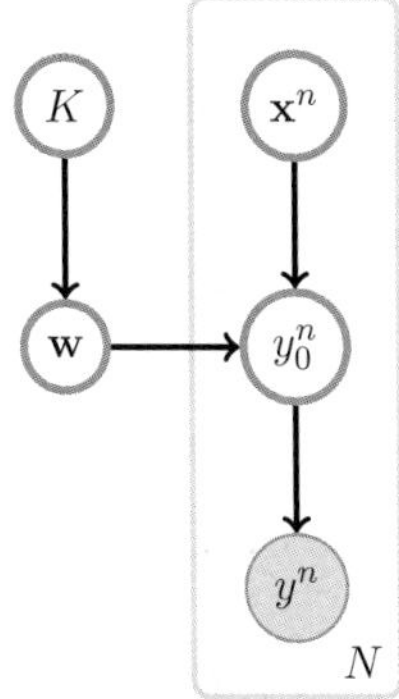

Figure 12.5 Belief network representation of a hierarchical Bayesian model for regression under the i.i.d. data assumption. Note that the intermediate nodes on y_0^n are included to highlight the role of the 'clean' underlying model. Since $p(y|\mathbf{w}, \mathbf{x}) = \int_{y_0} p(y|y_0)p(y_0|\mathbf{w}, \mathbf{x}) = \int_{y_0} \mathcal{N}(y|y_0, \sigma^2)\,\delta(y_0 - \mathbf{w}^\mathsf{T}\mathbf{x}) = \mathcal{N}(y|\mathbf{w}^\mathsf{T}\mathbf{x}, \sigma^2)$, we can if desired do away with the intermediate node y_0 and place directly arrows from $\mathbf{w}$ and $\mathbf{x}^n$ to y^n.

This can be conveniently written in vector form

$$y_0(x) \equiv \mathbf{w}^\mathsf{T}\boldsymbol{\phi}(x) \tag{12.4.2}$$

where $\boldsymbol{\phi}(x)$ is a $K + 1$ dimensional vector with elements

$$\boldsymbol{\phi}(x) \equiv (1, \cos(x), \cos(2x), \ldots, \cos(Kx))^\mathsf{T} \tag{12.4.3}$$

and the vector $\mathbf{w}$ contains the weights of the additive function. We are given a set of data $\mathcal{D} = \{(x^n, y^n), n = 1, \ldots, N\}$ drawn from this distribution, where y^n is the clean $y^0(x^n)$ corrupted with additive zero mean Gaussian noise with variance σ^2,

$$y^n = y_0(x^n) + \epsilon^n, \quad \epsilon^n \sim \mathcal{N}\left(\epsilon^n|0, \sigma^2\right) \tag{12.4.4}$$

see Fig. 12.5 and Fig. 12.6. Assuming i.i.d. data, we are interested in the posterior probability of the number of coefficients, given the observed data:

$$p(K|\mathcal{D}) = \frac{p(\mathcal{D}|K)p(K)}{p(\mathcal{D})} = \frac{p(K)\prod_n p(x^n)}{p(\mathcal{D})} p(y^1, \ldots, y^N|x^1, \ldots, x^N, K). \tag{12.4.5}$$

We will assume that a priori we have no preference for the number of frequency components in the model, $p(K) = \text{const}$. The likelihood term above is given by the integral

$$p(y^1, \ldots, y^N|x^1, \ldots, x^N, K) = \int_{\mathbf{w}} p(\mathbf{w}|K)\prod_{n=1}^{N} p(y^n|x^n, \mathbf{w}, K). \tag{12.4.6}$$

For $p(\mathbf{w}|K) = \mathcal{N}(\mathbf{w}|0, \mathbf{I}_K/\alpha)$, the integrand is a Gaussian in $\mathbf{w}$ for which it is straightforward to evaluate the integral, (see Section 8.4 and Exercise 12.3)

$$2\log p(y^1, \ldots, y^N|x^1, \ldots, x^N, K)$$
$$= N\log\left(2\pi\sigma^2\right) - \sum_{n=1}^{N}\frac{(y^n)^2}{\sigma^2} + \mathbf{b}^\mathsf{T}\mathbf{A}^{-1}\mathbf{b} - \log\det(2\pi\mathbf{A}) + K\log(2\pi\alpha) \tag{12.4.7}$$

where

$$\mathbf{A} \equiv \alpha\mathbf{I} + \frac{1}{\sigma^2}\sum_{n=1}^{N}\boldsymbol{\phi}(x^n)\boldsymbol{\phi}^\mathsf{T}(x^n), \qquad \mathbf{b} \equiv \frac{1}{\sigma^2}\sum_{n=1}^{N} y^n\boldsymbol{\phi}(x^n). \tag{12.4.8}$$

Assuming $\alpha = 1$ and $\sigma = 0.5$, we sampled some data from a model with $K = 5$ components, Fig. 12.6(a). Given then this data, and assuming that we know the correct noise level σ and prior precision $\alpha = 1$, the task is to infer the number of components K that were used to generate this

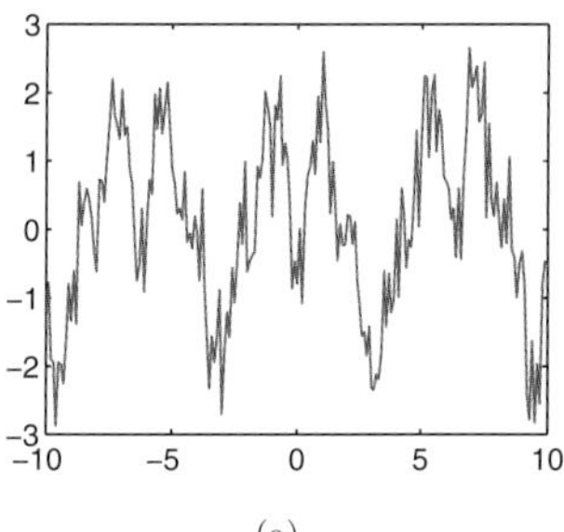

(a)

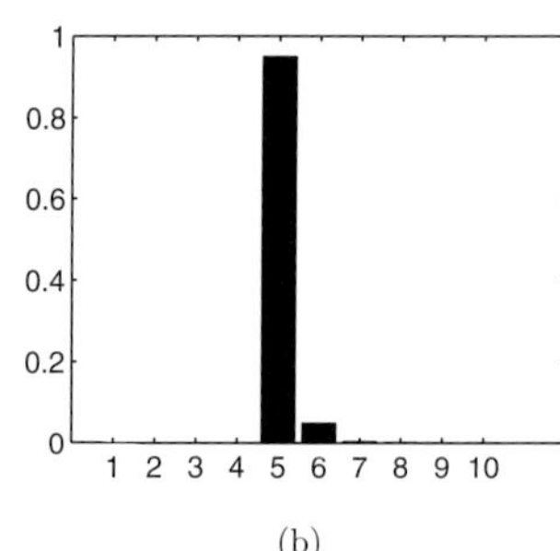

(b)

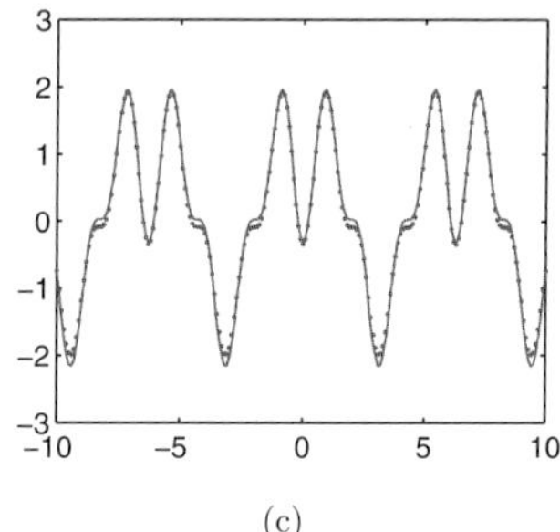

(c)

Figure 12.6 **(a)** The data generated with additive Gaussian noise $\sigma = 0.5$ from a $K = 5$ component model. **(b)** The posterior $p(K|\mathcal{D})$. **(c)** The reconstruction of the data using $\langle \mathbf{w} \rangle^{\mathsf{T}} \boldsymbol{\phi}(x)$ where $\langle \mathbf{w} \rangle$ is the mean posterior vector of the optimal dimensional model $p(\mathbf{w}|\mathcal{D}, K = 5)$. Plotted in the continuous line is the reconstruction. Plotted in dots is the true underlying clean data.

data. The posterior $p(K|\mathcal{D})$ plotted in Fig. 12.6(b) is sharply peaked at $K = 5$, which is the value used to generate the data. The clean posterior mean reconstructions $\langle y_0^n|\mathcal{D}\rangle$ for $K = 5$ are plotted in Fig. 12.6(c).

12.5 Approximating the model likelihood

For a model with continuous parameter vector $\boldsymbol{\theta}$, $\dim(\boldsymbol{\theta}) = K$ and data $\mathcal{D}$, the model likelihood is

$$p(\mathcal{D}|M) = \int p(\mathcal{D}|\boldsymbol{\theta}, M)p(\boldsymbol{\theta}|M)d\boldsymbol{\theta}. \tag{12.5.1}$$

For a generic expression

$$p(\mathcal{D}|\boldsymbol{\theta}, M)p(\boldsymbol{\theta}|M) = \exp(-f(\boldsymbol{\theta})) \tag{12.5.2}$$

unless f is of a particularly simple form (quadratic in $\boldsymbol{\theta}$ for example), for large K, the integral in (12.5.1) is high dimensional and cannot be exactly evaluated. In order to implement Bayesian model comparison methods in practice, therefore, typically we need to use some form of approximation for the model likelihood.

12.5.1 Laplace's method

A simple approximation of (12.5.1) is given by Laplace's method, Section 28.2, which finds the optimum $\boldsymbol{\theta}^*$ of the posterior and then fits a Gaussian at this point based on the local curvature, giving

$$\log p(\mathcal{D}|M) \approx \log p(\mathcal{D}|\boldsymbol{\theta}^*, M) + \log p(\boldsymbol{\theta}^*|M) + \frac{1}{2}\log\det\left(2\pi\mathbf{H}^{-1}\right) \tag{12.5.3}$$

where $\boldsymbol{\theta}^*$ is the MAP solution

$$\boldsymbol{\theta}^* = \underset{\boldsymbol{\theta}}{\operatorname{argmax}}\; p(\mathcal{D}|\boldsymbol{\theta}, M)p(\boldsymbol{\theta}|M) \tag{12.5.4}$$

and $\mathbf{H}$ is the Hessian of $f(\boldsymbol{\theta}) \equiv -\log p(\mathcal{D}|\boldsymbol{\theta}, M)p(\boldsymbol{\theta}|M)$ evaluated at $\boldsymbol{\theta}^*$.

For data $\mathcal{D} = \{x^1, \ldots, x^N\}$ that is i.i.d. generated the above specialises to

$$p(\mathcal{D}|M) = \int p(\boldsymbol{\theta}|M) \prod_{n=1}^{N} p(x^n|\boldsymbol{\theta}, M) d\boldsymbol{\theta}. \quad (12.5.5)$$

In this case Laplace's method computes the optimum of the function

$$-f(\boldsymbol{\theta}) = \log p(\boldsymbol{\theta}|M) + \sum_{n=1}^{N} \log p(x^n|\boldsymbol{\theta}, M). \quad (12.5.6)$$

A partial justification for Laplace's approximation is that as the number of datapoints N increases, the posterior typically becomes increasingly peaked around a single most likely explanation for the data. This means that a narrow width Gaussian will tend to be a good approximation in the large data limit. Quantifying how well an approximation works though is typically rather difficult. The Laplace method's popularity stems from it simplicity although clearly there weil be cases where the posterior is known to be strongly non-Gaussian, in which case Laplace's method should be used with some caution.

12.5.2 Bayes information criterion

The Bayes information criterion is a simpler version of Laplace's method that replaces the exact Hessian with a crude approximation. For i.i.d. data the Hessian scales with the number of training examples, N, and a somewhat severe approximation is to set $\mathbf{H} \approx N\mathbf{I}_K$ where $K = \dim \boldsymbol{\theta}$. Continuing with the notation from Laplace's method, this gives the approximation

$$\log p(\mathcal{D}|M) \approx \log p(\mathcal{D}|\boldsymbol{\theta}^*, M) + \log p(\boldsymbol{\theta}^*|M) + \frac{K}{2} \log 2\pi - \frac{K}{2} \log N. \quad (12.5.7)$$

For a simple prior that penalises the length of the parameter vector, $p(\boldsymbol{\theta}|M) = \mathcal{N}(\boldsymbol{\theta}|\mathbf{0}, \mathbf{I})$, the above reduces to

$$\log p(\mathcal{D}|M) \approx \log p(\mathcal{D}|\boldsymbol{\theta}^*, M) - \frac{1}{2} (\boldsymbol{\theta}^*)^{\mathsf{T}} \boldsymbol{\theta}^* - \frac{K}{2} \log N. \quad (12.5.8)$$

The Bayes Information Criterion (BIC) [261] approximates (12.5.8) by ignoring the penalty term, giving

$$BIC = \log p(\mathcal{D}|\boldsymbol{\theta}^*, M) - \frac{K}{2} \log N. \quad (12.5.9)$$

Typically the BIC criterion is used when no specific prior is specified on $\boldsymbol{\theta}$, in which case $\boldsymbol{\theta}^*$ is given by the maximum likelihood setting. The BIC criterion may be used as an approximate way to compare models, where the term $-\frac{K}{2} \log N$ penalises model complexity. In general, the Laplace approximation, Equation (12.5.3), is to be preferred to the BIC criterion since it more correctly accounts for the uncertainty in the posterior parameter estimate. Other techniques that aim to improve on the Laplace method are discussed in Section 28.3 and Section 28.8.

12.6 Bayesian hypothesis testing for outcome analysis

In outcome analysis we wish to analyse the results of some experimental data. We assume however, that we make no detailed model of the data generating mechanism, asking rather generic questions such as whether the results support some basic hypothesis such as whether two classifiers are performing differently. The techniques we discuss are quite general, but we phrase them in terms of classifier analysis for concreteness. The central question we consider here therefore is how to assess whether two classifiers are performing differently. For techniques which are based on Bayesian classifiers there will always be, in principle, a direct way to estimate the suitability of the model M by computing $p(M|\mathcal{D}) \propto p(M) \int_\theta p(\mathcal{D}|\theta, M)p(\theta|\mathcal{D}, M)$. We consider here the less fortunate situation where the only information presumed available is the test performance of the two classifiers.

To outline the basic issue, we consider two classifiers A and B which predict the class of 55 test examples. Classifier A makes 20 errors, and 35 correct classifications, whereas classifier B makes 23 errors and 32 correct classifications. Is classifier A better than classifier B? Our lack of confidence in pronouncing that A is better than B results from the small number of test examples. On the other hand if classifier A makes 200 errors and 350 correct classifications, whilst classifier B makes 230 errors and 320 correct classifications, intuitively, we would be more confident that classifier A is better than classifier B. Perhaps the most practically relevant question from a machine learning perspective is the probability that classifier A outperforms classifier B, given the available test information. Whilst this question can be addressed using a Bayesian procedure, Section 12.6.5, we first focus on a simpler question, namely whether classifier A and B are the same [15].

12.6.1 Outcome analysis

Consider a situation where two classifiers A and B have been tested on some data, so that we have, for each example in the test set, an outcome pair

$$(o_a(n), o_b(n)), n = 1, \ldots, N \tag{12.6.1}$$

where N is the number of test data points, and $o_a \in \{1, \ldots, Q\}$ (and similarly for o_b). That is, there are Q possible types of outcomes that can occur. For example, for binary classification we will typically have the four cases

$$\text{dom}(o) = \{\text{TruePositive, FalsePositive, TrueNegative, FalseNegative}\}. \tag{12.6.2}$$

If the classifier predicts class $c \in \{\text{true, false}\}$ and the truth is class $t \in \{\text{true, false}\}$ these are defined as

$$\begin{array}{lll} \text{TruePositive} & c = \text{true} & t = \text{true} \\ \text{FalsePositive} & c = \text{true} & t = \text{false} \\ \text{TrueNegative} & c = \text{false} & t = \text{false} \\ \text{FalseNegative} & c = \text{false} & t = \text{true}. \end{array} \tag{12.6.3}$$

We call $\mathbf{o}_a = \{o_a(n), n = 1, \ldots, N\}$, the outcomes for classifier A, and similarly $\mathbf{o}_b = \{o_b(n), n = 1, \ldots, N\}$ for classifier B. To be specific we have two hypotheses we wish to test:

1. H_{indep}: $\mathbf{o}_a$ and $\mathbf{o}_b$ are from different categorical distributions.
2. H_{same}: $\mathbf{o}_a$ and $\mathbf{o}_b$ are from the same categorical distribution.

In both cases we will use categorical models $p(\mathbf{o}_c = q|\boldsymbol{\gamma}, H) = \gamma_q^c$, with unknown parameters $\boldsymbol{\gamma}^c$. Hypothesis 2 will correspond to using the same parameters $\boldsymbol{\gamma}^a = \boldsymbol{\gamma}^b$ for both classifiers, and hypothesis 1 to using different parameters, as we will discuss below. In the Bayesian framework we want to find how likely it is that a model/hypothesis is responsible for generating the data. For any hypothesis H this is given by

$$p(H|\mathbf{o}_a, \mathbf{o}_b) = \frac{p(\mathbf{o}_a, \mathbf{o}_b|H)p(H)}{p(\mathbf{o}_a, \mathbf{o}_b)} \tag{12.6.4}$$

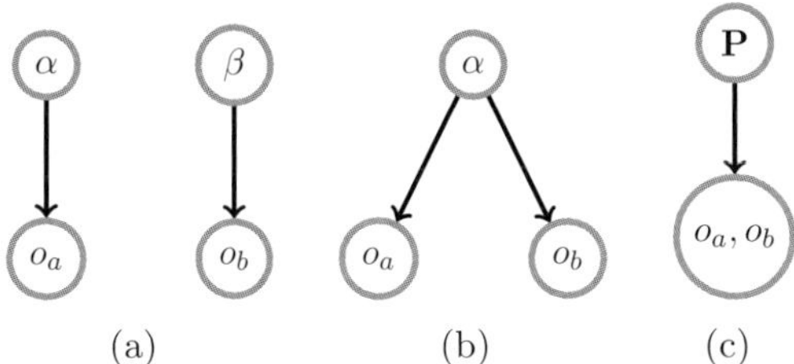

Figure 12.7 (**a**) H_{indep}: corresponds to the outcomes for the two classifiers being independently generated. (**b**) H_{same}: both outcomes are generated from the same distribution. (**c**) H_{dep}: the outcomes are dependent ('correlated').

where $p(H)$ is the prior belief that H is the correct hypothesis. Note that the normalising constant $p(\mathbf{o}_a, \mathbf{o}_b)$ does not depend on the hypothesis. For all hypotheses we make the *independence of trials assumption*

$$p(\mathbf{o}_a, \mathbf{o}_b|H) = \prod_{n=1}^{N} p(o_a(n), o_b(n)|H). \tag{12.6.5}$$

To make further progress we need to clarify the meaning of the hypotheses.

12.6.2 H_{indep}: model likelihood

From Bayes' rule we may write the posterior hypothesis probability as

$$p(H_{\text{indep}}|\mathbf{o}_a, \mathbf{o}_b) = \frac{p(\mathbf{o}_a, \mathbf{o}_b, H_{\text{indep}})}{p(\mathbf{o}_a, \mathbf{o}_b)} = \frac{p(\mathbf{o}_a, \mathbf{o}_b|H_{\text{indep}})p(H_{\text{indep}})}{p(\mathbf{o}_a, \mathbf{o}_b)}. \tag{12.6.6}$$

The outcome model for classifier A is specified using continuous parameters, $\boldsymbol{\alpha}$, giving $p(\mathbf{o}_a|\boldsymbol{\alpha}, H_{\text{indep}})$, and similarly we use $\boldsymbol{\beta}$ for classifier B. The finite amount of data means that we are uncertain as to these parameter values and therefore the joint term in the numerator above is

$$p(\mathbf{o}_a, \mathbf{o}_b, H_{\text{indep}}) = \int p(\mathbf{o}_a, \mathbf{o}_b|\boldsymbol{\alpha}, \boldsymbol{\beta}, H_{\text{indep}})p(\boldsymbol{\alpha}, \boldsymbol{\beta}|H_{\text{indep}})p(H_{\text{indep}})d\boldsymbol{\alpha}d\boldsymbol{\beta} \tag{12.6.7}$$

$$= p(H_{\text{indep}}) \int p(\mathbf{o}_a|\boldsymbol{\alpha}, H_{\text{indep}})p(\boldsymbol{\alpha}|H_{\text{indep}})d\boldsymbol{\alpha} \int p(\mathbf{o}_b|\boldsymbol{\beta}, H_{\text{indep}})p(\boldsymbol{\beta}|H_{\text{indep}})d\boldsymbol{\beta} \tag{12.6.8}$$

where we assumed

$$p(\boldsymbol{\alpha}, \boldsymbol{\beta}|H_{\text{indep}}) = p(\boldsymbol{\alpha}|H_{\text{indep}})p(\boldsymbol{\beta}|H_{\text{indep}}) \quad \text{and} \quad p(\mathbf{o}_a, \mathbf{o}_b|\boldsymbol{\alpha}, \boldsymbol{\beta}, H_{\text{indep}}) = p(\mathbf{o}_a|\boldsymbol{\alpha}, H_{\text{indep}})p(\mathbf{o}_b|\boldsymbol{\beta}, H_{\text{indep}}). \tag{12.6.9}$$

See Fig. 12.7(a) for a depiction of these independence assumptions. Note that one might expect there to be a specific constraint that the two models A and B are different. However since the models are assumed independent and each has parameters sampled from an effectively infinite set ($\boldsymbol{\alpha}$ and $\boldsymbol{\beta}$ are continuous), the a priori probability that values of randomly sampled $\boldsymbol{\alpha}$ and $\boldsymbol{\beta}$ are the same is zero, and we may consider H_{indep} as equivalent to $H_{\text{different}}$.

Since we are dealing with categorical distributions, it is convenient to use the Dirichlet prior, which is conjugate to the categorical distribution:

$$p(\boldsymbol{\alpha}|H_{\text{indep}}) = \frac{1}{Z(\mathbf{u})}\prod_q \alpha_q^{u_q-1}, \qquad Z(\mathbf{u}) = \frac{\prod_{q=1}^{Q}\Gamma(u_q)}{\Gamma\left(\sum_{q=1}^{Q} u_q\right)}. \tag{12.6.10}$$

The prior hyperparameter **u** controls how strongly the mass of the distribution is pushed to the corners of the simplex, see Fig. 8.6. Setting $u_q = 1$ for all q corresponds to a uniform prior. The likelihood of observing $\mathbf{o}_a$ is given by

$$\int p(\mathbf{o}_a|\boldsymbol{\alpha}, H_{\text{indep}})p(\boldsymbol{\alpha}|H_{\text{indep}})d\boldsymbol{\alpha} = \int \prod_q \alpha_q^{\sharp_q^a} \frac{1}{Z(\mathbf{u})} \prod_q \alpha_q^{u_q - 1} d\boldsymbol{\alpha} = \frac{Z(\mathbf{u} + \sharp^a)}{Z(\mathbf{u})} \tag{12.6.11}$$

where $\sharp^a$ is a vector with components $\sharp_q^a$ being the number of times that variable a is in state q in the data. Hence

$$p(\mathbf{o}_a, \mathbf{o}_b, H_{\text{indep}}) = p(H_{\text{indep}}) \frac{Z(\mathbf{u} + \sharp^a)}{Z(\mathbf{u})} \frac{Z(\mathbf{u} + \sharp^b)}{Z(\mathbf{u})} \tag{12.6.12}$$

where $Z(\mathbf{u})$ is given by Equation (12.6.10).

12.6.3 H_{same}: model likelihood

In H_{same}, the hypothesis is that the outcomes for the two classifiers are generated from the same categorical distribution, see Fig. 12.7b. Hence

$$p(\mathbf{o}_a, \mathbf{o}_b, H_{\text{same}}) = p(H_{\text{same}}) \int p(\mathbf{o}_a|\boldsymbol{\alpha}, H_{\text{same}})p(\mathbf{o}_b|\boldsymbol{\alpha}, H_{\text{same}})p(\boldsymbol{\alpha}|H_{\text{same}})d\boldsymbol{\alpha} \tag{12.6.13}$$

$$= p(H_{\text{same}}) \frac{Z(\mathbf{u} + \sharp^a + \sharp^b)}{Z(\mathbf{u})}. \tag{12.6.14}$$

Bayes' factor

If we assume no prior preference for either hypothesis, $p(H_{\text{indep}}) = p(H_{\text{same}})$, then

$$\frac{p(H_{\text{indep}}|\mathbf{o}_a, \mathbf{o}_b)}{p(H_{\text{same}}|\mathbf{o}_a, \mathbf{o}_b)} = \frac{Z(\mathbf{u} + \sharp^a)Z(\mathbf{u} + \sharp^b)}{Z(\mathbf{u})Z(\mathbf{u} + \sharp^a + \sharp^b)}. \tag{12.6.15}$$

The higher this ratio is, the more we belive that the data were generated by two different categorical distributions.

Example 12.3

Two people classify the expression of each image into happy, sad or normal, using states 1, 2, 3 respectively. Each column of the data below represents an image classified by the two people (person 1 is the top row and person 2 the second row). Are the two people essentially in agreement?

1	3	1	3	1	1	3	2	2	3	1	1	1	1	1	1	1	1	1	2
1	3	1	2	2	3	3	3	2	3	3	2	2	2	2	1	2	1	3	2

To help answer this question, we perform a H_{indep} versus H_{same} test. From this data, the count vector for person 1 is [13, 3, 4] and for person 2, [4, 9, 7]. Based on a flat prior for the categorical distribution and assuming no prior preference for either hypothesis, we have the posterior Bayes' factor

$$\frac{p(\text{persons 1 and 2 classify differently})}{p(\text{persons 1 and 2 classify the same})} = \frac{Z([14, 4, 5])Z([5, 10, 8])}{Z([1, 1, 1])Z([18, 13, 12])} = 12.87 \tag{12.6.16}$$

where the Z function is given in Equation (12.6.10). This is strong evidence the two people are classifying the images differently.

Below we discuss some further examples for the H_{indep} versus H_{same} test. As above, the only quantities we need for this test are the vector counts from the data. We assume that there are three kinds of outcomes, $Q = 3$, for example $\text{dom}(o) = \{\text{good, bad, ugly}\}$, and we want to test if two classifiers are essentially producing the same outcome distributions, or different. Throughout we assume a flat prior on the table entries, $u = 1$.

Example 12.4 H_{indep} **versus** H_{same}

- We have the two outcome counts $\sharp^a = [39, 26, 35]$ and $\sharp^b = [63, 12, 25]$. The posterior Bayes' factor equation (12.6.15) is 20.7 – strong evidence in favour of the two classifiers being different.
- Alternatively, consider the two outcome counts $\sharp^a = [52, 20, 28]$ and $\sharp^b = [44, 14, 42]$. Then, the posterior Bayes' factor equation (12.6.15) is 0.38 – weak evidence against the two classifiers being different.
- As a final example, consider counts $\sharp^a = [459, 191, 350]$ and $\sharp^b = [465, 206, 329]$. This gives a posterior Bayes' factor equation (12.6.15) of 0.008 – strong evidence that the two classifiers are statistically the same.

In all cases the results are consistent with the actual model in fact used to generate the count data.

12.6.4 Dependent outcome analysis

Here we consider the case that outcomes are dependent. For example, it may be the case that when classifier A works well, classifier B will also work well. Our interest is to evaluate the hypothesis:

$$H_{\text{dep}}: \text{ the outcomes that the two classifiers make are dependent.} \tag{12.6.17}$$

To do so we assume a categorical distribution over the joint states, see Fig. 12.7(c):

$$p(o_a(n), o_b(n)|\mathbf{P}, H_{\text{dep}}). \tag{12.6.18}$$

Here $\mathbf{P}$ is a $Q \times Q$ matrix of probabilities:

$$[P]_{ij} = p(o_a = i, o_b = j) \tag{12.6.19}$$

so $[P]_{ij}$ is the probability that A makes outcome i and B makes outcome j. Then,

$$p(\mathbf{o}|H_{\text{dep}}) = \int p(\mathbf{o}, \mathbf{P}|H_{\text{dep}})d\mathbf{P} = \int p(\mathbf{o}|\mathbf{P}, H_{\text{dep}})p(\mathbf{P}|H_{\text{dep}})d\mathbf{P}$$

where, for convenience, we write $\mathbf{o} = (\mathbf{o}_a, \mathbf{o}_b)$. Assuming a Dirichlet prior on $\mathbf{P}$, with hyperparameters $\mathbf{U}$, we have

$$p(\mathbf{o}, H_{\text{dep}}) = p(H_{\text{dep}})\frac{Z(vec\,(\mathbf{U} + \sharp))}{Z(vec(\mathbf{U}))} \tag{12.6.20}$$

where $vec(\mathbf{D})$ is a vector formed from concatenating the rows of the matrix $\mathbf{D}$. Here $\sharp$ is the count matrix, with $[\sharp]_{ij}$ equal to the number of times that joint outcome $(o_a = i, o_b = j)$ occurred in the N datapoints. We assume the uniform prior, $[U]_{ij} = 1, \forall i, j$.

Testing for dependencies in the outcomes: H_{dep} versus H_{indep}

To test whether or not the outcomes of the classifiers are dependent H_{dep} against the hypothesis that they are independent H_{indep} we may use, assuming $p(H_{\text{indep}}) = p(H_{\text{dep}})$,

$$\frac{p(H_{\text{indep}}|\mathbf{o})}{p(H_{\text{dep}}|\mathbf{o})} = \frac{Z(\mathbf{u}+\sharp^a)}{Z(\mathbf{u})}\frac{Z(\mathbf{u}+\sharp^b)}{Z(\mathbf{u})}\frac{Z(vec(\mathbf{U}))}{Z(vec(\mathbf{U}+\sharp))}. \tag{12.6.21}$$

Example 12.5 H_{dep} **versus** H_{indep}

- Consider the outcome count matrix $\sharp$

$$\begin{pmatrix} 98 & 7 & 93 \\ 168 & 13 & 163 \\ 245 & 12 & 201 \end{pmatrix} \tag{12.6.22}$$

so that $\sharp^a = [511, 32, 457]$, and $\sharp^b = [198, 344, 458]$. Then

$$\frac{p(H_{\text{indep}}|\mathbf{o})}{p(H_{\text{dep}}|\mathbf{o})} = 3020 \tag{12.6.23}$$

– strong evidence that the classifiers perform independently.

- Consider the outcome count matrix $\sharp$

$$\begin{pmatrix} 82 & 120 & 83 \\ 107 & 162 & 4 \\ 170 & 203 & 70 \end{pmatrix} \tag{12.6.24}$$

so that $\sharp^a = [359, 485, 156]$, and $\sharp^b = [284, 273, 443]$. Then

$$\frac{p(H_{\text{indep}}|\mathbf{o})}{p(H_{\text{dep}}|\mathbf{o})} = 2 \times 10^{-18} \tag{12.6.25}$$

– strong evidence that the classifiers perform dependently.

These results are in fact consistent with the way the data was generated in each case.

12.6.5 Is classifier A better than B?

We return to the question with which we began this outcome analysis. Given the common scenario of observing a number of (binary) errors for classifier A on a test set and a number for B, can we say which classifier is better? This corresponds to the special case of binary classes $Q = 2$ with $\text{dom}(e) = \{\text{correct, incorrect}\}$. Then for θ_a being the probability that classifier A generates a correct label, and similarly for θ_b, one way to judge this is to compare the hypotheses:

1. $H_{a>b}$: $\mathbf{o}_a$ and $\mathbf{o}_b$ are from different binomial distributions with corresponding probabilities θ_a, θ_b and $\theta_a > \theta_b$.
2. H_{same}: $\mathbf{o}_a$ and $\mathbf{o}_b$ are from the same binomial distribution.

Writing $\mathcal{D} = \{\mathbf{o}_A, \mathbf{o}_B\}$, and assuming independent parameter priors, we have

$$p(\mathcal{D}|H_{a>b}) = \int_{\theta_a>\theta_b} p(\mathbf{o}_A|\theta_a)p(\mathbf{o}_B|\theta_b)p(\theta_a)p(\theta_b). \tag{12.6.26}$$

Using

$$p(\mathbf{o}_A|\theta_a) = \theta_a^{\sharp^a_{\text{correct}}} (1-\theta_a)^{\sharp^a_{\text{incorrect}}}, \qquad p(\mathbf{o}_B|\theta_b) = \theta_b^{\sharp^b_{\text{correct}}} (1-\theta_b)^{\sharp^b_{\text{incorrect}}} \tag{12.6.27}$$

and Beta distribution priors

$$p(\theta_a) = B(\theta_a|u_1, u_2), \qquad p(\theta_b) = B(\theta_b|u_1, u_2) \tag{12.6.28}$$

then one may readily show, using the Beta function $B(x, y)$:

$$p(\mathcal{D}|H_{a>b}) = \frac{B(u_1 + \sharp^a_{\text{correct}}, u_2 + \sharp^a_{\text{incorrect}}) B(u_1 + \sharp^b_{\text{correct}}, u_2 + \sharp^b_{\text{incorrect}})}{(B(u_1, u_2))^2} \int_{\theta_a > \theta_b} p(\theta_a > \theta_b|\mathcal{D}, H_{a>b}) \tag{12.6.29}$$

where

$$p(\theta_a > \theta_b|\mathcal{D}, H_{a>b}) = \int_{\theta_a > \theta_b} B(\theta_a|u_1 + \sharp^a_{\text{correct}}, u_2 + \sharp^a_{\text{incorrect}}) B(\theta_b|u_1 + \sharp^b_{\text{correct}}, u_2 + \sharp^b_{\text{incorrect}}). \tag{12.6.30}$$

The integral above needs to be computed numerically – see `betaXbiggerY.m`. For the H_{same} hypothesis, using $\theta = \theta_a = \theta_b$:

$$p(\mathcal{D}|H_{\text{same}}) = \frac{1}{B(u_1, u_2)} \int_\theta \theta^{u_1 + \sharp^a_{\text{correct}} + \sharp^b_{\text{correct}}} (1-\theta)^{u_2 + \sharp^a_{\text{incorrect}} + \sharp^b_{\text{incorrect}}} \tag{12.6.31}$$

$$= \frac{B(u_1 + \sharp^a_{\text{correct}} + \sharp^b_{\text{correct}}, u_2 + \sharp^a_{\text{incorrect}} + \sharp^b_{\text{incorrect}})}{B(u_1, u_2)}. \tag{12.6.32}$$

The question of whether A is better than B can then be addressed by computing

$$\frac{p(\mathcal{D}|H_{a>b})}{p(\mathcal{D}|H_{\text{same}})} = \frac{B(u_1 + \sharp^a_{\text{correct}}, u_2 + \sharp^a_{\text{incorrect}}) B(u_1 + \sharp^b_{\text{correct}}, u_2 + \sharp^b_{\text{incorrect}})}{B(u_1, u_2) B(u_1 + \sharp^a_{\text{correct}} + \sharp^b_{\text{correct}}, u_2 + \sharp^a_{\text{incorrect}} + \sharp^b_{\text{incorrect}})} p(\theta_a > \theta_b|\mathcal{D}, H_{a>b}). \tag{12.6.33}$$

Examining the quotient term, we see that this is related to the H_{indep} hypothesis via

$$\frac{p(\mathcal{D}|H_{a>b})}{p(\mathcal{D}|H_{\text{same}})} = \frac{p(\mathcal{D}|H_{\text{indep}})}{p(\mathcal{D}|H_{\text{same}})} p(\theta_a > \theta_b|\mathcal{D}, H_{a>b}) \tag{12.6.34}$$

where the second term decreases the H_{indep} versus H_{same} Bayes' factor. This is intuitive since $H_{a>b}$ places more constraints on the parameter space than H_{indep}.

Example 12.6

Classifier A makes 20 errors, and 35 correct classifications, whereas classifier B makes 27 errors and 28 correct classifications. Using a flat prior $u_1 = u_2 = 1$ this gives

$$p(\theta_a > \theta_b|\mathbf{o}_A, \mathbf{o}_B, H_{\text{indep}}) = \texttt{betaXbiggerY(1+35,1+20,1+28,1+27)} = 0.909. \tag{12.6.35}$$

The Bayes' factor is then

$$\frac{p(\mathcal{D}|H_{a>b})}{p(\mathcal{D}|H_{\text{same}})} = \frac{B(1+35, 1+20) B(1+28, 1+27)}{B(1,1) B(1+35+28, 1+20+27)} 0.909 = 0.516. \tag{12.6.36}$$

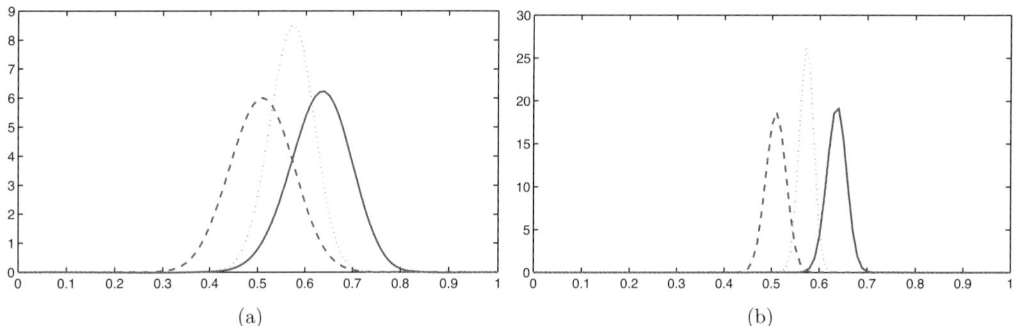

(a) (b)

Figure 12.8 Two classifiers A and B and their posterior distributions of the probability that they classify correctly (using a uniform Beta prior). (**a**) For A with 35 correct and 20 incorrect labels, $B(x|1+35, 1+20)$ (solid curve); B with 28 correct 27 incorrect $B(y|1+28, 1+27)$ (dashed curve). Also plotted is the posterior assuming that both classifiers are the same, $B(x|1+35+28, 1+20+27)$, (dotted curve). Whilst the posterior overlap of the two classifiers A and B is small, they both overlap with the posterior for the assumption that the classifiers are the same. For this reason, there is no significant evidence that A is better than B. (**b**) For A with 350 correct and 200 incorrect labels (solid curve), $B(x|1+350, 1+200)$; B with 280 correct 270 incorrect $B(y|1+280, 1+270)$ (dashed curve). As the amount of data increases the overlap between the distributions decreases and the certainty that one classifier is better than the other correspondingly increases.

On the other hand if classifier A makes 200 errors and 350 correct classifications, whilst classifier B makes 270 errors and 280 correct classifications, we have

$$p(\theta_a > \theta_b|\mathbf{o}_A, \mathbf{o}_B, H_{\text{same}}) = \texttt{betaXbiggerY(1+350,1+200,1+280,1+270)} = 1.0 \tag{12.6.37}$$

and

$$\frac{p(\mathcal{D}|H_{a>b})}{p(\mathcal{D}|H_{\text{same}})} = \frac{B(1+350, 1+200)B(1+280, 1+270)}{B(1,1)B(1+350+280, 1+200+270)} 1.0 = 676. \tag{12.6.38}$$

This demonstrates the intuitive effect that even though the proportion of correct/incorrect classifications doesn't change for the two scenarios, our confidence in determining which is the better classifier increases with the amount of data. See also Fig. 12.8.

12.7 Summary

- Bayes' rule enables us to evaluate models based on how well they fit the data via the model likelihood.
- There is no need to explicitly penalise 'complex' models in the Bayesian approach since it automatically incorporates an Occam's razor effect due to the integral over the posterior parameter distribution.
- Computing the model likelihood can be a complex task. In continuous parameter models, Laplace's method provides a simple approximation, the BIC being a cruder version of Laplace's approximation. .
- Assessing performance on the basis of a limited amount of data can be achieved using simple Bayesian hypothesis testing.

12.8 Code

`demoBayesErrorAnalysis.m`: Demo for Bayesian error analysis
`betaXbiggerY.m`: $p(x > y)$ for $x \sim B(x|a,b)$, $y \sim B(y|c,d)$

12.9 Exercises

12.1 Write a program to implement the fair/biased coin tossing model selection example of Section 12.2.1 using a discrete domain for θ. Explain how to overcome potential numerical issues in dealing with large N_H and N_T (of the order of 1000).

12.2 You work at Dodder's *hedge fund* and the manager wants to model next day 'returns' y_{t+1} based on current day information $\mathbf{x}_t$. The vector of 'factors' each day, $\mathbf{x}_t$ captures essential aspects of the market. He argues that a simple linear model

$$y_{t+1} = \sum_{k=1}^{K} w_k x_{kt} \tag{12.9.1}$$

should be reasonable and asks you to find the weight vector $\mathbf{w}$, based on historical information $\mathcal{D} = \{(\mathbf{x}_t, y_{t+1}), t = 1, \ldots, T-1\}$. In addition he also gives you a measure of the 'volatility' σ_t^2 for each day.

1. Under the assumption that the returns are i.i.d. Gaussian distributed

$$p(y_{1:T}|\mathbf{x}_{1:T}, \mathbf{w}) = \prod_{t=2}^{T} p(y_t|\mathbf{x}_{t-1}, \mathbf{w}) = \prod_{t=2}^{T} \mathcal{N}\left(y_t \middle| \mathbf{w}^\mathsf{T}\mathbf{x}_{t-1}, \sigma_t^2\right) \tag{12.9.2}$$

explain how to set the weight vector $\mathbf{w}$ by maximum likelihood.

2. Your hedge fund manager is however convinced that some of the factors are useless for prediction and wishes to remove as many as possible. To do this you decide to use a Bayesian model selection method in which you use a prior

$$p(\mathbf{w}|M) = \mathcal{N}(\mathbf{w}|\mathbf{0}, \mathbf{I}) \tag{12.9.3}$$

where $M = 1, \ldots, 2^K - 1$ indexes the model. Each model uses only a subset of the factors. By translating the integer M into a binary vector representation, the model describes which factors are to be used. For example if $K = 3$, there would be seven models

$$\{0,0,1\}, \{0,1,0\}, \{1,0,0\}, \{0,1,1\}, \{1,0,1\}, \{1,1,0\}, \{1,1,1\} \tag{12.9.4}$$

where the first model is $y_t = w_3 x_3$ with weight prior $p(w_3) = \mathcal{N}(w_3|0,1)$. Similarly model 7 would be $y_t = w_1x_1 + w_2x_2 + w_3x_3$ with $p(w_1, w_2, w_3) = \mathcal{N}((w_1, w_2, w_3)|(0,0,0), \mathbf{I}_3)$. You decide to use a flat prior $p(M) = \text{const}$. Draw the hierarchical Bayesian network for this model and explain how to find the best model for the data using Bayesian model selection by suitably adapting Equation (12.4.7).

3. Using the data `dodder.mat`, perform Bayesian model selection as above for $K = 6$ and find which of the factors $x_1, \ldots, x_6$ are most likely to explain the data.

12.3 Here we will derive the expression (12.4.7) and also an alternative form.

1. Starting from

$$p(\mathbf{w})\prod_{n=1}^{N} p(y^n|\mathbf{w}, x^n, K) = \mathcal{N}(\mathbf{w}|\mathbf{0}, \mathbf{I}/\alpha)\prod_{n}\mathcal{N}\left(y^n|\mathbf{w}^{\mathsf{T}}\boldsymbol{\phi}(x^n), \sigma^2\right) \tag{12.9.5}$$

$$= \frac{1}{\sqrt{2\pi\alpha^{-1}}}e^{-\frac{\alpha}{2}\mathbf{w}^{\mathsf{T}}\mathbf{w}}\frac{1}{(2\pi\sigma^2)^{N/2}}e^{-\frac{1}{2\sigma^2}\sum_n\left(y^n-\mathbf{w}^{\mathsf{T}}\boldsymbol{\phi}(x^n)\right)^2}. \tag{12.9.6}$$

Show that this can be expressed as

$$\frac{1}{\sqrt{2\pi\alpha^{-1}}}\frac{1}{(2\pi\sigma^2)^{N/2}}e^{-\frac{1}{2\sigma^2}\sum_n(y^n)^2}e^{-\frac{1}{2}\mathbf{w}^{\mathsf{T}}\mathbf{A}\mathbf{w}+\mathbf{b}^{\mathsf{T}}\mathbf{w}} \tag{12.9.7}$$

where

$$\mathbf{A} = \alpha\mathbf{I} + \frac{1}{\sigma^2}\sum_n \boldsymbol{\phi}(x^n)\boldsymbol{\phi}^{\mathsf{T}}(x^n) \qquad \mathbf{b} = \frac{1}{\sigma^2}\sum_n y^n\boldsymbol{\phi}(x^n). \tag{12.9.8}$$

2. By completing the square (see Section 8.4.1), derive (12.4.7).
3. Since each y^n, $n = 1, \ldots, N$ is linearly related through $\mathbf{w}$ and $\mathbf{w}$ is Gaussian distributed, the joint vector $y^1, \ldots, y^N$ is Gaussian distributed. Using Gaussian propagation, Result 8.3, derive an alternative expression for $\log p(y^1, \ldots, y^N|x^1, \ldots, x^N)$.

12.4 Similar to Example 12.3, three people classify images into one of three categories. Each column in the table below represents the classifications of each image, with the top row being the class from person 1, the middle from person 2 and the bottom from person 3. You wish to estimate p (class of image|person $= i$), assuming that for person i each image class is drawn independently from this distribution.

1	3	1	3	1	1	3	2	2	3	1	1	1	1	1	1	1	1	1	2
1	3	1	2	2	3	3	3	2	3	3	2	2	2	2	1	2	1	3	2
1	2	1	1	1	3	2	2	2	3	1	2	1	2	1	1	2	3	3	2

Assuming no prior preference amongst hypotheses and a uniform prior on counts, compute

$$\frac{p(\text{persons 1, 2 and 3 classify differently})}{p(\text{persons 1, 2 and 3 classify the same})}. \tag{12.9.9}$$

12.5 Consider a classifier that makes R correct classifications and W wrong classifications. Is the classifier better than random guessing? Let $\mathcal{D}$ represent the fact that there are R right and W wrong answers. Assume also that the classifications are i.i.d.

1. Show that under the hypothesis that the data is generated purely at random, the likelihood is

$$p(\mathcal{D}|\mathcal{H}_{\text{random}}) = 0.5^{R+W}. \tag{12.9.10}$$

2. Define θ to be the probability that the classifier makes an error. Then

$$p(\mathcal{D}|\theta) = \theta^R(1-\theta)^W. \tag{12.9.11}$$

Now consider

$$p(\mathcal{D}|\mathcal{H}_{\text{non-random}}) = \int_\theta p(\mathcal{D}|\theta)p(\theta). \tag{12.9.12}$$

Show that for a Beta prior, $p(\theta) = B(\theta|a, b)$

$$p(\mathcal{D}|\mathcal{H}_{\text{non-random}}) = \frac{B(R+a, W+b)}{B(a, b)} \tag{12.9.13}$$

where $B(a, b)$ is the Beta-function.

3. Considering the random and non-random hypotheses as *a priori* equally likely, show that

$$p(\mathcal{H}_{\text{random}}|\mathcal{D}) = \frac{0.5^{R+W}}{0.5^{R+W} + \frac{B(R+a,W+b)}{B(a,b)}}. \tag{12.9.14}$$

4. For a flat prior $a = b = 1$ compute the probability that for 10 correct and 12 incorrect classifications, the data is from a purely random distribution (according to Equation (12.9.14)). Repeat this for 100 correct and 120 incorrect classifications.

5. Show that the standard deviation in the number of errors of a random classifier is $0.5\sqrt{R+W}$ and relate this to the above computation.

Part III

Machine learning

Machine learning is fundamentally about extracting value from large datasets. Often the motivation is ultimately to produce an algorithm that can either mimic or enhance human/biological performance.

In Part III we begin by discussing some of the basic concepts in machine learning, namely supervised and unsupervised learning. We then move on to discuss some standard models in machine learning and related areas.

13 Machine learning concepts

Machine learning is the body of research related to automated large-scale data analysis. Historically, the field was centred around biologically inspired models and the long-term goals of much of the community are oriented to producing models and algorithms that can process information as well as biological systems. The field also encompasses many of the traditional areas of statistics with, however, a strong focus on mathematical models and also prediction. Machine learning is now central to many areas of interest in computer science and related large-scale information processing domains.

13.1 Styles of learning

Broadly speaking the main two subfields of machine learning are *supervised learning* and *unsupervised learning*. In supervised learning the focus is on accurate prediction, whereas in unsupervised learning the aim is to find compact descriptions of the data. In both cases, one is interested in methods that generalise well to previously unseen data. In this sense, one distinguishes between data that is used to train a model and data that is used to test the performance of the trained model, see Fig. 13.1. We discuss first the basic characteristics of some learning frameworks before discussing supervised learning in more detail.

13.1.1 Supervised learning

Consider a database of face images, each represented by a vector $\mathbf{x}$.[1] Along with each image $\mathbf{x}$ is an output class $y \in \{\text{male}, \text{female}\}$ that states if the image is of a male or female. A database of 10 000 such image–class pairs is available, $\mathcal{D} = \{(\mathbf{x}^n, y^n), n = 1, \ldots, 10\,000\}$. The task is to make an accurate predictor $y(\mathbf{x}^*)$ of the sex of a novel image $\mathbf{x}^*$. This is an example application that would be hard to program in a traditional manner since formally specifying a rule that differentiates male from female faces is difficult. An alternative is to give example faces and their gender labels and let a machine automatically 'learn' such a rule.

Definition 13.1 Supervised learning Given a set of data $\mathcal{D} = \{(x^n, y^n), n = 1, \ldots, N\}$ the task is to learn the relationship between the input x and output y such that, when given a novel input x^* the predicted output y^* is accurate. The pair (x^*, y^*) is not in $\mathcal{D}$ but assumed to be generated by the same unknown process that generated $\mathcal{D}$. To specify explicitly what accuracy means one defines a loss function $L(y^{pred}, y^{true})$ or, conversely, a utility function $U = -L$.

In supervised learning our interest is describing y conditioned on knowing x. From a probabilistic modelling perspective, we are therefore concerned primarily with the conditional distribution

[1] For an $m \times n$ face image with elements F_{mn} we can form a vector by stacking the entries of the matrix.

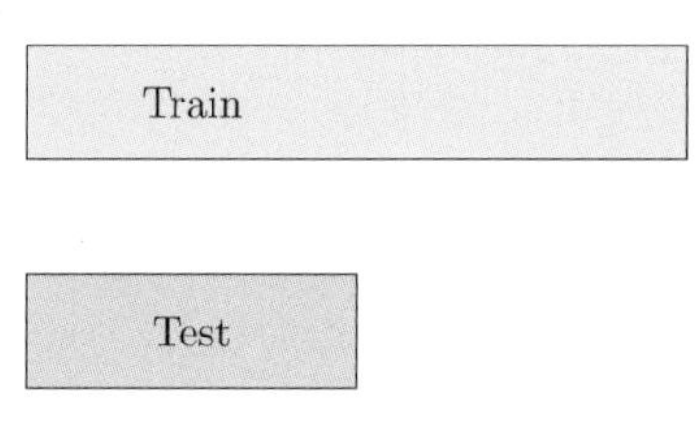

Figure 13.1 In training and evaluating a model, conceptually there are two sources of data. The parameters of the model are set on the basis of the train data only. If the test data is generated from the same underlying process that generated the train data, an unbiased estimate of the generalisation performance can be obtained by measuring the test data performance of the trained model. Importantly, the test performance should not be used to adjust the model parameters since we would then no longer have an independent measure of the performance of the model.

$p(y|x, \mathcal{D})$. The term 'supervised' indicates that there is a notional 'supervisor' specifying the output y for each input x in the available data $\mathcal{D}$. The output is also called a 'label', particularly when discussing classification.

Predicting tomorrow's stock price $y(T+1)$ based on past observations $y(1), \ldots, y(T)$ is a form of supervised learning. We have a collection of times and prices $\mathcal{D} = \{(t, y(t)), t = 1, \ldots, T\}$ where time t is the input and the price $y(t)$ is the output.

Example 13.1

A father decides to teach his young son what a sports car is. Finding it difficult to explain in words, he decides to give some examples. They stand on a motorway bridge and, as each car passes underneath, the father cries out 'that's a sports car!' when a sports car passes by. After ten minutes, the father asks his son if he's understood what a sports car is. The son says, 'sure, it's easy'. An old red VW Beetle passes by, and the son shouts – 'that's a sports car!'. Dejected, the father asks – 'why do you say that?'. 'Because all sports cars are red!', replies the son.

This is an example scenario for supervised learning. Here the father plays the role of the supervisor, and his son is the 'student' (or 'learner'). It's indicative of the kinds of problems encountered in machine learning in that it is not easy to formally specify what a sports car is – if we knew that, then we wouldn't need to go through the process of learning. This example also highlights the issue that there is a difference between performing well on training data and performing well on novel test data. The main interest in supervised learning is to discover an underlying rule that will generalise well, leading to accurate prediction on new inputs. If there is insufficient train data then, as in this scenario, generalisation performance may be disappointing.

If the output is one of a discrete number of possible 'classes', this is called a *classification problem*. In classification problems we will generally use c for the output. If the output is continuous, this is called a *regression problem*. For example, based on historical information of demand for suncream in your supermarket, you are asked to predict the demand for the next month. In some cases it is possible to discretise a continuous output and then consider a corresponding classification problem. However, in other cases it is impractical or unnatural to do this, for example if the output y is a high-dimensional continuous valued vector.

13.1.2 Unsupervised learning

Definition 13.2 Unsupervised learning Given a set of data $\mathcal{D} = \{x^n, n = 1, \ldots, N\}$ in unsupervised learning we aim to find a plausible compact description of the data. An objective is used to quantify the accuracy of the description. In unsupervised learning there is no special prediction variable so that, from a probabilistic perspective, we are interested in modelling the distribution $p(x)$. The likelihood of the model to generate the data is a popular measure of the accuracy of the description.

Example 13.2

A supermarket chain wishes to discover how many different basic consumer buying behaviours there are based on a large database of supermarket checkout data. Items brought by a customer on a visit to a checkout are represented by a (very sparse) 10 000 dimensional vector $\mathbf{x}$ which contains a 1 in the ith element if the customer bought product i and 0 otherwise. Based on 10 million such checkout vectors from stores across the country, $\mathcal{D} = \{\mathbf{x}^n, n = 1, \ldots, 10^7\}$ the supermarket chain wishes to discover patterns of buying behaviour.

In the table each column represents the products bought by a customer (7 customer records with the first 6 of the 10 000 products are shown). A 1 indicates that the customer bought that item. We wish to find common patterns in the data, such as if someone buys diapers they are also likely to buy aspirin.

coffee	1	0	0	1	0	0	0	..
tea	0	0	1	0	0	0	0	..
milk	1	0	1	1	0	1	1	..
beer	0	0	0	1	1	0	1	..
diapers	0	0	1	0	1	0	1	..
aspirin	0	1	1	0	1	0	1	..

Example 13.3 Clustering

x_1	−2	−6	−1	11	−1	46	33	42	32	45
x_2	7	22	1	1	−8	52	40	33	54	39

The table on the right represents a collection of unlabelled two-dimensional points. By simply eye-balling the data, we can see that there are two apparent clusters, one centred around (0,5) and the other around (35,45). A reasonable compact description of the data is that is has two clusters, one centred at (0,0) and one at (35,45), each with a standard deviation of 10.

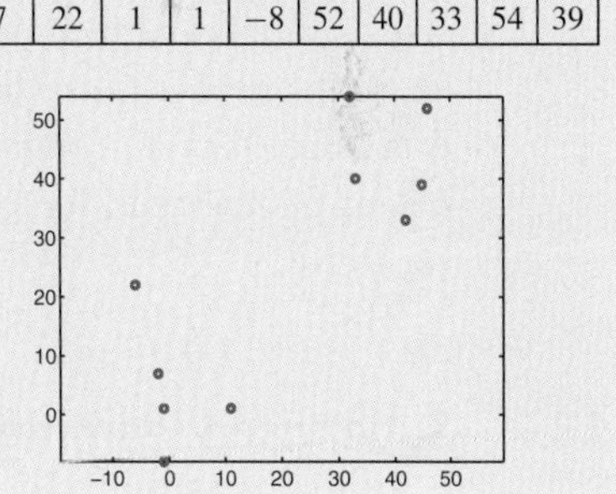

13.1.3 Anomaly detection

A baby processes a mass of initially confusing sensory data. After a while the baby begins to understand her environment so that sensory data from the same environment is familiar or expected. When a strange face presents itself, the baby recognises that this is not familiar and becomes upset. The baby has learned a representation of the environment and can distinguish the expected from the unexpected; this is an example of unsupervised learning. Detecting anomalous events in industrial processes (*plant monitoring*), engine monitoring and unexpected buying behaviour patterns in customers all fall under the area of anomaly detection. This is also known as 'novelty' detection.

13.1.4 Online (sequential) learning

In the above situations we assumed that the data $\mathcal{D}$ was given beforehand. In *online learning* data arrives sequentially and we continually update our model as new data becomes available. Online learning may occur in either a supervised or unsupervised context.

13.1.5 Interacting with the environment

In certain situations, an agent may be able to interact in some manner with its environment. This interaction can complicate but also enrich the potential for learning.

Query (active) learning Here the agent has the ability to request data from the environment. For example, a predictor might recognise that it is less confidently able to predict in certain regions of the space x and therefore requests more training data in this region. Active learning can also be considered in an unsupervised context in which the agent might request information in regions where $p(x)$ is currently uninformative.

Reinforcement learning In reinforcement learning an agent inhabits an environment in which it may take actions. Some actions may eventually be beneficial (lead to food for example), whilst others may be disastrous (lead to being eaten for example). Based on accumulated experience, the agent needs to learn which action to take in a given situation in order to maximise the probability of obtaining a desired long-term goal (long-term survival, for example). Actions that lead to long-term rewards need to be reinforced. Reinforcement learning has connections with control theory, Markov decision processes and game theory. Whilst we discussed MDPs and briefly mentioned how an environment can be learned based on delayed rewards in Section 7.9.2, we will not discuss this topic further and refer the reader to specialised texts, for example [283].

13.1.6 Semi-supervised learning

In machine learning, a common scenario is to have a small amount of labelled and a large amount of unlabelled data. For example, it may be that we have access to many images of faces; however, only a small number of them may have been labelled as instances of known faces. In semi-supervised learning, one tries to use the unlabelled data to make a better classifier than that based on the labelled data alone. This is a common issue in many examples since often gathering unlabelled data is cheap (taking photographs, for example). However, typically the labels are assigned by humans, which is expensive.

13.2 Supervised learning

Supervised and unsupervised learning are mature fields with a wide range of practical tools and associated theoretical analyses. Our aim here is to give a brief introduction to the issues and 'philosophies' behind the approaches. We focus here on supervised learning and classification in particular.

13.2.1 Utility and loss

Given a new input x^*, the optimal prediction depends on how costly making an error is. This can be quantified using a loss function (or conversely a utility). In forming a *decision function* $c(x^*)$ that will produce a class label for the new input x^*, we don't know the true class, only our surrogate for this, the predictive distribution $p(c|x^*)$. If $U(c^{true}, c^{pred})$ represents the utility of making a decision c^{pred} when the truth is c^{true}, the expected utility for the decision function is

$$U(c(x^*)) = \sum_{c^{true}} U(c^{true}, c(x^*))p(c^{true}|x^*) \tag{13.2.1}$$

and the optimal decision function $c(x^*)$ is that which maximises the expected utility,

$$c(x^*) = \underset{c(x^*)}{\text{argmax}}\, U(c(x^*)). \tag{13.2.2}$$

One may also consider equivalently a loss $L(c^{true}, c(x))$, for which the expected loss with respect to $p(c, x)$ is then termed the *risk*. The optimal decision function is then that which minimises the risk with respect to θ.

Zero-one loss/utility

A 'count the correct predictions' measure of prediction performance is based on the zero-one utility (or conversely the *zero-one loss*):

$$U(c^{true}, c^*) = \begin{cases} 1 & \text{if} \quad c^* = c^{true} \\ 0 & \text{if} \quad c^* \neq c^{true} \end{cases}. \tag{13.2.3}$$

For the two-class case, the expected utility Equation (13.2.1) given by

$$U(c(x^*)) = \begin{cases} p(c^{true} = 1|x^*) & \text{for} \quad c(x^*) = 1 \\ p(c^{true} = 2|x^*) & \text{for} \quad c(x^*) = 2 \end{cases}. \tag{13.2.4}$$

Hence, in order to have the highest expected utility, the decision function $c(x^*)$ should correspond to selecting the highest class probability $p(c|x^*)$:

$$c(x^*) = \begin{cases} 1 & \text{if} \quad p(c = 1|x^*) > 0.5 \\ 2 & \text{if} \quad p(c = 2|x^*) > 0.5 \end{cases} \tag{13.2.5}$$

In the case of a tie, either class is selected at random with equal probability.

General loss/utility functions

In general, for a two-class problem, we have

$$U(c(x^*)) = \begin{cases} U(c^{true} = 1, c^* = 1)p(c^{true} = 1|x^*) + U(c^{true} = 2, c^* = 1)p(c^{true} = 2|x^*) \text{ for } c(x^*) = 1 \\ U(c^{true} = 1, c^* = 2)p(c^{true} = 1|x^*) + U(c^{true} = 2, c^* = 2)p(c^{true} = 2|x^*) \text{ for } c(x^*) = 2 \end{cases} \tag{13.2.6}$$

and the optimal decision function $c(x^*)$ chooses that class with highest expected utility. One can readily generalise this to multiple-class situations using a *utility matrix* with elements

$$U_{ij} = U(c^{true} = i, c^{pred} = j) \tag{13.2.7}$$

where the i, j element of the matrix contains the utility of predicting class j when the true class is i. Conversely one could think of a loss-matrix with entries $L_{ij} = -U_{ij}$. In some applications the utility matrix is highly non-symmetric. Consider a medical scenario in which we are asked to predict whether or not the patient has cancer dom $(c) = \{\text{cancer}, \text{benign}\}$. If the true class is cancer yet we predict benign, this could have terrible consequences for the patient. On the other hand, if the class is benign yet we predict cancer, this may be less disastrous for the patient. Such asymmetric utilities can favour conservative decisions – in the cancer case, we would be more inclined to decide the sample is cancerous than benign, even if the predictive probability of the two classes is equal.

In solving for the optimal decision function $c(x^*)$ in Equation (13.2.5) we are assuming that the model $p(c, x)$ is correct. However, in practice we typically don't know the correct model underlying the data – all we have is a dataset of examples $\mathcal{D} = \{(x^n, c^n), n = 1, \ldots, N\}$ and our domain knowledge. We therefore need to form a distribution $p(c, x|\mathcal{D})$ which should ideally be close to the true but unknown joint data distribution $p^{true}(c, x)$. Only then can our decisions be expected to generalise well to examples outside of the train data. Communities of researchers in machine learning form around different strategies to address the lack of knowledge about $p^{true}(c, x)$.

Squared loss/utilty

In regression problems, for a real-valued prediction y^{pred} and truth y^{true}, a common loss function is the squared loss

$$L(y^{true}, y^{pred}) = \left(y^{true} - y^{pred}\right)^2. \tag{13.2.8}$$

The above decision framework then follows through, replacing summation with integration for the continuous variables.

13.2.2 Using the empirical distribution

A direct approach to not knowing the correct model $p^{true}(c, x)$ is to replace it with the *empirical distribution*

$$p(c, x|\mathcal{D}) = \frac{1}{N}\sum_{n=1}^{N} \delta(c, c^n)\,\delta(x, x^n). \tag{13.2.9}$$

That is, we assume that the underlying distribution is approximated by placing equal mass on each of the points (x^n, c^n) in the dataset. Using this gives the empirical expected utility

$$\langle U(c, c(x))\rangle_{p(c,x|\mathcal{D})} = \frac{1}{N}\sum_n U(c^n, c(x^n)) \tag{13.2.10}$$

or conversely the *empirical risk*

$$R = \frac{1}{N}\sum_n L(c^n, c(x^n)). \tag{13.2.11}$$

Assuming the loss is minimal when the correct class is predicted, the optimal decision $c(x)$ for any input in the train set is given by $c(x^n) = c^n$. However, for any new x^* not contained in $\mathcal{D}$ then $c(x^*)$ is undefined. In order to define the class of a novel input, one may use a parametric function $c(x|\theta)$. For example for a two-class problem $\mathrm{dom}(c) = \{1, 2\}$, a linear decision function is given by

$$c(\mathbf{x}|\theta) = \begin{cases} 1 & \text{if } \boldsymbol{\theta}^{\mathsf{T}}\mathbf{x} + \theta_0 \geq 0 \\ 2 & \text{if } \boldsymbol{\theta}^{\mathsf{T}}\mathbf{x} + \theta_0 < 0 \end{cases}. \tag{13.2.12}$$

If the vector input $\mathbf{x}$ is on the positive side of a hyperplane defined by the vector $\boldsymbol{\theta}$ and bias θ_0, we assign it to class 1, otherwise to class 2. (We return to the geometric interpretation of this in Chapter 17.) The empirical risk then becomes a function of the parameters $\theta = \{\boldsymbol{\theta}, \theta_0\}$,

$$R(\theta|\mathcal{D}) = \frac{1}{N}\sum_n L(c^n, c(x^n|\theta)). \tag{13.2.13}$$

The optimal parameters θ are given by minimising the empirical risk with respect to θ,

$$\theta_{opt} = \underset{\theta}{\mathrm{argmin}}\; R(\theta|\mathcal{D}). \tag{13.2.14}$$

The decision for a new datapoint x^* is then given by $c(x^*|\theta_{opt})$.

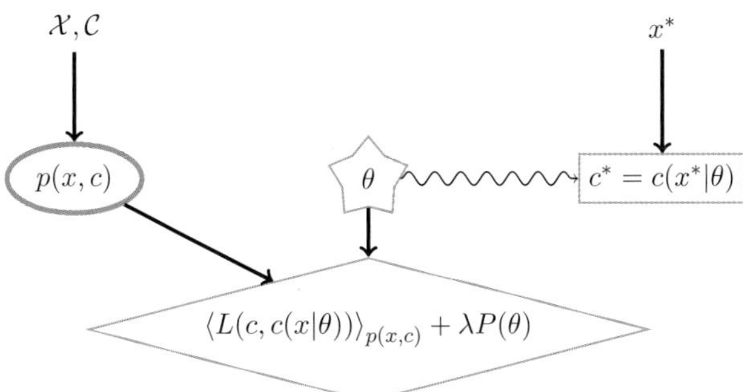

Figure 13.2 Empirical risk approach. Given the dataset $\mathcal{X}$, $\mathcal{C}$, a model of the data $p(x, c)$ is made, usually using the empirical distribution. For a classifier $c(x|\theta)$, the parameter θ is learned by minimising the penalised empirical risk with respect to θ. The penalty parameter λ is set by validation. A novel input x^* is then assigned to class $c(x^*|\theta)$, given this optimal θ.

In this *empirical risk minimisation* approach, as we make the decision function $c(x|\theta)$ more flexible, the empirical risk goes down. However, if we make $c(x|\theta)$ too flexible we will have little confidence that $c(x|\theta)$ will perform well on a novel input x^*. The reason for this is that a flexible decision function $c(x|\theta)$ is one for which the class label can change for only a small change in x. Such flexibility seems good since it means that we will be able to find a parameter setting θ so that the train data is fitted well. However, since we are only constraining the decision function on the known training points, a flexible $c(x|\theta)$ may change rapidly as we move away from the train data, leading to poor generalisation. To constrain the complexity of $c(x|\theta)$ we may minimise the *penalised empirical risk*

$$R'(\theta|\mathcal{D}) = R(\theta|\mathcal{D}) + \lambda P(\theta) \tag{13.2.15}$$

where $P(\theta)$ is a function that penalises complex functions $c(x|\theta)$. The *regularisation constant*, λ, determines the strength of this penalty and is typically set by validation – see below. The empirical risk approach is summarised in Fig. 13.2.

For the linear decision function above, it is reasonable to penalise wildly changing classifications in the sense that if we change the input $\mathbf{x}$ by only a small amount we expect (on average) minimal change in the class label. The squared difference in $\boldsymbol{\theta}^\mathsf{T}\mathbf{x} + \theta_0$ for two inputs $\mathbf{x}_1$ and $\mathbf{x}_2$ is $(\boldsymbol{\theta}^\mathsf{T}\Delta\mathbf{x})^2$ where $\Delta\mathbf{x} \equiv \mathbf{x}_2 - \mathbf{x}_1$. By constraining the length of $\boldsymbol{\theta}$ to be small we limit the ability of the classifier to change class for only a small change in the input space. Assuming the distance between two datapoints is distributed according to an isotropic multivariate Gaussian with zero mean and covariance $\sigma^2\mathbf{I}$, the average squared change is $\left\langle (\boldsymbol{\theta}^\mathsf{T}\Delta\mathbf{x})^2 \right\rangle = \sigma^2\boldsymbol{\theta}^\mathsf{T}\boldsymbol{\theta}$, motivating the choice of the Euclidean squared length of the parameter $\boldsymbol{\theta}$ as the penalty term, $P(\theta) = \boldsymbol{\theta}^\mathsf{T}\boldsymbol{\theta}$.

Validation

In penalised empirical risk minimisation we need to set the regularisation constant λ. This can be achieved by evaluating the performance of the learned classifier $c(x|\theta)$ on validation data $\mathcal{D}_{validate}$ for several different λ values, and choosing the λ which gave rise to the classifier with the best performance. It's important that the validation data is not the data on which the model was trained since we know that the optimal setting for λ in that case is zero, and again we will have little confidence in the generalisation ability.

Given a dataset $\mathcal{D}$ we split this into disjoint parts, $\mathcal{D}_{train}$, $\mathcal{D}_{validate}$, where the size of the validation set is usually chosen to be smaller than the train set, see Fig. 13.3. For each parameter λ_a one then finds the minimal empirical risk parameter θ_a. The optimal λ is chosen as that which gives rise to

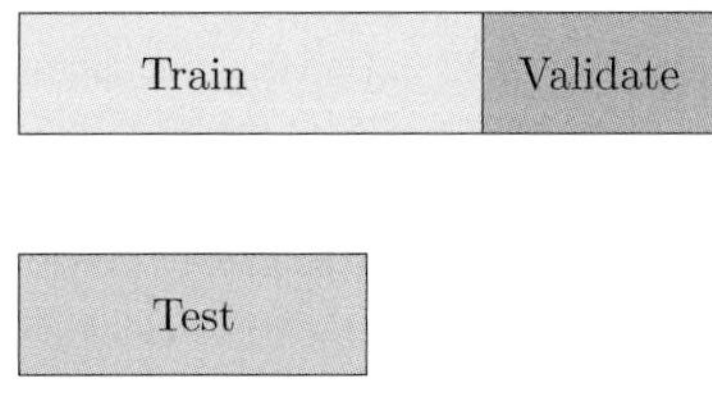

Figure 13.3 Models can be trained using the train data based on different regularisation parameters. The optimal regularisation parameter is determined by the empirical performance on the validation data. An independent measure of the generalisation performance is obtained by using a separate test set.

Algorithm 13.1 Setting regularisation parameters using cross-validation.

Choose a set of regularisation parameters $\lambda_1, \ldots, \lambda_A$
Choose a set of training and validation set splits $\left\{\mathcal{D}^i_{train}, \mathcal{D}^i_{validate}\right\}$, $i = 1, \ldots, K$
for $a = 1$ to A **do**
    for $i = 1$ to K **do**
        $\theta^i_a = \underset{\theta}{\text{argmin}} \left[R\left(\theta|\mathcal{D}^i_{train}\right) + \lambda_a P\left(\theta\right)\right]$
    end for
    $L\left(\lambda_a\right) = \frac{1}{K}\sum_{i=1}^{K} R\left(\theta^i_a|\mathcal{D}^i_{validate}\right)$
end for
$\lambda_{opt} = \underset{\lambda_a}{\text{argmin}}\, L\left(\lambda_a\right)$

---

the model with the minimal validation risk. Using the optimal regularisation parameter λ, many practitioners retrain θ on the basis of the whole dataset $\mathcal{D}$.

In cross-validation the dataset is partitioned into training and validation sets multiple times with validation results obtained for each partition. Each partition produces a different training $\mathcal{D}^i_{train}$ and validation $\mathcal{D}^i_{validate}$ set, along with an optimal penalised empirical risk parameter θ^i_a and associated (unregularised) validation performance $R(\theta^i_a|\mathcal{D}^i_{validate})$. The performance of regularisation parameter λ_a is taken as the average of the validation performances over i. The best regularisation parameter is then given as that with the minimal average validation error, see Algorithm 13.1. More specifically, in K-fold cross-validation the data $\mathcal{D}$ is split into K equal-sized disjoint parts $\mathcal{D}_1, \ldots, \mathcal{D}_K$. Then $\mathcal{D}^i_{validate} = \mathcal{D}_i$ and $\mathcal{D}^i_{train} = \mathcal{D}\backslash\mathcal{D}^i_{validate}$. This gives a total of K different training-validation sets over which performance is averaged, see Fig. 13.4. In practice 10-fold cross-validation is popular, as is leave-one-out cross-validation in which the validation sets consist of only a single example.

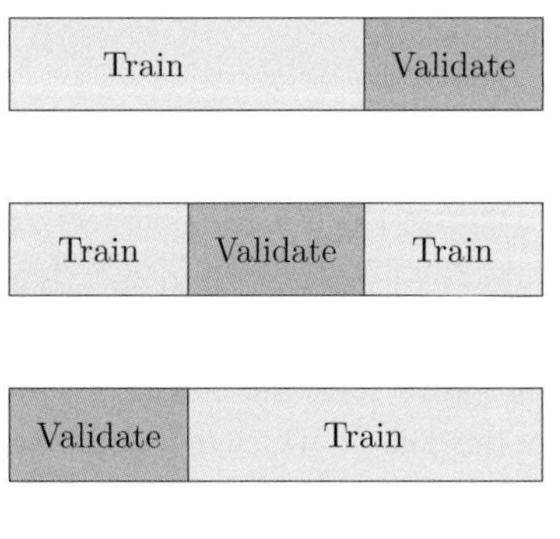

Figure 13.4 In cross-validation the dataset is split into several train-validation sets. Depicted is 3-fold cross-validation. For a range of regularisation parameters, the optimal regularisation parameter is found based on the empirical validation performance averaged across the different splits.

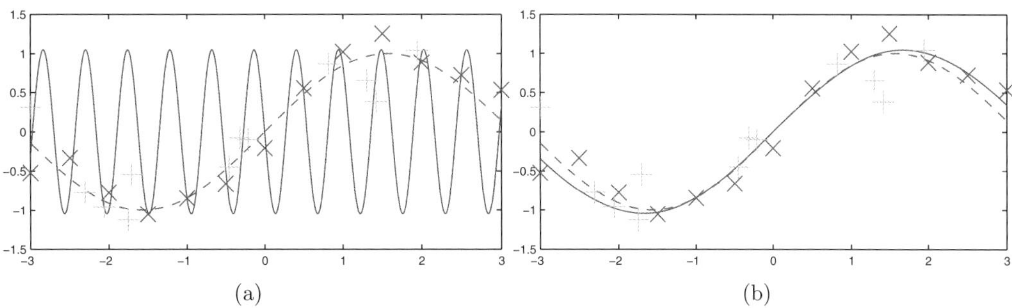

(a) (b)

Figure 13.5 The true function which generated the noisy data is the dashed line; the function learned from the data is given by the solid line. (**a**) The unregularised fit ($\lambda = 0$) to training given by $\times$. Whilst the training data is well fitted, the error on the validation examples, denoted by $+$, is high. (**b**) The regularised fit ($\lambda = 0.5$). Whilst the train error is high, the validation error is low.

Example 13.4 Finding a good regularisation parameter

In Fig. 13.5, we fit the function $a\sin(wx)$ to the plotted data, learning the parameters a, w based on minimising the squared loss. The unregularised solution Fig. 13.5(a) badly overfits the data, and has a high validation error. To encourage a smoother solution, a regularisation term w^2 is used. The validation error based on several different values of the regularisation parameter λ was computed, and $\lambda = 0.5$ gives the lowest validation error. The resulting fit to the data, found by retraining a and w using the validation-optimal λ, is reasonable, see Fig. 13.5(b).

Benefits of the empirical risk approach

- In the limit of a large amount of training data the empirical distribution tends to the correct distribution.
- The discriminant function is chosen on the basis of minimal risk, which is the quantity we are ultimately interested in.
- The procedure is conceptually straightforward.

Drawbacks of the empirical risk approach

- It seems extreme to assume that the data follows the empirical distribution, particularly for small amounts of training data. More reasonable assumptions for $p(x)$ would take into account likely x that could arise, not just those in the train data.
- If the loss function changes, the discriminant function needs to be retrained.
- Some problems require an estimate of the confidence of the prediction. Whilst there may be heuristic ways to evaluating confidence in the prediction, this is not inherent in the framework.
- When there are many penalty parameters, performing cross-validation in a discretised grid of the parameters becomes infeasible.
- During validation, many models are trained, and all but one subsequently discarded.

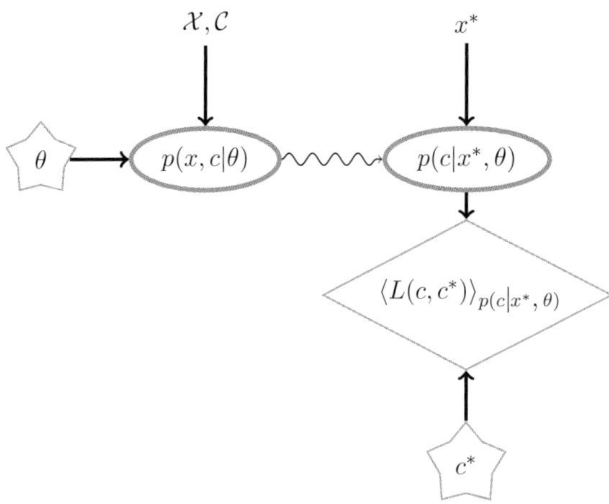

Figure 13.6 Bayesian decision approach. A model $p(x, c|\theta)$ is fitted to the data. After learning the optimal model parameters θ, we compute $p(c|x, \theta)$. For a novel x^*, the distribution of the assumed 'truth' is $p(c|x^*, \theta)$. The prediction (decision) is then given by that c^* which minimises the expected risk $\langle L(c, c^*)\rangle_{p(c|x^*, \theta)}$.

13.2.3 Bayesian decision approach

An alternative to using the empirical distribution is to first fit a model $p(c, x|\theta)$ to the train data $\mathcal{D}$. Given this model, the decision function $c(x)$ is automatically determined from the maximal expected utility (or minimal risk) with respect to this model, as in Equation (13.2.6), in which the unknown $p(c^{true}|x)$ is replaced with $p(c|x, \theta)$. See Fig. 13.6 for a schematic depiction of the Bayesian decision approach.

There are two main approaches to fitting $p(c, x|\theta)$ to data $\mathcal{D}$, see Fig. 13.7. We could parameterise the joint distribution using

$$p(c, x|\theta) = p(c|x, \theta_{c|x})p(x|\theta_x) \qquad \textit{discriminative approach} \tag{13.2.16}$$

or

$$p(c, x|\theta) = p(x|c, \theta_{x|c})p(c|\theta_c) \qquad \textit{generative approach.} \tag{13.2.17}$$

We'll consider these two approaches below in the context of trying to make a system that can distinguish between a male and female face. The setup is that we have a database of face images in which each image is represented as a real-valued vector $\mathbf{x}^n$, $n = 1, \ldots, N$, along with a label $c^n \in \{0, 1\}$ stating if the image is male or female.

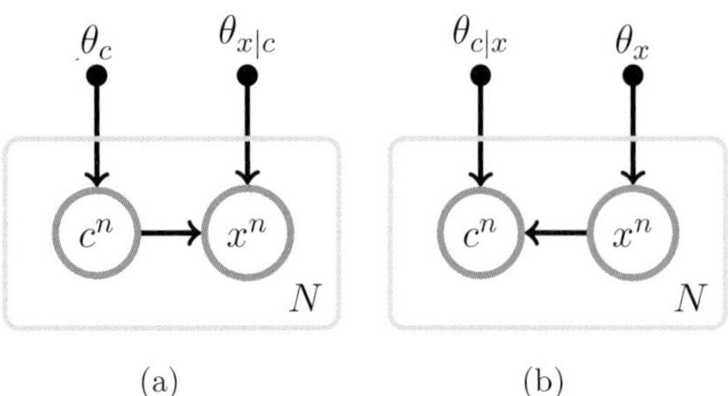

Figure 13.7 Two generic strategies for probabilistic classification. **(a)** Class-dependent generative model of x. After learning parameters, classification is obtained by making x evidential and inferring $p(c|x)$. **(b)** A discriminative classification method $p(c|x)$.

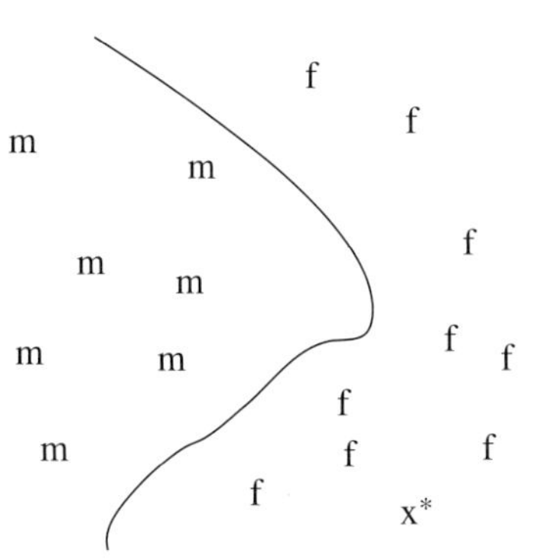

Figure 13.8 Each point represents a high-dimensional vector with an associated class label, either male or female. The point $\mathbf{x}^*$ is a new point for which we would like to predict whether this should be male or female. In the generative approach, a male model $p(\mathbf{x}|\text{male})$ generates data similar to the 'm' points. Similarly, the female model $p(\mathbf{x}|\text{female})$ generates points that are similar to the 'f' points above. We then use Bayes' rule to calculate the probability $p(\text{male}|\mathbf{x}^*)$ using the two fitted models, as given in the text. In the discriminative approach, we directly make a model of $p(\text{male}|\mathbf{x}^*)$, which cares less about how the points 'm' or 'f' are distributed, but more about describing the boundary which can separate the two classes, as given by the line. In this case, modelling the distribution of the data is not required since our decisions are only related to which side of the decision boundary a point lies.

Generative approach $p(\mathbf{x}, c|\theta) = p(\mathbf{x}|c, \theta_{x|c})p(c|\theta_c)$

For simplicity we use maximum likelihood training for the parameters θ. Assuming the data $\mathcal{D}$ is i.i.d., we have a log likelihood

$$\log p(\mathcal{D}|\theta) = \sum_n \log p(\mathbf{x}^n|c^n, \theta_{x|c}) + \sum_n \log p(c^n|\theta_c). \tag{13.2.18}$$

As we see the dependence on $\theta_{x|c}$ occurs only in the first term, and θ_c only occurs in the second. This means that learning the optimal parameters is equivalent to isolating the data for the male class and fitting a model $p(\mathbf{x}|c = \text{male}, \theta_{x|\text{male}})$. We may similarly isolate the female data and fit a separate model $p(\mathbf{x}|c = \text{female}, \theta_{x|\text{female}})$. The class distribution $p(c|\theta_c)$ is set according to the ratio of males/females in the set of training data.

To make a classification of a new image $\mathbf{x}^*$ as either male or female, we use Bayes' rule:

$$p(c = \text{male}|\mathbf{x}^*) = \frac{p(\mathbf{x}^*, c = \text{male}|\theta_{x|\text{male}})}{p(\mathbf{x}^*, c = \text{male}|\theta_{x|\text{male}}) + p(\mathbf{x}^*, c = \text{female}|\theta_{x|\text{female}})}. \tag{13.2.19}$$

Based on zero-one loss, if this probability is greater than 0.5 we classify $\mathbf{x}^*$ as male, otherwise female. For a general loss function, we use this probability as part of a decision process, as in Equation (13.2.6).

Advantages Prior information about the structure of the data is often most naturally specified through a generative model $p(x|c)$. For example, for male faces, we would expect to see heavier eyebrows, a squarer jaw, etc.

Disadvantages The generative approach does not directly target the classification model $p(c|x)$ since the goal of generative training is rather to model $p(x|c)$. If the data x is complex, finding a suitable generative data model $p(x|c)$ is a difficult task. Furthermore, since each generative model is separately trained for each class, there is no competition amongst the models to explain the x data. On the other hand it might be that making a model of $p(c|x)$ is simpler, particularly if the decision boundary between the classes has a simple form, even if the data distribution of each class is complex, see Fig. 13.8.

Discriminative approach $p(\mathbf{x}, c|\theta) = p(c|\mathbf{x}, \theta_{c|x})p(\mathbf{x}|\theta_x)$

Assuming i.i.d. data, the log likelihood is

$$\log p(\mathcal{D}|\theta) = \sum_n \log p(c^n|\mathbf{x}^n, \theta_{c|x}) + \sum_n \log p(\mathbf{x}^n|\theta_x). \tag{13.2.20}$$

The parameters are isolated in the two terms so that maximum likelihood training is equivalent to finding the parameters of $\theta_{c|x}$ that will best predict the class c for a given training input x. The parameters θ_x for modelling the data occur only in the second term above, and setting them can therefore be treated as a separate unsupervised learning problem. This approach consequently isolates modelling the *decision boundary* from modelling the input distribution, see Fig. 13.8.

Classification of a new point $\mathbf{x}^*$ is based on

$$p(c|\mathbf{x}, \theta_{c|x}^{opt}). \tag{13.2.21}$$

As for the generative case, this approach still learns a joint distribution $p(c, x) = p(c|x)p(x)$ which can be used as part of a decision process if required, Equation (13.2.6).

Advantages The discriminative approach directly addresses finding an accurate classifier $p(c|x)$ based on modelling the decision boundary, as opposed to the class conditional data distribution in the generative approach. Whilst the data from each class may be distributed in a complex way, it could be that the decision boundary between them is relatively easy to model.

Disadvantages Discriminative approaches are usually trained as 'black-box' classifiers, with little prior knowledge built used to describe how data for a given class is distributed. Domain knowledge is often more easily expressed using the generative framework.

Hybrid generative–discriminative approaches

One could use a generative description, $p(x|c)$, building in prior information, and use this to form a joint distribution $p(x, c)$, from which a discriminative model $p(c|x)$ may be formed, using Bayes' rule. Specifically, we can use

$$p(c|x, \theta) = \frac{p(x|c, \theta_{x|c})p(c|\theta_c)}{\sum_c p(x|c, \theta_{x|c})p(c|\theta_c)}. \tag{13.2.22}$$

Subsequently the parameters $\theta = (\theta_{x|c}, \theta_c)$, for this hybrid model can be found by maximising the probability of being in the correct class. A separate model is learned for $p(x|\theta_x)$. This approach would appear to leverage the advantages of both the discriminative and generative frameworks since we can more readily incorporate domain knowledge in the generative model $p(x|c, \theta_{x|c})$ yet train this in a discriminative way. This approach is rarely taken in practice since the resulting functional form of the likelihood depends in a complex manner on the parameters. In this case no parameter separation between θ_c and $\theta_{x|c}$ occurs (as was previously the case for the generative and discriminative approaches).

Features and preprocessing

It is often the case that in discriminative training, transforming the raw input x into a form that more directly captures the relevant label information can greatly improve performance. For example, in the male–female classification case, it might be that building a classifier directly in terms of the elements of the face vector $\mathbf{x}$ is difficult. However, using 'features' which contain geometric information such

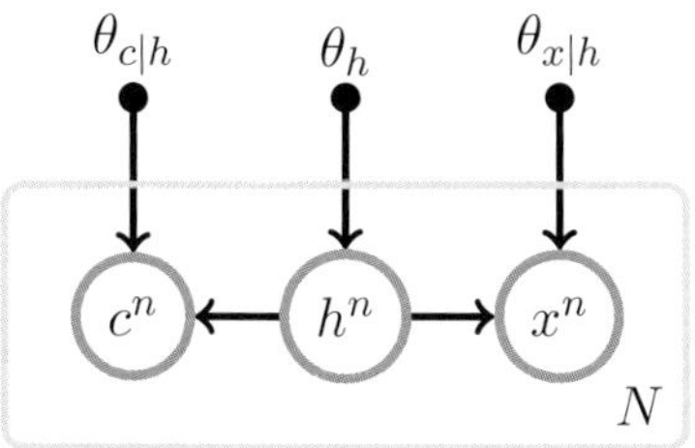

Figure 13.9 A strategy for semi-supervised learning. When c^n is missing, the term $p(c^n|h^n)$ is absent. The large amount of training data helps the model learn a good lower dimension/compressed representation h of the data x. Fitting then a classification model $p(c|h)$ using this lower-dimensional representation may be much easier than fitting a model directly from the complex data to the class, $p(c|x)$.

as the distance between eyes, width of mouth, etc. may make finding a classifier easier. In practice data is also often preprocessed to remove noise, centre an image etc.

Learning lower-dimensional representations in semi-supervised learning

One way to exploit a large amount of unlabelled training data to improve classification is to first find a lower-dimensional representation h of the data x. Based on this, the mapping from h to c may be rather simpler to learn than a mapping from x to c directly. We use $c^n = \emptyset$ to indicate that the class for datapoint n is missing. We can then form the likelihood on the visible data using, see Fig. 13.9,

$$p(\mathcal{C}, \mathcal{X}, \mathcal{H}|\theta) = \prod_n \left\{p(c^n|h^n, \theta_{c|h})\right\}^{\mathbb{I}[c^n \neq \emptyset]} p(x^n|h^n, \theta_{x|h})p(h|\theta_h) \tag{13.2.23}$$

and set any parameters for example by using maximum likelihood

$$\theta^{opt} = \underset{\theta}{\operatorname{argmax}} \sum_{\mathcal{H}} p(\mathcal{C}, \mathcal{X}, \mathcal{H}|\theta). \tag{13.2.24}$$

Benefits of the Bayesian decision approach

- This is a conceptually 'clean' approach, in which one tries one's best to model the environment (using either a generative or discriminative approach), independent of the subsequent decision process. In this case learning the environment is separated from the effect this will have on the expected utility.
- The decision c^* for a novel input x^* can be a highly complex function of x^* due to the maximisation operation.
- If $p(x, c|\theta)$ is the 'true' model of the data, this approach is optimal.

Drawbacks of the Bayesian decision approach

- If the environment model $p(c, x|\theta)$ is poor, the prediction c^* could be highly inaccurate since modelling the environment is divorced from prediction.
- To avoid fully divorcing the learning of the model $p(c, x|\theta)$ from its effect on decisions, in practice one often includes regularisation terms in the environment model $p(c, x|\theta)$ which are set by validation based on an empirical loss.

13.3 Bayes versus empirical decisions

The empirical risk and Bayesian approaches are at the extremes of the philosophical spectrum. In the empirical risk approach one makes a seemingly over-simplistic data generating assumption. However decision function parameters are set based on the task of making decisions. On the other hand, the Bayesian approach attempts to learn meaningful $p(c, x)$ without regard to its ultimate use as part of a larger decision process. What 'objective' criterion can we use to learn $p(c, x)$, particularly if we are only interested in classification with a low test-risk? The following example is intended to recapitulate the two generic Bayes and empirical risk approaches we've been considering. Note that we've previously written utilities suggesting that they are both for example class labels; however the theory applies more generally, for example to utilities $u(c, d)$ where d is some decision (which is not necessarily of the form of the class label c).

Example 13.5 The two generic decision strategies

Consider a situation in which, based on patient information $\mathbf{x}$, we need to take a decision d as whether or not to operate. The utility of operating $u(c, d)$ depends on whether or not the patient has cancer, c. For example

$$\begin{array}{ll} u(\text{cancer, operate}) = 100 & u(\text{benign, operate}) = 30 \\ u(\text{cancer, don't operate}) = 0 & u(\text{benign, don't operate}) = 70. \end{array} \tag{13.3.1}$$

We have independent true assessments of whether or not a patient had cancer, giving rise to a set of historical records $\mathcal{D} = \{(\mathbf{x}^n, c^n), n = 1, \dots, N\}$. Faced with a new patient with information $\mathbf{x}$, we need to make a decision whether or not to operate.

In the Bayesian decision approach one would first make a model $p(c|\mathbf{x}, \mathcal{D})$ (for example using a discriminative model such as logistic regression, Section 17.4.1). Using this model the decision is given by that which maximises the expected utility

$$d = \underset{d}{\operatorname{argmax}} \left[p(\text{cancer}|\mathbf{x}, \mathcal{D}) u(\text{cancer}, d) + p(\text{benign}|\mathbf{x}, \mathcal{D}) u(\text{benign}, d) \right]. \tag{13.3.2}$$

In this approach learning the model $p(c|\mathbf{x}, \mathcal{D})$ is divorced from the ultimate use of the model in the decision making process. An advantage of this approach is that, from the viewpoint of expected utility, it is optimal – provided the model $p(c|\mathbf{x}, \mathcal{D})$ is 'correct'. Unfortunately, this is rarely the case. Given the limited model resources, it might make sense to focus on ensuring the prediction of cancer is correct since this has a more significant effect on the utility. However, formally, this would require a corruption of this framework.

The alternative empirical utility approach recognises that the task can be stated as to translate patient information $\mathbf{x}$ into an operation decision d. To do so one could parameterise this as $d(\mathbf{x}) = f(\mathbf{x}|\boldsymbol{\theta})$ and then learn $\boldsymbol{\theta}$ under maximising the empirical utility

$$u(\boldsymbol{\theta}) = \sum_n u(f(x^n|\boldsymbol{\theta}), c^n). \tag{13.3.3}$$

For example, if $\mathbf{x}$ is a vector representing the patient information and $\boldsymbol{\theta}$ the parameter, we might use a linear decision function such as

$$f(\mathbf{x}|\boldsymbol{\theta}) = \begin{cases} \boldsymbol{\theta}^\mathsf{T}\mathbf{x} \geq 0 & d = \text{operate} \\ \boldsymbol{\theta}^\mathsf{T}\mathbf{x} < 0 & d = \text{don't operate} \end{cases}. \tag{13.3.4}$$

The advantage of this approach is that the parameters of the decision are directly related to the utility of making the decision. However, it may be that we have a good model of $p(c|\mathbf{x})$ and would wish to make use of this. A disadvantage is that we cannot easily incorporate such domain knowledge into the decision function.

Both approaches are heavily used in practice and which is to be preferred depends very much on the problem. Whilst the Bayesian approach appears formally optimal, it is prone to model mis-specification. A pragmatic alternative Bayesian approach is to fit a parameterised distribution $p(c, x|\lambda)$ to the data $\mathcal{D}$, where λ penalises complexity of the fitted distribution, setting λ using validation on the risk. This has the potential advantage of allowing one to incorporate sensible prior information about $p(c, x)$ whilst assessing competing models in the light of their actual predictive risk. Similarly, for the empirical risk approach, one can modify the extreme empirical distribution assumption by using a more plausible model $p(c, x)$ of the data.

13.4 Summary

- Supervised and unsupervised learning are the two main branches of machine learning considered in this book.
- The two classical approaches in supervised learning are empirical risk minimisation and Bayesian decision theory.
- In the empirical risk minimisation, there is typically no explicit model of the data, and the focus is on the end use of the predictor.
- In the Bayesian decision approach, an explicit model of the data is made, with the end decision/classification being computed independently of the fitting of the model to the data.

A general introduction to machine learning is given in [215]. An excellent reference for Bayesian decision theory is [33]. Approaches based on empirical risk are discussed in [302].

13.5 Exercises

13.1 Given the distributions $p(x|\text{class1}) = \mathcal{N}\left(x\,|\,\mu_1, \sigma_1^2\right)$ and $p(x|\text{class2}) = \mathcal{N}\left(x\,|\,\mu_2, \sigma_2^2\right)$, with corresponding prior occurrence of classes p_1 and p_2 ($p_1 + p_2 = 1$), calculate the decision boundary $p(\text{class1}|x) = 0.5$ explicitly as a function of $\mu_1, \mu_2, \sigma_1^2, \sigma_2^2, p_1, p_2$. How many solutions are there to the decision boundary and are they all reasonable?

13.2 Under zero-one loss, the Bayes' decision rule chooses class k if $p(\text{class } k|\mathbf{x}) > p(\text{class } j|\mathbf{x})$ for all $j \neq k$. Imagine instead we use a randomized decision rule, choosing class j with probability $q(\text{class } j|\mathbf{x})$. Calculate the error for this decision rule, and show that the error is minimised by using Bayes' decision rule.

13.3 For a novel input x, a predictive model of the class c is given by $p(c = 1|x) = 0.7$, $p(c = 2|x) = 0.2$, $p(c = 3|x) = 0.1$. The corresponding utility matrix $U(c^{true}, c^{pred})$ has elements

$$\begin{pmatrix} 5 & 3 & 1 \\ 0 & 4 & -2 \\ -3 & 0 & 10 \end{pmatrix}. \tag{13.5.1}$$

In terms of maximal expected utility, which is the best decision to take?

13.4 Consider datapoints generated from two different classes. Class 1 has the distribution $p(x|c = 1) \sim \mathcal{N}\left(x\,|\,m_1, \sigma^2\right)$ and class 2 has the distribution $p(x|c = 2) \sim \mathcal{N}\left(x\,|\,m_2, \sigma^2\right)$. The prior probabilities of each class are $p(c=1) = p(c=2) = 1/2$. Show that the posterior probability $p(c=1|x)$ is of the form

$$p(c=1|x) = \frac{1}{1+\exp -(ax+b)} \tag{13.5.2}$$

and determine a and b in terms of m_1, m_2 and σ^2.

13.5 WowCo.com is a new startup prediction company. After years of failures, they eventually find a neural network with a trillion hidden units that achieves zero test error on every learning problem posted on the Internet up to last week. Each learning problem included a train and test set. Proud of their achievement, they market their product aggressively with the claim that it 'predicts perfectly on all known problems'. Discuss whether or not these claims would justify buying this product.

13.6 For a prediction model $\tilde{p}(y|x)$ and true data generating distribution $p(x, y)$, one may define a measure of the accuracy as

$$A = \int_{x,y} p(x, y)\tilde{p}(y|x) \tag{13.5.3}$$

which is the average overlap between the true and predicting distributions.

1. By defining

$$\hat{p}(x, y) \equiv \frac{p(x, y)\tilde{p}(y|x)}{A} \tag{13.5.4}$$

and considering

$$\mathrm{KL}(q(x, y)|\hat{p}(x, y)) \geq 0 \tag{13.5.5}$$

show that for any distribution $q(x, y)$,

$$\log A \geq \langle \log \tilde{p}(y|x)\rangle_{q(x,y)} - \mathrm{KL}(q(x, y)|p(x, y)). \tag{13.5.6}$$

2. Consider a set of train data $\mathcal{D} = \{(x^n, y^n), n = 1, \ldots, N\}$ and define the empirical distribution

$$q(x, y) = \frac{1}{N}\sum_{n=1}^{N} \delta(x, x^n)\,\delta(y, y^n). \tag{13.5.7}$$

Show that

$$\log A \geq \frac{1}{N}\sum_{n=1}^{N} \log \tilde{p}(y^n|x^n) - \mathrm{KL}(q(x, y)|p(x, y)). \tag{13.5.8}$$

This shows that the log prediction accuracy is lower bounded by the training accuracy and the 'gap' between the empirical distribution and the unknown true data generating mechanism. According to this naive bound (which doesn't account for possible overfitting), the best thing to do to increase the prediction accuracy is to increase the training accuracy (since the Kullback–Leibler term is independent of the predictor). As N increases, the empirical distribution tends to the true distribution and the Kullback–Leibler term becomes small, justifying minimising the train error.

Assuming that the train outputs are drawn from a distribution $p(y|x) = \delta(y, f(x))$ which is deterministic, show that

$$\log A \geq \frac{1}{N}\sum_{n=1}^{N} \log \tilde{p}(y^n|x^n) - \mathrm{KL}(q(x)|p(x)) \tag{13.5.9}$$

and hence that, provided the train data is correctly predicted with full certainty, the accuracy can be related to the empirical and true input distribution by

$$A \geq \exp\left(-\mathrm{KL}(q(x)|p(x))\right). \tag{13.5.10}$$

13.7 You wish to make a classifier for a variable c based on two kinds of inputs, x and y. You have a generative model $p(y|c)$ and a discriminative model $p(c|x)$. Explain how to combine these to make a model $p(c|x, y)$.

14 Nearest neighbour classification

Often when faced with a classification problem it is useful to first employ a simple method to produce a baseline against which more complex methods can be compared. In this chapter we discuss the simple nearest neighbour method. The nearest neighbour methods are extremely popular and can perform surprisingly well. We also discuss how these methods are related to probabilistic mixture models.

14.1 Do as your neighbour does

Successful prediction typically relies on smoothness in the data – if the class label can change as we move a small amount in the input space, the problem is essentially random and no algorithm will generalise well. In machine learning one constructs appropriate measures of smoothness for the problem at hand and hopes to exploit this to obtain good generalisation. Nearest neighbour methods are a useful starting point since they readily encode basic smoothness intuitions and are easy to program.

In a classification problem each input vector $\mathbf{x}$ has a corresponding class label, $c^n \in \{1, \ldots, C\}$. Given a dataset of N train examples, $\mathcal{D} = \{\mathbf{x}^n, c^n\}, n = 1, \ldots, N$, and a novel $\mathbf{x}$, we aim to return the correct class $c(\mathbf{x})$. A simple, but often effective, strategy for this supervised learning problem can be stated as: for novel $\mathbf{x}$, find the nearest input in the train set and use the class of this nearest input, Algorithm 14.1. For vectors $\mathbf{x}$ and $\mathbf{x}'$ representing two different datapoints, we measure 'nearness' using a *dissimilarity function* $d(\mathbf{x}, \mathbf{x}')$. A common dissimilarity is the *squared Euclidean distance*

$$d(\mathbf{x}, \mathbf{x}') = (\mathbf{x} - \mathbf{x}')^\mathsf{T}(\mathbf{x} - \mathbf{x}') \tag{14.1.1}$$

which can be more conveniently written $(\mathbf{x} - \mathbf{x}')^2$. Based on the squared Euclidean distance, the decision boundary is determined by the perpendicular bisectors of the closest training points with different training labels, see Fig. 14.1. This partitions the input space into regions classified equally and is called a *Voronoi tessellation*.

The nearest neighbour algorithm is simple and intuitive. There are, however, some issues:

- How should we measure the distance between points? Whilst the Euclidean square distance is popular, this may not always be appropriate. A fundamental limitation of the Euclidean distance is that it does not take into account how the data is distributed. For example if the length scales of the components of the vector $\mathbf{x}$ vary greatly, largest length scale will dominate the squared distance, with potentially useful class-specific information in other components of $\mathbf{x}$ lost. The *Mahalanobis distance*

$$d(\mathbf{x}, \mathbf{x}') = (\mathbf{x} - \mathbf{x}')^\mathsf{T} \boldsymbol{\Sigma}^{-1} (\mathbf{x} - \mathbf{x}') \tag{14.1.2}$$

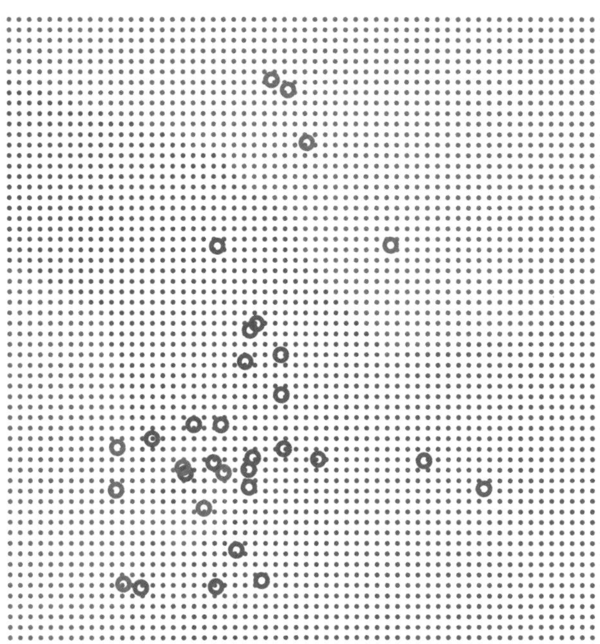

Figure 14.1 In nearest neighbour classification a new vector is assigned the label of the nearest vector in the training set. Here there are three classes, with training points given by the circles, along with their class. The dots indicate the class of the nearest training vector. The decision boundary is piecewise linear with each segment corresponding to the perpendicular bisector between two datapoints belonging to different classes, giving rise to a Voronoi tessellation of the input space. See plate section for colour version.

Algorithm 14.1 Nearest neighbour algorithm to classify a vector $\mathbf{x}$, given train data $\mathcal{D} = \{(\mathbf{x}^n, c^n), n = 1, \ldots, N\}$.

1: Calculate the dissimilarity of the test point $\mathbf{x}$ to each of the train points, $d^n = d(\mathbf{x}, \mathbf{x}^n)$, $n = 1, \ldots, N$.

2: Find the train point $\mathbf{x}^{n^*}$ which is nearest to $\mathbf{x}$:

$$n^* = \underset{n}{\operatorname{argmin}}\, d(\mathbf{x}, \mathbf{x}^n)$$

3: Assign the class label $c(\mathbf{x}) = c^{n^*}$.

4: In the case that there are two or more nearest neighbours with different class labels, the most numerous class is chosen. If there is no one single most numerous class, we use the K-nearest neighbours.

---

where $\boldsymbol{\Sigma}$ is the covariance matrix of the inputs (from all classes) can overcome some of these problems since it effectively rescales the input vector components.

- The whole dataset needs to be stored to make a classification since the novel point must be compared to all of the train points. This can be partially addressed by a method called data editing in which datapoints which have little or no effect on the decision boundary are removed from the training dataset. Depending on the geometry of the training points, finding the nearest neighbour can also be accelerated by examining the values of each of the components x_i of $\mathbf{x}$ in turn. Such an axis-aligned space-split is called a *KD-tree* [218] and can reduce the possible set of candidate nearest neighbours in the training set to the novel $\mathbf{x}^*$, particularly in low dimensions.
- Each distance calculation can be expensive if the datapoints are high dimensional. Principal Components Analysis (PCA), see Chapter 15, is one way to address this and replaces $\mathbf{x}$ with a low-dimensional projection $\mathbf{p}$. The Euclidean distance of two datapoints $(\mathbf{x}^a - \mathbf{x}^b)^2$ is then approximately given by $(\mathbf{p}^a - \mathbf{p}^b)^2$, see Section 15.2.4. This is both faster to compute and can also improve classification accuracy since only the large-scale characteristics of the data are retained in the PCA projections.
- It is not clear how to deal with missing data or incorporate prior beliefs and domain knowledge.

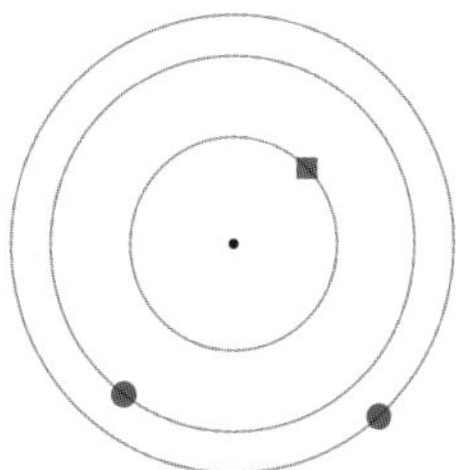

Figure 14.2 In K-nearest neighbours, we centre a hypersphere around the point we wish to classify (here the central dot). The inner circle corresponds to the nearest neighbour, a square. However, using the three nearest neighbours, we find that there are two round-class neighbours and one square-class neighbour– and we would therefore classify the central point as round-class. In the case of a tie, one may increase K until the tie is broken.

14.2 K-nearest neighbours

If your neighbour is simply mistaken (has an incorrect training class label), or is not a particularly representative example of his class, then these situations will typically result in an incorrect classification. By including more than the single nearest neighbour, we hope to make a more robust classifier with a smoother decision boundary (less swayed by single neighbour opinions). If we assume the Euclidean distance as the dissimilarity measure, the K-nearest neighbour algorithm considers a hypersphere centred on the test point $\mathbf{x}$. The radius of the hypersphere is increased until it contains exactly K train inputs. The class label $c(\mathbf{x})$ is then given by the most numerous class within the hypersphere, see Fig. 14.2.

Choosing K

Whilst there is some sense in making $K > 1$, there is certainly little sense in making $K = N$ (N being the number of training points). For K very large, all classifications will become the same – simply assign each novel $\mathbf{x}$ to the most numerous class in the train data. This suggests that there is an optimal intermediate setting of K which gives the best generalisation performance. This can be determined using cross-validation, as described in Section 13.2.2.

Example 14.1 Handwritten digit example

Consider two classes of handwritten digits, zeros and ones. Each digit contains $28 \times 28 = 784$ pixels. The train data consists of 300 zeros, and 300 ones, a subset of which are plotted in Fig. 14.3(a,b). To test the performance of the nearest neighbour method (based on Euclidean distance) we use an independent test set containing a further 600 digits. The nearest neighbour method,

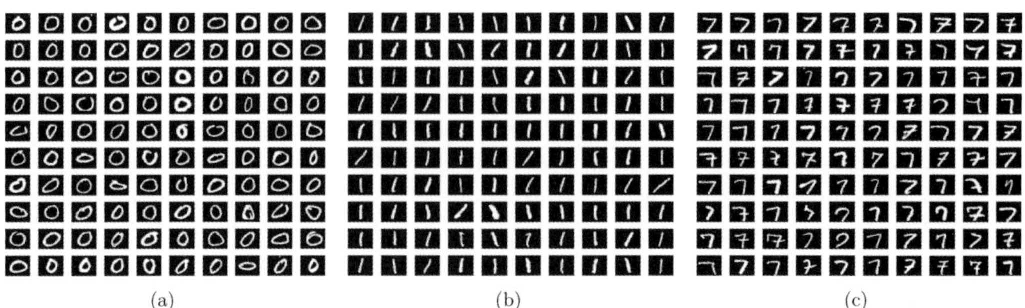

Figure 14.3 Some of the train examples of the digit zero (a), one (b) and seven (c). There are 300 train examples of each of these three digit classes.

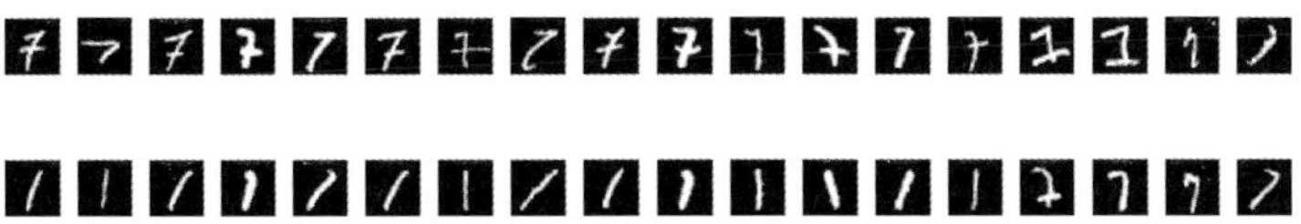

Figure 14.4 '1' versus '7' classification using the NN method. (Top) The 18 out of 600 test examples that are incorrectly classified; (Bottom) the nearest neighbours in the training set corresponding to each testpoint above.

applied to this data, correctly predicts the class label of all 600 test points. The reason for the high success rate is that examples of zeros and ones are sufficiently different that they can be easily distinguished.

A more difficult task is to distinguish between ones and sevens. We repeat the above experiment, now using 300 training examples of ones, and 300 training examples of sevens, Fig. 14.3(b,c). Again, 600 new test examples (containing 300 ones and 300 sevens) were used to assess the performance. This time, 18 errors are found using nearest neighbour classification – a 3 per cent error rate for this two-class problem. The 18 test points on which the nearest neighbour method makes errors are plotted in Fig. 14.4. If we use $K = 3$ nearest neighbours, the classification error reduces to 14 – a slight improvement. As an aside, the best machine learning methods classify real world digits (over all 10 classes) to an error of less than 1 per cent – better than the performance of an 'average' human.

14.3 A probabilistic interpretation of nearest neighbours

Consider the situation where we have data from two classes – class 0 and class 1. We make the following mixture model for data from class 0 which places a Gaussian on each datapoint:

$$p(\mathbf{x}|c=0) = \frac{1}{N_0}\sum_{n\in\text{ class }0}\mathcal{N}\left(\mathbf{x}|\mathbf{x}^n,\sigma^2\mathbf{I}\right) = \frac{1}{N_0}\frac{1}{\left(2\pi\sigma^2\right)^{D/2}}\sum_{n\in\text{ class }0}e^{-(\mathbf{x}-\mathbf{x}^n)^2/(2\sigma^2)} \tag{14.3.1}$$

where D is the dimension of a datapoint $\mathbf{x}$ and N_0 are the number of train points of class 0, and σ^2 is the variance. This is a *Parzen estimator*, and models the data as a uniform weighted sum of Gaussian distributions centred on the training points, Fig. 14.5.

Similarly, for data from class 1:

$$p(\mathbf{x}|c=1) = \frac{1}{N_1}\sum_{n\in\text{ class }1}\mathcal{N}\left(\mathbf{x}|\mathbf{x}^n,\sigma^2\mathbf{I}\right) = \frac{1}{N_1}\frac{1}{\left(2\pi\sigma^2\right)^{D/2}}\sum_{n\in\text{ class }1}e^{-(\mathbf{x}-\mathbf{x}^n)^2/(2\sigma^2)}. \tag{14.3.2}$$

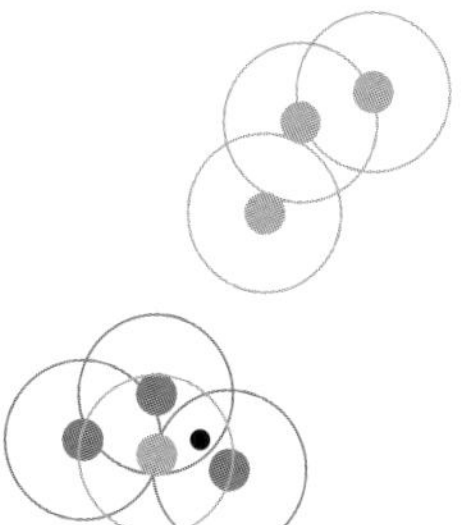

Figure 14.5 A probabilistic interpretation of nearest neighbours. For each class we use a mixture of Gaussians to model the data from that class $p(\mathbf{x}|c)$, placing at each training point an isotropic Gaussian of width σ^2. The width of each Gaussian is represented by the circle. In the limit $\sigma^2 \to 0$ a novel point (small black dot) is assigned the class of its nearest neighbour. For finite $\sigma^2 > 0$ the influence of non-nearest neighbours has an effect, resulting in a soft version of nearest neighbours.

To classify a new datapoint $\mathbf{x}^*$, we use Bayes' rule

$$p(c = 0|\mathbf{x}^*) = \frac{p(\mathbf{x}^*|c = 0)p(c = 0)}{p(\mathbf{x}^*|c = 0)p(c = 0) + p(\mathbf{x}^*|c = 1)p(c = 1)}. \tag{14.3.3}$$

The maximum likelihood setting of $p(c = 0)$ is $N_0/(N_0 + N_1)$, and $p(c = 1) = N_1/(N_0 + N_1)$. An analogous expression to Equation (14.3.3) holds for $p(c = 1|\mathbf{x}^*)$. To see which class is most likely we may use the ratio

$$\frac{p(c = 0|\mathbf{x}^*)}{p(c = 1|\mathbf{x}^*)} = \frac{p(\mathbf{x}^*|c = 0)p(c = 0)}{p(\mathbf{x}^*|c = 1)p(c = 1)}. \tag{14.3.4}$$

If this ratio is greater than one, we classify $\mathbf{x}^*$ as 0, otherwise 1.

Equation (14.3.4) is a complicated function of $\mathbf{x}^*$. However, if σ^2 is very small, the numerator, which is a sum of exponential terms, will be dominated by that term for which datapoint $\mathbf{x}^{n_0}$ in class 0 is closest to the point $\mathbf{x}^*$. Similarly, the denominator will be dominated by that datapoint $\mathbf{x}^{n_1}$ in class 1 which is closest to $\mathbf{x}^*$. In this case, therefore,

$$\frac{p(c = 0|\mathbf{x}^*)}{p(c = 1|\mathbf{x}^*)} \approx \frac{e^{-(\mathbf{x}^*-\mathbf{x}^{n_0})^2/(2\sigma^2)}p(c = 0)/N_0}{e^{-(\mathbf{x}^*-\mathbf{x}^{n_1})^2/(2\sigma^2)}p(c = 1)/N_1} = \frac{e^{-(\mathbf{x}^*-\mathbf{x}^{n_0})^2/(2\sigma^2)}}{e^{-(\mathbf{x}^*-\mathbf{x}^{n_1})^2/(2\sigma^2)}}. \tag{14.3.5}$$

Taking the limit $\sigma^2 \to 0$, with certainty we classify $\mathbf{x}^*$ as class 0 if $\mathbf{x}^*$ is closer to $\mathbf{x}^{n_0}$ than to $\mathbf{x}^{n_1}$. The nearest (single) neighbour method is therefore recovered as the limiting case of a probabilistic generative model, see Fig. 14.5.

The motivation for K nearest neighbours is to produce a classification that is robust against unrepresentative single nearest neighbours. To ensure a similar kind of robustness in the probabilistic interpretation, we may use a finite value $\sigma^2 > 0$. This smoothes the extreme probabilities of classification and means that more points (not just the nearest) will have an effective contribution in Equation (14.3.4). The extension to more than two classes is straightforward, requiring a class conditional generative model for each class.

By using a richer generative model of the data we may go beyond the Parzen estimator approach. We will examine such cases in some detail in later chapters, in particular Chapter 20.

14.3.1 When your nearest neighbour is far away

For a novel input $\mathbf{x}^*$ that is far from all training points, nearest neighbours, and its soft probabilistic variant will confidently classify $\mathbf{x}^*$ as belonging to the class of the nearest training point. This is arguably opposite to what we would like, namely that the classification should tend to the prior probabilities of the class based on the number of training data per class. A way to avoid this problem is, for each class, to include a fictitious large-variance mixture component at the mean of all the data, one for each class. For novel inputs close to the training data, this extra fictitious component will have no appreciable effect. However, as we move away from the high density regions of the training data, this additional fictitious component will dominate since it has larger variance than any of the other components. As the distance from $\mathbf{x}^*$ to each fictitious class point is the same, in the limit that

$\mathbf{x}^*$ is far from the training data, the effect is that no class information from the position of $\mathbf{x}^*$ occurs. See Section 20.3.3 for an example.

14.4 Summary

- Nearest neighbour methods are general classification methods.
- The NN method can be understood as a class conditional mixture of Gaussians in the limit of a vanishingly small covariance for each mixture component model.

14.5 Code

`nearNeigh.m`: K nearest neighbour
`majority.m`: Find the majority entry in each column of a matrix
`demoNearNeigh.m`: K nearest neighbour demo

14.6 Exercises

14.1 The file `NNdata.mat` contains training and test data for the handwritten digits 5 and 9. Using leave one out cross-validation, find the optimal K in K-nearest neighours, and use this to compute the classification accuracy of the method on the test data.

14.2 Write a routine `SoftNearNeigh(xtrain,xtest,trainlabels,sigma)` to implement soft nearest neighbours, analogous to `nearNeigh.m`. Here `sigma` is the variance σ^2 in Equation (14.3.1). The file `NNdata.mat` contains training and test data for the handwritten digits 5 and 9. Using leave one out cross-validation, find the optimal σ^2 and use this to compute the classification accuracy of the method on the test data. Hint: you may have numerical difficulty with this method. To avoid this, consider using the logarithm, and how to numerically compute $\log\left(e^a + e^b\right)$ for large (negative) a and b. See also `logsumexp.m`.

14.3 The editor at *YoMan!* (a 'men's' magazine) has just had a great idea. Based on the success of a recent national poll to test IQ, she decides to make a 'Beauty Quotient' (BQ) test. She collects as many images of male faces as she can, taking care to make sure that all the images are scaled to roughly the same size and under the same lighting conditions. She then gives each male face a BQ score from 0 ('Severely Aesthetically Challenged') to 100 ('Generously Aesthetically Gifted'). Thus, for each real-valued D-dimensional image $\mathbf{x}$, there is an associated value b in the range 0 to 100. In total she collects N images and associated scores, $\{(\mathbf{x}^n, b^n), n = 1, \ldots, N\}$. One morning, she bounces into your office and tells you the good news : it is your task to make a test for the male nation to determine their Beauty Quotient. The idea, she explains, is that a man can send online an image of their face $\mathbf{x}^*$, to *YoMan!* and will immediately receive an automatic BQ response b^*.

1. As a first step, you decide to use the K-nearest neighbour method (KNN) to assign a BQ score b^* to a novel test image $\mathbf{x}^*$. Describe how to determine the optimal number of neighbours K to use.
2. Your line manager is pleased with your algorithm but is disappointed that it does not provide any simple explanation of Beauty that she can present in a future version of *YoMan!* magazine. To address

this, you decide to make a model based on linear regression. That is

$$b = \mathbf{w}^{\mathsf{T}}\mathbf{x} \tag{14.6.1}$$

where $\mathbf{w}$ is a parameter vector chosen to minimise

$$E(\mathbf{w}) = \sum_n \left(b^n - \mathbf{w}^{\mathsf{T}}\mathbf{x}^n\right)^2.$$

After training (finding a suitable $\mathbf{w}$), how can *YoMan!* explain to its readership in a simple way what facial features are important for determining one's BQ?

15 Unsupervised linear dimension reduction

High-dimensional data is prevalent in machine learning and related areas. Indeed, there often arises the situation in which there are more data dimensions than there are data examples. In such cases we seek a lower-dimensional representation of the data. In this chapter we discuss some standard methods which can also improve the prediction performance by removing 'noise' from the representation.

15.1 High-dimensional spaces – low-dimensional manifolds

In machine learning problems data is often high dimensional – images, bag-of-word descriptions, gene-expressions etc. In such cases we cannot expect the training data to densely populate the space, meaning that there will be large parts in which little is known about the data. For the hand written digits from Chapter 14, the data is 784 dimensional and for binary valued pixels the number of possible images is $2^{784} \approx 10^{236}$. Nevertheless, we would expect that only a handful of examples of a digit should be sufficient (for a human) to understand how to recognise a 7. Digit-like images must therefore occupy a highly constrained volume in the 784 dimensions and we expect only a small number of degrees of freedom to be required to describe the data to a reasonable accuracy. Whilst the data vectors may be very high dimensional, they will therefore typically lie close to a much lower-dimensional 'manifold' (informally, a two-dimensional manifold corresponds to a warped sheet of paper embedded in a high-dimensional space), meaning that the distribution of the data is heavily constrained. Here we concentrate on computationally efficient linear dimension reduction techniques in which a high-dimensional datapoint $\mathbf{x}$ is projected down to a lower-dimensional vector $\mathbf{y}$ by

$$\mathbf{y} = \mathbf{F}\mathbf{x} + \text{const.} \tag{15.1.1}$$

The non-square matrix $\mathbf{F}$ has dimensions $\dim(\mathbf{y}) \times \dim(\mathbf{x})$, with $\dim(\mathbf{y}) < \dim(\mathbf{x})$. The methods in this chapter are largely non-probabilistic, although many have natural probabilistic interpretations. For example, PCA is closely related to factor analysis, as described in Chapter 21.

15.2 Principal components analysis

If data lies close to a linear subspace, as in Fig. 15.1 we can accurately approximate each data point by using vectors that span the linear subspace alone. In such cases we aim to discover a

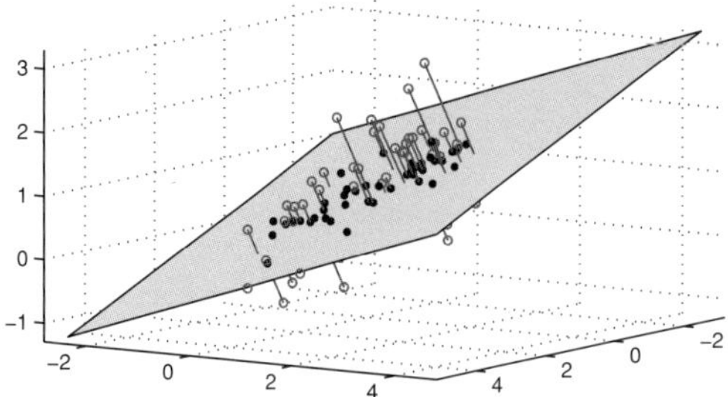

Figure 15.1 In linear dimension reduction a linear subspace is fitted such that the average squared distance between datapoints (rings) and their projections onto the plane (black dots) is minimal.

low-dimensional coordinate system in which we can approximately represent the data. We express the approximation for datapoint $\mathbf{x}^n$ as

$$\mathbf{x}^n \approx \mathbf{c} + \sum_{j=1}^{M} y_j^n \mathbf{b}^j \equiv \tilde{\mathbf{x}}^n. \tag{15.2.1}$$

Here the vector $\mathbf{c}$ is a constant and defines a point in the linear subspace and the $\mathbf{b}^j$ are 'basis' vectors that span the linear subspace (also known as 'principal component coefficients' or 'loadings'). Note that some authors define PCA without the constant $\mathbf{c}$. Collectively we can write $\mathbf{B} = \left[\mathbf{b}^1, \ldots, \mathbf{b}^M\right]$. The y_i^n are the low-dimensional coordinates of the data, forming a lower dimension $\mathbf{y}^n$ for each datapoint n; collectively we can write these lower dimensional vectors as $\mathbf{Y} = \left[\mathbf{y}^1, \ldots, \mathbf{y}^N\right]$. Equation (15.2.1) expresses how to find the reconstruction $\tilde{\mathbf{x}}^n$ given the lower-dimensional representation $\mathbf{y}^n$ (which has components $y_i^n, i = 1, \ldots, M$). For a data space of dimension $\dim(\mathbf{x}) = D$, we hope to accurately describe the data using only a small number $M \ll D$ of coordinates $\mathbf{y}$.

To determine the best lower-dimensional representation it is convenient to use the squared distance error between $\mathbf{x}$ and its reconstruction $\tilde{\mathbf{x}}$:

$$E(\mathbf{B}, \mathbf{Y}, \mathbf{c}) = \sum_{n=1}^{N} \sum_{i=1}^{D} \left[x_i^n - \tilde{x}_i^n\right]^2. \tag{15.2.2}$$

It is straightforward to show that the optimal bias $\mathbf{c}$ is given by the mean of the data $\sum_n \mathbf{x}^n / N$, Exercise 15.1. We therefore assume that the data has been centred (has zero mean $\sum_n \mathbf{x}^n = \mathbf{0}$), so that we can set $\mathbf{c}$ to zero, and concentrate on finding the optimal basis $\mathbf{B}$ below.

15.2.1 Deriving the optimal linear reconstruction

To find the best basis vectors $\mathbf{B}$ (defining $[B]_{i,j} = b_i^j$) and corresponding low-dimensional coordinates $\mathbf{Y}$, we wish to minimise the sum of squared differences between each vector $\mathbf{x}$ and its reconstruction $\tilde{\mathbf{x}}$:

$$E(\mathbf{B}, \mathbf{Y}) = \sum_{n=1}^{N} \sum_{i=1}^{D} \left[x_i^n - \sum_{j=1}^{M} y_j^n b_i^j\right]^2 = \operatorname{trace}\left((\mathbf{X} - \mathbf{BY})^{\mathsf{T}} (\mathbf{X} - \mathbf{BY})\right) \tag{15.2.3}$$

where $\mathbf{X} = \left[\mathbf{x}^1, \ldots, \mathbf{x}^N\right]$.

An important observation is that the optimal solution for $\mathbf{B}$ and $\mathbf{Y}$ is not unique since the reconstruction error $E(\mathbf{B}, \mathbf{Y})$ depends only on the product $\mathbf{BY}$. Indeed, without loss of generality, we may constrain $\mathbf{B}$ to be an orthonormal matrix. To see this, consider an invertible transformation $\mathbf{Q}$ of the basis $\mathbf{B}$ so that $\tilde{\mathbf{B}} \equiv \mathbf{BQ}$ is an orthonormal matrix, $\tilde{\mathbf{B}}^{\mathsf{T}}\tilde{\mathbf{B}} = \mathbf{I}$. Since $\mathbf{Q}$ is invertible, we may write

$\mathbf{BY} = \tilde{\mathbf{B}}\tilde{\mathbf{Y}}$ on defining $\tilde{\mathbf{Y}} = \mathbf{Q}^{-1}\mathbf{Y}$. Since $\tilde{\mathbf{Y}}$ is unconstrained (because $\mathbf{Y}$ is unconstrained), without loss of generality, we may consider Equation (15.2.3) under the orthonormality constraint $\mathbf{B}^{\mathsf{T}}\mathbf{B} = \mathbf{I}$, namely that the basis vectors are mutually orthogonal and of unit length.

By differentiating Equation (15.2.3) with respect to y_k^n we obtain (using the orthonormality constraint on $\mathbf{B}$)

$$-\frac{1}{2}\frac{\partial}{\partial y_k^n}E(\mathbf{B},\mathbf{Y}) = \sum_i \left[x_i^n - \sum_j y_j^n b_i^j\right] b_i^k = \sum_i x_i^n b_i^k - \sum_j y_j^n \underbrace{\sum_i b_i^j b_i^k}_{\delta_{jk}} = \sum_i x_i^n b_i^k - y_k^n.$$

The squared error $E(\mathbf{B},\mathbf{Y})$ therefore has zero derivative when

$$y_k^n = \sum_i b_i^k x_i^n, \qquad \text{which can be written as} \quad \mathbf{Y} = \mathbf{B}^{\mathsf{T}}\mathbf{X}. \tag{15.2.4}$$

We now substitute this solution into Equation (15.2.3) to write the squared error as a function of $\mathbf{B}$ alone. Using

$$(\mathbf{X}-\mathbf{BY})^{\mathsf{T}}(\mathbf{X}-\mathbf{BY}) = \mathbf{X}^{\mathsf{T}}\mathbf{X} - \mathbf{X}^{\mathsf{T}}\mathbf{B}\mathbf{B}^{\mathsf{T}}\mathbf{X} - \mathbf{X}^{\mathsf{T}}\mathbf{B}\mathbf{B}^{\mathsf{T}}\mathbf{X} + \mathbf{X}^{\mathsf{T}}\mathbf{B}\underbrace{\mathbf{B}^{\mathsf{T}}\mathbf{B}}_{\mathbf{I}}\mathbf{B}^{\mathsf{T}}\mathbf{X}. \tag{15.2.5}$$

The last two terms above therefore cancel. Using then trace $(\mathbf{ABC}) =$ trace $(\mathbf{CAB})$ we obtain

$$E(\mathbf{B}) = \text{trace}\left(\mathbf{X}\mathbf{X}^{\mathsf{T}}\left(\mathbf{I}-\mathbf{B}\mathbf{B}^{\mathsf{T}}\right)\right). \tag{15.2.6}$$

Hence the objective becomes

$$E(\mathbf{B}) = (N-1)\left[\text{trace}\,(\mathbf{S}) - \text{trace}\left(\mathbf{S}\mathbf{B}\mathbf{B}^{\mathsf{T}}\right)\right] \tag{15.2.7}$$

where $\mathbf{S}$ is the sample covariance matrix of the data.[1] Since we assumed the data is zero mean, this is

$$\mathbf{S} = \frac{1}{N-1}\mathbf{X}\mathbf{X}^{\mathsf{T}} = \frac{1}{N-1}\sum_{n=1}^{N}\mathbf{x}^n(\mathbf{x}^n)^{\mathsf{T}}. \tag{15.2.8}$$

More generally, for non-zero mean data, we have

$$\mathbf{S} = \frac{1}{N-1}\sum_{n=1}^{N}(\mathbf{x}^n-\mathbf{m})(\mathbf{x}^n-\mathbf{m})^{\mathsf{T}}, \qquad \mathbf{m} = \frac{1}{N}\sum_{n=1}^{N}\mathbf{x}^n. \tag{15.2.9}$$

To minimise Equation (15.2.7) under the constraint $\mathbf{B}^{\mathsf{T}}\mathbf{B} = \mathbf{I}$ we use a set of Lagrange multipliers $\mathbf{L}$, so that the objective is to minimise

$$-\text{trace}\left(\mathbf{S}\mathbf{B}\mathbf{B}^{\mathsf{T}}\right) + \text{trace}\left(\mathbf{L}\left(\mathbf{B}^{\mathsf{T}}\mathbf{B}-\mathbf{I}\right)\right) \tag{15.2.10}$$

(neglecting the constant prefactor $N-1$ and the trace $(\mathbf{S})$ term). Since the constraint is symmetric, we can assume that $\mathbf{L}$ is also symmetric. Differentiating with respect to $\mathbf{B}$ and equating to zero we obtain that at the optimum

$$\mathbf{SB} = \mathbf{BL}. \tag{15.2.11}$$

[1] Here we use the unbiased sample covariance, simply because this is standard in the literature. If we were to replace this with the sample covariance as defined in Chapter 8, the only change required is to replace $N-1$ by N throughout, which has no effect on the form of the solutions found by PCA.

We need to find matrices **B** and **L** that satisfy this equation. One solution is given when **L** is diagonal, in which case this is a form of eigen-equation and the columns of **B** are the corresponding eigenvectors of **S**. In this case, trace $(\mathbf{S}\mathbf{B}\mathbf{B}^{\mathsf{T}}) = \text{trace}(\mathbf{L})$, which is the sum of the eigenvalues corresponding to the eigenvectors forming **B**. For this eigen solution, therefore

$$\frac{1}{N-1}E(\mathbf{B}) = -\text{trace}(\mathbf{L}) + \text{trace}(\mathbf{S}) = -\sum_{i=1}^{M}\lambda_i + \text{const.} \tag{15.2.12}$$

Since we wish to minimise $E(\mathbf{B})$, we therefore define the basis using the eigenvectors with largest corresponding eigenvalues. If we order the eigenvalues $\lambda_1 \geq \lambda_2, \ldots$, the squared error is then given by, from Equation (15.2.7),

$$\frac{1}{N-1}E(\mathbf{B}) = \text{trace}(\mathbf{S}) - \text{trace}(\mathbf{L}) = \sum_{i=1}^{D}\lambda_i - \sum_{i=1}^{M}\lambda_i = \sum_{i=M+1}^{D}\lambda_i. \tag{15.2.13}$$

Whilst the solution to this eigen-problem is unique, this only serves to define the solution subspace since one may rotate and scale **B** and **Y** such that the value of the squared loss is exactly the same (since the least squares objective depends only on the product **BY**). The justification for choosing the non-rotated eigen solution is given by the additional requirement that the basis (columns of **B**) correspond to directions of maximal variance, as explained in Section 15.2.2.

15.2.2 Maximum variance criterion

To break the invariance of least squares projection with respect to rotations and rescaling, we need an additional criterion. One such is given by first searching for the single direction **b** such that the variance of the data projected onto this direction is maximal amongst all possible such projections. This makes sense since we are looking for 'interesting' directions along which the data varies a lot. Using Equation (15.2.4) for a single vector **b** we have

$$y^n = \sum_i b_i x_i^n. \tag{15.2.14}$$

The projection of a datapoint onto a direction **b** is $\mathbf{b}^{\mathsf{T}}\mathbf{x}^n$ for a unit length vector **b**. Hence the sum of squared projections is

$$\sum_n \left(\mathbf{b}^{\mathsf{T}}\mathbf{x}^n\right)^2 = \mathbf{b}^{\mathsf{T}}\left[\sum_n \mathbf{x}^n\left(\mathbf{x}^n\right)^{\mathsf{T}}\right]\mathbf{b} = (N-1)\mathbf{b}^{\mathsf{T}}\mathbf{S}\mathbf{b}. \tag{15.2.15}$$

Ignoring constants, this is the negative of Equation (15.2.7) for a single basis vector **b**. Since, optimally, **b** is an eigenvector with $\mathbf{S}\mathbf{b} = \lambda\mathbf{b}$, and the squared projection becomes $\lambda(N-1)$. Hence the optimal single **b** which maximises the projection variance is given by the eigenvector corresponding to the largest eigenvalue of **S**. Under the criterion that the next optimal direction $\mathbf{b}^{(2)}$ should be orthonormal to the first, one can readily show that $\mathbf{b}^{(2)}$ is given by the second largest eigenvector, and so on. This explains why, despite the squared loss equation (15.2.7) being invariant with respect to arbitrary rotation (and scaling) of the basis vectors, the ones given by the eigen-decomposition have the additional property that they correspond to directions of maximal variance. These maximal variance directions found by PCA are called the *principal directions*.

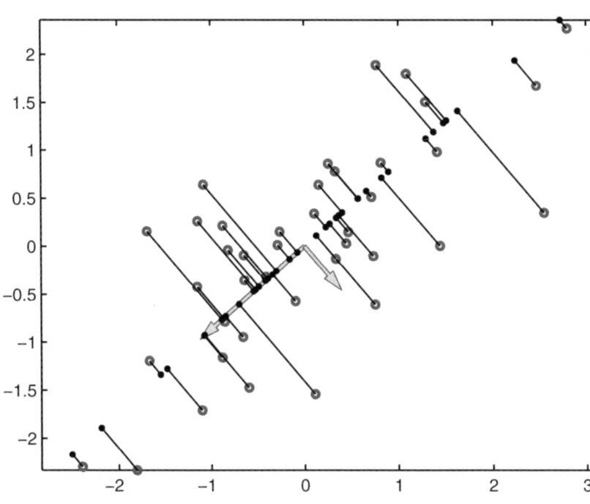

Figure 15.2 Projection of two-dimensional data using one-dimensional PCA. Plotted are the original datapoints **x** (larger rings) and their reconstructions $\tilde{\mathbf{x}}$ (small dots) using one-dimensional PCA. The lines represent the orthogonal projection of the original datapoint onto the first eigenvector. The arrows are the two eigenvectors scaled by the square root of their corresponding eigenvalues. The data has been centred to have zero mean. For each 'high-dimensional' datapoint **x**, the 'low-dimensional' representation **y** is given in this case by the distance (possibly negative) from the origin along the first eigenvector direction to the corresponding orthogonal projection point.

15.2.3 PCA algorithm

The routine for PCA is presented in Algorithm 15.1. In the notation of $\mathbf{y} = \mathbf{F}\mathbf{x}$, the projection matrix $\mathbf{F}$ corresponds to $\mathbf{E}^\mathsf{T}$. Similarly for the reconstruction equation (15.2.1), the coordinate $\mathbf{y}^n$ corresponds to $\mathbf{E}^\mathsf{T}\mathbf{x}^n$ and $\mathbf{b}^i$ corresponds to $\mathbf{e}^i$. The PCA reconstructions are orthogonal projections of the data onto the subspace spanned by the eigenvectors corresponding to the M largest eigenvalues of the covariance matrix, see Fig. 15.2.

Example 15.1 Reducing the dimension of digits

We have 892 examples of handwritten 5's, where each image consists of 28×28 real-values pixels, see Fig. 15.3. Each image matrix is stacked to form a 784-dimensional vector, giving a 784×892 dimensional data matrix $\mathbf{X}$. The covariance matrix of this data has eigenvalue spectrum as plotted in Fig. 15.4, where we plot only the 100 largest eigenvalues. Note how after around 40 components, the mean squared reconstruction error is small, indicating that the data lies close to a 40-dimensional linear subspace. The eigenvalues are computed using `pca.m`. The reconstructions using different numbers of eigenvectors (100, 30 and 5) are plotted in Fig. 15.3. Note how using only a small number of eigenvectors, the reconstruction more closely resembles the mean image.

Example 15.2 Eigenfaces

In Fig. 15.5 we present example images for which we wish to find a lower-dimensional representation. Using PCA the mean and first 48 'eigenfaces' are presented along with reconstructions of the original data using these eigenfaces, see Fig. 15.6. The PCA respresentation was found using the SVD techniques, as described in Section 15.3.2.

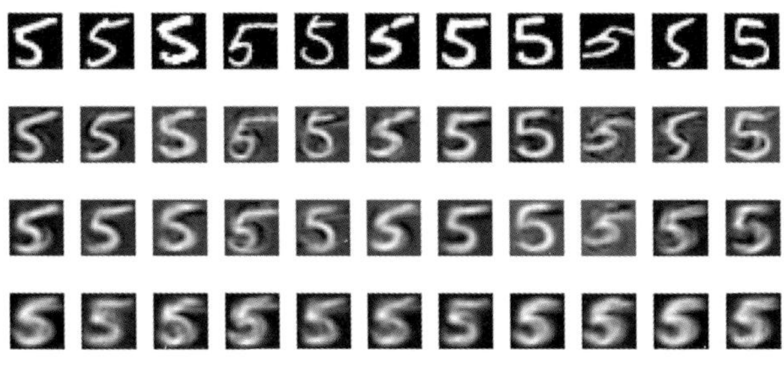

Figure 15.3 Top row: a selection of the digit 5 taken from the database of 892 examples. Plotted beneath each digit is the reconstruction using 100, 30 and 5 eigenvectors (from top to bottom). Note how the reconstructions for fewer eigenvectors express less variability from each other, and resemble more a mean 5 digit.

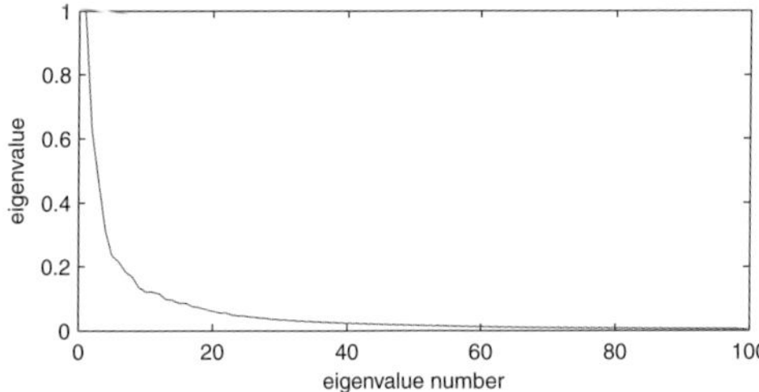

Figure 15.4 The digits data consists of 892 examples of the digit 5, each image being represented by a 784-dimensional vector. Plotted are 100 largest eigenvalues (scaled so that the largest eigenvalue is 1) of the sample covariance matrix.

Algorithm 15.1 Principal components analysis to form an M-dimensional approximation of a dataset $\{\mathbf{x}^n, n = 1, \dots, N\}$, with $\dim(\mathbf{x}^n) = D$.

1: Find the $D \times 1$ sample mean vector and $D \times D$ covariance matrix

$$\mathbf{m} = \frac{1}{N}\sum_{n=1}^{N}\mathbf{x}^n, \quad \mathbf{S} = \frac{1}{N-1}\sum_{n=1}^{N}(\mathbf{x}^n - \mathbf{m})(\mathbf{x}^n - \mathbf{m})^{\mathsf{T}}.$$

2: Find the eigenvectors $\mathbf{e}^1, \dots, \mathbf{e}^D$ of the covariance matrix $\mathbf{S}$, sorted so that the eigenvalue of $\mathbf{e}^i$ is larger than $\mathbf{e}^j$ for $i < j$. Form the matrix $\mathbf{E} = [\mathbf{e}^1, \dots, \mathbf{e}^M]$.

3: The lower-dimensional representation of each data point $\mathbf{x}^n$ is given by

$$\mathbf{y}^n = \mathbf{E}^{\mathsf{T}}(\mathbf{x}^n - \mathbf{m}). \tag{15.2.16}$$

4: The approximate reconstruction of the original datapoint $\mathbf{x}^n$ is

$$\mathbf{x}^n \approx \mathbf{m} + \mathbf{E}\mathbf{y}^n. \tag{15.2.17}$$

5: The total squared error over all the training data made by the approximation is

$$\sum_{n=1}^{N}(\mathbf{x}^n - \tilde{\mathbf{x}}^n)^2 = (N-1)\sum_{j=M+1}^{D}\lambda_j \tag{15.2.18}$$

where $\lambda_{M+1} \dots \lambda_N$ are the eigenvalues discarded in the projection.

15.2.4 PCA and nearest neighbours classification

In nearest neighbours classification, Chapter 14, we need to compute the distance between datapoints. For high-dimensional data computing the squared Euclidean distance between vectors can be expensive, and also sensitive to noise. It is therefore often useful to project the data to a lower-dimensional representation first. For example, in making a classifier to distinguish between the digit 1 and the digit 7, Example 14.1, we can form a lower-dimensional representation and use this as a more robust representation of the data. To do so we first ignore the class label to make a dataset of 1200 training points. Each of the training points $\mathbf{x}^n$ is then projected to a lower-dimensional PCA representation $\mathbf{y}^n$. Subsequently, any distance calculations $(\mathbf{x}^a - \mathbf{x}^b)^2$ are replaced by $(\mathbf{y}^a - \mathbf{y}^b)^2$. To justify this, consider

$$\begin{aligned}(\mathbf{x}^a - \mathbf{x}^b)^{\mathsf{T}}(\mathbf{x}^a - \mathbf{x}^b) &\approx (\mathbf{E}\mathbf{y}^a + \mathbf{m} - \mathbf{E}\mathbf{y}^b - \mathbf{m})^{\mathsf{T}}(\mathbf{E}\mathbf{y}^a + \mathbf{m} - \mathbf{E}\mathbf{y}^b - \mathbf{m})\\ &= (\mathbf{y}^a - \mathbf{y}^b)^{\mathsf{T}}\mathbf{E}^{\mathsf{T}}\mathbf{E}(\mathbf{y}^a - \mathbf{y}^b)\\ &= (\mathbf{y}^a - \mathbf{y}^b)^{\mathsf{T}}(\mathbf{y}^a - \mathbf{y}^b)\end{aligned} \tag{15.2.19}$$

where the last equality is due to the orthonormality of eigenvectors, $\mathbf{E}^{\mathsf{T}}\mathbf{E} = \mathbf{I}$.

Figure 15.5 100 training images. Each image consists of $92 \times 112 = 10\,304$ greyscale pixels. The train data is scaled so that, represented as an image, the components of each image sum to 1. The average value of each pixel across all images is 9.70×10^{-5}. This is a subset of the 400 images in the full Olivetti Research Face Database.

Using 19 principal components (see Example 15.3 as to why this number was chosen) and the nearest neighbour rule to classify 1's and 7's gave a test-set error of 14 in 600 examples, compared to 18 from the standard method on the non-projected data. A plausible explanation for this improvement is that the new PCA representation of the data is more robust since only the 'interesting' directions in the space are retained, with low variance directions discarded.

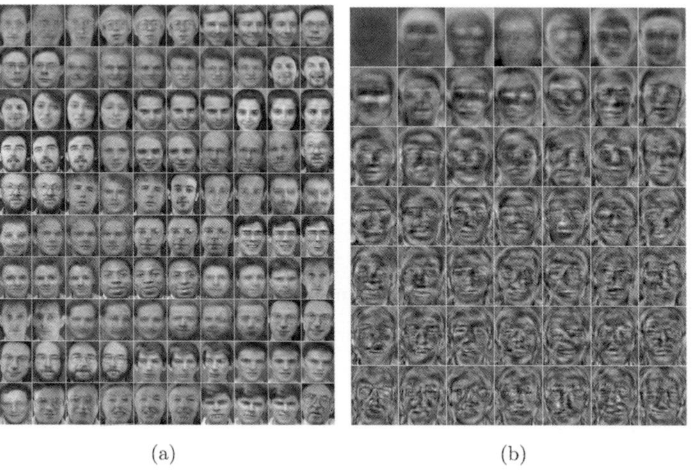

Figure 15.6 (**a**) SVD reconstruction of the images in Fig. 15.5 using a combination of the 49 eigen-images. (**b**) The eigen-images are found using SVD of the images in Fig. 15.5 and taking the mean and 48 eigenvectors with largest corresponding eigenvalue. The images corresponding to the largest eigenvalues are contained in the first row, and the next 7 in the row below, etc. The root mean square reconstruction error is 1.121×10^{-5}, a small improvement over PLSA (see Fig. 15.16).

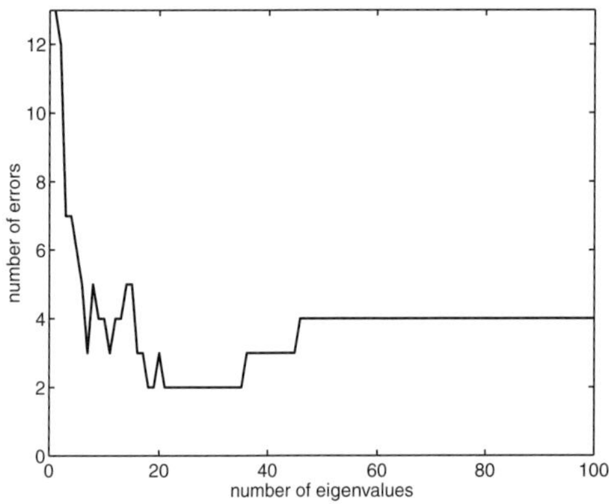

Figure 15.7 Finding the optimal PCA dimension to use for classifying hand-written digits using nearest neighbours: 400 training examples are used, and the validation error plotted on 200 further examples. Based on the validation error, we see that a dimension of 19 is reasonable.

Example 15.3 Finding the best PCA dimension

There are 600 examples of the digit 1 and 600 examples of the digit 7. We will use half the data for training and the other half for testing. The 600 training examples were further split into a training set of 400 examples and a separate validation set of 200 examples. PCA was used to reduce the dimensionality of the inputs, and then nearest neighbours used to classify the 200 validation examples. Different reduced dimensions were investigated and, based on the validation results, 19 was selected as the optimal number of PCA components retained, see Fig. 15.7. The independent test error on 600 independent examples using 19 dimensions is 14.

15.2.5 Comments on PCA

The 'intrinsic' dimension of data

How many dimensions should the linear subspace have? From Equation (15.2.13), the reconstruction error is proportional to the sum of the discarded eigenvalues. If we plot the eigenvalue spectrum (the set of eigenvalues ordered by decreasing value), we might hope to see a few large values and many small values. If the data does lie close to an M-dimensional linear subspace, we would see M large eigenvalues with the rest being very small. This gives an indication of the number of degrees of freedom in the data, or the intrinsic dimensionality. Directions corresponding to the small eigenvalues are then interpreted as 'noise'.

Non-linear dimension reduction

In PCA we are presupposing that the data lies close to a linear subspace. Is this really a good description? More generally, we would expect data to lie on low-dimensional non-linear subspace. Also, data is often clustered – examples of handwritten 4's look similar to each other and form a cluster, separate from the 8's cluster. Nevertheless, since linear dimension reduction is computationally relatively straightforward, this is one of the most common dimensionality reduction techniques.

15.3 High-dimensional data

The computational complexity of computing the eigen-decomposition of a $D \times D$ matrix is $O\left(D^3\right)$. You might be wondering therefore how it is possible to perform PCA on high-dimensional data.

For example, if we have 500 images each of $1000 \times 1000 = 10^6$ pixels, the covariance matrix will be a $10^6 \times 10^6$ square matrix. It would appear to be a significant computational challenge to find the eigen-decomposition of this matrix directly. In this case, however, since there are only 500 such vectors, the number of non-zero eigenvalues cannot exceed 500. One can exploit this fact to reduce the $O(D^3)$ complexity of the naive approach, as described below.

15.3.1 Eigen-decomposition for $N < D$

First note that for zero mean data, the sample covariance matrix can be expressed as

$$[\mathbf{S}]_{ij} = \frac{1}{N-1} \sum_{n=1}^{N} x_i^n x_j^n. \tag{15.3.1}$$

In matrix notation this can be written

$$\mathbf{S} = \frac{1}{N-1} \mathbf{X}\mathbf{X}^{\mathsf{T}} \tag{15.3.2}$$

where the $D \times N$ matrix $\mathbf{X}$ contains all the data vectors:

$$\mathbf{X} = \left[\mathbf{x}^1, \ldots, \mathbf{x}^N\right]. \tag{15.3.3}$$

Since the eigenvectors of a matrix $\mathbf{M}$ are equal to those of $\gamma\mathbf{M}$ for scalar γ, one can consider more simply the eigenvectors of $\mathbf{X}\mathbf{X}^{\mathsf{T}}$. Writing the $D \times N$ matrix of eigenvectors as $\mathbf{E}$ and the eigenvalues as an $N \times N$ diagonal matrix $\mathbf{\Lambda}$, the eigen-decomposition of the scaled covariance $\mathbf{S}$ satisfies

$$\mathbf{X}\mathbf{X}^{\mathsf{T}}\mathbf{E} = \mathbf{E}\mathbf{\Lambda} \Rightarrow \mathbf{X}^{\mathsf{T}}\mathbf{X}\mathbf{X}^{\mathsf{T}}\mathbf{E} = \mathbf{X}^{\mathsf{T}}\mathbf{E}\mathbf{\Lambda} \Rightarrow \mathbf{X}^{\mathsf{T}}\mathbf{X}\tilde{\mathbf{E}} = \tilde{\mathbf{E}}\mathbf{\Lambda} \tag{15.3.4}$$

where we defined $\tilde{\mathbf{E}} = \mathbf{X}^{\mathsf{T}}\mathbf{E}$. The final expression above represents the eigenvector equation for $\mathbf{X}^{\mathsf{T}}\mathbf{X}$. This is a matrix of dimensions $N \times N$ so that calculating the eigen-decomposition takes $O(N^3)$ operations, compared with $O(D^3)$ operations in the original high-dimensional space. We can therefore calculate the eigenvectors $\tilde{\mathbf{E}}$ and eigenvalues $\mathbf{\Lambda}$ of this matrix more easily. Once found, we use the fact that the eigenvalues of $\mathbf{S}$ are given by the diagonal entries of $\mathbf{\Lambda}$ and the eigenvectors by

$$\mathbf{E} = \mathbf{X}\tilde{\mathbf{E}}\mathbf{\Lambda}^{-1}. \tag{15.3.5}$$

15.3.2 PCA via singular value decomposition

An alternative to using an eigen-decomposition routine to find the PCA solution is to make use of the *Singular Value Decomposition* (SVD) of a $D \times N$ dimensional matrix $\mathbf{X}$. This is given by

$$\mathbf{X} = \mathbf{U}\mathbf{D}\mathbf{V}^{\mathsf{T}} \tag{15.3.6}$$

where $\mathbf{U}^{\mathsf{T}}\mathbf{U} = \mathbf{I}_D$ and $\mathbf{V}^{\mathsf{T}}\mathbf{V} = \mathbf{I}_N$ and $D \times N$ is a diagonal matrix of the (positive) singular values. We assume that the decomposition has ordered the singular values so that the upper left diagonal element of $\mathbf{D}$ contains the largest singular value. The matrix $\mathbf{XX}^\mathsf{T}$ can then be written as

$$\mathbf{XX}^\mathsf{T} = \mathbf{UDV}^\mathsf{T}\mathbf{VD}^\mathsf{T}\mathbf{U}^\mathsf{T} = \mathbf{U}\tilde{\mathbf{D}}^2\mathbf{U}^\mathsf{T} \tag{15.3.7}$$

where $\tilde{\mathbf{D}} \equiv \mathbf{DD}^\mathsf{T}$ is a $D \times D$ diagonal matrix with the N squared singular values on the first diagonal entries, and zero elsewhere. Since $\mathbf{U}\tilde{\mathbf{D}}\mathbf{U}^\mathsf{T}$ is in the form of an eigen-decomposition, the PCA solution is equivalently given by performing the SVD decomposition of $\mathbf{X}$, for which the eigenvectors are then given by $\mathbf{U}$, and corresponding eigenvalues by the square of the singular values.

Equation (15.3.6) shows that PCA is a form of matrix decomposition method:

$$\mathbf{X} = \mathbf{UDV}^\mathsf{T} \approx \mathbf{U}_M\mathbf{D}_M\mathbf{V}_M^\mathsf{T} \tag{15.3.8}$$

where $\mathbf{U}_M, \mathbf{D}_M, \mathbf{V}_M$ correspond to taking only the first M singular values of the full matrices.

15.4 Latent semantic analysis

In the document analysis literature PCA is also called Latent Semantic Analysis (LSA) and is concerned with analysing a set of N documents. Each document is represented by a vector

$$\mathbf{x}^n = (x_1^n, \ldots, x_D^n)^\mathsf{T} \tag{15.4.1}$$

of word occurrences. For example the first element x_1^n might count how many times the word 'cat' appears in document n, x_2^n the number of occurrences of 'dog', etc. This *bag of words*[2] is formed by first choosing a dictionary of D words. The vector element x_i^n is the (possibly normalised) number of occurrences of the word i in the document n. Typically D will be large, of the order 10^6, and $\mathbf{x}$ will be very sparse since any document contains only a small fraction of the available words in the dictionary. Using $\sharp_{i,n}$ to represent the number of times that term i occurs in document n, the term-frequency is defined as

$$\mathrm{tf}_i^n \equiv \frac{\sharp_{i,n}}{\sum_i \sharp_{i,n}}. \tag{15.4.2}$$

An issue with this representation is that frequently occurring words such as 'the' will dominate. To counter this one can measure how unique a term i is by seeing how many documents contain the term, and define the inverse-document frequency

$$\mathrm{idf}_i \equiv \log \frac{N}{\text{number of documents that contain term } i}. \tag{15.4.3}$$

An alternative to the above term-frequency representation is the term frequency-inverse document frequency (TF-IDF) representation which is given by

$$x_i^n = \mathrm{tf}_i^n \times \mathrm{idf}_i \tag{15.4.4}$$

which gives high weight to terms that appear often in a document, but rarely amongst documents.

Given a set of documents $\mathcal{D}$, the aim in LSA is to form a lower-dimensional representation of each document. The whole document database is represented by the so-called *term-document matrix*

$$\mathbf{X} = \left[\mathbf{x}^1, \ldots, \mathbf{x}^N\right] \tag{15.4.5}$$

[2] More generally one can consider term-counts, in which terms can can be single words, or sets of words, or even sub-words.

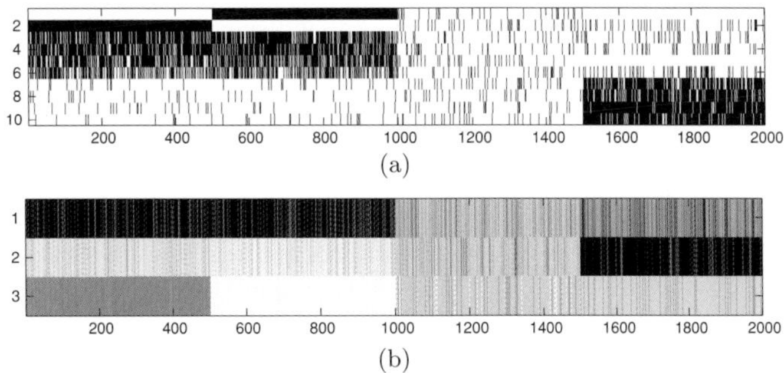

Figure 15.8 (**a**) Document data for a dictionary containing 10 words and 2000 documents. Black indicates that a word was present in a document. The data consists of two distinct topics and a random background topic. The first topic contains two sub-topics which differ only in their usage of the first two words, 'influenza' and 'flu'. (**b**) The projections of each datapoint onto the two principal components.

which has dimension $D \times N$, see for example Fig. 15.8, with entries typically defined by either the term-frequency, or TF-IDF representation. An interpretation of PCA in this case is that the principal directions define 'topics'. Principal components analysis is arguably suboptimal for document analysis since we would expect the presence of a latent topic to contribute only positive counts to the data. A related version of PCA in which the decomposition is constrained to have positive elements is called PLSA, and discussed in Section 15.6.

Example 15.4 Latent topic

We have a small dictionary containing the words *influenza, flu, headache, nose, temperature, bed, cat, dog, rabbit, pet.* The database contains a large number of articles that discuss ailments, and articles which seem to talk about the effects of influenza, in addition to some background documents that are not specific to ailments; other documents also discuss pet related issues. Some of the more formal documents exclusively use the term *influenza*, whereas the other more 'tabloid' documents use the informal term *flu*. Each document is represented by a 10-dimensional vector in which element i of that vector is set to 1 if word i occurs in the document, and 0 otherwise. The data is represented in Fig. 15.8. The data is generated using the artificial mechanism described in `demoLSI.m`.

The result of using PCA on this data is represented in Fig. 15.9 where we plot the eigenvectors, scaled by their eigenvalue. To aid interpretability, we do not use the bias term $\mathbf{c}$ in Equation (15.2.1). The first eigenvector groups all the 'ailment' words together, the second the 'pet' words and the third deals with the different usage of the terms *influenza* and *flu*. Note that unlike clustering models (see Section 20.3 for example) in PCA (and related methods such as PLSA) a datapoint can in principle be constructed from many basis vectors, so that a document could represent a mixture of different topics.

Rescaling

In LSA it is common to scale the transformation so that the projected vectors have approximately unit covariance (assuming centred data). Using

$$\mathbf{y} = \sqrt{N-1}\mathbf{D}_M^{-1}\mathbf{U}_M^{\mathsf{T}}\mathbf{x} \tag{15.4.6}$$

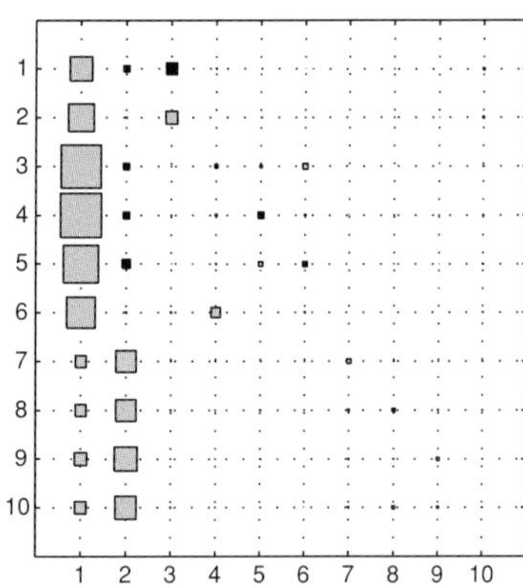

Figure 15.9 Hinton diagram of the eigenvector matrix **E** where each eigenvector column is scaled by the corresponding eigenvalue. The dark-shaded squares indicates positive and light-shaded squares negative values (the area of each square corresponds to the magnitude), showing that there are only a few large eigenvalues. Note that the overall sign of any eigenvector is irrelevant. The first eigenvector corresponds to a topic in which the words *influenza, flu, headache, nose, temperature, bed* are prevalent. The second eigenvector denotes the 'pet' topic words. The third eigenvector shows that there is negative correlation between the occurrence of *influenza* and *flu*. The interpretation of the eigenvectors as 'topics' can be awkward since the basis eigenvectors are by definition orthogonal. Contrast this basis with that found using PSLA with two components, Fig. 15.14.

the covariance of the projections is obtained from

$$\frac{1}{N-1}\sum_n \mathbf{y}^n\left(\mathbf{y}^n\right)^\mathsf{T} = \mathbf{D}_M^{-1}\mathbf{U}_M^\mathsf{T}\underbrace{\sum_n \mathbf{x}^n\left(\mathbf{x}^n\right)^\mathsf{T}}_{\mathbf{X}\mathbf{X}^\mathsf{T}}\mathbf{U}_M\mathbf{D}_M^{-1} = \mathbf{D}_M^{-1}\mathbf{U}_M^\mathsf{T}\mathbf{U}\mathbf{D}\mathbf{D}^\mathsf{T}\mathbf{U}^\mathsf{T}\mathbf{U}_M\mathbf{D}_M^{-1} \approx \mathbf{I}.$$

Given $\mathbf{y}$, the approximate reconstruction $\tilde{\mathbf{x}}$ is

$$\tilde{\mathbf{x}} = \frac{1}{\sqrt{N-1}}\mathbf{U}_M\mathbf{D}_M\mathbf{y}. \tag{15.4.7}$$

The Euclidean distance between two points $\mathbf{x}^a$ and $\mathbf{x}^b$ is then approximately

$$d\left(\tilde{\mathbf{x}}^a, \tilde{\mathbf{x}}^b\right) = \frac{1}{N-1}\left(\mathbf{y}^a - \mathbf{y}^b\right)^\mathsf{T}\mathbf{D}_M\mathbf{U}_M^\mathsf{T}\mathbf{U}_M\mathbf{D}_M\left(\mathbf{y}^a - \mathbf{y}^b\right) \approx \frac{1}{N-1}\left(\mathbf{y}^a - \mathbf{y}^b\right)^\mathsf{T}\mathbf{D}_M^2\left(\mathbf{y}^a - \mathbf{y}^b\right).$$

It is common to ignore the $\mathbf{D}_M^2$ term (and $1/(N-1)$ factor), and to consider a measure of dissimilarity in the projected space to be the Euclidean distance between the $\mathbf{y}$ vectors.

15.4.1 Information retrieval

Consider a large collection of documents from the web, creating a database $\mathcal{D}$. Our interest it to find the most similar document to a specified query document. Using a bag-of-words style representation for document n, $\mathbf{x}^n$, and similarly for the query document, $\mathbf{x}^*$, we address this task by first defining a measure of dissimilarity between documents, for example

$$d(\mathbf{x}^n, \mathbf{x}^m) = \left(\mathbf{x}^n - \mathbf{x}^m\right)^\mathsf{T}\left(\mathbf{x}^n - \mathbf{x}^m\right). \tag{15.4.8}$$

One then searches for the document that minimises this dissimilarity:

$$n_{opt} = \underset{n}{\operatorname{argmin}}\, d(\mathbf{x}^n, \mathbf{x}^*) \tag{15.4.9}$$

and returns document $\mathbf{x}^{n_{opt}}$ as the result of the search query. The squared difference between two documents can also be written

$$\left(\mathbf{x} - \mathbf{x}'\right)^\mathsf{T}\left(\mathbf{x} - \mathbf{x}'\right) = \mathbf{x}^\mathsf{T}\mathbf{x} + \mathbf{x}'^\mathsf{T}\mathbf{x}' - 2\mathbf{x}^\mathsf{T}\mathbf{x}'. \tag{15.4.10}$$

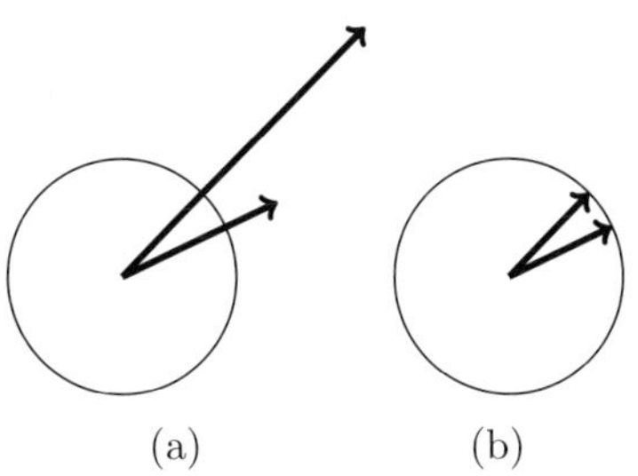

Figure 15.10 (**a**) Two bag-of-word vectors. The Euclidean distance between the two is large. (**b**) Normalised vectors. The Euclidean distance is now related directly to the angle between the vectors. In this case two documents which have the same relative frequency of words will both have the same dissimilarity, even though the number of occurrences of the words is different.

If, as is commonly done, the bag-of-words representations are scaled to have unit length,

$$\hat{\mathbf{x}} = \frac{\mathbf{x}}{\sqrt{\mathbf{x}^{\mathsf{T}}\mathbf{x}}} \tag{15.4.11}$$

so that $\hat{\mathbf{x}}^{\mathsf{T}}\hat{\mathbf{x}} = 1$, the distance is

$$\left(\hat{\mathbf{x}} - \hat{\mathbf{x}}'\right)^{\mathsf{T}}\left(\hat{\mathbf{x}} - \hat{\mathbf{x}}'\right) = 2\left(1 - \hat{\mathbf{x}}^{\mathsf{T}}\hat{\mathbf{x}}'\right) \tag{15.4.12}$$

and one may equivalently consider the *cosine similarity*

$$s(\hat{\mathbf{x}}, \hat{\mathbf{x}}') = \hat{\mathbf{x}}^{\mathsf{T}}\hat{\mathbf{x}}' = \cos(\theta) \tag{15.4.13}$$

where θ is the angle between the unit vectors $\hat{\mathbf{x}}$ and $\hat{\mathbf{x}}'$, Fig. 15.10.

A difficulty with using a bag-of-words representation is that the representation will have mostly zeros. Hence differences may be due to 'noise' rather than any real similarity between the query and database document. Latent semantic analysis helps alleviate this problem somewhat by using a lower-dimensional representation $\mathbf{y}$ of the high-dimensional $\mathbf{x}$. The $\mathbf{y}$ capture the main variations in the data and are less sensitive to random uncorrelated noise. Using the dissimilarity defined in terms of the lower-dimensional $\mathbf{y}$ is therefore more robust and likely to result in the retrieval of more useful documents.

Example 15.5

Continuing the Influenza example, someone who uploads a query document which uses the term 'flu' might also be interested in documents about 'influenza'. However, the search query term 'flu' does not contain the word 'influenza', so how can one retrieve such documents? Since the first component using PCA (LSA) groups all 'influenza' terms together, if we use only the first component of the representation $\mathbf{y}$ to compare documents, this will retrieve documents independent of whether the term 'flu' or 'influenza' is used.

15.5 PCA with missing data

When values of the data matrix $\mathbf{X}$ are missing, the standard PCA algorithm as described cannot be applied. Unfortunately, there is no 'quick fix' PCA solution when some of the x_i^n are missing and more complex numerical procedures need to invoked. A simple approach in this case is to require the squared reconstruction error to be small only for the existing elements of $\mathbf{X}$. That is[3]

$$E(\mathbf{B}, \mathbf{Y}) = \sum_{n=1}^{N}\sum_{i=1}^{D} \gamma_i^n \left[x_i^n - \sum_j y_j^n b_i^j \right]^2 \tag{15.5.1}$$

where $\gamma_i^n = 1$ if the ith entry of the nth vector is available, and is zero otherwise. Differentiating, as before, we find that the optimal weights satisfy (assuming $\mathbf{B}^\mathsf{T}\mathbf{B} = \mathbf{I}$),

$$y_n^k = \sum_i \gamma_i^n x_i^n b_i^k. \tag{15.5.2}$$

One then substitutes this expression into the squared error, and minimises the error with respect to $\mathbf{B}$ under the orthonormality constraint. An alternative iterative optimisation procedure is as follows: First select a random $D \times M$ matrix $\hat{\mathbf{B}}$. Then iterate until convergence the following two steps:

Optimize Y for fixed B

$$E(\hat{\mathbf{B}}, \mathbf{Y}) = \sum_{n=1}^{N}\sum_{i=1}^{D} \gamma_i^n \left[x_i^n - \sum_j y_j^n \hat{b}_i^j \right]^2. \tag{15.5.3}$$

For fixed $\hat{\mathbf{B}}$ the above $E(\hat{\mathbf{B}}, \mathbf{Y})$ is a quadratic function of the matrix $\mathbf{Y}$, which can be optimised directly. By differentiating and equating to zero, one obtains the fixed-point condition

$$\sum_i \gamma_i^n \left(x_i^n - \sum_l y_l^n \hat{b}_i^l \right) \hat{b}_i^k = 0. \tag{15.5.4}$$

Defining

$$\left[\mathbf{y}^{(n)}\right]_l = y_n^l, \qquad \left[\mathbf{M}^{(n)}\right]_{kl} = \sum_i \hat{b}_i^l \hat{b}_i^k \gamma_i^n, \qquad [\mathbf{c}^n]_k = \sum_i \gamma_i^n x_i^n \hat{b}_i^k, \tag{15.5.5}$$

in matrix notation, we then have a set of linear systems:

$$\mathbf{c}^{(n)} = \mathbf{M}^{(n)}\mathbf{y}^{(n)}, \qquad n = 1, \ldots, N. \tag{15.5.6}$$

One may solve each linear system for $\mathbf{y}^n$ using Gaussian elimination.[4] It can be that one or more of the above linear systems is underdetermined – this can occur when there are less observed values in the nth data column of $\mathbf{X}$ than there are components M. In this case one may use the pseudo-inverse to provide a minimal length solution.

Optimize B for fixed Y

One now freezes $\hat{\mathbf{Y}}$ and considers the function

$$E(\mathbf{B}, \hat{\mathbf{Y}}) = \sum_{n=1}^{N}\sum_{i=1}^{D} \gamma_i^n \left[x_i^n - \sum_j \hat{y}_j^n b_i^j \right]^2. \tag{15.5.7}$$

[3] For simplicity we assume that there is no mean term included.

[4] One can avoid explicit matrix inversion by using the \ operator in MATLAB.

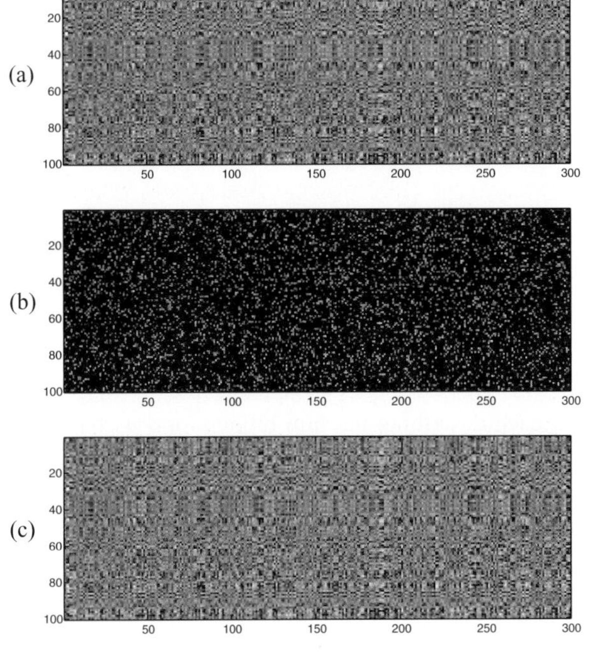

Figure 15.11 (**a**) Original data matrix **X**. Black is missing, white present. The data is constructed from a set of only five basis vectors. (**b**) **X** with missing data (80 per cent sparsity). (**c**) Reconstruction found using `svdm.m`, SVD for missing data. This problem is essentially easy since, despite there being many missing elements, the data is indeed constructed from a model for which SVD is appropriate. Such techniques have application in collaborative filtering and recommender systems where one wishes to 'fill in' missing values in a matrix.

For fixed $\hat{\mathbf{Y}}$ the above expression is quadratic in the matrix **B**, which can again be optimised using linear algebra. This corresponds to solving a set of linear systems for the ith row of **B**:

$$\mathbf{m}^{(i)} = \mathbf{F}^{(i)}\mathbf{b}^{(i)} \tag{15.5.8}$$

where

$$\left[\mathbf{m}^{(i)}\right]_k = \sum_n \gamma_i^n x_i^n \hat{y}_k^n, \qquad \left[\mathbf{F}^{(i)}\right]_{kj} = \sum_n \gamma_i^n \hat{y}_j^n \hat{y}_k^n. \tag{15.5.9}$$

Mathematically, this is $\mathbf{b}^{(i)} = \mathbf{F}^{(i)^{-1}}\mathbf{m}^{(i)}$.

In this manner one is guaranteed to iteratively decrease the value of the squared error loss until a minimum is reached. This technique is implemented in `svdm.m` – see also Fig. 15.11. Efficient techniques based on updating the solution as a new column of **X** arrives one at a time ('online' updating) are also available, see for example [52].

15.5.1 Finding the principal directions

For the missing data case the basis **B** found using the above technique is based only on minimising the squared reconstruction error and therefore does not necessarily satisfy the maximal variance (or principal directions) criterion, namely that the columns of **B** point along the eigen-directions. For a given **B**, **Y** with approximate decomposition $\mathbf{X} \approx \mathbf{BY}$ we can return a new orthonormal basis **U** by performing SVD on the completed data, $\mathbf{BY} = \mathbf{USV}^\mathsf{T}$ to return an orthonormal basis **U**.

An alternative is to explicitly transform the solution **B**. Forming the SVD of **B**,

$$\mathbf{B} = \mathbf{UDV}^\mathsf{T} \tag{15.5.10}$$

the principal directions $\tilde{\mathbf{B}}$ are given by

$$\tilde{\mathbf{B}} = \mathbf{B}\mathbf{V}\mathbf{D}^{-1}. \tag{15.5.11}$$

If the $D \times M$ matrix $\mathbf{B}$ is non-square $M < D$, then the matrix $\mathbf{D}$ will be non-square and non-invertible. To make the above well defined, one may append $\mathbf{D}$ with the columns of the identity:

$$\mathbf{D}' = [\mathbf{D}, \mathbf{I}_{M+1}, \ldots, \mathbf{I}_D] \tag{15.5.12}$$

where $\mathbf{I}_K$ is the Kth column of the identity matrix, and we use $\mathbf{D}'$ in place of $\mathbf{D}$ in Equation (15.5.11) above.

15.5.2 Collaborative filtering using PCA with missing data

A database contains a set of vectors, each describing the film ratings for a user in the database. The entry x_i^n in the vector $\mathbf{x}^n$ specifies the rating the user n gives to the ith film. The matrix $\mathbf{X} = \left[\mathbf{x}^1, \ldots, \mathbf{x}^N\right]$ contains the ratings for all the N users and has many missing values since any single user will only have given a rating for a small selection of the possible D films. In a practical example one might have $D = 10^4$ films and $N = 10^6$ users. For any user n the task is to predict reasonable values for the missing entries of their rating vector $\mathbf{x}^n$, thereby providing a suggestion as to which films they might like to view. Viewed as a missing data problem, one can fit $\mathbf{B}$ and $\mathbf{Y}$ using `svdm.m` as above. Given $\mathbf{B}$ and $\mathbf{Y}$ we can form a reconstruction on all the entries of $\mathbf{X}$, by using

$$\tilde{\mathbf{X}} = \mathbf{B}\mathbf{Y} \tag{15.5.13}$$

giving therefore a prediction for the missing values.

15.6 Matrix decomposition methods

Given a data matrix $\mathbf{X}$ for which each column represents a datapoint, an approximate matrix decomposition is of the form $\mathbf{X} \approx \mathbf{B}\mathbf{Y}$ into a basis matrix $\mathbf{B}$ and weight (or coordinate) matrix $\mathbf{Y}$. Symbolically, matrix decompositions are of the form

$$\underbrace{\Bigg(\quad X : \text{Data} \quad \Bigg)}_{D\times N} \approx \underbrace{\Bigg(\; B : \text{Basis} \; \Bigg)}_{D\times M} \underbrace{\bigg(\quad Y : \text{Weights/Components} \quad \bigg)}_{M\times N}. \tag{15.6.1}$$

By considering the SVD of the data matrix, we see that PCA is in this class. In this section we will consider some further common matrix decomposition methods. The form of the decomposition we have previously considered has been under-complete, although over-complete decompositions are also of interest, as described below.

Under-complete decompositions

When $M < D$, there are fewer basis vectors than dimensions, Fig. 15.12(a). The matrix $\mathbf{B}$ is then called 'tall' or 'thin'. In this case the matrix $\mathbf{Y}$ forms a lower-dimensional approximate representation of the data $\mathbf{X}$, PCA being a classic example.

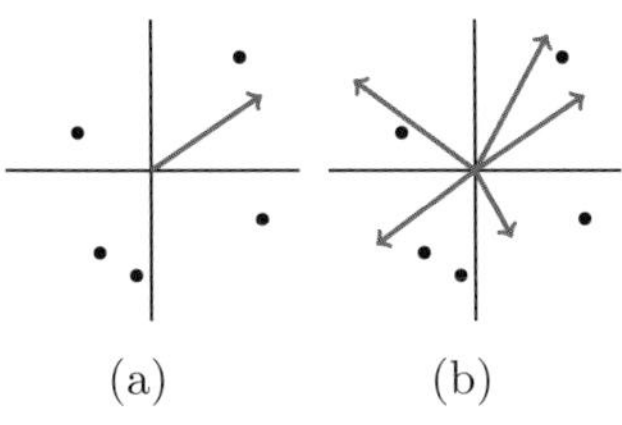

Figure 15.12 (**a**) Under-complete representation. There are too few basis vectors to represent the datapoints exactly. (**b**) Over-complete representation. There are too many basis vectors to form a unique representation of a datapoint in terms of a linear combination of the basis vectors.

Over-complete decompositions

For $M > D$ the basis is over-complete, there being more basis vectors than dimensions, Fig. 15.12(b). In such cases additional constraints are placed on either the basis or components. For example, one might require that only a small number of the large number of available basis vectors is used to form the representation for any given $\mathbf{x}$. Other popular constraints are that the basis vectors themselves should be sparse. Such sparse-representations are common in theoretical neurobiology where issues of energy efficiency, rapidity of processing and robustness are of interest [230, 168, 268].

Below we discuss some popular constrained matrix factorisation methods, in particular including positivity constraints on both the basis vectors and the components.

15.6.1 Probabilistic latent semantic analysis

Consider two objects, x and y, where $\mathrm{dom}(x) = \{1, \ldots, I\}$, $\mathrm{dom}(y) = \{1, \ldots, J\}$ and a dataset $\{(x^n, y^n), n = 1, \ldots, N\}$. We have a count matrix with elements C_{ij} which describes the number of times the joint state $x = i, y = j$ was observed in the dataset. We can transform this count matrix into a frequency matrix p with elements

$$p(x = i, y = j) = \frac{C_{ij}}{\sum_{ij} C_{ij}}. \tag{15.6.2}$$

Our interest is to find a decomposition of this frequency matrix of the form in Fig. 15.13(a)

$$\underbrace{p(x = i, y = j)}_{X_{ij}} \approx \sum_k \underbrace{\tilde{p}(x = i|z = k)}_{B_{ik}} \underbrace{\tilde{p}(y = j|z = k)\tilde{p}(z = k)}_{Y_{kj}} \equiv \tilde{p}(x = i, y = j) \tag{15.6.3}$$

where all quantities $\tilde{p}$ are distributions. This is then a form of matrix decomposition into a positive basis $\mathbf{B}$ and positive coordinates $\mathbf{Y}$. This has the interpretation of discovering latent features/topics z that describe the joint behaviour of x and y. After training, the term $\tilde{p}(z)$ can be used to rank the basis vectors or 'topics' (the columns on $\mathbf{B}$) in terms of importance, if desired. Note that PLSA is not a sequential solver in the sense that the optimal two basis vectors solution is not generally equivalent to the taking the highest ranked (according to $\tilde{p}(z)$) columns of the three basis vector solution – see Fig. 15.14.

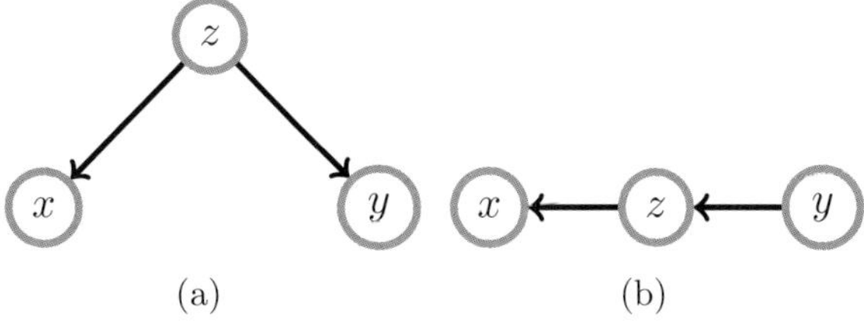

Figure 15.13 (**a**) Joint PLSA. (**b**) Conditional PLSA.

An EM-style training algorithm

In order to find the approximate decomposition we first need a measure of difference between the matrix with elements p_{ij} and the approximation with elements $\tilde{p}_{ij}$. Since all elements are bounded between 0 and 1 and sum to 1, we may interpret p as a joint probability and $\tilde{p}$ as an approximation to this. For probabilities, a useful measure of discrepancy is the Kullback–Leibler divergence

$$\mathrm{KL}(p|\tilde{p}) = \langle \log p \rangle_p - \langle \log \tilde{p} \rangle_p. \tag{15.6.4}$$

Since p is fixed, minimising the Kullback–Leibler divergence with respect to the approximation $\tilde{p}$ is equivalent to maximising the 'likelihood' term $\langle \log \tilde{p} \rangle_p$. This is

$$\sum_{x,y} p(x, y) \log \tilde{p}(x, y). \tag{15.6.5}$$

where $\sum_z$ implies summation over all states of the variable z. It's convenient to derive an EM-style algorithm to learn $\tilde{p}(x|z)$, $\tilde{p}(y|z)$ and $\tilde{p}(z)$. To do this, consider

$$\mathrm{KL}(q(z|x, y)|\tilde{p}(z|x, y)) = \sum_z q(z|x, y) \log q(z|x, y) - \sum_z q(z|x, y) \log \tilde{p}(z|x, y) \geq 0. \tag{15.6.6}$$

Using

$$\tilde{p}(z|x, y) = \frac{\tilde{p}(x, y, z)}{\tilde{p}(x, y)} \tag{15.6.7}$$

and rearranging, this gives the bound,

$$\log \tilde{p}(x, y) \geq -\sum_z q(z|x, y) \log q(z|x, y) + \sum_z q(z|x, y) \log \tilde{p}(z, x, y). \tag{15.6.8}$$

Plugging this into the 'likelihood' term above, we have the bound

$$\begin{aligned}\sum_{x,y} p(x, y) \log \tilde{p}(x, y) \geq & -\sum_{x,y} p(x, y) \sum_z q(z|x, y) \log q(z|x, y) \\ & + \sum_{x,y} p(x, y) \sum_z q(z|x, y) \left[\log \tilde{p}(x|z) + \log \tilde{p}(y|z) + \log \tilde{p}(z)\right].\end{aligned} \tag{15.6.9}$$

M-step

For fixed $\tilde{p}(x|z)$, $\tilde{p}(y|z)$, the contribution to the bound from $\tilde{p}(z)$ is

$$\sum_{x,y} p(x, y) \sum_z q(z|x, y) \log \tilde{p}(z). \tag{15.6.10}$$

It is straightforward to see that the optimal setting of $\tilde{p}(z)$ is

$$\tilde{p}(z) = \sum_{x,y} q(z|x, y) p(x, y) \tag{15.6.11}$$

since Equation (15.6.10) is, up to a constant, $\mathrm{KL}\left(\sum_{x,y} q(z|x, y) p(x, y) | \tilde{p}(z)\right)$. Similarly, for fixed $\tilde{p}(y|z)$, $\tilde{p}(z)$, the contribution to the bound from $\tilde{p}(x|z)$ is

$$\sum_{x,y} p(x, y) \sum_z q(z|x, y) \log \tilde{p}(y|z). \tag{15.6.12}$$

Algorithm 15.2 PLSA: Given a frequency matrix $p(x = i, y = j)$, return a decomposition $\sum_k \tilde{p}(x = i|z = k)\tilde{p}(y = j|z = k)\tilde{p}(z = k)$. See `plsa.m`.

Initialise $\tilde{p}(z)$, $\tilde{p}(x|z)$, $\tilde{p}(y|z)$.
while Not Converged **do**
    Set $q(z|x, y) = \tilde{p}(z|x, y)$ ▷ E-step
    Set $\tilde{p}(x|z) \propto \sum_y p(x, y)q(z|x, y)$ ▷ M-steps
    Set $\tilde{p}(y|z) \propto \sum_x p(x, y)q(z|x, y)$
end while
Set $\tilde{p}(z) = \sum_{x,y} p(x, y)q(z|x, y)$.

Therefore, optimally

$$\tilde{p}(x|z) \propto \sum_y p(x, y)q(z|x, y) \tag{15.6.13}$$

and similarly,

$$\tilde{p}(y|z) \propto \sum_x p(x, y)q(z|x, y). \tag{15.6.14}$$

E-step

The optimal setting for the q distribution at each iteration is

$$q(z|x, y) = \tilde{p}(z|x, y) \tag{15.6.15}$$

which is fixed throughout the M-step.

The 'likelihood' equation (15.6.5) is guaranteed to increase (and the Kullback–Leibler divergence equation (15.6.4) decrease) under iterating between the E- and M-steps, since the method is analogous to an EM procedure. The procedure is given in Algorithm 15.2 and a demonstration is in `demoPLSA.m`. Generalisations, such as using simpler q distributions, (corresponding to generalised EM procedures) are immediate based on modifying the above derivation.

Algorithm 15.3 Conditional PLSA: Given a frequency matrix $p(x = i|y = j)$, return a decomposition $\sum_k \tilde{p}(x = i|z = k)\tilde{p}(z = k|y = j)$. See `plsaCond.m`.

Initialise $\tilde{p}(x|z)$, $\tilde{p}(z|y)$.
while Not Converged **do**
    Set $q(z|x, y) = \tilde{p}(z|x, y)$ ▷ E-step
    Set $\tilde{p}(x|z) \propto \sum_y p(x|y)q(z|x, y)$ ▷ M-steps
    Set $\tilde{p}(z|y) \propto \sum_x p(x|y)q(z|x, y)$
end while

Example 15.6 PLSA for documents

We repeated the analysis of the toy document data in Fig. 15.8, now using PLSA. As we see from Fig. 15.14, the basis found is interpretable and intuitive. Also, the 'projections' onto these basis

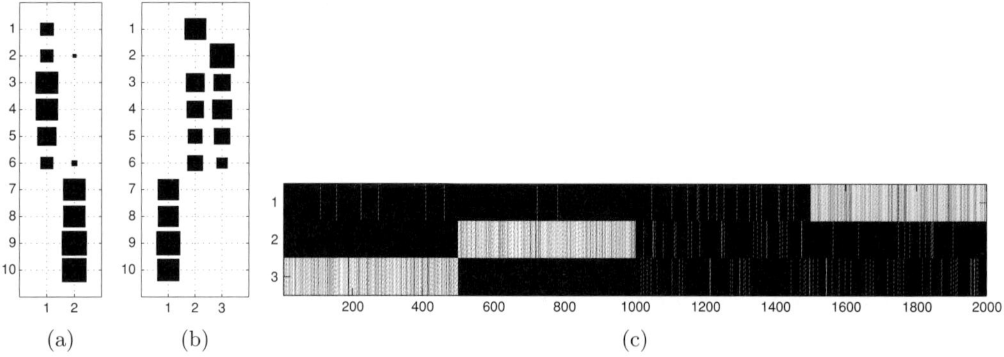

Figure 15.14 PLSA for the document data in Fig. 15.8. (**a**) Hinton diagram for two basis vectors. (**b**) Hinton diagram for three basis vectors. (**c**) The projections for the three basis vectors case. The solution is quite satisfactory since the first 1000 documents are clearly considered to be from the similar 'ailments' topics, the next 500 from some other non-specific 'background' topic, and the last 500 from a separate 'pet' topic.

vectors is also reasonable, and corresponds to what we would expect. The limited expressibility of the two-basis model causes the two 'influenza' and 'flu' terms to be placed in the same basis vector and each basis vector clearly represents two non-overlapping topics. Note that there is no requirement in general for the topics to be non-overlapping; this just happens to be the case for this example only. For the richer three-basis vector model, the model distinguishes clearly two similar topics, differing in only a single word.

Conditional PLSA

In some cases it is more natural to consider a conditional frequency matrix

$$p(x = i|y = j) \tag{15.6.16}$$

and seek an approximate decomposition

$$\underbrace{p(x = i|y = j)}_{X_{ij}} \approx \sum_k \underbrace{\tilde{p}(x = i|z = k)}_{B_{ik}} \underbrace{\tilde{p}(z = k|y = j)}_{Y_{kj}} \tag{15.6.17}$$

as depicted in Fig. 15.13(b). Deriving an EM-style algorithm for this is straightforward, Exercise 15.9, and is presented in Algorithm 15.3.

Example 15.7 Discovering the basis

A set of images is given in Fig. 15.15(a). These were created by first defining four base images Fig. 15.15(b). Each base image is positive and scaled so that the sum of the pixels is unity, $\sum_i p(x = i|z = k) = 1$, where $k = 1, \ldots, 4$ and x indexes the pixels, see Fig. 15.15. We then summed each of these images using a randomly chosen positive set of four weights (under the constraint that the weights sum to 1) to generate a training image with elements $p(x = i|y = j)$ and j indexes the training image. This was repeated 144 times to form the full train set, Fig. 15.15(a). The task is, given only the training set images, to reconstruct the basis from which the images were formed. We assume that we know the correct number of base images, namely four. The results of using

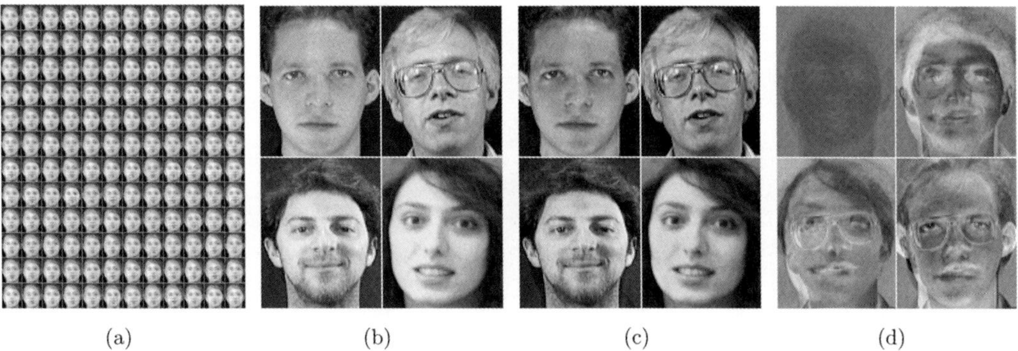

(a) (b) (c) (d)

Figure 15.15 (**a**) Training data, consisting of a positive (convex) combination of the base images. (**b**) The chosen base images from which the training data is derived. (**c**) Basis learned using conditional PLSA on the training data. This is virtually indistinguishable from the true basis. (**d**) Eigenbasis (sometimes called 'eigenfaces').

conditional PLSA on this task are presented in Fig. 15.15(c) and using SVD in Fig. 15.15(d). In this case PLSA finds the correct 'natural' basis, corresponding to the way the images were generated. The eigenbasis is better in terms of mean squared reconstruction error of the training images, but in this case does not correspond to the constraints under which the data was generated.

Example 15.8 Eigenfaces verus PLSA faces

We return to Example 15.2 and now rerun the experiment, seeking a PLSA basis, rather than an eigenbases. In Fig. 15.16 we show the reconstruction of the original 100 images and the corresponding PLSA basis. The reconstruction error is necessarily higher for the PLSA solution since the optimal mean squared error solution is given by PCA (PLSA has more constraints on the form of the solution than PCA). However, the basis found by PLSA is arguably more interpretable since the positive features are positively summed to produce an image. Because of this, the PLSA basis vectors tend to be rather sparse.

15.6.2 Extensions and variations

A fully probabilistic interpretation of PLSA can be made via Poisson processes [58]. A related probabilistic model is Latent Dirichlet Allocation, which is described in Section 20.6.1.

Non-negative matrix factorisation

Non-negative Matrix Factorisation (NMF) considers a decomposition in which both the basis and weight matrices have non-negative entries; this can be considered as constrained factor analysis [233]. Closely related works are [185] which is a generalisation of PLSA (with no requirement that the basis or components sum to unity). In all cases EM-style training algorithms exist, although their convergence can be slow. We will encounter similar models in the discussion on Independent Component Analysis, Section 21.6.

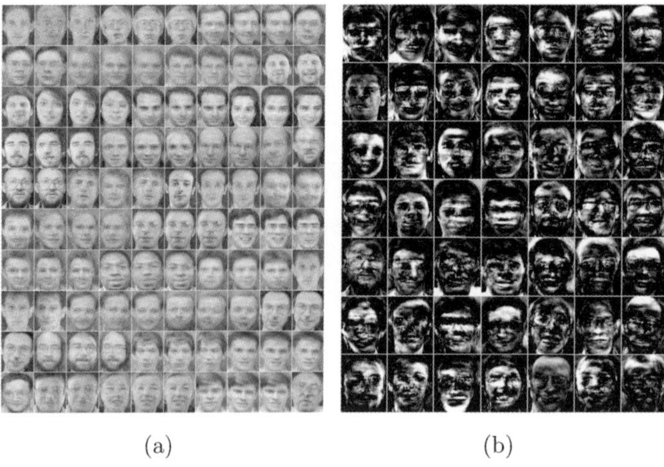

Figure 15.16 (**a**) Conditional PLSA reconstruction of the images in Fig. 15.5 using a positive convex combination of the 49 positive base images in (**b**). The root mean square reconstruction error is 1.391×10^{-5}. The base images tend to be more 'localised' than the corresponding eigen-images Fig. 15.6(b). Here one sees local structure such as foreheads, chins, etc.

Gradient-based training

Expectation maximisation style algorithms are easy to derive and implement but can exhibit poor convergence. Gradient-based methods to simultaneously optimise with respect to the basis and the components have been developed, but require a parameterisation that ensures positivity of the solutions [233].

Array decompositions

It is straightforward to extend PLSA to the decomposition of multidimensional arrays. For example

$$p(s, t, u) \approx \sum_{v,w} \tilde{p}(s, t, u|v, w)\tilde{p}(v, w) = \sum_{v,w} \tilde{p}(s, t|u, v)\tilde{p}(u|w)\tilde{p}(v)\tilde{p}(w). \tag{15.6.18}$$

Such extensions require only additional bookkeeping.

15.6.3 Applications of PLSA/NMF

Modelling citations

We have a collection of research documents which cite other documents. For example, document 1 might cite documents 3, 2, 10, etc. Given only the list of citations for each document, can we identify key research papers and the communities that cite them? Note that this is not the same question as finding the most cited documents – rather we want to identify documents with communities and find their relevance for a community.

We use the variable $d \in \{1, \dots, D\}$ to index documents and $c \in \{1, \dots, D\}$ to index citations (both d and c have the same domain, namely the index of a research article). If document $d = i$ cites article $c = j$ then we set the entry of the matrix $C_{ij} = 1$. If there is no citation, C_{ij} is set to zero. We can form a 'distribution' over documents and citations using

$$p(d = i, c = j) = \frac{C_{ij}}{\sum_{ij} C_{ij}} \tag{15.6.19}$$

and use PLSA to decompose this matrix into citation-topics, see the example below.

Table 15.1 Highest ranked documents according to $p(c|z)$. The factor topic labels are manual assignments based on similarity to the Cora topics. Reproduced from [66].

factor 1	(Reinforcement Learning)
0.0108	Learning to predict by the methods of temporal differences. Sutton.
0.0066	Neuronlike adaptive elements that can solve difficult learning control problems. Barto *et al.*
0.0065	Practical Issues in Temporal Difference Learning. Tesauro.
factor 2	(Rule Learning)
0.0038	Explanation-based generalization: a unifying view. Mitchell *et al.*
0.0037	Learning internal representations by error propagation. Rumelhart *et al.*
0.0036	Explanation-Based Learning: An Alternative View. DeJong *et al.*
factor 3	(Neural Networks)
0.0120	Learning internal representations by error propagation. Rumelhart *et al.*
0.0061	Neural networks and the bias-variance dilemma. Geman *et al.*
0.0049	The Cascade-Correlation learning architecture. Fahlman *et al.*
factor 4	(Theory)
0.0093	Classification and Regression Trees. Breiman *et al.*
0.0066	Learnability and the Vapnik-Chervonenkis dimension. Blumer *et al.*
0.0055	Learning Quickly when Irrelevant Attributes Abound. Littlestone.
factor 5	(Probabilistic Reasoning)
0.0118	Probabilistic Reasoning in Intelligent Systems: Networks of Plausible Inference. Pearl.
0.0094	Maximum likelihood from incomplete data via the em algorithm. Dempster *et al.*
0.0056	Local computations with probabilities on graphical structures. Lauritzen *et al.*
factor 6	(Genetic Algorithms)
0.0157	Genetic Algorithms in Search, Optimization, and Machine Learning. Goldberg.
0.0132	Adaptation in Natural and Artificial Systems. Holland.
0.0096	Genetic Programming: On the Programming of Computers by Means of Natural Selection. Koza.
factor 7	(Logic)
0.0063	Efficient induction of logic programs. Muggleton *et al.*
0.0054	Learning logical definitions from relations. Quinlan.
0.0033	Inductive Logic Programming Techniques and Applications. Lavrac *et al.*

Example 15.9 Modelling citations

The Cora corpus [201] contains an archive of around 30 000 computer science research papers. From this archive the authors in [66] extracted the papers in the machine learning category, consisting of 4220 documents and 38 372 citations. Using these the distribution equation (15.6.19) was formed. The documents have additionally been categorised by hand into seven topics: *Case-based reasoning, Genetic Algorithms, Neural Networks, Probabilistic methods, Reinforcement Learning, Rule Learning and Theory*. In [66] the joint PLSA method is fitted to the data using $\dim(z) = 7$ topics. From the trained model the expression $p(c = j|z = k)$ defines how authoritative paper j is according to community $z = k$. The method discovers intuitively meaningful topics, as presented in Table 15.1.

Modelling the web

Consider a collection of websites, indexed by i. If website j points to website i, set $C_{ij} = 1$, otherwise set $C_{ij} = 0$. This gives a directed graph of website-to-website links. Since a website will discuss usually only a small number of 'topics' we might be able to explain why there is a link between two websites using a PLSA decomposition. These algorithms have proved useful for Internet search for example to determine the latent topics of websites and identify the most authoritative websites. See [67] for a discussion.

Physical models

Non-negative decompositions can arise naturally in physical situations. For example, in acoustics, positive amounts of energy combine linearly from different signal sources to form the observed signal. If we consider that two kinds of signals are present in an acoustic signal, say a piano and a singer then using NMF one can learn two separate bases, one for each 'instrument', and then reconstruct a given signal using only one of the bases. This means that one could potentially remove the singer from a recording, leaving only the piano. This is analogous to reconstructing the images in Fig. 15.15(a) using say only one of the learned basis images, see Example 15.7. See [305] for a related model in acoustics.

15.7 Kernel PCA

Kernel PCA is a non-linear extension of PCA designed to discover non-linear subspace. Here we only briefly describe the approach and refer the reader to [259] for details. In kernel PCA, we replace each $\mathbf{x}$ by a 'feature' vector $\tilde{\mathbf{x}} \equiv \boldsymbol{\phi}(\mathbf{x})$. Note that the use of $\tilde{\mathbf{x}}$ here does not have the interpretation we used before as the approximate reconstruction. Rather, the *feature map* $\boldsymbol{\phi}$ takes a vector $\mathbf{x}$ and produces a higher-dimensional vector $\tilde{\mathbf{x}}$. For example we could map a two-dimensional vector $\mathbf{x} = [x_1, x_2]^{\mathsf{T}}$ using

$$\boldsymbol{\phi}(\mathbf{x}) = \left[x_1, x_2, x_1^2, x_2^2, x_1x_2, x_1^3, \ldots\right]^{\mathsf{T}}. \tag{15.7.1}$$

The idea is then to perform PCA on these higher-dimensional feature vectors, subsequently mapping back the eigenvectors to the original space $\mathbf{x}$. The main challenge is to write this without explicitly computing PCA in the potentially very high dimensional feature vector space. As a reminder, in standard PCA, for zero mean data, one forms an eigen-decomposition of the sample matrix[5]

$$\mathbf{S} = \frac{1}{N}\tilde{\mathbf{X}}\tilde{\mathbf{X}}^{\mathsf{T}}. \tag{15.7.2}$$

For simplicity, we concentrate here on finding the first principal component $\tilde{\mathbf{e}}$ which satisfies

$$\tilde{\mathbf{X}}\tilde{\mathbf{X}}^{\mathsf{T}}\tilde{\mathbf{e}} = \lambda'\tilde{\mathbf{e}} \tag{15.7.3}$$

for corresponding eigenvalue λ (writing $\lambda' = N\lambda$). The 'dual' representation is obtained by pre-multiplying by $\tilde{\mathbf{X}}^{\mathsf{T}}$, so that in terms of $\tilde{\mathbf{f}} \equiv \tilde{\mathbf{X}}^{\mathsf{T}}\tilde{\mathbf{e}}$, the standard PCA eigen-problem reduces to solving:

$$\tilde{\mathbf{X}}^{\mathsf{T}}\tilde{\mathbf{X}}\tilde{\mathbf{f}} = \lambda'\tilde{\mathbf{f}}. \tag{15.7.4}$$

The feature eigenvector $\tilde{\mathbf{e}}$ is then recovered using

$$\tilde{\mathbf{X}}\tilde{\mathbf{f}} = \lambda'\tilde{\mathbf{e}}. \tag{15.7.5}$$

We note that matrix $\tilde{\mathbf{X}}^{\mathsf{T}}\tilde{\mathbf{X}}$ has elements

$$\left[\tilde{\mathbf{X}}^{\mathsf{T}}\tilde{\mathbf{X}}\right]_{mn} = \boldsymbol{\phi}(\mathbf{x}^m)^{\mathsf{T}}\boldsymbol{\phi}(\mathbf{x}^n) \tag{15.7.6}$$

[5] We use the normalisation N as opposed to $N-1$ just for notational convenience – in practice, there is little difference.

and recognise this as the scalar product between vectors. This means that the matrix is positive semidefinite and we may equivalently use a covariance function kernel, see Section 19.3,

$$\left[\tilde{\mathbf{X}}^{\mathsf{T}}\tilde{\mathbf{X}}\right]_{mn} = k(\mathbf{x}^m, \mathbf{x}^n) = K_{mn}. \tag{15.7.7}$$

Then Equation (15.7.4) can be written as

$$\mathbf{K}\tilde{\mathbf{f}} = \lambda'\tilde{\mathbf{f}}. \tag{15.7.8}$$

One then solves this eigen-equation to find the N-dimensional principal dual feature vector $\tilde{\mathbf{f}}$. The projection of the feature $\tilde{\mathbf{x}}$ is given by

$$y = \tilde{\mathbf{x}}^{\mathsf{T}}\tilde{\mathbf{e}} = \frac{1}{\lambda}\tilde{\mathbf{x}}^{\mathsf{T}}\tilde{\mathbf{X}}\tilde{\mathbf{f}}. \tag{15.7.9}$$

More generally, for a larger number of components, the ith kernel PCA projection y_i can be expressed in terms of the kernel directly as

$$y_i = \frac{1}{N\lambda^i}\sum_{n=1}^{N} k(\mathbf{x}, \mathbf{x}^n)\tilde{f}_n^i \tag{15.7.10}$$

where i is the eigenvalue label and $\tilde{f}_n^i$ is the nth component of the ith eigenvector of $\mathbf{K}$.

The above derivation implicitly assumed zero mean features $\tilde{\mathbf{x}}$. Even if the original data $\mathbf{x}$ is zero mean, due to the non-linear mapping, however, the features may not be zero mean. To correct for this one may show that the only modification required is to replace the matrix $\mathbf{K}$ in Equation (15.7.8) above with

$$K'_{mn} = k(\mathbf{x}^m, \mathbf{x}^n) - \frac{1}{N}\sum_{d=1}^{N} k(\mathbf{x}^d, \mathbf{x}^n) - \frac{1}{N}\sum_{d=1}^{N} k(\mathbf{x}^m, \mathbf{x}^d) + \frac{1}{N^2}\sum_{d=1,d'=1}^{N} k(\mathbf{x}^{d'}, \mathbf{x}^d). \tag{15.7.11}$$

Finding the reconstructions

Through Equation (15.7.10), the above gives a procedure for finding the KPCA projection $\mathbf{y}$. However, in many cases we would also like to have an approximate reconstruction $\mathbf{x}'$ using the lower-dimensional $\mathbf{y}$. This is not straightforward since the mapping from $\mathbf{y}$ to $\mathbf{x}$ is in general highly non-linear. Here we outline a procedure for achieving this. First we find the reconstruction $\tilde{\mathbf{x}}^*$ of the feature space vector $\tilde{\mathbf{x}}$, using

$$\tilde{\mathbf{x}}^* = \sum_i y_i \tilde{\mathbf{e}}^i = \sum_i y_i \frac{1}{\lambda_i}\sum_n \tilde{f}_i^n \boldsymbol{\phi}(\mathbf{x}^n). \tag{15.7.12}$$

Given $\tilde{\mathbf{x}}^*$ we try to find that point $\mathbf{x}'$ in the original data space that maps to $\tilde{\mathbf{x}}^*$. This can be found by minimising

$$E(\mathbf{x}') = \left(\boldsymbol{\phi}(\mathbf{x}') - \tilde{\mathbf{x}}^*\right)^2. \tag{15.7.13}$$

Up to negligible constants this is

$$E(\mathbf{x}') = k(\mathbf{x}', \mathbf{x}') - 2\sum_i \frac{y_i}{\lambda_i}\sum_n \tilde{f}_i^n k(\mathbf{x}^n, \mathbf{x}'). \tag{15.7.14}$$

One then finds $\mathbf{x}'$ by minimising $E(\mathbf{x}')$ numerically. The resulting procedure gives a way to form a non-linear extension of PCA; however it is computationally relatively demanding and results in a complex optimisation problem. See [259] for details and example applications.

15.8 Canonical correlation analysis

Consider variables $\mathbf{x}$ and $\mathbf{y}$ being 'different views' of the same underlying object. For example $\mathbf{x}$ might represent a segment of video and $\mathbf{y}$ the corresponding audio. Given then a collection $\{(\mathbf{x}^n, \mathbf{y}^n), n = 1, \ldots, N\}$, an interesting challenge is to identify which parts of the audio and video are strongly correlated. One might expect, for example, that the mouth region of the video is strongly correlated with the audio.

One way to achieve this is to project each $\mathbf{x}$ and $\mathbf{y}$ to one dimension using $\mathbf{a}^\mathsf{T}\mathbf{x}$ and $\mathbf{b}^\mathsf{T}\mathbf{y}$ such that the correlation between the projections is maximal. The unnormalised correlation between the projections $\mathbf{a}^\mathsf{T}\mathbf{x}$ and $\mathbf{b}^\mathsf{T}\mathbf{y}$ is

$$\sum_n \mathbf{a}^\mathsf{T}\mathbf{x}^n\mathbf{b}^\mathsf{T}\mathbf{y}^n = \mathbf{a}^\mathsf{T}\left[\sum_n \mathbf{x}^n\mathbf{y}^{n\mathsf{T}}\right]\mathbf{b}. \tag{15.8.1}$$

Defining

$$\mathbf{S}_{xy} \equiv \frac{1}{N}\sum_n \mathbf{x}^n\mathbf{y}^{n\mathsf{T}} \tag{15.8.2}$$

and similarly for $\mathbf{S}_{yx}$, $\mathbf{S}_{xx}$, $\mathbf{S}_{yy}$, the normalised correlation is

$$\frac{\mathbf{a}^\mathsf{T}\mathbf{S}_{xy}\mathbf{b}}{\sqrt{\mathbf{a}^\mathsf{T}\mathbf{S}_{xx}\mathbf{a}}\sqrt{\mathbf{b}^\mathsf{T}\mathbf{S}_{yy}.\mathbf{b}}}. \tag{15.8.3}$$

Since Equation (15.8.3) is invariant with respect to rescaling $\mathbf{a}$ and also $\mathbf{b}$, we can consider the equivalent objective

$$E(\mathbf{a}, \mathbf{b}) = \mathbf{a}^\mathsf{T}\mathbf{S}_{xy}\mathbf{b} \tag{15.8.4}$$

subject to $\mathbf{a}^\mathsf{T}\mathbf{S}_{xx}\mathbf{a} = 1$ and $\mathbf{b}^\mathsf{T}\mathbf{S}_{yy}\mathbf{b} = 1$. To find the optimal projections $\mathbf{a}$, $\mathbf{b}$, under the constraints, we use the Lagrangian,

$$\mathcal{L}(\mathbf{a}, \mathbf{b}, \lambda_a, \lambda_b) \equiv \mathbf{a}^\mathsf{T}\mathbf{S}_{xy}\mathbf{b} + \frac{\lambda_a}{2}\left(1 - \mathbf{a}^\mathsf{T}\mathbf{S}_{xx}\mathbf{a}\right) + \frac{\lambda_b}{2}\left(1 - \mathbf{b}^\mathsf{T}\mathbf{S}_{yy}\mathbf{b}\right) \tag{15.8.5}$$

from which we obtain the zero derivative criteria

$$\mathbf{S}_{xy}\mathbf{b} = \lambda_a\mathbf{S}_{xx}\mathbf{a}, \qquad \mathbf{S}_{yx}\mathbf{a} = \lambda_b\mathbf{S}_{yy}\mathbf{b}. \tag{15.8.6}$$

Hence

$$\mathbf{a}^\mathsf{T}\mathbf{S}_{xy}\mathbf{b} = \lambda_a\mathbf{a}^\mathsf{T}\mathbf{S}_{xx}\mathbf{a} = \lambda_a, \qquad \mathbf{b}^\mathsf{T}\mathbf{S}_{yx}\mathbf{a} = \lambda_b\mathbf{b}^\mathsf{T}\mathbf{S}_{yy}\mathbf{b} = \lambda_b. \tag{15.8.7}$$

Since $\mathbf{a}^\mathsf{T}\mathbf{S}_{xy}\mathbf{b} = \mathbf{b}^\mathsf{T}\mathbf{S}_{yx}\mathbf{a}$ we must have $\lambda_a = \lambda_b = \lambda$ at the optimum. If we assume that $\mathbf{S}_{yy}$ is invertible we can write,

$$\mathbf{b} = \frac{1}{\lambda}\mathbf{S}_{yy}^{-1}\mathbf{S}_{yx}\mathbf{a} \tag{15.8.8}$$

and use this to eliminate $\mathbf{b}$ in Equation (15.8.6), giving

$$\mathbf{S}_{xy}\mathbf{S}_{yy}^{-1}\mathbf{S}_{yx}\mathbf{a} = \lambda^2\mathbf{S}_{xx}\mathbf{a} \tag{15.8.9}$$

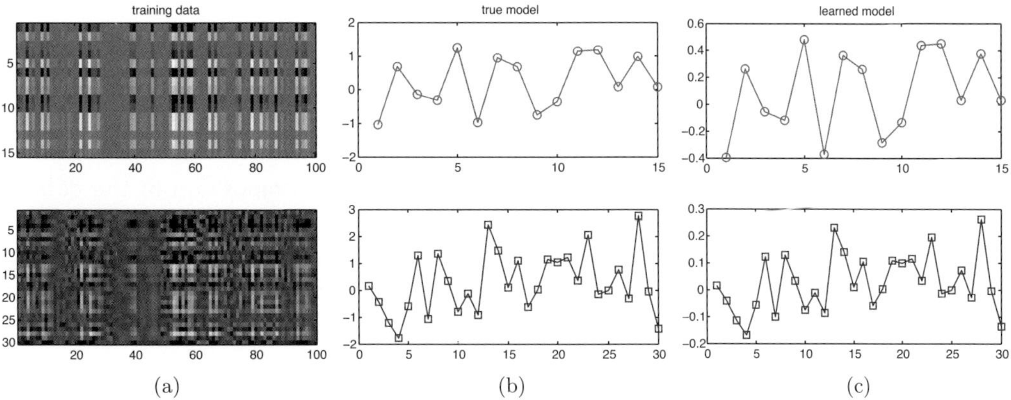

Figure 15.17 Canonical Correlation Analysis (CCA). (**a**) Training data. The top panel contains the **X** matrix of 100, 15-dimensional points, and the bottom the corresponding 30-dimensional **Y** matrix. (**b**) The data in (a) was produced using $\mathbf{X} = \mathbf{Ah}$, $\mathbf{Y} = \mathbf{Bh}$ where **A** is a 15×1 matrix, and **B** is a 30×1 matrix. The underlying latent **h** is a 1×100 dimensional randomly chosen vector. (**c**) Matrices **A** and **B** learned by CCA. Note that they are close to the true **A** and **B** up to rescaling and sign changes. See `demoCCA.m`.

which is a generalised eigen-problem. Assuming that $\mathbf{S}_{xx}$ is invertible we can equivalently write

$$\mathbf{S}_{xx}^{-1}\mathbf{S}_{xy}\mathbf{S}_{yy}^{-1}\mathbf{S}_{yx}\mathbf{a} = \lambda^2\mathbf{a} \tag{15.8.10}$$

which is a standard eigen-problem (albeit with λ^2 as the eigenvalue). Once this is solved we can find **b** using Equation (15.8.8).

15.8.1 SVD formulation

It is straightforward to show that we can find **a** (the optimal projection of **x**) by first computing the SVD of

$$\mathbf{S}_{xx}^{-\frac{1}{2}}\mathbf{S}_{xy}\mathbf{S}_{yy}^{-\frac{1}{2}} \tag{15.8.11}$$

in the form $\mathbf{UDV}^\mathsf{T}$ and extracting the maximal singular vector $\mathbf{u}_1$ of **U** (the first column of **U**). Then **a** is optimally $\mathbf{S}_{xx}^{-\frac{1}{2}}\mathbf{u}_1$, and similarly, **b** is optimally $\mathbf{S}_{yy}^{-\frac{1}{2}}\mathbf{v}_1$, where $\mathbf{v}_1$ is the first column of **V**. In this way, the extension to finding M multiple directions $\mathbf{A} = \left[\mathbf{a}^1, \ldots, \mathbf{a}^M\right]$ and $\mathbf{B} = \left[\mathbf{b}^1, \ldots, \mathbf{b}^M\right]$ is clear – one takes the corresponding first M singular values accordingly. Doing so maximises the criterion

$$\frac{\operatorname{trace}\left(\mathbf{A}^\mathsf{T}\mathbf{S}_{xy}\mathbf{B}\right)}{\sqrt{\operatorname{trace}\left(\mathbf{A}^\mathsf{T}\mathbf{S}_{xx}\mathbf{A}\right)}\sqrt{\operatorname{trace}\left(\mathbf{B}^\mathsf{T}\mathbf{S}_{yy}\mathbf{B}\right)}}. \tag{15.8.12}$$

This approach is taken in `cca.m` – see Fig. 15.17 for a demonstration. One can also show that CCA corresponds to factor analysis under a block restriction on the form of the factor loadings, see Section 21.2.1.

Canonical correlation analysis and related kernel extensions have been applied in machine learning contexts, for example to model the correlation between images and text in order to improve image retrieval from text queries, see [138].

15.9 Summary

- Principal components analysis is a classical linear dimension reduction method and assumes that the data lies close to a linear subspace.
- The PCA representation can be found by an eigen-decomposition of the data covariance matrix, or alternatively using an SVD decomposition of the data matrix.
- More generally, PCA is special case of a matrix decomposition method. Other standard methods include PLSA and non-negative matrix factorisation, which can be considered as constrained forms of PCA (positivity constraints).
- Canonical correlation analysis attempts to find a low-dimensional representation that jointly models the two related data spaces. Canonical correlation analysis is a special case of the probabilistic factor analysis model.

Principal components analysis appears in many different research communities and can be referred to differently. For example it is also known as the Karhunen–Loève decomposition and proper orthogonal decomposition.

Another important use for dimension reduction is in data visualisation. Methods such as PCA can be used in this context, though are not designed to produce visually interpretable results. See [252] and [300] for discussions of work in this area.

15.10 Code

`pca.m`: Principal components analysis
`demoLSI.m`: Demo of latent semantic indexing/analysis
`svdm.m`: Singular value decomposition with missing data
`demoSVDmissing.m`: Demo SVD with missing data
`plsa.m`: Probabilistic latent semantic analysis
`plsaCond.m`: Conditional probabilistic latent semantic analysis
`demoPLSA.m`: Demo of PLSA
`cca.m`: Canonical correlation analysis (CCA)
`demoCCA.m`: Demo of canonical correlation analysis

15.11 Exercises

15.1 As described in Section 15.2, we wish to show that the optimal bias $\mathbf{c}$ is equal to the sample mean of the data.

1. Explain why, when considering a bias $\mathbf{c}$, and carrying out the derivation in Section 15.2.1, we will obtain, analogously to Equation (15.2.1):

$$E(\mathbf{B}, \mathbf{c}) = \sum_n (\mathbf{x}^n - \mathbf{c})^{\mathsf{T}} \left(\mathbf{I} - \mathbf{B}\mathbf{B}^{\mathsf{T}}\right) (\mathbf{x}^n - \mathbf{c}). \tag{15.11.1}$$

2. Show that for a matrix $\mathbf{M}$

$$\frac{\partial}{\partial \mathbf{c}} \mathbf{c}^{\mathsf{T}}\mathbf{M}\mathbf{c} = \mathbf{M}\mathbf{c} + \mathbf{M}^{\mathsf{T}}\mathbf{c}. \tag{15.11.2}$$

3. Using this derivative result, show that the optimal bias $\mathbf{c}$ satisfies

$$\mathbf{0} = \left(\mathbf{I} - \mathbf{B}\mathbf{B}^{\mathsf{T}}\right) \sum_n (\mathbf{x}^n - \mathbf{c}) \tag{15.11.3}$$

and hence determine that the optimal bias is given by the mean of the data, $\mathbf{c} = \sum_{n=1}^{N} \mathbf{x}^n/N$.

15.2 Consider a dataset in two dimensions where the data lies on the circumference of a circle of unit radius. What would be the effect of using PCA on this dataset, in which we attempt to reduce the dimensionality to 1? Suggest an alternative one-dimensional representation of the data.

15.3 Consider two vectors $\mathbf{x}^a$ and $\mathbf{x}^b$ and their corresponding PCA approximations $\mathbf{c} + \sum_{i=1}^{M} a_i \mathbf{e}^i$ and $\mathbf{c} + \sum_{i=1}^{M} b_i \mathbf{e}^i$, where the eigenvectors $\mathbf{e}^i, i = 1, \ldots, M$ are mutually orthogonal and have unit length. The eigenvector $\mathbf{e}^i$ has corresponding eigenvalue λ^i. Approximate $(\mathbf{x}^a - \mathbf{x}^b)^2$ by using the PCA representations of the data, and show that this is equal to $(\mathbf{a} - \mathbf{b})^2$.

15.4 Show how the solution for $\mathbf{a}$ to the CCA problem in Equation (15.8.9) can be transformed into the form expressed by Equation (15.8.11), as claimed in the text.

15.5 Let $\mathbf{S}$ be the covariance matrix of the data. The Mahalanobis distance between $\mathbf{x}^a$ and $\mathbf{x}^b$ is defined as

$$\left(\mathbf{x}^a - \mathbf{x}^b\right)^{\mathsf{T}} \mathbf{S}^{-1} \left(\mathbf{x}^a - \mathbf{x}^b\right). \tag{15.11.4}$$

Explain how to approximate this distance using M-dimensional PCA.

15.6 (PCA with external inputs) In some applications, one may suspect that certain external variables $\mathbf{v}$ have a strong influence on how the data $\mathbf{x}$ is distributed. For example, if $\mathbf{x}$ represents an image, it might be that we know the lighting condition $\mathbf{v}$ under which the image was made – this will have a large effect on the image. It would make sense therefore to include the known lighting condition in forming a lower-dimensional representation of the image. Note that we don't want to form a lower-dimensional representation of the joint $(\mathbf{x}, \mathbf{v})$, rather we want to form a lower-dimensional representation of $\mathbf{x}$ alone, bearing in mind that some of the variability observed may be due to $\mathbf{v}$. We therefore assume an approximation

$$\mathbf{x}^n \approx \sum_j y_j^n \mathbf{b}^j + \sum_k v_k^n \mathbf{c}^k \tag{15.11.5}$$

where the coefficients y_i^n, $i = 1, \ldots, N$, $n = 1, \ldots, N$, basis vectors $\mathbf{b}^j$, $j = 1, \ldots, J$ and $\mathbf{c}^k$, $k = 1, \ldots, K$ are to be determined. The external inputs $\mathbf{v}^1, \ldots, \mathbf{v}^N$ are given. The sum squared error loss between the $\mathbf{x}^n$ and their linear reconstruction Equation (15.11.5) is

$$E = \sum_{n,i} \left(x_i^n - \sum_j y_j^n b_i^j - \sum_k v_k^n c_i^k \right)^2. \tag{15.11.6}$$

Find the parameters $\left\{\mathbf{b}^j, \mathbf{c}^k\right\}$, $j = 1, \ldots, J, k = 1, \ldots, K$ that minimise E.

15.7 Consider the following three-dimensional datapoints:

$$(1.3, 1.6, 2.8)(4.3, -1.4, 5.8)(-0.6, 3.7, 0.7)(-0.4, 3.2, 5.8)(3.3, -0.4, 4.3)(-0.4, 3.1, 0.9) \tag{15.11.7}$$

Perform principal components analysis by:

1. Calculating the mean, $\mathbf{c}$, of the data.
2. Calculating the covariance matrix $S = \frac{1}{6}\sum_{n=1}^{6} \mathbf{x}^n (\mathbf{x}^n)^{\mathsf{T}} - \mathbf{c}\mathbf{c}^{\mathsf{T}}$ of the data.
3. Finding the eigenvalues and eigenvectors $\mathbf{e}_i$ of the covariance matrix.

4. You should find that only two eigenvalues are large, and therefore that the data can be well represented using two components only. Let $\mathbf{e}_1$ and $\mathbf{e}_2$ be the two eigenvectors with largest eigenvalues. Calculate the two-dimensional representation of each datapoint $(\mathbf{e}_1^\mathsf{T}(\mathbf{x}^n - \mathbf{c}), \mathbf{e}_2^\mathsf{T}(\mathbf{x}^n - \mathbf{c})), n = 1, \ldots, 6$.
5. Calculate the reconstruction of each datapoint$\mathbf{c} + (\mathbf{e}_1^\mathsf{T}(\mathbf{x}^n - \mathbf{c}))\mathbf{e}_1 + (\mathbf{e}_2^\mathsf{T}(\mathbf{x}^n - \mathbf{c}))\mathbf{e}_2, n = 1, \ldots, 6$.

15.8 Show that for the missing data case, the transformed solution $\tilde{\mathbf{B}}$ given in Equation (15.5.11) satisfies $\tilde{\mathbf{B}}^\mathsf{T}\tilde{\mathbf{B}} = \mathbf{I}$.

15.9 Consider a 'conditional frequency matrix'

$$p(x = i|y = j). \tag{15.11.8}$$

Following Section 15.6.1, show how to derive an EM-style algorithm for an approximate decomposition of this matrix in the form

$$p(x = i|y = j) \approx \sum_k \tilde{p}(x = i|z = k)\tilde{p}(z = k|y = j) \tag{15.11.9}$$

where $k = 1, \ldots, Z, i = 1, \ldots, X, j = 1, \ldots, Y$.

16 Supervised linear dimension reduction

Principal components analysis is a popular and very useful method. However, if we subsequently use the projected data in a classification problem, by not making use of the class labels of the data, we are potentially forming lower-dimensional representations that are suboptimal in terms of how well separated they are amongst the different classes. In this chapter we discuss some classical methods that reduce the data dimension such that the resulting data is well separated between the classes.

16.1 Supervised linear projections

In Chapter 15 we discussed dimension reduction using an unsupervised procedure. In cases where class information is available, and our ultimate interest is to reduce dimensionality for improved classification, it makes sense to use the available class information in forming the projection. We consider data from two different classes. For class 1, we have a set of N_1 datapoints,

$$\mathcal{X}_1 = \left\{\mathbf{x}_1^1, \ldots, \mathbf{x}_1^{N_1}\right\} \tag{16.1.1}$$

and similarly for class 2, we have a set of N_2 datapoints

$$\mathcal{X}_2 = \left\{\mathbf{x}_2^1, \ldots, \mathbf{x}_2^{N_2}\right\}. \tag{16.1.2}$$

Our interest is then to find a linear projection,

$$\mathbf{y} = \mathbf{W}^{\mathsf{T}}\mathbf{x} \tag{16.1.3}$$

where $\dim \mathbf{W} = D \times L, L < D$, such that for two datapoints $\mathbf{x}^i$ and $\mathbf{x}^j$ in the same class, the distance between their projections $\mathbf{y}^i$ and $\mathbf{y}^j$ should be small. Conversely, for datapoints in different classes, the distance between their projections should be large. This may be useful for classification purposes since for a novel point $\mathbf{x}^*$, if its projection

$$\mathbf{y}^* = \mathbf{W}^{\mathsf{T}}\mathbf{x}^* \tag{16.1.4}$$

is close to class 1 projected data, we would expect $\mathbf{x}^*$ to belong to class 1. In forming the supervised projection, only the class discriminative parts of the data are retained, so that the procedure can be considered a form of supervised feature extraction.

16.2 Fisher's linear discriminant

We first restrict our attention to binary class data. Also, for simplicity, we project the data down to one dimension. The canonical variates algorithm of Section 16.3 deals with the generalisations.

Gaussian assumption

We model the data from each class with a Gaussian. That is

$$p(\mathbf{x}_1) = \mathcal{N}(\mathbf{x}_1 | \mathbf{m}_1, \mathbf{S}_1), \qquad p(\mathbf{x}_2) = \mathcal{N}(\mathbf{x}_2 | \mathbf{m}_2, \mathbf{S}_2) \tag{16.2.1}$$

where $\mathbf{m}_1$ is the sample mean of class 1 data, and $\mathbf{S}_1$ the sample covariance; similarly for class 2. The projections of the points from the two classes are then given by

$$y_1^n = \mathbf{w}^\mathsf{T}\mathbf{x}_1^n, \qquad y_2^n = \mathbf{w}^\mathsf{T}\mathbf{x}_2^n. \tag{16.2.2}$$

Because the projections are linear, the projected distributions are also Gaussian,

$$p(y_1) = \mathcal{N}\left(y_1 | \mu_1, \sigma_1^2\right), \qquad \mu_1 = \mathbf{w}^\mathsf{T}\mathbf{m}_1, \qquad \sigma_1^2 = \mathbf{w}^\mathsf{T}\mathbf{S}_1\mathbf{w}, \tag{16.2.3}$$

$$p(y_2) = \mathcal{N}\left(y_2 | \mu_2, \sigma_2^2\right), \qquad \mu_2 = \mathbf{w}^\mathsf{T}\mathbf{m}_2, \qquad \sigma_2^2 = \mathbf{w}^\mathsf{T}\mathbf{S}_2\mathbf{w}. \tag{16.2.4}$$

We search for a projection $\mathbf{w}$ such that the projected distributions have minimal overlap. This can be achieved if the projected Gaussian means are maximally separated, that is $(\mu_1 - \mu_2)^2$ is large. However, if the variances σ_1^2, σ_2^2 are also large, there could still be a large overlap still in the classes. A useful objective function therefore is

$$\frac{(\mu_1 - \mu_2)^2}{\pi_1\sigma_1^2 + \pi_2\sigma_2^2} \tag{16.2.5}$$

where π_i represents the fraction of the dataset in class i. In terms of the projection $\mathbf{w}$, the objective equation (16.2.5) is

$$F(\mathbf{w}) = \frac{\mathbf{w}^\mathsf{T}(\mathbf{m}_1 - \mathbf{m}_2)(\mathbf{m}_1 - \mathbf{m}_2)^\mathsf{T}\mathbf{w}}{\mathbf{w}^\mathsf{T}(\pi_1\mathbf{S}_1 + \pi_2\mathbf{S}_2)\mathbf{w}} = \frac{\mathbf{w}^\mathsf{T}\mathbf{A}\mathbf{w}}{\mathbf{w}^\mathsf{T}\mathbf{B}\mathbf{w}} \tag{16.2.6}$$

where

$$\mathbf{A} = (\mathbf{m}_1 - \mathbf{m}_2)(\mathbf{m}_1 - \mathbf{m}_2)^\mathsf{T}, \qquad \mathbf{B} = \pi_1\mathbf{S}_1 + \pi_2\mathbf{S}_2. \tag{16.2.7}$$

The optimal $\mathbf{w}$ can be found by differentiating Equation (16.2.6) with respect to $\mathbf{w}$. This gives

$$\frac{\partial}{\partial\mathbf{w}}\frac{\mathbf{w}^\mathsf{T}\mathbf{A}\mathbf{w}}{\mathbf{w}^\mathsf{T}\mathbf{B}\mathbf{w}} = \frac{2}{(\mathbf{w}^\mathsf{T}\mathbf{B}\mathbf{w})^2}\left[\left(\mathbf{w}^\mathsf{T}\mathbf{B}\mathbf{w}\right)\mathbf{A}\mathbf{w} - \left(\mathbf{w}^\mathsf{T}\mathbf{A}\mathbf{w}\right)\mathbf{B}\mathbf{w}\right] \tag{16.2.8}$$

and therefore the zero derivative requirement is

$$\left(\mathbf{w}^\mathsf{T}\mathbf{B}\mathbf{w}\right)\mathbf{A}\mathbf{w} = \left(\mathbf{w}^\mathsf{T}\mathbf{A}\mathbf{w}\right)\mathbf{B}\mathbf{w}. \tag{16.2.9}$$

Multiplying by the inverse of $\mathbf{B}$ we have

$$\mathbf{B}^{-1}(\mathbf{m}_1 - \mathbf{m}_2)(\mathbf{m}_1 - \mathbf{m}_2)^\mathsf{T}\mathbf{w} = \frac{\mathbf{w}^\mathsf{T}\mathbf{A}\mathbf{w}}{\mathbf{w}^\mathsf{T}\mathbf{B}\mathbf{w}}\mathbf{w}. \tag{16.2.10}$$

Since $(\mathbf{m}_1 - \mathbf{m}_2)^\mathsf{T}\mathbf{w}$ is a scalar, the optimal projection is explicitly given by

$$\mathbf{w} \propto \mathbf{B}^{-1}(\mathbf{m}_1 - \mathbf{m}_2). \tag{16.2.11}$$

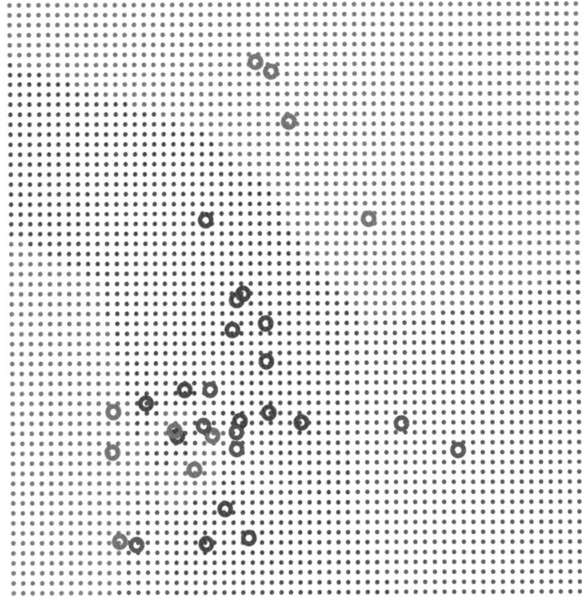

Figure 14.1 In nearest neighbour classification a new vector is assigned the label of the nearest vector in the training set. Here there are three classes, with training points given by the circles, along with their class. The dots indicate the class of the nearest training vector. The decision boundary is piecewise linear with each segment corresponding to the perpendicular bisector between two datapoints belonging to different classes, giving rise to a Voronoi tessellation of the input space.

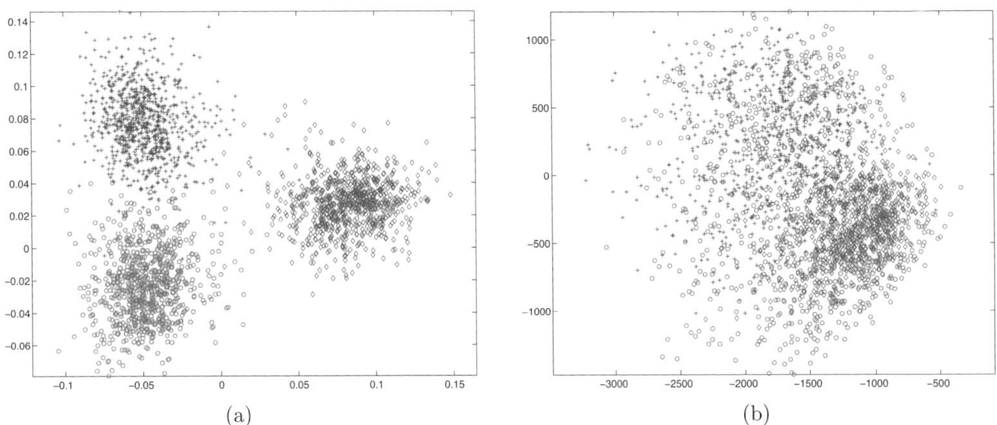

Figure 16.3 (**a**) Canonical variates projection of examples of handwritten digits 3('+'), 5('o') and 7(diamond). There are 800 examples from each digit class. Plotted are the projections down to two dimensions. (**b**) PCA projections for comparison.

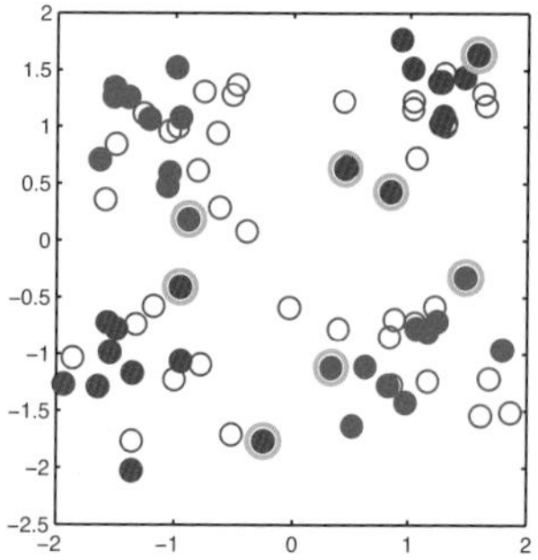

Figure 17.15 SVM training. The solid red and solid blue circles represent train data from different classes. The support vectors are highlighted in green. For the unfilled test points, the class assigned to them by the SVM is given by the colour. See `demoSVM.m`.

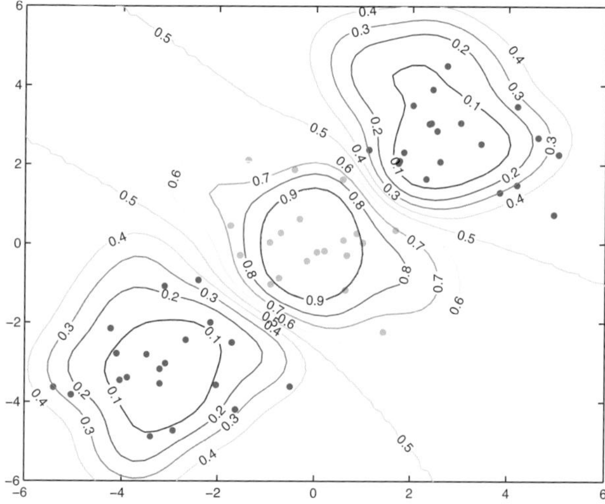

Figure 18.5 Bayesian logistic regression using RBF functions $\phi_i(\mathbf{x}) = \exp\left(-\lambda(\mathbf{x} - \mathbf{m}_i)^2\right)$, placing the centres $\mathbf{m}_i$ on a subset of the training points. The green points are training data from class 1, and the red points are training data from class 0. The contours represent the probability of being in class 1. The optimal value of α found by ML-II is 0.45 (λ is set by hand to 2). See `demoBayesLogRegression.m`.

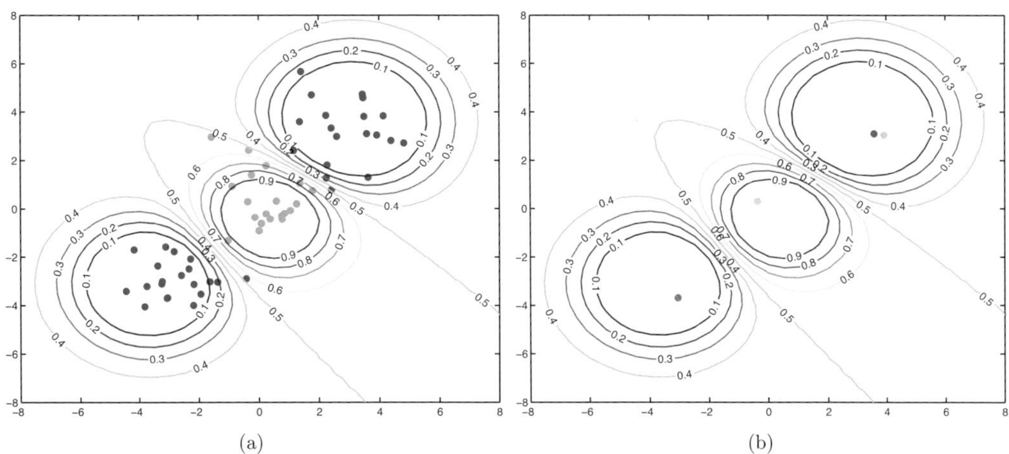

Figure 18.8 Classification using the RVM with RBF $e^{-\lambda(\mathbf{x}-\mathbf{m})^2}$, placing a basis function on a subset of the training data points. The green points are training data from class 1, and the red points are training data from class 0. The contours represent the probability of being in class 1. (**a**) Training points. (**b**) The training points weighted by their relevance value $1/\alpha_n$. Nearly all the points have a value so small that they effectively vanish. See `demoBayesLogRegRVM.m`.

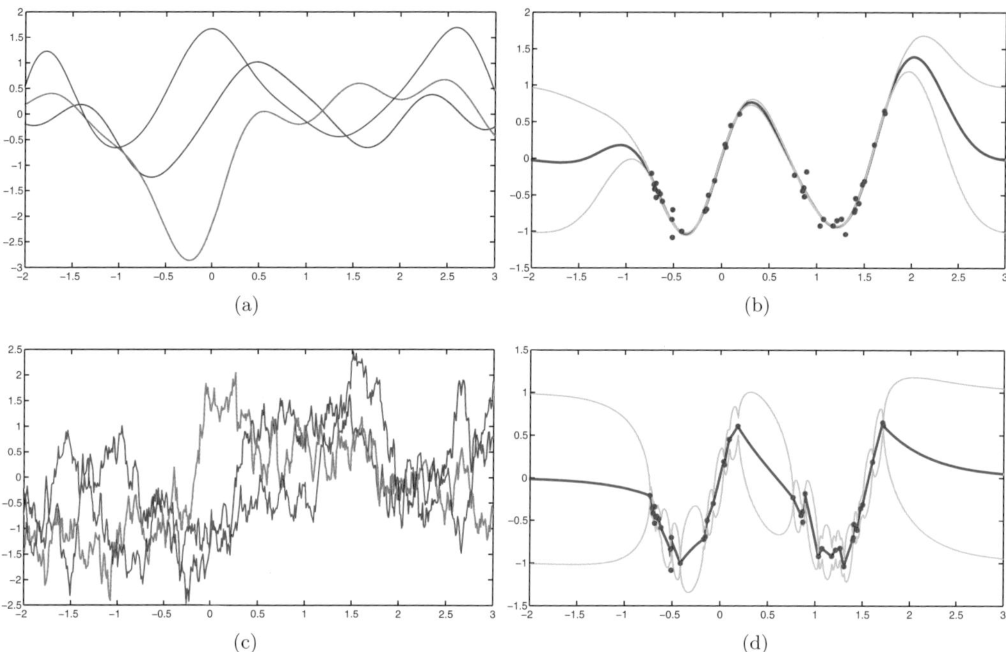

Figure 19.2 The input space from -2 to 3 is split evenly into 1000 points $x^1, \ldots, x^{1000}$. (**a**) Three samples from a GP prior with squared exponential covariance function, $\lambda = 2$. The 1000×1000 covariance matrix $\mathbf{K}$ is defined using the SE kernel, from which the samples are drawn using `mvrandn(zeros(1000,1),K,3)`. (**b**) Prediction based on training points. Plotted is the posterior predicted function based on the SE covariance. The central line is the mean prediction, with standard errors bars on either side. The log marginal likelihood is ≈ 70. (**c**) Three samples from the Ornstein–Uhlenbeck GP prior with $\lambda = 2$. (**d**) Posterior prediction for the OU covariance. The log marginal likelihood is ≈ 3, meaning that the SE covariance is much more heavily supported by the data than the rougher OU covariance.

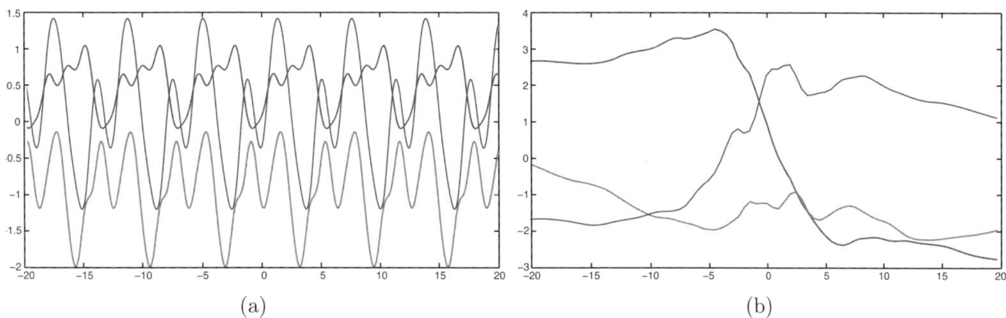

Figure 19.4 Samples from a GP prior for 500 x points uniformly placed from -20 to 20. (**a**) Samples from the periodic covariance function $\exp\left(-2\sin^2 0.5(x-x')\right)$. (**b**) Samples from the neural network covariance function with bias $b=5$ and $\lambda=1$.

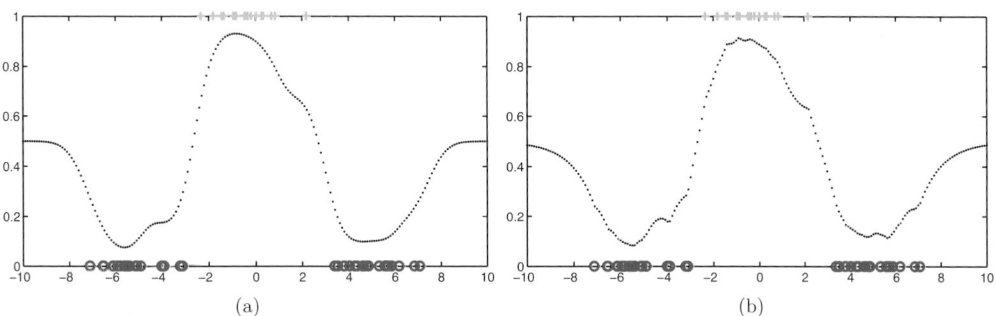

Figure 19.6 Gaussian process classification. The x-axis are the inputs, and the class is the y-axis. Green points are training points from class 1 and red from class 0. The dots are the predictions $p(c=1|x^*)$ for points x^* ranging across the x axis. (**a**) Square exponential covariance ($\gamma=2$). (**b**) OU covariance ($\gamma=1$). See `demoGPclass1D.m`.

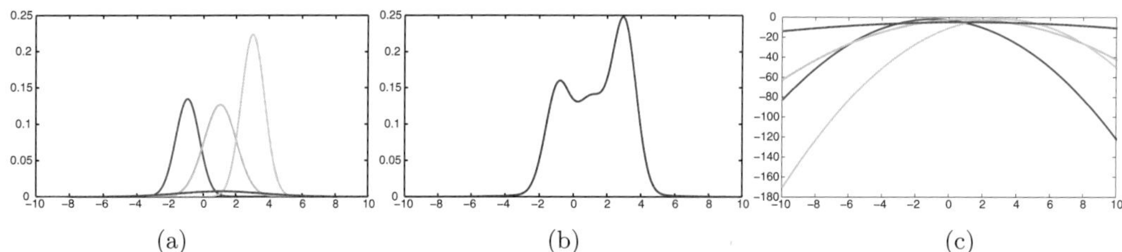

(a) (b) (c)

Figure 20.8 (**a**) A Gaussian mixture model with $H = 4$ components. There is a component (purple) with large variance and small weight that has little effect on the distribution close to where the other three components have appreciable mass. As we move further away this additional component gains in influence. (**b**) The GMM probability density function from (a). (**c**) Plotted on a log scale, the influence of each Gaussian far from the origin becomes clearer.

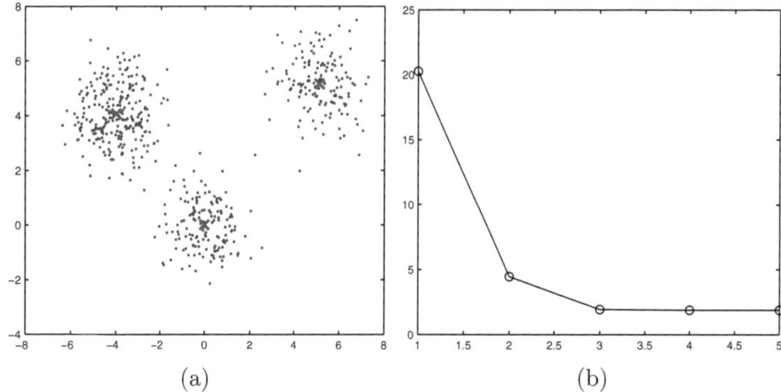

(a) (b)

Figure 20.10 (**a**) 550 datapoints clustered using K-means with three components. The means are given by the red crosses. (**b**) Evolution of the mean square distance to the nearest centre against iterations of the algorithm. The means were initialised to be close to the overall mean of the data. See `demoKmeans.m`.

Arts	Budgets	Children	Education
new	million	children	school
film	tax	women	students
show	program	people	schools
music	budget	child	education
movie	billion	years	teachers
play	federal	families	high
musical	year	work	public
best	spending	parents	teacher
actor	new	says	bennett
first	state	family	manigat
york	plan	welfare	namphy
opera	money	men	state
theater	programs	percent	president
actress	government	care	elementary
love	congress	life	haiti

(a)

The William Randolph Hearst Foundation will give $ 1.25 million to Lincoln Center, Metropolitan Opera Co., New York Philharmonic and Juilliard School. Our board felt that we had a real opportunity to make a mark on the future of the performing arts with these grants an act every bit as important as our traditional areas of support in health, medical research, education and the social services, Hearst Foundation President Randolph A. Hearst said Monday in announcing the grants. Lincoln Centers share will be $200,000 for its new building, which will house young artists and provide new public facilities. The Metropolitan Opera Co. and New York Philharmonic will receive $400,000 each. The Juilliard School, where music and the performing arts are taught, will get $250,000. The Hearst Foundation, a leading supporter of the Lincoln Center Consolidated Corporate Fund, will make its usual annual $100,000 donation, too.

(b)

Figure 20.15 (**a**) A subset of the latent topics discovered by LDA and the high probability words associated with each topic. Each column represents a topic, with the topic name such as 'arts' assigned by hand after viewing the most likely words corresponding to the topic. (**b**) A document from the training data in which the words are coloured according to the most likely latent topic. This demonstrates the mixed membership nature of the model, assigning the datapoint (document in this case) to several clusters (topics). Reproduced from [46].

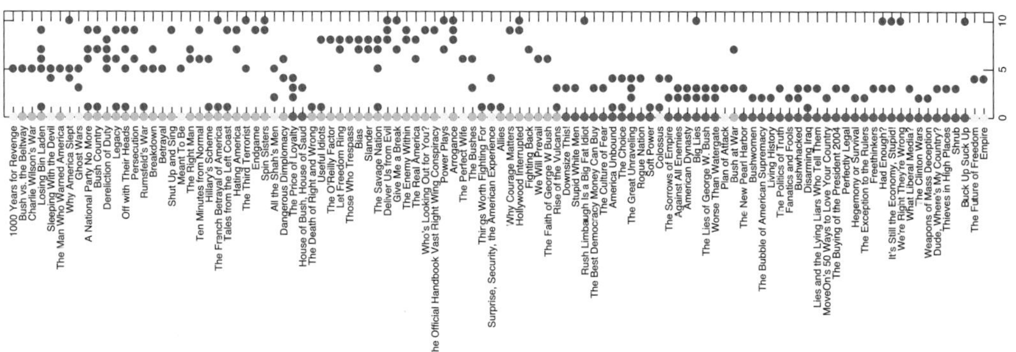

Figure 20.22 Political books. 105 $\times$ 10 dimensional clique matrix broken into three groups by a politically astute reader. A black square indicates $q(\mathbf{f}_{ic}) > 0.5$. Liberal books (red), conservative books (green), neutral books (yellow). By inspection, cliques 5,6,7,8,9 largely correspond to 'conservative' books.

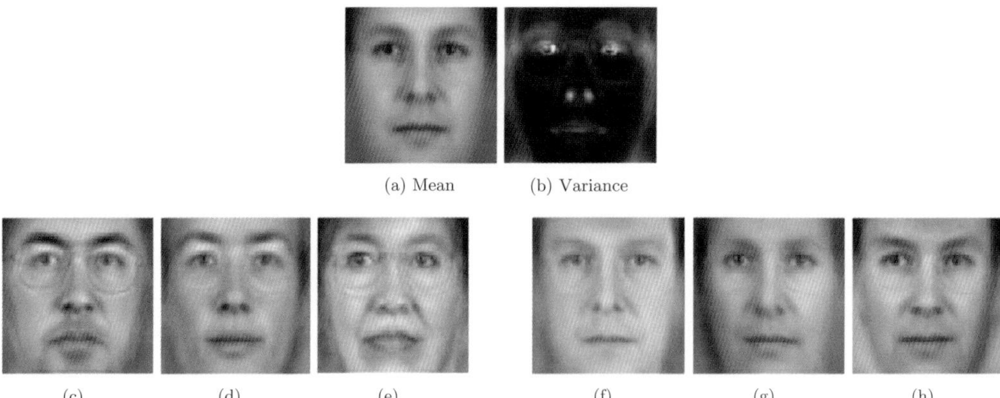

Figure 21.5 Latent identity model of face images. Each image is represented by a $70 \times 70 \times 3$ vector (the 3 comes from the RGB colour coding). There are $I = 195$ individuals in the database and $J = 4$ images per person. (**a**) Mean of the data. (**b**) Per pixel standard deviation – black is low, white is high. (**c,d,e**) Three directions from the between-individual subspace **F**. (**f,g,h**) Three samples from the model with **h** fixed and drawing randomly from **w** in the within-individual subspace **G**. Reproduced from [245] © 2007 IEEE.

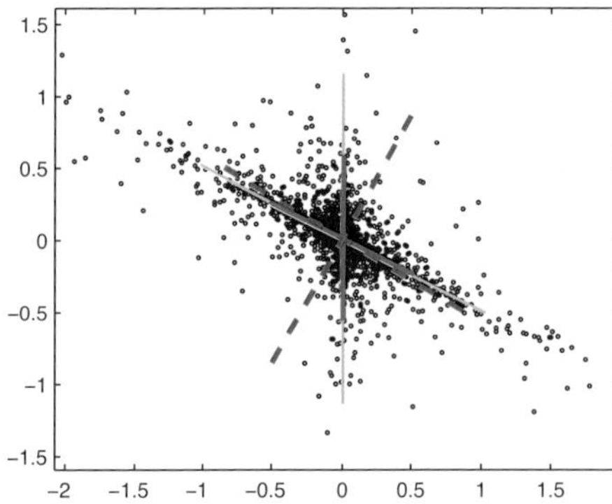

Figure 21.10 Latent data is sampled from the prior $p(x_i) \propto \exp(-5\sqrt{|x_i|})$ with the mixing matrix **A** shown in green to create the observed two-dimensional vectors $\mathbf{y} = \mathbf{A}\mathbf{x}$. The red lines are the mixing matrix estimated by `ica.m` based on the observations. For comparison, PCA produces the blue (dashed) components. Note that the components have been scaled to improve visualisation. As expected, PCA finds the orthogonal directions of maximal variation; ICA however, correctly estimates the directions in which the components were independently generated. See `demoICA.m`.

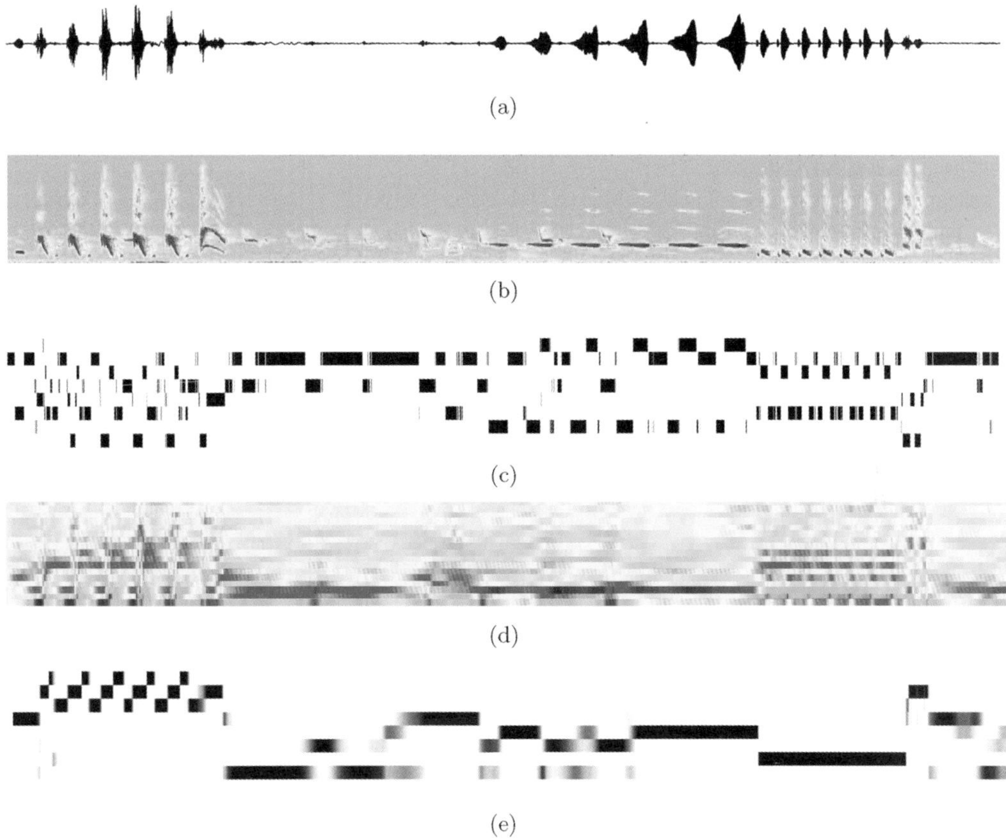

Figure 24.3 (**a**) The raw recording of 5 seconds of a nightingale song (with additional background birdsong). (**b**) Spectrogram of (a) up to 20 000 Hz. (**c**) Clustering of the results in panel (b) using an 8 component Gaussian mixture model. Plotted at each time vertically is the distribution over the cluster indices (from 1 to 8), so that the darker the component, the more responsible that component is for the spectrogram slice at that timepoint. (**d**) The 20 time-varying AR coefficients learned using $\sigma_v^2 = 0.001$, $\sigma_h^2 = 0.001$, see `ARlds.m`. (**e**) Clustering the results in panel (d) using a Gaussian mixture model with 8 components. The AR components group roughly according to the different song regimes.

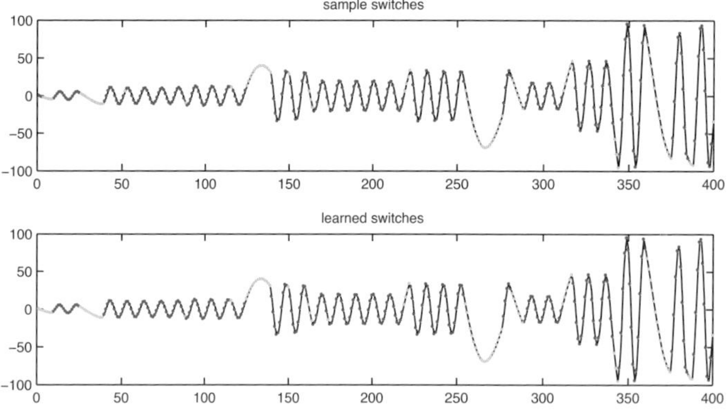

Figure 24.9 Learning a switching AR model. The upper plot shows the train data. The colour indicates which of the two AR models is active at that time. Whilst this information is plotted here, this is assumed unknown to the learning algorithm, as are the coefficients $\mathbf{a}(s)$. We assume that the order $L = 2$ and number of switches $S = 2$ however is known. In the bottom plot we show the timeseries again after training in which we colour the points according to the most likely smoothed AR model at each timestep. See `demoSARlearn.m`.

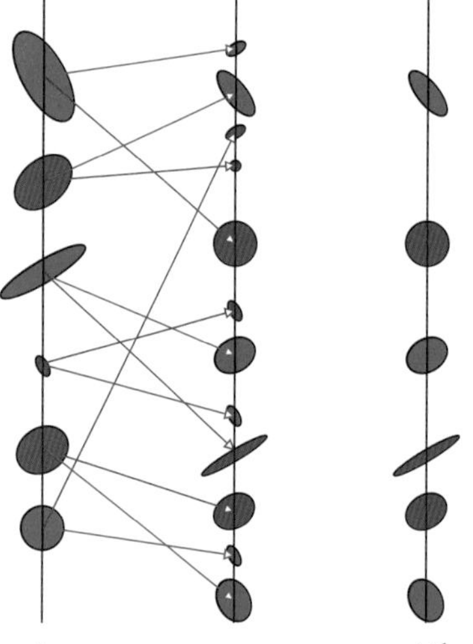

Figure 25.2 Gaussian sum filtering. The leftmost column depicts the previous Gaussian mixture approximation $q(\mathbf{h}_t, i_t|\mathbf{v}_{1:t})$ for two states $S = 2$ (red and blue) and three mixture components $I = 3$, with the mixture weight represented by the area of each oval. There are $S = 2$ different linear systems which take each of the components of the mixture into a new filtered state, the colour of the arrow indicating which dynamic system is used. After one timestep each mixture component branches into a further S components so that the joint approximation $q(\mathbf{h}_{t+1}, s_{t+1}|\mathbf{v}_{1:t+1})$ contains S^2I components (middle column). To keep the representation computationally tractable the mixture of Gaussians for each state s_{t+1} is collapsed back to I components. This means that each coloured set of Gaussians needs to be approximated by a smaller I component mixture of Gaussians. There are many ways to achieve this. A naive but computationally efficient approach is to simply ignore the lowest weight components, as depicted on the right column, see `mix2mix.m`.

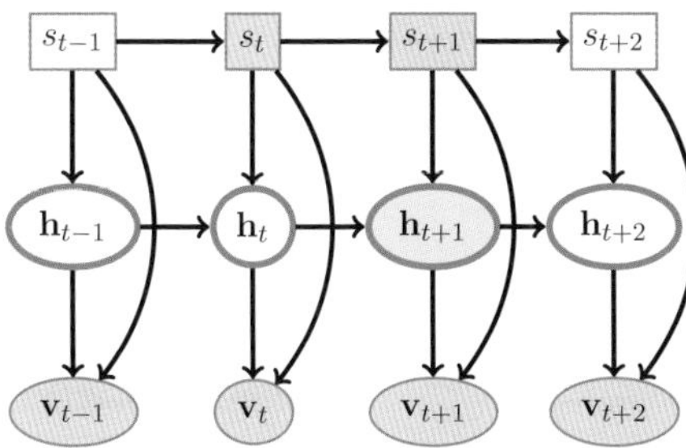

Figure 25.3 The EC backpass approximates $p(\mathbf{h}_{t+1}|s_{t+1}, s_t, \mathbf{v}_{1:T})$ by $p(\mathbf{h}_{t+1}|s_{t+1}, \mathbf{v}_{1:T})$. The motivation for this is that s_t influences $\mathbf{h}_{t+1}$ only indirectly through $\mathbf{h}_t$. However, $\mathbf{h}_t$ will most likely be heavily influenced by $\mathbf{v}_{1:t}$, so that not knowing the state of s_t is likely to be of secondary importance. The green shaded node is the variable we wish to find the posterior for. The values of the blue shaded nodes are known, and the red shaded node indicates a known variable which is assumed unknown in forming the approximation.

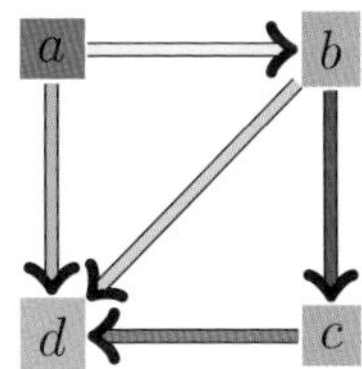

Figure 25.4 A representation of the traffic flow between junctions at a, b, c, d, with traffic lights at a and b. If $s_a = 1$ $a \to d$ and $a \to b$ carry 0.75 and 0.25 of the flow out of a respectively. If $s_a = 2$ all the flow from a goes through $a \to d$; for $s_a = 3$, all the flow goes through $a \to b$. For $s_b = 1$ the flow out of b is split equally between $b \to d$ and $b \to c$. For $s_b = 2$ all flow out of b goes along $b \to c$.

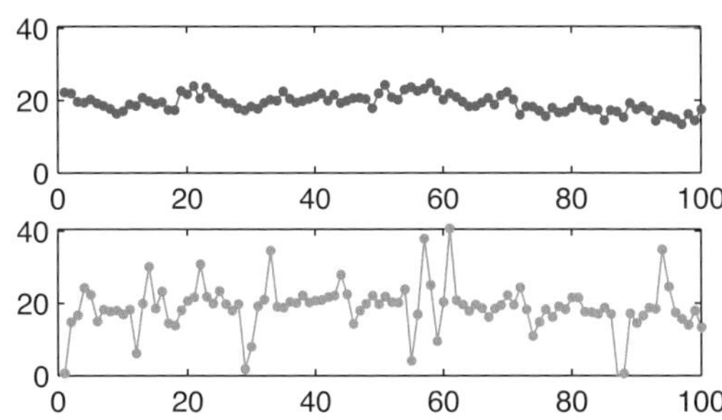

Figure 25.5 Time evolution of the traffic flow measured at two points in the network. Sensors measure the total flow into the network (upper panel) $\phi_a(t)$ and the total flow out of the network (lower panel), $\phi_d(t) = \phi_{a\to d}(t) + \phi_{b\to d}(t) + \phi_{c\to d}(t)$. The total inflow at a undergoes a random walk. Note that the flow measured at d can momentarily drop to zero if all traffic is routed through $a \to b \to c$ in two consecutive timesteps.

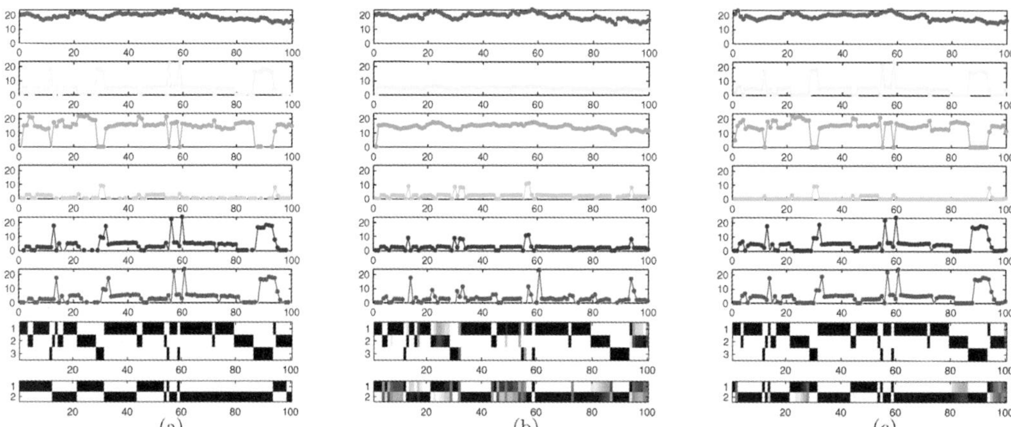

Figure 25.6 Given the observations from Fig. 25.5 we infer the flows and switch states of all the latent variables. (**a**) The correct latent flows through time along with the switch variable state used to generate the data. The colours corresponds to the flows at the corresponding coloured edges/nodes in Fig. 25.4. (**b**) Filtered flows based on a $I = 2$ Gaussian sum forward pass approximation. Plotted are the six components of the vector $\langle \mathbf{h}_t | \mathbf{v}_{1:t} \rangle$ with the posterior distribution of the s_a and s_b traffic light states $p(s_t^a | \mathbf{v}_{1:t})$, $p(s_t^b | \mathbf{v}_{1:t})$ plotted below. (**c**) Smoothed flows $\langle \mathbf{h}_t | \mathbf{v}_{1:T} \rangle$ and corresponding smoothed switch states $p(s_t | \mathbf{v}_{1:T})$ using a Gaussian sum smoothing approximation (EC with $J = 1$).

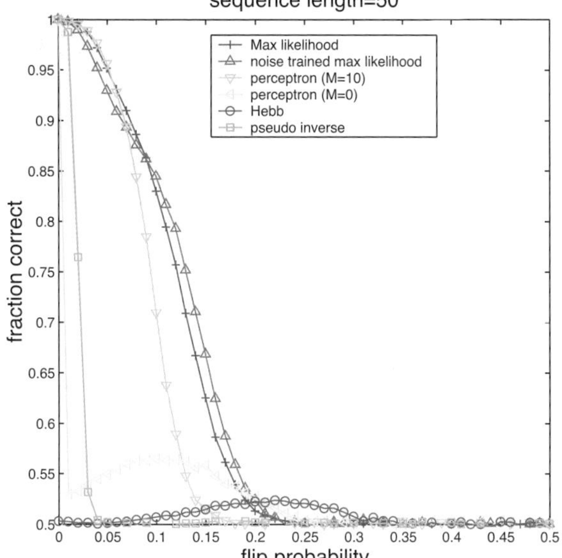

Figure 26.4 The fraction of neurons correct for the final state of the network $T = 50$ for a 100 neuron Hopfield network trained to store a length 50 sequence of patterns. After initialisation in the correct initial state at $t = 1$, the Hopfield network is updated deterministically, with a randomly chosen percentage of the neurons flipped after updating. The correlated sequence of length $T = 50$ was produced by flipping with probability 0.5, 20 per cent of the previous state of the network. A fraction correct value of 1 indicates perfect recall of the final state, and a value of 0.5 indicates a performance no better than random guessing of the final state. For maximum likelihood 50 epochs of training were used with $\eta = 0.02$. During recall, deterministic updates $\beta = \infty$ were used. The results presented are averages over 5000 simulations, resulting in standard errors of the order of the symbol sizes.

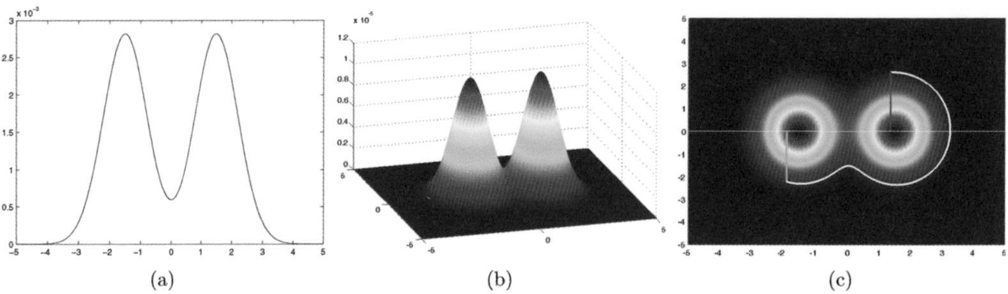

Figure 27.9 Hybrid Monte Carlo. (**a**) Multi-modal distribution $p(x)$ for which we desire samples. (**b**) HMC forms the joint distribution $p(x)p(y)$ where $p(y)$ is Gaussian. (**c**) This is a plot of (b) from above. Starting from the point x, we first draw a y from the Gaussian $p(y)$, giving a point (x, y), given by the green line. Then we use Hamiltonian dynamics (white line) to traverse the distribution at roughly constant energy for a fixed number of steps, giving x', y'. We accept this point if $H(x', y') > H(x, y')$ and make the new sample x' (red line). Otherwise this candidate is accepted with probability $\exp(H(x', y') - H(x, y'))$. If rejected the new sample x' is taken as a copy of x.

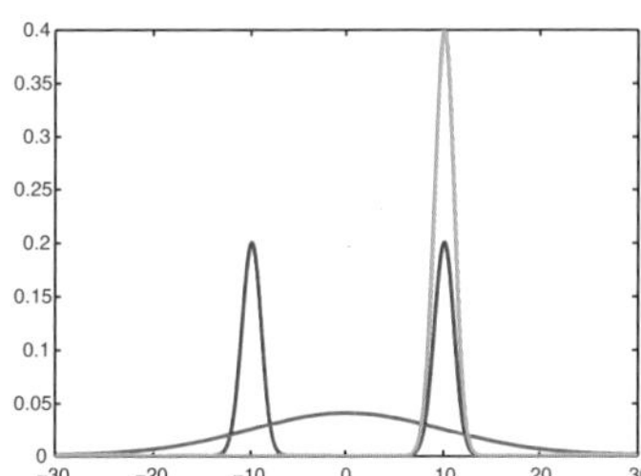

Figure 28.1 Fitting a mixture of Gaussians $p(x)$ (blue) with a single Gaussian. The green curve minimises $\mathrm{KL}(q|p)$ corresponding to fitting a local model. The red curve minimises $\mathrm{KL}(p|q)$ corresponding to moment matching.

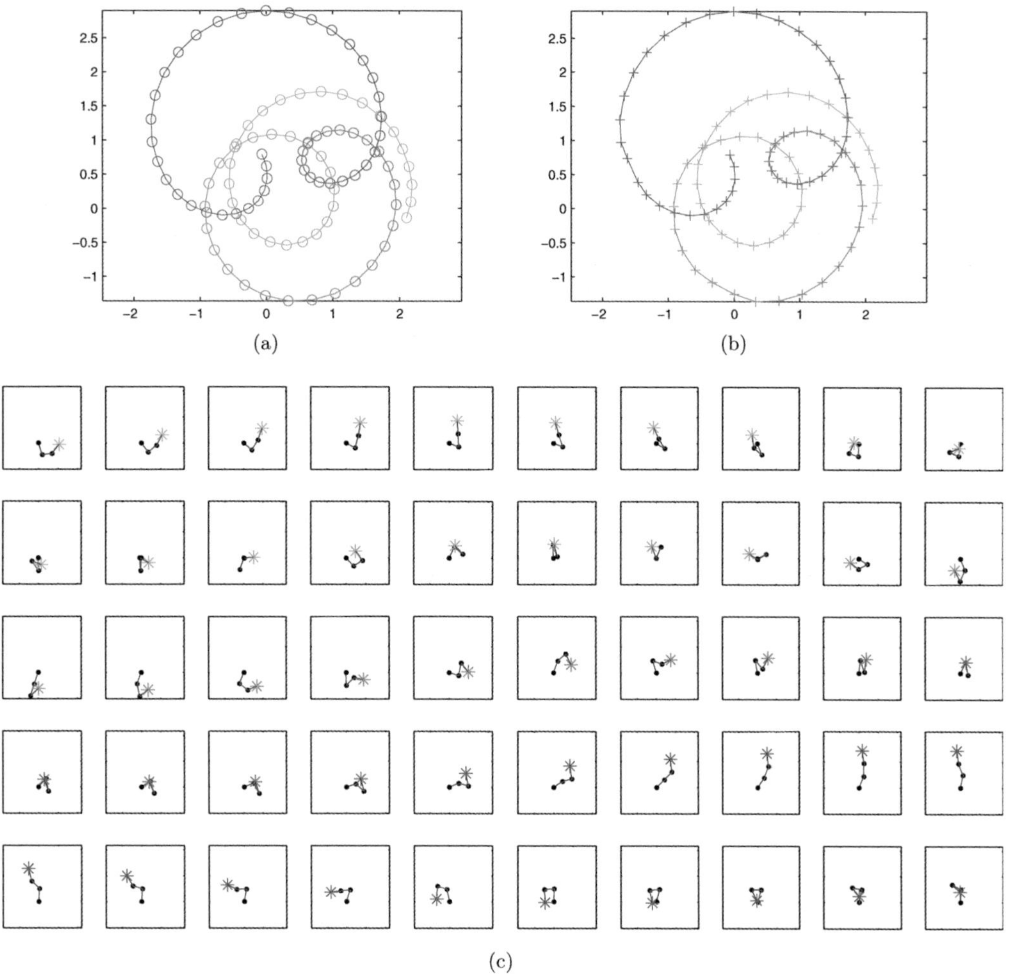

Figure 28.6 (**a**) The desired trajectory of the end point of a three link robot arm. Green denotes time 1 and red time 100. (**b**) The learned trajectory based on a fully factorised KL variational approximation. (**c**) The robot arm sections every 2nd timestep, from time 1 (top left) to time 100 (bottom right). The control problem of matching the trajectory using a smoothly changing angle set is solved using this simple approximation.

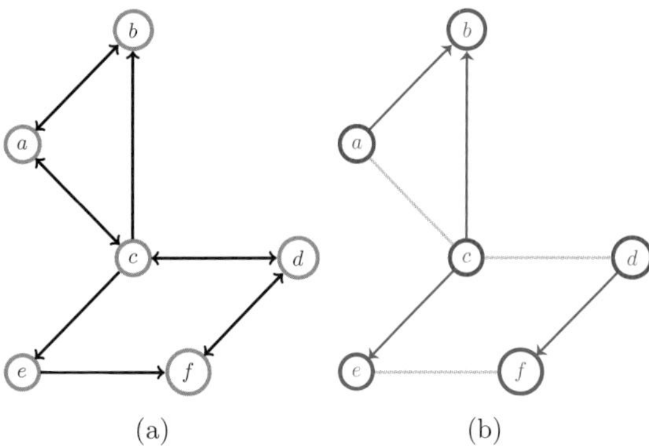

Figure 28.13 (**a**) A directed graph with edge weights w_{ij} from node i to j with $w_{ij} = 0$ if no edge exists from i to j. (**b**) A graph cut partitions the nodes into two groups $\mathcal{S}$ (blue) and $\mathcal{T}$ (red). The weight of the cut is the sum of the weights of edges that leave $\mathcal{S}$ (blue) and land in $\mathcal{T}$ (red). Intuitively, it is clear that after assigning nodes to state 1 (for blue) and 0 (red) that the weight of the cut corresponds to the summed weights of neighbours in different states. Here we highlight those weight contributions. The non-highlighted edges do not contribute to the cut weight. Note that only one of the edge directions contributes to the cut.

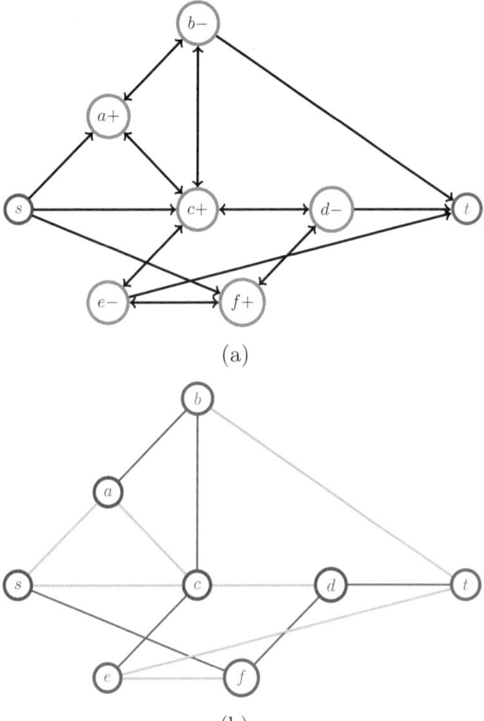

Figure 28.14 (**a**) A graph with bidirectional weights $w_{ij} = w_{ji}$ augmented with a source node s and sink node t. Each node has a corresponding bias whose sign is indicated. The source node is linked to the nodes corresponding to positive bias, and the nodes with negative bias to the sink. (**b**) A graph cut partitions the nodes into two groups $\mathcal{S}$ (blue) and $\mathcal{T}$ (red), where $\mathcal{S}$ is the union of the source node s and nodes in state 1, $\mathcal{T}$ is the union of the sink node t and nodes in state 0. The weight of the cut is the sum of the edge weights from $\mathcal{S}$ (blue) to $\mathcal{T}$ (red). The red lines indicate contributions to the cut, and can be considered penalties since we wish to find the minimal cut.

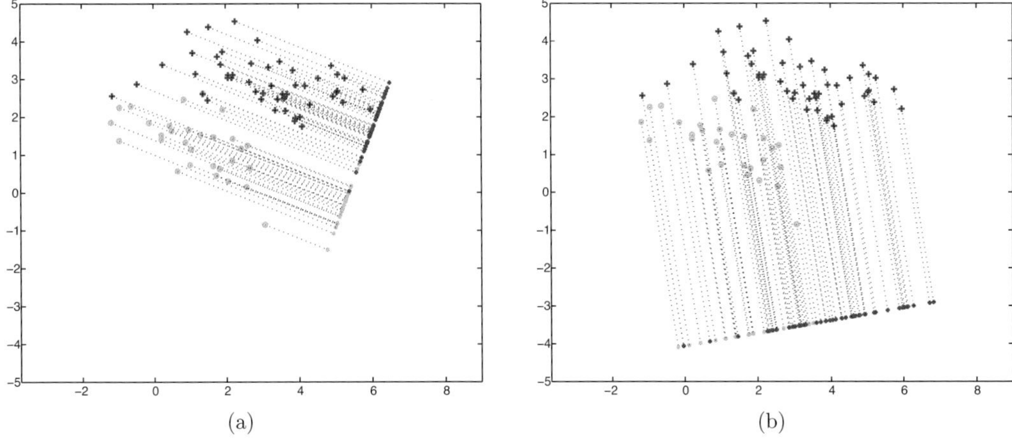

Figure 16.1 The large crosses represent data from class 1, and the large circles from class 2. Their projections onto 1 dimension are represented by their small counterparts. (**a**) Fisher's Linear Discriminant Analysis (LDA). Here there is little class overlap in the projections. (**b**) Unsupervised dimension reduction using principal components analysis for comparison. There is considerable class overlap in the projection. In both (a) and (b) the one-dimensional projection is the distance along the line, measured from an arbitrary chosen fixed point on the line.

Although the proportionality factor depends on $\mathbf{w}$, we may take it to be constant since the objective function $F(\mathbf{w})$ in Equation (16.2.6) is invariant to rescaling of $\mathbf{w}$. We may therefore take

$$\mathbf{w} = k\mathbf{B}^{-1}(\mathbf{m}_1 - \mathbf{m}_2). \tag{16.2.12}$$

It is common to rescale $\mathbf{w}$ to have unit length, $\mathbf{w}^\mathsf{T}\mathbf{w} = 1$, such that

$$k = \frac{1}{\sqrt{(\mathbf{m}_1 - \mathbf{m}_2)^\mathsf{T}\mathbf{B}^{-2}(\mathbf{m}_1 - \mathbf{m}_2)}}. \tag{16.2.13}$$

An illustration of the method is given in Fig. 16.1, which demonstrates how supervised dimension reduction can produce lower-dimensional representations more suitable for subsequent classification than an unsupervised method such as PCA.

One can also arrive at Equation (16.2.12) from a different starting objective. By treating the projection as a regression problem $y = \mathbf{w}^\mathsf{T}\mathbf{x} + b$ in which the outputs y are defined as y_1 and y_2 for classes 1 and class 2 respectively, one may show that, for suitably chosen y_1 and y_2, the solution using a least squares criterion is given by Equation (16.2.12) [88, 43]. This also suggests a way to regularise LDA, see Exercise 16.3. Kernel extensions of LDA are possible, see for example [82, 264].

When the naive method breaks down

The above derivation relied on the existence of the inverse of $\mathbf{B}$. In practice, however, $\mathbf{B}$ may not be invertible, and the above procedure requires modification. A case where $\mathbf{B}$ is not invertible is when there are fewer datapoints $N_1 + N_2$ than dimensions D. A related problematic case is when there are elements of the input vectors that never vary. For example, in the hand-written digits case, the pixels at the corner edges are actually always zero. Let's call such a pixel z. The matrix $\mathbf{B}$ will then have a zero entry for $[B]_{z,z}$ (indeed the whole zth row and column of $\mathbf{B}$ will be zero) so that for any vector of the form

$$\mathbf{w}^{\mathsf{T}} = (0, 0, \ldots, w_z, 0, 0, \ldots, 0) \Rightarrow \mathbf{w}^{\mathsf{T}}\mathbf{B}\mathbf{w} = 0. \tag{16.2.14}$$

This shows that the denominator of Fisher's objective can become zero, and the objective ill defined. We will address these issues in Section 16.3.1.

16.3 Canonical variates

Canonical variates generalises Fisher's method to projections of more than one dimension and more than two classes. The projection of any point is given by

$$\mathbf{y} = \mathbf{W}^{\mathsf{T}}\mathbf{x} \tag{16.3.1}$$

where $\mathbf{W}$ is a $D \times L$ matrix. Assuming that the data $\mathbf{x}$ from class c is Gaussian distributed,

$$p(\mathbf{x}) = \mathcal{N}(\mathbf{x}|\mathbf{m}_c, \mathbf{S}_c) \tag{16.3.2}$$

the projections $\mathbf{y}$ are also Gaussian

$$p(\mathbf{y}) = \mathcal{N}\left(\mathbf{y}|\mathbf{W}^{\mathsf{T}}\mathbf{m}_c, \mathbf{W}^{\mathsf{T}}\mathbf{S}_c\mathbf{W}\right). \tag{16.3.3}$$

By analogy with Equation (16.2.7), we define the following matrices:

Between class scatter Find the mean $\mathbf{m}$ of the whole dataset and $\mathbf{m}_c$, the mean of the each class c. Form

$$\mathbf{A} \equiv \sum_{c=1}^{C} N_c (\mathbf{m}_c - \mathbf{m})(\mathbf{m}_c - \mathbf{m})^{\mathsf{T}} \tag{16.3.4}$$

where N_c is the number of datapoints in class c, $c = 1, \ldots, C$.

Within class scatter Compute the covariance matrix $\mathbf{S}_c$ of the data for each class c. Define

$$\mathbf{B} \equiv \sum_{c=1}^{C} N_c \mathbf{S}_c. \tag{16.3.5}$$

Assuming $\mathbf{B}$ is invertible (see Section 16.3.1 otherwise), we can define the Cholesky factor $\tilde{\mathbf{B}}$, with

$$\tilde{\mathbf{B}}^{\mathsf{T}}\tilde{\mathbf{B}} = \mathbf{B}. \tag{16.3.6}$$

A natural objective is then to maximise the *Raleigh quotient*

$$F(\mathbf{W}) \equiv \frac{\operatorname{trace}\left(\mathbf{W}^{\mathsf{T}}\tilde{\mathbf{B}}^{-\mathsf{T}}\mathbf{A}\tilde{\mathbf{B}}^{-1}\mathbf{W}\right)}{\operatorname{trace}\left(\mathbf{W}^{\mathsf{T}}\mathbf{W}\right)}. \tag{16.3.7}$$

If we assume an orthonormality constraint on $\mathbf{W}$, then we equivalently require the maximisation of

$$F(\mathbf{W}) \equiv \operatorname{trace}\left(\mathbf{W}^{\mathsf{T}}\mathbf{C}\mathbf{W}\right), \text{ subject to } \mathbf{W}^{\mathsf{T}}\mathbf{W} = \mathbf{I} \tag{16.3.8}$$

where

$$\mathbf{C} \equiv \frac{1}{D}\tilde{\mathbf{B}}^{-\mathsf{T}}\mathbf{A}\tilde{\mathbf{B}}^{-1}. \tag{16.3.9}$$

Algorithm 16.1 Canonical variates

Compute the between and within class scatter matrices $\mathbf{A}$, Equation (16.3.4) and $\mathbf{B}$, Equation (16.3.5).
Compute the Cholesky factor $\tilde{\mathbf{B}}$ of $\mathbf{B}$.
Compute the L principal eigenvectors $[\mathbf{e}_1, \ldots, \mathbf{e}_L]$ of $\tilde{\mathbf{B}}^{-\mathsf{T}}\mathbf{A}\tilde{\mathbf{B}}^{-1}$.
Return $\mathbf{W} = [\mathbf{e}_1, \ldots, \mathbf{e}_L]$ as the projection matrix.

Since $\mathbf{C}$ is symmetric and positive semidefinite, it has a real eigen-decomposition

$$\mathbf{C} = \mathbf{E}\mathbf{\Lambda}\mathbf{E}^{\mathsf{T}} \tag{16.3.10}$$

where $\mathbf{\Lambda} = \text{diag}(\lambda_1, \lambda_2, \ldots, \lambda_D)$ is diagonal with non-negative entries containing the eigenvalues, sorted by decreasing order, $\lambda_1 \geq \lambda_2 \geq \ldots$ and $\mathbf{E}^{\mathsf{T}}\mathbf{E} = \mathbf{I}$. Hence

$$F(\mathbf{W}) = \text{trace}\left(\mathbf{W}^{\mathsf{T}}\mathbf{E}\mathbf{\Lambda}\mathbf{E}^{\mathsf{T}}\mathbf{W}\right). \tag{16.3.11}$$

By setting $\mathbf{W} = [\mathbf{e}_1, \ldots, \mathbf{e}_L]$, where $\mathbf{e}_l$ is the lth eigenvector, the objective $F(\mathbf{W})$ becomes the sum of the first L eigenvalues. This setting maximises the objective function since forming $\mathbf{W}$ from any other columns of $\mathbf{E}$ would give a lower sum. The procedure is outlined in Algorithm 16.1. Note that since $\mathbf{A}$ has rank C, there can be no more than $C - 1$ non-zero eigenvalues and corresponding directions.

16.3.1 Dealing with the nullspace

The above derivation of canonical variates (and also Fisher's LDA) requires the invertibility of the matrix $\mathbf{B}$. However, as we discussed in Section 16.2, one may encounter situations where $\mathbf{B}$ is not invertible. A solution is to require that $\mathbf{W}$ lies only in the subspace spanned by the data (that is there can be no contribution from the nullspace). To do this we first concatenate the training data from all classes into one large matrix $\mathbf{X}$. A basis for $\mathbf{X}$ can be found using, for example, the thin-SVD technique which returns an orthonormal non-square basis matrix $\mathbf{Q}$. We then require the solution $\mathbf{W}$ to be expressed in this basis, see Fig. 16.2:

$$\mathbf{W} = \mathbf{Q}\mathbf{W}' \tag{16.3.12}$$

for some matrix $\mathbf{W}'$. Substituting this in the canonical variates objective equation (16.3.7), we obtain

$$F(\mathbf{W}') \equiv \frac{\text{trace}\left(\mathbf{W}'^{\mathsf{T}}\mathbf{Q}^{\mathsf{T}}\mathbf{A}\mathbf{Q}\mathbf{W}'\right)}{\text{trace}\left(\mathbf{W}'^{\mathsf{T}}\mathbf{Q}^{\mathsf{T}}\mathbf{B}\mathbf{Q}\mathbf{W}'\right)}. \tag{16.3.13}$$

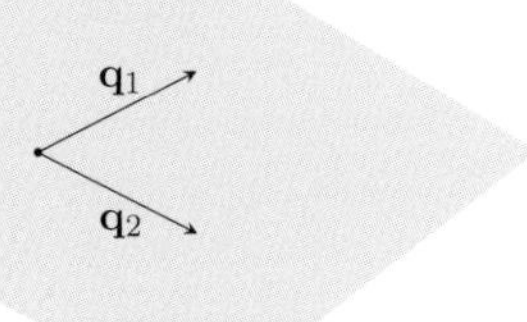

Figure 16.2 Each three-dimensional datapoint lies in a two-dimensional plane, meaning that the matrix $\mathbf{B}$ is not full rank, and therefore not invertible. A solution is given by finding vectors $\mathbf{q}_1$, $\mathbf{q}_2$ that span the plane, and expressing the canonical variates solution in terms of these vectors alone.

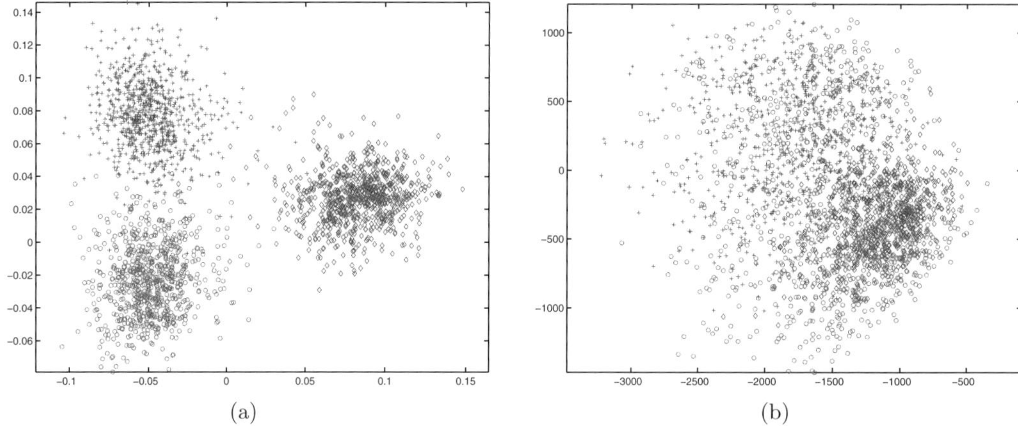

Figure 16.3 (**a**) Canonical variates projection of examples of handwritten digits 3('+'), 5('o') and 7(diamond). There are 800 examples from each digit class. Plotted are the projections down to two dimensions. (**b**) PCA projections for comparison. See plate section for colour version.

This is of the same form as the standard quotient, Equation (16.3.7), on replacing the between-scatter $\mathbf{A}$ with

$$\mathbf{A}' \equiv \mathbf{Q}^{\mathsf{T}}\mathbf{A}\mathbf{Q} \tag{16.3.14}$$

and the within-scatter $\mathbf{B}$ with

$$\mathbf{B}' \equiv \mathbf{Q}^{\mathsf{T}}\mathbf{B}\mathbf{Q}. \tag{16.3.15}$$

In this case $\mathbf{B}'$ is guaranteed invertible since $\mathbf{B}$ is projected down to the basis that spans the data. One may then carry out canonical variates, as in Section 16.3 above, which returns the matrix $\mathbf{W}'$. Transforming, back, $\mathbf{W}$ is then given by Equation (16.3.12). See also `CanonVar.m`.

Example 16.1 Using canonical variates on the digit data

We apply canonical variates to project the digit data onto two dimensions, see Fig. 16.3. There are 800 examples of a three, 800 examples of a five and 800 examples of a seven. Thus, overall, there are 2400 examples lying in a 784 (28×28 pixels) dimensional space. The canonical variates projected data onto two dimensions has very little class overlap, see Fig. 16.3(a). In comparison the projections formed from PCA, which discards the class information, displays a high degree of class overlap. The different scales of the canonical variates and PCA projections is due to the different constraints on the projection matrices $\mathbf{W}$. In PCA $\mathbf{W}$ is unitary; in canonical variates $\mathbf{W}^{\mathsf{T}}\mathbf{B}\mathbf{W} = \mathbf{I}$, meaning that $\mathbf{W}$ will scale with the inverse square root of the largest eigenvalues of the within class scatter matrix. Since the canonical variates objective is independent of linear scaling, $\mathbf{W}$ can be rescaled with an arbitrary scalar prefactor $\gamma\mathbf{W}$, as desired.

16.4 Summary

- Fisher's linear discriminant seeks a scalar projection that is maximally different for data from each of two classes.

- Canonical variates generalises Fisher's method to multiple classes and multiple projected dimensions.
- Fisher's method and Canonical variates are related to standard eigen-problems.

The applicability of canonical variates depends on our assumption that a Gaussian is a good description of the data. Clearly, if the data is multimodal, using a single Gaussian to model the data in each class is a poor assumption. This may result in projections with a large class overlap. In principle, there is no conceptual difficulty in using more complex distributions, and a more general criteria such as maximal Kullback–Leibler divergence between projected distributions. However, such criteria typically result in difficult optimisation problems. Canonical variates is popular due to its simplicity and lack of local optima issues in constructing the projection.

16.5 Code

`CanonVar.m`: Canonical variates
`demoCanonVarDigits.m`: Demo for canonical variates

16.6 Exercises

16.1 What happens to Fisher's linear discriminant if there are less datapoints than dimensions?

16.2 Modify `demoCanonVarDigits.m` to project and visualise the digits data in three dimensions.

16.3 Consider N_1 class 1 datapoints $\mathbf{x}_{n_1}, n_1 = 1, \ldots, N_1$ and N_2 class 2 datapoints $\mathbf{x}_{n_2}, n_2 = 1, \ldots, N_2$. We define a linear predictor for the data,

$$y = \mathbf{w}^\mathsf{T}\mathbf{x} + b \tag{16.6.1}$$

with the aim to predict value y_1 for data from class 1 and y_2 for data from class 2. A measure of the fit is given by

$$E(\mathbf{w}, b|y_1, y_2) = \sum_{n_1=1}^{N_1} \left(y_1 - \mathbf{w}^\mathsf{T}\mathbf{x}_{n_1} - b\right)^2 + \sum_{n_2=1}^{N_2} \left(y_2 - \mathbf{w}^\mathsf{T}\mathbf{x}_{n_2} - b\right)^2. \tag{16.6.2}$$

Show that by setting $y_1 = (N_1 + N_2)/N_1$ and $y_2 = (N_1 + N_2)/N_2$ the $\mathbf{w}$ which minimises E corresponds to Fisher's LDA solution. Hint: first show that the two zero derivative conditions are

$$\sum_{n_1} \left(y_1 - b - \mathbf{w}^\mathsf{T}\mathbf{x}_{n_1}\right) + \sum_{n_2} \left(y_2 - b - \mathbf{w}^\mathsf{T}\mathbf{x}_{n_2}\right) = 0 \tag{16.6.3}$$

and

$$\sum_{n_1} \left(y_1 - b - \mathbf{w}^\mathsf{T}\mathbf{x}_{n_1}\right)\mathbf{x}_{n_1}^\mathsf{T} + \sum_{n_2} \left(y_2 - b - \mathbf{w}^\mathsf{T}\mathbf{x}_{n_2}\right)\mathbf{x}_{n_2}^\mathsf{T} = 0 \tag{16.6.4}$$

which can be reduced to the single equation

$$N\left(\mathbf{m}_1 - \mathbf{m}_2\right) = \left(N\mathbf{B} + \frac{N_1 N_2}{N}\left(\mathbf{m}_1 - \mathbf{m}_2\right)\left(\mathbf{m}_1 - \mathbf{m}_2\right)^\mathsf{T}\right)\mathbf{w} \tag{16.6.5}$$

where $\mathbf{B}$ is as defined for LDA in the text, Equation (16.2.7).

Note that this suggests a way to regularise LDA, namely by adding on a term $\lambda \mathbf{w}^\mathsf{T}\mathbf{w}$ to $E(\mathbf{w}, b|y_1, y_2)$. This can be absorbed into redefining Equation (16.3.5) as

$$\mathbf{B}' = \mathbf{B} + \lambda \mathbf{I}. \tag{16.6.6}$$

That is, we increase the covariance $\mathbf{B}$ by an additive amount $\lambda\mathbf{I}$. The optimal regularising constant λ may be set by cross-validation.

16.4 Consider the digit data of 892 fives `digit5.mat` and 1028 sevens `digit7.mat`. Make a training set which consists of the first 500 examples from each digit class. Use canonical variates to first project the data down to 10 dimensions and compute the nearest neighbour performance on the remaining digits. Alternatively, use PCA to reduce the data to 10 dimensions, and compare the resulting nearest neighbour classification performance. Visualise also the 10 directions found by canonical variates and the 10 principal directions of PCA.

16.5 Consider an objective function of the form

$$F(w) \equiv \frac{A(w)}{B(w)} \tag{16.6.7}$$

where $A(w)$ and $B(w)$ are positive functions, and our task is to maximise $F(w)$ with respect to w. It may be that this objective does not have a simple algebraic solution, even though $A(w)$ and $B(w)$ are simple functions. We can consider an alternative objective, namely

$$J(w, \lambda) = A(w) - \lambda B(w) \tag{16.6.8}$$

where λ is a constant scalar. Choose an initial point w^{old} at random and set

$$\lambda^{old} \equiv A(w^{old})/B(w^{old}). \tag{16.6.9}$$

In that case $J(w^{old}, \lambda^{old}) = 0$. Now choose a w such that

$$J(w, \lambda^{old}) = A(w) - \lambda^{old} B(w) \geq 0. \tag{16.6.10}$$

This is certainly possible since $J(w^{old}, \lambda^{old}) = 0$. If we can find a w such that $J(w, \lambda^{old}) > 0$, then

$$A(w) - \lambda^{old} B(w) > 0. \tag{16.6.11}$$

Show that for such a w, $F(w) > F(w^{old})$, and suggest an iterative optimisation procedure for objective functions of the form $F(w)$.

17 Linear models

In this chapter we discuss some classical methods for prediction based on fitting simple linear models to data. These include standard methods such as linear and logistic regression, and also their kernelised variants. We also discuss the popular support vector machine and related methods for ensuring good generalisation performance.

17.1 Introduction: fitting a straight line

Given training data $\{(x^n, y^n), n = 1, \ldots, N\}$, for scalar input x^n and scalar output y^n, a linear regression fit is

$$y(x) = a + bx. \tag{17.1.1}$$

To determine the best parameters a, b, we use a measure of the discrepancy between the observed outputs and the linear regression fit such as the sum squared training error. This is also called *ordinary least squares* and minimises the average vertical projection of the points y to the fitted line, Fig. 17.1(a):

$$E(a, b) = \sum_{n=1}^{N} [y^n - y(x^n)]^2 = \sum_{n=1}^{N} (y^n - a - bx^n)^2. \tag{17.1.2}$$

Our task is to find the parameters a and b that minimise $E(a, b)$. Differentiating with respect to a and b we obtain

$$\frac{\partial}{\partial a} E(a, b) = -2 \sum_{n=1}^{N} (y^n - a - bx^n), \qquad \frac{\partial}{\partial b} E(a, b) = -2 \sum_{n=1}^{N} (y^n - a - bx^n)x^n. \tag{17.1.3}$$

Dividing by N and equating to zero, the optimal parameters are given from the solution to the two linear equations

$$\langle y \rangle - a - b \langle x \rangle = 0, \qquad \langle xy \rangle - a \langle x \rangle - b \langle x^2 \rangle = 0 \tag{17.1.4}$$

where we used the notation $\langle f(x, y) \rangle$ to denote $\frac{1}{N} \sum_{n=1}^{N} f(x^n, y^n)$. We can readily solve the Equations (17.1.4) to determine a and b:

$$a = \langle y \rangle - b \langle x \rangle \tag{17.1.5}$$

$$b \langle x^2 \rangle = \langle yx \rangle - \langle x \rangle (\langle y \rangle - b \langle x \rangle) \Rightarrow b \left[\langle x^2 \rangle - \langle x \rangle^2 \right] = \langle xy \rangle - \langle x \rangle \langle y \rangle. \tag{17.1.6}$$

Hence

$$b = \frac{\langle xy \rangle - \langle x \rangle \langle y \rangle}{\langle x^2 \rangle - \langle x \rangle^2} \tag{17.1.7}$$

and a is found by substituting this value for b into Equation (17.1.5).

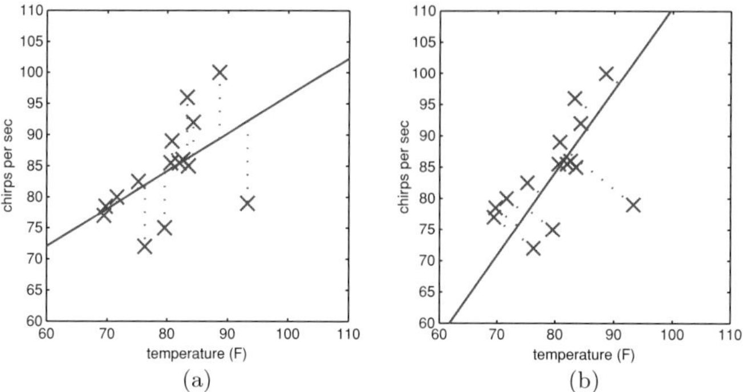

Figure 17.1 Data from singbats – the number of chirps per second, versus the temperature in Fahrenheit. (**a**) Straight line regression fit to the singbat data. (**b**) PCA fit to the data. In regression we minimise the *residuals* – the vertical distances from datapoints to the line. In PCA the fit minimises the orthogonal projections to the line. Both lines go through the mean of the data.

In contrast to ordinary least squares regression, PCA from Chapter 15 minimises the orthogonal projection of y to the line and is known as *orthogonal least squares* – see Example 17.1.

Example 17.1

In Fig. 17.1 we plot the number of chirps c per second for singbats, versus the temperature t in degrees Fahrenheit. A biologist believes that there is a simple relation between the number of chirps and the temperature of the form

$$c = a + bt \tag{17.1.8}$$

where she needs to determine the parameters a and b. For the singbat data, the fit is plotted in Fig. 17.1(a). For comparison we plot the fit from the PCA, Fig. 17.1(b), which minimises the sum of the squared orthogonal projections from the data to the line.

17.2 Linear parameter models for regression

We can generalise the above to fitting linear functions of vector inputs $\mathbf{x}$. For a dataset $\{(\mathbf{x}^n, y^n), n = 1, \ldots, N\}$, a linear parameter regression model (LPM) is defined by[1]

$$y(\mathbf{x}) = \mathbf{w}^{\mathsf{T}}\boldsymbol{\phi}(\mathbf{x}) \tag{17.2.1}$$

where $\boldsymbol{\phi}(\mathbf{x})$ is a vector valued function of the input vector $\mathbf{x}$. For example, in the case of a straight line fit, with scalar input and output, Equation (17.1.1), we have

$$\boldsymbol{\phi}(x) = (1, x)^{\mathsf{T}}, \qquad \mathbf{w} = (a, b)^{\mathsf{T}}. \tag{17.2.2}$$

We define the train error as the sum of squared differences between the observed outputs and the predictions under the linear model:

$$E(\mathbf{w}) = \sum_{n=1}^{N} (y^n - \mathbf{w}^{\mathsf{T}}\boldsymbol{\phi}^n)^2, \qquad \text{where } \boldsymbol{\phi}^n \equiv \boldsymbol{\phi}(\mathbf{x}^n). \tag{17.2.3}$$

[1] Note that the model is linear in the parameter $\mathbf{w}$ – not necessarily linear in $\mathbf{x}$.

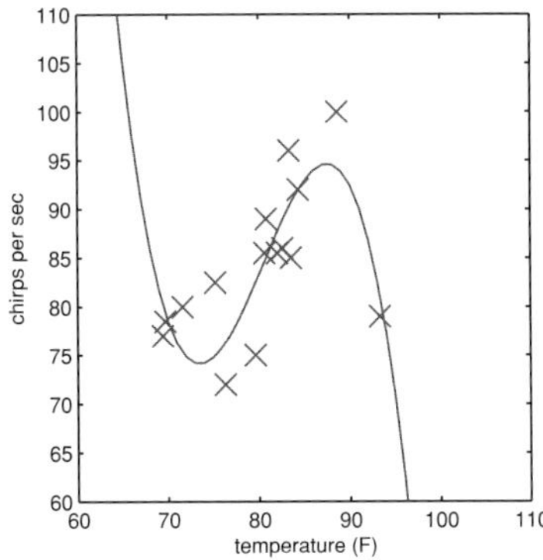

Figure 17.2 Cubic polynomial fit to the singbat data.

We now wish to determine the parameter vector $\mathbf{w}$ that minimises $E(\mathbf{w})$. In terms of the components of $\mathbf{w}$, the squared error is

$$E(\mathbf{w}) = \sum_{n=1}^{N} (y^n - \sum_i w_i \phi_i^n)(y^n - \sum_j w_j \phi_j^n). \tag{17.2.4}$$

Differentiating with respect to w_k, and equating to zero gives

$$\sum_{n=1}^{N} y^n \phi_k^n = \sum_i w_i \sum_{n=1}^{N} \phi_i^n \phi_k^n \tag{17.2.5}$$

or, in matrix notation,

$$\sum_{n=1}^{N} y^n \boldsymbol{\phi}^n = \sum_{n=1}^{N} \boldsymbol{\phi}^n (\boldsymbol{\phi}^n)^{\mathsf{T}} \mathbf{w}. \tag{17.2.6}$$

These are called the *normal equations*, for which the solution is

$$\mathbf{w} = \left(\sum_{n=1}^{N} \boldsymbol{\phi}^n (\boldsymbol{\phi}^n)^{\mathsf{T}} \right)^{-1} \sum_{n=1}^{N} y^n \boldsymbol{\phi}^n. \tag{17.2.7}$$

Although we write the solution using matrix inversion, in practice one finds the numerical solution using Gaussian elimination [129] since this is faster and numerically more stable.

Example 17.2 A cubic polynomial fit

A cubic polynomial is given by

$$y(x) = w_1 + w_2 x + w_3 x^2 + w_4 x^3. \tag{17.2.8}$$

As an LPM, this can be expressed using

$$\boldsymbol{\phi}(x) = \left(1, x, x^2, x^3\right)^{\mathsf{T}}. \tag{17.2.9}$$

The ordinary least squares solution has the form given in Equation (17.2.18). The fitted cubic polynomial is plotted in Fig. 17.2. See also `demoCubicPoly.m`.

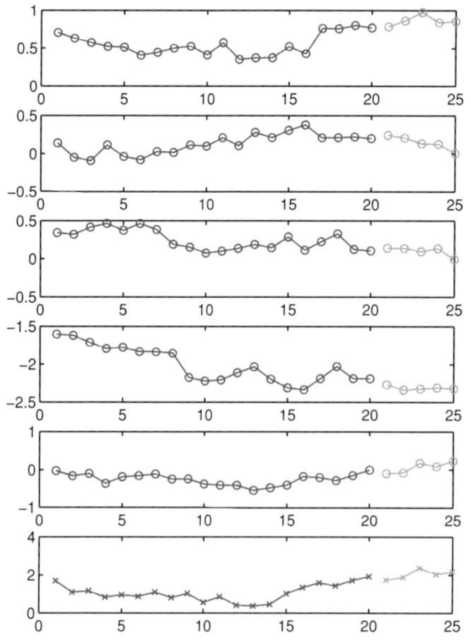

Figure 17.3 Predicting stock return using a linear LPM. The top five panels present the inputs $x_1, \ldots, x_5$ for 20 train days and 5 test days. The corresponding train output (stock return) y for each day is given in the bottom panel. The predictions $y_{21}, \ldots, y_{25}$ are the predictions based on $y_t = \sum_i w_i x_{it}$ with $\mathbf{w}$ trained using ordinary least squares. With a regularisation term $0.01\mathbf{w}^\mathsf{T}\mathbf{w}$, the OLS learned $\mathbf{w}$ is $[1.42, 0.62, 0.27, -0.26, 1.54]$. Despite the simplicity of these models, their application in the finance industry is widespread, with significant investment made on finding factors $\mathbf{x}$ that may be indicative of future return. See `demoLPMhedge.m`.

Example 17.3 Predicting return

In Fig. 17.3 we fit an LPM with vector inputs $\mathbf{x}$ to a scalar output y. The vector $\mathbf{x}$ represents factors that are believed to affect the stock price of a company, with the stock price return given by the scalar y. A hedge fund manager believes that the returns may be linearly related to the factors:

$$y_t = \sum_{i=1}^{5} w_i x_{it} \tag{17.2.10}$$

and wishes to fit the parameters $\mathbf{w}$ in order to use the model to predict future stock returns. This is straightforward using ordinary least squares, this being simply an LPM with a linear ϕ function. See Fig. 17.3 for an example. Such models also form the basis for more complex models in finance, see for example [209].

17.2.1 Vector outputs

It is straightforward to generalise the above framework to vector outputs $\mathbf{y}$. Using a separate weight vector $\mathbf{w}_i$ for each output component y_i, we have

$$y_i(\mathbf{x}) = \mathbf{w}_i^\mathsf{T}\boldsymbol{\phi}(\mathbf{x}). \tag{17.2.11}$$

The mathematics follows similarly to before, and we may define a train error per output as

$$E(\mathbf{w}_i) = \sum_n \left(y_i^n - \mathbf{w}_i^\mathsf{T}\boldsymbol{\phi}^n\right)^2, \qquad E(\mathbf{w}) = \sum_i E(\mathbf{w}_i). \tag{17.2.12}$$

Since the training error decomposes into individual terms, one for each output, the weights for each output can be trained separately. In other words, the problem decomposes into a set of independent scalar output problems. In case the parameters $\mathbf{w}$ are tied or shared amongst the outputs, the training is still straightforward since the objective function remains linear in the parameters, and this is left as an exercise for the interested reader.

17.2.2 Regularisation

For most purposes, our interest is not just to find the function that best fits the train data but one that will generalise well. To control the complexity of the fitted function we may add an extra regularising term $R(\mathbf{w})$ to the train error to penalise rapid changes in the output

$$E'(\mathbf{w}) = E(\mathbf{w}) + \lambda R(\mathbf{w}) \tag{17.2.13}$$

where λ is a scalar amount that adjusts the strength of the regularisation term. For example a regularising term that can be added to Equation (17.2.3) is

$$R(\mathbf{w}) = \sum_{n=1}^{N}\sum_{n'=1}^{N} e^{-\gamma\left(\mathbf{x}^n - \mathbf{x}^{n'}\right)^2}\left[y(\mathbf{x}^n) - y(\mathbf{x}^{n'})\right]^2. \tag{17.2.14}$$

The factor $\left[y(\mathbf{x}^n) - y(\mathbf{x}^{n'})\right]^2$ penalises large differences in the outputs corresponding to two inputs. The factor $\exp\left(-\gamma\left(\mathbf{x}^n - \mathbf{x}^{n'}\right)^2\right)$ has the effect of weighting more heavily terms for which two input vectors $\mathbf{x}^n$ and $\mathbf{x}^{n'}$ are close together; γ is a fixed length-scale parameter. Since $y = \mathbf{w}^{\mathsf{T}}\boldsymbol{\phi}(\mathbf{x})$, expression (17.2.14) can be written as

$$\mathbf{w}^{\mathsf{T}}\mathbf{R}\mathbf{w} \tag{17.2.15}$$

where

$$\mathbf{R} \equiv \sum_{n=1}^{N}\sum_{n'=1}^{N} e^{-\gamma\left(\mathbf{x}^n - \mathbf{x}^{n'}\right)^2}\left(\boldsymbol{\phi}^n - \boldsymbol{\phi}^{n'}\right)\left(\boldsymbol{\phi}^n - \boldsymbol{\phi}^{n'}\right)^{\mathsf{T}}. \tag{17.2.16}$$

The regularised train error is then

$$E'(\mathbf{w}) = \sum_{n=1}^{N}(y^n - \mathbf{w}^{\mathsf{T}}\boldsymbol{\phi}^n)^2 + \lambda\mathbf{w}^{\mathsf{T}}\mathbf{R}\mathbf{w}. \tag{17.2.17}$$

By differentiating the regularised training error and equating to zero, we find the optimal $\mathbf{w}$ is given by

$$\mathbf{w} = \left(\sum_{n}\boldsymbol{\phi}^n(\boldsymbol{\phi}^n)^{\mathsf{T}} + \lambda\mathbf{R}\right)^{-1}\sum_{n=1}^{N} y^n\boldsymbol{\phi}^n. \tag{17.2.18}$$

In practice it is common to use a regulariser that penalises the sum squared length of the weights

$$R(\mathbf{w}) = \mathbf{w}^{\mathsf{T}}\mathbf{w} = \sum_{i} w_i^2 \tag{17.2.19}$$

which corresponds to setting $\mathbf{R} = \mathbf{I}$. This is known as *ridge regression*. Regularising pararameters such as λ, γ may be determined using a validation set, Section 13.2.2.

17.2.3 Radial basis functions

A popular LPM is given by the non-linear function $\boldsymbol{\phi}(\mathbf{x})$ with components

$$\phi_i(\mathbf{x}) = \exp\left(-\frac{1}{2\alpha^2}\left(\mathbf{x} - \mathbf{m}^i\right)^2\right). \tag{17.2.20}$$

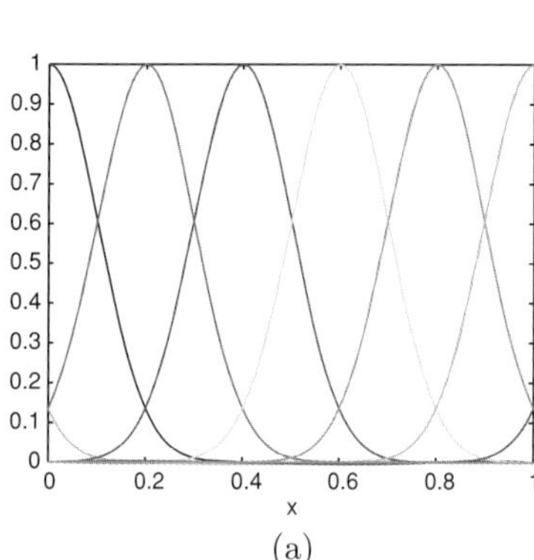

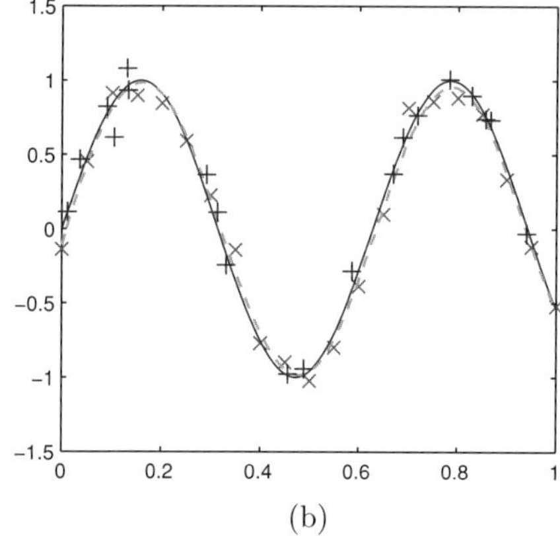

Figure 17.4 (**a**) A set of fixed-width ($\alpha = 1$) radial basis functions, $\exp\left(-\frac{1}{2}(x - m^i)^2\right)$, with the centres m^i evenly spaced. By taking a linear combination of these functions we can form a flexible function class. (**b**) The $\times$ are the training points, and the $+$ are the validation points. The solid line is the correct underlying function $\sin(10x)$ which is corrupted with a small amount of additive noise to form the train data. The dashed line is the best predictor based on the validation set.

These basis functions are bump shaped, with the centre of bump i being given by $\mathbf{m}^i$ and the width by α. An example is given in Fig. 17.4 in which several RBFs are plotted with different centres. In LPM regression we can then use a linear combination of these bumps to fit the data. One can apply the same approach using vector inputs. For vector $\mathbf{x}$ and centre $\mathbf{m}$, the radial basis function depends on the distance between $\mathbf{x}$ and the centre $\mathbf{m}$, giving a bump in input space, Fig. 17.6.

Example 17.4 Setting α

Consider fitting the data in Fig. 17.4(b) using 16 radial basis functions uniformly spread over the input space, with width parameter α and regularising term $\lambda\mathbf{w}^\mathsf{T}\mathbf{w}$. The generalisation performance on the test data depends heavily on the width and regularising parameter λ. In order to find reasonable values for these parameters we may use a validation set. For simplicity we set the regularisation parameter to $\lambda = 0.0001$ and use the validation set to determine a suitable α. In Fig. 17.5 we plot the validation error $E(\mathbf{w})$ as a function of α, choosing then the α with the lowest validation error. The predictions for this optimal α are also given in Fig. 17.4(b).

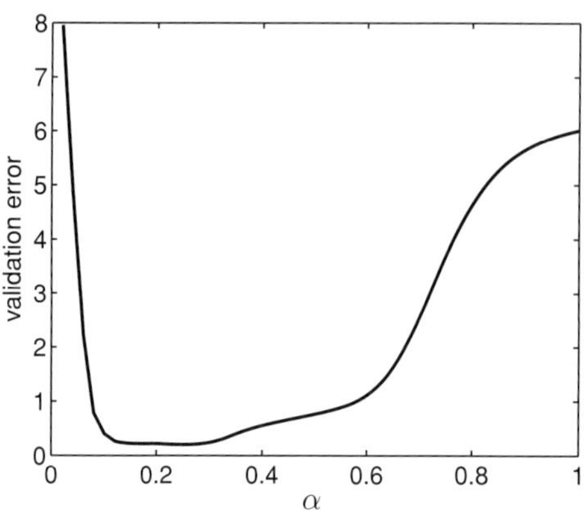

Figure 17.5 The validation error as a function of the basis function width for the validation data in Fig. 17.4(b) and RBFs in Fig. 17.4(a). Based on the validation error, the optimal setting of the basis function width parameter is $\alpha = 0.25$.

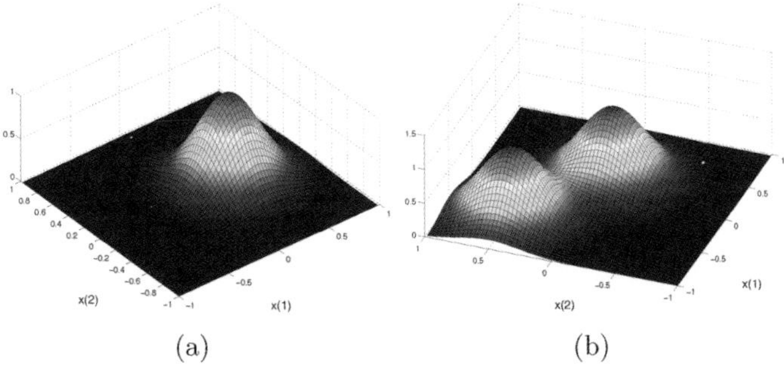

Figure 17.6 (**a**) The output of an RBF function $\exp(-\frac{1}{2}(\mathbf{x}-\mathbf{m}^1)^2/\alpha^2)$. Here $\mathbf{m}^1 = (0, 0.3)^\mathsf{T}$ and $\alpha = 0.25$. (**b**) The combined output for two RBFs with $\mathbf{m}^1$ as above and $\mathbf{m}^2 = (0.5, -0.5)^\mathsf{T}$.

A curse of dimensionality

If the data has non-trivial behaviour over some input region, then we need to cover this region input space fairly densely with bump type functions. In the above case, we used 16 basis functions for a one dimensional input space. In two dimensions if we wish to cover each dimension to the same discretisation level, we would need $16^2 = 256$ basis functions. Similarly, for 10 dimensions we would need $16^{10} \approx 10^{12}$ functions. To fit such an LPM would require solving a linear system in more than 10^{12} variables. This explosion in the number of basis functions with the input dimension is a 'curse of dimensionality'.

A possible remedy is to make the basis functions very broad so that each covers more of the high-dimensional space. However, this will mean a lack of flexibility of the fitted function since it is constrained to be smooth. Another approach is to place basis functions centred on the training input points and add some more basis functions randomly placed close to the training inputs. The rationale behind this is that when we come to do prediction, we will most likely see novel $\mathbf{x}$ that are close to the training points – we do not need to make accurate predictions over all the space. A further approach is to make the positions of the basis functions adaptive, allowing them to be moved around in the space to minimise the error. This approach is used in neural network models [42]. An alternative is to reexpress the problem of fitting an LPM by reparameterising the problem, as discussed below.

17.3 The dual representation and kernels

Consider a set of training data with inputs, $\mathcal{X} = \{\mathbf{x}^n, n = 1, \ldots, N\}$ and corresponding outputs $y^n, n = 1, \ldots, N$. For an LPM of the form

$$f(\mathbf{x}) = \mathbf{w}^\mathsf{T}\mathbf{x} \tag{17.3.1}$$

our interest is to find the 'best fit' parameters $\mathbf{w}$. We assume that we have found an optimal parameter $\mathbf{w}_*$. The nullspace of $\mathcal{X}$ are those $\mathbf{x}^\perp$ which are orthogonal to all the inputs in $\mathcal{X}$. That is, $\mathbf{x}^\perp$ is in the nullspace if

$$\left(\mathbf{x}^\perp\right)^\mathsf{T}\mathbf{x}^n = 0, \qquad \text{for all } n = 1, \ldots, N. \tag{17.3.2}$$

If we then consider the vector $\mathbf{w}_*$ with an additional component in the nullspace,

$$\left(\mathbf{w}_* + \mathbf{x}^\perp\right)^\mathsf{T}\mathbf{x}^n = \mathbf{w}_*^\mathsf{T}\mathbf{x}^n. \tag{17.3.3}$$

This means that adding a contribution to $\mathbf{w}_*$ outside of the space spanned by $\mathcal{X}$, has no effect on the predictions on the train data. If the training criterion depends only on how well the LPM predicts the train data, there is therefore no need to consider contributions to $\mathbf{w}$ from outside of $\mathcal{X}$. That is, without loss of generality we may consider the representation

$$\mathbf{w} = \sum_{m=1}^{N} a_m \mathbf{x}^m. \tag{17.3.4}$$

The parameters $\mathbf{a} = (a_1, \ldots, a_N)$ are called the *dual parameters*. We can then write the output of the LPM directly in terms of the dual parameters,

$$\mathbf{w}^\mathsf{T}\mathbf{x}^n = \sum_{m=1}^{N} a_m \left(\mathbf{x}^m\right)^\mathsf{T} \mathbf{x}^n. \tag{17.3.5}$$

More generally, for a vector function $\boldsymbol{\phi}(\mathbf{x})$, the solution will lie in the space spanned by $\boldsymbol{\phi}(\mathbf{x}^1), \ldots, \boldsymbol{\phi}(\mathbf{x}^N)$,

$$\mathbf{w} = \sum_{n=1}^{N} a_n \boldsymbol{\phi}\left(\mathbf{x}^n\right) \tag{17.3.6}$$

and we may write

$$\mathbf{w}^\mathsf{T}\boldsymbol{\phi}(\mathbf{x}^n) = \sum_{m=1}^{N} a_m \boldsymbol{\phi}\left(\mathbf{x}^m\right)^\mathsf{T} \boldsymbol{\phi}\left(\mathbf{x}^n\right) = \sum_{m=1}^{N} a_m K\left(\mathbf{x}^m, \mathbf{x}^n\right) \tag{17.3.7}$$

where we have defined a *kernel* function

$$K\left(\mathbf{x}^m, \mathbf{x}^n\right) \equiv \boldsymbol{\phi}\left(\mathbf{x}^m\right)^\mathsf{T} \boldsymbol{\phi}\left(\mathbf{x}^n\right) \equiv \left[\mathbf{K}\right]_{m,n}. \tag{17.3.8}$$

In matrix form, the output of the LPM on a training input $\mathbf{x}$ is then

$$\mathbf{w}^\mathsf{T}\boldsymbol{\phi}(\mathbf{x}^n) = \left[\mathbf{K}\mathbf{a}\right]_n = \mathbf{a}^\mathsf{T}\mathbf{k}^n \tag{17.3.9}$$

where $\mathbf{k}^n$ is the nth column of the *Gram matrix* $\mathbf{K}$. By construction, the Gram matrix must be positive semidefinite, and the kernel a covariance function, see Section 19.3.

17.3.1 Regression in the dual space

For ordinary least squares regression, using Equation (17.3.9), we have a train error

$$E(\mathbf{a}) = \sum_{n=1}^{N} \left(y^n - \mathbf{a}^\mathsf{T}\mathbf{k}^n\right)^2. \tag{17.3.10}$$

Equation (17.3.10) is analogous to the standard regression Equation (17.2.3) on interchanging $\mathbf{a}$ for $\mathbf{w}$ and $\mathbf{k}^n$ for $\boldsymbol{\phi}(\mathbf{x}^n)$. Similarly, the regularisation term can be expressed as

$$\mathbf{w}^\mathsf{T}\mathbf{w} = \sum_{n,m=1}^{N} a_n a_m \boldsymbol{\phi}\left(\mathbf{x}^n\right) \boldsymbol{\phi}\left(\mathbf{x}^m\right) = \mathbf{a}^\mathsf{T}\mathbf{K}\mathbf{a}. \tag{17.3.11}$$

By direct analogy the optimal solution for $\mathbf{a}$ is therefore

$$\mathbf{a} = \left(\sum_{n=1}^{N} \mathbf{k}^n \left(\mathbf{k}^n\right)^\mathsf{T} + \lambda\mathbf{K}\right)^{-1} \sum_{n=1}^{N} y^n \mathbf{k}^n. \tag{17.3.12}$$

We can express the above solution more conveniently by first writing

$$\mathbf{a} = \left(\sum_{n=1}^{N} \mathbf{K}^{-1}\mathbf{k}^n \left(\mathbf{k}^n\right)^\mathsf{T} + \lambda \mathbf{I} \right)^{-1} \sum_{n=1}^{N} y^n \mathbf{K}^{-1}\mathbf{k}^n. \tag{17.3.13}$$

Since $\mathbf{k}^n$ is the nth column of $\mathbf{K}$ then $\mathbf{K}^{-1}\mathbf{k}^n$ is the nth column of the identity matrix. With a little manipulation, we can therefore rewrite Equation (17.3.13) more simply as

$$\mathbf{a} = \left(\mathbf{K} + \lambda \mathbf{I}\right)^{-1} \mathbf{y} \tag{17.3.14}$$

where $\mathbf{y}$ is the vector with components formed from the training inputs $y^1, \ldots, y^N$. Using this, the prediction for a new input $\mathbf{x}^*$ is given by

$$y(\mathbf{x}^*) = \mathbf{k}_*^\mathsf{T} \left(\mathbf{K} + \lambda \mathbf{I}\right)^{-1} \mathbf{y} \tag{17.3.15}$$

where the vector $\mathbf{k}_*$ has components

$$\left[\mathbf{k}_*\right]_m = K\left(\mathbf{x}^*, \mathbf{x}^m\right). \tag{17.3.16}$$

This dual space solution shows that predictions can be expressed purely in terms of the kernel $K\left(\mathbf{x}, \mathbf{x}'\right)$. This means that we may dispense with defining the vector functions $\boldsymbol{\phi}(\mathbf{x})$ and define a kernel function directly. This approach is also used in Gaussian processes, Chapter 19 and enables us to use effectively very large (even infinite) dimensional vectors $\boldsymbol{\phi}$ without ever explicitly needing to compute them. Note that the Gram matrix $\mathbf{K}$ has dimension $N \times N$, which means that the computational complexity of performing the matrix inversion in Equation (17.3.16) is $O\left(N^3\right)$. For moderate to large N (greater than 5000), this will be prohibitively expensive, and numerical approximations are required. This is in contrast to the computational complexity of solving the normal equations in the original weight space viewpoint which is $O\left(\dim\left(\boldsymbol{\phi}\right)^3\right)$. The dual parameterisation therefore helps us with the curse of dimensionality since the complexity of learning in the dual parameterisation scales cubically with the number of training points – not cubically with the dimension of the $\boldsymbol{\phi}$ vector.

17.4 Linear parameter models for classification

In a binary classification problem we are given train data, $\mathcal{D} = \{(\mathbf{x}^n, c^n), n = 1 \ldots, N\}$, where the targets $c \in \{0, 1\}$. Inspired by the LPM regression model, we can assign the probability that a novel input $\mathbf{x}$ belongs to class 1 using

$$p(c = 1|\mathbf{x}) = f(\mathbf{x}^\mathsf{T}\mathbf{w}) \tag{17.4.1}$$

where $0 \leq f(x) \leq 1$. In the statistics literature, $f(x)$ is termed a mean function – the inverse function $f^{-1}(x)$ is the link function.[2] Two popular choices for the function $f(x)$ are the logit and probit functions. The *logit* is given by

$$f(x) = \frac{e^x}{1 + e^x} = \frac{1}{1 + e^{-x}} \tag{17.4.2}$$

[2] These models are part of the 'generalised linear models' class in the statistics literature which includes the regression model and classification models as special cases.

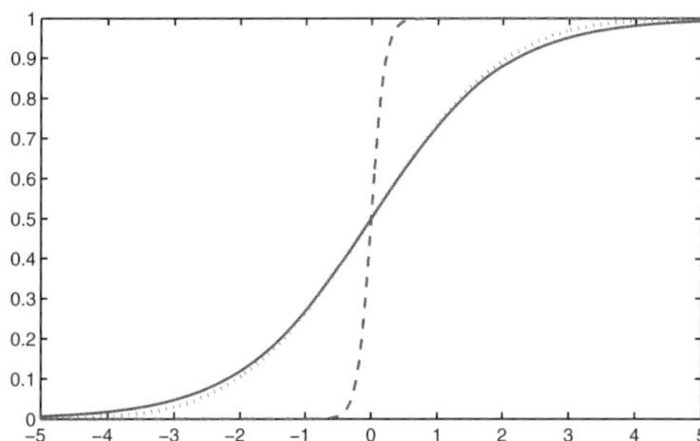

Figure 17.7 The logistic sigmoid function $\sigma_\beta(x) = 1/(1 + e^{-\beta x})$. The parameter β determines the steepness of the sigmoid. The full line is for $\beta = 1$ and the dashed for $\beta = 10$. As $\beta \to \infty$, the logistic sigmoid tends to a Heaviside step function. The dotted curve is the error function (probit) $0.5\,(1 + \text{erf}(\lambda x))$ for $\lambda = \sqrt{\pi}/4$, which closely matches the standard logistic sigmoid with $\beta = 1$.

which is also called the *logistic sigmoid* and written $\sigma(x)$, Fig. 17.7. The scaled version is defined as

$$\sigma_\beta(x) = \sigma(\beta x). \tag{17.4.3}$$

A closely related model is *probit regression* which uses in place of the logistic sigmoid the cumulative distribution of the standard normal distribution

$$f(x) = \frac{1}{\sqrt{2\pi}} \int_{-\infty}^{x} e^{-\frac{1}{2}t^2} dt = \frac{1}{2}\left(1 + \text{erf}(x)\right). \tag{17.4.4}$$

where the standard *error function*, is

$$\text{erf}(x) \equiv \frac{2}{\sqrt{\pi}} \int_{0}^{x} e^{-t^2} dt. \tag{17.4.5}$$

The shape of the probit and logistic functions are similar under rescaling, see Fig. 17.7. We focus below on the logit function.

17.4.1 Logistic regression

Logistic regression corresponds to the model

$$p(c = 1|\mathbf{x}) = \sigma(b + \mathbf{x}^\mathsf{T}\mathbf{w}) \tag{17.4.6}$$

where b is a scalar, and $\mathbf{w}$ is a vector.

The decision boundary

The decision boundary is defined as that set of $\mathbf{x}$ for which $p(c = 1|\mathbf{x}) = p(c = 0|\mathbf{x}) = 0.5$. This is given by the hyperplane

$$b + \mathbf{x}^\mathsf{T}\mathbf{w} = 0. \tag{17.4.7}$$

On the side of the hyperplane for which $b + \mathbf{x}^\mathsf{T}\mathbf{w} > 0$, inputs $\mathbf{x}$ are classified as 1's, and on the other side they are classified as 0's. The 'bias' parameter b simply shifts the decision boundary by a constant amount. The orientation of the decision boundary is determined by $\mathbf{w}$, the normal to the hyperplane, see Fig. 17.8. To clarify the geometric interpretation, let $\mathbf{x}$ be a point on the decision boundary and consider a new point $\mathbf{x}^* = \mathbf{x} + \mathbf{w}^\perp$, where $\mathbf{w}^\perp$ is a vector perpendicular to $\mathbf{w}$, so that $\mathbf{w}^\mathsf{T}\mathbf{w}^\perp = 0$. Then

$$b + \mathbf{w}^\mathsf{T}\mathbf{x}^* = b + \mathbf{w}^\mathsf{T}\left(\mathbf{x} + \mathbf{w}^\perp\right) = b + \mathbf{w}^\mathsf{T}\mathbf{x} + \mathbf{w}^\mathsf{T}\mathbf{w}^\perp = b + \mathbf{w}^\mathsf{T}\mathbf{x} = 0. \tag{17.4.8}$$

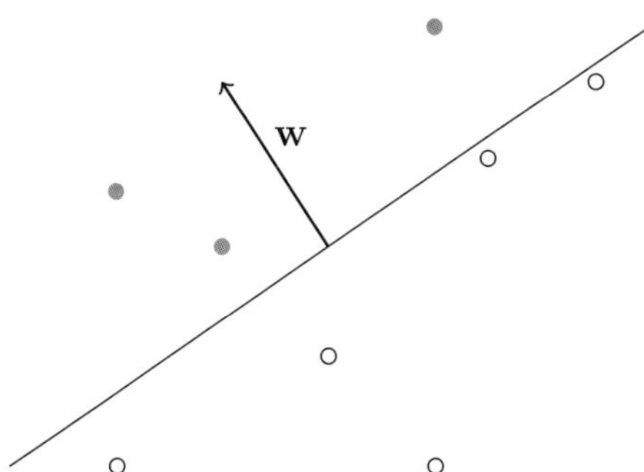

Figure 17.8 The decision boundary $p(c = 1|\mathbf{x}) = 0.5$ (solid line). For two-dimensional data, the decision boundary is a line. If all the training data for class 1 (filled circles) lie on one side of the line, and for class 0 (open circles) on the other, the data is said to be *linearly separable*. More generally, $\mathbf{w}$ defines the normal to a hyperplane and data is linearly separable if data from each of the two classes lies on opposite sides of the hyperplane.

Thus if $\mathbf{x}$ is on the decision boundary, so is $\mathbf{x}$ plus any vector perpendicular to $\mathbf{w}$. In D dimensions, the space of vectors that are perpendicular to $\mathbf{w}$ occupy a $D - 1$ dimensional hyperplane. For example, if the data is two dimensional, the decision boundary is a one-dimensional hyperplane, a line, as depicted in Fig. 17.8.

Definition 17.1 Linear separability If all the train data for class 1 lies on one side of a hyperplane, and for class 0 on the other, the data is said to be linearly separable.

For D-dimensional data, provided there are no more than D training points, then these are linearly separable if they are linearly independent. To see this, let $c^n = +1$ if $\mathbf{x}^n$ is in class 1, and $c^n = -1$ if $\mathbf{x}^n$ is in class 0. For the data to be linearly separable we require

$$\mathbf{w}^\mathsf{T}\mathbf{x}^n + b = \epsilon c^n, \qquad n = 1, \ldots, N \tag{17.4.9}$$

where ϵ is an arbitrary positive constant. The above equations state that each input is just the correct side of the decision boundary. If there are $N = D$ datapoints, the above can be written in matrix form as

$$\mathbf{X}\mathbf{w} + \mathbf{b} = \epsilon\mathbf{c} \tag{17.4.10}$$

where $\mathbf{X}$ is a square matrix whose nth column contains $\mathbf{x}^n$ and $[\mathbf{b}]_i = b$. Provided that $\mathbf{X}$ is invertible the solution is

$$\mathbf{w} = \mathbf{X}^{-1}(\epsilon\mathbf{c} - \mathbf{b}). \tag{17.4.11}$$

The bias b can be set arbitrarily. This shows that provided the $\mathbf{x}^n$ are linearly independent, we can always find a hyperplane that linearly separates the data. Provided the data are not-collinear (all occupying the same $D - 1$ dimensional subspace) the additional bias enables $D + 1$ arbitrarily labelled points to be linearly separated in D dimensions.

An example dataset that is not linearly separable is given by the following four training points and class labels

$$\{([0, 0], 0), ([0, 1], 1), ([1, 0], 1), ([1, 1], 0)\}. \tag{17.4.12}$$

This data represents the XOR function, and is plotted in Fig. 17.9. This function is not linearly separable since no straight line has all inputs from one class on one side and the other class on

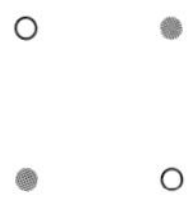

Figure 17.9 The XOR problem. This is not linearly separable.

the other. Classifying data which is not linearly separable can only be achieved using a non-linear decision boundary. It might be that data is non-linearly separable in the original data space. An alternative is to map the data to a higher dimension using a non-linear vector function; this creates a set of non-linearly dependent high-dimensional vectors which can then be separated using a high-dimensional hyperplane. We discuss this in Section 17.4.5.

The perceptron

We briefly describe here the perceptron, an important early model in the field of AI, see for example [42]. The perceptron deterministically assigns $\mathbf{x}$ to class 1 if $b + \mathbf{w}^{\mathsf{T}}\mathbf{x} \geq 0$, and to class 0 otherwise. That is

$$p(c = 1|\mathbf{x}) = \theta(b + \mathbf{x}^{\mathsf{T}}\mathbf{w}) \tag{17.4.13}$$

where the step function is defined as

$$\theta(x) = \begin{cases} 1 & x > 0 \\ 0 & x \leq 0. \end{cases} \tag{17.4.14}$$

If we consider the logistic regression model

$$p(c = 1|\mathbf{x}) = \sigma_{\beta}\left(b + \mathbf{x}^{\mathsf{T}}\mathbf{w}\right) \tag{17.4.15}$$

and take the limit $\beta \to \infty$, we have the perceptron like classifier

$$p(c = 1|\mathbf{x}) = \begin{cases} 1 & b + \mathbf{x}^{\mathsf{T}}\mathbf{w} > 0 \\ 0.5 & b + \mathbf{x}^{\mathsf{T}}\mathbf{w} = 0 \\ 0 & b + \mathbf{x}^{\mathsf{T}}\mathbf{w} < 0. \end{cases} \tag{17.4.16}$$

The only difference between this 'probabilistic perceptron' and the standard perceptron is in the technical definition of the value of the step function at 0. The perceptron may therefore essentially be viewed as a limiting case of logistic regression.

Maximum likelihood training

For this class discriminative model, we do not model the input distribution $p(\mathbf{x})$ so that we may equivalently consider the likelihood of the set of output class variables $\mathcal{C}$ conditioned on the set of training inputs $\mathcal{X}$. If we assume that each data point has been drawn independently from the same distribution that generates the data (the standard i.i.d. assumption), the likelihood is (writing explicitly the conditional dependence on the parameters b, $\mathbf{w}$)

$$\begin{aligned} p(\mathcal{C}|b, \mathbf{w}, \mathcal{X}) &= \prod_{n=1}^{N} p(c^n|\mathbf{x}^n, b, \mathbf{w})p(\mathbf{x}^n) \\ &= \prod_{n=1}^{N} p(c = 1|\mathbf{x}^n, b, \mathbf{w})^{c^n} \left(1 - p(c = 1|\mathbf{x}^n, b, \mathbf{w})\right)^{1-c^n} p(\mathbf{x}^n) \end{aligned} \tag{17.4.17}$$

where we have used the fact that $c^n \in \{0, 1\}$. For logistic regression this gives the log likelihood as

$$L(\mathbf{w}, b) = \sum_{n=1}^{N} c^n \log \sigma(b + \mathbf{w}^{\mathsf{T}}\mathbf{x}^n) + (1 - c^n) \log\left(1 - \sigma(b + \mathbf{w}^{\mathsf{T}}\mathbf{x}^n)\right). \tag{17.4.18}$$

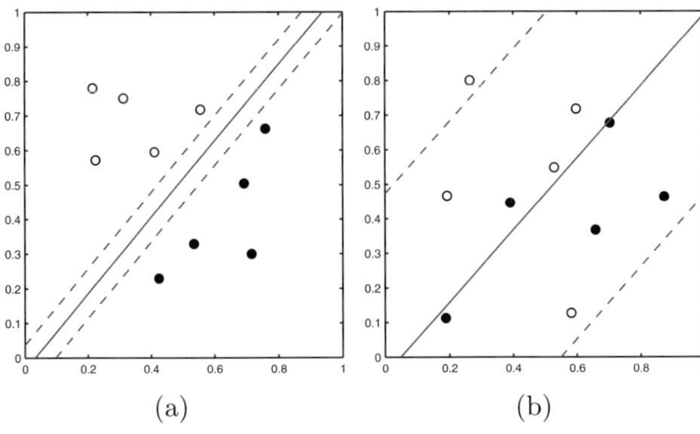

Figure 17.10 The decision boundary $p(c = 1|\mathbf{x}) = 0.5$ (solid line) and confidence boundaries $p(c = 1|\mathbf{x}) = 0.9$ and $p(c = 1|\mathbf{x}) = 0.1$ after 10 000 iterations of batch gradient ascent with $\eta = 0.1$. **(a)** Linearly separable data. **(b)** Non-linearly separable data. Note how the confidence interval remains broad, see `demoLogReg.m`.

Gradient ascent

There is no closed form solution to the maximisation of $L(\mathbf{w}, b)$ which needs to be carried out numerically. One of the simplest methods is gradient ascent for which the gradient is given by

$$\nabla_{\mathbf{w}} L = \sum_{n=1}^{N} (c^n - \sigma(\mathbf{w}^{\mathsf{T}}\mathbf{x}^n + b))\mathbf{x}^n. \tag{17.4.19}$$

Here we made use of the derivative relation for the logistic sigmoid

$$d\sigma(x)/dx = \sigma(x)(1 - \sigma(x)). \tag{17.4.20}$$

The derivative with respect to the bias is

$$\frac{dL}{db} = \sum_{n=1}^{N} (c^n - \sigma(\mathbf{w}^{\mathsf{T}}\mathbf{x}^n + b)). \tag{17.4.21}$$

The gradient ascent procedure then corresponds to updating the weights and bias using

$$\mathbf{w}^{new} = \mathbf{w} + \eta \nabla_{\mathbf{w}} L, \qquad b^{new} = b + \eta \frac{dL}{db} \tag{17.4.22}$$

where η, the *learning rate* is a scalar chosen small enough to ensure convergence.[3] The application of the above rule will lead to a gradual increase in the log likelihood.

Batch training

Writing the updates (17.4.22) explicitly gives

$$\mathbf{w}^{new} = \mathbf{w} + \eta \sum_{n=1}^{N} (c^n - \sigma(\mathbf{w}^{\mathsf{T}}\mathbf{x}^n + b))\mathbf{x}^n, \quad b^{new} = b + \eta \sum_{n=1}^{N} (c^n - \sigma(\mathbf{w}^{\mathsf{T}}\mathbf{x}^n + b)). \tag{17.4.23}$$

This is called a *batch update* since the parameters $\mathbf{w}$ and b are updated only after passing through the whole (batch) of train data.

[3] In principle one may use a different learning rate for each parameter.

For linearly separable data, we can also show that the weights must become infinite at convergence. Taking the scalar product of Equation (17.4.19) with $\mathbf{w}$, we have the zero gradient requirement

$$\sum_{n=1}^{N}(c^n - \sigma^n)\,\mathbf{w}^{\mathsf{T}}\mathbf{x}^n = 0 \tag{17.4.24}$$

where $\sigma^n \equiv \sigma\left(\mathbf{w}^{\mathsf{T}}\mathbf{x}^n + b\right)$. For simplicity we assume $b = 0$. For linearly separable data we have

$$\mathbf{w}^{\mathsf{T}}\mathbf{x}^n \begin{cases} >0 & \text{if } c^n = 1 \\ <0 & \text{if } c^n = 0. \end{cases} \tag{17.4.25}$$

Then, using the fact that $0 \le \sigma^n \le 1$, we have

$$(c^n - \sigma^n)\,\mathbf{w}^{\mathsf{T}}\mathbf{x}^n \begin{cases} \ge 0 & \text{if } c^n = 1 \\ \ge 0 & \text{if } c^n = 0. \end{cases} \tag{17.4.26}$$

Each term $(c^n - \sigma^n)\,\mathbf{w}^{\mathsf{T}}\mathbf{x}^n$ is therefore non-negative and the zero gradient condition requires the sum of these terms to be zero. This can only happen if all the terms are zero, implying that $c^n = \sigma^n$, requiring the sigmoid to saturate and the weights to be infinite.

Online training

In practice it is common to update the parameters after each training example pair $(\mathbf{x}^n, c^n)$ has been considered:

$$\mathbf{w}^{new} = \mathbf{w} + \frac{\eta}{N}(c^n - \sigma(\mathbf{w}^{\mathsf{T}}\mathbf{x}^n + b))\mathbf{x}^n, \qquad b^{new} = b + \frac{\eta}{N}(c^n - \sigma(\mathbf{w}^{\mathsf{T}}\mathbf{x}^n + b)). \tag{17.4.27}$$

An advantage of online training is that the dataset need not be stored since only the performance on the current input is required. Provided that the data is linearly separable, the above online procedure converges (provided η is not too large). However, if the data is not linearly separable, the online version will not converge since the opposing class labels will continually pull the weights one way and then the other as each conflicting example is used to form an update. For the limiting case of the perceptron (replacing $\sigma(x)$ with $\theta(x)$) and linearly separable data, online updating converges in a finite number of steps [228, 42], but does not converge for non-linearly separable data.

Geometry of the error surface

The Hessian of the log likelihood $L(\mathbf{w})$ is the matrix with elements[4]

$$H_{ij} \equiv \frac{\partial^2 L}{\partial w_i w_j} = -\sum_n x_i^n x_j^n \sigma^n(1 - \sigma^n). \tag{17.4.28}$$

This is negative semidefinite since, for any $\mathbf{z}$,

$$\sum_{ij} z_i H_{ij} z_j = -\sum_{i,j,n} z_i x_i^n z_j x_j^n \sigma^n(1 - \sigma^n) \le -\sum_n \left(\sum_i z_i x_i^n\right)^2 \le 0. \tag{17.4.29}$$

This means that the error surface is concave (an upside down bowl) and batch gradient ascent converges to the optimal solution, provided the learning rate η is small enough.

[4] For simplicity we ignore the bias b. This can readily be dealt with by extending $\mathbf{x}$ to a $D+1$ dimensional vector $\hat{\mathbf{x}}$ with a 1 in the $D+1$ component. Then for a $D+1$ dimensional $\hat{\mathbf{w}} = \left(\mathbf{w}^{\mathsf{T}}, w_{D+1}\right)^{\mathsf{T}}$, we have $\hat{\mathbf{w}}^{\mathsf{T}}\hat{\mathbf{x}} = \mathbf{w}^{\mathsf{T}}\mathbf{x} + w_{D+1}$.

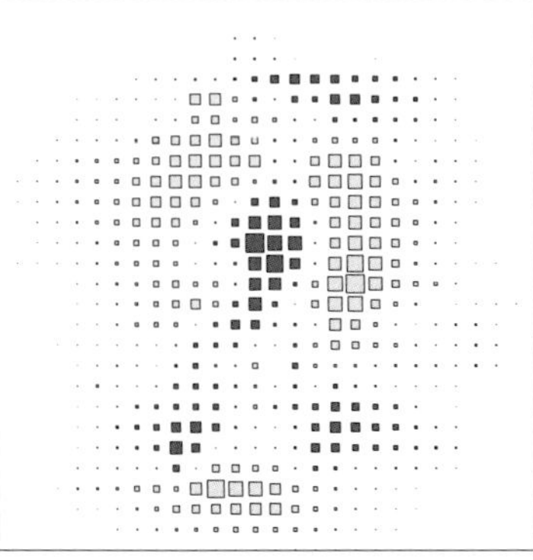

Figure 17.11 Logistic regression for classifying handwritten digits 1 and 7. Displayed is a Hinton diagram of the 784 learned weight vector **w**, plotted as a 28×28 image for visual interpretation. Light squares are positive weights and an input **x** with a (positive) value in this component will tend to increase the probability that the input is classed as a 7. Similarly, inputs with positive contributions in the dark regions tend to increase the probability as being classed as a 1 digit. Note that the elements of each input **x** are either positive or zero.

Example 17.5 Classifying handwritten digits

We apply logistic regression to the 600 handwritten digits of Example 14.1, in which there are 300 ones and 300 sevens in the train data. Using gradient ascent training with a suitably chosen stopping criterion, the number of errors made on the 600 test points is 12, compared with 14 errors using nearest neighbour methods. See Fig. 17.11 for a visualisation of the learned **w**.

17.4.2 Beyond first-order gradient ascent

Since the surface has a single optimum, a Newton update

$$\mathbf{w}^{new} = \mathbf{w}^{old} + \eta \mathbf{H}^{-1} \mathbf{w}^{old} \tag{17.4.30}$$

where $\mathbf{H}$ is the Hessian matrix as above and $0 < \eta < 1$, will typically converge much faster than gradient ascent. However, for large scale problems with $\dim(\mathbf{w}) \gg 1$, the inversion of the Hessian is computationally demanding and limited memory BFGS or conjugate gradient methods are more practical alternatives, see Section A.4.

17.4.3 Avoiding overconfident classification

Provided the data is linearly separable the weights will continue to increase and the classifications will become extreme. This is undesirable since the resulting classifications will be over-confident. One way to prevent this is *early stopping* in which only a limited number of gradient updates are performed. An alternative method is to add a penalty term to the objective function

$$L'(\mathbf{w}, b) = L(\mathbf{w}, b) - \alpha \mathbf{w}^{\mathsf{T}} \mathbf{w}. \tag{17.4.31}$$

The scalar constant $\alpha > 0$ encourages smaller values of $\mathbf{w}$ (remember that we wish to maximise the log likelihood). An appropriate value for α can be determined using validation data.

17.4.4 Multiple classes

For more than two classes, one may use the *softmax function*

$$p(c = i|\mathbf{x}) = \frac{e^{\mathbf{w}_i^{\mathsf{T}} \mathbf{x} + b_i}}{\sum_{j=1}^{C} e^{\mathbf{w}_j^{\mathsf{T}} \mathbf{x} + b_j}} \tag{17.4.32}$$

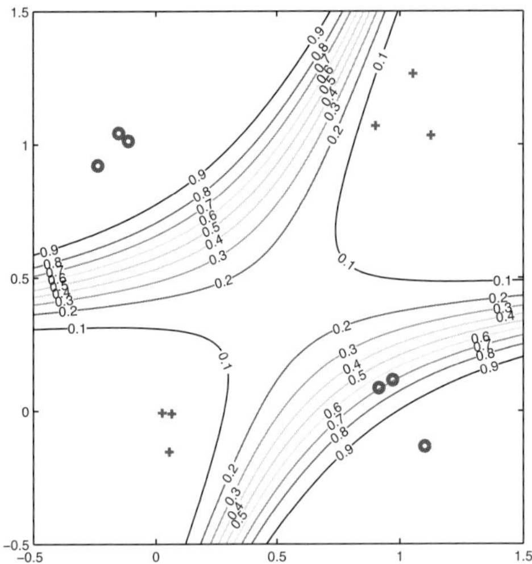

Figure 17.12 Logistic regression $p(c = 1|\mathbf{x}) = \sigma(\mathbf{w}^{\mathsf{T}}\boldsymbol{\phi}(\mathbf{x}))$ using a quadratic function $\boldsymbol{\phi}(\mathbf{x}) = (1, x_1, x_2, x_1^2, x_2^2, x_1x_2)^{\mathsf{T}}$; 1000 iterations of gradient ascent training were performed with a learning rate $\eta = 0.1$. Plotted are the datapoints for the two classes (cross) and (circle) and the equal probability contours. The decision boundary is the 0.5-probability contour. See `demoLogRegNonLinear.m`.

where C is the number of classes. When $C = 2$ this can be reduced to the logistic sigmoid model. One can show that the likelihood for this case is also concave, see Exercise 17.3 and [318]. Gradient-based training methods then can be applied to training these models, as a straightforward extension of the two-class case.

17.4.5 The kernel trick for classification

A drawback of logistic regression as described above is the simplicity of the decision surface – a hyperplane. Analogous to the regression case, one way to achieve more complex non-linear decision boundaries is to map the inputs $\mathbf{x}$ in a non-linear way to a higher-dimensional $\boldsymbol{\phi}(\mathbf{x})$ and use

$$p(c = 1|\mathbf{x}) = \sigma\left(\mathbf{w}^{\mathsf{T}}\boldsymbol{\phi}(\mathbf{x}) + b\right). \tag{17.4.33}$$

Mapping into a higher-dimensional space makes it easier to find a separating hyperplane since any set of points that are linearly independent can be linearly separated provided we have as many dimensions as datapoints. For the maximum likelihood criterion, we may use exactly the same algorithm as before on replacing $\mathbf{x}$ with $\boldsymbol{\phi}(\mathbf{x})$. See Fig. 17.12 for a demonstration using a quadratic function. Since only the scalar product between the $\boldsymbol{\phi}$ vectors plays a role the dual representation Section 17.3 may again be used in which we assume the weight can be expressed in the form

$$\mathbf{w} = \sum_n \alpha_m \boldsymbol{\phi}(\mathbf{x}^n). \tag{17.4.34}$$

We then subsequently find a solution in terms of the dual parameters α_n. This is potentially advantageous since there may be less training points than dimensions of $\boldsymbol{\phi}$. The classifier depends only on the scalar product $\mathbf{w}^{\mathsf{T}}\boldsymbol{\phi}(\mathbf{x}) = \sum_n \alpha_n \boldsymbol{\phi}(\mathbf{x}^n)^{\mathsf{T}}\boldsymbol{\phi}(\mathbf{x})$ and we can write more generally, using a positive definite kernel, $K(\mathbf{x}, \mathbf{x}')$

$$p(c = 1|\mathbf{x}) = \sigma\left(\sum_n a_n K(\mathbf{x}, \mathbf{x}^n)\right). \tag{17.4.35}$$

For convenience, we can write the above as

$$p(c = 1|\mathbf{x}) = \sigma\left(\mathbf{a}^{\mathsf{T}}\mathbf{k}(\mathbf{x})\right) \tag{17.4.36}$$

where the N-dimensional vector $\mathbf{k}(\mathbf{x})$ has elements $[\mathbf{k}(\mathbf{x})]_m = K(\mathbf{x}, \mathbf{x}^m)$. Then the above is of exactly the same form as the original specification of logistic regression, namely as a function of a linear combination of vectors. Hence the same training algorithm to maximise the likelihood can be employed, simply on replacing $\mathbf{x}^n$ with $\mathbf{k}(\mathbf{x}^n)$. The details are left to the interested reader and follow closely the treatment of Gaussian processes for classification, Section 19.5.

17.5 Support vector machines

Like kernel logistic regression, Support Vector Machines (SVMs) are a form of kernel linear classifier. However, the SVM uses an objective which more explicitly encourages good generalisation performance. Support vector machines do not fit comfortably within a probabilistic framework and as such we describe them here only briefly, referring the reader to the wealth of excellent literature on this topic.[5] The description here is inspired largely by [75].

17.5.1 Maximum margin linear classifier

In the SVM literature it is common to use $+1$ and -1 to denote the two classes. For a hyperplane defined by weight $\mathbf{w}$ and bias b, a linear discriminant is given by

$$\mathbf{w}^{\mathsf{T}}\mathbf{x} + b \begin{cases} \geq 0 & \text{class } +1 \\ < 0 & \text{class } -1. \end{cases} \tag{17.5.1}$$

For a point $\mathbf{x}$ that is close to the decision boundary at $\mathbf{w}^{\mathsf{T}}\mathbf{x} + b = 0$, a small change in $\mathbf{x}$ can lead to a change in classification. To make the classifier more robust we therefore impose that for the train data at least, the decision boundary should be separated from the data by some finite amount ϵ^2 (assuming in the first instance that the data is linearly separable):

$$\mathbf{w}^{\mathsf{T}}\mathbf{x} + b \begin{cases} \geq \epsilon^2 & \text{class } +1 \\ < -\epsilon^2 & \text{class } -1. \end{cases} \tag{17.5.2}$$

Since $\mathbf{w}$, b and ϵ^2 can all be rescaled arbitrary, we need to fix the scale of the above to break this invariance. It is convenient to set $\epsilon = 1$ so that a point $\mathbf{x}_+$ from class $+1$ that is closest to the decision boundary satisfies

$$\mathbf{w}^{\mathsf{T}}\mathbf{x}_+ + b = 1 \tag{17.5.3}$$

and a point $\mathbf{x}_-$ from class -1 that is closest to the decision boundary satisfies

$$\mathbf{w}^{\mathsf{T}}\mathbf{x}_- + b = -1. \tag{17.5.4}$$

From vector algebra, Fig. 17.13, the distance from the origin along the direction $\mathbf{w}$ to a point $\mathbf{x}$ is given by

$$\frac{\mathbf{w}^{\mathsf{T}}\mathbf{x}}{\sqrt{\mathbf{w}^{\mathsf{T}}\mathbf{w}}}. \tag{17.5.5}$$

[5] www.support-vector.net

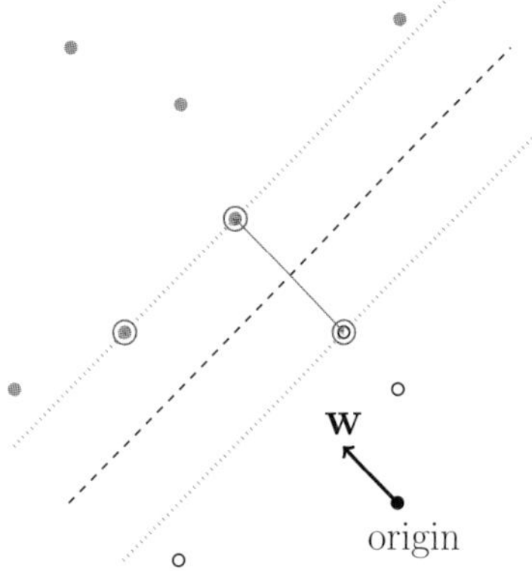

Figure 17.13 SVM classification of data from two classes (open circles and filled circles). The decision boundary $\mathbf{w}^\mathsf{T}\mathbf{x} + b = 0$ (dashed line). For linearly separable data the maximum margin hyperplane is equidistant from the closest opposite class points. These support vectors are highlighted with an outer circle and the margin is given by the solid line. The distance of the decision boundary from the origin is $-b/\sqrt{\mathbf{w}^\mathsf{T}\mathbf{w}}$, and the distance of a general point $\mathbf{x}$ from the origin along the direction $\mathbf{w}$ is $\mathbf{x}^\mathsf{T}\mathbf{w}/\sqrt{\mathbf{w}^\mathsf{T}\mathbf{w}}$.

The *margin* between the hyperplanes for the two classes is then the difference between the two distances along the direction $\mathbf{w}$ which is

$$\frac{\mathbf{w}^\mathsf{T}}{\sqrt{\mathbf{w}^\mathsf{T}\mathbf{w}}}\left(\mathbf{x}_+ - \mathbf{x}_-\right) = \frac{2}{\sqrt{\mathbf{w}^\mathsf{T}\mathbf{w}}}. \tag{17.5.6}$$

To set the distance between the two hyperplanes to be maximal, we therefore need to minimise the length $\mathbf{w}^\mathsf{T}\mathbf{w}$. Given that for each $\mathbf{x}^n$ we have a corresponding label $y^n \in \{+1, -1\}$, in order to classify the training labels correctly and maximise the margin, the optimisation problem is equivalent to:

$$\text{minimise } \frac{1}{2}\mathbf{w}^\mathsf{T}\mathbf{w} \quad \text{subject to } y^n\left(\mathbf{w}^\mathsf{T}\mathbf{x}^n + b\right) \geq 1, \quad n = 1, \ldots, N. \tag{17.5.7}$$

This is a *quadratic programming* problem. The factor 0.5 is just for convenience.

To account for potentially mislabelled training points (or for data that is not linearly separable), we relax the exact classification constraint and use instead

$$y^n\left(\mathbf{w}^\mathsf{T}\mathbf{x}^n + b\right) \geq 1 - \xi^n \tag{17.5.8}$$

where the 'slack variables' are $\xi^n \geq 0$. Here each ξ^n measures how far $\mathbf{x}^n$ is from the correct margin, see Fig. 17.14. For $0 < \xi^n < 1$ datapoint $\mathbf{x}^n$ is on the correct side of the decision boundary. However for $\xi^n > 1$, the datapoint is assigned the opposite class to its training label. Ideally we want to limit the size of these 'violations' ξ^n. Here we briefly describe two standard approaches.

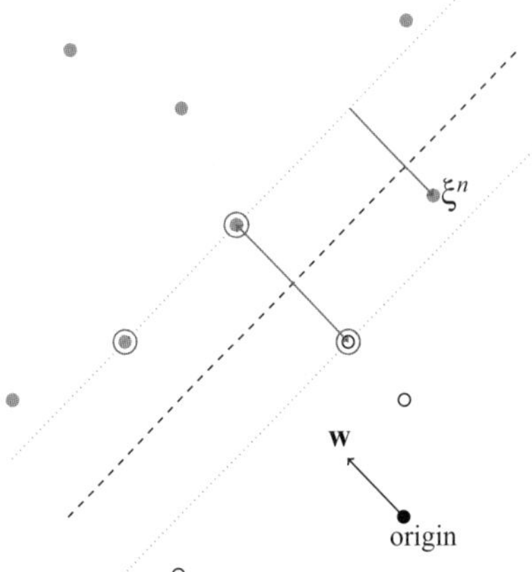

Figure 17.14 Slack margin. The term ξ^n measures how far a variable is from the correct side of the margin for its class. If $\xi^n > 1$ then the point will be misclassified and treated as an outlier.

2-norm soft-margin

The 2-norm soft-margin objective is

$$\text{minimise } \frac{1}{2}\mathbf{w}^{\mathsf{T}}\mathbf{w} + \frac{C}{2}\sum_n (\xi^n)^2 \qquad \text{subject to} \quad y^n\left(\mathbf{w}^{\mathsf{T}}\mathbf{x}^n + b\right) \geq 1 - \xi^n, \quad n = 1, \ldots, N \tag{17.5.9}$$

where C controls the number of mislabellings of the train data. The constant C needs to be determined empirically using a validation set. The optimisation problem expressed by (17.5.9) can be formulated using the Lagrangian

$$L(\mathbf{w}, b, \xi, \alpha) = \frac{1}{2}\mathbf{w}^{\mathsf{T}}\mathbf{w} + \frac{C}{2}\sum_n (\xi^n)^2 - \sum_n \alpha^n\left[y^n\left(\mathbf{w}^{\mathsf{T}}\mathbf{x}^n + b\right) - 1 + \xi^n\right], \qquad \alpha^n \geq 0, \xi^n \geq 0 \tag{17.5.10}$$

which is to be minimised with respect to $\mathbf{x}, b, \xi$ and maximised with respect to α. For points $\mathbf{x}^n$ on the 'correct' side of the decision boundary $y^n\left(\mathbf{w}^{\mathsf{T}}\mathbf{x}^n + b\right) - 1 + \xi^n > 0$ so that maximising L with respect to α requires the corresponding α^n to be set to zero. Only training points that are *support vectors* lying on the decision boundary have non-zero α^n. Differentiating the Lagrangian and equating to zero, we have the conditions

$$\frac{\partial}{\partial w_i}L(\mathbf{w}, b, \xi, \alpha) = w_i - \sum_n \alpha^n y^n x_i^n = 0, \tag{17.5.11}$$

$$\frac{\partial}{\partial b}L(\mathbf{w}, b, \xi, \alpha) = -\sum_n \alpha^n y^n = 0, \tag{17.5.12}$$

$$\frac{\partial}{\partial \xi^n}L(\mathbf{w}, b, \xi, \alpha) = C\xi^n - \alpha^n = 0. \tag{17.5.13}$$

From this we see that the solution for $\mathbf{w}$ is given by

$$\mathbf{w} = \sum_n \alpha^n y^n \mathbf{x}^n. \tag{17.5.14}$$

Since only the support vectors have non-zero α^n, the solution for $\mathbf{w}$ will typically depend on only a small number of the training data. Using these conditions and substituting back into the original problem, the objective is equivalent to minimising

$$L(\alpha) = \sum_n \alpha^n - \frac{1}{2}\sum_{n,m} y^n y^m \alpha^n \alpha^m \left(\mathbf{x}^n\right)^{\mathsf{T}}\mathbf{x}^m - \frac{1}{2C}\sum_n (\alpha^n)^2$$

$$\text{subject to} \qquad \sum_n y^n \alpha^n = 0, \qquad \alpha^n \geq 0. \tag{17.5.15}$$

If we define

$$K\left(\mathbf{x}^n, \mathbf{x}^m\right) = \left(\mathbf{x}^n\right)^{\mathsf{T}}\mathbf{x}^m. \tag{17.5.16}$$

The optimisation problem is

$$\begin{aligned} &\text{maximize} \qquad \sum_n \alpha^n - \frac{1}{2}\sum_{n,m} y^n y^m \alpha^n \alpha^m \left(K\left(\mathbf{x}^n, \mathbf{x}^m\right) + \frac{1}{C}\delta_{n,m}\right) \\ &\text{subject to} \qquad \sum_n y^n \alpha^n = 0, \qquad \alpha^n \geq 0. \end{aligned} \tag{17.5.17}$$

Optimising this objective is discussed in Section 17.5.3.

1-norm soft-margin (box constraint)

In the 1-norm soft-margin version, one uses a 1-norm penalty

$$C \sum_n \xi^n \tag{17.5.18}$$

to give the optimisation problem:

$$\text{minimise } \frac{1}{2}\mathbf{w}^\mathsf{T}\mathbf{w} + C\sum_n \xi^n \qquad \text{subject to } y^n\left(\mathbf{w}^\mathsf{T}\mathbf{x}^n + b\right) \geq 1 - \xi^n, \xi^n \geq 0, \qquad n = 1, \ldots, N \tag{17.5.19}$$

where C is an empirically determined penalty factor that controls the number of mislabellings of the train data. To reformulate the optimisation problem we use the Lagrangian

$$L(\mathbf{w}, b, \xi) = \frac{1}{2}\mathbf{w}^\mathsf{T}\mathbf{w} + C\sum_n \xi^n - \sum_n \alpha^n \left[y^n\left(\mathbf{w}^\mathsf{T}\mathbf{x}^n + b\right) - 1 + \xi^n\right] - \sum_n r^n\xi^n, \qquad \alpha^n \geq 0, \xi^n \geq 0, r^n \geq 0. \tag{17.5.20}$$

The variables r^n are introduced in order to give a non-trivial solution (otherwise $\alpha^n = C$). Following a similar argument as for the 2-norm case, by differentiating the Lagrangian and equating to zero, we arrive at the optimisation problem

$$\begin{aligned} &\text{maximize} && \sum_n \alpha^n - \frac{1}{2}\sum_{n,m} y^n y^m \alpha^n \alpha^m K(\mathbf{x}^n, \mathbf{x}^m) \\ &\text{subject to} && \sum_n y^n \alpha^n = 0, \qquad 0 \leq \alpha^n \leq C \end{aligned} \tag{17.5.21}$$

which is closely related to the 2-norm problem except that we now have the box-constraint $0 \leq \alpha^n \leq C$.

17.5.2 Using kernels

The final objectives (17.5.17) and (17.5.21) depend on the inputs $\mathbf{x}^n$ only via the scalar product $(\mathbf{x}^n)^\mathsf{T}\mathbf{x}^n$. If we map $\mathbf{x}$ to a vector function of $\mathbf{x}$, then we can write

$$K(\mathbf{x}^n, \mathbf{x}^m) = \boldsymbol{\phi}(\mathbf{x}^n)^\mathsf{T}\boldsymbol{\phi}(\mathbf{x}^m). \tag{17.5.22}$$

This means that we can use any positive semidefinite kernel K and make a non-linear classifier. See also Section 19.3.

17.5.3 Performing the optimisation

Both of the above soft-margin SVM optimisation problems (17.5.17) and (17.5.21) are quadratic programs for which the exact computational cost scales as $O\left(N^3\right)$. Whilst these can be solved with general purpose routines, specifically tailored routines that exploit the structure of the problem are preferred in practice. Of particular practical interest are 'chunking' techniques that optimise over a subset of the α. In the limit of updating only two components of α, this can be achieved analytically, resulting in the Sequential Minimal Optimisation algorithm [241], whose practical performance

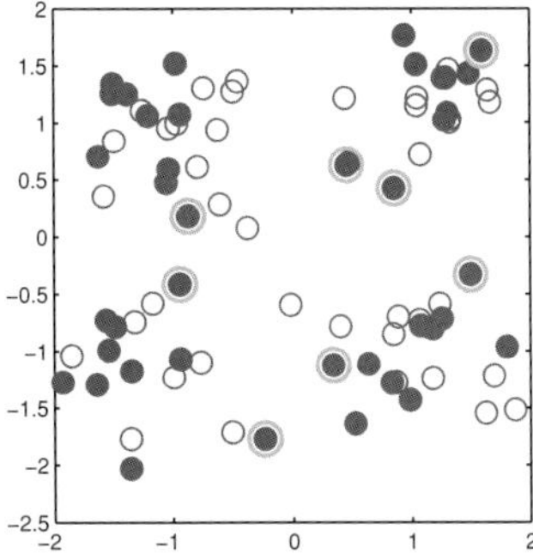

Figure 17.15 SVM training. The solid red and solid blue circles represent train data from different classes. The support vectors are highlighted in green. For the unfilled test points, the class assigned to them by the SVM is given by the colour. See `demoSVM.m`. See plate section for colour version.

is typically $O\left(N^2\right)$ or better. A variant of this algorithm [99] is provided in `SVMtrain.m`. See Fig. 17.15 for a demonstration.

Once the optimal solution $\alpha_*^1, \ldots, \alpha_*^N$ is found the decision function for a new point $\mathbf{x}$ is

$$\sum_n \alpha_*^n y^n K(\mathbf{x}^n, \mathbf{x}) + b_* \begin{cases} > 0 & \text{assign to class } 1 \\ < 0 & \text{assign to class } -1. \end{cases} \tag{17.5.23}$$

The optimal b_* is determined using the maximum margin condition, Equations (17.5.3)–(17.5.4):

$$b_* = \frac{1}{2}\left[\min_{y^n=1} \sum_m \alpha_*^m y^m K(\mathbf{x}^m, \mathbf{x}^n) - \max_{y^n=-1} \sum_m \alpha_*^m y^m K(\mathbf{x}^m, \mathbf{x}^n)\right]. \tag{17.5.24}$$

17.5.4 Probabilistic interpretation

Kernelised logistic-regression has some of the characteristics of the SVM but does not express the large margin requirement. Also the sparse data usage of the SVM is similar to that of the relevance vector machine we discuss in Section 18.2.5. However, a probabilistic model whose MAP assignment matches exactly the SVM is hampered by the normalisation requirement for a probability distribution. Whilst, arguably, no fully satisfactory direct match between the SVM and a related probabilistic model has been achieved, approximate matches have been obtained [271].

17.6 Soft zero-one loss for outlier robustness

Both the support vector machine and logistic regression are potentially misled by outliers. For the SVM, a mislabelled datapoint that is far from the correct side of the decision boundary would require a large slack ξ. However, since exactly such large ξ are discouraged, it is unlikely that the SVM would admit such a solution. For logistic regression, the probability of generating a mislabelled point far from the correct side of the decision boundary is so exponentially small that this will never happen in practice. This means that the model trained with maximum likelihood will never present such a solution. In both cases therefore mislabelled points (or outliers) potentially have a significant impact on the location of the decision boundary.

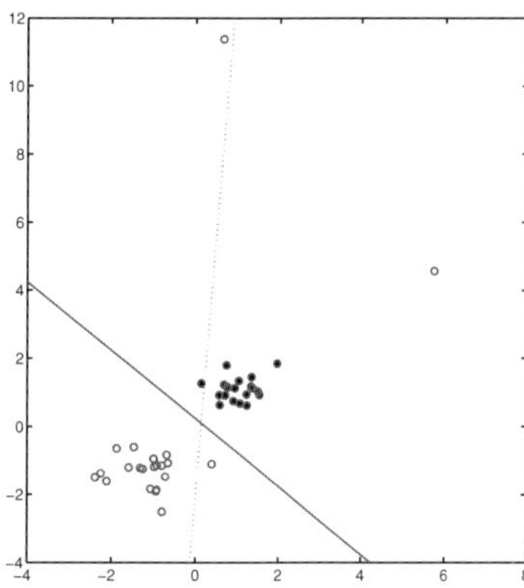

Figure 17.16 Soft zero-one loss decision boundary (solid line) versus logistic regression (dotted line). The number of mis-classified training points using the soft zero-one loss is 2, compared to 3 for logistic regression. The penalty $\lambda = 0.01$ was used for the soft-loss, with $\beta = 10$. For logistic regression, no penalty term was used. The outliers have a significant impact on the decision boundary for logistic regression, whilst the soft zero-one loss essentially gives up on the outliers and fits a classifier to the remaining points. See `demoSoftLoss.m`.

A robust technique to deal with outliers is to use the zero-one loss in which a mislabelled point contributes only a relatively small loss. Soft variants of this are obtained by using the objective

$$\sum_{n=1}^{N} \left[\sigma_\beta(b + \mathbf{w}^\mathsf{T} x^n) - c^n\right]^2 + \lambda \mathbf{w}^\mathsf{T}\mathbf{w} \tag{17.6.1}$$

which is to be minimised with respect to $\mathbf{w}$ and b. For $\beta \to \infty$ the first term above tends to the zero-one loss. The second term represents a penalty on the length of $\mathbf{w}$ and prevents overfitting. Kernel extensions of this soft zero-one loss are straightforward.

Unfortunately, the objective (17.6.1) is non-convex and finding the optimal $\mathbf{w}$, b is computationally difficult. A simple-minded scheme is to fix all components of $\mathbf{w}$ except one and then perform a numerical one-dimensional optimisation over this single parameter w_i. At the next step, another parameter w_j is chosen, and the procedure repeated until convergence. As usual, λ can be set using validation. The practical difficulties of minimising non-convex high-dimensional objective functions means that these approaches are rarely used in practice. A discussion of practical attempts in this area is given in [306].

An illustration of the difference between logistic regression and this soft zero-one loss is given in Fig. 17.16, which demonstrates how logistic regression is influenced by the mass of the data points, whereas the zero-one loss attempts to minimise the number of mis-classifications whilst maintaining a large margin.

17.7 Summary

- Fitting linear regression models based on least squares is straightforward and requires only the solution of a linear system.
- In classification, the maximum likelihood criterion typically results in a simple concave function of the parameters, for which simple gradient-based learning methods are suitable for training.
- The well-known and historically important perceptron can be viewed as a limiting case of logistic regression.
- The kernel extensions of these linear models enable one to find non-linear decision boundaries in the classification case. These techniques are closely related to Gaussian Processes.

Historical note

The perceptron has a long history in artificial intelligence and machine learning. Rosenblatt discussed the perceptron as a model for human learning, arguing that its distributive nature (the input–output 'patterns' are stored in the weight vector) is closely related to the kind of information storage believed to be present in biological systems [251]. To deal with non-linear decision boundaries, the main thrust of research in the ensuing neural network community was on the use of multi-layered structures in which the outputs of perceptrons are used as the inputs to other perceptrons, resulting in potentially highly non-linear discriminant functions. This line of research was largely inspired by analogies to biological information processing in which layered structures are prevalent. Such multilayered artificial neural networks are fascinating and, once trained, are extremely fast in forming their decisions. However, reliably training these systems is a highly complex task and probabilistic generalisations in which priors are placed on the parameters lead to computational difficulties. Whilst perhaps less inspiring from a biological viewpoint, the alternative route of using the kernel trick to boost the power of a linear classifier has the advantage of ease of training and generalisation to probabilistic variants. More recently, however, there has been a resurgence of interest in multilayer systems, with new heuristics aimed at improving the difficulties in training, see for example [147].

17.8 Code

`demoCubicPoly.m`: Demo of fitting a cubic polynomial
`demoLogReg.m`: Demo of logistic regression
`LogReg.m`: Logistic regression gradient ascent training
`demoLogRegNonLinear.m`: Demo of logistic regression with a non-linear $\phi(x)$
`SVMtrain.m`: SVM training using the SMO algorithm
`demoSVM.m`: SVM demo
`demoSoftLoss.m`: softloss demo
`softloss.m`: softloss function

17.9 Exercises

17.1
1. Give an example of a two-dimensional dataset for which the data are linearly separable, but not linearly independent.
2. Can you find a dataset which is linearly independent but not linearly separable?

17.2 Show that for both ordinary and orthogonal least squares regression fits to data $(x^n, y^n), n = 1, \ldots, N)$ the fitted lines go through the point $\sum_{n=1}^{N}(x^n, y^n)/N$.

17.3 Consider the softmax function for classifying an input vector $\mathbf{x}$ into one of $c = 1, \ldots, C$ classes using

$$p(c|\mathbf{x}) = \frac{e^{\mathbf{w}_c^\mathsf{T}\mathbf{x}}}{\sum_{c'=1}^{C} e^{\mathbf{w}_{c'}^\mathsf{T}\mathbf{x}}}. \tag{17.9.1}$$

A set of input-class examples is given by $\mathcal{D} = \{(\mathbf{x}^n, c^n), n = 1, \ldots, N\}$.

1. Relate this model to logistic regression when $C = 2$.
2. Write down the log likelihood L of the classes conditional on the inputs, assuming that the data is i.i.d.
3. Compute the Hessian with elements

$$H_{ij} = \frac{\partial^2 L(\mathcal{D})}{\partial w_i w_j} \tag{17.9.2}$$

where $\mathbf{w}$ is the stacked vector

$$\mathbf{w} = \left(\mathbf{w}_1^\mathsf{T}, \ldots, \mathbf{w}_C^\mathsf{T}\right)^\mathsf{T} \tag{17.9.3}$$

and show that the Hessian is negative semidefinite, that is $\mathbf{z}^\mathsf{T}\mathbf{H}\mathbf{z} \leq 0$ for any $\mathbf{z}$. Hint: at some point you need to use the result that the variance is non-negative.

17.4 Derive from Equation (17.5.9) the dual optimisation problem Equation (17.5.15).

17.5 A datapoint $\mathbf{x}$ is projected to a lower-dimensional vector $\acute{\mathbf{x}}$ using

$$\acute{\mathbf{x}} = \mathbf{M}\mathbf{x} \tag{17.9.4}$$

where $\mathbf{M}$ is a given 'fat' (short and wide) matrix. For a set of data $\{\mathbf{x}^n, n = 1, \ldots, N\}$ and corresponding binary class labels $y^n \in \{0, 1\}$, using logistic regression on the projected datapoints $\acute{\mathbf{x}}^n$ corresponds to a form of constrained logistic regression in the original higher-dimensional space $\mathbf{x}$. Explain if it is reasonable to use an algorithm such as PCA to first reduce the data dimensionality before using logistic regression.

17.6 The logistic sigmoid function is defined as $\sigma(x) = e^x/(1 + e^x)$. What is the inverse function, $\sigma^{-1}(x)$?

17.7 Given a dataset $\mathcal{D} = \{(\mathbf{x}^n, c^n), n = 1, \ldots, N\}$, where $c^n \in \{0, 1\}$, logistic regression uses the model $p(c = 1|\mathbf{x}) = \sigma(\mathbf{w}^\mathsf{T}\mathbf{x} + b)$. Assuming the data is drawn independently and identically, show that the derivative of the log likelihood L with respect to $\mathbf{w}$ is

$$\nabla_{\mathbf{w}} L = \sum_{n=1}^{N} \left(c^n - \sigma\left(\mathbf{w}^\mathsf{T}\mathbf{x}^n + b\right)\right)\mathbf{x}^n. \tag{17.9.5}$$

17.8 Consider a dataset $\mathcal{D} = \{(\mathbf{x}^n, c^n), n = 1, \ldots, N\}$, where $c^n \in \{0, 1\}$, and $\mathbf{x}$ is a D-dimensional vector.

1. Show that if the training data is linearly separable with the hyperplane $\mathbf{w}^\mathsf{T}\mathbf{x} + b$, the data is also separable with the hyperplane $\tilde{\mathbf{w}}^\mathsf{T}\mathbf{x} + \tilde{b}$, where $\tilde{\mathbf{w}} = \lambda\mathbf{w}$, $\tilde{b} = \lambda b$ for any scalar $\lambda > 0$.
2. What consequence does the above result have for maximum likelihood training of logistic regression for linearly separable data?

17.9 Consider a dataset $\mathcal{D} = \{(\mathbf{x}^n, c^n), n = 1, \ldots, N\}$, where $c^n \in \{0, 1\}$, and $\mathbf{x}$ is an N-dimensional vector. Hence we have N datapoints in an N-dimensional space. In the text we showed that to find a hyperplane (parameterised by $\mathbf{w}$ and b) that linearly separates this data we need, for each datapoint $\mathbf{x}^n$, $\mathbf{w}^\mathsf{T}\mathbf{x}^n + b = \epsilon^n$ where $\epsilon^n > 0$ for $c^n = 1$ and $\epsilon^n < 0$ for $c^n = 0$. Furthermore, we suggested an algorithm to find such a hyperplane. Comment on the relation between maximum likelihood training of logistic regression and the algorithm suggested above.

17.10 Given training data $\mathcal{D} = \{(\mathbf{x}^n, c^n), n = 1, \ldots, N\}, c^n \in \{0, 1\}$, where $\mathbf{x}$ are vector inputs, a discriminative model is

$$p(c = 1|\mathbf{x}) = \sigma(b_0 + v_1 g(\mathbf{w}_1^\mathsf{T}\mathbf{x} + b_1) + v_2 g(\mathbf{w}_2^\mathsf{T}\mathbf{x} + b_2)) \tag{17.9.6}$$

where $g(x) = \exp(-0.5x^2)$ and $\sigma(x) = e^x/(1 + e^x)$ (this is a *neural network* [42] with a single hidden layer and two hidden units).

1. Write down the log likelihood for the class conditioned on the inputs, based on the usual i.i.d. assumption.
2. Calculate the derivatives of the log likelihood as a function of the network parameters, $\mathbf{w}_1$, $\mathbf{w}_2$, b_1, b_2, v_0, v_1, v_2.
3. Comment on the relationship between this model and logistic regression.
4. Comment on the decision boundary of this model.

18 Bayesian linear models

The previous chapter discussed the use of linear models in classification and regression. In this chapter we discuss using priors on the parameters and the resulting posterior distribution over parameters. This represents a powerful extension since it enables us to specify in a principled way our prior knowledge and takes into account that when data is limited there will be considerable uncertainty as to which is the 'best' parameter estimate.

18.1 Regression with additive Gaussian noise

The linear models in Chapter 17 were trained under maximum likelihood and do not deal with the issue that, from a probabilistic perspective, parameter estimates are inherently uncertain due to the limited available training data. Regression refers to inferring a mapping on the basis of observed data $\mathcal{D} = \{(\mathbf{x}^n, y^n), n = 1, \dots, N\}$, where $(\mathbf{x}^n, y^n)$ represents an input–output pair. We discuss here the scalar output case (and vector inputs $\mathbf{x}$) with the extension to the vector output case $\mathbf{y}$ being straightforward. We assume that each (clean) output is generated from a model $f(\mathbf{x}; \mathbf{w})$ where the parameters $\mathbf{w}$ of the function f are unknown. An observed output y is generated by the addition of noise η to the clean model output,

$$y = f(\mathbf{x}; \mathbf{w}) + \eta. \tag{18.1.1}$$

If the noise is Gaussian distributed, $\eta \sim \mathcal{N}(\eta|0, \sigma^2)$, the model generates an output y for input $\mathbf{x}$ with probability

$$p(y|\mathbf{w}, \mathbf{x}) = \mathcal{N}\left(y \middle| f(\mathbf{x}; \mathbf{w}), \sigma^2\right) = \frac{1}{\sqrt{2\pi\sigma^2}} \exp\left(-\frac{1}{2\sigma^2}\left[y - f(\mathbf{x}; \mathbf{w})\right]^2\right). \tag{18.1.2}$$

Here our interest is only in modelling this output distribution, and not the distribution of the inputs. As such no parameters are used to model the inputs. If we assume that each data input–output pair is generated identically and independently, the likelihood the model generates the data is

$$p(\mathcal{D}|\mathbf{w}) = \prod_{n=1}^{N} p(y^n|\mathbf{w}, \mathbf{x}^n) p(\mathbf{x}^n). \tag{18.1.3}$$

We may use a prior weight distribution $p(\mathbf{w})$ to quantify our a priori belief in the suitability of each parameter setting. Writing $\mathcal{D} = \{\mathcal{D}_x, \mathcal{D}_y\}$, the posterior weight distribution is then given by

$$p(\mathbf{w}|\mathcal{D}) \propto p(\mathcal{D}|\mathbf{w}) p(\mathbf{w}) \propto p(\mathcal{D}_y|\mathbf{w}, \mathcal{D}_x) p(\mathbf{w}). \tag{18.1.4}$$

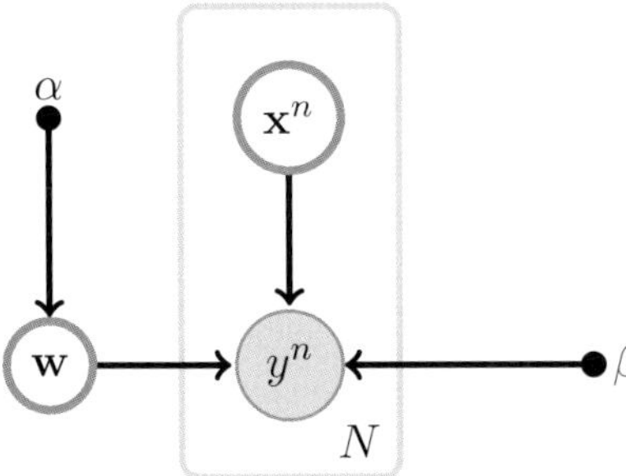

Figure 18.1 Belief network representation of a Bayesian model for regression under the i.i.d. data assumption. The hyperparameter α acts as a form of regulariser, controlling the flexibility of the prior on the weights $\mathbf{w}$. The hyperparameter β controls the level of noise on the observations.

Using the Gaussian noise assumption, and for convenience defining $\beta = 1/\sigma^2$, this gives

$$\log p(\mathbf{w}|\mathcal{D}) = -\frac{\beta}{2}\sum_{n=1}^{N}\left[y^n - f(\mathbf{x}^n;\mathbf{w})\right]^2 + \log p(\mathbf{w}) + \frac{N}{2}\log\beta + \text{const.} \tag{18.1.5}$$

Note the similarity between Equation (18.1.5) and the regularised training error equation (17.2.17). In the probabilistic framework, we identify the choice of a sum squared error with the assumption of additive Gaussian noise. Similarly, the regularising term is identified with $\log p(\mathbf{w})$.

18.1.1 Bayesian linear parameter models

Linear Parameter Models (LPMs), as discussed in Chapter 17, have the form

$$f(\mathbf{x};\mathbf{w}) = \sum_{i=1}^{B} w_i\phi_i(\mathbf{x}) \equiv \mathbf{w}^{\mathsf{T}}\boldsymbol{\phi}(\mathbf{x}) \tag{18.1.6}$$

where the parameters w_i are also called 'weights' and the number of basis functions is $\dim(\mathbf{w}) = B$. Such models have a linear parameter dependence, but may represent a non-linear input–output mapping if the basis functions $\phi_i(\mathbf{x})$ are non-linear in $\mathbf{x}$. Since the output scales linearly with $\mathbf{w}$, we can discourage extreme output values by penalising large weight values. A natural weight prior is thus

$$p(\mathbf{w}|\alpha) = \mathcal{N}\left(\mathbf{w}|\mathbf{0}, \alpha^{-1}\mathbf{I}\right) = \left(\frac{\alpha}{2\pi}\right)^{\frac{B}{2}}\exp\left(-\frac{\alpha}{2}\mathbf{w}^{\mathsf{T}}\mathbf{w}\right) \tag{18.1.7}$$

where the *precision* α is the inverse variance. If α is large, the total squared length of the weight vector $\mathbf{w}$ is encouraged to be small. The full model $p(\mathcal{D}, \mathbf{w}|\alpha, \beta)$ is then specified, see Fig. 18.1. Under the Gaussian noise assumption, the posterior distribution is

$$\log p(\mathbf{w}|\Gamma, \mathcal{D}) = -\frac{\beta}{2}\sum_{n=1}^{N}\left[y^n - \mathbf{w}^{\mathsf{T}}\boldsymbol{\phi}(\mathbf{x}^n)\right]^2 - \frac{\alpha}{2}\mathbf{w}^{\mathsf{T}}\mathbf{w} + \text{const.} \tag{18.1.8}$$

where $\Gamma = \{\alpha, \beta\}$ represents the hyperparameter set. Parameters that determine the functions ϕ may also be included in the hyperparameter set. Completing the square, Section 8.4.1, the weight posterior is therefore a Gaussian distribution,

$$p(\mathbf{w}|\Gamma, \mathcal{D}) = \mathcal{N}(\mathbf{w}|\mathbf{m}, \mathbf{S}) \tag{18.1.9}$$

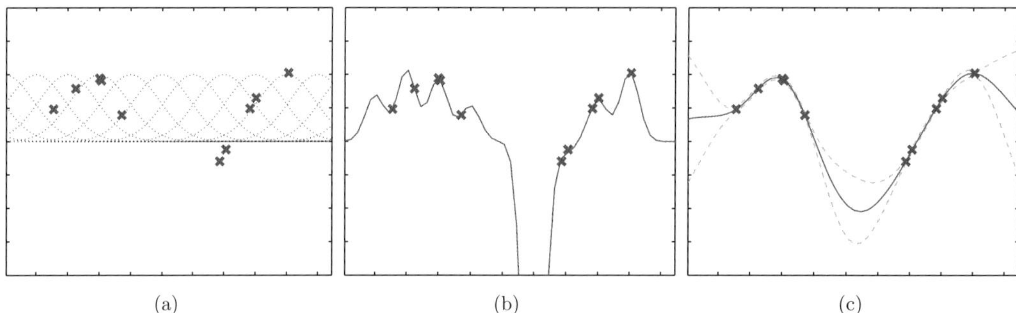

Figure 18.2 Along the horizontal axis we plot the input x and along the vertical axis the output y. (**a**) The raw input–output training data and basis functions $\phi_i(x)$. (**b**) Prediction using regularised training and (poorly chosen) fixed hyperparameters. (**c**) Prediction using ML-II optimised hyperparameters. Also plotted are standard error bars on the clean underlying function, $\bar{f}(x) \pm \sqrt{\text{var}(f(x))}$.

where the covariance and mean are given by

$$\mathbf{S} = \left(\alpha\mathbf{I} + \beta\sum_{n=1}^{N}\boldsymbol{\phi}(\mathbf{x}^n)\boldsymbol{\phi}^{\mathsf{T}}(\mathbf{x}^n)\right)^{-1}, \qquad \mathbf{m} = \beta\mathbf{S}\sum_{n=1}^{N} y^n\boldsymbol{\phi}(\mathbf{x}^n). \tag{18.1.10}$$

The mean prediction for an input $\mathbf{x}$ is then given by

$$\bar{f}(\mathbf{x}) \equiv \int f(\mathbf{x};\mathbf{w})p(\mathbf{w}|\mathcal{D},\Gamma)d\mathbf{w} = \mathbf{m}^{\mathsf{T}}\boldsymbol{\phi}(\mathbf{x}). \tag{18.1.11}$$

Similarly, the variance of the underlying estimated clean function is

$$\text{var}(f(\mathbf{x})) = \left\langle\left[\mathbf{w}^{\mathsf{T}}\boldsymbol{\phi}(\mathbf{x})\right]^2\right\rangle_{p(\mathbf{w}|\mathcal{D},\Gamma)} - \bar{f}(\mathbf{x})^2 = \boldsymbol{\phi}^{\mathsf{T}}(\mathbf{x})\mathbf{S}\boldsymbol{\phi}(\mathbf{x}). \tag{18.1.12}$$

The output variance $\text{var}(f(\mathbf{x}))$ depends only on the input variables and not on the training outputs y. Since the additive noise η is uncorrelated with the model outputs, the *predictive variance* is

$$\text{var}(y(\mathbf{x})) = \text{var}(f(\mathbf{x})) + \sigma^2 \tag{18.1.13}$$

and represents the variance of the 'noisy' output for an input $\mathbf{x}$.

Example 18.1

In Fig. 18.2(b), we show the mean prediction on the data in Fig. 18.2(a) using 15 Gaussian basis functions

$$\phi_i(x) = \exp\left(-0.5(x - c_i)^2/\lambda^2\right) \tag{18.1.14}$$

with width $\lambda = 0.03^2$ and centres c_i spread out evenly over the one-dimensional input space from -2 to 2. We set the other hyperparameters by hand to $\beta = 100$ and $\alpha = 1$. The prediction severely overfits the data, a result of a poor choice of hyperparameter settings. This is resolved in Fig. 18.2(c) using the ML-II parameters, as described below.

18.1.2 Determining hyperparameters: ML-II

The hyperparameter posterior distribution is

$$p(\Gamma|\mathcal{D}) \propto p(\mathcal{D}|\Gamma)p(\Gamma). \tag{18.1.15}$$

A simple summarisation of the posterior is given by the MAP assignment which takes the single 'optimal' setting:

$$\Gamma^* = \underset{\Gamma}{\text{argmax}}\ p(\Gamma|\mathcal{D}). \tag{18.1.16}$$

If the prior belief about the hyperparameters is weak ($p(\Gamma) \approx \text{const.}$), this is equivalent to using the Γ that maximises the *marginal likelihood*

$$p(\mathcal{D}|\Gamma) = \int p(\mathcal{D}|\Gamma, \mathbf{w})p(\mathbf{w}|\Gamma)d\mathbf{w}. \tag{18.1.17}$$

This approach to setting hyperparameters is called 'ML-II' [33] or the *evidence procedure* [195].

In the case of Bayesian linear parameter models under Gaussian additive noise, computing the marginal likelihood equation (18.1.17) involves only Gaussian integration. A direct approach to deriving an expression for the marginal likelihood is to consider

$$p(\mathcal{D}|\Gamma, \mathbf{w})p(\mathbf{w}) = \exp\left(-\frac{\beta}{2}\left[y^n - \mathbf{w}^{\mathsf{T}}\boldsymbol{\phi}(\mathbf{x}^n)\right]^2 - \frac{\alpha}{2}\mathbf{w}^{\mathsf{T}}\mathbf{w}\right)(2\pi\beta)^{N/2}(2\pi\alpha)^{B/2}. \tag{18.1.18}$$

By collating terms in $\mathbf{w}$ (completing the square, Section 8.4.1), the above represents a Gaussian in $\mathbf{w}$ with additional factors. After integrating over this Gaussian we have

$$2\log p(\mathcal{D}|\Gamma) = -\beta\sum_{n=1}^{N}(y^n)^2 + \mathbf{d}^{\mathsf{T}}\mathbf{S}^{-1}\mathbf{d} - \log\det(\mathbf{S}) + B\log\alpha + N\log\beta - N\log(2\pi) \tag{18.1.19}$$

where

$$\mathbf{d} = \beta\sum_{n}\boldsymbol{\phi}(\mathbf{x}^n)y^n. \tag{18.1.20}$$

See Exercise 18.2 for an alternative expression.

Example 18.2

We return to the example in Fig. 18.2 and try to find a more appropriate setting for the hyperparameters. Using the hyperparameters α, β, λ that optimise expression (18.1.19) gives the results in Fig. 18.2(c) where we plot both the mean predictions and standard predictive error bars. This demonstrates that an acceptable setting for the hyperparameters can be obtained by maximising the marginal likelihood. Generally speaking, provided the number of hyperparameters is low compared to the number of datapoints, setting hyperparameters using ML-II will not be at risk of overfitting.

18.1.3 Learning the hyperparameters using EM

As described above, we can set hyperparameters Γ by maximising the marginal likelihood equation (18.1.17). A convenient computational procedure to achieve this is to interpret the $\mathbf{w}$ as latent variables and apply the EM algorithm, Section 11.2. From Equation (18.1.17), the energy term is

$$E \equiv \langle \log p(\mathcal{D}|\mathbf{w}, \Gamma) p(\mathbf{w}|\Gamma) \rangle_{p(\mathbf{w}|\mathcal{D},\Gamma^{old})}. \tag{18.1.21}$$

According to the general EM procedure we need to maximise the energy term. For a hyperparameter Γ the derivative of the energy is given by

$$\frac{\partial}{\partial \Gamma} E \equiv \left\langle \frac{\partial}{\partial \Gamma} \log p(\mathcal{D}|\mathbf{w}, \Gamma) p(\mathbf{w}|\Gamma) \right\rangle_{p(\mathbf{w}|\mathcal{D},\Gamma^{old})}. \tag{18.1.22}$$

For the Bayesian LPM with Gaussian weight and noise distributions, we obtain

$$\frac{\partial}{\partial \beta} E = \frac{N}{2\beta} - \frac{1}{2} \sum_{n=1}^{N} \left\langle \left[y^n - \mathbf{w}^\mathsf{T} \boldsymbol{\phi}(\mathbf{x}^n) \right]^2 \right\rangle_{p(\mathbf{w}|\Gamma^{old},\mathcal{D})} \tag{18.1.23}$$

$$= \frac{N}{2\beta} - \frac{1}{2} \sum_{n=1}^{N} \left[y^n - \mathbf{m}^\mathsf{T} \boldsymbol{\phi}(\mathbf{x}^n) \right]^2 - \frac{1}{2} \text{trace} \left(\mathbf{S} \sum_{n=1}^{N} \boldsymbol{\phi}(\mathbf{x}^n) \boldsymbol{\phi}^\mathsf{T}(\mathbf{x}^n) \right). \tag{18.1.24}$$

where $\mathbf{S}$ and $\mathbf{m}$ are given in Equation (18.1.10). Solving for the zero derivatives gives the M-step update

$$\frac{1}{\beta^{new}} = \frac{1}{N} \sum_{n=1}^{N} \left[y^n - \mathbf{m}^\mathsf{T} \boldsymbol{\phi}(\mathbf{x}^n) \right]^2 + \text{trace} \left(\mathbf{S} \hat{\mathbf{S}} \right) \tag{18.1.25}$$

where

$$\hat{\mathbf{S}} \equiv \frac{1}{N} \sum_{n=1}^{N} \boldsymbol{\phi}(\mathbf{x}^n) \boldsymbol{\phi}^\mathsf{T}(\mathbf{x}^n). \tag{18.1.26}$$

Similarly, for α,

$$\frac{\partial}{\partial \alpha} E = \frac{B}{2\alpha} - \frac{1}{2} \left\langle \mathbf{w}^\mathsf{T} \mathbf{w} \right\rangle_{p(\mathbf{w}|\Gamma^{old},\mathcal{D})} = \frac{B}{2\alpha} - \frac{1}{2} \left(\text{trace}(\mathbf{S}) + \mathbf{m}^\mathsf{T} \mathbf{m} \right)$$

which, on equating to zero, gives the update

$$\frac{1}{\alpha^{new}} = \frac{1}{B} \left(\text{trace}(\mathbf{S}) + \mathbf{m}^\mathsf{T} \mathbf{m} \right). \tag{18.1.27}$$

An alternative fixed-point procedure that can be more rapidly convergent than EM is given in Equation (18.1.37). Closed form updates for other hyperparameters, such as the width of the basis functions, are generally not available, and the corresponding energy term needs to be optimised numerically.

18.1.4 Hyperparameter optimisation: using the gradient

To maximise Equation (18.1.17) with respect to hyperparameters Γ, we can make use of the general identity from Equation (11.6.3) which, in this context, is

$$\frac{\partial}{\partial \Gamma} \log p(\mathcal{D}|\Gamma) = \left\langle \frac{\partial}{\partial \Gamma} \log p(\mathcal{D}|\mathbf{w}, \Gamma) p(\mathbf{w}|\Gamma) \right\rangle_{p(\mathbf{w}|\mathcal{D},\Gamma)}. \tag{18.1.28}$$

Since the likelihood is independent of α,

$$\frac{\partial}{\partial \alpha} \log p(\mathcal{D}|\Gamma) = \left\langle \frac{\partial}{\partial \alpha} \log p(\mathbf{w}|\alpha) \right\rangle_{p(\mathbf{w}|\Gamma,\mathcal{D})}. \tag{18.1.29}$$

Using

$$\log p(\mathbf{w}|\alpha) = -\frac{\alpha}{2}\mathbf{w}^{\mathsf{T}}\mathbf{w} + \frac{B}{2}\log \alpha + \text{const.} \tag{18.1.30}$$

we obtain

$$\frac{\partial}{\partial \alpha} \log p(\mathcal{D}|\Gamma) = \frac{1}{2}\left\langle -\mathbf{w}^{\mathsf{T}}\mathbf{w} + \frac{B}{\alpha} \right\rangle_{p(\mathbf{w}|\Gamma,\mathcal{D})}. \tag{18.1.31}$$

Setting the derivative to zero, the optimal α satisfies

$$0 = -\left\langle \mathbf{w}^{\mathsf{T}}\mathbf{w} \right\rangle_{p(\mathbf{w}|\Gamma,\mathcal{D})} + \frac{B}{\alpha}. \tag{18.1.32}$$

One may now form a fixed-point equation

$$\alpha^{new} = \frac{B}{\left\langle \mathbf{w}^{\mathsf{T}}\mathbf{w} \right\rangle_{p(\mathbf{w}|\Gamma,\mathcal{D})}} \tag{18.1.33}$$

which is equivalent to an EM update, Equation (18.1.27), for this model. For a Gaussian posterior, $p(\mathbf{w}|\Gamma, \mathcal{D}) = \mathcal{N}(\mathbf{w}|\mathbf{m}, \mathbf{S})$,

$$\left\langle \mathbf{w}^{\mathsf{T}}\mathbf{w} \right\rangle = \text{trace}\left(\left\langle \mathbf{w}\mathbf{w}^{\mathsf{T}} \right\rangle - \langle \mathbf{w} \rangle \langle \mathbf{w} \rangle^{\mathsf{T}} + \langle \mathbf{w} \rangle \langle \mathbf{w} \rangle^{\mathsf{T}} \right) = \text{trace}\left(\mathbf{S}\right) + \mathbf{m}^{\mathsf{T}}\mathbf{m}, \tag{18.1.34}$$

$$\alpha^{new} = \frac{B}{\text{trace}\left(\mathbf{S}\right) + \mathbf{m}^{\mathsf{T}}\mathbf{m}}. \tag{18.1.35}$$

One may similarly find the gradient and associated fixed point update for β which, again is equivalent to the EM update for this model.

Gull–MacKay fixed-point iteration

From Equation (18.1.32) we have

$$0 = -\alpha \left\langle \mathbf{w}^{\mathsf{T}}\mathbf{w} \right\rangle_{p(\mathbf{w}|\Gamma,\mathcal{D})} + B = -\alpha \mathbf{S} - \alpha \mathbf{m}^{\mathsf{T}}\mathbf{m} + B \tag{18.1.36}$$

so that an alternative fixed-point equation [135, 194] is

$$\alpha^{new} = \frac{B - \alpha \text{trace}\left(\mathbf{S}\right)}{\mathbf{m}^{\mathsf{T}}\mathbf{m}}. \tag{18.1.37}$$

In practice this update converges more rapidly than Equation (18.1.35). Similarly, one can form an alternative update for β

$$\beta^{new} = \frac{1 - \beta \text{trace}\left(\mathbf{S}\hat{\mathbf{S}}\right)}{\frac{1}{N}\sum_{n=1}^{N}\left[y^n - \mathbf{m}^{\mathsf{T}}\boldsymbol{\phi}(\mathbf{x}^n)\right]^2}. \tag{18.1.38}$$

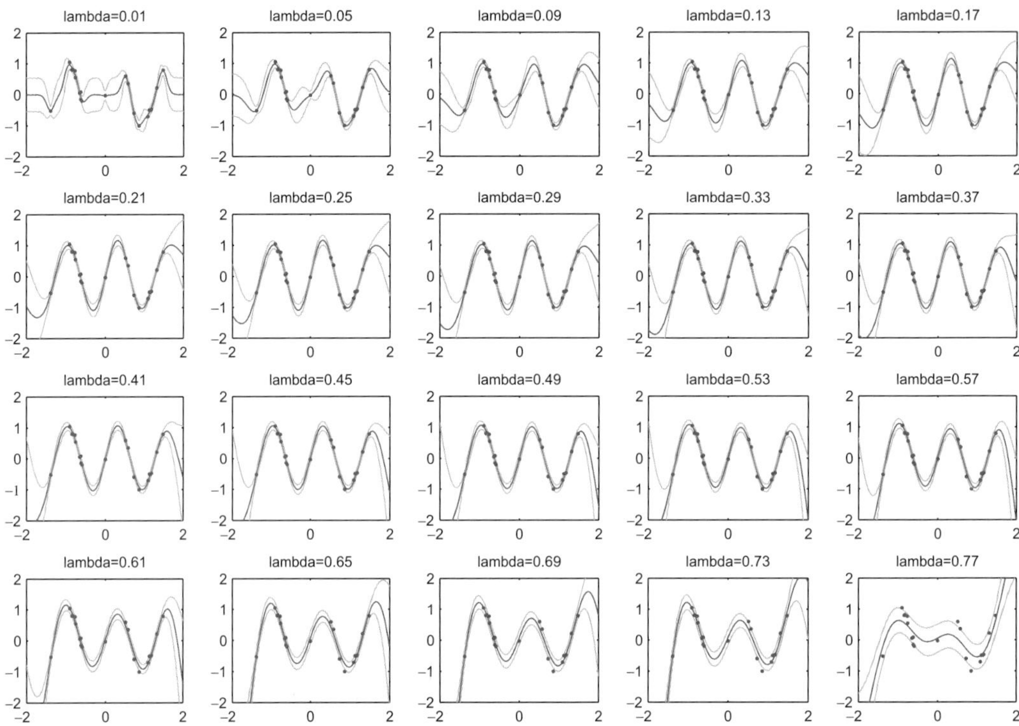

Figure 18.3 Predictions for an RBF for different widths λ. For each λ the ML-II optimal α, β are obtained by running the EM procedure to convergence and subsequently used to form the predictions. In each panel the dots represent the training points, with x along the horizontal axis and y along the vertical axis. Mean predictions are plotted, along with predictive error bars of one standard deviation. According to ML-II, the best model corresponds to $\lambda = 0.37$, see Fig. 18.4. The smaller values of λ overfit the data, giving rise to too 'rough' functions. The largest values of λ underfit, giving too 'smooth' functions. See `demoBayesLinReg.m`.

Example 18.3 Learning the basis function widths

In Fig. 18.3 we plot the training data for a regression problem using a Bayesian LPM. A set of 10 radial basis functions (RBFs) is used,

$$\phi_i(x) = \exp\left(-0.5(x - c_i)^2/\lambda^2\right) \tag{18.1.39}$$

with c_i, $i = 1, \ldots, 10$ spread out evenly between -2 and 2. The hyperparameters α and β are learned by ML-II under EM updating. For a fixed width λ we then present the predictions, each time finding the optimal α and β for this width. The optimal joint α, β, λ hyperparameter setting is obtained as described in Fig. 18.4 which shows the marginal log likelihood for a range of widths. The fit resulting from the jointly optimal α, β, λ hyperparameter is reasonable.

18.1.5 Validation likelihood

The hyperparameters found by ML-II are those which are best at explaining the training data. In principle, this is different from those that are best for prediction and, in practice therefore, it is reasonable to set hyperparameters also by validation techniques. One such method is to set hyperparameters by

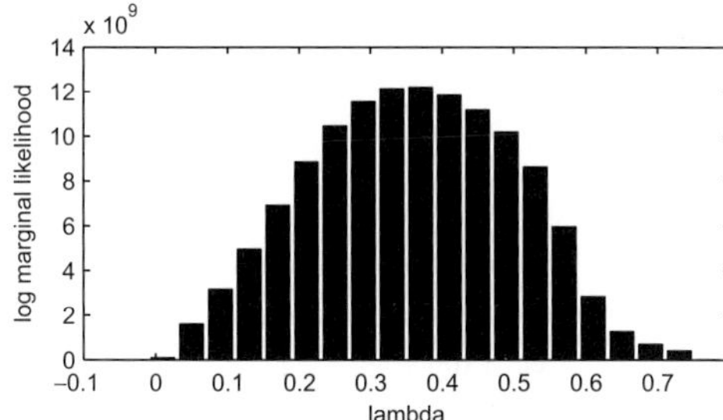

Figure 18.4 The log marginal likelihood $\log p(\mathcal{D}|\lambda, \alpha^*(\lambda), \beta^*(\lambda))$ having found the optimal values of the hyperparameters α and β using ML-II. These optimal values are dependent on λ. According to ML-II, the best model corresponds to $\lambda = 0.37$. From Fig. 18.3 we see that this gives a reasonable fit to the data.

minimal prediction error on a validation set. Another common technique is to set hyperparameters Γ by their likelihood on a validation set $\{\mathcal{X}_{val}, \mathcal{Y}_{val}\} \equiv \{(\mathbf{x}^m_{val}, y^m_{val}), m = 1, \ldots, M\}$:

$$p(\mathcal{Y}_{val}|\Gamma, \mathcal{X}_{train}, \mathcal{Y}_{train}, \mathcal{X}_{val}) = \int_{\mathbf{w}} p(\mathcal{Y}_{val}|\mathbf{w}, \Gamma)p(\mathbf{w}|\Gamma, \mathcal{X}_{train}, \mathcal{Y}_{train}) \tag{18.1.40}$$

from which we obtain (see Exercise 18.3)

$$\log p(\mathcal{Y}_{val}|\Gamma, \mathcal{D}_{train}, \mathcal{X}_{val}) = -\frac{1}{2}\log\det(2\pi\mathbf{C}_{val}) - \frac{1}{2}(\mathbf{y}_{val} - \mathbf{\Phi}_{val}\mathbf{m})^{\mathsf{T}}\mathbf{C}_{val}^{-1}(\mathbf{y}_{val} - \mathbf{\Phi}_{val}\mathbf{m}) \tag{18.1.41}$$

where $\mathbf{y}_{val} = \left[y^1_{val}, \ldots, y^M_{val}\right]^{\mathsf{T}}$, covariance

$$\mathbf{C}_{val} \equiv \mathbf{\Phi}_{val}\mathbf{S}\mathbf{\Phi}^{\mathsf{T}}_{val} + \sigma^2\mathbf{I}_M \tag{18.1.42}$$

and the *design matrix* of explanatory variables

$$\mathbf{\Phi}^{\mathsf{T}}_{val} = \left[\boldsymbol{\phi}(\mathbf{x}^1_{val}), \ldots, \boldsymbol{\phi}(\mathbf{x}^M_{val})\right]. \tag{18.1.43}$$

The optimal hyperparameters Γ^* can then be found by maximising (18.1.41) with respect to Γ.

18.1.6 Prediction and model averaging

For fixed hyperparameters, the Bayesian LPM defines a Gaussian posterior distribution on the weights $\mathbf{w}$. The distribution can be used to compute the expected predictor and also the variance of the predictor. More generally, however, we can place a prior distribution on the hyperparameters themselves and obtain a corresponding posterior

$$p(\Gamma|\mathcal{D}) \propto p(\mathcal{D}|\Gamma)p(\Gamma). \tag{18.1.44}$$

The mean function predictor is then given by integrating over both the posterior weights and the hyperparameters

$$\bar{f}(\mathbf{x}) = \int f(\mathbf{x};\mathbf{w})p(\mathbf{w},\Gamma|\mathcal{D})d\mathbf{w}d\Gamma = \int\left\{\int f(\mathbf{x};\mathbf{w})p(\mathbf{w}|\Gamma,\mathcal{D})d\mathbf{w}\right\}p(\Gamma|\mathcal{D})d\Gamma. \tag{18.1.45}$$

The term in curly brackets is the mean predictor for fixed hyperparameters. Equation (18.1.45) then weights each mean predictor by the posterior probability of the hyperparameter $p(\Gamma|\mathcal{D})$. This is a general recipe for combining model predictions, where each model is weighted by its posterior probability. However, computing the integral over the hyperparameter posterior is numerically challenging and approximations are usually required. Provided the hyperparameters are well determined by the data, we may instead approximate the above hyperparameter integral by finding the MAP hyperparameters and use

$$\bar{f}(\mathbf{x}) \approx \int f(\mathbf{x};\mathbf{w})p(\mathbf{w}|\Gamma^*,\mathcal{D})d\mathbf{w}. \tag{18.1.46}$$

Under a flat prior $p(\Gamma) = \text{const.}$, this is equivalent to using the mean predictor with hyperparameters set by ML-II. An alternative is to draw samples $\Gamma^l, l = 1, \ldots, L$ from the posterior distribution $p(\Gamma|\mathcal{D})$ and form then a predictor by averaging over the samples

$$\bar{f}(\mathbf{x}) \approx \frac{1}{L}\sum_{l=1}^{L} \int f(\mathbf{x};\mathbf{w})p(\mathbf{w}|\Gamma^l,\mathcal{D})\, d\mathbf{w} \tag{18.1.47}$$

18.1.7 Sparse linear models

A common interest is to attempt to explain data using as few of the inputs as possible. More generally, we can try to find the most parsimonious explanation using a limited number of features $\phi_i(\mathbf{x})$. From a Bayesian LPM perspective, we require a prior that strongly encourages only a limited number of weights w_i to be active, with the rest being set to zero. Formally, this corresponds to a non-Gaussian prior on the weights which hampers the use of exact Bayesian methods. Non-Bayesian methods make use of penalty terms such as L_1 (lasso) regularisation $\sum_i |w_i|$ for which the objective of the LPM remains concave [291]l; this is closely related to using Laplace priors in the Bayesian setting. Here we briefly discuss some approximate methods for sparse linear regression.

The relevance vector machine

The *relevance vector machine* assumes that only a small number of components of the basis function vector are relevant in determining the solution for $\mathbf{w}$. For a predictor,

$$f(\mathbf{x};\mathbf{w}) = \sum_{i=1}^{B} w_i\phi_i(\mathbf{x}) \equiv \mathbf{w}^{\mathsf{T}}\boldsymbol{\phi}(\mathbf{x}) \tag{18.1.48}$$

it is often the case that some basis functions will be redundant in the sense that a linear combination of the other basis functions can reproduce the training outputs with insignificant loss in accuracy. To exploit this effect and seek a parsimonious solution we may use a more refined prior that encourages each w_i itself to be small:

$$p(\mathbf{w}|\boldsymbol{\alpha}) = \prod_i p(w_i|\alpha_i). \tag{18.1.49}$$

For computational convenience, in the RVM one typically chooses a Gaussian

$$p(w_i|\alpha_i) = \mathcal{N}\left(w_i\middle|0,\alpha_i^{-1}\right) = \left(\frac{\alpha_i}{2\pi}\right)^{\frac{1}{2}} \exp\left(-\frac{\alpha_i}{2}w_i^2\right). \tag{18.1.50}$$

Sparsity is then achieved by optimising over the hyperparameters α_i, with large α_i effectively forcing a weight w_i to be zero. The modifications required to the description of Section 18.1.1 are to replace $\mathbf{S}$ with

$$\mathbf{S} = \left(\text{diag}\,(\boldsymbol{\alpha}) + \beta\sum_{n=1}^{N}\boldsymbol{\phi}\left(\mathbf{x}^n\right)\boldsymbol{\phi}^{\mathsf{T}}\left(\mathbf{x}^n\right)\right)^{-1}. \tag{18.1.51}$$

The marginal likelihood is then given by

$$2\log p(\mathcal{D}|\Gamma) = -\beta\sum_{n=1}^{N}(y^n)^2 + \mathbf{d}^\mathsf{T}\mathbf{S}^{-1}\mathbf{d} - \log\det(\mathbf{S}) + \sum_{i=1}^{B}\log\alpha_i + N\log\beta - N\log(2\pi). \tag{18.1.52}$$

The EM update for β is unchanged, and the EM update for each α_i is

$$\frac{1}{\alpha_i^{new}} = [\mathbf{S}]_{ii} + m_i^2. \tag{18.1.53}$$

A potential difficulty with this approach is that there are as many hyperparameters as there are parameters and finding the optimal hyperparameters by ML-II can be problematic, resulting in overly aggressive pruning of the weights. This can be ameliorated by using a more fully Bayesian approach [294].

Spike and slab priors

A natural alternative approach to sparse linear regression is to use binary indicators $s_i \in \{0, 1\}$

$$f(\mathbf{x};\mathbf{w}) = \sum_{i=1}^{B} s_i w_i \phi_i(\mathbf{x}), \qquad p(\mathbf{w}) = \prod_i \mathcal{N}\left(w_i|0,\sigma^2\right) \tag{18.1.54}$$

so that only those weights w_i with $s_i = 1$ will contribute to the function. One can specify a level of sparsity by choosing a prior on the joint set $p(s_1, \ldots, s_B)$ that encourages only a small number of the s_i to be 1, the rest being zero. This can be achieved using a product of Bernoulli distributions

$$p(\mathbf{s}) = \prod_{i=1}^{B}\theta^{s_i}(1-\theta)^{1-s_i} \tag{18.1.55}$$

where $0 \le \theta \le 1$ specifies the prior level of sparsity. This is equivalent to using the original LPM

$$f(\mathbf{x};\mathbf{w}) = \sum_{i=1}^{B} w_i \phi_i(\mathbf{x}), \tag{18.1.56}$$

with the 'spike and slab' weight prior

$$p(\mathbf{w}|\mathbf{s}) = \prod_i \left\{s_i\mathcal{N}\left(w_i|0,\sigma^2\right) + (1-s_i)\delta(w_i)\right\} \tag{18.1.57}$$

which places either a spike at 0 (when $s_i = 0$) or a broader Gaussian 'slab' $\mathcal{N}\left(w_i|0,\sigma^2\right)$ when $s_i = 1$. These two formulations are equivalent and result in a non-Gaussian posterior for the weights, for which approximation methods are required. Popular approaches include Gibbs sampling, Chapter 27, and variational methods Chapter 28.

18.2 Classification

For the logistic regression model

$$p(c = 1|\mathbf{w},\mathbf{x}) = \sigma\left(\sum_{i=1}^{B} w_i\phi_i(\mathbf{x})\right) \tag{18.2.1}$$

Algorithm 18.1 Evidence procedure for Bayesian logistic regression.

1: Initialise **w** and α.
2: **while** Not Converged **do**
3: Find optimal $\mathbf{w}^*$ by iterating Equation (18.2.16), Equation (18.2.15) to convergence. ▷ E-step
4: Update α according to Equation (18.2.9). ▷ M-step
5: **end while**

the maximum likelihood method returns only a single optimal **w**. To deal with the inevitable uncertainty in estimating **w** we need to determine the posterior distribution. To do so we first define a prior on the weights $p(\mathbf{w})$. As for the regression case, a convenient choice is a Gaussian

$$p(\mathbf{w}|\alpha) = \mathcal{N}\left(\mathbf{w}|\mathbf{0}, \alpha^{-1}\mathbf{I}\right) = \frac{\alpha^{B/2}}{(2\pi)^{B/2}} \exp\left(-\alpha\mathbf{w}^{\mathsf{T}}\mathbf{w}/2\right) \tag{18.2.2}$$

where α is the inverse variance (precision). Given a dataset of input-class labels, $\mathcal{D} = \{(\mathbf{x}^n, c^n), n = 1, \ldots, N\}$, the parameter posterior is (assuming we make no model of the input distribution)

$$p(\mathbf{w}|\alpha, \mathcal{D}) = \frac{p(\mathcal{D}|\mathbf{w}, \alpha)p(\mathbf{w}|\alpha)}{p(\mathcal{D}|\alpha)} = \frac{1}{p(\mathcal{D}|\alpha)} p(\mathbf{w}|\alpha) \prod_{n=1}^{N} p(c^n|\mathbf{x}^n, \mathbf{w}). \tag{18.2.3}$$

Unfortunately, this distribution is not of any standard form and exactly inferring statistics such as the mean is formally computationally intractable.

18.2.1 Hyperparameter optimisation

Analogous to the regression case, hyperparameters such as α can be set by maximising the marginal likelihood

$$p(\mathcal{D}|\alpha) = \int p(\mathcal{D}|\mathbf{w})p(\mathbf{w}|\alpha)d\mathbf{w} = \int \prod_{n=1}^{N} p(c^n|\mathbf{x}^n, \mathbf{w}) \left(\frac{\alpha}{2\pi}\right)^{B/2} \exp\left(-\frac{\alpha}{2}\mathbf{w}^{\mathsf{T}}\mathbf{w}\right) d\mathbf{w}. \tag{18.2.4}$$

There are several approaches one could take to approximate this integral and below we discuss the Laplace and a variational technique. Common to all approaches, however, is the form of the gradient, differing only in the statistics under an approximation to the posterior. For this reason we derive first generic hyperparameter update formulae that apply under both approximations.

To find the optimal α, we search for the zero derivative of $\log p(\mathcal{D}|\alpha)$. This is equivalent to the linear regression case, and we immediately obtain

$$\frac{\partial}{\partial\alpha} \log p(\mathcal{D}|\alpha) = \frac{1}{2}\left\langle -\mathbf{w}^{\mathsf{T}}\mathbf{w} + \frac{B}{\alpha}\right\rangle_{p(\mathbf{w}|\alpha,\mathcal{D})}. \tag{18.2.5}$$

Setting the derivative to zero, an exact equation is that the optimal α satisfies

$$0 = -\left\langle \mathbf{w}^{\mathsf{T}}\mathbf{w}\right\rangle_{p(\mathbf{w}|\alpha,\mathcal{D})} + \frac{B}{\alpha}. \tag{18.2.6}$$

One may now form a fixed-point equation

$$\alpha^{new} = \frac{B}{\left\langle \mathbf{w}^{\mathsf{T}}\mathbf{w}\right\rangle_{p(\mathbf{w}|\alpha,\mathcal{D})}}. \tag{18.2.7}$$

The averages in the above expression cannot be computed exactly and are replaced by averages with respect to an approximation of the posterior $q(\mathbf{w}|\alpha, \mathcal{D})$. For a Gaussian approximation of the posterior, $q(\mathbf{w}|\alpha, \mathcal{D}) = \mathcal{N}(\mathbf{w}|\mathbf{m}, \mathbf{S})$

$$\langle \mathbf{w}^\mathsf{T}\mathbf{w}\rangle = \text{trace}\left(\langle \mathbf{w}\mathbf{w}^\mathsf{T}\rangle - \langle \mathbf{w}\rangle \langle \mathbf{w}\rangle^\mathsf{T} + \langle \mathbf{w}\rangle \langle \mathbf{w}\rangle^\mathsf{T}\right) = \text{trace}(\mathbf{S}) + \mathbf{m}^\mathsf{T}\mathbf{m}, \tag{18.2.8}$$

$$\alpha^{new} = \frac{B}{\text{trace}(\mathbf{S}) + \mathbf{m}^\mathsf{T}\mathbf{m}}. \tag{18.2.9}$$

In this case the Gull–Mackay alternative fixed-point equation [135, 194] is

$$\alpha^{new} = \frac{B - \alpha\mathbf{S}}{\mathbf{m}^\mathsf{T}\mathbf{m}}. \tag{18.2.10}$$

The hyperparameter updates (18.2.9) and (18.2.10) have the same form as for the regression model. The mean $\mathbf{m}$ and covariance $\mathbf{S}$ of the posterior in the regression and classification cases are however different. In the classification case we need to approximate the mean and covariance, as discussed below.

18.2.2 Laplace approximation

The Laplace approximation, Section 28.2 is a simple approximation made by fitting a Gaussian locally around the most probable point of the posterior. The weight posterior for the logistic regression model is given by

$$p(\mathbf{w}|\alpha, \mathcal{D}) \propto \exp(-E(\mathbf{w})) \tag{18.2.11}$$

where

$$E(\mathbf{w}) = \frac{\alpha}{2}\mathbf{w}^\mathsf{T}\mathbf{w} - \sum_{n=1}^{N} \log\sigma\left(\mathbf{w}^\mathsf{T}\mathbf{h}^n\right), \qquad \mathbf{h}^n \equiv (2c^n - 1)\boldsymbol{\phi}^n. \tag{18.2.12}$$

By approximating $E(\mathbf{w})$ by a quadratic function in $\mathbf{w}$, we obtain a Gaussian approximation $q(\mathbf{w}|\mathcal{D}, \alpha)$ to $p(\mathbf{w}|\mathcal{D}, \alpha)$. To do so we first find the minimum of $E(\mathbf{w})$. Differentiating, we obtain

$$\nabla E = \alpha\mathbf{w} - \sum_{n=1}^{N}(1 - \sigma^n)\mathbf{h}^n, \qquad \sigma^n \equiv \sigma\left(\mathbf{w}^\mathsf{T}\mathbf{h}^n\right). \tag{18.2.13}$$

It is convenient to use a Newton method to find the optimum. The Hessian matrix with elements

$$H_{ij} \equiv \frac{\partial^2}{\partial w_i \partial w_j}E(\mathbf{w}) \tag{18.2.14}$$

is given by

$$\mathbf{H} = \alpha\mathbf{I} + \underbrace{\sum_{n=1}^{N}\sigma^n(1 - \sigma^n)\boldsymbol{\phi}^n(\boldsymbol{\phi}^n)^\mathsf{T}}_{\mathbf{J}}. \tag{18.2.15}$$

Note that the Hessian is positive semidefinite (see Exercise 18.4) so that the function $E(\mathbf{w})$ is convex (bowl shaped), and finding a minimum of $E(\mathbf{w})$ is numerically unproblematic. A Newton update then is

$$\mathbf{w}^{new} = \mathbf{w} - \mathbf{H}^{-1}\nabla E. \tag{18.2.16}$$

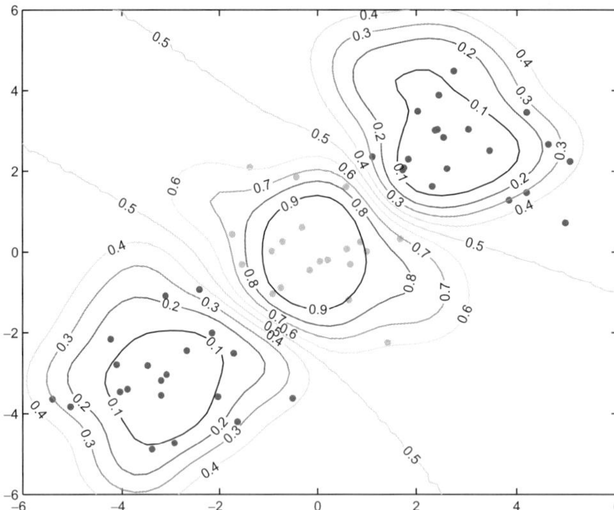

Figure 18.5 Bayesian logistic regression using RBF functions $\phi_i(\mathbf{x}) = \exp\left(-\lambda(\mathbf{x} - \mathbf{m}_i)^2\right)$, placing the centres $\mathbf{m}_i$ on a subset of the training points. The green points are training data from class 1, and the red points are training data from class 0. The contours represent the probability of being in class 1. The optimal value of α found by ML-II is 0.45 (λ is set by hand to 2). See `demoBayesLogRegression.m`. See plate section for colour version.

Given a converged $\mathbf{w}$, the posterior approximation is given by

$$q(\mathbf{w}|\mathcal{D}, \alpha) = \mathcal{N}(\mathbf{w}|\mathbf{m}, \mathbf{S}), \qquad \mathbf{S} \equiv \mathbf{H}^{-1} \tag{18.2.17}$$

where $\mathbf{m} = \mathbf{w}^*$ is the converged estimate of the minimum point of $E(\mathbf{w})$ and $\mathbf{H}$ is the Hessian of $E(\mathbf{w})$ at this point.

Approximating the marginal likelihood

Using the Laplace approximation, the marginal likelihood is given by

$$p(\mathcal{D}|\alpha) = \int_{\mathbf{w}} p(\mathcal{D}|\mathbf{w})p(\mathbf{w}|\alpha) = \int_{\mathbf{w}} \prod_{n=1}^{N} p(c^n|\mathbf{x}^n, \mathbf{w}) \left(\frac{\alpha}{2\pi}\right)^{B/2} e^{-\frac{\alpha}{2}\mathbf{w}^\mathsf{T}\mathbf{w}} \propto \int_{\mathbf{w}} e^{-E(\mathbf{w})}. \tag{18.2.18}$$

For an optimum value $\mathbf{m} = \mathbf{w}^*$, we approximate the marginal likelihood using (see Section 28.2)

$$\log p(\mathcal{D}|\alpha) \approx L(\alpha) \equiv -\frac{\alpha}{2}(\mathbf{w}^*)^\mathsf{T}\mathbf{w}^* + \sum_n \log \sigma\left((\mathbf{w}^*)^\mathsf{T}\mathbf{h}^n\right) - \frac{1}{2}\log\det(\alpha\mathbf{I} + \mathbf{J}) + \frac{B}{2}\log\alpha. \tag{18.2.19}$$

Given this approximation $L(\alpha)$ to the marginal likelihood, an alternative strategy for hyperparameter optimisation is to optimise $L(\alpha)$ with respect to α. By differentiating $L(\alpha)$ directly, the reader may show that the resulting updates are in fact equivalent to using the general condition equation (18.2.6) under a Laplace approximation to the posterior statistics. See Fig. 18.5 for an example.

Making predictions

Ultimately, our interest is to classify in novel situations, averaging over posterior weight uncertainty (assuming α is fixed to a suitable value),

$$p(c = 1|\mathbf{x}, \mathcal{D}) = \int p(c = 1|\mathbf{x}, \mathbf{w})p(\mathbf{w}|\mathcal{D})d\mathbf{w}. \tag{18.2.20}$$

The B-dimensional integrals over $\mathbf{w}$ cannot be computed analytically and numerical approximation is required. Using the Laplace approximation, we replace the exact posterior $p(\mathbf{w}|\mathcal{D})$ with our Laplace's method Gaussian approximation $q(\mathbf{w}|\mathcal{D}) = \mathcal{N}(\mathbf{w}|\mathbf{m}, \mathbf{S})$

$$p(c = 1|\mathbf{x}, \mathcal{D}) \approx \int p(c = 1|\mathbf{x}, \mathbf{w})q(\mathbf{w}|\mathcal{D})d\mathbf{w} = \int \sigma\left(\tilde{\mathbf{x}}^{\mathsf{T}}\mathbf{w}\right)\mathcal{N}(\mathbf{w}|\mathbf{m}, \mathbf{S})\,d\mathbf{w} \tag{18.2.21}$$

where, for notational convenience, we write $\tilde{\mathbf{x}} \equiv \boldsymbol{\phi}(\mathbf{x})$. To compute the predictions it would appear that we need to carry out an integral in B dimensions. However, since the term $\sigma\left(\tilde{\mathbf{x}}^{\mathsf{T}}\mathbf{w}\right)$ depends on $\mathbf{w}$ via the scalar product $\tilde{\mathbf{x}}^{\mathsf{T}}\mathbf{w}$, we only require the integral over the one-dimensional projection $h \equiv \tilde{\mathbf{x}}^{\mathsf{T}}\mathbf{w}$, see Exercise 18.5. That is

$$p(c = 1|\mathbf{x}, \mathcal{D}) \approx \int \sigma(h)\,q(h|\mathbf{x}, \mathcal{D})dh. \tag{18.2.22}$$

Since under the Laplace approximation $\mathbf{w}$ is Gaussian distributed, then so is the linear projection h

$$q(h|\mathbf{x}, \mathcal{D}) = \mathcal{N}\left(h|\tilde{\mathbf{x}}^{\mathsf{T}}\mathbf{m}, \tilde{\mathbf{x}}^{\mathsf{T}}\boldsymbol{\Sigma}\tilde{\mathbf{x}}\right). \tag{18.2.23}$$

Predictions may then be made by numerically evaluating the one-dimensional integral over the Gaussian distribution in h, Equation (18.2.22). Fast approximate methods for computing this are discussed below.

Approximating the Gaussian average of a logistic sigmoid

Predictions under a Gaussian posterior approximation require the computation of

$$I \equiv \langle\sigma(x)\rangle_{\mathcal{N}(x|\mu,\sigma^2)} \tag{18.2.24}$$

Gaussian quadrature is an obvious numerical candidate [244]. An alternative is to replace the logistic sigmoid by a suitably transformed erf function [195], the reason being that the Gaussian average of an erf function is another erf function. Using a single erf, an approximation is[1]

$$\sigma(x) \approx \frac{1}{2}(1 + \text{erf}(\nu x)). \tag{18.2.25}$$

These two functions agree at $-\infty, 0, \infty$. A reasonable criterion is that the derivatives of these two should agree at $x = 0$ since then they have locally the same slope around the origin and have globally similar shape. Using $\sigma(0) = 0.5$ and that the derivative is $\sigma(0)(1 - \sigma(0))$, this requires

$$\frac{1}{4} = \frac{\nu}{\sqrt{\pi}} \Rightarrow \nu = \frac{\sqrt{\pi}}{4}. \tag{18.2.26}$$

A more accurate approximation can be obtained by taking a convex combination of scaled erf functions [22], see `logsigapp.m`.

18.2.3 Variational Gaussian approximation

An alternative to Laplace's method is to use a so-called variational method. Since the marginal likelihood is a key quantity that can be used for example for hyperparameter selection, it is useful

[1] Note that the definition of the erf function used here is taken to be consistent with MATLAB, namely that $\text{erf}(x) \equiv \frac{2}{\sqrt{\pi}}\int_0^x e^{-t^2}dt$. Other authors define it to be the cumulative density function of a standard Gaussian, $\frac{2}{\sqrt{\pi}}\int_{-\infty}^x e^{-\frac{1}{2}t^2}dt$.

to have a lower bound on the log marginal likelihood. Like in EM, one can then find the best hyperparameters by maximising this lower bound, rather than the likelihood itself. To keep the notation reasonably simple, we drop the conditioning on hyperparameters throughout and attempt to find a lower bound on the log marginal likelihood $p(\mathcal{D})$. One approach to obtaining a bound is based on the Kullback–Leibler divergence

$$\mathrm{KL}(q(\mathbf{w})|p(\mathbf{w}|\mathcal{D})) \geq 0. \tag{18.2.27}$$

Since $p(\mathbf{w}|\mathcal{D}) = p(\mathcal{D}|\mathbf{w})p(\mathbf{w})/p(\mathcal{D})$ we obtain

$$\log p(\mathcal{D}) \geq \langle \log p(\mathcal{D}|\mathbf{w})p(\mathbf{w})\rangle_{q(\mathbf{w})} - \langle \log q(\mathbf{w})\rangle_{q(\mathbf{w})} \tag{18.2.28}$$

which holds for any distribution $q(\mathbf{w})$. The angled brackets $\langle\cdot\rangle_q$ denote expectation with respect to q. Using the explicit form for the logistic regression model, the right-hand side is given by[2]

$$\mathcal{B}_{KL} \equiv \sum_{n=1}^{N} \left\langle \log \sigma\left(s_n \mathbf{w}^{\mathsf{T}}\tilde{\mathbf{x}}_n\right)\right\rangle_{q(\mathbf{w})} - \mathrm{KL}(q(\mathbf{w})|p(\mathbf{w})). \tag{18.2.29}$$

To form a tractable lower bound, we need to choose a class of distributions $q(\mathbf{w})$ for which the above expression can be evaluated, for example a Gaussian $q(\mathbf{w}) = \mathcal{N}(\mathbf{w}|\mathbf{m}, \mathbf{S})$. For a Gaussian prior $p(\mathbf{w}) = \mathcal{N}(\mathbf{w}|\mathbf{0}, \mathbf{\Sigma})$ then $\mathrm{KL}(q(\mathbf{w})|p(\mathbf{w}))$ is straightforward. For numerical convenience, we parameterise the covariance of the approximation using a Cholesky decomposition $\mathbf{S} = \mathbf{C}^{\mathsf{T}}\mathbf{C}$ for upper triangular $\mathbf{C}$. This gives

$$-2\mathrm{KL}(q(\mathbf{w})|p(\mathbf{w})) = 4\sum_i \log C_{ii} - \log\det(\mathbf{\Sigma}) + \mathrm{trace}\left(\mathbf{C}^{\mathsf{T}}\mathbf{C}\mathbf{\Sigma}^{-1}\right) + \mathbf{m}^{\mathsf{T}}\mathbf{\Sigma}^{-1}\mathbf{m} + B \tag{18.2.30}$$

where $B = \dim(\tilde{\mathbf{x}})$. In computing the bound (18.2.29), the problematic remaining terms are

$$I_n \equiv \left\langle \log \sigma\left(s_n \mathbf{w}^{\mathsf{T}}\tilde{\mathbf{x}}_n\right)\right\rangle_{\mathcal{N}(\mathbf{w}|\mathbf{m},\mathbf{S})}. \tag{18.2.31}$$

We define the activation $a_n \equiv s_n \mathbf{w}^{\mathsf{T}}\tilde{\mathbf{x}}_n$. Since $\mathbf{w}$ is Gaussian distributed, so is the activation,

$$p(a_n) = \mathcal{N}\left(a_n \middle| \tilde{\mu}_n, \tilde{\sigma}_n^2\right), \qquad \tilde{\mu}_n = s_n \tilde{\mathbf{x}}_n^{\mathsf{T}}\mathbf{m}, \quad \tilde{\sigma}_n^2 = \tilde{\mathbf{x}}_n^{\mathsf{T}}\mathbf{C}^{\mathsf{T}}\mathbf{C}\tilde{\mathbf{x}}_n \tag{18.2.32}$$

so that

$$I_n = \langle \log \sigma(a_n)\rangle_{\mathcal{N}(a_n|\tilde{\mu}_n,\tilde{\sigma}_n^2)} = \langle \log \sigma(\tilde{\mu}_n + z\tilde{\sigma}_n)\rangle_z$$

where $\langle\cdot\rangle_z$ denotes expectation with respect to the standard normal distribution $z \sim \mathcal{N}(z|0, 1)$. In this way I_n can be computed by any standard one-dimensional numerical integration method, such as Gaussian quadrature. Since the bound (18.2.29) is therefore numerically accessible for any parameters $\mathbf{m}, \mathbf{C}$ of the approximating Gaussian, we may proceed to find the optimal parameters by direct numerical maximisation of the lower bound. The gradient of the bound with respect to $\mathbf{m}$ is

$$\frac{\partial \mathcal{B}_{KL}}{\partial \mathbf{m}} = -\mathbf{\Sigma}^{-1}\mathbf{m} + \sum_{n=1}^{N} s_n \tilde{\mathbf{x}}_n \left(1 - \langle \sigma(\tilde{\mu}_n + z\tilde{\sigma}_n)\rangle_z\right). \tag{18.2.33}$$

Similarly, one may show that

$$\frac{\partial \mathcal{B}_{KL}}{\partial \mathbf{C}} = \mathbf{C}^{-\mathsf{T}} - \mathbf{C}\mathbf{\Sigma}^{-1} + \mathbf{C}\sum_{n=1}^{N} \frac{\tilde{\mathbf{x}}_n\tilde{\mathbf{x}}_n^{\mathsf{T}}}{\tilde{\sigma}_n}\langle z\sigma(\tilde{\mu}_n + z\tilde{\sigma}_n)\rangle_z \tag{18.2.34}$$

[2] The generalisation to using $\boldsymbol{\phi}(x)$ in the below follows from simply replacing $\mathbf{x}$ with $\boldsymbol{\phi}(\mathbf{x})$ throughout.

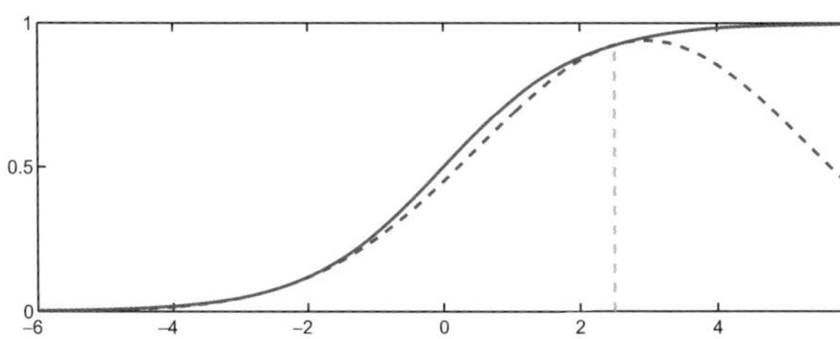

Figure 18.6 The logistic sigmoid $\sigma(x) = 1/(1 + \exp(-x))$ (solid curve) and a Gaussian lower bound (dashed curve) with operating point $\xi = 2.5$.

with the understanding that only the upper triangular part of the matrix expression is to be taken. One may show that the bound equation (18.2.29) is concave in the mean and covariance [60]. These gradients may then be used as part of a general purpose optimisation routine to find the best **m** and **C** approximation parameters.

18.2.4 Local variational approximation

An alternative to the KL bounding method above is to use a so-called local method that bounds each term in the integrand. To lower bound

$$p(\mathcal{D}) = \int \prod_n \sigma\left(s_n \mathbf{w}^\mathsf{T} \tilde{\mathbf{x}}_n\right) p(\mathbf{w}) d\mathbf{w} \tag{18.2.35}$$

we may bound the logistic sigmoid function [155], see Fig. 18.6,

$$\sigma(x) \geq \sigma(\xi)\left(\frac{1}{2}(x-\xi) - \lambda(\xi)\left(x^2-\xi^2\right)\right), \qquad \lambda(\xi) \equiv \frac{1}{2\xi}\left(\sigma(\xi) - \frac{1}{2}\right). \tag{18.2.36}$$

Hence

$$\log\sigma\left(s_n \mathbf{w}^\mathsf{T} \tilde{\mathbf{x}}_n\right) \geq \log\sigma(\xi_n) + \frac{1}{2}s_n \mathbf{w}^\mathsf{T}\tilde{\mathbf{x}}_n - \frac{1}{2}\xi_n - \lambda(\xi_n)\left[\left(\mathbf{w}^\mathsf{T}\tilde{\mathbf{x}}_n\right)^2 - \xi_n^2\right]. \tag{18.2.37}$$

Using this we can write

$$p(\mathcal{D}) \geq \int d\mathbf{w}\mathcal{N}(\mathbf{w}|\mathbf{0}, \boldsymbol{\Sigma}) \prod_n e^{\log\sigma(\xi_n) + \frac{1}{2}s_n \mathbf{w}^\mathsf{T}\tilde{\mathbf{x}}_n - \frac{1}{2}\xi_n - \lambda(\xi_n)\left[\left(\mathbf{w}^\mathsf{T}\tilde{\mathbf{x}}_n\right)^2 - \xi_n^2\right]}. \tag{18.2.38}$$

For fixed $\xi_n, n = 1, \ldots, N$, the right-hand side can be analytically integrated over **w**, resulting in the bound

$$\log p(\mathcal{D}) \geq \frac{1}{2}\log\frac{\det(\mathbf{S})}{\det(\boldsymbol{\Sigma})} + \frac{1}{2}\mathbf{m}^\mathsf{T}\mathbf{S}^{-1}\mathbf{m} + \sum_{n=1}^{N}\left[\log\sigma(\xi_n) - \frac{\xi_n}{2} + \lambda(\xi_n)\xi_n^2\right] \tag{18.2.39}$$

where

$$\mathbf{A} = \boldsymbol{\Sigma}^{-1} + 2\sum_{n=1}^{N}\lambda(\xi_n)\tilde{\mathbf{x}}_n\tilde{\mathbf{x}}_n^\mathsf{T}, \quad \mathbf{b} = \sum_{n=1}^{N}\frac{1}{2}s_n\tilde{\mathbf{x}}_n, \quad \hat{\mathbf{S}} \equiv \mathbf{A}^{-1}, \quad \hat{\mathbf{m}} \equiv \mathbf{A}^{-1}\mathbf{b}. \tag{18.2.40}$$

The bound equation (18.2.39) may then be maximised with respect to the variational parameters ξ_n. At convergence, we may take the Gaussian $\mathcal{N}\left(\mathbf{w}|\hat{\mathbf{m}}, \hat{\mathbf{S}}\right)$ as an approximation to the posterior.

Relation to KL variational procedure

As an alternative to the numerical integration in the KL procedure described in Section 18.2.3, we may instead bound the problematic term $\left\langle\log\sigma\left(s_n\mathbf{w}^\mathsf{T}\tilde{\mathbf{x}}_n\right)\right\rangle_{q(\mathbf{w})}$ in Equation (18.2.29) using (18.2.37).

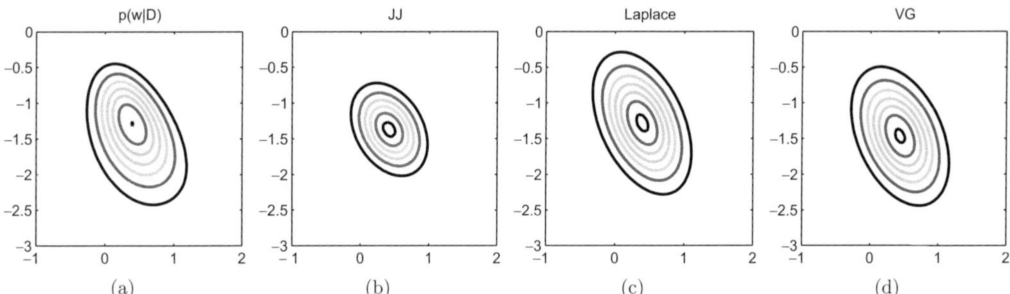

Figure 18.7 Posterior approximations for a two-dimensional Bayesian logistic regression posterior based on $N = 20$ datapoints. (**a**) True posterior. (**b**) The Gaussian from the Jaakola–Jordan local approximation. (**c**) The Laplace Gaussian approximation. (**d**) The variational Gaussian approximation from the KL approach.

As we discuss in Section 28.5, this enables us to relate the KL and the local bounding procedures [60], showing that for unconstrained Cholesky parameterisation $\mathbf{C}$ the KL approach results in a provably tighter lower bound than the local approach.

As an illustration of these approximations, for two-dimensional data, $D = 2$, we plot contours of the posterior and approximations in Fig. 18.7 which again demonstrates the over-compact nature of the local approximation. The Laplace approximation, which does not yield a bound, is plotted for comparison.

18.2.5 Relevance vector machine for classification

It is straightforward to apply the sparse linear model methods of Section 18.1.7 to classification. For example, in adopting the RVM prior to classification, as before we encourage individual weights to be small using

$$p(\mathbf{w}|\boldsymbol{\alpha}) = \prod_i p(w_i|\alpha_i), \qquad p(w_i|\alpha_i) = \mathcal{N}\left(w_i \middle| 0, \frac{1}{\alpha_i}\right). \tag{18.2.41}$$

The only alterations to the previous ML-II approach is to replace Equation (18.2.13) and Equation (18.2.15) with

$$[\nabla E]_i = \alpha_i w_i - \sum_n (1 - \sigma^n) h_i^n, \qquad \mathbf{H} = \text{diag}(\boldsymbol{\alpha}) + \mathbf{J}. \tag{18.2.42}$$

These are used in the Newton update formula as before. The update equation for the α's is given by

$$\alpha_i^{new} = \frac{1}{m_i^2 + S_{ii}}. \tag{18.2.43}$$

Similarly, the Gull–MacKay update is given by

$$\alpha_i^{new} = \frac{1 - \alpha_i S_{ii}}{m_i^2}. \tag{18.2.44}$$

Running this procedure, one typically finds that many of the α's tend to infinity and the corresponding weights are pruned from the system. The remaining weights typically correspond to basis

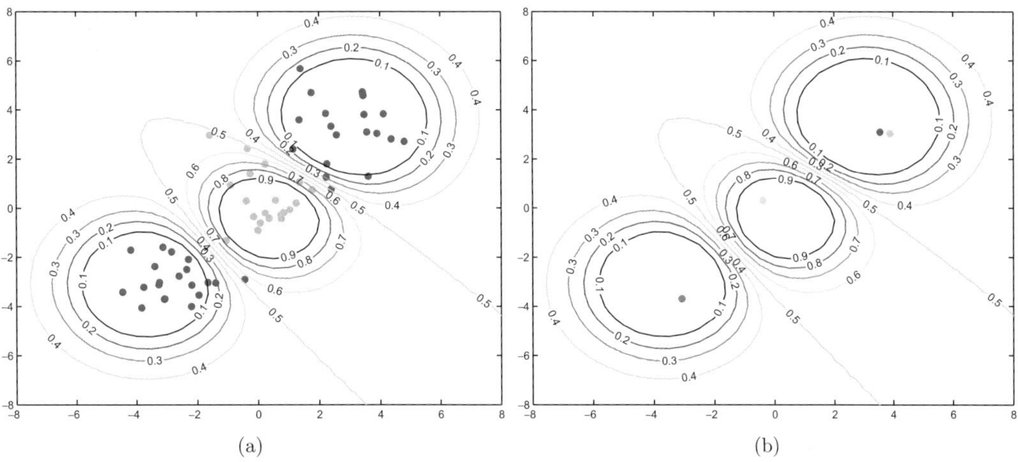

Figure 18.8 Classification using the RVM with RBF $e^{-\lambda(\mathbf{x}-\mathbf{m})^2}$, placing a basis function on a subset of the training data points. The green points are training data from class 1, and the red points are training data from class 0. The contours represent the probability of being in class 1. (**a**) Training points. (**b**) The training points weighted by their relevance value $1/\alpha_n$. Nearly all the points have a value so small that they effectively vanish. See `demoBayesLogRegRVM.m`. See plate section for colour version.

functions (in the RBF case) in the centres of mass of clusters of datapoints of the same class, see Fig. 18.8. Contrast this with the situation in SVMs, where the retained datapoints tend to be on the decision boundaries. The number of training points retained by the RVM tends to be very small – smaller indeed than the number retained in the SVM framework. Whilst the RVM does not support large margins, and hence may be a less robust classifier, it does retain the advantages of a probabilistic framework [295]. A potential critique of the RVM, coupled with an ML-II procedure for learning the α_i is that it is overly aggressive in terms of pruning. Indeed, as one may verify running `demoBayesLogRegRVM.m` it is common to find an instance of a problem for which there exists a set of α_i such that the training data can be classified perfectly; however, after using ML-II, so many of the α_i are set to zero that the training data can no longer be classified perfectly. An alternative is to apply the spike-and-slab prior technique which suffers less from overly aggressive pruning, although requires more sophisticated approximation methods.

18.2.6 Multi-class case

We briefly note that the multi-class case can be treated by using the softmax function under a one-of-m class coding scheme. The class probabilities are

$$p(c = m|y) = \frac{e^{y_m}}{\sum_{m'} e^{y_{m'}}} \tag{18.2.45}$$

which automatically enforces the constraint $\sum_m p(c = m) = 1$. Naively it would appear that for C classes, the cost of the Laplace approximation scales as $O\left(C^3N^3\right)$. However, one may show by careful implementation that the cost may be reduced to only $O\left(CN^3\right)$, analogous to the cost savings possible in the Gaussian process classification model [318, 247].

18.3 Summary

- A simple extension of linear regression is achieved by using a Gaussian prior on the parameters. Coupled with the assumption of additive Gaussian noise on the output, the posterior distribution is Gaussian, for which predictions can be computed readily.
- In the case of classification, no closed form Bayesian solution is obtained by using simple Gaussian priors on the parameters, and approximations are required. The parameter posterior is nevertheless well-behaved so that simple unimodal approximations may be adequate.

18.4 Code

`demoBayesLinReg.m`: Demo of Bayesian linear regression
`BayesLinReg.m`: Bayesian linear regression
`demoBayesLogRegRVM.m`: Demo of Bayesian logistic regression (RVM)
`BayesLogRegressionRVM.m`: Bayesian logistic regression (RVM)
`avsigmaGauss.m`: Approximation of the Gaussian average of a logistic sigmoid
`logsigapp.m`: Approximation of the logistic sigmoid using mixture of erfs

18.5 Exercises

18.1 The exercise concerns Bayesian regression.

1. Show that for $f = \mathbf{w}^\mathsf{T}\mathbf{x}$ and $p(\mathbf{w}) \sim \mathcal{N}(\mathbf{w}|\mathbf{0}, \mathbf{\Sigma})$, $p(f|\mathbf{x})$ is Gaussian distributed. Furthermore, find the mean and covariance of this Gaussian.
2. Consider a target point $t = f + \epsilon$, where $\epsilon \sim \mathcal{N}(\epsilon|0, \sigma^2)$. What is $p(f|t, \mathbf{x})$?

18.2 A Bayesian linear parameter regression model is given by

$$y^n = \mathbf{w}^\mathsf{T}\boldsymbol{\phi}(\mathbf{x}^n) + \eta^n. \tag{18.5.1}$$

In vector notation $\mathbf{y} = \left(y^1, \ldots, y^N\right)^\mathsf{T}$ this can be written

$$\mathbf{y} = \mathbf{\Phi}\mathbf{w} + \boldsymbol{\eta} \tag{18.5.2}$$

with $\mathbf{\Phi}^\mathsf{T} = \left[\boldsymbol{\phi}(\mathbf{x}^1), \ldots, \boldsymbol{\phi}(\mathbf{x}^N)\right]$ and $\boldsymbol{\eta}$ is a zero mean Gaussian distributed vector with covariance $\beta^{-1}\mathbf{I}$. An expression for the marginal likelihood of a dataset is given in Equation (18.1.19). We aim to find a more compact expression for the likelihood given the hyperparameters Γ

$$p(y^1, \ldots, y^N|\mathbf{x}^1, \ldots, \mathbf{x}^N, \Gamma). \tag{18.5.3}$$

Since y^n is linearly related to $\mathbf{w}$ and $p(\mathbf{w}) = \mathcal{N}\left(\mathbf{w}|\mathbf{0}, \alpha^{-1}\mathbf{I}\right)$, then $\mathbf{y}$ is Gaussian distributed with mean

$$\langle \mathbf{y} \rangle = \mathbf{\Phi}\langle \mathbf{w} \rangle = \mathbf{0} \tag{18.5.4}$$

and covariance matrix

$$\mathbf{C} = \left\langle \mathbf{y}\mathbf{y}^\mathsf{T} \right\rangle - \langle \mathbf{y} \rangle \langle \mathbf{y} \rangle^\mathsf{T} = \left\langle (\mathbf{\Phi}\mathbf{w} + \boldsymbol{\eta})(\mathbf{\Phi}\mathbf{w} + \boldsymbol{\eta})^\mathsf{T} \right\rangle. \tag{18.5.5}$$

1. Show that the covariance matrix can be expressed as

$$\mathbf{C} = \frac{1}{\beta}\mathbf{I} + \frac{1}{\alpha}\boldsymbol{\Phi}\boldsymbol{\Phi}^{\mathsf{T}}. \tag{18.5.6}$$

2. Hence show that the log marginal likelihood can be written as

$$\log p(y^1, \ldots, y^N|\mathbf{x}^1, \ldots, \mathbf{x}^N, \Gamma) = -\frac{1}{2}\log\det(2\pi\mathbf{C}) - \frac{1}{2}\mathbf{y}^{\mathsf{T}}\mathbf{C}^{-1}\mathbf{y}. \tag{18.5.7}$$

18.3 Using Exercise 18.2 as a basis, derive expression (18.1.41) for the log likelihood on a validation set.

18.4 Consider the function $E(\mathbf{w})$ as defined in Equation (18.2.12).

1. Show that the Hessian matrix which has elements,

$$H_{ij} \equiv \frac{\partial^2}{\partial w_i \partial w_j}E(\mathbf{w}) = \left[\alpha\mathbf{I} + \sum_{n=1}^{N}\sigma^n\left(1-\sigma^n\right)\boldsymbol{\phi}^n\left(\boldsymbol{\phi}^n\right)^{\mathsf{T}}\right]_{ij}. \tag{18.5.8}$$

2. Show that the Hessian is positive definite.

18.5 Show that for any function $f(\cdot)$,

$$\int f(\mathbf{x}^{\mathsf{T}}\mathbf{w})p(\mathbf{w})d\mathbf{w} = \int f(h)p(h)dh \tag{18.5.9}$$

where $p(h)$ is the distribution of the scalar $\mathbf{x}^{\mathsf{T}}\mathbf{w}$. The significance is that any high-dimensional integral of the above form can be reduced to a one-dimensional integral over the distribution of the 'field' h [22].

18.6 This exercise concerns Bayesian logistic regression. Our interest is to derive the optimal regularisation parameter α based on the Laplace approximation to the marginal log likelihood given by

$$\log p(\mathcal{D}|\alpha) \approx L(\alpha) \equiv -\frac{\alpha}{2}(\mathbf{w})^{\mathsf{T}}\mathbf{w} + \sum_n \log\sigma\left((\mathbf{w})^{\mathsf{T}}\mathbf{h}^n\right) - \frac{1}{2}\log\det(\alpha\mathbf{I}+\mathbf{J}) + \frac{B}{2}\log\alpha. \tag{18.5.10}$$

The Laplace procedure finds first an optimal $\mathbf{w}^*$ that minimises $\alpha\mathbf{w}^{\mathsf{T}}\mathbf{w}/2 - \sum_n \log\sigma\left(\mathbf{w}^{\mathsf{T}}\mathbf{h}^n\right)$, as in Equation (18.2.12) which will depend on the setting of α. Formally, therefore, in finding the α that optimises $L(\alpha)$ we should make use of the total derivative formula

$$\frac{dL}{d\alpha} = \frac{\partial L}{\partial\alpha} + \sum_i \frac{\partial L}{\partial w_i}\frac{\partial w_i}{\partial\alpha}. \tag{18.5.11}$$

However, when evaluated at $\mathbf{w} = \mathbf{w}^*$, $\frac{\partial L}{\partial\mathbf{w}} = \mathbf{0}$. This means that in order to compute the derivative with respect to α, we only need consider the terms with an explicit α dependence. Equating the derivative to zero and using

$$\partial\log\det(\mathbf{M}) = \text{trace}\left(\mathbf{M}^{-1}\partial\mathbf{M}\right) \tag{18.5.12}$$

show that the optimal α satisfies the fixed-point equation

$$\alpha^{new} = \frac{N}{(\mathbf{w}^*)^{\mathsf{T}}\mathbf{w}^* + \text{trace}\left((\alpha\mathbf{I}+\mathbf{J})^{-1}\right)}. \tag{18.5.13}$$

19 Gaussian processes

In Bayesian linear parameter models, we saw that the only relevant quantities are related to the scalar product of data vectors. In Gaussian processes we use this to motivate a prediction method that does not necessarily correspond to any 'parametric' model of the data. Such models are flexible Bayesian predictors.

19.1 Non-parametric prediction

Gaussian Processes (GPs) are flexible Bayesian models that fit well within the probabilistic modelling framework. In developing GPs it is useful to first step back and see what information we need to form a predictor. Given a set of training data

$$\mathcal{D} = \{(x^n, y^n), n = 1, \ldots, N\} = \mathcal{X} \cup \mathcal{Y} \tag{19.1.1}$$

where x^n is the input for datapoint n and y^n the corresponding output (a continuous variable in the regression case and a discrete variable in the classification case), our aim is to make a prediction y^* for a new input x^*. In the discriminative framework no model of the inputs x is assumed and only the outputs are modelled, conditioned on the inputs. Given a joint model

$$p(y^1, \ldots, y^N, y^*|x^1, \ldots, x^N, x^*) = p(\mathcal{Y}, y^*|\mathcal{X}, x^*) \tag{19.1.2}$$

we may subsequently use conditioning to form a predictor $p(y^*|x^*, \mathcal{D})$. In previous chapters we've made much use of the i.i.d. assumption that each datapoint is independently sampled from the same generating distribution. In this context, this might appear to suggest the assumption

$$p(y^1, \ldots, y^N, y^*|x^1, \ldots, x^N, x^*) = p(y^*|\mathcal{X}, x^*) \prod_n p(y^n|\mathcal{X}, x^*). \tag{19.1.3}$$

However, this is clearly of little use since the predictive conditional is simply $p(y^*|\mathcal{D}, x^*) = p(y^*|\mathcal{X}, x^*)$ meaning the predictions make no use of the training outputs. For a non-trivial predictor we therefore need to specify a joint non-factorised distribution over outputs.

19.1.1 From parametric to non-parametric

If we revisit our i.i.d. assumptions for parametric models, we used a parameter θ to make a model of the input–output distribution $p(y|x, \theta)$. For a parametric model predictions are formed using

$$p(y^*|x^*, \mathcal{D}) \propto p(y^*, x^*, \mathcal{D}) = \int_\theta p(y^*, \mathcal{Y}, x^*, \mathcal{X}, \theta) \propto \int_\theta p(y^*, \mathcal{Y}|\theta, x^*, \mathcal{X}) p(\theta|\cancel{x^*, \mathcal{X}}). \tag{19.1.4}$$

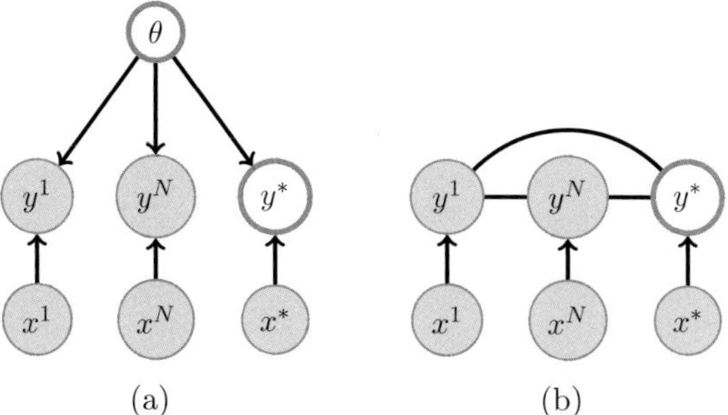

Figure 19.1 (**a**) A parametric model for prediction assuming i.i.d. data. (**b**) The form of the model after integrating out the parameters θ. Our non-parametric model will have this structure.

Under the assumption that, given θ, the data is i.i.d., we obtain

$$p(y^*|x^*, \mathcal{D}) \propto \int_\theta p(y^*|x^*, \theta)p(\theta) \prod_n p(y^n|\theta, x^n) \propto \int_\theta p(y^*|x^*, \theta)p(\theta|\mathcal{D}) \tag{19.1.5}$$

where

$$p(\theta|\mathcal{D}) \propto p(\theta) \prod_n p(y^n|\theta, x^n). \tag{19.1.6}$$

After integrating over the parameters θ, the joint data distribution is given by

$$p(y^*, \mathcal{Y}|x^*, \mathcal{X}) = \int_\theta p(y^*|x^*, \theta)p(\theta) \prod_n p(y^n|\theta, x^n) \tag{19.1.7}$$

which does not in general factorise into individual datapoint terms, see Fig. 19.1. The idea of a non-parametric approach is to specify the form of the dependencies $p(y^*, \mathcal{Y}|x^*, \mathcal{X})$ without reference to an explicit parametric model. One route towards a non-parametric model is to start with a parametric model and integrate out the parameters. In order to make this tractable, we use a simple linear parameter predictor with a Gaussian parameter prior. For regression this leads to closed form expressions, although the classification case will require numerical approximation.

19.1.2 From Bayesian linear models to Gaussian processes

To develop the GP, we briefly revisit the Bayesian linear parameter model of Section 18.1.1. For parameters $\mathbf{w}$ and basis functions $\phi_i(x)$ the output is given by (assuming zero output noise)

$$y = \sum_i w_i \phi_i(x). \tag{19.1.8}$$

If we stack all the $y^1, \ldots, y^N$ into a vector $\mathbf{y}$, then we can write the predictors as

$$\mathbf{y} = \mathbf{\Phi}\mathbf{w} \tag{19.1.9}$$

where $\mathbf{\Phi} = \left[\boldsymbol{\phi}(x^1), \ldots, \boldsymbol{\phi}(x^N)\right]^\mathsf{T}$ is the design matrix. Assuming a Gaussian weight prior

$$p(\mathbf{w}) = \mathcal{N}(\mathbf{w}|\mathbf{0}, \mathbf{\Sigma}_\mathbf{w}) \tag{19.1.10}$$

the joint output

$$p(\mathbf{y}|\mathbf{x}) = \int_\mathbf{w} \delta(\mathbf{y} - \mathbf{\Phi}\mathbf{w})\, p(\mathbf{w}) \tag{19.1.11}$$

is Gaussian distributed with mean

$$\langle \mathbf{y} \rangle = \mathbf{\Phi} \langle \mathbf{w} \rangle_{p(\mathbf{w})} = \mathbf{0} \tag{19.1.12}$$

and covariance

$$\left\langle \mathbf{y}\mathbf{y}^{\mathsf{T}} \right\rangle = \mathbf{\Phi} \left\langle \mathbf{w}\mathbf{w}^{\mathsf{T}} \right\rangle_{p(\mathbf{w})} \mathbf{\Phi}^{\mathsf{T}} = \mathbf{\Phi}\mathbf{\Sigma}_{\mathbf{w}}\mathbf{\Phi}^{\mathsf{T}} = \left(\mathbf{\Phi}\mathbf{\Sigma}_{\mathbf{w}}^{\frac{1}{2}}\right)\left(\mathbf{\Phi}\mathbf{\Sigma}_{\mathbf{w}}^{\frac{1}{2}}\right)^{\mathsf{T}}. \tag{19.1.13}$$

From this we see that the $\mathbf{\Sigma}_{\mathbf{w}}$ can be absorbed into $\mathbf{\Phi}$ using its Cholesky decomposition. In other words, without loss of generality we may assume $\mathbf{\Sigma}_{\mathbf{w}} = \mathbf{I}$. Hence, after integrating out the weights, the Bayesian linear regression model induces a Gaussian distribution on any set of outputs $\mathbf{y}$ as

$$p(\mathbf{y}|\mathbf{x}) = \mathcal{N}(\mathbf{y}|\mathbf{0}, \mathbf{K}) \tag{19.1.14}$$

where the covariance matrix $\mathbf{K}$ depends on the training inputs alone via

$$[\mathbf{K}]_{n,n'} = \boldsymbol{\phi}(x^n)^{\mathsf{T}}\boldsymbol{\phi}(x^{n'}), \qquad n, n' = 1, \ldots, N. \tag{19.1.15}$$

Since the matrix $\mathbf{K}$ is formed as the scalar product of vectors, it is by construction positive semidefinite, see Section 19.4.2. After integrating out the weights, the only thing the model directly depends on is the covariance matrix $\mathbf{K}$. In a Gaussian process we directly specify the joint output covariance $\mathbf{K}$ as a function of two inputs, rather than specifying a linear model with parameters $\mathbf{w}$. Specifically we need to define the n, n' element of the covariance matrix for any two inputs x^n and $x^{n'}$. This is achieved using a *covariance function* $k(x^n, x^{n'})$

$$[\mathbf{K}]_{n,n'} = k(x^n, x^{n'}). \tag{19.1.16}$$

The matrix $\mathbf{K}$ formed from a covariance function k is called the Gram matrix. The required form of the function $k(x^n, x^{n'})$ is very special – when applied to create the elements of the matrix $\mathbf{K}$ it must produce a positive definite matrix. We discuss how to create such covariance functions in Section 19.3. One explicit straightforward construction is to form the covariance function from the scalar product of the basis vector $\boldsymbol{\phi}(x^n)$ and $\boldsymbol{\phi}(x^{n'})$. For finite-dimensional $\boldsymbol{\phi}$ this is known as a *finite-dimensional Gaussian process*. Given any covariance function we can always find a corresponding basis vector representation – that is, for any GP, we can always relate this back to a parametric Bayesian LPM. However, for many commonly used covariance functions, the basis functions corresponds to infinite-dimensional vectors. It is in such cases that the advantages of using the GP framework are particularly evident since we would not be able to compute efficiently with the corresponding infinite-dimensional parametric model.

19.1.3 A prior on functions

The nature of many machine learning applications is such that the knowledge about the true underlying mechanism behind the data generation process is limited. Instead one relies on generic 'smoothness' assumptions; for example we might wish that for two inputs x and x' that are close, the corresponding outputs y and y' should be similar. Many generic techniques in machine learning can be viewed as different characterisations of smoothness. An advantage of the GP framework in this respect is that the mathematical smoothness properties of the functions are well understood, giving confidence in the procedure.

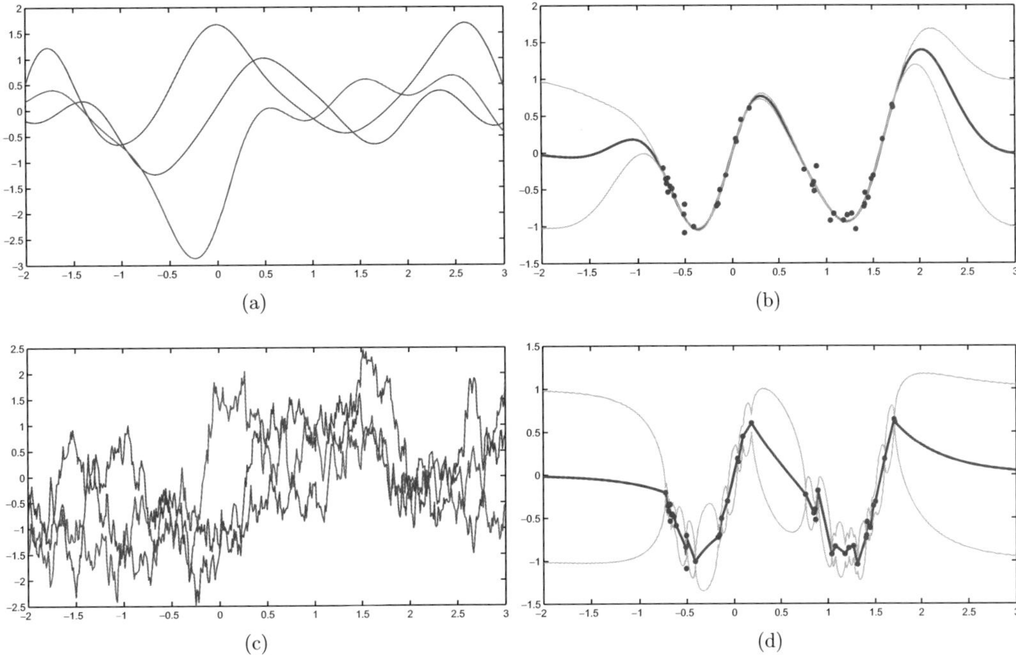

Figure 19.2 The input space from -2 to 3 is split evenly into 1000 points $x^1, \ldots, x^{1000}$. (**a**) Three samples from a GP prior with squared exponential covariance function, $\lambda = 2$. The 1000×1000 covariance matrix **K** is defined using the SE kernel, from which the samples are drawn using `mvrandn(zeros(1000,1),K,3)`. (**b**) Prediction based on training points. Plotted is the posterior predicted function based on the SE covariance. The central line is the mean prediction, with standard errors bars on either side. The log marginal likelihood is ≈ 70. (**c**) Three samples from the Ornstein–Uhlenbeck GP prior with $\lambda = 2$. (**d**) Posterior prediction for the OU covariance. The log marginal likelihood is ≈ 3, meaning that the SE covariance is much more heavily supported by the data than the rougher OU covariance. See plate section for colour version.

For a given covariance matrix $\mathbf{K}$, Equation (19.1.14) specifies a distribution on functions[1] in the following sense: we specify a set of input points $\mathbf{x} = (x^1, \ldots, x^N)$ and an $N \times N$ covariance matrix $\mathbf{K}$. Then we draw a vector $\mathbf{y} = \left(y^1, \ldots, y^N\right)$ from the Gaussian defined by Equation (19.1.14). We can then plot the sampled 'function' at the finite set of points $(x^n, y^n), n = 1, \ldots, N$. What kind of function does a GP correspond to? In Fig. 19.2(a) we show three sample functions drawn from a Squared Exponential covariance function defined over 500 points uniformly spaced from -2 to 3. Each sampled function looks reasonably smooth. Conversely, for the Ornstein Uhlenbeck covariance function, the sampled functions Fig. 19.2(c) look locally rough. These smoothness properties are related to the form of the covariance function, as discussed in Section 19.4.1.

Consider two scalar inputs, x^i and x^j and corresponding sampled outputs y^i and y^j. For a covariance function with large $k(x^i, x^j)$, we expect y^i and y^j to be very similar since they are highly correlated. Conversely, for a covariance function that has low $k(x^i, x^j)$, we expect y^i and y^j to be

[1] The term 'function' is potentially confusing since we do not have an explicit functional form for the input–output mapping. For any finite set of inputs $x^1, \ldots, x^N$ the values for the 'function' are given by the outputs at those points $y^1, \ldots, y^N$.

effectively independent. In general, we would expect the correlation between y_i and y_j to decrease the further apart x_i and x_j are.[2]

The zero mean assumption implies that if we were to draw a large number of such 'functions', the mean across these functions at a given point x tends to zero. Similarly, for any two points x and x' if we compute the sample covariance between the corresponding y and y' for all such sampled functions, this will tend to the covariance function value $k(x, x')$. The zero mean assumption can be easily relaxed by defining a mean function $m(x)$ to give $p(\mathbf{y}|\mathbf{x}) = \mathcal{N}(\mathbf{y}|\mathbf{m}, \mathbf{K})$. In many practical situations one typically deals with 'detrended' data in which such mean trends have been already removed. For this reason much of the development of GPs in the machine learning literature is for the zero mean case.

19.2 Gaussian process prediction

For a dataset $\mathcal{D} = \{\mathbf{x}, \mathbf{y}\}$ and novel input x^*, a zero mean GP makes a Gaussian model of the joint outputs $y^1, \ldots, y^N, y^*$ given the joint inputs $x^1, \ldots, x^N, x^*$. For convenience we write this as

$$p(\mathbf{y}, y^*|\mathbf{x}, x^*) = \mathcal{N}\left(\mathbf{y}, y^*|\mathbf{0}_{N+1}, \mathbf{K}^+\right) \tag{19.2.1}$$

where $\mathbf{0}_{N+1}$ is an $N+1$ dimensional zero-vector. The covariance matrix $\mathbf{K}^+$ is a block matrix with elements

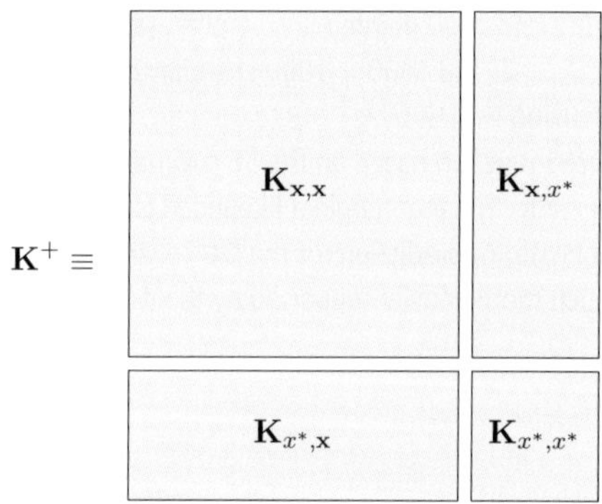

where $\mathbf{K}_{\mathbf{x},\mathbf{x}}$ is the covariance matrix of the training inputs $\mathbf{x} = \left(x^1, \ldots, x^N\right)$ – that is

$$\left[\mathbf{K}_{\mathbf{x},\mathbf{x}}\right]_{n,n'} \equiv k(x^n, x^{n'}), \qquad n, n' = 1, \ldots, N. \tag{19.2.2}$$

The $N \times 1$ vector $\mathbf{K}_{\mathbf{x},x^*}$ has elements

$$\left[\mathbf{K}_{\mathbf{x},x^*}\right]_{n,*} \equiv k(x^n, x^*) \qquad n = 1, \ldots, N. \tag{19.2.3}$$

Here $\mathbf{K}_{x^*,\mathbf{x}}$ is the transpose of the above vector. The scalar covariance is given by

$$\mathbf{K}_{x^*,x^*} \equiv k(x^*, x^*). \tag{19.2.4}$$

The predictive distribution $p(y^*|x^*, \mathbf{x}, \mathbf{y})$ is obtained by Gaussian conditioning using Result 8.4, giving a Gaussian distribution

$$p(y^*|x^*, \mathcal{D}) = \mathcal{N}\left(y^*\left|\mathbf{K}_{x^*,\mathbf{x}}\mathbf{K}_{\mathbf{x},\mathbf{x}}^{-1}\mathbf{y}, \mathbf{K}_{x^*,x^*} - \mathbf{K}_{x^*,\mathbf{x}}\mathbf{K}_{\mathbf{x},\mathbf{x}}^{-1}\mathbf{K}_{\mathbf{x},x^*}\right.\right). \tag{19.2.5}$$

[2] For periodic functions one can have high correlation even if the inputs are far apart.

GP regression is an exact method and there are no issues with local minima. Furthermore, GPs are attractive since they automatically model uncertainty in the predictions. However, the computational complexity for making a prediction is $O\left(N^3\right)$ due to the requirement of performing the matrix inversion (or solving the corresponding linear system by Gaussian elimination). This can be prohibitively expensive for large datasets and a large body of research on efficient approximations exists. A discussion of these techniques is beyond the scope of this book, and the reader is referred to [247].

19.2.1 Regression with noisy training outputs

To prevent overfitting to noisy data it is useful to assume that a training output y^n is the result of some clean Gaussian process f^n corrupted by independent additive Gaussian noise,

$$y^n = f^n + \epsilon^n, \quad \text{where} \quad \epsilon^n \sim \mathcal{N}\left(\epsilon^n | 0, \sigma^2\right). \tag{19.2.6}$$

In this case our interest is to predict the clean signal f^* for a novel input x^*. Then the distribution $p(\mathbf{y}, f^*|\mathbf{x}, x^*)$ is a zero mean Gaussian with block covariance matrix

$$\begin{pmatrix} \mathbf{K}_{\mathbf{x},\mathbf{x}} + \sigma^2\mathbf{I} & \mathbf{K}_{\mathbf{x},x^*} \\ \mathbf{K}_{x^*,\mathbf{x}} & \mathbf{K}_{x^*,x^*} \end{pmatrix} \tag{19.2.7}$$

so that $\mathbf{K}_{\mathbf{x},\mathbf{x}}$ is replaced by $\mathbf{K}_{\mathbf{x},\mathbf{x}} + \sigma^2\mathbf{I}$ in forming the prediction, Equation (19.2.5). This follows since

$$\langle y^n \rangle = \langle f^n \rangle + \langle \epsilon^n \rangle = 0 + 0 \tag{19.2.8}$$

and, using the assumed independence of the noise with the clean signal, $f^m \perp\!\!\!\perp \epsilon^n$ and the independence of two noise components, $\epsilon^m \perp\!\!\!\perp \epsilon^n, m \neq n$, we have

$$\begin{aligned}\langle y^m y^n \rangle &= \langle (f^m + \epsilon^m)(f^n + \epsilon^n) \rangle \\ &= \underbrace{\langle f^m f^n \rangle}_{k(x^m,x^n)} + \underbrace{\langle f^m \epsilon^n \rangle}_{\langle f^m \rangle \langle \epsilon^n \rangle} + \langle f^n \epsilon^m \rangle_{\langle f^n \rangle \langle \epsilon^m \rangle} + \langle \epsilon^m \epsilon^n \rangle_{\sigma^2 \delta_{m,n}}.\end{aligned} \tag{19.2.9}$$

Using $\langle \epsilon^m \rangle = 0$ we obtain the form in Equation (19.2.7).

Example 19.1

Training data from a one-dimensional input x and one-dimensional output y are plotted in Fig. 19.2(b,d), along with the mean regression function fit, based on two different covariance functions. Note how the smoothness of the prior translates into smoothness of the prediction. The smoothness of the function space prior is a consequence of the choice of covariance function. Naively, we can partially understand this by the behaviour of the covariance function at the origin, Section 19.4.1. An intuitive way to think about GP regression is to sample an 'infinite' number of functions from the prior; these are then 'filtered' by how well they fit the data by the likelihood term, leaving a posterior distribution on the functions. See `demoGPreg.m`.

The marginal likelihood and hyperparameter learning

For a set of N one-dimensional training inputs represented by the $N \times 1$ dimensional vector $\mathbf{y}$ and a covariance matrix $\mathbf{K}$ defined on the inputs $\mathbf{x} = (x^1, \ldots, x^N)$, the log marginal likelihood is

$$\log p(\mathbf{y}|\mathbf{x}) = -\frac{1}{2}\mathbf{y}^{\mathsf{T}}\mathbf{K}^{-1}\mathbf{y} - \frac{1}{2}\log\det(2\pi\mathbf{K}). \tag{19.2.10}$$

One can learn any free (hyper) parameters of the covariance function by maximising the marginal likelihood. For example, a squared exponential covariance function may have parameters λ, v_0:

$$k(x, x') = v_0 \exp\left\{-\frac{1}{2}\lambda\left(x - x'\right)^2\right\}. \tag{19.2.11}$$

The λ parameter in Equation (19.2.12) specifies the appropriate length scale of the inputs, and v_0 the variance of the function. The dependence of the marginal likelihood (19.2.10) on the parameters is typically complex and no closed form expression for the maximum likelihood optimum exists; in this case one resorts to numerical optimisation techniques such as conjugate gradients.

Vector inputs

For regression with vector inputs and scalar outputs we need to define a covariance as a function of the two vectors, $k(\mathbf{x}, \mathbf{x}')$. Using the multiplicative property of covariance functions, Definition 19.3, a simple way to do this is to define

$$k(\mathbf{x}, \mathbf{x}') = \prod_i k(x_i, x_i'). \tag{19.2.12}$$

For example, for the squared exponential covariance function this gives

$$k(\mathbf{x}, \mathbf{x}') = e^{-(\mathbf{x}-\mathbf{x}')^2} \tag{19.2.13}$$

though 'correlated' forms are possible as well, see Exercise 19.6. We can generalise the above using parameters:

$$k(\mathbf{x}, \mathbf{x}') = v_0 \exp\left\{-\frac{1}{2}\sum_{l=1}^{D}\lambda_l\left(x_l - x_l'\right)^2\right\} \tag{19.2.14}$$

where x_l is the lth component of $\mathbf{x}$ and $\theta = (v_0, \lambda_1, \ldots, \lambda_D)$ are the parameters. The λ_l in Equation (19.2.14) allow a different length scale on each input dimension and can be learned by numerically maximising the marginal likelihood. For irrelevant inputs, the corresponding λ_l will become small, and the model will ignore the lth input dimension.

19.3 Covariance functions

Covariance functions $k(x, x')$ are special in that they define elements of a positive definite matrix. These functions are also referred to as 'kernels', particulary in the machine learning literature.

Definition 19.1 Covariance function Given any collection of points $x^1, \ldots, x^M$, a covariance function $k(x^i, x^j)$ defines the elements of an $M \times M$ matrix

$$[\mathbf{C}]_{i,j} = k(x^i, x^j)$$

such that $\mathbf{C}$ is positive semidefinite.

19.3.1 Making new covariance functions from old

The following rules (see Exercise 19.1) generate new covariance functions from existing covariance functions k_1, k_2 [196], [247].

Definition 19.2 Sum

$$k(\mathbf{x}, \mathbf{x}') = k_1(\mathbf{x}, \mathbf{x}') + k_2(\mathbf{x}, \mathbf{x}'). \tag{19.3.1}$$

Definition 19.3 Product

$$k(\mathbf{x}, \mathbf{x}') = k_1(\mathbf{x}, \mathbf{x}')k_2(\mathbf{x}, \mathbf{x}'). \tag{19.3.2}$$

Definition 19.4 Product spaces For $\mathbf{z} = \begin{pmatrix} \mathbf{x} \\ \mathbf{y} \end{pmatrix}$,

$$k(\mathbf{z}, \mathbf{z}') = k_1(\mathbf{x}, \mathbf{x}') + k_2(\mathbf{y}, \mathbf{y}') \tag{19.3.3}$$

and

$$k(\mathbf{z}, \mathbf{z}') = k_1(\mathbf{x}, \mathbf{x}')k_2(\mathbf{y}, \mathbf{y}'). \tag{19.3.4}$$

Definition 19.5 Vertical rescaling

$$k(\mathbf{x}, \mathbf{x}') = a(\mathbf{x})k_1(\mathbf{x}, \mathbf{x}')a(\mathbf{x}') \tag{19.3.5}$$

for any function $a(\mathbf{x})$.

Definition 19.6 Warping and embedding

$$k(\mathbf{x}, \mathbf{x}') = k_1\left(\mathbf{u}(\mathbf{x}), \mathbf{u}(\mathbf{x}')\right) \tag{19.3.6}$$

for any mapping $\mathbf{x} \to \mathbf{u}(\mathbf{x})$, where the mapping $\mathbf{u}(\mathbf{x})$ has arbitrary dimension.

A small collection of covariance functions commonly used in machine learning is given below. We refer the reader to [247] and [117] for further popular covariance functions.

19.3.2 Stationary covariance functions

Definition 19.7 Stationary kernel A kernel $k(x, x')$ is stationary if the kernel depends only on the separation $\mathbf{x} - \mathbf{x}'$. That is

$$k(\mathbf{x}, \mathbf{x}') = k(\mathbf{x} - \mathbf{x}'). \tag{19.3.7}$$

For a stationary covariance function we may write $k(\mathbf{d})$, where $\mathbf{d} = \mathbf{x} - \mathbf{x}'$. This means that for functions drawn from the GP, on average, the functions depend only on the distance between inputs and not on the absolute position of an input. In other words, the functions are on average translation invariant. For *isotropic covariance functions*, the covariance is defined as a function of the distance $|\mathbf{d}|$. Such covariance functions are, by construction, rotationally invariant.

Definition 19.8 Squared exponential

$$k(\mathbf{d}) = \exp\left(-|\mathbf{d}|^2\right). \tag{19.3.8}$$

The squared exponential is one of the most common covariance functions. There are many ways to show that this is a covariance function. An elementary technique is to consider

$$\exp\left(-\frac{1}{2}\left(\mathbf{x}^n-\mathbf{x}^{n'}\right)^{\mathsf{T}}\left(\mathbf{x}^n-\mathbf{x}^{n'}\right)\right)=\exp\left(-\frac{1}{2}|\mathbf{x}^n|^2\right)\exp\left(-\frac{1}{2}\left|\mathbf{x}^{n'}\right|^2\right)\exp\left((\mathbf{x}^n)^{\mathsf{T}}\mathbf{x}^{n'}\right). \quad (19.3.9)$$

The first two factors on the right above form a kernel of the form $\phi(\mathbf{x}^n)\phi(\mathbf{x}^{n'})$. In the final term $k_1(\mathbf{x}^n,\mathbf{x}^{n'})=(\mathbf{x}^n)^{\mathsf{T}}\mathbf{x}^{n'}$ is the linear kernel. Taking the exponential and writing the power series expansion of the exponential, we have

$$\exp\left(k_1(\mathbf{x}^n,\mathbf{x}^{n'})\right)=\sum_{i=1}^{\infty}\frac{1}{i!}k_1^i(\mathbf{x}^n,\mathbf{x}^{n'}) \quad (19.3.10)$$

this can be expressed as a series of integer powers of k_1, with positive coefficients. By the product (with itself) and sum rules above, this is therefore a kernel as well. We then use the fact that Equation (19.3.9) is the product of two kernels, and hence also a kernel.

Definition 19.9 **γ-Exponential**

$$k(\mathbf{d})=\exp\left(-|\mathbf{d}|^{\gamma}\right), \qquad 0<\gamma\leq 2. \quad (19.3.11)$$

When $\gamma=2$ we have the squared exponential covariance function. When $\gamma=1$ this is the *Ornstein–Uhlenbeck* covariance function.

Definition 19.10 **Matérn**

$$k(\mathbf{d})=|\mathbf{d}|^{\nu}K_{\nu}\left(|\mathbf{d}|\right) \quad (19.3.12)$$

where K_ν is a modified Bessel function, $\nu>0$.

Definition 19.11 **Rational quadratic**

$$k(\mathbf{d})=\left(1+|\mathbf{d}|^2\right)^{-\alpha}, \qquad \alpha>0. \quad (19.3.13)$$

Definition 19.12 **Periodic** For one-dimensional x and x', a stationary (and isotropic) covariance function can be obtained by first mapping x to the two-dimensional vector $\mathbf{u}(x)=(\cos(x),\sin(x))$ and then using the SE covariance $\exp\left(-\left(\mathbf{u}(x)-\mathbf{u}(x')\right)^2\right)$ [196]

$$k(x-x')=\exp\left(-\lambda\sin^2\left(\omega(x-x')\right)\right), \qquad \lambda>0. \quad (19.3.14)$$

See Fig. 19.4(a).

19.3.3 Non-stationary covariance functions

Definition 19.13 **Linear**

$$k(\mathbf{x},\mathbf{x}')=\mathbf{x}^{\mathsf{T}}\mathbf{x}'. \quad (19.3.15)$$

Definition 19.14 **Neural network (NN)**

$$k(\mathbf{x},\mathbf{x}')=\arcsin\left(\frac{2\mathbf{x}^{\mathsf{T}}\mathbf{x}'}{\sqrt{1+2\mathbf{x}^{\mathsf{T}}\mathbf{x}}\sqrt{1+2\mathbf{x}'^{\mathsf{T}}\mathbf{x}'}}\right). \quad (19.3.16)$$

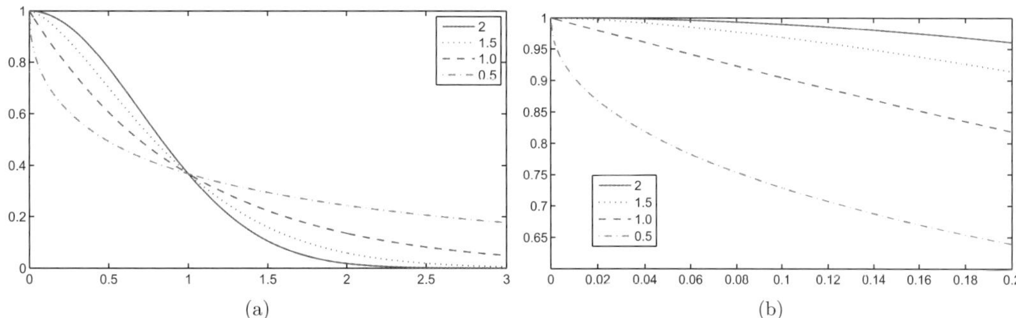

Figure 19.3 (**a**) Plots of the gamma-exponential covariance $e^{-|x|^\gamma}$ versus x. The case $\gamma = 2$ corresponds to the SE covariance function. The drop in the covariance is much more rapid as a function of the separation x for small γ, suggesting that the functions corresponding to smaller γ will be locally rough (though possess relatively higher long-range correlation). (**b**) As for (a) but zoomed in towards the origin. For the SE case, $\gamma = 2$, the derivative of the covariance function is zero, whereas the OU covariance $\gamma = 1$ has a first-order contribution to the drop in the covariance, suggesting that locally OU sampled functions will be much rougher than SE functions.

The functions defined by this covariance always go through the origin. To shift this, one may use the embedding $\mathbf{x} \to (1, \mathbf{x})$ where the 1 has the effect of a 'bias' from the origin. To change the scale of the bias and non-bias contributions one may use additional parameters $\mathbf{x} \to (b, \lambda\mathbf{x})$. The NN covariance function can be derived as a limiting case of a neural network with infinite hidden units [317], and making use of exact integral results in [21]. See Fig. 19.4(b).

Definition 19.15 **Gibbs**

$$k(\mathbf{x}, \mathbf{x}') = \prod_i \left(\frac{r_i(\mathbf{x}) r_i(\mathbf{x}')}{r_i^2(\mathbf{x}) + r_i^2(\mathbf{x}')} \right)^{\frac{1}{2}} \exp\left(-\frac{(x_i - x_i')^2}{r_i^2(\mathbf{x}) + r_i^2(\mathbf{x}')} \right) \tag{19.3.17}$$

for functions $r_i(\mathbf{x}) > 0$ [122].

19.4 Analysis of covariance functions

19.4.1 Smoothness of the functions

We examine local smoothness for a translation invariant kernel $k(x, x') = k(x - x')$. For two one-dimensional points x and x', separated by a small amount $\delta \ll 1$, $x' = x + \delta$, the covariance between the outputs y and y' is, by Taylor expansion,

$$k(x, x') \approx k(0) + \delta \frac{dk}{dx}|_{x=0} + O\left(\delta^2\right) \tag{19.4.1}$$

so that the change in the covariance at the local level is dominated by the first derivative of the covariance function. For the SE covariance $k(x) = e^{-x^2}$,

$$\frac{dk}{dx} = -2xe^{-x^2} \tag{19.4.2}$$

is zero at $x = 0$. This means that for the SE covariance function, the first-order change in the covariance is zero, and only higher-order δ^2 terms contribute.

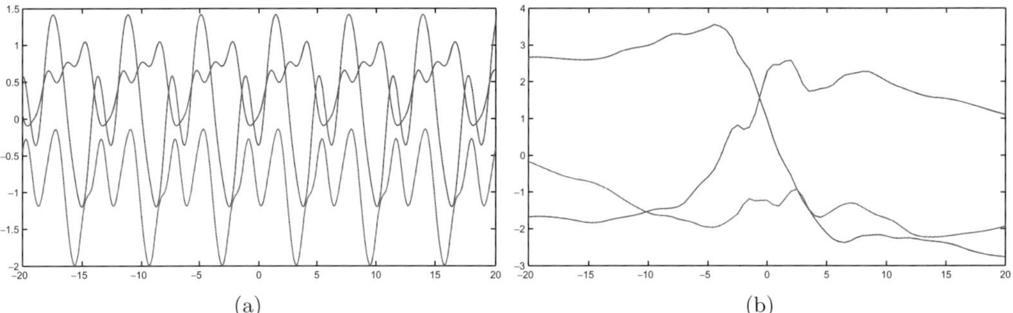

Figure 19.4 Samples from a GP prior for 500 x points uniformly placed from -20 to 20. (**a**) Samples from the periodic covariance function $\exp\left(-2\sin^2 0.5(x-x')\right)$. (**b**) Samples from the neural network covariance function with bias $b=5$ and $\lambda=1$. See plate section for colour version.

For the Ornstein-Uhlenbeck covariance, $k(x)=e^{-|x|}$, the right derivative at the origin is

$$\lim_{\delta\to 0}\frac{k(\delta)-k(0)}{\delta}=\lim_{\delta\to 0}\frac{e^{-\delta}-1}{\delta}=-1 \tag{19.4.3}$$

where this result is obtained using L'Hôpital's rule. Hence for the OU covariance function, there is a first-order negative change in the covariance; at the local level, this decrease in the covariance is therefore much more rapid than for the SE covariance, see Fig. 19.3. Since low covariance implies low dependence (in Gaussian distributions), locally the functions generated from the OU process are rough, whereas they are smooth in the SE case. A more formal treatment for the stationary case can be obtained by examining the eigenvalue-frequency plot of the covariance function (spectral density), Section 19.4.3. For rough functions the density of eigenvalues for high-frequency components is higher than for smooth functions.

19.4.2 Mercer kernels

Consider the function

$$k(x,x')=\boldsymbol{\phi}(x)^{\mathsf{T}}\boldsymbol{\phi}(x')=\sum_{s=1}^{B}\phi_s(x)\phi_s(x') \tag{19.4.4}$$

where $\boldsymbol{\phi}(x)$ is a vector with component functions $\phi_1(x),\phi_2(x),\ldots,\phi_B(x)$. Then for a set of points $x^1,\ldots,x^P$, we construct the matrix $\mathbf{K}$ with elements

$$[\mathbf{K}]_{ij}=k(x^i,x^j)=\sum_{s=1}^{B}\phi_s(x^i)\phi_s(x^j). \tag{19.4.5}$$

We claim that the matrix $\mathbf{K}$ so constructed is positive semidefinite and hence a valid covariance matrix. Recalling that a matrix is positive semidefinite if for any non zero vector $\mathbf{z}$, $\mathbf{z}^{\mathsf{T}}\mathbf{K}\mathbf{z}\geq 0$. Using the definition of $\mathbf{K}$ above we have

$$\mathbf{z}^{\mathsf{T}}\mathbf{K}\mathbf{z}=\sum_{i,j=1}^{P}z_iK_{ij}z_j=\sum_{s=1}^{B}\underbrace{\left[\sum_{i=1}^{P}z_i\phi_s(x^i)\right]}_{\gamma_s}\underbrace{\left[\sum_{j=1}^{P}\phi_s(x^j)z_j\right]}_{\gamma_s}=\sum_{s=1}^{B}\gamma_s^2\geq 0. \tag{19.4.6}$$

Hence any function of the form Equation (19.4.4) is a covariance function. We can generalise the Mercer kernel to complex functions $\boldsymbol{\phi}(x)$ using

$$k(x, x') = \boldsymbol{\phi}(x)^{\mathsf{T}}\boldsymbol{\phi}^{\dagger}(x') \tag{19.4.7}$$

where † represents the complex conjugate. Then the matrix $\mathbf{K}$ formed from inputs $x^i, i = 1, \ldots, P$ is positive semidefinite since for any real vector $\mathbf{z}$,

$$\mathbf{z}^{\mathsf{T}}\mathbf{K}\mathbf{z} = \sum_{s=1}^{B} \underbrace{\left[\sum_{i=1}^{P} z_i \phi_s(x^i)\right]}_{\gamma_s} \underbrace{\left[\sum_{j=1}^{P} \phi_s^{\dagger}(x^j) z_j\right]}_{\gamma_s^{\dagger}} = \sum_{s=1}^{B} |\gamma_s|^2 \geq 0 \tag{19.4.8}$$

where we made use of the general result for a complex variable $xx^{\dagger} = |x|^2$. A further generalisation is to write

$$k(x, x') = \int f(s)\phi(x, s)\phi^{\dagger}(x', s)ds \tag{19.4.9}$$

for real $f(s) \geq 0$, and scalar complex functions $\phi(x, s)$. Then replacing summations with integration (and assuming we can interchange the sum over the components of $\mathbf{z}$ with the integral over s), we obtain

$$\mathbf{z}^{\mathsf{T}}\mathbf{K}\mathbf{z} = \int f(s) \underbrace{\left[\sum_{i=1}^{P} z_i \phi(x^i, s)\right]}_{\gamma(s)} \underbrace{\left[\sum_{j=1}^{P} \phi^{\dagger}(x^j, s) z_j\right]}_{\gamma^{\dagger}(s)} ds = \int f(s)|\gamma(s)|^2 ds \geq 0. \tag{19.4.10}$$

19.4.3 Fourier analysis for stationary kernels

For a function $g(x)$ with Fourier transform $\tilde{g}(s)$, we may use the inverse Fourier transform to write

$$g(x) = \frac{1}{2\pi}\int \tilde{g}(s)e^{-\mathrm{i}xs}ds \tag{19.4.11}$$

where $\mathrm{i} \equiv \sqrt{-1}$. For a stationary kernel $k(x)$ with Fourier transform $\tilde{k}(s)$, we can therefore write

$$k(x - x') = \frac{1}{2\pi}\int \tilde{k}(s)e^{-\mathrm{i}(x-x')s}ds = \frac{1}{2\pi}\int \tilde{k}(s)e^{-\mathrm{i}xs}e^{\mathrm{i}x's}ds \tag{19.4.12}$$

which is of the same form as Equation (19.4.9) where the Fourier transform $\tilde{k}(s)$ is identified with $f(s)$ and $\phi(x, s) = e^{-\mathrm{i}sx}$. Hence, provided the Fourier transform $\tilde{k}(s)$ is positive, the translation invariant kernel $k(x - x')$ is a covariance function. Bochner's theorem [247] asserts the converse that any translation invariant covariance function must have such a Fourier representation.

Application to the squared exponential kernel

For the translation invariant squared exponential kernel, $k(x) = e^{-\frac{1}{2}x^2}$, its Fourier transform is

$$\tilde{k}(s) = \int_{-\infty}^{\infty} e^{-\frac{1}{2}x^2+\mathrm{i}sx}dx = e^{-\frac{s^2}{2}}\int_{-\infty}^{\infty} e^{-\frac{1}{2}(x+\mathrm{i}s)^2}dx = \sqrt{2\pi}e^{-\frac{s^2}{2}}. \tag{19.4.13}$$

Hence the Fourier transform of the SE kernel is a Gaussian. Since this is positive the SE kernel is a covariance function.

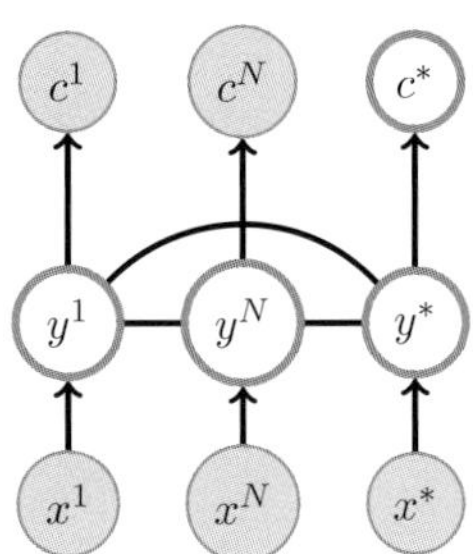

Figure 19.5 GP classification. The GP induces a Gaussian distribution on the latent activations $y_1, \ldots, y^N, y^*$, given the observed values of $c^1, \ldots, c^N$. The classification of the new input x^* is then given via the correlation induced by the training points on the latent activation y^*.

19.5 Gaussian processes for classification

Adapting the GP framework to classification requires replacing the Gaussian regression term $p(y|x)$ with a corresponding classification term $p(c|x)$ for a discrete label c. To do so we will use the GP to define a latent continuous space y which will then be mapped to a class probability using

$$p(c|x) = \int p(c|y, \not{x})p(y|x)dy = \int p(c|y)p(y|x)dy. \tag{19.5.1}$$

Given training data inputs $\mathcal{X} = \{x^1, \ldots, x^N\}$, corresponding class labels $\mathcal{C} = \{c^1, \ldots, c^N\}$, and a novel input x^*, then

$$p(c^*|x^*, \mathcal{C}, \mathcal{X}) = \int p(c^*|y^*)p(y^*|\mathcal{X}, \mathcal{C})dy^* \tag{19.5.2}$$

where

$$\begin{aligned} p(y^*|\mathcal{X}, \mathcal{C}) &\propto p(y^*, \mathcal{C}|\mathcal{X}) \\ &= \int p(y^*, \mathcal{Y}, \mathcal{C}|\mathcal{X}, x^*)d\mathcal{Y} \\ &= \int p(\mathcal{C}|\mathcal{Y})p(y^*, \mathcal{Y}|\mathcal{X}, x^*)d\mathcal{Y} \\ &= \int \underbrace{\left\{\prod_{n=1}^{N} p(c^n|y^n)\right\}}_{\text{class mapping}} \underbrace{p(y^1, \ldots, y^N, y^*|x^1, \ldots, x^N, x^*)}_{\text{Gaussian process}} dy^1, \ldots, dy^N. \end{aligned} \tag{19.5.3}$$

The graphical structure of the joint class and latent y distribution is depicted in Fig. 19.5. The posterior marginal $p(y^*|\mathcal{X}, \mathcal{C})$ is the marginal of a Gaussian process, multiplied by a set of non-Gaussian maps from the latent activations to the class probabilities. We can reformulate the prediction problem more conveniently as follows:

$$p(y^*, \mathcal{Y}|x^*, \mathcal{X}, \mathcal{C}) \propto p(y^*, \mathcal{Y}, \mathcal{C}|x^*, \mathcal{X}) \propto p(y^*|\mathcal{Y}, x^*, \mathcal{X})p(\mathcal{Y}|\mathcal{C}, \mathcal{X}) \tag{19.5.4}$$

where

$$p(\mathcal{Y}|\mathcal{C}, \mathcal{X}) \propto \left\{\prod_{n=1}^{N} p(c^n|y^n)\right\} p(y^1, \ldots, y^N|x^1, \ldots, x^N). \tag{19.5.5}$$

In Equation (19.5.4) the term $p(y^*|\mathcal{Y}, x^*, \mathcal{X})$ does not contain any class label information and is simply a conditional Gaussian. The advantage of the above description is that we can therefore form an approximation to $p(\mathcal{Y}|\mathcal{C}, \mathcal{X})$ and then reuse this approximation in the prediction for many different x^* without needing to rerun the approximation [318, 247].

19.5.1 Binary classification

For the binary class case we will use the convention that $c \in \{1, 0\}$. We therefore need to specify $p(c = 1|y)$ for a real-valued activation y. A convenient choice is the logistic transfer function[3]

$$\sigma(x) = \frac{1}{1 + e^{-x}}. \tag{19.5.6}$$

Then

$$p(c|y) = \sigma((2c - 1)y) \tag{19.5.7}$$

is a valid distribution since $\sigma(-x) = 1 - \sigma(x)$, ensuring that the sum over the class states is 1. A difficulty is that the non-linear class mapping term makes the computation of the posterior distribution equation (19.5.3) difficult since the integrals over $y^1, \ldots, y^N$ cannot be carried out analytically. There are many approximate techniques one could apply in this case, including variational methods analogous to that described in Section 18.2.3. Below we describe the straightforward Laplace method, leaving the more sophisticated methods for further reading [247].

19.5.2 Laplace's approximation

In the Laplace method, Section 28.2, we approximate the non-Gaussian distribution (19.5.5) by a Gaussian[4] $q(\mathcal{Y}|\mathcal{C}, \mathcal{X})$,

$$p(\mathcal{Y}|\mathcal{C}, \mathcal{X}) \approx q(\mathcal{Y}|\mathcal{C}, \mathcal{X}). \tag{19.5.8}$$

From Equation (19.5.4), approximate predictions can then be formed through the joint Gaussian

$$p(y^*, \mathcal{Y}|x^*, \mathcal{X}, \mathcal{C}) \approx p(y^*|\mathcal{Y}, x^*, \mathcal{X})q(\mathcal{Y}|\mathcal{C}, \mathcal{X}). \tag{19.5.9}$$

We will then marginalise this Gaussian to find the Gaussian distribution on y^* alone, and then use this to form the prediction via $p(c^*|y^*)$.

For compactness we define the class label vector, and outputs

$$\mathbf{c} = \left(c^1, \ldots, c^N\right)^\mathsf{T}, \qquad \mathbf{y} = \left(y^1, \ldots, y^N\right)^\mathsf{T} \tag{19.5.10}$$

and notationally drop the (ever present) conditioning on the inputs x. Also for convenience, we define

$$\boldsymbol{\sigma} = \left(\sigma(y^1), \ldots, \sigma(y^N)\right)^\mathsf{T}. \tag{19.5.11}$$

Finding the mode

The Laplace approximation, Section 28.2, corresponds to a second-order expansion around the mode of the distribution. Our task is therefore to find the maximum of

$$p(\mathbf{y}|\mathbf{c}) \propto p(\mathbf{y}, \mathbf{c}) = \exp(\Psi(\mathbf{y})) \tag{19.5.12}$$

[3] We will also refer to this as 'the sigmoid function'. More strictly a sigmoid function refers to any 's-shaped' function (from the Greek for 's').

[4] Some authors use the term Laplace approximation solely for approximating an integral. Here we use the term to refer to a Gaussian approximation of a non-Gaussian distribution.

where

$$\Psi(\mathbf{y}) = \mathbf{c}^{\mathsf{T}}\mathbf{y} - \sum_{n=1}^{N} \log(1 + e^{y_n}) - \frac{1}{2}\mathbf{y}^{\mathsf{T}}\mathbf{K}_{\mathbf{x},\mathbf{x}}^{-1}\mathbf{y} - \frac{1}{2}\log\det(\mathbf{K}_{\mathbf{x},\mathbf{x}}) - \frac{N}{2}\log 2\pi. \tag{19.5.13}$$

The maximum needs to be found numerically, and it is convenient to use the Newton method [132, 318, 247],

$$\mathbf{y}^{new} = \mathbf{y} - (\nabla\nabla\Psi)^{-1}\nabla\Psi. \tag{19.5.14}$$

Differentiating Equation (19.5.13) with respect to $\mathbf{y}$ we obtain the gradient and Hessian

$$\nabla\Psi = (\mathbf{c} - \boldsymbol{\sigma}) - \mathbf{K}_{\mathbf{x},\mathbf{x}}^{-1}\mathbf{y} \tag{19.5.15}$$

$$\nabla\nabla\Psi = -\mathbf{K}_{\mathbf{x},\mathbf{x}}^{-1} - \mathbf{D} \tag{19.5.16}$$

where the 'noise' matrix is given by

$$\mathbf{D} = \operatorname{diag}(\sigma_1(1-\sigma_1), \ldots, \sigma_N(1-\sigma_N)). \tag{19.5.17}$$

Using these expressions in the Newton update, (19.5.14) gives

$$\mathbf{y}^{new} = \mathbf{y} + \left(\mathbf{K}_{\mathbf{x},\mathbf{x}}^{-1} + \mathbf{D}\right)^{-1}\left(\mathbf{c} - \boldsymbol{\sigma} - \mathbf{K}_{\mathbf{x},\mathbf{x}}^{-1}\mathbf{y}\right). \tag{19.5.18}$$

To avoid unnecessary inversions, one may rewrite this in the form

$$\mathbf{y}^{new} = \mathbf{K}_{\mathbf{x},\mathbf{x}}(\mathbf{I} + \mathbf{D}\mathbf{K}_{\mathbf{x},\mathbf{x}})^{-1}(\mathbf{D}\mathbf{y} + \mathbf{c} - \boldsymbol{\sigma}). \tag{19.5.19}$$

For an initial guess of $\mathbf{y}$, we repeatedly apply Equation (19.5.19) until convergence. This is guaranteed to converge since the Hessian is negative definite and has a unique maximum.

Making predictions

Given a converged solution $\tilde{\mathbf{y}}$ we have found a Gaussian approximation

$$q(\mathbf{y}|\mathcal{X}, x^*, \mathcal{C}) = \mathcal{N}\left(\mathbf{y}\middle|\tilde{\mathbf{y}}, \left(\mathbf{K}_{\mathbf{x},\mathbf{x}}^{-1} + \mathbf{D}\right)^{-1}\right). \tag{19.5.20}$$

We now have Gaussians for $p(y^*|\mathbf{y})$ and $q(\mathbf{y}|\mathcal{X}, x^*, \mathcal{C})$ in Equation (19.5.9). Predictions are then made using

$$p(y^*|x^*, \mathcal{X}, \mathcal{C}) \approx \int p(y^*|x^*, \mathcal{X}, \mathbf{y})q(\mathbf{y}|\mathcal{X}, x^*, \mathcal{C})d\mathbf{y} \tag{19.5.21}$$

where, by conditioning, Section 8.4.2,

$$p(y^*|\mathbf{y}, x^*, \mathcal{X}) = \mathcal{N}\left(y^*\middle|\mathbf{K}_{x^*,\mathbf{x}}\mathbf{K}_{\mathbf{x},\mathbf{x}}^{-1}\mathbf{y}, \mathbf{K}_{x^*,x^*} - \mathbf{K}_{x^*,\mathbf{x}}\mathbf{K}_{\mathbf{x},\mathbf{x}}^{-1}\mathbf{K}_{\mathbf{x},x^*}\right). \tag{19.5.22}$$

We can also write this as a linear system

$$y^* = \mathbf{K}_{x^*,\mathbf{x}}\mathbf{K}_{\mathbf{x},\mathbf{x}}^{-1}\mathbf{y} + \eta \tag{19.5.23}$$

where $\eta \sim \mathcal{N}\left(\eta\middle|0, \mathbf{K}_{x^*,x^*} - \mathbf{K}_{x^*,\mathbf{x}}\mathbf{K}_{\mathbf{x},\mathbf{x}}^{-1}\mathbf{K}_{\mathbf{x},x^*}\right)$. Using Equation (19.5.23) and Equation (19.5.20) and averaging over $\mathbf{y}$ and the noise η, we obtain

$$\langle y^*|x^*, \mathcal{X}, \mathcal{C}\rangle \approx \mathbf{K}_{x^*,\mathbf{x}}\mathbf{K}_{\mathbf{x},\mathbf{x}}^{-1}\tilde{\mathbf{y}} = \mathbf{K}_{x^*,\mathbf{x}}(\mathbf{c} - \boldsymbol{\sigma}(\tilde{\mathbf{y}})). \tag{19.5.24}$$

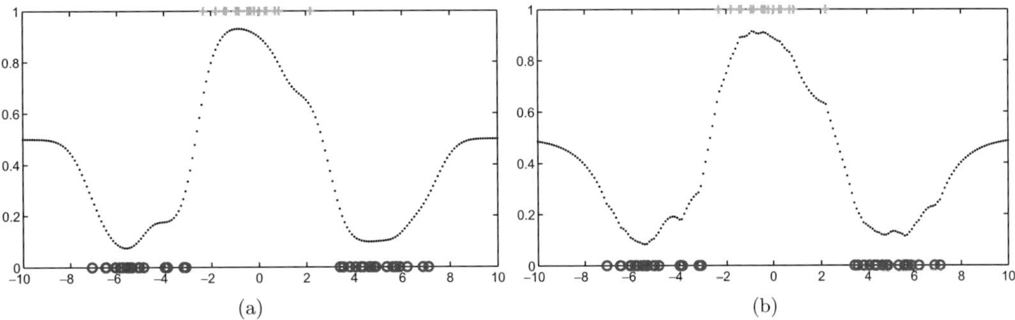

Figure 19.6 Gaussian process classification. The x-axis are the inputs, and the class is the y-axis. Green points are training points from class 1 and red from class 0. The dots are the predictions $p(c = 1|x^*)$ for points x^* ranging across the x axis. **(a)** Square exponential covariance ($\gamma = 2$). **(b)** OU covariance ($\gamma = 1$). See `demoGPclass1D.m`. See plate section for colour version.

Similarly, the variance of the latent prediction is

$$\text{var}(y^*|x^*, \mathcal{X}, \mathcal{C}) \approx \mathbf{K}_{x^*,\mathbf{x}}\mathbf{K}_{\mathbf{x},\mathbf{x}}^{-1}\left(\mathbf{K}_{\mathbf{x},\mathbf{x}}^{-1} + \mathbf{D}\right)^{-1}\mathbf{K}_{\mathbf{x},\mathbf{x}}^{-1}\mathbf{K}_{\mathbf{x},x^*} + \mathbf{K}_{x^*,x^*} - \mathbf{K}_{x^*,\mathbf{x}}\mathbf{K}_{\mathbf{x},\mathbf{x}}^{-1}\mathbf{K}_{\mathbf{x},x^*} \tag{19.5.25}$$

$$= \mathbf{K}_{x^*,x^*} - \mathbf{K}_{x^*,\mathbf{x}}\left(\mathbf{K}_{\mathbf{x},\mathbf{x}} + \mathbf{D}^{-1}\right)^{-1}\mathbf{K}_{\mathbf{x},x^*} \tag{19.5.26}$$

where the last line is obtained using the matrix inversion lemma, Definition A.11.

The class prediction for a new input x^* is then given by

$$p(c^* = 1|x^*, \mathcal{X}, \mathcal{C}) \approx \langle \sigma(y^*) \rangle_{\mathcal{N}(y^*|\langle y^* \rangle, \text{var}(y^*))}. \tag{19.5.27}$$

In order to calculate the Gaussian integral over the logistic sigmoid function, we use an approximation of the sigmoid function based on the error function erf(x), see Section 18.2.2 and `avsigmaGauss.m`.

Example 19.2

An example of binary classification is given in Fig. 19.6 in which one-dimensional input training data with binary class labels is plotted along with the class probability predictions on a range of input points. In both cases the covariance function is of the form $2\exp\left(|x_i - x_j|^\gamma\right) + 0.001\delta_{ij}$. The square exponential covariance produces a smoother class prediction than the Ornstein–Uhlenbeck covariance function. See `demoGPclass1D.m` and `demoGPclass.m`.

Marginal likelihood

The marginal likelihood is given by

$$p(\mathcal{C}|\mathcal{X}) = \int_{\mathcal{Y}} p(\mathcal{C}|\mathcal{Y})p(\mathcal{Y}|\mathcal{X}). \tag{19.5.28}$$

Under the Laplace approximation, the marginal likelihood is approximated by

$$p(\mathcal{C}|\mathcal{X}) \approx \int_{\mathbf{y}} \exp\left(\Psi(\tilde{\mathbf{y}})\right)\exp\left(-\frac{1}{2}\left(\mathbf{y} - \tilde{\mathbf{y}}\right)^{\mathsf{T}}\mathbf{A}\left(\mathbf{y} - \tilde{\mathbf{y}}\right)\right) \tag{19.5.29}$$

where $\mathbf{A} = -\nabla\nabla\Psi$. Integrating over $\mathbf{y}$ gives

$$\log p(\mathcal{C}|\mathcal{X}) \approx \log q(\mathcal{C}|\mathcal{X}) \tag{19.5.30}$$

where

$$\log q(\mathcal{C}|\mathcal{X}) = \Psi(\tilde{\mathbf{y}}) - \frac{1}{2}\log\det(2\pi\mathbf{A}) \tag{19.5.31}$$

$$= \Psi(\tilde{\mathbf{y}}) - \frac{1}{2}\log\det\left(\mathbf{K}_{\mathbf{x},\mathbf{x}}^{-1} + \mathbf{D}\right) + \frac{N}{2}\log 2\pi \tag{19.5.32}$$

$$= \mathbf{c}^{\mathsf{T}}\tilde{\mathbf{y}} - \sum_{n=1}^{N}\log(1+\exp(\tilde{y}_n)) - \frac{1}{2}\tilde{\mathbf{y}}^{\mathsf{T}}\mathbf{K}_{\mathbf{x},\mathbf{x}}^{-1}\tilde{\mathbf{y}} - \frac{1}{2}\log\det(\mathbf{I} + \mathbf{K}_{\mathbf{x},\mathbf{x}}\mathbf{D}) \tag{19.5.33}$$

where $\tilde{\mathbf{y}}$ is the converged iterate of Equation (19.5.18). One can also simplify the above using that at convergence $\mathbf{K}_{\mathbf{x},\mathbf{x}}^{-1}\tilde{\mathbf{y}} = \mathbf{c} - \boldsymbol{\sigma}(\mathbf{y})$.

19.5.3 Hyperparameter optimisation

The approximate marginal likelihood can be used to assess hyperparameters θ of the kernel. A little care is required in computing derivatives of the approximate marginal likelihood since the optimum $\tilde{\mathbf{y}}$ depends on θ. We use the total derivative formula [25]

$$\frac{d}{d\theta}\log q(\mathcal{C}|\mathcal{X}) = \frac{\partial}{\partial\theta}\log q(\mathcal{C}|\mathcal{X}) + \sum_i \frac{\partial}{\partial\tilde{y}_i}\log q(\mathcal{C}|\mathcal{X})\frac{d}{d\theta}\tilde{y}_i \tag{19.5.34}$$

$$\frac{\partial}{\partial\theta}\log q(\mathcal{C}|\mathcal{X}) = -\frac{1}{2}\frac{\partial}{\partial\theta}\left[\mathbf{y}^{\mathsf{T}}\mathbf{K}_{\mathbf{x},\mathbf{x}}^{-1}\mathbf{y} + \log\det(\mathbf{I} + \mathbf{K}_{\mathbf{x},\mathbf{x}}\mathbf{D})\right] \tag{19.5.35}$$

which can be evaluated using the standard results for the derivative of a matrix determinant and inverse. Since the derivative of Ψ is zero at $\tilde{\mathbf{y}}$, and noting that $\mathbf{D}$ depends explicitly on $\tilde{\mathbf{y}}$,

$$\frac{\partial}{\partial\tilde{y}_i}\log q(\mathcal{C}|\mathcal{X}) = -\frac{1}{2}\frac{\partial}{\partial\tilde{y}_i}\log\det(\mathbf{I} + \mathbf{K}_{\mathbf{x},\mathbf{x}}\mathbf{D}). \tag{19.5.36}$$

The implicit derivative is obtained from using the fact that at convergence

$$\tilde{\mathbf{y}} = \mathbf{K}_{\mathbf{x},\mathbf{x}}(\mathbf{c} - \boldsymbol{\sigma}(\mathbf{y})) \tag{19.5.37}$$

to give

$$\frac{d}{d\theta}\tilde{\mathbf{y}} = (\mathbf{I} + \mathbf{K}_{\mathbf{x},\mathbf{x}}\mathbf{D})^{-1}\frac{\partial}{\partial\theta}\mathbf{K}_{\mathbf{x},\mathbf{x}}(\mathbf{c} - \boldsymbol{\sigma}). \tag{19.5.38}$$

These results are substituted into Equation (19.5.34) to find an explicit expression for the derivative. See Exercise 19.7.

19.5.4 Multiple classes

The extension of the preceding framework to multiple classes is essentially straightforward and may be achieved using the softmax function

$$p(c = m|y) = \frac{e^{y_m}}{\sum_{m'} e^{y_{m'}}} \tag{19.5.39}$$

which automatically enforces the constraint $\sum_m p(c = m) = 1$. Naively it would appear that for C classes, the cost of implementing the Laplace approximation for the multiclass case scales as $O\left(C^3N^3\right)$. However, one may show by careful implementation that the cost is only $O\left(CN^3\right)$, and we refer the reader to [318, 247] for details.

19.6 Summary

- Gaussian processes are powerful regression models and mathematically well understood.
- The computational complexity of the prediction is cubic in the number of datapoints. This can be prohibitive for large datasets and approximate implementations are required.
- Gaussian process classification is analytically intractable and approximations are required. The posterior is log concave so that simple unimodal approximation schemes can provide satisfactory results.
- Many classical models in statistics and physics are related to Gaussian processes. For example, one can view linear dynamical systems , Chapter 24, as specially constrained GPs.

Gaussian processes have been heavily developed within the machine learning community over recent years and finding efficient approximations for both regression and classification remains an active research topic. We direct the interested reader to [262] and [247] for further discussion.

19.7 Code

`GPreg.m`: Gaussian process regression
`demoGPreg.m`: Demo GP regression
`covfnGE.m`: Gamma-exponential covariance function
`GPclass.m`: Gaussian process classification
`demoGPclass.m`: Demo Gaussian process classification

19.8 Exercises

19.1 The Gram matrix $\mathbf{K}$ of a covariance function $k(x, x')$ is positive semidefinite and hence expressible as

$$K_{ij} = \sum_l u_{il} u_{jl} \tag{19.8.1}$$

for suitable u_{il}.

1. The Gram matrix of the sum of two covariance functions, $k^+(x, x') = k_1(x, x') + k_2(x, x')$, is of the form

$$\mathbf{K}^+ = \mathbf{K}^1 + \mathbf{K}^2 \tag{19.8.2}$$

for suitable Gram matrices $\mathbf{K}^1$ and $\mathbf{K}^2$. Show that $k^+(x, x')$ is a covariance function.

2. Consider the element-wise (Hadamard) product of two positive semidefinite matrices. That is

$$K^*_{ij} = K^1_{ij} K^2_{ij}. \tag{19.8.3}$$

Using $K^1_{ij} = \sum_l u_{il} u_{jl}$ and $K^2_{ij} = \sum_m v_{im} v_{jm}$, show that $\mathbf{K}^*$ is positive semidefinite, and hence that the product of two covariance functions, $k^*(x, x') = k_1(x, x') k_2(x, x')$, is a covariance function.

19.2 Show that the sample covariance matrix with elements $S_{ij} = \sum_{n=1}^N x_i^n x_j^n / N - \bar{x}_i \bar{x}_j$, where $\bar{x}_i = \sum_{n=1}^N x_i^n / N$, is positive semidefinite.

19.3 Show that

$$k(x - x') = \exp\left(-|\sin\left(x - x'\right)|\right) \tag{19.8.4}$$

is a covariance function.

19.4 Consider the function

$$f(x_i, x_j) = \exp\left(-\frac{1}{2}\left(x_i - x_j\right)^2\right) \tag{19.8.5}$$

for one-dimensional inputs x_i. Show that

$$f(x_i, x_j) = \exp\left(-\frac{1}{2}x_i^2\right)\exp\left(x_i x_j\right)\exp\left(-\frac{1}{2}x_j^2\right). \tag{19.8.6}$$

By Taylor expanding the central term, show that $\exp\left(-\frac{1}{2}\left(x_i - x_j\right)^2\right)$ is a kernel and find an explicit representation for the kernel $f(x_i, x_j)$ as the scalar product of two infinite-dimensional vectors.

19.5 Show that for a covariance function $k_1(\mathbf{x}, \mathbf{x}')$ then

$$k(\mathbf{x}, \mathbf{x}') = f\left(k_1\left(\mathbf{x}, \mathbf{x}'\right)\right) \tag{19.8.7}$$

is also a covariance function for any polynomial $f(x)$ with positive coefficients. Show therefore that $\exp\left(k_1\left(\mathbf{x}, \mathbf{x}'\right)\right)$ and $\tan\left(k_1\left(\mathbf{x}, \mathbf{x}'\right)\right)$ are covariance functions.

19.6 For a covariance function

$$k_1(\mathbf{x}, \mathbf{x}') = f\left(\left(\mathbf{x} - \mathbf{x}'\right)^{\mathsf{T}}\left(\mathbf{x} - \mathbf{x}'\right)\right) \tag{19.8.8}$$

show that

$$k_2(\mathbf{x}, \mathbf{x}') = f\left(\left(\mathbf{x} - \mathbf{x}'\right)^{\mathsf{T}}\mathbf{A}\left(\mathbf{x} - \mathbf{x}'\right)\right) \tag{19.8.9}$$

is also a valid covariance function for a positive definite symmetric matrix $\mathbf{A}$.

19.7 Show that the derivative of the Laplace approximation to the marginal likelihood equation (19.5.34) is given by

$$\frac{d}{d\theta}\log q(\mathcal{C}|\mathcal{X}) = \frac{1}{2}\mathbf{y}^{\mathsf{T}}\mathbf{K}_{\mathbf{x},\mathbf{x}}^{-1}\mathbf{K}'_{\mathbf{x},\mathbf{x}}\mathbf{K}_{\mathbf{x},\mathbf{x}}^{-1}\mathbf{y} - \frac{1}{2}\text{trace}\left(\mathbf{L}^{-1}\mathbf{K}'_{\mathbf{x},\mathbf{x}}\mathbf{D}\right) - \frac{1}{2}\sum_i M_{ii}D'_{ii}\left[\mathbf{L}^{-1}\mathbf{K}'_{\mathbf{x},\mathbf{x}}\left(\mathbf{c} - \boldsymbol{\sigma}\right)\right]_i \tag{19.8.10}$$

where

$$\mathbf{K}'_{\mathbf{x},\mathbf{x}} \equiv \frac{\partial}{\partial\theta}\mathbf{K}_{\mathbf{x},\mathbf{x}}, \quad \mathbf{L} \equiv \mathbf{I} + \mathbf{K}_{\mathbf{x},\mathbf{x}}\mathbf{D}, \quad \mathbf{M} \equiv \mathbf{L}^{-1}\mathbf{K}_{\mathbf{x},\mathbf{x}}, \quad \mathbf{D}' \equiv \text{diag}\left(\frac{\partial}{\partial y_1}D_{11}, \frac{\partial}{\partial y_2}D_{22}, \ldots\right). \tag{19.8.11}$$

Hint: You will need to make use of the general derivative results

$$\frac{\partial}{\partial x}\mathbf{A}^{-1} = -\mathbf{A}^{-1}\left(\frac{\partial}{\partial x}\mathbf{A}\right)\mathbf{A}^{-1}, \qquad \frac{\partial}{\partial x}\log\det\left(\mathbf{A}\right) = \text{trace}\left(\mathbf{A}^{-1}\frac{\partial}{\partial x}\mathbf{A}\right). \tag{19.8.12}$$

19.8 (String kernel) Let x and x' be two strings of characters and $\phi_s(x)$ be the number of times that substring s appears in string x. Then

$$k(x, x') = \sum_s w_s\phi_s(x)\phi_s(x') \tag{19.8.13}$$

is a (string kernel) covariance function, provided the weight of each substring w_s is positive.

1. Given a collection of strings about politics and another collection about sport, explain how to form a GP classifier using a string kernel.

2. Explain how the weights w_s can be adjusted to improve the fit of the classifier to the data and give an explicit formula for the derivative with respect to w_s of the log marginal likelihood under the Laplace approximation.

19.9 (Vector regression) Consider predicting a vector output $\mathbf{y}$ given training data $\mathcal{X} \cup \mathcal{Y} = \{\mathbf{x}^n, \mathbf{y}^n, n = 1, \ldots, n\}$. To make a GP predictor

$$p(\mathbf{y}^* | \mathbf{x}^*, \mathcal{X}, \mathcal{Y}) \tag{19.8.14}$$

we need a Gaussian model

$$p(\mathbf{y}^1, \ldots, \mathbf{y}^N, \mathbf{y}^* | \mathbf{x}^1, \ldots, \mathbf{x}^n, \mathbf{x}^*). \tag{19.8.15}$$

A GP requires then a specification of the covariance $c(y_i^m, y_j^n | \mathbf{x}^n, \mathbf{x}^m)$ of the components of the outputs for two different input vectors. Show that under the dimension independence assumption

$$c(y_i^m, y_j^n | \mathbf{x}^n, \mathbf{x}^m) = c_i(y_i^m, y_i^n | \mathbf{x}^n, \mathbf{x}^m) \delta_{i,j} \tag{19.8.16}$$

where $c_i(y_i^m, y_i^n | \mathbf{x}^n, \mathbf{x}^m)$ is a covariance function for the ith dimension, that separate GP predictors can be constructed independently, one for each output dimension i.

19.10 Consider the Markov update of a linear dynamical system, Section 24.1,

$$\mathbf{x}_t = \mathbf{A}\mathbf{x}_{t-1} + \boldsymbol{\eta}_t, \qquad t \geq 2 \tag{19.8.17}$$

where $\mathbf{A}$ is a given matrix and $\boldsymbol{\eta}_t$ is zero mean Gaussian noise with covariance $\langle \eta_{i,t} \eta_{j,t'} \rangle = \sigma^2 \delta_{i,j} \delta_{t,t'}$. Also, $p(\mathbf{x}_1) = \mathcal{N}(\mathbf{x}_1 | \mathbf{0}, \boldsymbol{\Sigma})$.

1. Show that $\mathbf{x}_1, \ldots, \mathbf{x}_t$ is Gaussian distributed.
2. Show that the covariance matrix of $\mathbf{x}_1, \ldots, \mathbf{x}_t$ has elements

$$\left\langle \mathbf{x}_{t'} \mathbf{x}_t^{\mathsf{T}} \right\rangle = \mathbf{A}^{t'-t} \boldsymbol{\Sigma} \left(\mathbf{A}^{t-1}\right)^{\mathsf{T}} + \sigma^2 \sum_{\tau=2}^{\min(t,t')} \mathbf{A}^{t'-\tau} \left(\mathbf{A}^{t-1}\right)^{\mathsf{T}} \tag{19.8.18}$$

and explain why a linear dynamical system is a (constrained) Gaussian process.

3. Consider

$$\mathbf{y}_t = \mathbf{B}\mathbf{x}_t + \boldsymbol{\epsilon}_t \tag{19.8.19}$$

where $\boldsymbol{\epsilon}_t$ is zero mean Gaussian noise with covariance $\langle \epsilon_{i,t} \epsilon_{j,t'} \rangle = \nu^2 \delta_{i,j} \delta_{t,t'}$. The vectors $\boldsymbol{\epsilon}$ are uncorrelated with the vectors $\boldsymbol{\eta}$. Show that the sequence of vectors $\mathbf{y}_1, \ldots, \mathbf{y}_t$ is a Gaussian process with a suitably defined covariance function.

20 Mixture models

Mixture models assume that the data is essentially clustered with each component in the mixture representing a cluster. In this chapter we view mixture models from the viewpoint of learning with missing data and discuss some of the classical algorithms, such as EM training of Gaussian mixture models. We also discuss more powerful models which allow for the possibility that an object can be a member of more than one cluster. These models have applications in areas such as document modelling.

20.1 Density estimation using mixtures

A mixture model is one in which a set of component models is combined to produce a richer model:

$$p(v) = \sum_{h=1}^{H} p(v|h)p(h). \tag{20.1.1}$$

The variable v is 'visible' or 'observable' and the discrete variable h with $\text{dom}(h) = \{1, \ldots, H\}$ indexes each component model $p(v|h)$, along with its weight $p(h)$. The variable v can be either discrete or continuous. Mixture models have natural application in clustering data, where h indexes the cluster. This interpretation can be gained from considering how to generate a sample datapoint v from the model Equation (20.1.1). First we sample a cluster h from $p(h)$, and then draw a visible state v from $p(v|h)$.

For a set of i.i.d. data $v^1, \ldots, v^N$, a mixture model is of the form, Fig. 20.1,

$$p(v^1, \ldots, v^N, h^1, \ldots, h^n) = \prod_{n=1}^{N} p(v^n|h^n)p(h^n) \tag{20.1.2}$$

from which the observation likelihood is given by

$$p(v^1, \ldots, v^N) = \prod_{n=1}^{N} \sum_{h^n} p(v^n|h^n)p(h^n). \tag{20.1.3}$$

Finding the most likely assignment of datapoints to clusters is achieved by inference of

$$\underset{h^1,\ldots,h^N}{\text{argmax}}\ p(h^1, \ldots, h^N|v^1, \ldots, v^N) \tag{20.1.4}$$

which, thanks to the factorised form of the distribution is equivalent to computing $\arg\max_{h^n} p(h^n|v^n)$ for each datapoint.

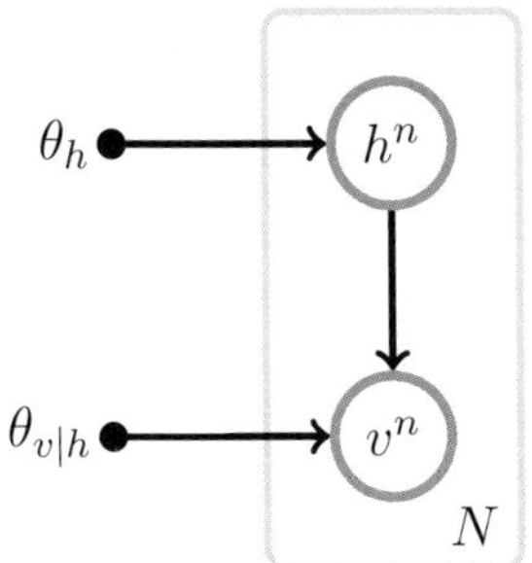

Figure 20.1 A mixture model has a graphical representation as a DAG with a single hidden node, h which indexes the mixture component; given a setting of h, we then generate an observation v from $p(v|h)$. Independence of the N observations means the model is replicated by the plate. The parameters are assumed common across all datapoints.

In most applications, however, the 'location' of the clusters is a priori unknown and the parameters θ of the model need to be learned to locate where these clusters are. Explicitly writing the dependence on the parameters, the model for a single datapoint v and its corresponding cluster index h is

$$p(v, h|\theta) = p(v|h, \theta_{v|h})p(h|\theta_h). \tag{20.1.5}$$

The optimal parameters $\theta_{v|h}, \theta_h$ of a mixture model are then most commonly set by maximum likelihood,

$$\theta_{opt} = \underset{\theta}{\text{argmax}}\ p(v^1, \ldots, v^N|\theta) = \underset{\theta}{\text{argmax}} \prod_n p(v^n|\theta). \tag{20.1.6}$$

Numerically this can be achieved using an optimisation procedure such as gradient-based approaches. Alternatively, by treating the component indices as latent variables, one may apply the EM algorithm, as described in the following section, which in many classical models produces simple update formulae.

Example 20.1

The data in Fig. 20.2 naturally has two clusters and can be modelled with a mixture of two two-dimensional Gaussians, each Gaussian describing one of the clusters. Here there is a clear visual interpretation of the meaning of 'cluster', with the mixture model placing two datapoints in the same cluster if they are both likely to be generated by the same model component. A priori we don't know the location of these two clusters and need to find the parameters; the Gaussian mean and covariance for each cluster $\mathbf{m}_h, \mathbf{C}_h, h = 1, 2$. This can be achieved using maximum likelihood.

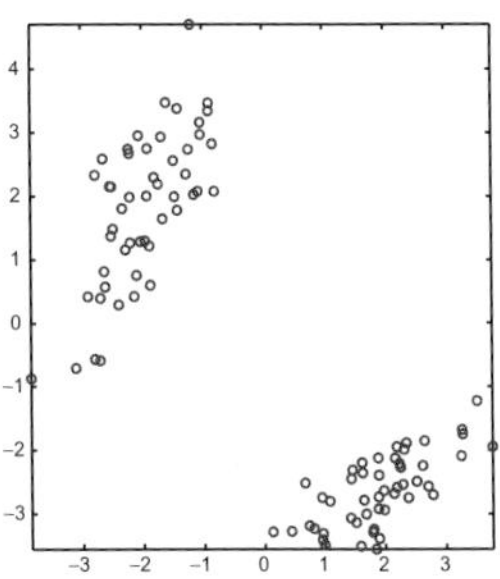

Figure 20.2 Two-dimensional data which displays clusters. In this case a Gaussian mixture model $1/2\mathcal{N}(\mathbf{x}|\mathbf{m}_1, \mathbf{C}_1) + 1/2\mathcal{N}(\mathbf{x}|\mathbf{m}_2, \mathbf{C}_2)$ would fit the data well for suitable means $\mathbf{m}_1, \mathbf{m}_2$ and covariances $\mathbf{C}_1, \mathbf{C}_2$. To the human eye, identifying these clusters is an easy task; however, we will be interested in automatic methods that can cluster potentially very high dimensional data, for which the cluster solutions may be far less obvious.

20.2 Expectation maximisation for mixture models

Our task is to find the parameters θ that maximise the likelihood of the observations $v^1, \dots, v^N$

$$p(v^1, \dots, v^N|\theta) = \prod_{n=1}^{N} \left\{ \sum_h p(v^n|h, \theta)p(h|\theta) \right\}. \tag{20.2.1}$$

By treating the index h as a missing variable, mixture models can be trained using the EM algorithm, Section 11.2. There are two sets of parameters – $\theta_{v|h}$ for each component model $p(v|h, \theta_{v|h})$ and θ_h for the mixture weights $p(h|\theta_h)$. According to the general approach for i.i.d. data of Section 11.2, for the M-step we need to consider the energy term:

$$E(\theta) = \sum_{n=1}^{N} \langle \log p(v^n, h|\theta) \rangle_{p^{old}(h|v^n)} \tag{20.2.2}$$

$$= \sum_{n=1}^{N} \langle \log p(v^n|h, \theta_{v|h}) \rangle_{p^{old}(h|v^n)} + \sum_{n=1}^{N} \langle \log p(h|\theta_h) \rangle_{p^{old}(h|v^n)} \tag{20.2.3}$$

and maximise (20.2.3) with respect to the parameters $\theta_{v|h}, \theta_h, h = 1, \dots, H$. The E-step results in the update

$$p^{new}(h|v^n) \propto p(v^n|h, \theta_{v|h}^{old}) p(h|\theta_h^{old}). \tag{20.2.4}$$

For initial parameters θ, one then updates the E and M-steps until convergence. This is a general approach for training mixture models. Below we flesh out how these updates work for some specific models.

20.2.1 Unconstrained discrete tables

Here we consider training a simple belief network $p(v|h, \theta_{v|h})p(h|\theta_h)$, $\mathrm{dom}(v) = \{1, \dots, V\}$, $\mathrm{dom}(h) = \{1, \dots, H\}$, in which the tables are unconstrained. This is a special case of the more general framework discussed in Section 11.2, although it is instructive to see how the EM algorithm can be derived for this specific case.

M-step: $p(h)$

If no constraint is placed on $p(h|\theta_h)$ we may write the parameters as simply $p(h)$, with the understanding that $0 \le p(h) \le 1$ and $\sum_h p(h) = 1$. Isolating the dependence of Equation (20.2.3) on $p(h)$ we obtain

$$\sum_{n=1}^{N} \langle \log p(h) \rangle_{p^{old}(h|v^n)} = \sum_h \log p(h) \sum_{n=1}^{N} p^{old}(h|v^n). \tag{20.2.5}$$

We now wish to maximise Equation (20.2.5) with respect to $p(h)$ under the constraint that $\sum_h p(h) = 1$. There are different ways to perform this constrained optimisation. One approach is to use Lagrange multipliers, see Exercise 20.4. Another, arguably more elegant approach is to use the techniques described in Section 11.2 based on the similarity of the above to a Kullback–Leibler divergence. First we define the distribution

$$\tilde{p}(h) \equiv \frac{\sum_{n=1}^{N} p^{old}(h|v^n)}{\sum_h \sum_{n=1}^{N} p^{old}(h|v^n)} = \frac{1}{N}\sum_{n=1}^{N} p^{old}(h|v^n). \tag{20.2.6}$$

Then maximising Equation (20.2.5) is equivalent to maximising

$$\langle \log p(h)\rangle_{\tilde{p}(h)} = \underbrace{\langle \log p(h)\rangle_{\tilde{p}(h)} - \langle \log \tilde{p}(h)\rangle_{\tilde{p}(h)}}_{-\mathrm{KL}(\tilde{p}|p)} + \langle \log \tilde{p}(h)\rangle_{\tilde{p}(h)} \tag{20.2.7}$$

since Equation (20.2.5) is related to $\langle \log p(h)\rangle_{\tilde{p}(h)}$ by the constant factor N. By subtracting the θ independent term $\langle \log \tilde{p}(h)\rangle_{\tilde{p}(h)}$ from Equation (20.2.7), we obtain the negative Kullback–Leibler divergence $\mathrm{KL}(\tilde{p}|p)$. This means that the optimal $p(h)$ is that distribution which minimises the Kullback–Leibler divergence. Optimally, therefore $p(h) = \tilde{p}(h)$, so that the M-step is given by

$$p^{new}(h) = \frac{1}{N}\sum_{n=1}^{N} p^{old}(h|v^n). \tag{20.2.8}$$

M-step: $p(v|h)$

The dependence of Equation (20.2.3) on $p(v|h)$ is

$$\sum_{n=1}^{N} \langle \log p(v^n|h, \theta_{v|h})\rangle_{p^{old}(h|v^n)} = \sum_v \sum_{n=1}^{N} \sum_{h=1}^{H} \mathbb{I}[v^n = v]\, p^{old}(h|v^n) \log p(v|h). \tag{20.2.9}$$

If the distributions $p(v|h, \theta_{v|h})$ are not constrained, we can apply a similar Kullback–Leibler method, as we did in Section 11.2 and above for $p(h)$. As an alternative to that approach, we describe here how the Lagrange method works in this case. We need to ensure that $p(v|h)$ is a distribution for each of the mixture states $h = 1, \ldots, H$. This can be achieved using a set of Lagrange multipliers, giving the Lagrangian:

$$\mathcal{L} \equiv \sum_{v=1}^{V} \sum_{n=1}^{N} \sum_{h=1}^{H} \mathbb{I}[v^n = v]\, p^{old}(h|v^n) \log p(v|h) + \sum_{h=1}^{H} \lambda(h)\left(1 - \sum_{v=1}^{V} p(v|h)\right). \tag{20.2.10}$$

Differentiating with respect to $p(v = i|h = j)$ and equating to zero,

$$\frac{\partial \mathcal{L}}{\partial p(v = i|h = j)} = \sum_{n=1}^{N} \frac{\mathbb{I}[v^n = i]\, p^{old}(h = j|v^n = i)}{p(v = i|h = j)} - \lambda(h = j) = 0. \tag{20.2.11}$$

Solving this, we have

$$p(v = i|h = j) = \frac{1}{\lambda(h = j)} \sum_{n=1}^{N} \mathbb{I}[v^n = i]\, p^{old}(h = j|v^n = i). \tag{20.2.12}$$

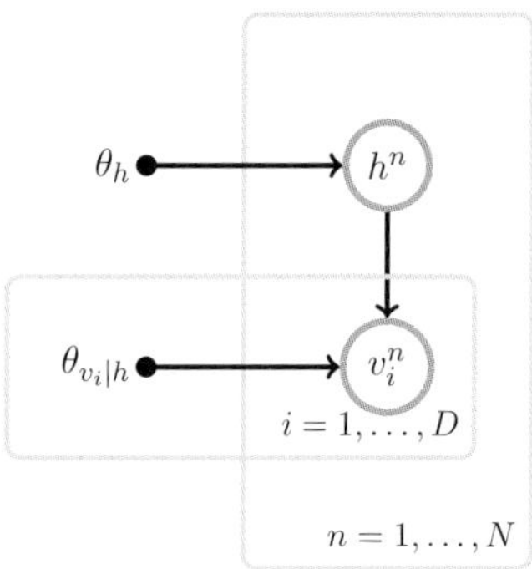

Figure 20.3 Mixture of a product of Bernoulli distributions. In a Bayesian treatment, a parameter prior is used. In the text we simply set the parameters using maximum likelihood.

Using the normalisation requirement, $\sum_v p(v = i|h = j) = 1$ shows that $\lambda(h = j)$ is just the numerator of the above equation, summed over v. Hence the M-step update is given by

$$p^{new}(v = i|h = j) = \frac{\sum_{n=1}^{N} \mathbb{I}[v^n = i]\, p^{old}(h = j|v^n = i)}{\sum_{i=1}^{V}\sum_{n=1}^{N} \mathbb{I}[v^n = i]\, p^{old}(h = j|v^n = i)}. \tag{20.2.13}$$

E-step

According to the general EM procedure, Section 11.2, optimally we set $p^{new}(h|v^n) = p^{old}(h|v^n)$:

$$p^{new}(h|v^n) = \frac{p^{old}(v^n|h)p^{old}(h)}{\sum_h p^{old}(v^n|h)p^{old}(h)}. \tag{20.2.14}$$

Equations (20.2.8), (20.2.13), (20.2.14) are repeated until convergence and guarantee that the likelihood Equation (20.2.1) cannot decrease. The initialisation of the tables and mixture probabilities can severely affect the quality of the solution found since the likelihood often has local optima. If random initialisations are used, it is recommended to record the converged value of the likelihood itself, to see which parameters have the higher likelihood. The solution with the highest likelihood is to be preferred.

20.2.2 Mixture of product of Bernoulli distributions

As an example mixture model, and one that can be used for practical clustering, see Example 20.2, we describe a simple mixture model that can be used to cluster binary vectors, $\mathbf{v} = (v_1, \ldots, v_D)^\mathsf{T}$, $v_i \in \{0, 1\}$. The mixture of Bernoulli products[1] model is given by

$$p(\mathbf{v}) = \sum_{h=1}^{H} p(h) \prod_{i=1}^{D} p(v_i|h) \tag{20.2.15}$$

where each term $p(v_i|h)$ is a Bernoulli distribution. The model is depicted in Fig. 20.3 and has parameters $p(h)$ and $p(v_i = 1|h)$, $\text{dom}(h) = \{1 \ldots, H\}$. One way to understand the model is to imagine drawing samples. In this case, for each datapoint n, we draw a cluster index $h \in \{1, \ldots, H\}$ from $p(h)$. Then for each $i = 1, \ldots, D$, we draw a state $v_i \in \{0, 1\}$ from $p(v_i|h)$.

[1] This is similar to the naive Bayes classifier in which the class labels are always hidden.

EM training

To train the model under maximum likelihood it is convenient to use the EM algorithm which, as usual, may be derived by writing down the energy:

$$\sum_n \langle \log p(\mathbf{v}^n, h)\rangle_{p^{old}(h|\mathbf{v}^n)} = \sum_n \sum_i \langle \log p(v_i^n|h)\rangle_{p^{old}(h|\mathbf{v}^n)} + \sum_n \langle \log p(h)\rangle_{p^{old}(h|\mathbf{v}^n)} \tag{20.2.16}$$

and then performing the maximisation over the table entries. From our general results, Section 11.2, we know that the M-step is equivalent to maximum likelihood when all variables are observed, and then replacing the unobserved variables h by the conditional distribution $p(h|v)$. Using this we can write down immediately the M-step as

$$\begin{aligned} p^{new}(v_i = 1|h = j) &= \frac{\sum_n \mathbb{I}[v_i^n = 1]\, p^{old}(h = j|\mathbf{v}^n)}{\sum_n \mathbb{I}[v_i^n = 1]\, p^{old}(h = j|\mathbf{v}^n) + \sum_n \mathbb{I}[v_i^n = 0]\, p^{old}(h = j|\mathbf{v}^n)} \\ p^{new}(h = j) &= \frac{\sum_n p^{old}(h = j|\mathbf{v}^n)}{\sum_{h'} \sum_n p^{old}(h'|\mathbf{v}^n)} \end{aligned} \tag{20.2.17}$$

and the E-step by

$$p^{new}(h = j|\mathbf{v}^n) \propto p^{old}(h = j) \prod_{i=1}^{D} p^{old}(v_i^n|h = j). \tag{20.2.18}$$

Equations (20.2.17)–(20.2.18) are iterated until convergence.

If an attribute i is missing for datapoint n, one needs to sum over the states of the corresponding v_i^n. The effect of performing the summation for this model is simply to remove the corresponding factor $p(v_i^n|h)$ from the algorithm, see Exercise 20.1.

Initialisation

The EM algorithm can be very sensitive to initial conditions. Consider the following initialisation: $p(v_i = 1|h = j) = 0.5$, with $p(h)$ set arbitrarily. This means that at the first iteration, $p^{old}(h = j|\mathbf{v}^n) = p(h = j)$. The subsequent M-step updates are

$$p^{new}(h) = p^{old}(h), \qquad p^{new}(v_i|h = j) = p^{new}(v_i|h = j') \tag{20.2.19}$$

for any j, j'. This means that the parameters $p(v|h)$ immediately become independent of h and the model is numerically trapped in a symmetric solution. It makes sense, therefore, to initialise the parameters in a non-symmetric fashion.

The model is readily extendable to more than two output class, and this is left as an exercise for the interested reader.

Example 20.2 Questionnaire

A company sends out a questionnaire containing a set of D 'yes/no' questions to a set of customers. The binary responses of a customer are stored in a vector $\mathbf{v} = (v_1, \ldots, v_D)^\mathsf{T}$. In total N customers send back their questionnaires, $\mathbf{v}^1, \ldots, \mathbf{v}^N$, and the company wishes to perform an analysis to find what kinds of customers it has. The company assumes there are H essential types of customer for which the profile of responses is defined by only the customer type.

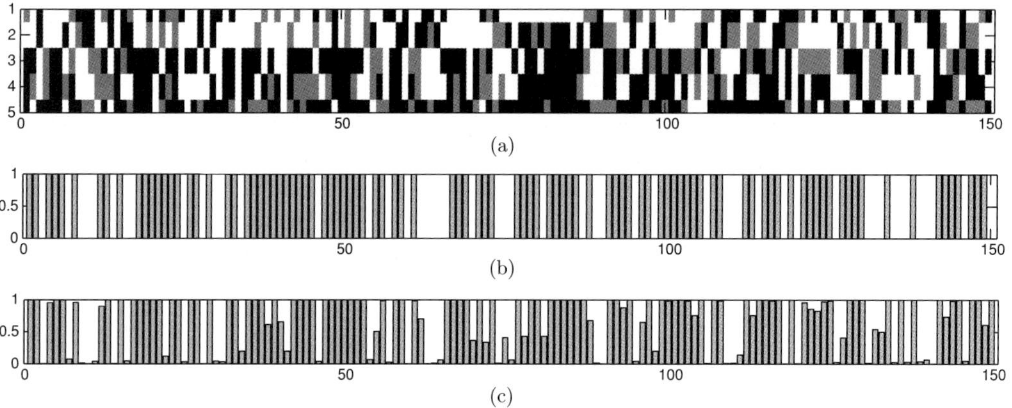

Figure 20.4 **(a)** Data from questionnaire responses. 150 people were each asked 5 questions, with 'yes' (white) and 'no' (black) answers. Grey denotes that the absence of a response (missing data). This training data was generated by a two-component product of Bernouilli model. Missing data was simulated by randomly removing values from the dataset. **(b)** the 'correct' h values sampled from the data. A '0' denotes $h^n = 1$ and '1' denotes $h^n = 2$. **(c)** The estimated $p(h_i^n = 2|\mathbf{v}^n)$ values.

Data from a questionnaire containing five questions, with 150 respondents is presented in Fig. 20.4. The data has a large number of missing values. We assume there are $H = 2$ kinds of respondents and attempt to assign each respondent into one of the two clusters. Running the EM algorithm on this data, with random initial values for the tables, produces the results in Fig. 20.5. Based on assigning each datapoint $\mathbf{v}^n$ to the cluster with maximal posterior probability $h^n = \arg\max_h p(h|\mathbf{v}^n)$, given a trained model $p(\mathbf{v}|h)p(h)$, the model assigns 90 per cent of the data to the correct cluster (which is known in this simulated case). See `MIXprodBern.m`.

Example 20.3 Handwritten digits

We have a collection of 5000 handwritten digits which we wish to cluster into 20 groups, Fig. 20.6. Each digit is a $28 \times 28 = 784$-dimensional binary vector. Using a mixture of Bernoulli products, trained with 50 iterations of EM (with random initialisation), the clusters are presented in Fig. 20.6. As we see, the method captures natural clusters in the data – for example, there are two kinds of 1, one slightly more slanted than the other, two kinds of 4, etc.

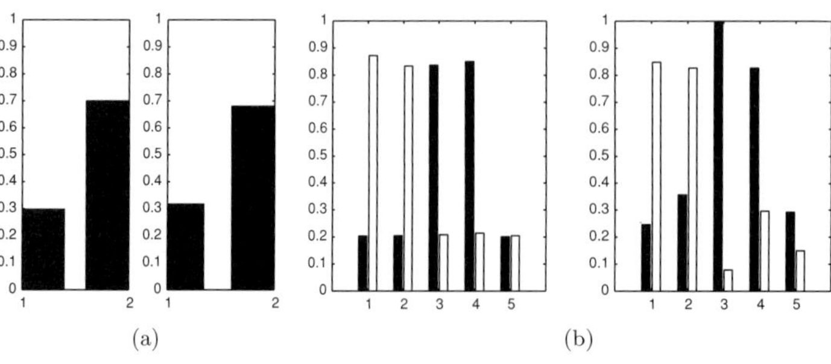

Figure 20.5 EM learning of a mixture of Bernoulli products. **(a)** True $p(h)$ (left) and learned $p(h)$ (right) for $h = 1,2$. **(b)** True $p(v|h)$ (left) and learned $p(v|h)$ (right) for $v = 1, \ldots, 5$. Each column pair corresponds to $p(v_i|h = 1)$ (right column) and $p(v_i|h = 2)$ (left column) with $i = 1, \ldots, 5$. The learned probabilities are reasonably close to the true values.

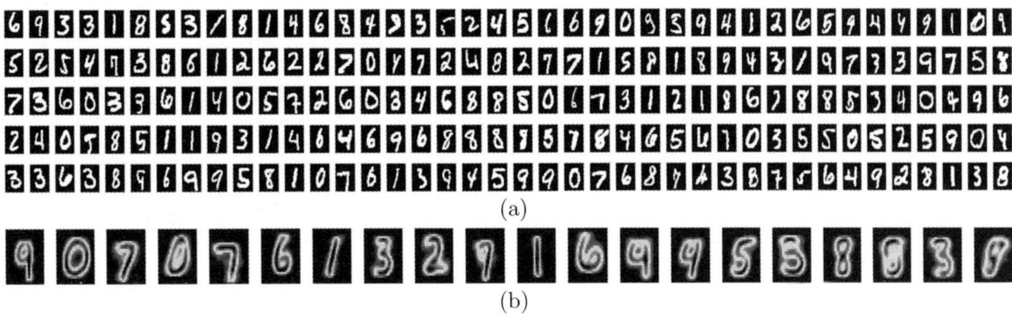

Figure 20.6 **(a)** a selection of 200 of the 5000 handwritten digits in the training set. **(b)** the trained cluster outputs $p(v_i = 1|h)$ for $h = 1, \dots, 20$ mixtures. See `demoMixBernoulliDigits.m`.

20.3 The Gaussian mixture model

We turn our attention now to modelling continuous vector observations $\mathbf{x}$ ($\mathbf{x}$ plays the role of the 'visible' variable v previously). Gaussians are particularly convenient continuous mixture components since they constitute 'bumps' of probability mass, aiding an intuitive interpretation of the model. As a reminder, a D-dimensional Gaussian distribution for a continuous variable $\mathbf{x}$ is

$$p(\mathbf{x}|\mathbf{m}, \mathbf{S}) = \frac{1}{\sqrt{\det(2\pi\mathbf{S})}} \exp\left\{-\frac{1}{2}(\mathbf{x}-\mathbf{m})^{\mathsf{T}}\mathbf{S}^{-1}(\mathbf{x}-\mathbf{m})\right\} \tag{20.3.1}$$

where $\mathbf{m}$ is the mean and $\mathbf{S}$ is the covariance matrix. A mixture of Gaussians is then

$$p(\mathbf{x}) = \sum_{i=1}^{H} p(\mathbf{x}|\mathbf{m}_i, \mathbf{S}_i)p(i) \tag{20.3.2}$$

where $p(i)$ is the mixture weight for component i. For a set of data $\mathcal{X} = \left\{\mathbf{x}^1, \dots, \mathbf{x}^N\right\}$ and under the usual i.i.d. assumption, the log likelihood is

$$\log p(\mathcal{X}|\theta) = \sum_{n=1}^{N} \log \sum_{i=1}^{H} p(i) \frac{1}{\sqrt{\det(2\pi\mathbf{S}_i)}} \exp\left\{-\frac{1}{2}(\mathbf{x}^n-\mathbf{m}_i)^{\mathsf{T}}\mathbf{S}_i^{-1}(\mathbf{x}^n-\mathbf{m}_i)\right\} \tag{20.3.3}$$

where the parameters are $\theta = \{\mathbf{m}_i, \mathbf{S}_i, p(i), i = 1, \dots, H\}$. The optimal parameters θ can be set using maximum likelihood, bearing in mind the constraint that the $\mathbf{S}_i$ must be symmetric positive definite matrices, in addition to $0 \leq p(i) \leq 1, \sum_i p(i) = 1$. Gradient-based optimisation approaches are feasible under a parameterisation of the $\mathbf{S}_i$ (e.g. Cholesky decomposition) and $p(i)$ (e.g. softmax) that enforce the constraints. An alternative is the EM approach which in this case is particularly convenient since it automatically provides parameter updates that ensure these constraints.

20.3.1 EM algorithm

From the general approach, Section 11.2, for the M-step we need to consider the energy. Using the fact that the component index i plays the role of the latent variable, the energy is given by

$$\sum_{n=1}^{N} \left\langle \log p(\mathbf{x}^n, i)\right\rangle_{p^{old}(i|\mathbf{x}^n)} = \sum_{n=1}^{N} \left\langle \log\left[p(\mathbf{x}^n|i)p(i)\right]\right\rangle_{p^{old}(i|\mathbf{x}^n)}. \tag{20.3.4}$$

Plugging in the definition of the Gaussian components, we have

$$\sum_{n=1}^{N}\sum_{i=1}^{H} p^{old}(i|\mathbf{x}^n)\sum_{n=1}^{N}\left\{-\frac{1}{2}\left(\mathbf{x}^n-\mathbf{m}_i\right)^{\mathsf{T}}\mathbf{S}_i^{-1}\left(\mathbf{x}^n-\mathbf{m}_i\right)-\frac{1}{2}\log\det\left(2\pi\mathbf{S}_i\right)+\log p(i)\right\}. \quad (20.3.5)$$

The M-step requires the maximisation of the above with respect to $\mathbf{m}_i$, $\mathbf{S}_i$, $p(i)$.

M-step: optimal $\mathbf{m}_i$

Maximising Equation (20.3.5) with respect to $\mathbf{m}_i$ is equivalent to minimising

$$\sum_{n=1}^{N}\sum_{i=1}^{H} p^{old}(i|\mathbf{x}^n)\left(\mathbf{x}^n-\mathbf{m}_i\right)^{\mathsf{T}}\mathbf{S}_i^{-1}\left(\mathbf{x}^n-\mathbf{m}_i\right). \quad (20.3.6)$$

Differentiating with respect to $\mathbf{m}_i$ and equating to zero we have

$$-2\sum_{n=1}^{N} p^{old}(i|\mathbf{x}^n)\mathbf{S}_i^{-1}\left(\mathbf{x}^n-\mathbf{m}_i\right)=\mathbf{0}. \quad (20.3.7)$$

Hence, optimally,

$$\mathbf{m}_i=\frac{\sum_{n=1}^{N} p^{old}(i|\mathbf{x}^n)\mathbf{x}^n}{\sum_{n=1}^{N} p^{old}(i|\mathbf{x}^n)}. \quad (20.3.8)$$

By defining the membership distribution

$$p^{old}(n|i)\equiv\frac{p^{old}(i|\mathbf{x}^n)}{\sum_{n=1}^{N} p^{old}(i|\mathbf{x}^n)} \quad (20.3.9)$$

which quantifies the membership of datapoints to cluster i, we can write Equation (20.3.8) more compactly as the update

$$\mathbf{m}_i^{new}=\sum_{n=1}^{N} p^{old}(n|i)\mathbf{x}^n. \quad (20.3.10)$$

Intuitively, this updates the mean for cluster i as the average over all datapoints weighted by their membership to cluster i.

M-step: optimal $\mathbf{S}_i$

Optimising Equation (20.3.5) with respect to $\mathbf{S}_i$ is equivalent to minimising

$$\sum_{n=1}^{N}\left\langle(\Delta_i^n)^{\mathsf{T}}\mathbf{S}_i^{-1}\Delta_i^n-\log\det\left(\mathbf{S}_i^{-1}\right)\right\rangle_{p^{old}(i|\mathbf{x}^n)} \quad (20.3.11)$$

where $\Delta_i^n\equiv\mathbf{x}^n-\mathbf{m}_i$. To aid the matrix calculus, we isolate the dependency on $\mathbf{S}_i$ to give

$$\operatorname{trace}\left(\mathbf{S}_i^{-1}\sum_{n=1}^{N} p^{old}(i|\mathbf{x}^n)\Delta_i^n\left(\Delta_i^n\right)^{\mathsf{T}}\right)-\log\det\left(\mathbf{S}_i^{-1}\right)\sum_{n=1}^{N} p^{old}(i|\mathbf{x}^n). \quad (20.3.12)$$

Differentiating with respect to $\mathbf{S}_i^{-1}$ and equating to zero, we obtain

$$\sum_{n=1}^{N} p^{old}(i|\mathbf{x}^n)\Delta_i^n (\Delta_i^n)^{\mathsf{T}} - \mathbf{S}_i \sum_{n=1}^{N} p^{old}(i|\mathbf{x}^n) = \mathbf{0}. \tag{20.3.13}$$

Using the membership distribution $p^{old}(n|i)$, the resulting update is given by

$$\mathbf{S}_i^{new} = \sum_{n=1}^{N} p^{old}(n|i)\,(\mathbf{x}^n - \mathbf{m}_i)\,.\,(\mathbf{x}^n - \mathbf{m}_i)^{\mathsf{T}}. \tag{20.3.14}$$

As for the mean, this essentially softly 'filters' those datapoints that belong to cluster i and takes their covariance. This update also ensures that $\mathbf{S}_i$ is symmetric positive semidefinite. A special case is to constrain the covariances $\mathbf{S}_i$ to be diagonal for which the update is, see Exercise 20.2,

$$\mathbf{S}_i = \sum_{n=1}^{N} p^{old}(n|i)\mathrm{diag}\left((\mathbf{x}^n - \mathbf{m}_i)(\mathbf{x}^n - \mathbf{m}_i)^{\mathsf{T}}\right) \tag{20.3.15}$$

where above diag $(\mathbf{M})$ means forming a new matrix from the matrix $\mathbf{M}$ with zero entries except for the diagonal entries of $\mathbf{M}$. A more extreme case is that of *isotropic* Gaussians $\mathbf{S}_i = \sigma_i^2\mathbf{I}$. The reader may show that the optimal update for σ_i^2 in this case is given by taking the average of the diagonal entries of the diagonally constrained covariance update,

$$\sigma_i^2 = \frac{1}{D}\sum_{n=1}^{N} p^{old}(n|i)(\mathbf{x}^n - \mathbf{m}_i)^2. \tag{20.3.16}$$

M-step: optimal mixture coefficients

If no constraint is placed on the weights, the update follows the general formula given in Equation (20.2.8),

$$p^{new}(i) = \frac{1}{N}\sum_{n=1}^{N} p^{old}(i|\mathbf{x}^n). \tag{20.3.17}$$

E-step

From the general theory, Section 11.2, the E-step is given by

$$p(i|\mathbf{x}^n) \propto p(\mathbf{x}^n|i)p(i). \tag{20.3.18}$$

Explicitly, this is given by the *responsibility*

$$p(i|\mathbf{x}^n) = \frac{p(i)\exp\left\{-\frac{1}{2}(\mathbf{x}^n - \mathbf{m}_i)^{\mathsf{T}}\mathbf{S}_i^{-1}(\mathbf{x}^n - \mathbf{m}_i)\right\}\det(\mathbf{S}_i)^{-\frac{1}{2}}}{\sum_{i'} p(i')\exp\left\{-\frac{1}{2}(\mathbf{x}^n - \mathbf{m}_{i'})^{\mathsf{T}}\mathbf{S}_{i'}^{-1}(\mathbf{x}^n - \mathbf{m}_{i'})\right\}\det(\mathbf{S}_{i'})^{-\frac{1}{2}}}. \tag{20.3.19}$$

The above Equations (20.3.8), (20.3.14), (20.3.17), (20.3.19) are iterated in sequence until convergence. Note that this means that the 'new' means are used in the update for the covariance, see Algorithm 20.1.

The performance of EM for Gaussian mixtures can be strongly dependent on the initialisation, which we discuss below. In addition, constraints on the covariance matrix are required in order to find sensible solutions.

Algorithm 20.1 EM training for the GMM.

Initialise the centres $\mathbf{m}_i$, covariances $\mathbf{S}_i$ and weights $p(i) > 0, \sum_i p(i) = 1$ $i = 1, \ldots, H$.
while Likelihood not converged or termination criterion not reached **do**
  for $n = 1, \ldots N$ **do**
    for $i = 1, \ldots, H$ **do**
      $p(i|\mathbf{x}^n) = p(i) \exp\left\{-\frac{1}{2}(\mathbf{x}^n - \mathbf{m}_i)^{\mathsf{T}} \mathbf{S}_i^{-1} (\mathbf{x}^n - \mathbf{m}_i)\right\} \det(\mathbf{S}_i)^{-\frac{1}{2}}$ ▷ responsibility
    end for
    Normalise $p(i|\mathbf{x}^n)$ so that $\sum_i p(i|\mathbf{x}^n) = 1$
    $p(n|i) = p(i|\mathbf{x}^n)$ ▷ membership
  end for
  Normalise $p(n|i)$ so that $\sum_n p(n|i) = 1$ for each i.
  for $i = 1, \ldots, H$ **do**
    $\mathbf{m}_i = \sum_{n=1}^{N} p(n|i)\mathbf{x}^n$ ▷ M-step for means
    $\mathbf{S}_i = \sum_{n=1}^{N} p(n|i)(\mathbf{x}^n - \mathbf{m}_i)(\mathbf{x}^n - \mathbf{m}_i)^{\mathsf{T}}$ ▷ M-step for covariances
    $p(i) = \frac{1}{N}\sum_{n=1}^{N} p(i|\mathbf{x}^n)$ ▷ M-step for weights
  end for
  $L = \sum_{n=1}^{N} \log \sum_{i=1}^{H} p(i) \frac{1}{\sqrt{\det(2\pi\mathbf{S}_i)}} \exp\left\{-\frac{1}{2}(\mathbf{x}^n - \mathbf{m}_i)^{\mathsf{T}} \mathbf{S}_i^{-1} (\mathbf{x}^n - \mathbf{m}_i)\right\}$ ▷ Log likelihood
end while

20.3.2 Practical issues

Infinite troubles

A difficulty arises with using maximum likelihood to fit a Gaussian mixture model. Consider placing a component $p(\mathbf{x}|\mathbf{m}_i, \mathbf{S}_i)$ with mean $\mathbf{m}_i$ set to one of the datapoints $\mathbf{m}_i = \mathbf{x}^n$. The contribution from that Gaussian for datapoint $\mathbf{x}^n$ will be

$$p(\mathbf{x}^n|\mathbf{m}_i, \mathbf{S}_i) = \frac{1}{\sqrt{\det(2\pi\mathbf{S}_i)}} e^{-\frac{1}{2}(\mathbf{x}^n - \mathbf{x}^n)^{\mathsf{T}}\mathbf{S}_i^{-1}(\mathbf{x}^n - \mathbf{x}^n)} = \frac{1}{\sqrt{\det(2\pi\mathbf{S}_i)}}. \tag{20.3.20}$$

In the limit that the 'width' of the covariance goes to zero (the eigenvalues of $\mathbf{S}_i$ tend to zero), this probability density becomes infinite. This means that one can obtain a maximum likelihood solution by placing zero-width Gaussians on a selection of the datapoints, resulting in an infinite likelihood. This is clearly undesirable and arises because, in this case, the maximum likelihood solution does not constrain the parameters in a sensible way. Note that this is not related to the EM algorithm, but a property of the maximum likelihood method itself. All computational methods which aim to fit unconstrained mixtures of Gaussians using maximum likelihood therefore succeed in finding 'reasonable' solutions merely by getting trapped in favourable local maxima. A remedy is to include an additional constraint on the width of the Gaussians, ensuring that they cannot become too small. One approach is to monitor the eigenvalues of each covariance matrix and if an update would result in a new eigenvalue smaller than a desired threshold, the update is rejected. In `GMMem.m` we use a similar approach in which we constrain the determinant (the product of the eigenvalues) of the covariances to be greater than a desired specified minimum value. One can view the formal failure of maximum likelihood in the case of Gaussian mixtures as a result of an inappropriate prior. Maximum likelihood is equivalent to MAP in which a flat prior is placed on each matrix $\mathbf{S}_i$. This

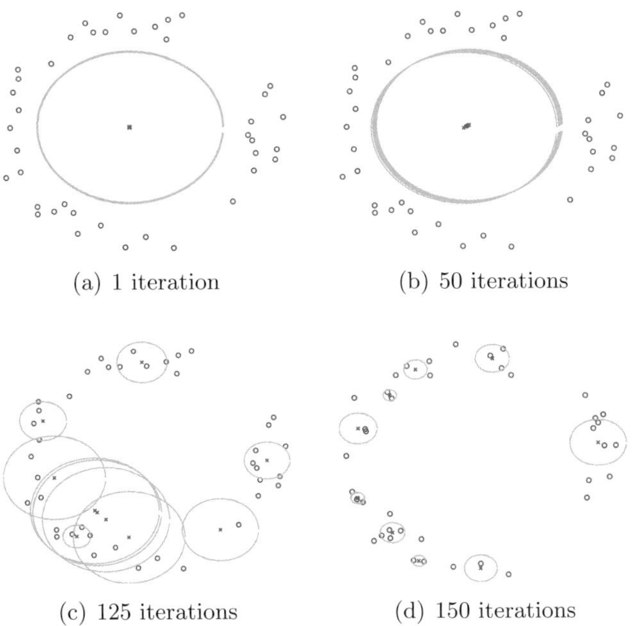

Figure 20.7 Training a mixture of 10 isotropic Gaussians (**a**) If we start with large variances for the Gaussians, even after one iteration, the Gaussians are centred close to the mean of the data. (**b**) The Gaussians begin to separate. (**c**) One by one, the Gaussians move towards appropriate parts of the data. (**d**) The final converged solution. The Gaussians are constrained to have variances greater than a set amount. See `demoGMMem.m`.

is unreasonable since the matrices are required to be positive definite and of non-vanishing width. A Bayesian solution to this problem is possible, placing a prior on covariance matrices. The natural prior in this case is the Wishart Distribution, or a Gamma distribution in the case of a diagonal covariance.

Initialisation

A useful initialisation strategy is to set the covariances to be diagonal with large variances. This gives the components a chance to 'sense' where data lies. An illustration of the performance of the algorithm is given in Fig. 20.7.

Symmetry breaking

If the covariances are initialised to large values, the EM algorithm appears to make little progress in the beginning as each component jostles with the others to try to explain the data. Eventually one Gaussian component breaks away and takes responsibility for explaining the data in its vicinity, see Fig. 20.7. The origin of this initial jostling is an inherent symmetry in the solution – it makes no difference to the likelihood if we relabel what the components are called. The symmetries can severely handicap EM in fitting a large number of component models in the mixture since the number of permutations increases dramatically with the number of components. A heuristic is to begin with a small number of components, say two, for which symmetry breaking is less problematic. Once a local broken solution has been found, more models are included into the mixture, initialised close to the currently found solutions. In this way, a hierarchical scheme is envisaged. Another popular method for initialisation is to centre the means to those found by the K-means algorithm, see Section 20.3.5 – however, this itself requires a heuristic initialisation.

20.3.3 Classification using Gaussian mixture models

We can use GMMs as part of a class conditional generative model, in order to make a powerful classifier. Consider data drawn from two classes, $c \in \{1, 2\}$. We can fit a GMM $p(\mathbf{x}|c = 1, \mathcal{X}_1)$ to the data $\mathcal{X}_1$ from class 1, and another GMM $p(\mathbf{x}|c = 2, \mathcal{X}_2)$ to the data $\mathcal{X}_2$ from class 2. This gives rise to two class-conditional GMMs,

$$p(\mathbf{x}|c, \mathcal{X}_c) = \sum_{i=1}^{H} p(i|c)\mathcal{N}(\mathbf{x}|\mathbf{m}_i^c, \mathbf{S}_i^c). \tag{20.3.21}$$

For a novel point $\mathbf{x}^*$, the posterior class probability is

$$p(c|\mathbf{x}^*, \mathcal{X}) \propto p(\mathbf{x}^*|c, \mathcal{X}_c)p(c) \tag{20.3.22}$$

where $p(c)$ is the prior class probability. The maximum likelihood setting is that $p(c)$ is proportional to the number of training points in class c.

Overconfident classification

Consider a testpoint $\mathbf{x}^*$ a long way from the training data for both classes. For such a point, the probability that either of the two class models generated the data is very low. Nevertheless, one probability will be exponentially higher than the other (since the Gaussians drop exponentially quickly at different rates), meaning that the posterior probability will be confidently close to 1 for that class which has a component closest to $\mathbf{x}^*$. This is an unfortunate property since we would end up confidently predicting the class of novel data that is not similar to anything we've seen before. We would prefer the opposite effect that for novel data far from the training data, the classification confidence drops and all classes become equally likely.

A remedy for this situation is to include an additional component in the Gaussian mixture for each class that is very broad. We first collect the input data from all classes into a dataset $\mathcal{X}$, and let $\mathbf{m}$ be the mean of all this data and $\mathbf{S}$ the covariance. Then for the model of each class c data we include an additional Gaussian (dropping the notational dependency on $\mathcal{X}$)

$$p(\mathbf{x}|c) = \sum_{i=1}^{H} \tilde{p}_i^c \mathcal{N}(\mathbf{x}|\mathbf{m}_i^c, \mathbf{S}_i^c) + \tilde{p}_{H+1}^c \mathcal{N}(\mathbf{x}|\mathbf{m}, \lambda\mathbf{S}) \tag{20.3.23}$$

where

$$\tilde{p}_i^c \propto \begin{cases} p_i^c & i \leq H \\ \delta & i = H+1 \end{cases} \tag{20.3.24}$$

where δ is a small positive value and λ inflates the covariance (we take $\delta = 0.0001$ and $\lambda = 10$ in `demoGMMclass.m`). The effect of the additional component on the training likelihood is negligible since it has small weight and large variance compared to the other components, see Fig. 20.8. However, as we move away from the region where the first H components have appreciable mass, the additional component gains in influence since it has a higher variance. If we include the same additional component in the GMM for each class c then the influence of this additional component will be the same for each class, dominating as we move far from the influence of the other components. For a point far from the training data the likelihood will be roughly equal for each class since in this region the additional broad component dominates each class with equal measure. The posterior distribution will then tend to the prior class probability $p(c)$, mitigating the deleterious effect of a single GMM dominating when a testpoint is far from the training data.

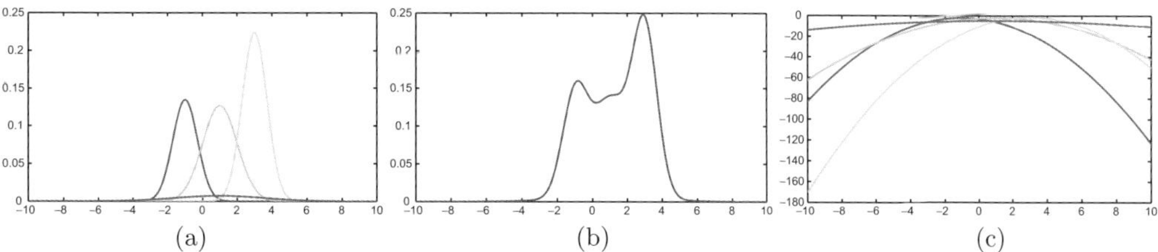

Figure 20.8 (**a**) A Gaussian mixture model with $H = 4$ components. There is a component (purple) with large variance and small weight that has little effect on the distribution close to where the other three components have appreciable mass. As we move further away this additional component gains in influence. (**b**) The GMM probability density function from (a). (**c**) Plotted on a log scale, the influence of each Gaussian far from the origin becomes clearer. See plate section for colour version.

Example 20.4

The data in Fig. 20.9(a) has a cluster structure for each class. Based on fitting a GMM to each of the two classes, a test point (diamond) far from the training data is confidently classified as belonging to class 1. This is an undesired effect since we would prefer that points far from the training data are not classified with any certainty. By including an additional large variance Gaussian component for each class this has little effect on the class probabilities of the training data, yet has the desired effect of making the class probability for the test point maximally uncertain, Fig. 20.9(b).

20.3.4 The Parzen estimator

The Parzen density estimator is formed by placing a 'bump of mass', $\rho(\mathbf{x}|\mathbf{x}^n)$, on each datapoint,

$$p(\mathbf{x}) = \frac{1}{N}\sum_{n=1}^{N}\rho(\mathbf{x}|\mathbf{x}^n). \tag{20.3.25}$$

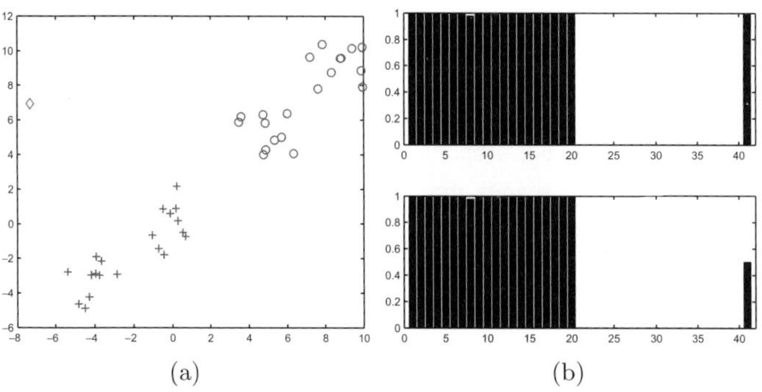

Figure 20.9 Class-conditional GMM training and classification. (**a**) Data from two different classes. We fit a GMM with two components to the data from each class. The diamond is a test point far from the training data we wish to classify. (**b**) Upper subpanel are the class probabilities $p(c = 1|n)$ for the 40 training points, and the 41st point, being the test point. This shows how the test point is confidently placed in class 1. The lower subpanel are the class probabilities but including the additional large variance Gaussian term. The class label for the test point is now maximally uncertain. See `demoGMMclass.m`.

Algorithm 20.2 K-means.

Initialise the centres $\mathbf{m}_i$, $i = 1, \ldots, K$.
while not converged **do**
    For each centre i, find all the $\mathbf{x}^n$ for which i is the nearest (in Euclidean sense) centre.
    Call this set of points $\mathcal{N}_i$. Let N_i be the number of datapoints in set $\mathcal{N}_i$.
    Update the means

$$\mathbf{m}_i^{new} = \frac{1}{N_i} \sum_{n \in \mathcal{N}_i} \mathbf{x}^n.$$

end while

A popular choice is (for a D-dimensional $\mathbf{x}$)

$$p(\mathbf{x}|\mathbf{x}^n) = \mathcal{N}\left(\mathbf{x}|\mathbf{x}^n, \sigma^2 \mathbf{I}_D\right) \tag{20.3.26}$$

giving the mixture of Gaussians

$$p(\mathbf{x}) = \frac{1}{N} \sum_{n=1}^{N} \frac{1}{(2\pi\sigma^2)^{D/2}} \exp\left(-\frac{1}{2\sigma^2}(\mathbf{x} - \mathbf{x}^n)^2\right). \tag{20.3.27}$$

There is no training required for a Parzen estimator – only the positions of the N datapoints need storing. Whilst the Parzen technique is a reasonable and cheap way to form a density estimator, it does not enable us to form any simpler description of the data. In particular, we cannot perform clustering since there is no lower number of clusters assumed to underly the data generating process. This is in contrast to GMMs trained using maximum likelihood on a fixed number $H \leq N$ of components.

20.3.5 K-means

Consider a mixture of K isotropic Gaussians in which each covariance is constrained to be equal to $\sigma^2 \mathbf{I}$, with mixture weights $p_i \geq 0$, $\sum_i p_i = 1$

$$p(\mathbf{x}) = \sum_{i=1}^{K} p_i \mathcal{N}\left(\mathbf{x}|\mathbf{m}_i, \sigma^2 \mathbf{I}\right). \tag{20.3.28}$$

Whilst the EM algorithm breaks down if a Gaussian component is allowed to set $\mathbf{m}_i$ equal to a datapoint with $\sigma^2 \to 0$, by constraining all components to have the same variance σ^2, the algorithm has a well-defined limit as $\sigma^2 \to 0$. The reader may show, Exercise 20.3, that in this case the membership distribution equation (20.3.9) becomes deterministic

$$p(n|i) \propto \begin{cases} 1 & \text{if } \mathbf{m}_i \text{ is closest to } \mathbf{x}^n \\ 0 & \text{otherwise.} \end{cases} \tag{20.3.29}$$

In this limit the EM update (20.3.10) for the mean $\mathbf{m}_i$ is given by taking the average of the points closest to $\mathbf{m}_i$. This limiting and constrained GMM then reduces to the so-called K-means algorithm, Algorithm 20.2. Despite its simplicity the K-means algorithm converges quickly and often gives a reasonable clustering, provided the centres are initialised sensibly. See Fig. 20.10.

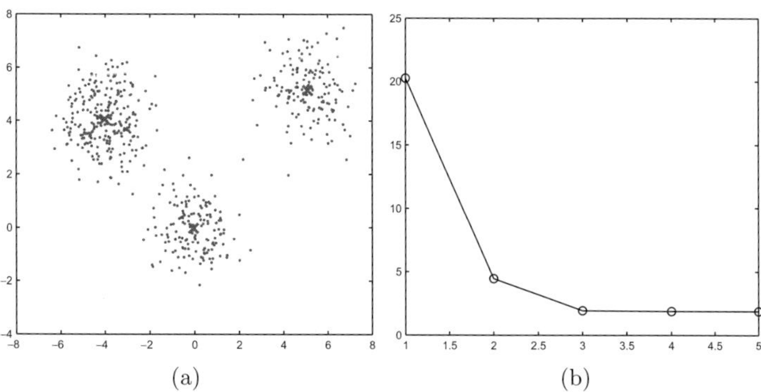

Figure 20.10 (**a**) 550 datapoints clustered using K-means with three components. The means are given by the red crosses. (**b**) Evolution of the mean square distance to the nearest centre against iterations of the algorithm. The means were initialised to be close to the overall mean of the data. See `demoKmeans.m`. See plate section for colour version.

K-means is often used as a simple form of data compression. Rather than sending the datapoint $\mathbf{x}^n$, one sends instead the index of the centre to which it is associated. This is called *vector quantisation* and is a form of lossy compression. To improve the quality, more information can be transmitted such as an approximation of the difference between $\mathbf{x}^n$ and the corresponding closest mean $\mathbf{m}$, which can be used to improve the reconstruction of the compressed datapoint.

20.3.6 Bayesian mixture models

Bayesian extensions include placing priors on the parameters of each model in the mixture, and also on the component mixture weights. In most cases this will give rise to an intractable integral for the marginal likelihood. Methods that approximate the integral include sampling techniques [105]. See also [119, 70] for an approximate variational treatment focussed on Bayesian Gaussian mixture models.

20.3.7 Semi-supervised learning

In some cases we may know to which mixture component certain datapoints belong. For example, given a collection of images that we wish to cluster, it may be that we already have cluster labels for a subset of the images. Given this information we want to fit a mixture model with a specified number of components H and parameters θ. We write (v_*^m, h_*^m), $m = 1, \ldots, M$ for the M known datapoints and corresponding components, and (v^n, h^n), $n = 1, \ldots, N$ for the remaining datapoints whose components h^n are unknown. We aim then to maximise the likelihood

$$p(v_*^{1:M}, v^{1:N}|h_*^{1:M}, \theta) = \left\{\prod_m p(v_*^m|h_*^m, \theta)\right\}\left\{\prod_n \sum_{h^n} p(v^n|h^n, \theta)p(h^n)\right\}. \tag{20.3.30}$$

If we were to lump all the datapoints together, this is essentially equivalent to the standard unsupervised case, expect that some of the h are fixed into known states. The only effect on the EM algorithm is therefore in the terms $p(h|v_*^m)$ for the labelled datapoints which are delta functions $p(h|v_*^m) = \delta_{h,h_*^m}$ in the known state, resulting in a minor modification of the standard algorithm, Exercise 20.6.

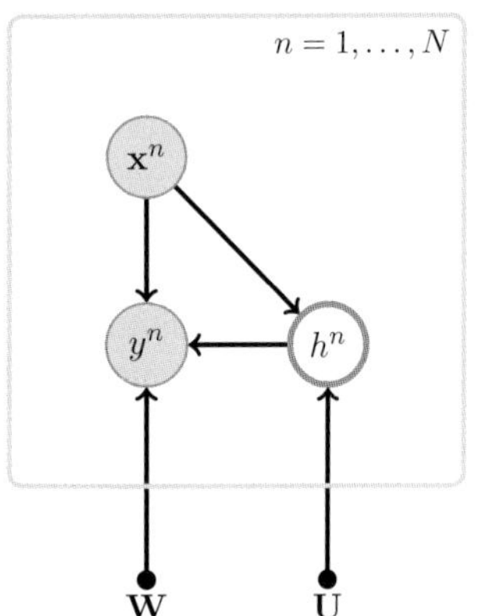

Figure 20.11 Mixture of experts model. The prediction of the output y^n (real or continuous) given the input $\mathbf{x}^n$ is averaged over individual experts $p(y^n|\mathbf{x}^n, \mathbf{w}_{h^n})$. The expert h^n is selected by the gating mechanism with probability $p(h^n|\mathbf{x}^n, \mathbf{U})$, so that some experts will be more responsible for predicting the output for $\mathbf{x}^n$ in 'their' part of the input space. The parameters $\mathbf{W}$, $\mathbf{U}$ can be learned by maximum likelihood after marginalising over the hidden expert indices $h^1, \dots, h^N$.

20.4 Mixture of experts

The mixture of experts model [162] is an extension to input-dependent mixture weights. For an output y (a discrete class or continuous regression variable) and input $\mathbf{x}$, this has the general form, see Fig. 20.11,

$$p(y|\mathbf{x}, \mathbf{W}, \mathbf{U}) = \sum_{h=1}^{H} p(y|\mathbf{x}, \mathbf{w}_h)p(h|\mathbf{x}, \mathbf{U}). \tag{20.4.1}$$

Here h indexes the mixture component. Each expert h has parameters $\mathbf{w}_h$ with $\mathbf{W} = [\mathbf{w}_1, \dots, \mathbf{w}_H]$ and corresponding gating parameters $\mathbf{u}_h$ with $\mathbf{U} = [\mathbf{u}_1, \dots, \mathbf{u}_H]$. Unlike a standard mixture model, the component distribution $p(h|\mathbf{x}, \mathbf{U})$ is dependent on the input $\mathbf{x}$. This so-called gating distribution is conventionally taken to be of the softmax form

$$p(h|\mathbf{x}, \mathbf{U}) = \frac{e^{\mathbf{u}_h^\mathsf{T}\mathbf{x}}}{\sum_h e^{\mathbf{u}_h^\mathsf{T}\mathbf{x}}}. \tag{20.4.2}$$

The idea is that we have a set of H predictive models (experts), $p(y|\mathbf{x}, \mathbf{w}_h)$, each with a different parameter $\mathbf{w}_h$, $h = 1, \dots, H$. How suitable model h is for predicting the output for input $\mathbf{x}$ is determined by the alignment of input $\mathbf{x}$ with the weight vector $\mathbf{u}_h$. In this way the input $\mathbf{x}$ is softly assigned to the appropriate experts.

Learning the parameters

Maximum likelihood training can be achieved using a form of EM. We will not derive the EM algorithm for the mixture of experts model in full, merely pointing the direction along which the derivation would continue. For a single datapoint $\mathbf{x}$, the EM energy term is

$$\left\langle \log p(y|\mathbf{x}, \mathbf{w}_h)p(h|\mathbf{x}, \mathbf{U})\right\rangle_{p(h|\mathbf{x}, \mathbf{W}^{old}, \mathbf{U}^{old})}. \tag{20.4.3}$$

For regression a simple choice is

$$p(y|\mathbf{x}, \mathbf{w}_h) = \mathcal{N}\left(y|\mathbf{x}^\mathsf{T}\mathbf{w}_h, \sigma^2\right) \tag{20.4.4}$$

and for (binary) classification

$$p(y = 1|\mathbf{x}, \mathbf{w}_h) = \sigma(\mathbf{x}^\mathsf{T}\mathbf{w}_h). \tag{20.4.5}$$

In both cases computing the derivatives of the energy with respect to the parameters $\mathbf{W}$ is straightforward, so that an EM algorithm is readily available. An alternative to EM is to compute the gradient of the likelihood directly using the standard approach discussed in Section 11.6.

A Bayesian treatment is to consider

$$p(y, \mathbf{W}, \mathbf{U}, h|\mathbf{x}) = p(y|\mathbf{x}, \mathbf{w}_h)p(h|\mathbf{x}, \mathbf{u})p(\mathbf{W})p(\mathbf{U}) \tag{20.4.6}$$

where it is conventional to assume $p(\mathbf{W}) = \prod_h p(\mathbf{w}_h)$, $p(\mathbf{U}) = \prod_h p(\mathbf{u}_h)$. The integrals required to calculate the marginal likelihood are generally intractable and approximations are required. See [310] for a variational treatment for regression and [44] for a variational treatment of classification. An extension to Bayesian model selection in which the number of experts is estimated is considered in [156].

20.5 Indicator models

Indicator models generalise our previous mixture models by allowing a more general prior distribution on cluster assignments. For consistency with the literature we use an indicator z, as opposed to a hidden variable h, although they play the same role. A clustering model with parameters θ on the component models and joint indicator prior $p(z^{1:N})$ takes the form, see Fig. 20.12(a),

$$p(v^{1:N}|\theta) = \sum_{z^{1:N}} p(v^{1:N}|z^{1:N}, \theta)p(z^{1:N}). \tag{20.5.1}$$

Since the z^n indicate cluster membership,

$$p(v^{1:N}|\theta) = \sum_{z^{1:N}} p(z^{1:N}) \prod_{n=1}^{N} p(v^n|z^n, \theta). \tag{20.5.2}$$

Below we discuss the role of different indicator priors $p(z^{1:N})$ in clustering.

20.5.1 Joint indicator approach: factorised prior

Assuming prior independence of indicators,

$$p(z^{1:N}) = \prod_{n=1}^{N} p(z^n), \qquad z^n \in \{1, \ldots, K\} \tag{20.5.3}$$

we obtain from Equation (20.5.2)

$$p(v^{1:N}|\theta) = \sum_{z^{1:N}} \prod_{n=1}^{N} p(v^n|z^n, \theta)p(z^n) = \prod_{n=1}^{N} \sum_{z^n} p(v^n|z^n, \theta)p(z^n) \tag{20.5.4}$$

which recovers the standard mixture model equation (20.1.3). As we discuss below, more sophisticated joint indicator priors can be used to explicitly control the complexity of the indicator assignments and open the path to essentially 'infinite-dimensional' models.

20.5.2 Polya prior

For a large number of available clusters (mixture components) $K \gg 1$, using a factorised joint indicator distribution could potentially lead to overfitting, resulting in little or no meaningful clustering.

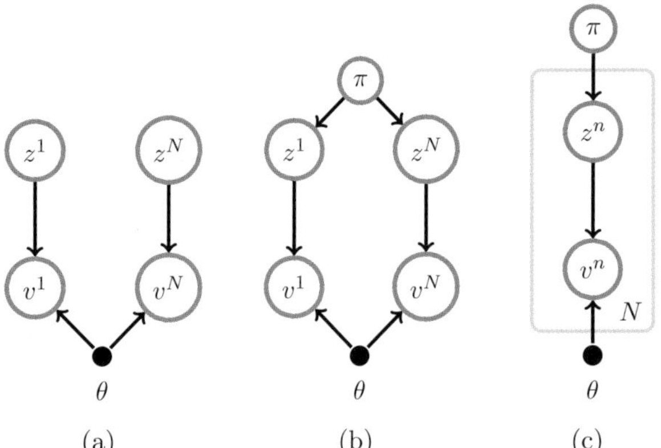

Figure 20.12 (**a**) A generic mixture model for data $v^{1:N}$. Each z^n indicates the cluster of each datapoint; θ is a set of parameters and $z^n = k$ selects parameter θ^k for datapoint v^n. (**b**) For a potentially large number of clusters one way to control complexity is to constrain the joint indicator distribution. (**c**) Plate notation of (b).

One way to control the effective number of components that are used is via a parameter π that regulates the complexity, see Fig. 20.12(b,c),

$$p(z^{1:N}) = \int_{\pi} \left\{ \prod_n p(z^n|\pi) \right\} p(\pi) \tag{20.5.5}$$

where $p(z|\pi)$ is a categorical distribution,

$$p(z^n = k|\pi) = \pi_k. \tag{20.5.6}$$

This means, for example, that if π_l is low, we are therefore unlikely to select cluster k for any datapoint n. A convenient choice for $p(\pi)$ is the Dirichlet distribution (since this is conjugate to the categorical distribution),

$$p(\pi) = \text{Dirichlet}\,(\pi|\alpha) \propto \prod_{k=1}^{K} \pi_k^{\alpha/K-1}. \tag{20.5.7}$$

The integral over π in Equation (20.5.5) can be performed analytically to give a Polya distribution:

$$p(z^{1:N}) = \frac{\Gamma(\alpha)}{\Gamma(N+\alpha)} \prod_{k=1}^{K} \frac{\Gamma(N_k + \alpha/K)}{\Gamma(\alpha/K)}, \qquad N_k \equiv \sum_n \mathbb{I}[z^n = k]. \tag{20.5.8}$$

The number of unique clusters used is then given by $U = \sum_k \mathbb{I}[N_k > 0]$. The distribution over likely cluster numbers is controlled by the parameter α. The scaling α/K in Equation (20.5.7) ensures a sensible limit as $K \to \infty$, see Fig. 20.13, in which limit the models are known as *Dirichlet process mixture models*. This approach means that we do not need to explicitly constrain the number of possible components K since the number of active components U remains limited even for very large K.

Clustering is achieved by considering $\underset{z^{1:N}}{\text{argmax}}\; p(z^{1:N}|v^{1:N})$. In practice it is common to consider

$$\underset{z^n}{\text{argmax}}\; p(z^n|v^{1:N}). \tag{20.5.9}$$

Unfortunately, posterior inference of $p(z^n|v^{1:N})$ for this class of models is formally computationally intractable and approximate inference techniques are required. A detailed discussion of these techniques is beyond the scope of this book and we refer the reader to [179] for a deterministic (variational) approach and [221] for a discussion of sampling approaches.

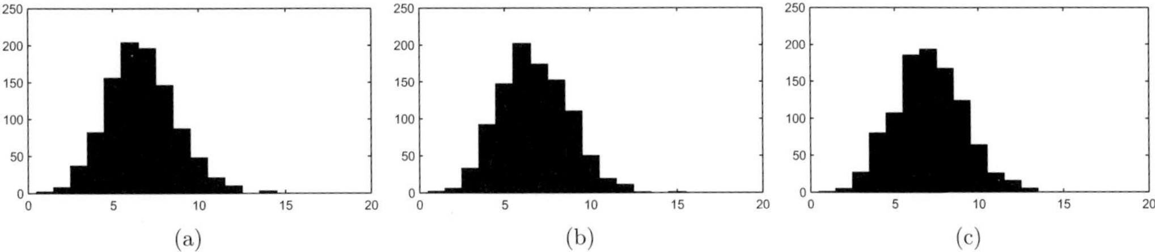

Figure 20.13 The distribution of the number of unique clusters U when indicators are sampled from a Polya distribution equation (20.5.8), with $\alpha = 2$, and $N = 50$ datapoints. (**a**) $K = 50$, (**b**) $K = 100$, (**c**) $K = 1000$. Even though the number of available clusters K is larger than the number of datapoints, the number of used clusters U remains constrained. See `demoPolya.m`.

20.6 Mixed membership models

Unlike standard mixture models in which each object is assumed to have been generated from a single cluster, in mixed membership models an object may be a member of more than one group. Latent Dirichlet Allocation (LDA) discussed below is an example of such a mixed membership model, and is one of a number of models developed in recent years [4, 98].

20.6.1 Latent Dirichlet allocation

Latent Dirichlet Allocation [46] considers that each datapoint may belong to more than a single cluster. A typical application is to identify topic clusters in a collection of documents. A single document contains a sequence of words, for example

$$v = (\text{the, cat, sat, on, the, mat}). \tag{20.6.1}$$

If each word in the available dictionary of D words is assigned to a unique state (say dog $= 1$, tree $= 2$, cat $= 3, \ldots$), we can represent then the nth document as a vector of word indices

$$v^n = \left(v_1^n, \ldots, v_{W_n}^n\right), \qquad v_i^n \in \{1, \ldots, D\} \tag{20.6.2}$$

where W_n is the number of words in the nth document. The number of words W_n in each document can vary although the overall dictionary from which they came is fixed.

The aim is to find common topics in documents, assuming that any document could potentially contain more than one topic. It is useful to think first of an underlying generative model of words, including latent topics (which we will later integrate out). For each document n we have a distribution of topics $\boldsymbol{\pi}^n$ with $\sum_{k=1}^{K} \pi_k^n = 1$ which gives a latent description of the document in terms of its topic membership. For example, document n (which discusses issues related to wildlife conservation) might have a topic distribution with high mass on the latent 'animals' and 'environment', topics. Note that the topics are indeed latent – the name 'animal' would be given post-hoc based on the kinds of words that the latent topic would generate, $\theta_{i|k}$. As in Section 20.5.2, to control complexity one may use a Dirichlet prior to limit the number of topics active in any particular document:

$$p(\boldsymbol{\pi}^n|\boldsymbol{\alpha}) = \text{Dirichlet}\left(\boldsymbol{\pi}^n|\boldsymbol{\alpha}\right) \tag{20.6.3}$$

where $\boldsymbol{\alpha}$ is a vector of length the number of topics.

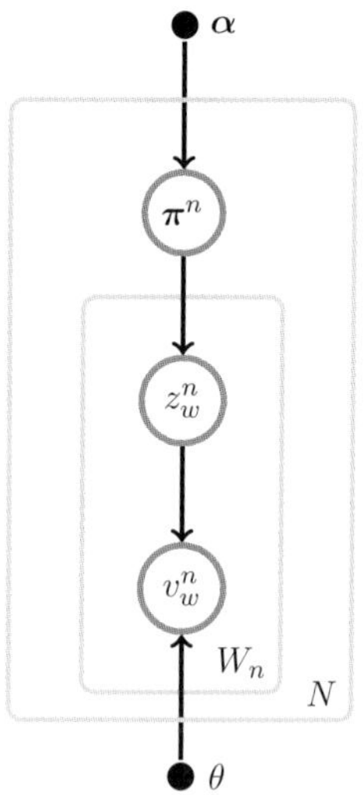

Figure 20.14 Latent Dirichlet allocation. For document n we first sample a distribution of topics $\boldsymbol{\pi}^n$. Then for each word position $w = 1, \ldots, W_n$ in the document we sample a topic z_w^n from the topic distribution. Given the topic we then sample a word from the word distribution of that topic. The parameters of the model are the word distributions for each topic θ, and the parameters of the topic distribution $\boldsymbol{\alpha}$.

We first sample a probability distribution (histogram) $\boldsymbol{\pi}^n$ that represents the topics likely to occur for this document. Then, for each word-position in the document, sample a topic and subsequently a word from the distribution of words for that topic. For document n and the wth word-position in the document, v_w^n, we use $z_w^n \in \{1, \ldots, K\}$ to indicate to which of the K possible topics that word belongs. For each topic k, one then has a categorical distribution over all the words $i = 1, \ldots, D$, in the dictionary:

$$p(v_w^n = i | z_w^n = k, \theta) = \theta_{i|k}. \tag{20.6.4}$$

For example, the 'animal' topic has high probability to emit animal-like words, etc.

A generative model for sampling a document v^n with W_n word positions is then given by, see Fig. 20.14:

1. Choose $\boldsymbol{\pi}^n \sim \text{Dirichlet}\left(\boldsymbol{\pi}^n | \boldsymbol{\alpha}\right)$
2. For each of word position v_w^n, $w = 1, \ldots, W_n$:
   (a) Choose a topic $z_w^n \sim p\left(z_w^n | \boldsymbol{\pi}^n\right)$
   (b) Choose a word $v_w^n \sim p\left(v_w^n | \theta_{\cdot | z_w^n}\right)$.

Training the LDA model corresponds to learning the parameters $\boldsymbol{\alpha}$, which relates to the number of topics, and θ, which describes the distribution of words within each topic. Unfortunately, finding the requisite marginals for learning from the posterior is formally computationally intractable. Efficient approximate inference for this class of models is a topic of research interest and both variational and sampling approaches have recently been developed [46, 289, 242].

There are close similarities between LDA and PLSA [125], Section 15.6.1, both of which describe a document in terms of a distribution over latent topics: LDA is a probabilistic model for which issues such as setting hyperparameters can be addressed using maximum likelihood; PLSA on the other hand is essentially a matrix decomposition technique (such as PCA). Issues such as hyperparameters setting for PLSA are therefore addressed using validation data. Whilst PLSA is a description only of the training data, LDA is a generative data model and can in principle be used to synthesise new documents.

Arts	Budgets	Children	Education
new	million	children	school
film	tax	women	students
show	program	people	schools
music	budget	child	education
movie	billion	years	teachers
play	federal	families	high
musical	year	work	public
best	spending	parents	teacher
actor	new	says	bennett
first	state	family	manigat
york	plan	welfare	namphy
opera	money	men	state
theater	programs	percent	president
actress	government	care	elementary
love	congress	life	haiti

(a)

The William Randolph Hearst Foundation will give $ 1.25 million to Lincoln Center, Metropolitan Opera Co., New York Philharmonic and Juilliard School. Our board felt that we had a real opportunity to make a mark on the future of the performing arts with these grants an act every bit as important as our traditional areas of support in health, medical research, education and the social services, Hearst Foundation President Randolph A. Hearst said Monday in announcing the grants. Lincoln Centers share will be $200,000 for its new building, which will house young artists and provide new public facilities. The Metropolitan Opera Co. and New York Philharmonic will receive $400,000 each. The Juilliard School, where music and the performing arts are taught, will get $250,000. The Hearst Foundation, a leading supporter of the Lincoln Center Consolidated Corporate Fund, will make its usual annual $100,000 donation, too.

(b)

Figure 20.15 (**a**) A subset of the latent topics discovered by LDA and the high probability words associated with each topic. Each column represents a topic, with the topic name such as 'arts' assigned by hand after viewing the most likely words corresponding to the topic. (**b**) A document from the training data in which the words are coloured according to the most likely latent topic. This demonstrates the mixed membership nature of the model, assigning the datapoint (document in this case) to several clusters (topics). Reproduced from [46]. See plate section for colour version.

Example 20.5

An illustration of the use of LDA is given in Fig. 20.15 [46]. The documents are taken from the TREC Associated Press corpus containing 16 333 newswire articles with 23 075 unique terms. After removing a standard list of *stop words* (frequent words such as 'the','a' etc. that would otherwise dominate the statistics), the EM algorithm (with variational approximate inference) was used to find the Dirichlet and conditional categorical parameters for a 100-topic LDA model. The top words from four resulting categorical distributions $\theta_{i|k}$ are illustrated Fig. 20.15(a). These distributions capture some of the underlying topics in the corpus. An example document from the corpus is presented along with the words coloured by the most probable latent topic they correspond to.

20.6.2 Graph-based representations of data

Mixed membership models are used in a variety of contexts and are distinguished also by the form of data available. Here we focus on analysing a representation of the interactions amongst a collection of objects; in particular, the data has been processed such that all the information of interest is characterised by an interaction matrix. For graph-based representations of data, two objects are similar if they are neighbours on a graph representing the data objects. In the field of social-networks, for example, each individual is represented as a node in a graph, with a link between two nodes if the individuals are friends. Given a graph one might wish to identify communities of closely linked friends. Interpreted as a social network, in Fig. 20.16(a), individual 3 is a member of his work group $(1, 2, 3)$ and also the poker group $(3, 4, 5)$. These two groups of individuals are otherwise disjoint. Discovering such groupings contrasts with *graph partitioning* in which each node is assigned to only one of a set of subgraphs, Fig. 20.16(b), for which a typical criterion is that each subgraph should be roughly of the same size and that there are few connections between the subgraphs [169].

Another example is that nodes in the graph represent products and a link between nodes i and j indicates that customers who buy product i frequently also buy product j. The aim is to decompose the graph into groups, each corresponding to products that are commonly co-bought by customers

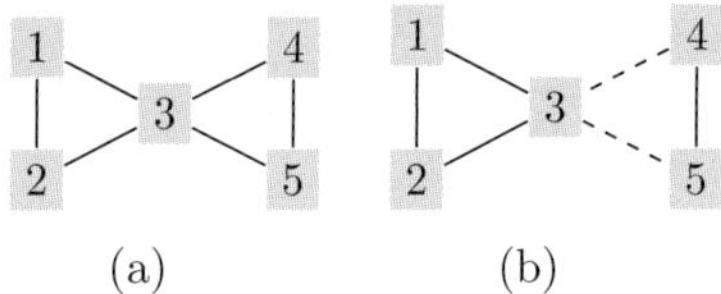

Figure 20.16 **(a)** The social network of a set of five individuals, represented as an undirected graph. Here individual 3 belongs to the group (1, 2, 3) and also (3, 4, 5). **(b)** By contrast, in graph partitioning, one breaks the graph into roughly equally sized disjoint partitions such that each node is a member of only a single partition, with a minimal number of edges between partitions.

[128]. A growing area of application of graph-based representations is in bioinformatics in which nodes represent genes, and a link between them representing that the two genes have similar activity profiles. The task is then to identify groups of similarly behaving genes [5].

20.6.3 Dyadic data

Consider two kinds of objects, for example, films and customers. Each film is indexed by $f = 1, \ldots, F$ and each user by $u = 1, \ldots, U$. The interaction of user u with film f can be described by the element of a matrix M_{uf} representing the rating a user gives to a film. A dyadic dataset consists of such a matrix and the aim is to decompose this matrix to explain the ratings by finding types of films and types of user.

Another example is to consider a collection of documents, summarised by an interaction matrix in which M_{wd} is 1 if word w appears in document d and zero otherwise. This matrix can be represented as a bipartite graph, as in Fig. 20.17(a). The upper nodes represent documents, and the lower nodes words, with a link between them if that word occurs in that document. One then seeks assignments of documents to groups or latent 'topics' to succinctly explain the link structure of the bipartite graph via a small number of latent nodes, as schematically depicted in Fig. 20.17(b). One may view this as a form of matrix factorisation, as in PLSA Section 15.6.1 [148, 204]

$$M_{wd} \approx \sum_t U_{wt} V_{td}^{\mathsf{T}} \tag{20.6.5}$$

where t indexes the topics and the feature matrices $\mathbf{U}$ and $\mathbf{V}$ control the word-to-topic mapping and the topic-to-document mapping. This differs from latent Dirichlet allocation which has a probabilistic interpretation of first generating a topic and then a word, conditional on the chosen topic. Here the interaction between document-topic matrix $\mathbf{V}$ and word-topic matrix $\mathbf{U}$ is non-probabilistic. In [204], real-valued data is modelled using

$$p(\mathbf{M}|\mathbf{U}, \mathbf{W}, \mathbf{V}) = \mathcal{N}\left(\mathbf{M}|\mathbf{U}\mathbf{W}\mathbf{V}^{\mathsf{T}}, \sigma^2\mathbf{I}\right) \tag{20.6.6}$$

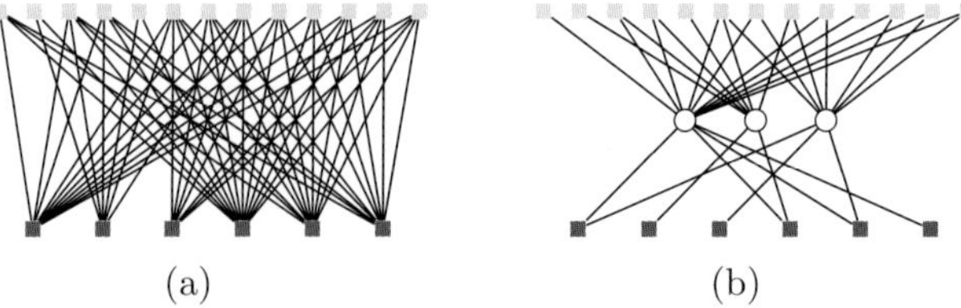

Figure 20.17 Graphical representation of dyadic data. **(a)** There are 6 documents and 13 words. A link represents that a particular word–document pair occurs in the dataset. **(b)** A latent decomposition of (a) using 3 'topics'. A topic corresponds to a collection of words, and each document a collection of topics. The open nodes indicate latent variables.

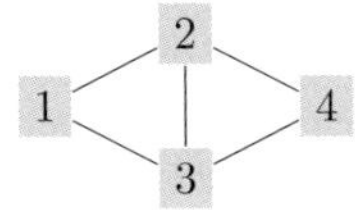

Figure 20.18 The minimal clique cover is (1, 2, 3), (2, 3, 4).

where **U** and **V** are assumed binary and the real-valued **W** is a topic-interaction matrix. In this viewpoint learning then consists of inferring **U**,**W**,**V**, given the dyadic observation matrix **M**. Assuming factorised priors, the posterior over the matrices is

$$p(\mathbf{U}, \mathbf{W}, \mathbf{V}|\mathbf{M}) \propto p(\mathbf{M}|\mathbf{U}, \mathbf{W}, \mathbf{V})p(\mathbf{U})p(\mathbf{W})p(\mathbf{V}). \tag{20.6.7}$$

A convenient choice is a Gaussian prior distribution for **W**, with the feature matrices **U** and **V** sampled from Beta-Bernoulli priors. The resulting posterior distribution is formally computationally intractable, and in [204] this is addressed using a sampling approximation.

20.6.4 Monadic data

In monadic data there is only one type of object and the interaction between the objects is represented by a square interaction matrix. For example one might have a matrix with elements $A_{ij} = 1$ if proteins i and j can bind to each other and 0 otherwise. A depiction of the interaction matrix is given by a graph in which an edge represents an interaction, for example Fig. 20.18. In the following section we discuss a particular mixed membership model and highlight potential applications. The method is based on clique decompositions of graphs and as such we require a short digression into clique-based graph representations.

20.6.5 Cliques and adjacency matrices for monadic binary data

A symmetric adjacency matrix has elements $A_{ij} \in \{0, 1\}$, with a 1 indicating a link between nodes i and j. For the graph in Fig. 20.18, the adjacency matrix is

$$\mathbf{A} = \begin{pmatrix} 1 & 1 & 1 & 0 \\ 1 & 1 & 1 & 1 \\ 1 & 1 & 1 & 1 \\ 0 & 1 & 1 & 1 \end{pmatrix} \tag{20.6.8}$$

where we include self-connections on the diagonal. Given **A**, our aim is to find a 'simpler' description that reveals the underlying cluster structure, such as $(1, 2, 3)$ and $(2, 3, 4)$ in Fig. 20.18. Given the undirected graph in Fig. 20.18, the incidence matrix $\mathbf{F}_{inc}$ is an alternative description of the adjacency structure [86]. Given the V nodes in the graph, we construct $\mathbf{F}_{inc}$ as follows: For each link $i \sim j$ in the graph, form a column of the matrix $\mathbf{F}_{inc}$ with zero entries except for a 1 in the ith and jth row. The column ordering is arbitrary. For example, for the graph in Fig. 20.18 an incidence matrix is

$$\mathbf{F}_{inc} = \begin{pmatrix} 1 & 1 & 0 & 0 & 0 \\ 1 & 0 & 1 & 1 & 0 \\ 0 & 1 & 1 & 0 & 1 \\ 0 & 0 & 0 & 1 & 1 \end{pmatrix}. \tag{20.6.9}$$

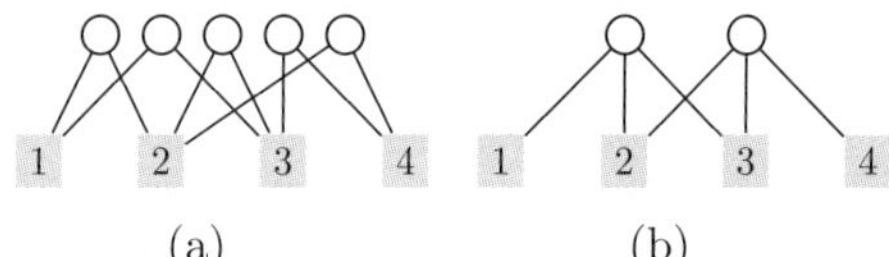

Figure 20.19 Bipartite representations of the decompositions of Fig. 20.18. Shaded nodes represent observed variables, and open nodes latent variables. **(a)** Incidence matrix representation. **(b)** Minimal clique decomposition.

The incidence matrix has the property that the adjacency structure of the original graph is given by the outer product of the incidence matrix with itself. The diagonal entries contain the degree (number of links) of each node. For our example, this gives

$$\mathbf{F}_{inc}\mathbf{F}_{inc}^{\mathsf{T}} = \begin{pmatrix} 2 & 1 & 1 & 0 \\ 1 & 3 & 1 & 1 \\ 1 & 1 & 3 & 1 \\ 0 & 1 & 1 & 2 \end{pmatrix} \tag{20.6.10}$$

so that

$$\mathbf{A} = H\left(\mathbf{F}_{inc}\mathbf{F}_{inc}^{\mathsf{T}}\right). \tag{20.6.11}$$

Here $H(\cdot)$ is the element-wise Heaviside step function, $[H(\mathbf{M})]_{ij} = 1$ if $M_{ij} > 0$ and is 0 otherwise. A useful viewpoint of the incidence matrix is that it identifies 2-cliques in the graph (here we are using the term 'clique' in the non-maximal sense). There are five 2-cliques in Fig. 20.18, and each column of $\mathbf{F}_{inc}$ specifies which elements are in each 2-clique. Graphically we can depict this incidence decomposition as a bipartite graph, as in Fig. 20.19(a) where the open nodes represent the five 2-cliques. The incidence matrix can be generalised to describe larger cliques. Consider the following matrix as a decomposition for Fig. 20.18, and its outer-product:

$$\mathbf{F} = \begin{pmatrix} 1 & 0 \\ 1 & 1 \\ 1 & 1 \\ 0 & 1 \end{pmatrix}, \qquad \mathbf{F}\mathbf{F}^{\mathsf{T}} = \begin{pmatrix} 1 & 1 & 1 & 0 \\ 1 & 2 & 2 & 1 \\ 1 & 2 & 2 & 1 \\ 0 & 1 & 1 & 1 \end{pmatrix}. \tag{20.6.12}$$

The interpretation is that $\mathbf{F}$ represents a decomposition into two 3-cliques. As in the incidence matrix, each column represents a clique, and the rows containing a '1' express which elements are in the clique defined by that column. This decomposition can be represented as the bipartite graph of Fig. 20.19(b). For the graph of Fig. 20.18, both $\mathbf{F}_{inc}$ and $\mathbf{F}$ satisfy

$$\mathbf{A} = H\left(\mathbf{F}\mathbf{F}^{\mathsf{T}}\right) = H\left(\mathbf{F}_{inc}\mathbf{F}_{inc}^{\mathsf{T}}\right). \tag{20.6.13}$$

One can view Equation (20.6.13) as a form of matrix factorisation of binary matrix factorisation of the binary square (symmetric) matrix $\mathbf{A}$ into non-square binary matrices. For our clustering purposes, the decomposition using $\mathbf{F}$ is to be preferred to the incidence decomposition since $\mathbf{F}$ decomposes the graph into a smaller number of larger cliques. A formal specification of the problem of finding a minimum number of maximal fully connected subsets is the computationally hard problem `MIN CLIQUE COVER` [113, 267].

Definition 20.1 Clique matrix Given an adjacency matrix $[A]_{ij}, i, j = 1, \ldots, V$ $(A_{ii} = 1)$, a clique matrix $\mathbf{F}$ has elements $\mathbf{F}_{ic} \in \{0, 1\}, i = 1, \ldots, V, c = 1, \ldots, C$ such that $\mathbf{A} = H(\mathbf{F}\mathbf{F}^{\mathsf{T}})$.

Diagonal elements $\left[\mathbf{F}\mathbf{F}^{\mathsf{T}}\right]_{ii}$ express the number of cliques/columns that node i occurs in. Off-diagonal elements $\left[\mathbf{F}\mathbf{F}^{\mathsf{T}}\right]_{ij}$ contain the number of cliques/columns that nodes i and j jointly inhabit [18].

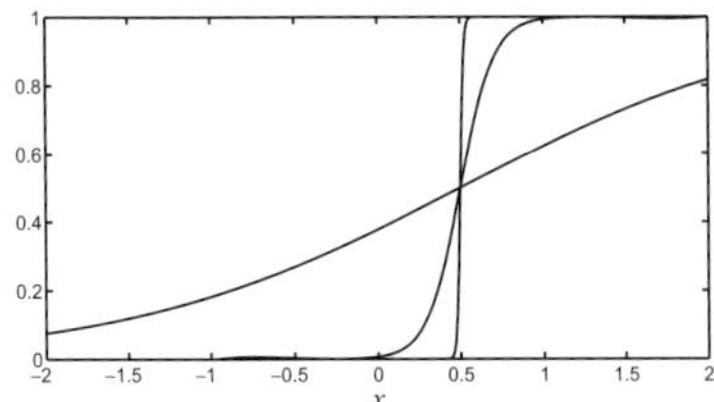

Figure 20.20 The function $\sigma(x) \equiv \left(1 + e^{\beta(0.5-x)}\right)^{-1}$ for $\beta = 1, 10, 100$. As β increases, this sigmoid function tends to a step function.

Whilst finding a clique matrix $\mathbf{F}$ is easy (use the incidence matrix for example), finding a clique matrix with the minimal number of columns, i.e. solving `MIN CLIQUE COVER`, is NP-Hard [113, 9]. In [130] the cliques are required to be maximal although in our definition the cliques may be non-maximal.

A generative model of adjacency matrices

Given an adjacency matrix $\mathbf{A}$ and a prior on clique matrices $\mathbf{F}$, our interest is the posterior

$$p(\mathbf{F}|\mathbf{A}) \propto p(\mathbf{A}|\mathbf{F})p(\mathbf{F}). \tag{20.6.14}$$

We first concentrate on the generative term $p(\mathbf{A}|\mathbf{F})$. To find 'well-connected' clusters, we relax the constraint that the decomposition is in the form of perfect cliques in the original graph and view the absence of links as statistical fluctuations away from a perfect clique. Given a $V \times C$ matrix $\mathbf{F}$, we desire that the higher the overlap between rows[2] $\mathbf{f}_i$ and $\mathbf{f}_j$ is, the greater the probability of a link between i and j. This may be achieved using, for example,

$$p(A_{ij} = 1|\mathbf{F}) = \sigma\left(\mathbf{f}_i\mathbf{f}_j^{\mathsf{T}}\right) \tag{20.6.15}$$

with

$$\sigma(x) \equiv \left(1 + e^{\beta(0.5-x)}\right)^{-1} \tag{20.6.16}$$

where β controls the steepness of the function, see Fig. 20.20. The 0.5 shift in Equation (20.6.16) ensures that σ approximates the step-function since the argument of σ is an integer. Under Equation (20.6.15), if $\mathbf{f}_i$ and $\mathbf{f}_j$ have at least one '1' in the same position, $\mathbf{f}_i\mathbf{f}_j^{\mathsf{T}} - 0.5 > 0$ and $p(A_{ij} = 1|\mathbf{F})$ is high. Absent links contribute $p(A_{ij} = 0|\mathbf{F}) = 1 - p(A_{ij} = 1|\mathbf{F})$. The parameter β controls how strictly $\sigma(\mathbf{F}\mathbf{F}^{\mathsf{T}})$ matches $\mathbf{A}$; for large β, very little flexibility is allowed and only cliques will be identified. For small β, subsets that would be cliques if it were not for a small number of missing links, are clustered together. The setting of β is user and problem dependent.

Assuming each element of the adjacency matrix is sampled independently from the generating process, the joint probability of observing $\mathbf{A}$ is (neglecting its diagonal elements),

$$p(\mathbf{A}|\mathbf{F}) = \prod_{i,j}\left[\sigma\left(\mathbf{f}_i\mathbf{f}_j^{\mathsf{T}}\right)\right]^{A_{ij}}\left[1 - \sigma\left(\mathbf{f}_i\mathbf{f}_j^{\mathsf{T}}\right)\right]^{1-A_{ij}}. \tag{20.6.17}$$

The ultimate quantity of interest is the posterior distribution of clique structure, Equation (20.6.14), for which we now specify a prior $p(\mathbf{F})$ over clique matrices.

[2] We use lower indices $\mathbf{f}_i$ to denote the ith row of $\mathbf{F}$.

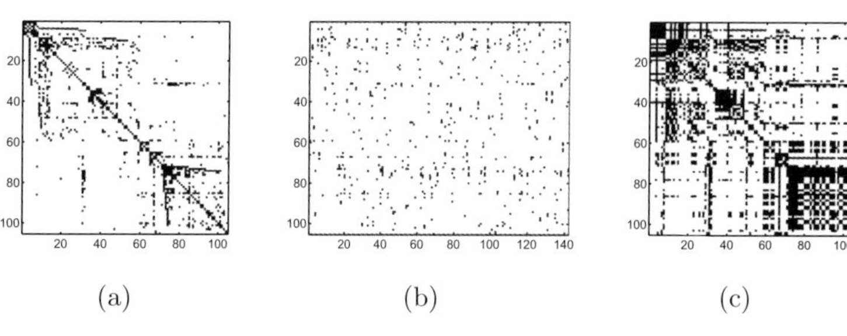

Figure 20.21 (**a**) Adjacency matrix of 105 political books (black = 1). (**b**) Clique matrix: 521 non-zero entries. (**c**) Adjacency reconstruction using an approximate clique matrix with 10 cliques – see also Fig. 20.22 and `demoCliqueDecomp.m`.

Clique matrix prior $p(\mathbf{F})$

Since we are interested in clustering, ideally we want to place as many nodes in the graph as possible in a cluster. This means that we wish to bias the contributions to the adjacency matrix $\mathbf{A}$ to occur from a small number of columns of $\mathbf{F}$. To achieve this we first reparameterise $\mathbf{F}$ as

$$\mathbf{F} = \left(\alpha_1 \mathbf{f}^1, \ldots, \alpha_{C_{max}} \mathbf{f}^{C_{max}}\right) \tag{20.6.18}$$

where $\alpha_c \in \{0, 1\}$ play the role of indicators and $\mathbf{f}^c$ is column c of $\mathbf{F}$; C_{max} is an assumed maximal number of clusters. Ideally, we would like to find an $\mathbf{F}$ with a low number of indicators $\alpha_1, \ldots, \alpha_{C_{max}}$ in state 1. To achieve this we define a prior distribution on the binary hypercube $\boldsymbol{\alpha} = (\alpha_1, \ldots, \alpha_{C_{max}})$,

$$p(\boldsymbol{\alpha}|\nu) = \prod_c \nu^{\alpha_c} (1-\nu)^{1-\alpha_c}. \tag{20.6.19}$$

To encourage a small number of the α_c's to be 1, we use a Beta prior $p(\nu)$ with suitable parameters to ensure that ν is less than 0.5. This gives rise to a Beta-Bernoulli distribution

$$p(\boldsymbol{\alpha}) = \int_\nu p(\alpha|\nu)p(\nu) = \frac{B(a+N, b+C_{max}-N)}{B(a,b)} \tag{20.6.20}$$

where $B(a, b)$ is the Beta function and $N = \sum_{c=1}^{C_{max}} \alpha_c$ is the number of indicators in state 1. To encourage that only a small number of components should be active, we set $a = 1, b = 3$. The distribution (20.6.20) is on the vertices of the binary hypercube $\{0, 1\}^{C_{max}}$ with a bias towards vertices close to the origin $(0, \ldots, 0)$. Through Equation (20.6.18), the prior on $\boldsymbol{\alpha}$ induces a prior on $\mathbf{F}$. The resulting distribution $p(\mathbf{F}, \boldsymbol{\alpha}|\mathbf{A}) \propto p(\mathbf{F}|\boldsymbol{\alpha})p(\boldsymbol{\alpha})$ is formally intractable and in [18] this is addressed using a variational technique.

Clique matrices also play a natural role in the parameterisation of positive definite matrices under the constraint of specified zeros in the matrix, see Exercise 20.7 [18].

Example 20.6 Political books clustering

The data consists of 105 books on US politics sold by the online bookseller Amazon. The adjacency matrix with element $A_{ij} = 1$ Fig. 20.21(a), represents frequent co-purchasing of books i and j (from Valdis Krebs). Additionally, books are labelled 'liberal', 'neutral', or 'conservative' according to the judgement of a politically astute reader. The interest is to assign books to clusters, using $\mathbf{A}$ alone, and then see if these clusters correspond in some way to the ascribed political leanings of each book. Note that the information here is minimal – all that is known to the clustering algorithm is

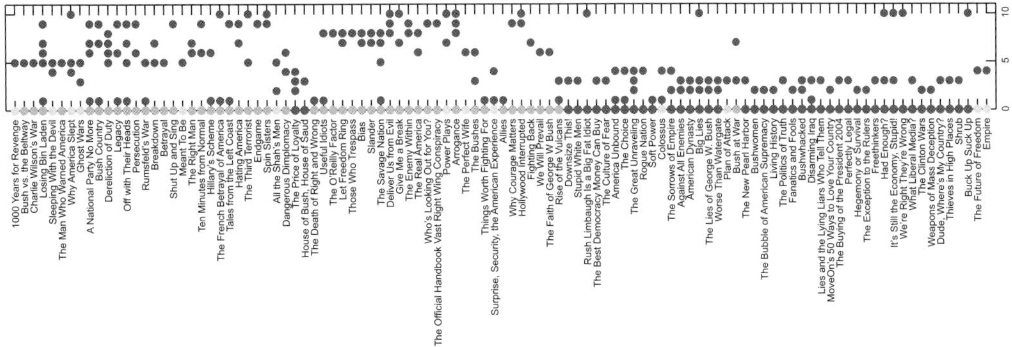

Figure 20.22 Political books. 105 $\times$ 10 dimensional clique matrix broken into three groups by a politically astute reader. A black square indicates $q(\mathbf{f}_{ic}) > 0.5$. Liberal books (red), conservative books (green), neutral books (yellow). By inspection, cliques 5,6,7,8,9 largely correspond to 'conservative' books. See plate section for colour version.

which books were co-bought (matrix $\mathbf{A}$); no other information on the content or title of the books are exploited by the algorithm. With an initial $C_{max} = 200$ cliques, Beta parameters $a = 1, b = 3$ and steepness $\beta = 10$, the most probable posterior marginal solution contains 142 cliques Fig. 20.21(b), giving a perfect reconstruction of the adjacency $\mathbf{A}$. For comparison, the incidence matrix has 441 2-cliques. However, this clique matrix is too large to provide a compact interpretation of the data – indeed there are more clusters than books. To cluster the data more aggressively, we fix $C_{max} = 10$ and re-run the algorithm. This results only in an approximate clique decomposition, $\mathbf{A} \approx H(\mathbf{F}\mathbf{F}^{\mathsf{T}})$, as plotted in Fig. 20.21(c). The resulting 105 $\times$ 10 approximate clique matrix is plotted in Fig. 20.22 and demonstrates how individual books are present in more than one cluster. Interestingly, the clusters found only on the basis of the adjacency matrix have some correspondence with the ascribed political leanings of each book; cliques 5, 6, 7, 8, 9 correspond to largely 'conservative' books. Most books belong to more than a single clique/cluster, suggesting that they are not single topic books, consistent with the assumption of a mixed membership model.

20.7 Summary

- Mixture models are discrete latent variable models and can be trained using maximum likelihood.
- A classical approach to training is to use the EM algorithm, though gradient-based approaches are also possible.
- Standard mixture models assume that a priori each object (datapoint) can be a member of only a single cluster.
- In mixed membership models, an object may a priori belong to more than a single cluster. Models such as latent Dirichlet allocation have interesting application for example to text modelling including the automatic discovery of latent topics.
- Mixed membership models may also be considered for monadic or dyadic data.

The literature on mixture modelling is extensive, and a good overview and entrance to the literature is contained in [203].

20.8 Code

`MIXprodBern.m`: EM training of a mixture of product Bernoulli distributions
`demoMixBernoulli.m`: Demo of a mixture of product Bernoulli distributions

`GMMem.m`: EM training of a mixture of Gaussians
`GMMloglik.m`: GMM log likelihood
`demoGMMem.m`: Demo of an EM for mixture of Gaussians
`demoGMMclass.m`: Demo GMM for classification

`Kmeans.m`: K-means
`demoKmeans.m`: Demo of K-means

`demoPolya.m`: Demo of the number of active clusters from a Polya distribution
`dirrnd.m`: Dirichlet random distribution generator

`cliquedecomp.m`: Clique matrix decomposition
`cliquedecomp.c`: Clique matrix decomposition (C-code)
`DemoCliqueDecomp.m`: Demo clique matrix decomposition

20.9 Exercises

20.1 Consider a mixture of factorised models for vector observations $\mathbf{v}$

$$p(\mathbf{v}) = \sum_h p(h) \prod_i p(v_i|h). \tag{20.9.1}$$

For assumed i.i.d. data $\mathbf{v}^n, n = 1, \ldots, N$, some observation components may be missing so that, for example the third component of the fifth datapoint, v_3^5 is unknown. Show that maximum likelihood training on the observed data corresponds to ignoring components v_i^n that are missing.

20.2 Derive the optimal EM update for fitting a mixture of Gaussians under the constraint that the covariances are diagonal.

20.3 Consider a mixture of K isotropic Gaussians, each with the same covariance, $\mathbf{S}_i = \sigma^2\mathbf{I}$. In the limit $\sigma^2 \to 0$ show that the EM algorithm tends to the K-means clustering algorithm.

20.4 Consider the term

$$\sum_{n=1}^{N} \langle \log p(h) \rangle_{p^{old}(h|v^n)}. \tag{20.9.2}$$

We wish to optimise the above with respect to the distribution $p(h)$. This can be achieved by defining the Lagrangian

$$L = \sum_{n=1}^{N} \langle \log p(h) \rangle_{p^{old}(h|v^n)} + \lambda \left(1 - \sum_h p(h)\right). \tag{20.9.3}$$

By differentiating the Lagrangian with respect to $p(h)$ and using the normalisation constraint $\sum_h p(h) = 1$, show that, optimally

$$p(h) = \frac{1}{N}\sum_{n=1}^{N} p^{old}(h|v^n). \tag{20.9.4}$$

20.5 We showed that fitting an unconstrained mixture of Gaussians using maximum likelihood is problematic since, by placing one of the Gaussians over a datapoint and letting the covariance determinant go to zero, we obtain an infinite likelihood. In contrast, when fitting a single Gaussian $\mathcal{N}(\mathbf{x}|\boldsymbol{\mu}, \boldsymbol{\Sigma})$ to i.i.d. data $\mathbf{x}^1, \mathbf{x}^2, \ldots, \mathbf{x}^N$ show that the maximum likelihood optimum for $\boldsymbol{\Sigma}$ has non-zero determinant, and that the optimal likelihood remains finite.

20.6 Modify `GMMem.m` suitably so that it can deal with the semi-supervised scenario in which the mixture component h of some of the observations v is known.

20.7 You wish to parameterise covariance matrices $\mathbf{S}$ under the constraint that specified elements are zero. The constraints are specified using a matrix $\mathbf{A}$ with elements $A_{ij} = 0$ if $S_{ij} = 0$ and $A_{ij} = 1$ otherwise. Consider a clique matrix $\mathbf{Z}$, for which

$$\mathbf{A} = H(\mathbf{Z}\mathbf{Z}^{\mathsf{T}}) \tag{20.9.5}$$

and matrix

$$\mathbf{S}_* = \mathbf{Z}_*\mathbf{Z}_*^{\mathsf{T}} \tag{20.9.6}$$

with

$$[\mathbf{Z}_*]_{ij} = \begin{cases} 0 & \text{if } Z_{ij} = 0 \\ \theta_{ij} & \text{if } Z_{ij} = 1 \end{cases} \tag{20.9.7}$$

for parameters θ. Show that for any θ, $\mathbf{S}_*$ is positive semidefinite and parameterises covariance matrices under the zero constraints specified by $\mathbf{A}$.

21 Latent linear models

In this chapter we discuss some simple continuous latent variable models. The factor analysis model is a classical statistical model and is essentially a probabilistic version of PCA. Such models can be used to form simple low-dimensional generative models of data. As an example we consider an application to face recognition. By extending the model to use non-Gaussian priors on the latent variables, independent dimensions underlying the data can be discovered, and can give rise to radically different low-dimensional representations of the data than afforded by PCA.

21.1 Factor analysis

In Chapter 15 we discussed principal components analysis which forms lower-dimensional representations of data based on assuming that the data lies close to a linear subspace. Here we describe a related probabilistic model for which extensions to Bayesian methods can be envisaged. Any probabilistic model may also be used as a component of a larger more complex model, such as a mixture model, enabling natural generalisations.

We use $\mathbf{v}$ to describe a real data vector to emphasise that this is a visible (observable) quantity. The dataset is then given by a set of vectors,

$$\mathcal{V} = \left\{\mathbf{v}^1, \ldots, \mathbf{v}^N\right\} \tag{21.1.1}$$

where $\dim(\mathbf{v}) = D$. Our interest is to find a lower-dimensional probabilistic description of this data. If data lies close to a H-dimensional linear subspace we may accurately approximate each datapoint by a low H-dimensional coordinate system. In general, datapoints will not lie exactly on the linear subspace and we model this discrepancy with Gaussian noise. Mathematically, the Factor Analysis (FA) model generates an observation $\mathbf{v}$ according to, see Fig. 21.1,

$$\mathbf{v} = \mathbf{F}\mathbf{h} + \mathbf{c} + \boldsymbol{\epsilon} \tag{21.1.2}$$

where the noise $\boldsymbol{\epsilon}$ is Gaussian distributed, with zero mean and covariance $\boldsymbol{\Psi}$

$$\boldsymbol{\epsilon} \sim \mathcal{N}(\boldsymbol{\epsilon}|\mathbf{0}, \boldsymbol{\Psi}). \tag{21.1.3}$$

The constant bias $\mathbf{c}$ sets the origin of the coordinate system.[1] The $D \times H$ *factor loading* matrix $\mathbf{F}$ plays a similar role as the basis matrix in PCA. Similarly, the hidden coordinates $\mathbf{h}$ plays the role of the components we used in Section 15.2. The difference between PCA and factor analysis is in the choice of $\boldsymbol{\Psi}$:

[1] Depending on the application, it can be sometimes useful to force the origin to be zero to aid the interpretation of the factors; this results in only a minor modification of the framework.

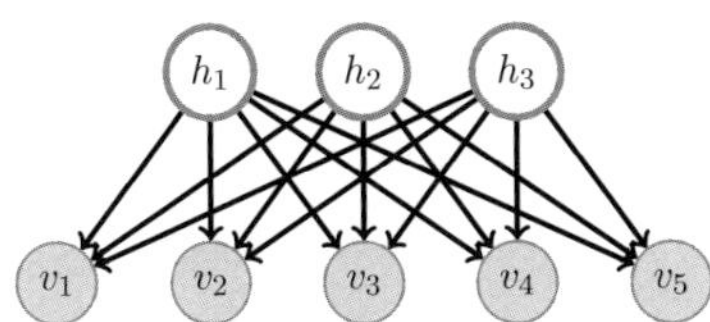

Figure 21.1 Factor analysis. The visible vector variable **v** is related to the vector hidden variable **h** by a linear mapping, with independent additive Gaussian noise on each visible variable. The prior on the hidden variable may be taken to be an isotropic Gaussian, thus being independent across its components.

Probabilistic PCA

$$\boldsymbol{\Psi} = \sigma^2\mathbf{I}. \tag{21.1.4}$$

Factor analysis

$$\boldsymbol{\Psi} = \text{diag}\,(\psi_1, \ldots, \psi_D). \tag{21.1.5}$$

Factor analysis therefore differs from probabilistic PCA in that it has a richer description for the off-subspace noise $\boldsymbol{\Psi}$.

A probabilistic description

From Equation (21.1.2) and Equation (21.1.3), given $\mathbf{h}$, the data is Gaussian distributed with mean $\mathbf{Fh} + \mathbf{c}$ and covariance $\boldsymbol{\Psi}$

$$p\,(\mathbf{v}|\mathbf{h}) = \mathcal{N}\,(\mathbf{v}|\mathbf{Fh} + \mathbf{c}, \boldsymbol{\Psi}) \propto \exp\left(-\frac{1}{2}\,(\mathbf{v} - \mathbf{Fh} - \mathbf{c})^{\mathsf{T}}\,\boldsymbol{\Psi}^{-1}\,(\mathbf{v} - \mathbf{Fh} - \mathbf{c})\right). \tag{21.1.6}$$

To complete the model, we need to specify the hidden distribution $p(\mathbf{h})$. A convenient choice is a Gaussian

$$p\,(\mathbf{h}) = \mathcal{N}\,(\mathbf{h}|\mathbf{0}, \mathbf{I}) \propto \exp\left(-\mathbf{h}^{\mathsf{T}}\mathbf{h}/2\right). \tag{21.1.7}$$

Under this prior the coordinates $\mathbf{h}$ will be preferentially concentrated around values close to $\mathbf{0}$. If we sample a $\mathbf{h}$ vector from $p(\mathbf{h})$ and then draw a value for $\mathbf{v}$ using $p(\mathbf{v}|\mathbf{h})$, the sampled $\mathbf{v}$ vectors would produce a saucer or 'pancake' of points in the $\mathbf{v}$ space, see Fig. 21.2. Using a correlated Gaussian prior $p(\mathbf{h}) = \mathcal{N}\,(\mathbf{h}|\mathbf{0}, \boldsymbol{\Sigma}_H)$ has no effect on the flexibility of the model since $\boldsymbol{\Sigma}_H$ can be

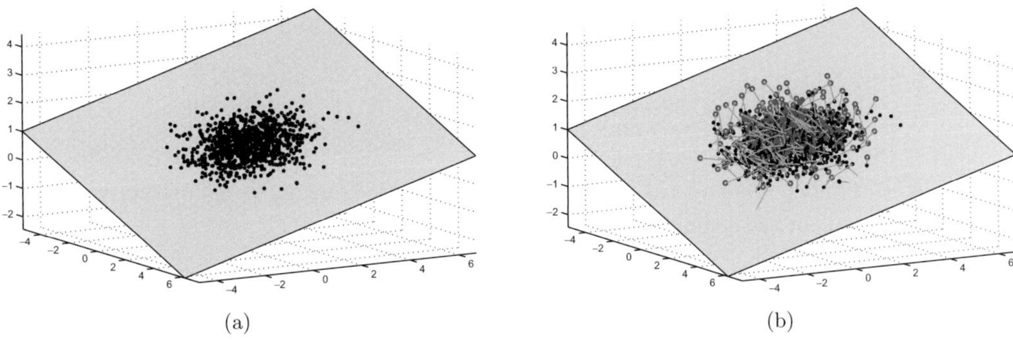

Figure 21.2 Factor analysis: 1000 points generated from the model. (**a**) 1000 latent two-dimensional points $\mathbf{h}^n$ sampled from $\mathcal{N}\,(\mathbf{h}|\mathbf{0}, \mathbf{I})$. These are transformed to a point on the three-dimensional plane by $\mathbf{x}_0^n = \mathbf{c} + \mathbf{Fh}^n$. The covariance of $\mathbf{x}_0$ is degenerate, with covariance matrix $\mathbf{FF}^{\mathsf{T}}$. (**b**) For each point $\mathbf{x}_0^n$ on the plane a random noise vector is drawn from $\mathcal{N}\,(\boldsymbol{\epsilon}|\mathbf{0}, \boldsymbol{\Psi})$ and added to the in-plane vector to form a sample $\mathbf{x}^n$, plotted in grey. The distribution of points forms a 'pancake' in space. Points 'underneath' the plane are not shown.

absorbed into $\mathbf{F}$, Exercise 21.3. Since $\mathbf{v}$ is linearly related to $\mathbf{h}$ through Equation (21.1.2) and both $\boldsymbol{\epsilon}$ and $\mathbf{h}$ are Gaussian, then $\mathbf{v}$ is Gaussian distributed. The mean and covariance can be computed using propagation, Result 8.3:

$$p(\mathbf{v}) = \int p(\mathbf{v}|\mathbf{h})\, p(\mathbf{h})\, d\mathbf{h} = \mathcal{N}\left(\mathbf{v}|\mathbf{c}, \mathbf{F}\mathbf{F}^{\mathsf{T}} + \boldsymbol{\Psi}\right). \tag{21.1.8}$$

What this says is that our model for the data is a Gaussian centred on $\mathbf{c}$ with covariance matrix constrained to be of the form $\mathbf{F}\mathbf{F}^{\mathsf{T}} + \boldsymbol{\Psi}$. The number of free parameters for factor analysis is therefore $D(H+1)$. Compared to an unconstrained covariance on $\mathbf{v}$ which has $D(D+1)/2$ free parameters, by choosing $H \ll D$, we have significantly fewer parameters to estimate in factor analysis than in unconstrained covariance case.

Invariance of the likelihood under factor rotation

Since the matrix $\mathbf{F}$ only appears in the final model $p(\mathbf{v})$ through $\mathbf{F}\mathbf{F}^{\mathsf{T}} + \boldsymbol{\Psi}$, the likelihood is unchanged if we rotate $\mathbf{F}$ using $\mathbf{F}\mathbf{R}$, with $\mathbf{R}\mathbf{R}^{\mathsf{T}} = \mathbf{I}$:

$$\mathbf{F}\mathbf{R}(\mathbf{F}\mathbf{R})^{\mathsf{T}} + \boldsymbol{\Psi} = \mathbf{F}\mathbf{R}\mathbf{R}^{\mathsf{T}}\mathbf{F}^{\mathsf{T}} + \boldsymbol{\Psi} = \mathbf{F}\mathbf{F}^{\mathsf{T}} + \boldsymbol{\Psi}. \tag{21.1.9}$$

The solution space for $\mathbf{F}$ is therefore not unique – we can arbitrarily rotate the matrix $\mathbf{F}$ and produce an equally likely model of the data. Some care is therefore required when interpreting the entries of $\mathbf{F}$. *Varimax* provides a more interpretable $\mathbf{F}$ by using a suitable rotation matrix $\mathbf{R}$. The aim is to produce a rotated $\mathbf{F}$ for which each column has only a small number of large values. Finding a suitable rotation results in a non-linear optimisation problem and needs to be solved numerically. See [199] for details.

21.1.1 Finding the optimal bias

For a set of data $\mathcal{V}$ and using the usual i.i.d. assumption, the log likelihood is

$$\log p(\mathcal{V}|\mathbf{F}, \boldsymbol{\Psi}, \mathbf{c}) = \sum_{n=1}^{N} \log p(\mathbf{v}^n) = -\frac{1}{2}\sum_{n=1}^{N} (\mathbf{v}^n - \mathbf{c})^{\mathsf{T}} \boldsymbol{\Sigma}_D^{-1} (\mathbf{v}^n - \mathbf{c}) - \frac{N}{2}\log\det(2\pi\boldsymbol{\Sigma}_D) \tag{21.1.10}$$

where

$$\boldsymbol{\Sigma}_D \equiv \mathbf{F}\mathbf{F}^{\mathsf{T}} + \boldsymbol{\Psi}. \tag{21.1.11}$$

Differentiating Equation (21.1.10) with respect to $\mathbf{c}$ and equating to zero, we arrive at the maximum likelihood optimal setting that the bias $\mathbf{c}$ is the mean of the data,

$$\mathbf{c} = \frac{1}{N}\sum_{n=1}^{N} \mathbf{v}^n \equiv \bar{\mathbf{v}}. \tag{21.1.12}$$

We will use this setting throughout. With this setting the log likelihood equation (21.1.10) can be written

$$\log p(\mathcal{V}|\mathbf{F}, \boldsymbol{\Psi}) = -\frac{N}{2}\left(\mathrm{trace}\left(\boldsymbol{\Sigma}_D^{-1}\mathbf{S}\right) + \log\det(2\pi\boldsymbol{\Sigma}_D)\right) \tag{21.1.13}$$

where $\mathbf{S}$ is the sample covariance matrix

$$\mathbf{S} = \frac{1}{N}\sum_{n=1}^{N}(\mathbf{v}-\bar{\mathbf{v}})(\mathbf{v}-\bar{\mathbf{v}})^{\mathsf{T}}. \tag{21.1.14}$$

21.2 Factor analysis: maximum likelihood

We now specialise to the assumption that $\boldsymbol{\Psi} = \text{diag}(\psi_1, \ldots, \psi_D)$. We consider two methods for learning the factor loadings $\mathbf{F}$: the 'eigen' approach[2] of Section 21.2.1 and the EM approach, Section 21.2.2. The eigen-approach is common in statistics and software packages, whilst the EM approach is more common in machine learning.

21.2.1 Eigen-approach likelihood optimisation

As we will show, if the noise matrix $\boldsymbol{\Psi}$ is given, we can find the optimal factor matrix $\mathbf{F}$ by solving an eigen-problem. If the $\boldsymbol{\Psi}$ is unknown, from a starting guess for $\boldsymbol{\Psi}$, we can find the optimal $\mathbf{F}$ and use this to reestimate the noise $\boldsymbol{\Psi}$, iterating this two-step process until convergence. This section is necessarily rather technical and can be skipped on first reading.

Optimal F for fixed $\boldsymbol{\Psi}$

To find the maximum likelihood setting of $\mathbf{F}$ we differentiate the log likelihood equation (21.1.13) with respect to $\mathbf{F}$ and equate to zero. This gives

$$\mathbf{0} = \text{trace}\left(\boldsymbol{\Sigma}_D^{-1}(\partial_{\mathbf{F}}\boldsymbol{\Sigma}_D)\boldsymbol{\Sigma}_D^{-1}\mathbf{S}\right) - \text{trace}\left(\boldsymbol{\Sigma}_D^{-1}\partial_{\mathbf{F}}\boldsymbol{\Sigma}_D\right). \tag{21.2.1}$$

Using

$$\partial_{\mathbf{F}}(\boldsymbol{\Sigma}_D) = \partial_{\mathbf{F}}(\mathbf{F}\mathbf{F}^{\mathsf{T}}) = \mathbf{F}(\partial_{\mathbf{F}}\mathbf{F}^{\mathsf{T}}) + (\partial_{\mathbf{F}}\mathbf{F})\mathbf{F}^{\mathsf{T}} \tag{21.2.2}$$

a stationary point is given when

$$\boldsymbol{\Sigma}_D^{-1}\mathbf{F} = \boldsymbol{\Sigma}_D^{-1}\mathbf{S}\boldsymbol{\Sigma}_D^{-1}\mathbf{F}. \tag{21.2.3}$$

The optimal $\mathbf{F}$ therefore satisfies

$$\mathbf{F} = \mathbf{S}\boldsymbol{\Sigma}_D^{-1}\mathbf{F}. \tag{21.2.4}$$

Using the definition of $\boldsymbol{\Sigma}_D$, Equation (21.1.11), one can rewrite $\boldsymbol{\Sigma}_D^{-1}\mathbf{F}$ as (see Exercise 21.4)

$$\boldsymbol{\Sigma}_D^{-1}\mathbf{F} = \boldsymbol{\Psi}^{-1}\mathbf{F}\left(\mathbf{I} + \mathbf{F}^{\mathsf{T}}\boldsymbol{\Psi}^{-1}\mathbf{F}\right)^{-1}. \tag{21.2.5}$$

Plugging this into the zero derivative condition, Equation (21.2.4) can be rearranged to

$$\mathbf{F}\left(\mathbf{I} + \mathbf{F}^{\mathsf{T}}\boldsymbol{\Psi}^{-1}\mathbf{F}\right) = \mathbf{S}\boldsymbol{\Psi}^{-1}\mathbf{F}. \tag{21.2.6}$$

Using the reparameterisations

$$\tilde{\mathbf{F}} \equiv \boldsymbol{\Psi}^{-\frac{1}{2}}\mathbf{F}, \qquad \tilde{\mathbf{S}} = \boldsymbol{\Psi}^{-\frac{1}{2}}\mathbf{S}\boldsymbol{\Psi}^{-\frac{1}{2}}, \tag{21.2.7}$$

[2] The presentation here follows closely that of [323].

Equation (21.2.6) can be written in the 'isotropic' form

$$\tilde{\mathbf{F}}\left(\mathbf{I}+\tilde{\mathbf{F}}^{\mathsf{T}}\tilde{\mathbf{F}}\right)=\tilde{\mathbf{S}}\tilde{\mathbf{F}}. \tag{21.2.8}$$

We assume that the transformed factor matrix $\tilde{\mathbf{F}}$ has a thin SVD decomposition

$$\tilde{\mathbf{F}}=\mathbf{U}_H\mathbf{L}\mathbf{W}^{\mathsf{T}} \tag{21.2.9}$$

where $\dim(\mathbf{U}_H)=D\times H$, $\dim(\mathbf{L})=H\times H$, $\dim(\mathbf{W})=H\times H$ and

$$\mathbf{U}_H^{\mathsf{T}}\mathbf{U}_H=\mathbf{I}_H, \qquad \mathbf{W}^{\mathsf{T}}\mathbf{W}=\mathbf{I}_H \tag{21.2.10}$$

and $\mathbf{L}=\operatorname{diag}(l_1,\ldots,l_H)$ are the singular values of $\tilde{\mathbf{F}}$. Plugging this assumption into Equation (21.2.8) we obtain

$$\mathbf{U}_H\mathbf{L}\mathbf{W}^{\mathsf{T}}\left(\mathbf{I}_H+\mathbf{W}\mathbf{L}^2\mathbf{W}^{\mathsf{T}}\right)=\tilde{\mathbf{S}}\mathbf{U}_H\mathbf{L}\mathbf{W}^{\mathsf{T}} \tag{21.2.11}$$

which gives

$$\mathbf{U}_H\left(\mathbf{I}_H+\mathbf{L}^2\right)=\tilde{\mathbf{S}}\mathbf{U}_H, \qquad \mathbf{L}^2=\operatorname{diag}\left(l_1^2,\ldots,l_H^2\right). \tag{21.2.12}$$

Equation (21.2.12) is then an eigen-equation for $\mathbf{U}_H$. Intuitively, it's clear that we need to find then the eigen-decomposition of $\tilde{\mathbf{S}}$ and then set the columns of $\mathbf{U}_H$ to those eigenvectors corresponding to the largest eigenvalues. This is derived more formally below.

Determining the appropriate eigenvalues

We can relate the form of the solution to the eigen-decomposition of $\tilde{\mathbf{S}}$

$$\tilde{\mathbf{S}}=\mathbf{U}\boldsymbol{\Lambda}\mathbf{U}^{\mathsf{T}}, \qquad \mathbf{U}=[\mathbf{U}_H|\mathbf{U}_r] \tag{21.2.13}$$

where $\mathbf{U}_r$ are arbitrary additional columns chosen to complete $\mathbf{U}_H$ to form an orthogonal $\mathbf{U}$, $\mathbf{U}^{\mathsf{T}}\mathbf{U}=\mathbf{U}\mathbf{U}^{\mathsf{T}}=\mathbf{I}$. Using $\boldsymbol{\Lambda}=\operatorname{diag}(\lambda_1,\ldots,\lambda_D)$, Equation (21.2.12) stipulates $1+l_i^2=\lambda_i$, or $l_i=\sqrt{\lambda_i-1}$, $i=1,\ldots,H$. Given the solution for $\tilde{\mathbf{F}}$, the solution for $\mathbf{F}$ is found from Equation (21.2.7). To determine the optimal λ_i we write the log likelihood in terms of the λ_i as follows. Using the new parameterisation,

$$\boldsymbol{\Sigma}_D=\boldsymbol{\Psi}^{\frac{1}{2}}\left(\tilde{\mathbf{F}}\tilde{\mathbf{F}}^{\mathsf{T}}+\mathbf{I}\right)\boldsymbol{\Psi}^{\frac{1}{2}} \tag{21.2.14}$$

and $\mathbf{S}=\boldsymbol{\Psi}^{\frac{1}{2}}\tilde{\mathbf{S}}\boldsymbol{\Psi}^{\frac{1}{2}}$, we have

$$\operatorname{trace}\left(\boldsymbol{\Sigma}_D^{-1}\mathbf{S}\right)=\operatorname{trace}\left(\left(\tilde{\mathbf{F}}\tilde{\mathbf{F}}^{\mathsf{T}}+\mathbf{I}_D\right)^{-1}\tilde{\mathbf{S}}\right). \tag{21.2.15}$$

The log likelihood equation (21.1.10) in this new parameterisation is

$$-\frac{2}{N}\log p(\mathcal{V}|\mathbf{F},\boldsymbol{\Psi})=\operatorname{trace}\left(\left(\mathbf{I}_D+\tilde{\mathbf{F}}\tilde{\mathbf{F}}^{\mathsf{T}}\right)^{-1}\tilde{\mathbf{S}}\right)+\log\det\left(\mathbf{I}_D+\tilde{\mathbf{F}}\tilde{\mathbf{F}}^{\mathsf{T}}\right)+\log\det\left(2\pi\boldsymbol{\Psi}\right). \tag{21.2.16}$$

Using $\lambda_i=1+l_i^2$, and Equation (21.2.9) we can write

$$\mathbf{I}_D+\tilde{\mathbf{F}}\tilde{\mathbf{F}}^{\mathsf{T}}=\mathbf{I}_D+\mathbf{U}_H\mathbf{L}^2\mathbf{U}_H^{\mathsf{T}}=\mathbf{U}\operatorname{diag}\left(\lambda_1,\ldots,\lambda_H,1,\ldots,1\right)\mathbf{U}^{\mathsf{T}} \tag{21.2.17}$$

so that the inverse of this matrix is given by $\mathbf{U}\operatorname{diag}\left(\lambda_1^{-1},\ldots,\lambda_H^{-1},1,\ldots,1\right)\mathbf{U}^{\mathsf{T}}$ and hence

$$\operatorname{trace}\left(\left(\mathbf{I}_D+\tilde{\mathbf{F}}\tilde{\mathbf{F}}^{\mathsf{T}}\right)^{-1}\tilde{\mathbf{S}}\right)=\sum_i\frac{\lambda_i}{\lambda_i'}, \qquad \lambda_i'=\begin{cases}\lambda_i & i\leq H\\ 1 & i>H.\end{cases} \tag{21.2.18}$$

Similarly

$$\log\det\left(\mathbf{I}_D + \tilde{\mathbf{F}}\tilde{\mathbf{F}}^{\mathsf{T}}\right) = \sum_{i=1}^{H} \log \lambda_i. \tag{21.2.19}$$

Using this we can write the log likelihood as a function of the eigenvalues (for fixed $\boldsymbol{\Psi}$) as

$$-\frac{2}{N}\log p(\mathcal{V}|\mathbf{F}, \boldsymbol{\Psi}) = \sum_{i=1}^{H} \log \lambda_i + H + \sum_{i=H+1}^{D} \lambda_i + \log\det(2\pi\boldsymbol{\Psi}). \tag{21.2.20}$$

To maximise the likelihood we need to minimise the right-hand side of the above. Since $\log \lambda < \lambda$ we should place the largest H eigenvalues in the $\sum_i \log \lambda_i$ term. A solution for fixed $\boldsymbol{\Psi}$ is therefore

$$\mathbf{F} = \boldsymbol{\Psi}^{\frac{1}{2}} \mathbf{U}_H \left(\boldsymbol{\Lambda}_H - \mathbf{I}_H\right)^{\frac{1}{2}} \mathbf{R} \tag{21.2.21}$$

where

$$\boldsymbol{\Lambda}_H \equiv \text{diag}\left(\lambda_1, \ldots, \lambda_H\right) \tag{21.2.22}$$

are the H largest eigenvalues of $\boldsymbol{\Psi}^{-\frac{1}{2}}\mathbf{S}\boldsymbol{\Psi}^{-\frac{1}{2}}$, with $\mathbf{U}_H$ being the matrix of the corresponding eigenvectors. $\mathbf{R}$ is an arbitrary orthogonal matrix.

SVD-based approach

Rather than finding the eigen-decomposition of $\boldsymbol{\Psi}^{-\frac{1}{2}}\mathbf{S}\boldsymbol{\Psi}^{-\frac{1}{2}}$ we can avoid forming the covariance matrix by considering the thin SVD decomposition of

$$\tilde{\mathbf{X}} = \frac{1}{\sqrt{N}} \boldsymbol{\Psi}^{-\frac{1}{2}} \mathbf{X} \tag{21.2.23}$$

where the centred data matrix is

$$\mathbf{X} \equiv \left[\mathbf{v}^1 - \bar{\mathbf{v}}, \ldots, \mathbf{x}^N - \bar{\mathbf{v}}\right]. \tag{21.2.24}$$

Given a thin decomposition

$$\tilde{\mathbf{X}} = \mathbf{U}_H \tilde{\boldsymbol{\Lambda}} \tilde{\mathbf{W}}^{\mathsf{T}} \tag{21.2.25}$$

we obtain the eigenvalues $\lambda_i = \tilde{\Lambda}_{ii}^2$. When the matrix $\mathbf{X}$ is too large to store in memory, online SVD methods are available [52].

Finding the optimal $\boldsymbol{\Psi}$

The zero derivative of the log likelihood equation (21.1.13) with respect to $\boldsymbol{\Psi}$ occurs when

$$\boldsymbol{\Psi} = \text{diag}\left(\mathbf{S} - \mathbf{F}\mathbf{F}^{\mathsf{T}}\right) \tag{21.2.26}$$

where $\mathbf{F}$ is given by Equation (21.2.21). There is no closed form solution to Equations (21.2.26), (21.2.21). A simple iterative scheme is to first guess values for the diagonal entries of $\boldsymbol{\Psi}$ and then find the optimal $\mathbf{F}$ using Equation (21.2.21). Subsequently $\boldsymbol{\Psi}$ is updated using

$$\boldsymbol{\Psi}^{new} = \text{diag}\left(\mathbf{S} - \mathbf{F}\mathbf{F}^{\mathsf{T}}\right). \tag{21.2.27}$$

We update $\mathbf{F}$ using Equation (21.2.21) and $\boldsymbol{\Psi}$ using Equation (21.2.27) until convergence, see Algorithm 21.1.

Algorithm 21.1 Factor analysis training using SVD for N D-dimensional datapoints $\mathbf{v}^1, \dots, \mathbf{v}^N$. H is the latent number of factors required.

```
Initialise the diagonal noise Ψ
Find the mean v̄ of the data v^1, ..., v^N
Find the variance σ_i^2 for each component i of the data v_i^1, ..., v_i^N
Compute the centred matrix X = [v^1 − v̄, ..., x^N − v̄]
while Likelihood not converged or termination criterion not reached do
    Form the scaled data matrix X̃ = Ψ^{-1/2} X/√N
    Perform SVD for X̃ = U Λ̃ W̃^T and set Λ = Λ̃^2
    Set U_H to the first H columns of U and set Λ_H to contain the first H diagonal entries of Λ.
    F = Ψ^{1/2} U_H (Λ_H − I_H)^{1/2}                                          ▷ factor update
    L = −(N/2) { Σ_{i=1}^{H} log λ_i + H + Σ_{i=H+1}^{D} λ_i + log det(2πΨ) }   ▷ log likelihood
    Ψ = diag(σ^2) − diag(FF^T)                                                ▷ noise update
end while
```

Alternative schemes for updating the noise matrix $\mathbf{\Psi}$ can improve convergence considerably. For example updating only a single component of $\mathbf{\Psi}$ with the rest fixed can be achieved using a closed form expression [323].

21.2.2 Expectation maximisation

An alternative way way to train factor analysis that is popular in machine learning is to use EM. We assume that the bias $\mathbf{c}$ has been optimally set to the data mean $\bar{\mathbf{v}}$.

M-step

As usual, we need to consider the energy which, neglecting constants, is

$$E(\mathbf{F}, \mathbf{\Psi}) = -\sum_{n=1}^{N} \left\langle \frac{1}{2} (\mathbf{d}^n - \mathbf{F}\mathbf{h})^{\mathsf{T}} \mathbf{\Psi}^{-1} (\mathbf{d}^n - \mathbf{F}\mathbf{h}) \right\rangle_{q(\mathbf{h}|\mathbf{v}^n)} - \frac{N}{2} \log\det(\mathbf{\Psi}) \tag{21.2.28}$$

where $\mathbf{d}^n \equiv \mathbf{v}^n - \bar{\mathbf{v}}$. The optimal variational distribution $q(\mathbf{h}|\mathbf{v}^n)$ is determined by the E-step below. Maximising $E(\mathbf{F}, \mathbf{\Psi})$ with respect to $\mathbf{F}$ gives

$$\mathbf{F} = \mathbf{A}\mathbf{H}^{-1} \tag{21.2.29}$$

where

$$\mathbf{A} \equiv \frac{1}{N} \sum_n \mathbf{d}^n \langle \mathbf{h} \rangle^{\mathsf{T}}_{q(\mathbf{h}|\mathbf{v}^n)}, \qquad \mathbf{H} \equiv \frac{1}{N} \sum_n \langle \mathbf{h}\mathbf{h}^{\mathsf{T}} \rangle_{q(\mathbf{h}|\mathbf{v}^n)}. \tag{21.2.30}$$

Finally

$$\mathbf{\Psi} = \frac{1}{N} \sum_n \operatorname{diag}\left(\left\langle (\mathbf{d}^n - \mathbf{F}\mathbf{h})(\mathbf{d}^n - \mathbf{F}\mathbf{h})^{\mathsf{T}} \right\rangle_{q(\mathbf{h}|\mathbf{v}^n)} \right) = \operatorname{diag}\left(\frac{1}{N} \sum_n \mathbf{d}^n (\mathbf{d}^n)^{\mathsf{T}} - 2\mathbf{F}\mathbf{A}^{\mathsf{T}} + \mathbf{F}\mathbf{H}\mathbf{F}^{\mathsf{T}} \right). \tag{21.2.31}$$

Note that the new $\mathbf{F}$ is used in the above update for the covariance.

E-step

The above updates depend on the statistics $\langle \mathbf{h} \rangle_{q(\mathbf{h}|\mathbf{v}^n)}$ and $\langle \mathbf{h}\mathbf{h}^{\mathsf{T}} \rangle_{q(\mathbf{h}|\mathbf{v}^n)}$. Using the EM optimal choice for the E-step we have

$$q(\mathbf{h}|\mathbf{v}^n) \propto p(\mathbf{v}^n|\mathbf{h})p(\mathbf{h}) = \mathcal{N}(\mathbf{h}|\mathbf{m}^n, \mathbf{\Sigma}) \tag{21.2.32}$$

with

$$\mathbf{m}^n = \langle \mathbf{h} \rangle_{q(\mathbf{h}|\mathbf{v}^n)} = \left(\mathbf{I} + \mathbf{F}^{\mathsf{T}}\mathbf{\Psi}^{-1}\mathbf{F}\right)^{-1}\mathbf{F}^{\mathsf{T}}\mathbf{\Psi}^{-1}\mathbf{d}^n, \qquad \mathbf{\Sigma} = \left(\mathbf{I} + \mathbf{F}^{\mathsf{T}}\mathbf{\Psi}^{-1}\mathbf{F}\right)^{-1}. \tag{21.2.33}$$

Using these results we can express the statistics in Equation (21.2.30) as

$$\mathbf{H} = \mathbf{\Sigma} + \frac{1}{N}\sum_n \mathbf{m}^n(\mathbf{m}^n)^{\mathsf{T}}. \tag{21.2.34}$$

Equations (21.2.29), (21.2.31), (21.2.33) are iterated till convergence. As for any EM algorithm, the likelihood Equation (21.1.10) (under the diagonal constraint on $\mathbf{\Psi}$) increases at each iteration. Convergence using this EM technique can be slower than that of the eigen-approach of Section 21.2.1. Provided however that a reasonable initialisation is used, the performance of the two training algorithms can be similar. A useful initialisation is to use PCA and then set $\mathbf{F}$ to the principal directions.

Mixtures of FA

An advantage of probabilistic models is that they may be used as components in more complex models, such as mixtures of FA [293]. Training can then be achieved using EM or gradient-based approaches. Bayesian extensions are clearly of interest; whilst formally intractable they can be addressed using approximate methods, for example [105, 192, 119].

21.3 Interlude: modelling faces

Factor analysis has widespread application in statistics and machine learning. As an inventive application of FA, highlighting the probabilistic nature of the model, we describe a face modelling technique that has as its heart a latent linear model [245]. Consider a gallery of face images $\mathcal{X} = \{\mathbf{x}_{ij}, i = 1, \ldots, I; j = 1, \ldots, J\}$ so that the vector $\mathbf{x}_{ij}$ represents the jth image of the ith person. As a latent linear model of faces we consider

$$\mathbf{x}_{ij} = \boldsymbol{\mu} + \mathbf{F}\mathbf{h}_i + \mathbf{G}\mathbf{w}_{ij} + \boldsymbol{\epsilon}_{ij}. \tag{21.3.1}$$

Here $\mathbf{F}$ ($\dim \mathbf{F} = D \times F$) is used to model variability between people, and $\mathbf{G}$ ($\dim \mathbf{G} = D \times G$) models variability related to pose, illumination etc. within the different images of each person. The contribution

$$\mathbf{f}_i \equiv \boldsymbol{\mu} + \mathbf{F}\mathbf{h}_i \tag{21.3.2}$$

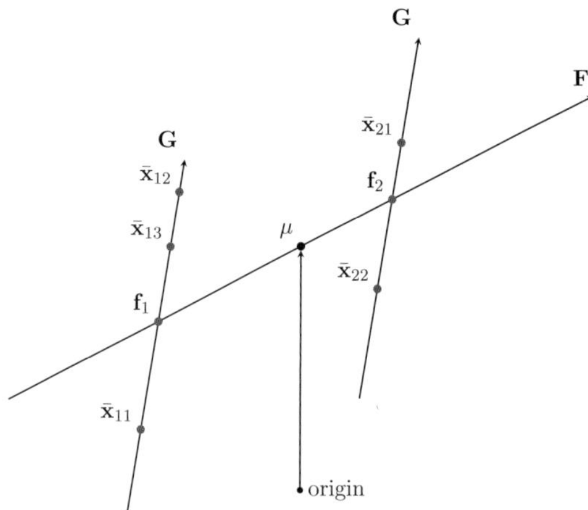

Figure 21.3 Latent identity model. The mean $\boldsymbol{\mu}$ represents the mean of the faces. The subspace **F** represents the directions of variation of different faces so that $\mathbf{f}_1 = \boldsymbol{\mu} + \mathbf{F}\mathbf{h}_1$ is a mean face for individual 1, and similarly for $\mathbf{f}_2 = \boldsymbol{\mu} + \mathbf{F}\mathbf{h}_2$. The subspace **G** denotes the directions of variability for any individual face, caused by pose, lighting etc. This variability is assumed the same for each person. A particular mean face is then given by the mean face of the person plus pose/illumination variation, for example $\bar{\mathbf{x}}_{12} = \mathbf{f}_1 + \mathbf{G}\mathbf{w}_{12}$. A sample face is then given by a mean face $\bar{\mathbf{x}}_{ij}$ plus Gaussian noise from $(\mathcal{N}\,\boldsymbol{\epsilon}_{ij}\,|\mathbf{0}, \boldsymbol{\Sigma})$.

accounts for variability between different people, being constant for individual i. For fixed i, the contribution

$$\mathbf{G}\mathbf{w}_{ij} + \boldsymbol{\epsilon}_{ij}, \qquad \text{with } \boldsymbol{\epsilon}_{ij} \sim \mathcal{N}\left(\boldsymbol{\epsilon}_{ij}\,|\mathbf{0}, \boldsymbol{\Sigma}\right) \tag{21.3.3}$$

accounts for the variability over the images of person i, explaining why two images of the same person do not look identical. See Fig. 21.3 for a graphical representation. As a probabilistic linear latent variable model, we have for an image $\mathbf{x}_{ij}$:

$$p(\mathbf{x}_{ij}|\mathbf{h}_i, \mathbf{w}_{ij}, \theta) = \mathcal{N}\left(\mathbf{x}_{ij}\,|\boldsymbol{\mu} + \mathbf{F}\mathbf{h}_i + \mathbf{G}\mathbf{w}_{ij}, \boldsymbol{\Sigma}\right) \tag{21.3.4}$$

$$p(\mathbf{h}_i) = \mathcal{N}\left(\mathbf{h}_i\,|\mathbf{0}, \mathbf{I}\right), \qquad p(\mathbf{w}_{ij}) = \mathcal{N}\left(\mathbf{w}_{ij}\,|\mathbf{0}, \mathbf{I}\right). \tag{21.3.5}$$

The parameters are $\theta = \{\mathbf{F}, \mathbf{G}, \boldsymbol{\mu}, \boldsymbol{\Sigma}\}$. For the collection of images, assuming i.i.d. data,

$$p(\mathcal{X}, \mathbf{w}, \mathbf{h}|\theta) = \prod_{i=1}^{I}\left\{\prod_{j=1}^{J} p(\mathbf{x}_{ij}|\mathbf{h}_i, \mathbf{w}_{ij}, \theta)p(\mathbf{w}_{ij})\right\} p(\mathbf{h}_i) \tag{21.3.6}$$

for which the graphical model is depicted in Fig. 21.4. The task of learning is then to maximise the likelihood

$$p(\mathcal{X}|\theta) = \int_{\mathbf{w},\mathbf{h}} p(\mathcal{X}, \mathbf{w}, \mathbf{h}|\theta). \tag{21.3.7}$$

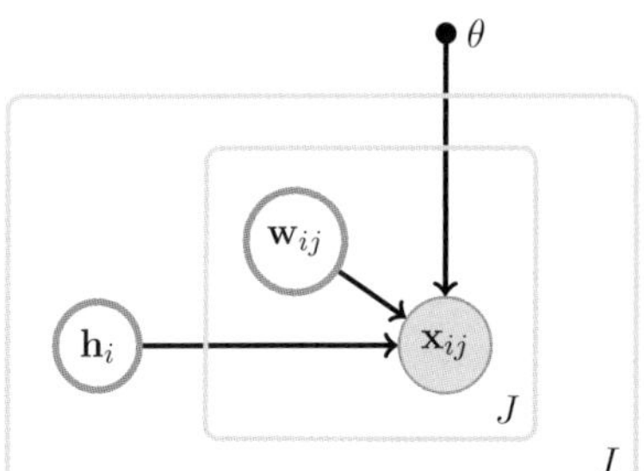

Figure 21.4 The jth image of the ith person, $\mathbf{x}_{ij}$, is modelled using a linear latent model with parameters θ.

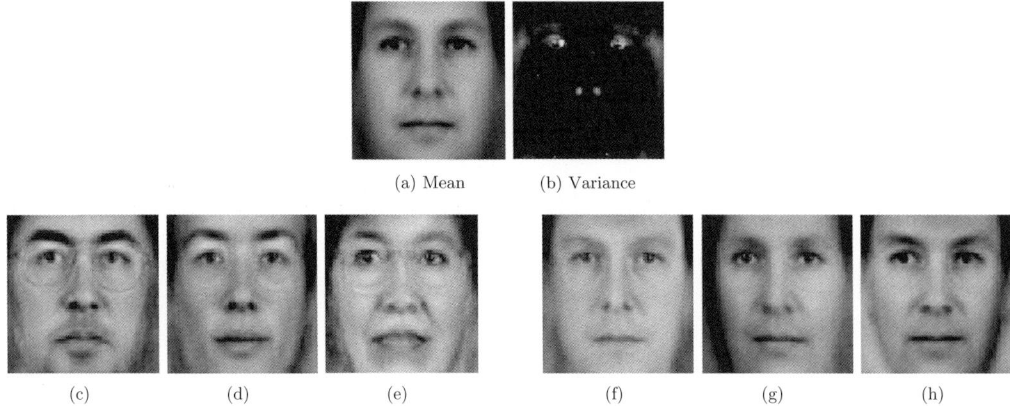

Figure 21.5 Latent identity model of face images. Each image is represented by a $70 \times 70 \times 3$ vector (the 3 comes from the RGB colour coding). There are $I = 195$ individuals in the database and $J = 4$ images per person. (**a**) Mean of the data. (**b**) Per pixel standard deviation – black is low, white is high. (**c,d,e**) Three directions from the between-individual subspace **F**. (**f,g,h**) Three samples from the model with **h** fixed and drawing randomly from **w** in the within-individual subspace **G**. Reproduced from [245] © 2007 IEEE. See plate section for colour version.

This model can be seem as a constrained version of factor analysis by using stacked vectors (here for only a single individual, $I = 1$)

$$\begin{pmatrix} \mathbf{x}_{11} \\ \mathbf{x}_{12} \\ \vdots \\ \mathbf{x}_{1J} \end{pmatrix} = \begin{pmatrix} \boldsymbol{\mu} \\ \boldsymbol{\mu} \\ \vdots \\ \boldsymbol{\mu} \end{pmatrix} + \begin{pmatrix} \mathbf{F} & \mathbf{G} & \mathbf{0} & \dots & \mathbf{0} \\ \mathbf{F} & \mathbf{0} & \mathbf{G} & \dots & \mathbf{0} \\ \vdots & \vdots & \vdots & \ddots & \vdots \\ \mathbf{F} & \mathbf{0} & \mathbf{0} & \dots & \mathbf{G} \end{pmatrix} \begin{pmatrix} \mathbf{h}_1 \\ \mathbf{w}_{11} \\ \mathbf{w}_{12} \\ \vdots \\ \mathbf{w}_{1J} \end{pmatrix} + \begin{pmatrix} \boldsymbol{\epsilon}_{11} \\ \boldsymbol{\epsilon}_{12} \\ \vdots \\ \boldsymbol{\epsilon}_{1J}. \end{pmatrix}. \tag{21.3.8}$$

The generalisation to multiple individuals $I > 1$ is straightforward. The model can be trained using either a constrained form of the eigen method, or EM as described in [245]. Example images from the trained model are presented in Fig. 21.5.

Recognition

Using the above constrained factor analysis models for faces, one can extend their application to classification, as we now briefly describe. In closed set face recognition a new 'probe' face $\mathbf{x}_*$ is to be matched to a person n in the gallery of training faces. In model $\mathcal{M}_n$ the nth gallery face is forced to share its latent identity variable $\mathbf{h}_n$ with the test face, indicating that these faces belong to the same person, see Fig. 21.6.[3] Assuming a single exemplar per person ($J = 1$),

$$p(\mathbf{x}_1, \dots, \mathbf{x}_I, \mathbf{x}_* | \mathcal{M}_n) = p(\mathbf{x}_n, \mathbf{x}_*) \prod_{i=1, i \neq n}^{I} p(\mathbf{x}_i). \tag{21.3.9}$$

Bayes' rule then gives the posterior class assignment

$$p(\mathcal{M}_n | \mathbf{x}_1, \dots, \mathbf{x}_I, \mathbf{x}_*) \propto p(\mathbf{x}_1, \dots, \mathbf{x}_I, \mathbf{x}_* | \mathcal{M}_n) p(\mathcal{M}_n). \tag{21.3.10}$$

[3] This is analogous to Bayesian outcome analysis in Section 12.6 in which the hypotheses assume that either the errors were generated from the same or a different model.

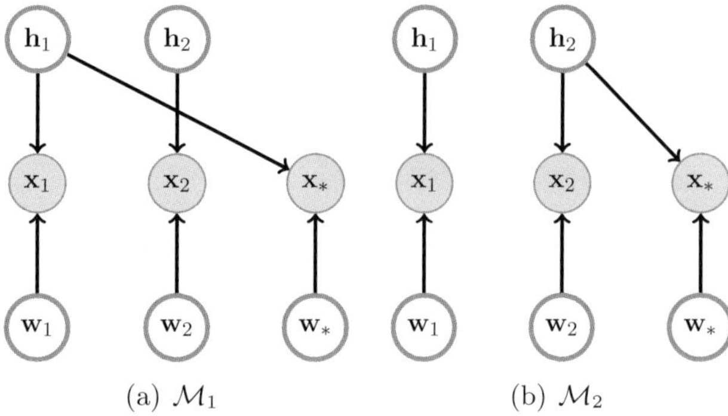

Figure 21.6 Face recognition model (depicted only for a single exemplar per person, $J = 1$). (**a**) In model $\mathcal{M}_1$ the test image (or 'probe') $\mathbf{x}_*$ is assumed to be from person 1, albeit with a different pose/illumination. (**b**) For model $\mathcal{M}_2$ the test image is assumed to be from person 2. One calculates $p(\mathbf{x}_1, \mathbf{x}_2, \mathbf{x}_*|\mathcal{M}_1)$ and $p(\mathbf{x}_1, \mathbf{x}_2, \mathbf{x}_*|\mathcal{M}_2)$ and then uses Bayes' rule to infer to which person the test image $\mathbf{x}_*$ most likely belongs.

For a uniform prior, the term $p(\mathcal{M}_n)$ is constant and can be neglected. All these marginal quantities are straightforward to derive since they are simply marginals of a Gaussian.

In practice, the best results are obtained using a between-individual subspace dimension F and within-individual subspace dimension G both equal to 128. This model then has performance competitive with the state of the art [245]. A benefit of the probabilistic model is that the extension to mixtures of this model is essentially straightforward, which boosts performance further. Related models can also be used for the 'open set' face recognition problem in which the probe face may or may not belong to one of the individuals in the database [245].

21.4 Probabilistic principal components analysis

Probabilistic Principal Components Analysis (PPCA) [296] corresponds to factor analysis under the restriction $\mathbf{\Psi} = \sigma^2\mathbf{I}_D$. Plugging this assumption into the eigen-solution equation (21.2.21) gives

$$\mathbf{F} = \sigma\mathbf{U}_H\left(\mathbf{\Lambda}_H - \mathbf{I}_H\right)^{\frac{1}{2}}\mathbf{R} \tag{21.4.1}$$

where the eigenvalues (diagonal entries of $\mathbf{\Lambda}_H$) and corresponding eigenvectors (columns of $\mathbf{U}_H$) are the largest eigenvalues of $\sigma^{-2}\mathbf{S}$. Since the eigenvalues of $\sigma^{-2}\mathbf{S}$ are those of $\mathbf{S}$ simply scaled by σ^{-2} (and the eigenvectors are unchanged), we can equivalently write

$$\mathbf{F} = \mathbf{U}_H\left(\mathbf{\Lambda}_H - \sigma^2\mathbf{I}_H\right)^{\frac{1}{2}}\mathbf{R} \tag{21.4.2}$$

where $\mathbf{R}$ is an arbitrary orthogonal matrix with $\mathbf{R}^\mathsf{T}\mathbf{R} = \mathbf{I}$ and $\mathbf{U}_H$, $\mathbf{\Lambda}_H$ are the eigenvectors and corresponding eigenvalues of the sample covariance $\mathbf{S}$. Classical PCA, Section 15.2, is recovered in the limit $\sigma^2 \to 0$. Note that for a full correspondence with PCA, one needs to set $\mathbf{R} = \mathbf{I}$, which points $\mathbf{F}$ along the principal directions.

Optimal σ^2

A particular convenience of PPCA is that the optimal noise σ^2 can be found immediately. We order the eigenvalues of $\mathbf{S}$ so that $\lambda_1 \geq \lambda_2, \ldots \geq \lambda_D$. In Equation (21.2.20) an expression for the log likelihood is given in which the eigenvalues are those $\sigma^{-2}\mathbf{S}$. On replacing λ_i with λ_i/σ^2 we can therefore write an explicit expression for the log likelihood in terms of σ^2 and the eigenvalues of the

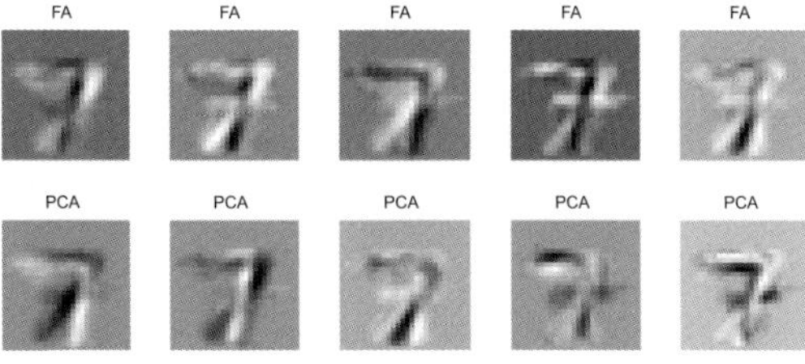

Figure 21.7 For a five hidden unit model, here are plotted the results of training PPCA and FA on 100 examples of the handwritten digit seven. The top row contains the five Factor Analysis factors and the bottom row the five largest eigenvectors from PPCA are plotted.

sample covariance $\mathbf{S}$,

$$L(\sigma^2) = -\frac{N}{2}\left(D\log(2\pi) + \sum_{i=1}^{H}\log\lambda_i + \frac{1}{\sigma^2}\sum_{i=H+1}^{D}\lambda_i + (D-H)\log\sigma^2 + H\right). \tag{21.4.3}$$

By differentiating $L(\sigma^2)$ and equating to zero, the maximum likelihood optimal setting for σ^2 is

$$\sigma^2 = \frac{1}{D-H}\sum_{j=H+1}^{D}\lambda_j. \tag{21.4.4}$$

In summary PPCA is obtained by taking the H principal eigenvalues and corresponding eigenvectors of the sample covariance matrix $\mathbf{S}$, and setting the variance by Equation (21.4.4). The single-shot training nature of PPCA makes it an attractive algorithm and also gives a useful initialisation for factor analysis.

Example 21.1 A comparison of FA and PPCA

We trained both PPCA and FA to model handwritten digits of the number 7. From a database of 100 such images, we fitted both PPCA and FA (100 iterations of EM in each case from the same random initialisation) using five hidden units. The learned factors for these models are in Fig. 21.7. To get a feeling for how well each of these models the data, we drew 25 samples from each model, as given in Fig. 21.8(a). Compared with PPCA, in FA the individual noise on each observation pixel enables a cleaner representation of the regions of zero sample variance.

21.5 Canonical correlation analysis and factor analysis

We outline how Canonical Correlation Analysis (CCA), as discussed in Section 15.8, is related to a constrained form of FA. As a brief reminder, CCA considers two spaces X and Y where, for example, X might represent an audio sequence of a person speaking and Y the corresponding video sequence of the face of the person speaking. The two streams of data are dependent since we would expect the parts around the mouth region to be correlated with the speech signal. The aim in CCA is to find a low-dimensional representation that explains the correlation between the X and Y spaces.

A model that achieves a similar effect to CCA is to use a latent factor h to underlie the data in both the X and Y spaces, see Fig. 21.5. That is

$$p(\mathbf{x}, \mathbf{y}) = \int p(\mathbf{x}|h)p(\mathbf{y}|h)p(h)dh \tag{21.5.1}$$

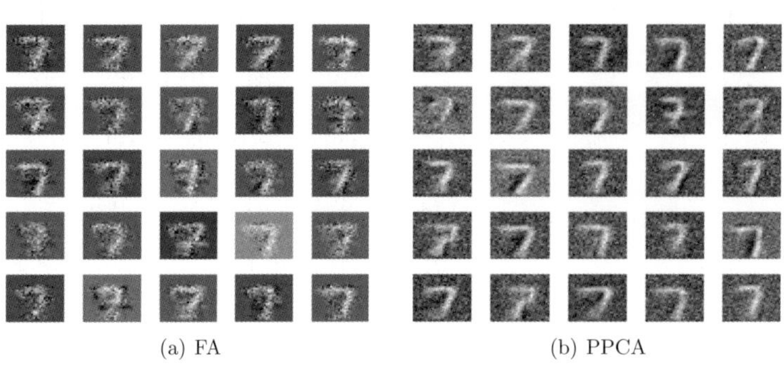

Figure 21.8 (**a**) 25 samples from the learned FA model. Note how the noise variance depends on the pixel, being zero for pixels on the boundary of the image. (**b**) 25 samples from the learned PPCA model with the same noise variance on each pixel.

where

$$p(\mathbf{x}|h) = \mathcal{N}(\mathbf{x}|h\mathbf{a}, \mathbf{\Psi}_x), \qquad p(\mathbf{y}|h) = \mathcal{N}(\mathbf{y}|h\mathbf{b}, \mathbf{\Psi}_y), \qquad p(h) = \mathcal{N}(h|0, 1). \quad (21.5.2)$$

We can express Equation (21.5.2) as a form of factor analysis by writing

$$\begin{pmatrix} \mathbf{x} \\ \mathbf{y} \end{pmatrix} = \begin{pmatrix} \mathbf{a} \\ \mathbf{b} \end{pmatrix} h + \begin{pmatrix} \boldsymbol{\epsilon}_x \\ \boldsymbol{\epsilon}_y \end{pmatrix}, \qquad \boldsymbol{\epsilon}_x \sim \mathcal{N}(\boldsymbol{\epsilon}_x|\mathbf{0}, \mathbf{\Psi}_x), \quad \boldsymbol{\epsilon}_y \sim \mathcal{N}(\boldsymbol{\epsilon}_y|\mathbf{0}, \mathbf{\Psi}_y). \quad (21.5.3)$$

By using the stacked vectors

$$\mathbf{z} = \begin{pmatrix} \mathbf{x} \\ \mathbf{y} \end{pmatrix}, \qquad \mathbf{f} = \begin{pmatrix} \mathbf{a} \\ \mathbf{b} \end{pmatrix}, \quad (21.5.4)$$

and integrating out the latent variable h, we obtain

$$p(\mathbf{z}) = \mathcal{N}(\mathbf{z}|\mathbf{0}, \mathbf{\Sigma}), \qquad \mathbf{\Sigma} = \mathbf{f}\mathbf{f}^{\mathsf{T}} + \mathbf{\Psi}, \qquad \mathbf{\Psi} = \begin{pmatrix} \mathbf{\Psi}_x & \mathbf{0} \\ \mathbf{0} & \mathbf{\Psi}_y \end{pmatrix}. \quad (21.5.5)$$

This is therefore clearly simply a factor analysis model, in this case with a single latent factor. We can learn the best **a** and **b** by maximising the likelihood on a set of data. From the FA results equation (21.2.6) the optimal **f** is given by (with **S** being the sample covariance matrix)

$$\mathbf{f}\left(1 + \mathbf{f}^{\mathsf{T}}\mathbf{\Psi}^{-1}\mathbf{f}\right) = \mathbf{S}\mathbf{\Psi}^{-1}\mathbf{f} \Rightarrow \mathbf{f} \propto \mathbf{S}\mathbf{\Psi}^{-1}\mathbf{f} \quad (21.5.6)$$

so that optimally **f** is given by the principal eigenvector of $\mathbf{S}\mathbf{\Psi}^{-1}$. By imposing $\mathbf{\Psi}_x = \sigma_x^2\mathbf{I}$, $\mathbf{\Psi}_y = \sigma_y^2\mathbf{I}$ the above equation can be expressed as the coupled equations

$$\mathbf{a} \propto \frac{1}{\sigma_x^2}\mathbf{S}_{xx}\mathbf{a} + \frac{1}{\sigma_y^2}\mathbf{S}_{xy}\mathbf{b}, \qquad \mathbf{b} \propto \frac{1}{\sigma_x^2}\mathbf{S}_{yx}\mathbf{a} + \frac{1}{\sigma_y^2}\mathbf{S}_{yy}\mathbf{b}. \quad (21.5.7)$$

Eliminating **b** we have, for an arbitrary proportionality constant γ,

$$\left(\mathbf{I} - \frac{\gamma}{\sigma_x^2}\mathbf{S}_{xx}\right)\mathbf{a} = \frac{\gamma^2}{\sigma_x^2\sigma_y^2}\mathbf{S}_{xy}\left(\mathbf{I} - \frac{\gamma}{\sigma_y^2}\mathbf{S}_{yy}\right)^{-1}\mathbf{S}_{yx}\mathbf{a}. \quad (21.5.8)$$

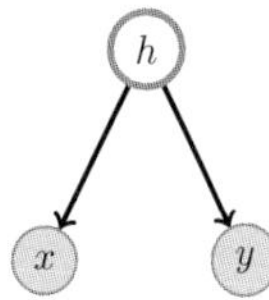

Figure 21.9 Canonical correlation analysis corresponds to the latent variable model in which a common latent variable generates both the observed x and y variables. This is therefore a formed of constrained factor analysis.

In the limit $\sigma_x^2, \sigma_y^2 \to 0$, this tends to the zero derivative condition equation (15.8.9) so that CCA can be seen as in fact a limiting form of FA (see [11] for a more thorough correspondence). By viewing CCA in this manner extensions to using more than a single latent dimension H become clear, see Exercise 21.2, in addition to the benefits of a probabilistic interpretation.

As we've indicated, CCA corresponds to training a form of FA by maximising the joint likelihood $p(\mathbf{x}, \mathbf{y}|\mathbf{w}, \mathbf{u})$. If the $\mathbf{x}$ represents rather an input and $\mathbf{y}$ the output, we are more interested in finding a good predictive representation. In this case, training based on maximising the conditional $p(\mathbf{y}|\mathbf{x}, \mathbf{w}, \mathbf{u})$ corresponds to a special case of a technique called *Partial Least Squares*, see for example [82]. This correspondence is left as an exercise for the interested reader.

21.6 Independent components analysis

Independent Components Analysis (ICA) seeks a representation of data $\mathbf{v}$ using a coordinate system $\mathbf{h}$ in which the components h_i are independent [238, 151]. Such independent coordinate systems arguably form a natural representation of the data. In ICA it is common to assume that the observations are linearly related to the latent variables $\mathbf{h}$. For technical reasons, the most convenient practical choice is to use[4]

$$\mathbf{v} = \mathbf{A}\mathbf{h} \tag{21.6.1}$$

where $\mathbf{A}$ is a square *mixing matrix* so that the likelihood of an observation $\mathbf{v}$ is

$$p(\mathbf{v}|\mathbf{A}) = \int p(\mathbf{v}|\mathbf{h}, \mathbf{A}) \prod_i p(h_i) d\mathbf{h} = \int \delta\left(\mathbf{v} - \mathbf{A}\mathbf{h}\right) \prod_i p(h_i) d\mathbf{h} = \frac{1}{|\det\left(\mathbf{A}\right)|} \prod_i p\left(\left[\mathbf{A}^{-1}\mathbf{v}\right]_i\right). \tag{21.6.2}$$

For a given set of data $\mathcal{V} = \left(\mathbf{v}^1, \ldots, \mathbf{v}^N\right)$ and prior $p(h)$, our aim is to find $\mathbf{A}$. For i.i.d. data, the log likelihood is conveniently written in terms of $\mathbf{B} = \mathbf{A}^{-1}$,

$$L(\mathbf{B}) = N \log\det\left(\mathbf{B}\right) + \sum_n \sum_i \log p\left(\left[\mathbf{B}\mathbf{v}^n\right]_i\right). \tag{21.6.3}$$

Note that for a Gaussian prior

$$p(h) \propto \exp\left(-h^2\right) \tag{21.6.4}$$

the log likelihood becomes

$$L(\mathbf{B}) = N \log\det\left(\mathbf{B}\right) - \sum_n \left(\mathbf{v}^n\right)^\mathsf{T} \mathbf{B}^\mathsf{T}\mathbf{B}\mathbf{v}^n + \text{const.} \tag{21.6.5}$$

which is invariant with respect to an orthogonal rotation $\mathbf{B} \to \mathbf{R}\mathbf{B}$, with $\mathbf{R}^\mathsf{T}\mathbf{R} = \mathbf{I}$. This means that for a Gaussian prior $p(h)$, we cannot estimate uniquely the mixing matrix. To break this rotational invariance we therefore need to use a non-Gaussian prior. Assuming we have a non-Gaussian prior $p(h)$, taking the derivative w.r.t. B_{ab} we obtain

$$\frac{\partial}{\partial B_{ab}} L(\mathbf{B}) = N A_{ba} + \sum_n \phi(\left[\mathbf{B}\mathbf{v}\right]_a) v_b^n \tag{21.6.6}$$

[4] This treatment follows that presented in [197].

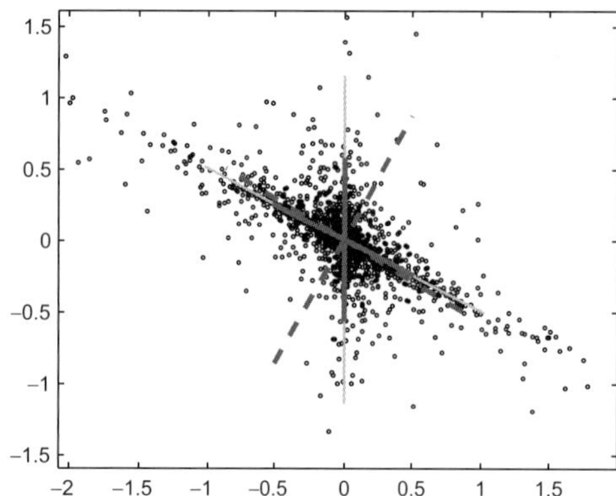

Figure 21.10 Latent data is sampled from the prior $p(x_i) \propto \exp(-5\sqrt{|x_i|})$ with the mixing matrix $\mathbf{A}$ shown in green to create the observed two-dimensional vectors $\mathbf{y} = \mathbf{A}\mathbf{x}$. The red lines are the mixing matrix estimated by `ica.m` based on the observations. For comparison, PCA produces the blue (dashed) components. Note that the components have been scaled to improve visualisation. As expected, PCA finds the orthogonal directions of maximal variation; ICA however, correctly estimates the directions in which the components were independently generated. See `demoICA.m`. See plate section for colour version.

where

$$\phi(x) \equiv \frac{d}{dx} \log p(x) = \frac{1}{p(x)} \frac{d}{dx} p(x). \tag{21.6.7}$$

A simple gradient ascent learning rule for $\mathbf{B}$ is then

$$\mathbf{B}^{new} = \mathbf{B} + \eta \left(\mathbf{B}^{-\mathsf{T}} + \frac{1}{N} \sum_n \boldsymbol{\phi}(\mathbf{B}\mathbf{v}^n) \left(\mathbf{v}^n\right)^{\mathsf{T}} \right). \tag{21.6.8}$$

An alternative 'natural gradient' algorithm [7, 197] that approximates a Newton update is given by multiplying the gradient by $\mathbf{B}^{\mathsf{T}}\mathbf{B}$ on the right to give the update

$$\mathbf{B}^{new} = \mathbf{B} + \eta \left(\mathbf{I} + \frac{1}{N} \sum_n \boldsymbol{\phi}(\mathbf{B}\mathbf{v}^n) \left(\mathbf{B}\mathbf{v}^n\right)^{\mathsf{T}} \right) \mathbf{B}. \tag{21.6.9}$$

Here η is a learning rate which in the code `ica.m` we nominally set to 0.5. The performance of the algorithm is relatively insensitive to the choice of the prior function $\phi(x)$. In `ica.m` we use the tanh function. An example is given in Fig. 21.10 in which the data clearly has an underlying 'X' shape, although the axes of the 'X' are not orthogonal. In this case, the ICA and PCA representations are very different, see Fig. 21.10. A natural extension is to consider noise on the outputs, Exercise 21.6, for which an EM algorithm is readily available. However, in the limit of low output noise, the EM formally fails, an effect which is related to the general discussion in Section 11.4.

A popular alternative estimation method is FastICA[5] and can be related to an iterative maximum likelihood optimisation procedure. Independent components analysis can also be motivated from several alternative directions, including information theory [29]. We refer the reader to [151] for an in-depth discussion of ICA and related extensions.

21.7 Summary

- Factor analysis is a classical probabilistic method for finding low-dimensional representations of the data.
- There is no closed form solution in general and iterative procedures are typically used to find the maximum likelihood parameters.

[5] See `www.cis.hut.fi/projects/ica/fastica/`

- Canonical correlation analysis is a special case of factor analysis.
- Under the assumption of non-Gaussian latent variable priors, one is able to discover independent directions in the data.

21.8 Code

`FA.m`: Factor analysis
`demoFA.m`: Demo of factor analysis
`ica.m`: Independent components analysis
`demoIca.m`: Demo ICA

21.9 Exercises

21.1 Factor analysis and scaling. Assume that a H-factor model holds for $\mathbf{x}$. Now consider the transformation $\mathbf{y} = \mathbf{C}\mathbf{x}$, where $\mathbf{C}$ is a non-singular square diagonal matrix. Show that factor analysis is scale invariant, i.e. that the H-factor model also holds for $\mathbf{y}$, with the factor loadings appropriately scaled. How must the specific factors be scaled?

21.2 For the constrained factor analysis model

$$\mathbf{x} = \begin{pmatrix} \mathbf{A} & \mathbf{0} \\ \mathbf{0} & \mathbf{B} \end{pmatrix} \mathbf{h} + \boldsymbol{\epsilon}, \qquad \boldsymbol{\epsilon} \sim \mathcal{N}\left(\boldsymbol{\epsilon} \,|\, \mathbf{0}, \text{diag}\left(\psi_1, \ldots, \psi_n\right)\right), \qquad \mathbf{h} \sim \mathcal{N}\left(\mathbf{h} \,|\, \mathbf{0}, \mathbf{I}\right) \tag{21.9.1}$$

derive a maximum likelihood EM algorithm for the matrices $\mathbf{A}$ and $\mathbf{B}$, assuming the datapoints $\mathbf{x}^1, \ldots, \mathbf{x}^N$ are i.i.d.

21.3 An apparent extension of FA analysis is to consider a correlated prior

$$p(\mathbf{h}) = \mathcal{N}\left(\mathbf{h} \,|\, \mathbf{0}, \boldsymbol{\Sigma}_H\right). \tag{21.9.2}$$

Show that, provided no constraints are placed on the factor loading matrix $\mathbf{F}$, using a correlated prior $p(\mathbf{h})$ is an equivalent model to the original uncorrelated FA model.

21.4 Using the Woodbury identity and the definition of $\boldsymbol{\Sigma}_D$ in Equation (21.2.3), show that one can rewrite $\boldsymbol{\Sigma}_D^{-1}\mathbf{F}$ as

$$\boldsymbol{\Sigma}_D^{-1}\mathbf{F} = \boldsymbol{\Psi}^{-1}\mathbf{F}\left(\mathbf{I} + \mathbf{F}^\mathsf{T}\boldsymbol{\Psi}^{-1}\mathbf{F}\right)^{-1}. \tag{21.9.3}$$

21.5 For the log likelihood function

$$L(\sigma^2) = -\frac{N}{2}\left(D\log(2\pi) + \sum_{i=1}^{H}\log\lambda_i + \frac{1}{\sigma^2}\sum_{i=H+1}^{D}\lambda_i + (D-H)\log\sigma^2 + H\right), \tag{21.9.4}$$

show $L(\sigma^2)$ is maximal for

$$\sigma^2 = \frac{1}{D-H}\sum_{j=H+1}^{D}\lambda_j. \tag{21.9.5}$$

21.6 Consider an ICA model in which $\mathbf{y}$ represents the outputs and $\mathbf{x}$ the latent components

$$p(\mathbf{y}, \mathbf{x}|\mathbf{W}) = \prod_j p(y_j|\mathbf{x}, \mathbf{W}) \prod_i p(x_i), \qquad \mathbf{W} = [\mathbf{w}_1, \ldots, \mathbf{w}_J] \tag{21.9.6}$$

with

$$p(y_j|\mathbf{x}, \mathbf{W}) = \mathcal{N}\left(y_j \middle| \mathbf{w}_j^\mathsf{T}\mathbf{x}, \sigma^2\right). \tag{21.9.7}$$

1. For the above model derive an EM algorithm for a set of i.i.d. data $\mathbf{y}^1, \ldots, \mathbf{y}^N$ and show that the required statistics for the M-step are $\langle \mathbf{x} \rangle_{p(\mathbf{x}|\mathbf{y}^n, \mathbf{W})}$ and $\langle \mathbf{x}\mathbf{x}^\mathsf{T} \rangle_{p(\mathbf{x}|\mathbf{y}^n, \mathbf{W})}$.
2. Show that for a non-Gaussian prior $p(x_i)$, the posterior

$$p(\mathbf{x}|\mathbf{y}, \mathbf{W}) \tag{21.9.8}$$

is non-factorised, non-Gaussian and generally intractable (its normalisation constant cannot be computed efficiently).

3. Show that in the limit $\sigma^2 \to 0$, the EM algorithm fails.

22 Latent ability models

In this chapter we discuss an application of latent variable models to ascertaining the ability of players in games. These models are applicable in a variety of contexts from exam performance to football match prediction to online gaming analysis.

22.1 The Rasch model

Consider an exam in which student s answers question q either correctly $x_{qs} = 1$ or incorrectly $x_{qs} = 0$. For a set of N students and Q questions, the performance of all students is given in the $Q \times N$ binary matrix $\mathbf{X}$. Based on this data alone we wish to evaluate the ability of each student. One approach is to define the ability a_s as the fraction of questions student s answered correctly. A more subtle analysis is to accept that some questions are more difficult than others so that a student who answered difficult questions should be awarded more highly than a student who answered the same number of easy questions. A priori, however, we do not know which are the difficult questions and this needs to be estimated based on $\mathbf{X}$. To account for inherent differences in question difficulty we may model the probability that a student s gets a question q correct based on the student's latent ability α_s and the latent difficulty of the question δ_q. A simple generative model of the response is, see Fig. 22.1,

$$p(x_{qs} = 1|\boldsymbol{\alpha}, \boldsymbol{\delta}) = \sigma\left(\alpha_s - \delta_q\right) \tag{22.1.1}$$

where $\sigma\left(x\right) = 1/(1 + e^{-x})$. Under this model, the higher the latent ability is above the latent difficulty of the question, the more likely it is that the student will answer the question correctly.

22.1.1 Maximum likelihood training

We may use maximum likelihood to find the best parameters $\boldsymbol{\alpha}, \boldsymbol{\delta}$. Making the i.i.d. assumption, the likelihood of the data $\mathbf{X}$ under this model is

$$p(\mathbf{X}|\boldsymbol{\alpha}, \boldsymbol{\delta}) = \prod_{s=1}^{S}\prod_{q=1}^{Q} \sigma\left(\alpha_s - \delta_q\right)^{x_{qs}}\left(1 - \sigma\left(\alpha_s - \delta_q\right)\right)^{1-x_{qs}}. \tag{22.1.2}$$

The log likelihood is then

$$L \equiv \log p(\mathbf{X}|\boldsymbol{\alpha}, \boldsymbol{\delta}) = \sum_{q,s} x_{qs} \log \sigma\left(\alpha_s - \delta_q\right) + (1 - x_{qs}) \log\left(1 - \sigma\left(\alpha_s - \delta_q\right)\right) \tag{22.1.3}$$

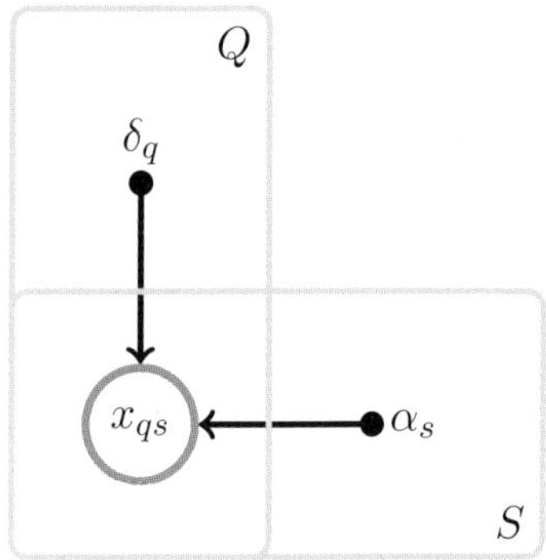

Figure 22.1 The Rasch model for analysing questions. Each element of the binary matrix **X**, with $x_{qs} = 1$ if student s gets question q correct, is generated using the latent ability of the student α_s and the latent difficulty of the question δ_q.

with derivatives

$$\frac{\partial L}{\partial \alpha_s} = \sum_{q=1}^{Q} (x_{qs} - \sigma(\alpha_s - \delta_q)), \qquad \frac{\partial L}{\partial \delta_q} = -\sum_{s=1}^{S} (x_{qs} - \sigma(\alpha_s - \delta_q)). \tag{22.1.4}$$

A simple way to learn the parameters is to use gradient ascent, see `demoRasch.m`, with extensions to Newton methods being straightforward.

The generalisation to more than two responses $x_{qs} \in \{1, 2, \ldots\}$ can be achieved using a softmax-style function. More generally, the Rasch model falls under *item response theory*, a subject dealing with the analysis of questionnaires [101].

Missing data

Assuming the data is missing at random, missing data can be treated by computing the likelihood of only the observed elements of **X**. In `rasch.m` missing data is assumed to be coded as `nan` so that the likelihood and gradients are straightforward to compute based on summing only over terms containing non `nan` entries.

Example 22.1

We display an example of the use of the Rasch model in Fig. 22.2, estimating the latent abilities of 20 students based on a set of 50 questions. Based on using the number of questions each student answered correctly, the best students are (ranked from first) 8, 6, 1, 19, 4, 17, 20, 7, 15, 5, 12, 16, 2, 3, 18, 9, 11, 14, 10, 13. Alternatively, ranking students according to the latent ability gives 8, 6, 19, 1, 20, 4, 17, 7, 15, 12, 5, 16, 2, 3, 18, 9, 11, 14, 10, 13. This differs (only slightly in this case) from the number-correct ranking since the Rasch model takes into account the fact that some students answered difficult questions correctly. For example student 20 answered some difficult questions correctly.

22.1.2 Bayesian Rasch models

The Rasch model will potentially overfit the data especially when there is only a small amount of data. For this case a natural extension is to use a Bayesian technique, placing independent priors on

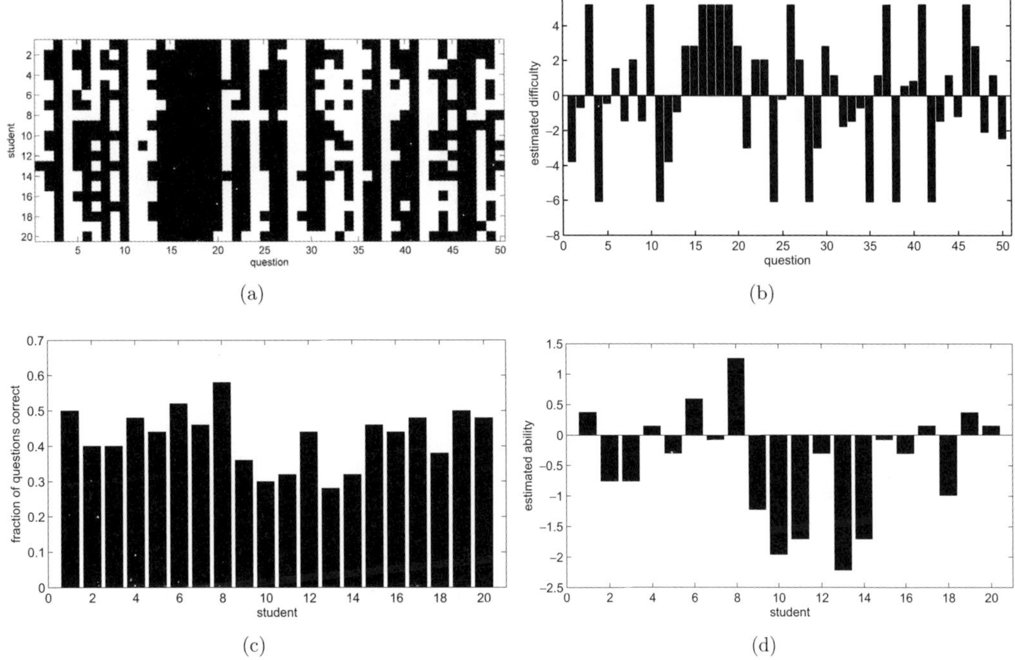

Figure 22.2 Rasch model. (**a**) The data of correct answers (white) and incorrect answers (black). (**b**) The estimated latent difficulty of each question. (**c**) The fraction of questions each student answered correctly. (**d**) The estimated latent ability.

the ability and question difficulty, so that the posterior ability and question difficulty is given by

$$p(\boldsymbol{\alpha}, \boldsymbol{\delta}|\mathbf{X}) \propto p(\mathbf{X}|\boldsymbol{\alpha}, \boldsymbol{\delta})p(\boldsymbol{\alpha})p(\boldsymbol{\delta}). \tag{22.1.5}$$

Natural priors are those that discourage very large values of the parameters, such as Gaussians

$$p(\boldsymbol{\alpha}) = \prod_s \mathcal{N}\left(\alpha_s|0, \sigma^2\right), \qquad p(\boldsymbol{\delta}) = \prod_q \mathcal{N}\left(\delta_q|0, \tau^2\right) \tag{22.1.6}$$

where σ^2 and τ^2 are hyperparameters that can be learned by maximising $p(\mathbf{X}|\sigma^2, \tau^2)$. Even using Gaussian priors, however, the posterior distribution $p(\boldsymbol{\alpha}, \boldsymbol{\delta}|\mathbf{X})$ is not of a standard form and approximations are required. In this case, however, the posterior is log concave so that approximation methods based on variational or Laplace techniques are potentially adequate, Chapter 28; alternatively one may use sampling approximations, Chapter 27.

22.2 Competition models

22.2.1 Bradley–Terry–Luce model

The Bradley–Terry–Luce model assesses the ability of players based on one-on-one matches. Here we describe games in which only win/lose outcomes arise, leaving aside the complicating possibility of draws. For this win/lose scenario, the BTL model is a straightforward modification of the Rasch

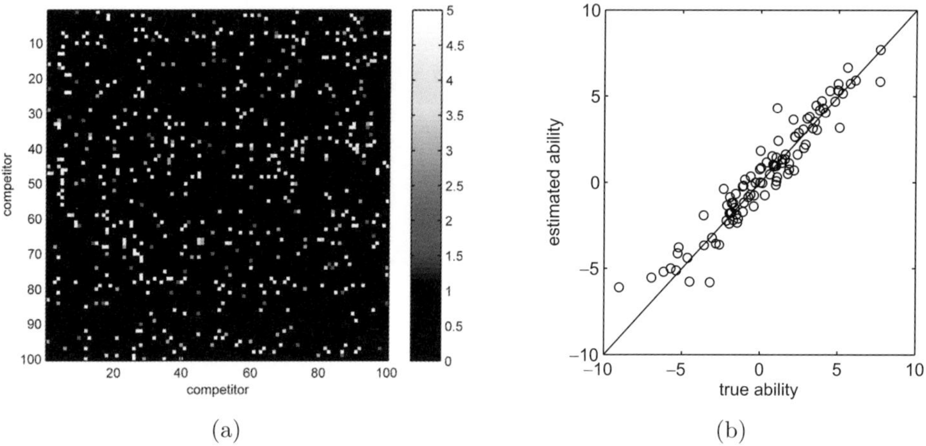

Figure 22.3 BTL model. (**a**) The data **M** with M_{ij} being the number of times that competitor i beat competitor j. (**b**) The true versus estimated ability of the 100 competitors (unlabelled). Even though the data is quite sparse, a reasonable estimate of the latent ability of each competitor is found.

model so that for latent ability α_i of player i and latent ability α_j of player j, the probability that i beats j is given by

$$p(i \rhd j|\boldsymbol{\alpha}) = \sigma\left(\alpha_i - \alpha_j\right) \tag{22.2.1}$$

where $i \rhd j$ stands for player i beats player j. Based on a matrix of games data $\mathbf{X}$ with

$$x_{ij}^n = \begin{cases} 1 & \text{if } i \rhd j \text{ in game } n \\ 0 & \text{otherwise} \end{cases} \tag{22.2.2}$$

the likelihood of the model is given by

$$p(\mathbf{X}|\boldsymbol{\alpha}) = \prod_n \prod_{ij} \left[\sigma\left(\alpha_i - \alpha_j\right)\right]^{x_{ij}^n} = \prod_{ij} \left[\sigma\left(\alpha_i - \alpha_j\right)\right]^{M_{ij}} \tag{22.2.3}$$

where $M_{ij} = \sum_n x_{ij}^n$ is the number of times player i beat player j. Training using maximum likelihood or a Bayesian technique can then proceed as for the Rasch model.

These models are also called *pairwise comparison models* and pioneered by Thurstone in the 1920s who applied such models to a wide range of data [77].

Example 22.2

An example application of the BTL model is given in Fig. 22.3 in which a matrix **M** containing the number of times that competitor i beat competitor j is given. The matrix entries **M** were drawn from a BTL model based on 'true abilities'. Using **M** alone the maximum likelihood estimate of these latent abilities is in close agreement with the true abilities.

22.2.2 Elo ranking model

The Elo system [95] used in chess ranking is closely related to the BTL model above, though there is the added complication of the possibility of draws. In addition, the Elo system takes into account a measure of the variability in performance. For a given ability α_i, the actual performance π_i of player i in a game is given by

$$\pi_i = \alpha_i + \epsilon_i \tag{22.2.4}$$

where $\epsilon_i \sim \mathcal{N}\left(\epsilon_i \mid 0, \sigma^2\right)$. The variance σ^2 is fixed across all players and thus takes into account intrinsic variability in the performance. More formally the Elo model modifies the BTL model to give

$$p(\mathbf{X}|\boldsymbol{\alpha}) = \int_{\boldsymbol{\pi}} p(\mathbf{X}|\boldsymbol{\pi})p(\boldsymbol{\pi}|\boldsymbol{\alpha}), \qquad p(\boldsymbol{\pi}|\boldsymbol{\alpha}) = \mathcal{N}\left(\boldsymbol{\pi}\,|\boldsymbol{\alpha}, \sigma^2\mathbf{I}\right) \tag{22.2.5}$$

where $p(\mathbf{X}|\boldsymbol{\pi})$ is given by Equation (22.2.3) on replacing $\boldsymbol{\alpha}$ with $\boldsymbol{\pi}$.

22.2.3 Glicko and TrueSkill

Glicko [126] and TrueSkill [142] are essentially Bayesian versions of the Elo model with the refinement that the latent ability is modelled, not by a single number, but by a Gaussian distribution

$$p(\alpha_i|\theta_i) = \mathcal{N}\left(\alpha_i \middle| \mu_i, \sigma_i^2\right). \tag{22.2.6}$$

This can capture the fact that a player may be consistently reasonable (quite high μ_i and low σ_i^2) or an erratic genius (high μ_i but with large σ_i^2). The parameters of the model are then

$$\theta = \left\{\mu_i, \sigma_i^2, i = 1, \ldots, S\right\} \tag{22.2.7}$$

for a set of S players. The interaction model $p(\mathbf{X}|\boldsymbol{\alpha})$ is as for the win/lose Elo model, Equation (22.2.1). The likelihood for the model given the parameters is

$$p(\mathbf{X}|\theta) = \int_{\boldsymbol{\alpha}} p(\mathbf{X}|\boldsymbol{\alpha})p(\boldsymbol{\alpha}|\theta). \tag{22.2.8}$$

This integral is formally intractable and numerical approximations are required. In this context expectation propagation, Section 28.8, has proven to be a useful technique [210]. The TrueSkill system is used for example to assess the abilities of players in online gaming, also taking into account the abilities of teams of individuals in tournaments. A temporal extension has recently been used to reevaluate the change in ability of chess players with time [76].

22.3 Summary

- The Rasch model is a simple model of latent student ability and question difficulty. In principle it is better able to assess student performance than simply counting the number of correct questions since it implicitly takes into account the fact that some questions are more difficult than others.
- Related models can be used to assess the underlying ability of players in games.

22.4 Code

`rasch.m`: Rasch model training
`demoRasch.m`: Demo for the Rasch model

22.5 Exercises

22.1 (Bucking bronco) `bronco.mat` contains information about a bucking bronco competition. There are 500 competitors and 20 bucking broncos. A competitor j attempts to stay on a bucking bronco i for a minute. If the competitor succeeds, the entry X_{ij} is 1, otherwise 0. Each competitor gets to ride three bucking broncos only (the missing data is coded as `nan`). Having viewed all the 500 amateurs, Desperate Dan enters the competition and bribes the organisers into letting him avoid having to ride the difficult broncos. Based on using a Rasch model, which are the top 10 most difficult broncos, in order of the most difficult first?

22.2 (BTL training)

1. Show that the log likelihood for the Bradley–Terry–Luce model is given by

$$L(\boldsymbol{\alpha}) = \sum_{ij} M_{ij} \log \sigma\left(\alpha_i - \alpha_j\right) \tag{22.5.1}$$

   where M_{ij} is the number of times that player i beats player j in a set of games.
2. Compute the gradient of $L(\boldsymbol{\alpha})$.
3. Compute the Hessian of the BTL model and verify that it is negative semidefinite.

22.3 (La Reine)

1. Program a simple gradient ascent routine to learn the latent abilities of competitors based on a series of win/lose outcomes.
2. In a modified form of Swiss cow 'fighting', a set of cows compete by pushing each other until submission. At the end of the competition one cow is deemed to be 'la reine'. Based on the data in `BTL.mat` (for which X_{ij} contains the number of times cow i beat cow j), fit a BTL model and return a ranked list of the top 10 best fighting cows, 'la reine' first.

22.4 An extension of the BTL model is to consider additional factors that describe the state of the competitors when they play. For example, we have a set of S football teams, and a set of matrices $\mathbf{X}^1, \ldots, \mathbf{X}^N$, with $X^n_{ij} = 1$ if team i beat team j in match n. In addition we have for each match n and team i a vector of binary factors $f^n_{h,i} \in \{0, 1\}, h = 1, \ldots, H$ that describes the team. For example, for the team $i = 1$ (Madchester United), the factor $f^n_{1,1} = 1$ if Bozo is playing in match n, 0 if not. It is suggested that the ability of team i in game n is measured by

$$\alpha^n_i = d_i + \sum_{h=1}^{H} w_{h,i} f^n_{h,i}. \tag{22.5.2}$$

Here d_i is a default latent ability of the team which is assumed constant across all games. We have such a set of factors for each match.

1. Using the above definition of the latent ability in the BTL model, our interest is to find the weights $\mathbf{W}$ and abilities $\mathbf{d}$ that best describe the ability of the team, given that we have a set of historical plays $(\mathbf{X}^n, \mathbf{F}^n), n = 1, \ldots, N$. Write down the likelihood for the BTL model as a function of the set of all team weights $\mathbf{W}, \mathbf{d}$.
2. Compute the gradient of the log likelihood of this model.

3. Explain how this model can be used to assess the importance of Bozo's contribution to Madchester United's ability.
4. Given learned $\mathbf{W}$, $\mathbf{d}$ and the knowledge that Madchester United (team 1) will play Chelski (team 2) tomorrow explain how, given the list of factors $\mathbf{f}$ for Chelski (which includes issues such as who will be playing in the team), one can select the best Madchester United team to maximise the probability of winning the game.

Part IV

Dynamical models

Natural organisms inhabit a dynamical environment and arguably a large part of natural intelligence is in modelling causal relations and consequences of actions. In this sense, modelling temporal data is of fundamental interest. In a more artificial environment, there are many instances where predicting the future is of interest, particularly in areas such as finance and also in tracking of moving objects.

In Part IV, we discuss some of the classical models of timeseries that may be used to represent temporal data and also to make predictions of the future. Many of these models are well known in different branches of science from physics to engineering and are heavily used in areas such as speech recognition, financial prediction and control. We also discuss some more sophisticated models in Chapter 25, which may be skipped at first reading.

As an allusion to the fact that natural organisms inhabit a temporal world, we also address in Chapter 26 some basic models of how information processing might be achieved in distributed systems.

23 Discrete-state Markov models

Timeseries require specialised models since the number of variables can be very large and typically increases as new datapoints arrive. In this chapter we discuss models in which the process generating the observed data is fundamentally discrete. These models give rise to classical models with interesting applications in many fields from finance to speech processing and website ranking.

23.1 Markov models

Timeseries are datasets for which the constituent datapoints can be naturally ordered. This order often corresponds to an underlying single physical dimension, typically time, though any other single dimension may be used. The timeseries models we consider are probability models over a collection of random variables $v_1, \ldots, v_T$ with individual variables v_t indexed by discrete time t. A probabilistic timeseries model requires a specification of the joint distribution $p(v_1, \ldots, v_T)$. For the case in which the observed data v_t are discrete, the joint probability table for $p(v_1, \ldots, v_T)$ has exponentially many entries. We therefore cannot expect to independently specify all the exponentially many entries and need to make simplified models under which these entries can be parameterised in a lower-dimensional manner. Such simplifications are at the heart of timeseries modelling and we will discuss some classical models in the following sections.

Definition 23.1 Timeseries notation

$$x_{a:b} \equiv x_a, x_{a+1}, \ldots, x_b, \qquad \text{with } x_{a:b} = x_a \text{ for } b \le a. \tag{23.1.1}$$

For timeseries data $v_1, \ldots, v_T$, we need a model $p(v_{1:T})$. For consistency with the causal nature of time, it is natural to consider the cascade decomposition

$$p(v_{1:T}) = \prod_{t=1}^{T} p(v_t | v_{1:t-1}) \tag{23.1.2}$$

with the convention $p(v_t | v_{1:t-1}) = p(v_1)$ for $t = 1$. It is often useful to assume that the influence of the immediate past is more relevant than the remote past and in Markov models only a limited number of previous observations are required to predict the future, see Fig. 23.1.

Definition 23.2 Markov chain A Markov chain defined on either discrete or continuous variables $v_{1:T}$ is one in which the following conditional independence assumption holds:

$$p(v_t | v_1, \ldots, v_{t-1}) = p(v_t | v_{t-L}, \ldots, v_{t-1}) \tag{23.1.3}$$

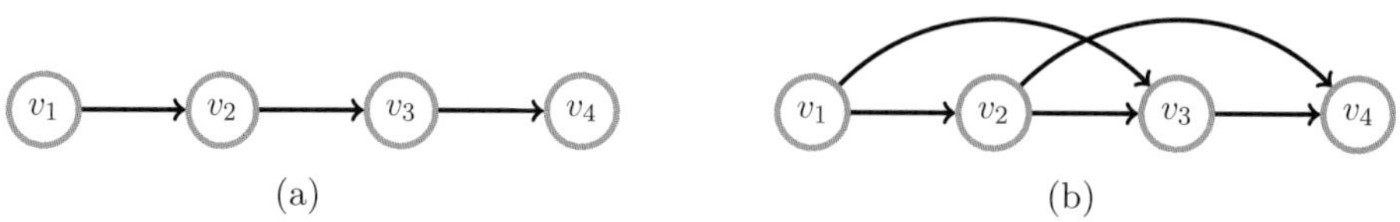

Figure 23.1 (**a**) First-order Markov chain. (**b**) Second-order Markov chain.

where $L \geq 1$ is the *order* of the Markov chain and $v_t = \emptyset$ for $t < 1$. For a first-order Markov chain,

$$p(v_{1:T}) = p(v_1)p(v_2|v_1)p(v_3|v_2)\dots p(v_T|v_{T-1}). \tag{23.1.4}$$

For a *stationary Markov chain* the transitions $p(v_t = s'|v_{t-1} = s) = f(s', s)$ are time-independent. Otherwise the chain is non-stationary, $p(v_t = s'|v_{t-1} = s) = f(s', s, t)$.

For a discrete state first-order time-independent Markov chain one can visualise the transition $p(v_t|v_{t-1})$ using a state-transition diagram, as in Fig. 23.2.

23.1.1 Equilibrium and stationary distribution of a Markov chain

For a transition $p(x_t|x_{t-1})$, it is interesting to know how the marginal $p(x_t)$ evolves through time. For a discrete state system, this is given by

$$p(x_t = i) = \sum_j \underbrace{p(x_t = i|x_{t-1} = j)}_{M_{ij}} p(x_{t-1} = j). \tag{23.1.5}$$

For an initial distribution $p(x_1)$, the above recursively defines the marginal for all future timepoints. The marginal $p(x_t = i)$ has the interpretation of the frequency that we visit state i at time t, given we started with a sample from $p(x_1)$ and subsequently repeatedly drew samples from the transition $p(x_\tau|x_{\tau-1})$. That is, by drawing a state $x_1 = \mathrm{x}_1$, from $p(x_1)$ we can draw samples $\mathrm{x}_2, \dots, \mathrm{x}_t$ from the Markov chain by first drawing a sample from $p(x_2|x_1 = \mathrm{x}_1)$, and then from $p(x_3|x_2 = \mathrm{x}_2)$ etc. As we repeatedly sample a new state from the chain, the marginal distribution at time t, represented by the vector $[\mathbf{p}_t]_i = p(x_i = i)$ and initial distribution $\mathbf{p}_1$ is

$$\mathbf{p}_t = \mathbf{M}\mathbf{p}_{t-1} = \mathbf{M}^{t-1}\mathbf{p}_1. \tag{23.1.6}$$

If, for $t \to \infty$, $\mathbf{p}_\infty$ is independent of the initial distribution $\mathbf{p}_1$, then $\mathbf{p}_\infty$ is called the equilibrium distribution of the chain. See Exercise 23.2 for an example of a Markov chain which does not have an equilibrium distribution. The so-called stationary distribution of a Markov chain is defined by the

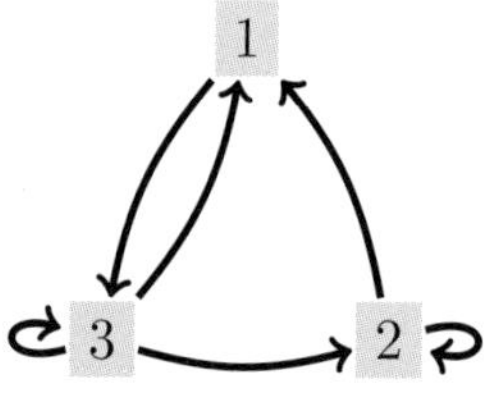

Figure 23.2 A state-transition diagram for a three-state Markov chain. Note that a state-transition diagram is not a graphical model – it simply displays the non-zero entries of the transition matrix $p(i|j)$. The absence of a link from j to i indicates that $p(i|j) = 0$.

condition

$$p_\infty(i) = \sum_j p(x_t = i|x_{t-1} = j)p_\infty(j). \tag{23.1.7}$$

In matrix notation this can be written as the vector equation

$$\mathbf{p}_\infty = \mathbf{M}\mathbf{p}_\infty \tag{23.1.8}$$

so that the stationary distribution is proportional to the eigenvector with unit eigenvalue of the transition matrix. Note that there may be more than one stationary distribution. See Exercise 23.1 and [134].

Example 23.1 ***PageRank***

Despite their apparent simplicity, Markov chains have been put to interesting use in information retrieval and search engines. Define the matrix

$$A_{ij} = \begin{cases} 1 & \text{if website } j \text{ has a hyperlink to website } i \\ 0 & \text{otherwise.} \end{cases} \tag{23.1.9}$$

From this we can define a Markov transition matrix with elements

$$M_{ij} = \frac{A_{ij}}{\sum_{i'} A_{i'j}}. \tag{23.1.10}$$

The equilibrium distribution of this Markov chain has the interpretation: If we follow links at random, jumping from website to website, the equilibrium distribution component $p_\infty(i)$ is the relative number of times we will visit website i. This has a natural interpretation as the 'importance' of website i; if a website is isolated in the web, it will be visited infrequently by random hopping; if a website is linked by many others it will be visited more frequently.

A crude *search engine* works as follows. For each website i a list of words associated with that website is collected. After doing this for all websites, one can make an 'inverse' list of which websites contain word w. When a user searches for word w, the list of websites that contain that word is then returned, ranked according to the importance of the site (as defined by the equilibrium distribution).

23.1.2 Fitting Markov models

Given a sequence $v_{1:T}$, fitting a stationary first-order Markov chain by maximum likelihood corresponds to setting the transitions by counting the number of observed (first-order) transitions in the sequence:

$$p(v_\tau = i|v_{\tau-1} = j) \propto \sum_{t=2}^{T} \mathbb{I}[v_t = i, v_{t-1} = j]. \tag{23.1.11}$$

To show this, for convenience we write $p(v_\tau = i|v_{\tau-1} = j) \equiv \theta_{i|j}$, so that the likelihood is (assuming v_1 is known):

$$p(v_{2:T}|\theta, v_1) = \prod_{t=2}^{T} \theta_{v_t|v_{t-1}} = \prod_{t=2}^{T} \prod_{i,j} \theta_{i|j}^{\mathbb{I}[v_t=i, v_{t-1}=j]}. \tag{23.1.12}$$

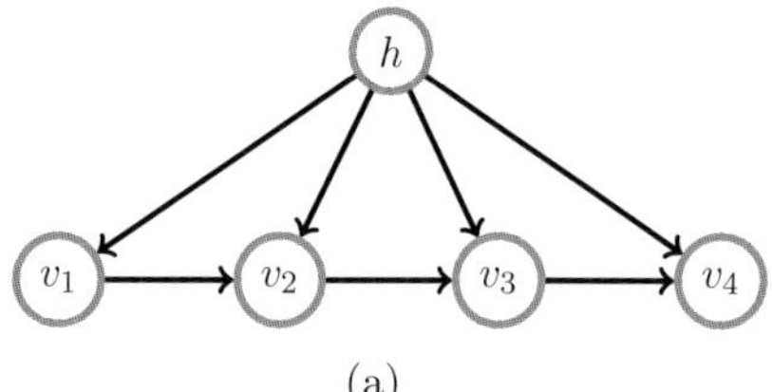

Figure 23.3 Mixture of first-order Markov chains. The discrete hidden variable $\mathrm{dom}(h) = \{1, \dots, H\}$ indexes the Markov chain $\prod_t p(v_t|v_{t-1}, h)$. Such models can be useful as simple sequence clustering tools.

Taking logs and adding the Lagrange constraint for the normalisation,

$$L(\theta) = \sum_{t=2}^{T} \sum_{i,j} \mathbb{I}[v_t = i, v_{t-1} = j] \log \theta_{i|j} + \sum_j \lambda_j \left(1 - \sum_i \theta_{i|j}\right). \tag{23.1.13}$$

Differentiating with respect to $\theta_{i|j}$ and equating to zero, we immediately arrive at the intuitive setting, Equation (23.1.11). For a set of timeseries, $v^n_{1:T_n}, n = 1, \dots, N$, the transition is given by counting all transitions across time and datapoints. The maximum likelihood setting for the initial first timestep distribution is $p(v_1 = i) \propto \sum_n \mathbb{I}[v^n_1 = i]$.

Bayesian fitting

For simplicity, we assume a factorised prior on the transition

$$p(\theta) = \prod_j p(\theta_{\cdot|j}). \tag{23.1.14}$$

A convenient choice for each conditional transition is a Dirichlet distribution with hyperparameters $\mathbf{u}_j$, $p(\theta_{\cdot|j}) = \mathrm{Dirichlet}(\theta_{\cdot|j}|\mathbf{u}_j)$, since this is conjugate to the categorical transition, giving

$$p(\theta|v_{1:T}) \propto p(v_{1:T}|\theta)p(\theta) \propto \prod_t \prod_{i,j} \theta_{i|j}^{\mathbb{I}[v_t=i, v_{t-1}=j]} \theta_{i|j}^{u_{ij}-1} = \prod_j \mathrm{Dirichlet}(\theta_{\cdot|j}|\hat{\mathbf{u}}_j) \tag{23.1.15}$$

where $\hat{\mathbf{u}}_j = \sum_{t=2}^{T} \mathbb{I}[v_{t-1} = j, v_t = i]$, being the number of $j \to i$ transitions in the dataset.

23.1.3 Mixture of Markov models

Given a set of sequences $\mathcal{V} = \{v^n_{1:T}, n = 1, \dots, N\}$, how might we cluster them? To keep the notation less cluttered, we assume that all sequences are of the same length T with the extension to differing lengths being straightforward. One simple approach is to fit a mixture of Markov models. Assuming the data is i.i.d., $p(\mathcal{V}) = \prod_n p(v^n_{1:T})$, we define a mixture model for a single sequence $v_{1:T}$. Here we assume each component model is first-order Markov

$$p(v_{1:T}) = \sum_{h=1}^{H} p(h)p(v_{1:T}|h) = \sum_{h=1}^{H} p(h) \prod_{t=1}^{T} p(v_t|v_{t-1}, h). \tag{23.1.16}$$

The graphical model is depicted in Fig. 23.3. Clustering can then be achieved by finding the maximum likelihood parameters $p(h)$, $p(v_t|v_{t-1}, h)$ and subsequently assigning the clusters according to $p(h|v^n_{1:T})$.

EM algorithm

The EM algorithm, Section 11.2, is particularly convenient for finding the maximum likelihood solution in this case since the M-step can be performed simply. Under the i.i.d. data assumption, the log likelihood is

$$\log p(\mathcal{V}) = \sum_{n=1}^{N} \log \sum_{h=1}^{H} p(h) \prod_{t=1}^{T} p(v_t^n | v_{t-1}^n, h). \tag{23.1.17}$$

For the M-step, our task is to maximise the energy

$$E = \sum_{n=1}^{N} \left\langle \log p(v_{1:T}^n, h) \right\rangle_{p^{old}(h|v_{1:T}^n)} = \sum_{n=1}^{N} \left\{ \left\langle \log p(h) \right\rangle_{p^{old}(h|v_{1:T}^n)} + \sum_{t=1}^{T} \left\langle \log p(v_t | v_{t-1}, h) \right\rangle_{p^{old}(h|v_{1:T}^n)} \right\}.$$

The contribution to the energy from the parameter $p(h)$ is

$$\sum_{n=1}^{N} \left\langle \log p(h) \right\rangle_{p^{old}(h|v_{1:T}^n)}. \tag{23.1.18}$$

By defining

$$\hat{p}^{old}(h) \propto \sum_{n=1}^{N} p^{old}(h|v_{1:T}^n) \tag{23.1.19}$$

one can view maximising (23.1.18) as equivalent to minimising

$$\mathrm{KL}\left(\hat{p}^{old}(h) | p(h)\right) \tag{23.1.20}$$

so that the optimal choice from the M-step is to set $p^{new} = \hat{p}^{old}$, namely

$$p^{new}(h) \propto \sum_{n=1}^{N} p^{old}(h|v_{1:T}^n). \tag{23.1.21}$$

For those less comfortable with this argument, a direct maximisation including a Lagrange term to ensure normalisation of $p(h)$ can be used to derive the same result.

Similarly, the M-step for $p(v_t|v_{t-1}, h)$ is

$$p^{new}(v_t = i | v_{t-1} = j, h = k) \propto \sum_{n=1}^{N} p^{old}(h = k | v_{1:T}^n) \sum_{t=2}^{T} \mathbb{I}\left[v_t^n = i\right] \mathbb{I}\left[v_{t-1}^n = j\right]. \tag{23.1.22}$$

The initial term $p(v_1|h)$ is updated using

$$p^{new}(v_1 = i | h = k) \propto \sum_{n=1}^{N} p^{old}(h = k | v_{1:T}^n) \mathbb{I}\left[v_1^n = i\right]. \tag{23.1.23}$$

Finally, the E-step sets

$$p^{old}(h|v_{1:T}^n) \propto p(h)p(v_{1:T}^n|h) = p(h)\prod_{t=1}^{T} p(v_t^n|v_{t-1}^n, h). \tag{23.1.24}$$

Given an initialisation, the EM algorithm then iterates (23.1.21), (23.1.22), (23.1.23) and (23.1.24) until convergence.

For long sequences, explicitly computing the product of many terms may lead to numerical underflow issues. In practice it is therefore best to work with logs,

$$\log p^{old}(h|v_{1:T}^n) = \log p(h) + \sum_{t=1}^{T} \log p(v_t^n|v_{t-1}^n, h) + \text{const.} \tag{23.1.25}$$

In this way any large constants common to all h can be removed and the distribution may be computed accurately. See `mixMarkov.m`.

Example 23.2 Gene clustering

Consider the 20 fictitious gene sequences below presented in an arbitrarily chosen order. Each sequence consists of 20 symbols from the set $\{A, C, G, T\}$. The task is to try to cluster these sequences into two groups, based on the assumption that gene sequences in the same cluster follow a stationary Markov chain.

```
CATAGGCATTCTATGTGCTG   CCAGTTACGGACGCCGAAAG   TGGAACCTTAAAAAAAAAAA   GTCTCCTGCCCTCTCTGAAC
GTGCCTGGACCTGAAAAGCC   CGGCCGCGCCTCCGGGAACG   AAAGTGCTCTGAAAACTCAC   ACATGAACTACATAGTATAA
GTTGGTCAGCACACGGACTG   CCTCCCCTCCCCTTTCCTGC   CACTACGGCTACCTGGGCAA   CGGTCCGTCCGAGGCACTC
TAAGTGTCCTCTGCTCCTAA   CACCATCACCCTTGCTAAGG   AAAGAACTCCCCTCCCTGCC   CAAATGCCTCACGCGTCTCA
GCCAAGCAGGGTCTCAACTT   CATGGACTGCTCCACAAAGG   AAAAAAACGAAAAACCTAAG   GCGTAAAAAAAGTCCTGGGT
```

(23.1.26)

A simple approach is to assume that the sequences are generated from a two-component $H = 2$ mixture of Markov models and train the model using maximum likelihood. The likelihood has local optima so that the procedure needs to be run several times and the solution with the highest likelihood chosen. One can then assign each of the sequences by examining $p(h = 1|v_{1:T}^n)$. If this posterior probability is greater than 0.5, we assign it to cluster 1, otherwise to cluster 2. Using this procedure, we find the following clusters:

```
CATAGGCATTCTATGTGCTG   TGGAACCTTAAAAAAAAAAA
CCAGTTACGGACGCCGAAAG   GTCTCCTGCCCTCTCTGAAC
CGGCCGCGCCTCCGGGAACG   GTGCCTGGACCTGAAAAGCC
ACATGAACTACATAGTATAA   AAAGTGCTCTGAAAACTCAC
GTTGGTCAGCACACGGACTG   CCTCCCCTCCCCTTTCCTGC
CACTACGGCTACCTGGGCAA   TAAGTGTCCTCTGCTCCTAA
CGGTCCGTCCGAGGCACTCG   AAAGAACTCCCCTCCCTGCC
CACCATCACCCTTGCTAAGG   AAAAAAACGAAAAACCTAAG
CAAATGCCTCACGCGTCTCA   GCGTAAAAAAAGTCCTGGGT
GCCAAGCAGGGTCTCAACTT
CATGGACTGCTCCACAAAGG
```

(23.1.27)

where sequences in the first column are assigned to cluster 1, and sequences in the second column to cluster 2. In this case the data in (23.1.26) were in fact generated by a two-component Markov mixture and the posterior assignment (23.1.27) is in agreement with the known clusters. See `demoMixMarkov.m`.

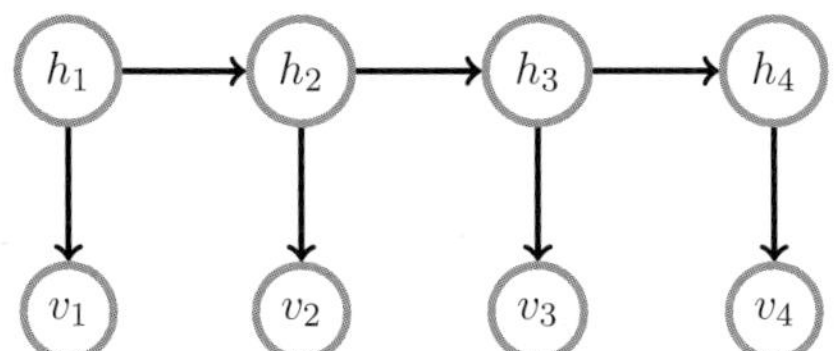

Figure 23.4 A first-order hidden Markov model with 'hidden' variables $\text{dom}(h_t) = \{1, \ldots, H\}$, $t = 1 : T$. The 'visible' variables v_t can be either discrete or continuous.

23.2 Hidden Markov models

The Hidden Markov Model (HMM) defines a Markov chain on hidden (or 'latent') variables $h_{1:T}$. The observed (or 'visible') variables are dependent on the hidden variables through an emission $p(v_t|h_t)$. This defines a joint distribution

$$p(h_{1:T}, v_{1:T}) = p(v_1|h_1)p(h_1)\prod_{t=2}^{T} p(v_t|h_t)p(h_t|h_{t-1}) \tag{23.2.1}$$

for which the graphical model is depicted in Fig. 23.4. For a stationary HMM the transition $p(h_t|h_{t-1})$ and emission $p(v_t|h_t)$ distributions are constant through time. The use of the HMM is widespread and a subset of the many applications of HMMs is given in Section 23.5.

Definition 23.3 Transition distribution For a stationary HMM the transition distribution $p(h_{t+1}|h_t)$ is defined by the $H \times H$ transition matrix

$$A_{i',i} = p(h_{t+1} = i'|h_t = i) \tag{23.2.2}$$

and an initial distribution

$$a_i = p(h_1 = i). \tag{23.2.3}$$

Definition 23.4 Emission distribution For a stationary HMM and emission distribution $p(v_t|h_t)$ with discrete states $v_t \in \{1, \ldots, V\}$, we define a $V \times H$ emission matrix

$$B_{i,j} = p(v_t = i|h_t = j). \tag{23.2.4}$$

For continuous outputs, h_t selects one of H possible output distributions $p(v_t|h_t)$, $h_t \in \{1, \ldots, H\}$.

In the engineering and machine learning communities, the term HMM typically refers to the case of discrete variables h_t, a convention that we adopt here. In statistics the term HMM often refers to any model with the independence structure in Equation (23.2.1), regardless of the form of the variables h_t (see for example [57]).

23.2.1 The classical inference problems

The common inference problems in HMMs are summarised below:

Filtering	(Inferring the present)	$p(h_t|v_{1:t})$	
Prediction	(Inferring the future)	$p(h_t|v_{1:s})$	$t > s$
Smoothing	(Inferring the past)	$p(h_t|v_{1:u})$	$t < u$
Likelihood		$p(v_{1:T})$	
Most likely hidden path	(Viterbi alignment)	$\underset{h_{1:T}}{\text{argmax}}\ p(h_{1:T}|v_{1:T})$	

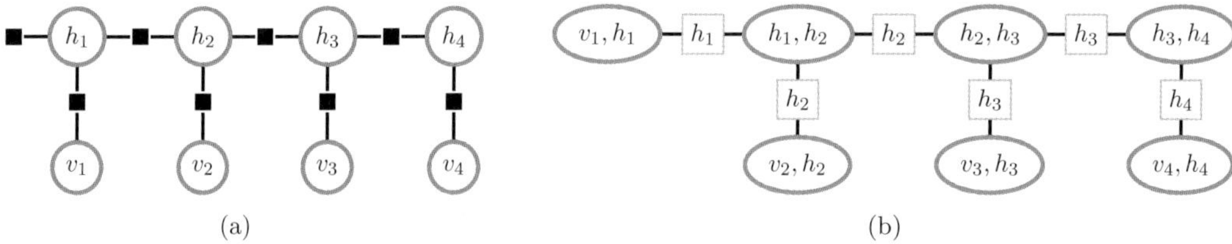

Figure 23.5 (**a**) Factor graph for the first-order HMM of Fig. 23.4. (**b**) Junction tree for Fig. 23.4.

The most likely hidden path problem is termed *Viterbi alignment* in the engineering and speech recognition literature. All these classical inference problems are computationally straightforward since the distribution is singly connected, so that any standard inference method can be adopted for these problems. The factor graph and junction trees for the first-order HMM are given in Fig. 23.5. In both cases, after suitable setting of the factors and clique potentials, filtering corresponds to passing messages from left to right and upwards; smoothing corresponds to a valid schedule of message passing/absorption both forwards and backwards along all edges. It is also straightforward to derive appropriate recursions directly, as we will do below. This is both instructive and also useful in constructing compact and numerically stable algorithms. The algorithms we derive below only exploit the conditional independence statements in the belief network structure so that analogous procedures hold for all models which have these conditional independencies; for example for continuous states on replacing summation with integration.

23.2.2 Filtering $p(h_t|v_{1:t})$

Filtering refers to ascertaining the distribution of the latent variable h_t given all information up to the present $v_{1:t}$. To do so, we first compute the joint marginal $p(h_t, v_{1:t})$ from which the conditional marginal $p(h_t|v_{1:t})$ can subsequently be obtained by normalisation. A recursion for $p(h_t, v_{1:t})$ is obtained by considering:

$$p(h_t, v_{1:t}) = \sum_{h_{t-1}} p(h_t, h_{t-1}, v_{1:t-1}, v_t) \tag{23.2.5}$$

$$= \sum_{h_{t-1}} p(v_t|\cancel{v_{1:t-1}}, h_t, \cancel{h_{t-1}})p(h_t|\cancel{v_{1:t-1}}, h_{t-1})p(v_{1:t-1}, h_{t-1}) \tag{23.2.6}$$

$$= \sum_{h_{t-1}} p(v_t|h_t)p(h_t|h_{t-1})p(h_{t-1}, v_{1:t-1}). \tag{23.2.7}$$

The cancellations follow from the conditional independence assumptions of the model. Hence if we define

$$\alpha(h_t) = p(h_t, v_{1:t}), \tag{23.2.8}$$

Equation (23.2.7) above gives the α*-recursion*

$$\alpha(h_t) = \underbrace{p(v_t|h_t)}_{\text{corrector}} \underbrace{\sum_{h_{t-1}} p(h_t|h_{t-1})\alpha(h_{t-1})}_{\text{predictor}}, \qquad t > 1 \tag{23.2.9}$$

with

$$\alpha(h_1) = p(h_1, v_1) = p(v_1|h_1)p(h_1). \tag{23.2.10}$$

This recursion has the interpretation that the filtered distribution $\alpha(h_{t-1})$ is propagated forwards by the dynamics for one timestep to reveal a new 'prior' distribution at time t. This distribution is then modulated by the observation v_t, incorporating the new evidence into the filtered distribution (this is also referred to as a predictor–corrector method). Since each α is smaller than 1, and the recursion involves multiplication by terms less than 1, the α's can become very small. To avoid numerical problems it is therefore advisable to work with $\log \alpha(h_t)$, see `HMMforward.m`.

Normalisation gives the *filtered posterior*

$$p(h_t|v_{1:t}) \propto \alpha(h_t). \tag{23.2.11}$$

If we only require the filtered posterior we are free to rescale the α's as we wish. In this case an alternative to working with $\log \alpha$ messages is to work with normalised α messages so that $\sum_{h_t} \alpha(h_t) = 1$.

We can write Equation (23.2.7) above directly as a recursion for the filtered distribution

$$p(h_t|v_{1:t}) \propto \sum_{h_{t-1}} p(v_t|h_t)p(h_t|h_{t-1})p(h_{t-1}|v_{1:t-1}) \qquad t > 1. \tag{23.2.12}$$

Intuitively, the term $p(h_{t-1}|v_{1:t-1})$ has the effect of removing all nodes in the graph before time $t-1$ and replacing their influence by a modified 'prior' distribution on h_t. One may interpret $p(v_t|h_t)p(h_t|h_{t-1})$ as a likelihood, giving rise to the joint posterior $p(h_t, h_{t-1}|v_{1:t})$ under Bayesian updating. At the next timestep the previous posterior becomes the new prior.

23.2.3 Parallel smoothing $p(h_t|v_{1:T})$

There are two main approaches to computing $p(h_t|v_{1:T})$. Perhaps the most common in the HMM literature is the parallel method which is equivalent to message passing on factor graphs. In this one separates the smoothed posterior into contributions from the past and future:

$$p(h_t, v_{1:T}) = p(h_t, v_{1:t}, v_{t+1:T}) = \underbrace{p(h_t, v_{1:t})}_{\text{past}} \underbrace{p(v_{t+1:T}|h_t, \cancel{v_{1:t}})}_{\text{future}} = \alpha(h_t)\beta(h_t). \tag{23.2.13}$$

The cancellation above occurs due to the fact that h_t d-separates the past from the future. The term $\alpha(h_t)$ is obtained from the 'forward' α recursion, (23.2.9). The $\beta(h_t)$ term may be obtained using a 'backward' β recursion as we show below. The forward and backward recursions are independent and may therefore be run in parallel, with their results combined to obtain the smoothed posterior.

The β recursion

$$p(v_{t:T}|h_{t-1}) = \sum_{h_t} p(v_t, v_{t+1:T}, h_t|h_{t-1}) \tag{23.2.14}$$

$$= \sum_{h_t} p(v_t|\cancel{v_{t+1:T}}, h_t, \cancel{h_{t-1}})p(v_{t+1:T}, h_t|h_{t-1}) \tag{23.2.15}$$

$$= \sum_{h_t} p(v_t|h_t)p(v_{t+1:T}|h_t, \cancel{h_{t-1}})p(h_t|h_{t-1}). \tag{23.2.16}$$

Defining

$$\beta(h_t) \equiv p(v_{t+1:T}|h_t), \tag{23.2.17}$$

Equation (23.2.16) above gives the β*-recursion*

$$\beta(h_{t-1}) = \sum_{h_t} p(v_t|h_t)p(h_t|h_{t-1})\beta(h_t), \qquad 2 \le t \le T \tag{23.2.18}$$

with $\beta(h_T) = 1$. As for the forward pass, working in log space is recommended to avoid numerical difficulties. If one only desires posterior distributions, one can also perform local normalisation at each stage to give $\sum_{h_t} \beta(h_t) = 1$ since only the relative magnitude of the components of β are of importance. The smoothed posterior is then given by

$$p(h_t|v_{1:T}) \equiv \gamma(h_t) = \frac{\alpha(h_t)\beta(h_t)}{\sum_{h_t} \alpha(h_t)\beta(h_t)}. \tag{23.2.19}$$

Together the $\alpha - \beta$ recursions are called the *forward-backward* algorithm.

23.2.4 Correction smoothing

An alternative to the parallel method is to form a recursion directly for the smoothed posterior. This can be achieved by recognising that conditioning on the present makes the future redundant:

$$p(h_t|v_{1:T}) = \sum_{h_{t+1}} p(h_t, h_{t+1}|v_{1:T}) = \sum_{h_{t+1}} p(h_t|h_{t+1}, v_{1:t}, \cancel{v_{t+1:T}})p(h_{t+1}|v_{1:T}). \tag{23.2.20}$$

This gives a recursion for $\gamma(h_t) \equiv p(h_t|v_{1:T})$:

$$\gamma(h_t) = \sum_{h_{t+1}} p(h_t|h_{t+1}, v_{1:t})\gamma(h_{t+1}) \tag{23.2.21}$$

with $\gamma(h_T) \propto \alpha(h_T)$. The term $p(h_t|h_{t+1}, v_{1:t})$ may be computed using the filtered results $p(h_t|v_{1:t})$:

$$p(h_t|h_{t+1}, v_{1:t}) = \frac{p(h_{t+1}, h_t|v_{1:t})}{p(h_{t+1}|v_{1:t})} = \frac{p(h_{t+1}|h_t)p(h_t|v_{1:t})}{p(h_{t+1}|v_{1:t})} \tag{23.2.22}$$

where the term $p(h_{t+1}|v_{1:t}) = \sum_{h_t} p(h_{t+1}|h_t)p(h_t|v_{1:t})$ can be found by normalisation. This is a form of *dynamics reversal*, as if we are reversing the direction of the hidden to hidden arrow in the HMM. This procedure, also termed the *Rauch–Tung–Striebel* smoother[1], is sequential since we need to first complete the α recursions, after which the γ recursion may begin. This is a so-called *correction smoother* since it 'corrects' the filtered result. Interestingly, once filtering has been carried out, the evidential states $v_{1:T}$ are not needed during the subsequent γ recursion. The $\alpha - \beta$ and $\alpha - \gamma$ recursions are related through

$$\gamma(h_t) \propto \alpha(h_t)\beta(h_t). \tag{23.2.23}$$

Computing the pairwise marginal $p(h_t, h_{t+1}|v_{1:T})$

To implement the EM algorithm for learning, Section 23.3.1, we require terms such as $p(h_t, h_{t+1}|v_{1:T})$. These can be obtained by message passing on either a factor graph or junction tree (for which the pairwise marginals are contained in the cliques, see Fig. 23.4(b)). Alternatively,

[1] It is most common to use this terminology for the continuous variable case, though we adopt it here also for the discrete variable case.

an explicit recursion is as follows:

$$
\begin{aligned}
p(h_t, h_{t+1}|v_{1:T}) &\propto p(v_{1:t}, v_{t+1}, v_{t+2:T}, h_{t+1}, h_t) \\
&= p(v_{t+2:T}|\cancel{v_{1:t}, v_{t+1}, h_t}, h_{t+1})\, p(v_{1:t}, v_{t+1}, h_{t+1}, h_t) \\
&= p(v_{t+2:T}|h_{t+1})\, p(v_{t+1}|\cancel{v_{1:t}, h_t}, h_{t+1})\, p(v_{1:t}, h_{t+1}, h_t) \\
&= p(v_{t+2:T}|h_{t+1})\, p(v_{t+1}|h_{t+1})\, p(h_{t+1}|\cancel{v_{1:t}}, h_t)\, p(v_{1:t}, h_t).
\end{aligned}
\tag{23.2.24}
$$

Rearranging, we therefore have

$$
p(h_t, h_{t+1}|v_{1:T}) \propto \alpha(h_t)\, p(v_{t+1}|h_{t+1})\, p(h_{t+1}|h_t)\, \beta(h_{t+1}). \tag{23.2.25}
$$

See HMMsmooth.m.

The likelihood $p(v_{1:T})$

The likelihood of a sequence of observations can be computed from

$$
p(v_{1:T}) = \sum_{h_T} p(h_T, v_{1:T}) = \sum_{h_T} \alpha(h_T). \tag{23.2.26}
$$

An alternative computation can be found by making use of the decomposition

$$
p(v_{1:T}) = \prod_{t=1}^{T} p(v_t|v_{1:t-1}). \tag{23.2.27}
$$

Each factor can be computed using

$$
p(v_t|v_{1:t-1}) = \sum_{h_t} p(v_t, h_t|v_{1:t-1}) \tag{23.2.28}
$$

$$
= \sum_{h_t} p(v_t|h_t, \cancel{v_{1:t-1}})\, p(h_t|v_{1:t-1}) \tag{23.2.29}
$$

$$
= \sum_{h_t} p(v_t|h_t) \sum_{h_{t-1}} p(h_t|h_{t-1}, \cancel{v_{1:t-1}})\, p(h_{t-1}|v_{1:t-1}) \tag{23.2.30}
$$

where the final term $p(h_{t-1}|v_{1:t-1})$ is the filtered result.

In both approaches the likelihood of an output sequence requires only a forward computation (filtering). If required, one can also compute the likelihood using Equation (23.2.13),

$$
p(v_{1:T}) = \sum_{h_t} \alpha(h_t)\beta(h_t) \tag{23.2.31}
$$

which is valid for any $1 \le t \le T$.

23.2.5 Sampling from $p(h_{1:T}|v_{1:T})$

Sometimes one wishes to sample joint trajectories $h_{1:T}$ from the posterior $p(h_{1:T}|v_{1:T})$. A general purpose method is described in Section 27.2.2 which can be applied in this case by noting that conditioned on the observations $v_{1:T}$, one can write the latent distribution as a Markov network. This means that the posterior distribution $p(h_{1:T}|v_{1:T})$ is a simple linear Markov chain and we can reexpress the distribution as

$$
p(h_{1:T}|v_{1:T}) = p(h_1|h_2, v_{1:T}) \ldots p(h_{T-1}|h_T, v_{1:T})\, p(h_T|v_{1:T}) \tag{23.2.32}
$$

where, from Equation (23.2.25),

$$p(h_{t-1}|h_t, v_{1:T}) \propto p(h_{t-1}, h_t|v_{1:T}) \propto \alpha(h_{t-1})p(h_t|h_{t-1}). \tag{23.2.33}$$

Sampling then begins by first drawing a state h_T from $p(h_T|v_{1:T})$. Given this state, one then draws from $p(h_{T-t}|h_T, v_{1:T})$ using Equation (23.2.33). This procedure is known as forward-filtering-backward-sampling since one first needs to run filtering to compute the required 'time-reversed' transitions $p(h_{t-1}|h_t, v_{1:T})$.

23.2.6 Most likely joint state

The most likely path $h_{1:T}$ of $p(h_{1:T}|v_{1:T})$ is the same as the most likely state (for fixed $v_{1:T}$) of

$$p(h_{1:T}, v_{1:T}) = \prod_t p(v_t|h_t)p(h_t|h_{t-1}). \tag{23.2.34}$$

The most likely path can be found using the max-product version of the factor graph or max-absorption on the junction tree. Alternatively, an explicit derivation can be obtained by considering:

$$\max_{h_T} \prod_{t=1}^{T} p(v_t|h_t)p(h_t|h_{t-1}) = \left\{\prod_{t=1}^{T-1} p(v_t|h_t)p(h_t|h_{t-1})\right\} \underbrace{\max_{h_T} p(v_T|h_T)p(h_T|h_{T-1})}_{\mu(h_{T-1})}. \tag{23.2.35}$$

The message $\mu(h_{T-1})$ conveys information from the end of the chain to the penultimate timestep. We can continue in this manner, defining the recursion

$$\mu(h_{t-1}) = \max_{h_t} p(v_t|h_t)p(h_t|h_{t-1})\mu(h_t), \qquad 2 \le t \le T \tag{23.2.36}$$

with $\mu(h_T) = 1$. This means that the effect of maximising over $h_2, \ldots, h_T$ is compressed into a message $\mu(h_1)$ so that the most likely state h_1^* is given by

$$h_1^* = \underset{h_1}{\text{argmax}}\ p(v_1|h_1)p(h_1)\mu(h_1). \tag{23.2.37}$$

Once computed, backtracking gives

$$h_t^* = \underset{h_t}{\text{argmax}}\ p(v_t|h_t)p(h_t|h_{t-1}^*)\mu(h_t). \tag{23.2.38}$$

This special case of the max-product algorithm is called the *Viterbi algorithm*. Similarly, one may use the N-max-product algorithm, Section 5.2.1, to obtain the N-most likely hidden paths.

23.2.7 Prediction

The one-step ahead predictive distribution is given by

$$p(v_{t+1}|v_{1:t}) = \sum_{h_t, h_{t+1}} p(v_{t+1}|h_{t+1})p(h_{t+1}|h_t)p(h_t|v_{1:t}). \tag{23.2.39}$$

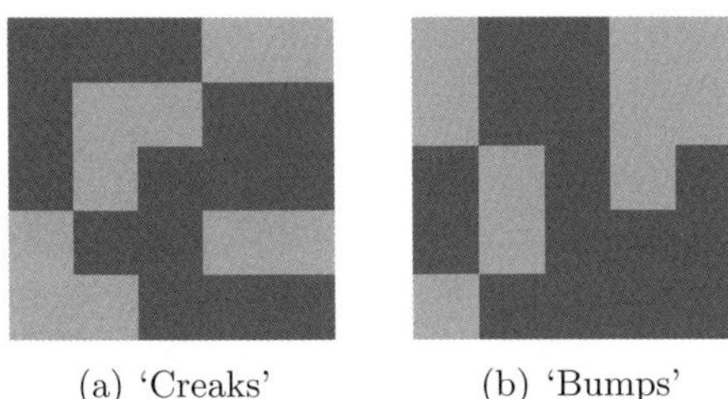

(a) 'Creaks' (b) 'Bumps'

Figure 23.6 Localising the burglar. The latent variable $h_t \in \{1, \ldots, 25\}$ denotes the positions, defined over the 5×5 grid of the ground floor of the house. (**a**) A representation of the probability that the 'floor will creak' at each of the 25 positions, $p(v^{creak}|h)$. Light squares represent probability 0.9 and dark squares 0.1. (**b**) A representation of the probability $p(v^{bump}|h)$ that the burglar will bump into something in each of the 25 positions.

Example 23.3 A localisation example

You're asleep upstairs in your house and awoken by noises from downstairs. You realise that a burglar is on the ground floor and attempt to understand where he is from listening to his movements. You mentally partition the ground floor into a 5×5 grid. For each grid position you know the probability that if someone is in that position the floorboard will creak, Fig. 23.6(a). Similarly you know for each position the probability that someone will bump into something in the dark, Fig. 23.6(b). The floorboard creaking and bumping into objects can occur independently. In addition you assume that the burglar will move only one grid square – forwards, backwards, left or right – in a single timestep. Based on a series of bump/no bump and creak/no creak information, Fig. 23.7(a), you try to figure out based on your knowledge of the ground floor, where the burglar might be.

We can represent the scenario using an HMM where $h \in \{1, \ldots, 25\}$ denotes the grid square. The visible variable has a composite form $v = v^{creak} \otimes v^{bump}$ where v^{creak} and v^{bump} each take two states. To use our standard code, we form a new visible variable v with four states using

$$p(v|h) = p(v^{creak}|h)p(v^{bump}|h). \tag{23.2.40}$$

Based on the past information, our belief as to where the burglar might be is represented by the filtered distribution $p(h_t|v_{1:t})$, Fig. 23.7. In the beginning the filtered distribution has significant mass in many states since we don't yet have sufficient information to establish where the burglar is. As time goes along and we gather more information, the filtered distribution becomes more concentrated in a small number of states. After the burglar has left at $T = 10$, the police arrive and try to piece together where the burglar went, based on the sequence of creaks and bumps you provide. At any time t, the information as to where the burglar could have been is represented by the smoothed distribution $p(h_t|v_{1:10})$. The smoothed distribution is generally more concentrated in a few states than the filtered distribution since we have more information (from the past and future) to help establish the burglar's position at that time. The police's single best-guess for the trajectory the burglar took is provided by the most likely joint hidden state $\arg\max_{h_{1:10}} p(h_{1:10}|v_{1:10})$. See `demoHMMburglar.m`.

23.2.8 Self-localisation and kidnapped robots

A robot has an internal grid-based map of its environment and for each location $h \in \{1, \ldots, H\}$ knows the likely sensor readings he would expect in that location. The robot is 'kidnapped' and placed somewhere in the environment. The robot then starts to move, gathering sensor information. Based on these readings $v_{1:t}$ and intended movements $m_{1:t}$, the robot attempts to figure out his location by comparing his actual sensor readings with his internal map of expected sensor readings

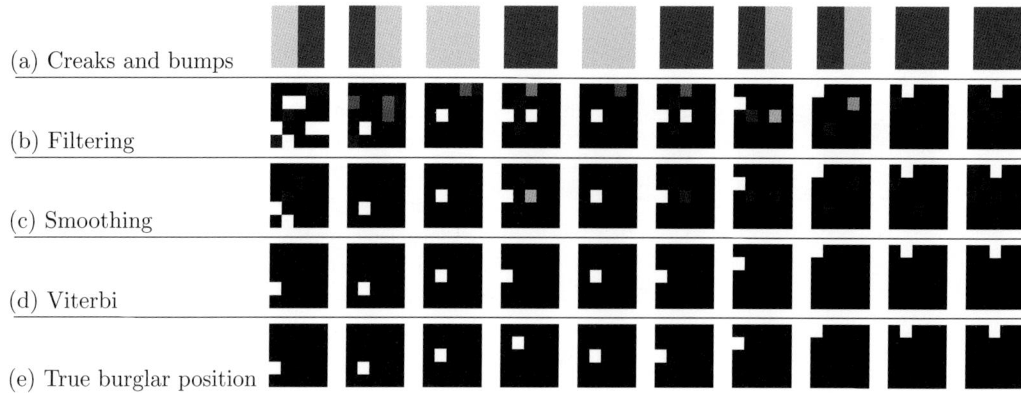

Figure 23.7 Localising the burglar through time for 10 timesteps. (**a**) Each panel represents the visible information $v_t = \left(v_t^{creak}, v_t^{bump}\right)$, where $v_t^{creak} = 1$ means that there was a 'creak in the floorboard' ($v_t^{creak} = 2$ otherwise) and $v_t^{bump} = 1$ meaning 'bumped into something' (and is in state 2 otherwise). There are 10 panels, one for each time $t = 1, \ldots, 10$. The left half of the panel represents v_t^1 and the right half v_t^2. The lighter shade represents the occurrence of a creak or bump, the darker shade the absence. (**b**) The filtered distribution $p(h_t|v_{1:t})$ representing where we think the burglar is. (**c**) The smoothed distribution $p(h_t|v_{1:10})$ that represents the distribution of the burglar's position given that we know both the past and future observations. (**d**) The most likely (Viterbi) burglar path $\arg\max_{h_{1:10}} p(h_{1:10}|v_{1:10})$. (**e**) The actual path of the burglar.

for each location. Due to wheel slippage on the floor an intended action by the robot, such as 'move forwards', might not be successful. Given all the information the robot has, he would like to infer $p(h_t|v_{1:t}, m_{1:t})$. This problem differs from the burglar scenario in that the robot now has knowledge of the intended movements he makes. This should give more information as to where he could be. One can view this as extra 'visible' information, though it is more natural to think of this as additional input information. A model of this scenario is, see Fig. 23.9,

$$p(v_{1:T}, m_{1:T}, h_{1:T}) = \prod_{t=1}^{T} p(v_t|h_t)p(h_t|h_{t-1}, m_{t-1})p(m_t). \tag{23.2.41}$$

The visible variables $v_{1:T}$ are known, as are the intended movements $m_{1:T}$. The model expresses that the movements selected by the robot are random (hence no decision making in terms of where to go next). We assume that the robot has full knowledge of the conditional distributions defining the model (he knows the 'map' of his environment and all state transition and emission probabilities).

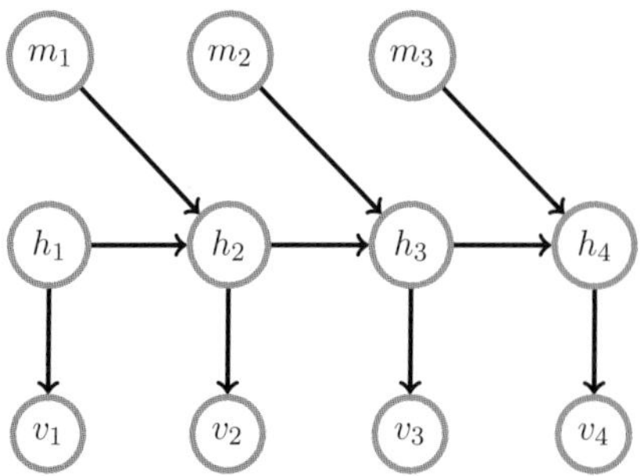

Figure 23.8 A model for robot self-localisation. At each time the robot makes an intended movement, m_t. As a generative model, knowing the intended movement m_t and the current grid position h_t, the robot has an idea of where he should be at the next time step and what sensor reading v_{t+1} he would expect there. Based on only the sensor information $v_{1:T}$ and the intended movements $m_{1:T}$, the task is to infer a distribution over robot locations $p(h_{1:T}|m_{1:T}, v_{1:T})$.

If our interest is only in localising the robot, since the inputs m are known, this model is in fact a form of time-dependent HMM:

$$p(v_{1:T}, h_{1:T}) = \prod_{t=1}^{T} p(v_t|h_t)p(h_t|h_{t-1}, t) \tag{23.2.42}$$

for a time-dependent transition $p(h_t|h_{t-1}, t)$ defined by the intended movement m_{t-1}. Any inference task required then follows the standard stationary HMM algorithms, albeit on replacing the time-independent transitions $p(h_t|h_{t-1})$ with the known time-dependent transitions.

In *self-localisation and mapping* (SLAM) the robot does not know the map of his environment. This corresponds to having to learn the transition and emission distributions on-the-fly as he explores the environment.

Example 23.4 Robot localisation (Robot Localisation)

Consider the following toy tracking problem (from Taylan Cemgil). A robot is moving around a circular corridor and at any time occupies one of S possible locations, as indicated. At each timestep t, the robot stays where it is with probability ϵ, or moves to the next point in a counter-clockwise direction with probability $1 - \epsilon$.

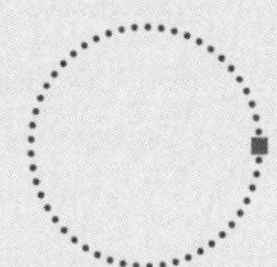

This can be conveniently represented by an $S \times S$ matrix $\mathbf{A}$ with elements $A_{ji} = p(h_t = j|h_{t-1} = i)$. For example, for $S = 3$, we have

$$\mathbf{A} = \epsilon \begin{pmatrix} 1 & 0 & 0 \\ 0 & 1 & 0 \\ 0 & 0 & 1 \end{pmatrix} + (1 - \epsilon) \begin{pmatrix} 0 & 0 & 1 \\ 1 & 0 & 0 \\ 0 & 1 & 0 \end{pmatrix}. \tag{23.2.43}$$

At each timestep t, the robot sensors measure its position, obtaining either the correct location with probability w or a uniformly random location with probability $1 - w$. For example, for $S = 3$, we have

$$\mathbf{B} = w \begin{pmatrix} 1 & 0 & 0 \\ 0 & 1 & 0 \\ 0 & 0 & 1 \end{pmatrix} + \frac{(1 - w)}{3} \begin{pmatrix} 1 & 1 & 1 \\ 1 & 1 & 1 \\ 1 & 1 & 1 \end{pmatrix}. \tag{23.2.44}$$

A typical realisation $y_{1:T}$ from the process defined by this HMM with $S = 50$, $\epsilon = 0.5$, $T = 30$ and $w = 0.3$ is depicted in Fig. 23.9(a). We are interested in inferring the true locations of the robot from the noisy measured locations. At each time t, the true location can be inferred from the filtered posterior $p(h_t|v_{1:t})$, Fig. 23.9(b), which uses measurements up to t; or from the smoothed posterior $p(h_t|v_{1:T})$, Fig. 23.9(c), which uses both past and future observations and is therefore generally more accurate.

23.2.9 Natural language models

A simple generative model of language can be obtained from the letter-to-letter transitions (a so-called *bigram*). In the example below, we use this in an HMM to clean up mis-typings.

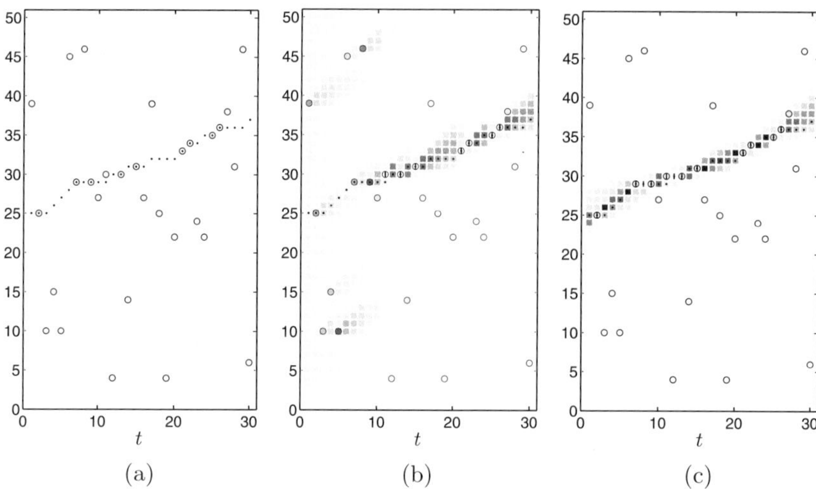

Figure 23.9 Filtering and smoothing for robot tracking using an HMM with $S = 50$. (**a**) A realisation from the HMM example described in the text. The dots indicate the true latent locations of the robot, whilst the open circles indicate the noisy measured locations. (**b**) The squares indicate the filtering distribution at each timestep t, $p(h_t|v_{1:t})$. This probability is proportional to the grey level with black corresponding to 1 and white to 0. Note that the posterior for the first timesteps is multimodal, therefore the true position cannot be accurately estimated. (**c**) The squares indicate the smoothing distribution at each timestep t, $p(t|v_{1:T})$. Note that, for $t < T$, we estimate the position retrospectively and the uncertainty is significantly lower when compared to the filtered estimates.

Example 23.5 Stubby fingers

A 'stubby fingers' typist has the tendency to hit either the correct key or a single neighbouring key. For simplicity we assume that there are 27 keys: lower case a to lower case z and the space bar. To model this we use an emission distribution $B_{ij} = p(v = i|h = j)$ where $i = 1, \ldots, 27$, $j = 1, \ldots, 27$, as depicted in Fig. 23.10. A database of letter-to-next-letter frequencies, yields the transition matrix $A_{ij} = p(h' = i|h = j)$ in English. For simplicity we assume that $p(h_1)$ is uniform. Also we assume that each intended key press results in a single press. Given a typed sequence `kezrninh` what is the most likely word that this corresponds to? By listing the 200 most likely hidden sequences (using the N-max-product algorithm) and discarding those that are not in a standard English dictionary, the most likely word that was intended is `learning`. See `demoHMMbigram.m`.

23.3 Learning HMMs

Given a set of data $\mathcal{V} = \{\mathbf{v}^1, \ldots, \mathbf{v}^N\}$ of N sequences, where sequence $\mathbf{v}^n = v^n_{1:T_n}$ is of length T_n, we seek the HMM transition matrix $\mathbf{A}$, emission matrix $\mathbf{B}$ and initial vector $\mathbf{a}$ most likely to have have generated $\mathcal{V}$. We make the i.i.d. assumption so that each sequence is independently generated and assume that we know the number of hidden states H. For simplicity we concentrate here on the case of discrete visible variables, assuming also we know the number of states V. Whilst implementing either EM or gradient-based maximum likelihood is straightforward for the HMM, the likelihood has many local optima, and care needs to be taken with initialisation.

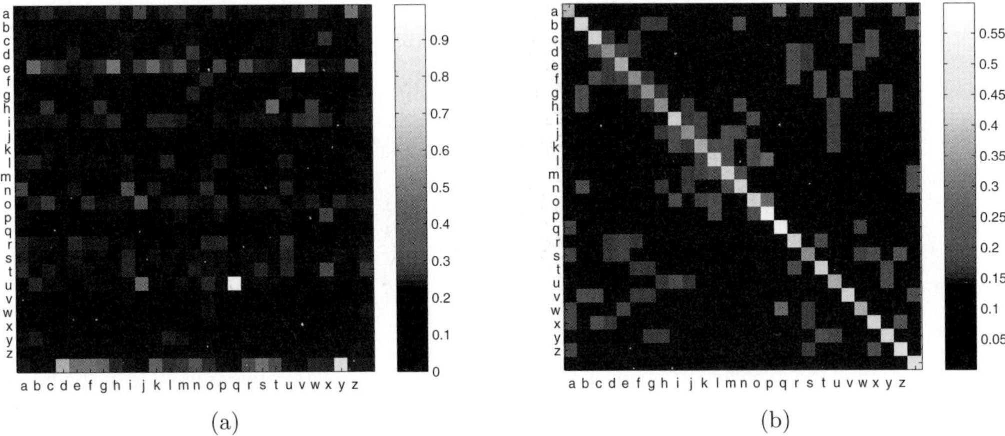

Figure 23.10 (**a**) The letter-to-letter transition matrix for English $p(h' = i|h = j)$. (**b**) The letter emission matrix for a typist with 'stubby fingers' in which the key or a neighbour on the keyboard is likely to be hit.

23.3.1 EM algorithm

The application of EM to the HMM model is called the *Baum–Welch* algorithm and follows the general strategy outlined in Section 11.2. The EM algorithm is convenient in this case and leads to closed form expressions for the M-step.

M-step

Assuming i.i.d. data, the M-step is given by maximising the 'energy':

$$\sum_{n=1}^{N} \langle \log p(v_1^n, v_2^n \ldots, v_{T^n}^n, h_1^n, h_2^n, \ldots, h_{T^n}^n) \rangle_{p^{old}(\mathbf{h}^n|\mathbf{v}^n)} \tag{23.3.1}$$

with respect to the parameters $\mathbf{A}, \mathbf{B}, \mathbf{a}$; $\mathbf{h}^n$ denotes $h_{1:T_n}$. Using the form of the HMM, we obtain

$$\sum_{n=1}^{N} \left\{ \langle \log p(h_1) \rangle_{p^{old}(h_1|\mathbf{v}^n)} + \sum_{t=1}^{T_n-1} \langle \log p(h_{t+1}|h_t) \rangle_{p^{old}(h_t,h_{t+1}|\mathbf{v}^n)} + \sum_{t=1}^{T_n} \langle \log p(v_t^n|h_t) \rangle_{p^{old}(h_t|\mathbf{v}^n)} \right\} \tag{23.3.2}$$

where for compactness we drop the sequence index from the h variables. To avoid potential confusion, we write $p^{new}(h_1 = i)$ to denote the (new) table entry for the probability that the initial hidden variable is in state i. Optimising Equation (23.3.2) with respect to $p(h_1)$, (and enforcing $p(h_1)$ to be a distribution) we obtain

$$a_i^{new} \equiv p^{new}(h_1 = i) = \frac{1}{N} \sum_{n=1}^{N} p^{old}(h_1 = i|\mathbf{v}^n). \tag{23.3.3}$$

which is the average number of times (with respect to p^{old}) that the first hidden variable is in state i. Similarly, the M-step for the transition is

$$A_{i',i}^{new} \equiv p^{new}(h_{t+1} = i'|h_t = i) \propto \sum_{n=1}^{N} \sum_{t=1}^{T_n-1} p^{old}(h_t = i, h_{t+1} = i'|\mathbf{v}^n) \tag{23.3.4}$$

which is the number of times that a transition from hidden state i to hidden state i' occurs, averaged over all times (since we assumed stationarity) and training sequences. Normalising, we obtain

$$A^{new}_{i',i} = \frac{\sum_{n=1}^{N}\sum_{t=1}^{T_n-1} p^{old}(h_t = i, h_{t+1} = i'|\mathbf{v}^n)}{\sum_{i'}\sum_{n=1}^{N}\sum_{t=1}^{T_n-1} p^{old}(h_t = i, h_{t+1} = i'|\mathbf{v}^n)}. \tag{23.3.5}$$

Finally, the M-step update for the emission is

$$B^{new}_{j,i} \equiv p^{new}(v_t = j|h_t = i) \propto \sum_{n=1}^{N}\sum_{t=1}^{T_n} \mathbb{I}\left[v_t^n = j\right] p^{old}(h_t = i|\mathbf{v}^n) \tag{23.3.6}$$

which is the expected number of times that, for the observation being in state j, the hidden state is i. The proportionality constant is determined by the normalisation requirement.

E-step

In computing the M-step above the quantities $p^{old}(h_1 = i|\mathbf{v}^n)$, $p^{old}(h_t = i, h_{t+1} = i'|\mathbf{v}^n)$ and $p^{old}(h_t = i|\mathbf{v}^n)$ are obtained by smoothed inference using the techniques described in Section 23.2.1.

Equations (23.3.3), (23.3.5), (23.3.6) are repeated until convergence. See `HMMem.m` and `demoHMMlearn.m`.

Parameter initialisation

The EM algorithm converges to a local maximum of the likelihood and, in general, there is no guarantee that the algorithm will find the global maximum. How best to initialise the parameters is a thorny issue, with a suitable initialisation of the emission distribution often being critical for success [246]. A practical strategy is to initialise the emission $p(v|h)$ based on first fitting a simpler non-temporal mixture model $\sum_h p(v|h)p(h)$ to the data.

Continuous observations

For a continuous vector observation $\mathbf{v}_t$, with $\dim(\mathbf{v}_t) = D$, we require a model $p(\mathbf{v}_t|h_t)$ mapping the discrete state h_t to a distribution over outputs. Using a continuous output does not change any of the standard inference message-passing equations so that inference can be carried out for essentially arbitrarily complex emission distributions. Indeed, for filtering, smoothing and Viterbi inference, the normalisation Z of the emission $p(\mathbf{v}|h) = \phi(\mathbf{v}, h)/Z$ is not required. For learning, however, the emission normalisation constant is required since this is dependent on the parameters of the model.

23.3.2 Mixture emission

To make a richer emission model (particularly for continuous observations), one approach is to use a mixture

$$p(v_t|h_t) = \sum_{k_t} p(v_t|k_t, h_t)p(k_t|h_t) \tag{23.3.7}$$

where k_t is a discrete summation variable. For learning, it is useful to consider the k_t as additional latent variables; the EM algorithm then carries through in a straightforward way. Using the notation q as shorthand for p^{old}, the E-step sets:

$$q(k_t|h_t^n) \propto p(v^n|h_t^n, k_t)p(k_t|h_t). \tag{23.3.8}$$

The energy is given by

$$E = \sum_n \sum_{t=1}^{T} \left\langle -\langle \log q(k_t|h_t^n) \rangle_{q(k_t|h_t^n)} + \langle \log p(v_t^n|k_t, h_t^n) \rangle_{q(k_t|h_t^n)} + \langle \log p(k_t|h_t^n) \rangle_{q(k_t|h_t^n)} \right\rangle_{q(h_t^n|v_{1:T}^n)}. \tag{23.3.9}$$

The contribution from each emission component $p(v = \mathsf{v}|h = \mathsf{h}, k = \mathsf{k})$ is

$$\sum_n \sum_{t=1}^{T} q(k_t = \mathsf{k}|h_t^n = \mathsf{h})q(h_t^n = \mathsf{h}|v_{1:T}^n) \log p(v_t^n|h = \mathsf{h}, k = \mathsf{k}). \tag{23.3.10}$$

For fixed $q(k_t = \mathsf{k}|h_t^n = \mathsf{h})$, one needs to numerically optimise the above expression with respect to the emission parameters. Similarly, the contribution to the energy bound from the mixture weights is given by

$$\log p(k = \mathsf{k}|h = \mathsf{h}) \sum_n \sum_{t=1}^{T} q(k_t = \mathsf{k}|h_t^n = \mathsf{h})q(h_t^n = \mathsf{h}|v_{1:T}^n) \tag{23.3.11}$$

so that the M-step update for the mixture weights is,

$$p(k = \mathsf{k}|h = \mathsf{h}) \propto \sum_n \sum_{t=1}^{T} q(k_t = \mathsf{k}|h_t^n = \mathsf{h})q(h_t^n = \mathsf{h}|v_{1:T}^n). \tag{23.3.12}$$

In this case the EM algorithm is composed of an 'emission' EM loop in which the transitions and $q(h_t^n = \mathsf{h}|v_{1:T}^n)$ are fixed, during which the emissions $p(v|h, k)$ are learned, along with updating $q(k_t = \mathsf{k}|h_t^n = \mathsf{h})$. The 'transition' EM loop fixes the emission distribution $p(v|h)$ and learns the best transition $p(h_t|h_{t-1})$.

23.3.3 The HMM-GMM

A common continuous observation mixture emission model component is a Gaussian

$$p(\mathbf{v}_t|k_t, h_t) = \mathcal{N}\left(\mathbf{v}_t \,|\, \boldsymbol{\mu}_{k_t,h_t}, \boldsymbol{\Sigma}_{k_t,h_t}\right) \tag{23.3.13}$$

so that k_t, h_t indexes the $K \times H$ mean vectors and covariance matrices. Expectation maximisation updates for these means and covariances are straightforward to derive from Equation (23.3.9), see Exercise 23.14. These models are common in tracking applications and speech recognition (usually under the constraint that the covariances are diagonal).

23.3.4 Discriminative training

Hidden Markov models can be used for supervised learning of sequences. That is, for each sequence $v_{1:T}^n$, we have a corresponding class label c^n. For example, we might associate a particular composer $c \in \{1, \ldots, C\}$ with a sequence $v_{1:T}$ and wish to make a model that will predict the composer for a novel music sequence. A generative approach to using HMMs for classification is to train a separate

HMM for each class, $p(v_{1:T}|c)$ and subsequently use Bayes' rule to form the classification for a novel sequence $v^*_{1:T}$ using

$$p(c^*|v^*_{1:T}) = \frac{p(v^*_{1:T}|c^*)p(c^*)}{\sum_{c'=1}^{C} p(v^*_{1:T}|c')p(c')}. \tag{23.3.14}$$

If the data are noisy and difficult to model, however, this generative approach may not work well since much of the expressive power of each model is used to model the complex data, rather than focussing on the decision boundary. In applications such as speech recognition, improvements in performance are often reported when the models are trained in a discriminative way. In discriminative training, see for example [163], one defines a new single discriminative model, formed from the C HMMs using

$$p(c|v_{1:T}) = \frac{p(v_{1:T}|c)p(c)}{\sum_{c'=1}^{C} p(v_{1:T}|c')p(c')} \tag{23.3.15}$$

and then maximises the likelihood of a set of observed classes and corresponding observations $v_{1:T}$. For a single data pair, $(c^n, v^n_{1:T})$, the log likelihood is

$$\log p(c^n|v^n_{1:T}) = \underbrace{\log p(v^n_{1:T}|c^n)}_{\text{generative likelihood}} + \log p(c^n) - \log \sum_{c'=1}^{C} p(v^n_{1:T}|c')p(c'). \tag{23.3.16}$$

The first term above represents the generative likelihood term, with the last term accounting for the discrimination. Whilst deriving EM-style updates is hampered by the discriminative terms, computing the gradient is straightforward using the technique described in Section 11.6.

23.4 Related models

23.4.1 Explicit duration model

For an HMM with self-transition $p(h_t = i|h_{t-1} = i) \equiv \theta_i$, the probability that the latent dynamics stays in state i for τ timesteps is θ_i^τ, which decays exponentially with time. In practice, however, we would often like to constrain the dynamics to remain in the same state for a minimum number of timesteps, or to have a specified duration distribution. A way to enforce this is to use a latent counter variable c_t which at the beginning is initialised to a duration sampled from the duration distribution $p_{dur}(c_t)$ with maximal duration D_{max}. Then at each timestep the counter decrements by 1, until it reaches 1, after which a new duration is sampled:

$$p(c_t|c_{t-1}) = \begin{cases} \delta\left(c_t, c_{t-1} - 1\right) & c_{t-1} > 1 \\ p_{dur}(c_t) & c_{t-1} = 1. \end{cases} \tag{23.4.1}$$

The state h_t can transition only when $c_t = 1$:

$$p(h_t|h_{t-1}, c_t) = \begin{cases} \delta\left(h_t, h_{t-1}\right) & c_t > 1 \\ p_{tran}(h_t|h_{t-1}) & c_t = 1. \end{cases} \tag{23.4.2}$$

Including the counter variable c defines a joint latent distribution $p(c_{1:T}, h_{1:T})$ that ensures h remains in a desired minimal number of timesteps, see Fig. 23.11. Since $\dim\left(c_t \otimes h_t\right) = D_{max}H$, naively the computational complexity of inference in this model scales as $O\left(TH^2D^2_{max}\right)$. However, when one runs the forward and backward recursions, the deterministic nature of the transitions means that this can be reduced to $O\left(TH^2D_{max}\right)$[214] – see also Exercise 23.15.

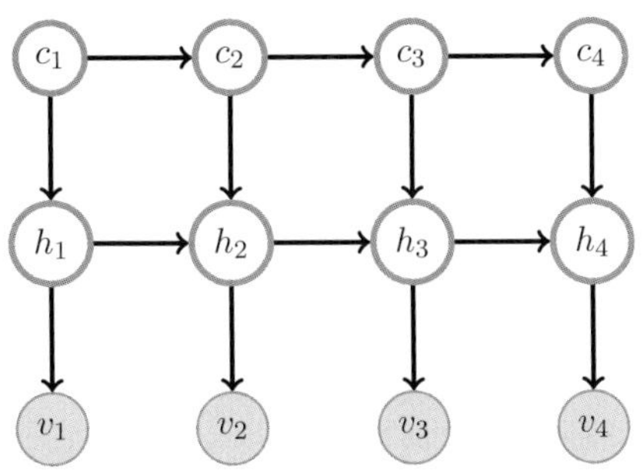

Figure 23.11 An explicit duration HMM. The counter variables c_t deterministically count down to zero. When they reach one, a h transition is allowed, and a new value for the duration c_t is sampled.

The hidden semi-Markov model generalises the explicit duration model in that once a new duration c_t is sampled, the model emits a distribution $p(v_{t:t+c_t-1}|h_t)$ defined on a segment of the next c_t observations [232].

23.4.2 Input–output HMM

The IOHMM [31] is an HMM with additional input variables $x_{1:T}$, see Fig. 23.12. Each input can be continuous or discrete and modulates the transitions

$$p(v_{1:T}, h_{1:T}|x_{1:T}) = \prod_t p(v_t|h_t, x_t)p(h_t|h_{t-1}, x_t). \tag{23.4.3}$$

The IOHMM may be used as a conditional predictor, where the outputs v_t represent the prediction at time t. In the case of continuous inputs and discrete outputs, the tables $p(v_t|h_t, x_t)$ and $p(h_t|h_{t-1}, x_t)$ are usually parameterised using a non-linear function, for example

$$p(v_t = y|h_t = h, x_t = x, \mathbf{w}) \propto \exp\left(\mathbf{w}_{h,y}^{\mathsf{T}} x\right). \tag{23.4.4}$$

Inference then follows in a similar manner as for the standard HMM. Defining

$$\alpha(h_t) \equiv p(h_t, v_{1:t}|x_{1:t}) \tag{23.4.5}$$

the forward pass is given by

$$\alpha(h_t) = \sum_{h_{t-1}} p(h_t, h_{t-1}, v_{1:t-1}, v_t|x_{1:t}) \tag{23.4.6}$$

$$= \sum_{h_{t-1}} p(v_t|v_{1:t-1}, x_{1:t}, h_t, h_{t-1})p(h_t|v_{1:t-1}, x_{1:t}, h_{t-1})p(v_{1:t-1}, h_{t-1}|x_{1:t}) \tag{23.4.7}$$

$$= p(v_t|x_t, h_t)\sum_{h_{t-1}} p(h_t|h_{t-1}, x_t)\alpha(h_{t-1}). \tag{23.4.8}$$

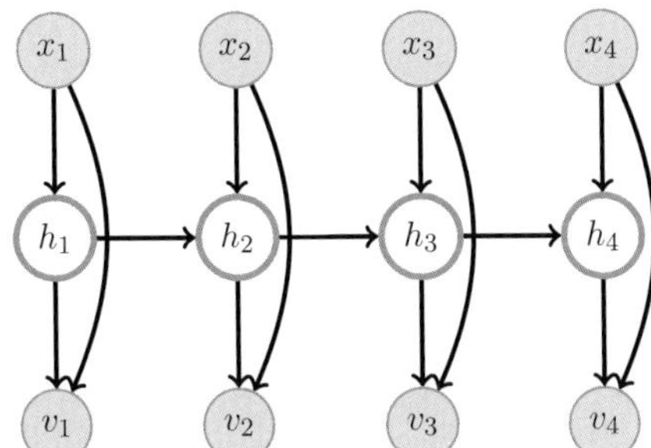

Figure 23.12 A first-order input–output hidden Markov model. The input x and output v nodes are shaded to emphasise that their states are known during training. During testing, the inputs are known and the outputs are predicted.

The γ backward pass is

$$p(h_t|x_{1:T}, v_{1:T}) = \sum_{h_{t+1}} p(h_t, h_{t+1}|x_{1:t+1}, x_{t+2:T}, v_{1:T}) = \sum_{h_{t+1}} p(h_t|h_{t+1}, x_{1:t+1}, v_{1:t})p(h_{t+1}|x_{1:T}, v_{1:T}) \tag{23.4.9}$$

for which we need

$$p(h_t|h_{t+1}, x_{1:t+1}, v_{1:t}) = \frac{p(h_{t+1}, h_t|x_{1:t+1}, v_{1:t})}{p(h_{t+1}|x_{1:t+1}, v_{1:t})} = \frac{p(h_{t+1}|h_t, x_{t+1})p(h_t|x_{1:t}, v_{1:t})}{\sum_{h_t} p(h_{t+1}|h_t, x_{t+1})p(h_t|x_{1:t}, v_{1:t})}. \tag{23.4.10}$$

The likelihood can be found from $\sum_{h_T} \alpha(h_T)$.

Direction bias

Consider predicting the output distribution $p(v_t|x_{1:T})$ given both past and future input information $x_{1:T}$. Because the hidden states are unobserved we have $p(v_t|x_{1:T}) = p(v_t|x_{1:t})$. Thus the IOHMM prediction uses only past information and discards any future contextual information. This 'direction bias' is sometimes considered problematic (particularly in natural language modelling) and motivates the use of undirected models, such as conditional random fields.

23.4.3 Linear chain CRFs

Linear chain Conditional Random Fields (CRFs) are an extension of the unstructured CRFs we briefly discussed in Section 9.6.5 and have application to modelling the distribution of a set of outputs $y_{1:T}$ given an input vector $\mathbf{x}$. For example, $\mathbf{x}$ might represent a sentence in English, and $y_{1:T}$ should represent the translation into French. Note that the vector $\mathbf{x}$ does not have to have dimension T. A first-order linear chain CRF has the form

$$p(y_{1:T}|\mathbf{x}, \boldsymbol{\lambda}) = \frac{1}{Z(\mathbf{x}, \boldsymbol{\lambda})} \prod_{t=2}^{T} \phi_t(y_t, y_{t-1}, \mathbf{x}, \boldsymbol{\lambda}) \tag{23.4.11}$$

where $\boldsymbol{\lambda}$ are the free parameters of the potentials. In practice it is common to use potentials of the form

$$\exp\left(\sum_{k=1}^{K} \lambda_k f_{k,t}(y_t, y_{t-1}, \mathbf{x})\right) \tag{23.4.12}$$

where $f_{k,t}(y_t, y_{t-1}, x)$ are 'features', see also Section 9.6.5. Given a set of input–output sequence pairs, $\{(\mathbf{x}^n, y^n_{1:T}), n = 1, \ldots, N\}$ (assuming all sequences have equal length T for simplicity), we can learn the parameters $\boldsymbol{\lambda}$ by maximum likelihood. Under the standard i.i.d. data assumption, the log likelihood is

$$L(\boldsymbol{\lambda}) = \sum_{t,n} \sum_{k} \lambda_k f_k(y^n_t, y^n_{t-1}, \mathbf{x}^n) - \sum_{n} \log Z(\mathbf{x}^n, \boldsymbol{\lambda}). \tag{23.4.13}$$

The reader may readily check that the log likelihood is concave so that the objective function has no local optima. The gradient is given by

$$\frac{\partial}{\partial \lambda_i} L(\boldsymbol{\lambda}) = \sum_{n,t} \left(f_i(y^n_t, y^n_{t-1}, \mathbf{x}^n) - \langle f_i(y_t, y_{t-1}, \mathbf{x}^n) \rangle_{p(y_t, y_{t-1}|\mathbf{x}^n, \lambda)} \right). \tag{23.4.14}$$

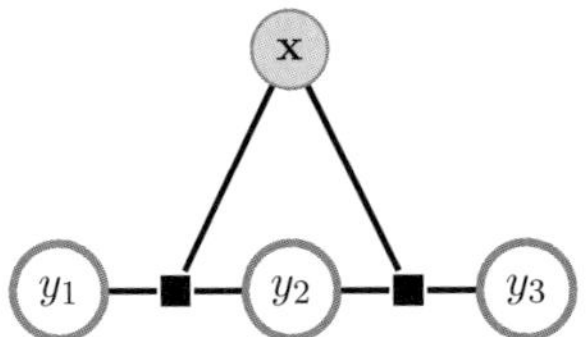

Figure 23.13 Linear chain CRF. Since the input x is observed, the distribution is just a linear chain factor graph. The inference of pairwise marginals $p(y_t, y_{t-1}|x)$ is therefore straightforward using message passing.

Learning therefore requires inference of the marginal terms $p(y_t, y_{t-1}|\mathbf{x}, \boldsymbol{\lambda})$. Since Equation (23.4.11) corresponds to a linear chain factor graph, see Fig. 23.13, inference of pairwise marginals is straightforward using message passing. This can be achieved using either the standard factor graph message passing or by deriving an explicit algorithm, see Exercise 23.10. Given the gradient, one may use any standard numerical optimisation routine to learn the parameters $\boldsymbol{\lambda}$. In some applications, particularly in natural language processing, the dimension K of the vector of features $f_1, \ldots, f_K$ may be many hundreds of thousands. This means that the storage of the Hessian is not feasible for Newton-based training and either limited memory methods or conjugate gradient techniques are typically preferred [308].

After training we can use the model to find the most likely output sequence for a novel input $\mathbf{x}^*$. This is straightforward since

$$y_{1:T}^* = \underset{y_{1:T}}{\text{argmax}} \prod_t \phi_t(y_t, y_{t-1}, \mathbf{x}^*, \boldsymbol{\lambda}) \tag{23.4.15}$$

corresponds again to a simple linear chain, for which max-product inference yields the required result, see also Exercise 23.9. See Example 9.11 for a small example.

23.4.4 Dynamic Bayesian networks

A Dynamic Bayesian Network (DBN) is defined as a belief network replicated through time. For a multivariate $\mathbf{x}_t$, with $\dim(\mathbf{x}_t) = D$, the DBN defines a joint model

$$p(\mathbf{x}_1, \ldots, \mathbf{x}_T) = \prod_{t=1}^{T} \prod_{i=1}^{D} p(x_i(t)|\mathbf{x}_{\setminus i}(t), \mathbf{x}(t-1)) \tag{23.4.16}$$

where $\mathbf{x}_{\setminus i}(t)$ denotes the set of variables at time t, except for $x_i(t)$. The form of each $p(x_i(t)|\mathbf{x}_{\setminus i}(t), \mathbf{x}(t-1))$ is chosen such that the overall distribution remains acyclic. At each timestep t there is a set of variables $x_i(t), i = 1, \ldots, D$, some of which may be observed. In a first-order DBN, each variable $x_i(t)$ has parental variables taken from the set of variables in the previous time-slice, $\mathbf{x}_{t-1}$, or from the present time-slice. In most applications, the model is temporally homogeneous so that one may fully describe the distribution in terms of a two-time-slice model, Fig. 23.14. The generalisation to higher-order models is straightforward. A *coupled HMM* is a special DBN that may be used to model coupled 'streams' of information, for example video and audio, see Fig. 23.15 [224].

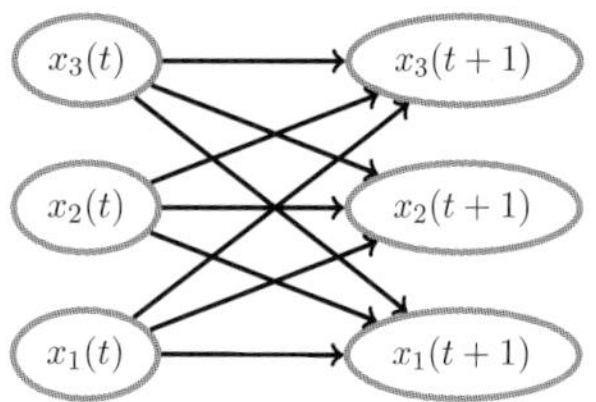

Figure 23.14 A dynamic Bayesian network. Possible transitions between variables at the same time-slice have not been shown.

23.5 Applications

23.5.1 Object tracking

Hidden Markov models are used to track moving objects, based on an understanding of the dynamics of the object (encoded in the transition distribution) and an understanding of how an object with a known position would be observed (encoded in the emission distribution). Given an observed sequence, the hidden position can then be inferred. The burglar, Example 3.1 is a case in point. Hidden Markov models have been applied in many tracking contexts, including tracking people in videos, musical pitch, and many more [57, 246, 54].

23.5.2 Automatic speech recognition

Many speech recognition systems make use of HMMs [321]. Roughly speaking, the raw scalar speech signal $x_{1:T}$ is first translated into a stream of continuous acoustic vectors $\mathbf{v}_{1:T}$ where at time t, $\mathbf{v}_t$ represents which frequencies are present in the speech signal in a small window around time t. These acoustic vectors are typically formed from taking a discrete Fourier transform of the speech signal over a small window around time t, with additional transformations to mimic human auditory processing. Alternatively, related forms of linear coding of the observed acoustic waveform may be used [143].

The corresponding discrete latent state h_t represents a phoneme – a basic unit of human speech (for which there are 44 in standard English). Training data is painstakingly constructed by a human linguist who determines the phoneme h_t for each time t and many different observed sequences $x_{1:T}$. Given then each acoustic vector $\mathbf{v}_t$ and an associated phoneme h_t, one may use maximum likelihood to fit a mixture of (usually isotropic) Gaussians $p(\mathbf{v}_t|h_t)$ to $\mathbf{v}_t$. This forms the emission distribution for an HMM.

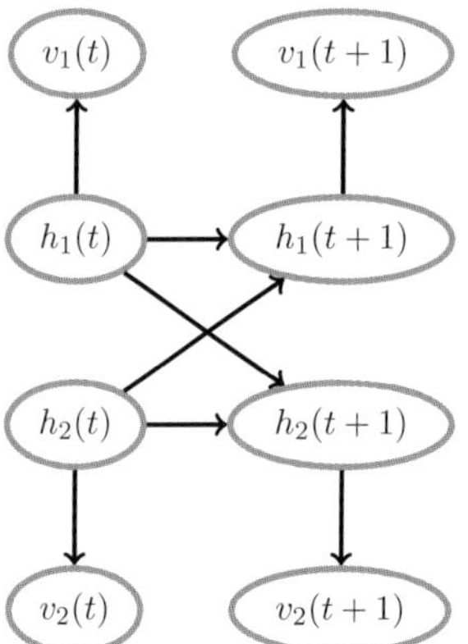

Figure 23.15 A coupled HMM. For example the upper HMM might model speech, and the lower the corresponding video sequence. The upper hidden units then correspond to phonemes, and the lower to mouth positions; this model therefore captures the expected coupling between mouth positions and phonemes.

Using the database of labelled phonemes, the phoneme transition $p(h_t|h_{t-1})$ can be learned (by simple counting) and forms the transition distribution for an HMM. Note that in this case, since the 'hidden' variable h and observation v are known during training, training the HMM is straightforward and boils down to training the emission and transition distributions independently using the observed acoustic vectors and associated phonemes.

For a new sequence of acoustic vectors $\mathbf{v}_{1:T}$ we can then use the HMM to infer the most likely phoneme sequence through time, $\arg\max_{h_{1:T}} p(h_{1:T}|\mathbf{v}_{1:T})$, which takes into account both the way that phonemes generate acoustic vectors, and also the prior language constraints of phoneme of phoneme transitions. The fact that people speak at different speeds can be addressed using *time-warping* in which the latent phoneme remains in the same state for a number of timesteps. If the HMM is used to model a single word, it is natural to constrain the hidden state sequence to only go 'forwards' through the set of available phonemes (i.e. one cannot revisit a state, except possibly the current state). In this case the structure of the transition matrices corresponds to a DAG state-transition diagram; under suitable labelling of the states, this can always be represented by a triangular *left-to-right transition matrix*.

23.5.3 Bioinformatics

In the field of bioinformatics HMMs have been widely applied to modelling genetic sequences. Multiple sequence alignment using forms of constrained HMMs have been particularly successful. Other applications involve gene finding and protein family modelling [177, 90].

23.5.4 Part-of-speech tagging

Consider the sentence below in which each word has been linguistically tagged

```
hospitality_NN is_BEZ an_AT excellent_JJ virtue_NN ,_,
but_CC not_XNOT when_WRB the_ATI guests_NNS have_HV
to_TO sleep_VB in_IN rows_NNS in_IN the_ATI cellar_NN !_!
```

The linguistic tags are denoted at the end of each word, for example NN is the singular common noun tag, ATI is the article tag etc. Given a training set of such tagged sentences, the task is to tag a novel sentence. One approach is to use h_t to be a tag, and v_t to be a word and fit an HMM to this data. For the training data, both the tags and words are observed so that maximum likelihood training of the transition and emission distributions can be achieved by simple counting. Given a new sequence of words, the most likely tag sequence can be inferred using the Viterbi algorithm.

More recent part-of-speech taggers tend to use conditional random fields in which the input sequence $x_{1:T}$ is the sentence and the output sequence $y_{1:T}$ is the tag sequence. One possible parameterisation of a linear chain CRF is to use a potential of the form $\phi(y_{t-1}, y_t)\phi(y_t, \mathbf{x})$, see Section 9.6.5, in which the first factor encodes the grammatical structure of the language and the second the a priori likely tag y_t [180].

23.6 Summary

- Timeseries require simplifying assumptions such as the Markov assumption which makes it feasible to specify a model for the process.

- A discrete-state Markov chain is a generalisation of deterministic finite-state transitions to stochastic transitions between states.
- Mixtures of Markov models and extensions thereof can be used as simple timeseries clustering models.
- Hidden Markov models are popular timeseries models in which the latent process is a discrete-state Markov chain. The observations can be either discrete or continuous and the classical inference tasks of filtering, smoothing and computing the joint most likely latent sequence are computationally straightforward.
- Dynamic Bayes nets are essentially structured HMMs with conditional independencies encoded in their transition and emission distributions.
- HMMs have widespread application in a variety of tracking scenarios, from speech recognition to genetic sequence analysis.
- Undirected linear chain structures such as the conditional random field are popular in areas such as natural language processing for translating an input sequence to a structured output sequence.

23.7 Code

`demoMixMarkov.m`: Demo for mixture of Markov models
`mixMarkov.m`: Mixture of Markov models
`demoHMMinference.m`: Demo of HMM inference
`HMMforward.m`: Forward α recursion
`HMMbackward.m`: Forward β recursion
`HMMgamma.m`: RTS γ 'correction' recursion
`HMMsmooth.m`: Single and pairwise $\alpha - \beta$ smoothing
`HMMviterbi.m`: Most likely state (Viterbi) algorithm
`demoHMMburglar.m`: Demo of burglar localisation
`demoHMMbigram.m`: Demo of stubby fingers typing
`HMMem.m`: EM algorithm for HMM (Baum-Welch)
`demoHMMlearn.m`: Demo of EM algorithm for HMM (Baum-Welch)
`demoLinearCRF.m`: Demo of learning a linear chain CRF
`linearCRFpotential.m`: Linear CRF potential
`linearCRFgrad.m`: Linear CRF gradient
`linearCRFloglik.m`: Linear CRF log likelihood

23.8 Exercises

23.1 A stochastic matrix M_{ij} has non-negative entries with $\sum_i M_{ij} = 1$. Consider an eigenvalue λ and eigenvector $\mathbf{e}$ such that $\sum_j M_{ij} e_j = \lambda e_i$. By summing over i show that, provided $\sum_i e_i > 0$, then λ must be equal to 1.

23.2 Consider the Markov chain with transition matrix

$$\mathbf{M} = \begin{pmatrix} 0 & 1 \\ 1 & 0 \end{pmatrix}. \tag{23.8.1}$$

Show that this Markov chain does not have an equilibrium distribution and state a stationary distribution for this chain.

23.3 Consider an HMM with three states ($M = 3$) and two output symbols, with a left-to-right state transition matrix

$$\mathbf{A} = \begin{pmatrix} 0.5 & 0.0 & 0.0 \\ 0.3 & 0.6 & 0.0 \\ 0.2 & 0.4 & 1.0 \end{pmatrix} \tag{23.8.2}$$

where $A_{ij} \equiv p(h_{t+1} = i | h_t = j)$, emission matrix $B_{ij} \equiv p(v_t = i | h_t = j)$

$$\mathbf{B} = \begin{pmatrix} 0.7 & 0.4 & 0.8 \\ 0.3 & 0.6 & 0.2 \end{pmatrix} \tag{23.8.3}$$

and initial state probability vector $\mathbf{a} = (0.9\ 0.1\ 0.0)^\mathsf{T}$. Given the observed symbol sequence is $v_{1:3} = (1, 2, 1)$:

1. Compute $p(v_{1:3})$.
2. Compute $p(h_1 | v_{1:3})$.
3. Find the most probable hidden state sequence $\arg\max_{h_{1:3}} p(h_{1:3} | v_{1:3})$.

23.4 This exercise follows from Example 23.5. Given the 27 long character string `rgenmonleunosbpnntje vrancg` typed with 'stubby fingers', what is the most likely correct English sentence intended? In the list of decoded sequences, what value is $\log p(h_{1:27} | v_{1:27})$ for this sequence? You will need to modify `demoHMMbigram.m` suitably.

23.5 Show that if an HMM transition matrix $\mathbf{A}$ and emission matrix $\mathbf{B}$ are initialised to uniformly constant values, then the EM algorithm fails to update the parameters meaningfully.

23.6 Consider the problem of finding the most likely joint output sequence $v_{1:T}$ for an HMM. That is,

$$v^*_{1:T} \equiv \underset{v_{1:T}}{\text{argmax}}\ p(v_{1:T}) \tag{23.8.4}$$

where

$$p(h_{1:T}, v_{1:T}) = \prod_{t=1}^{T} p(v_t | h_t) p(h_t | h_{t-1}). \tag{23.8.5}$$

1. Explain why a local message-passing algorithm cannot, in general, be found for this problem and discuss the computational complexity of finding an exact solution.
2. Explain how to adapt the expectation maximisation algorithm to form a recursive algorithm for finding an approximate $v^*_{1:T}$. Explain why your approach guarantees an improved solution at each iteration. Additionally, explain how the algorithm can be implemented using local message passing.

23.7 Explain how to train an HMM using EM (expectation maximisation), but with a constrained transition matrix. In particular, explain how to learn a transition matrix with a triangular structure.

23.8 Using the correspondence $A = 1, C = 2, G = 3, T = 4$ define a 4×4 transition matrix p that produces sequences of the form

$$\text{A, C, G, T, A, C, G, T, A, C, G, T, A, C, G, T, \ldots} \tag{23.8.6}$$

Now define a new transition matrix

$$\texttt{pnew} = \texttt{0.9} * \texttt{p} + \texttt{0.1} * \texttt{ones(4)/4}. \tag{23.8.7}$$

Define a 4×4 transition matrix q that produces sequences of the form

$$\text{T, G, C, A, T, G, C, A, T, G, C, A, T, G, C, A, \ldots} \tag{23.8.8}$$

Now define a new transition matrix

$$\texttt{qnew} = \texttt{0.9} * \texttt{q} + \texttt{0.1} * \texttt{ones(4)/4}. \tag{23.8.9}$$

Assume that the probability of being in the initial state of the Markov chain $p(h_1)$ is constant for all four states A, C, G, T.

1. What is the probability that the Markov chain `pnew` generated the sequence S given by

$$\text{S} \equiv \text{A, A, G, T, A, C, T, T, A, C, C, T, A, C, G, C.} \tag{23.8.10}$$

2. Similarly what is the probability that S was generated by `qnew`? Does it make sense that S has a higher likelihood under `pnew` compared with `qnew`?
3. Using the function `randgen.m`, generate 100 sequences of length 16 from the Markov chain defined by `pnew`. Similarly, generate 100 sequences each of length 16 from the Markov chain defined by `qnew`. Concatenate all these sequences into a cell array `v` so that `v{1}` contains the first sequence and `v{200}` the last sequence. Use `MixMarkov.m` to learn the maximum likelihood parameters that generated these sequences. Assume that there are $H = 2$ kinds of Markov chain. The result returned in `phgv` indicates the posterior probability of sequence assignment. Do you agree with the solution found?
4. Take the sequence S as defined in Equation (23.8.10). Define an emission distribution that has four output states such that

$$p(v = i|h = j) = \begin{cases} 0.7 & i = j \\ 0.1 & i \neq j. \end{cases} \tag{23.8.11}$$

Using this emission distribution and the transition given by `pnew` defined in Equation (23.8.7), adapt `demoHMMinferenceSimple.m` suitably to find the most likely hidden sequence $h^p_{1:16}$ that generated the observed sequence S. Repeat this computation but for the transition `qnew` to give $h^q_{1:16}$. Which hidden sequence – $h^p_{1:16}$ or $h^q_{1:16}$ is to be preferred? Justify your answer.

23.9 Derive an algorithm that will find the most likely joint state

$$\underset{h_{1:T}}{\text{argmax}} \prod_{t=2}^{T} \phi_t(h_{t-1}, h_t) \tag{23.8.12}$$

for arbitrarily defined potentials $\phi_t(h_{t-1}, h_t)$.

1. First consider

$$\max_{h_{1:T}} \prod_{t=2}^{T} \phi_t(h_{t-1}, h_t). \tag{23.8.13}$$

Show how the maximisation over h_T may be pushed inside the product and that the result of the maximisation can be interpreted as a message

$$\gamma_{T-1\leftarrow T}(h_{T-1}). \tag{23.8.14}$$

2. Derive the recursion

$$\gamma_{t-1\leftarrow t}(h_{t-1}) = \max_{h_t} \phi_t(h_t, h_{t-1})\gamma_{t\leftarrow t+1}(h_t). \tag{23.8.15}$$

3. Explain how the above recursion enables the computation of

$$\underset{h_1}{\text{argmax}} \prod_{t=2}^{T} \phi_t(h_t, h_{t-1}). \tag{23.8.16}$$

4. Explain how once the most likely state for h_1 is computed, one may efficiently compute the remaining optimal states $h_2, \dots, h_T$.

23.10 Derive an algorithm that will compute pairwise marginals

$$p(h_t, h_{t-1}) \tag{23.8.17}$$

from the joint distribution

$$p(h_{1:T}) \propto \prod_{t=2}^{T} \phi_t(h_{t-1}, h_t) \tag{23.8.18}$$

for arbitrarily defined potentials $\phi_t(h_{t-1}, h_t)$.

1. First consider

$$\sum_{h_1,\dots,h_T} \prod_{t=2}^{T} \phi_t(h_t, h_{t-1}). \tag{23.8.19}$$

Show how the summation over h_1 may be pushed inside the product and that the result of the maximisation can be interpreted as a message

$$\alpha_{1\to 2}(h_2) = \sum_{h_1} \phi_2(h_1, h_2). \tag{23.8.20}$$

2. Show that the summation over the variables $h_{1:t-1}$ can be accomplished via the recursion

$$\alpha_{t-1\to t}(h_t) = \sum_{h_{t-1}} \phi_t(h_{t-1}, h_t)\alpha_{t-2\to t-1}(h_{t-1}). \tag{23.8.21}$$

3. Similarly, show that one can push the summation of h_T inside the product to define

$$\beta_{T-1\leftarrow T}(h_{T-1}) = \sum_{h_T} \phi_T(h_{T-1}, h_T). \tag{23.8.22}$$

Show that the summation over the variables $h_{T:t+1}$ can be accomplished via the recursion

$$\beta_{t\leftarrow t+1}(h_t) = \sum_{h_{t+1}} \phi_{t+1}(h_t, h_{t+1})\beta_{t+1\leftarrow t+2}(h_{t+1}). \tag{23.8.23}$$

4. Show that

$$p(h_t, h_{t-1}) \propto \sum_{h_{t+1}} \alpha_{t-2\to t-1}(h_{t-1})\phi(h_{t-1}, h_t)\beta_{t\leftarrow t+1}(h_t). \tag{23.8.24}$$

23.11 A second-order HMM is defined as

$$p(h_{1:T}, v_{1:T}) = p(h_1)p(v_1|h_1)p(h_2|h_1)p(v_2|h_2)\prod_{t=3}^{T} p(h_t|h_{t-1}, h_{t-2})p(v_t|h_t). \tag{23.8.25}$$

Following a similar approach to the first-order HMM, derive explicitly a message-passing algorithm to compute the most likely joint state

$$\operatorname*{argmax}_{h_{1:T}} p(h_{1:T}|v_{1:T}). \tag{23.8.26}$$

23.12 Derive an algorithm to efficiently compute the gradient of the log likelihood for an HMM; assume unconstrained discrete transition and emission matrices.

23.13 Consider the HMM defined on hidden variables $\mathcal{H} = \{h_1, \ldots, h_T\}$ and observations $\mathcal{V} = \{v_1, \ldots, v_T\}$

$$p(\mathcal{V}, \mathcal{H}) = p(h_1)p(v_1|h_1)\prod_{t=2}^{T} p(h_t|h_{t-1})p(v_t|h_t). \tag{23.8.27}$$

Show that the posterior $p(\mathcal{H}|\mathcal{V})$ is a Markov chain

$$p(\mathcal{H}|\mathcal{V}) = \tilde{p}(h_1)\prod_{t=2}^{T} \tilde{p}(h_t|h_{t-1}) \tag{23.8.28}$$

where $\tilde{p}(h_t|h_{t-1})$ and $\tilde{p}(h_1)$ are suitably defined distributions.

23.14 For training an HMM with a Gaussian mixture emission (the HMM-GMM model) in Section 23.3.3, derive the following EM update formulae for the means and covariances:

$$\boldsymbol{\mu}^{new}_{\mathsf{k},\mathsf{h}} = \sum_{n=1}^{N}\sum_{t=1}^{T} \rho_{\mathsf{k},\mathsf{h}}(t, n)\mathbf{v}^n_t \tag{23.8.29}$$

and

$$\boldsymbol{\Sigma}^{new}_{\mathsf{k},\mathsf{h}} = \sum_{n=1}^{N}\sum_{t=1}^{T} \rho_{\mathsf{k},\mathsf{h}}(t, n)\left(\mathbf{v}^n_t - \boldsymbol{\mu}_{\mathsf{k},\mathsf{h}}\right)\left(\mathbf{v}^n_t - \boldsymbol{\mu}_{\mathsf{k},\mathsf{h}}\right)^{\mathsf{T}} \tag{23.8.30}$$

where

$$\rho_{\mathsf{k},\mathsf{h}}(t, n) = \frac{q(k_t = \mathsf{k}|h^n_t = \mathsf{h})q(h^n_t = \mathsf{h}|v^n_{1:T})}{\sum_n\sum_t q(k_t = \mathsf{k}|h^n_t = \mathsf{h})q(h^n_t = \mathsf{h}|v^n_{1:T})}. \tag{23.8.31}$$

23.15 Consider the HMM duration model defined by Equation (23.4.2) and Equation (23.4.1) with emission distribution $p(v_t|h_t)$. Our interest is to derive a recursion for the filtered distribution

$$\alpha_t(h_t, c_t) \equiv p(h_t, c_t, v_{1:t}). \tag{23.8.32}$$

1. Show that:

$$\alpha_t(h_t, c_t) = p(v_t|h_t)\sum_{h_{t-1}, c_{t-1}} p(h_t|h_{t-1}, c_t)p(c_t|c_{t-1})\alpha_{t-1}(h_{t-1}, c_{t-1}). \tag{23.8.33}$$

2. Using this derive

$$\frac{\alpha_t(h_t, c_t)}{p(v_t|h_t)} = \sum_{h_{t-1}} p(h_t|h_{t-1}, c)p(c_t|c_{t-1} = 1)\alpha_{t-1}(h_{t-1}, c_{t-1} = 1)$$
$$+ \sum_{h_{t-1}} p(h_t|h_{t-1}, c)\sum_{c_{t-1}=2}^{D_{max}} p(c|c_{t-1})\alpha_{t-1}(h_{t-1}, c_{t-1}). \tag{23.8.34}$$

3. Show that the right-hand side of the above can be written as

$$\sum_{h_{t-1}} p(h_t|h_{t-1}, c_t = c)p(c_t = c|c_{t-1} = 1)\alpha_{t-1}(h_{t-1}, 1)$$
$$+\mathbb{I}[c \neq D_{max}]\sum_{h_{t-1}} p(h_t|h_{t-1}, c)\alpha_{t-1}(h_{t-1}, c + 1). \tag{23.8.35}$$

4. Show that the recursion for α is then given by

$$\alpha_t(h,1) = p(v_t|h_t = h)p_{dur}(1)\sum_{h_{t-1}} p_{tran}(h|h_{t-1})\alpha_{t-1}(h_{t-1},1) + \mathbb{I}\left[D_{max} \neq 1\right] p(v_t|h_t = h)\sum_{h_{t-1}} p_{tran}(h_t|h_{t-1})\alpha_{t-1}(h_{t-1},2) \quad (23.8.36)$$

and for $c > 1$

$$\alpha_t(h,c) = p(v_t|h_t = h)\left\{p_{dur}(c)\alpha_{t-1}(h,1) + \mathbb{I}\left[c \neq D_{max}\right]\alpha_{t-1}(h,c+1)\right\}. \quad (23.8.37)$$

5. Explain why the computational complexity of filtered inference in the duration model is $O\left(TH^2D_{max}\right)$.
6. Derive an efficient smoothing algorithm for this duration model.

24 Continuous-state Markov models

Many physical systems can be understood as continuous variable models undergoing a transition that depends only on the state of the system at the previous time. In this chapter we discuss some of the classical models in this area which are highly specialised to retain tractability of inference. These models are found in a wide variety of fields from finance to signal processing in engineering.

24.1 Observed linear dynamical systems

In many practical timeseries applications the data is naturally continuous, particularly for models of the physical environment. In contrast to discrete-state Markov models, Chapter 23, parametric continuous state distributions are not automatically closed under operations such as products and marginalisation. To make practical algorithms for which inference and learning can be carried out efficiently, we therefore are heavily restricted in the form of the continuous transition $p(v_t|v_{t-1})$. A simple yet powerful class of such transitions are the linear dynamical systems. A deterministic Observed Linear Dynamical System[1] (OLDS) defines the temporal evolution of a vector $\mathbf{v}_t$ according to the discrete-time update equation

$$\mathbf{v}_t = \mathbf{A}_t \mathbf{v}_{t-1} \tag{24.1.1}$$

where $\mathbf{A}_t$ is the transition matrix at time t. For the case that $\mathbf{A}_t$ is invariant with t, the process is called stationary or time-invariant, which we assume throughout unless explicitly stated otherwise.

A motivation for studying OLDSs is that many equations that describe the physical world can be written as an OLDS. They are interesting since they may be used as simple prediction models: if $\mathbf{v}_t$ describes the state of the environment at time t, then $\mathbf{A}\mathbf{v}_t$ predicts the environment at time $t+1$. As such, these models have widespread application in many branches of science, from engineering and physics to economics.

The OLDS Equation (24.1.1) is deterministic so that if we specify $\mathbf{v}_1$, all future values $\mathbf{v}_2, \mathbf{v}_3, \ldots,$ are defined. For a $\dim(\mathbf{v}) = V$ dimensional vector, its evolution is described by (assuming $\mathbf{A}$ is diagonalisable)

$$\mathbf{v}_t = \mathbf{A}^{t-1}\mathbf{v}_1 = \mathbf{P}\boldsymbol{\Lambda}^{t-1}\mathbf{P}^{-1}\mathbf{v}_1 \tag{24.1.2}$$

where $\boldsymbol{\Lambda} = \text{diag}(\lambda_1, \ldots, \lambda_V)$ is the diagonal eigenvalue matrix, and $\mathbf{P}$ is the corresponding eigenvector matrix of $\mathbf{A}$. If any $\lambda_i > 1$ then for large t, $\mathbf{v}_t$ will explode. On the other hand, if $\lambda_i < 1$, then λ_i^{t-1} will tend to zero. For stable systems we require therefore no eigenvalues of magnitude greater

[1] We use the terminology 'observed' LDS to differentiate from the more general LDS state-space model. In some texts, however, the term LDS is applied to the models under discussion in this chapter.

than 1 and only unit eigenvalues $|\lambda_i = 1|$ will contribute in the long term. Note that the eigenvalues may be complex which corresponds to rotational behaviour, see Exercise 24.1.

More generally, we may consider additive noise on $\mathbf{v}$ and define a stochastic OLDS, as defined below.

Definition 24.1 Observed linear dynamical system

$$\mathbf{v}_t = \mathbf{A}_t \mathbf{v}_{t-1} + \boldsymbol{\eta}_t \tag{24.1.3}$$

where $\boldsymbol{\eta}_t$ is a noise vector sampled from a Gaussian distribution,

$$\mathcal{N}(\boldsymbol{\eta}_t | \boldsymbol{\mu}_t, \boldsymbol{\Sigma}_t). \tag{24.1.4}$$

This is equivalent to a first-order Markov model with transition

$$p(\mathbf{v}_t|\mathbf{v}_{t-1}) = \mathcal{N}(\mathbf{v}_t | \mathbf{A}_t \mathbf{v}_{t-1} + \boldsymbol{\mu}_t, \boldsymbol{\Sigma}_t). \tag{24.1.5}$$

At $t = 1$ we have an initial distribution $p(\mathbf{v}_1) = \mathcal{N}(\mathbf{v}_1 | \boldsymbol{\mu}_1, \boldsymbol{\Sigma}_1)$. For $t > 1$ if the parameters are time-independent, $\boldsymbol{\mu}_t \equiv \boldsymbol{\mu}$, $\mathbf{A}_t \equiv \mathbf{A}$, $\boldsymbol{\Sigma}_t \equiv \boldsymbol{\Sigma}$, the process is called time-invariant.

24.1.1 Stationary distribution with noise

Consider the one-dimensional linear system with independent additive noise

$$v_t = a v_{t-1} + \eta_t, \qquad \eta_t \sim \mathcal{N}\left(\eta_t \middle| 0, \sigma_v^2\right). \tag{24.1.6}$$

If we start at some state v_1, and then for $t > 1$ recursively sample according to $v_t = a v_{t-1} + \eta_t$, what is the distribution of v_t? Since the transitions are linear and the noise is Gaussian, then v_t must also be Gaussian. Assuming that we can represent the distribution of v_{t-1} as a Gaussian with mean μ_{t-1} and variance σ_{t-1}^2, $v_{t-1} \sim \mathcal{N}\left(v_{t-1} \middle| \mu_{t-1}, \sigma_{t-1}^2\right)$, then using $\langle \eta_t \rangle = 0$ we have

$$\langle v_t \rangle = a \langle v_{t-1} \rangle + \langle \eta_t \rangle \Rightarrow \mu_t = a \mu_{t-1} \tag{24.1.7}$$

$$\left\langle v_t^2 \right\rangle = \left\langle (a v_{t-1} + \eta_t)^2 \right\rangle = a^2 \left\langle v_{t-1}^2 \right\rangle + 2a \langle v_{t-1} \rangle \langle \eta_t \rangle + \left\langle \eta_t^2 \right\rangle \tag{24.1.8}$$

$$\Rightarrow \sigma_t^2 = a^2 \sigma_{t-1}^2 + \sigma_v^2 \tag{24.1.9}$$

so that

$$v_t \sim \mathcal{N}\left(v_t \middle| a\mu_{t-1}, a^2\sigma_{t-1}^2 + \sigma_v^2\right). \tag{24.1.10}$$

Infinite time limit

Does the distribution of the $v_t, t \gg 1$ tend to a steady, fixed distribution? If $a \geq 1$ the variance increases indefinitely with t, as does the mean value.

For $a < 1$, and assuming there is a finite variance σ_∞^2 for the infinite time case, from Equation (24.1.9), the stationary distribution satisfies

$$\sigma_\infty^2 = a^2 \sigma_\infty^2 + \sigma_v^2 \quad \Rightarrow \sigma_\infty^2 = \frac{\sigma_v^2}{1 - a^2}. \tag{24.1.11}$$

Similarly, the mean is given by $\mu_\infty = a^\infty \mu_1$. Hence, for $a < 1$, the mean tends to zero yet the variance remains finite. Even though the magnitude of v_{t-1} is decreased by a factor of a at each iteration, the additive noise on average boosts the magnitude so that it remains steady in the long run. More generally for a system updating a vector $\mathbf{v}_t$ according to non-zero additive noise,

$$\mathbf{v}_t = \mathbf{A}\mathbf{v}_{t-1} + \boldsymbol{\eta}_t \tag{24.1.12}$$

for the existence of a steady state we require that all eigenvalues of $\mathbf{A}$ must be < 1.

24.2 Auto-regressive models

A scalar time-invariant Auto-Regressive (AR) model is defined by

$$v_t = \sum_{l=1}^{L} a_l v_{t-l} + \eta_t, \qquad \eta_t \sim \mathcal{N}\left(\eta_t \middle| \mu, \sigma^2\right) \tag{24.2.1}$$

where $\mathbf{a} = (a_1, \ldots, a_L)^{\mathsf{T}}$ are called the AR coefficients and σ^2 is called the *innovation noise*. The model predicts the future based on a linear combination of the previous L observations. As a belief network, the AR model can be written as an Lth-order Markov model:

$$p(v_{1:T}) = \prod_{t=1}^{T} p(v_t | v_{t-1}, \ldots, v_{t-L}), \qquad \text{with } v_i = \emptyset \text{ for } i \leq 0 \tag{24.2.2}$$

with

$$p(v_t | v_{t-1}, \ldots, v_{t-L}) = \mathcal{N}\left(v_t \middle| \sum_{l=1}^{L} a_l v_{t-l}, \sigma^2\right). \tag{24.2.3}$$

Introducing the vector of the L previous observations

$$\hat{\mathbf{v}}_{t-1} \equiv \left[v_{t-1}, v_{t-2}, \ldots, v_{t-L}\right]^{\mathsf{T}} \tag{24.2.4}$$

we can write more compactly

$$p(v_t | v_{t-1}, \ldots, v_{t-L}) = \mathcal{N}\left(v_t \middle| \mathbf{a}^{\mathsf{T}} \hat{\mathbf{v}}_{t-1}, \sigma^2\right). \tag{24.2.5}$$

Auto-regressive models are heavily used in financial timeseries prediction (see for example [288]), being able to capture simple trends in the data. Another common application area is in speech processing whereby for a one-dimensional speech signal partitioned into windows of length $T \gg L$, the AR coefficients best able to describe the signal in each window are found [231]. These AR coefficients then form a compressed representation of the signal and subsequently transmitted for each window, rather than the original signal itself. The signal can then be approximately reconstructed based on the AR coefficients. This is known as a linear predictive vocoder [273]. Note that an interesting property of the AR representation of a signal is that if we scale the signal by a constant amount ρ, then

$$\rho v_t = \sum_{l=1}^{L} a_l \rho v_{t-l} + \rho \eta_t, \tag{24.2.6}$$

so that provided we scale the noise suitably, the same AR coefficients can be used to represent the signal; the AR coefficients are therefore to a degree amplitude invariant.

24.2.1 Training an AR model

Maximum likelihood training of the AR coefficients is straightforward based on

$$\log p(v_{1:T}) = \sum_{t=1}^{T} \log p(v_t|\hat{\mathbf{v}}_{t-1}) = -\frac{1}{2\sigma^2}\sum_{t=1}^{T}\left(v_t - \hat{\mathbf{v}}_{t-1}^{\mathsf{T}}\mathbf{a}\right)^2 - \frac{T}{2}\log(2\pi\sigma^2). \tag{24.2.7}$$

Differentiating w.r.t. $\mathbf{a}$ and equating to zero we arrive at

$$\sum_t \left(v_t - \hat{\mathbf{v}}_{t-1}^{\mathsf{T}}\mathbf{a}\right)\hat{\mathbf{v}}_{t-1} = 0 \tag{24.2.8}$$

so that optimally

$$\mathbf{a} = \left(\sum_t \hat{\mathbf{v}}_{t-1}\hat{\mathbf{v}}_{t-1}^{\mathsf{T}}\right)^{-1}\sum_t v_t\hat{\mathbf{v}}_{t-1}. \tag{24.2.9}$$

These equations can be solved by Gaussian elimination. The linear system has a Toeplitz form that can be more efficiently solved using the Levinson–Durbin method [89]. Similarly, optimally,

$$\sigma^2 = \frac{1}{T}\sum_{t=1}^{T}\left(v_t - \hat{\mathbf{v}}_{t-1}^{\mathsf{T}}\mathbf{a}\right)^2. \tag{24.2.10}$$

Above we assume that 'negative' timesteps are available in order to keep the notation simple. If times before the window over which we learn the coefficients are not available, a minor adjustment is required to start the summations from $t = L + 1$. Given a trained $\mathbf{a}$, future predictions can be made using $v_{t+1} = \hat{\mathbf{v}}_t^{\mathsf{T}}\mathbf{a}$.

Example 24.1 Fitting a trend

We illustrate with a simple example how AR models can be used to estimate trends underlying timeseries data. A third-order AR model was fit to the set of 100 observations shown in Fig. 24.1 using maximum likelihood. A prediction for the mean $\langle y\rangle_t$ was then recursively generated as

$$\langle y\rangle_t = \begin{cases} \sum_{i=1}^{3} a_i \langle y\rangle_{t-i} & \text{for } t > 100, \\ y_t & \text{for } t \leq 100. \end{cases}$$

As we can see (solid line in Fig. 24.1), the predicted means for time $t > 100$ capture an underlying trend in the data. Whilst this example is very simple, AR models are quite powerful and can model complex signal behaviour.

24.2.2 AR model as an OLDS

We can write Equation (24.2.1) as an OLDS using

$$\begin{pmatrix} v_t \\ v_{t-1} \\ \vdots \\ v_{t-L+1} \end{pmatrix} = \begin{pmatrix} a_1 & a_2 & \dots & a_L \\ 1 & 0 & \dots & 0 \\ \vdots & 1 & \dots & 0 \\ 0 & \dots & 1 & 0 \end{pmatrix} \begin{pmatrix} v_{t-1} \\ v_{t-2} \\ \vdots \\ v_{t-L} \end{pmatrix} + \begin{pmatrix} \eta_t \\ 0 \\ \vdots \\ 0 \end{pmatrix}. \tag{24.2.11}$$

which in vector notation is

$$\hat{\mathbf{v}}_t = \mathbf{A}\hat{\mathbf{v}}_{t-1} + \boldsymbol{\eta}_t, \qquad \boldsymbol{\eta}_t \sim \mathcal{N}(\boldsymbol{\eta}_t|\mathbf{0}, \boldsymbol{\Sigma}) \tag{24.2.12}$$

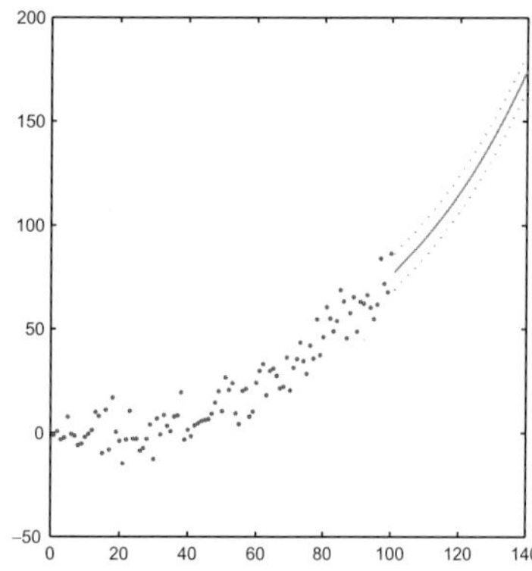

Figure 24.1 Fitting an order 3 AR model to the training points. The x axis represents time, and the y axis the value of the timeseries. The dots represent the 100 observations $y_{1:100}$. The solid line indicates the mean predictions $\langle y \rangle_t$, $t > 100$, and the dashed lines $\langle y \rangle_t \pm \sigma$. See `demoARtrain.m`.

where we define the block matrices

$$\mathbf{A} = \left(\begin{array}{c|c} a_{1:L-1} & a_L \\ \hline \mathbf{I} & \mathbf{0} \end{array} \right), \qquad \boldsymbol{\Sigma} = \left(\begin{array}{c|c} \sigma^2 & 0_{1,1:L-1} \\ \hline 0_{1:L-1,1} & 0_{1:L-1,1:L-1} \end{array} \right). \tag{24.2.13}$$

In this representation, the first component of the vector is updated according to the standard AR model, with the remaining components being copies of the previous values.

24.2.3 Time-varying AR model

An alternative to maximum likelihood is to view learning the AR coefficients as a problem in inference in a latent LDS, a model which is discussed in detail in Section 24.3. If $\mathbf{a}_t$ are the latent AR coefficients, the term

$$v_t = \hat{\mathbf{v}}_{t-1}^{\mathsf{T}} \mathbf{a}_t + \eta_t, \qquad \eta_t \sim \mathcal{N}\left(\eta_t \middle| 0, \sigma^2\right) \tag{24.2.14}$$

can be viewed as the emission distribution of a latent LDS in which the hidden variable is $\mathbf{a}_t$ and the time-dependent emission matrix is given by $\hat{\mathbf{v}}_{t-1}^{\mathsf{T}}$. By placing a simple latent transition

$$\mathbf{a}_t = \mathbf{a}_{t-1} + \boldsymbol{\eta}_t^a, \qquad \boldsymbol{\eta}_t^a \sim \mathcal{N}\left(\eta_t^a \middle| 0, \sigma_a^2 \mathbf{I}\right) \tag{24.2.15}$$

we encourage the AR coefficients to change slowly with time. This defines a model, see Fig. 24.2,

$$p(v_{1:T}, \mathbf{a}_{1:T}) = \prod_t p(v_t | \mathbf{a}_t, \hat{\mathbf{v}}_{t-1}) p(\mathbf{a}_t | \mathbf{a}_{t-1}). \tag{24.2.16}$$

Our interest is then in the conditional $p(\mathbf{a}_{1:T} | v_{1:T})$ from which we can compute the a-posteriori most likely sequence of AR coefficients. Standard smoothing algorithms can then be applied to yield the time-varying AR coefficients, see `demoARlds.m`.

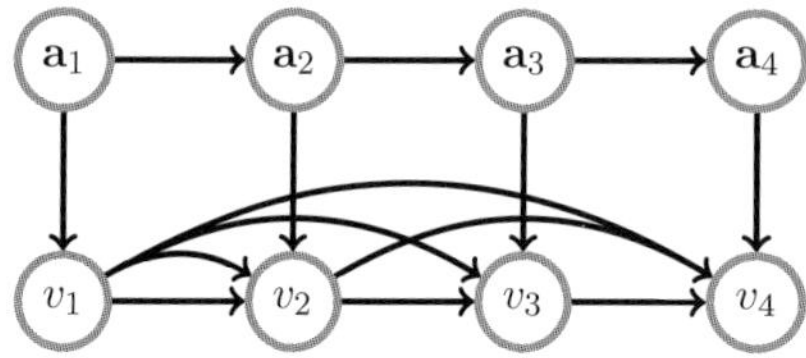

Figure 24.2 A time-varying AR model as a latent LDS. Since the observations are known, this model is a time-varying latent LDS, for which smoothed inference determines the time-varying AR coefficients.

Definition 24.2 **Discrete Fourier Transform (DFT)** For a sequence $x_{0:N-1}$ the DFT $f_{0:N-1}$ is defined as

$$f_k = \sum_{n=0}^{N-1} x_n e^{-\frac{2\pi i}{N}kn}, \qquad k = 0, \ldots, N-1; \tag{24.2.17}$$

f_k is a (complex) representation as to how much frequency k is present in the sequence $x_{0:N-1}$. The power of component k is defined as the absolute length of the complex f_k.

Definition 24.3 **Spectrogram** Given a timeseries $x_{1:T}$ the spectrogram at time t is a representation of the frequencies present in a window localised around t. For each window one computes the discrete Fourier transform, from which we obtain a vector of log power in each frequency. The window is then moved (usually) one step forward and the DFT recomputed. Note that by taking the logarithm, small values in the original signal can translate to visibly appreciable values in the spectrogram.

Example 24.2 Nightingale

In Fig. 24.3(a) we plot the raw acoustic recording for a 5 second fragment of a nightingale song (`freesound.org`, sample 17185). The spectrogram is also plotted and gives an indication of which frequencies are present in the signal as a function of time. The nightingale song is very complicated but at least locally can be very repetitive. A crude way to find which segments repeat is to cluster the time-slices of the spectrogram. In Fig. 24.3(c) we show the results of fitting a Gaussian mixture model, Section 20.3, with eight components, from which we see there is some repetition of components locally in time. An alternative representation of the signal is given by the time-varying AR coefficients, Section 24.2.3, as plotted in Fig. 24.3(d). A GMM clustering with eight components Fig. 24.3(e) in this case produces a somewhat clearer depiction of the different phases of the nightingale singing than that afforded by the spectrogram.

24.2.4 Time-varying variance AR models

In the standard AR model, Equation (24.2.1), the variance σ^2 is assumed fixed throughout time. For some applications, particularly in finance, this is undesirable since the 'volatility' can change dramatically with time. A simple extension of the AR model is to write

$$v_t = \sum_{l=1}^{L} a_l v_{t-l} + \eta_t, \qquad \eta_t \sim \mathcal{N}\left(\eta_t \middle| \mu, \sigma_t^2\right) \tag{24.2.18}$$

$$\bar{v}_t = \sum_{l=1}^{L} a_l v_{t-l} \tag{24.2.19}$$

$$\sigma_t^2 = \alpha_0 + \sum_{i=1}^{Q} \alpha_i \left(v_{t-i} - \bar{v}_{t-i}\right)^2 \tag{24.2.20}$$

where $\alpha_i \geq 0$. The motivation is that Equation (24.2.20) represents an estimate of the variance of the noise, based on a weighted sum of the squared discrepancies between the mean prediction $\bar{v}$ and the

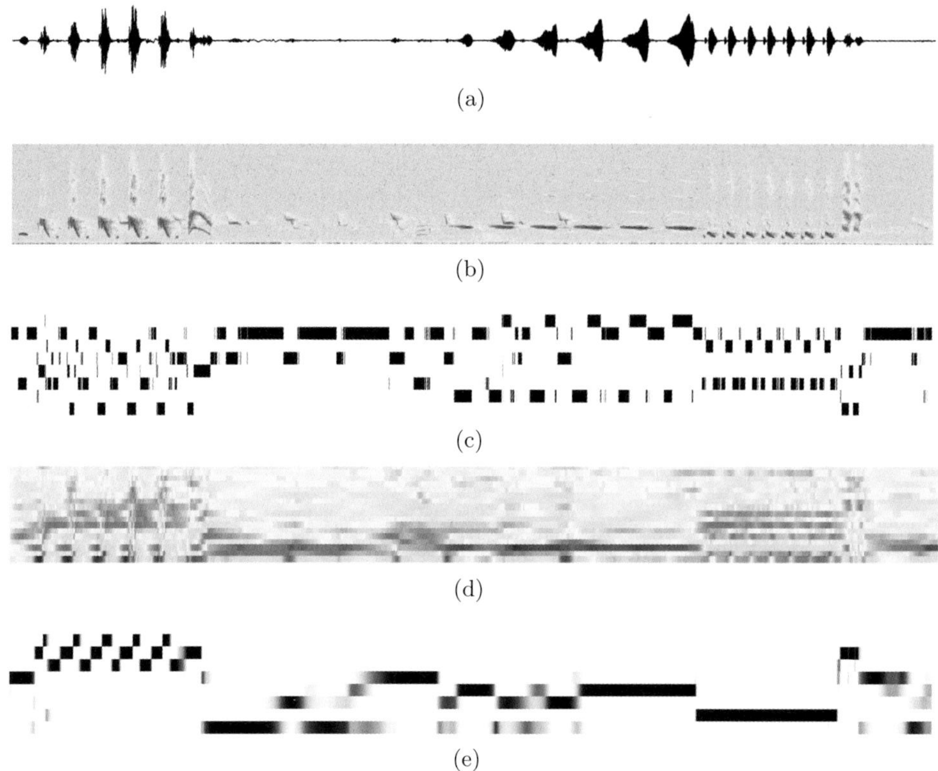

Figure 24.3 (**a**) The raw recording of 5 seconds of a nightingale song (with additional background birdsong). (**b**) Spectrogram of (a) up to 20 000 Hz. (**c**) Clustering of the results in panel (b) using an 8 component Gaussian mixture model. Plotted at each time vertically is the distribution over the cluster indices (from 1 to 8), so that the darker the component, the more responsible that component is for the spectrogram slice at that timepoint. (**d**) The 20 time-varying AR coefficients learned using $\sigma_v^2 = 0.001$, $\sigma_h^2 = 0.001$, see `ARlds.m`. (**e**) Clustering the results in panel (d) using a Gaussian mixture model with 8 components. The AR components group roughly according to the different song regimes. See plate section for colour version.

actual observation v over the previous Q timesteps. This is called an AutoRegressive Conditional Heteroskedasticity (ARCH) model [99], see Fig. 24.4(a). A further extension is to the generalised ARCH (GARCH) model, see Fig. 24.4(b), for which

$$\sigma_t^2 = \alpha_0 + \sum_{i=1}^{Q} \alpha_i \left(v_{t-i} - \bar{v}_{t-i}\right)^2 + \sum_{i=1}^{P} \beta_i \sigma_{t-i}^2 \tag{24.2.21}$$

where $\beta_i \geq 0$.

One can interpret these as deterministic latent variable models, see Section 26.4, albeit with the extension to a higher-order Markov process. In this sense, learning of the parameters by maximum likelihood is straightforward since derivatives of the log likelihood can be computed by deterministic propagation, as described in Section 26.4. Indeed, based on this insight, a whole range of possible non-linear 'volatility' models come into view.

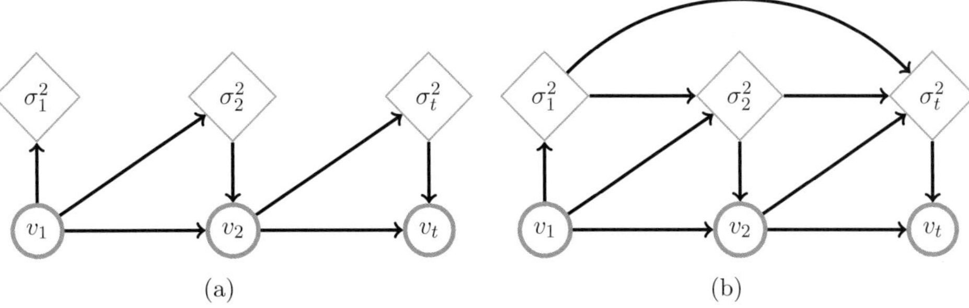

Figure 24.4 (**a**) A first-order $L = 1$, $Q = 1$ ARCH model, in which the observations are dependent on the previous observation, and the variance is dependent on the previous observations in a deterministic manner. (**b**) An $L = 1$, $Q = 1$, $P = 2$ GARCH model, in which the observations are dependent on the previous observation, and the variance is dependent on the previous observations and previous two variances in a deterministic manner. These are special cases of the general deterministic latent variable models, Section 26.4.

24.3 Latent linear dynamical systems

The latent LDS defines a stochastic linear dynamical system in a latent (or 'hidden') space on a sequence of vectors $\mathbf{h}_{1:T}$. Each observation $\mathbf{v}_t$ is as linear function of the latent vector $\mathbf{h}_t$. This model is also called a *linear Gaussian state space model*.[2] The model can also be considered a form of LDS on the joint variables $x_t = (v_t, h_t)$, with parts of the vector x_t missing. For this reason we will also sometimes refer to this model as a linear dynamical system (without the 'latent' prefix). These models are powerful models of timeseries and their use is widespread. Their latent nature means that we can use the latent variable $\mathbf{h}_t$ to track and explain the observation $\mathbf{t}$. The formal definition of the model is given below.

Definition 24.4 Latent linear dynamical system

$$\begin{array}{lll} \mathbf{h}_t = \mathbf{A}_t\mathbf{h}_{t-1} + \boldsymbol{\eta}_t^h & \boldsymbol{\eta}_t^h \sim \mathcal{N}\left(\boldsymbol{\eta}_t^h \middle| \bar{\mathbf{h}}_t, \boldsymbol{\Sigma}_t^h\right) & \text{transition model} \\ \mathbf{v}_t = \mathbf{B}_t\mathbf{h}_t + \boldsymbol{\eta}_t^v & \boldsymbol{\eta}_t^v \sim \mathcal{N}\left(\boldsymbol{\eta}_t^v \middle| \bar{\mathbf{v}}_t, \boldsymbol{\Sigma}_t^v\right) & \text{emission model} \end{array} \tag{24.3.1}$$

where $\boldsymbol{\eta}_t^h$ and $\boldsymbol{\eta}_t^v$ are noise vectors; $\mathbf{A}_t$ is called the *transition matrix* and $\mathbf{B}_t$ the *emission matrix*. The terms $\bar{\mathbf{h}}_t$ and $\bar{\mathbf{v}}_t$ are the hidden and output bias respectively. The transition and emission models define a first-order Markov model

$$p(\mathbf{h}_{1:T}, \mathbf{v}_{1:T}) = p(\mathbf{h}_1)p(\mathbf{v}_1|\mathbf{h}_1)\prod_{t=2}^{T} p(\mathbf{h}_t|\mathbf{h}_{t-1})p(\mathbf{v}_t|\mathbf{h}_t) \tag{24.3.2}$$

with the transitions and emissions given by Gaussian distributions

$$p(\mathbf{h}_t|\mathbf{h}_{t-1}) = \mathcal{N}\left(\mathbf{h}_t \middle| \mathbf{A}_t\mathbf{h}_{t-1} + \bar{\mathbf{h}}_t, \boldsymbol{\Sigma}_t^h\right), \qquad p(\mathbf{h}_1) = \mathcal{N}\left(\mathbf{h}_1 \middle| \boldsymbol{\mu}_\pi, \boldsymbol{\Sigma}_\pi\right) \tag{24.3.3}$$

$$p(\mathbf{v}_t|\mathbf{h}_t) = \mathcal{N}\left(\mathbf{v}_t \middle| \mathbf{B}_t\mathbf{h}_t + \bar{\mathbf{v}}_t, \boldsymbol{\Sigma}_t^v\right). \tag{24.3.4}$$

The model is represented as a belief network in Fig. 24.5 with the extension to higher orders being intuitive. One may also include an external input $\mathbf{o}_t$ at each time, which will add $\mathbf{C}\mathbf{o}_t$ to the mean of the hidden variable and $\mathbf{D}\mathbf{o}_t$ to the mean of the observation.

[2] These models are also often called Kalman Filters. We avoid this terminology here since the word 'filter' refers to a specific kind of inference and runs the risk of confusing a filtering algorithm with the model itself.

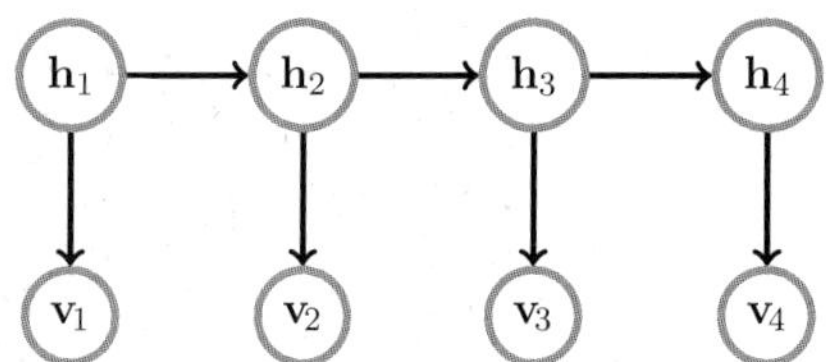

Figure 24.5 A (latent) LDS. Both hidden and visible variables are Gaussian distributed.

Explicit expressions for the transition and emission distributions are given below for the time-invariant case $\mathbf{A_t} \equiv \mathbf{A}$, $\mathbf{B_t} \equiv \mathbf{B}$, $\boldsymbol{\Sigma}_t^h \equiv \boldsymbol{\Sigma}_h$, $\boldsymbol{\Sigma}_t^v \equiv \boldsymbol{\Sigma}_v$ with zero biases $\bar{\mathbf{v}}_t = \mathbf{0}$, $\bar{\mathbf{h}}_t = \mathbf{0}$. Each hidden variable is a multidimensional Gaussian distributed vector $\mathbf{h}_t$, with transition

$$p(\mathbf{h}_t|\mathbf{h}_{t-1}) = \frac{1}{\sqrt{|2\pi\boldsymbol{\Sigma}_h|}} \exp\left(-\frac{1}{2}\left(\mathbf{h}_t - \mathbf{A}\mathbf{h}_{t-1}\right)^{\mathsf{T}} \boldsymbol{\Sigma}_h^{-1} \left(\mathbf{h}_t - \mathbf{A}\mathbf{h}_{t-1}\right)\right) \tag{24.3.5}$$

which states that $\mathbf{h}_t$ has a mean $\mathbf{A}\mathbf{h}_{t-1}$ and covariance $\boldsymbol{\Sigma}_h$. Similarly,

$$p(\mathbf{v}_t|\mathbf{h}_t) = \frac{1}{\sqrt{|2\pi\boldsymbol{\Sigma}_v|}} \exp\left(-\frac{1}{2}\left(\mathbf{v}_t - \mathbf{B}\mathbf{h}_t\right)^{\mathsf{T}} \boldsymbol{\Sigma}_v^{-1} \left(\mathbf{v}_t - \mathbf{B}\mathbf{h}_t\right)\right) \tag{24.3.6}$$

describes an output $\mathbf{v}_t$ with mean $\mathbf{B}\mathbf{h}_t$ and covariance $\boldsymbol{\Sigma}_v$.

Example 24.3

Consider a dynamical system defined on two-dimensional vectors $\mathbf{h}_t$:

$$\mathbf{h}_{t+1} = \mathbf{R}_\theta \mathbf{h}_t, \qquad \text{with } \mathbf{R}_\theta = \begin{pmatrix} \cos\theta & -\sin\theta \\ \sin\theta & \cos\theta \end{pmatrix} \tag{24.3.7}$$

which rotates the vector $\mathbf{h}_t$ through angle θ in one timestep. Under this LDS we trace out points on a circle, $\mathbf{h}_1, \ldots, \mathbf{h}_t$ through time. By taking a scalar projection of $\mathbf{h}_t$, for example,

$$v_t = [\mathbf{h}_t]_1 = [1 \;\; 0]^{\mathsf{T}}\mathbf{h}_t, \tag{24.3.8}$$

the elements $v_t, t = 1, \ldots, T$ describe a sinusoid through time, see Fig. 24.6. By using a block diagonal $\mathbf{R} = \text{blkdiag}\left(\mathbf{R}_{\theta_1}, \ldots, \mathbf{R}_{\theta_m}\right)$ and taking a scalar projection of the extended $m \times 2$ dimensional $\mathbf{h}_t$ vector, one can construct a representation of a signal in terms of m sinusoidal components. Hence we see that LDSs can represent potentially highly complex period behaviour.

24.4 Inference

Given an observation sequence $\mathbf{v}_{1:T}$ we here consider filtering and smoothing, as we did for the HMM, Section 23.2.1. For the HMM, in deriving the various message-passing recursions, we used only the

Figure 24.6 A single phasor plotted as a damped two-dimensional rotation $\mathbf{h}_{t+1} = \gamma\mathbf{R}_\theta\mathbf{h}_t$ with a damping factor $0 < \gamma < 1$. By taking a projection onto the y axis, the phasor generates a damped sinusoid.

independence structure encoded by the belief network. Since the LDS has the same independence structure as the HMM, we can use the same independence assumptions in deriving the updates for the LDS. However, in implementing them we need to deal with the issue that we now have continuous hidden variables, rather than discrete states. The fact that the distributions are Gaussian means that we can deal with continuous messages exactly. In translating the HMM message-passing equations, we first replace summation with integration. For example, the filtering recursion (23.2.7) becomes

$$p(\mathbf{h}_t|\mathbf{v}_{1:t}) \propto \int_{\mathbf{h}_{t-1}} p(\mathbf{v}_t|\mathbf{h}_t)p(\mathbf{h}_t|\mathbf{h}_{t-1})p(\mathbf{h}_{t-1}|\mathbf{v}_{1:t-1}), \qquad t > 1. \tag{24.4.1}$$

Since the product of two Gaussians is another Gaussian, and the integral of a Gaussian is another Gaussian, the resulting $p(\mathbf{h}_t|\mathbf{v}_{1:t})$ is also Gaussian. This closure property of Gaussians means that we may represent $p(\mathbf{h}_{t-1}|\mathbf{v}_{1:t-1}) = \mathcal{N}(\mathbf{h}_{t-1}|\mathbf{f}_{t-1}, \mathbf{F}_{t-1})$ with mean $\mathbf{f}_{t-1}$ and covariance $\mathbf{F}_{t-1}$. The effect of Equation (24.4.1) is equivalent to updating the mean $\mathbf{f}_{t-1}$ and covariance $\mathbf{F}_{t-1}$ into a mean $\mathbf{f}_t$ and covariance $\mathbf{F}_t$ for $p(\mathbf{h}_t|\mathbf{v}_{1:t})$. Our task below is to find explicit algebraic formulae for these updates.

Numerical stability

Translating the message-passing inference techniques we developed for the HMM into the LDS is largely straightforward. Indeed, one could simply run a standard sum-product algorithm (albeit for continuous variables), see `demoSumprodGaussCanonLDS.m`. In long timeseries, however, numerical instabilities can build up and may result in grossly inaccurate results, depending on the transition and emission distribution parameters and the method of implementing the message updates. For this reason specialised routines have been developed that are numerically stable under certain parameter regimes [303]. For the HMM in Section 23.2.1, we discussed two alternative methods for smoothing, the parallel β approach, and the sequential γ approach. The β recursion is suitable when the emission and transition covariance entries are large, and the γ recursion preferable in the more standard case of small covariance values.

Analytical shortcuts

In deriving the inference recursions we need to frequently multiply and integrate Gaussians. Whilst in principle straightforward, this can be algebraically tedious and, wherever possible, it is useful to appeal to known shortcuts. For example, one can exploit the general result that the linear transform of a Gaussian random variable is another Gaussian random variable. Similarly it is convenient to make use of the conditioning formulae, as well as the dynamics reversal intuition. These results are stated in Section 8.4, and below we derive the most useful for our purposes here. This will also explain how the equations for filtering can be derived.

Consider a linear transformation of a Gaussian random variable:

$$\mathbf{y} = \mathbf{M}\mathbf{x} + \boldsymbol{\eta}, \qquad \boldsymbol{\eta} \sim \mathcal{N}(\boldsymbol{\eta}|\boldsymbol{\mu}, \boldsymbol{\Sigma}), \qquad \mathbf{x} \sim \mathcal{N}(\mathbf{x}|\boldsymbol{\mu}_x, \boldsymbol{\Sigma}_x) \tag{24.4.2}$$

where $\mathbf{x}$ and $\boldsymbol{\eta}$ are assumed to be generated from independent processes. To find the distribution $p(\mathbf{y})$, one approach would be to write this formally as

$$p(\mathbf{y}) = \int \mathcal{N}(\mathbf{y}|\mathbf{M}\mathbf{x} + \boldsymbol{\mu}, \boldsymbol{\Sigma}) \mathcal{N}(\mathbf{x}|\boldsymbol{\mu}_x, \boldsymbol{\Sigma}_x)\, d\mathbf{x} \tag{24.4.3}$$

Algorithm 24.1 LDS forward pass. Compute the filtered posteriors $p(\mathbf{h}_t|\mathbf{v}_{1:t}) \equiv \mathcal{N}(\mathbf{f}_t, \mathbf{F}_t)$ for a LDS with parameters $\theta_t = \left\{\mathbf{A}, \mathbf{B}, \boldsymbol{\Sigma}^h, \boldsymbol{\Sigma}^v, \bar{\mathbf{h}}, \bar{\mathbf{v}}\right\}_t$. The log likelihood $L = \log p(\mathbf{v}_{1:T})$ is also returned.

$\{\mathbf{f}_1, \mathbf{F}_1, p_1\} = \text{LDSFORWARD}(\mathbf{0}, \mathbf{0}, \mathbf{v}_1; \theta_1)$
$L \leftarrow \log p_1$
for $t \leftarrow 2, T$ **do**
  $\{\mathbf{f}_t, \mathbf{F}_t, p_t\} = \text{LDSFORWARD}(\mathbf{f}_{t-1}, \mathbf{F}_{t-1}, \mathbf{v}_t; \theta_t)$
  $L \leftarrow L + \log p_t$
end for
function LDSFORWARD($\mathbf{f}, \mathbf{F}, \mathbf{v}; \theta$)
  $\boldsymbol{\mu}_h \leftarrow \mathbf{A}\mathbf{f} + \bar{\mathbf{h}}, \quad \boldsymbol{\mu}_v \leftarrow \mathbf{B}\boldsymbol{\mu}_h + \bar{\mathbf{v}}$ ▷ Mean of $p(\mathbf{h}_t, \mathbf{v}_t|\mathbf{v}_{1:t-1})$
  $\boldsymbol{\Sigma}_{hh} \leftarrow \mathbf{A}\mathbf{F}\mathbf{A}^\mathsf{T} + \boldsymbol{\Sigma}_h, \quad \boldsymbol{\Sigma}_{vv} \leftarrow \mathbf{B}\boldsymbol{\Sigma}_{hh}\mathbf{B}^\mathsf{T} + \boldsymbol{\Sigma}_v, \quad \boldsymbol{\Sigma}_{vh} \leftarrow \mathbf{B}\boldsymbol{\Sigma}_{hh}$ ▷ Covariance of $p(\mathbf{h}_t, \mathbf{v}_t|\mathbf{v}_{1:t-1})$
  $\mathbf{f}' \leftarrow \boldsymbol{\mu}_h + \boldsymbol{\Sigma}_{vh}^\mathsf{T}\boldsymbol{\Sigma}_{vv}^{-1}(\mathbf{v} - \boldsymbol{\mu}_v), \quad \mathbf{F}' \leftarrow \boldsymbol{\Sigma}_{hh} - \boldsymbol{\Sigma}_{vh}^\mathsf{T}\boldsymbol{\Sigma}_{vv}^{-1}\boldsymbol{\Sigma}_{vh}$ ▷ Find $p(\mathbf{h}_t|\mathbf{v}_{1:t})$ by conditioning
  $p' \leftarrow \exp\left(-\frac{1}{2}(\mathbf{v} - \boldsymbol{\mu}_v)^\mathsf{T}\boldsymbol{\Sigma}_{vv}^{-1}(\mathbf{v} - \boldsymbol{\mu}_v)\right)/\sqrt{\det(2\pi\boldsymbol{\Sigma}_{vv})}$ ▷ Compute $p(\mathbf{v}_t|\mathbf{v}_{1:t-1})$
  return $\mathbf{f}', \mathbf{F}', p'$
end function

---

and carry out the integral (by completing the square). However, since a Gaussian variable under linear transformation is another Gaussian, we can take a shortcut and just find the mean and covariance of the transformed variable. Its mean is given by

$$\langle \mathbf{y} \rangle = \mathbf{M} \langle \mathbf{x} \rangle + \langle \boldsymbol{\eta} \rangle = \mathbf{M}\boldsymbol{\mu}_x + \boldsymbol{\mu}. \tag{24.4.4}$$

To find the covariance of $p(\mathbf{y})$, consider the displacement of a variable $\mathbf{x}$ from its mean, which we write as

$$\Delta\mathbf{x} \equiv \mathbf{x} - \langle \mathbf{x} \rangle. \tag{24.4.5}$$

The covariance is, by definition, $\langle \Delta\mathbf{x}\Delta\mathbf{x}^\mathsf{T} \rangle$. For $\mathbf{y}$, the displacement is

$$\Delta\mathbf{y} = \mathbf{M}\Delta\mathbf{x} + \Delta\boldsymbol{\eta}, \tag{24.4.6}$$

so that the covariance is

$$\begin{aligned}\langle \Delta\mathbf{y}\Delta\mathbf{y}^\mathsf{T} \rangle &= \left\langle (\mathbf{M}\Delta\mathbf{x} + \Delta\boldsymbol{\eta})(\mathbf{M}\Delta\mathbf{x} + \Delta\boldsymbol{\eta})^\mathsf{T} \right\rangle \\ &= \mathbf{M}\langle \Delta\mathbf{x}\Delta\mathbf{x}^\mathsf{T} \rangle \mathbf{M}^\mathsf{T} + \mathbf{M}\langle \Delta\mathbf{x}\Delta\boldsymbol{\eta}^\mathsf{T} \rangle + \langle \Delta\boldsymbol{\eta}\Delta\mathbf{x}^\mathsf{T} \rangle \mathbf{M}^\mathsf{T} + \langle \Delta\boldsymbol{\eta}\Delta\boldsymbol{\eta}^\mathsf{T} \rangle.\end{aligned}$$

Since the noises $\boldsymbol{\eta}$ and $\mathbf{x}$ are assumed independent, $\langle \Delta\boldsymbol{\eta}\Delta\mathbf{x}^\mathsf{T} \rangle = \mathbf{0}$ we have

$$\boldsymbol{\Sigma}_y = \mathbf{M}\boldsymbol{\Sigma}_x\mathbf{M}^\mathsf{T} + \boldsymbol{\Sigma}. \tag{24.4.7}$$

24.4.1 Filtering

We represent the filtered distribution as a Gaussian with mean $\mathbf{f}_t$ and covariance $\mathbf{F}_t$,

$$p(\mathbf{h}_t|\mathbf{v}_{1:t}) \sim \mathcal{N}(\mathbf{h}_t|\mathbf{f}_t, \mathbf{F}_t). \tag{24.4.8}$$

This is called the *moment representation*. Our task is then to find a recursion for $\mathbf{f}_t, \mathbf{F}_t$ in terms of $\mathbf{f}_{t-1}, \mathbf{F}_{t-1}$. A convenient approach is to first find the joint distribution $p(\mathbf{h}_t, \mathbf{v}_t|\mathbf{v}_{1:t-1})$ and then condition on $\mathbf{v}_t$ to find the distribution $p(\mathbf{h}_t|\mathbf{v}_{1:t})$. The term $p(\mathbf{h}_t, \mathbf{v}_t|\mathbf{v}_{1:t-1})$ is a Gaussian whose statistics can be found from the relations

$$\mathbf{v}_t = \mathbf{B}\mathbf{h}_t + \boldsymbol{\eta}_t^v, \qquad \mathbf{h}_t = \mathbf{A}\mathbf{h}_{t-1} + \boldsymbol{\eta}_t^h. \tag{24.4.9}$$

Using the above, and assuming time-invariance and zero biases, we readily find

$$\left\langle \Delta\mathbf{h}_t \Delta\mathbf{h}_t^\mathsf{T} | \mathbf{v}_{1:t-1} \right\rangle = \mathbf{A}\mathbf{F}_{t-1}\mathbf{A}^\mathsf{T} + \boldsymbol{\Sigma}_h, \tag{24.4.10}$$

$$\left\langle \Delta\mathbf{v}_t \Delta\mathbf{h}_t^\mathsf{T} | \mathbf{v}_{1:t-1} \right\rangle = \mathbf{B}\left(\mathbf{A}\mathbf{F}_{t-1}\mathbf{A}^\mathsf{T} + \boldsymbol{\Sigma}_h\right), \tag{24.4.11}$$

$$\left\langle \Delta\mathbf{v}_t \Delta\mathbf{v}_t^\mathsf{T} | \mathbf{v}_{1:t-1} \right\rangle = \mathbf{B}\left(\mathbf{A}\mathbf{F}_{t-1}\mathbf{A}^\mathsf{T} + \boldsymbol{\Sigma}_h\right)\mathbf{B}^\mathsf{T} + \boldsymbol{\Sigma}_v, \tag{24.4.12}$$

$$\left\langle \mathbf{v}_t | \mathbf{v}_{1:t-1} \right\rangle = \mathbf{B}\mathbf{A}\left\langle \mathbf{h}_{t-1} | \mathbf{v}_{1:t-1} \right\rangle, \tag{24.4.13}$$

$$\left\langle \mathbf{h}_t | \mathbf{v}_{1:t-1} \right\rangle = \mathbf{A}\left\langle \mathbf{h}_{t-1} | \mathbf{v}_{1:t-1} \right\rangle. \tag{24.4.14}$$

In the above, using our moment representation of the forward messages

$$\left\langle \mathbf{h}_{t-1} | \mathbf{v}_{1:t-1} \right\rangle \equiv \mathbf{f}_{t-1}, \qquad \left\langle \Delta\mathbf{h}_{t-1} \Delta\mathbf{h}_{t-1}^\mathsf{T} | \mathbf{v}_{1:t-1} \right\rangle \equiv \mathbf{F}_{t-1}. \tag{24.4.15}$$

Then, using conditioning[3] $p(\mathbf{h}_t|\mathbf{v}_t, \mathbf{v}_{1:t-1})$ will have mean

$$\mathbf{f}_t \equiv \left\langle \mathbf{h}_t | \mathbf{v}_{1:t-1} \right\rangle + \left\langle \Delta\mathbf{h}_t \Delta\mathbf{v}_t^\mathsf{T} | \mathbf{v}_{1:t-1} \right\rangle \left\langle \Delta\mathbf{v}_t \Delta\mathbf{v}_t^\mathsf{T} | \mathbf{v}_{1:t-1} \right\rangle^{-1} \left(\mathbf{v}_t - \left\langle \mathbf{v}_t | \mathbf{v}_{1:t-1} \right\rangle\right) \tag{24.4.16}$$

and covariance

$$\mathbf{F}_t \equiv \left\langle \Delta\mathbf{h}_t \Delta\mathbf{h}_t^\mathsf{T} | \mathbf{v}_{1:t-1} \right\rangle - \left\langle \Delta\mathbf{h}_t \Delta\mathbf{v}_t^\mathsf{T} | \mathbf{v}_{1:t-1} \right\rangle \left\langle \Delta\mathbf{v}_t \Delta\mathbf{v}_t^\mathsf{T} | \mathbf{v}_{1:t-1} \right\rangle^{-1} \left\langle \Delta\mathbf{v}_t \Delta\mathbf{h}_t^\mathsf{T} | \mathbf{v}_{1:t-1} \right\rangle. \tag{24.4.17}$$

Writing out the above explicitly we have for the mean and covariance:

$$\mathbf{f}_t = \mathbf{A}\mathbf{f}_{t-1} + \mathbf{P}\mathbf{B}^\mathsf{T}\left(\mathbf{B}\mathbf{P}\mathbf{B}^\mathsf{T} + \boldsymbol{\Sigma}_v\right)^{-1}\left(\mathbf{v}_t - \mathbf{B}\mathbf{A}\mathbf{f}_{t-1}\right) \tag{24.4.18}$$

$$\mathbf{F}_t = \mathbf{P} - \mathbf{P}\mathbf{B}^\mathsf{T}\left(\mathbf{B}\mathbf{P}\mathbf{B}^\mathsf{T} + \boldsymbol{\Sigma}_v\right)^{-1}\mathbf{B}\mathbf{P} \tag{24.4.19}$$

where

$$\mathbf{P} \equiv \mathbf{A}\mathbf{F}_{t-1}\mathbf{A}^\mathsf{T} + \boldsymbol{\Sigma}_h. \tag{24.4.20}$$

The recursion is initialised with $\mathbf{f}_0 = \mathbf{0}$, $\mathbf{F}_0 = \mathbf{0}$. The filtering procedure is presented in Algorithm 24.1 with a single update in `LDSforwardUpdate.m`.

One can write the covariance update as

$$\mathbf{F}_t = \left(\mathbf{I} - \mathbf{K}\mathbf{B}\right)\mathbf{P} \tag{24.4.21}$$

where we define the *Kalman gain* matrix

$$\mathbf{K} = \mathbf{P}\mathbf{B}^\mathsf{T}\left(\boldsymbol{\Sigma}_V + \mathbf{B}\mathbf{P}\mathbf{B}^\mathsf{T}\right)^{-1}. \tag{24.4.22}$$

Symmetrising the updates

A potential numerical issue with the covariance update (24.4.21) is that it is the difference of two positive definite matrices. If there are numerical errors, the $\mathbf{F}_t$ may not be numerically positive definite, nor symmetric. Using the Woodbury identity, Definition A.11, Equation (24.4.19) can be written more compactly as

$$\mathbf{F}_t = \left(\mathbf{P}^{-1} + \mathbf{B}^\mathsf{T}\boldsymbol{\Sigma}_v^{-1}\mathbf{B}\right)^{-1}. \tag{24.4.23}$$

[3] $p(\mathbf{x}|\mathbf{y})$ is a Gaussian with mean $\boldsymbol{\mu}_x + \boldsymbol{\Sigma}_{xy}\boldsymbol{\Sigma}_{yy}^{-1}\left(\mathbf{y} - \boldsymbol{\mu}_y\right)$ and covariance $\boldsymbol{\Sigma}_{xx} - \boldsymbol{\Sigma}_{xy}\boldsymbol{\Sigma}_{yy}^{-1}\boldsymbol{\Sigma}_{yx}$.

Whilst this is positive semidefinite, this is numerically expensive since it involves two matrix inversions. An alternative is to use the definition of $\mathbf{K}$, from which we can write

$$\mathbf{K}\boldsymbol{\Sigma}_v\mathbf{K}^\mathsf{T} = (\mathbf{I} - \mathbf{K}\mathbf{B})\,\mathbf{P}\mathbf{B}^\mathsf{T}\mathbf{K}^\mathsf{T}. \tag{24.4.24}$$

Hence we arrive at *Joseph's symmetrised update* [114]

$$\mathbf{F}_t = (\mathbf{I} - \mathbf{K}\mathbf{B})\,\mathbf{P}\,(\mathbf{I} - \mathbf{K}\mathbf{B})^\mathsf{T} + \mathbf{K}\boldsymbol{\Sigma}_v\mathbf{K}^\mathsf{T}. \tag{24.4.25}$$

The right-hand side of the above is the addition of two positive definite matrices so that the resulting update for the covariance is more numerically stable. A similar method can be used in the backward pass below. An alternative is to avoid using covariance matrices directly and use their square root as the parameter, deriving updates for these instead [243, 39].

Prediction

From the dynamics, Definition 24.4, the distribution of the future visible variable is given by propagating the filtered distribution forwards one timestep (written here for the time-independent case)

$$p(\mathbf{v}_{t+1}|\mathbf{v}_{1:t}) = \int_{\mathbf{h}_t,\mathbf{h}_{t+1}} p(\mathbf{v}_{t+1}|\mathbf{h}_{t+1})p(\mathbf{h}_{t+1}|\mathbf{h}_t)p(\mathbf{h}_t|\mathbf{v}_{1:t}) \tag{24.4.26}$$

$$= \mathcal{N}\left(\mathbf{v}_{t+1}\middle|\mathbf{B}\left(\mathbf{A}\mathbf{f}_t + \bar{\mathbf{h}}\right) + \bar{\mathbf{v}}, \mathbf{B}\left(\mathbf{A}\mathbf{F}_t\mathbf{A}^\mathsf{T} + \boldsymbol{\Sigma}_h\right)\mathbf{B}^\mathsf{T} + \boldsymbol{\Sigma}_v\right). \tag{24.4.27}$$

24.4.2 Smoothing: Rauch–Tung–Striebel correction method

The smoothed posterior $p(\mathbf{h}_t|\mathbf{v}_{1:T})$ is necessarily Gaussian since it is the conditional marginal of a larger Gaussian. By representing the posterior as a Gaussian with mean $\mathbf{g}_t$ and covariance $\mathbf{G}_t$,

$$p(\mathbf{h}_t|\mathbf{v}_{1:T}) \sim \mathcal{N}(\mathbf{h}_t|\mathbf{g}_t, \mathbf{G}_t) \tag{24.4.28}$$

we can form a recursion for $\mathbf{g}_t$ and $\mathbf{G}_t$ as follows:

$$p(\mathbf{h}_t|\mathbf{v}_{1:T}) = \int_{\mathbf{h}_{t+1}} p(\mathbf{h}_t, \mathbf{h}_{t+1}|\mathbf{v}_{1:T}) \tag{24.4.29}$$

$$= \int_{\mathbf{h}_{t+1}} p(\mathbf{h}_t|\mathbf{v}_{1:T}, \mathbf{h}_{t+1})p(\mathbf{h}_{t+1}|\mathbf{v}_{1:T}) = \int_{\mathbf{h}_{t+1}} p(\mathbf{h}_t|\mathbf{v}_{1:t}, \mathbf{h}_{t+1})p(\mathbf{h}_{t+1}|\mathbf{v}_{1:T}). \tag{24.4.30}$$

The term $p(\mathbf{h}_t|\mathbf{v}_{1:t}, \mathbf{h}_{t+1})$ can be found by conditioning the joint distribution

$$p(\mathbf{h}_t, \mathbf{h}_{t+1}|\mathbf{v}_{1:t}) = p(\mathbf{h}_{t+1}|\mathbf{h}_t, \cancel{\mathbf{v}_{1:t}})p(\mathbf{h}_t|\mathbf{v}_{1:t}) \tag{24.4.31}$$

which is obtained in the usual manner by finding its mean and covariance: The term $p(\mathbf{h}_t|\mathbf{v}_{1:t})$ is a known Gaussian from filtering with mean $\mathbf{f}_t$ and covariance $\mathbf{F}_t$. Hence the joint distribution $p(\mathbf{h}_t, \mathbf{h}_{t+1}|\mathbf{v}_{1:t})$ has means

$$\langle \mathbf{h}_t|\mathbf{v}_{1:t}\rangle = \mathbf{f}_t, \qquad \langle \mathbf{h}_{t+1}|\mathbf{v}_{1:t}\rangle = \mathbf{A}\mathbf{f}_t \tag{24.4.32}$$

and covariance elements

$$\left\langle \Delta \mathbf{h}_t \Delta \mathbf{h}_t^{\mathsf{T}} | \mathbf{v}_{1:t} \right\rangle = \mathbf{F}_t, \quad \left\langle \Delta \mathbf{h}_t \Delta \mathbf{h}_{t+1}^{\mathsf{T}} | \mathbf{v}_{1:t} \right\rangle = \mathbf{F}_t \mathbf{A}^{\mathsf{T}}, \quad \left\langle \Delta \mathbf{h}_{t+1} \Delta \mathbf{h}_{t+1}^{\mathsf{T}} | \mathbf{v}_{1:t} \right\rangle = \mathbf{A} \mathbf{F}_t \mathbf{A}^{\mathsf{T}} + \boldsymbol{\Sigma}_h. \quad (24.4.33)$$

To find $p(\mathbf{h}_t | \mathbf{v}_{1:t}, \mathbf{h}_{t+1})$ we may use the conditioned Gaussian results, Result 8.4. However, it will turn out to be useful to use the system reversal result, Section 8.4.2, which interprets $p(\mathbf{h}_t | \mathbf{v}_{1:t}, \mathbf{h}_{t+1})$ as an equivalent linear system going backwards in time:

$$\mathbf{h}_t = \overleftarrow{\mathbf{A}}_t \mathbf{h}_{t+1} + \overleftarrow{\mathbf{m}}_t + \overleftarrow{\boldsymbol{\eta}}_t \quad (24.4.34)$$

where

$$\overleftarrow{\mathbf{A}}_t \equiv \left\langle \Delta \mathbf{h}_t \Delta \mathbf{h}_{t+1}^{\mathsf{T}} | \mathbf{v}_{1:t} \right\rangle \left\langle \Delta \mathbf{h}_{t+1} \Delta \mathbf{h}_{t+1}^{\mathsf{T}} | \mathbf{v}_{1:t} \right\rangle^{-1} \quad (24.4.35)$$

$$\overleftarrow{\mathbf{m}}_t \equiv \langle \mathbf{h}_t | \mathbf{v}_{1:t} \rangle - \left\langle \Delta \mathbf{h}_t \Delta \mathbf{h}_{t+1}^{\mathsf{T}} | \mathbf{v}_{1:t} \right\rangle \left\langle \Delta \mathbf{h}_{t+1} \Delta \mathbf{h}_{t+1}^{\mathsf{T}} | \mathbf{v}_{1:t} \right\rangle^{-1} \langle \mathbf{h}_{t+1} | \mathbf{v}_{1:t} \rangle \quad (24.4.36)$$

and $\overleftarrow{\boldsymbol{\eta}}_t \sim \mathcal{N}\left(\overleftarrow{\boldsymbol{\eta}}_t \middle| \mathbf{0}, \overleftarrow{\boldsymbol{\Sigma}}_t\right)$, with

$$\overleftarrow{\boldsymbol{\Sigma}}_t \equiv \left\langle \Delta \mathbf{h}_t \Delta \mathbf{h}_t^{\mathsf{T}} | \mathbf{v}_{1:t} \right\rangle - \left\langle \Delta \mathbf{h}_t \Delta \mathbf{h}_{t+1}^{\mathsf{T}} | \mathbf{v}_{1:t} \right\rangle \left\langle \Delta \mathbf{h}_{t+1} \Delta \mathbf{h}_{t+1}^{\mathsf{T}} | \mathbf{v}_{1:t} \right\rangle^{-1} \left\langle \Delta \mathbf{h}_{t+1} \Delta \mathbf{h}_t^{\mathsf{T}} | \mathbf{v}_{1:t} \right\rangle. \quad (24.4.37)$$

Using dynamics reversal, Equation (24.4.34) and assuming that $\mathbf{h}_{t+1}$ is Gaussian distributed, it is then straightforward to work out the statistics of $p(\mathbf{h}_t | \mathbf{v}_{1:T})$. The mean is given by

$$\mathbf{g}_t \equiv \langle \mathbf{h}_t | \mathbf{v}_{1:T} \rangle = \overleftarrow{\mathbf{A}}_t \langle \mathbf{h}_{t+1} | \mathbf{v}_{1:T} \rangle + \overleftarrow{\mathbf{m}}_t = \overleftarrow{\mathbf{A}}_t \mathbf{g}_{t+1} + \overleftarrow{\mathbf{m}}_t \quad (24.4.38)$$

and covariance

$$\mathbf{G}_t \equiv \left\langle \Delta \mathbf{h}_t \Delta \mathbf{h}_t^{\mathsf{T}} | \mathbf{v}_{1:T} \right\rangle = \overleftarrow{\mathbf{A}}_t \left\langle \Delta \mathbf{h}_{t+1} \Delta \mathbf{h}_{t+1}^{\mathsf{T}} | \mathbf{v}_{1:T} \right\rangle \overleftarrow{\mathbf{A}}_t^{\mathsf{T}} + \overleftarrow{\boldsymbol{\Sigma}}_t = \overleftarrow{\mathbf{A}}_t \mathbf{G}_{t+1} \overleftarrow{\mathbf{A}}_t^{\mathsf{T}} + \overleftarrow{\boldsymbol{\Sigma}}_t. \quad (24.4.39)$$

This procedure is the Rauch–Tung–Striebel Kalman smoother [248]. This is called a 'correction' method since it takes the filtered estimate $p(\mathbf{h}_t | \mathbf{v}_{1:t})$ and 'corrects' it to form a smoothed estimate $p(\mathbf{h}_t | \mathbf{v}_{1:T})$. The procedure is outlined in Algorithm 24.2 and is detailed in `LDSbackwardUpdate.m`. See also `LDSsmooth.m`.

Sampling a trajectory from $p(\mathbf{h}_{1:T} | \mathbf{v}_{1:T})$

One may use Equation (24.4.34) to draw a sample trajectory $\mathbf{h}_{1:T}$ from the posterior $p(\mathbf{h}_{1:T} | \mathbf{v}_{1:T})$. We start by first drawing a sample $\mathbf{h}_T$ from the Gaussian posterior $p(\mathbf{h}_T | \mathbf{v}_{1:T}) = \mathcal{N}(\mathbf{h}_T | \mathbf{f}_T, \mathbf{F}_T)$. Given this value, we write

$$\mathbf{h}_{T-1} = \overleftarrow{\mathbf{A}}_{T-1} \mathbf{h}_T + \overleftarrow{\mathbf{m}}_{T-1} + \overleftarrow{\boldsymbol{\eta}}_{T-1}. \quad (24.4.40)$$

By drawing a sample from the zero mean Gaussian $\mathcal{N}\left(\overleftarrow{\boldsymbol{\eta}}_{T-1} \middle| \mathbf{0}, \overleftarrow{\boldsymbol{\Sigma}}_{T-1}\right)$, we then have a value for $\mathbf{h}_{T-1}$. We continue in this way, reversing backwards in time, to build up the sample trajectory $\mathbf{h}_T, \mathbf{h}_{T-1}, \mathbf{h}_{T-2}, \ldots, \mathbf{h}_1$. This is equivalent to the forward-filtering-backward-sampling approach described in Section 23.2.5.

Algorithm 24.2 LDS backward pass. Compute the smoothed posteriors $p(\mathbf{h}_t|\mathbf{v}_{1:T})$. This requires the filtered results from Algorithm 24.1.

$\mathbf{G}_T \leftarrow \mathbf{F}_T, \mathbf{g}_T \leftarrow \mathbf{f}_T$
for $t \leftarrow T-1, 1$ **do**
  $\{\mathbf{g}_t, \mathbf{G}_t\} = \text{LDSBACKWARD}(\mathbf{g}_{t+1}, \mathbf{G}_{t+1}, \mathbf{f}_t, \mathbf{F}_t; \theta_t)$
end for
function LDSBACKWARD($\mathbf{g}, \mathbf{G}, \mathbf{f}, \mathbf{F}; \theta$)
  $\boldsymbol{\mu}_h \leftarrow \mathbf{A}\mathbf{f} + \bar{\mathbf{h}}$, $\boldsymbol{\Sigma}_{h'h'} \leftarrow \mathbf{A}\mathbf{F}\mathbf{A}^\mathsf{T} + \boldsymbol{\Sigma}_h$, $\boldsymbol{\Sigma}_{h'h} \leftarrow \mathbf{A}\mathbf{F}$ ▷ Statistics of $p(\mathbf{h}_t, \mathbf{h}_{t+1}|\mathbf{v}_{1:t})$
  $\overleftarrow{\boldsymbol{\Sigma}} \leftarrow \mathbf{F} - \boldsymbol{\Sigma}^\mathsf{T}_{h'h}\boldsymbol{\Sigma}^{-1}_{h'h'}\boldsymbol{\Sigma}_{h'h}$, $\overleftarrow{\mathbf{A}} \leftarrow \boldsymbol{\Sigma}^\mathsf{T}_{h'h}\boldsymbol{\Sigma}^{-1}_{h'h'}$, $\overleftarrow{\mathbf{m}} \leftarrow \mathbf{f} - \overleftarrow{\mathbf{A}}\boldsymbol{\mu}_h$ ▷ Dynamics Reversal $p(\mathbf{h}_t|\mathbf{h}_{t+1}, \mathbf{v}_{1:t})$
  $\mathbf{g}' \leftarrow \overleftarrow{\mathbf{A}}\mathbf{g} + \overleftarrow{\mathbf{m}}$, $\mathbf{G}' \leftarrow \overleftarrow{\mathbf{A}}\mathbf{G}\overleftarrow{\mathbf{A}}^\mathsf{T} + \overleftarrow{\boldsymbol{\Sigma}}$ ▷ Backward propagation
  return $\mathbf{g}', \mathbf{G}'$
end function

The cross moment

An advantage of the dynamics reversal interpretation given above is that the cross moment (which is required for learning) is immediately obtained from

$$\left\langle \Delta\mathbf{h}_t \Delta\mathbf{h}^\mathsf{T}_{t+1}|\mathbf{v}_{1:T}\right\rangle = \overleftarrow{\mathbf{A}}_t\mathbf{G}_{t+1} \Rightarrow \left\langle \mathbf{h}_t\mathbf{h}^\mathsf{T}_{t+1}|\mathbf{v}_{1:T}\right\rangle = \overleftarrow{\mathbf{A}}_t\mathbf{G}_{t+1} + \mathbf{g}_t\mathbf{g}^\mathsf{T}_{t+1}. \tag{24.4.41}$$

24.4.3 The likelihood

For the discrete HMM in Section 23.2, we showed how the likelihood can be computed directly from the filtered messages $\sum_{h_T} \alpha(h_T)$. We cannot apply that technique here since the message distributions we are passing are conditional distributions $p(\mathbf{h}_t|\mathbf{v}_{1:t})$, rather than joint distributions $p(\mathbf{h}_t, \mathbf{v}_{1:t})$. However, help is at hand and we may compute the likelihood using the decomposition

$$p(\mathbf{v}_{1:T}) = \prod_{t=1}^{T} p(\mathbf{v}_t|\mathbf{v}_{1:t-1}) \tag{24.4.42}$$

in which $p(\mathbf{v}_t|\mathbf{v}_{1:t-1}) = \mathcal{N}(\mathbf{v}_t|\boldsymbol{\mu}_t, \boldsymbol{\Sigma}_t)$ with

$$\begin{array}{lll} \boldsymbol{\mu}_1 \equiv \mathbf{B}\boldsymbol{\mu}_\pi & \boldsymbol{\Sigma}_1 \equiv \mathbf{B}\boldsymbol{\Sigma}\mathbf{B}^\mathsf{T} + \boldsymbol{\Sigma}_\pi & t = 1 \\ \boldsymbol{\mu}_t \equiv \mathbf{B}\mathbf{A}\mathbf{f}_{t-1} & \boldsymbol{\Sigma}_t \equiv \mathbf{B}\left(\mathbf{A}\mathbf{F}_{t-1}\mathbf{A}^\mathsf{T} + \boldsymbol{\Sigma}_h\right)\mathbf{B}^\mathsf{T} + \boldsymbol{\Sigma}_v & t > 1. \end{array} \tag{24.4.43}$$

The log likelihood is then given by

$$\log p(\mathbf{v}_{1:T}) = -\frac{1}{2}\sum_{t=1}^{T}\left[(\mathbf{v}_t - \boldsymbol{\mu}_t)^\mathsf{T}\boldsymbol{\Sigma}_t^{-1}(\mathbf{v}_t - \boldsymbol{\mu}_t) + \log\det(2\pi\boldsymbol{\Sigma}_t)\right]. \tag{24.4.44}$$

24.4.4 Most likely state

Since the mode of a Gaussian is equal to its mean, there is no difference between the most probable joint posterior state

$$\underset{\mathbf{h}_{1:T}}{\operatorname{argmax}}\ p(\mathbf{h}_{1:T}|\mathbf{v}_{1:T}) \tag{24.4.45}$$

and the set of most probable marginal states

$$h_t = \underset{\mathbf{h}_t}{\text{argmax}}\ p(\mathbf{h}_t|\mathbf{v}_{1:T}), \qquad t = 1, \ldots, T. \tag{24.4.46}$$

Hence the most likely hidden state sequence is equivalent to the smoothed mean sequence.

24.4.5 Time independence and Riccati equations

Both the filtered $\mathbf{F}_t$ and smoothed $\mathbf{G}_t$ covariance recursions are independent of the observations $\mathbf{v}_{1:T}$, depending only on the parameters of the model. This is a general characteristic of linear Gaussian systems. Typically the covariance recursions converge quickly to values that are constant throughout the dynamics, with only appreciable differences close to the boundaries $t = 1$ and $t = T$. In practice therefore one often drops the time-dependence of the covariances and approximates them with a single time-independent covariance. This approximation dramatically reduces storage requirements. The converged filtered $\mathbf{F}$ satisfies the recursion

$$\mathbf{F} = \mathbf{AFA}^\mathsf{T} + \boldsymbol{\Sigma}_h - \left(\mathbf{AFA}^\mathsf{T} + \boldsymbol{\Sigma}_h\right)\mathbf{B}^\mathsf{T}\left(\mathbf{B}\left(\mathbf{AFA}^\mathsf{T} + \boldsymbol{\Sigma}_h\right)\mathbf{B}^\mathsf{T} + \boldsymbol{\Sigma}_v\right)^{-1}\mathbf{B}\left(\mathbf{AFA}^\mathsf{T} + \boldsymbol{\Sigma}_h\right) \tag{24.4.47}$$

which is a form of *algebraic Riccati equation*. A technique to solve these equations is to initialise the covariance $\mathbf{F}$ to $\boldsymbol{\Sigma}$. With this, a new $\mathbf{F}$ is found using the right-hand side of (24.4.47), and subsequently recursively updated. Alternatively, using the Woodbury identity, the converged covariance satisfies

$$\mathbf{F} = \left(\left(\mathbf{AFA}^\mathsf{T} + \boldsymbol{\Sigma}_h\right)^{-1} + \mathbf{B}^\mathsf{T}\boldsymbol{\Sigma}_v^{-1}\mathbf{B}\right)^{-1} \tag{24.4.48}$$

although this form is less numerically convenient in forming an iterative solver for $\mathbf{F}$ since it requires two matrix inversions.

Example 24.4 Newtonian trajectory analysis

A toy rocket with unknown mass and initial velocity is launched in the air. In addition, the constant accelerations from the rocket's propulsion system are unknown. It is known that Newton's laws apply and an instrument can make very noisy measurements of the horizontal distance $x(t)$ and vertical height $y(t)$ of the rocket at each time t. Based on these noisy measurements, our task is to infer the position of the rocket at each time.

Although this is perhaps most appropriately considered using continuous time dynamics, we will translate this into a discrete time approximation. Newton's law states that

$$\frac{d^2}{dt^2}x = \frac{f_x(t)}{m}, \qquad \frac{d^2}{dt^2}y = \frac{f_y(t)}{m} \tag{24.4.49}$$

where m is the mass of the object and $f_x(t)$, $f_y(t)$ are the horizontal and vertical forces respectively. As they stand, these equations are not in a form directly usable in the LDS framework. A naive approach is to reparameterise time to use the variable $\tilde{t}$ such that $t \equiv \tilde{t}\Delta$, where $\tilde{t}$ is integer and Δ is a unit of time. The dynamics is then

$$x((\tilde{t}+1)\Delta) = x(\tilde{t}\Delta) + \Delta x'(\tilde{t}\Delta), \quad y((\tilde{t}+1)\Delta) = y(\tilde{t}\Delta) + \Delta y'(\tilde{t}\Delta) \tag{24.4.50}$$

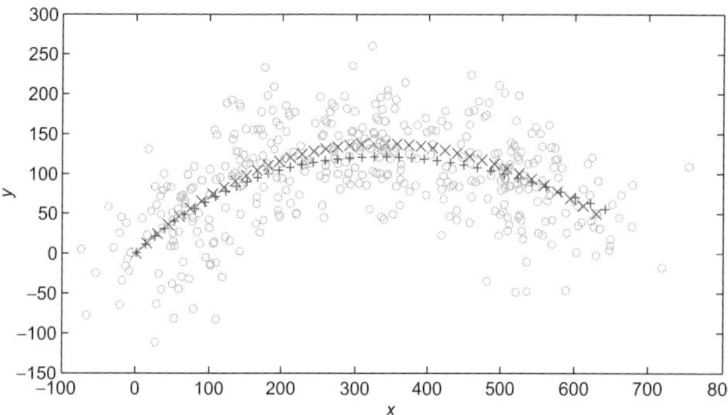

Figure 24.7 Estimate of the trajectory of a Newtonian ballistic object based on noisy observations (small circles). All time labels are known but omitted in the plot. The 'x' points are the true positions of the object, and the crosses '+' are the estimated smoothed mean positions $\langle x_t, y_t | \mathbf{v}_{1:T} \rangle$ of the object plotted every several timesteps. See `demoLDStracking.m`.

where $y'(t) \equiv dy/dt$. We can write an update equation for the x' and y' as

$$x'((\tilde{t}+1)\Delta) = x'(\tilde{t}\Delta) + f_x(\tilde{t}\Delta)\Delta/m, \qquad y'((\tilde{t}+1)\Delta) = y'(\tilde{t}\Delta) + f_x(\tilde{t}\Delta)\Delta/m. \tag{24.4.51}$$

These two sets of coupled discrete time difference equations approximate Newton's law equation (24.4.49). For simplicity, we relabel $a_x(t) = f_x(t)/m(t)$, $a_y(t) = f_y(t)/m(t)$. These accelerations are unknown but assumed to change slowly over time

$$a_x((\tilde{t}+1)\Delta) = a_x(\tilde{t}\Delta) + \eta_x, \quad a_y((\tilde{t}+1)\Delta) = a_y(\tilde{t}\Delta) + \eta_y, \tag{24.4.52}$$

where η_x and η_y are small noise terms. The initial distributions for the accelerations are assumed vague, using a zero mean Gaussian with large variance. We describe the above model by defining

$$\mathbf{h}_t \equiv \left[x'(t), x(t), y'(t), y(t), a_x(t), a_y(t)\right]^{\mathsf{T}} \tag{24.4.53}$$

as the hidden variable, giving rise to a $H = 6$ dimensional LDS with transition and emission matrices as below:

$$\mathbf{A} = \begin{pmatrix} 1 & 0 & 0 & 0 & \Delta & 0 \\ \Delta & 1 & 0 & 0 & 0 & 0 \\ 0 & 0 & 1 & 0 & 0 & \Delta \\ 0 & 0 & \Delta & 1 & 0 & 0 \\ 0 & 0 & 0 & 0 & 1 & 0 \\ 0 & 0 & 0 & 0 & 0 & 1 \end{pmatrix}, \qquad \mathbf{B} = \begin{pmatrix} 0 & 1 & 0 & 0 & 0 & 0 \\ 0 & 0 & 0 & 1 & 0 & 0 \end{pmatrix}. \tag{24.4.54}$$

We use large a covariance $\boldsymbol{\Sigma}_\pi$ to state that little is known about the latent state initial values. Based then on noisy observations $\mathbf{v}_t = \mathbf{B}\mathbf{h}_t + \boldsymbol{\eta}_t$ we attempt to infer the unknown trajectory using smoothing. A demonstration is given in Fig. 24.7. Despite the significant observation noise, the object trajectory can be accurately inferred.

24.5 Learning linear dynamical systems

Whilst in many applications, particularly of underlying known physical processes, the parameters of the LDS are known, in many machine learning tasks we need to learn the parameters of the LDS based on $\mathbf{v}_{1:T}$. For simplicity we assume that we know the dimensionality H of the LDS.

24.5.1 Identifiability issues

An interesting question is whether we can uniquely identify (learn) the parameters of an LDS. There are always trivial redundancies in the solution obtained by permuting the hidden variables arbitrarily and flipping their signs. To show that there are potentially many more equivalent solutions, consider the following LDS

$$\mathbf{v}_t = \mathbf{B}\mathbf{h}_t + \eta_t^v, \qquad \mathbf{h}_t = \mathbf{A}\mathbf{h}_{t-1} + \eta_t^h. \tag{24.5.1}$$

We now attempt to transform this original system to a new form which will produce exactly the same outputs $\mathbf{v}_{1:T}$. For an invertible matrix $\mathbf{R}$ we consider

$$\mathbf{R}\mathbf{h}_t = \mathbf{R}\mathbf{A}\mathbf{R}^{-1}\mathbf{R}\mathbf{h}_{t-1} + \mathbf{R}\eta_t^h \tag{24.5.2}$$

which is representable as a new latent dynamics

$$\hat{\mathbf{h}}_t = \hat{\mathbf{A}}\hat{\mathbf{h}}_{t-1} + \hat{\eta}_t^h \tag{24.5.3}$$

where $\hat{\mathbf{A}} \equiv \mathbf{R}\mathbf{A}\mathbf{R}^{-1}$, $\hat{\mathbf{h}}_t \equiv \mathbf{R}\mathbf{h}_t$, $\hat{\eta}_t^h \equiv \mathbf{R}\eta_t^h$. In addition, we can reexpress the outputs to be a function of the transformed $\mathbf{h}$:

$$\mathbf{v}_t = \mathbf{B}\mathbf{R}^{-1}\mathbf{R}\mathbf{h}_t + \eta_t^v = \hat{\mathbf{B}}\hat{\mathbf{h}}_t + \eta_t^v. \tag{24.5.4}$$

Hence, provided we place no constraints on $\mathbf{A}$, $\mathbf{B}$ and $\mathbf{\Sigma}_h$ there exists an infinite space of equivalent solutions, $\hat{\mathbf{A}} = \mathbf{R}\mathbf{A}\,\mathbf{R}^{-1}$, $\hat{\mathbf{B}} = \mathbf{B}\mathbf{R}^{-1}$, $\hat{\mathbf{\Sigma}}_H = \mathbf{R}\mathbf{\Sigma}_h\mathbf{R}^{\mathsf{T}}$, all with the same likelihood value. This means that interpreting the learned parameters needs to be done with some care.

24.5.2 EM algorithm

For simplicity, we assume we have a single sequence $\mathbf{v}_{1:T}$, to which we wish to fit a LDS using maximum likelihood. Since the LDS contains latent variables one approach is to use the EM algorithm. As usual, the M-step of the EM algorithm requires us to maximise the energy

$$\langle \log p(\mathbf{v}_{1:T}, \mathbf{h}_{1:T}) \rangle_{p^{old}(\mathbf{h}_{1:T}|\mathbf{v}_{1:T})} \tag{24.5.5}$$

with respect to the parameters $\mathbf{A}$, $\mathbf{B}$, $\mathbf{a}$, $\mathbf{\Sigma}$, $\mathbf{\Sigma}_v$, $\mathbf{\Sigma}_h$. Thanks to the form of the LDS the energy decomposes as

$$\langle \log p(\mathbf{h}_1) \rangle_{p^{old}(\mathbf{h}_1|\mathbf{v}_{1:T})} + \sum_{t=2}^{T} \langle \log p(\mathbf{h}_t|\mathbf{h}_{t-1}) \rangle_{p^{old}(\mathbf{h}_t,\mathbf{h}_{t-1}|\mathbf{v}_{1:T})} + \sum_{t=1}^{T} \langle \log p(\mathbf{v}_t|\mathbf{h}_t) \rangle_{p^{old}(\mathbf{h}_t|\mathbf{v}_{1:T})}. \tag{24.5.6}$$

It is straightforward to derive that the M-step for the parameters is given by (angled brackets $\langle \cdot \rangle$ denote expectation with respect to the smoothed posterior $p^{old}(\mathbf{h}_{1:T}|\mathbf{v}_{1:T})$):

$$\boldsymbol{\mu}_\pi^{new} = \langle \mathbf{h}_1 \rangle \tag{24.5.7}$$

$$\boldsymbol{\Sigma}_\pi^{new} = \left\langle \mathbf{h}_1 \mathbf{h}_1^\mathsf{T} \right\rangle - \langle \mathbf{h}_1 \rangle \langle \mathbf{h}_1 \rangle^\mathsf{T} \tag{24.5.8}$$

$$\mathbf{A}^{new} = \sum_{t=1}^{T-1} \left\langle \mathbf{h}_{t+1} \mathbf{h}_t^\mathsf{T} \right\rangle \left(\sum_{t=1}^{T-1} \left\langle \mathbf{h}_t \mathbf{h}_t^\mathsf{T} \right\rangle \right)^{-1} \tag{24.5.9}$$

$$\mathbf{B}^{new} = \sum_{t=1}^{T} \mathbf{v}_t \langle \mathbf{h}_t \rangle^\mathsf{T} \left(\sum_{t=1}^{T} \left\langle \mathbf{h}_t \mathbf{h}_t^\mathsf{T} \right\rangle \right)^{-1} \tag{24.5.10}$$

$$\boldsymbol{\Sigma}_v^{new} = \frac{1}{T} \sum_{t=1}^{T} \left(\mathbf{v}_t \mathbf{v}_t^\mathsf{T} - \mathbf{v}_t \langle \mathbf{h}_t \rangle^\mathsf{T} \mathbf{B}^{new\mathsf{T}} - \mathbf{B}^{new} \langle \mathbf{h}_t \rangle \mathbf{v}_t^\mathsf{T} + \mathbf{B}^{new} \left\langle \mathbf{h}_t \mathbf{h}_t^\mathsf{T} \right\rangle \mathbf{B}^{new\mathsf{T}} \right) \tag{24.5.11}$$

$$\boldsymbol{\Sigma}_h^{new} = \frac{1}{T-1} \sum_{t=1}^{T-1} \left(\left\langle \mathbf{h}_{t+1} \mathbf{h}_{t+1}^\mathsf{T} \right\rangle - \mathbf{A}^{new} \left\langle \mathbf{h}_t \mathbf{h}_{t+1}^\mathsf{T} \right\rangle - \left\langle \mathbf{h}_{t+1} \mathbf{h}_t^\mathsf{T} \right\rangle \mathbf{A}^{new\mathsf{T}} + \mathbf{A}^{new} \left\langle \mathbf{h}_t \mathbf{h}_t^\mathsf{T} \right\rangle \mathbf{A}^{new\mathsf{T}} \right). \tag{24.5.12}$$

The above can be simplified to

$$\boldsymbol{\Sigma}_v^{new} = \frac{1}{T} \sum_t \left(\mathbf{v}_t \mathbf{v}_t^\mathsf{T} - \mathbf{v}_t \langle \mathbf{h}_t \rangle^\mathsf{T} \mathbf{B}^{new\mathsf{T}} \right). \tag{24.5.13}$$

Similarly,

$$\boldsymbol{\Sigma}_h^{new} = \frac{1}{T-1} \sum_{t=1}^{T-1} \left(\left\langle \mathbf{h}_{t+1} \mathbf{h}_{t+1}^\mathsf{T} \right\rangle - \mathbf{A}^{new} \left\langle \mathbf{h}_t \mathbf{h}_{t+1}^\mathsf{T} \right\rangle \right). \tag{24.5.14}$$

The statistics required therefore include smoothed means, covariances and cross moments. The extension to learning multiple timeseries is straightforward since the energy is simply summed over the individual sequences.

The performance of the EM algorithm for the LDS often depends heavily on the initialisation. If we remove the hidden to hidden links, the model is closely related to factor analysis (the LDS can be considered a temporal extension of factor analysis). One initialisation technique therefore is to learn the **B** matrix using factor analysis by treating the observations as temporally independent.

Note that whilst the LDS model in not identifiable, as described in Section 24.5.1, the M-step for the EM algorithm is unique. This apparent contradiction is resolved when one considers that the EM algorithm is a conditional method, updating depending on the previous parameters and ultimately the initialisation. It is this initialisation that breaks the invariance.

24.5.3 Subspace methods

An alternative to maximum likelihood training is to use a subspace method [301, 265]. The chief benefit of these techniques is that they avoid the convergence difficulties of EM. To motivate subspace techniques, consider a deterministic LDS

$$\mathbf{h}_t = \mathbf{A}\mathbf{h}_{t-1}, \qquad \mathbf{v}_t = \mathbf{B}\mathbf{h}_t. \tag{24.5.15}$$

Under this assumption, $\mathbf{v}_t = \mathbf{B}\mathbf{h}_t = \mathbf{B}\mathbf{A}\mathbf{h}_{t-1}$ and, more generally, $\mathbf{v}_t = \mathbf{B}\mathbf{A}^{t-1}\mathbf{h}_1$. This means that a H-dimensional system underlies all visible information since all points $\mathbf{A}^t\mathbf{h}_1$ lie in an H-dimensional subspace, which is then projected to form the observation. This suggests that some form of subspace identification technique will enable us to learn $\mathbf{A}$ and $\mathbf{B}$.

Given a set of observation vectors $\mathbf{v}_1, \ldots, \mathbf{v}_t$, consider the block *Hankel matrix* formed from stacking L consecutive observation vectors. For example, for $T = 6$ and $L = 3$, this is

$$\mathbf{M} = \begin{pmatrix} \mathbf{v}_1 & \mathbf{v}_2 & \mathbf{v}_3 & \mathbf{v}_4 \\ \mathbf{v}_2 & \mathbf{v}_3 & \mathbf{v}_4 & \mathbf{v}_5 \\ \mathbf{v}_3 & \mathbf{v}_4 & \mathbf{v}_5 & \mathbf{v}_6 \end{pmatrix}. \tag{24.5.16}$$

If the $\mathbf{v}$ are generated from a (noise-free) LDS, we can write

$$\mathbf{M} = \begin{pmatrix} \mathbf{B}\mathbf{h}_1 & \mathbf{B}\mathbf{h}_2 & \mathbf{B}\mathbf{h}_3 & \mathbf{B}\mathbf{h}_4 \\ \mathbf{B}\mathbf{A}\mathbf{h}_1 & \mathbf{B}\mathbf{A}\mathbf{h}_2 & \mathbf{B}\mathbf{A}\mathbf{h}_3 & \mathbf{B}\mathbf{A}\mathbf{h}_4 \\ \mathbf{B}\mathbf{A}^2\mathbf{h}_1 & \mathbf{B}\mathbf{A}^2\mathbf{h}_2 & \mathbf{B}\mathbf{A}^2\mathbf{h}_3 & \mathbf{B}\mathbf{A}^2\mathbf{h}_4 \end{pmatrix} = \begin{pmatrix} \mathbf{B} \\ \mathbf{B}\mathbf{A} \\ \mathbf{B}\mathbf{A}^2 \end{pmatrix} \begin{pmatrix} \mathbf{h}_1 & \mathbf{h}_2 & \mathbf{h}_3 & \mathbf{h}_4 \end{pmatrix}. \tag{24.5.17}$$

We now find the SVD of $\mathbf{M}$,

$$\mathbf{M} = \hat{\mathbf{U}} \underbrace{\hat{\mathbf{S}}\hat{\mathbf{V}}^{\mathsf{T}}}_{\mathbf{W}} \tag{24.5.18}$$

where $\mathbf{W}$ is termed the *extended observability matrix*. The matrix $\hat{\mathbf{S}}$ will contain the singular values up to the dimension of the hidden variables H, with the remaining singular values 0. From Equation (24.5.17), this means that the emission matrix $\mathbf{B}$ is contained in $\hat{\mathbf{U}}_{1:V,1:H}$. The estimated hidden variables are then contained in the submatrix $\mathbf{W}_{1:H,1:T-L+1}$,

$$\begin{pmatrix} \mathbf{h}_1 & \mathbf{h}_2 & \mathbf{h}_3 & \mathbf{h}_4 \end{pmatrix} = \mathbf{W}_{1:H,1:T-L+1}. \tag{24.5.19}$$

Based on the relation $\mathbf{h}_t = \mathbf{A}\mathbf{h}_{t-1}$ one can then find the best least squares estimate for $\mathbf{A}$ by minimising

$$\sum_{t=2}^{T} (\mathbf{h}_t - \mathbf{A}\mathbf{h}_{t-1})^2 \tag{24.5.20}$$

for which the optimal solution is

$$\mathbf{A} = \begin{pmatrix} \mathbf{h}_2 & \mathbf{h}_3 & \ldots & \mathbf{h}_t \end{pmatrix} \begin{pmatrix} \mathbf{h}_1 & \mathbf{h}_2 & \ldots & \mathbf{h}_{T-1} \end{pmatrix}^{\dagger} \tag{24.5.21}$$

where † denotes the pseudo inverse, see `LDSsubspace.m`. Estimates for the covariance matrices can also be obtained from the residual errors in fitting the block Hankel matrix and extended observability matrix. Whilst this derivation formally holds only for the noise-free case one can nevertheless apply this in the case of non-zero noise and hope to gain an estimate for $\mathbf{A}$ and $\mathbf{B}$ that is correct in the mean. In addition to forming a solution in its own right, the subspace method forms a potentially useful way to initialise the EM algorithm.

24.5.4 Structured LDSs

Many physical equations are local both in time and space. For example in weather models the atmosphere is partitioned into cells $h_i(t)$ each containing the pressure at that location. The equations describing how the pressure updates only depend on the pressure at the current cell and small number of neighbouring cells at the previous time $t - 1$. If we use a linear model and measure some aspects of the cells at each time, then the weather is describable by an LDS with a highly structured sparse transition matrix $\mathbf{A}$. In practice, the weather models are non-linear but local linear approximations

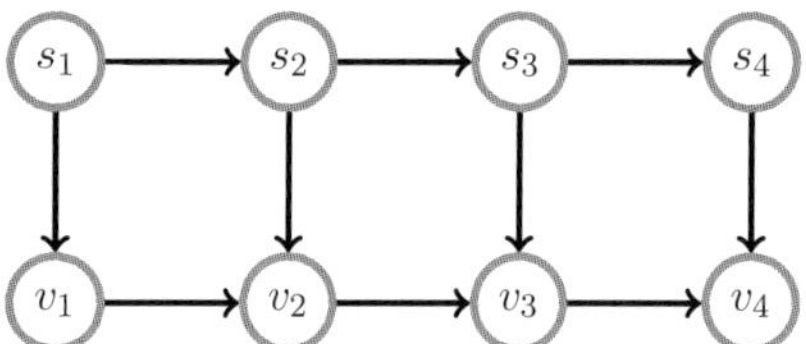

Figure 24.8 A first-order switching AR model. In terms of inference, conditioned on $v_{1:T}$, this is an HMM.

are often employed [270]. A similar situation arises in brain imaging in which voxels (local cubes of activity) depend only on their neighbours from the previous timestep [111].

Another application of structured LDSs is in temporal independent component analysis. This is defined as the discovery of a set of independent latent dynamical processes, from which the data is a projected observation. If each independent dynamical process can itself be described by an LDS, this gives rise to a structured LDS with a block diagonal transition matrix $\mathbf{A}$. Such models can be used to extract independent components under prior knowledge of the likely underlying frequencies in each of the temporal compoments [62].

24.5.5 Bayesian LDSs

The extension to placing priors on the transition and emission parameters of the LDS leads in general to computational difficulties in computing the likelihood. For example, for a prior on $\mathbf{A}$, the likelihood is $p(\mathbf{v}_{1:T}) = \int_{\mathbf{A}} p(\mathbf{v}_{1:T}|\mathbf{A})p(\mathbf{A})$ which is difficult to evaluate since the dependence of the likelihood on the matrix $\mathbf{A}$ is a complicated function. Approximate treatments of this case are beyond the scope of this book, although we briefly note that sampling methods [57, 105] are popular in this context, in addition to deterministic variational approximations [27, 23, 62].

24.6 Switching auto-regressive models

Whilst the linear dynamical models considered so far in this chapter are powerful, they nevertheless have some inherent restrictions. For example, they cannot model abrupt changes in the observation. Here we describe an extension of the AR model. We consider a set of S different AR models, each with associated coefficients $\mathbf{a}(s)$, $s = 1, \ldots, d$, and allow the model to select one of these AR models at each time. For a timeseries of scalar values $v_{1:T}$ an Lth-order switching AR model can be written as

$$v_t = \hat{\mathbf{v}}_{t-1}^{\mathsf{T}}\mathbf{a}(s_t) + \eta_t, \qquad \eta_t \sim \mathcal{N}\left(\eta_t|0, \sigma^2(s_t)\right) \tag{24.6.1}$$

where we now have a set of AR coefficients $\theta = \left\{\mathbf{a}(s), \sigma^2(s), s \in \{1, \ldots, S\}\right\}$. The discrete switch variables themselves have a Markov transition $p(s_{1:T}) = \prod_t p(s_t|s_{t-1})$ so that the full model is, see Fig. 24.8,

$$p(v_{1:T}, s_{1:T}|\theta) = \prod_t p(v_t|v_{t-1}, \ldots, v_{t-L}, s_t, |\theta)p(s_t|s_{t-1}). \tag{24.6.2}$$

24.6.1 Inference

Given an observed sequence $v_{1:T}$ and parameters θ inference is straightforward since this is a form of HMM. To make this more apparent we may write

$$p(v_{1:T}, s_{1:T}) = \prod_t \hat{p}(v_t|s_t)p(s_t|s_{t-1}) \tag{24.6.3}$$

where

$$\hat{p}(v_t|s_t) \equiv p(v_t|v_{t-1}, \ldots, v_{t-L}, s_t) = \mathcal{N}\left(v_t \middle| \hat{\mathbf{v}}_{t-1}^{\mathsf{T}}\mathbf{a}(s_t), \sigma^2(s_t)\right). \tag{24.6.4}$$

Note that the emission distribution $\hat{p}(v_t|s_t)$ is time-dependent. The filtering recursion is then

$$\alpha(s_t) = \sum_{s_{t-1}} \hat{p}(v_t|s_t)p(s_t|s_{t-1})\alpha(s_{t-1}). \tag{24.6.5}$$

Smoothing can be achieved using the standard recursions, modified to use the time-dependent emissions, see `demoSARinference.m`.

With high-frequency data it is unlikely that a change in the switch variable is reasonable at each time t. A simple constraint to account for this is to use a modified transition

$$\hat{p}(s_t|s_{t-1}) = \begin{cases} p(s_t|s_{t-1}) & \text{mod}\,(t, T_{skip}) = 0 \\ \delta\,(s_t - s_{t-1}) & \text{otherwise.} \end{cases} \tag{24.6.6}$$

24.6.2 Maximum likelihood learning using EM

To fit the set of AR coefficients and innovation variances, $\mathbf{a}(s), \sigma^2(s), s = 1, \ldots, S$, using maximum likelihood training for a set of data $v_{1:T}$, we may make use of the EM algorithm.

M-step

Up to negligible constants, the energy is given by

$$E = \sum_t \langle \log p(v_t|\hat{\mathbf{v}}_{t-1}, \mathbf{a}(s_t))\rangle_{p^{old}(s_t|v_{1:T})} + \sum_t \langle \log p(s_t|s_{t-1})\rangle_{p^{old}(s_t,s_{t-1})} \tag{24.6.7}$$

which we need to maximise with respect to the parameters θ. Using the definition of the emission and isolating the dependency on $\mathbf{a}$, we have

$$-2E = \sum_t \left\langle \frac{1}{\sigma^2(s_t)}\left(v_t - \hat{\mathbf{v}}_{t-1}^{\mathsf{T}}\mathbf{a}(s_t)\right)^2 + \log\sigma^2(s_t)\right\rangle_{p^{old}(s_t|v_{1:T})} + \text{const.} \tag{24.6.8}$$

On differentiating with respect to $\mathbf{a}(\mathsf{s})$ and equating to zero, the optimal $\mathbf{a}(\mathsf{s})$ satisfies the linear equation

$$\sum_t p^{old}(s_t = \mathsf{s}|v_{1:T})\frac{v_t\hat{\mathbf{v}}_{t-1}}{\sigma^2(\mathsf{s})} = \left[\sum_t p^{old}(s_t = \mathsf{s}|v_{1:T})\frac{\hat{\mathbf{v}}_{t-1}\hat{\mathbf{v}}_{t-1}^{\mathsf{T}}}{\sigma^2(\mathsf{s})}\right]\mathbf{a}(\mathsf{s}) \tag{24.6.9}$$

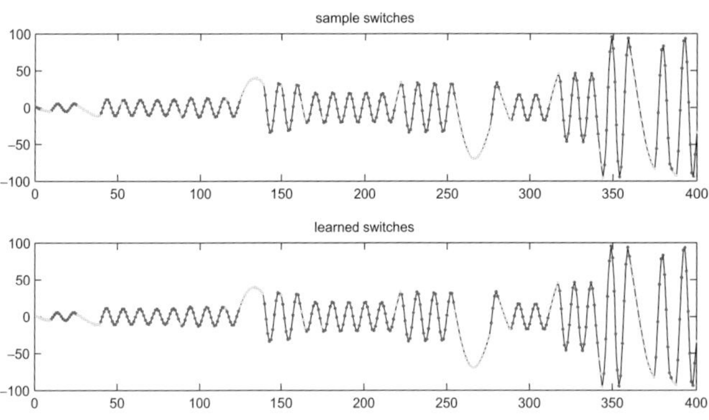

Figure 24.9 Learning a switching AR model. The upper plot shows the train data. The colour indicates which of the two AR models is active at that time. Whilst this information is plotted here, this is assumed unknown to the learning algorithm, as are the coefficients $\mathbf{a}(s)$. We assume that the order $L = 2$ and number of switches $S = 2$ however is known. In the bottom plot we show the timeseries again after training in which we colour the points according to the most likely smoothed AR model at each timestep. See `demoSARlearn.m`. See plate section for colour version.

which may be solved using Gaussian elimination. Similarly one may show that updates that maximise the energy with respect to σ^2 are

$$\sigma^2(\mathrm{s}) = \frac{1}{\sum_{t'} p^{old}(s'_t = \mathrm{s}|v_{1:T})} \sum_t p^{old}(s_t = \mathrm{s}|v_{1:T}) \left[v_t - \hat{\mathbf{v}}_{t-1}^{\mathsf{T}}\mathbf{a}(\mathrm{s})\right]^2. \tag{24.6.10}$$

The update for $p(s_t|s_{t-1})$ follows the standard EM for HMM rule, Equation (23.3.5), see `SARlearn.m`. Here we don't include an update for the prior $p(s_1)$ since there is insufficient information at the start of the sequence and assume $p(s_1)$ is flat.

E-step

The M-step requires the smoothed statistics $p^{old}(s_t = \mathrm{s}|v_{1:T})$ and $p^{old}(s_t = \mathrm{s}, s_{t-1} = \mathrm{s}'|v_{1:T})$ which can be obtained from HMM inference.

Example 24.5 Learning a switching AR model

In Fig. 24.9 the train data is generated by a switching AR model so that we know the ground truth as to which model generated which parts of the data. Based on the train data (assuming the labels s_t are unknown), a switching AR model is fitted using EM. In this case the problem is straightforward so that a good estimate is obtained of both the sets of AR parameters and which switches were used at which time.

Example 24.6 Modelling parts of speech

In Fig. 24.10 a segment of a speech signal (corresponding to the spoken digit 'four') is shown. We model this data using a switching AR model with $S = 10$ states. Each of the 10 available AR models is responsible for modelling the dynamics of a basic subunit of speech [97, 207]. The model was trained on many example clean spoken digit sequences using $S = 10$ states with a left-to-right transition matrix. An additional complexity is that we wish to use the model to clean up a noisy speech signal. A simple model for the noise is that it is Gaussian and additive on the original speech

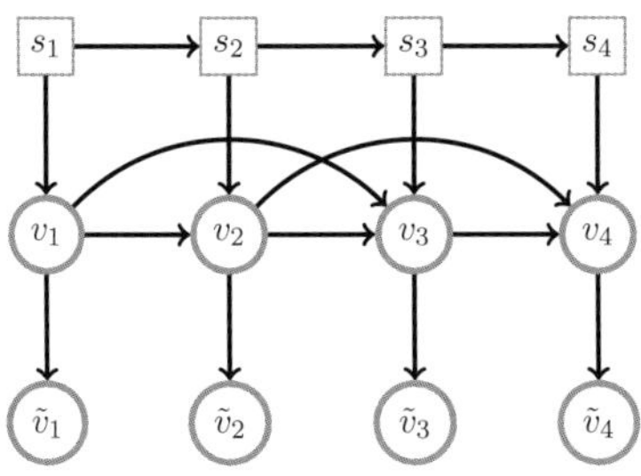

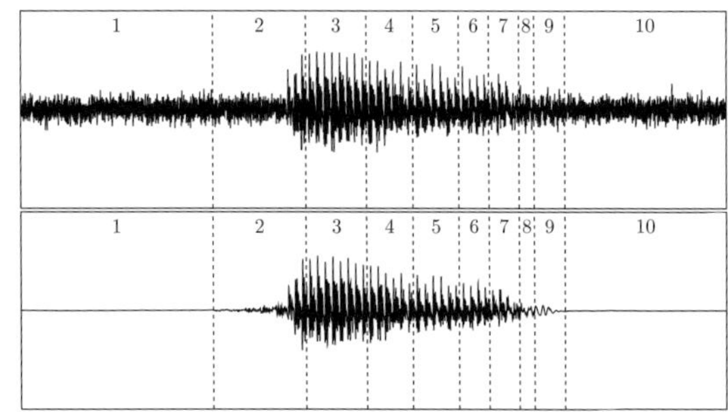

Figure 24.10 (**a**) A latent switching (second order) AR model. Here the s_t indicates which of a set of 10 available AR models is active at time t. The square nodes emphasise that these are discrete variables. The 'clean' AR signal v_t, which is not observed, is corrupted by additive noise to form the noisy observations $\tilde{v}_t$. In terms of inference, conditioned on $\tilde{v}_{1:T}$, this can be expressed as a Switching LDS, chapter(25). (**b**) Signal reconstruction using the latent switching AR model in (a). Top: noisy signal $\tilde{v}_{1:T}$; bottom: reconstructed clean signal $v_{1:T}$. The dashed lines and the numbers show the most-likely state segmentation $\arg\max_{s_{1:T}} p(s_{1:T}|\tilde{v}_{1:T})$ of the 10 states, from left (1) to right (10).

signal v_t, forming now a new noisy observation $\tilde{v}_t$. Based then on a sequence of noisy $\tilde{v}_{1:T}$ we wish to infer the switch states and the clean signal $v_{1:T}$. Unfortunately, this task is no longer in the form of an SAR since we now have both continuous and discrete latent states. Formally this model falls in the class of the switching linear dynamical systems, as described in the following chapter. The results using this more complex model show how denoising of complex signals can be achieved and are a prelude to the more advanced material in the following chapter.

24.7 Summary

- Continuous observations can be modelled using auto-regressive models.
- Observed linear dynamical systems are the vector versions of auto-regressive models.
- Latent continuous dynamical processes can be used to model many physical systems. In order for these to be computationally tractable, one needs to restrict the transition and emission distributions. The latent linear dynamical system is such as restriction to linear Gaussian transitions and emissions.
- The latent linear dynamical system is a powerful timeseries model with widespread application in tracking and signal representation.

24.8 Code

In the linear dynamical system code below only the simplest form of the recursions is given. No attempt has been made to ensure numerical stability.

`LDSforwardUpdate.m`: LDS forward
`LDSbackwardUpdate.m`: LDS backward
`LDSsmooth.m`: Linear dynamical system: filtering and smoothing

`LDSforward.m`: Alternative LDS forward algorithm (see SLDS chapter)
`LDSbackward.m`: Alternative LDS backward algorithm (see SLDS chapter)
`demoSumprodGaussCanonLDS.m`: Sum-product algorithm for smoothed inference
`demoLDStracking.m`: Demo of tracking in a Newtonian system
`LDSsubspace.m`: Subspace learning (Hankel matrix method)
`demoLDSsubspace.m`: Demo of subspace learning method

24.8.1 Auto-regressive models

Note that in the code the auto-regressive vector **a** has as its last entry the first AR coefficient (i.e. in reverse order to that presented in the text).

`ARtrain.m`: Learn AR coefficients (Gaussian Elimination)
`demoARtrain.m`: Demo of fitting an AR model to data
`ARlds.m`: Learn time-varying AR coefficients using a LDS
`demoARlds.m`: Demo of learning AR coefficients using an LDS
`demoSARinference.m`: Demo for inference in a switching autoregressive model
`SARlearn.m`: Learning of a SAR using EM
`demoSARlearn.m`: Demo of SAR learning
`HMMforwardSAR.m`: Switching autoregressive HMM forward pass
`HMMbackwardSAR.m`: Switching autoregressive HMM backward pass

24.9 Exercises

24.1 Consider the two-dimensional linear model

$$\mathbf{h}_t = \mathbf{R}_\theta \mathbf{h}_{t-1}, \qquad \mathbf{R}_\theta = \begin{pmatrix} \cos\theta & -\sin\theta \\ \sin\theta & \cos\theta \end{pmatrix} \tag{24.9.1}$$

where $\mathbf{R}_\theta$ is a rotation matrix which rotates the vector $\mathbf{h}_t$ through angle θ in one timestep.

1. Explain why the eigenvalues of a rotation matrix are (in general) imaginary.
2. Explain how to model a sinusoid, rotating with angular velocity ω using a two-dimensional LDS.
3. By writing

$$\begin{pmatrix} x_t \\ y_t \end{pmatrix} = \begin{pmatrix} R_{11} & R_{12} \\ R_{21} & R_{22} \end{pmatrix} \begin{pmatrix} x_{t-1} \\ y_{t-1} \end{pmatrix} \tag{24.9.2}$$

   eliminate y_t to write an equation for x_{t+1} in terms of x_t and x_{t-1}.
4. Explain how to model a sinusoid using an AR model.
5. Explain the relationship between the second-order differential equation $\ddot{x} = -\lambda x$, which describes a harmonic oscillator, and the second-order difference equation which approximates this differential equation. Is it possible to find a difference equation which exactly matches the solution of the differential equation at particular points?

24.2 Show that for any square anti-symmetric matrix **M**,

$$\mathbf{M} = -\mathbf{M}^\mathsf{T} \tag{24.9.3}$$

the matrix exponential (in MATLAB this is `expm`)

$$\mathbf{A} = \exp(\mathbf{M}) \tag{24.9.4}$$

is orthogonal, namely

$$\mathbf{A}^{\mathsf{T}}\mathbf{A} = \mathbf{I}. \tag{24.9.5}$$

Explain how to construct random orthogonal matrices with some control over the angles of the complex eigenvalues.

24.3 Run `demoLDStracking.m` which tracks a ballistic object using a linear dynamical system, see Example 24.4. Modify `demoLDStracking.m` so that in addition to the x and y positions, the x speed is also observed. Compare and contrast the accuracy of the tracking with and without this extra information.

24.4 `nightsong.mat` contains a small stereo segment nightingale song sampled at 44100 Hertz.

1. Plot the original waveform using `plot(x(:,1))`
2. Plot the spectrogram using

```
y=myspecgram(x(:,1),1024,44100); imagesc(log(abs(y)))
```

3. The routine `demoGMMem.m` demonstrates fitting a mixture of Gaussians to data. The mixture assignment probabilities are contained in `phgn`. Write a routine to cluster the data `v=log(abs(y))` using eight Gaussian components, and explain how one might segment the series `x` into different regions.
4. Examine `demoARlds.m` which fits auto-regressive coefficients using an interpretation as a linear dynamical system. Adapt the routine `demoARlds.m` to learn the AR coefficients of the data `x`. You will almost certainly need to subsample the data `x` – for example by taking every fourth datapoint. With the learned AR coefficients (use the smoothed results) fit a Gaussian mixture with eight components. Compare and contrast your results with those obtained from the Gaussian mixture model fit to the spectrogram.

24.5 Consider a supervised learning problem in which we make a linear model of the scalar output y_t based on vector input $\mathbf{x}_t$:

$$y_t = \mathbf{w}_t^{\mathsf{T}}\mathbf{x}_t + \eta_t^y \tag{24.9.6}$$

where η_t^y is zero mean Gaussian noise with variance σ_y^2. Train data $\mathcal{D} = \{(\mathbf{x}_t, y_t), t = 1, \ldots, T\}$ is available.

1. For a time-invariant weight vector $\mathbf{w}_t \equiv \mathbf{w}$, explain how to find the single weight vector $\mathbf{w}$ and the noise variance σ_y^2 by maximum likelihood.
2. Extend the above model to include a transition

$$\mathbf{w}_t = \mathbf{w}_{t-1} + \boldsymbol{\eta}_t^w \tag{24.9.7}$$

where $\boldsymbol{\eta}_t^w$ is zero mean Gaussian noise with a given covariance $\boldsymbol{\Sigma}_w$; $\mathbf{w}_1$ has zero mean. Explain how to cast finding $\langle \mathbf{w}_t | \mathcal{D} \rangle$ as smoothing in a related linear dynamical system. Write a routine `W = LinPredAR(X,Y,SigmaW,SigmaY)` that takes an input data matrix $\mathbf{X} = [\mathbf{x}_1, \ldots, \mathbf{x}_T]$ where each column contains an input, and vector $Y = [y_1, \ldots, y_T]^{\mathsf{T}}$; `SigmaW` is the additive weight noise and `SigmaY` is an assumed known time-invariant output noise. The returned `W` contains the smoothed mean weights.

24.6 This exercise relates to forming an α-β style smoothing approach, as described in Section 23.2.3, but applied to the LDS. Note that the derivations in Section 23.2.3 hold for continuous variables as well simply on replacing summation with integration.

1. By virtue of the fact that the smoothed posterior for a LDS, $\gamma(\mathbf{h}_t) \equiv p(\mathbf{h}_t|\mathbf{v}_{1:T})$ is Gaussian, and using the relation $\gamma(\mathbf{h}_t) = \alpha(\mathbf{h}_t)\beta(\mathbf{h}_t)$, explain why the β message for an LDS can be represented in the form

$$\beta(\mathbf{h}_t) = z_t \exp\left(-\frac{1}{2}\mathbf{h}_t^\mathsf{T}\mathbf{Z}_t\mathbf{h}_t + \mathbf{h}_t^\mathsf{T}\mathbf{z}_t\right) \tag{24.9.8}$$

where $\mathbf{Z}_t$ is a (not necessarily full rank) matrix.

2. Based on the recursion

$$\beta(\mathbf{h}_{t-1}) = \int_{\mathbf{h}_t} p(\mathbf{v}_t|\mathbf{h}_t)p(\mathbf{h}_t|\mathbf{h}_{t-1})\beta(\mathbf{h}_t) \tag{24.9.9}$$

derive the recursion (ignoring the prefactor z_t)

$$\mathbf{L}_t = \mathbf{Q}_t^{-1} + \mathbf{B}_t^\mathsf{T}\mathbf{R}_t^{-1}\mathbf{B}_t + \mathbf{Z}_t \tag{24.9.10}$$

$$\mathbf{Z}_{t-1} = \mathbf{A}_t^\mathsf{T}\left(\mathbf{Q}_t^{-1} - \mathbf{Q}_t^{-1}\mathbf{L}_t^{-1}\mathbf{Q}_t^{-1}\right)\mathbf{A}_t \tag{24.9.11}$$

$$\mathbf{z}_{t-1} = \mathbf{A}_t^\mathsf{T}\mathbf{Q}_t^{-1}\mathbf{L}_t^{-1}\left(\mathbf{B}_t^\mathsf{T}\mathbf{R}_t^{-1} + \mathbf{z}_t\right) \tag{24.9.12}$$

with initialisation $\mathbf{Z}_T = \mathbf{0}$, $\mathbf{z}_T = \mathbf{0}$. The notation $\mathbf{Q}_t \equiv \mathbf{\Sigma}_t^h$ is the covariance matrix of the transition distribution $p(\mathbf{h}_t|\mathbf{h}_{t-1})$, and $\mathbf{R}_t \equiv \mathbf{\Sigma}_t^v$ is the covariance of the emission $p(\mathbf{v}_t|\mathbf{h}_t)$.

3. Show that the posterior covariance and mean are given by

$$\left(\mathbf{F}_t^{-1} + \mathbf{Z}_t\right)^{-1}, \qquad \left(\mathbf{F}_t^{-1} + \mathbf{Z}_t\right)^{-1}\left(\mathbf{F}_t^{-1}\mathbf{f}_t + \mathbf{z}_t\right) \tag{24.9.13}$$

where $\mathbf{F}_t$ and $\mathbf{f}_t$ are the filtered mean and covariance.

Note that this parallel smoothing recursion is not appropriate in the case of small covariance since, due to the explicit appearance of the inverse of the covariances, numerical stability issues can arise. However, it is possible to reexpress the recursion without explicit reference to inverse noise covariances, see [16].

25 Switching linear dynamical systems

Hidden Markov models assume that the underlying process is discrete; linear dynamical systems that the underlying process is continuous. However, there are scenarios in which the underlying system might jump from one continuous regime to another. In this chapter we discuss a class of models that can be used in this situation. Unfortunately the technical demands of this class of models are somewhat more involved than in previous chapters, although the models are correspondingly more powerful.

25.1 Introduction

Complex timeseries which are not well described globally by a single linear dynamical system may be divided into segments, each modelled by a potentially different LDS. Such models can handle situations in which the underlying model 'jumps' from one parameter setting to another. For example a single LDS might well represent the normal flows in a chemical plant. When a break in a pipeline occurs, the dynamics of the system changes from one set of linear flow equations to another. This scenario can be modelled using a set of two linear systems, each with different parameters. The discrete latent variable at each time $s_t \in \{\text{normal}, \text{pipe broken}\}$ indicates which of the LDSs is most appropriate at the current time. This is called a Switching LDS (SLDS) and is used in many disciplines, from econometrics to machine learning [12, 63, 59, 235, 324, 189].

25.2 The switching LDS

At each time t, a switch variable $s_t \in 1, \ldots, S$ describes which of a set of LDSs is to be used. The continuous observation (or 'visible') variable $\mathbf{v}_t$, $\dim(\mathbf{v}_t) = V$ is linearly related to the continuous hidden variable $\mathbf{h}_t$, $\dim(\mathbf{h}_t) = H$ by

$$\mathbf{v}_t = \mathbf{B}(s_t)\mathbf{h}_t + \boldsymbol{\eta}^v(s_t), \qquad \boldsymbol{\eta}^v(s_t) \sim \mathcal{N}(\boldsymbol{\eta}^v(s_t)|\bar{\mathbf{v}}(s_t), \boldsymbol{\Sigma}_v(s_t)). \tag{25.2.1}$$

Here s_t describes which one from the set of emission matrices $\{\mathbf{B}(1), \ldots, \mathbf{B}(S)\}$ is active at time t. The observation noise $\boldsymbol{\eta}^v(s_t)$ is drawn from a Gaussian with mean $\bar{\mathbf{v}}(s_t)$ and covariance $\boldsymbol{\Sigma}_v(s_t)$. The transition dynamics of the continuous hidden state $\mathbf{h}_t$ is linear,

$$\mathbf{h}_t = \mathbf{A}(s_t)\mathbf{h}_{t-1} + \boldsymbol{\eta}^h(s_t), \qquad \boldsymbol{\eta}^h(s_t) \sim \mathcal{N}\left(\boldsymbol{\eta}^h(s_t)|\bar{\mathbf{h}}(s_t), \boldsymbol{\Sigma}_h(s_t)\right) \tag{25.2.2}$$

and the switch variable s_t selects a single transition matrix from the available set $\{\mathbf{A}(1), \ldots, \mathbf{A}(S)\}$. The Gaussian transition noise $\boldsymbol{\eta}^h(s_t)$ also depends on the switch variable. The dynamics of s_t itself is Markovian, with transition $p(s_t|s_{t-1})$. For the more general 'augmented' aSLDS model the

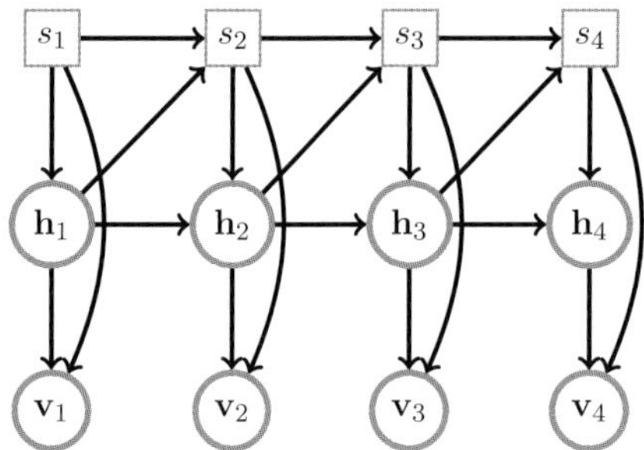

Figure 25.1 The independence structure of the aSLDS. Square nodes s_t denote discrete switch variables; $\mathbf{h}_t$ are continuous latent/hidden variables, and $\mathbf{v}_t$ continuous observed/visible variables. The discrete state s_t determines which linear dynamical system from a finite set of linear dynamical systems is operational at time t. In the SLDS links from h to s are not normally considered.

switch s_t is dependent on both the previous s_{t-1} and $\mathbf{h}_{t-1}$. The model defines a joint distribution (see Fig. 25.1)

$$p(\mathbf{v}_{1:T}, \mathbf{h}_{1:T}, s_{1:T}) = \prod_{t=1}^{T} p(\mathbf{v}_t|\mathbf{h}_t, s_t)p(\mathbf{h}_t|\mathbf{h}_{t-1}, s_t)p(s_t|\mathbf{h}_{t-1}, s_{t-1})$$

with

$$p(\mathbf{v}_t|\mathbf{h}_t, s_t) = \mathcal{N}\left(\mathbf{v}_t|\bar{\mathbf{v}}(s_t) + \mathbf{B}(s_t)\mathbf{h}_t, \boldsymbol{\Sigma}_v(s_t)\right), \quad p(\mathbf{h}_t|\mathbf{h}_{t-1}, s_t) = \mathcal{N}\left(\mathbf{h}_t|\bar{\mathbf{h}}(s_t) + \mathbf{A}(s_t)\mathbf{h}_t, \boldsymbol{\Sigma}_h(s_t)\right). \tag{25.2.3}$$

At time $t = 1$, $p(s_1|\mathbf{h}_0, s_0)$ denotes the initial switch distribution $p(s_1)$, and $p(\mathbf{h}_1|\mathbf{h}_0, s_1)$ denotes the initial Gaussians $p(\mathbf{h}_1|s_1) = \mathcal{N}\left(\mathbf{h}_1|\boldsymbol{\mu}_\pi(s_1), \boldsymbol{\Sigma}_\pi(s_1)\right)$.

The SLDS can be thought of as a marriage between a hidden Markov model and a linear dynamical system. The SLDS is also called a jump Markov model/process, switching Kalman filter, switching linear Gaussian state space model, conditional linear Gaussian model.

25.2.1 Exact inference is computationally intractable

Both exact filtered and smoothed inference in the SLDS is intractable, scaling exponentially with time. As an informal explanation, consider filtered posterior inference for which, by analogy with Equation (23.2.9), the forward pass is

$$p(s_{t+1}, \mathbf{h}_{t+1}|\mathbf{v}_{1:t+1}) = \sum_{s_t} \int_{\mathbf{h}_t} p(s_{t+1}, \mathbf{h}_{t+1}|s_t, \mathbf{h}_t, \mathbf{v}_{t+1})p(s_t, \mathbf{h}_t|\mathbf{v}_{1:t}). \tag{25.2.4}$$

At timestep 1, $p(s_1, \mathbf{h}_1|\mathbf{v}_1) = p(\mathbf{h}_1|s_1, \mathbf{v}_1)p(s_1|\mathbf{v}_1)$ is an indexed set of Gaussians. At timestep 2, due to the summation over the states s_1, $p(s_2, \mathbf{h}_2|\mathbf{v}_{1:2})$ will be an indexed set of S Gaussians; similarly at timestep 3, it will be S^2 and, in general, gives rise to S^{t-1} Gaussians at time t. Even for small t, the number of components required to exactly represent the filtered distribution is therefore computationally intractable. Analogously, smoothing is also intractable. The origin of the intractability of the SLDS differs from 'structural intractability' that we've previously encountered. In the SLDS, in terms of the cluster variables $x_{1:T}$, with $x_t \equiv (s_t, \mathbf{h}_t)$ and visible variables $\mathbf{v}_{1:T}$, the graph of the distribution is singly connected. From a purely graph-theoretic viewpoint, one would therefore envisage little difficulty in carrying out inference. Indeed, as we saw above, the derivation of the filtering algorithm is straightforward since the graph is singly connected. However, the numerical implementation of the algorithm is intractable since the description of the messages requires an exponentially increasing number of terms.

In order to deal with this intractability, several approximation schemes have been introduced [105, 120, 188, 174, 173]. Here we focus on techniques which approximate the switch conditional posteriors using a limited mixture of Gaussians. Since the exact posterior distributions are mixtures of Gaussians, albeit with an exponentially large number of components, the aim is to drop low-weight components such that the resulting approximation accurately represents the posterior.

25.3 Gaussian sum filtering

Equation (25.2.4) describes the exact filtering recursion and generates an exponentially increasing number of components with time. In general, however, the influence of ancient observations will be much less relevant than that of recent observations. This suggests that the 'effective time' is limited and that therefore a corresponding limited number of components in the Gaussian mixture may suffice to accurately represent the filtered posterior [6]. Our aim is to form a recursion for $p(s_t, \mathbf{h}_t|\mathbf{v}_{1:t})$ based on a Gaussian mixture approximation of $p(\mathbf{h}_t|s_t, \mathbf{v}_{1:t})$. Given an approximation of the filtered distribution $p(s_t, \mathbf{h}_t|\mathbf{v}_{1:t}) \approx q(s_t, \mathbf{h}_t|\mathbf{v}_{1:t})$, the exact recursion equation (25.2.4) is approximated by

$$q(s_{t+1}, \mathbf{h}_{t+1}|\mathbf{v}_{1:t+1}) = \sum_{s_t} \int_{\mathbf{h}_t} p(s_{t+1}, \mathbf{h}_{t+1}|s_t, \mathbf{h}_t, \mathbf{v}_{t+1}) q(s_t, \mathbf{h}_t|\mathbf{v}_{1:t}). \tag{25.3.1}$$

This approximation to the filtered posterior at the next timestep will contain S times more components than in the previous timestep and, to prevent an exponential explosion in mixture components, we will need to subsequently collapse the mixture $q(s_{t+1}, \mathbf{h}_{t+1}|\mathbf{v}_{1:t+1})$ in a suitable way. It is useful to break the filtered approximation for Equation (25.2.4) into continuous and discrete parts:

$$q(\mathbf{h}_t, s_t|\mathbf{v}_{1:t}) = q(\mathbf{h}_t|s_t, \mathbf{v}_{1:t}) q(s_t|\mathbf{v}_{1:t}) \tag{25.3.2}$$

and derive separate filtered update formulae, as described below.

25.3.1 Continuous filtering

The exact representation of $p(\mathbf{h}_t|s_t, \mathbf{v}_{1:t})$ is a mixture with $O\left(S^{t-1}\right)$ components. To retain computational feasibility we therefore approximate this with a limited I-component mixture

$$q(\mathbf{h}_t|s_t, \mathbf{v}_{1:t}) = \sum_{i_t=1}^{I} q(\mathbf{h}_t|i_t, s_t, \mathbf{v}_{1:t}) q(i_t|s_t, \mathbf{v}_{1:t}) \tag{25.3.3}$$

where $q(\mathbf{h}_t|i_t, s_t, \mathbf{v}_{1:t})$ is a Gaussian parameterised with mean $\mathbf{f}(i_t, s_t)$ and covariance $\mathbf{F}(i_t, s_t)$. Strictly speaking, we should use the notation $\mathbf{f}_t(i_t, s_t)$ since, for each time t, we have a set of means indexed by i_t, s_t, although we drop these dependencies in the notation used here.

An important remark is that many techniques approximate $p(\mathbf{h}_t|s_t, \mathbf{v}_{1:t})$ using a *single* Gaussian, one for each state of s_t. Naturally, this gives rise to a mixture of Gaussians for $p(\mathbf{h}_t|\mathbf{v}_{1:t}) = \sum_{s_t} p(\mathbf{h}_t|s_t, \mathbf{v}_{1:t}) p(s_t|\mathbf{v}_{1:t})$. However, in making a single Gaussian approximation to $p(\mathbf{h}_t|s_t, \mathbf{v}_{1:t})$ the representation of the posterior may be poor. Our aim here is to maintain an accurate approximation to $p(\mathbf{h}_t|s_t, \mathbf{v}_{1:t})$ by using a *mixture* of Gaussians.

To find a recursion for the approximating distribution we first assume that we know the filtered approximation $q(\mathbf{h}_t, s_t|\mathbf{v}_{1:t})$ and then propagate this forwards using the exact dynamics. To do so consider first the relation

$$q(\mathbf{h}_{t+1}|s_{t+1}, \mathbf{v}_{1:t+1}) = \sum_{s_t, i_t} q(\mathbf{h}_{t+1}, s_t, i_t|s_{t+1}, \mathbf{v}_{1:t+1})$$
$$= \sum_{s_t, i_t} q(\mathbf{h}_{t+1}|s_t, i_t, s_{t+1}, \mathbf{v}_{1:t+1}) q(s_t, i_t|s_{t+1}, \mathbf{v}_{1:t+1}). \tag{25.3.4}$$

Wherever possible we now substitute the exact dynamics and evaluate each of the two factors above. The usefulness of decomposing the update in this way is that the new filtered approximation is of the form of a Gaussian mixture, where $q(\mathbf{h}_{t+1}|s_t, i_t, s_{t+1}, \mathbf{v}_{1:t+1})$ is Gaussian and $q(s_t, i_t|s_{t+1}, \mathbf{v}_{1:t+1})$ are the weights or mixing proportions of the components. We describe below how to compute these terms explicitly. Equation (25.3.4) produces a new Gaussian mixture with $I \times S$ components which we will collapse back to I components at the end of the computation.

Evaluating $q(\mathbf{h}_{t+1}|s_t, i_t, s_{t+1}, \mathbf{v}_{1:t+1})$

We aim to find a filtering recursion for $q(\mathbf{h}_{t+1}|s_t, i_t, s_{t+1}, \mathbf{v}_{1:t+1})$. Since this is conditional on switch states and components, this corresponds to a single LDS forward step which can be evaluated by considering first the joint distribution

$$q(\mathbf{h}_{t+1}, \mathbf{v}_{t+1}|s_t, i_t, s_{t+1}, \mathbf{v}_{1:t}) = \int_{\mathbf{h}_t} p(\mathbf{h}_{t+1}, \mathbf{v}_{t+1}|\mathbf{h}_t, \cancel{s_t}, \cancel{i_t}, s_{t+1}, \mathbf{v}_{1:t}) q(\mathbf{h}_t|s_t, i_t, \cancel{s_{t+1}}, \mathbf{v}_{1:t}) \tag{25.3.5}$$

and subsequently conditioning on $\mathbf{v}_{t+1}$. In the above we use the exact dynamics where possible. To ease the burden on notation we derive this for $\bar{\mathbf{h}}_t, \bar{\mathbf{v}}_t \equiv 0$ for all t. The exact forward dynamics is then given by

$$\mathbf{h}_{t+1} = \mathbf{A}(s_{t+1})\mathbf{h}_t + \boldsymbol{\eta}^h(s_{t+1}), \qquad \mathbf{v}_{t+1} = \mathbf{B}(s_{t+1})\mathbf{h}_{t+1} + \boldsymbol{\eta}^v(s_{t+1}). \tag{25.3.6}$$

Given the mixture component index i_t,

$$q(\mathbf{h}_t|\mathbf{v}_{1:t}, i_t, s_t) = \mathcal{N}(\mathbf{h}_t|\mathbf{f}(i_t, s_t), \mathbf{F}(i_t, s_t)) \tag{25.3.7}$$

we propagate this Gaussian with the exact dynamics equation (25.3.6). Then $q(\mathbf{h}_{t+1}, \mathbf{v}_{t+1}|s_t, i_t, s_{t+1}, \mathbf{v}_{1:t})$ is a Gaussian with covariance and mean elements

$$\boldsymbol{\Sigma}_{hh} = \mathbf{A}(s_{t+1})\mathbf{F}(i_t, s_t)\mathbf{A}^{\mathsf{T}}(s_{t+1}) + \boldsymbol{\Sigma}_h(s_{t+1}), \quad \boldsymbol{\Sigma}_{vv} = \mathbf{B}(s_{t+1})\boldsymbol{\Sigma}_{hh}\mathbf{B}^{\mathsf{T}}(s_{t+1}) + \boldsymbol{\Sigma}_v(s_{t+1})$$
$$\boldsymbol{\Sigma}_{vh} = \mathbf{B}(s_{t+1})\boldsymbol{\Sigma}_{hh} = \boldsymbol{\Sigma}_{hv}^{\mathsf{T}}, \quad \boldsymbol{\mu}_v = \mathbf{B}(s_{t+1})\mathbf{A}(s_{t+1})\mathbf{f}(i_t, s_t), \quad \boldsymbol{\mu}_h = \mathbf{A}(s_{t+1})\mathbf{f}(i_t, s_t). \tag{25.3.8}$$

These results are obtained from integrating the forward dynamics, Equations (25.2.1)–(25.2.2) over $\mathbf{h}_t$, using Result 8.3. To find $q(\mathbf{h}_{t+1}|s_t, i_t, s_{t+1}, \mathbf{v}_{1:t+1})$ we now condition $q(\mathbf{h}_{t+1}, \mathbf{v}_{t+1}|s_t, i_t, s_{t+1}, \mathbf{v}_{1:t})$ on $\mathbf{v}_{t+1}$ using the standard Gaussian conditioning formulae, Result 8.4, to obtain

$$q(\mathbf{h}_{t+1}|s_t, i_t, s_{t+1}, \mathbf{v}_{1:t+1}) = \mathcal{N}\left(\mathbf{h}_{t+1}|\boldsymbol{\mu}_{h|v}, \boldsymbol{\Sigma}_{h|v}\right) \tag{25.3.9}$$

with

$$\boldsymbol{\mu}_{h|v} = \boldsymbol{\mu}_h + \boldsymbol{\Sigma}_{hv}\boldsymbol{\Sigma}_{vv}^{-1}(\mathbf{v}_{t+1} - \boldsymbol{\mu}_v), \qquad \boldsymbol{\Sigma}_{h|v} = \boldsymbol{\Sigma}_{hh} - \boldsymbol{\Sigma}_{hv}\boldsymbol{\Sigma}_{vv}^{-1}\boldsymbol{\Sigma}_{vh} \tag{25.3.10}$$

where the quantities required are defined in Equation (25.3.8).

Evaluating the mixture weights $q(s_t, i_t|s_{t+1}, \mathbf{v}_{1:t+1})$

Up to a normalisation constant the mixture weight in Equation (25.3.4) can be found from

$$q(s_t, i_t|s_{t+1}, \mathbf{v}_{1:t+1}) \propto q(\mathbf{v}_{t+1}|i_t, s_t, s_{t+1}, \mathbf{v}_{1:t})q(s_{t+1}|i_t, s_t, \mathbf{v}_{1:t})q(i_t|s_t, \mathbf{v}_{1:t})q(s_t|\mathbf{v}_{1:t}). \quad (25.3.11)$$

The first factor in Equation (25.3.11), $q(\mathbf{v}_{t+1}|i_t, s_t, s_{t+1}, \mathbf{v}_{1:t})$ is Gaussian with mean $\boldsymbol{\mu}_v$ and covariance $\boldsymbol{\Sigma}_{vv}$, as given in Equation (25.3.8). The last two factors $q(i_t|s_t, \mathbf{v}_{1:t})$ and $q(s_t|\mathbf{v}_{1:t})$ are given from the previous filtered iteration. Finally, $q(s_{t+1}|i_t, s_t, \mathbf{v}_{1:t})$ is found from

$$q(s_{t+1}|i_t, s_t, \mathbf{v}_{1:t}) = \begin{cases} \langle p(s_{t+1}|\mathbf{h}_t, s_t)\rangle_{q(\mathbf{h}_t|i_t, s_t, \mathbf{v}_{1:t})} & \text{augmented SLDS} \\ p(s_{t+1}|s_t) & \text{standard SLDS} \end{cases} \quad (25.3.12)$$

In the aSLDS, the term in Equation (25.3.12) will generally need to be computed numerically. A simple approximation is to evaluate Equation (25.3.12) at the mean value of the distribution $q(\mathbf{h}_t|i_t, s_t, \mathbf{v}_{1:t})$. To take covariance information into account an alternative would be to draw samples from the Gaussian $q(\mathbf{h}_t|i_t, s_t, \mathbf{v}_{1:t})$ and thus approximate the average of $p(s_{t+1}|\mathbf{h}_t, s_t)$ by sampling. Note that this does not equate Gaussian sum filtering for the augmented SLDS with a sequential sampling procedure, such as particle filtering, Section 27.6.2. The sampling here is exact, for which no convergence issues arise.

Closing the recursion

We are now in a position to calculate Equation (25.3.4). For each setting of the variable s_{t+1}, we have a mixture of $I \times S$ Gaussians. To prevent the number of components increasing exponentially with time, we numerically collapse $q(\mathbf{h}_{t+1}|s_{t+1}, \mathbf{v}_{1:t+1})$ back to I Gaussians to form

$$q(\mathbf{h}_{t+1}|s_{t+1}, \mathbf{v}_{1:t+1}) \to \sum_{i_{t+1}=1}^{I} q(\mathbf{h}_{t+1}|i_{t+1}, s_{t+1}, \mathbf{v}_{1:t+1})q(i_{t+1}|s_{t+1}, \mathbf{v}_{1:t+1}). \quad (25.3.13)$$

The numerical collapse then generates the new Gaussian components and corresponding mixture weights. Any method of choice may be supplied to collapse a mixture to a smaller mixture. A straightforward approach is to repeatedly merge low-weight components, as explained in Section 25.3.4. In this way the new mixture coefficients $q(i_{t+1}|s_{t+1}, \mathbf{v}_{1:t+1})$, $i_{t+1} \in 1, \ldots, I$ are defined. This completes the description of how to form a recursion for the continuous filtered posterior approximation $q(\mathbf{h}_{t+1}|s_{t+1}, \mathbf{v}_{1:t+1})$ in Equation (25.3.2).

25.3.2 Discrete filtering

A recursion for the switch variable distribution in Equation (25.3.2) is

$$q(s_{t+1}|\mathbf{v}_{1:t+1}) \propto \sum_{i_t, s_t} q(s_{t+1}, i_t, s_t, \mathbf{v}_{t+1}, \mathbf{v}_{1:t}). \quad (25.3.14)$$

The r.h.s. of the above equation is proportional to

$$\sum_{s_t, i_t} q(\mathbf{v}_{t+1}|s_{t+1}, i_t, s_t, \mathbf{v}_{1:t})q(s_{t+1}|i_t, s_t, \mathbf{v}_{1:t})q(i_t|s_t, \mathbf{v}_{1:t})q(s_t|\mathbf{v}_{1:t}) \quad (25.3.15)$$

for which all terms have been computed during the recursion for $q(\mathbf{h}_{t+1}|s_{t+1}, \mathbf{v}_{1:t+1})$. We therefore now have all the quantities required to compute the Gaussian sum approximation of the filtering forward pass. A schematic representation of Gaussian sum filtering is given in Fig. 25.2 and the pseudo code is presented in Algorithm 25.1. See also `SLDSforward.m`.

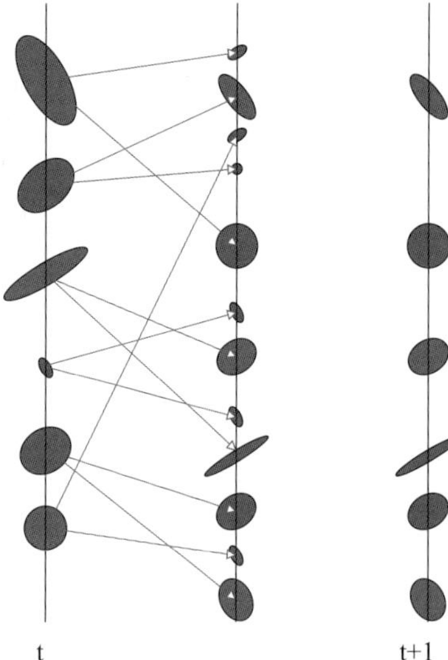

Figure 25.2 Gaussian sum filtering. The leftmost column depicts the previous Gaussian mixture approximation $q(\mathbf{h}_t, i_t|\mathbf{v}_{1:t})$ for two states $S = 2$ (red and blue) and three mixture components $I = 3$, with the mixture weight represented by the area of each oval. There are $S = 2$ different linear systems which take each of the components of the mixture into a new filtered state, the colour of the arrow indicating which dynamic system is used. After one timestep each mixture component branches into a further S components so that the joint approximation $q(\mathbf{h}_{t+1}, s_{t+1}|\mathbf{v}_{1:t+1})$ contains $S^2 I$ components (middle column). To keep the representation computationally tractable the mixture of Gaussians for each state s_{t+1} is collapsed back to I components. This means that each coloured set of Gaussians needs to be approximated by a smaller I component mixture of Gaussians. There are many ways to achieve this. A naive but computationally efficient approach is to simply ignore the lowest weight components, as depicted on the right column, see `mix2mix.m`. See plate section for colour version.

Algorithm 25.1 aSLDS forward pass. Approximate the filtered posterior $p(s_t|\mathbf{v}_{1:t}) \equiv \alpha_t$, $p(\mathbf{h}_t|s_t, \mathbf{v}_{1:t}) \equiv \sum_{i_t} w_t(i_t, s_t)\mathcal{N}(\mathbf{h}_t|\mathbf{f}_t(i_t, s_t), \mathbf{F}_t(i_t, s_t))$. Also return the approximate log likelihood $L \equiv \log p(\mathbf{v}_{1:T})$. I_t are the number of components in each Gaussian mixture approximation. We require $I_1 = 1$, $I_2 \leq S$, $I_t \leq S \times I_{t-1}$. $\theta(s) = \{\mathbf{A}(s), \mathbf{B}(s), \mathbf{\Sigma}^h(s), \mathbf{\Sigma}^v(s), \bar{\mathbf{h}}(s), \bar{\mathbf{v}}(s)\}$. The routine LDSFORWARD is found in Algorithm 24.1.

---

for $s_1 \leftarrow 1$ **to** S **do**
  $\{\mathbf{f}_1(1, s_1), \mathbf{F}_1(1, s_1), \hat{p}\} = \text{LDSFORWARD}(0, 0, \mathbf{v}_1; \theta(s_1))$
  $\alpha_1 \leftarrow p(s_1)\hat{p}$
end for

for $t \leftarrow 2$ **to** T **do**
  for $s_t \leftarrow 1$ **to** S **do**
    for $i \leftarrow 1$ **to** I_{t-1}, **and** $s \leftarrow 1$ **to** S **do**
      $\{\boldsymbol{\mu}_{x|y}(i, s), \mathbf{\Sigma}_{x|y}(i, s), \hat{p}\} = \text{LDSFORWARD}(\mathbf{f}_{t-1}(i, s), \mathbf{F}_{t-1}(i, s), \mathbf{v}_t; \theta(s_t))$
      $p^*(s_t|i, s) \equiv \langle p(s_t|\mathbf{h}_{t-1}, s_{t-1} = s)\rangle_{p(\mathbf{h}_{t-1}|i_{t-1}=i, s_{t-1}=s, \mathbf{v}_{1:t-1})}$
      $p'(s_t, i, s) \leftarrow w_{t-1}(i, s)p^*(s_t|i, s)\alpha_{t-1}(s)\hat{p}$
    end for
    Collapse the $I_{t-1} \times S$ mixture of Gaussians defined by $\boldsymbol{\mu}_{x|y}$, $\mathbf{\Sigma}_{x|y}$, and weights $p(i, s|s_t) \propto p'(s_t, i, s)$ to a Gaussian with I_t components, $p(\mathbf{h}_t|s_t, \mathbf{v}_{1:t}) \approx \sum_{i_t=1}^{I_t} p(i_t|s_t, \mathbf{v}_{1:t}) \times p(\mathbf{h}_t|s_t, i_t, \mathbf{v}_{1:t})$. This defines the new means $\mathbf{f}_t(i_t, s_t)$, covariances $\mathbf{F}_t(i_t, s_t)$ and mixture weights $w_t(i_t, s_t) \equiv p(i_t|s_t, \mathbf{v}_{1:t})$.
    Compute $\alpha_t(s_t) \propto \sum_{i,s} p'(s_t, i, s)$
  end for
  normalise α_t
  $L \leftarrow L + \log \sum_{s_t, i, s} p'(s_t, i, s)$
end for

25.3.3 The likelihood $p(\mathbf{v}_{1:T})$

The likelihood $p(\mathbf{v}_{1:T})$ may be found from

$$p(\mathbf{v}_{1:T}) = \prod_{t=0}^{T-1} p(\mathbf{v}_{t+1}|\mathbf{v}_{1:t}) \tag{25.3.16}$$

where

$$p(\mathbf{v}_{t+1}|\mathbf{v}_{1:t}) \approx \sum_{i_t, s_t, s_{t+1}} q(\mathbf{v}_{t+1}|i_t, s_t, s_{t+1}, \mathbf{v}_{1:t}) q(s_{t+1}|i_t, s_t, \mathbf{v}_{1:t}) q(i_t|s_t, \mathbf{v}_{1:t}) q(s_t|\mathbf{v}_{1:t}).$$

In the above expression, all terms have been computed in forming the recursion for the filtered posterior $q(\mathbf{h}_{t+1}, s_{t+1}|\mathbf{v}_{1:t+1})$.

25.3.4 Collapsing Gaussians

A central part of the above filtering recursion is the collapse of a mixture of Gaussians to a smaller number of Gaussians. That is, given a mixture N Gaussians

$$p(\mathbf{x}) = \sum_{i=1}^{N} p_i \mathcal{N}(\mathbf{x}|\boldsymbol{\mu}_i, \boldsymbol{\Sigma}_i) \tag{25.3.17}$$

we wish to collapse this to a smaller $K < N$ mixture of Gaussians. We describe a simple method which has the advantage of computational efficiency, but the disadvantage that no spatial information about the mixture is used [297]. First we describe how to collapse a mixture to a single Gaussian. This can be achieved by finding the mean and covariance of the mixture distribution (25.3.17). These are

$$\boldsymbol{\mu} = \sum_i p_i \boldsymbol{\mu}_i, \qquad \boldsymbol{\Sigma} = \sum_i p_i \left(\boldsymbol{\Sigma}_i + \boldsymbol{\mu}_i \boldsymbol{\mu}_i^{\mathsf{T}}\right) - \boldsymbol{\mu}\boldsymbol{\mu}^{\mathsf{T}}. \tag{25.3.18}$$

To collapse a mixture then to a K-component mixture we may first retain the $K-1$ Gaussians with the largest mixture weights. The remaining $N-K+1$ Gaussians are simply merged to a single Gaussian using the above method. Alternative heuristics such as recursively merging the two Gaussians with the lowest mixture weights are also reasonable.

More sophisticated methods which retain some spatial information would clearly be potentially useful. The method presented in [188] is a suitable approach which considers removing Gaussians which are spatially similar (and not just low-weight components), thereby retaining a sense of diversity over the possible solutions. In applications with many thousands of timesteps, speed can be a factor in determining which method of collapsing Gaussians is to be preferred.

25.3.5 Relation to other methods

Gaussian sum filtering can be considered a form of 'analytical particle filtering', Section 27.6.2, in which instead of point distributions (delta functions) being propagated, Gaussians are propagated. The collapse operation to a smaller number of Gaussians is analogous to resampling in particle filtering. Since a Gaussian is more expressive than a delta function, the Gaussian sum filter is generally an improved approximation technique over using point particles. See [17] for a numerical comparison.

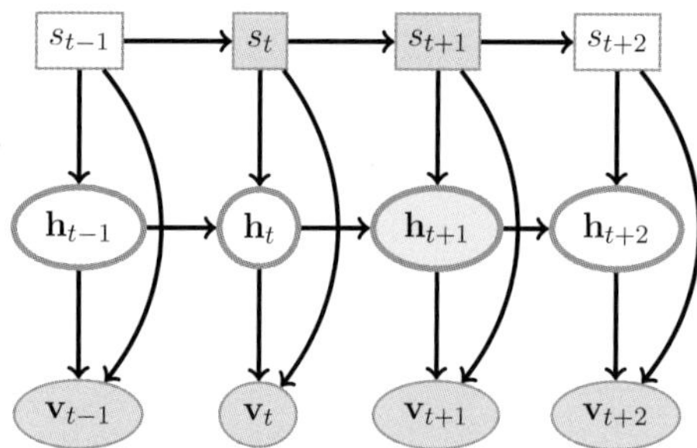

Figure 25.3 The EC backpass approximates $p(\mathbf{h}_{t+1}|s_{t+1}, s_t, \mathbf{v}_{1:T})$ by $p(\mathbf{h}_{t+1}|s_{t+1}, \mathbf{v}_{1:T})$. The motivation for this is that s_t influences $\mathbf{h}_{t+1}$ only indirectly through $\mathbf{h}_t$. However, $\mathbf{h}_t$ will most likely be heavily influenced by $\mathbf{v}_{1:t}$, so that not knowing the state of s_t is likely to be of secondary importance. The green shaded node is the variable we wish to find the posterior for. The values of the blue shaded nodes are known, and the red shaded node indicates a known variable which is assumed unknown in forming the approximation. See plate section for colour version.

25.4 Gaussian sum smoothing

Approximating the smoothed posterior $p(\mathbf{h}_t, s_t|\mathbf{v}_{1:T})$ is more involved than filtering and requires additional approximations. For this reason smoothing is more prone to failure since there are more assumptions that need to be satisfied for the approximations to hold. The route we take here is to assume that a Gaussian sum filtered approximation has been carried out, and then approximate the γ backward pass, analogous to that of Section 23.2.4. By analogy with the RTS smoothing recursion Equation (23.2.20), the exact backward pass for the SLDS reads

$$p(\mathbf{h}_t, s_t|\mathbf{v}_{1:T}) = \sum_{s_{t+1}} \int_{\mathbf{h}_{t+1}} p(\mathbf{h}_t, s_t|\mathbf{h}_{t+1}, s_{t+1}, \mathbf{v}_{1:t}) p(\mathbf{h}_{t+1}, s_{t+1}|\mathbf{v}_{1:T}) \tag{25.4.1}$$

where $p(\mathbf{h}_{t+1}, s_{t+1}|\mathbf{v}_{1:T}) = p(s_{t+1}|\mathbf{v}_{1:T}) p(\mathbf{h}_{t+1}|s_{t+1}, \mathbf{v}_{1:T})$ is composed of the discrete and continuous components of the smoothed posterior at the next timestep. The recursion runs backwards in time, beginning with the initialisation $p(\mathbf{h}_T, s_T|\mathbf{v}_{1:T})$ set by the filtered result (at time $t = T$, the filtered and smoothed posteriors coincide). Apart from the fact that the number of mixture components will increase at each step, computing the integral over $\mathbf{h}_{t+1}$ in Equation (25.4.1) is problematic since the conditional distribution term is non-Gaussian in $\mathbf{h}_{t+1}$. For this reason it is more useful to derive an approximate recursion by beginning with the exact relation

$$p(\mathbf{h}_t, s_t|\mathbf{v}_{1:T}) = \sum_{s_{t+1}} p(s_{t+1}|\mathbf{v}_{1:T}) p(\mathbf{h}_t|s_t, s_{t+1}, \mathbf{v}_{1:T}) p(s_t|s_{t+1}, \mathbf{v}_{1:T}) \tag{25.4.2}$$

which can be expressed more directly in terms of the SLDS dynamics as

$$p(\mathbf{h}_t, s_t|\mathbf{v}_{1:T}) = \sum_{s_{t+1}} p(s_{t+1}|\mathbf{v}_{1:T}) \left\langle p(\mathbf{h}_t|\mathbf{h}_{t+1}, s_t, s_{t+1}, \mathbf{v}_{1:t}, \cancel{\mathbf{v}_{t+1:T}})\right\rangle_{p(\mathbf{h}_{t+1}|s_t, s_{t+1}, \mathbf{v}_{1:T})}$$
$$\times \left\langle p(s_t|\mathbf{h}_{t+1}, s_{t+1}, \mathbf{v}_{1:T})\right\rangle_{p(\mathbf{h}_{t+1}|s_{t+1}, \mathbf{v}_{1:T})}. \tag{25.4.3}$$

In forming the recursion we assume access to the distribution $p(\mathbf{h}_{t+1}, s_{t+1}|\mathbf{v}_{1:T})$ from the future timestep. However, we also require the distribution $p(\mathbf{h}_{t+1}|s_t, s_{t+1}, \mathbf{v}_{1:T})$ which is not directly known and needs to be inferred, in itself a computationally challenging task. In the *Expectation Correction* (EC) approach [17] one assumes the approximation (see Fig. 25.3)

$$p(\mathbf{h}_{t+1}|s_t, s_{t+1}, \mathbf{v}_{1:T}) \approx p(\mathbf{h}_{t+1}|s_{t+1}, \mathbf{v}_{1:T}) \tag{25.4.4}$$

resulting in an approximate recursion for the smoothed posterior,

$$p(\mathbf{h}_t, s_t|\mathbf{v}_{1:T}) \approx \sum_{s_{t+1}} p(s_{t+1}|\mathbf{v}_{1:T}) \left\langle p(\mathbf{h}_t|\mathbf{h}_{t+1}, s_t, s_{t+1}, \mathbf{v}_{1:t})\right\rangle_{\mathbf{h}_{t+1}} \left\langle p(s_t|\mathbf{h}_{t+1}, s_{t+1}, \mathbf{v}_{1:T})\right\rangle_{\mathbf{h}_{t+1}} \tag{25.4.5}$$

where $\langle\cdot\rangle_{\mathbf{h}_{t+1}}$ represents averaging with respect to the distribution $p(\mathbf{h}_{t+1}|s_{t+1}, \mathbf{v}_{1:T})$. In carrying out the approximate recursion, (25.4.5), we will end up with a mixture of Gaussians that grows at each timestep. To avoid the exponential explosion problem, we use a finite mixture approximation, $q(\mathbf{h}_{t+1}, s_{t+1}|\mathbf{v}_{1:T})$:

$$p(\mathbf{h}_{t+1}, s_{t+1}|\mathbf{v}_{1:T}) \approx q(\mathbf{h}_{t+1}, s_{t+1}|\mathbf{v}_{1:T}) = q(\mathbf{h}_{t+1}|s_{t+1}, \mathbf{v}_{1:T})q(s_{t+1}|\mathbf{v}_{1:T}) \tag{25.4.6}$$

and plug this into the approximate recursion above. From Equation (25.4.5) a recursion for the approximation is given by

$$q(\mathbf{h}_t, s_t|\mathbf{v}_{1:T}) = \sum_{s_{t+1}} q(s_{t+1}|\mathbf{v}_{1:T}) \underbrace{\langle q(\mathbf{h}_t|\mathbf{h}_{t+1}, s_t, s_{t+1}, \mathbf{v}_{1:t})\rangle_{q(\mathbf{h}_{t+1}|s_{t+1},\mathbf{v}_{1:T})}}_{q(\mathbf{h}_t|s_t,s_{t+1},\mathbf{v}_{1:T})} \times \underbrace{\langle q(s_t|\mathbf{h}_{t+1}, s_{t+1}, \mathbf{v}_{1:t})\rangle_{q(\mathbf{h}_{t+1}|s_{t+1},\mathbf{v}_{1:T})}}_{q(s_t|s_{t+1},\mathbf{v}_{1:T})}. \tag{25.4.7}$$

As for filtering, wherever possible, we replace approximate terms by their exact counterparts and parameterise the posterior using

$$q(\mathbf{h}_{t+1}, s_{t+1}|\mathbf{v}_{1:T}) = q(\mathbf{h}_{t+1}|s_{t+1}, \mathbf{v}_{1:T})q(s_{t+1}|\mathbf{v}_{1:T}). \tag{25.4.8}$$

To reduce the notational burden here we outline the method only for the case of using a single component approximation in both the forward and backward passes. The extension to using a mixture to approximate each $p(\mathbf{h}_{t+1}|s_{t+1}, \mathbf{v}_{1:T})$ is conceptually straightforward and deferred to Section 25.4.4. In the single Gaussian case we assume we have a Gaussian approximation available for

$$q(\mathbf{h}_{t+1}|s_{t+1}, \mathbf{v}_{1:T}) = \mathcal{N}(\mathbf{h}_{t+1}|\mathbf{g}(s_{t+1}), \mathbf{G}(s_{t+1})). \tag{25.4.9}$$

25.4.1 Continuous smoothing

For given s_t, s_{t+1}, an RTS-style recursion for the smoothed continuous distribution is obtained from Equation (25.4.7), giving

$$q(\mathbf{h}_t|s_t, s_{t+1}, \mathbf{v}_{1:T}) = \int_{\mathbf{h}_{t+1}} p(\mathbf{h}_t|\mathbf{h}_{t+1}, s_t, s_{t+1}, \mathbf{v}_{1:t})q(\mathbf{h}_{t+1}|s_{t+1}, \mathbf{v}_{1:T}). \tag{25.4.10}$$

To compute Equation (25.4.10) we then perform a single update of the LDS backward recursion, Section 24.4.2.

25.4.2 Discrete smoothing

The second average in Equation (25.4.7) corresponds to a recursion for the discrete variable and is given by

$$\langle q(s_t|\mathbf{h}_{t+1}, s_{t+1}, \mathbf{v}_{1:t})\rangle_{q(\mathbf{h}_{t+1}|s_{t+1},\mathbf{v}_{1:T})} \equiv q(s_t|s_{t+1}, \mathbf{v}_{1:T}). \tag{25.4.11}$$

The average of $q(s_t|\mathbf{h}_{t+1}, s_{t+1}, \mathbf{v}_{1:t})$ with respect to $q(\mathbf{h}_{t+1}|s_{t+1}, \mathbf{v}_{1:T})$ cannot be achieved in closed form. A simple approach is to approximate the average by evaluation at the mean[1]

$$\langle q(s_t|\mathbf{h}_{t+1}, s_{t+1}\mathbf{v}_{1:t})\rangle_{q(\mathbf{h}_{t+1}|s_{t+1},\mathbf{v}_{1:T})} \approx q(s_t|\mathbf{h}_{t+1}, s_{t+1}, \mathbf{v}_{1:t})\Big|_{\mathbf{h}_{t+1}=\langle\mathbf{h}_{t+1}|s_{t+1},\mathbf{v}_{1:T}\rangle} \tag{25.4.12}$$

where $\langle\mathbf{h}_{t+1}|s_{t+1}, \mathbf{v}_{1:T}\rangle$ is the mean of $\mathbf{h}_{t+1}$ with respect to $q(\mathbf{h}_{t+1}|s_{t+1}, \mathbf{v}_{1:T})$.

[1] In general this approximation has the form $\langle f(x)\rangle \approx f(\langle x\rangle)$.

Replacing $\mathbf{h}_{t+1}$ by its mean gives the approximation

$$\langle q(s_t|\mathbf{h}_{t+1}, s_{t+1}, \mathbf{v}_{1:t})\rangle_{q(\mathbf{h}_{t+1}|s_{t+1},\mathbf{v}_{1:T})} \approx \frac{1}{Z}\frac{e^{-\frac{1}{2}\mathbf{z}_{t+1}^{\mathsf{T}}(s_t,s_{t+1})\boldsymbol{\Sigma}^{-1}(s_t,s_{t+1}|\mathbf{v}_{1:t})\mathbf{z}_{t+1}(s_t,s_{t+1})}}{\sqrt{\det\left(\boldsymbol{\Sigma}(s_t, s_{t+1}|\mathbf{v}_{1:t})\right)}} q(s_t|s_{t+1}, \mathbf{v}_{1:t}) \tag{25.4.13}$$

where

$$\mathbf{z}_{t+1}(s_t, s_{t+1}) \equiv \langle \mathbf{h}_{t+1}|s_{t+1}, \mathbf{v}_{1:T}\rangle - \langle \mathbf{h}_{t+1}|s_t, s_{t+1}, \mathbf{v}_{1:t}\rangle \tag{25.4.14}$$

and Z ensures normalisation over s_t. Here $\boldsymbol{\Sigma}(s_t, s_{t+1}|\mathbf{v}_{1:t})$ is the filtered covariance of $\mathbf{h}_{t+1}$ given s_t, s_{t+1} and the observations $\mathbf{v}_{1:t}$, which may be taken from $\boldsymbol{\Sigma}_{hh}$ in Equation (25.3.8). Approximations which take covariance information into account can also be considered, although the above simple (and fast) method may suffice in practice [17, 207].

25.4.3 Collapsing the mixture

From Section 25.4.1 and Section 25.4.2 we now have all the terms in Equation (25.4.8) to compute the approximation to Equation (25.4.7). Due to the summation over s_{t+1} in Equation (25.4.7), the number of mixture components is multiplied by S at each iteration. To prevent an exponential explosion of components, the mixture equation (25.4.7) is then collapsed to a single Gaussian

$$q(\mathbf{h}_t, s_t|\mathbf{v}_{1:T}) \rightarrow q(\mathbf{h}_t|s_t, \mathbf{v}_{1:T})q(s_t|\mathbf{v}_{1:T}) \tag{25.4.15}$$

The collapse to a mixture is discussed in Section 25.4.4.

25.4.4 Using mixtures in smoothing

The extension to the mixture case is straightforward based on the representation

$$p(\mathbf{h}_t|s_t, \mathbf{v}_{1:T}) \approx \sum_{j_t=1}^{J} q(j_t|s_t, \mathbf{v}_{1:T})q(\mathbf{h}_t|s_t, j_t, \mathbf{v}_{1:T}). \tag{25.4.16}$$

Analogously to the case with a single component,

$$q(\mathbf{h}_t, s_t|\mathbf{v}_{1:T}) = \sum_{i_t, j_{t+1}, s_{t+1}} p(s_{t+1}|\mathbf{v}_{1:T})p(j_{t+1}|s_{t+1}, \mathbf{v}_{1:T})q(\mathbf{h}_t|j_{t+1}, s_{t+1}, i_t, s_t, \mathbf{v}_{1:T}) \\ \times \langle q(i_t, s_t|\mathbf{h}_{t+1}, j_{t+1}, s_{t+1}, \mathbf{v}_{1:t})\rangle_{q(\mathbf{h}_{t+1}|j_{t+1},s_{t+1},\mathbf{v}_{1:T})}. \tag{25.4.17}$$

The average in the last line of the above equation can be tackled using the same techniques as outlined in the single Gaussian case. To approximate $q(\mathbf{h}_t|j_{t+1}, s_{t+1}, i_t, s_t, \mathbf{v}_{1:T})$ we consider this as the marginal of the joint distribution

$$q(\mathbf{h}_t, \mathbf{h}_{t+1}|i_t, s_t, j_{t+1}, s_{t+1}, \mathbf{v}_{1:T}) = q(\mathbf{h}_t|\mathbf{h}_{t+1}, i_t, s_t, j_{t+1}, s_{t+1}, \mathbf{v}_{1:t})q(\mathbf{h}_{t+1}|i_t, s_t, j_{t+1}, s_{t+1}, \mathbf{v}_{1:T}). \tag{25.4.18}$$

As in the case of a single mixture, the problematic term is $q(\mathbf{h}_{t+1}|i_t, s_t, j_{t+1}, s_{t+1}, \mathbf{v}_{1:T})$. Analogously to Equation (25.4.4), we make the assumption

$$q(\mathbf{h}_{t+1}|i_t, s_t, j_{t+1}, s_{t+1}, \mathbf{v}_{1:T}) \approx q(\mathbf{h}_{t+1}|j_{t+1}, s_{t+1}, \mathbf{v}_{1:T}) \tag{25.4.19}$$

Algorithm 25.2 aSLDS: EC backward pass. Approximates $p(s_t|\mathbf{v}_{1:T})$ and $p(\mathbf{h}_t|s_t,\mathbf{v}_{1:T}) \equiv \sum_{j_t=1}^{J_t} u_t(j_t,s_t)\mathcal{N}(\mathbf{g}_t(j_t,s_t),\mathbf{G}_t(j_t,s_t))$ using a mixture of Gaussians. $J_T = I_T$, $J_t \le S \times I_t \times J_{t+1}$. This routine needs the results from Algorithm 25.1. The routine `LDSBACKWARD` is found in Algorithm 24.2.

$\mathbf{G}_T \leftarrow \mathbf{F}_T, \mathbf{g}_T \leftarrow \mathbf{f}_T, u_T \leftarrow w_T$
for $t \leftarrow T-1$ **to** 1 **do**
  for $s \leftarrow 1$ **to** S, $s' \leftarrow 1$ **to** S, $i \leftarrow 1$ **to** I_t, $j' \leftarrow 1$ **to** J_{t+1} **do**
    $(\boldsymbol{\mu},\boldsymbol{\Sigma})(i,s,j',s') = \text{LDSFORWARD}(\mathbf{g}_{t+1}(j',s'),\mathbf{G}_{t+1}(j',s'),\mathbf{f}_t(i,s),\mathbf{F}_t(i,s),\theta(s'))$
    $p(i_t,s_t|j_{t+1},s_{t+1},\mathbf{v}_{1:T}) = \langle p(s_t=s,i_t=i|\mathbf{h}_{t+1},s_{t+1}=s',j_{t+1}=j',\mathbf{v}_{1:t})\rangle_{p(\mathbf{h}_{t+1}|s_{t+1}=s',j_{t+1}=j',\mathbf{v}_{1:T})}$
    $p(i,s,j',s'|\mathbf{v}_{1:T}) \leftarrow p(s_{t+1}=s'|\mathbf{v}_{1:T})u_{t+1}(j',s')p(i_t,s_t|j_{t+1},s_{t+1},\mathbf{v}_{1:T})$
  end for
  for $s_t \leftarrow 1$ **to** S **do**
    Collapse the mixture defined by weights $p(i_t=i,s_{t+1}=s',j_{t+1}=j'|s_t,\mathbf{v}_{1_T}) \propto p(i,s_t,j',s'|\mathbf{v}_{1:T})$, means $\boldsymbol{\mu}(i_t,s_t,j_{t+1},s_{t+1})$ and covariances $\boldsymbol{\Sigma}(i_t,s_t,j_{t+1},s_{t+1})$ to a mixture with J_t components. This defines the new means $\mathbf{g}_t(j_t,s_t)$, covariances $\mathbf{G}_t(j_t,s_t)$ and mixture weights $u_t(j_t,s_t)$.
    $p(s_t|\mathbf{v}_{1:T}) \leftarrow \sum_{i_t,j',s'} p(i_t,s_t,j',s'|\mathbf{v}_{1:T})$
  end for
end for

---

meaning that information about the current switch state s_t, i_t is ignored. We can then form

$$p(\mathbf{h}_t|s_t,\mathbf{v}_{1:T}) = \sum_{i_t,j_{t+1},s_{t+1}} p(i_t,j_{t+1},s_{t+1}|s_t,\mathbf{v}_{1:T})p(\mathbf{h}_t|i_t,s_t,j_{t+1},s_{t+1},\mathbf{v}_{1:T}). \tag{25.4.20}$$

This mixture can then be collapsed to a smaller mixture using any method of choice, to give

$$p(\mathbf{h}_t|s_t,\mathbf{v}_{1:T}) \approx \sum_{j_t} q(j_t|s_t,\mathbf{v}_{1:T})q(\mathbf{h}_t|j_t,s_t,\mathbf{v}_{1:T}). \tag{25.4.21}$$

The resulting procedure is sketched in Algorithm 25.2, including using mixtures in both the forward and backward passes.

25.4.5 Relation to other methods

A classical smoothing approximation for the SLDS is *Generalised Pseudo Bayes* (GPB) [12, 173, 172]. In GPB one starts from the exact recursion

$$p(s_t|\mathbf{v}_{1:T}) = \sum_{s_{t+1}} p(s_t,s_{t+1}|\mathbf{v}_{1:T}) = \sum_{s_{t+1}} p(s_t|s_{t+1},\mathbf{v}_{1:T})p(s_{t+1}|\mathbf{v}_{1:T}). \tag{25.4.22}$$

The quantity $p(s_t|s_{t+1},\mathbf{v}_{1:T})$ is difficult to obtain and GPB makes the approximation

$$p(s_t|s_{t+1},\mathbf{v}_{1:T}) \approx p(s_t|s_{t+1},\mathbf{v}_{1:t}). \tag{25.4.23}$$

Plugging this into Equation (25.4.22) we have

$$p(s_t|\mathbf{v}_{1:T}) \approx \sum_{s_{t+1}} p(s_t|s_{t+1},\mathbf{v}_{1:t})p(s_{t+1}|\mathbf{v}_{1:T}) \tag{25.4.24}$$

$$= \sum_{s_{t+1}} \frac{p(s_{t+1}|s_t)p(s_t|\mathbf{v}_{1:t})}{\sum_{s_t} p(s_{t+1}|s_t)p(s_t|\mathbf{v}_{1:t})} p(s_{t+1}|\mathbf{v}_{1:T}). \tag{25.4.25}$$

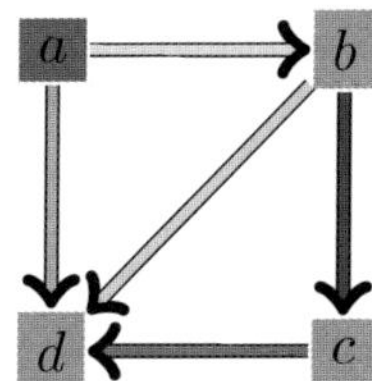

Figure 25.4 A representation of the traffic flow between junctions at *a*, *b*, *c*, *d*, with traffic lights at *a* and *b*. If $s_a = 1$ $a \to d$ and $a \to b$ carry 0.75 and 0.25 of the flow out of *a* respectively. If $s_a = 2$ all the flow from *a* goes through $a \to d$; for $s_a = 3$, all the flow goes through $a \to b$. For $s_b = 1$ the flow out of *b* is split equally between $b \to d$ and $b \to c$. For $s_b = 2$ all flow out of *b* goes along $b \to c$. See plate section for colour version.

The recursion is initialised with the approximate filtered $p(s_T|\mathbf{v}_{1:T})$. Computing the smoothed recursion for the switch states in GPB is then equivalent to running the RTS backward pass on a hidden Markov model, independently of the backward recursion for the continuous variables. The only information the GPB method uses to form the smoothed distribution $p(s_t|\mathbf{v}_{1:T})$ from the filtered distribution $p(s_t|\mathbf{v}_{1:t})$ is the Markov switch transition $p(s_{t+1}|s_t)$. This approximation drops information from the future since information passed via the continuous variables is not taken into account. In contrast to GPB, the EC Gaussian smoothing technique preserves future information passing through the continuous variables. GPB forms an approximation for $p(\mathbf{h}_t|s_t, \mathbf{v}_{1:T})$ by using the recursion (25.4.8) where $q(s_t|s_{t+1}, \mathbf{v}_{1:T})$ is replaced by $q(s_t|s_{t+1}, \mathbf{v}_{1:t})$. In `SLDSbackward.m` one may choose to use either EC or GBP.

Example 25.1 Traffic flow

A illustration of modelling and inference with a SLDS is to consider a simple network of traffic flow, Fig. 25.4. Here there are four junctions a, b, c, d and traffic flows along the roads in the direction indicated. Traffic flows into the junction at a and then goes via different routes to d. Flow out of a junction must match the flow into a junction (up to noise). There are traffic light switches at junctions a and b which, depending on their state, route traffic differently along the roads. Using ϕ to denote the clean (noise free) flow, we model the flows using the switching linear system:

$$\left.\begin{array}{r} \phi_a(t) \\ \phi_{a\to d}(t) \\ \phi_{a\to b}(t) \\ \phi_{b\to d}(t) \\ \phi_{b\to c}(t) \\ \phi_{c\to d}(t) \end{array}\right\} = \left\{\begin{array}{l} \phi_a(t-1) \\ \phi_a(t-1)\left(0.75 \times \mathbb{I}\left[s_a(t)=1\right] + 1 \times \mathbb{I}\left[s_a(t)=2\right]\right) \\ \phi_a(t-1)\left(0.25 \times \mathbb{I}\left[s_a(t)=1\right] + 1 \times \mathbb{I}\left[s_a(t)=3\right]\right) \\ \phi_{a\to b}(t-1)0.5 \times \mathbb{I}\left[s_b(t)=1\right] \\ \phi_{a\to b}(t-1)\left(0.5 \times \mathbb{I}\left[s_b(t)=1\right] + 1 \times \mathbb{I}\left[s_b(t)=2\right]\right) \\ \phi_{b\to c}(t-1). \end{array}\right. \tag{25.4.26}$$

By identifying the flows at time t with a six-dimensional vector hidden variable $\mathbf{h}_t$, we can write the above flow equations as

$$\mathbf{h}_t = \mathbf{A}(s_t)\mathbf{h}_{t-1} + \boldsymbol{\eta}_t^h \tag{25.4.27}$$

for a set of suitably defined matrices $\mathbf{A}(s)$ indexed by the switch variable $s = s_a \bigotimes s_b$, which takes $3 \times 2 = 6$ states. We additionally include noise terms to model cars parking or de-parking during a single timestep. The covariance $\boldsymbol{\Sigma}_h$ is diagonal with a larger variance at the inflow point a to model that the total volume of traffic entering the system can vary.

Noisy measurements of the flow into the network are taken at a

$$v_{1,t} = \phi_a(t) + \eta_1^v(t) \tag{25.4.28}$$

along with a noisy measurement of the total flow out of the system at d,

$$v_{2,t} = \phi_{a\to d}(t) + \phi_{b\to d}(t) + \phi_{c\to d}(t) + \eta_2^v(t). \tag{25.4.29}$$

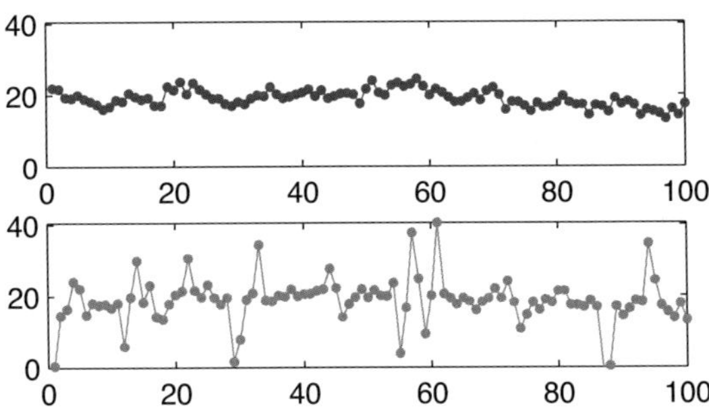

Figure 25.5 Time evolution of the traffic flow measured at two points in the network. Sensors measure the total flow into the network (upper panel) $\phi_a(t)$ and the total flow out of the network (lower panel), $\phi_d(t) = \phi_{a\to d}(t) + \phi_{b\to d}(t) + \phi_{c\to d}(t)$. The total inflow at a undergoes a random walk. Note that the flow measured at d can momentarily drop to zero if all traffic is routed through $a \to b \to c$ in two consecutive timesteps. See plate section for colour version.

The observation model can be represented by $\mathbf{v}_t = \mathbf{B}\mathbf{h}_t + \boldsymbol{\eta}_t^v$ using a constant 2×6 projection matrix $\mathbf{B}$. The switch variables follow a simple Markov transition $p(s_t|s_{t-1})$ which biases the switches to remain in the same state in preference to jumping to another state. See `demoSLDStraffic.m` for details.

Given the above system and a prior which initialises all flow at a, we draw samples from the model using forward (ancestral) sampling which form the observations $\mathbf{v}_{1:100}$, Fig. 25.5. Using only the observations and the known model structure we then attempt to infer the latent switch variables and traffic flows using Gaussian sum filtering and smoothing (EC method) with two mixture components per switch state, Fig. 25.6.

We note that a naive HMM approximation based on discretising each continuous flow into 20 bins would contain $2 \times 3 \times 20^6$ or 384 million states. Even for modest size problems, a naive approximation based on discretisation is therefore impractical.

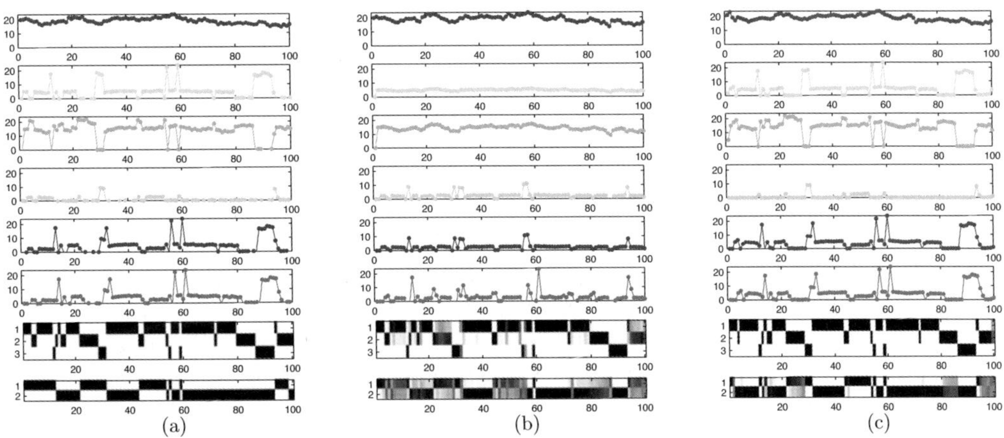

Figure 25.6 Given the observations from Fig. 25.5 we infer the flows and switch states of all the latent variables. **(a)** The correct latent flows through time along with the switch variable state used to generate the data. The colours corresponds to the flows at the corresponding coloured edges/nodes in Fig. 25.4. **(b)** Filtered flows based on a $I = 2$ Gaussian sum forward pass approximation. Plotted are the six components of the vector $\langle \mathbf{h}_t|\mathbf{v}_{1:t}\rangle$ with the posterior distribution of the s_a and s_b traffic light states $p(s_t^a|\mathbf{v}_{1:t})$, $p(s_t^b|\mathbf{v}_{1:t})$ plotted below. **(c)** Smoothed flows $\langle \mathbf{h}_t|\mathbf{v}_{1:T}\rangle$ and corresponding smoothed switch states $p(s_t|\mathbf{v}_{1:T})$ using a Gaussian sum smoothing approximation (EC with $J = 1$). See plate section for colour version.

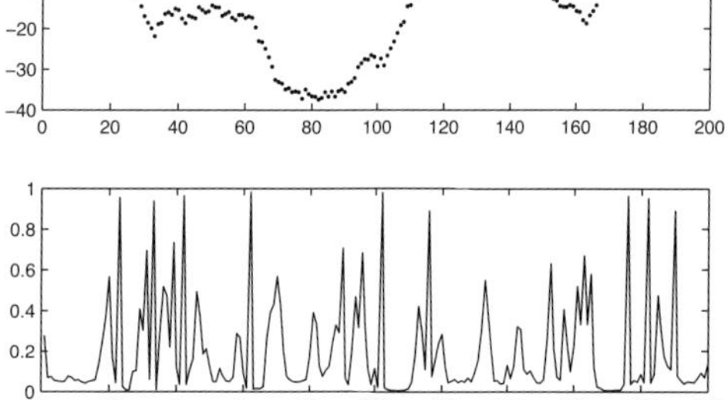

Figure 25.7 The top panel is a timeseries of 'prices'. The prices tend to keep going up or down with infrequent changes in the direction. Based on fitting a simple SLDS model to capture this kind of behaviour, the probability of a significant change in the price direction is given in the panel below based on the smoothed distribution $p(s_t = 2|v_{1:T})$.

Example 25.2 Following the price trend

The following is a simple model of the price trend of a stock, which assumes that the price tends to continue going up (or down) for a while before it reverses direction:

$$h_{1,t} = h_{1,t-1} + h_{2,t-1} + \eta_1^h(s_t) \tag{25.4.30}$$

$$h_2(t) = \mathbb{I}[s_t = 1]\, h_{2,t-1} + \eta_2^h(s_t) \tag{25.4.31}$$

$$v_t = h_{1,t} + \eta^v(s_t) \tag{25.4.32}$$

here h_1 represents the 'clean' price and h_2 the direction. There is only a single observation variable at each time, which is the clean price plus a small amount of noise. There are two switch states, $\text{dom}(s_t) = \{1, 2\}$. When $s_t = 1$, the model functions normally, with the direction being equal to the previous direction plus a small amount of noise $\eta_2^h(s_t = 1)$. When $s_t = 2$ however, the direction is sampled from a Gaussian with a large variance. The transition $p(s_t|s_{t-1})$ is set so that normal dynamics is more likely, and when $s_t = 2$ it is likely to go back to normal dynamics the next timestep. Full details are in `SLDSpricemodel.mat`. In Fig. 25.7 we plot some samples from the model and also smoothed inference of the switch distribution, showing how we can analyse the series to infer the points of likely change in the stock price direction. See also Exercise 25.1.

25.5 Reset models

Reset models are special switching models in which the switch state isolates the present from the past, resetting the position of the latent dynamics (these are also known as changepoint models). Whilst these models are rather general, it can be helpful to consider a specific model, and here we consider the SLDS changepoint model with two states. We use the state $s_t = 0$ to denote that the LDS continues with the standard dynamics. With $s_t = 1$, however, the continuous dynamics is reset to a prior:

$$p(\mathbf{h}_t|\mathbf{h}_{t-1}, s_t) = \begin{cases} p^0(\mathbf{h}_t|\mathbf{h}_{t-1}) & s_t = 0 \\ p^1(\mathbf{h}_t) & s_t = 1 \end{cases} \tag{25.5.1}$$

where

$$p^0(\mathbf{h}_t|\mathbf{h}_{t-1}) = \mathcal{N}\left(\mathbf{h}_t|\mathbf{A}\mathbf{h}_{t-1} + \boldsymbol{\mu}^0, \boldsymbol{\Sigma}^0\right), \qquad p^1(\mathbf{h}_t) = \mathcal{N}\left(\mathbf{h}_t|\boldsymbol{\mu}^1, \boldsymbol{\Sigma}^1\right). \tag{25.5.2}$$

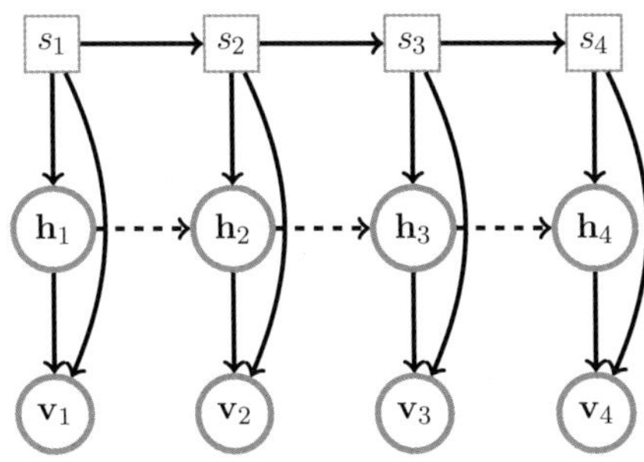

Figure 25.8 The independence structure of a reset model. Square nodes s_t denote the binary reset variables and $\mathbf{h}_t$ the continuous state. The $\mathbf{h}_t$ are continuous variables, and $\mathbf{v}_t$ continuous observations. If the dynamics resets, $s_t = 1$, the dependence of the continuous $\mathbf{h}_t$ on the past is cut.

Similarly we write

$$p(\mathbf{v}_t|\mathbf{h}_t, s_t) = \begin{cases} p^0(\mathbf{v}_t|\mathbf{h}_t) & s_t = 0 \\ p^1(\mathbf{v}_t|\mathbf{h}_t) & s_t = 1. \end{cases} \tag{25.5.3}$$

For simplicity we assume the switch dynamics are first-order Markov with transition $p(s_t|s_{t-1})$, see Fig. 25.8. Under this model the dynamics follows a standard LDS, but when $s_t = 1$, $\mathbf{h}_t$ is reset to a value drawn from a Gaussian distribution, independent of the past. Such models are of interest in prediction where the timeseries is following a trend but suddenly changes and the past is forgotten. Whilst this may not seem like a big change to the model, this model is computationally more tractable, exact filtered inference scaling with $O\left(T^2\right)$, compared to $O\left(T2^T\right)$ in the general two-state SLDS. To see this, consider the filtering recursion

$$\alpha(\mathbf{h}_t, s_t) \propto \int_{\mathbf{h}_{t-1}} \sum_{s_{t-1}} p(\mathbf{v}_t|\mathbf{h}_t, s_t) p(\mathbf{h}_t|\mathbf{h}_{t-1}, s_t) p(s_t|s_{t-1}) \alpha(\mathbf{h}_{t-1}, s_{t-1}). \tag{25.5.4}$$

We now consider the two cases

$$\alpha(\mathbf{h}_t, s_t = 0) \propto \int_{\mathbf{h}_{t-1}} \sum_{s_{t-1}} p^0(\mathbf{v}_t|\mathbf{h}_t) p^0(\mathbf{h}_t|\mathbf{h}_{t-1}) p(s_t = 0|s_{t-1}) \alpha(\mathbf{h}_{t-1}, s_{t-1}) \tag{25.5.5}$$

$$\begin{aligned} \alpha(\mathbf{h}_t, s_t = 1) &\propto p^1(\mathbf{v}_t|\mathbf{h}_t) p^1(\mathbf{h}_t) \int_{\mathbf{h}_{t-1}} \sum_{s_{t-1}} p(s_t = 1|s_{t-1}) \alpha(\mathbf{h}_{t-1}, s_{t-1}) \\ &\propto p^1(\mathbf{v}_t|\mathbf{h}_t) p^1(\mathbf{h}_t) \sum_{s_{t-1}} p(s_t = 1|s_{t-1}) \alpha(s_{t-1}). \end{aligned} \tag{25.5.6}$$

Equation (25.5.6) shows that $p(\mathbf{h}_t, s_t = 1|\mathbf{v}_{1:t})$ is not a mixture model in $\mathbf{h}_t$, but contains only a single component proportional to $p^1(\mathbf{v}_t|\mathbf{h}_t)p^1(\mathbf{h}_t)$. If we use this information in Equation (25.5.5) we have

$$\begin{aligned} \alpha(\mathbf{h}_t, s_t = 0) \propto & \int_{\mathbf{h}_{t-1}} p^0(\mathbf{v}_t|\mathbf{h}_t) p^0(\mathbf{h}_t|\mathbf{h}_{t-1}) p(s_t = 0|s_{t-1} = 0) \alpha(\mathbf{h}_{t-1}, s_{t-1} = 0) \\ & + \int_{\mathbf{h}_{t-1}} p^0(\mathbf{v}_t|\mathbf{h}_t) p^0(\mathbf{h}_t|\mathbf{h}_{t-1}) p(s_t = 0|s_{t-1} = 1) \alpha(\mathbf{h}_{t-1}, s_{t-1} = 1). \end{aligned} \tag{25.5.7}$$

Assuming $\alpha(\mathbf{h}_{t-1}, s_{t-1} = 0)$ is a mixture distribution with K components, then $\alpha(\mathbf{h}_t, s_t = 0)$ will be a mixture with $K + 1$ components. In general, therefore, $\alpha(\mathbf{h}_t, s_t = 0)$ will contain T components and $\alpha(\mathbf{h}_t, s_t = 1)$ a single component. As opposed to the full SLDS case, the number of components therefore grows only linearly with time, as opposed to exponentially. This means that the computational effort to perform exact filtering scales as $O\left(T^2\right)$. Smoothing can be achieved using the $\alpha - \beta$ approach, see Exercise 25.3. Despite this reduction in complexity over the SLDS, for long timeseries

$T \gg 1$, filtering and smoothing for these reset models can still be computationally expensive. See [51] for approximations based on retaining only a limited number of mixture components, reducing the complexity to linear in T.

Run-length formalism

One may also describe reset models using a 'run-length' formalism defining at each time t a latent variable r_t which describes the length of the current segment [3]. If there is a change, the run-length variable is reset to zero, otherwise it is increased by 1:

$$p(r_t|r_{t-1}) = \begin{cases} P_{cp} & r_t = 0 \\ 1 - P_{cp} & r_t = r_{t-1} + 1 \end{cases} \tag{25.5.8}$$

where P_{cp} is the probability of a reset (or 'changepoint'). The joint distribution is given by

$$p(v_{1:T}, r_{1:T}) = \prod_t p(r_t|r_{t-1})p(v_t|v_{1:t-1}, r_t), \qquad p(v_t|v_{1:t-1}, r_t) = p(v_t|v_{t-r_t:t-1}) \tag{25.5.9}$$

with the understanding that if $r_t = 0$ then $p(v_t|v_{t-r_t:t-1}) = p(v_t)$. The graphical model of this distribution is awkward to draw since the number of links depends on the run-length r_t. Predictions can be made using

$$p(v_{t+1}|v_{1:t}) = \sum_{r_t} p(v_{t+1}|v_{t-r_t:t})p(r_t|v_{1:t}) \tag{25.5.10}$$

where the filtered 'run-length' $p(r_t|v_{1:t})$ is given by the forward recursion:

$$\begin{aligned} p(r_t, v_{1:t}) &= \sum_{r_{t-1}} p(r_t, r_{t-1}, v_{1:t-1}, v_t) = \sum_{r_{t-1}} p(r_t, v_t|r_{t-1}, v_{1:t-1})p(r_{t-1}, v_{1:t-1}) \\ &= \sum_{r_{t-1}} p(v_t|r_t, \cancel{r_{t-1}}, v_{1:t-1})p(r_t|r_{t-1}, \cancel{v_{1:t-1}})p(r_{t-1}, v_{1:t-1}) \\ &= \sum_{r_{t-1}} p(r_t|r_{t-1})p(v_t|v_{t-r_t:t-1})p(r_{t-1}, v_{1:t-1}) \end{aligned}$$

which shows that filtered inference scales with $O\left(T^2\right)$.

25.5.1 A Poisson reset model

The changepoint structure is not limited to conditionally Gaussian cases only. To illustrate this, we consider the following model:[2] At each time t, we observe a count y_t which we assume is Poisson distributed with an unknown positive intensity h. The intensity is constant, but at certain unknown times t, it jumps to a new value. The indicator variable c_t denotes whether time t is such a changepoint or not. Mathematically, the model is:

$$p(h_0) = \mathcal{G}(h_0; a_0, b_0) \tag{25.5.11}$$

$$p(c_t) = \mathcal{BE}(c_t; \pi) \tag{25.5.12}$$

$$p(h_t|h_{t-1}, c_t) = \mathbb{I}[c_t = 0]\, \delta(h_t, h_{t-1}) + \mathbb{I}[c_t = 1]\, \mathcal{G}(h_t; \nu, b) \tag{25.5.13}$$

$$p(v_t|h_t) = \mathcal{PO}(v_t; h_t). \tag{25.5.14}$$

[2] This example is due to Taylan Cemgil.

The symbols $\mathcal{G}$, $\mathcal{BE}$ and $\mathcal{PO}$ denote the Gamma, Bernoulli and the Poisson distributions respectively:

$$\mathcal{G}(h; a, b) = \exp\left((a-1)\log h - bh - \log\Gamma(a) + a\log b\right) \tag{25.5.15}$$

$$\mathcal{BE}(c; \pi) = \exp\left(c\log\pi + (1-c)\log(1-\pi)\right) \tag{25.5.16}$$

$$\mathcal{PO}(v; h) = \exp\left(v\log h - h - \log\Gamma(v+1)\right). \tag{25.5.17}$$

Given observed counts $v_{1:T}$, the task is to find the posterior probability of a change and the associated intensity levels for each region between two consecutive changepoints. Plugging the above definitions in the generic updates Equation (25.5.5) and Equation (25.5.6), we see that $\alpha(h_t, c_t = 0)$ is a Gamma potential, and that $\alpha(g_t, c_t = 1)$ is a mixture of Gamma potentials, where a Gamma potential is defined as

$$\phi(h) = e^l \mathcal{G}(h; a, b) \tag{25.5.18}$$

via the triple (a, b, l). For the corrector update step we need to calculate the product of a Poisson term with the observation model $p(v_t|h_t) = \mathcal{PO}(v_t; h_t)$. A useful property of the Poisson distribution is that, given the observation, the latent variable is Gamma distributed:

$$\mathcal{PO}(v; h) = v\log h - h - \log\Gamma(v+1) \tag{25.5.19}$$

$$= (v+1-1)\log h - h - \log\Gamma(v+1) \tag{25.5.20}$$

$$= \mathcal{G}(h; v+1, 1). \tag{25.5.21}$$

Hence, the update equation requires multiplication of two Gamma potentials. A nice property of the Gamma density is that the product of two Gamma densities is also a Gamma potential:

$$(a_1, b_1, l_1) \times (a_2, b_2, l_2) = (a_1 + a_2 - 1, b_1 + b_2, l_1 + l_2 + g(a_1, b_1, a_2, b_2)) \tag{25.5.22}$$

where

$$g(a_1, b_1, a_2, b_2) \equiv \log\frac{\Gamma(a_1 + a_2 - 1)}{\Gamma(a_1)\Gamma(a_2)} + \log(b_1 + b_2) + a_1\log(b_1/(b_1 + b_2)) + a_2\log(b_2/(b_1 + b_2)). \tag{25.5.23}$$

The α recursions for this reset model are therefore closed in the space of a mixture of Gamma potentials, with an additional Gamma potential in the mixture at each timestep. A similar approach can be used to form the smoothing recursions.

Example 25.3 Coal mining disasters

We illustrate the Poisson reset model on the coal mining disaster dataset [157]. The dataset consists of the number of deadly coal mining disasters in England per year over a time span of 112 years from 1851 to 1962. It is widely agreed in the statistical literature that a change in the intensity (the expected value of the number of disasters) occurs around the year 1890, after new health and safety regulations were introduced. In Fig. 25.9 we show the marginals $p(h_t|y_{1:T})$ along with the filtering density. Note that we are not constraining the number of changepoints and in principle allow any number. The smoothed density suggests a sharp decrease around $t = 1890$.

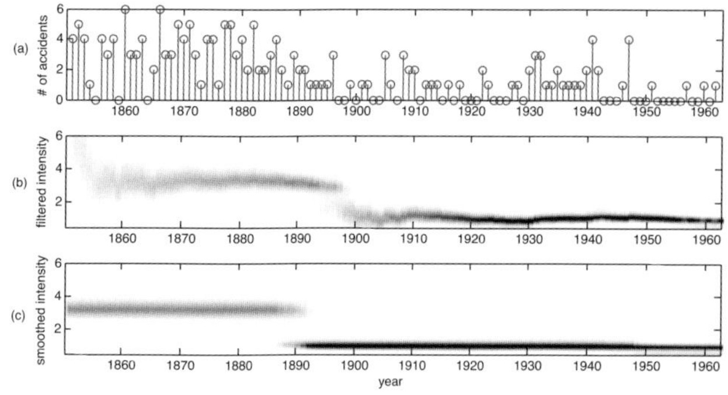

Figure 25.9 Estimation of change points. (**a**) Coal mining disaster dataset. (**b**) Filtered estimate of the marginal intensity $p(h_t|v_{1:t})$ and (**c**) smoothed estimate $p(h_t|v_{1:T})$. Here, darker shade means higher probability.

25.5.2 Reset-HMM-LDS

The reset model defined by Equations (25.5.1), (25.5.3) above is useful in many applications, but is limited since only a single dynamical model is considered. An extension is to consider a set of available dynamical models, indexed by $s_t \in \{1, \ldots, S\}$, with a reset that cuts dependency of the continuous variable on the past [100, 59]:

$$p(\mathbf{h}_t|\mathbf{h}_{t-1}, s_t, c_t) = \begin{cases} p^0(\mathbf{h}_t|\mathbf{h}_{t-1}, s_t) & c_t = 0 \\ p^1(\mathbf{h}_t|s_t) & c_t = 1. \end{cases} \tag{25.5.24}$$

The states s_t follow a Markovian dynamics $p(s_t|s_{t-1}, c_{t-1})$, see Fig. 25.10. A reset occurs if the state s_t changes, otherwise, no reset occurs:

$$p(c_t = 1|s_t, s_{t-1}) = \mathbb{I}[s_t \neq s_{t-1}]. \tag{25.5.25}$$

The computational complexity of filtering for this model is $O\left(S^2T^2\right)$ which can be understood by analogy with the reset α recursions, Equations (25.5.5)–(25.5.6) on replacing h_t by (h_t, s_t). To see

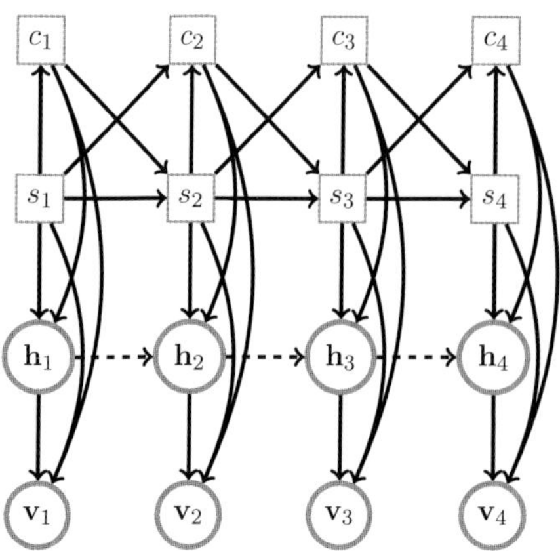

Figure 25.10 The independence structure of a reset-HMM-LDS model. Square nodes $c_t \in \{0, 1\}$ denote reset variables; $\mathbf{h}_t$ are continuous latent variables, and $\mathbf{v}_t$ continuous observations. The discrete state $s_t \in \{1, \ldots, S\}$ determines which linear dynamical system from a finite set of linear dynamical systems is operational at time t.

this we consider the filtering recursion for the two cases

$$\alpha(\mathbf{h}_t, s_t, c_t = 0) \\ = \int_{\mathbf{h}_{t-1}} \sum_{s_{t-1}, c_{t-1}} p^0(\mathbf{v}_t|\mathbf{h}_t, s_t) p^0(\mathbf{h}_t|\mathbf{h}_{t-1}, s_t) p(s_t|s_{t-1}, c_{t-1}) p(c_t = 0|s_t, s_{t-1}) \alpha(\mathbf{h}_{t-1}, c_{t-1}) \tag{25.5.26}$$

$$\alpha(\mathbf{h}_t, s_t, c_t = 1) \\ = \int_{\mathbf{h}_{t-1}} \sum_{s_{t-1}, c_{t-1}} p^1(\mathbf{v}_t|\mathbf{h}_t, s_t) p^1(\mathbf{h}_t|s_t) p(s_t|s_{t-1}, c_t) p(c_t = 1|s_t, s_{t-1}) \alpha(\mathbf{h}_{t-1}, s_{t-1}, c_{t-1}) \\ = p^1(\mathbf{v}_t|\mathbf{h}_t, s_t) p^1(\mathbf{h}_t|s_t) \sum_{s_{t-1}, c_{t-1}} p(c_t = 1|s_t, s_{t-1}) p(s_t|s_{t-1}, c_{t-1}) \alpha(s_{t-1}, c_{t-1}). \tag{25.5.27}$$

From Equation (25.5.27) we see that $\alpha(\mathbf{h}_t, s_t, c_t = 1)$ contains only a single component proportional to $p^1(\mathbf{v}_t|\mathbf{h}_t, s_t)p^1(\mathbf{h}_t|s_t)$. This is therefore exactly analogous to the standard reset model, except that we need now to index a set of messages with s_t, therefore each message taking $O(S)$ steps to compute. The computational effort to perform exact filtering scales as $O\left(S^2T^2\right)$.

25.6 Summary

- The switching linear dynamical system is a marriage of a discrete state HMM with the continuous latent state linear dynamical system. It is able to model discrete jumps in an underlying continuous process, finding application in a large variety of domains from finance to speech processing.
- The classical inference problems in the SLDS are formally intractable since representing the messages requires an exponential amount of space.
- Many approximation methods have been developed for the SLDS and in this chapter we described a robust deterministic method based on a mixture of Gaussians representation.
- Reset models are such that the continuous variable forgets the past when reset. Unlike the SLDS such models are much more amenable to exact inference. Extensions include the reset-HMM which allows for a set of discrete and continuous states in which a special discrete state resets the continuous states.

25.7 Code

`SLDSforward.m`: SLDS forward
`SLDSbackward.m`: SLDS backward (Expectation Correction)
`mix2mix.m`: Collapse a mixture of Gaussians to a smaller mixture of Gaussians
`SLDSmargGauss.m`: Marginalise an SLDS Gaussian mixture
`logeps.m`: Logarithm with offset to deal with log(0)
`demoSLDStraffic.m`: Demo of traffic flow using a switching linear dynamical system

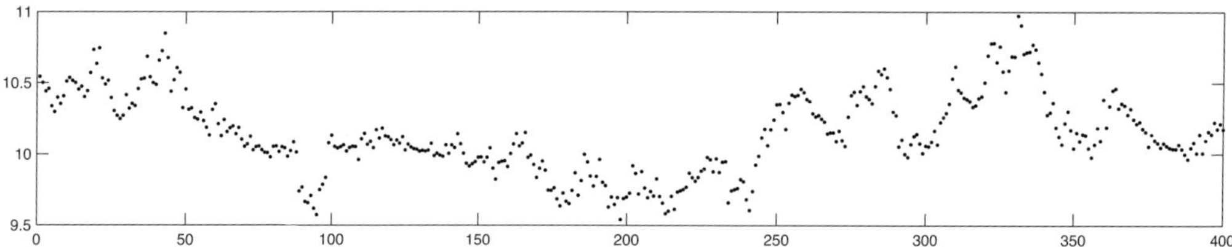

Figure 25.11 Data from an intermittent mean-reverting process. See Exercise 25.2.

25.8 Exercises

25.1 Consider the setup described in Example 25.2, for which the full SLDS model is given in `SLDSprice-model.mat`, following the notation used in `demoSLDStraffic.m`. Given the data in the vector `v` your task is to fit a prediction model to the data. To do so, approximate the filtered distribution $p(h_t, s_t|v_{1:t})$ using a mixture of $I = 2$ components. The prediction of the mean price at the next day is then

$$v_{t+1}^{pred} = \langle h_{1,t} + h_{2,t} \rangle_{p(h_t|v_{1:t})} \tag{25.8.1}$$

where $p(h_t|v_{1:t}) = \sum_{s_t} p(h_t, s_t|v_{1:t})$.

1. Compute the mean prediction error
`mean_abs_pred_error=mean(abs(vpred(2:end)-v(2:end)))`
2. Compute the mean naive prediction error
`mean_abs_pred_error_naive=mean(abs(v(1:end-1)-v(2:end)))`
which corresponds to saying that tomorrow's price will be the same as today's.

Hint: you might find `SLDSmargGauss.m` of interest.

25.2 The data in Fig. 25.11 are observed prices from an intermittent mean-reverting process, contained in `meanrev.mat`. There are two states $S = 2$. There is a true (latent) price p_t and an observed price v_t (which is plotted). When $s = 1$, the true underlying price reverts back towards the mean $m = 10$ with rate $r = 0.9$. Otherwise the true price follows a random walk:

$$p_t = \begin{cases} r(p_{t-1} - m) + m + \eta_t^p & s_t = 1 \\ p_{t-1} + \eta_t^p & s_t = 2 \end{cases} \tag{25.8.2}$$

where

$$\eta_t^p \sim \begin{cases} \mathcal{N}\left(\eta_t^p|0, 0.0001\right) & s_t = 1 \\ \mathcal{N}\left(\eta_t^p|0, 0.01\right) & s_t = 2. \end{cases} \tag{25.8.3}$$

The observed price v_t is related to the unknown price p_t by

$$v_t \sim \mathcal{N}\left(v_t|p_t, 0.001\right). \tag{25.8.4}$$

It is known that 95 per cent of the time s_{t+1} is in the same state as at time $t > 1$ and that at time $t = 1$ either state of s_1 is equally likely. Also at $t = 1$, $p_1 \sim \mathcal{N}\left(p_1|m, 0.1\right)$. Based on this information, and using Gaussian sum filtering with $I = 2$ components (use `SLDSforward.m`), what is the probability at time $t = 280$ that the dynamics is following a random walk, $p(s_{280} = 2|v_{1:280})$? Repeat this computation for smoothing $p(s_{280} = 2|v_{1:400})$ based on using expectation correction with $I = J = 2$ components.

25.3 We here derive a smoothing recursion based on the $\alpha - \beta$ approach for the reset-LDS described in Section 25.5. Smoothing can be achieved using

$$p(\mathbf{h}_t, s_t|\mathbf{v}_{1:T}) \propto \underbrace{p(\mathbf{h}_t, s_t|\mathbf{v}_{1:t})}_{\alpha(\mathbf{h}_t,s_t)} \underbrace{p(\mathbf{v}_{t+1:T}|\mathbf{h}_t, s_t)}_{\beta(\mathbf{h}_t,s_t)}. \tag{25.8.5}$$

From the formal β recursion, we have

$$\beta(\mathbf{h}_{t-1}, s_{t-1}) = \sum_{s_t} \int_{\mathbf{h}_t} p(\mathbf{v}_t|\mathbf{h}_t, s_t) p(\mathbf{h}_t|\mathbf{h}_{t-1}, s_t) p(s_t|s_{t-1}) \beta(\mathbf{h}_t, s_t). \tag{25.8.6}$$

1. Show that the right-hand side of Equation (25.8.6) can be written as

$$\underbrace{p(s_t = 0|s_{t-1}) \int_{\mathbf{h}_t} p^0(\mathbf{v}_t|\mathbf{h}_t) p^0(\mathbf{h}_t|\mathbf{h}_{t-1}) \beta(\mathbf{h}_t, s_t = 0)}_{\beta^0(\mathbf{h}_{t-1}, s_{t-1})} + \underbrace{p(s_t = 1|s_{t-1}) \int_{\mathbf{h}_t} p^1(\mathbf{v}_t|\mathbf{h}_t) p^1(\mathbf{h}_t) \beta(\mathbf{h}_t, s_t = 1)}_{\beta^1(s_{t-1})}. \tag{25.8.7}$$

2. Writing

$$\beta(\mathbf{h}_t, s_t) = \beta^0(\mathbf{h}_t, s_t) + \beta^1(s_t) \tag{25.8.8}$$

derive then the recursions

$$\beta^0(\mathbf{h}_{t-1}, s_{t-1}) = p(s_t = 0|s_{t-1}) \int_{\mathbf{h}_t} p^0(\mathbf{v}_t|\mathbf{h}_t) p^0(\mathbf{h}_t|\mathbf{h}_{t-1}) \left[\beta^0(\mathbf{h}_t, s_t = 0) + \beta^1(s_t = 0)\right] \tag{25.8.9}$$

and

$$\beta^1(s_{t-1}) = p(s_t = 1|s_{t-1}) \int_{\mathbf{h}_t} p^1(\mathbf{v}_t|\mathbf{h}_t) p^1(\mathbf{h}_t) \left[\beta^0(\mathbf{h}_t, s_t = 1) + \beta^1(s_t = 1)\right]. \tag{25.8.10}$$

The β^1 contribution is simply a scalar, so that its complexity of representation is fixed. According to the above β^0 recursion, we include an additional component in the representation of β^0 with each timestep that we go backwards in time. Thus the number of components to represent $\beta^0(\mathbf{h}_t, s_t)$ will be $O(T - t)$, since at time T, we may define $\beta(h_T, s_t) = 1$. This means that the term $p(\mathbf{h}_t, s_t, \mathbf{v}_{1:T}) = \alpha(\mathbf{h}_t, s_t)\beta(\mathbf{h}_t, s_t)$ will contain $O(t(T - t))$ components. To form a complete smoothing pass over all time therefore takes $O(T^3)$ time.

26 Distributed computation

In this chapter we discuss from a probabilistic perspective models that are loosely based on a crude understanding of neural systems in biology. This is a fascinating area and we show how patterns can be stored and recalled by reference to our standard tools from learning probabilistic models. We also discuss a general model that enables us to consider non-linear latent continuous dynamics whilst retaining computational tractability.

26.1 Introduction

How natural organisms process information is a fascinating subject and one of the grand challenges of science. Whilst this subject is still in its early stages, loosely speaking, there are some generic properties that most such systems are believed to possess: patterns are stored in a set of neurons; recall of patterns is robust to noise; neural activity is essentially binary; information processing is distributed and highly modular. In this chapter we discuss some of the classical toy models that have been developed as a test bed for analysing such properties [65, 80, 68, 144].

26.2 Stochastic Hopfield networks

Hopfield networks are models of biological memory in which a pattern is represented by the activity of a set of V interconnected neurons. The term 'network' here refers to the set of neurons, see Fig. 26.1, and not the belief network representation of distribution of neural states unrolled through time, Fig. 26.2. At time t neuron i fires $v_i(t) = +1$ or is quiescent $v_i(t) = -1$ (not firing) depending on the states of the neurons at the preceding time $t-1$. Explicitly, neuron i fires depending on the potential

$$a_i(t) \equiv b_i + \sum_{j=1}^{V} w_{ij} v_j(t) \tag{26.2.1}$$

where w_{ij} characterises the efficacy with which neuron j transmits a binary signal to neuron i. The bias b_i relates to the neuron's predisposition to firing. Writing the state of the network at time t as $\mathbf{v}(t) \equiv (v_1(t), \ldots, v_V(t))^{\mathsf{T}}$, the probability that neuron i fires at time $t+1$ is modelled as

$$p(v_i(t+1) = 1|\mathbf{v}(t)) = \sigma_\beta\left(a_i(t)\right) \tag{26.2.2}$$

where $\sigma_\beta(x) = 1/(1+e^{-\beta x})$ and β controls the level of stochastic behaviour of the neuron. The probability of being in the quiescent state is given by normalisation

$$p(v_i(t+1) = -1|\mathbf{v}(t)) = 1 - p(v_i(t+1) = 1|\mathbf{v}(t)) = 1 - \sigma_\beta\left(a_i(t)\right). \tag{26.2.3}$$

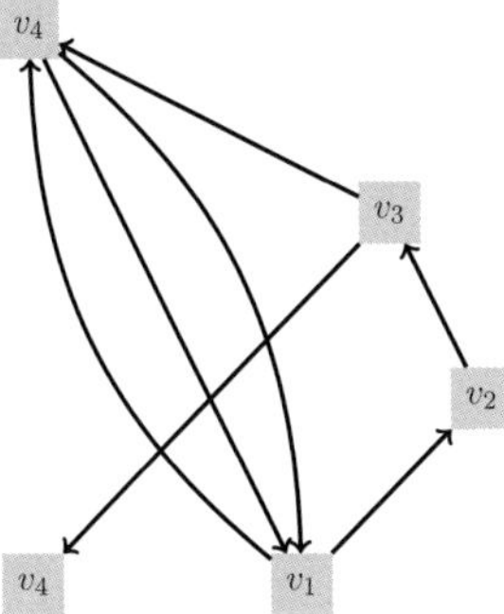

Figure 26.1 A depiction of a Hopfield network (for five neurons). The connectivity of the neurons is described by a weight matrix with elements w_{ij}. The graph represents a snapshot of the state of all neurons at time t which simultaneously update as functions of the network at the previous time $t-1$.

These two rules can be compactly written as

$$p(v_i(t+1)|\mathbf{v}(t)) = \sigma_\beta\left(v_i(t+1)a_i(t)\right) \tag{26.2.4}$$

which follows directly from $1-\sigma_\beta(x) = \sigma_\beta(-x)$. In the limit $\beta \to \infty$, the neuron updates deterministically

$$v_i(t+1) = \text{sgn}\left(a_i(t)\right). \tag{26.2.5}$$

In a synchronous Hopfield network all neurons update independently and simultaneously, and we can represent the temporal evolution of the neurons as a dynamic belief network, Fig. 26.2

$$p(\mathbf{v}(t+1)|\mathbf{v}(t)) = \prod_{i=1}^{V} p(v_i(t+1)|\mathbf{v}(t)). \tag{26.2.6}$$

Given this description of how neurons update, we wish to use the network to do interesting things, for example to store pattern sequences and recall them under some cue. The patterns will be stored in the weights and biases and in the following section we address how to learn suitable settings based on simple local learning rules.

26.3 Learning sequences

26.3.1 A single sequence

Given a sequence of network states, $\mathcal{V} = \{\mathbf{v}(1), \ldots, \mathbf{v}(T)\}$, we would like the network to store this sequence such that it can be later recalled under some cue. That is, if the network is initialised in the

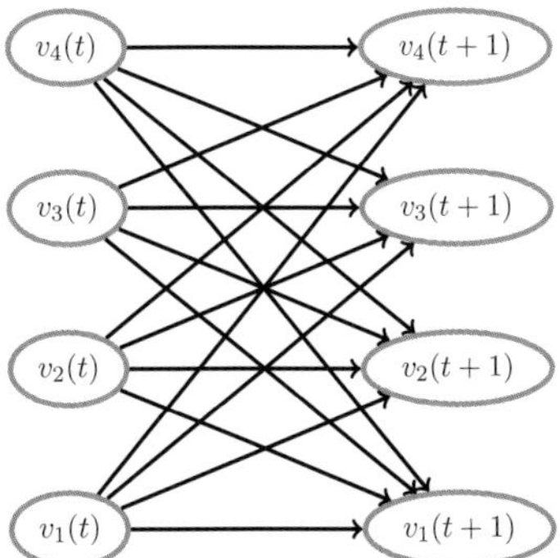

Figure 26.2 A dynamic belief network representation of a Hopfield network. The network operates by simultaneously generating a new set of neuron states from the previous set. Equation (26.2.6) defines a Markov transition matrix, modelling the transition probability $\mathbf{v}(t) \to \mathbf{v}(t+1)$ and furthermore imposes the constraint that the neurons are conditionally independent given the previous state of the network.

correct starting state of the training sequence $\mathbf{v}(t = 1)$, the remainder of the training sequence for $t > 1$ should be reproduced under the deterministic dynamics equation (26.2.5), without error. Two classical approaches to learning a temporal sequence are the *Hebb* and *Pseudo Inverse* (*PI*) rules [144]. In both the standard Hebb and PI cases, the biases b_i are usually set to zero.

Standard Hebb rule

The standard Hebb rule sets the weights according to[1]

$$w_{ij} = \frac{1}{V}\sum_{t=1}^{T-1} v_i(t+1)v_j(t). \tag{26.3.1}$$

The Hebb rule can be motivated mathematically by considering

$$\sum_j w_{ij}v_j(t) = \frac{1}{V}\sum_{\tau=1}^{T-1} v_i(\tau+1)\sum_j v_j(\tau)v_j(t) \tag{26.3.2}$$

$$= \frac{1}{V}v_i(t+1)\sum_j v_j^2(t) + \frac{1}{V}\sum_{\tau\neq t}^{T-1} v_i(\tau+1)\sum_j v_j(\tau)v_j(t) \tag{26.3.3}$$

$$= v_i(t+1) + \frac{1}{V}\sum_{\tau\neq t}^{T-1} v_i(\tau+1)\sum_j v_j(\tau)v_j(t). \tag{26.3.4}$$

If the patterns are uncorrelated then the 'interference' term

$$\Omega \equiv \frac{1}{V}\sum_{\tau\neq t}^{T-1} v_i(\tau+1)\sum_j v_j(\tau)v_j(t) \tag{26.3.5}$$

will be relatively small. To see this, we first note that for uniform randomly drawn patterns, the mean of Ω is zero, since the patterns are randomly ± 1. The variance is therefore given by

$$\langle\Omega^2\rangle = \frac{1}{V^2}\sum_{\tau,\tau'\neq t}^{T-1}\sum_{j,k}\langle v_i(\tau+1)v_i(\tau'+1)v_j(\tau)v_j(t)v_k(\tau')v_k(t)\rangle. \tag{26.3.6}$$

For $j \neq k$, all the terms are independent and contribute zero on average. Therefore

$$\langle\Omega^2\rangle = \frac{1}{V^2}\sum_{\tau,\tau'=1}^{T-1}\sum_j\left\langle v_i(\tau+1)v_i(\tau'+1)v_j(\tau)v_j(\tau')v_j^2(t)\right\rangle. \tag{26.3.7}$$

When $\tau \neq \tau'$ all the terms are independent zero mean and contribute zero. Hence

$$\langle\Omega^2\rangle = \frac{1}{V^2}\sum_{\tau\neq t}\sum_j\left\langle v_i^2(\tau+1)v_j^2(\tau)v_j^2(t)\right\rangle = \frac{T-1}{V}. \tag{26.3.8}$$

[1] Donald Hebb, a neurobiologist actually stated [139]

> Let us assume that the persistence or repetition of a reverberatory activity (or 'trace') tends to induce lasting cellular changes that add to its stability. . . When an axon of cell A is near enough to excite a cell B and repeatedly or persistently takes part in firing it, some growth process or metabolic change takes place in one or both cells such that A's efficiency, as one of the cells firing B, is increased.

This statement is sometimes misinterpreted to mean that weights are exclusively of the correlation form Equation (26.3.1) (see [286] for a discussion). This can severely limit the performance and introduce adverse storage artifacts including local minima [144].

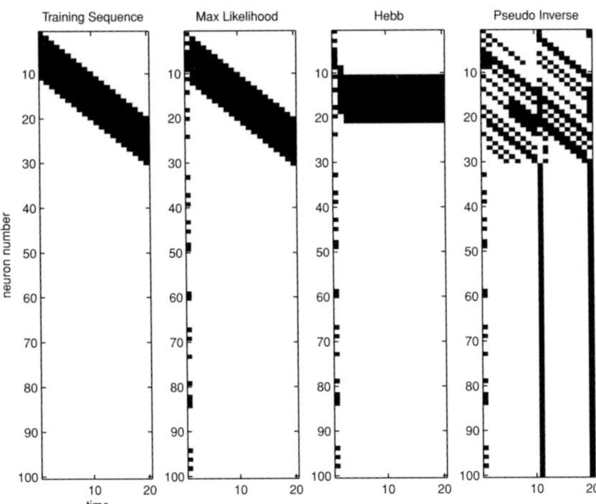

Figure 26.3 Leftmost panel: The highly correlated training sequence we desire to store. The other panels show the temporal evolution of the network after initialisation in the correct starting state but corrupted with 30 per cent noise. During recall, deterministic updates $\beta = \infty$ were used. The maximum likelihood rule was trained using 10 batch epochs with $\eta = 0.1$. See also `demoHopfield.m`.

Provided that the number of neurons V is significantly larger than the length of the sequence, T, the average size of the interference will therefore be small. In this case the term $v_i(t+1)$ in Equation (26.3.4) dominates, meaning that the sign of $\sum_j w_{ij} v_j(t)$ will be that of $v_i(t+1)$, and the correct pattern sequence recalled. A careful analysis beyond our scope shows that the Hebb rule is capable of storing a random (uncorrelated) temporal sequence of length $0.269V$ timesteps [91]. However, the Hebb rule performs poorly for the case of correlated patterns since interference from the other patterns becomes significant [144, 68].

Pseudo inverse rule

The PI rule finds a matrix $[\mathbf{W}]_{ij} = w_{ij}$ that solves the linear equations

$$\sum_j w_{ij} v_j(t) = v_i(t+1), \qquad t = 1, \ldots, T-1. \tag{26.3.9}$$

Under this condition $\text{sgn}\left(\sum_j w_{ij} v_j(t)\right) = \text{sgn}\left(v_i(t+1)\right) = v_i(t+1)$ so that patterns will be correctly recalled. In matrix notation we require

$$\mathbf{W}\mathbf{V} = \hat{\mathbf{V}} \tag{26.3.10}$$

where

$$[\mathbf{V}]_{it} = v_i(t), \quad t = 1, \ldots, T-1, \qquad [\hat{\mathbf{V}}]_{it} = v_i(t+1), \quad t = 2, \ldots, T. \tag{26.3.11}$$

For $T < V$ the problem is under-determined so that multiple solutions exist. One solution is given by the pseudo inverse:

$$\mathbf{W} = \hat{\mathbf{V}} \left(\mathbf{V}^{\mathsf{T}}\mathbf{V}\right)^{-1} \mathbf{V}^{\mathsf{T}}. \tag{26.3.12}$$

The pseudo inverse rule can store any sequence of V linearly independent patterns. Whilst attractive compared to the standard Hebb rule in terms of its ability to store longer correlated sequences, this rule suffers from very small basins of attraction for temporally correlated patterns, see Fig. 26.3.

The maximum likelihood Hebb rule

An alternative to the above classical algorithms is to view this as a problem of pattern storage in the DBN, Equation (26.2.6) [19]. First, we need to clarify what we mean by 'store'. Given that we initialise the network in a state $\mathbf{v}(t = 1)$, we wish that the remaining sequence will be generated with high probability. That is, we wish to adjust the network parameters such that the probability

$$p(\mathbf{v}(T), \mathbf{v}(T-1), \ldots, \mathbf{v}(2)|\mathbf{v}(1)) \tag{26.3.13}$$

is maximal.[2] Furthermore, we might hope that the sequence will be recalled with high probability not just when initialised in the correct state but also for states close (in Hamming distance) to the correct initial state $\mathbf{v}(1)$.

Due to the Markov nature of the dynamics, the conditional likelihood is

$$p(\mathbf{v}(T), \mathbf{v}(T-1), \ldots, \mathbf{v}(2)|\mathbf{v}(1)) = \prod_{t=1}^{T-1} p(\mathbf{v}(t+1)|\mathbf{v}(t)). \tag{26.3.14}$$

This is a product of transitions from given states to given states. Since these transition probabilities are known, Equation (26.2.6) and Equation (26.2.2), the conditional likelihood can be easily evaluated. The sequence log (conditional) likelihood is

$$L(\mathbf{w}, b) \equiv \log \prod_{t=1}^{T-1} p(\mathbf{v}(t+1)|\mathbf{v}(t)) = \sum_{t=1}^{T-1} \log p(\mathbf{v}(t+1)|\mathbf{v}(t)) = \sum_{t=1}^{T-1}\sum_{i=1}^{V} \log \sigma_\beta\left(v_i(t+1)a_i(t)\right). \tag{26.3.15}$$

Our task is then to find weights $\mathbf{w}$ and biases b that maximise $L(\mathbf{w}, b)$. There is no closed form solution and the parameters need to be determined numerically. Nevertheless, this corresponds to a straightforward computational problem since the log likelihood is a convex function. To show this, we compute the Hessian (neglecting b for expositional clarity):

$$\frac{d^2 L}{dw_{ij}dw_{kl}} = -\beta^2 \sum_{t=1}^{T-1} v_i(t+1)v_j(t)\gamma_i(t)(1-\gamma_i(t))v_k(t+1)v_l(t)\delta_{ik} \tag{26.3.16}$$

where we defined

$$\gamma_i(t) \equiv 1 - \sigma_\beta\left(v_i(t+1)a_i(t)\right). \tag{26.3.17}$$

It is straightforward to show that the Hessian is negative semidefinite (see Exercise 26.4) and hence the likelihood has a single global maximum. To increase the likelihood of the sequence, we can use a simple method such as gradient ascent[3]

$$w_{ij}^{new} = w_{ij} + \eta \frac{dL}{dw_{ij}}, \qquad b_i^{new} = b_i + \eta \frac{dL}{db_i} \tag{26.3.18}$$

where

$$\frac{dL}{dw_{ij}} = \beta \sum_{t=1}^{T-1} \gamma_i(t) v_i(t+1) v_j(t), \qquad \frac{dL}{db_i} = \beta \sum_{t=1}^{T-1} \gamma_i(t) v_i(t+1). \tag{26.3.19}$$

[2] Static patterns can also be considered in this framework as a set of patterns that map to each other.

[3] Naturally, one can use more sophisticated methods such as the Newton method, or conjugate gradients. In theoretical neurobiology the emphasis is on gradient-style updates since these are deemed to be biologically more plausible.

The learning rate η is chosen empirically to be sufficiently small to ensure convergence. The maximum likelihood learning rule, Equation (26.3.19), can be seen as a modified Hebb learning rule, the basic Hebb rule being given when $\gamma_i(t) \equiv 1$. As learning progresses, the factors $\gamma_i(t)$ will typically tend to values close to either 1 or 0, and hence the learning rule can be seen as asymptotically equivalent to making an update only in the case of disagreement ($a_i(t)$ and $v_i(t+1)$ are of different signs). This batch training procedure can be readily converted to an online process in which an update occurs immediately after the presentation of two consecutive patterns.

Storage capacity of the ML Hebb rule

The ML Hebb rule is capable of storing a sequence of V linearly independent patterns. To see this, we first form an input–output training set for each neuron i, $\{(\mathbf{v}(t), v_i(t+1)), t = 1, \ldots, T-1\}$. Each neuron has an associated weight vector $\mathbf{w}^i \equiv w_{ij}, j = 1, \ldots, V$, which forms a logistic regressor or, in the limit $\beta = \infty$, a perceptron [144]. For perfect recall of the patterns, we therefore need only that the vectors constituting the pattern sequence be linearly separable. This will be the case if the patterns are linearly independent, regardless of the outputs $v_i(t+1), t = 1, \ldots, T-1$, see Section 17.4.1.

Relation to the perceptron rule

In the limit that the activation is large, $|a_i| \gg 1$

$$\gamma_i(t) \approx \begin{cases} 1 & v_i(t+1)a_i < 0 \\ 0 & v_i(t+1)a_i \geq 0. \end{cases} \tag{26.3.20}$$

Provided the activation and desired next output are the same sign, no update is made for neuron i. In this limit, Equation (26.3.19) is called the perceptron rule [144, 85]. For an activation a that is close to the decision boundary, a small change can lead to a different sign of the neural firing. To guard against this it is common to include a stability criterion

$$\gamma_i(t) = \begin{cases} 1 & v_i(t+1)a_i < M \\ 0 & v_i(t+1)a_i \geq M \end{cases} \tag{26.3.21}$$

where M is an empirically chosen positive threshold.

Example 26.1 Storing a correlated sequence

In Fig. 26.3 we consider storage of a temporal sequence of length $T = 20$ of 100 neurons using the three learning rules: Hebb, maximum likelihood and pseudo inverse. The sequence is highly correlated and therefore represents a difficult learning task. The biases b_i are set to zero throughout to facilitate comparison. The initial state of the training sequence, corrupted by 30 per cent noise is presented to the trained networks, and we desire that the remaining training sequence will be recalled from this initial noisy state. Whilst the Hebb rule is operating in a feasible limit for uncorrelated patterns, the strong correlations in this training sequence give rise to poor results. The PI rule is capable of storing a sequence of length 100 yet is not robust to perturbations from the correct initial state. The maximum likelihood rule performs well after a small amount of training.

Stochastic interpretation

By straightforward manipulations, the weight update rule in Equation (26.3.19) can be written as

$$\frac{dL}{dw_{ij}} = \sum_{t=1}^{T-1} \frac{1}{2} \left(v_i(t+1) - \langle v_i(t+1) \rangle_{p(v_i(t+1)|a_i(t))} \right) v_j(t). \tag{26.3.22}$$

A stochastic, online learning rule is therefore

$$\Delta w_{ij}(t) = \eta \left(v_i(t+1) - \tilde{v}_i(t+1) \right) v_j(t) \tag{26.3.23}$$

where $\tilde{v}_i(t+1)$ is sampled in state 1 with probability $\sigma_\beta(a_i(t))$, and -1 otherwise. Provided that the learning rate η is small, this stochastic updating will approximate the learning rule (26.3.18)–(26.3.19).

Example 26.2 Recalling sequences under perpetual noise

We consider 50 neurons storing a $T = 50$ length sequence (with zero biases thresholds θ) and compare the performance of the maximum likelihood learning rule with the Hebb, pseudo inverse, and perceptron rule. The training sequences are produced by starting from a random initial state, $\mathbf{v}(1)$, and then choosing at random 20 per cent of the neurons to flip, each of the chosen neurons being flipped with probability 0.5, giving a random training sequence with a high degree of temporal correlation.

After training, the network is initialised to a noise-corrupted version of the correct initial state $\mathbf{v}(t = 1)$ from the training sequence. The dynamics is then run (at $\beta = \infty$) for the same number of steps as the length of the training sequence. The fraction of bits of the recalled final state which are the same as the training sequence final state $\mathbf{v}(T)$ is then measured, Fig. 26.4. At each stage in the dynamics (except the last), the state of the network is corrupted with noise by flipping each neuron state with the specified flip probability.

The standard Hebb rule performs relatively poorly, particularly for small flip rates, whilst the other methods perform relatively well, being robust at small flip rates. As the flip rate increases, the pseudo inverse rule becomes unstable, especially for the longer temporal sequence which places more demands on the network. The perceptron rule can perform as well as the maximum likelihood rule, although its performance is critically dependent on an appropriate choice of the threshold M. The results for $M = 0$ perceptron training are poor for small flip rates. An advantage of the maximum likelihood rule is that it performs well without the need for fine tuning of parameters.

A similar example for a larger network is given in Fig. 26.5 which consists of highly correlated sequences. The weights are learned using the maximum likelihood procedure. For such short sequences the basin of attraction is very large and the video sequence can be stored robustly.

26.3.2 Multiple sequences

We now address learning a set of sequences $\{\mathcal{V}^n, n = 1, \ldots, N\}$. If we assume that the sequences are independent, the log likelihood of a set of sequences is the sum of the individual sequences. The gradient is given by

$$\frac{dL}{dw_{ij}} = \beta \sum_{n=1}^{N} \sum_{t=1}^{T-1} \gamma_i^n(t) v_i^n(t+1) v_j^n(t), \quad \frac{dL}{db_i} = \beta \sum_{n=1}^{N} \sum_{t=1}^{T-1} \gamma_i^n(t) v_i^n(t+1) \tag{26.3.24}$$

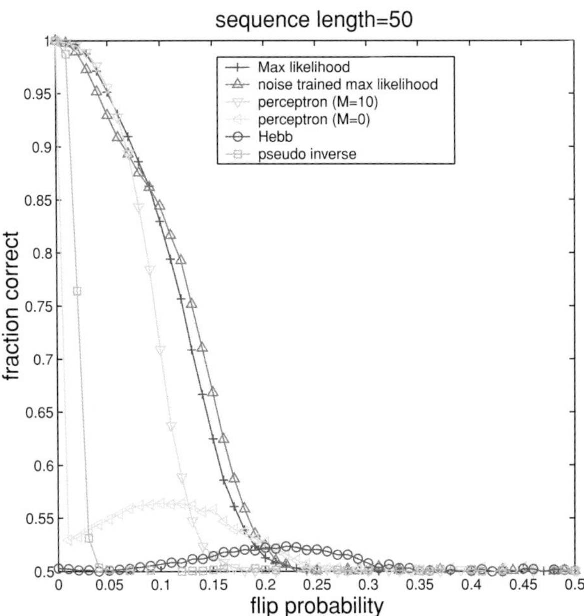

Figure 26.4 The fraction of neurons correct for the final state of the network $T = 50$ for a 100 neuron Hopfield network trained to store a length 50 sequence of patterns. After initialisation in the correct initial state at $t = 1$, the Hopfield network is updated deterministically, with a randomly chosen percentage of the neurons flipped after updating. The correlated sequence of length $T = 50$ was produced by flipping with probability 0.5, 20 per cent of the previous state of the network. A fraction correct value of 1 indicates perfect recall of the final state, and a value of 0.5 indicates a performance no better than random guessing of the final state. For maximum likelihood 50 epochs of training were used with $\eta = 0.02$. During recall, deterministic updates $\beta = \infty$ were used. The results presented are averages over 5000 simulations, resulting in standard errors of the order of the symbol sizes. See plate section for colour version.

where

$$\gamma_i^n(t) \equiv 1 - \sigma_\beta\left(v_i^n(t+1)a_i^n(t)\right), \quad a_i^n(t) = b_i + \sum_j w_{ij}v_j^n(t). \tag{26.3.25}$$

The log likelihood remains convex since it is a sum of convex functions, so that the standard gradient-based learning algorithms can be used successfully here as well.

26.3.3 Boolean networks

The Hopfield network is one particular parameterisation of the table $p(v_i(t+1) = 1|\mathbf{v}(t))$. However, less constrained parameters may be considered. In the fully unconstrained case each neuron i has an associated 2^V parental states. However, to specify this exponentially large number of states

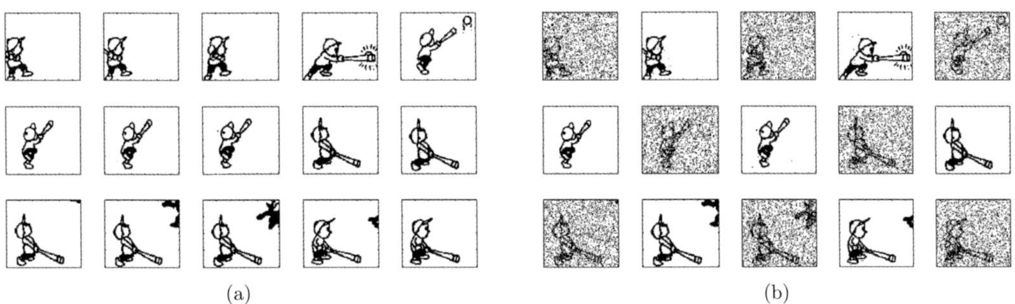

Figure 26.5 (**a**) Original $T = 15$ binary video sequence on a set of $81 \times 111 = 8991$ neurons. (**b**) The reconstructions beginning from a 20 per cent noise perturbed initial state. Every odd time reconstruction is also randomly perturbed. Despite the high level of noise the basin of attraction of the pattern sequence is very broad and the patterns immediately fall back close to the pattern sequence even after a single timestep.

is impractical and an interesting restriction is to consider that each neuron has only K parents, so that each table contains 2^K entries. Learning the table parameters by maximum likelihood is straightforward since the log likelihood is a convex function of the table entries. Hence, for any given sequence (or set of sequences) one may readily find parameters that maximise the sequence reconstruction probability. The maximum likelihood method also produces large basins of attraction for the associated stochastic dynamical system. Such models are of interest in *Artificial Life* and *Random Boolean networks* in which emergent macroscopic behaviour appears from local update rules. Such systems are also used to study the robustness of chemical and gene regulatory networks [171].

26.3.4 Sequence disambiguation

A limitation of time-independent first-order networks defined on visible variables alone (such as the Hopfield network) is that the observation transition $p(\mathbf{v}_{t+1}|\mathbf{v}_t = \mathsf{v})$ is the same every time the joint state v is encountered. This means that if the sequence contains a subsequence such as $\mathsf{a}, \mathsf{b}, \mathsf{a}, \mathsf{c}$ this cannot be recalled with high probability since a joint state a transitions to different states at different times. Whilst one could attempt to resolve this sequence disambiguation problem using a higher-order Markov model to account for a longer temporal context, or by using a time-dependent model, we would lose biological plausibility. Using latent variables is an alternative way to sequence disambiguation. In the Hopfield model the recall capacity can be increased using latent variables by making a sequence in the joint latent-visible space that is linearly independent, even if the visible variable sequence alone is not. In Section 26.4 we discuss a general method that extends dynamic belief networks defined on visible variables alone, such as the Hopfield network, to include non-linearly updating latent variables.

26.4 Tractable continuous latent variable models

A dynamic belief network with hidden (latent) variables h and visible variables (observations) v takes the form

$$p(v(1:T), h(1:T)) = p(v(1))p(h(1)|v(1)) \prod_{t=1}^{T-1} p(v(t+1)|v(t), h(t))p(h(t+1)|v(t), v(t+1), h(t)). \quad (26.4.1)$$

As we saw in Chapter 23, provided all hidden variables are discrete, inference in these models is straightforward. However, in many physical systems it is more natural to assume continuous $h(t)$. In Chapter 24 we saw that one such tractable continuous $h(t)$ model is given by linear Gaussian transitions and emissions – the LDS. Whilst this is useful, we cannot represent non-linear changes in the latent process using an LDS alone. The switching LDS of Chapter 25 is able to model non-linear continuous dynamics (via switching) although we saw that this leads to computational difficulties. For computational reasons we therefore seem limited to either purely discrete h (with no limitation on the discrete transitions) or purely continuous h (but be forced to use simple linear dynamics). Is there a way to have a continuous state with non-linear dynamics for which posterior inference remains tractable? The answer is yes, provided that we assume the hidden transitions are deterministic [13]. When conditioned on the visible variables, this renders the hidden unit distribution trivial. This allows the consideration of rich non-linear dynamics in the hidden space. Note that such models are

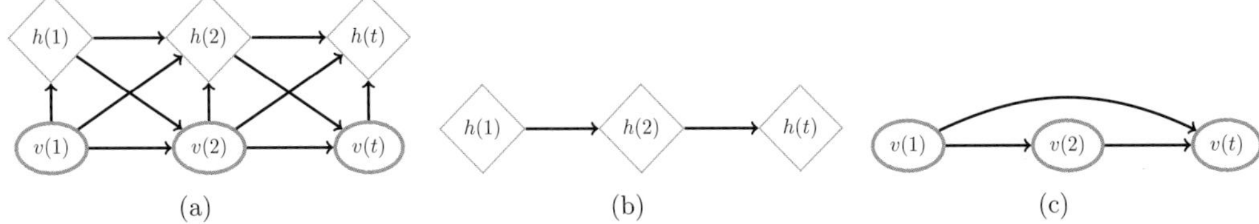

Figure 26.6 (**a**) A first-order dynamic belief network with deterministic hidden transitions (represented by diamonds) that is, each hidden node is certainly in a single state, determined by its parents. (**b**) Conditioning on the visible variables forms a directed chain in the hidden space which is deterministic. Hidden unit inference can be achieved by forward propagation alone. (**c**) Integrating out hidden variables gives a cascade style directed visible graph so that each $v(t)$ depends on all $v(1:t-1)$.

limited to the distributed computation context of this chapter; for example the ARCH and GARCH models of Chapter 24 are special cases.

26.4.1 Deterministic latent variables

Consider a belief network defined on a sequence of visible variables $v(1:T)$. To enrich the model we include additional continuous latent variables $h(1:T)$ that follow a non-linear Markov transition. To retain tractability of inference, we constrain the latent dynamics to be deterministic, described by

$$p(h(t+1)|v(t+1), v(t), h(t)) = \delta\left(h(t+1) - f\left(v(t+1), v(t), h(t), \theta_h\right)\right). \tag{26.4.2}$$

The (possibly non-linear) function f parameterises the conditional probability table. Whilst the restriction to deterministic transitions appears severe, the model retains some attractive features: The marginal $p(v(1:T))$ is non-Markovian, coupling all the variables in the sequence, see Fig. 26.6(c), whilst hidden unit inference $p(h(1:T)|v(1:T))$ is deterministic. See also Fig. 26.6.

The adjustable parameters of the hidden and visible distributions are represented by θ_h and θ_v respectively. For learning, the log likelihood of a single training sequence $v(1:T)$ is

$$L = \log p(v(1)|\theta_v) + \sum_{t=1}^{T-1} \log p(v(t+1)|v(t), h(t), \theta_v) \tag{26.4.3}$$

where the hidden unit values are calculated recursively using

$$h(t+1) = f\left(v(t+1), v(t), h(t), \theta_h\right). \tag{26.4.4}$$

To maximise the log likelihood using gradient techniques we need the derivatives with respect to the model parameters. These can be calculated recursively as follows:

$$\frac{dL}{d\theta_v} = \frac{\partial}{\partial\theta_v}\log p(v(1)|\theta_v) + \sum_{t=1}^{T-1}\frac{\partial}{\partial\theta_v}\log p(v(t+1)|v(t), h(t), \theta_v) \tag{26.4.5}$$

$$\frac{dL}{d\theta_h} = \sum_{t=1}^{T-1}\frac{\partial}{\partial h(t)}\log p(v(t+1)|v(t), h(t), \theta_v)\frac{dh(t)}{d\theta_h} \tag{26.4.6}$$

$$\frac{dh(t)}{d\theta_h} = \frac{\partial f(t)}{\partial\theta_h} + \frac{\partial f(t)}{\partial h(t-1)}\frac{dh(t-1)}{d\theta_h} \tag{26.4.7}$$

where we use the shorthand

$$f(t) \equiv f(v(t), v(t-1), h(t-1), \theta_h). \tag{26.4.8}$$

Hence the derivatives can be calculated by deterministic forward propagation. The case of training multiple independently generated sequences is a straightforward extension obtained by summing the above over the individual sequences.

Whilst the deterministic latent variable models are very general, in the context of this chapter it is interesting to apply them to some simple neurobiological models, enriching the Hopfield model with more powerful internal dynamics.

26.4.2 An augmented Hopfield network

To make the deterministic latent variable model more explicit, we consider the case of continuous vector hidden variables $\mathbf{h}(t)$ and discrete, binary vector visible variables with components $v_i(t) \in \{-1, 1\}$. In particular, we restrict attention to the Hopfield model augmented with latent variables that have a simple linear dynamics (see Exercise 26.5 for a non-linear extension):

$$\mathbf{h}(t+1) = 2\sigma(\mathbf{A}\mathbf{h}(t) + \mathbf{B}\mathbf{v}(t)) - \mathbf{1} \quad \text{deterministic latent transition} \tag{26.4.9}$$

$$p(\mathbf{v}(t+1)|\mathbf{v}(t), \mathbf{h}(t)) = \prod_{i=1}^{V} \sigma\left(v_i(t+1)\phi_i(t)\right), \quad \boldsymbol{\phi}(t) \equiv \mathbf{C}\mathbf{h}(t) + \mathbf{D}\mathbf{v}(t). \tag{26.4.10}$$

This model generalises a recurrent stochastic heteroassociative Hopfield network [144] to include deterministic hidden units dependent on previous network states. The parameters of the model are $\mathbf{A}, \mathbf{B}, \mathbf{C}, \mathbf{D}$. For gradient-based training we require the derivatives with respect to each of these parameters. The derivative of the log likelihood for a generic parameter θ is

$$\frac{d}{d\theta}L = \sum_i \nu_i(t)\frac{d}{d\theta}\phi_i(t), \quad \nu_i(t) \equiv \left(1 - \sigma(v_i(t+1)\phi_i(t))\right) v_i(t+1). \tag{26.4.11}$$

This gives:

$$\frac{d}{dA_{\alpha\beta}}\phi_i(t) = \sum_j C_{ij}\frac{d}{dA_{\alpha\beta}}h_j(t), \quad \frac{d}{dB_{\alpha\beta}}\phi_i(t) = \sum_j C_{ij}\frac{d}{dB_{\alpha\beta}}h_j(t) \tag{26.4.12}$$

$$\frac{d}{dC_{\alpha\beta}}\phi_i(t) = \delta_{i\alpha}h_\beta(t), \quad \frac{d}{dD_{\alpha\beta}}\phi_i(t) = \delta_{i\alpha}v_\beta(t) \tag{26.4.13}$$

$$\frac{d}{dA_{\alpha\beta}}h_i(t+1) = 2\sigma_i'(t+1)\sum_j A_{ij}\frac{d}{dA_{\alpha\beta}}h_j(t) + \delta_{i\alpha}h_\beta(t) \tag{26.4.14}$$

$$\frac{d}{dB_{\alpha\beta}}h_i(t+1) = 2\sigma_i'(t+1)\sum_j A_{ij}\frac{d}{dB_{\alpha\beta}}h_j(t) + \delta_{i\alpha}v_\beta(t) \tag{26.4.15}$$

$$\sigma_i'(t) \equiv \sigma(h_i(t))\left(1 - \sigma(h_i(t))\right). \tag{26.4.16}$$

If we assume that $\mathbf{h}(1)$ is a given fixed value (say $\mathbf{0}$), we can compute the derivatives recursively by forward propagation. Gradient-based training for this augmented Hopfield network is therefore straightforward to implement. This model extends the power of the original Hopfield model, being capable of resolving ambiguous transitions in sequences such as a, b, a, c, see Example 26.3. In terms of a dynamic system, the learned network is an attractor with the training sequence as a stable point

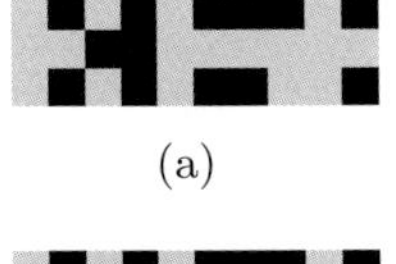

(a)

(b)

Figure 26.7 (**a**) The training sequence consists of a random set of vectors ($V = 3$) over $T = 10$ timesteps. (**b**) The reconstruction using $H = 7$ hidden units. The initial state $\mathbf{v}(t = 1)$ for the recalled sequence was set to the correct initial training value albeit with one of the values flipped. Note that the method is capable of sequence disambiguation in the sense that transitions of the form a, b, . . . , a, c can be recalled.

and demonstrates that such models are capable of learning attractor networks more powerful than those without hidden units.

Example 26.3 Sequence disambiguation

The sequence in Fig. 26.7(a) contains repeated patterns and therefore cannot be reliably recalled with a first-order model containing visible variables alone. To deal with this we consider a Hopfield network with three visible units and seven additional hidden units with deterministic (linear) latent dynamics. The model was trained with gradient ascent to maximise the likelihood of the binary sequence in Fig. 26.7(a). See `demoHopfieldLatent.m`. As shown in Fig. 26.7(b), the learned network is capable of recalling the sequence correctly, even when initialised in an incorrect state, having no difficulty with the fact that the sequence transitions are ambiguous.

26.5 Neural models

The tractable deterministic latent variable model introduced in Section 26.4 presents an opportunity to extend models such as the Hopfield network to include more biologically realistic processes without losing computational tractability. First we discuss a general framework for learning in a class of neural models [14, 240], this being a special case of the deterministic latent variable models [13] and a generalisation of the spike-response model of theoretical neurobiology [118].

26.5.1 Stochastically spiking neurons

We assume that neuron i fires depending on the membrane potential $a_i(t)$ through

$$p(v_i(t+1) = 1|\mathbf{v}(t), \mathbf{h}(t)) = p(v_i(t+1) = 1|a_i(t)). \tag{26.5.1}$$

To be specific, we take throughout

$$p(v_i(t+1) = 1|a_i(t)) = \sigma(a_i(t)). \tag{26.5.2}$$

Here we define the quiescent state as $v_i(t+1) = 0$, so that

$$p(v_i(t+1)|a_i(t)) = \sigma((2v_i(t+1) - 1)a_i(t)). \tag{26.5.3}$$

The use of the sigmoid function $\sigma(x)$ is not fundamental and is chosen merely for analytical convenience. The log likelihood of a sequence of visible states $\mathcal{V} = \{\mathbf{v}(1), \dots, \mathbf{v}(T)\}$ is

$$L = \sum_{t=1}^{T-1} \sum_{i=1}^{V} \log \sigma((2v_i(t+1) - 1)a_i(t)) \tag{26.5.4}$$

for which the gradient is

$$\frac{dL}{dw_{ij}} = \sum_{t=1}^{T-1} (v_i(t+1) - \sigma(a_i(t))) \frac{da_i(t)}{dw_{ij}} \tag{26.5.5}$$

where we used the fact that $v_i \in \{0, 1\}$. Here w_{ij} are parameters of the membrane potential (see below). We take Equation (26.5.5) as common in the following models in which the membrane potential $a_i(t)$ is described with increasing sophistication.

26.5.2 Hopfield membrane potential

As a first step, we show how the Hopfield maximum likelihood training rule, as described in Section 26.3.1, can be recovered as a special case of the above framework. The Hopfield membrane potential is

$$a_i(t) \equiv \sum_{j=1}^{V} w_{ij} v_j(t) - b_i \tag{26.5.6}$$

where w_{ij} characterises the efficacy of information transmission from neuron j to neuron i, and b_i is a bias. Applying the maximum likelihood framework to this model to learn a temporal sequence $\mathcal{V}$ by adjustment of the parameters w_{ij} (the b_i are fixed for simplicity), we obtain the (batch) learning rule (using $da_i/dw_{ij} = v_j(t)$ from Equation (26.5.5))

$$w_{ij}^{new} = w_{ij} + \eta \frac{dL}{dw_{ij}}, \qquad \frac{dL}{dw_{ij}} = \sum_{t=1}^{T-1} (v_i(t+1) - \sigma(a_i(t))) \, v_j(t), \tag{26.5.7}$$

where the learning rate η is chosen empirically to be sufficiently small to ensure convergence. Equation (26.5.7) matches Equation (26.3.19) (which uses the ± 1 encoding).

26.5.3 Dynamic synapses

In more realistic synaptic models, neurotransmitter generation depends on a finite rate of cell subcomponent production and the quantity of vesicles released is affected by the history of firing [1]. Loosely speaking, when a neuron fires it releases a chemical substance from a local reservoir. If the neuron fires several times in short succession, its ability to continue firing weakens since the reservoir of release chemical is depleted. This phenomenon can be modelled by using a depression mechanism that reduces the membrane potential

$$a_i(t) = w_{ij} x_j(t) v_j(t) \tag{26.5.8}$$

for depression factors $x_j(t) \in [0, 1]$. A simple dynamics for these depression factors is [299]

$$x_j(t+1) = x_j(t) + \delta t \left(\frac{1 - x_j(t)}{\tau} - U x_j(t) v_j(t) \right) \tag{26.5.9}$$

where δt, τ, and U represent time scales, recovery times and spiking effect parameters respectively. Note that these depression factor dynamics are exactly of the form of deterministic hidden variables. It is therefore straightforward to include these dynamic synapses in a principled way using the

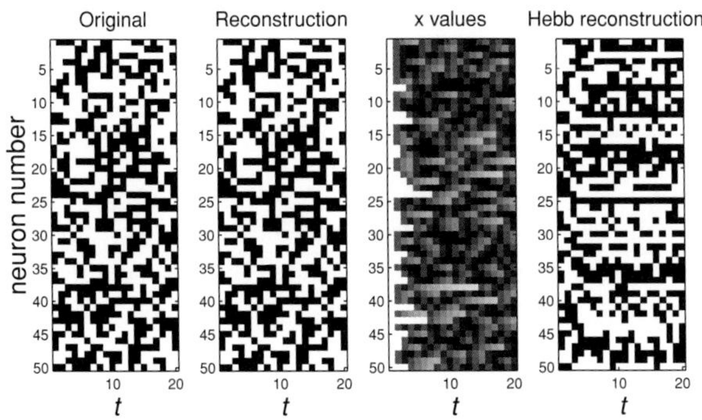

Figure 26.8 Learning with depression: $U = 0.5$, $\tau = 5$, $\delta t = 1$, $\eta = 0.25$. Despite the apparent complexity of the dynamics, learning appropriate neural connection weights is straightforward using maximum likelihood. The reconstruction using the standard Hebb rule by contrast is poor [14].

maximum likelihood learning framework. For the Hopfield potential, the learning dynamics is simply given by Equations (26.5.5), (26.5.9), with

$$\frac{da_i(t)}{dw_{ij}} = x_j(t)v_j(t). \tag{26.5.10}$$

Example 26.4 Learning with depression

In Fig. 26.8 we demonstrate learning a random temporal sequence of 20 timesteps for 50 neurons with dynamic depressive synapses. After learning w_{ij} the trained network is initialised in the first state of the training sequence. The remaining states of the sequence were then correctly recalled by forward sampling of the learned model. The corresponding generated factors $x_i(t)$ are also plotted during the reconstruction; we see the characteristic drop in x after a neuron fires with gradual recovery. For comparison, we plot the results of using the dynamics having set the w_{ij} using the temporal Hebb rule, Equation (26.3.1). The poor performance of the correlation-based Hebb rule demonstrates the necessity, in general, to tailor the learning rule to the dynamical system it attempts to control.

26.5.4 Leaky integrate and fire models

Leaky integrate and fire models move a step further towards biological realism in which the membrane potential increments if it receives an excitatory stimulus ($w_{ij} > 0$), and decrements if it receives an inhibitory stimulus ($w_{ij} < 0$). After firing, the membrane potential is reset to a low value below the firing threshold, and thereafter steadily increases to a resting level (see for example [65, 118]). A model that incorporates such effects is

$$a_i(t) = \left(\alpha a_i(t-1) + \sum_j w_{ij}v_j(t) + \theta^{rest}(1-\alpha)\right)(1 - v_i(t-1)) + v_i(t-1)\theta^{fired}. \tag{26.5.11}$$

Since $v_i \in \{0, 1\}$, if neuron i fires at time $t-1$ the potential is reset to θ^{fired} at time t. Similarly, with no synaptic input, the potential equilibrates to θ^{rest} with time constant $-1/\log\alpha$ [14].

Despite the increase in complexity of the membrane potential over the Hopfield case, deriving appropriate learning dynamics for this new system is straightforward since, as before, the hidden variables (here the membrane potentials) update in a deterministic fashion. The membrane potential derivatives are

$$\frac{da_i(t)}{dw_{ij}} = (1 - v_i(t-1))\left(\alpha \frac{da_i(t-1)}{dw_{ij}} + v_j(t)\right). \tag{26.5.12}$$

By initialising the derivative $da_i(t=1)/dw_{ij} = 0$, Equations (26.5.5), (26.5.11), (26.5.12) define a first-order recursion for the gradient which can be used to adapt w_{ij} in the usual manner $w_{ij}^{new} = w_{ij} + \eta dL/dw_{ij}$. We could also apply synaptic dynamics to this case by replacing the term $v_j(t)$ in Equation (26.5.12) by $x_j(t)v_j(t)$.

Although a detailed discussion of the properties of the neuronal responses for networks trained in this way is beyond our scope here, an interesting consequence of the learning rule Equation (26.5.12) is a spike-time dependent learning window in qualitative agreement with experimental observation in real biological systems [240, 200].

26.6 Summary

- Classical models such as the Hopfield network can be trained to learn temporal sequences using maximum likelihood. This results in a robust storage mechanism in which the patterns have a large basin of attraction.
- We can form tractable non-linear continuous latent systems provided the latent dynamics is deterministic. These deterministic latent variable models are powerful yet inference is straightforward.
- We demonstrated how complex models in neurobiology can be considered within the deterministic latent variable framework, and also how learning rules can be derived in a straightforward manner. It is important that the learning rule is derived with the particular neural dynamics in mind – otherwise undesirable effects in pattern storage can occur.

26.7 Code

`demoHopfield.m`: Demo of Hopfield sequence learning
`HebbML.m`: Gradient ascent training of a set of sequences using maximum likelihood
`HopfieldHiddenNL.m`: Hopfield network with additional non-linear latent variables
`demoHopfieldLatent.m`: Demo of Hopfield net with deterministic latent variables
`HopfieldHiddenLikNL.m`: Hopfield network with hidden variables sequence likelihood

26.8 Exercises

26.1 Consider a very large $V \gg 1$ stochastic Hopfield network, Section 26.2, used to store a single temporal sequence $\mathbf{v}(1:T)$ of length $T \ll V$. In this case the weight matrix with elements w_{ij} may be computationally difficult to store. Explain how to justify the assumption

$$w_{ij} = \sum_{t=1}^{T-1} u_i(t) v_i(t+1) v_j(t) \tag{26.8.1}$$

where $u_i(t)$ are the dual parameters and derive a maximum likelihood update rule for the dual parameters $u_i(t)$.

26.2 A Hopfield network is used to store a raw uncompressed binary video sequence. Each image in the sequence contains 10^6 binary pixels. At a rate of 10 frames per second, how many hours of video can 10^6 neurons store?

26.3 Derive the update equation (26.3.22).

26.4 Show that the Hessian equation (26.3.16) is negative semidefinite. That is

$$\sum_{i,j,k,l} x_{ij} x_{kl} \frac{d^2 L}{dw_{ij} dw_{kl}} \leq 0 \tag{26.8.2}$$

for any $x \neq 0$.

26.5 For the augmented Hopfield network of Section 26.4.2, with latent dynamics

$$h_i(t+1) = 2\sigma \left(\sum_j A_{ij} h_j(t) + B_{ij} v_j(t) \right) - 1 \tag{26.8.3}$$

derive the derivative recursions described in Section 26.4.2.

26.6 The storage of a static pattern $\mathbf{v}$ can be considered equivalent to the requirement that, under temporal dynamics, the probability $p(\mathbf{v}(t+1) = \mathbf{v} | \mathbf{v}(t) = \mathbf{v})$ is high. Based on this, estimate numerically how many such static patterns a 100 neuron stochastic Hopfield network can robustly recover when 10 per cent of the elements of a pattern are flipped.

Part V

Approximate inference

In Part I we discussed inference and showed that for certain models this is computationally tractable. However, for many models of interest, one cannot perform inference exactly and approximations are required.

In Part V we discuss approximate inference methods, beginning with sampling-based approaches. These are popular and well known in many branches of the mathematical sciences, having their origins in chemistry and physics. We also discuss alternative deterministic approximate inference methods which in some cases can have remarkably accurate performance.

It is important to bear in mind that no single algorithm is going to be best on all inference tasks. For this reason, we attempt throughout to explain the assumptions behind the techniques so that one may select an appropriate technique for the problem at hand.

27 Sampling

In cases where exact results cannot be obtained, a general purpose approach is to draw samples from the distribution. In this chapter we discuss classical exact sampling methods that are typically limited to a small number of variables or models with a high degree of structure. When these can no longer be applied, we discuss approximate sampling methods including Markov chain Monte Carlo.

27.1 Introduction

Sampling concerns drawing realisations (samples) $\mathcal{X} = \{x^1, \ldots, x^L\}$ of a variable x from a distribution $p(x)$. For a discrete variable x, in the limit of a large number of samples, the fraction of samples in state x tends to $p(x = \mathsf{x})$. That is,

$$\lim_{L\to\infty} \frac{1}{L}\sum_{l=1}^{L} \mathbb{I}\left[x^l = \mathsf{x}\right] = p(x = \mathsf{x}). \tag{27.1.1}$$

In the continuous case, one can consider a region R such that the probability that the samples occupy R tends to the integral of $p(x)$ over R. Given a finite set of samples, one can then approximate expectations using

$$\langle f(x)\rangle_{p(x)} \approx \frac{1}{L}\sum_{l=1}^{L} f(x^l) \equiv \hat{f}_{\mathcal{X}}. \tag{27.1.2}$$

The subscript in $\hat{f}_{\mathcal{X}}$ emphasises that the approximation is dependent on the set of samples drawn. This sample approximation holds for both discrete and continuous variables.

A sampling procedure produces realisations of the set $\mathcal{X}$ and can itself be considered as generating a distribution $\tilde{p}(\mathcal{X})$. Provided the marginals of the sampling distribution are equal to the marginals of the target distribution, $\tilde{p}(x^l) = p(x^l)$, then the average of the approximation $\hat{f}_{\mathcal{X}}$ with respect to draws of the sample set $\mathcal{X}$ is

$$\left\langle \hat{f}_{\mathcal{X}}\right\rangle_{\tilde{p}(\mathcal{X})} = \frac{1}{L}\sum_{l=1}^{L}\left\langle f(x^l)\right\rangle_{\tilde{p}(x^l)} = \langle f(x)\rangle_{p(x)}. \tag{27.1.3}$$

Hence the mean of the sample approximation is the exact mean of f provided only that the marginals of $\tilde{p}(\mathcal{X})$ correspond to the required marginals $p(x)$; that is, using $\tilde{p}(\mathcal{X})$ then $\hat{f}_{\mathcal{X}}$ is an unbiased estimator for $\langle f(x)\rangle_{p(x)}$. Note that this holds, even if the individual samples $x^1, \ldots, x^L$ are dependent, that is $\tilde{p}(\mathcal{X})$ does not factorise into $\prod_l \tilde{p}(x^l)$.

For any sampling method, an important issue is the variance of the sample estimate. If this is low then only a small number of samples are required since the sample mean must be close to the true mean (assuming it is unbiased). Defining

$$\Delta \hat{f}_{\mathcal{X}} = \hat{f}_{\mathcal{X}} - \left\langle \hat{f}_{\mathcal{X}} \right\rangle_{\tilde{p}(\mathcal{X})}, \qquad \Delta f(x) = f(x) - \langle f(x) \rangle_{p(x)} \tag{27.1.4}$$

the variance of the approximation is (assuming $\tilde{p}(x^l) = p(x^l)$, for all l)

$$\left\langle \left[\Delta \hat{f}_{\mathcal{X}}\right]^2 \right\rangle_{\tilde{p}(\mathcal{X})} = \frac{1}{L^2} \sum_{l,l'} \left\langle \Delta f(x^l) \Delta f(x^{l'}) \right\rangle_{\tilde{p}(x^l, x^{l'})} \tag{27.1.5}$$

$$= \frac{1}{L^2} \left(L \left\langle [\Delta f(x)]^2 \right\rangle_{\tilde{p}(x)} + \sum_{l \neq l'} \left\langle \Delta f(x^l) \Delta f(x^{l'}) \right\rangle_{\tilde{p}(x^l, x^{l'})} \right). \tag{27.1.6}$$

Provided the samples are independent

$$\tilde{p}(\mathcal{X}) = \prod_{l=1}^{L} \tilde{p}(x^l)$$

and $\tilde{p}(x) = p(x)$, then $\tilde{p}(x^l, x^{l'}) = p(x^l)p(x^{l'})$. The second term in Equation (27.1.6) above is composed of $\left\langle \Delta f(x^l) \right\rangle \left\langle \Delta f(x^{l'}) \right\rangle$ which is zero since $\langle \Delta f(x) \rangle = 0$. Hence

$$\left\langle \left[\Delta \hat{f}_{\mathcal{X}}\right]^2 \right\rangle_{\tilde{p}(\mathcal{X})} = \frac{1}{L} \left\langle [\Delta f(x)]^2 \right\rangle_{p(x)} \tag{27.1.7}$$

and the variance of the approximation scales inversely with the number of samples. In principle, therefore, provided the samples are independently drawn from $p(x)$, only a small number of samples is required to accurately estimate the expectation. Importantly, this result is independent of the dimension of x. However, the critical difficulty is in actually generating independent samples from $p(x)$. Drawing samples from high-dimensional distributions is generally difficult and few guarantees exist to ensure that in a practical timeframe the samples produced are independent. Whilst a dependent sampling scheme may be unbiased, the variance of the resulting estimate can be high such that a large number of samples may be required for expectations to be approximated accurately. There are many different sampling algorithms, all of which work in principle, but each working in practice only when the distribution satisfies particular properties [123]; for example Markov chain Monte Carlo methods do not produce independent samples and a large number of samples may be necessary to produce a satisfactory approximation. Before we develop schemes for multivariate distributions, we consider the univariate case.

27.1.1 Univariate sampling

In the following, we assume that a random number generator exists which is able to produce a value uniformly at random from the unit interval $[0, 1]$. We will make use of this uniform sampler to draw samples from non-uniform distributions.

1 ×	2	3

Figure 27.1 A representation of the discrete distribution equation (27.1.8). The unit interval from 0 to 1 is partitioned in parts whose lengths are equal to 0.6, 0.1 and 0.3.

Algorithm 27.1 Sampling from a univariate discrete distribution p with K states.

Label the K states as $i = 1, \ldots, K$, with associated probabilities p_i.

Calculate the *cumulant*

$$c_i = \sum_{j \le i} p_j$$

and set $c_0 = 0$.

Draw a value u uniformly at random from the unit interval $[0,1]$.

Find that i for which $c_{i-1} < u \le c_i$.

Return state i as a sample from p.

Discrete case

Consider the one-dimensional discrete distribution $p(x)$ where $\text{dom}(x) = \{1, 2, 3\}$, with

$$p(x) = \begin{cases} 0.6 & x = 1 \\ 0.1 & x = 2 \\ 0.3 & x = 3. \end{cases} \tag{27.1.8}$$

This represents a partitioning of the unit interval $[0, 1]$ in which the interval $[0, 0.6]$ has been labelled as state 1, $(0.6, 0.7]$ as state 2, and $(0.7, 1.0]$ as state 3, Fig. 27.1. If we were to drop a point $\times$ anywhere at random, uniformly in the interval $[0, 1]$, the chance that $\times$ would land in interval 1 is 0.6, and the chance that it would be in interval 2 is 0.1 and similarly, for interval 3, 0.3. This therefore defines a valid sampling procedure for discrete one-dimensional distributions in which we draw from a uniform distribution and then identify the partition of the unit interval in which it lies. This can easily be found using the cumulant, see Algorithm 27.1. Sampling from a discrete univariate distribution is straightforward since computing the cumulant takes only $O(K)$ steps for a K state discrete variable. In our example, we have $(c_0, c_1, c_2, c_3) = (0, 0.6, 0.7, 1)$. We then draw a sample uniformly from $[0, 1]$, say $u = 0.66$. Then the sampled state would be state 2, since this is in the interval $(c_1, c_2]$. Since the samples are independent, the number of samples required to accurately represent a marginal is reasonably small, see Fig. 27.2.

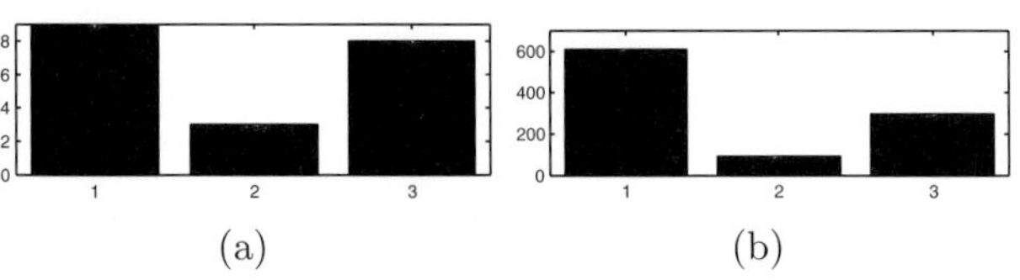

Figure 27.2 Histograms of the samples from the three-state distribution $p(x) = \{0.6, 0.1, 0.3\}$. **(a)** 20 samples. **(b)** 1000 samples. As the number of samples increases, the relative frequency of the samples tends to the distribution $p(x)$.

Algorithm 27.2 Rejection sampling to draw L independent samples from $p(x) = p^*(x)/Z$.

Given $p^*(x)$ and $q(x)$, find M such that $p^*(x)/q(x) \leq M$ for all x.
for $l = 1$ to L **do**
    repeat
        Draw a candidate sample x^{cand} from $q(x)$.
        Let $a = \frac{p^*(x^{cand})}{Mq(x^{cand})}$.
        Draw a value u uniformly between 0 and 1.
    until $u \leq a$
    $x^l = x^{cand}$ ▷ Accept the candidate
end for

Continuous case

Intuitively, the generalisation from the discrete to the continuous case is clear. First we calculate the cumulant density function

$$C(y) = \int_{-\infty}^{y} p(x)dx. \tag{27.1.9}$$

Then we sample u uniformly from $[0, 1]$, and obtain the corresponding sample x by solving $C(x) = u \Rightarrow x = C^{-1}(u)$. Formally, therefore, sampling of a continuous univariate variable is straightforward provided we can compute the integral of the corresponding probability density function.

For special distributions, however, one may avoid explicit use of the cumulant of $p(x)$ by using alternative procedures based on coordinate transformations. For the Gaussian, for example, one may avoid the use of the cumulant, see Exercise 27.1.

27.1.2 Rejection sampling

Consider that we have an efficient sampling procedure for a distribution $q(x)$. Can we use this to help us sample from another distribution $p(x)$? We assume $p(x)$ is known only up to a normalisation constant Z, $p(x) = p^*(x)/Z$. One way to sample from $p(x)$ is to use a binary auxiliary variable $y \in \{0, 1\}$ and define $q(x, y) = q(x)q(y|x)$ with

$$q(x, y = 1) = q(x)q(y = 1|x). \tag{27.1.10}$$

We can use the term $q(y = 1|x)$ to our advantage if we set $q(y = 1|x) \propto p(x)/q(x)$ since then $q(x, y = 1) \propto p(x)$ and sampling from $q(x, y)$ gives us a procedure for sampling from $p(x)$. To achieve this we assume we can find a positive M such that

$$q(y = 1|x) = \frac{p^*(x)}{Mq(x)} \leq 1 \quad \forall x. \tag{27.1.11}$$

To sample y given x we then draw a value u uniformly between 0 and 1. If this value is less then $q(y = 1|x)$, we set $y = 1$, otherwise we set $y = 0$. To draw a sample from $p(x)$ we first draw a candidate x^{cand} from $q(x)$, and then a y from $q(y|x^{cand})$. If $y = 1$ we take x^{cand} as an independent sample from $p(x)$ – otherwise no sample is made, see Algorithm 27.2. Note that the samples are drawn only proportionally to $p(x)$ – however, since this proportionality constant is common to all x, this is equivalent to drawing from $p(x)$.

The expected rate that we accept a sample is

$$q(y = 1) = \int_x q(y = 1|x)q(x) = \frac{Z}{M} \tag{27.1.12}$$

so that, to increase the acceptance rate, we seek the minimal M subject to $p^*(x) \leq Mq(x)$. In cases where $q(x)$ has free parameters $q(x|\beta)$, the parameter β can be adjusted to minimise M. If we set $q(x) = p(x)$ and $M = Z$ then $q(y = 1|x) = 1$ and sampling is efficient. In general, however, $q(y = 1|x)$ will be less than 1 and sampling less than ideally efficient. In high dimensions for vector $\mathbf{x}$, $q(y = 1|\mathbf{x})$ will often be much less than 1 so that rejection sampling can be extremely inefficient. To see this, consider a simple scenario in which the distributions $p(\mathbf{x})$ and $q(\mathbf{x})$ are factorised, $p(\mathbf{x}) = \prod_{i=1}^{D} p(x_i)$ and $q(\mathbf{x}) = \prod_{i=1}^{D} q(x_i)$. Then

$$q(y = 1|\mathbf{x}) = \prod_{i=1}^{D} \frac{p^*(x_i)}{M_i q(x_i)} = \prod_{i=1}^{D} q(y = 1|x_i) = O\left(\gamma^D\right) \tag{27.1.13}$$

where $0 \leq \gamma \leq 1$ is the typical value of $q(y = 1|x_i)$ for each dimension. Hence the probability of accepting $\mathbf{x}$ may decrease exponentially with the number of dimensions of $\mathbf{x}$. Rejection sampling is therefore a potentially useful method of drawing independent samples in very low dimensions, but is likely to be impractical in higher dimensions.

27.1.3 Multivariate sampling

One way to generalise the one-dimensional (univariate) discrete case to a higher-dimensional (multivariate) distribution $p(x_1, \ldots, x_n)$ is to translate this into an equivalent one-dimensional distribution. This can be achieved by enumerating all the possible joint states $(x_1, \ldots, x_n)$, giving each a unique integer i from 1 to the total number of states, and constructing a univariate distribution with probability $p(i)$. This then transforms the multivariate distribution into an equivalent univariate distribution, and sampling can be achieved as before. In general, of course, this procedure is impractical since the number of states grows exponentially with the number of variables $x_1, \ldots, x_n$.

An alternative exact approach, that holds for both discrete and continuous variables is to capitalise on the relation

$$p(x_1, x_2) = p(x_2|x_1)p(x_1). \tag{27.1.14}$$

We can sample from the joint distribution $p(x_1, x_2)$ by first sampling a state for x_1 from the one-dimensional $p(x_1)$, and then, with x_1 clamped to this state, sampling a state for x_2 from the one-dimensional $p(x_2|x_1)$. It is clear how to generalise this to more variables by using a cascade decomposition:

$$p(x_1, \ldots, x_n) = p(x_n|x_{n-1}, \ldots, x_1)p(x_{n-1}|x_{n-2}, \ldots, x_1) \ldots p(x_2|x_1)p(x_1). \tag{27.1.15}$$

However, in order to apply this technique, we need to know the conditionals $p(x_i|x_{i-1}, \ldots, x_1)$. Unless these are explicitly given we need to compute these from the joint distribution $p(x_1, \ldots, x_n)$. Computing such conditionals will, in general, require the summation over an exponential number of states and, except for small n, generally also be impractical. For belief networks, however, by construction the conditionals are specified so that this technique becomes practical, as we discuss in Section 27.2.

Drawing samples from a multivariate distribution is in general therefore a complex task and one seeks to exploit any structural properties of the distribution to make this computationally more feasible. A common approach is to seek to transform the distribution into a product of lower-dimensional distributions, for which the general change of variables method for continuous variables, Definition 8.1, is required. A classic example of this is sampling from a multivariate Gaussian, which can be reduced to sampling from a set of univariate Gaussians by a suitable coordinate transformation, as discussed in Example 27.1. For much of the remaining chapter we discuss methods that are appropriate for drawing from multivariate distributions when no obvious transformation exists to reduce the problem to a univariate form. Note that if there nevertheless exist transformations that result even in approximately independent variables, this can still be a very useful preprocessing step.

Example 27.1 Sampling from a multivariate Gaussian

Our interest is to draw a sample from the multivariate Gaussian $p(\mathbf{x}) = \mathcal{N}(\mathbf{x}|\mathbf{m}, \mathbf{S})$. For a general covariance matrix $\mathbf{S}$, $p(\mathbf{x})$ does not factorise into a product of univariate distributions. However, consider the transformation

$$\mathbf{y} = \mathbf{C}^{-1}(\mathbf{x} - \mathbf{m}) \tag{27.1.16}$$

where $\mathbf{C}$ is chosen so that $\mathbf{C}\mathbf{C}^{\mathsf{T}} = \mathbf{S}$. Since this is a linear transformation, $\mathbf{y}$ is also Gaussian distributed with mean

$$\langle \mathbf{y} \rangle = \left\langle \mathbf{C}^{-1}(\mathbf{x} - \mathbf{m}) \right\rangle_{p(\mathbf{x})} = \mathbf{C}^{-1}\left(\langle \mathbf{x} \rangle_{p(\mathbf{x})} - \mathbf{m} \right) = \mathbf{C}^{-1}(\mathbf{m} - \mathbf{m}) = \mathbf{0}. \tag{27.1.17}$$

Since the mean of $\mathbf{y}$ is zero, the covariance is given by

$$\left\langle \mathbf{y}\mathbf{y}^{\mathsf{T}} \right\rangle_{p(\mathbf{x})} = \mathbf{C}^{-1} \left\langle (\mathbf{x} - \mathbf{m})(\mathbf{x} - \mathbf{m})^{\mathsf{T}} \right\rangle_{p(\mathbf{x})} \mathbf{C}^{-\mathsf{T}} = \mathbf{C}^{-1}\mathbf{S}\mathbf{C}^{-\mathsf{T}} = \mathbf{C}^{-1}\mathbf{C}\mathbf{C}^{\mathsf{T}}\mathbf{C}^{-\mathsf{T}} = \mathbf{I}. \tag{27.1.18}$$

Hence

$$p(\mathbf{y}) = \mathcal{N}(\mathbf{y}|\mathbf{0}, \mathbf{I}) = \prod_i \mathcal{N}(y_i|0, 1). \tag{27.1.19}$$

A sample from $\mathbf{y}$ can then be obtained by independently drawing a sample from each of the univariate zero mean unit variance Gaussians. Given a sample for $\mathbf{y}$, a sample for $\mathbf{x}$ is obtained using

$$\mathbf{x} = \mathbf{C}\mathbf{y} + \mathbf{m}. \tag{27.1.20}$$

Drawing samples from a univariate Gaussian is a well-studied topic, with a popular method being the Box–Muller technique, Exercise 27.1.

27.2 Ancestral sampling

Belief networks take the general form:

$$p(x) = \prod_i p(x_i|\mathrm{pa}(x_i)) \tag{27.2.1}$$

where we assume that each of the conditional distributions $p(x_i|\mathrm{pa}(x_i))$ is specified. Provided that no variables are evidential, we can sample from this distribution in a straightforward manner. For convenience, we first rename the variable indices so that parent variables always come before their children (*ancestral ordering*), for example (see Fig. 27.3)

$$p(x_1, \ldots, x_6) = p(x_1)p(x_2)p(x_3|x_1, x_2)p(x_4|x_3)p(x_5|x_3)p(x_6|x_4, x_5). \tag{27.2.2}$$

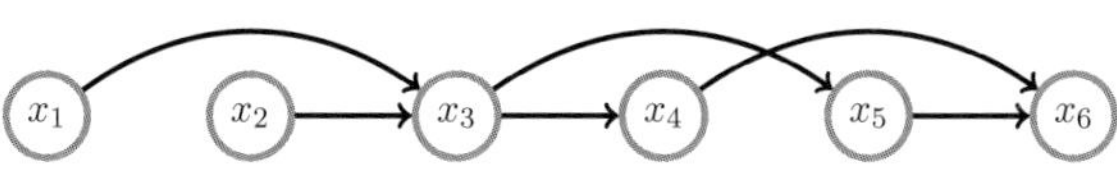

Figure 27.3 An ancestral belief network without any evidential variables. To sample from this distribution, we draw a sample from variable 1, and then variables, 2, . . . , 6 in order.

One can sample first from those nodes that do not have any parents (here, x_1 and x_2). Given these values, one can then sample x_3, and then x_4 and x_5 and finally x_6. Despite the presence of loops in the graph, such a *forward sampling* procedure is straightforward. This procedure holds for both discrete and continuous variables. If one attempted to carry out an exact marginal inference scheme in a complex multiply connected graph, the moralisation and triangulation steps can result in very large cliques, so that exact inference becomes intractable. However, regardless of the loop structure, ancestral sampling remains straightforward. Ancestral or 'forward' sampling is a case of *perfect sampling* (also termed *exact sampling*) since each sample is indeed independently drawn from the required distribution. This is in contrast to Markov chain Monte Carlo methods, Sections 27.3, 27.4, for which (dependent) samples are drawn from $p(x)$ only in the limit of a large number of iterations.

27.2.1 Dealing with evidence

How can we sample from a distribution in which a subset of variables $x_{\mathcal{E}}$ are clamped to evidential states? Writing $x = x_{\mathcal{E}} \cup x_{\backslash\mathcal{E}}$, formally we wish to sample from

$$p(x_{\backslash\mathcal{E}}|x_{\mathcal{E}}) = \frac{p(x_{\backslash\mathcal{E}}, x_{\mathcal{E}})}{p(x_{\mathcal{E}})}. \tag{27.2.3}$$

If an evidential variable x_i has no parents, then one can simply set the variable into this state and continue forward sampling as before. For example, to compute a sample from $p(x_1, x_3, x_4, x_5, x_6|x_2)$ defined in Equation (27.2.2), one simply clamps x_2 into its evidential state and continues forward sampling. The reason this is straightforward is that conditioning on x_2 merely defines a new distribution on a subset of the variables, for which the belief network representation of the distribution is immediately known and remains ancestral.

On the other hand, consider sampling from $p(x_1, x_2, x_3, x_4, x_5|x_6)$. Using Bayes' rule, we have

$$p(x_1, x_2, x_3, x_4, x_5|x_6) = \frac{p(x_1)p(x_2)p(x_3|x_1, x_2)p(x_4|x_3)p(x_5|x_3)p(x_6|x_4, x_5)}{\sum_{x_1,x_2,x_3,x_4,x_5} p(x_1)p(x_2)p(x_3|x_1, x_2)p(x_4|x_3)p(x_5|x_3)p(x_6|x_4, x_5)}. \tag{27.2.4}$$

The conditioning on x_6 means that the structure of the distribution on the non-evidential variables changes – for example x_4 and x_5 become coupled (conditioned on x_3, x_4 and x_5 are independent; however, conditioned on x_3 and x_6, x_4 and x_5 are dependent). One could attempt to work out an equivalent new forward sampling structure, see Exercise 27.3, although generally this will be as complex as running an exact inference approach.

An alternative is to proceed with forward sampling from the non-evidential distribution, and then discard any samples which do not match the evidential states, see Exercise 27.8 for an analogous situation that justifies this procedure. However, this is generally not recommended since the probability that a sample from $p(x)$ will be consistent with the evidence is roughly $O\left(1/\prod_i \dim x_i^e\right)$ where $\dim x_i^e$ is the number of states of evidential variable i. In principle one can ease this effect by discarding the sample as soon as any variable state is inconsistent with the evidence. Nevertheless, the number of re-starts required to obtain a valid sample would, on average, be very large. For this reason, alternative non-exact procedures are more common, as we discuss in Section 27.3.

27.2.2 Perfect sampling for a Markov network

For a Markov network we can draw exact samples by forming an equivalent directed representation of the graph, see Section 6.8, and subsequently using ancestral sampling on this directed graph. This is achieved by first choosing a root clique and then consistently orienting edges away from this clique. An exact sample can then be drawn from the Markov network by first sampling from the root clique and then recursively from the children of this clique. See `potsample.m`, `JTsample.m` and `demoJTreeSample.m`.

27.3 Gibbs sampling

The inefficiency of methods such as ancestral sampling under evidence motivates alternative techniques. An important and widespread technique is Gibbs sampling which is generally straightforward to implement.

No evidence

Assume we have a joint sample state x^1 from the multivariate distribution $p(x)$. We then consider a particular variable, x_i, for which we wish to draw a sample. Using conditioning we may write

$$p(x) = p(x_i|x_1, \ldots, x_{i-1}, x_{i+1}, \ldots, x_n)p(x_1, \ldots, x_{i-1}, x_{i+1}, \ldots, x_n). \tag{27.3.1}$$

Given a joint initial state x^1, from which we can read off the 'parental' state $x_1^1, \ldots, x_{i-1}^1, x_{i+1}^1, \ldots, x_n^1$, we then draw a sample x_i^2 from

$$p(x_i|x_1^1, \ldots, x_{i-1}^1, x_{i+1}^1, \ldots, x_n^1) \equiv p(x_i|x_{\setminus i}). \tag{27.3.2}$$

We assume this distribution is easy to sample from since it is univariate. We call this new joint sample (in which only x_i has been updated) $x^2 = \left(x_1^1, \ldots, x_{i-1}^1, x_i^2, x_{i+1}^1, \ldots, x_n^1\right)$. One then selects another variable x_j to sample and, by continuing this procedure, generates a set $x^1, \ldots, x^L$ of samples in which each x^{l+1} differs from x^l in only a single component. Clearly, this is not an exact sampler since the resulting samples are highly dependent. Whilst Gibbs sampling is therefore generally straightforward to implement, a drawback is that the samples are strongly dependent. Nevertheless, as discussed in Section 27.1, provided the marginal of the sampling distribution is correct, then this is still a valid sampler. We outline in Section 27.3.1 why in the limit of a large number of samples, this holds and the sampler becomes valid.

For a general distribution, the conditional $p(x_i|x_{\setminus i})$ depends only on the *Markov blanket* of the variable x_i. For a belief network, the Markov blanket of x_i is

$$p(x_i|x_{\setminus i}) = \frac{1}{Z}p(x_i|\text{pa}\,(x_i)) \prod_{j\in\text{ch}(i)} p(x_j|\text{pa}\,(x_j)) \tag{27.3.3}$$

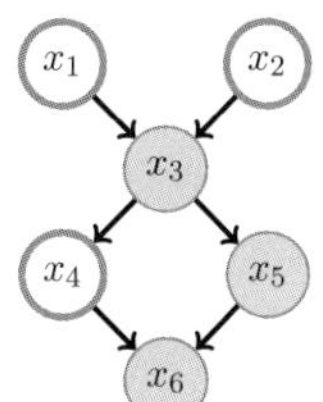

Figure 27.4 The shaded nodes are the Markov blanket of x_4 for the belief network of Fig. 27.3. To draw a sample from $p(x_4|x_{\setminus 4})$ we clamp x_3, x_5, x_6 into their evidential states and draw a sample from $p(x_4|x_3)p(x_6|x_4, x_5)/Z$ where Z is a normalisation constant.

see for example, Fig. 27.4. The normalisation constant for this univariate distribution is straightforward to work out from the requirement:

$$Z = \sum_{x_i} p(x_i|\text{pa}(x_i)) \prod_{j \in \text{ch}(i)} p(x_j|\text{pa}(x_j)). \tag{27.3.4}$$

In the case of a continuous variable x_i the summation above is replaced with integration. Due to the local structure of a belief network, only the parental and parents-of-children states are required in forming the sample update.

Evidence

Evidence is readily dealt with by clamping for all samples the evidential variables into their evidential states. There is also no need to sample for these variables, since their states are known. One then proceeds as before, selecting a non-evidential variable and determining its distribution conditioned on its Markov blanket, and subsequently drawing a sample from this variable.

27.3.1 Gibbs sampling as a Markov chain

In Gibbs sampling we have a sample of the joint variables x^l at stage l. Based on this we produce a new joint sample x^{l+1}. This means that we can write Gibbs sampling as a procedure that draws from

$$x^{l+1} \sim q(x^{l+1}|x^l) \tag{27.3.5}$$

for some distribution $q(x^{l+1}|x^l)$. If we choose the variable to update, x_i, at random from a distribution $q(i)$, then Gibbs sampling corresponds to drawing samples using the Markov transition

$$q(x^{l+1}|x^l) = \sum_i q(x^{l+1}|x^l, i)q(i), \quad q(x^{l+1}|x^l, i) = p(x_i^{l+1}|x_{\setminus i}^l) \prod_{j \neq i} \delta\left(x_j^{l+1}, x_j^l\right) \tag{27.3.6}$$

with $q(i) > 0$, $\sum_i q(i) = 1$. That is, we select a variable, then sample from its conditional, copying across the states of the other variables from the previous sample. Our interest is to show that the stationary distribution of $q(x'|x)$ is $p(x)$. We carry this out assuming x is continuous – the discrete

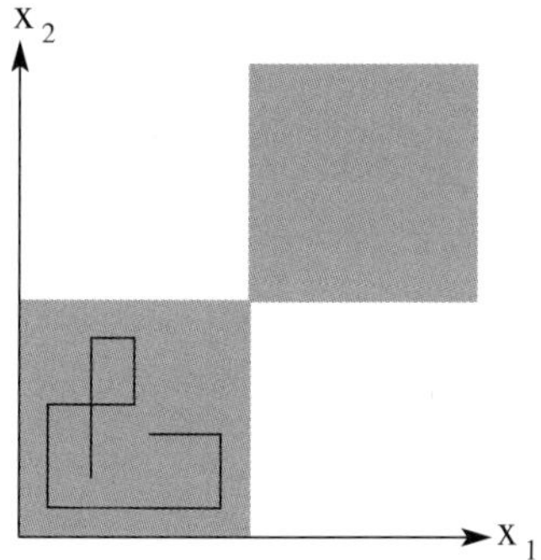

Figure 27.5 A two-dimensional distribution for which Gibbs sampling fails. The distribution has mass only in the shaded quadrants. Gibbs sampling proceeds from the lth sample state (x_1^l, x_2^l) and then sampling from $p(x_2|x_1^l)$, which we write (x_1^{l+1}, x_2^{l+1}) where $x_1^{l+1} = x_1^l$. One then continues with a sample from $p(x_1|x_2 = x_2^{l+1})$, etc. If we start in the lower left quadrant and proceed this way, the upper right region is never explored.

case is analogous:

$$\int_x q(x'|x)p(x) = \sum_i q(i) \int_x q(x'|x_{\setminus i})p(x) \tag{27.3.7}$$

$$= \sum_i q(i) \int_x \prod_{j \neq i} \delta\left(x'_j, x_j\right) p(x'_i|x_{\setminus i})p(x_i, x_{\setminus i}) \tag{27.3.8}$$

$$= \sum_i q(i) \int_{x_i} p(x'_i|x'_{\setminus i})p(x_i, x'_{\setminus i}) \tag{27.3.9}$$

$$= \sum_i q(i)p(x'_i|x'_{\setminus i})p(x'_{\setminus i}) = \sum_i q(i)p(x') = p(x'). \tag{27.3.10}$$

Hence, as long as we continue to draw samples according to the distribution $q(x'|x)$, in the limit of a large number of samples we will ultimately tend to draw (dependent) samples from $p(x)$. Any distribution $q(i)$ suffices so that visiting all variables equally often is a valid choice. Technically, we also require that $q(x'|x)$ has $p(x)$ as its equilibrium distribution, so that no matter in which state we start, we always converge to $p(x)$; see Fig. 27.5 and Section 27.3.3 for a discussion of this issue.

27.3.2 Structured Gibbs sampling

One can extend Gibbs sampling by using conditioning to reveal a tractable distribution on the remaining variables. For example, consider the distribution, Fig. 27.6(a)

$$p(x_1, x_2, x_3, x_4) = \phi(x_1, x_2)\phi(x_2, x_3)\phi(x_3, x_4)\phi(x_4, x_1)\phi(x_1, x_3). \tag{27.3.11}$$

In single-site Gibbs sampling we would condition on three of the four variables, and sample from the remaining variable. For example, using x to emphasise known states,

$$p(x_1|\mathrm{x}_2, \mathrm{x}_3, \mathrm{x}_4) \propto \phi(x_1, \mathrm{x}_2)\phi(\mathrm{x}_4, x_1)\phi(x_1, \mathrm{x}_3). \tag{27.3.12}$$

However, we may use more limited conditioning as long as the conditioned distribution is easy to sample from. In the case of Equation (27.3.11) we can condition on x_3 alone to give

$$p(x_1, x_2, x_4|\mathrm{x}_3) \propto \phi(x_1, x_2)\phi(x_2, \mathrm{x}_3)\phi(\mathrm{x}_3, x_4)\phi(x_4, x_1)\phi(x_1, \mathrm{x}_3). \tag{27.3.13}$$

This can be written as a modified distribution, Fig. 27.6(b)

$$p(x_1, x_2, x_4|\mathrm{x}_3) \propto \phi'(x_1, x_2)\phi'(x_4, x_1). \tag{27.3.14}$$

As a distribution on x_1, x_2, x_4 this is a singly connected linear chain Markov network from which samples can be drawn exactly, as explained in Section 27.2.2. A simple approach is to compute

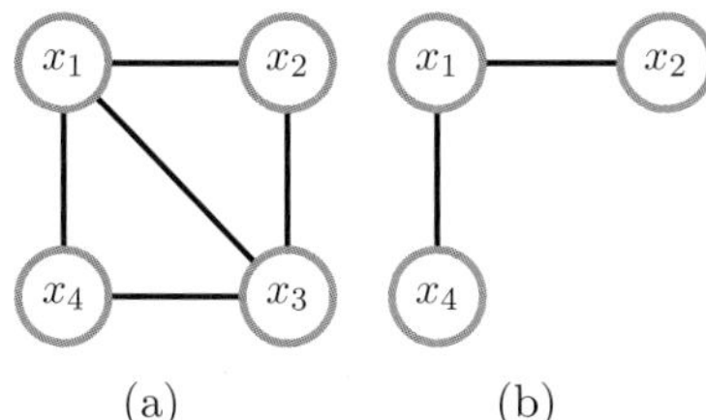

Figure 27.6 (**a**) A toy 'intractable' distribution. Gibbs sampling by conditioning on all variables except one leads to a simple univariate conditional distribution. (**b**) Conditioning on x_3 yields a new distribution that is singly connected, for which exact sampling is straightforward.

the normalisation constant by any of the standard techniques, for example, using the factor graph method. One may then convert this undirected linear chain to a directed graph, and use ancestral sampling. These operations are linear in the number of variables in the conditioned distribution. Alternatively, one may form a junction tree from a set of potentials, choose a root and then form a set chain by reabsorption on the junction tree. Ancestral sampling can then be performed on the resulting oriented clique tree. This is the approach taken in `GibbsSample.m`.

In the above example one can also reveal a tractable distribution by conditioning on x_1,

$$p(x_3, x_2, x_4|\mathrm{x}_1) \propto \phi(\mathrm{x}_1, x_2)\phi(x_2, x_3)\phi(x_3, x_4)\phi(x_4, \mathrm{x}_1)\phi(\mathrm{x}_1, x_3) \tag{27.3.15}$$

and then draw a sample of x_2, x_3, x_4 from this distribution using another exact sampler. A structured Gibbs sampling procedure is then to first draw a sample x_1, x_2, x_4 from Equation (27.3.13) and then a sample x_3, x_2, x_4 from Equation (27.3.15). These two steps (of drawing exact conditional samples) are then iterated. Note that x_2 and x_4 are not constrained to be equal to their values in the previous sample. This procedure is generally to be preferred to the single-site Gibbs updating since the samples are less dependent from one sample to the next.

See `demoGibbsSample.m` for a comparison of unstructured and structured sampling from a set of potentials.

27.3.3 Remarks

If the initial sample x^1 is in a part of the state space that has very low probability, it may take some time for the samples to become representative, as only a single component of x is updated at each iteration. This motivates a so-called *burn in* stage in which the initial samples are discarded.

In single-site Gibbs sampling there will be a high degree of dependence in any two successive samples, since only one variable (in the single-site updating version) is updated at each stage. This motivates *subsampling* in which, say, every 10th, sample $x^K, x^{K+10}, x^{K+20}, \ldots$, is taken, and the rest discarded.

Due to its simplicity, Gibbs sampling is one of the most popular sampling methods and is particularly convenient when applied to belief networks due to the Markov blanket property.[1] Gibbs sampling is a special case of the MCMC framework and, as with all MCMC methods, one should bear in mind that convergence can be an issue since it is generally unknown how many samples are needed to be reasonably sure that a sample estimate is accurate.

Gibbs sampling assumes that we can move throughout the space effectively by only single coordinate updates. We also require that every state can be visited infinitely often. In Fig. 27.5, we show a two-dimensional continuous distribution that has mass only in the lower left and upper right regions. In that case, if we start in the lower left region, we will always remain there, and

[1] The BUGS package `www.mrc-bsu.cam.ac.uk/bugs` is general purpose software for sampling from belief networks.

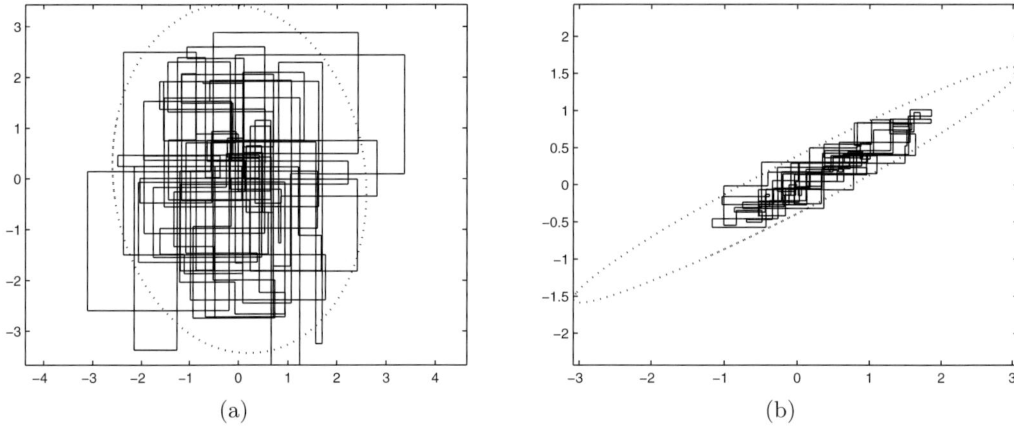

Figure 27.7 Two hundred Gibbs samples for a two-dimensional Gaussian. At each stage only a single component is updated. (**a**) For a Gaussian with low correlation, Gibbs sampling can move through the likely regions effectively. (**b**) For a strongly correlated Gaussian, Gibbs sampling is less effective and does not rapidly explore the likely regions, see `demoGibbsGauss.m`.

never explore the upper right region. This problem occurs when two regions are not connected by a 'probable' Gibbs path.

A Gibbs sampler is a perfect sampler (provided we subsample appropriately) when the distribution is factorised – that is the variables are independent. This suggests that in general Gibbs sampling will be less effective when variables are strongly correlated. For example, if we consider Gibbs sampling from a strongly correlated two-variable Gaussian distribution, then updates will move very slowly in space, see Fig. 27.7. It is useful therefore to find variable transformations that render the new variables approximately independent, since then one may apply Gibbs sampling more effectively.

27.4 Markov chain Monte Carlo (MCMC)

We assume we have a multivariate distribution in the form

$$p(x) = \frac{1}{Z}p^*(x) \tag{27.4.1}$$

where $p^*(x)$ is the unnormalised distribution and $Z = \int_x p^*(x)$ is the (computationally intractable) normalisation constant. We assume we are able to evaluate $p^*(x = \mathsf{x})$, for any state x, but not $p(x = \mathsf{x})$ since Z is intractable. The idea in MCMC sampling is to sample, not directly from $p(x)$, but from a different distribution such that, in the limit of a large number of samples, effectively the samples will be from $p(x)$. To achieve this we forward sample from a Markov transition whose stationary distribution is equal to $p(x)$.

27.4.1 Markov chains

Consider the conditional distribution $q(x^{l+1}|x^l)$. If we are given an initial sample x^1, then we can recursively generate samples $x^1, x^2, \ldots, x^L$. After a long time $L \gg 1$, (and provided the Markov chain is 'irreducible', meaning that we can eventually get from any state to any other state) the samples are from the *stationary* distribution $q_\infty(x)$ which is defined as (for a continuous variable)

$$q_\infty(x') = \int_x q(x'|x)q_\infty(x). \tag{27.4.2}$$

The condition for a discrete variable is analogous on replacing integration with summation. The idea in MCMC is, for a given distribution $p(x)$, to find a transition $q(x'|x)$ which has $p(x)$ as its stationary distribution. If we can do so, then we can draw samples from the Markov chain by forward sampling and take these as samples from $p(x)$ as the chain converges towards its stationary distribution.

Note that for every distribution $p(x)$ there will be more than one transition $q(x'|x)$ with $p(x)$ as its stationary distribution. This is why there are many different MCMC sampling methods, each with different characteristics and varying suitability for the particular distribution at hand. We've already encountered one class of samplers from the MCMC family, namely Gibbs sampling which corresponds to a particular transition $q(x'|x)$. Below we discuss more general members of this family.

27.4.2 Metropolis–Hastings sampling

Consider the following transition

$$q(x'|x) = \tilde{q}(x'|x)f(x', x) + \delta(x', x)\left(1 - \int_{x''} \tilde{q}(x''|x)f(x'', x)\right) \tag{27.4.3}$$

where $\tilde{q}(x'|x)$ is a so-called *proposal distribution* and $0 < f(x', x) \leq 1$ a positive function. This defines a valid distribution $q(x'|x)$ since it is non-negative and

$$\int_{x'} q(x'|x) = \int_{x'} \tilde{q}(x'|x)f(x', x) + 1 - \int_{x''} \tilde{q}(x''|x)f(x'', x) = 1. \tag{27.4.4}$$

Our interest is to set $f(x', x)$ such that the stationary distribution of $q(x'|x)$ is equal to $p(x)$ for any proposal $\tilde{q}(x'|x)$. That is

$$p(x') = \int_x q(x'|x)p(x) = \int_x \tilde{q}(x'|x)f(x', x)p(x) + p(x')\left(1 - \int_{x''} \tilde{q}(x''|x')f(x'', x')\right). \tag{27.4.5}$$

In order that this holds, we require (changing the integral variable from x'' to x)

$$\int_x \tilde{q}(x'|x)f(x', x)p(x) = \int_x \tilde{q}(x|x')f(x, x')p(x'). \tag{27.4.6}$$

Now consider the *Metropolis–Hastings acceptance function*

$$f(x', x) = \min\left(1, \frac{\tilde{q}(x|x')p(x')}{\tilde{q}(x'|x)p(x)}\right) = \min\left(1, \frac{\tilde{q}(x|x')p^*(x')}{\tilde{q}(x'|x)p^*(x)}\right) \tag{27.4.7}$$

which is defined for all x, x' and has the 'detailed balance' property

$$f(x', x)\tilde{q}(x'|x)p(x) = \min\left(\tilde{q}(x'|x)p(x), \tilde{q}(x|x')p(x')\right) \tag{27.4.8}$$

$$= \min\left(\tilde{q}(x|x')p(x'), \tilde{q}(x'|x)p(x)\right) = f(x, x')\tilde{q}(x|x')p(x'). \tag{27.4.9}$$

Hence the function $f(x', x)$ as defined above ensures Equation (27.4.6) holds and that $q(x'|x)$ has $p(x)$ as its stationary distribution.

Algorithm 27.3 Metropolis–Hastings MCMC sampling.

Choose a starting point x^1.
for $i = 2$ to L **do**
  Draw a candidate sample x^{cand} from the proposal $\tilde{q}(x'|x^{l-1})$.
  Let $a = \frac{\tilde{q}(x^{l-1}|x^{cand})p(x^{cand})}{\tilde{q}(x^{cand}|x^{l-1})p(x^{l-1})}$.
  if $a \geq 1$ **then** $x^l = x^{cand}$ ▷ Accept the candidate
  else
    draw a random value u uniformly from the unit interval $[0, 1]$.
    if $u < a$ **then** $x^l = x^{cand}$ ▷ Accept the candidate
    else
      $x^l = x^{l-1}$ ▷ Reject the candidate
    end if
  end if
end for

How do we sample from $q(x'|x)$? Equation (27.4.3) can be interpreted as a mixture of two distributions, one proportional to $\tilde{q}(x'|x)f(x', x)$ and the other $\delta(x', x)$ with mixture coefficient $1 - \int_{x''} \tilde{q}(x''|x)f(x'', x)$. To draw a sample from this, we draw a sample from $\tilde{q}(x'|x)$ and accept this with probability $f(x', x)$. Since drawing from $\tilde{q}(x'|x)$ and accepting are performed independently, the probability of accepting the drawn candidate is the product of these probabilities, namely $\tilde{q}(x'|x)f(x', x)$. Otherwise the candidate is rejected and we take the sample $x' = x$. Using the properties of the acceptance function, Equation (27.4.7), the following is equivalent to the above procedure: When

$$\tilde{q}(x|x')p^*(x') > \tilde{q}(x'|x)p^*(x) \tag{27.4.10}$$

we accept the sample from $\tilde{q}(x'|x)$. Otherwise we accept the sample x' from $q(x'|x)$ with probability $\tilde{q}(x|x')p^*(x')/\tilde{q}(x'|x)p^*(x)$. If we reject the candidate we take $x' = x$. Note that if the candidate x' is rejected, we take the original x as the new sample. Hence each iteration of the algorithm produces a sample – either a copy of the current sample, or the candidate sample, see Algorithm 27.3. A rough rule of thumb is to choose a proposal distribution for which the acceptance rate is between 50 per cent and 85 per cent [115].

Gaussian proposal distribution

A common proposal distribution for vector $\mathbf{x}$ is

$$\tilde{q}(\mathbf{x}'|\mathbf{x}) = \mathcal{N}\left(\mathbf{x}'|\mathbf{x}, \sigma^2\mathbf{I}\right) \propto e^{-\frac{1}{2\sigma^2}(\mathbf{x}'-\mathbf{x})^2} \tag{27.4.11}$$

for which $\tilde{q}(\mathbf{x}'|\mathbf{x}) = \tilde{q}(\mathbf{x}|\mathbf{x}')$ and the acceptance criterion equation (27.4.7) becomes

$$f(\mathbf{x}', \mathbf{x}) = \min\left(1, \frac{p^*(\mathbf{x}')}{p^*(\mathbf{x})}\right). \tag{27.4.12}$$

If the unnormalised probability $p^*(x')$ of the candidate state is higher than the current state, $p^*(x)$, we therefore accept the candidate. Otherwise, we accept the candidate only with probability

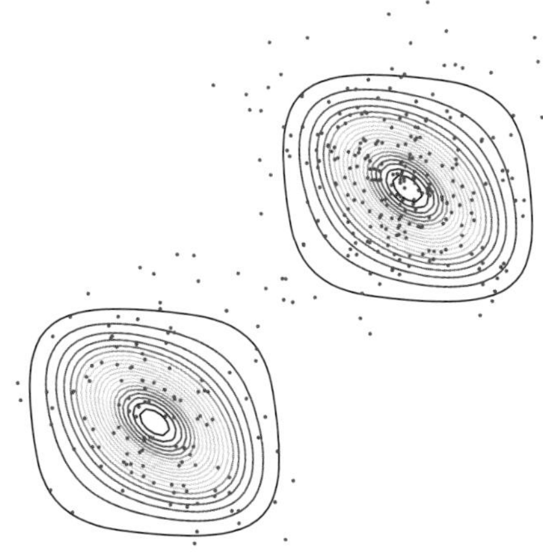

Figure 27.8 Metropolis–Hastings samples from a bi-variate distribution $p(x_1, x_2)$ using a proposal $\tilde{q}(\mathbf{x}'|\mathbf{x}) = \mathcal{N}(\mathbf{x}'|\mathbf{x}, \mathbf{I})$. We also plot the iso-probability contours of p. Although $p(x)$ is multi-modal, the dimensionality is low enough and the modes sufficiently close such that a simple Gaussian proposal distribution is able to bridge the two modes. In higher dimensions, such multi-modality is more problematic. See `demoMetropolis.m`.

$p^*(\mathbf{x}')/p^*(\mathbf{x})$. If the candidate is rejected, the new sample is taken to be a copy of the previous sample $\mathbf{x}$. See Fig. 27.8 for a demonstration.

In high dimensions it is unlikely that a random candidate sampled from a Gaussian will result in a candidate probability higher than the current value, Exercise 27.5. Because of this, only very small jumps (σ^2 small) are likely to be accepted. This limits the speed at which we explore the space $\mathbf{x}$ and increases the dependency between samples. As an aside, the acceptance function (27.4.12) highlights that sampling is different from finding the optimum. Provided $\mathbf{x}'$ has a higher probability than $\mathbf{x}$, we accept $\mathbf{x}'$. However, we may also accept candidates that have a *lower* probability than the current sample.

27.5 Auxiliary variable methods

A practical concern in MCMC methods is ensuring that one moves effectively through the significant probability regions of the distribution. For methods such as Metropolis-Hastings with local proposal distributions (local in the sense they are unlikely to propose a candidate far from the current sample), if the target distribution has isolated islands of high density, then the chance that we would move from one island to the other is very small. Conversely, if we attempt to make the proposal less local by using one with a high variance the chance then of landing at random on a high density island is remote. Auxiliary variable methods use additional dimensions to aid exploration and in certain cases to provide a bridge between isolated high-density islands. See also [213] for the use of auxiliary variables in perfect sampling.

Consider drawing samples from $p(x)$. For an auxiliary variable y we introduce a distribution $p(y|x)$ to form the joint distribution

$$p(x, y) = p(y|x)p(x). \tag{27.5.1}$$

If we draw samples (x^l, y^l) from this joint distribution then a valid set of samples from $p(x)$ is given by taking the x^l alone. If we sampled x directly from $p(x)$ and then y from $p(y|x)$, introducing y is pointless since there is no effect on the x sampling procedure. In order for this to be useful, therefore, the auxiliary variable must influence how we sample x. Below we discuss some of the common auxiliary variable schemes.

27.5.1 Hybrid Monte Carlo (HMC)

Hybrid MC is a method for continuous variables that aims to make non-local jumps in the sample space and, in so doing, to jump potentially from one mode to another. We define the distribution from which we wish to sample as

$$p(\mathbf{x}) = \frac{1}{Z_{\mathbf{x}}} e^{H_{\mathbf{x}}(\mathbf{x})} \tag{27.5.2}$$

for some given 'Hamiltonian' $H_{\mathbf{x}}(\mathbf{x})$. We then define another, 'easy' auxiliary distribution from which we can readily generate samples,

$$p(\mathbf{y}) = \frac{1}{Z_{\mathbf{y}}} e^{H_{\mathbf{y}}(\mathbf{y})} \tag{27.5.3}$$

so that the joint distribution is given by

$$p(\mathbf{x}, \mathbf{y}) = p(\mathbf{x})p(\mathbf{y}) = \frac{1}{Z} e^{H_{\mathbf{x}}(\mathbf{x})+H_{\mathbf{y}}(\mathbf{y})} = \frac{1}{Z} e^{H(\mathbf{x},\mathbf{y})}, \quad H(\mathbf{x}, \mathbf{y}) \equiv H(\mathbf{x}) + H(\mathbf{y}). \tag{27.5.4}$$

In the standard form of the algorithm, a multi-dimensional Gaussian is chosen for the auxiliary distribution with $\dim(\mathbf{y}) = \dim(\mathbf{x})$, so that

$$H_{\mathbf{y}}(\mathbf{y}) = -\frac{1}{2}\mathbf{y}^{\mathsf{T}}\mathbf{y}. \tag{27.5.5}$$

The HMC algorithm first draws from $p(\mathbf{y})$ and subsequently from $p(\mathbf{x}, \mathbf{y})$. For a Gaussian $p(\mathbf{y})$, sampling from this is straightforward. In the next 'dynamic' step, a sample is drawn from $p(\mathbf{x}, \mathbf{y})$ using a Metropolis MCMC sampler. The idea is to go from one point of the space $\mathbf{x}, \mathbf{y}$ to a new point $\mathbf{x}', \mathbf{y}'$ that is a non-trivial distance from $\mathbf{x}, \mathbf{y}$ and which will be accepted with a high probability. The candidate $(\mathbf{x}', \mathbf{y}')$ will have a good chance to be accepted if $H(\mathbf{x}', \mathbf{y}')$ is close to $H(\mathbf{x}, \mathbf{y})$ – this can be achieved by following a contour of equal 'energy' H, as described in the next section.

Hamiltonian dynamics

We wish to make an update $\mathbf{x}' = \mathbf{x} + \Delta\mathbf{x}, \mathbf{y}' = \mathbf{y} + \Delta\mathbf{y}$ for small $\Delta\mathbf{x}$ and $\Delta\mathbf{y}$ such that the Hamiltonian $H(\mathbf{x}, \mathbf{y}) \equiv H_{\mathbf{x}}(\mathbf{x}) + H_{\mathbf{y}}(\mathbf{y})$ is conserved,

$$H(\mathbf{x}', \mathbf{y}') \approx H(\mathbf{x}, \mathbf{y}). \tag{27.5.6}$$

We can satisfy this (up to first order) by considering the Taylor expansion

$$\begin{aligned} H(\mathbf{x}', \mathbf{y}') &= H(\mathbf{x} + \Delta\mathbf{x}, \mathbf{y} + \Delta\mathbf{y}) \\ &\approx H(\mathbf{x}, \mathbf{y}) + \Delta\mathbf{x}^{\mathsf{T}}\nabla_{\mathbf{x}}H(\mathbf{x}, \mathbf{y}) + \Delta\mathbf{y}^{\mathsf{T}}\nabla_{\mathbf{y}}H(\mathbf{x}, \mathbf{y}) + O\left(|\Delta\mathbf{x}|^2\right) + O\left(|\Delta\mathbf{y}|^2\right). \end{aligned} \tag{27.5.7}$$

Conservation, up to first order, therefore requires

$$\Delta\mathbf{x}^{\mathsf{T}}\nabla_{\mathbf{x}}H(\mathbf{x}, \mathbf{y}) + \Delta\mathbf{y}^{\mathsf{T}}\nabla_{\mathbf{y}}H(\mathbf{x}, \mathbf{y}) = 0. \tag{27.5.8}$$

This is a single scalar requirement, and there are therefore many different solutions for $\Delta\mathbf{x}$ and $\Delta\mathbf{y}$ that satisfy this single condition. It is customary to use Hamiltonian dynamics, which corresponds to the setting:

$$\Delta\mathbf{x} = \epsilon\nabla_{\mathbf{y}}H(\mathbf{x}, \mathbf{y}), \qquad \Delta\mathbf{y} = -\epsilon\nabla_{\mathbf{x}}H(\mathbf{x}, \mathbf{y}) \tag{27.5.9}$$

Algorithm 27.4 Hybrid Monte Carlo sampling.

```
Start from x^1
for i = 1 to L do
    Draw a new sample y from p(y).
    Choose a random (forwards or backwards) trajectory direction.
    Starting from x^i, y, follow Hamiltonian dynamics for a fixed number of steps, giving a candidate x', y'.
    Accept the candidate x^{i+1} = x' if H(x', y') > H(x, y), otherwise accept it with probability exp(H(x', y') − H(x, y)).
    If rejected, we take the sample as x^{i+1} = x^i.
end for
```

where ϵ is a small value to ensure that the Taylor expansion is accurate. Hence

$$\mathbf{x}(t+1) = \mathbf{x}(t) + \epsilon \nabla_{\mathbf{y}} H_{\mathbf{y}}(\mathbf{y}), \qquad \mathbf{y}(t+1) = \mathbf{y}(t) - \epsilon \nabla_{\mathbf{x}} H_{\mathbf{x}}(\mathbf{x}). \tag{27.5.10}$$

For the HMC method, $\nabla_{\mathbf{x}} H(\mathbf{x}, \mathbf{y}) = \nabla_{\mathbf{x}} H_{\mathbf{x}}(\mathbf{x})$ and $\nabla_{\mathbf{y}} H(\mathbf{x}, \mathbf{y}) = \nabla_{\mathbf{y}} H_{\mathbf{y}}(\mathbf{y})$. For the Gaussian case, $\nabla_{\mathbf{y}} H_{\mathbf{y}}(\mathbf{y}) = -\mathbf{y}$ so that

$$\mathbf{x}(t+1) = \mathbf{x}(t) - \epsilon \mathbf{y}, \qquad \mathbf{y}(t+1) = \mathbf{y}(t) - \epsilon \nabla_{\mathbf{x}} H(\mathbf{x}). \tag{27.5.11}$$

There are specific ways to implement the Hamiltonian dynamics called *Leapfrog discretisation* that are more accurate than the simple time-discretisation used above and we refer the reader to [220] for details.

In order to make a symmetric proposal distribution, at the start of the dynamic step, we choose $\epsilon = +\epsilon_0$ or $\epsilon = -\epsilon_0$ uniformly. We then follow the Hamiltonian dynamics for many timesteps (usually of the order of several hundred) to reach a candidate point $\mathbf{x}', \mathbf{y}'$. If the Hamiltonian dynamics is numerically accurate, $H(\mathbf{x}', \mathbf{y}')$ will have roughly the same value as $H(\mathbf{x}, \mathbf{y})$. We then do a Metropolis step, and accept the point $\mathbf{x}', \mathbf{y}'$ if $H(\mathbf{x}', \mathbf{y}') > H(\mathbf{x}, \mathbf{y})$ and otherwise accept it with probability $\exp(H(\mathbf{x}', \mathbf{y}') - H(\mathbf{x}, \mathbf{y}))$. If rejected, we take the initial point $\mathbf{x}, \mathbf{y}$ as the sample. Combined with the $p(\mathbf{y})$ sample step, we then have the general procedure as described in Algorithm 27.4.

In HMC we use not just the potential $H_{\mathbf{x}}(\mathbf{x})$ to define candidate samples, but the gradient of $H_{\mathbf{x}}(\mathbf{x})$ as well. An intuitive explanation for the success of the algorithm is that it is less myopic than straightforward Metropolis since the gradient enables the algorithm to feel its way to other regions of high probability by contouring around paths in the augmented space. One can also view the auxiliary variables as momentum variables – it is as if the sample has now a momentum which can carry it through the low-density $\mathbf{x}$-regions. Provided this momentum is high enough, we can escape local regions of significant probability, see Fig. 27.9.

27.5.2 Swendson–Wang (SW)

Originally, the SW method was introduced to alleviate the problems encountered in sampling from Ising models close to their critical temperature [284]. At this point large islands of same-state variables form so that strong correlations appear in the distribution – the scenario under which, for example, Gibbs sampling is not well suited. The method has since been generalised to other models [94], although here we outline the procedure for the Ising model only, referring the reader to more specialised text for the extensions [38].

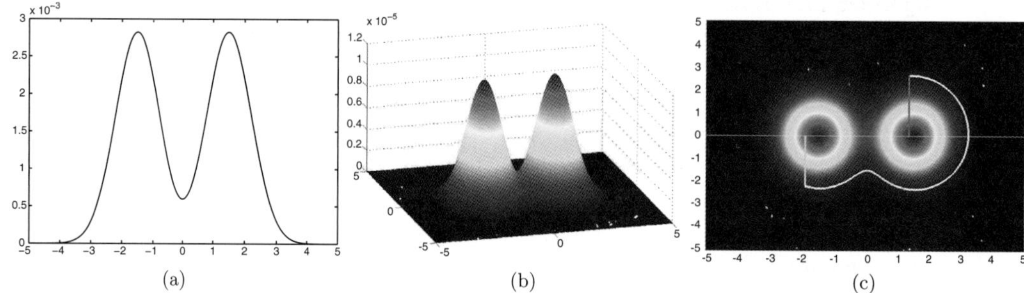

Figure 27.9 Hybrid Monte Carlo. (**a**) Multi-modal distribution $p(x)$ for which we desire samples. (**b**) HMC forms the joint distribution $p(x)p(y)$ where $p(y)$ is Gaussian. (**c**) This is a plot of (b) from above. Starting from the point x, we first draw a y from the Gaussian $p(y)$, giving a point (x, y), given by the green line. Then we use Hamiltonian dynamics (white line) to traverse the distribution at roughly constant energy for a fixed number of steps, giving x', y'. We accept this point if $H(x', y') > H(x, y')$ and make the new sample x' (red line). Otherwise this candidate is accepted with probability $\exp(H(x', y') - H(x, y'))$. If rejected the new sample x' is taken as a copy of x. See plate section for colour version.

The Ising model with no external fields is defined on variables $x = (x_1, \ldots, x_n)$, $x_i \in \{0, 1\}$ and takes the form

$$p(x) = \frac{1}{Z} \prod_{i \sim j} e^{\beta \mathbb{I}[x_i = x_j]} \tag{27.5.12}$$

which means that this is a pairwise Markov network with a potential contribution e^{β} if neighbouring nodes i and j on a square lattice are in the same state, and a contribution 1 otherwise. We assume that $\beta > 0$ which encourages neighbours to be in the same state. The lattice-based neighbourhood structure makes this difficult to sample from, and especially when $\beta \approx 0.9$ which encourages large-scale islands of same-state variables to form.

The aim is to remove the problematic terms $e^{\beta \mathbb{I}[x_i = x_j]}$ by the use of auxiliary real-valued 'bond' variables, y_{ij}, one for each edge on the lattice, making the conditional $p(x|y)$ easy to sample from. This is given by

$$p(x|y) \propto p(y|x)p(x) \propto p(y|x) \prod_{i \sim j} e^{\beta \mathbb{I}[x_i = x_j]}. \tag{27.5.13}$$

Using $p(y|x)$ we can cancel the terms $e^{\beta \mathbb{I}[x_i = x_j]}$ by setting

$$p(y|x) = \prod_{i \sim j} p(y_{ij}|x_i, x_j) = \prod_{i \sim j} \frac{1}{z_{ij}} \mathbb{I}\left[0 < y_{ij} < e^{\beta \mathbb{I}[x_i = x_j]}\right] \tag{27.5.14}$$

where $\mathbb{I}\left[0 < y_{ij} < e^{\beta \mathbb{I}[x_i = x_j]}\right]$ denotes a uniform distribution between 0 and $e^{\beta \mathbb{I}[x_i = x_j]}$; z_{ij} is the normalisation constant $z_{ij} = e^{\beta \mathbb{I}[x_i = x_j]}$. Hence

$$p(x|y) \propto p(y|x)p(x) \tag{27.5.15}$$

$$\propto \prod_{i \sim j} \frac{1}{e^{\beta \mathbb{I}[x_i = x_j]}} \mathbb{I}\left[0 < y_{ij} < e^{\beta \mathbb{I}[x_i = x_j]}\right] e^{\beta \mathbb{I}[x_i = x_j]} \tag{27.5.16}$$

$$\propto \prod_{i \sim j} \mathbb{I}\left[0 < y_{ij} < e^{\beta \mathbb{I}[x_i = x_j]}\right]. \tag{27.5.17}$$

Algorithm 27.5 Swendson–Wang sampling.

Start from a random configuration of all $x_1^1, \ldots, x_n^1$.
for $l = 2$ to L **do**
  for each i, j in the edge set **do**
    If $x_i^{l-1} = x_j^{l-1}$, we bind variables x_i and x_j with probability $1 - e^{-\beta}$.
  end for
  For each cluster formed from the above bonds, set the state of the cluster uniformly at random.
  This gives a new joint configuration $x_1^l, \ldots, x_n^l$.
end for

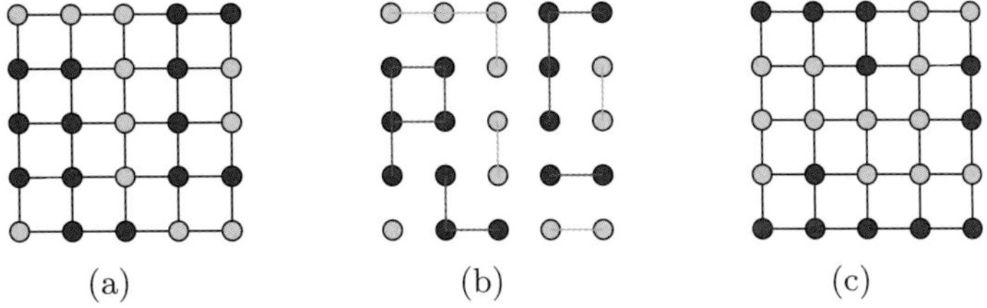

Figure 27.10 Swendson–Wang updating for $p(x) \propto \prod_{i\sim j} \exp \beta\mathbb{I}[x_i = x_j]$. **(a)** Current sample of states (here on a nearest neighbour lattice). **(b)** Like-shaded neighbours are bonded together with probability $1 - e^{-\beta}$, forming clusters of variables. **(c)** Each cluster is given a random shade, forming the new sample.

We first assume we have a sample for all the bond variables $\{y_{ij}\}$. If $y_{ij} > 1$, then to draw a sample from $p(x|y)$, we must have $1 < e^{\beta\mathbb{I}[x_i=x_j]}$, which means that x_i and x_j are constrained to be in the same state. Otherwise, if $y_{ij} < 1$, then this introduces no constraint on x_i and x_j. Hence, wherever $y_{ij} > 1$, we bind x_i and x_j to be in the same state, otherwise not.

To sample from the bond variables $p(y_{ij}|x_i, x_j)$ consider first the situation that x_i and x_j are in the same state. Then $p(y_{ij}|x_i = x_j) = U\left(y_{ij}|\left[0, e^{\beta}\right]\right)$. A bond will occur if $y_{ij} > 1$, which occurs with probability

$$p(y_{ij} > 1|x_i = x_j) = \int_{y_{ij}=1}^{\infty} \frac{1}{z_{ij}} \mathbb{I}\left[0 < y_{ij} < e^{\beta}\right] = \frac{e^{\beta} - 1}{e^{\beta}} = 1 - e^{-\beta}. \tag{27.5.18}$$

Hence, if $x_i = x_j$, we bind x_i and x_j to be in the same state with probability $1 - e^{-\beta}$. On the other hand if x_i and x_j are in different states, $p(y_{ij}|x_i \neq x_j) = U\left(y_{ij}|\left[0, 1\right]\right)$, and y_{ij} is uniformly distributed between 0 and 1.

After doing this for all the x_i and x_j pairs, we will end up with a graph in which we have clusters of like-state bonded variables. The algorithm then simply chooses a random state for each cluster – that is, with probability 0.5 all variables in the cluster are in state 1. This is useful since we are able to update variables, even if they are strongly dependent. This is in contrast to say Gibbs sampling which when the variables are strongly dependent will only very rarely change the state of a variable from its neighbours since it is strongly encouraged to agree with them; this results in a critical slowing down effect and Gibbs sampling essentially freezes. See Algorithm 27.5, Fig. 27.10 and Fig. 27.11. This technique has found application in spatial statistics, particularly image restoration [146].

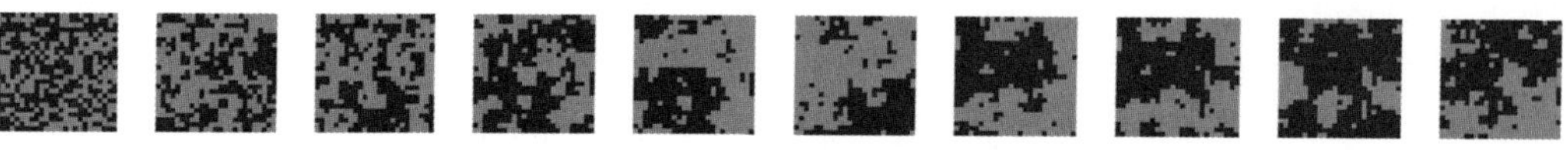

Figure 27.11 Ten successive samples from a 25 × 25 Ising model $p(x) \propto \exp\left(\sum_{i\sim j} \beta \mathbb{I}[x_i = x_j]\right)$, with $\beta = 0.88$, close to the critical temperature. The Swendson–Wang procedure is used. Starting in a random initial configuration, the samples quickly move away from this initial state. The samples display the characteristic long-range correlations close to the critical temperature.

27.5.3 Slice sampling

Slice sampling [222] is an auxiliary variable technique that aims to overcome some of the difficulties in choosing an appropriate length scale in methods such as Metropolis sampling. The brief discussion here follows that presented in [197] and [43]. We want to draw samples from $p(x) = \frac{1}{Z}p^*(x)$ where the normalisation constant Z is unknown. By introducing the auxiliary variable y and defining the distribution

$$p(x, y) = \begin{cases} 1/Z & \text{for } 0 \le y \le p^*(x) \\ 0 & \text{otherwise} \end{cases} \tag{27.5.19}$$

we have

$$\int p(x, y)dy = \int_0^{p^*(x)} \frac{1}{Z}dy = \frac{1}{Z}p^*(x) = p(x) \tag{27.5.20}$$

which shows that the marginal of $p(x, y)$ over y is equal to the distribution we wish to draw samples from. Hence if we draw samples from $p(x, y)$, we can ignore the y samples and we will have a valid sampling scheme for $p(x)$.

To draw from $p(x, y)$ we use Gibbs sampling, first drawing from $p(y|x)$ and then from $p(x|y)$. Drawing a sample from $p(y|x)$ means that we draw a value y from the uniform distribution $U(y|\,[0, p^*(x)])$. Given a sample y, one then draws a sample x from $p(x|y)$. Using $p(x|y) \propto p(x, y)$ we see that $p(x|y)$ is the distribution over x such that $p^*(x) > y$:

$$p(x|y) \propto \mathbb{I}[p^*(x) > y]. \tag{27.5.21}$$

That is, x is uniformly distributed from the 'slice' that satisfies $p^*(x) > y$, Fig. 27.12. Computing the normalisation of this distribution is in general non-trivial since we would in principle need to search over all x to find those for which $p^*(x) > y$. The challenge in slice sampling is therefore to sample from the slice. This can be addressed using MCMC techniques. Ideally we would like to get as much of the slice as feasible, since this will improve the 'mixing' of the chain (the rate that we converge to the stationary distribution). If we concentrate on the part of the slice only very local to the current x, then the samples move through the space very slowly. If we attempt to guess at random a point a long way from x and check if it is in the slice, this will be mostly unsuccessful.

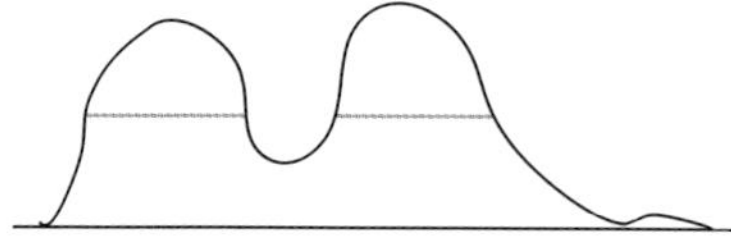

Figure 27.12 The full slice for a given y. Ideally slice sampling would draw an x sample from anywhere on the full slice. In general this is intractable for a complex distribution and a local approximate slice is formed instead, see Fig. 27.13.

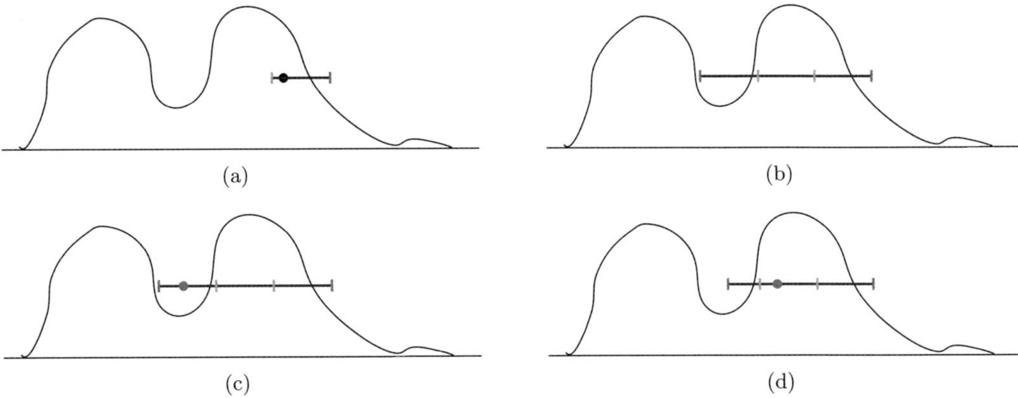

Figure 27.13 (**a**) For the current sample x, a point y is sampled between 0 and $p^*(x)$, giving a point (x, y) (black circle). Then an interval of width w is placed around x, the horizontal bar. The ends of the bar denote if the point is in the slice (light shade) or out of the slice (dark shade). (**b**) The interval is increased by w until it hits a point out of the slice. (**c**) Given an interval a sample x' is taken uniformly in the interval. If the candidate x' is not in the slice (dark shade), $p(x') < y$, the candidate is rejected and the interval is shrunk. (**d**) The sampling from the interval is repeated until a candidate is in the slice (light circle), and is subsequently accepted.

We will not discuss how to do this in general and highlight only how this can be achieved for a univariate slice. The happy compromise presented in Algorithm 27.6 [222] and described in Fig. 27.13 determines an appropriate incremental widening of an initial interval. Once the largest potential interval is determined we attempt to sample from this. If the sample point within the interval is in fact not in the slice, this is rejected and the interval is shrunk.

27.6 Importance sampling

Importance sampling is a technique to approximate averages with respect to an intractable distribution $p(x)$. The term 'sampling' is arguably a misnomer since the method does not attempt to draw samples from $p(x)$. Rather the method draws samples from a simpler *importance distribution* $q(x)$ and then reweights them such that averages with respect to $p(x)$ can be approximated using the samples from $q(x)$. Consider $p(x) = p^*(x)/Z$ where $p^*(x)$ can be evaluated but $Z = \int_x p^*(x)$ is an intractable normalisation constant. The average of $f(x)$ with respect to $p(x)$ is given by

$$\int_x f(x)p(x) = \frac{\int_x f(x)p^*(x)}{\int_x p^*(x)} = \frac{\int_x f(x)\frac{p^*(x)}{q(x)}q(x)}{\int_x \frac{p^*(x)}{q(x)}q(x)}. \tag{27.6.1}$$

Let $x^1, \ldots, x^L$ be samples from $q(x)$. We can then approximate the above average by

$$\int_x f(x)p(x) \approx \frac{\sum_{l=1}^L f(x^l)\frac{p^*(x^l)}{q(x^l)}}{\sum_{l=1}^L \frac{p^*(x^l)}{q(x^l)}} = \sum_{l=1}^L f(x^l)w_l \tag{27.6.2}$$

where we define the *normalised importance weights*

$$w_l = \frac{p^*(x^l)/q(x^l)}{\sum_{l=1}^L p^*(x^l)/q(x^l)}, \qquad \text{with } \sum_{l=1}^L w_l = 1. \tag{27.6.3}$$

Algorithm 27.6 Slice sampling (univariate).

```
Choose a starting point x^1 and step size w.
for i = 1 to L do
    Draw a vertical coordinate y uniformly from the interval (0,p*(x^i))
    Create a horizontal interval (x_left, x_right) that contains x^i as follows:
    Draw r ~ U(r|(0, 1)).
    x_left = x^i - rw, x_right = x^i + (1 - r)w                ▷ Create an initial interval
    while p*(x_left) > y do
        x_left = x_left - w                                    ▷ Step out left
    end while
    while p*(x_right) > y do
        x_right = x_right + w                                  ▷ Step out right
    end while
    accept = false
    while accept = false do
        draw a random value x' uniformly from the unit interval (x_left, x_right).
        if p*(x') > y then
            accept = true                                      ▷ Found a valid sample
        else
            modify the interval (x_left, x_right) as follows:
            if x' > x^i then
                x_right = x'                                   ▷ Shrinking
            else
                x_left = x'
            end if
        end if
    end while
    x^{i+1} = x'
end for
```

In principle, reweighing the samples from q will give the correct result for the average with respect to p.

The importance weight vector $\mathbf{w}$ can be seen as a measure of how well q fits p since for $q = p$, the weight vector has uniform values, $\mathbf{w} = \mathbf{1}/L$. Hence the more variable the components of the weight vector are, the less well-matched q is to p. Since the weight is a measure of how well q matches p, unless q and p are well-matched, there will typically be only a small number of dominant weights. This is particularly evident in high dimensions. As an indication of this effect, consider a D-dimensional multivariate $\mathbf{x}$. Using $\mathbf{u}$ as the vector of unnormalised importance weights with $u_i = p(\mathbf{x}^i)/q(\mathbf{x}^i)$, a measure of the variability of two components of $\mathbf{u}$ is given by (dropping momentarily the notational dependence on $\mathbf{x}$)

$$\left\langle (u_i - u_j)^2 \right\rangle = \left\langle u_i^2 \right\rangle + \left\langle u_j^2 \right\rangle - 2 \left\langle u_i \right\rangle \left\langle u_j \right\rangle \tag{27.6.4}$$

where the averages are with respect to q. The mean unnormalised weights are

$$\langle u_i \rangle = \langle u_j \rangle = \int_{\mathbf{x}} \frac{p(\mathbf{x})}{q(\mathbf{x})} q(\mathbf{x}) = 1 \tag{27.6.5}$$

and

$$\langle u_i^2 \rangle = \langle u_j^2 \rangle = \left\langle \frac{p^2(\mathbf{x})}{q^2(\mathbf{x})} \right\rangle_{q(\mathbf{x})} = \left\langle \frac{p(\mathbf{x})}{q(\mathbf{x})} \right\rangle_{p(\mathbf{x})}. \tag{27.6.6}$$

For simplicity we assume that $q(\mathbf{x})$ and $p(\mathbf{x})$ both factorise, $p(\mathbf{x}) = \prod_{d=1}^{D} p(x_d), q(\mathbf{x}) = \prod_{d=1}^{D} q(x_d)$ and further that the distributions are axis-aligned, being the same for each co-ordinate d. Then

$$\langle u_i^2 \rangle = \left\langle \frac{p(x)}{q(x)} \right\rangle_{p(x)}^{D}. \tag{27.6.7}$$

Since $\left\langle \frac{p(x)}{q(x)} \right\rangle_{p(x)} > 1$ for $q \neq p$ (this is the 2-divergence, Exercise 8.37), the variability of the weights is

$$\left\langle (u_i - u_j)^2 \right\rangle = 2 \left(\left\langle \frac{p(x)}{q(x)} \right\rangle_{p(x)}^{D} - 1 \right) \tag{27.6.8}$$

which grows exponentially with the dimension D. This means that a single unnormalised importance weight is likely to dominate. After normalisation, typically, therefore in high dimensions the weight vector $\mathbf{w}$ will have only a single significantly non-zero component.

A method that can help address this weight dominance is *resampling*. Given the weight distribution $w_1, \ldots, w_L$, one draws a set of L sample indices. This new set of indices will almost certainly contain repeats since any of the original low-weight samples will most likely not be included. The weight of each of these new samples is set uniformly to $1/L$. This procedure helps select only the 'fittest' of the samples and is known as *Sampling Importance Resampling* [253].

27.6.1 Sequential importance sampling

Our interest is to apply importance sampling to temporal distributions $p(x_{1:t})$ for which the importance samples from $q(x_{1:t})$ are paths $x_{1:t}$. When a new observation at time t arrives, we require a set of sample paths $x_{1:t}^l$ from $q(x_{1:t})$. If we assume that for the previous time, we have a set of paths $x_{1:t-1}^l$ along with their importance weights w_{t-1}^l, we can find the new importance weights w_t^l by simply sampling from the transition $q(x_t|x_{1:t-1})$ and updating the weights, without needing to explicitly sample whole new paths. To see this, consider the unnormalised importance weights for a sample path $x_{1:t}^l$

$$\tilde{w}_t^l = \frac{p^*(x_{1:t}^l)}{q(x_{1:t}^l)} = \frac{p^*(x_{1:t-1}^l)}{q(x_{1:t-1}^l)} \frac{p^*(x_{1:t}^l)}{p^*(x_{1:t-1}^l) q(x_t^l|x_{1:t-1}^l)}, \qquad \tilde{w}_1^l = \frac{p^*(x_1^l)}{q(x_1^l)}. \tag{27.6.9}$$

Using $p(x_{1:t}) = p(x_t|x_{1:t-1})p(x_{1:t-1})$, we can ignore constants and equivalently define the unnormalised weights recursively using

$$\tilde{w}_t^l = \tilde{w}_{t-1}^l \alpha_t^l, \qquad t > 1. \tag{27.6.10}$$

where

$$\alpha_t^l \equiv \frac{p^*(x_t^l|x_{1:t-1}^l)}{q(x_t^l|x_{1:t-1}^l)}. \tag{27.6.11}$$

This means that in Sequential Importance Sampling (SIS) we need only define the conditional importance distribution $q(x_t|x_{1:t-1})$. The ideal setting of the sequential importance distribution is $q(x_t|x_{1:t-1}) = p(x_t|x_{1:t-1})$, although this choice is impractical in most cases, as we discuss below. Sequential importance sampling is also known as *particle filtering*.

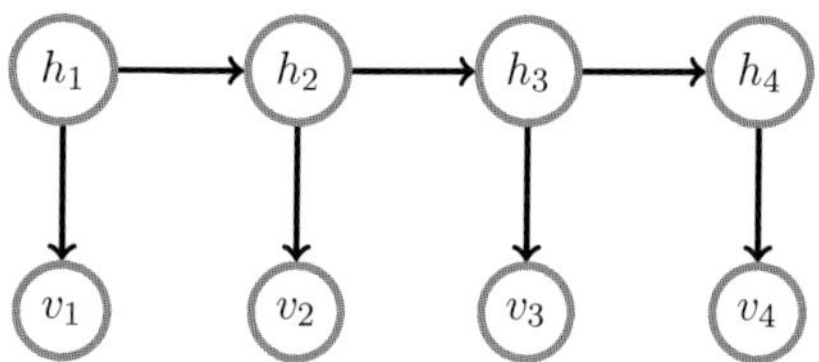

Figure 27.14 A dynamic belief network. In many applications of interest, the emission distribution $p(v_t|h_t)$ is non-Gaussian, leading to the formal intractability of filtering/smoothing.

Dynamic belief networks

Consider distributions with a hidden Markov independence structure, see Fig. 27.14,

$$p(v_{1:t}, h_{1:t}) = p(v_1|h_1)p(h_1)\prod_{t=2}^{t} \underbrace{p(v_t|h_t)}_{\text{emission}} \underbrace{p(h_t|h_{t-1})}_{\text{transition}} \tag{27.6.12}$$

where $v_{1:t}$ are observations and $h_{1:t}$ are the random variables. Our interest is to draw sample paths $h_{1:t}$ given the observations $v_{1:t}$. In some models, such as the HMM, this is straightforward. However, in other cases, for example when the emission $p(v_t|h_t)$ is intractable to normalise, we can use SIS to draw samples instead. For dynamic belief networks, Equation (27.6.11) simplifies to

$$\alpha_t^l \equiv \frac{p(v_t|h_t^l)p(h_t^l|h_{t-1}^l)}{q(h_t^l|h_{1:t-1}^l)}. \tag{27.6.13}$$

The optimal importance distribution is achieved by using the importance transition

$$q(h_t|h_{1:t-1}) \propto p(v_t|h_t)p(h_t|h_{t-1}). \tag{27.6.14}$$

It is often the case, however, that drawing samples from this optimal $q(h_t|h_{1:t-1})$ is difficult, usually because the normalisation constant of the emission distribution $p(v_t|h_t)$ is unknown. In cases where the transition is easy to sample from, a common sequential importance distribution is

$$q(h_t|h_{1:t-1}) = p(h_t|h_{t-1}) \tag{27.6.15}$$

in which case, from Equation (27.6.11), $\alpha_t^l = p(v_t|h_t)$ and the unnormalised weights are recursively defined by

$$\tilde{w}_t^l = \tilde{w}_{t-1}^l p(v_t|h_t^l). \tag{27.6.16}$$

A drawback of this procedure is that after a small number of iterations only very few particle weights will be significantly non-zero due to the mismatch between the importance distribution q and the target distribution p. This can be addressed using resampling, as described in Section 27.6 [153, 87].

27.6.2 Particle filtering as an approximate forward pass

Particle filtering (PF) can be viewed as an approximation to the exact filtering recursion. Using ρ to represent the filtered distribution,

$$\rho(h_t) \propto p(h_t|v_{1:t}) \tag{27.6.17}$$

the exact filtering recursion is

$$\rho(h_t) \propto p(v_t|h_t) \int_{h_{t-1}} p(h_t|h_{t-1})\rho(h_{t-1}). \tag{27.6.18}$$

A PF can be viewed as an approximation of Equation (27.6.18) in which the message $\rho(h_{t-1})$ is approximated by a sum of delta-spikes:

$$\rho(h_{t-1}) \approx \sum_{l=1}^{L} w_{t-1}^{l} \delta\left(h_{t-1}, h_{t-1}^{l}\right) \tag{27.6.19}$$

where w_{t-1}^l are the normalised importance weights $\sum_{l=1}^L w_{t-1}^l = 1$, and h_{t-1}^l are the particles. In other words, the ρ message is represented as a weighted mixture of delta-spikes where the weight and position of the spikes are the parameters of the distribution. Using Equation (27.6.19) in Equation (27.6.18), we have

$$\rho(h_t) \approx \frac{1}{Z} p(v_t|h_t) \sum_{l=1}^{L} p(h_t|h_{t-1}^l) w_{t-1}^l. \tag{27.6.20}$$

The constant Z is used to normalise the distribution $\rho(h_t)$. Although $\rho(h_{t-1})$ was a simple sum of delta-spikes, in general $\rho(h_t)$ will not be – the delta-spikes get 'broadened' by the transition and emission factors. Our task is then to approximate $\rho(h_t)$ as a new sum of delta-spikes. Below we discuss a method to achieve this for which explicit knowledge of the normalisation Z is not required. This is useful since in many tracking applications the normalisation of the emission $p(v_t|h_t)$ is unknown.

A Monte Carlo sampling approximation

A simple approach to forming an approximate mixture-of-delta functions representation of Equation (27.6.20) is to generate a set of points using sampling. In principle any sampling method can be used, including powerful MCMC approaches.

In particle filters, importance sampling is use to generate the new particles. That is we generate a set of samples $h_t^1, \ldots, h_t^L$ from some importance distribution $q(h_t)$ which gives the unnormalised importance weights

$$\tilde{w}_t^l = \frac{p(v_t|h_t^l) \sum_{l'=1}^{L} p(h_t^l|h_{t-1}^{l'}) w_{t-1}^{l'}}{q(h_t^l)}. \tag{27.6.21}$$

Defining the normalised weights:

$$w_t^l = \frac{\tilde{w}_t^l}{\sum_{l'} \tilde{w}_t^{l'}} \tag{27.6.22}$$

we obtain an approximation

$$\rho(h_t) \approx \sum_{l=1}^{L} w_t^l \delta\left(h_t, h_t^l\right). \tag{27.6.23}$$

Ideally one would use the importance distribution that makes the importance weights uniform, namely

$$q(h_t) \propto p(v_t|h_t) \sum_{l=1}^{L} p(h_t|h_{t-1}^l) w_{t-1}^l. \tag{27.6.24}$$

However, this is often difficult to sample from directly due to the unknown normalisation of the emission $p(v_t|h_t)$. A simpler alternative is to sample from the transition mixture:

$$q(h_t) = \sum_{l=1}^{L} p(h_t|h_{t-1}^l)w_{t-1}^l. \tag{27.6.25}$$

To do so, one first samples a component l^* from the histogram with weights $w_{t-1}^1, \ldots, w_{t-1}^L$. Given this sample index, say l^*, one then draws a sample from $p(h_t|h_{t-1}^{l^*})$. In this case the unnormalised weights become simply

$$\tilde{w}_t^l = p(v_t|h_t^l). \tag{27.6.26}$$

This *forward-sampling-resampling* procedure is used in `demoParticleFilter.m` and in the following toy example.

Example 27.2 A toy face-tracking example

At time t a binary face template is in a two-dimensional location $\mathbf{h}_t$, which describes the upper-left corner of the template. At time $t = 1$ the position of the face is known, see Fig. 27.15(a). In subsequent times the face moves randomly according to

$$\mathbf{h}_t = \mathbf{h}_{t-1} + \sigma \boldsymbol{\eta}_t \tag{27.6.27}$$

where $\boldsymbol{\eta}_t \sim \mathcal{N}(\boldsymbol{\eta}_t|\mathbf{0}, \mathbf{I})$ is a two-dimensional zero mean unit covariance noise vector. In addition, a fraction of the binary pixels in the whole image are selected at random and their states flipped. The aim is to try to track the upper-left corner of the face through time.

We need to define the emission distribution $p(\mathbf{v}_t|\mathbf{h}_t)$ on the binary pixels with $v_i \in \{0, 1\}$. Consider the following *compatibility function*

$$\phi(\mathbf{v}_t, \mathbf{h}_t) = \mathbf{v}_t^{\mathsf{T}}\tilde{\mathbf{v}}(\mathbf{h}_t) \tag{27.6.28}$$

where $\tilde{\mathbf{v}}(\mathbf{h}_t)$ is the vector representing the whole image with a clean face placed at position $\mathbf{h}_t$ and zeros outside of the face template. Then $\phi(\mathbf{v}_t, \mathbf{h}_t)$ measures the overlap between the face template at a specific location and the noisy image restricted to the template pixels. The compatibility function is maximal when the observed image $\mathbf{v}_t$ has the face placed at position $\mathbf{h}_t$. We can therefore tentatively define

$$p(\mathbf{v}_t|\mathbf{h}_t) \propto \phi(\mathbf{v}_t, \mathbf{h}_t). \tag{27.6.29}$$

A subtlety is that $\mathbf{h}_t$ is continuous, and in the compatibility function we first map $\mathbf{h}_t$ to the nearest integer pixel representation. The normalisation constant of $p(\mathbf{v}_t|\mathbf{h}_t)$ is difficult to work out. An advantage of the sampling approach is that this normalisation is not required if we use forward-sampling-resampling. In Fig. 27.15(a) 50 particles are used to track the face. The particles are plotted along with their corresponding weights. For each $t > 1$, 5 per cent of the pixels are selected at random in the image and their states flipped. Using the forward-sampling-resampling method we can successfully track the face despite the presence of the background clutter.

Real tracking applications involve complex issues, including tracking multiple objects, transformations of the object (scaling, rotation, morphology changes). Nevertheless, the principles are largely the same and many tracking applications work by seeking compatibility functions, often based on the colour histogram in a template.

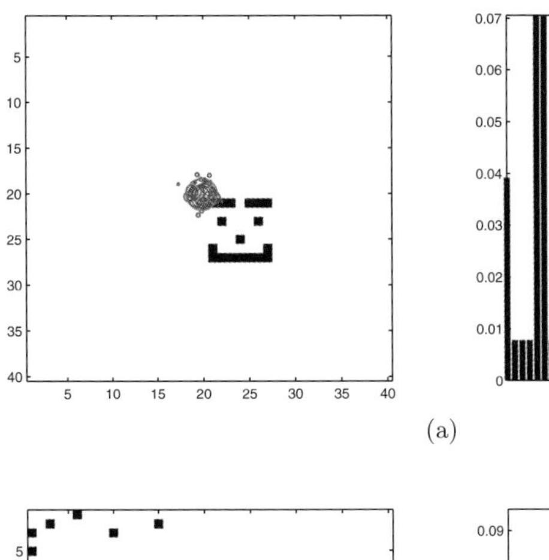

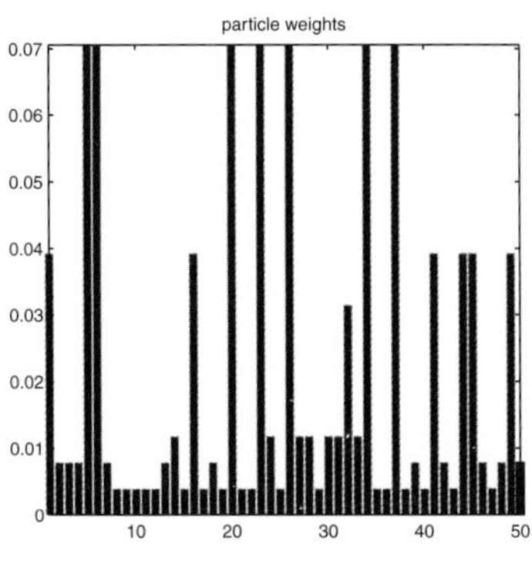

(a)

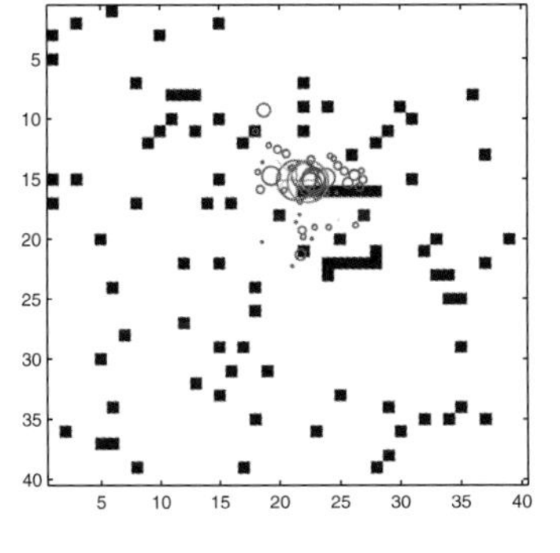

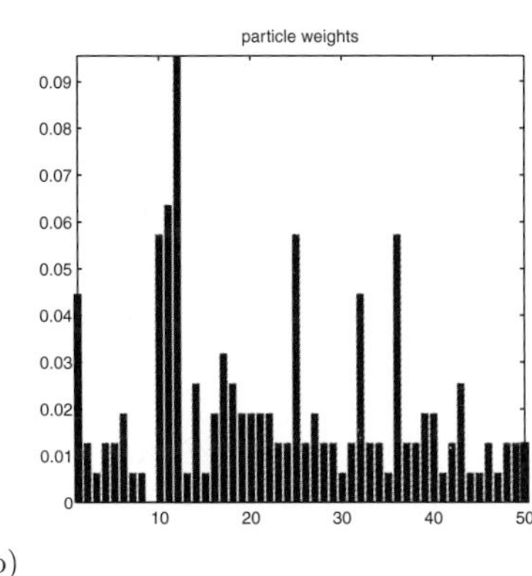

(b)

Figure 27.15 Tracking an object with a particle filter containing 50 particles. The small circles are the particles, scaled by their weights. The correct corner position of the face is given by the '$\times$', the filtered average by the large circle 'o', and the most likely particle by '$+$'. (**a**) Initial position of the face without noise and corresponding weights of the particles. (**b**) Face with noisy background and the tracked corner position after 20 timesteps. The forward-sampling-resampling PF method is used to maintain a healthy proportion of non-zero weights. See `demoParticleFilter.m`.

27.7 Summary

- Exact sampling can be achieved for models such as belief networks, although forward sampling in the case of evidence can be inefficient.
- Provided independent samples are drawn from a distribution, only a small number of samples is required to obtain a good estimate of an expectation. However, drawing independent samples from high-dimensional non-standard distributions is computationally extremely difficult.
- Markov chain Monte Carlo methods are approximate sampling methods which converge to drawing samples from the correct distribution in the limit of a large number of samples. Whilst powerful, assessing convergence of the method can be difficult. Also, samples are often highly dependent, so that a great number of samples may be required to obtain a reliable estimate of an expectation.

27.8 Code

`potsample.m`: Exact sample from a set of potentials
`ancestralsample.m`: Ancestral sample from a belief network
`JTsample.m`: Sampling from a consistent junction tree
`GibbsSample.m`: Gibbs sampling from a set of potentials

`demoMetropolis.m`: Demo of Metropolis sampling for a bimodal distribution
`metropolis.m`: Metropolis sample
`logp.m`: Log of a bimodal distribution
`demoParticleFilter.m`: Demo of particle filtering (forward-sampling-resampling method)
`placeobject.m`: Place an object in a grid
`compat.m`: Compatibility function
`demoSampleHMM.m`: Naive Gibbs sampling for an HMM

27.9 Exercises

27.1 (Box–Muller method) Let $x_1 \sim \mathcal{U}(x_1|[0,1])$, $x_2 \sim \mathcal{U}(x_2|[0,1])$ and

$$y_1 = \sqrt{-2\log x_1}\cos 2\pi x_2, \qquad y_2 = \sqrt{-2\log x_1}\sin 2\pi x_2. \tag{27.9.1}$$

Show that

$$p(y_1, y_2) = \int p(y_1|x_1, x_2)p(y_2|x_1, x_2)p(x_1)p(x_2)dx_1dx_2 = \mathcal{N}(y_1|0,1)\mathcal{N}(y_2|0,1) \tag{27.9.2}$$

and suggest an algorithm to sample from a univariate normal distribution. Hint: Use the change of variable result, Result 8.1, for vectors $\mathbf{y} = (y_1, y_2)$ and $\mathbf{x} = (x_1, x_2)$.

27.2 Consider the distribution $p(x) \propto \exp(\sin(x))$ for $-\pi \le x \le \pi$. Using rejection sampling with $q(x) = \mathcal{N}(x|0, \sigma^2)$ show that a suitable value for M such that $p^*(s)/q(x) \le M$ is

$$M = e^{1+\frac{\pi^2}{2\sigma^2}}\sqrt{2\pi\sigma^2}. \tag{27.9.3}$$

For a suitably chosen σ^2 draw 10 000 samples from $p(x)$ and plot the resulting histogram of the samples.

27.3 Consider the distribution

$$p(x_1, \ldots, x_6) = p(x_1)p(x_2)p(x_3|x_1, x_2)p(x_4|x_3)p(x_5|x_3)p(x_6|x_4, x_5). \tag{27.9.4}$$

For x_5 fixed in a given state x_5, write down a distribution on the remaining variables $p'(x_1, x_2, x_3, x_4, x_6)$ and explain how forward (ancestral) sampling can be carried out for this new distribution.

27.4 Consider an Ising model on an $M \times M$ square lattice with nearest neighbour interactions:

$$p(x) \propto \exp \beta \sum_{i \sim j} \mathbb{I}\left[x_i = x_j\right]. \tag{27.9.5}$$

Now consider the $M \times M$ grid as a checkerboard, and give each white square a label w_i, and each black square a label b_j, so that each square is associated with a particular variable. Show that

$$p(b_1, b_2, \ldots, |w_1, w_2, \ldots) = p(b_1|w_1, w_2, \ldots)p(b_2|w_1, w_2, \ldots)\ldots \tag{27.9.6}$$

That is, conditioned on the white variables, the black variables are independent. The converse is also true, that conditioned on the black variables, the white variables are independent. Explain how this can be exploited by a Gibbs sampling procedure. This procedure is known as *checkerboard* or *black and white sampling*.

27.5 Consider the symmetric Gaussian proposal distribution

$$\tilde{q}(\mathbf{x}'|\mathbf{x}) = \mathcal{N}\left(\mathbf{x}'|\mathbf{x}, \sigma_q^2\mathbf{I}\right) \tag{27.9.7}$$

and the target distribution

$$p(\mathbf{x}) = \mathcal{N}\left(\mathbf{x}|\mathbf{0}, \sigma_p^2\mathbf{I}\right) \tag{27.9.8}$$

where $\dim(\mathbf{x}) = N$. Show that

$$\left\langle \log \frac{p(\mathbf{x}')}{p(\mathbf{x})} \right\rangle_{\tilde{q}(\mathbf{x}'|\mathbf{x})} = -\frac{N\sigma_q^2}{2\sigma_p^2}. \tag{27.9.9}$$

Discuss how this result relates to the probability of accepting a Metropolis–Hastings update under a Gaussian proposal distribution in high dimensions.

27.6 The file `demoSampleHMM.m` performs naive Gibbs sampling of the posterior $p(h_{1:T}|v_{1:T})$ for an HMM for $T = 10$. At each Gibbs update a single variable h_t is chosen, with the remaining h variables clamped. The procedure starts from $t = 1$ and sweeps forwards through time. When the end time $t = T$ is reached, the joint state $h_{1:T}$ is taken as a sample from the posterior. The parameter λ controls how deterministic the hidden transition matrix $p(h_t|h_{t-1})$ will be. Adjust `demoSampleHMM.m` to run 100 times for the same λ, computing a mean absolute error for the posterior marginal $p(h_t|v_{1:T})$ over these 100 runs. Then repeat this for $\lambda = 0.1, 1, 10, 20$. Finally, repeat this whole procedure 20 times for different random draws of the transition and emission matrices, and average the errors in computing the smoothed posterior marginal by Gibbs sampling. Discuss why the performance of this Gibbs sampling routine deteriorates with increasing λ.

27.7 Consider the following MATLAB code snippet:

```
c=p(1); i=1; r=rand;
while r>c && i<n
    i=i+1; c=c+p(i);
end
sample=i;
```

1. Explain why this draws a sample state i from a discrete distribution with probability $p(i), i = 1, \ldots, n$.
2. Explain how to effectively sample from the distribution $p(i) = e^{-\lambda}\lambda^i/i!$, $0 < \lambda < 1$, $i = 0, \ldots, \infty$ which contains an infinite number of discrete states.

27.8 Consider drawing samples from a posterior $p(\theta|\mathcal{D}) \propto p(\mathcal{D}|\theta)p(\theta)$.

1. Show that for

$$q(\mathcal{D}, \mathcal{D}', \theta) = q(\mathcal{D}|\mathcal{D}')p(\mathcal{D}'|\theta)p(\theta), \text{ where } q(\mathcal{D}|\mathcal{D}') = \delta\left(\mathcal{D} - \mathcal{D}'\right) \tag{27.9.10}$$

the marginal distribution is

$$q(\theta|\mathcal{D}) = p(\theta|\mathcal{D}) \tag{27.9.11}$$

2. Hence show that the following procedure generates a sample from $p(\theta|\mathcal{D})$:
   (a) Sample θ from $p(\theta)$
   (b) Sample a 'candidate' dataset $\mathcal{D}'$ from $p(\mathcal{D}'|\theta)$
   (c) If $\mathcal{D}' = \mathcal{D}$ accept the candidate as a sample, otherwise make no sample and go to (a).
3. One may relax the delta-function constraint and use, for example, $q(\mathcal{D}|\mathcal{D}') = \mathcal{N}\left(\mathcal{D}|\mathcal{D}', \sigma^2\mathbf{I}\right)$ for some chosen σ^2. Then

$$q(\theta|\mathcal{D}) = \sum_l w_l \delta\left(\theta - \theta^l\right) \text{ where } w_l \equiv \frac{q(\mathcal{D}|\mathcal{D}^l)}{\sum_{l=1}^{L} q(\mathcal{D}|\mathcal{D}^l)}. \tag{27.9.12}$$

   Explain how this approximate sampling procedure is related to the Parzen estimator.
4. By considering a single D-dimensional datapoint $\mathbf{x}$ and sampled datapoint $\mathbf{x}^i$, both generated from the same underlying distribution $\mathcal{N}\left(\mathbf{x}|\mathbf{0}, \nu^2\mathbf{I}_{D\times D}\right)$ show that for the unnormalised weight

$$u_i = \exp\left(-\frac{1}{2\sigma^2}\left(\mathbf{x} - \mathbf{x}^i\right)^2\right) \tag{27.9.13}$$

the typical ratio of the weights can be assessed using

$$\left\langle \left(\log \frac{u_i}{u_j} \right)^2 \right\rangle_{\mathcal{N}(\mathbf{x}|\mathbf{0},\nu^2\mathbf{I})\mathcal{N}(\mathbf{x}^i|\mathbf{0},\nu^2\mathbf{I})\mathcal{N}(\mathbf{x}^j|\mathbf{0},\nu^2\mathbf{I})} = 12D\frac{\nu^4}{\sigma^4}. \tag{27.9.14}$$

Explain why the normalised weights will typically be dominated by a single component, rendering the sampling method described in part (3) above generally impractical.

28 Deterministic approximate inference

Sampling methods are popular and well known for approximate inference. In this chapter we give an introduction to the less well known class of deterministic approximation techniques. These have been spectacularly successful in branches of the information sciences and many have their origins in the study of large-scale physical systems.

28.1 Introduction

Deterministic approximate inference methods are an alternative to the sampling techniques discussed in Chapter 27. Drawing exact independent samples is typically computationally intractable and assessing the quality of the sample estimates is difficult. In this chapter we discuss some alternatives. The first, Laplace's method, is a simple perturbation technique. The second class of methods are those that produce rigorous bounds on quantities of interest. Such methods are interesting since they provide certain knowledge – it may be sufficient, for example, to show that a marginal probability is greater than 0.1 in order to make an informed decision. A further class of methods are the consistency methods, such as loopy belief propagation. Such methods have revolutionised certain fields, including error correction [197]. It is important to bear in mind that no single approximation technique, deterministic or stochastic, is going to beat all others on all problems, given the same computational resources. In this sense, insight as to the properties of the various approximations is useful in matching an approximation method to the problem at hand.

28.2 The Laplace approximation

Consider a distribution on a continuous variable of the form

$$p(\mathbf{x}) = \frac{1}{Z} e^{-E(\mathbf{x})}. \tag{28.2.1}$$

The Laplace method makes a Gaussian approximation of $p(\mathbf{x})$ based on a local perturbation expansion around a mode $\mathbf{x}^*$. First we find the mode numerically, giving

$$\mathbf{x}^* = \underset{\mathbf{x}}{\operatorname{argmin}}\ E(\mathbf{x}). \tag{28.2.2}$$

Then a Taylor expansion up to second order around this mode gives

$$E(\mathbf{x}) \approx E(\mathbf{x}^*) + (\mathbf{x} - \mathbf{x}^*)^{\mathsf{T}} \nabla E|_{\mathbf{x}^*} + \frac{1}{2} (\mathbf{x} - \mathbf{x}^*)^{\mathsf{T}} \mathbf{H} (\mathbf{x} - \mathbf{x}^*) \tag{28.2.3}$$

where $\mathbf{H} \equiv \nabla\nabla E(\mathbf{x})|_{\mathbf{x}^*}$ is the Hessian evaluated at the mode. At the mode, $\nabla E|_{\mathbf{x}^*} = \mathbf{0}$, and an approximation of the distribution is given by the Gaussian

$$q(\mathbf{x}) = \frac{1}{Z_q} e^{-\frac{1}{2}(\mathbf{x}-\mathbf{x}^*)^{\mathsf{T}}\mathbf{H}(\mathbf{x}-\mathbf{x}^*)} = \mathcal{N}\left(\mathbf{x}|\mathbf{x}^*, \mathbf{H}^{-1}\right) \tag{28.2.4}$$

which has mean $\mathbf{x}^*$ and covariance $\mathbf{H}^{-1}$, with $Z_q = \sqrt{\det(2\pi\mathbf{H}^{-1})}$. We can use the above expansion to estimate the integral

$$\int_{\mathbf{x}} e^{-E(\mathbf{x})} \approx \int_{\mathbf{x}} e^{-E(\mathbf{x}^*)-\frac{1}{2}(\mathbf{x}-\mathbf{x}^*)^{\mathsf{T}}\mathbf{H}(\mathbf{x}-\mathbf{x}^*)} = e^{-E(\mathbf{x}^*)}\sqrt{\det(2\pi\mathbf{H}^{-1})}. \tag{28.2.5}$$

The Laplace Gaussian fit to a distribution is not necessarily the 'best' Gaussian approximation. As we'll see below, other criteria, such as those based on minimal KL divergence between $p(\mathbf{x})$ and a Gaussian approximation may be more appropriate, depending on the context. A benefit of Laplace's method is its relative simplicity compared with other approximate inference techniques.

28.3 Properties of Kullback–Leibler variational inference

Variational methods can be used to approximate a complex distribution $p(x)$ by a simpler distribution $q(x)$. Given a definition of discrepancy between an approximation $q(x)$ to $p(x)$, any free parameters of $q(x)$ are then set by minimising the discrepancy. This class of techniques is also called 'mean field' methods in the physics literature.

A particularly popular measure of the discrepancy between an approximation $q(x)$ and the intractable distribution $p(x)$ is the Kullback–Leibler divergence

$$\mathrm{KL}(q|p) = \langle \log q \rangle_q - \langle \log p \rangle_q. \tag{28.3.1}$$

It is straightforward to show that $\mathrm{KL}(q|p) \geq 0$ and is zero if and only if the distributions p and q are identical, see Section 8.2.1. Note that whilst the KL divergence cannot be negative, there is no upper bound on the value it can potentially take so that the discrepancy can be 'infinitely' large.

28.3.1 Bounding the normalisation constant

For a distribution of the form

$$p(x) = \frac{1}{Z} e^{\phi(x)} \tag{28.3.2}$$

we have

$$\mathrm{KL}(q|p) = \langle \log q(x) \rangle_{q(x)} - \langle \log p(x) \rangle_{q(x)} = \langle \log q(x) \rangle_{q(x)} - \langle \phi(x) \rangle_{q(x)} + \log Z. \tag{28.3.3}$$

Since $\mathrm{KL}(q|p) \geq 0$ this immediately gives the bound

$$\log Z \geq \underbrace{-\langle \log q(x) \rangle_{q(x)}}_{\text{entropy}} + \underbrace{\langle \phi(x) \rangle_{q(x)}}_{\text{energy}} \tag{28.3.4}$$

which is called the 'free energy' bound in the physics community [254]. The $\mathrm{KL}(q|p)$ method provides therefore a lower bound on the normalisation constant. The art is then to choose a class of approximating distributions q such that both its entropy and the energy term are tractably computable.

28.3.2 Bounding the marginal likelihood

In Bayesian modelling the likelihood of the model $\mathcal{M}$ with parameters θ generating data $\mathcal{D}$ is given by

$$p(\mathcal{D}|\mathcal{M}) = \int_\theta \underbrace{p(\mathcal{D}|\theta,\mathcal{M})}_{\text{likelihood}} \underbrace{p(\theta|\mathcal{M})}_{\text{prior}}. \tag{28.3.5}$$

This quantity is fundamental to model comparison. However, in cases where θ is high-dimensional, the integral over θ is often difficult to perform. Using Bayes' rule,

$$p(\theta|\mathcal{D},\mathcal{M}) = \frac{p(\mathcal{D}|\theta,\mathcal{M})p(\theta|\mathcal{M})}{p(\mathcal{D}|\mathcal{M})} \tag{28.3.6}$$

and considering

$$\text{KL}(q(\theta)|p(\theta|\mathcal{D},\mathcal{M})) = \langle \log q(\theta)\rangle_{q(\theta)} - \langle \log p(\theta|\mathcal{D},\mathcal{M})\rangle_{q(\theta)} \tag{28.3.7}$$

$$= \langle \log q(\theta)\rangle_{q(\theta)} - \langle \log p(\mathcal{D}|\theta,\mathcal{M})p(\theta|\mathcal{M})\rangle_{q(\theta)} + \log p(\mathcal{D}|\mathcal{M}) \tag{28.3.8}$$

the non-negativity of the Kullback–Leibler divergence gives the bound

$$\log p(\mathcal{D}|\mathcal{M}) \geq -\langle \log q(\theta)\rangle_{q(\theta)} + \langle \log p(\mathcal{D}|\theta,\mathcal{M})p(\theta|\mathcal{M})\rangle_{q(\theta)} \tag{28.3.9}$$

$$= \langle \log p(\mathcal{D}|\theta,\mathcal{M})\rangle_{q(\theta)} - \text{KL}(q(\theta)|p(\theta|\mathcal{M})). \tag{28.3.10}$$

This bound holds for any distribution $q(\theta)$ and becomes equality when $q(\theta) = p(\theta|\mathcal{D},\mathcal{M})$. Since using the optimal setting is assumed computationally intractable, the idea in variational bounding is to choose a distribution family for $q(\theta)$ for which the bound is computationally tractable, and then maximise the bound with respect to any free parameters of $q(\theta)$. The resulting bound then can be used as a surrogate for the exact marginal likelihood in model comparison.

28.3.3 Bounding marginal quantities

The Kullback–Leibler approach provides a lower bound on normalisation constants. Combined with an upper bound, obtained using alternative methods, see for example [307] and Exercise 28.6, we are able to bracket marginals $l \leq p(x_i) \leq u$, see Exercise 28.9. The tightness of the resulting bracket gives an indication as to how tight the bounding procedures are. Even in cases where the resulting bracket is weak – for example it might be that the result is that $0.1 < p(cancer = \text{true}) < 0.99$, this may be sufficient for decision making purposes since the probability of cancer is sufficiently large to merit action.

28.3.4 Gaussian approximations using KL divergence

Minimising KL$(q|p)$

Using a simple approximation $q(x)$ of a more complex distribution $p(x)$ by minimising KL$(q|p)$ tends to give a solution for $q(x)$ that focusses on a local mode of $p(x)$, thereby underestimating the variance of $p(x)$. To show this, consider approximating a mixture of two Gaussians with equal variance σ^2,

$$p(x) = \frac{1}{2}\left(\mathcal{N}(x|-\mu,\sigma^2) + \mathcal{N}(x|\mu,\sigma^2)\right) \tag{28.3.11}$$

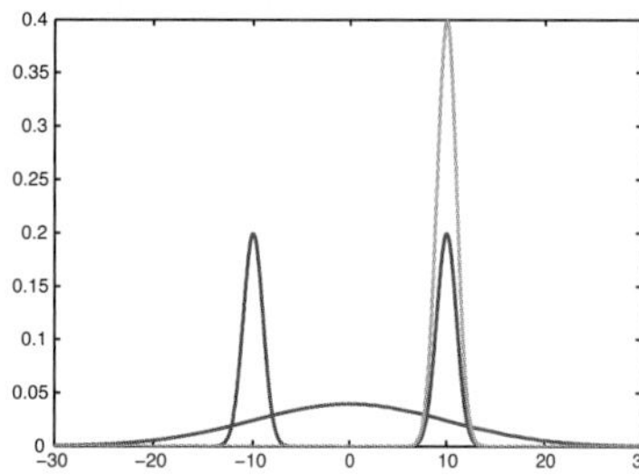

Figure 28.1 Fitting a mixture of Gaussians $p(x)$ (blue) with a single Gaussian. The green curve minimises $\mathrm{KL}(q|p)$ corresponding to fitting a local model. The red curve minimises $\mathrm{KL}(p|q)$ corresponding to moment matching. See plate section for colour version.

see Fig. 28.1, with a single Gaussian

$$q(x) = \mathcal{N}\left(x|m, s^2\right). \tag{28.3.12}$$

We wish to find the optimal m, s^2 that minimise

$$\mathrm{KL}(q|p) = \langle \log q(x)\rangle_{q(x)} - \langle \log p(x)\rangle_{q(x)}. \tag{28.3.13}$$

If we consider the case that the two Gaussian components of $p(x)$ are well separated, $\mu \gg \sigma$, then by setting $q(x)$ to be centred on the left mode at $-\mu$ the Gaussian $q(x)$ only has appreciable mass close to $-\mu$, so that the second mode at μ has negligible contribution to the Kullback–Leibler divergence. In this sense one can approximate $p(x) \approx \frac{1}{2}q(x)$, so that

$$\mathrm{KL}(q|p) \approx \langle \log q(x)\rangle_{q(x)} - \langle \log p(x)\rangle_{q(x)} = \log 2. \tag{28.3.14}$$

On the other hand, setting $m = 0$, which is the correct mean of the distribution $p(x)$, very little of the mass of the mixture is captured unless s^2 is large, giving a poor fit and large KL divergence. Another way to view this is to consider $\mathrm{KL}(q|p) = \langle \log q(x)/p(x)\rangle_{q(x)}$; provided q is close to p around where q has significant mass, the ratio $q(x)/p(x)$ will be order 1 and the KL divergence small. Setting $m = 0$ means that $q(x)/p(x)$ is large where q has significant mass, and is therefore a poor fit. The optimal solution in this case is therefore to place the Gaussian close to a single mode. However, for two modes that are less well separated, the optimal solution will not necessarily be to place the Gaussian around a local mode. In general, the optimal Gaussian fit needs to be determined numerically – that is, there is no closed form solution to finding the optimal mean and (co)variance parameters.

Minimising KL$(p|q)$

Bearing in mind that in general $\mathrm{KL}(q|p) \neq \mathrm{KL}(p|q)$, it is also useful to understand the properties of $\mathrm{KL}(p|q)$. For fitting a Gaussian $q(x) = \mathcal{N}\left(x|m, s^2\right)$ to p based on $\mathrm{KL}(p|q)$, we have

$$\mathrm{KL}(p|q) = \langle \log p(x)\rangle_{p(x)} - \langle \log q(x)\rangle_{p(x)} = -\frac{1}{2s^2}\left\langle (x-m)^2\right\rangle_{p(x)} - \frac{1}{2}\log s^2 + \text{const.} \tag{28.3.15}$$

Minimising this with respect to m and σ^2 we obtain:

$$m = \langle x\rangle_{p(x)}, \qquad s^2 = \left\langle (x-m)^2\right\rangle_{p(x)} \tag{28.3.16}$$

so that the optimal Gaussian fit matches the first and second moments of $p(x)$.

In the case of Fig. 28.1, the mean of $p(x)$ is a zero, and the variance of $p(x)$ is large. This solution is therefore dramatically different from that produced by fitting the Gaussian using $\mathrm{KL}(q|p)$. The fit found using $\mathrm{KL}(q|p)$ focusses on making q fit p well locally, see also Exercise 28.17, whereas

KL$(p|q)$ focusses on making q fit p well to the global statistics of the distribution (possibly at the expense of a good local match).

28.3.5 Marginal and moment matching properties of minimising KL$(p|q)$

For simplicity, consider a factorised approximation $q(x) = \prod_i q(x_i)$. Then

$$\mathrm{KL}(p|q) = \langle \log p(x) \rangle_{p(x)} - \sum_i \langle \log q(x_i) \rangle_{p(x_i)}. \tag{28.3.17}$$

The first entropic term is independent of $q(x)$ so that, up to a constant independent of $q(x)$, the above is

$$\sum_i \mathrm{KL}(p(x_i)|q(x_i)) \tag{28.3.18}$$

so that optimally $q(x_i) = p(x_i)$. That is, the optimal factorised approximation is to set the factors of $q(x_i)$ to the marginals of $p(x_i)$, Exercise 28.13.

Another approximating distribution class that yields a known form for the approximation is the exponential family. In this case minimising KL$(p|q)$ corresponds to moment matching, see Exercise 28.13. In practice, one generally cannot compute the moments of $p(x)$ (since the distribution $p(x)$ is considered 'intractable'), so that fitting q to p based only on KL$(p|q)$ does not itself lead to a practical algorithm for approximate inference. Nevertheless, as we will see, it is a useful subroutine for local approximations, in particular expectation propagation.

28.4 Variational bounding using KL$(q|p)$

In this section we discuss how to fit a distribution $q(x)$ from some assumed family to an 'intractable' distribution $p(x)$. As we saw above for the case of fitting Gaussians, the optimal q needs to be found numerically. This itself can be a complex task (indeed, formally this can be just as difficult as performing inference directly with the intractable p) and the reader may wonder why we trade a difficult inference task for a potentially difficult optimisation problem. The general idea is that the optimisation problem has some local smoothness properties that enable one to rapidly find a reasonable optimum based on generic optimisation methods. To make these ideas more concrete, we discuss a particular case of fitting q to a formally intractable p in Section 28.4.1 below.

28.4.1 Pairwise Markov random field

A canonical intractable distribution is the pairwise Markov Random Field[1] (MRF) defined on binary variables $x_i \in \{+1, -1\}, i = 1, \ldots, D$,

$$p(x) = \frac{1}{Z(w, b)} e^{\sum_{i,j} w_{ij} x_i x_j + \sum_i b_i x_i}. \tag{28.4.1}$$

[1] Whilst inference with a general MRF is formally computationally intractable (no exact polynomial time methods are known), two celebrated results that we mention in passing are that for the planar MRF model with pure interactions ($b = 0$), the partition function is computable in polynomial time [170, 102, 191, 127, 260], as is the MAP state for attractive planar Ising models $w > 0$ [133], see Section 28.9.

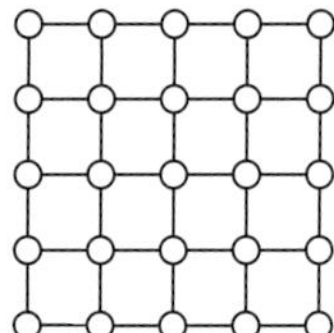

Figure 28.2 A planar pairwise Markov random field on a set of variables $x_1, \ldots, x_{25}$, representing a distribution of the form $\prod_{i\sim j} \phi(x_i, x_j)$. In statistical physics such lattice models include the Ising model on binary 'spin' variables $x_i \in \{+1, -1\}$ with $\phi(x_i, x_j) = e^{w_{ij} x_i x_j}$.

Here the partition function $Z(w, b)$ ensures normalisation,

$$Z(w, b) = \sum_x e^{\sum_{i,j} w_{ij} x_i x_j + \sum_i b_i x_i}. \tag{28.4.2}$$

Since $x_i^2 = 1$, the terms $w_{ii} x_i^2$ are constant and without loss of generality we may set w_{ii} to zero. A motivational example for this model is described below.

Example 28.1 Bayesian image denoising

Consider a binary image y generated by corrupting a clean image x; our interest is to recover the clean image given the corrupted image. We assume a noisy pixel generating process that takes each clean pixel $x_i \in \pm 1$ and flips its binary state:

$$p(y|x) = \prod_i p(y_i|x_i), \qquad p(y_i|x_i) \propto e^{\gamma y_i x_i}. \tag{28.4.3}$$

The probability that y_i and x_i are in the same state is $e^{\gamma}/(e^{\gamma} + e^{-\gamma})$. Our interest is the posterior distribution on clean pixels $p(x|y)$. We assume that clean images are reasonably smooth and can be described using an MRF prior defined on a lattice, Fig. 28.2,

$$p(x) \propto e^{\sum_{ij} w_{ij} x_i x_j} \tag{28.4.4}$$

where $w_{ij} > 0$, for neighbouring i and j, and $w_{ij} = 0$ otherwise. This encodes the assumption that clean images tend to have neighbouring pixels in the same state. An isolated pixel in a different state to its neighbours is unlikely under this prior. We now have the joint distribution

$$p(x, y) = p(x) \prod_i p(y_i|x_i) = \frac{1}{Z} e^{\sum_{ij} w_{ij} x_i x_j + \sum_i \gamma y_i x_i} \tag{28.4.5}$$

see Fig. 28.3, from which the posterior is given by

$$p(x|y) = \frac{p(y|x)p(x)}{\sum_x p(y|x)p(x)} \propto e^{\sum_{ij} w_{ij} x_i x_j + \sum_i \gamma y_i x_i}. \tag{28.4.6}$$

Quantities such as the MAP state (most a posteriori probable image), marginals $p(x_i|y)$ and the normalisation constant are of interest. This example is equivalent to the Markov network in

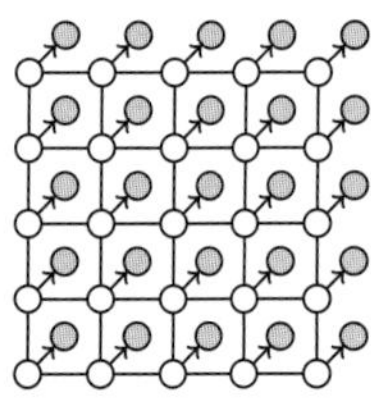

Figure 28.3 A distribution on pixels. The filled nodes indicate observed noisy pixels, the unshaded nodes a Markov random field on latent clean pixels. The task is to infer the clean pixels given the noisy pixels. The MRF encourages the posterior distribution on the clean pixels to contain neighbouring pixels in the same state.

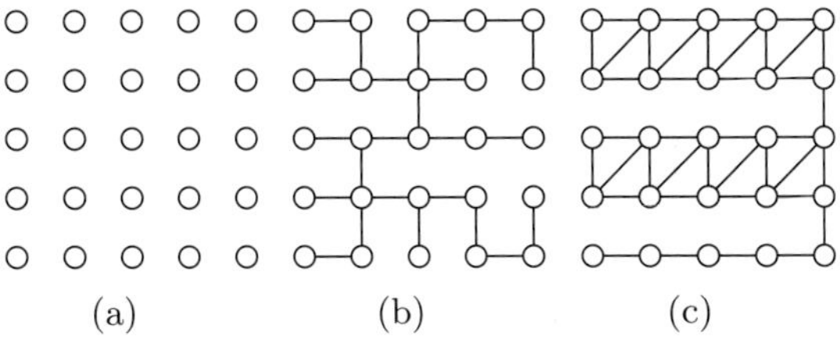

Figure 28.4 (**a**) Naive mean field approximation $q(x) = \prod_i q_i(x_i)$. (**b**) A spanning tree approximation. (**c**) A decomposable (hypertree) approximation.

Example 4.2. On the left below is the clean image, the middle is the noisy image, and on the right is the most likely posterior clean image $\arg\max_x p(x|y)$ found using iterated conditional modes, Section 28.9.1.

We discuss how to compute the MAP state for Example 28.1 in Section 28.9 and concentrate first on a technique that can bound the normalisation constant Z, a quantity that is useful in model comparison.

Kullback–Leibler based methods

For the MRF we have

$$\mathrm{KL}(q|p) = \langle \log q \rangle_q - \sum_{ij} w_{ij} \langle x_i x_j \rangle_q - \sum_i b_i \langle x_i \rangle_q + \log Z \geq 0. \tag{28.4.7}$$

Rewriting, this gives a bound on the log-partition function

$$\log Z \geq \underbrace{- \langle \log q \rangle_q}_{\text{entropy}} + \underbrace{\sum_{ij} w_{ij} \langle x_i x_j \rangle_q + \sum_i b_i \langle x_i \rangle_q}_{\text{energy}}. \tag{28.4.8}$$

The bound saturates when $q = p$. This is of little help, however, since we cannot compute the averages $\langle x_i x_j \rangle_p, \langle x_i \rangle_p$ with respect to this intractable distribution p. The idea of a variational method is to assume a simpler tractable distribution q for which these averages can be computed, along with the entropy of q. Minimising the KL divergence with respect to any free parameters of $q(x)$ is then equivalent to maximising the lower bound on the log partition function.

Factorised approximation

A 'naive' assumption is the fully factorised distribution

$$q(x) = \prod_i q_i(x_i). \tag{28.4.9}$$

The graphical model of this approximation is given in Fig. 28.4(a). In this case

$$\log Z \geq -\sum_i \langle \log q_i \rangle_{q_i} + \sum_{ij} w_{ij} \langle x_i x_j \rangle_{q(x_i,x_j)} + \sum_i b_i \langle x_i \rangle_{q(x_i)}. \tag{28.4.10}$$

For a factorised distribution $q(x) = \prod_i q(x_i)$, and $\langle x_i x_j \rangle = \langle x_i \rangle \langle x_j \rangle$, $i \neq j$. For a binary variable, one may use the convenient parametrization

$$q_i(x_i = 1) = \frac{e^{\alpha_i}}{e^{\alpha_i} + e^{-\alpha_i}} \tag{28.4.11}$$

so that for $x_i \in \{-1, +1\}$

$$\langle x_i \rangle_{q_i} = +1 \times q(x_i = 1) - 1 \times q(x_i = -1) = \tanh(\alpha_i). \tag{28.4.12}$$

This gives the following lower bound on the log partition function:

$$\log Z \geq \mathcal{B}(\alpha) \equiv \sum_i H(\alpha_i) + \sum_{i \neq j} w_{ij} \tanh(\alpha_i) \tanh(\alpha_j) + \sum_i b_i \tanh(\alpha_i) \tag{28.4.13}$$

where $H(\alpha_i)$ is the *binary entropy* of a distribution parameterised according to Equation (28.4.11):

$$H(\alpha_i) = \log\left(e_i^{\alpha} + e^{-\alpha_i}\right) - \alpha_i \tanh(\alpha_i). \tag{28.4.14}$$

Finding the best factorised approximation in the minimal Kullback–Leibler divergence sense then corresponds to maximising the bound $\mathcal{B}(\alpha)$ with respect to the variational parameters α. The bound $\mathcal{B}$, Equation (28.4.13), is generally non-convex in α and riddled with local optima. Finding the globally optimal α is therefore typically a computationally hard problem. It seems that we have simply replaced the computationally hard problem of computing $\log Z$ by an equally hard computational problem of maximising $\mathcal{B}(\alpha)$. Indeed, written as a factor graph in α, the structure of this optimisation problem matches exactly that of the original MRF. However, the hope is that by approximating a difficult discrete summation by a continuous optimisation problem, we will be able to bring to the table effective continuous variable optimisation techniques. A particularly simple optimisation technique is to solve for the zero derivative of the bound Equation (28.4.13). Differentiating and equating to zero, a little algebra leads to the requirement that the optimal solution satisfies the equations

$$\alpha_i = b_i + \sum_{i,j} w_{ij} \tanh(\alpha_j), \quad \forall i. \tag{28.4.15}$$

One may show that sequentially updating any α_i according to Equation (28.4.15) increases $\mathcal{B}(\alpha)$. This is called *asychronous updating* and is guaranteed to lead to a (local) minimum of the KL divergence, see Section 28.4.3. Once a converged solution α has been identified, in addition to a bound on $\log Z$, we can approximate

$$\langle x_i \rangle_p \approx \langle x_i \rangle_q = \tanh(\alpha_i). \tag{28.4.16}$$

Validity of the factorised approximation

When might one expect such a naive factorised approximation to work well? Clearly, for Equation (28.4.1), if w_{ij} is very small, the distribution p will be effectively factorised and the approximation will be accurate. A more interesting case is when each variable x_i has many neighbours. In this case it is useful to write the MRF as (ignoring the bias terms b_i for simplicity)

$$p(x) = \frac{1}{Z} e^{\sum_{ij} w_{ij} x_i x_j} = \frac{1}{Z} e^{D \sum_i x_i \frac{1}{D} \sum_j w_{ij} x_j} = \frac{1}{Z} e^{D \sum_i x_i z_i} \tag{28.4.17}$$

where the local 'fields' are defined as

$$z_i \equiv \frac{1}{D} \sum_j w_{ij} x_j. \tag{28.4.18}$$

An interesting question is how z_i is distributed. We now invoke a circular (but self-consistent) argument: Let's assume that $p(x)$ is factorised. Assuming that each w_{ij} is $O(1)$, the mean of z_i is

$$\langle z_i \rangle = \frac{1}{D} \sum_j w_{ij} \langle x_j \rangle = O(1). \tag{28.4.19}$$

The variance is

$$\langle z_i^2 \rangle - \langle z_i \rangle^2 = \frac{1}{D^2} \sum_{k=1}^{D} w_{ik}^2 \left(1 - \langle x_k \rangle^2\right) = O(1/D). \tag{28.4.20}$$

Hence for large D the variance of the field z_i is much smaller than its mean value. Since each of the terms x_j in the summation $\sum_j w_{ij} x_j$ is independent, provided the w_{ij} are not extreme, the conditions of validity of the central limit theorem hold [134], and z_i will be Gaussian distributed. In particular, as D increases the fluctuations around the mean diminish, and we may write

$$p(x) \approx \frac{1}{Z} e^{D \sum_i x_i \langle z_i \rangle} \approx \prod_i p(x_i). \tag{28.4.21}$$

The assumption that p is approximately factorised is therefore self-consistent in the limit of MRFs with a large number of neighbours. Hence the factorised approximation would appear to be reasonable in the extreme limits of (i) a very weakly connected system $w_{ij} \approx 0$, or (ii) a large densely connected system with random weights. The fully factorised approximation is also called the *naive mean field* theory since for the MRF case it assumes that we can replace the effect of the neighbours by a mean of the field at each site.

28.4.2 General mean-field equations

For a general intractable distribution $p(x)$ on discrete or continuous x, the KL divergence between a factorised approximation $q(x) = \prod_i q(x_i)$ and $p(x)$ is

$$\text{KL}(q(x)|p(x)) = \sum_i \langle \log q(x_i) \rangle_{q(x_i)} - \langle \log p(x) \rangle_{\prod_i q(x_i)}. \tag{28.4.22}$$

Isolating the dependency of the above on a single factor $q(x_i)$ we have

$$\langle \log q(x_i) \rangle_{q(x_i)} - \left\langle \langle \log p(x) \rangle_{\prod_{j \neq i} q(x_j)} \right\rangle_{q(x_i)}. \tag{28.4.23}$$

Up to a normalisation constant, this is therefore the KL divergence between $q(x_i)$ and a distribution proportional to $\exp\left(\langle \log p(x) \rangle_{\prod_{j \neq i} q(x_j)}\right)$ so that the optimal setting for $q(x_i)$ satisfies

$$q(x_i) \propto \exp\left(\langle \log p(x) \rangle_{\prod_{j \neq i} q(x_j)}\right). \tag{28.4.24}$$

These are known as the mean-field equations and define a new approximation factor in terms of the previous approximation factors. Note that if the normalisation constant of $p(x)$ is unknown, this presents no problem since this constant is simply absorbed into the normalisation of the factors $q(x_i)$. In other words one may replace $p(x)$ with the unnormalised $p^*(x)$ in Equation (28.4.24). Beginning with an initial randomly chosen set of distributions $q(x_i)$, the mean-field equations are iterated until convergence. Asynchronous updating is guaranteed to decrease the KL divergence at each stage, as we show below.

28.4.3 Asynchronous updating guarantees approximation improvement

For a factorised variational approximation equation (28.4.22), we claim that each update Equation (28.4.24) reduces the Kullback–Leibler approximation error. To show this we write a single updated distribution as

$$q_i^{new} = \frac{1}{Z_i} \exp \langle \log p(x) \rangle_{\prod_{j \neq i} q_j^{old}}. \tag{28.4.25}$$

The joint distribution under this single update is

$$q^{new} = q_i^{new} \prod_{j \neq i} q_j^{old}. \tag{28.4.26}$$

Our interest is the change in the approximation error under this single mean-field update:

$$\Delta \equiv \mathrm{KL}(q^{new}|p) - \mathrm{KL}(q^{old}|p). \tag{28.4.27}$$

Using

$$\mathrm{KL}(q^{new}|p) = \langle \log q_i^{new} \rangle_{q_i^{new}} + \sum_{j \neq i} \langle \log q_j^{old} \rangle_{q_j^{old}} - \left\langle \langle \log p(x) \rangle_{\prod_{j \neq i} q_j^{old}} \right\rangle_{q_i^{new}} \tag{28.4.28}$$

and defining the un-normalised distribution

$$q_i^*(x_i) = \exp \langle \log p(x) \rangle_{\prod_{j \neq i} q_j^{old}} = Z_i q_i^{new} \tag{28.4.29}$$

then

$$\begin{aligned} \Delta &= \langle \log q_i^{new} \rangle_{q_i^{new}} - \langle \log q_i^{old} \rangle_{q_i^{old}} - \left\langle \langle \log p \rangle_{\prod_{j \neq i} q_j^{old}} \right\rangle_{q_i^{new}} + \left\langle \langle \log p \rangle_{\prod_{j \neq i} q_j^{old}} \right\rangle_{q_i^{old}} && (28.4.30) \\ &= \langle \log q_i^* \rangle_{q_i^{new}} - \log Z_i - \langle \log q_i^{old} \rangle_{q_i^{old}} - \langle \log q_i^* \rangle_{q_i^{new}} + \langle \log q_i^* \rangle_{q_i^{old}} && (28.4.31) \\ &= -\log Z_i - \langle \log q_i^{old} \rangle_{q_i^{old}} + \langle \log q_i^* \rangle_{q_i^{old}} && (28.4.32) \\ &= -\mathrm{KL}(q_i^{old}|q_i^{new}) \leq 0. && (28.4.33) \end{aligned}$$

Hence

$$\mathrm{KL}(q^{new}|p) \leq \mathrm{KL}(q^{old}|p) \tag{28.4.34}$$

so that updating a single component of q at a time is guaranteed to improve the approximation. Note that this result is quite general, holding for any distribution $p(x)$. In the case of a Markov network the guaranteed approximation improvement is equivalent to a guaranteed increase (strictly speaking a non-decrease) in the lower bound on the partition function.

Remark 28.1 (Intractable energy) Even for a fully factorised approximation the mean-field equations may not be tractably implementable. For this we need to be able to compute $\langle \log p^*(x) \rangle_{\prod_{j \neq i} q(x_j)}$. For some models of interest this is still not possible and additional approximations are required.

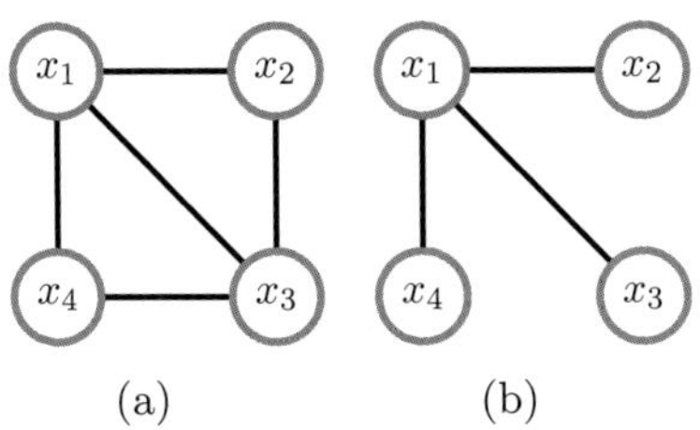

Figure 28.5 (**a**) A toy 'intractable' distribution. (**b**) A structured singly connected approximation.

28.4.4 Structured variational approximation

One can extend the factorised KL variational approximation by using non-factorised $q(x)$ [256, 24]. Those for which averages of the variables can be computed in linear time include spanning trees, Fig. 28.4(b), and decomposable graphs, Fig. 28.4(c). For example, for the distribution, Fig. 28.5(a),

$$p(x_1, x_2, x_3, x_4) = \frac{1}{Z}\phi(x_1, x_2)\phi(x_2, x_3)\phi(x_3, x_4)\phi(x_4, x_1)\phi(x_1, x_3) \tag{28.4.35}$$

a tractable q distribution would be, Fig. 28.5(b),

$$q(x_1, x_2, x_3, x_4) = \frac{1}{\tilde{Z}}\tilde{\phi}(x_1, x_2)\tilde{\phi}(x_1, x_3)\tilde{\phi}(x_1, x_4). \tag{28.4.36}$$

In this case we have

$$\mathrm{KL}(q|p) = H_q(x_1, x_2) + H_q(x_1, x_3) + H_q(x_1, x_4) - 3H_q(x_1) + \sum_{i\sim j}\langle \log\phi(x_i, x_j)\rangle_{q(x_i,x_j)}, \tag{28.4.37}$$

where $H_q(\mathcal{X})$ is the entropy of $q(\mathcal{X})$. Since q is singly connected, computing the marginals and entropy is straightforward (since the entropy requires only pairwise marginals on graph neighbours). In this case, however, we cannot apply directly the standard mean field update equations since there are constraints $\sum_{x_j} q(x_i, x_j) = q(x_j)$. We can either deal with these using Lagrange multipliers, or ensure that in performing a mean-field style update, we are including the contributions from coupled terms.

More generally one can exploit any structural approximation by use of, for example, the junction tree algorithm to compute the required moments. However, the computational expense typically increases exponentially with the hypertree width [315].

Example 28.2 Robot arm: control via inference

Control problems can also be cast as inference problems, see for example [165]. Consider the position $\mathbf{v}_t = (x_t, y_t)^\mathsf{T}$ of an n-link robot arm in a two-dimensional place, where each link $i \in \{1, \ldots, n\}$ in the arm is of unit length and angle $h_{i,t}$:

$$x_t = \sum_{i=1}^{n} \cos h_{i,t}, \qquad y_t = \sum_{i=1}^{n} \sin h_{i,t}. \tag{28.4.38}$$

Our interest is to use the robot arm to track a given sequence $\mathbf{v}_{1:T}$ such that the joint angles $\mathbf{h}_t$ do not change much from one time to the next. This is a classical control problem that we can formulate as an inference problem using a model

$$p(\mathbf{v}_{1:T}, \mathbf{h}_{1:T}) = p(\mathbf{v}_1|\mathbf{h}_1)p(\mathbf{h}_1)\prod_{t=2}^{T} p(\mathbf{v}_t|\mathbf{h}_t)p(\mathbf{h}_t|\mathbf{h}_{t-1}) \tag{28.4.39}$$

where the terms are

$$p(\mathbf{v}_t|\mathbf{h}_t) = \mathcal{N}\left(\mathbf{v}_t \middle| \left(\sum_{i=1}^n \cos h_{i,t}, \sum_{i=1}^n \sin h_{i,t}\right)^\mathsf{T}, \sigma^2\mathbf{I}\right), \qquad p(\mathbf{h}_t|\mathbf{h}_{t-1}) = \mathcal{N}\left(\mathbf{h}_t \middle| \mathbf{h}_{t-1}, \nu^2\mathbf{I}\right). \tag{28.4.40}$$

One solution to the control problem is then given by the most likely posterior sequence $\arg\max_{\mathbf{h}_{1:T}} p(\mathbf{h}_{1:T}|\mathbf{v}_{1:T})$. Here we consider an alternative, the maximum posterior marginal solution at each time $\arg\max_{\mathbf{h}_t} p(\mathbf{h}_t|\mathbf{v}_{1:T})$. Due to the non-linear observation, this posterior marginal cannot be computed exactly. A simple approximation is to use a fully factorised variational distribution $p(\mathbf{h}_{1:T}|\mathbf{v}_{1:T}) \approx q(\mathbf{h}_{1:T})$ where

$$q(\mathbf{h}_{1:T}) = \prod_{t=1}^T \prod_{i=1}^n q(h_{i,t}). \tag{28.4.41}$$

From the general form of the mean-field equations, the update for $q(h_{i,t})$ is given by (for $1 < t < T$)

$$-2\log q(h_{i,t}) = \frac{1}{\nu^2}\left(h_{i,t} - \bar{h}_{i,t-1}\right)^2 + \frac{1}{\nu^2}\left(h_{i,t} - \bar{h}_{i,t+1}\right)^2 + \frac{1}{\sigma^2}\left(\cos h_{i,t} - \alpha_{i,t}\right)^2 + \frac{1}{\sigma^2}\left(\sin h_{i,t} - \beta_{i,t}\right)^2 + \text{const.} \tag{28.4.42}$$

where

$$\bar{h}_{i,t+1} \equiv \langle h_{i,t+1}\rangle, \quad \alpha_{i,t} \equiv x_t - \sum_{j\neq i}\langle\cos h_{j,t}\rangle, \quad \beta_{i,t} \equiv y_t - \sum_{j\neq i}\langle\sin h_{j,t}\rangle \tag{28.4.43}$$

and the above averages are with respect to the q marginal distribution. Due to the non-linearities, the above marginal distributions are non-Gaussian. However, since they are only one-dimensional, the required averages can readily be computed using quadrature. The above mean-field equations are iterated to convergence. See `demoRobotArm.m` for further details and Fig. 28.6 for a demonstration. Note that the planning problem of starting from a point (x_1, y_1) to smoothly move the arm to a desired end point (x_T, y_T) is a special case of this framework. One can achieve this either by removing the observation terms for the intermediate times or, equivalently, making the observation variances for those intermediate times extremely large.

28.5 Local and KL variational approximations

In fitting a model parameterised by $\mathbf{w}$ to data $\mathcal{D}$, one often encounters parameter posteriors of the form

$$p(\mathbf{w}|\mathcal{D}) = \frac{1}{Z}\mathcal{N}(\mathbf{w}|\boldsymbol{\mu}, \boldsymbol{\Sigma}) f(\mathbf{w}) \tag{28.5.1}$$

where

$$Z = \int \mathcal{N}(\mathbf{w}|\boldsymbol{\mu}, \boldsymbol{\Sigma}) f(\mathbf{w}) d\mathbf{w}. \tag{28.5.2}$$

A classical example is Bayesian logistic regression, Section 18.2 in which $\mathcal{N}(\mathbf{w}|\boldsymbol{\mu}, \boldsymbol{\Sigma})$ represents a prior on the weight $\mathbf{w}$, $f(\mathbf{w})$ represents the likelihood $p(\mathcal{D}|\mathbf{w})$ and $Z = p(\mathcal{D})$. In all but limited special cases, the function $f(\mathbf{w})$ is not a simple squared exponential, resulting in a posterior distribution

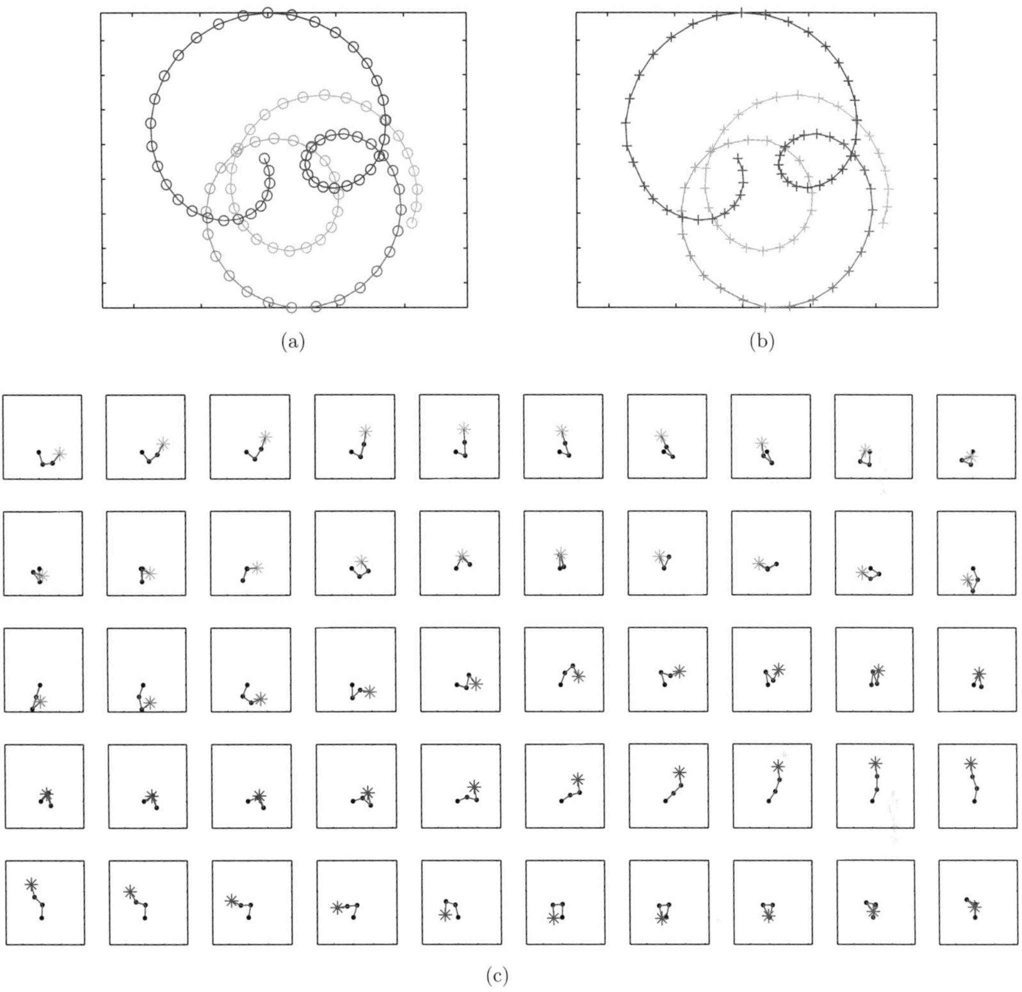

Figure 28.6 (**a**) The desired trajectory of the end point of a three link robot arm. Green denotes time 1 and red time 100. (**b**) The learned trajectory based on a fully factorised KL variational approximation. (**c**) The robot arm sections every 2nd timestep, from time 1 (top left) to time 100 (bottom right). The control problem of matching the trajectory using a smoothly changing angle set is solved using this simple approximation. See plate section for colour version.

of a non-standard form. Inevitably, therefore, approximations are required. When the dimension of the parameter vector $\dim(\mathbf{w}) = W$ is large, finding an accurate posterior approximation is in general non-trivial. Our particular interest here is to form an approximation of $p(\mathbf{w}|\mathcal{D})$ that also gives a principled lower bound on the marginal likelihood $p(\mathcal{D})$.

28.5.1 Local approximation

In a local method [225, 154, 124, 234], one replaces f by a suitable function for which the integral can be computed. Since in our case the integrand is composed of a Gaussian in $\mathbf{w}$, it is most convenient to bound $f(\mathbf{w})$ by an exponential quadratic function

$$f(\mathbf{w}) \geq c(\xi)e^{-\frac{1}{2}\mathbf{w}^{\mathsf{T}}\mathbf{F}(\xi)\mathbf{w}+\mathbf{w}^{\mathsf{T}}\mathbf{f}(\xi)} \tag{28.5.3}$$

where the matrix $\mathbf{F}(\xi)$, vector $\mathbf{f}(\xi)$ and scalar $c(\xi)$ depend on the specific function f; ξ is a variational parameter that enables one to find the tightest bound. We will discuss explicit c, $\mathbf{F}$ and $\mathbf{f}$ functions later, but for the moment leave them unspecified. Then from Equation (28.5.2)

$$Z \geq \frac{c(\xi)}{\sqrt{\det(2\pi\boldsymbol{\Sigma})}} \int \exp\left(-\frac{1}{2}(\mathbf{w}-\boldsymbol{\mu})^{\mathsf{T}}\boldsymbol{\Sigma}^{-1}(\mathbf{w}-\boldsymbol{\mu})\right)\exp\left(-\frac{1}{2}\mathbf{w}^{\mathsf{T}}\mathbf{F}(\xi)\mathbf{w}+\mathbf{w}^{\mathsf{T}}\mathbf{f}(\xi)\right)d\mathbf{w}$$

which can be expressed as

$$Z \geq c(\xi)\frac{e^{-\frac{1}{2}\boldsymbol{\mu}^{\mathsf{T}}\boldsymbol{\Sigma}^{-1}\boldsymbol{\mu}}}{\sqrt{\det(2\pi\boldsymbol{\Sigma})}} \int \exp\left(-\frac{1}{2}\mathbf{w}^{\mathsf{T}}\mathbf{A}\mathbf{w}+\mathbf{w}^{\mathsf{T}}\mathbf{b}\right)d\mathbf{w} \tag{28.5.4}$$

where

$$\mathbf{A} = \boldsymbol{\Sigma}^{-1} + \mathbf{F}(\xi), \quad \mathbf{b} = \boldsymbol{\Sigma}^{-1}\boldsymbol{\mu} + \mathbf{f}(\xi). \tag{28.5.5}$$

Whilst both $\mathbf{A}$ and $\mathbf{b}$ are functions of ξ, we notationally drop this dependency to keep the description more compact. Completing the square and integrating, we have $\log Z \geq B(\xi)$, with

$$\mathcal{B}(\xi) \equiv \log c(\xi) - \frac{1}{2}\boldsymbol{\mu}^{\mathsf{T}}\boldsymbol{\Sigma}^{-1}\boldsymbol{\mu} + \frac{1}{2}\mathbf{b}^{\mathsf{T}}\mathbf{A}\mathbf{b} - \frac{1}{2}\log\det(\boldsymbol{\Sigma}\mathbf{A}). \tag{28.5.6}$$

To obtain the tightest bound on $\log Z$, one maximises $B(\xi)$ with respect to ξ. In many practical problems of interest, $f(\mathbf{w}) = \prod_{s=1}^{M} f_s(\mathbf{w})$ for local site functions f_s. By bounding each site individually, we obtain a bound $\mathcal{B}(\xi_1, \ldots, \xi_M)$. The bound may be then optimised numerically with respect to the vector $\boldsymbol{\xi}$.

28.5.2 KL variational approximation

An alternative to the above local bounding method is to consider a KL approach based on fitting a Gaussian to the distribution. Defining

$$\tilde{p}(\mathbf{w}) \equiv \frac{\mathcal{N}(\mathbf{w}|\boldsymbol{\mu},\boldsymbol{\Sigma})\, f(\mathbf{w})}{Z}. \tag{28.5.7}$$

By fitting a Gaussian $q(\mathbf{w}) = \mathcal{N}(\mathbf{w}|\mathbf{m},\mathbf{S})$ based on minimising the $\mathrm{KL}(q(\mathbf{w})|\tilde{p}(\mathbf{w}))$, we obtain the bound $\log Z \geq \mathcal{B}_{KL}(\mathbf{m},\mathbf{S})$ with

$$\mathcal{B}_{KL}(\mathbf{m},\mathbf{S}) \equiv -\langle \log q(\mathbf{w})\rangle - \frac{1}{2}\log\det(2\pi\boldsymbol{\Sigma}) - \frac{1}{2}\left\langle (\mathbf{w}-\boldsymbol{\mu})^{\mathsf{T}}\boldsymbol{\Sigma}^{-1}(\mathbf{w}-\boldsymbol{\mu})\right\rangle + \langle \log f(\mathbf{w})\rangle.$$

where $\langle\cdot\rangle$ denotes expectation with respect to $q(\mathbf{w})$. One then numerically finds the best parameters $\mathbf{m}$, $\mathbf{S}$ that maximise the bound. Since the entropy of a Gaussian is trivial, the only potentially problematic term in evaluating this bound is $\langle \log f(\mathbf{w})\rangle$. A class of functions for which $\langle \log f(\mathbf{w})\rangle_{\mathcal{N}(\mathbf{w}|\mathbf{m},\mathbf{S})}$ is computationally tractable is when $f(\mathbf{w}) = f(\mathbf{w}^{\mathsf{T}}\mathbf{h})$ for some fixed vector $\mathbf{h}$. In this case, the projection $\mathbf{w}^{\mathsf{T}}\mathbf{h}$ is also Gaussian distributed and

$$\left\langle \log f(\mathbf{w}^{\mathsf{T}}\mathbf{h})\right\rangle_{\mathcal{N}(\mathbf{w}|\mathbf{m},\mathbf{S})} = \langle \log f(a)\rangle_{\mathcal{N}(a|\mathbf{m}^{\mathsf{T}}\mathbf{h},\mathbf{h}^{\mathsf{T}}\mathbf{S}\mathbf{h})} \tag{28.5.8}$$

which can be readily computed using any one-dimensional integration routine. Explicitly, as a function of $\mathbf{m}$, $\mathbf{S}$, we have

$$\begin{aligned} 2\mathcal{B}_{KL}(\mathbf{m},\mathbf{S}) \equiv & -\log\det(\mathbf{S}) + W + \log\det(\boldsymbol{\Sigma}) \\ & - \mathrm{trace}\left(\boldsymbol{\Sigma}^{-1}\left(\mathbf{S} + (\mathbf{m}-\boldsymbol{\mu})(\mathbf{m}-\boldsymbol{\mu})^{\mathsf{T}}\right)\right) + 2\langle \log f(a)\rangle_{\mathcal{N}(a|\mathbf{m}^{\mathsf{T}}\mathbf{h},\mathbf{h}^{\mathsf{T}}\mathbf{S}\mathbf{h})}. \end{aligned} \tag{28.5.9}$$

Whilst, in general, the variational bounds are non-concave in their variational parameters, provided f is log-concave then $\mathcal{B}_{KL}(\mathbf{m}, \mathbf{S})$ is jointly concave in $\mathbf{m}$ and $\mathbf{S}$. By using structured covariances $\mathbf{S}$ the method is scalable to very high dimensional problems [60].

Relation between the KL and local bounds

The KL and local variational methods both provide a lower bound on the normalisation term Z in Equation (28.5.2). It is interesting therefore to understand what relation there is between these bounds. Using the bound on $f(\mathbf{w})$, we obtain a new bound

$$\mathcal{B}_{KL}(\mathbf{m}, \mathbf{S}) \geq \tilde{\mathcal{B}}_{KL}(\mathbf{m}, \mathbf{S}, \xi) \tag{28.5.10}$$

where

$$\begin{aligned}\tilde{\mathcal{B}}_{KL} \equiv & -\langle \log q(\mathbf{w}) \rangle - \frac{1}{2} \log \det (2\pi \boldsymbol{\Sigma}) - \frac{1}{2} \left\langle (\mathbf{w} - \boldsymbol{\mu})^{\mathsf{T}} \boldsymbol{\Sigma}^{-1} (\mathbf{w} - \boldsymbol{\mu}) \right\rangle \\ & + \log c(\xi) - \frac{1}{2} \left\langle \mathbf{w}^{\mathsf{T}} \mathbf{F}(\xi) \mathbf{w} \right\rangle + \left\langle \mathbf{w}^{\mathsf{T}} \mathbf{f}(\xi) \right\rangle\end{aligned}$$

which, using Equation (28.5.5), can be written as

$$\tilde{\mathcal{B}}_{KL} = -\langle \log q(\mathbf{w}) \rangle - \frac{1}{2} \log \det (2\pi \boldsymbol{\Sigma}) + \log c(\xi) - \frac{1}{2} \boldsymbol{\mu}^{\mathsf{T}} \boldsymbol{\Sigma}^{-1} \boldsymbol{\mu} - \frac{1}{2} \left\langle \mathbf{w}^{\mathsf{T}} \mathbf{A} \mathbf{w} \right\rangle + \left\langle \mathbf{w}^{\mathsf{T}} \mathbf{b} \right\rangle. \tag{28.5.11}$$

By defining

$$\tilde{q}(\mathbf{w}) = \mathcal{N}\left(\mathbf{w} | \mathbf{A}^{-1}\mathbf{b}, \mathbf{A}^{-1}\right) \tag{28.5.12}$$

then

$$\begin{aligned}\tilde{\mathcal{B}}_{KL} = & -\mathrm{KL}(q(\mathbf{w}) | \tilde{q}(\mathbf{w})) - \frac{1}{2} \log \det (2\pi \boldsymbol{\Sigma}) + \log c(\xi) - \frac{1}{2} \boldsymbol{\mu}^{\mathsf{T}} \boldsymbol{\Sigma}^{-1} \boldsymbol{\mu} \\ & + \frac{1}{2} \mathbf{b}^{\mathsf{T}} \mathbf{A}^{-1} \mathbf{b} + \frac{1}{2} \log \det \left(2\pi \mathbf{A}^{-1}\right).\end{aligned}$$

Since $\mathbf{m}, \mathbf{S}$ only appear via $q(\mathbf{w})$ in the KL term, the tightest bound is given when $\mathbf{m}, \mathbf{S}$ are set such that $q(\mathbf{w}) = \tilde{q}(\mathbf{w})$. At this setting the KL term in $\tilde{\mathcal{B}}_{KL}$ disappears and $\mathbf{m}$ and $\mathbf{S}$ are given by

$$\mathbf{S}_{\xi} = \left(\boldsymbol{\Sigma}^{-1} + \mathbf{F}(\xi)\right)^{-1}, \qquad \mathbf{m}_{\xi} = \mathbf{S}_{\xi} \left(\boldsymbol{\Sigma}^{-1} \boldsymbol{\mu} + \mathbf{f}(\xi)\right). \tag{28.5.13}$$

For this setting of the variational parameters the bound matches the local bound (28.5.6). Since $\mathcal{B}_{KL}(\mathbf{m}, \mathbf{S}) \geq \tilde{\mathcal{B}}_{KL}(\mathbf{m}, \mathbf{S}, \xi)$ we therefore have that,

$$\mathcal{B}_{KL}(\mathbf{m}_{\xi}, \mathbf{S}_{\xi}) \geq \tilde{\mathcal{B}}_{KL}(\mathbf{m}_{\xi}, \mathbf{S}_{\xi}, \xi) = \mathcal{B}(\xi). \tag{28.5.14}$$

Importantly, the VG bound can be tightened beyond this setting:

$$\max_{\mathbf{m}, \mathbf{S}} \mathcal{B}_{KL}(\mathbf{m}, \mathbf{S}) \geq \mathcal{B}_{KL}(\mathbf{m}_{\xi}, \mathbf{S}_{\xi}). \tag{28.5.15}$$

Thus the optimal KL bound is provably tighter than both the local variational bound (28.5.6) and the KL bound calculated using the optimal local moments $\mathbf{m}_{\xi}$ and $\mathbf{S}_{\xi}$.

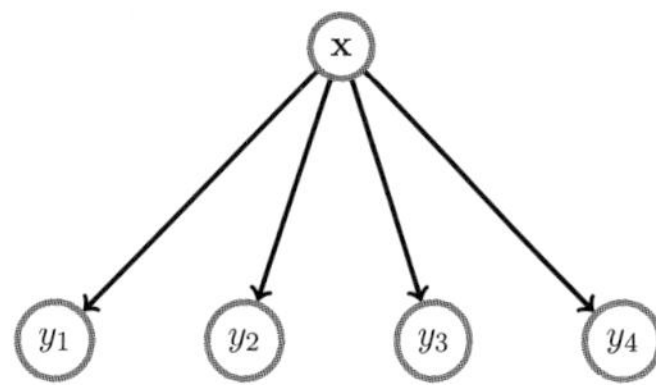

Figure 28.7 An information transfer problem. For a fixed distribution $p(\mathbf{x})$ and parameterised distributions $p(y_j|\mathbf{x}) = \sigma(\mathbf{w}_i^T\mathbf{x})$, find the optimal parameters $\mathbf{w}_i$ that maximise the mutual information between the variables $\mathbf{x}$ and $\mathbf{y}$. Such considerations are popular in theoretical neuroscience and aim to understand how the receptive fields $\mathbf{w}_i$ of a neuron relate to the statistics of the environment $p(\mathbf{x})$.

28.6 Mutual information maximisation: a KL variational approach

Here we take a short interlude to discuss an application of the Kullback–Leibler variational approach in information theory. A common goal is to maximise information transfer, measured by the mutual information (see also Definition 8.13)

$$I(X, Y) \equiv H(X) - H(X|Y) \tag{28.6.1}$$

where the entropy and conditional entropy are defined

$$H(X) \equiv -\langle \log p(x) \rangle_{p(x)}, \qquad H(X|Y) \equiv -\langle \log p(x|y) \rangle_{p(x,y)}. \tag{28.6.2}$$

Here we are interested in the situation in which $p(x)$ is fixed, but $p(y|x, \theta)$ has adjustable parameters θ that we wish to set in order to maximise $I(X, Y)$. In this case $H(X)$ is constant and the optimisation problem is equivalent to minimising the conditional entropy $H(X|Y)$. Unfortunately, in many cases of practical interest $H(X|Y)$ is computationally intractable. We discuss in Section 28.6.1 a general procedure based on the Kullback–Leibler divergence to approximately maximise the mutual information.

Example 28.3

Consider a neural transmission system in which $x_i \in \{0, 1\}$ denotes an emitting neuron in a non-firing state (0) or firing state (1), and $y_j \in \{0, 1\}$ a receiving neuron. If each receiving neuron fires independently, depending only on the emitting neurons, we have

$$p(\mathbf{y}|\mathbf{x}) = \prod_i p(y_i|\mathbf{x}) \tag{28.6.3}$$

where for example we could use

$$p(y_i = 1|\mathbf{x}) = \sigma\left(\mathbf{w}_i^T\mathbf{x}\right). \tag{28.6.4}$$

Given an empirical distribution on neural firings $p(\mathbf{x})$, our interest is to set the weights $\{\mathbf{w}_i\}$ to maximise information transfer, see Fig. 28.7. Since $p(\mathbf{x})$ is fixed, this requires maximising

$$\langle \log p(\mathbf{x}|\mathbf{y}) \rangle_{p(\mathbf{y}|\mathbf{x})p(\mathbf{x})}. \tag{28.6.5}$$

The quantity $p(\mathbf{x}|\mathbf{y}) = p(\mathbf{y}|\mathbf{x})p(\mathbf{x})/p(\mathbf{y})$ is a non-factorised function of $\mathbf{y}$ (due to the term $p(\mathbf{y})$. This means that the conditional entropy is typically intractable to compute and we require an approximation.

Algorithm 28.1 IM algorithm for maximising mutual information $I(X, Y)$ for fixed $p(x)$ and adjustable parameters are $p(y|x, \theta)$.

1: Choose a class of approximating distributions Q (for example factorised).
2: Initialise the parameters θ.
3: **repeat**
4: $\quad \theta^{new} = \underset{\theta}{\text{argmax}} \langle \log q(x|y) \rangle_{p(x)p(y|x,\theta)}$
5: $\quad q^{new}(x|y) = \underset{q(x|y) \in Q}{\text{argmax}} \langle \log q(x|y) \rangle_{p(x)p(y|x,\theta^{new})}$
6: **until** converged

28.6.1 The information maximisation algorithm

Consider

$$\text{KL}(p(x|y)|q(x|y)) \geq 0. \tag{28.6.6}$$

This immediately gives a bound

$$\sum_x p(x|y) \log p(x|y) - \sum_x p(x|y) \log q(x|y) \geq 0. \tag{28.6.7}$$

Multiplying both sides by $p(y)$, we obtain

$$\sum_{x,y} p(y)p(x|y) \log p(x|y) \geq \sum_{x,y} p(x, y) \log q(x|y). \tag{28.6.8}$$

From the definition, the left side of the above bound is $-H(X|Y)$. Hence

$$I(X, Y) \geq H(X) + \langle \log q(x|y) \rangle_{p(x,y)} \equiv \tilde{I}(X, Y). \tag{28.6.9}$$

From this lower bound on the mutual information we arrive at the *information maximisation* (IM) algorithm [20]. Given a distribution $p(x)$ and a parameterised distribution $p(y|x, \theta)$, we seek to maximise $\tilde{I}(X, Y)$ with respect to θ. A coordinate wise optimisation procedure is presented in Algorithm 28.1. The *Blahut–Arimoto algorithm* in information theory (see for example [198]) is a special case in which the optimal decoder

$$q(x|y) \propto p(y|x, \theta)p(x) \tag{28.6.10}$$

is used. In applications where the Blahut–Arimoto algorithm is intractable to implement, the IM algorithm can provide an alternative by restricting q to a tractable family of distributions (tractable in the sense that the lower bound can be computed). The Blahut–Arimoto algorithm is analogous to the EM algorithm for maximum likelihood and guarantees a non-decrease of the mutual information at each stage of the update, see Section 11.2.2. Similarly, the IM procedure is analogous to a variational EM procedure and each step of the procedure cannot decrease the lower bound on the mutual information.

28.6.2 Linear Gaussian decoder

A special case of the IM framework is to use a linear Gaussian decoder

$$q(\mathbf{x}|\mathbf{y}) = \mathcal{N}(\mathbf{x}|\mathbf{U}\mathbf{y}, \boldsymbol{\Sigma}) \Rightarrow \log q(\mathbf{x}|\mathbf{y}) = -\frac{1}{2}(\mathbf{x} - \mathbf{U}\mathbf{y})^{\mathsf{T}} \Sigma^{-1} (\mathbf{x} - \mathbf{U}\mathbf{y}) - \frac{1}{2} \log \det (2\pi \boldsymbol{\Sigma}). \tag{28.6.11}$$

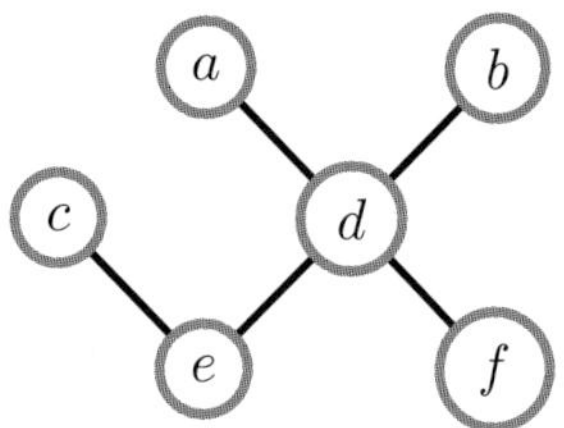

Figure 28.8 Belief propagation can be derived by considering how to compute the marginal of a variable on an MRF. In this case the marginal $p(d)$ depends on messages transmitted via the neighbours of d. By defining local messages on the links of the graph, a recursive algorithm for computing all marginals can be derived, see text.

Plugging this into the bound, Equation (28.6.9), and optimising with respect to $\mathbf{\Sigma}$, and $\mathbf{U}$, we obtain

$$\mathbf{\Sigma} = \left\langle (\mathbf{x} - \mathbf{U}\mathbf{y})(\mathbf{x} - \mathbf{U}\mathbf{y})^{\mathsf{T}} \right\rangle, \qquad \mathbf{U} = \left\langle \mathbf{x}\mathbf{y}^{\mathsf{T}} \right\rangle \left\langle \mathbf{y}\mathbf{y}^{\mathsf{T}} \right\rangle^{-1} \tag{28.6.12}$$

where $\langle \cdot \rangle \equiv \langle \cdot \rangle_{p(\mathbf{x},\mathbf{y})}$. Using this setting in the bound we obtain

$$I(X,Y) \geq H(X) - \frac{1}{2} \log \det \left(\left\langle \mathbf{x}\mathbf{x}^{\mathsf{T}} \right\rangle - \left\langle \mathbf{x}\mathbf{y}^{\mathsf{T}} \right\rangle \left\langle \mathbf{y}\mathbf{y}^{\mathsf{T}} \right\rangle^{-1} \left\langle \mathbf{y}\mathbf{x}^{\mathsf{T}} \right\rangle \right) - \frac{N}{2}(1 + \log 2\pi) \tag{28.6.13}$$

where $N = \dim(\mathbf{x})$. This is equivalent to *Linsker's as-if-Gaussian approximation* to the mutual information [190]. One can therefore view Linsker's approach as a special case of the IM algorithm restricted to linear Gaussian decoders. In principle, one can therefore improve on Linsker's method by considering more powerful non-linear Gaussian decoders. Applications of this technique to neural systems are discussed in [20].

28.7 Loopy belief propagation

Belief Propagation (BP) is a technique for exact inference of marginals $p(x_i)$ for singly connected distributions $p(x)$. There are different formulations of BP, the most modern treatment being the sum-product algorithm on the corresponding factor graph, as described in Section 5.1.2. An important observation is that the algorithm is purely local – the updates are unaware of the global structure of the graph. This means that even if the graph is multiply connected (it is loopy) one can still apply the algorithm and 'see what happens'. Provided the loops in the graph are relatively long, one may hope that 'loopy' BP will converge to a good approximation of the true marginals. When the method converges the results can be surprisingly accurate. In the following we will show how loopy BP can also be motivated by a variational objective. To do so, we make a connection to the classical BP algorithm (rather than the factor graph sum-product algorithm). For this reason we briefly describe below the classical BP approach.

28.7.1 Classical BP on an undirected graph

Belief propagation can be derived by considering how to calculate a marginal in terms of messages on an undirected graph. Consider calculating the marginal $p(d) = \sum_{a,b,c,e,f} p(a,b,c,d,e,f)$ for the pairwise Markov network in Fig. 28.8. We denote both a node and its state by the same symbol,

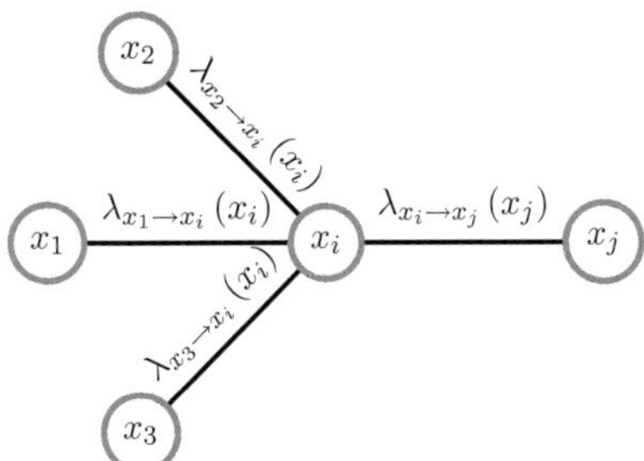

Figure 28.9 Loopy belief propagation. Once a node has received incoming messages from all neighbours (excluding the one it wants to send a message to), it may send an outgoing message to a neighbour: $\lambda_{x_i \to x_j}(x_j) = \sum_{x_i} \phi(x_i, x_j) \lambda_{x_1 \to x_i}(x_i) \lambda_{x_2 \to x_i}(x_i) \lambda_{x_3 \to x_i}(x_i)$.

so that $\sum_b \phi(d, b)$ denotes summation over the states of the variable b. To compute the summation efficiently we may distribute the summations as follows:

$$p(d) = \frac{1}{Z} \underbrace{\sum_b \phi(b, d)}_{\lambda_{b\to d}(d)} \underbrace{\sum_a \phi(a, d)}_{\lambda_{a\to d}(d)} \underbrace{\sum_f \phi(d, f)}_{\lambda_{f\to d}(d)} \underbrace{\sum_e \phi(d, e) \underbrace{\sum_c \phi(c, e)}_{\lambda_{c\to e}(e)}}_{\lambda_{e\to d}(d)} \tag{28.7.1}$$

where we define messages $\lambda_{n_1 \to n_2}(n_2)$ sending information from node n_1 to node n_2 as a function of the state of node n_2. In general, a node x_i passes a message to node x_j via

$$\lambda_{x_i \to x_j}(x_j) = \sum_{x_i} \phi(x_i, x_j) \prod_{k \in \text{ne}(i), k \neq j} \lambda_{x_k \to x_i}(x_i). \tag{28.7.2}$$

See also Fig. 28.9. At convergence the marginal $p(x_i)$ is then given by

$$q(x_i) \propto \prod_{i \in \text{ne}(j)} \lambda_{x_j \to x_i}(x_i) \tag{28.7.3}$$

the prefactor being determined by normalisation. The pairwise marginals are approximated by

$$q(x_i, x_j) \propto \left[\prod_{k \in \text{ne}(i) \setminus j} \lambda_{x_k \to x_i}(x_i) \right] \phi(x_i, x_j) \left[\prod_{k \in \text{ne}(j) \setminus i} \lambda_{x_k \to x_j}(x_j) \right]. \tag{28.7.4}$$

For a singly connected distribution p, this message-passing scheme converges and the marginal corresponds to the exact result. For multiply connected (loopy) structures, belief propagation will generally result in an approximation.

28.7.2 Loopy BP as a variational procedure

A variational procedure that corresponds to loopy BP can be derived by considering the terms of a standard variational approximation based on the Kullback–Leibler divergence $\text{KL}(q|p)$ [320]. We take as our example a pairwise Markov network defined on potentials $\phi(x_i, x_j)$,

$$p(x) = \frac{1}{Z} \prod_{i \sim j} \phi(x_i, x_j) \tag{28.7.5}$$

where $i \sim j$ denotes the unique neighbouring edges on the graph (each edge is counted only once). Using an approximating distribution $q(x)$, the Kullback–Leibler bound is

$$\log Z \geq \underbrace{- \langle \log q(x) \rangle_{q(x)}}_{\text{entropy}} + \underbrace{\sum_{i \sim j} \langle \log \phi(x_i, x_j) \rangle_{q(x)}}_{\text{energy}}. \tag{28.7.6}$$

Since

$$\langle \log \phi(x_i, x_j) \rangle_{q(x)} = \langle \log \phi(x_i, x_j) \rangle_{q(x_i, x_j)} \tag{28.7.7}$$

each contribution to the energy depends on $q(x)$ only via the pairwise marginals $q(x_i, x_j)$. This suggests that these marginals should form the natural parameters of any approximation. Can we then find an expression for the entropy $- \langle \log q(x) \rangle_{q(x)}$ in terms of these pairwise marginals? Consider a case in which the required marginals are

$$q(x_1, x_2), q(x_2, x_3), q(x_3, x_4). \tag{28.7.8}$$

Either by appealing to the junction tree representation, or by straightforward algebra, one can show that we can uniquely express q in terms of these marginals using

$$q(x) = \frac{q(x_1, x_2) q(x_2, x_3) q(x_3, x_4)}{q(x_2) q(x_3)}. \tag{28.7.9}$$

An intuitive way to arrive at this result is by examining the numerator of Equation (28.7.9). The variable x_2 appears twice, as does the variable x_3 and, since any joint distribution cannot have such replicated variables, we must compensate for 'overcounting' x_2 and x_3 by dividing by these marginals. In this case, the entropy of $q(x)$ can be written as

$$H_q(x) = - \langle \log q(x) \rangle_{q(x)} = H_q(x_1, x_2) + H_q(x_2, x_3) + H_q(x_3, x_4) - H_q(x_2) - H_q(x_3). \tag{28.7.10}$$

More generally, from Chapter 6, any decomposable graph can be represented as

$$q(x) = \frac{\prod_c q(\mathcal{X}_c)}{\prod_s q(\mathcal{X}_s)} \tag{28.7.11}$$

where the $q(\mathcal{X}_c)$ are the marginals defined on cliques of the graph, with $\mathcal{X}_c$ being the variables of the clique, and the $q(\mathcal{X}_s)$ are defined on the separators (intersections of neighbouring cliques). The expression for the entropy of the distribution is then given by a sum of marginal entropies minus the separator entropies.

Bethe free energy

Consider now a Markov network corresponding to a non-decomposable graph, for example the 4-cycle

$$p(x) = \frac{1}{Z} \phi(x_1, x_2) \phi(x_2, x_3) \phi(x_3, x_4) \phi(x_4, x_1). \tag{28.7.12}$$

The energy requires therefore that our approximating distribution defines the pairwise marginals

$$q(x_1, x_2), q(x_2, x_3), q(x_3, x_4), q(x_4, x_1). \tag{28.7.13}$$

Assuming that these marginals are given, can we find an expression for the entropy of the joint distribution $q(x)$ in terms of its pairwise marginals $q(x_i, x_j)$? In general this is not possible since the graph contains loops (so that the junction tree representation would result in cliques greater than size 2). However, a simple 'no overcounting' approximation is to write

$$q(x) \approx \frac{q(x_1, x_2)q(x_2, x_3)q(x_3, x_4)q(x_4, x_1)}{q(x_1)q(x_2)q(x_3)q(x_4)}. \tag{28.7.14}$$

Using this we can approximate the entropy as

$$H_q(x) \approx H_q(x_1, x_2) + H_q(x_2, x_3) + H_q(x_3, x_4) + H_q(x_1, x_4) - \sum_{i=1}^{4} H_q(x_i). \tag{28.7.15}$$

In general, to make the distribution 'dimensionally consistent' we need to compensate by a factor $q(x_i)^{c_i}$ where c_i is the number of neighbours of variable x_i minus 1. With this approximation the (negative) log partition function is known as the *Bethe free energy*. Our interest is then to maximise this expression with respect to the parameters $q(x_i, x_j)$ subject to marginal consistency constraints, $\sum_{x_j} q(x_i, x_j) = q(x_i)$. These constraints may be enforced using Lagrange multipliers $\gamma_{ij}(x_i)$. One can write the Bethe free energy (the approximated Kullback–Leibler divergence up to a constant) as

$$\mathcal{F}(q, \lambda) \equiv -\sum_{i\sim j} H_q(x_i, x_j) + \sum_i c_i H_q(x_i) - \sum_{i\sim j} \langle \log \phi(x_i, x_j)\rangle_{q(x_i,x_j)}$$
$$+ \sum_{i\sim j}\sum_{x_i} \gamma_{ij}(x_i)\left(q(x_i) - \sum_{x_j} q(x_i, x_j)\right). \tag{28.7.16}$$

We neglect including Lagrange terms to enforce normalisation of the q since these only add constant terms which can be later absorbed by explicitly normalising q. Expression (28.7.16) is no longer a bound on the log partition function since the entropy approximation is not a lower bound on the true entropy. The task is now to minimise Equation (28.7.16) with respect to the parameters, namely all the pairwise marginals $q(x_i, x_j)$ and the Lagrange multipliers γ. A simple scheme to optimise Equation (28.7.16) is to use a fixed-point iteration by equating the derivatives of the Bethe free energy with respect to the parameters $q(x_i, x_j)$ to zero, and likewise for the Lagrange multipliers. Differentiating with respect to $q(x_i, x_j)$ and equating to zero, we obtain

$$\log q(x_i, x_j) - \log \phi(x_i, x_j) - \gamma_{ij}(x_i) - \gamma_{ji}(x_j) + \text{const.} = 0 \tag{28.7.17}$$

so that

$$q(x_i, x_j) \propto \phi(x_i, x_j)\tilde{\gamma}_{ij}(x_i)\tilde{\gamma}_{ji}(x_j) \tag{28.7.18}$$

where $\tilde{\gamma}_{ij}(x_i) \equiv \exp \gamma_{ij}(x_i)$. Similarly, differentiating with respect to $q(x_i)$ and equating to zero, we obtain

$$-c_i \log q(x_i) + \sum_{j\in \text{ne}(i)} \gamma_{ij}(x_i) + \text{const.} = 0 \tag{28.7.19}$$

so that

$$q(x_i) \propto \prod_{j\in \text{ne}(i)} \tilde{\gamma}_{ij}^{1/c_i}(x_i). \tag{28.7.20}$$

From Equation (28.7.18) we can match Equation (28.7.4) by mapping

$$\tilde{\gamma}_{ij}(x_i) = \prod_{k\in \text{ne}(i)\setminus j} \lambda_{x_k\to x_i}(x_i). \tag{28.7.21}$$

We can verify that this assignment satisfies the single marginal requirements Equation (28.7.20) and Equation (28.7.3) since

$$\prod_{j\in\mathrm{ne}(i)} \tilde{\gamma}_{ij}^{1/c_i}(x_i) = \prod_{j\in\mathrm{ne}(i)} \prod_{k\in\mathrm{ne}(i)\backslash j} \lambda_{x_k\to x_i}(x_i)^{1/c_i} = \prod_{j\in\mathrm{ne}(i)} \lambda_{x_j\to x_i}(x_i). \tag{28.7.22}$$

Hence the fixed-point equations for minimising the Bethe free energy are equivalent to belief propagation [320]. The convergence of loopy belief propagation can be heavily dependent on the topology of the graph and also the message updating schedule [312, 216]. The potential benefit of the Bethe free energy viewpoint is that it opens up the possibility of using more general optimisation techniques than BP. The so-called double-loop techniques iteratively isolate convex contributions to the Bethe free energy, interleaved with concave contributions. At each stage, the resulting optimisiations can be carried out efficiently [322, 145, 320].

Validity of loopy belief propagation

For an Markov network which has a loop, a change in a variable on the loop eventually reverberates back to the same variable. However, if there are a large number of variables in the loop, and the individual neighbouring links are not all extremely strong, the numerical effect of the loop is small in the sense that the influence of the variable on itself will be small. In such cases one would expect the belief propagation approximation to be accurate. An area of particular success for loopy belief propagation inference is in error correction based on low-density parity check codes; these are usually explicitly designed to have this long-loop property [197] so that loopy belief propagation produces good results. In many examples of practical interest, however, loops can be very short (for example a Markov network on a lattice). In such cases a naive implementation of loopy BP will most likely fail. A natural extension is to cluster variables to alleviate strong local dependencies; this technique is called the *Kikuchi* or *Cluster Variation method* [167]. More elaborate ways of clustering variables can be considered using *region graphs* [320, 313].

Example 28.4

The file `demoMFBPGibbs.m` compares the performance of naive Mean Field (MF) theory, belief propagation and unstructured Gibbs sampling on marginal inference in a pairwise Markov network

$$p(w, x, y, z) = \phi_{wx}(w, x)\phi_{wy}(w, y)\phi_{wz}(w, z)\phi_{xy}(x, y)\phi_{xz}(x, z)\phi_{yz}(y, z) \tag{28.7.23}$$

in which all variables take 6 states. In the experiment the tables are selected from a uniform distribution raised to a power α. For α close to zero, all the tables are essentially flat and therefore the variables become independent, a situation for which MF, BP and Gibbs sampling are ideally suited. As α is increased to 5, the dependencies amongst the variables increase and the methods perform worse, especially MF and Gibbs. As α is increased to 25, the distribution becomes sharply peaked around a single state, such that the posterior is effectively factorised, see Fig. 28.10. This suggests that an MF approximation (and also Gibbs sampling) should work well. However, finding this state is computationally difficult and the methods often get stuck in local minima, see Fig. 28.11. Belief propagation seems less susceptible to being trapped in local minima in this regime and tends to outperform both MF and Gibbs sampling.

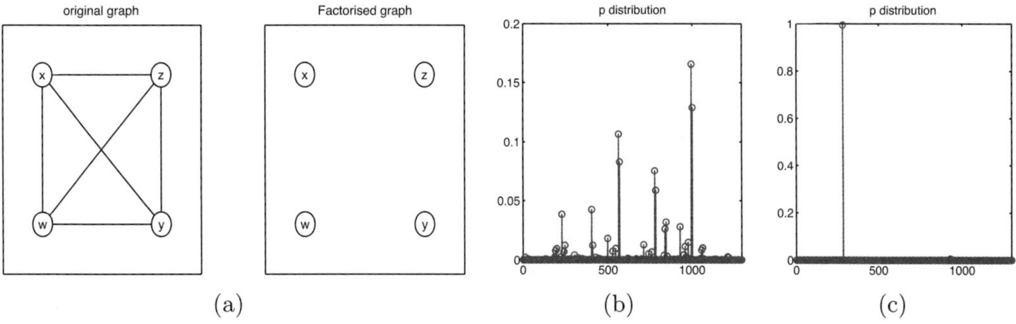

Figure 28.10 (**a**) The Markov network (left) that we wish to approximate the marginals $p(w)$, $p(x)$, $p(y)$, $p(z)$ for. All tables are drawn first from a uniform distribution and then raised to a power α and renormalised. On the right is shown the naive mean field approximation factorised structure. (**b**) There are $6^4 = 1296$ states of the distribution. Shown is a randomly sampled distribution for $\alpha = 5$ which has many isolated peaks, suggesting the distribution is far from factorised. In this case the MF and Gibbs sampling approximations may perform poorly. (**c**) As α is increased to 25, typically only one state of the distribution dominates. Whilst the distribution is then simple and essentially factorised, finding this maximal single state is numerically challenging. See `demoMFBPGibbs.m.` and Fig. 28.11.

28.8 Expectation propagation

The messages in schemes such as belief propagation are not always representable in a compact form. The switching linear dynamical system, as described in Chapter 25, is such an instance, with the messages requiring an exponential amount of storage. This limits BP to cases such as discrete networks, or more generally exponential family messages. Expectation Propagation (EP) extends the applicability of BP by projecting the messages back to a chosen distribution family at each stage. This projection is obtained by using a Kullback–Leibler measure [210, 263, 212].

Consider a distribution defined on subsets of variables $\mathcal{X}_i$ of the form

$$p(x) = \frac{1}{Z}\prod_i \phi_i(\mathcal{X}_i). \tag{28.8.1}$$

In EP one identifies those factors $\phi_i(\mathcal{X}_i)$ which, if replaced by simpler factors $\tilde{\phi}_i(\mathcal{X}_i)$, would render the distribution $\tilde{p}(x)$ tractable. One then sets any free parameters of $\tilde{\phi}_i(\mathcal{X}_i)$ by minimising the

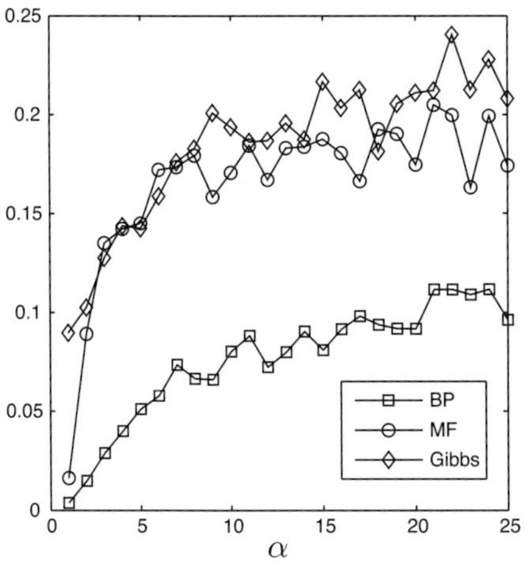

Figure 28.11 The absolute error in computing the marginal $p(x_i)$ for the graph in Fig. 28.10, averaged over all four marginals, for loopy belief propagation (BP), Gibbs sampling (Gibbs) and naive mean field using a factorised approximation (MF). Plotted along the horizontal axis is the parameter α that controls the 'complexity' of the true distribution, see Fig. 28.10. The vertical axis is the error averaged over 100 random realisations for the true distribution. For small α, the distribution is essentially factorised and all methods work reasonably well. As α increases the distribution becomes more peaked around a limited number of states, and finding these states becomes increasingly difficult. All methods use a similar amount of computation with 50 updates for each of the four variables.

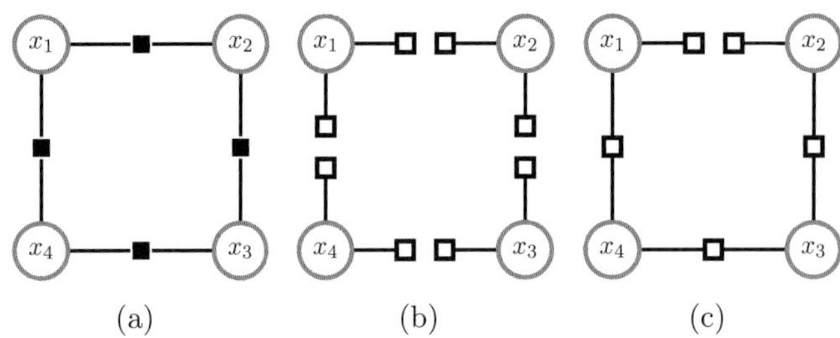

Figure 28.12 (**a**) Multiply connected factor graph representing $p(x)$. (**b**) Expectation propagation approximates (a) in terms of a tractable factor graph. The open squares indicate that the factors are parameters of the approximation. The basic EP approximation is to replace all factors in $p(x)$ by product factors. (**c**) Tree structured EP.

Kullback–Leibler divergence $\mathrm{KL}(p|\tilde{p})$. The general approach is outlined in Algorithm 28.2. To gain some intuition into the steps of the algorithm, we consider the specific example a pairwise Markov network

$$p(x) = \frac{1}{Z}\phi_{1,2}(x_1, x_2)\phi_{2,3}(x_2, x_3)\phi_{3,4}(x_3, x_4)\phi_{4,1}(x_4, x_1) \tag{28.8.2}$$

with factor graph as depicted in Fig. 28.12(a). If we replace all terms $\phi_{i,j}(x_i, x_j)$ by approximate factors $\tilde{\phi}_{i,j}(x_i)\tilde{\phi}_{i,j}(x_j)$ then the resulting joint distribution $\tilde{p}$ is factorised and hence tractable. Since the variable x_i appears in more than one term from p, we need to index the approximation factors appropriately. A convenient way to do this is

$$\tilde{p}(x) = \frac{1}{\tilde{Z}} \underbrace{\tilde{\phi}_{2\to1}(x_1)\,\tilde{\phi}_{1\to2}(x_2)}_{\approx\phi_{1,2}(x_1,x_2)}\,\underbrace{\tilde{\phi}_{3\to2}(x_2)\,\tilde{\phi}_{2\to3}(x_3)}_{\approx\phi_{2,3}(x_2,x_3)}\,\underbrace{\tilde{\phi}_{4\to3}(x_3)\,\tilde{\phi}_{3\to4}(x_4)}_{\approx\phi_{3,4}(x_3,x_4)}\,\underbrace{\tilde{\phi}_{1\to4}(x_4)\,\tilde{\phi}_{4\to1}(x_1)}_{\approx\phi_{4,1}(x_4,x_1)} \tag{28.8.3}$$

which is represented in Fig. 28.12(b). The idea in EP is now to determine the optimal approximation factors $\tilde{\phi}$ by the self-consistent requirement that, on replacing approximation factors by their exact counterparts, there is no difference to the marginals of $\tilde{p}$. Consider the approximation parameters $\tilde{\phi}_{3\to2}(x_2)$ and $\tilde{\phi}_{2\to3}(x_3)$. To set these we first replace the contribution $\tilde{\phi}_{3\to2}(x_2)\,\tilde{\phi}_{2\to3}(x_3)$ by the exact factor $\phi_{2,3}(x_2, x_3)$. This gives a modified approximation

$$\begin{aligned}\tilde{p}_* &= \frac{1}{\tilde{Z}_*}\tilde{\phi}_{2\to1}(x_1)\,\tilde{\phi}_{1\to2}(x_2)\,\phi(x_2, x_3)\tilde{\phi}_{4\to3}(x_3)\,\tilde{\phi}_{3\to4}(x_4)\,\tilde{\phi}_{1\to4}(x_4)\,\tilde{\phi}_{4\to1}(x_1) \\ &= \frac{\phi_{2,3}(x_2, x_3)\tilde{Z}\tilde{p}}{\tilde{\phi}_{3\to2}(x_2)\,\tilde{\phi}_{2\to3}(x_3)\,\tilde{Z}_*}.\end{aligned} \tag{28.8.4}$$

The intuition is that if all approximation parameters are set correctly, then replacing the approximation factors by the exact counterpart should not change the computation of the marginals. To measure how much using the modified $\tilde{p}^*$ changes from $\tilde{p}$ we use the Kullback–Leibler divergence between this distribution and our approximation,

$$\mathrm{KL}(\tilde{p}_*|\tilde{p}) = \langle\log\tilde{p}_*\rangle_{\tilde{p}_*} - \langle\log\tilde{p}\rangle_{\tilde{p}_*}. \tag{28.8.5}$$

We would like to set the parameters such that this Kullback–Leibler divergence is minimal. Since our interest is in updating $\tilde{\phi}_{3\to2}(x_2)$ and $\tilde{\phi}_{2\to3}(x_3)$, we isolate the contribution from these parameters to the Kullback–Leibler divergence which is

$$\mathrm{KL}(\tilde{p}_*|\tilde{p}) = \log\tilde{Z} - \left\langle\log\tilde{\phi}_{3\to2}(x_2)\,\tilde{\phi}_{2\to3}(x_3)\right\rangle_{\tilde{p}_*(x_2,x_3)} + \text{const}. \tag{28.8.6}$$

Also, since $\tilde{p}$ is factorised, up to a constant proportionality factor, the dependence of $\tilde{Z}$ on $\tilde{\phi}_{3\to 2}(x_2)$ and $\tilde{\phi}_{2\to 3}(x_3)$ is

$$\tilde{Z} \propto \sum_{x_2} \tilde{\phi}_{1\to 2}(x_2)\,\tilde{\phi}_{3\to 2}(x_2) \sum_{x_3} \tilde{\phi}_{2\to 3}(x_3)\,\tilde{\phi}_{4\to 3}(x_3). \tag{28.8.7}$$

Differentiating the Kullback–Leibler divergence equation (28.8.6) with respect to $\tilde{\phi}_{3\to 2}(x_2)$ and equating to zero, we obtain

$$\frac{\tilde{\phi}_{1\to 2}(x_2)\,\tilde{\phi}_{3\to 2}(x_2)}{\sum_{x_2} \tilde{\phi}_{1\to 2}(x_2)\,\tilde{\phi}_{3\to 2}(x_2)} = \tilde{p}_*(x_2). \tag{28.8.8}$$

Similarly, optimising w.r.t. $\tilde{\phi}_{2\to 3}(x_3)$ gives

$$\frac{\tilde{\phi}_{2\to 3}(x_3)\,\tilde{\phi}_{4\to 3}(x_3)}{\sum_{x_3} \tilde{\phi}_{2\to 3}(x_3)\,\tilde{\phi}_{4\to 3}(x_3)} = \tilde{p}_*(x_3). \tag{28.8.9}$$

Approximating Z

The above updates only determine the approximation factors up to a proportionality constant. This is fine if we only wish to find approximations for the marginals since any missing proportionality constants can be determined by the requirement that each marginal is normalised. However if we wish to also approximate Z, we care about such factors. To address this we write the optimal updates as

$$\tilde{\phi}_{3\to 2}(x_2) = z_{3\to 2}\frac{\tilde{p}_*(x_2)}{\tilde{\phi}_{1\to 2}(x_2)} \tag{28.8.10}$$

and

$$\tilde{\phi}_{2\to 3}(x_3) = z_{2\to 3}\frac{\tilde{p}_*(x_3)}{\tilde{\phi}_{4\to 3}(x_3)} \tag{28.8.11}$$

where $z_{3\to 2}$ and $z_{2\to 3}$ are proportionality terms. We can determine these proportionalities by the requirement that the term approximation $\tilde{\phi}_{3\to 2}(x_2)\,\tilde{\phi}_{2\to 3}(x_3)$ has the same effect on the normalisation of $\tilde{p}$ as it has on $\tilde{p}_*$. That is

$$\begin{aligned}&\sum_{x_1,x_2,x_3,x_4} \tilde{\phi}_{2\to 1}(x_1)\,\tilde{\phi}_{1\to 2}(x_2)\,\tilde{\phi}_{3\to 2}(x_2)\,\tilde{\phi}_{2\to 3}(x_3)\,\tilde{\phi}_{4\to 3}(x_3)\,\tilde{\phi}_{3\to 4}(x_4)\,\tilde{\phi}_{1\to 4}(x_4)\,\tilde{\phi}_{4\to 1}(x_1)\\ &\quad = \sum_{x_1,x_2,x_3,x_4} \tilde{\phi}_{2\to 1}(x_1)\,\tilde{\phi}_{1\to 2}(x_2)\,\phi(x_2,x_3)\tilde{\phi}_{4\to 3}(x_3)\,\tilde{\phi}_{3\to 4}(x_4)\,\tilde{\phi}_{1\to 4}(x_4)\,\tilde{\phi}_{4\to 1}(x_1)\end{aligned} \tag{28.8.12}$$

which, on substituting in the updates equation (28.8.10) and Equation (28.8.11), reduces to

$$z_{2\to 3}z_{3\to 2} = \frac{z^*_{2,3}}{\tilde{z}_{2,3}} \tag{28.8.13}$$

where

$$\tilde{z}_{2,3} = \sum_{x_2,x_3} \tilde{\phi}_{1\to 2}(x_2)\,\frac{\tilde{p}_*(x_2)}{\tilde{\phi}_{1\to 2}(x_2)}\,\frac{\tilde{p}_*(x_3)}{\tilde{\phi}_{4\to 3}(x_3)}\tilde{\phi}_{4\to 3}(x_3) \tag{28.8.14}$$

and

$$z^*_{2,3} = \sum_{x_2,x_3} \tilde{\phi}_{1\to 2}(x_2)\,\phi(x_2,x_3)\tilde{\phi}_{4\to 3}(x_3). \tag{28.8.15}$$

Algorithm 28.2 Expectation propagation: approximation of $p(x) = \frac{1}{Z}\prod_i \phi_i(\mathcal{X}_i)$.

1: Choose terms $\tilde{\phi}_i(\mathcal{X}_i)$ to give a tractable distribution:

$$\tilde{p}(x) = \frac{1}{\tilde{Z}}\prod_i \tilde{\phi}_i(\mathcal{X}_i). \tag{28.8.16}$$

2: Initialise all parameters $\tilde{\phi}_i(\mathcal{X}_i)$.
3: **repeat**
4: Select a term $\tilde{\phi}_i(\mathcal{X}_i)$ from $\tilde{p}$ to update.
5: Replace the term $\tilde{\phi}_i(\mathcal{X}_i)$ by the exact term $\phi_i(\mathcal{X}_i)$ to form

$$\tilde{p}_* \propto \phi_i(\mathcal{X}_i)\prod_{j\neq i} \tilde{\phi}_j(\mathcal{X}_j). \tag{28.8.17}$$

6: Find the parameters of $\tilde{\phi}_i(\mathcal{X}_i)$ by

$$\tilde{\phi}_i(\mathcal{X}_i) \propto \underset{\tilde{\phi}_i(\mathcal{X}_i)}{\text{argmin}}\ \text{KL}(\tilde{p}_*|\tilde{p})\,. \tag{28.8.18}$$

7: Set any proportionality terms of $\tilde{\phi}_i(\mathcal{X}_i)$ by requiring

$$\sum_x \phi_i(\mathcal{X}_i)\prod_{j\neq i}\tilde{\phi}_j(\mathcal{X}_j) = \sum_x\prod_j \tilde{\phi}_j(\mathcal{X}_j) \tag{28.8.19}$$

8: **until** converged
9: return

$$\tilde{p}(x) = \frac{1}{\tilde{Z}}\prod_i \tilde{\phi}_i(\mathcal{X}_i), \qquad \tilde{Z} = \sum_x\prod_i \tilde{\phi}_i(\mathcal{X}_i) \tag{28.8.20}$$

as an approximation to $p(x)$, where $\tilde{Z}$ approximates the normalisation constant Z.

Any choice of local normalisations $z_{2\to 3}$, $z_{3\to 2}$ that satisfies Equation (28.8.13) suffices to ensure that the scale of the term approximation matches. For example, one may set

$$z_{2\to 3} = z_{3\to 2} = \sqrt{\frac{z^*_{2,3}}{\tilde{z}_{2,3}}}. \tag{28.8.21}$$

Once set, an approximation for the global normalisation constant of p is

$$Z \approx \tilde{Z}. \tag{28.8.22}$$

The above gives a procedure for updating the terms $\tilde{\phi}_{3\to 2}(x_2)$ and $\tilde{\phi}_{2\to 3}(x_3)$. One then chooses another term and updates the corresponding approximation factors. We repeat this until all approximation parameters have converged (or a suitable termination criterion is reached in the case of non-convergence). The generic procedure is outlined in Algorithm 28.2.

Comments on EP

- For the Markov network example above, EP corresponds to belief propagation (the sum-product form on the factor graph). This is intuitively clear since in both EP and BP the product of messages incoming to a variable is proportional to the approximation of the marginal of that variable. A difference, however, is the schedule: in EP all messages corresponding to a term approximation are updated simultaneously (in the above $\tilde{\phi}_{3\to 2}(x_2)$ and $\tilde{\phi}_{2\to 3}(x_3)$), whereas in BP they are updated sequentially.

- Expectation propagation is a useful extension of BP to cases in which the BP messages cannot be easily represented; introducing the exact factors ϕ in the approximation $\tilde{p}$ increases the complexity of the approximation to $\tilde{p}_*$ which is resolved by projecting the approximation back to $\tilde{p}$. In the case that the approximating distribution $\tilde{p}$ is in the exponential family, the minimal Kullback–Leibler projection step equates to matching moments of the approximating distribution to p^*. See [263] for a more detailed discussion.
- In general there is no need to replace all terms in the joint distribution with factorised approximations. One only needs that the resulting approximating distribution is tractable; this results in a *structured expectation propagation* algorithm, see Fig. 28.12(c).
- Expectation propagation and its extensions are closely related to procedures such as tree-reweighting [307] and fractional EP [316] designed to compensate for message overcounting effects.

28.9 MAP for Markov networks

Consider a Markov network

$$p(x) = \frac{1}{Z} e^{E(x)}. \tag{28.9.1}$$

Then the most likely state is given by

$$x^* = \underset{x}{\text{argmax}}\ p(x) = \underset{x}{\text{argmax}}\ E(x). \tag{28.9.2}$$

For a general Markov network we cannot naively exploit dynamic programming intuitions to find an exact solution since the graph will generally be loopy. Below we consider some general techniques that can be used to approximate x^*.

Iterated conditional modes

A simple general approximate solution can be found as follows: first initialise all x at random. Then select a variable x_i and find the state of x_i that maximally improves $E(x)$, keeping all other variables fixed. One then repeats this selection and local maximal state computation until convergence. This axis aligned optimisation procedure is called *Iterated Conditional Modes* (ICM) [37]. Due to the Markov properties it's clear that we can improve on this ICM method by simultaneously optimising all variables conditioned on their respective Markov blankets (similar to the approach used in black-white sampling). Another improvement is to clamp a subset of the variables to reveal a singly connected structure on the un-clamped variables, and subsequently to find the exact MAP state on the un-clamped variables by a max-sum algorithm. One then chooses a new subset of variables to clamp, thus finding an approximate solution by solving a sequence of tractable problems.

Dual decomposition

A general approach is to decompose a difficult optimisation problem into a set of easier problems. In this approach we first identify tractable 'slave' objectives $E_s(x)$, $s = 1, \ldots, S$ such that the 'master' objective $E(x)$ decomposes as

$$E(x) = \sum_s E_s(x). \tag{28.9.3}$$

Then the x that optimises the master problem is equivalent to optimising each slave problem $E_s(x_s)$ under the constraint that the slaves agree $x_s = x$, $s = 1, \ldots, S$ [36]. This constraint can be be imposed by a Lagrangian

$$\mathcal{L}(x, \{x_s\}, \lambda) = \sum_s E_s(x_s) + \sum_s \lambda_s (x_s - x). \tag{28.9.4}$$

Finding the stationary point w.r.t. x gives the constraint $\sum_s \lambda_s = 0$, so that we may then consider

$$\mathcal{L}(\{x_s\}, \lambda) = \sum_s E_s(x_s) + \lambda_s x_s. \tag{28.9.5}$$

Given λ, we then optimise each slave problem

$$x_s^* = \underset{x_s}{\text{argmax}} \; (E_s(x_s) + \lambda_s x_s). \tag{28.9.6}$$

The Lagrange dual, Appendix A.6.1, is given by (noting here we have a maximisation problem)

$$\mathcal{L}_s(\lambda_s) = \max_{x_s} (E_s(x_s) + \lambda_s x_s). \tag{28.9.7}$$

In this case the dual bound on the primal is

$$\sum_s \mathcal{L}_s(\lambda_s) \geq E(x^*) \tag{28.9.8}$$

where x^* is the solution of the primal problem $x^* = \underset{x}{\text{argmax}}\, E(x)$. To update λ one may use a 'projected subgradient' method to minimise each $\mathcal{L}_s(\lambda_s)$

$$\lambda_s' = \lambda - \alpha x_s^* \tag{28.9.9}$$

where α is a chosen positive constant. Then we project,

$$\bar{\lambda} = \frac{1}{S} \sum_s \lambda_s', \qquad \lambda_s^{new} = \lambda_s' - \bar{\lambda} \tag{28.9.10}$$

which ensures that $\sum_s \lambda_s^{new} = 0$.

28.9.1 Pairwise Markov networks

Consider a pairwise Markov network $p(x) \propto e^{E(x)}$ with

$$E(x) \equiv \sum_{i \sim j} f_{ij}(x_i, x_j) + \sum_i g_i(x_i, x_i^0) \tag{28.9.11}$$

where $i \sim j$ denotes the set of neighbouring variables and $f(x_i, x_j) = f(x_j, x_i)$. This means that an undirected edge $i - j$ in the graph corresponding to the Markov network contributes a term

$f(x_i, x_j)$, not $2f(x_i, x_j)$. Here the terms $f(x_i, x_j)$ represent pairwise interactions. The terms $g(x_i, x_i^0)$ represent unary interactions, written for convenience in terms of a pairwise interaction with a fixed (non-variable) x^0. Typically the term $f(x_i, x_j)$ is used to ensure that neighbouring variables x_i and x_j are in similar states; the term $g_i(x_i, x_i^0)$ is used to bias x_i to be close to a desired state x_i^0.

Iterated conditional modes

Such models have application in image restoration in which an observed noisy image x^0 is to be cleaned, see Example 28.1 and Fig. 28.3. To do so we seek a clean image x for which each clean pixel value x_i is close to the observed noisy pixel value x_i^0, whilst being in a similar state to its clean neighbours. In Example 28.1 we used ICM to find the approximate most likely state by simply updating randomly chosen variables, one at a time.

Dual decomposition

For a binary Markov network

$$E(\mathbf{x}) = \frac{1}{2}\sum_{ij} x_i x_j w_{ij} + \sum_i c_i x_i = \frac{1}{2}\mathbf{x}^\mathsf{T}\mathbf{W}\mathbf{x} + \mathbf{x}^\mathsf{T}\mathbf{c} \tag{28.9.12}$$

we may define tractable slave problems

$$E_s(\mathbf{x}) = \frac{1}{2}\mathbf{x}^\mathsf{T}\mathbf{W}_s\mathbf{x} + \mathbf{x}^\mathsf{T}\mathbf{c}_s \tag{28.9.13}$$

by identifying a set of tree structured matrices $\mathbf{W}_s$ such that $\mathbf{W} = \sum_s \mathbf{W}_s$ and unary terms $\mathbf{c}_s$ such that $\mathbf{c} = \sum_s \mathbf{c}_s$. The dual decomposition technique then proceeds to solve each slave tree exactly, and subsequently updates λ to push the tree solutions towards agreement [176]. Similar general methods of solving trees under the constraint of agreement are discussed in [307].

28.9.2 Attractive binary Markov networks

Whilst, in general, no efficient exact solution exists for the general MAP Markov network problem, an important tractable special case is discussed below. Consider finding the MAP of a Markov network with binary variables $\mathrm{dom}(x_i) = \{0, 1\}$ and positive connections $w_{ij} = w_{ji} \geq 0$. In this case our task is to find the assignment x that maximises

$$E(x) \equiv \sum_{i\sim j} w_{ij}\mathbb{I}[x_i = x_j] + \sum_i c_i x_i \tag{28.9.14}$$

where $i \sim j$ denotes neighbouring variables. For this particular case an efficient exact MAP algorithm exists for arbitrary topology of the interactions w_{ij} [133]. The algorithm first translates the MAP assignment problem into an equivalent min s-t-cut problem [40], for which efficient algorithms exist. In min s-t-cut, we need a graph with positive weights on the edges. This is clearly satisfied if $w_{ij} > 0$, although the bias term $\sum_i c_i x_i$ needs to be addressed.

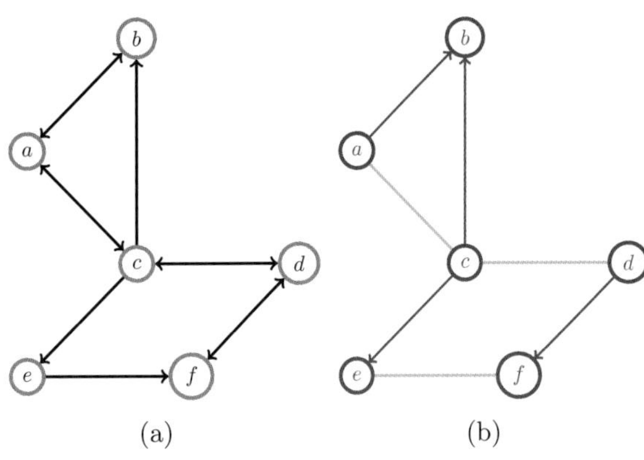

Figure 28.13 (**a**) A directed graph with edge weights w_{ij} from node i to j with $w_{ij} = 0$ if no edge exists from i to j. (**b**) A graph cut partitions the nodes into two groups $\mathcal{S}$ (blue) and $\mathcal{T}$ (red). The weight of the cut is the sum of the weights of edges that leave $\mathcal{S}$ (blue) and land in $\mathcal{T}$ (red). Intuitively, it is clear that after assigning nodes to state 1 (for blue) and 0 (red) that the weight of the cut corresponds to the summed weights of neighbours in different states. Here we highlight those weight contributions. The non-highlighted edges do not contribute to the cut weight. Note that only one of the edge directions contributes to the cut. See plate section for colour version.

Dealing with the bias terms

To translate the MAP assignment problem to a min-cut problem we need to deal with the additional term $\sum_i c_i x_i$. First consider the effect of including a new node x_* and connecting this to each existing node i with weight c_i. Using that for binary variables $x_i \in \{0, 1\}$,

$$\mathbb{I}[x_i = x_j] = x_i x_j + (1 - x_i)(1 - x_j) = 2x_i x_j - x_i - x_j + 1 \tag{28.9.15}$$

this then adds a term

$$\sum_i c_i \mathbb{I}[x_i = x_*] = \sum_i c_i (x_i x_* + (1 - x_i)(1 - x_*)). \tag{28.9.16}$$

If we set x_* in state 1, this contributes

$$\sum_i c_i x_i. \tag{28.9.17}$$

Otherwise, if we set x_* in state 0 we obtain

$$\sum_i c_i (1 - x_i) = -\sum_i c_i x_i + \text{const.} \tag{28.9.18}$$

Our requirement that the weights need to be positive can therefore be achieved by defining not a single additional node x_*, but rather two. We define a source node x_s, set to state 1 and connect it to those x_i which have positive c_i, defining $w_{si} = w_{is} = c_i$. In addition we define a sink node x_t set to state 0 and connect all nodes with negative c_i, to x_t, using weight $w_{it} = w_{ti} = -c_i$, (which is therefore positive). For the source node clamped to $x_s = 1$ and the sink node to $x_t = 0$, then including the source and sink, we have

$$E(x) = \sum_{i \sim j} w_{ij} \mathbb{I}[x_i = x_j] + \text{const.} \tag{28.9.19}$$

which is equal to the energy function, Equation (28.9.14), with positive weights.

Definition 28.1 Graph cut For a graph G with nodes $v_1, \ldots, v_D$, and weights $w_{ij} > 0$ a cut is a partition of the nodes into two disjoint groups, called $\mathcal{S}$ and $\mathcal{T}$. The weight of a cut is defined as the sum of the weights that leave $\mathcal{S}$ and land in $\mathcal{T}$, see Fig. 28.13.

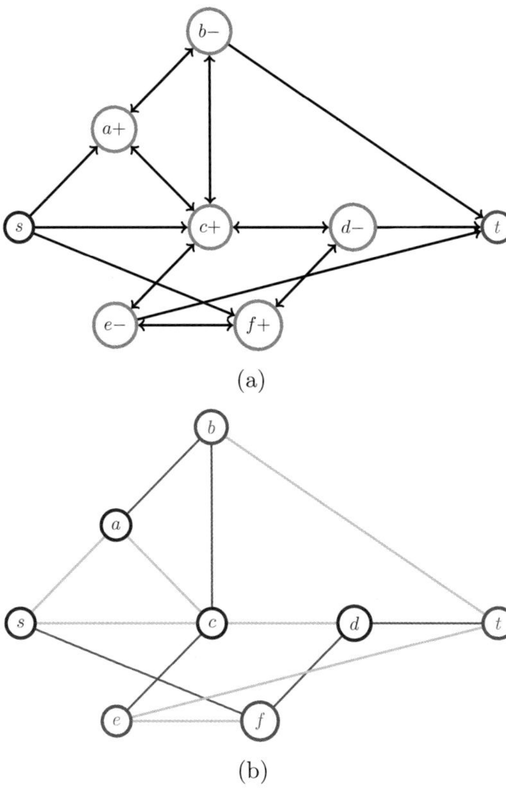

Figure 28.14 (**a**) A graph with bidirectional weights $w_{ij} = w_{ji}$ augmented with a source node *s* and sink node *t*. Each node has a corresponding bias whose sign is indicated. The source node is linked to the nodes corresponding to positive bias, and the nodes with negative bias to the sink. (**b**) A graph cut partitions the nodes into two groups $\mathcal{S}$ (blue) and $\mathcal{T}$ (red), where $\mathcal{S}$ is the union of the source node *s* and nodes in state 1, $\mathcal{T}$ is the union of the sink node *t* and nodes in state 0. The weight of the cut is the sum of the edge weights from $\mathcal{S}$ (blue) to $\mathcal{T}$ (red). The red lines indicate contributions to the cut, and can be considered penalties since we wish to find the minimal cut. See plate section for colour version.

For symmetric w, the weight of a cut corresponds to the sum of weights between mismatched neighbours, see Fig. 28.13(b). That is,

$$cut(x) = \sum_{i \sim j} w_{ij} \mathbb{I}\left[x_i \neq x_j\right]. \tag{28.9.20}$$

Since $\mathbb{I}\left[x_i \neq x_j\right] = 1 - \mathbb{I}\left[x_i = x_j\right]$, we can define the weight of the cut equivalently as

$$cut(x) = \sum_{i \sim j} w_{ij}\left(1 - \mathbb{I}\left[x_i = x_j\right]\right) = -\sum_{i \sim j} w_{ij} \mathbb{I}\left[x_i = x_j\right] + \text{const.} = -E(x) + \text{const.} \tag{28.9.21}$$

so that the minimal cut assignment will correspond to maximising $E(x)$. In the Markov network case, our translation into a weighted graph with positive interactions then requires that we identify the source and all other variables assigned to state 1 with $\mathcal{S}$, and the sink and all variables in state 0 with $\mathcal{T}$, see Fig. 28.14. Our task is then to find the minimal cut from $\mathcal{S}$ to $\mathcal{T}$. A fundamental result in discrete mathematics is that the min s-t-cut solution corresponds to the max-flow solution from the source s to the sink t [40]. There are efficient algorithms for max-flow, see for example [49], which take $O\left(D^3\right)$ operations or less, for a graph with D nodes. This means that one can find the exact MAP assignment of an attractive binary Markov network efficiently in $O\left(D^3\right)$ operations. In `MaxFlow.m` we implement the Ford–Fulkerson (Edmonds–Karp–Dinic breadth first search variant) [93].

28.9.3 Potts model

A Markov network defined on variables with more than two states, $x_i \in \{0, 1, 2 \ldots, S\}$ is called a *Potts model*:

$$E(x) = \sum_{i \sim j} w_{ij} \mathbb{I}[x_i = x_j] + \sum_i c_i \mathbb{I}[x_i = x_i^0] \tag{28.9.22}$$

where we assume $w_{ij} > 0$ and the x_i^0 are known. This model has immediate application in non-binary image restoration, and also in clustering based on a similarity score. This problem cannot be translated directly into a graph cuts problem and no efficient exact algorithm is known. A useful approach is to approximate the problem as a sequence of binary problems, as we describe below.

Potts to binary Markov network translation

Consider the *α-expansion* representation

$$x_i = s_i \alpha + (1 - s_i) x_i^{old} \tag{28.9.23}$$

where $s_i \in \{0, 1\}$ and $\alpha \in \{0, 1, 2, \ldots, S\}$. This restricts x_i to be either the state x_i^{old} or α, depending on the binary variable s_i. Using a new binary vector variable s we can therefore restrict x to a subpart of the full space and write a new objective function in terms of s alone (see below):

$$E(s) = \sum_{i \sim j} w'_{ij} \mathbb{I}[s_i = s_j] + \sum_i c'_i s_i + \text{const.} \tag{28.9.24}$$

for $w'_{ij} > 0$. This new problem is of the form of an attractive binary Markov network which can be solved exactly using the graph cuts procedure. This translation imposes a constraint since the x cannot access all the space, but enables us to solve the constrained problem efficiently. We then choose another α value (at random) and find the optimal s for the new α. In this way we are guaranteed to iteratively increase E.

For a given α and x^{old}, the transformation of the Potts model objective is given by using $s_i \in \{0, 1\}$ and considering

$$\begin{aligned} \mathbb{I}[x_i = x_j] &= \mathbb{I}\left[s_i \alpha + (1 - s_i) x_i^{old} = s_j \alpha + (1 - s_j) x_j^{old}\right] \\ &= (1 - s_i)(1 - s_j) \mathbb{I}\left[x_i^{old} = x_j^{old}\right] + (1 - s_i) s_j \mathbb{I}\left[x_i^{old} = \alpha\right] + s_i (1 - s_j) \mathbb{I}\left[x_j^{old} = \alpha\right] + s_i s_j \\ &= s_i s_j u_{ij} + a_i s_i + b_j s_j + \text{const.} \end{aligned} \tag{28.9.25}$$

with

$$u_{ij} \equiv 1 - \mathbb{I}[x_i^{old} = \alpha] - \mathbb{I}[x_j^{old} = \alpha] + \mathbb{I}[x_i^{old} = x_j^{old}] \tag{28.9.26}$$

with a_i and b_i defined in the obvious manner. By enumeration it is straightforward to show that u_{ij} is either 0, 1 or 2. Using the mathematical identity, for $s_i \in \{0, 1\}$,

$$s_i s_j = \frac{1}{2} \left(\mathbb{I}[s_i = s_j] + s_i + s_j - 1 \right) \tag{28.9.27}$$

we can write,

$$\mathbb{I}[x_i = x_j] = \frac{u_{ij}}{2} \left(\mathbb{I}[s_i = s_j] + s_i + s_j \right) + a_i s_i + b_j s_j + \text{const.} \tag{28.9.28}$$

(a)

(b)

Figure 28.15 (**a**) Noisy greyscale image defined using 244 intensity labels for each pixel. (**b**) Restored image. The α-expansion method was used, with suitable interactions *w* and bias *c* to ensure reasonable results. From [49] © 2004 IEEE.

Hence terms $w_{ij}\mathbb{I}[x_i = x_j]$ translate to positive interaction terms $\mathbb{I}[s_i = s_j]\, w_{ij}u_{ij}/2$. All the unary terms are easily exactly mapped into corresponding unary terms $c'_i s_i$ for c'_i defined as the sum of all unary terms in s_i. This shows that the positive interaction w_{ij} in terms of the original variables x maps to a positive interaction in the new variables s. Hence we can find the maximal state of s using a graph cuts algorithm. A related procedure is described in [50].

Example 28.5 Potts model for image reconstruction

An example image restoration problem for nearest neighbour interactions on a pixel lattice and suitably chosen w, c is given in Fig. 28.15. The images are non-binary so that the optimal MAP assignment cannot be computed exactly in an efficient way. The alpha-expansion technique was used here combined with an efficient min-cut approach to approximate the MAP assignment, see [49] for details.

28.10 Further reading

Approximate inference is a highly active research area and increasingly links to convex optimisation [48] are being developed. See [307] for a general overview.

28.11 Summary

- Deterministic methods offer an alternative to sampling techniques.
- For continuous distributions, perturbation approaches such as Laplace's method provide a simple approximation.
- Variational bounding approaches, such as minimal KL divergence, can provide bounds on quantities of interest, for example the normalisation constant of a distribution and the marginal likelihood. These are part of a larger class of methods derived from convex analysis.

- The deterministic bounding approaches can be applied to other areas such as bounding the mutual information.
- Consistency methods such as loopy belief propagation can work extremely well when the structure of the distribution is close to a tree. These methods have been very successful in information theory and error correction.
- Loopy belief propagation can also be motivated via the optimisation of the Bethe free energy objective function, although the method does not produce a bound on quantities of interest.
- For binary attractive Markov networks we can find the MAP state exactly in polynomial time. This method can be used as a subroutine in more complex multistate problems in which the MAP search problem is broken into a sequence of binary MAP problems.

28.12 Code

`LoopyBP.m`: Loopy belief propagation (factor graph formalism)
`demoLoopyBP.m`: Demo of loopy belief propagation
`demoMFBPGibbs.m`: Comparison of mean field, belief propagation and Gibbs sampling
`demoMRFclean.m`: Demo of analysing a dirty picture
`MaxFlow.m`: Max-flow min-cut algorithm (Ford–Fulkerson)
`binaryMRFmap.m`: Optimising a binary Markov network

28.13 Exercises

28.1 The file `p.mat` contains a distribution $p(x, y, z)$ on ternary state variables. Using BRMLToolbox, find the best approximation $q(x, y)q(z)$ that minimises the Kullback–Leibler divergence $\mathrm{KL}(q|p)$ and state the value of the minimal Kullback–Leibler divergence for the optimal q.

28.2 Consider the pairwise Markov network defined on a 2×2 lattice, as given in `pMRF.mat`. Using BRMLToolbox,

1. Find the optimal fully factorised approximation $\prod_{i=1}^{4} q_i^{BP}$ by loopy belief propagation, based on the factor graph formalism.
2. Find the optimal fully factorised approximation $\prod_{i=1}^{4} q_i^{MF}$ by solving the variational mean-field equations.
3. By pure enumeration, compute the exact marginals p_i.
4. Averaged over all four variables, compute the mean expected deviation in the marginals

$$\frac{1}{4}\sum_{i=1}^{4}\frac{1}{2}\sum_{j=1}^{2}|q_i(x=j)-p_i(x=j)|$$

for both the BP and MF approximations, and comment on your results.

28.3 In `LoopyBP.m` the message schedule is chosen at random. Modify the routine to choose a schedule using a forward-reverse elimination sequence on a random spanning tree.

28.4 (Double integration bounds) Consider a bound

$$f(x) \geq g(x). \tag{28.13.1}$$

Then for

$$\tilde{f}(x) \equiv \int_a^x f(x)dx, \qquad \tilde{g}(x) \equiv \int_a^x g(x)dx \tag{28.13.2}$$

show that:

1. $\tilde{f}(x) \geq \tilde{g}(x)$, for $x \geq a$.
2. $\hat{f}(x) \geq \hat{g}(x)$ for all x, where

$$\hat{f}(x) \equiv \int_a^x \tilde{f}(x)dx \qquad \hat{g}(x) \equiv \int_a^x \tilde{g}(x)dx. \tag{28.13.3}$$

The significance is that this double integration (or summation in the case of discrete variables) is a general procedure for generating a new bound from an existing bound [186].

28.5 This question concerns deriving both the standard mean-field bound and more powerful lower bounds for the Boltzmann machine.

1. Starting from

$$e^x \geq 0 \tag{28.13.4}$$

and using the double integration procedure, show that

$$e^x \geq e^a(1 + x - a).$$

2. By replacing $x \to \mathbf{s}^\mathsf{T}\mathbf{W}\mathbf{s}$ for $\mathbf{s} \in \{0, 1\}^D$, and $a \to \mathbf{h}^\mathsf{T}\mathbf{s} + \theta$ derive a bound on the partition function of a Boltzmann machine

$$Z = \sum_{\mathbf{s}} e^{\mathbf{s}^\mathsf{T}\mathbf{W}\mathbf{s}}. \tag{28.13.5}$$

3. Show that this bound is equivalent to a naive mean-field bound on the partition function. Hint: Optimise with respect to θ first.
4. Discuss how one can generate tighter bounds on the partition function of a Boltzmann distribution by further application of the double integration procedure.

28.6 Consider a pairwise Markov network

$$p(\mathbf{x}) = \frac{1}{Z} e^{\mathbf{x}^\mathsf{T}\mathbf{W}\mathbf{x} + \mathbf{b}^\mathsf{T}\mathbf{x}} \tag{28.13.6}$$

for symmetric $\mathbf{W}$. Consider the decomposition

$$\mathbf{W} = \sum_i q_i \mathbf{W}_i, \qquad i = 1, \ldots, I \tag{28.13.7}$$

where $0 \leq q_i \leq 1$ and $\sum_i q_i = 1$, and the graph corresponding to each matrix $\mathbf{W}_i$ is a tree. Explain how to form an upper bound on the normalisation Z and discuss a naive method to find the tightest upper bound. Hint: Consider $\langle e^x \rangle \geq e^{\langle x \rangle}$. See also [311].

28.7 Derive Linkser's bound on the mutual information, Equation (28.6.13).

28.8 Consider the average of a positive function $f(x)$ with respect to a distribution $p(x)$

$$J = \log \int_x p(x) f(x) \tag{28.13.8}$$

where $f(x) \geq 0$. The simplest version of Jensen's inequality states that

$$J \geq \int_x p(x) \log f(x). \tag{28.13.9}$$

1. By considering a distribution $r(x) \propto p(x)f(x)$, and $\text{KL}(q|r)$, for some variational distribution $q(x)$, show that

$$J \geq -\text{KL}(q(x)|p(x)) + \langle \log f(x) \rangle_{q(x)}. \tag{28.13.10}$$

The bound saturates when $q(x) \propto p(x)f(x)$. This shows that if we wish to approximate the average J, the optimal choice for the approximating distribution $q(x)$ depends on both the distribution $p(x)$ and integrand $f(x)$.

2. Furthermore, show that

$$J \geq -\text{KL}(q(x)|p(x)) - \text{KL}(q(x)|f(x)) - H(q(x)) \tag{28.13.11}$$

where $H(q(x))$ is the entropy of $q(x)$. The first term encourages q to be close to p. The second encourages q to be close to f, and the third encourages q to be sharply peaked.

28.9 For a Markov network defined over D binary variables $x_i \in \{0, 1\}, i = 1, \ldots, D$, we define

$$p(x) = \frac{1}{Z} e^{\mathbf{x}^\mathsf{T}\mathbf{W}\mathbf{x}} \tag{28.13.12}$$

show that

$$p(x_i) = \frac{Z_{\backslash i}}{Z} \tag{28.13.13}$$

where

$$Z_{\backslash i} \equiv \sum_{x_1,\ldots,x_{i-1},x_{i+1},\ldots,x_D} e^{\mathbf{x}^\mathsf{T}\mathbf{W}\mathbf{x}} \tag{28.13.14}$$

and explain why a bound on the marginal $p(x_i)$ requires both upper and lower bounds on partition functions Z.

28.10 Consider the model in Example 28.2. Implement a structured EP approximation based on replacing the observation factors $p(\mathbf{v}_t|\mathbf{h}_t)$ by terms of the form $c_t \exp\left(-\frac{1}{2}\mathbf{h}_t^\mathsf{T}\mathbf{A}_t\mathbf{h}_t + \mathbf{h}_t^\mathsf{T}\mathbf{b}_t\right)$.

28.11 Consider a directed graph such that the capacity of an edge $x \to y$ is $c(x, y) \geq 0$. The flow on an edge $f(x, y) \geq 0$ must not exceed the capacity of the edge. The aim is to maximise the flow from a defined source node s to a defined sink node t. In addition flow must be conserved such that for any node other than the source or sink ($y \neq s, y \neq t$),

$$\sum_x f(x, y) = \sum_x f(y, x). \tag{28.13.15}$$

A cut is defined as a partition of the nodes into two non-overlapping sets $\mathcal{S}$ and $\mathcal{T}$ such that s is in $\mathcal{S}$ and t in $\mathcal{T}$. Show that:

1. The net flow from s to t, $val(f)$, is the same as the net flow from $\mathcal{S}$ to $\mathcal{T}$:

$$val(f) = \sum_{x\in\mathcal{S},y\in\mathcal{T}} f(x, y) - \sum_{y\in\mathcal{T},x\in\mathcal{S}} f(y, x). \tag{28.13.16}$$

2. $val(f) \leq \sum_{x\in\mathcal{S},y\in\mathcal{T}} f(x, y)$ namely that the flow is upper bounded by the capacity of the cut.

The max-flow min-cut theorem further states that the maximal flow is actually equal to the capacity of the cut.

28.12 (Potts to Ising translation) Consider the function $E(x)$ defined on a set of multistate variables $\text{dom}(x_i) = \{0, 1, 2, \ldots, S\}$,

$$E(x) = \sum_{i\sim j} w_{ij}\mathbb{I}\left[x_i = x_j\right] + \sum_i c_i\mathbb{I}\left[x_i = x_i^0\right] \tag{28.13.17}$$

where $w_{ij} > 0$ and both the pixel states x_i^0 and c_i are known. Our interest is to find an approximate maximisation of $E(x)$. Using the restricted parameteristion

$$x_i = s_i\alpha + (1 - s_i)x_i^{old} \tag{28.13.18}$$

where $s_i \in \{0, 1\}$ and for a given $\alpha \in \{0, 1, 2, \ldots, N\}$, show how the maximisation of $E(x)$ is equivalent to maximising $\tilde{E}(s)$ over the binary variables s, where

$$\tilde{E}(s) = \sum_{i\sim j} w'_{ij}\mathbb{I}\left[s_i = s_j\right] + \sum_i c'_i s_i + \text{const.} \tag{28.13.19}$$

for $w'_{ij} > 0$. This new problem is of the form of an attractive binary Markov network which can be solved exactly using the graph cuts procedure.

28.13 Consider an approximating distribution in the exponential family,

$$q(x) = \frac{1}{Z(\boldsymbol{\phi})}e^{\boldsymbol{\phi}^\mathsf{T}\mathbf{g}(x)}. \tag{28.13.20}$$

We wish to use $q(x)$ to approximate a distribution $p(x)$ using the KL divergence $\text{KL}(p|q)$.

1. Show that optimally

$$\langle \mathbf{g}(x)\rangle_{p(x)} = \langle \mathbf{g}(x)\rangle_{q(x)}. \tag{28.13.21}$$

2. Show that a Gaussian can be written in the exponential form

$$\mathcal{N}\left(x\,|\,\mu, \sigma^2\right) = \frac{1}{Z(\boldsymbol{\phi})}e^{\boldsymbol{\phi}^\mathsf{T}\mathbf{g}(x)} \tag{28.13.22}$$

where $g_1(x) = x$, $g_2(x) = x^2$ for suitably chosen $\boldsymbol{\phi}$.

3. Hence show that the optimal Gaussian fit $\mathcal{N}\left(x\,|\,\mu, \sigma^2\right)$ to any distribution, in the minimal $\text{KL}(p|q)$ sense, matches the moments:

$$\mu = \langle x\rangle_{p(x)}, \qquad \sigma^2 = \left\langle x^2\right\rangle_{p(x)} - \langle x\rangle^2_{p(x)}. \tag{28.13.23}$$

28.14 For a pairwise binary Markov network, p, with partition function

$$Z(w, b) = \sum_x e^{\sum_{i,j} w_{ij}x_i x_j + \sum_i b_i x_i} \tag{28.13.24}$$

show that the mean $\langle x_i\rangle_p$ can be computed using a generating function approach

$$\frac{d}{db_i}\log Z(w, b) = \frac{1}{Z(w, b)}\sum_x x_i e^{\sum_{i\sim j} w_{ij}x_i x_j + \sum_i b_i x_i} = \langle x_i\rangle_p \tag{28.13.25}$$

and that similarly the covariance is given by

$$\langle x_i x_j\rangle_p - \langle x_i\rangle_p\langle x_j\rangle_p = \frac{d^2}{db_i db_j}\log Z(w, b). \tag{28.13.26}$$

By replacing $\log Z(w, b)$ by the mean-field bound $\mathcal{B}(\alpha)$ in Equation (28.4.13), show that the approximate mean and variance given by the naive mean-field theory is equivalent to those obtained on replacing $\log Z$ by the lower bound in the above generating function.

28.15 The naive mean field theory applied to a pairwise Markov network

$$p(x) \propto e^{\sum_{i,j} w_{ij}x_i x_j + \sum_i b_i x_i} \tag{28.13.27}$$

$\text{dom}(x_i) = \{0, 1\}$, gives a factorised approximation $q(x) = \prod_i q(x_i)$, based on minimising $\text{KL}(q|p)$. Using this we can approximate

$$\langle x_i x_j\rangle_p \approx \langle x_i\rangle_q\langle x_j\rangle_q, \qquad i \neq j. \tag{28.13.28}$$

To produce a better, non-factorised approximation to $\langle x_i x_j \rangle_p$ we could fit a non-factorised q. The linear-response method [166] may also be used, based on a perturbation expansion of the free energy. Alternatively, show that

$$\langle x_i x_j \rangle_p = p(x_i = 1, x_j = 1) = p(x_i = 1|x_j = 1)p(x_j = 1). \tag{28.13.29}$$

Explain how this can be used to form an improved non-factorised approximation to $\langle x_i x_j \rangle_p$.

28.16 Derive the EP updates Equation (28.8.8) and Equation (28.8.9).

28.17 Consider fitting a univariate Gaussian $q(x) = \mathcal{N}\left(x \mid \mu, \sigma^2\right)$ to a distribution $p(x)$ by minimising $\mathrm{KL}(q|p)$ with respect to μ, σ^2.

1. Show that, provided all quantities are well defined, the optimal variance and mean of the approximating Gaussian satisfy the implicit equations

$$\sigma^2 = -\frac{1}{\left\langle \frac{d^2}{dx^2} \log p(x) \right\rangle_{q(x)}}, \qquad \left\langle \frac{d}{dx} \log p(x) \right\rangle_{q(x)} = 0. \tag{28.13.30}$$

2. Hence relate the optimal variance to the maximal and minimal 'local curvature' of $p(x)$:

$$-\frac{1}{\max_x \frac{d^2}{dx^2} \log p(x)} \leq \sigma^2 \leq -\frac{1}{\min_x \frac{d^2}{dx^2} \log p(x)}. \tag{28.13.31}$$

3. Consider a distribution $p(x)$ that is a mixture of well-separated Gaussians, $p(x) = \sum_i p_i \mathcal{N}\left(x \mid \mu_i, \sigma_i^2\right)$. Show that, to a good approximation, the optimal choice is to set the mean of the approximating distribution to one of the components, $\mu = \mu_i$. Show furthermore that

$$\sigma^2_{min} \lesssim \sigma^2 \lesssim \sigma^2_{max} \tag{28.13.32}$$

where $\sigma^2_{min}, \sigma^2_{max}$ are the minimal and maximal variances of the Gaussian components of $p(x)$, and explain therefore why the optimal variance σ^2 will be smaller than the variance of $p(x)$.

APPENDIX

A Background mathematics

A.1 Linear algebra

A.1.1 Vector algebra

Let $\mathbf{x}$ denote the n-dimensional column vector with components

$$\begin{pmatrix} x_1 \\ x_2 \\ \vdots \\ x_n \end{pmatrix}.$$

The vector with all elements equal to 1 is written $\mathbf{1}$, and similarly the vector with all zero values is written $\mathbf{0}$.

Definition A.1 Scalar product The *scalar product* $\mathbf{w} \cdot \mathbf{x}$ is defined as:

$$\mathbf{w} \cdot \mathbf{x} = \sum_{i=1}^{n} w_i x_i = \mathbf{w}^{\mathsf{T}}\mathbf{x}. \tag{A.1.1}$$

The length of a vector is denoted $|\mathbf{x}|$, the squared length is given by

$$|\mathbf{x}|^2 = \mathbf{x}^{\mathsf{T}}\mathbf{x} = \mathbf{x}^2 = x_1^2 + x_2^2 + \cdots + x_n^2. \tag{A.1.2}$$

A *unit vector* $\mathbf{x}$ has $|\mathbf{x}| = 1$. The scalar product has a natural geometric interpretation as:

$$\mathbf{w} \cdot \mathbf{x} = |\mathbf{w}|\,|\mathbf{x}|\cos(\theta) \tag{A.1.3}$$

where θ is the angle between the two vectors. Thus if the lengths of two vectors are fixed their inner product is largest when $\theta = 0$, whereupon one vector is a constant multiple of the other. If the scalar product $\mathbf{x}^{\mathsf{T}}\mathbf{y} = 0$, then $\mathbf{x}$ and $\mathbf{y}$ are *orthogonal* (they are at right angles to each other). A set of vectors is orthonormal if they are mutually orthogonal and have unit length.

Definition A.2 Linear dependence A set of vectors $\mathbf{x}^1, \ldots, \mathbf{x}^n$ is linearly dependent if there exists a vector $\mathbf{x}^j$ that can be expressed as a linear combination of the other vectors. If the only solution to

$$\sum_{i=1}^{n} \alpha_i \mathbf{x}^i = \mathbf{0} \tag{A.1.4}$$

is for all $\alpha_i = 0$, $i = 1, \ldots, n$, the vectors $\mathbf{x}^1, \ldots, \mathbf{x}^n$ are linearly independent.

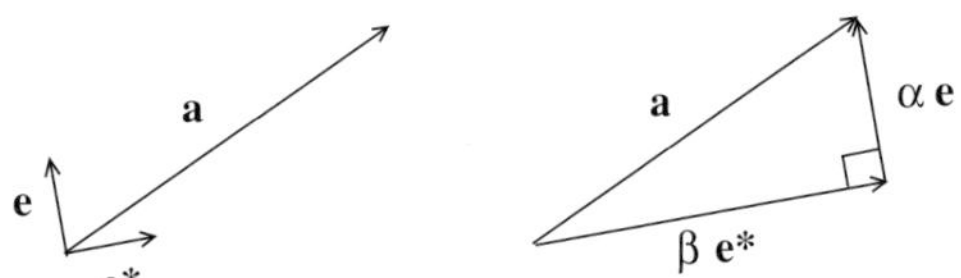

Figure A.1 Resolving a vector **a** into components along the orthogonal directions **e** and **e***. The projection of **a** onto these two directions are lengths α and β along the directions **e** and **e***.

A.1.2 The scalar product as a projection

Suppose that we wish to resolve the vector **a** into its components along the orthogonal directions specified by the unit vectors **e** and **e***, see Fig. A.1. That is $|e| = |e|^* = 1$ and $\mathbf{e} \cdot \mathbf{e^*} = 0$. We are required to find the scalar values α and β such that

$$\mathbf{a} = \alpha \mathbf{e} + \beta \mathbf{e}^*. \tag{A.1.5}$$

From this we obtain

$$\mathbf{a} \cdot \mathbf{e} = \alpha \mathbf{e} \cdot \mathbf{e} + \beta \mathbf{e^*} \cdot \mathbf{e}, \qquad \mathbf{a} \cdot \mathbf{e^*} = \alpha \mathbf{e} \cdot \mathbf{e^*} + \beta \mathbf{e^*} \cdot \mathbf{e^*}. \tag{A.1.6}$$

From the orthogonality and unit lengths of the vectors **e** and **e***, this becomes simply

$$\mathbf{a} \cdot \mathbf{e} = \alpha, \qquad \mathbf{a} \cdot \mathbf{e^*} = \beta. \tag{A.1.7}$$

This means that we can write the vector **a** in terms of the orthonormal components **e** and **e*** as

$$\mathbf{a} = (\mathbf{a} \cdot \mathbf{e})\, \mathbf{e} + (\mathbf{a} \cdot \mathbf{e}^*)\, \mathbf{e}^*. \tag{A.1.8}$$

The scalar product between **a** and **e** projects the vector **a** onto the (unit) direction **e**. The projection of a vector **a** onto a direction specified by general **f** is $\frac{\mathbf{a} \cdot \mathbf{f}}{|f|^2}\mathbf{f}$.

A.1.3 Lines in space

A line in two (or more) dimensions can be specified as follows. The vector of any point along the line is given, for some s, by the equation

$$\mathbf{p} = \mathbf{a} + s\mathbf{u}, \qquad s \in \mathcal{R}, \tag{A.1.9}$$

where **u** is parallel to the line, and the line passes through the point **a**, see Fig. A.2. An alternative specification can be given by realising that all vectors along the line are orthogonal to the normal of the line, **n** (**u** and **n** are orthonormal). That is

$$(\mathbf{p} - \mathbf{a}) \cdot \mathbf{n} = 0 \Leftrightarrow \mathbf{p} \cdot \mathbf{n} = \mathbf{a} \cdot \mathbf{n}. \tag{A.1.10}$$

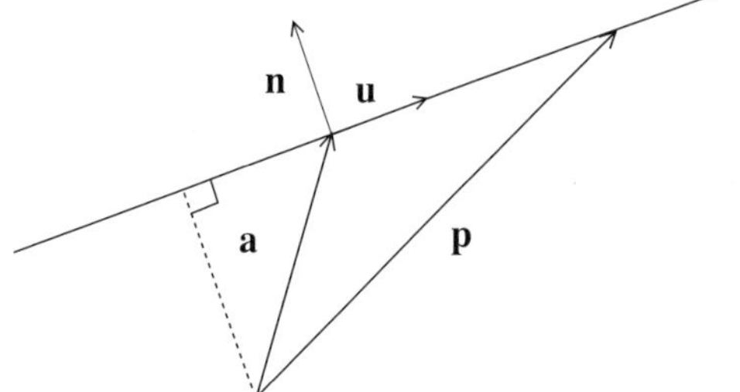

Figure A.2 A line can be specified by some position vector on the line, **a**, and a unit vector along the direction of the line, **u**. In two dimensions, there is a unique direction, **n**, perpendicular to the line. In three dimensions, the vectors perpendicular to the direction of the line lie in a plane, whose normal vector is in the direction of the line, **u**.

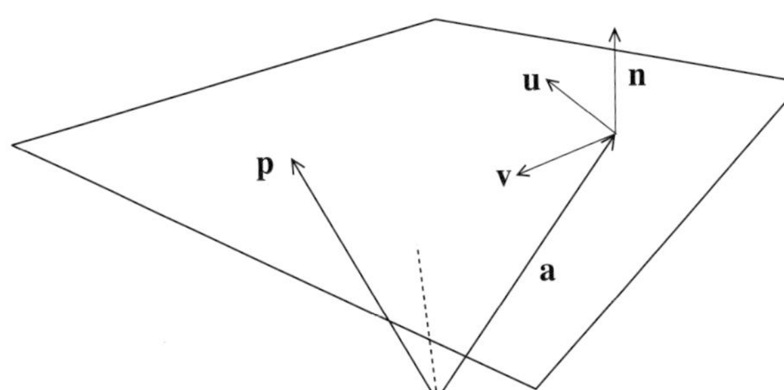

Figure A.3 A plane can be specified by a point in the plane, **a** and two, non-parallel directions in the plane, **u** and **v**. The normal to the plane is unique, and in the same direction as the directed line from the origin to the nearest point on the plane.

If the vector **n** is of unit length, the right-hand side of the above represents the shortest distance from the origin to the line, drawn by the dashed line in Fig. A.2 (since this is the projection of **a** onto the normal direction).

A.1.4 Planes and hyperplanes

To define a two-dimensional plane (in arbitrary dimensional space) one may specify two vectors **u** and **v** that lie in the plane (they need not be mutually orthogonal), and a position vector **a** in the plane, see Fig. A.3. Any vector **p** in the plane can then be written as

$$\mathbf{p} = \mathbf{a} + s\mathbf{u} + t\mathbf{v}, \qquad (s, t) \in \mathcal{R}. \tag{A.1.11}$$

An alternative definition is given by considering that any vector within the plane must be orthogonal to the normal of the plane **n**:

$$(\mathbf{p} - \mathbf{a}) \cdot \mathbf{n} = 0 \Leftrightarrow \mathbf{p} \cdot \mathbf{n} = \mathbf{a} \cdot \mathbf{n}. \tag{A.1.12}$$

The right-hand side of the above represents the shortest distance from the origin to the plane, drawn by the dashed line in Fig. A.3. The advantage of this representation is that it has the same form as a line. Indeed, this representation of (hyper)planes is independent of the dimension of the space. In addition, only two quantities need to be defined – the normal to the plane and the distance from the origin to the plane.

A.1.5 Matrices

An $m \times n$ matrix **A** is a collection of scalar values arranged in a rectangle of m rows and n columns. A vector can be considered as an $n \times 1$ matrix. The i, j element of matrix **A** can be written A_{ij} or more conventionally a_{ij}. Where more clarity is required, one may write $[\mathbf{A}]_{ij}$.

Definition A.3 Matrix addition For two matrices **A** and **B** of the same size,

$$[\mathbf{A} + \mathbf{B}]_{ij} = [\mathbf{A}]_{ij} + [\mathbf{B}]_{ij}. \tag{A.1.13}$$

Definition A.4 Matrix multiplication For an l by n matrix **A** and an n by m matrix B, the product **AB** is the l by m matrix with elements

$$[\mathbf{AB}]_{ik} = \sum_{j=1}^{n} [\mathbf{A}]_{ij} [\mathbf{B}]_{jk}; \qquad i = 1, \ldots, l \quad k = 1, \ldots, m. \tag{A.1.14}$$

Note that in general $\mathbf{BA} \neq \mathbf{AB}$. When $\mathbf{BA} = \mathbf{AB}$ we say that they $\mathbf{A}$ and $\mathbf{B}$ *commute*. The matrix $\mathbf{I}$ is the *identity matrix*, necessarily square, with 1's on the diagonal and 0's everywhere else. For clarity we may also write $\mathbf{I}_m$ for a square $m \times m$ identity matrix. Then for an $m \times n$ matrix $\mathbf{A}$, $\mathbf{I}_m\mathbf{A} = \mathbf{A}\mathbf{I}_n = \mathbf{A}$. The identity matrix has elements $[\mathbf{I}]_{ij} = \delta_{ij}$ given by the *Kronecker delta*:

$$\delta_{ij} \equiv \begin{cases} 1 & i = j \\ 0 & i \neq j \end{cases}. \tag{A.1.15}$$

Definition A.5 Transpose The transpose $\mathbf{B}^{\mathsf{T}}$ of the n by m matrix $\mathbf{B}$ is the m by n matrix with components

$$\left[\mathbf{B}^{\mathsf{T}}\right]_{kj} = \mathbf{B}_{jk}\,; \qquad k = 1, \ldots, m \quad j = 1, \ldots, n. \tag{A.1.16}$$

$\left(\mathbf{B}^{\mathsf{T}}\right)^{\mathsf{T}} = \mathbf{B}$ and $(\mathbf{AB})^{\mathsf{T}} = \mathbf{B}^{\mathsf{T}}\mathbf{A}^{\mathsf{T}}$. If the shapes of the matrices $\mathbf{A}$, $\mathbf{B}$ and $\mathbf{C}$ are such that it makes sense to calculate the product $\mathbf{ABC}$, then

$$(\mathbf{ABC})^{\mathsf{T}} = \mathbf{C}^{\mathsf{T}}\mathbf{B}^{\mathsf{T}}\mathbf{A}^{\mathsf{T}}. \tag{A.1.17}$$

A square matrix $\mathbf{A}$ is symmetric if $\mathbf{A}^{\mathsf{T}} = \mathbf{A}$. A square matrix is called *Hermitian* if $\mathbf{A} = \mathbf{A}^{\mathsf{T}*}$ where $*$ denotes the complex conjugate operator. For Hermitian matrices, the eigenvectors form an orthogonal set with real eigenvalues.

Definition A.6 Trace

$$\text{trace}\,(\mathbf{A}) = \sum_i A_{ii} = \sum_i \lambda_i \tag{A.1.18}$$

where λ_i are the eigenvalues of $\mathbf{A}$.

A.1.6 Linear transformations

If we define $\mathbf{u}_i$ to be the vector with zeros everywhere expect for the ith entry, then a vector can be expressed as $\mathbf{x} = \sum_i x_i \mathbf{u}_i$. Then a linear transformation of $\mathbf{x}$ is given by

$$\mathbf{Ax} = \sum_i x_i \mathbf{Au}_i = \sum_i x_i \mathbf{a}_i \tag{A.1.19}$$

where $\mathbf{a}_i$ is the ith column of $\mathbf{A}$.

Rotations

The unit vectors $(1, 0)^{\mathsf{T}}$ and $(0, 1)^{\mathsf{T}}$ under rotation by θ radians transform to the vectors

$$\begin{pmatrix} \cos\theta \\ \sin\theta \end{pmatrix}, \qquad \begin{pmatrix} -\sin\theta \\ \cos\theta \end{pmatrix} \tag{A.1.20}$$

which thus form the columns of the rotation matrix:

$$\mathbf{R} = \begin{pmatrix} \cos\theta & -\sin\theta \\ \sin\theta & \cos\theta \end{pmatrix}. \tag{A.1.21}$$

Multiplying a vector by $\mathbf{R}$, $\mathbf{Rx}$, rotates the vector through θ radians.

A.1.7 Determinants

Definition A.7 Determinant For a square matrix $\mathbf{A}$, the determinant is the volume of the transformation of the matrix $\mathbf{A}$ (up to a sign change). That is, we take a hypercube of unit volume and map each vertex under the transformation. The volume of the resulting object is defined as the determinant. Writing $[\mathbf{A}]_{ij} = a_{ij}$,

$$\det\begin{pmatrix} a_{11} & a_{12} \\ a_{21} & a_{22} \end{pmatrix} = a_{11}a_{22} - a_{21}a_{12}. \tag{A.1.22}$$

$$\det\begin{pmatrix} a_{11} & a_{12} & a_{13} \\ a_{21} & a_{22} & a_{23} \\ a_{31} & a_{32} & a_{33} \end{pmatrix} = a_{11}\left(a_{22}a_{33} - a_{23}a_{32}\right) - a_{12}\left(a_{21}a_{33} - a_{31}a_{23}\right) + a_{13}\left(a_{21}a_{32} - a_{31}a_{22}\right). \tag{A.1.23}$$

The determinant in the (3×3) case has the form

$$a_{11}\det\begin{pmatrix} a_{22} & a_{23} \\ a_{32} & a_{33} \end{pmatrix} - a_{12}\det\begin{pmatrix} a_{21} & a_{23} \\ a_{31} & a_{33} \end{pmatrix} + a_{13}\det\begin{pmatrix} a_{21} & a_{22} \\ a_{31} & a_{32} \end{pmatrix}. \tag{A.1.24}$$

The determinant of the (3×3) matrix $\mathbf{A}$ is given by the sum of terms $(-1)^{i+1}a_{1i}\det(\mathbf{A}_i)$ where $\mathbf{A}_i$ is the (2×2) matrix formed from $\mathbf{A}$ by removing the ith row and column. This form of the determinant generalises to any dimension. That is, we can define the determinant recursively as an expansion along the top row of determinants of reduced matrices. The absolute value of the determinant is the volume of the transformation.

$$\det\left(\mathbf{A}^{\mathsf{T}}\right) = \det(\mathbf{A}). \tag{A.1.25}$$

For square matrices $\mathbf{A}$ and $\mathbf{B}$ of equal dimensions,

$$\det(\mathbf{AB}) = \det(\mathbf{A})\det(\mathbf{B}), \qquad \det(\mathbf{I}) = 1 \Rightarrow \det\left(\mathbf{A}^{-1}\right) = 1/\det(\mathbf{A}). \tag{A.1.26}$$

Definition A.8 Orthogonal matrix A square matrix $\mathbf{A}$ is orthogonal if $\mathbf{A}\mathbf{A}^{\mathsf{T}} = \mathbf{I} = \mathbf{A}^{\mathsf{T}}\mathbf{A}$. From the properties of the determinant, we see therefore that an orthogonal matrix has determinant ± 1 and hence corresponds to a volume preserving transformation.

Definition A.9 Matrix rank For an $m \times n$ matrix $\mathbf{X}$ the rank of $\mathbf{X}$ is the maximum number of linearly independent columns (or equivalently rows). The matrix is full rank if it has rank equal to $\min(m, n)$ – otherwise the matrix is rank deficient. A square matrix that is rank deficient is singular.

A.1.8 Matrix inversion

Definition A.10 Matrix inversion For a square matrix $\mathbf{A}$, its inverse satisfies

$$\mathbf{A}^{-1}\mathbf{A} = \mathbf{I} = \mathbf{A}\mathbf{A}^{-1}. \tag{A.1.27}$$

It is not always possible to find a matrix $\mathbf{A}^{-1}$ such that $\mathbf{A}^{-1}\mathbf{A} = \mathbf{I}$, in which case $\mathbf{A}$ is *singular*. Geometrically, singular matrices correspond to projections: if we transform each of the vertices $\mathbf{v}$ of a binary hypercube using $\mathbf{Av}$, the volume of the transformed hypercube is zero. Hence if $\det(\mathbf{A}) = 0$, the matrix $\mathbf{A}$ is a form of projection or 'collapse' which means $\mathbf{A}$ is singular. Given a vector $\mathbf{y}$ and a singular transformation, $\mathbf{A}$, one cannot uniquely identify a vector $\mathbf{x}$ for which $\mathbf{y} = \mathbf{A}\mathbf{x}$. Provided the inverses exist

$$(\mathbf{AB})^{-1} = \mathbf{B}^{-1}\mathbf{A}^{-1}. \tag{A.1.28}$$

For a non-square matrix $\mathbf{A}$ such that $\mathbf{A}\mathbf{A}^{\mathsf{T}}$ is invertible, then the right pseudo inverse, defined as

$$\mathbf{A}^{\dagger} = \mathbf{A}^{\mathsf{T}}\left(\mathbf{A}\mathbf{A}^{\mathsf{T}}\right)^{-1} \tag{A.1.29}$$

satisfies $\mathbf{A}\mathbf{A}^{\dagger} = \mathbf{I}$. The left pseudo inverse is given by

$$\mathbf{A}^{\dagger} = \left(\mathbf{A}^{\mathsf{T}}\mathbf{A}\right)^{-1}\mathbf{A}^{\mathsf{T}} \tag{A.1.30}$$

and satisfies $\mathbf{A}^{\dagger}\mathbf{A} = \mathbf{I}$.

Definition A.11 Matrix inversion lemma (Woodbury formula) Provided the appropriate inverses exist:

$$\left(\mathbf{A} + \mathbf{U}\mathbf{V}^{\mathsf{T}}\right)^{-1} = \mathbf{A}^{-1} - \mathbf{A}^{-1}\mathbf{U}\left(\mathbf{I} + \mathbf{V}^{\mathsf{T}}\mathbf{A}^{-1}\mathbf{U}\right)^{-1}\mathbf{V}^{\mathsf{T}}\mathbf{A}^{-1}. \tag{A.1.31}$$

$$\det\left(\mathbf{A} + \mathbf{U}\mathbf{V}^{\mathsf{T}}\right) = \det\left(\mathbf{A}\right)\det\left(\mathbf{I} + \mathbf{V}^{\mathsf{T}}\mathbf{A}^{-1}\mathbf{U}\right). \tag{A.1.32}$$

Definition A.12 Block matrix inversion For matrices $\mathbf{A}, \mathbf{B}, \mathbf{C}, \mathbf{D}$, provided the appropriate inverses exist:

$$\begin{bmatrix} \mathbf{A} & \mathbf{B} \\ \mathbf{C} & \mathbf{D} \end{bmatrix}^{-1} = \begin{bmatrix} \left(\mathbf{A} - \mathbf{B}\mathbf{D}^{-1}\mathbf{C}\right)^{-1} & -\left(\mathbf{A} - \mathbf{B}\mathbf{D}^{-1}\mathbf{C}\right)^{-1}\mathbf{B}\mathbf{D}^{-1} \\ -\mathbf{D}^{-1}\mathbf{C}\left(\mathbf{A} - \mathbf{B}\mathbf{D}^{-1}\mathbf{C}\right)^{-1} & \mathbf{D}^{-1}\mathbf{C}\left(\mathbf{A} - \mathbf{B}\mathbf{D}^{-1}\mathbf{C}\right)^{-1}\mathbf{B}\mathbf{D}^{-1} \end{bmatrix}. \tag{A.1.33}$$

A.1.9 Computing the matrix inverse

For a 2×2 matrix, $\mathbf{A} = \begin{pmatrix} a & b \\ c & d \end{pmatrix}$, the inverse matrix has elements

$$\frac{1}{ad - bc}\begin{pmatrix} d & -b \\ -c & a \end{pmatrix} = \mathbf{A}^{-1}. \tag{A.1.34}$$

The quantity $ad - bc$ is the determinant of $\mathbf{A}$. There are many ways to compute the inverse of a general matrix, and we refer the reader to more specialised texts, such as [279, 129].

If one wants to solve only a linear system, $\mathbf{A}\mathbf{x} = \mathbf{b}$, algebraically, the solution is given by $\mathbf{x} = \mathbf{A}^{-1}\mathbf{b}$. This would suggest that one needs to compute the $n \times n$ matrix $\mathbf{A}^{-1}$. However, in practice, $\mathbf{A}^{-1}$ is not explicitly required – only $\mathbf{x}$ is needed. This can be obtained more rapidly and with greater numerical precision using Gaussian elimination [279, 129].

A.1.10 Eigenvalues and eigenvectors

The eigenvectors of a matrix correspond to a natural coordinate system in which the geometric transformation represented by $\mathbf{A}$ can be most easily understood.

Definition A.13 Eigenvalues and eigenvectors For an $n \times n$ square matrix $\mathbf{A}$, $\mathbf{e}$ is an eigenvector of $\mathbf{A}$ with eigenvalue λ if

$$\mathbf{A}\mathbf{e} = \lambda\mathbf{e}. \tag{A.1.35}$$

Geometrically, the eigenvectors are special directions such that the effect of the transformation **A** along a direction **e** is simply to scale the vector **e**. For a rotation matrix **R** in general there will be no direction preserved under the rotation so that the eigenvalues and eigenvectors are complex valued (which is why the Fourier representation, which corresponds to representation in a rotated basis, is necessarily complex).

For an $(n \times n)$ dimensional matrix, there are (including repetitions) n eigenvalues, each with a corresponding eigenvector. We can reform Equation (A.1.35) as

$$(\mathbf{A} - \lambda\mathbf{I})\,\mathbf{e} = \mathbf{0}. \tag{A.1.36}$$

We can write Equation (A.1.36) as $\mathbf{Be} = \mathbf{0}$, where $\mathbf{B} \equiv \mathbf{A} - \lambda\mathbf{I}$. If $\mathbf{B}$ has an inverse, then a solution is $\mathbf{e} = \mathbf{B}^{-1}\mathbf{0} = \mathbf{0}$, which trivially satisfies the eigen-equation. For any non-trivial solution to the problem $\mathbf{Be} = \mathbf{0}$, we therefore need $\mathbf{B}$ to be non-invertible. This is equivalent to the condition that $\mathbf{B}$ has zero determinant. Hence λ is an eigenvalue of $\mathbf{A}$ if

$$\det(\mathbf{A} - \lambda\mathbf{I}) = 0. \tag{A.1.37}$$

This is known as the characteristic equation. This determinant equation will be a polynomial in λ of degree n and the resulting equation is known as the characteristic polynomial. Once we have found an eigenvalue, the corresponding eigenvector can be found by substituting this value for λ in Equation (A.1.35) and solving the linear equations for **e**. It may be that for an eigenvalue λ the eigenvector is not unique and there is a space of corresponding vectors. An important relation between the determinant and the eigenvalues of a matrix is

$$\det(\mathbf{A}) = \prod_{i=1}^{n} \lambda_i. \tag{A.1.38}$$

Hence a matrix is singular if it has a zero eigenvalue. The trace of a matrix can be expressed as

$$\text{trace}(\mathbf{A}) = \sum_i \lambda_i. \tag{A.1.39}$$

For a real symmetric matrix $\mathbf{A} = \mathbf{A}^\mathsf{T}$, and eigenvectors $\mathbf{e}^i$, $\mathbf{e}^j$, then $(\mathbf{e}^i)^\mathsf{T}\mathbf{e}^j = 0$ if the eigenvalues λ_i and λ_j are different. This can be shown by considering:

$$\mathbf{A}\mathbf{e}^i = \lambda_i\mathbf{e}^i \Rightarrow (\mathbf{e}^j)^\mathsf{T}\mathbf{A}\mathbf{e}^i = \lambda_i(\mathbf{e}^j)^\mathsf{T}\mathbf{e}^i. \tag{A.1.40}$$

Since **A** is symmetric, then

$$((\mathbf{e}^j)^\mathsf{T}\mathbf{A})\mathbf{e}^i = (\mathbf{A}\mathbf{e}^j)^\mathsf{T}\mathbf{e}^i = \lambda_j(\mathbf{e}^j)^\mathsf{T}\mathbf{e}^i \Rightarrow \lambda_i(\mathbf{e}^j)^\mathsf{T}\mathbf{e}^i = \lambda_j(\mathbf{e}^j)^\mathsf{T}\mathbf{e}^i. \tag{A.1.41}$$

If $\lambda_i \neq \lambda_j$, this condition can be satisfied only if $(\mathbf{e}^j)^\mathsf{T}\mathbf{e}^i = 0$, namely that the eigenvectors are orthogonal.

Definition A.14 **Trace-log formula** For a positive definite matrix **A**,

$$\text{trace}(\log\mathbf{A}) \equiv \log\det(\mathbf{A}). \tag{A.1.42}$$

Note that the above logarithm of a matrix is not the element-wise logarithm. In MATLAB the required function is `logm`. In general for an analytic function $f(x)$, $f(\mathbf{M})$ is defined via the power-series expansion of the function. On the right, since $\det(\mathbf{A})$ is a scalar, the logarithm is the standard logarithm of a scalar.

A.1.11 Matrix decompositions

Definition A.15 Spectral decomposition A real $n \times n$ symmetric matrix $\mathbf{A}$ has an eigen-decomposition

$$\mathbf{A} = \sum_{i=1}^{n} \lambda_i \mathbf{e}_i \mathbf{e}_i^{\mathsf{T}} \tag{A.1.43}$$

where λ_i is the eigenvalue of eigenvector $\mathbf{e}_i$ and the eigenvectors form an orthogonal set,

$$\left(\mathbf{e}^i\right)^{\mathsf{T}} \mathbf{e}^j = \delta_{ij} \left(\mathbf{e}^i\right)^{\mathsf{T}} \mathbf{e}^i. \tag{A.1.44}$$

In matrix notation

$$\mathbf{A} = \mathbf{E}\boldsymbol{\Lambda}\mathbf{E}^{\mathsf{T}} \tag{A.1.45}$$

where $\mathbf{E} = \left[\mathbf{e}^1, \ldots, \mathbf{e}^n\right]$ is the matrix of eigenvectors and $\boldsymbol{\Lambda}$ the corresponding diagonal eigenvalue matrix. More generally, for a square non-symmetric diagonalisable $\mathbf{A}$ we can write

$$\mathbf{A} = \mathbf{E}\boldsymbol{\Lambda}\mathbf{E}^{-1}. \tag{A.1.46}$$

Definition A.16 Singular value decomposition The SVD decomposition of a $n \times p$ matrix $\mathbf{X}$ is

$$\mathbf{X} = \mathbf{U}\mathbf{S}\mathbf{V}^{\mathsf{T}} \tag{A.1.47}$$

where $\dim \mathbf{U} = n \times n$ with $\mathbf{U}^{\mathsf{T}}\mathbf{U} = \mathbf{I}_n$. Also $\dim \mathbf{V} = p \times p$ with $\mathbf{V}^{\mathsf{T}}\mathbf{V} = \mathbf{I}_p$.

The matrix $\mathbf{S}$ has $\dim \mathbf{S} = n \times p$ with zeros everywhere except on the diagonal entries. The singular values are the diagonal entries $[\mathbf{S}]_{ii}$ and are non-negative. The singular values are ordered so that the upper left diagonal element of $\mathbf{S}$ contains the largest singular value and $S_{ii} \geq S_{jj}$ for $i < j$. Assuming $n < p$ (otherwise transpose $\mathbf{X}$), the computational complexity of computing the SVD is $O\left(4n^2 p + 8np^2 + 9n^3\right)$ [129]. For the 'thin' SVD with $n > p$ only the first p columns of U and $\mathbf{S}$ are computed giving a decomposition

$$\mathbf{X} = \mathbf{U}_p \mathbf{S}_p \mathbf{V}^{\mathsf{T}} \tag{A.1.48}$$

where $\mathbf{U}_p$ has dimension $n \times p$, and $\mathbf{S}_p$ is the $p \times p$ diagonal matrix of singular values.

Definition A.17 Quadratic form

$$\mathbf{x}^{\mathsf{T}}\mathbf{A}\mathbf{x} + \mathbf{x}^{\mathsf{T}}\mathbf{b}. \tag{A.1.49}$$

Definition A.18 Positive definite matrix A symmetric matrix $\mathbf{A}$ with the property that $\mathbf{x}^{\mathsf{T}}\mathbf{A}\mathbf{x} \geq 0$ for any vector $\mathbf{x}$ is called positive semidefinite. A symmetric matrix $\mathbf{A}$, with the property that $\mathbf{x}^{\mathsf{T}}\mathbf{A}\mathbf{x} > 0$ for any vector $\mathbf{x} \neq \mathbf{0}$ is called positive definite. A positive definite matrix has full rank and is thus invertible. Using the eigen-decomposition of $\mathbf{A}$,

$$\mathbf{x}^{\mathsf{T}}\mathbf{A}\mathbf{x} = \sum_i \lambda_i \mathbf{x}^{\mathsf{T}}\mathbf{e}^i (\mathbf{e}^i)^{\mathsf{T}}\mathbf{x} = \sum_i \lambda_i \left(\mathbf{x}^{\mathsf{T}}\mathbf{e}^i\right)^2 \tag{A.1.50}$$

which is greater than zero if and only if all the eigenvalues are positive. Hence $\mathbf{A}$ is positive definite if and only if all its eigenvalues are positive.

Eigenfunctions

$$\int_x K(x', x)\phi_a(x) = \lambda_a \phi_a(x'). \tag{A.1.51}$$

The eigenfunctions of a real symmetric kernel, $K(x', x) = K(x, x')$ are orthogonal:

$$\int_x \phi_a(x)\phi_b^*(x) = \delta_{ab} \tag{A.1.52}$$

where $\phi^*(x)$ is the complex conjugate of $\phi(x)$. A kernel has a decomposition (provided the eigenvalues are countable)

$$K(x^i, x^j) = \sum_\mu \lambda_\mu \phi_\mu(x^i)\phi_\mu^*(x^j). \tag{A.1.53}$$

Then

$$\sum_{i,j} y_i K(x^i, x^j) y_j = \sum_{i,j,\mu} \lambda_\mu y_i \phi_\mu(x^i)\phi_\mu^*(x^j) y_j = \sum_\mu \lambda_\mu \underbrace{\left(\sum_i y_i \phi_\mu(x^i)\right)}_{z_i} \underbrace{\left(\sum_i y_i \phi_\mu^*(x^i)\right)}_{z_i^*} \tag{A.1.54}$$

which is greater than zero if the eigenvalues are all positive (since for complex z, $zz^* \geq 0$). If the eigenvalues are uncountable the appropriate decomposition is

$$K(x^i, x^j) = \int \lambda(s)\phi(x^i, s)\phi^*(x^j, s)ds. \tag{A.1.55}$$

A.2 Multivariate calculus

Definition A.19 Partial derivative Consider a function of n variables, $f(x_1, x_2, \ldots, x_n) \equiv f(\mathbf{x})$. The partial derivative of f w.r.t. x_i is defined as the following limit (when it exists)

$$\frac{\partial f}{\partial x_i} = \lim_{h \to 0} \frac{f(x_1, \ldots, x_{i-1}, x_i + h, x_{i+1}, \ldots, x_n) - f(\mathbf{x})}{h}. \tag{A.2.1}$$

The *gradient vector* of f is denoted ∇f or $\mathbf{g}$:

$$\nabla f(\mathbf{x}) \equiv \mathbf{g}(\mathbf{x}) \equiv \begin{pmatrix} \frac{\partial f}{\partial x_1} \\ \vdots \\ \frac{\partial f}{\partial x_n} \end{pmatrix}. \tag{A.2.2}$$

A.2.1 Interpreting the gradient vector

Consider a function $f(\mathbf{x})$ that depends on a vector $\mathbf{x}$. We are interested in how the function changes when the vector $\mathbf{x}$ changes by a small amount : $\mathbf{x} \to \mathbf{x} + \boldsymbol{\delta}$, where $\boldsymbol{\delta}$ is a vector whose length is very small. According to a Taylor expansion, the function f will change to

$$f(\mathbf{x} + \boldsymbol{\delta}) = f(\mathbf{x}) + \sum_i \delta_i \frac{\partial f}{\partial x_i} + O\left(\delta^2\right). \tag{A.2.3}$$

We can interpret the summation above as the scalar product between the vector ∇f with components $[\nabla f]_i = \partial f / \partial x_i$ and $\boldsymbol{\delta}$

$$f(\mathbf{x} + \boldsymbol{\delta}) = f(\mathbf{x}) + (\nabla f) \cdot \boldsymbol{\delta} + O\left(\delta^2\right). \tag{A.2.4}$$

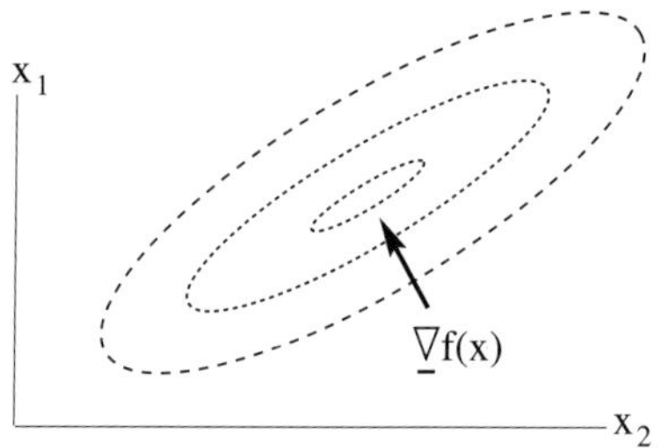

Figure A.4 Interpreting the gradient. The ellipses are contours of constant function value, $f = \text{const}$. At any point $\mathbf{x}$, the gradient vector $\nabla f(\mathbf{x})$ points along the direction of maximal increase of the function.

The gradient points along the direction in which the function increases most rapidly. To see this, consider a direction $\hat{\mathbf{p}}$ (a unit length vector). Then a displacement δ units along this direction changes the function value to

$$f(\mathbf{x} + \delta\hat{\mathbf{p}}) \approx f(\mathbf{x}) + \delta\nabla f(\mathbf{x}) \cdot \hat{\mathbf{p}}. \tag{A.2.5}$$

The direction $\hat{\mathbf{p}}$ for which the function has the largest change is that which maximises the overlap

$$\nabla f(\mathbf{x}) \cdot \hat{\mathbf{p}} = |\nabla f(\mathbf{x})||\hat{\mathbf{p}}| \cos\theta = |\nabla f(\mathbf{x})| \cos\theta \tag{A.2.6}$$

where θ is the angle between $\hat{\mathbf{p}}$ and $\nabla f(\mathbf{x})$. The overlap is maximised when $\theta = 0$, giving $\hat{\mathbf{p}} = \nabla f(\mathbf{x})/|\nabla f(\mathbf{x})|$. Hence, the direction along which the function changes the most rapidly is along $\nabla f(\mathbf{x})$.

A.2.2 Higher derivatives

The second derivative of an n-variable function is defined by

$$\frac{\partial}{\partial x_i}\left(\frac{\partial f}{\partial x_j}\right) \qquad i = 1, \ldots, n; \quad j = 1, \ldots, n. \tag{A.2.7}$$

which is usually written

$$\frac{\partial^2 f}{\partial x_i \partial x_j}, \quad i \neq j \qquad \frac{\partial^2 f}{\partial {x_i}^2}, \quad i = j. \tag{A.2.8}$$

If the partial derivatives $\partial^2 f/\partial x_i \partial x_j$ and $\partial^2 f/\partial x_j \partial x_i$ exist then

$$\partial^2 f/\partial x_i \partial x_j = \partial^2 f/\partial x_j \partial x_i \,. \tag{A.2.9}$$

This is also denoted by $\nabla\nabla f$. These n^2 second partial derivatives are represented by a square, symmetric matrix called the *Hessian* matrix of $f(\mathbf{x})$.

$$\mathbf{H}_f(\mathbf{x}) = \begin{pmatrix} \frac{\partial^2 f}{\partial {x_1}^2} & \cdots & \frac{\partial^2 f}{\partial x_1 \partial x_n} \\ \vdots & & \vdots \\ \frac{\partial^2 f}{\partial x_1 \partial x_n} & \cdots & \frac{\partial^2 f}{\partial {x_n}^2} \end{pmatrix}. \tag{A.2.10}$$

Definition A.20 **Chain rule** Let each x_j be parameterised by $u_1, \ldots, u_m$, i.e. $x_j = x_j(u_1, \ldots, u_m)$.

$$\frac{\partial f}{\partial u_\alpha} = \sum_{j=1}^{n} \frac{\partial f}{\partial x_j} \frac{\partial x_j}{\partial u_\alpha} \tag{A.2.11}$$

or in vector notation

$$\frac{\partial}{\partial u_\alpha} f(\mathbf{x}(\mathbf{u})) = \nabla f^{\mathsf{T}}(\mathbf{x}(\mathbf{u})) \frac{\partial \mathbf{x}(\mathbf{u})}{\partial u_\alpha}. \tag{A.2.12}$$

Definition A.21 Directional derivative Assume f is differentiable. We define the scalar directional derivative $(D_{\mathbf{v}} f)(\mathbf{x}^*)$ of f in a direction $\mathbf{v}$ at a point $\mathbf{x}^*$. Let $\mathbf{x} = \mathbf{x}^* + h\mathbf{v}$, then

$$(D_{\mathbf{v}} f)(\mathbf{x}^*) = \left. \frac{d}{dh} f(\mathbf{x}^* + h\mathbf{v}) \right|_{h=0} = \sum_j v_j \left. \frac{\partial f}{\partial x_j} \right|_{\mathbf{x}=\mathbf{x}^*} = \nabla f^{\mathsf{T}} \mathbf{v}. \tag{A.2.13}$$

A.2.3 Matrix calculus

Definition A.22 Derivative of a matrix trace For matrices $\mathbf{A}$ and $\mathbf{B}$

$$\frac{\partial}{\partial \mathbf{A}} \text{trace}(\mathbf{AB}) \equiv \mathbf{B}^{\mathsf{T}}. \tag{A.2.14}$$

Definition A.23 Derivative of $\log\det(\mathbf{A})$

$$\partial \log\det(\mathbf{A}) = \partial \text{trace}(\log \mathbf{A}) = \text{trace}\left(\mathbf{A}^{-1}\partial \mathbf{A}\right). \tag{A.2.15}$$

So that

$$\frac{\partial}{\partial \mathbf{A}} \log\det(\mathbf{A}) = \mathbf{A}^{-\mathsf{T}}. \tag{A.2.16}$$

Definition A.24 Derivative of a matrix inverse For an invertible matrix $\mathbf{A}$,

$$\partial \mathbf{A}^{-1} \equiv -\mathbf{A}^{-\mathsf{T}} \partial \mathbf{A} \mathbf{A}^{-1}. \tag{A.2.17}$$

A.3 Inequalities

A.3.1 Convexity

Definition A.25 Convex function A function $f(x)$ is defined as convex if for any x, y and $0 \le \lambda \le 1$

$$f(\lambda x + (1-\lambda)y) \le \lambda f(x) + (1-\lambda) f(y) \tag{A.3.1}$$

If $-f(x)$ is convex, $f(x)$ is called concave.

An intuitive picture is given by considering the quantity $\lambda x + (1-\lambda)y$. As we vary λ from 0 to 1, this traces points between x $(\lambda = 0)$ and y $(\lambda = 1)$. Hence for $\lambda = 0$ we start at the point $x, f(x)$ and as λ increases trace a straight line towards the point $y, f(y)$ at $\lambda = 1$. Convexity states that the function f always lies below this straight line. Geometrically this means that the function $f(x)$ is always always non-decreasing. Hence if $d^2 f(x)/dx^2 \ge 0$ the function is convex. As an example, the function $\log x$ is concave since its second derivative is negative:

$$\frac{d}{dx} \log x = \frac{1}{x}, \qquad \frac{d^2}{dx^2} \log x = -\frac{1}{x^2}. \tag{A.3.2}$$

A.3.2 Jensen's inequality

For a convex function, $f(x)$, it follows directly from the definition of convexity that

$$f(\langle x \rangle_{p(x)}) \leq \langle f(x) \rangle_{p(x)} \tag{A.3.3}$$

for any distribution $p(x)$.

A.4 Optimisation

Definition A.26 Critical point When all first-order partial derivatives at a point are zero (i.e. $\nabla f = \mathbf{0}$) then the point is said to be a stationary or critical point. A critical point can correspond to a minimum, maximum or saddle point of the function.

There is a minimum of f at $\mathbf{x}^*$ if $f(\mathbf{x}^*) \leq f(\mathbf{x})$ for all $\mathbf{x}$ sufficiently close to $\mathbf{x}^*$. This requires $\mathbf{x}^*$ to be a stationary point, $\nabla f(\mathbf{x}^*) = \mathbf{0}$. The Taylor expansion of f at the optimum is given by

$$f(\mathbf{x}^* + h\mathbf{v}) = f(\mathbf{x}^*) + h^2 \mathbf{v}^\mathsf{T} \mathbf{H}_f \mathbf{v} + O(h^3). \tag{A.4.1}$$

Thus the minimum condition requires that $\mathbf{v}^\mathsf{T} \mathbf{H}_f \mathbf{v} \geq 0$, i.e. the Hessian is non-negative definite.

Definition A.27 Conditions for a minimum Sufficient conditions for a minimum at $\mathbf{x}^*$ are (i) $\nabla f(\mathbf{x}^*) = 0$ and (ii) $\mathbf{H}_f(\mathbf{x}^*)$ is positive definite.

For a quadratic function $f(\mathbf{x}) = \frac{1}{2}\mathbf{x}^\mathsf{T}\mathbf{A}\mathbf{x} - \mathbf{b}^\mathsf{T}\mathbf{x} + c$, with symmetric $\mathbf{A}$ the condition $\nabla f(\mathbf{x}^*) = \mathbf{0}$ reads:

$$\mathbf{A}\mathbf{x}^* - \mathbf{b} = 0. \tag{A.4.2}$$

If $\mathbf{A}$ is invertible this equation has the unique solution $\mathbf{x}^* = \mathbf{A}^{-1}\mathbf{b}$. If $\mathbf{A}$ is positive definite then $\mathbf{x}^*$ corresponds to the minimum point.

A.5 Multivariate optimisation

In most cases the optima of functions cannot be found by algebraic means alone and numerical techniques are required. The search techniques that we consider here are iterative, i.e. we proceed towards the minimum $\mathbf{x}^*$ by a sequence of steps. Perhaps the simplest approach to minimising a multivariate function $f(\mathbf{x})$ is to break the problem into a sequence of one-dimensional problems. By initialising the elements of $\mathbf{x}$ at random, one then selects a component of $\mathbf{x}$ to update, keeping all others fixed. This coordinatewise optimisation decreases the function via a sequence of one-dimensional minimisations. Whilst such a procedure is simple, it can be inefficient in high dimensions, particularly when there are strong dependencies between the components in $\mathbf{x}$. For this reason, it is useful to use gradient-based procedures that take the local geometry of the objective into account. We will

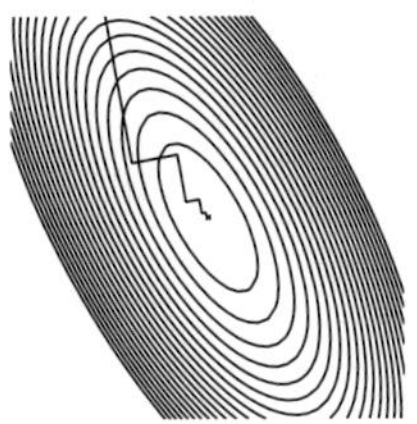

Figure A.5 Optimisation using line search along steepest descent directions. Following the steepest way downhill from a point (and continuing for a finite time in that direction) doesn't always result in the fastest way to get to the bottom.

consider a general class of iterative gradient-based method for which, on the kth step, we take a step of length α_k in the direction $\mathbf{p}_k$,

$$\mathbf{x}_{k+1} = \mathbf{x}_k + \alpha_k \mathbf{p}_k. \tag{A.5.1}$$

A.5.1 Gradient descent with fixed step size

Locally, if we are at point $\mathbf{x}_k$, we can decrease $f(\mathbf{x})$ by taking a step in the direction $-\mathbf{g}(\mathbf{x})$. To see why gradient descent works, consider the general update

$$\mathbf{x}_{k+1} = \mathbf{x}_k - \alpha \nabla_{\mathbf{x}} f. \tag{A.5.2}$$

For small α we can expand f around $\mathbf{x}_k$ using Taylor's theorem:

$$f(\mathbf{x}_k + \alpha_k \mathbf{p}_k) \approx f(\mathbf{x}_k) - \alpha ||\nabla_{\mathbf{x}} f|| \tag{A.5.3}$$

so that the change in f is $\Delta f = -\alpha ||\nabla_{\mathbf{x}} f||^2$. If α is non-infinitesimal, it is always possible that we will step over the true minimum. Making η very small guards against this, but means that the optimisation process will take a very long time to reach a minimum. A simple idea that can improve convergence of gradient descent is to include at each iteration a proportion of the change from the previous iteration, $\mathbf{p}_k = -\mathbf{g}_k - \beta \mathbf{g}_{k-1}$, where β is the *momentum coefficient*.

An unfortunate aspect of gradient descent is that the change in the function value depends on the coordinate system. Consider a new coordinate system $\mathbf{y} = \mathbf{Mx}$ for an invertible square matrix $\mathbf{M}$. Define $\hat{f}(\mathbf{y}) \equiv f(\mathbf{Mx})$. Then the change in the function $\hat{f}$ under a gradient update is

$$\Delta \hat{f} \equiv \hat{f}(\mathbf{y} - \alpha \nabla_{\mathbf{y}} \hat{f}) - \hat{f}(\mathbf{y}) \approx -\alpha ||\nabla_{\mathbf{y}} \hat{f}||^2. \tag{A.5.4}$$

Since $\nabla_{\mathbf{y}} \hat{f} = \mathbf{M} \nabla_{\mathbf{x}} f(\mathbf{x})$

$$\Delta \hat{f} = -\alpha \nabla_{\mathbf{x}} f(\mathbf{x})^{\mathsf{T}} \mathbf{M}^{\mathsf{T}} \mathbf{M} \nabla_{\mathbf{x}} f(\mathbf{x}) \tag{A.5.5}$$

which, except for an orthogonal $\mathbf{M}$, is not equal to $\Delta f = -\alpha ||\nabla_{\mathbf{x}} f||^2$.

A.5.2 Gradient descent with line searches

An extension to the idea of gradient descent is to choose the direction of steepest descent, as indicated by the gradient $\mathbf{g}$, but to calculate the value of the step to take which most reduces the value of f when moving in that direction. This involves solving the one-dimensional problem of minimising $f(\mathbf{x}_k + \alpha_k \mathbf{g}_k)$ with respect to α_k, and is known as a line search. To find the optimal step size at the kth step, we choose α_k to minimise $f(\mathbf{x}_k + \alpha_k \mathbf{p}_k)$. So setting $F(\lambda) = f(\mathbf{x}_k + \lambda \mathbf{p}_k)$, at this step we solve the one-dimensional minimisation problem for $F(\lambda)$. Thus our choice of $\alpha_k = \lambda^*$ will satisfy $F'(\alpha_k) = 0$. Now

$$F'(\alpha_k) = \frac{d}{dh}F(\alpha_k + h)_{|h=0} = \frac{d}{dh}f(\mathbf{x}_k + \alpha_k\mathbf{p}_k + h\mathbf{p}_k)_{|h=0}$$
$$= \frac{d}{dh}f(\mathbf{x}_{k+1} + h\mathbf{p}_k)_{|h=0} = (D_{\mathbf{p}_k}f)(\mathbf{x}_{k+1}) = \nabla f^{\mathsf{T}}(\mathbf{x}_{k+1})\mathbf{p}_k. \tag{A.5.6}$$

So $F'(\alpha_k) = 0$ means the directional derivative in the search direction must vanish at the new point and this gives condition $0 = \mathbf{g}_{k+1}^{\mathsf{T}}\mathbf{p}_k$. If the step size is chosen to reduce f as much as it can in that direction, then no further decrease in E can be made by moving in that direction for the moment. Thus the next step will have no component in that direction and will be at right angles to the previous just taken. This can lead to zig-zag type behaviour in the optimisation.

A.5.3 Minimising quadratic functions using line search

Consider minimising the quadratic function

$$f(\mathbf{x}) = \frac{1}{2}\mathbf{x}^{\mathsf{T}}\mathbf{A}\mathbf{x} - \mathbf{b}^{\mathsf{T}}\mathbf{x} + c \tag{A.5.7}$$

where $\mathbf{A}$ is positive definite and symmetric. Although we know where the minimum of this simple function, based on using linear algebra, we wish to use this function as a toy model for more complex functions. As we 'zoom in' to the minimum of a smooth function, it will increasingly appear quadratic. Hence at such small scales, methods that work for the quadratic case should work in general smooth functions. If the general function looks roughly quadratic on the larger scale, then these methods will also work well in that case. One approach is to search along a particular direction $\mathbf{p}$, and find a minimum along this direction. We can then search for a deeper minimum by looking in different directions. That is, we can search firstly along a line $\mathbf{x} + \lambda\mathbf{p}$ such that the function attains a minimum. This has solution,

$$\lambda = \frac{(\mathbf{b} - \mathbf{A}\mathbf{x})\cdot\mathbf{p}}{\mathbf{p}^{\mathsf{T}}\mathbf{A}\mathbf{p}} = \frac{-\nabla f(\mathbf{x})\cdot\mathbf{p}}{\mathbf{p}^{\mathsf{T}}\mathbf{A}\mathbf{p}}. \tag{A.5.8}$$

How should we now choose the next line search direction $\mathbf{p}^{new}$? It would seem sensible to choose successive line search directions $\mathbf{p}$ according to $\mathbf{p}^{new} = -\nabla f(\mathbf{x})$, so that each time we minimise the function along the line of steepest descent. However, this is generally not the optimal choice, see Fig. A.5. If the matrix $\mathbf{A}$ were diagonal, then the minimisation is straightforward and can be carried out independently for each dimension. If we could therefore find an invertible matrix $\mathbf{P}$ with the property that $\mathbf{P}^{\mathsf{T}}\mathbf{A}\mathbf{P}$ is diagonal then the solution is easy since for

$$\hat{f}(\hat{\mathbf{x}}) = \frac{1}{2}\hat{\mathbf{x}}^{\mathsf{T}}\mathbf{P}^{\mathsf{T}}\mathbf{A}\mathbf{P}\hat{\mathbf{x}} - \mathbf{b}^{\mathsf{T}}\mathbf{P}\hat{\mathbf{x}} + c \tag{A.5.9}$$

with $\mathbf{x} = \mathbf{P}\hat{\mathbf{x}}$ we can compute the minimum for each dimension of $\hat{\mathbf{x}}$ separately and then retransform to find $\mathbf{x}^* = \mathbf{P}\hat{\mathbf{x}}^*$. The columns of such a matrix $\mathbf{P}$ are called conjugate vectors.

Definition A.28 **Conjugate vectors** The vectors $\mathbf{p}_i, i = 1, \ldots, k$ are called conjugate to the matrix $\mathbf{A}$, if and only if for $i, j = 1, \ldots, k$ and $i \neq j$:

$$\mathbf{p}_i^{\mathsf{T}}\mathbf{A}\mathbf{p}_j = 0 \quad \text{and} \quad \mathbf{p}_i^{\mathsf{T}}\mathbf{A}\mathbf{p}_i > 0. \tag{A.5.10}$$

The two conditions guarantee that conjugate vectors are linearly independent: Assume that

$$\mathbf{0} = \sum_{j=1}^{k} \alpha_j \mathbf{p}_j = \sum_{j=1}^{i-1} \alpha_j \mathbf{p}_j + \alpha_i \mathbf{p}_i + \sum_{j=i+1}^{k} \alpha_j \mathbf{p}_j. \tag{A.5.11}$$

Now multiplying from the left with $\mathbf{p}_i^\mathsf{T}\mathbf{A}$ yields $0 = \alpha_i \mathbf{p}_i^\mathsf{T}\mathbf{A}\mathbf{p}_i$. So α_i is zero since we know that $\mathbf{p}_i^\mathsf{T}\mathbf{A}\mathbf{p}_i > 0$. As we can make this argument for any $i = 1, \ldots, k$, all of the α_i must be zero.

A.5.4 Gram–Schmidt construction of conjugate vectors

Assume we already have k conjugate vectors $\mathbf{p}_1, \ldots, \mathbf{p}_k$ and let $\mathbf{v}$ be a vector which is linearly independent of $\mathbf{p}_1, \ldots, \mathbf{p}_k$. We then use a Gram–Schmidt procedure:

$$\mathbf{p}_{k+1} = \mathbf{v} - \sum_{j=1}^{k} \frac{\mathbf{p}_j^\mathsf{T}\mathbf{A}\mathbf{v}}{\mathbf{p}_j^\mathsf{T}\mathbf{A}\mathbf{p}_j} \mathbf{p}_j \tag{A.5.12}$$

for which it is clear that the vectors $\mathbf{p}_1, \ldots, \mathbf{p}_{k+1}$ are conjugate if $\mathbf{A}$ is positive definite. We can construct n conjugate vectors for a positive definite matrix in the following way: We start with n linearly independent vectors $\mathbf{u}_1, \ldots, \mathbf{u}_n$. We then set $\mathbf{p}_1 = \mathbf{u}_1$ and use (A.5.12) to compute $\mathbf{p}_2$ from $\mathbf{p}_1$ and $\mathbf{v} = \mathbf{u}_2$. Next we set $\mathbf{v} = \mathbf{u}_3$ and compute $\mathbf{p}_3$ from $\mathbf{p}_1, \mathbf{p}_2$ and $\mathbf{v}$. Continuing in this manner we obtain n conjugate vectors. Note that at each stage of the procedure the vectors $\mathbf{u}_1, \ldots, \mathbf{u}_k$ span the same subspace as the vectors $\mathbf{p}_1, \ldots, \mathbf{p}_k$.

A.5.5 The conjugate vectors algorithm

Let us assume that when minimising $f(\mathbf{x}) = \frac{1}{2}\mathbf{x}^\mathsf{T}\mathbf{A}\mathbf{x} - \mathbf{b}^\mathsf{T}\mathbf{x} + c$ we first construct n vectors $\mathbf{p}_1, \ldots, \mathbf{p}_n$ conjugate to $\mathbf{A}$ which we use as our search directions. Using this our iterative solution takes the form

$$\mathbf{x}_{k+1} = \mathbf{x}_k + \alpha_k \mathbf{p}_k \tag{A.5.13}$$

where at each step we choose α_k by an exact line search with

$$\alpha_k = -\frac{\mathbf{p}_k^\mathsf{T}\mathbf{g}_k}{\mathbf{p}_k^\mathsf{T}\mathbf{A}\mathbf{p}_k}. \tag{A.5.14}$$

This conjugate vectors algorithm has the geometrical interpretation that not only is the directional derivative zero at the new point along the direction $\mathbf{p}_k$, it is zero along all the previous search directions $\mathbf{p}_1, \ldots, \mathbf{p}_k$, known as the Luenberger expanding subspace theorem. In particular $\nabla f^\mathsf{T}(\mathbf{x}_{n+1})\mathbf{p}_i = 0$, for $i = 1, \ldots, n$; that is

$$\nabla f^\mathsf{T}(\mathbf{x}_{n+1})(\mathbf{p}_1, \mathbf{p}_2, \ldots, \mathbf{p}_n) = \mathbf{0}. \tag{A.5.15}$$

The square matrix $\mathbf{P} = (\mathbf{p}_1, \mathbf{p}_2, \ldots \mathbf{p}_n)$ is invertible since the $\mathbf{p}_i$ are conjugate, so $\nabla f(\mathbf{x}_{n+1}) = \mathbf{0}$ and the point $\mathbf{x}_{n+1}$ is therefore the minimum $\mathbf{x}^*$ of the quadratic function f. So in contrast to gradient descent, for a quadratic function the conjugate vectors algorithm converges in a finite number of steps.

A.5.6 The conjugate gradients algorithm

The conjugate gradients algorithm is a special case of the conjugate vectors algorithm in which we construct the conjugate vectors on-the-fly. After k-steps of the conjugate vectors algorithm we need to construct a vector $\mathbf{p}_{k+1}$ which is conjugate to $\mathbf{p}_1, \ldots, \mathbf{p}_k$. In the conjugate gradients algorithm one makes the special choice $\mathbf{v} = -\nabla f(\mathbf{x}_{k+1})$. The gradient at the new point $\mathbf{x}_{k+1}$ is orthogonal to $\mathbf{p}_i$, $i = 1, \ldots, k$, so $\nabla f(\mathbf{x}_{k+1})$ is linearly independent of $\mathbf{p}_1, \ldots, \mathbf{p}_k$ and a valid choice for $\mathbf{v}$, unless $\nabla f(\mathbf{x}_{k+1}) = \mathbf{0}$. In the latter case $\mathbf{x}_{k+1}$ is our minimum and the algorithm terminates. Using the notation $\mathbf{g}_k = \nabla f(\mathbf{x}_k)$, the equation for the new search direction given by the Gram–Schmidt procedure is:

$$\mathbf{p}_{k+1} = -\mathbf{g}_{k+1} + \sum_{i=1}^{k} \frac{\mathbf{p}_i^{\mathsf{T}}\mathbf{A}\mathbf{g}_{k+1}}{\mathbf{p}_i^{\mathsf{T}}\mathbf{A}\mathbf{p}_i}\mathbf{p}_i. \tag{A.5.16}$$

Since $\mathbf{g}_{k+1}$ is orthogonal to $\mathbf{p}_i$, $i = 1, \ldots, k$, we have $\mathbf{p}_{k+1}^{\mathsf{T}}\mathbf{g}_{k+1} = -\mathbf{g}_{k+1}^{\mathsf{T}}\mathbf{g}_{k+1}$. So α_{k+1} can be written as

$$\alpha_{k+1} = \frac{\mathbf{g}_{k+1}^{\mathsf{T}}\mathbf{g}_{k+1}}{\mathbf{p}_{k+1}^{\mathsf{T}}\mathbf{A}\mathbf{p}_{k+1}}, \tag{A.5.17}$$

and in particular $\alpha_{k+1} \neq 0$. We now want to show that because we have been using the conjugate gradients algorithm at the previous steps as well, in Equation (A.5.16) all terms but the last in the sum over i vanish. We shall assume that $k > 0$ since in the first step ($k = 0$) we just set $\mathbf{p}_1 = -\mathbf{g}_1$. First note that

$$\mathbf{g}_{i+1} - \mathbf{g}_i = \mathbf{A}\mathbf{x}_{i+1} - \mathbf{b} - (\mathbf{A}\mathbf{x}_i - \mathbf{b}) = \mathbf{A}(\mathbf{x}_{i+1} - \mathbf{x}_i) = \alpha_i\mathbf{A}\mathbf{p}_i \tag{A.5.18}$$

and since $\alpha_i \neq 0$, then $\mathbf{A}\mathbf{p}_i = (\mathbf{g}_{i+1} - \mathbf{g}_i)/\alpha_i$. So in Equation (A.5.16):

$$\mathbf{p}_i^{\mathsf{T}}\mathbf{A}\mathbf{g}_{k+1} = \mathbf{g}_{k+1}^{\mathsf{T}}\mathbf{A}\mathbf{p}_i = \mathbf{g}_{k+1}^{\mathsf{T}}(\mathbf{g}_{i+1} - \mathbf{g}_i)/\alpha_i = (\mathbf{g}_{k+1}^{\mathsf{T}}\mathbf{g}_{i+1} - \mathbf{g}_{k+1}^{\mathsf{T}}\mathbf{g}_i)/\alpha_i. \tag{A.5.19}$$

Since the $\mathbf{p}_i$ were obtained by applying the Gram–Schmidt procedure to the gradients $\mathbf{g}_i$, we have $\mathbf{g}_{k+1}^{\mathsf{T}}\mathbf{p}_i = 0$ and $\mathbf{g}_{k+1}^{\mathsf{T}}\mathbf{g}_i = 0$ for $i = 1, \ldots, k$. This shows that

$$\mathbf{p}_i^{\mathsf{T}}\mathbf{A}\mathbf{g}_{k+1} = (\mathbf{g}_{k+1}^{\mathsf{T}}\mathbf{g}_{i+1} - \mathbf{g}_{k+1}^{\mathsf{T}}\mathbf{g}_i)/\alpha_i = \begin{cases} 0 & \text{if } 1 \le i < k \\ \mathbf{g}_{k+1}^{\mathsf{T}}\mathbf{g}_{k+1}/\alpha_k & \text{if } i = k \end{cases}. \tag{A.5.20}$$

Hence Equation (A.5.16) simplifies to

$$\mathbf{p}_{k+1} = -\mathbf{g}_{k+1} + \frac{\mathbf{g}_{k+1}^{\mathsf{T}}\mathbf{g}_{k+1}/\alpha_k}{\mathbf{p}_k^{\mathsf{T}}\mathbf{A}\mathbf{p}_k}\mathbf{p}_k. \tag{A.5.21}$$

This can be brought into an even simpler form by applying Equation (A.5.17) to α_k:

$$\mathbf{p}_{k+1} = -\mathbf{g}_{k+1} + \frac{\mathbf{g}_{k+1}^{\mathsf{T}}\mathbf{g}_{k+1}}{\mathbf{p}_k^{\mathsf{T}}\mathbf{A}\mathbf{p}_k}\frac{\mathbf{p}_k^{\mathsf{T}}\mathbf{A}\mathbf{p}_k}{\mathbf{g}_k^{\mathsf{T}}\mathbf{g}_k}\mathbf{p}_k = -\mathbf{g}_{k+1} + \frac{\mathbf{g}_{k+1}^{\mathsf{T}}\mathbf{g}_{k+1}}{\mathbf{g}_k^{\mathsf{T}}\mathbf{g}_k}\mathbf{p}_k. \tag{A.5.22}$$

We shall write this in the form

$$\mathbf{p}_{k+1} = -\mathbf{g}_{k+1} + \beta_k\mathbf{p}_k \quad \text{where } \beta_k = \frac{\mathbf{g}_{k+1}^{\mathsf{T}}\mathbf{g}_{k+1}}{\mathbf{g}_k^{\mathsf{T}}\mathbf{g}_k}. \tag{A.5.23}$$

The formula (A.5.23) for β_k is due to Fletcher and Reeves [244]. Since the gradients are orthogonal, β_k can also be written as

$$\beta_k = \frac{\mathbf{g}_{k+1}^{\mathsf{T}}(\mathbf{g}_{k+1} - \mathbf{g}_k)}{\mathbf{g}_k^{\mathsf{T}}\mathbf{g}_k}; \tag{A.5.24}$$

Algorithm A.1 Conjugate gradients for minimising a function $f(\mathbf{x})$.

$k = 1$
Choose $\mathbf{x}_1$.
$\mathbf{p}_1 = -\mathbf{g}_1$
while $\mathbf{g}_k \neq 0$ **do**
    $\alpha_k = \underset{\alpha_k}{\operatorname{argmin}} f(\mathbf{x}_k + \alpha_k \mathbf{p}_k)$ ▷ Line search
    $\mathbf{x}_{k+1} := \mathbf{x}_k + \alpha_k \mathbf{p}_k$
    $\beta_k := \mathbf{g}_{k+1}^{\mathsf{T}} \mathbf{g}_{k+1} / (\mathbf{g}_k^{\mathsf{T}} \mathbf{g}_k)$
    $\mathbf{p}_{k+1} := -\mathbf{g}_{k+1} + \beta_k \mathbf{p}_k$
    $k = k + 1$
end while

---

this is the Polak–Ribière formula. The choice between the two expressions for β_k can be of some importance if f is not quadratic with the Polak–Ribière formula the most commonly used. The important point here is that we derived the above algorithm for the particular case of minimising a quadratic function f. By writing the algorithm however only in terms of f and its gradients, we make no explicit reference to the fact that f is quadratic. This means that we can therefore apply this algorithm to non-quadratic functions as well. The more similar the function f is to a quadratic function, the more confident we can be that the algorithm will find the minimum.

A.5.7 Newton's method

Consider a function $f(\mathbf{x})$ that we wish to find the minimum of. A Taylor expansion up to second order gives

$$f(\mathbf{x} + \boldsymbol{\Delta}) = f(\mathbf{x}) + \boldsymbol{\Delta}^{\mathsf{T}} \nabla f + \frac{1}{2} \boldsymbol{\Delta}^{\mathsf{T}} \mathbf{H}_f \boldsymbol{\Delta} + O(|\boldsymbol{\Delta}|^3). \tag{A.5.25}$$

The matrix $\mathbf{H}_f$ is the Hessian. Differentiating the right-hand side with respect to $\boldsymbol{\Delta}$ (or, equivalently, completing the square), we find that the right-hand side (ignoring the $O(|\boldsymbol{\Delta}|^3)$ term) has its lowest value when

$$\nabla f = -\mathbf{H}_f \boldsymbol{\Delta} \Rightarrow \boldsymbol{\Delta} = -\mathbf{H}_f^{-1} \nabla f. \tag{A.5.26}$$

Hence, an optimisation routine to minimise f is given by the Newton update

$$\mathbf{x}_{k+1} = \mathbf{x}_k - \mathbf{H}_f^{-1} \nabla f. \tag{A.5.27}$$

A benefit of Newton's method over gradient descent is that the decrease in the objective function is invariant under a linear change of coordinates, $\mathbf{y} = \mathbf{M}\mathbf{x}$. Defining $\hat{f}(\mathbf{y}) \equiv f(\mathbf{M}\mathbf{x})$, the change in the function $\hat{f}$ under a Newton update is

$$\nabla_{\mathbf{y}} \hat{f}^{\mathsf{T}} \mathbf{H}_{\hat{f}}^{-1} \nabla_{\mathbf{y}} \hat{f}. \tag{A.5.28}$$

Since $\mathbf{H}_{\hat{f}} = \mathbf{M} \mathbf{H}_f \mathbf{M}^{\mathsf{T}}$ and $\nabla_{\mathbf{y}} \hat{f} = \mathbf{M}^{\mathsf{T}} \nabla_{\mathbf{x}} f$ this change is equal to

$$\nabla_{\mathbf{x}} f^{\mathsf{T}} \mathbf{H}_f^{-1} \nabla_{\mathbf{x}} f \tag{A.5.29}$$

so that the change in the function is independent (up to second order) of a linear coordinate transformation.

Algorithm A.2 Quasi-Newton for minimising a function $f(\mathbf{x})$.

$k = 1$
Choose $\mathbf{x}_1$.
$\tilde{\mathbf{H}}_1 = \mathbf{I}$
while $\mathbf{g}_k \neq 0$ **do**
    $\mathbf{p}_k = -\tilde{\mathbf{H}}_k \mathbf{g}_k$
    $\alpha_k = \underset{\alpha_k}{\text{argmin}}\, f(\mathbf{x}_k + \alpha_k \mathbf{p}_k)$ ▷ Line Search
    $\mathbf{x}_{k+1} := \mathbf{x}_k + \alpha_k \mathbf{p}_k$
    $\mathbf{s}_k = \mathbf{x}_{k+1} - \mathbf{x}_k$, $\mathbf{y}_k = \mathbf{g}_{k+1} - \mathbf{g}_k$, and update $\tilde{\mathbf{H}}_{k+1}$
    $k = k + 1$
end while

Quasi-Newton methods

For large-scale problems both storing the Hessian and solving the resulting linear system is computationally demanding, especially if the matrix is close to singular. An alternative is to set up the iteration

$$\mathbf{x}_{k+1} = \mathbf{x}_k - \alpha_k \mathbf{S}_k \mathbf{g}_k. \tag{A.5.30}$$

For $\mathbf{S}_k = \mathbf{A}^{-1}$ we have Newton's method, while if $\mathbf{S}_k = \mathbf{I}$ we have steepest descent. In general it would seem to be a good idea to choose $\mathbf{S}_k$ to be an approximation to the inverse Hessian. Also note that it is important that $\mathbf{S}_k$ be positive definite so that for small α_k we obtain a descent method. The idea behind most quasi-Newton methods is to try to construct an approximate inverse Hessian $\tilde{\mathbf{H}}_k$ using information gathered as the descent progresses, and to set $\mathbf{S}_k = \tilde{\mathbf{H}}_k$. As we have seen, for a quadratic optimisation problem we have the relationship

$$\mathbf{g}_{k+1} - \mathbf{g}_k = \mathbf{A}(\mathbf{x}_{k+1} - \mathbf{x}_k). \tag{A.5.31}$$

Defining

$$\mathbf{s}_k = \mathbf{x}_{k+1} - \mathbf{x}_k \qquad \text{and} \qquad \mathbf{y}_k = \mathbf{g}_{k+1} - \mathbf{g}_k \tag{A.5.32}$$

we see that Equation (A.5.31) becomes

$$\mathbf{y}_k = \mathbf{A}\mathbf{s}_k. \tag{A.5.33}$$

It is therefore reasonable to demand that

$$\tilde{\mathbf{H}}_{k+1}\mathbf{y}_i = \mathbf{s}_i \qquad 1 \leq i \leq k. \tag{A.5.34}$$

After n linearly independent steps we would then have $\tilde{\mathbf{H}}_{n+1} = \mathbf{A}^{-1}$. For $k < n$ there are an infinity of solutions for $\tilde{\mathbf{H}}_{k+1}$ satisfying Equation (A.5.34). A popular choice is the Broyden–Fletcher–Goldfarb–Shanno (or BFGS) update, given by

$$\tilde{\mathbf{H}}_{k+1} = \tilde{\mathbf{H}}_k + \left(1 + \frac{\mathbf{y}_k^{\mathsf{T}}\tilde{\mathbf{H}}_k\mathbf{y}_k}{\mathbf{y}_k^{\mathsf{T}}\mathbf{s}_k}\right)\frac{\mathbf{s}_k\mathbf{s}_k^{\mathsf{T}}}{\mathbf{s}_k^{\mathsf{T}}\mathbf{y}_k} - \frac{\mathbf{s}_k\mathbf{y}_k^{\mathsf{T}}\tilde{\mathbf{H}}_k + \tilde{\mathbf{H}}_k\mathbf{y}_k\mathbf{s}_k^{\mathsf{T}}}{\mathbf{s}_k^{\mathsf{T}}\mathbf{y}_k}. \tag{A.5.35}$$

This is a rank-2 correction to $\tilde{\mathbf{H}}_k$ constructed from the vectors $\mathbf{s}_k$ and $\tilde{\mathbf{H}}_k\mathbf{y}_k$. The direction vectors, $\mathbf{p}_k = -\tilde{\mathbf{H}}_k\mathbf{g}_k$, produced by the algorithm obey

$$\mathbf{p}_i^{\mathsf{T}}\mathbf{A}\mathbf{p}_j = 0 \qquad 1 \leq i < j \leq k, \qquad\qquad \tilde{\mathbf{H}}_{k+1}\mathbf{A}\mathbf{p}_i = \mathbf{p}_i \qquad 1 \leq i \leq k. \tag{A.5.36}$$

Since the $\mathbf{p}_k$'s are $\mathbf{A}$-conjugate the BFGS algorithm is a conjugate direction method. Indeed, with the choice of $\mathbf{H}_1 = \mathbf{I}$ it is in fact the conjugate gradient method. The storage requirements for quasi-Newton methods scale quadratically with the number of variables, and hence these methods tend to be used only for smaller problems. Limited memory BFGS reduces the storage by only using the l latest updates in computing the approximate Hessian inverse, Equation (A.5.35). In contrast, the memory requirements for pure conjugate gradient methods scale only linearly with the dimension of $\mathbf{x}$. As before, although the algorithm was derived with a quadratic function in mind, the final form of the algorithm depends only on f and its gradients and may therefore be applied to non-quadratic functions f.

A.6 Constrained optimisation using Lagrange multipliers

Consider first the problem of minimising $f(\mathbf{x})$ subject to a single constraint $c(\mathbf{x}) = 0$. A formal treatment of this problem is beyond the scope of these notes and requires understanding the conditions under which the optimum can be found [48]. As an informal argument, however, imagine that we have already identified an $\mathbf{x}$ that satisfies the constraint, that is $c(\mathbf{x}) = 0$. How can we tell if this $\mathbf{x}$ minimises the function f? We are only allowed to search for lower function values around this $\mathbf{x}$ in directions which are consistent with the constraint. For a small change $\boldsymbol{\delta}$, the change in the constraint is,

$$c(\mathbf{x} + \boldsymbol{\delta}) \approx c(\mathbf{x}) + \boldsymbol{\delta} \cdot \nabla c(\mathbf{x}). \tag{A.6.1}$$

Let us also explore the change in f along a direction $\boldsymbol{\delta}$ where $\boldsymbol{\delta} \cdot \nabla c(\mathbf{x}) = 0$,

$$f(\mathbf{x} + \boldsymbol{\delta}) \approx f(\mathbf{x}) + \nabla f(\mathbf{x}) \cdot \boldsymbol{\delta}. \tag{A.6.2}$$

We are looking for a point $\mathbf{x}$ and direction $\boldsymbol{\delta}$ such that the change in f and c is minimal. This dual requirement can be represented as to find $\mathbf{x}$ and $\boldsymbol{\delta}$ that minimise

$$\left|\boldsymbol{\delta} \cdot \nabla f(\mathbf{x})\right|^2 + \gamma \left|\boldsymbol{\delta} \cdot \nabla c(\mathbf{x})\right|^2 \tag{A.6.3}$$

where $\gamma > 0$. This is a simple quadratic form and optimising for $\boldsymbol{\delta}$ gives that

$$\nabla f(\mathbf{x}) = -\gamma \frac{\boldsymbol{\delta} \cdot \nabla c(\mathbf{x})}{\boldsymbol{\delta} \cdot \nabla f(\mathbf{x})} \nabla c(\mathbf{x}). \tag{A.6.4}$$

Hence at the constrained optimum

$$\nabla f(\mathbf{x}) = \lambda \nabla c(\mathbf{x}) \tag{A.6.5}$$

for some scalar λ. We can formulate this requirement as to look for $\mathbf{x}$ and λ that constitute a stationary point of the *Lagrangian*

$$\mathcal{L}(\mathbf{x}, \lambda) = f(\mathbf{x}) - \lambda c(\mathbf{x}). \tag{A.6.6}$$

Differentiating with respect to $\mathbf{x}$, we obtain the requirement $\nabla f(\mathbf{x}) = \lambda \nabla c(\mathbf{x})$, and differentiating with respect to λ, we get that $c(\mathbf{x}) = 0$.

In the multiple constraint case $\{c_i(\mathbf{x}) = 0\}$ we find the stationary point of the Lagrangian

$$\mathcal{L}(\mathbf{x}, \boldsymbol{\lambda}) = f(\mathbf{x}) - \sum_i \lambda_i c_i(\mathbf{x}). \tag{A.6.7}$$

A.6.1 Lagrange dual

Consider the 'primal' problem

$$\text{minimise } f(\mathbf{x}) \quad \text{subject to } c(\mathbf{x}) = 0. \tag{A.6.8}$$

The Lagrange dual is defined as

$$\mathcal{L}(\lambda) = \min_{\mathbf{x}} \left[f(\mathbf{x}) + \lambda c(\mathbf{x}) \right]. \tag{A.6.9}$$

By construction, for any $\mathbf{x}$,

$$\mathcal{L}(\lambda) \leq f(\mathbf{x}) + \lambda c(\mathbf{x}). \tag{A.6.10}$$

Now consider the optimal $\mathbf{x}^*$ that solves the primal problem Equation (A.6.8). Then

$$\mathcal{L}(\lambda) \leq f(\mathbf{x}^*) + \lambda c(\mathbf{x}^*) = f(\mathbf{x}^*) \tag{A.6.11}$$

where the last step follows since $\mathbf{x}^*$ solves the primal problem, meaning that $c(\mathbf{x}^*) = 0$. Since $\mathcal{L}(\lambda) \leq f(\mathbf{x}^*)$, the optimal λ is given by solving the unconstrained 'dual' problem

$$\max_{\lambda} \mathcal{L}(\lambda). \tag{A.6.12}$$

In addition to providing a bound that enables one to bracket the optimal primal value,

$$\mathcal{L}(\lambda) \leq f(\mathbf{x}^*) \leq f(\mathbf{x}), \qquad \text{for } c(\mathbf{x}) = 0 \tag{A.6.13}$$

the dual possesses the interesting property that it is concave, irrespective of whether f is convex. This follows since by construction the function $f(\mathbf{x}) + \lambda c(\mathbf{x})$ is concave in λ for any point $\mathbf{x}$. More explicitly, consider

$$\mathcal{L}(\lambda + \delta) = \min_{\mathbf{x}} \left[f(\mathbf{x}) + (\lambda + \delta) c(\mathbf{x}) \right] \leq f(\mathbf{x}) + \lambda c(\mathbf{x}) + \delta c(\mathbf{x}). \tag{A.6.14}$$

Similarly,

$$\mathcal{L}(\lambda - \delta) \leq f(\mathbf{x}) + \lambda c(\mathbf{x}) - \delta c(\mathbf{x}). \tag{A.6.15}$$

Averaging Equation (A.6.14) and Equation (A.6.15), and taking the minimum over $\mathbf{x}$ of both sides, we have

$$\frac{1}{2} \left(\mathcal{L}(\lambda - \delta) + \mathcal{L}(\lambda + \delta) \right) \leq \mathcal{L}(\lambda) \tag{A.6.16}$$

which shows that $\mathcal{L}$ is concave.

REFERENCES

[1] L. F. Abbott, J. A. Varela, K. Sen and S. B. Nelson. Synaptic depression and cortical gain control. *Science*, **275**:220–223, 1997.

[2] D. H. Ackley, G. E. Hinton and T. J. Sejnowski. A learning algorithm for Boltzmann machines. *Cognitive Science*, **9**:147–169, 1985.

[3] R. P. Adams and D. J. C. MacKay. Bayesian online changepoint detection. Cavendish Laboratory, Department of Physics, University of Cambridge, 2006.

[4] E. Airoldi, D. Blei, E. Xing and S. Fienberg. A latent mixed membership model for relational data. In *LinkKDD '05: Proceedings of the 3rd International Workshop on Link Discovery*, pages 82–89. ACM, 2005.

[5] E. M. Airoldi, D. M. Blei, S. E. Fienberg and E. P. Xing. Mixed membership stochastic blockmodels. *Journal of Machine Learning Research*, **9**:1981–2014, 2008.

[6] D. L. Alspach and H. W. Sorenson. Nonlinear Bayesian estimation using Gaussian sum approximations. *IEEE Transactions on Automatic Control*, **17**(4):439–448, 1972.

[7] S-i. Amari. Natural gradient learning for over and under-complete bases in ICA. *Neural Computation*, **11**:1875–1883, 1999.

[8] I. Androutsopoulos, J. Koutsias, K. V. Chandrinos and C. D. Spyropoulos. An experimental comparison of naive Bayesian and keyword-based anti-spam filtering with personal e-mail messages. In *Proceedings of the 23rd Annual International ACM SIGIR Conference on Research and Development in Information Retrieval*, pages 160–167. ACM 2000.

[9] S. Arora and C. Lund. Hardness of approximations. In *Approximation Algorithms for NP-Hard Problems*, pages 399–446. PWS Publishing Co., 1997.

[10] F. R. Bach and M. I. Jordan. Thin junction trees. In T. G. Dietterich, S. Becker and Z. Ghahramani, editors, *Advances in Neural Information Processing Systems (NIPS)*, number 14, pages 569–576. MIT Press, 2001.

[11] F. R. Bach and M. I. Jordan. A probabilistic interpretation of canonical correlation analysis. Computer Science Division and Department of Statistics 688, University of California Berkeley, Berkeley, USA, 2005.

[12] Y. Bar-Shalom and Xiao-Rong Li. *Estimation and Tracking: Principles, Techniques and Software*. Artech House, 1998.

[13] D. Barber. Dynamic Bayesian networks with deterministic tables. In S. Becker, S. Thrun and K. Obermayer, editors, *Advances in Neural Information Processing Systems (NIPS)*, number 15, pages 713–720. MIT Press, 2003.

[14] D. Barber. Learning in spiking neural assemblies. In S. Becker, S. Thrun and K. Obermayer, editors, *Advances in Neural Information Processing Systems (NIPS)*, number 15, pages 149–156. MIT Press, 2003.

[15] D. Barber. Are two classifiers performing equally? A treatment using Bayesian hypothesis testing. IDIAP-RR 57, IDIAP, Rue de Simplon 4, Martigny, CH-1920, Switzerland, May 2004. IDIAP-RR 04-57.

[16] D. Barber. The auxiliary variable trick for deriving Kalman smoothers. IDIAP-RR 87, IDIAP, Rue de Simplon 4, Martigny, CH-1920, Switzerland, December 2004. IDIAP-RR 04-87.

[17] D. Barber. Expectation correction for smoothing in switching linear Gaussian state space models. *Journal of Machine Learning Research*, **7**:2515–2540, 2006.

[18] D. Barber. Clique matrices for statistical graph decomposition and parameterising restricted positive definite matrices. In D. A. McAllester and P. Myllymaki, editors, *Uncertainty in Artificial Intelligence*, number 24, pages 26–33. AUAI Press, 2008.

[19] D. Barber and F. V. Agakov. Correlated sequence learning in a network of spiking neurons using maximum likelihood. Informatics Research Reports EDI-INF-RR-0149, Edinburgh University, 2002.

[20] D. Barber and F. V. Agakov. The IM algorithm: a variational approach to information maximization. In *Advances in Neural Information Processing Systems (NIPS)*, number 16, 2004.

[21] D. Barber and C. M. Bishop. Bayesian model comparison by Monte Carlo chaining. In M. C. Mozer, M. I. Jordan and T. Petsche, editors, *Advances in Neural Information Processing Systems (NIPS)*, number 9, pages 333–339. MIT Press, 1997.

[22] D. Barber and C. M. Bishop. Ensemble learning in Bayesian neural networks. In *Neural Networks and Machine Learning*, pages 215–237. Springer, 1998.

[23] D. Barber and S. Chiappa. Unified inference for variational Bayesian linear Gaussian state-space models. In B. Schölkopf, J. Platt and T. Hoffman, editors, *Advances in Neural Information Processing Systems (NIPS)*, number 19, pages 81–88. MIT Press, 2007.

[24] D. Barber and W. Wiegerinck. Tractable variational structures for approximating graphical models. In M. S. Kearns, S. A. Solla and D. A. Cohn, editors, *Advances in Neural Information Processing Systems (NIPS)*, number 11, pages 183–189. MIT Press, 1999.

[25] D. Barber and C. K. I. Williams. Gaussian processes for Bayesian classification via hybrid Monte Carlo. In M. C. Mozer, M. I. Jordan and T. Petsche, editors, *Advances in Neural Information Processing Systems NIPS 9*, pages 340–346. MIT Press, 1997.

[26] R. J. Baxter. *Exactly Solved Models in Statistical Mechanics*. Academic Press, 1982.

[27] M. J. Beal, F. Falciani, Z. Ghahramani, C. Rangel and D. L. Wild. A Bayesian approach to reconstructing genetic regulatory networks with hidden factors. *Bioinformatics*, **21**:349–356, 2005.

[28] A. Becker and D. Geiger. A sufficiently fast algorithm for finding close to optimal clique trees. *Artificial Intelligence*, **125**(1-2):3–17, 2001.

[29] A. J. Bell and T. J. Sejnowski. An information-maximization approach to blind separation and blind deconvolution. *Neural Computation*, **7**(6):1129–1159, 1995.

[30] R. E. Bellman. *Dynamic Programming*. Princeton University Press, 1957. Paperback edition by Dover Publications (2003).

[31] Y. Bengio and P. Frasconi. Input-output HMMs for sequence processing. *IEEE Transactions on Neural Networks*, **7**:1231–1249, 1996.

[32] A. L. Berger, S. D. Della Pietra and V. J. D. Della Pietra. A maximum entropy approach to natural language processing. *Computational Linguistics*, **22**(1):39–71, 1996.

[33] J. O. Berger. *Statistical Decision Theory and Bayesian Analysis*. Springer, second edition, 1985.

[34] D. P. Bertsekas. *Nonlinear Programming*. Athena Scientific, 2nd edition, 1999.

[35] D. P. Bertsekas. *Dynamic Programming and Optimal Control*. Athena Scientific, second edition, 2000.

[36] J. Besag. Spatial interactions and the statistical analysis of lattice systems. *Journal of the Royal Statistical Society, Series B*, **36**(2):192–236, 1974.

[37] J. Besag. On the statistical analysis of dirty pictures. *Journal of the Royal Statistical Society, Series B*, **48**:259–302, 1986.

[38] J. Besag and P. Green. Spatial statistics and Bayesian computation. *Journal of the Royal Statistical Society, Series B*, **55**:25–37, 1993.

[39] G. J. Bierman. Measurement updating using the U-D factorization. *Automatica*, **12**:375–382, 1976.

[40] N. L. Biggs. *Discrete Mathematics*. Oxford University Press, 1990.

[41] K. Binder and A. P. Young. Spin glasses: experimental facts, theoretical concepts, and open questions. *Reviews of Modern Physics*, **58**(4):801–976, Oct 1986.

[42] C. M. Bishop. *Neural Networks for Pattern Recognition*. Oxford University Press, 1995.

[43] C. M. Bishop. *Pattern Recognition and Machine Learning*. Springer, 2006.

[44] C. M. Bishop and M. Svensén. Bayesian hierarchical mixtures of experts. In U. Kjaerulff and C. Meek, editors, *Proceedings Nineteenth Conference on Uncertainty in Artificial Intelligence*, pages 57–64. Morgan Kaufmann, 2003.

[45] F. Black and M. Scholes. The pricing of options and corporate liabilities. *Journal of Political Economy*, **81**(3):637–654, 1973.

[46] D. Blei, A. Ng and M. Jordan. Latent Dirichlet allocation. *Journal of Machine Learning Research*, **3**:993–1022, 2003.

[47] R. R. Bouckaert. Bayesian belief networks: from construction to inference. PhD thesis, University of Utrecht, 1995.

[48] S. Boyd and L. Vandenberghe. *Convex Optimization*. Cambridge University Press, 2004.

[49] Y. Boykov and V. Kolmogorov. An experimental comparison of min-cut/max-flow algorithms for energy minimization in vision. *IEEE Transactions on Pattern Analysis Machine Intelligence*, **26**(9):1124–1137, 2004.

[50] Y. Boykov, O. Veksler and R. Zabih. Fast approximate energy minimization via graph cuts. *IEEE Transactions on Pattern Analysis Machine Intelligence*, **23**:1222–1239, 2001.

[51] C. Bracegirdle and D. Barber. Switch-reset models : Exact and approximate inference. In *Proceedings of The Fourteenth International Conference on Artificial Intelligence and Statistics (AISTATS)*, volume 10, 2011.

[52] M. Brand. Incremental singular value decomposition of uncertain data with missing values. In *European Conference on Computer Vision (ECCV)*, pages 707–720, 2002.

[53] J. Breese and D. Heckerman. Decision-theoretic troubleshooting: a framework for repair and experiment. In E. Horvitz and F. Jensen, editors, *Uncertainty in Artificial Intelligence*, number 12, pages 124–132. Morgan Kaufmann, 1996.

[54] H. Bunke and T. Caelli. *Hidden Markov Models: Applications in Computer Vision*. Machine Perception and Artificial Intelligence. World Scientific Publishing Co., Inc., 2001.

[55] W. Buntine. Theory refinement on Bayesian networks. In *Uncertainty in Artificial Intelligence*, number 7, pages 52–60, 1991. Morgan Kaufmann.

[56] A. Cano and S. Moral. Heuristic algorithms for the triangulation of graphs. In *Advances in Intelligent Computing – IPMU 1994*, pages 98–107. Number 945 in Lectures Notes in Computer Sciences. Springer-Verlag, 1995.

[57] O. Cappé, E. Moulines and T. Ryden. *Inference in Hidden Markov Models*. Springer, 2005.

[58] A. T. Cemgil. Bayesian inference in non-negative matrix factorisation models. Technical Report CUED/F-INFENG/TR.609, University of Cambridge, July 2008.

[59] A. T. Cemgil, B. Kappen and D. Barber. A generative model for music transcription. *IEEE Transactions on Audio, Speech and Language Processing*, **14**(2):679–694, 2006.

[60] E. Challis and D. Barber. Local and variational Gaussian approximations for Bayesian generalised linear models. Department of Computer Science, University College London, 2010.

[61] H. S. Chang, M. C. Fu, J. Hu and S. I. Marcus. *Simulation-based Algorithms for Markov Decision Processes*. Springer, 2007.

[62] S. Chiappa and D. Barber. Bayesian linear Gaussian state space models for biosignal decomposition. *Signal Processing Letters*, **14**(4):267–270, 2007.

[63] S. Chib and M. Dueker. Non-Markovian regime switching with endogenous states and time-varying state strengths. Econometric Society 2004 North American Summer Meetings 600, Econometric Society, August 2004.

[64] C. K. Chow and C. N. Liu. Approximating discrete probability distributions with dependence trees. *IEEE Transactions on Information Theory*, **14**(3):462–467, 1968.

[65] P. S. Churchland and T. J. Sejnowski. *The Computational Brain*. MIT Press, 1994.

[66] D. Cohn and H. Chang. Learning to probabilistically identify authoritative documents. In P. Langley, editor, *International Conference on Machine Learning*, number 17, pages 167–174. Morgan Kaufmann, 2000.

[67] D. Cohn and T. Hofmann. The missing link – a probabilistic model of document content and hypertext connectivity. *In Neural Information Processing Systems*, number 13, pages 430–436. MIT Press, 2001.

[68] A. C. C. Coolen, R. Kühn and P. Sollich. *Theory of Neural Information Processing Systems*. Oxford University Press, 2005.

[69] G. F. Cooper and E. Herskovits. A Bayesian method for the induction of probabilistic networks from data. *Machine Learning*, **9**(4):309–347, 1992.

[70] A. Corduneanu and C. M. Bishop. Variational Bayesian model selection for mixture distributions. In T. Jaakkola and T. Richardson, editors, *Artificial Intelligence and Statistics*, pages 27–34. Morgan Kaufmann, 2001.

[71] M. T. Cover and J. A. Thomas. *Elements of Information Theory*. Wiley, 1991.

[72] R. G. Cowell, A. P. Dawid, S. L. Lauritzen and D. J. Spiegelhalter. *Probabilistic Networks and Expert Systems*. Springer, 1999.

[73] D. R. Cox and N. Wermuth. *Multivariate Dependencies*. Chapman and Hall, 1996.

[74] J. C. Cox, S. A. Ross and M. Rubinstein. Option pricing: a simplified approach. *Journal of Financial Economics*, **7**:229–263, 1979.

[75] N. Cristianini and J. Shawe-Taylor. *An Introduction to Support Vector Machines*. Cambridge University Press, 2000.

[76] P. Dangauthier, R. Herbrich, T. Minka and T. Graepel. Trueskill through time: revisiting the history of chess. In B. Schölkopf, J. Platt and T. Hoffman, editors, *Advances in Neural Information Processing Systems (NIPS)*, number 19, pages 569–576. MIT Press, 2007.

[77] H. A. David. *The Method of Paired Comparisons*. Oxford University Press, 1988.

[78] A. P. Dawid. Influence diagrams for causal modelling and inference. *International Statistical Review*, **70**:161–189, 2002.

[79] A. P. Dawid and S. L. Lauritzen. Hyper Markov laws in the statistical analysis of decomposable graphical models. *Annals of Statistics*, **21**(3):1272–1317, 1993.

[80] P. Dayan and L. F. Abbott. *Theoretical Neuroscience*. MIT Press, 2001.

[81] P. Dayan and G. E. Hinton. Using expectation-maximization for reinforcement learning. *Neural Computation*, **9**:271–278, 1997.

[82] T. De Bie, N. Cristianini and R. Rosipal. Eigenproblems in pattern recognition. In *Handbook of Geometric Computing: Applications in Pattern Recognition, Computer Vision, Neuralcomputing, and Robotics*. Springer-Verlag, 2005.

[83] R. Dechter. Bucket elimination: a unifying framework for probabilistic inference algorithms. In E. Horvitz and F. Jensen, editors, *Uncertainty in Artificial Intelligence*, pages 211–219. Morgan Kaufmann, 1996.

[84] A. P. Dempster, N. M. Laird, and D. B. Rubin. Maximum Likelihood from Incomplete Data via the EM Algorithm. *Journal of the Royal Statistical Society. Series B (Methodological)*, 39(1):1–38, 1977.

[85] S. Diederich and M. Opper. Learning of correlated patterns in spin-glass networks by local learning rules. *Physical Review Letters*, **58**(9):949–952, 1986.

[86] R. Diestel. *Graph Theory*. Springer, 2005.

[87] A. Doucet and A. M. Johansen. A tutorial on particle filtering and smoothing: fifteen years later. In D. Crisan and B. Rozovsky, editors, *Oxford Handbook of Nonlinear Filtering*. Oxford University Press, 2009.

[88] R. O. Duda, P. E. Hart and D. G. Stork. *Pattern Classification*. Wiley-Interscience Publication, 2000.

[89] J. Durbin. The fitting of time series models. *Rev. Inst. Int. Stat.*, 28:233–243, 1960.

[90] R. Durbin, S. R. Eddy, A. Krogh and G. Mitchison. *Biological Sequence Analysis: Probabilistic Models of Proteins and Nucleic Acids*. Cambridge University Press, 1999.

[91] A. Düring, A. C. C. Coolen and D. Sherrington. Phase diagram and storage capacity of sequence processing neural networks. *Journal of Physics A*, **31**:8607–8621, 1998.

[92] J. M. Gutierrez, E. Castillo and A. S. Hadi. *Expert Systems and Probabilistic Network Models*. Springer-Verlag, 1997.

[93] J. Edmonds and R. M. Karp. Theoretical improvements in algorithmic efficiency for network flow problems. *Journal of the ACM*, **19**(2):248–264, 1972.

[94] R. Edwards and A. Sokal. Generalization of the Fortium-Kasteleyn-Swendson-Wang representation and Monte Carlo algorithm. *Physical Review D*, **38**:2009–2012, 1988.

[95] A. E. Elo. *The Rating of Chess Players, Past and Present*. Arco, second edition, 1986.

[96] R. F. Engel. GARCH 101: The Use of ARCH/GARCH Models in Applied Econometrics. *Journal of Economic Perspectives*, 15(4):157–168, 2001.

[97] Y. Ephraim and W. J. J. Roberts. Revisiting autoregressive hidden Markov modeling of speech signals. *IEEE Signal Processing Letters*, **12**(2):166–169, 2005.

[98] E. Erosheva, S. Fienberg and J. Lafferty. Mixed membership models of scientific publications. In *Proceedings of the National Academy of Sciences*, volume 101, pages 5220–5227, 2004.

[99] R-E. Fan, P-H. Chen and C-J. Lin. Working set selection using second order information for training support vector machines. *Journal of Machine Learning Research*, **6**:1889–1918, 2005.

[100] P. Fearnhead. Exact and efficient Bayesian inference for multiple changepoint problems. Technical report, Department of Mathematics and Statistics, Lancaster University, 2003.

[101] G. H. Fischer and I. W. Molenaar. *Rasch Models: Foundations, Recent Developments, and Applications*. Springer, 1995.

[102] M. E. Fisher. Statistical mechanics of dimers on a plane lattice. *Physical Review*, **124**:1664–1672, 1961.

[103] B. Frey. Extending factor graphs as to unify directed and undirected graphical models. In C. Meek and U. Kjærulff, editors, *Uncertainty in Artificial Intelligence*, number 19, pages 257–264. Morgan Kaufmann, 2003.

[104] N. Friedman, D. Geiger and M. Goldszmidt. Bayesian network classifiers. *Machine Learning*, **29**:131–163, 1997.

[105] S. Frühwirth-Schnatter. *Finite Mixture and Markov Switching Models*. Springer, 2006.

[106] M. Frydenberg. The chain graph Markov property. *Scandinavian Journal of Statistics*, **17**:333–353, 1990.

[107] T. Furmston and D. Barber. Solving deterministic policy (PO)MPDs using expectation-maximisation and antifreeze. In *First International Workshop on Learning and Data Mining for Robotics (LEMIR)*, September 2009. In conjunction with ECML/PKDD-2009.

[108] T. Furmston and D. Barber. Variational methods for reinforcement learning. In Y. W. Teh and M. Titterington, editors, *Proceedings of The Thirteenth International Conference on Artificial Intelligence and Statistics (AISTATS)*, volume 9, pages 241–248, Chia Laguna, Sardinia, Italy, May 13–15 2010. JMLR.

[109] T. Furmston and D. Barber. Efficient Inference in Markov Control Problems. In *Uncertainty in Artificial Intelligence*, number 27, Corvallis, Oregon, USA, 2011.

[110] T. Furmston and D. Barber. Lagrange Dual Decomposition for Finite Horizon Markov Decision Processes. In *European Conference on Machine Learning (ECML)*, 2011.

[111] A. Galka, O. Yamashita, T. Ozaki, R. Biscay and P. Valdes-Sosa. A solution to the dynamical inverse problem of EEG generation using spatiotemporal Kalman filtering. *NeuroImage*, **23**:435–453, 2004.

[112] P. Gandhi, F. Bromberg and D. Margaritis. Learning Markov network structure using few independence tests. In *Proceedings of the SIAM International Conference on Data Mining*, pages 680–691, 2008.

[113] M. R. Garey and D. S. Johnson. *Computers and Intractability, A Guide to the Theory of NP-Completeness*. W. H. Freeman and Company, 1979.

[114] A. Gelb. *Applied Optimal Estimation*. MIT Press, 1974.

[115] A. Gelman, G. O. Roberts and W. R. Gilks. Efficient Metropolis jumping rules. In J. O. Bernardo, J. M. Berger, A. P. Dawid and A. F. M. Smith, editors, *Bayesian Statistics*, volume 5, pages 599–607. Oxford University Press, 1996.

[116] S. Geman and D. Geman. Stochastic relaxation, Gibbs distributions, and the Bayesian restoration of images. In *Readings in Uncertain Reasoning*, pages 452–472. Morgan Kaufmann, 1990.

[117] M. G. Genton. Classes of kernels for machine learning: a statistics perspective. *Journal of Machine Learning Research*, **2**:299–312, 2001.

[118] W. Gerstner and W. M. Kistler. *Spiking Neuron Models*. Cambridge University Press, 2002.

[119] Z. Ghahramani and M. J. Beal. Variational inference for Bayesian mixtures of factor analysers. In S. A. Solla, T. K. Leen and K-R. Müller, editors, *Advances in Neural Information Processing Systems (NIPS)*, number 12, pages 449–455. MIT Press, 2000.

[120] Z. Ghahramani and G. E. Hinton. Variational learning for switching state-space models. *Neural Computation*, **12**(4):963–996, 1998.

[121] A. Gibbons. *Algorithmic Graph Theory*. Cambridge University Press, 1991.

[122] M. Gibbs. *Bayesian Gaussian processes for regression and classification*. PhD thesis, University of Cambridge, 1997.

[123] W. R. Gilks, S. Richardson and D. J. Spiegelhalter. *Markov Chain Monte Carlo in Practice*. Chapman and Hall, 1996.

[124] M. Girolami. A variational method for learning sparse and overcomplete representations. *Neural Computation*, **13**:2517–2532, 2001.

[125] M. Girolami and A. Kaban. On an equivalence between PLSI and LDA. In *Proceedings of the 26th Annual International ACM SIGIR Conference on Research and Development in Information Retrieval*, pages 433–434. ACM Press, 2003.

[126] M. E. Glickman. Parameter estimation in large dynamic paired comparison experiments. *Applied Statistics*, **48**:377–394, 1999.

[127] A. Globerson and T. Jaakkola. Approximate inference using planar graph decomposition. In B. Schölkopf, J. Platt and T. Hoffman, editors, *Advances in Neural Information Processing Systems (NIPS)*, number 19, pages 473–480. MIT Press, 2007.

[128] D. Goldberg, D. Nichols, B. M. Oki and D. Terry. Using collaborative filtering to weave an information tapestry. *Communications ACM*, **35**:61–70, 1992.

[129] G. H. Golub and C. F. van Loan. *Matrix Computations*. Johns Hopkins University Press, third edition, 1996.

[130] M. C. Golumbic and I. Ben-Arroyo Hartman. *Graph Theory, Combinatorics, and Algorithms*. Springer-Verlag, 2005.

[131] C. Goutis. A graphical method for solving a decision analysis problem. *IEEE Transactions on Systems, Man and Cybernetics*, **25**:1181–1193, 1995.

[132] P. J. Green and B. W. Silverman. *Nonparametric Regression and Generalized Linear Models*, volume 58 of Monographs on Statistics and Applied Probability. Chapman and Hall, 1994.

[133] D. M. Greig, B. T. Porteous and A. H. Seheult. Exact maximum a posteriori estimation for binary images. *Journal of the Royal Statistical Society, Series B*, **2**:271–279, 1989.

[134] G. Grimmett and D. Stirzaker. *Probability and Random Processes*. Oxford University Press, second edition, 1992.

[135] S. F. Gull. Bayesian data analysis: straight-line fitting. In J. Skilling, editor, *Maximum Entropy and Bayesian Methods (Cambridge 1988)*, pages 511–518. Kluwer, 1989.

[136] A. K. Gupta and D. K. Nagar. *Matrix Variate Distributions*. Chapman and Hall/CRC, 1999.

[137] D. J. Hand and K. Yu. Idiot's Bayes – not so stupid after all? *International Statistical Review*, **69**(3):385–398, 2001.

[138] D. R. Hardoon, S. Szedmak and J. Shawe-Taylor. Canonical correlation analysis: an overview with application to learning methods. *Neural Computation*, **16**(12):2639–2664, 2004.

[139] D. O. Hebb. *The Organization of Behavior*. Wiley, 1949.

[140] D. Heckerman. A tutorial on learning with Bayesian networks. Technical Report MSR-TR-95-06, Microsoft Research, March 1996. Revised November 1996.

[141] D. Heckerman, D. Geiger and D. Chickering. Learning Bayesian networks: the combination of knowledge and statistical data. *Machine Learning*, **20**(3):197–243, 1995.

[142] R. Herbrich, T. Minka and T. Graepel. TrueSkill™: a Bayesian skill rating system. In B. Schölkopf, J. Platt and T. Hoffman, editors, *Advances in Neural Information Processing Systems (NIPS)*, number 19, pages 569–576. MIT Press, 2007.

[143] H. Hermansky. Should recognizers have ears? *Speech Communication*, **25**:3–27, 1998.

[144] J. Hertz, A. Krogh and R. Palmer. *Introduction to the Theory of Neural Computation*. Addison-Wesley, 1991.

[145] T. Heskes. Convexity arguments for efficient minimization of the Bethe and Kikuchi free energies. *Journal of Artificial Intelligence Research*, **26**:153–190, 2006.

[146] D. M. Higdon. Auxiliary variable methods for Markov chain Monte Carlo with applications. *Journal of the American Statistical Association*, **93**(442):585–595, 1998.

[147] G. E. Hinton and R. R. Salakhutdinov. Reducing the dimensionality of data with neural networks. *Science*, **313**:504–507, 2006.

[148] T. Hofmann, J. Puzicha and M. I. Jordan. Learning from dyadic data. In M. S. Kearns, S. A. Solla and D. A. Cohn, editors, *Advances in Neural Information Processing Systems (NIPS)*, pages 466–472. MIT Press, 1999.

[149] R. A. Howard and J. E. Matheson. Influence diagrams. *Decision Analysis*, **2**(3), 2005. Republished version of the original 1981 report.

[150] J. C. Hull. *Options, Futures, and Other Derivatives*. Prentice Hall, 1997.

[151] A. Hyvärinen, J. Karhunen and E. Oja. *Independent Component Analysis*. Wiley, 2001.

[152] Aapo Hyvärinen. Consistency of pseudolikelihood estimation of fully visible Boltzmann machines. *Neural Computation*, **18**(10):2283–2292, 2006.

[153] M. Isard and A. Blake. CONDENSATION Conditional density propagation for visual tracking. *International Journal of Computer Vision*, **29**:5–28, 1998.

[154] T. S. Jaakkola and M. I. Jordan. Variational probabilistic inference and the QMR-DT network. *Journal of Artificial Intelligence Research*, **10**:291–322, 1999.

[155] T. S. Jaakkola and M. I. Jordan. Bayesian parameter estimation via variational methods. *Statistics and Computing*, **10**(1):25–37, 2000.

[156] R. A. Jacobs, F. Peng and M. A. Tanner. A Bayesian approach to model selection in hierarchical mixtures-of-experts architectures. *Neural Networks*, **10**(2):231–241, 1997.

[157] R. G. Jarrett. A note on the intervals between coal-mining disasters. *Biometrika*, **66**:191–193, 1979.

[158] E. T. Jaynes. *Probability Theory: The Logic of Science*. Cambridge University Press, 2003.

[159] F. Jensen, F. V. Jensen and D. Dittmer. From influence diagrams to junction trees. In *Proceedings of the 10th Annual Conference on Uncertainty in Artificial Intelligence (UAI-94)*, pages 367–373. Morgan Kaufmann, 1994.

[160] F. V. Jensen and F. Jensen. Optimal junction trees. In R. Lopez de Mantaras and D. Poole, editors, *Uncertainty in Artificial Intelligence*, number 10, pages 360–366. Morgan Kaufmann, 1994.

[161] F. V. Jensen and T. D. Nielson. *Bayesian Networks and Decision Graphs*. Springer-Verlag, second edition, 2007.

[162] M. I. Jordan and R. A. Jacobs. Hierarchical mixtures of experts and the EM algorithm. *Neural Computation*, **6**:181–214, 1994.

[163] B. H. Juang, W. Chou and C. H. Lee. Minimum classification error rate methods for speech recognition. *IEEE Transactions on Speech and Audio Processing*, **5**:257–265, 1997.

[164] L. P. Kaelbling, M. L. Littman and A. R. Cassandra. Planning and acting in partially observable stochastic domains. *Artificial Intelligence*, **101**(1–2):99–134, 1998.

[165] H. J. Kappen. An introduction to stochastic control theory, path integrals and reinforcement learning. In *Proceedings 9th Granada Seminar on Computational Physics: Computational and Mathematical Modeling of Cooperative Behavior in Neural Systems*, volume 887, pages 149–181. American Institute of Physics, 2007.

[166] H. J. Kappen and F. B. Rodríguez. Efficient learning in Boltzmann machines using linear response theory. *Neural Compution*, **10**(5):1137–1156, 1998.

[167] H. J. Kappen and W. Wiegerinck. Novel iteration schemes for the Cluster Variation Method. In T. G. Dietterich, S. Becker and Z. Ghahramani, editors, *Advances in Neural Information Processing Systems (NIPS)*, number 14, pages 415–422. MIT Press, 2002.

[168] Y. Karklin and M. S. Lewicki. Emergence of complex cell properties by learning to generalize in natural scenes. *Nature*, **457**:83–86, November 2008.

[169] G. Karypis and V. Kumar. A fast and high quality multilevel scheme for partitioning irregular graphs. *SIAM Journal on Scientific Computing*, **20**(1):359–392, 1998.

[170] P. W. Kasteleyn. Dimer statistics and phase transitions. *Journal of Mathematical Physics*, **4**(2):287–293, 1963.

[171] S. A. Kauffman. *At Home in the Universe: The Search for Laws of Self-Organization and Complexity*. Oxford University Press, 1995.

[172] C-J. Kim. Dynamic linear models with Markov-switching. *Journal of Econometrics*, **60**:1–22, 1994.

[173] C-J. Kim and C. R. Nelson. *State-Space Models with Regime Switching*. MIT Press, 1999.

[174] G. Kitagawa. The two-filter formula for smoothing and an implementation of the Gaussian-sum smoother. *Annals of the Institute of Statistical Mathematics*, **46**(4):605–623, 1994.

[175] U. B. Kjaerulff and A. L. Madsen. *Bayesian Networks and Influence Diagrams: A Guide to Construction and Analysis*. Springer, 2008.

[176] N. Komodakis, N. Paragios, and G. Tziritas. MRF Optimization via Dual Decomposition: Message-Passing Revisited. In *IEEE 11th International Conference on Computer Vision, ICCV*, pages 1–8, 2007.

[177] A. Krogh, M. Brown, I. Mian, K. Sjolander and D. Haussler. Hidden Markov models in computational biology: Applications to protein modeling. *Journal of Molecular Biology*, **235**:1501–1531, 1994.

[178] S. Kullback. *Information Theory and Statistics*. Dover, 1968.

[179] K. Kurihara, M. Welling and Y. W. Teh. Collapsed variational Dirichlet process mixture models. In *Proceedings of the International Joint Conference on Artificial Intelligence*, volume 20, pages 2796–2801, 2007.

[180] J. Lafferty, A. McCallum and F. Pereira. Conditional random fields: probabilistic models for segmenting and labeling sequence data. In C. E. Brodley and A. P. Danyluk, editors, *International Conference on Machine Learning*, number 18, pages 282–289. Morgan Kaufmann, 2001.

[181] H. Lass. *Elements of Pure and Applied Mathematics*. McGraw-Hill (reprinted by Dover), 1957.

[182] S. L. Lauritzen. *Graphical Models*. Oxford University Press, 1996.

[183] S. L. Lauritzen, A. P. Dawid, B. N. Larsen and H-G. Leimer. Independence properties of directed Markov fields. *Networks*, **20**:491–505, 1990.

[184] S. L. Lauritzen and D. J. Spiegelhalter. Local computations with probabilities on graphical structures and their application to expert systems. *Journal of Royal Statistical Society B*, **50**(2):157 – 224, 1988.

[185] D. D. Lee and H. S. Seung. Algorithms for non-negative matrix factorization. In T. K. Leen, T. G. Dietterich and V. Tresp, editors, *Advances in Neural Information Processing Systems (NIPS)*, number 13, pages 556–562, 2001. MIT Press.

[186] M. A. R. Leisink and H. J. Kappen. A tighter bound for graphical models. In *Neural Computation*, volume 13, pages 2149–2171. MIT Press, 2001.

[187] V. Lepar and P. P. Shenoy. A comparison of Lauritzen-Spiegelhalter, Hugin, and Shenoy-Shafer architectures for computing marginals of probability distributions. In G. Cooper and S. Moral, editors, *Uncertainty in Artificial Intelligence*, number 14, pages 328–333. Morgan Kaufmann, 1998.

[188] U. Lerner, R. Parr, D. Koller and G. Biswas. Bayesian fault detection and diagnosis in dynamic systems. In *Proceedings of the Seventeenth National Conference on Artificial Intelligence (AIII-00)*, pages 531–537, 2000.

[189] U. N. Lerner. *Hybrid Bayesian Networks for Reasoning about Complex Systems*. Computer Science Department, Stanford University, 2002.

[190] R. Linsker. Improved local learning rule for information maximization and related applications. *Neural Networks*, **18**(3):261–265, 2005.

[191] Y. L. Loh, E. W. Carlson and M. Y. J. Tan. Bond-propagation algorithm for thermodynamic functions in general two-dimensional Ising models. *Physical Review B*, **76**(1):014404, 2007.

[192] H. Lopes and M. West. Bayesian model assessment in factor analysis. *Statistica Sinica*, **14**:41–67, 2003.

[193] T. J. Loredo. From Laplace to supernova SN 1987A: Bayesian inference in astrophysics. In P. F. Fougere, editor, *Maximum Entropy and Bayesian Methods*, pages 81–142. Kluwer, 1990.

[194] D. J. C. MacKay. Bayesian interpolation. *Neural Computation*, **4**(3):415–447, 1992.

[195] D. J. C. MacKay. Probable networks and plausible predictions – a review of practical Bayesian methods for supervised neural networks. *Network: Computation in Neural Systems*, **6**(3):469–505, 1995.

[196] D. J. C. MacKay. Introduction to Gaussian processes. In *Neural Networks and Machine Learning*, volume 168 of NATO Advanced Study Institute on Generalization in Neural Networks and Machine Learning, pages 133–165. Springer, 1998.

[197] D. J. C. MacKay. *Information Theory, Inference and Learning Algorithms*. Cambridge University Press, 2003.

[198] U. Madhow. *Fundamentals of Digital Communication*. Cambridge University Press, 2008.

[199] K. V. Mardia, J. T. Kent and J. M. Bibby. *Multivariate Analysis*. Academic Press, 1997.

[200] H. Markram, J. Lubke, M. Frotscher and B. Sakmann. Regulation of synaptic efficacy by coincidence of postsynaptic APs and EPSPs. *Science*, **275**:213–215, 1997.

[201] A. McCallum, K. Nigam, J. Rennie, and K. Seymore. Automating the construction of internet portals with machine learning. *Information Retrieval Journal*, 3:127–163, 2000.

[202] G. McLachlan and T. Krishnan. *The EM Algorithm and Extensions*. John Wiley and Sons, 1997.

[203] G. McLachlan and D. Peel. *Finite Mixture Models*. Wiley Series in Probability and Statistics. Wiley-Interscience, 2000.

[204] E. Meeds, Z. Ghahramani, R. M. Neal and S. T. Roweis. Modeling dyadic data with binary latent factors. In B. Schölkopf, J. Platt and T. Hoffman, editors, *Advances in Neural Information Processing Systems (NIPS)*, volume 19, pages 977–984. MIT Press, 2007.

[205] M. Meila. An accelerated Chow and Liu algorithm: fitting tree distributions to high-dimensional sparse data. In I. Bratko, editor, *International Conference on Machine Learning*, pages 249–257. Morgan Kaufmann, 1999.

[206] M. Meila and M. I. Jordan. Triangulation by continuous embedding. In M. C. Mozer, M. I. Jordan and T. Petsche, editors, *Advances in Neural Information Processing Systems (NIPS)*, number 9, pages 557–563. MIT Press, 1997.

[207] B. Mesot and D. Barber. Switching linear dynamical systems for noise robust speech recognition. *IEEE Transactions of Audio, Speech and Language Processing*, **15**(6):1850–1858, 2007.

[208] N. Meuleau, M. Hauskrecht, K-E. Kim *et al.* Solving very large weakly coupled Markov decision processes. In *Proceedings of the Fifteenth National Conference on Artificial Intelligence*, pages 165–172, 1998.

[209] T. Mills. *The Econometric Modelling of Financial Time Series*. Cambridge University Press, 2000.

[210] T. Minka. Expectation propagation for approximate Bayesian inference. In J. Breese and D. Koller, editors, *Uncertainty in Artificial Intelligence*, number 17, pages 362–369. Morgan Kaufmann, 2001.

[211] T. Minka. A comparison of numerical optimizers for logistic regression. Technical report, Microsoft Research Ltd., 2003. research.microsoft.com/~minka/papers/logreg.

[212] T. Minka. Divergence measures and message passing. Technical Report MSR-TR-2005-173, Microsoft Research Ltd. December 2005.

[213] A. Mira, J. Møller and G. O. Roberts. Perfect slice samplers. *Journal of the Royal Statistical Society*, **63**(3):593–606, 2001. Series B (Statistical Methodology).

[214] C. Mitchell, M. Harper and L. Jamieson. On the complexity of explicit duration HMM's. *IEEE Transactions on Speech and Audio Processing*, **3**(3):213–217, 1995.

[215] T. Mitchell. *Machine Learning*. McGraw-Hill, 1997.

[216] J. Mooij and H. J. Kappen. Sufficient conditions for convergence of loopy belief propagation. *IEEE Information Theory*, **53**:4422–4437, 2007.

[217] J. W. Moon and L. Moser. On cliques in graphs. *Israel Journal of Mathematics*, (3):23–28, 1965.

[218] A. Moore. A tutorial on kd-trees. Technical report, 1991. Available from www.cs.cmu.edu/~awm/papers.html.

[219] J. Moussouris. Gibbs and Markov random systems with constraints. *Journal of Statistical Physics*, **10**:11–33, 1974.

[220] R. M. Neal. Probabilistic inference using Markov chain Monte Carlo methods. CRG-TR-93-1, Dept. of Computer Science, University of Toronto, 1993.

[221] R. M. Neal. Markov chain sampling methods for Dirichlet process mixture models. *Journal of Computational and Graphical Statistics*, **9**(2):249–265, 2000.

[222] R. M. Neal. Slice sampling. *Annals of Statistics*, **31**:705–767, 2003.

[223] R. E. Neapolitan. *Learning Bayesian Networks*. Prentice Hall, 2003.

[224] A. V. Nefian, L. Luhong, P. Xiaobo, X. Liu, C. Mao and K. Murphy. A coupled HMM for audio-visual speech recognition. In *IEEE International Conference on Acoustics, Speech, and Signal Processing*, volume 2, pages 2013–2016, 2002.

[225] H. Nickisch and M. Seeger. Convex variational Bayesian inference for large scale generalized linear models. *International Conference on Machine Learning*, **26**:761–768, 2009.

[226] D. Nilsson. An efficient algorithm for finding the m most probable configurations in a probabilistic expert system. *Statistics and Computing*, **8**:159–173, 1998.

[227] D. Nilsson and J. Goldberger. Sequentially finding the N-best list in hidden Markov models. *International Joint Conference on Artificial Intelligence (IJCAI)*, 17, 2001.

[228] A. B. Novikoff. On convergence proofs on perceptrons. In *Symposium on the Mathematical Theory of Automata (New York, 1962)*, volume 12, pages 615–622. Polytechnic Press of Polytechnic Institute of Brooklyn, 1963.

[229] F. J. Och and H. Ney. Discriminative training and maximum entropy models for statistical machine translation. In *Proceedings of the Annual Meeting of the Association for Computational Linguistics*, pages 295–302, Philadelphia, July 2002.

[230] B. A. Olshausen and D. J. Field. Sparse coding with an overcomplete basis set: a strategy employed by V1? *Vision Research*, **37**:3311–3325, 1998.

[231] A. V. Oppenheim, R. W. Shafer, M. T. Yoder and W. T. Padgett. *Discrete-Time Signal Processing*. Prentice Hall, third edition, 2009.

[232] M. Ostendorf, V. Digalakis and O. A. Kimball. From HMMs to segment models: a unified view of stochastic modeling for speech recognition. *IEEE Transactions on Speech and Audio Processing*, **4**:360–378, 1995.

[233] P. Paatero and U. Tapper. Positive matrix factorization: a non-negative factor model with optimal utilization of error estimates of data values. *Environmetrics*, **5**:111–126, 1994.

[234] A. Palmer, D. Wipf, K. Kreutz-Delgado and B. Rao. Variational EM algorithms for non-Gaussian latent variable models. In B. Schölkopf, J. Platt and T. Hoffman, editors, *Advances in Neural Information Processing Systems (NIPS)*, number 19, pages 1059–1066. MIT Press, 2006.

[235] V. Pavlovic, J. M. Rehg and J. MacCormick. Learning switching linear models of human motion. In T. K. Leen, T. G. Dietterich and V. Tresp, editors, *Advances in Neural Information Processing Systems (NIPS)*, number 13, pages 981–987. MIT Press, 2001.

[236] J. Pearl. *Probabilistic Reasoning in Intelligent Systems: Networks of Plausible Inference*. Morgan Kaufmann, 1988.

[237] J. Pearl. *Causality: Models, Reasoning and Inference*. Cambridge University Press, 2000.

[238] B. A. Pearlmutter and L. C. Parra. Maximum likelihood blind source separation: a context-sensitive generalization of ICA. In M. C. Mozer, M. I. Jordan and T. Petsche, editors, *Advances in Neural Information Processing Systems (NIPS)*, number 9, pages 613–619. MIT Press, 1997.

[239] K. B. Petersen and O. Winther. The EM algorithm in independent component analysis. In *IEEE International Conference on Acoustics, Speech, and Signal Processing*, volume 5, pages 169–172, 2005.

[240] J-P. Pfister, T. Toyiozumi, D. Barber and W. Gerstner. Optimal spike-timing dependent plasticity for precise action potential firing in supervised learning. *Neural Computation*, **18**:1309–1339, 2006.

[241] J. Platt. Fast training of support vector machines using sequential minimal optimization. In B. Schölkopf, C. J. C. Burges and A. J. Smola, editors, *Advances in Kernel Methods – Support Vector Learning*, pages 185–208. MIT Press, 1999.

[242] I. Porteous, D. Newman, A. Ihler, *et al.* Fast collapsed Gibbs sampling for latent Dirichlet allocation. In *KDD '08: Proceeding of the 14th ACM SIGKDD International Conference on Knowledge Discovery and Data Mining*, pages 569–577. ACM, 2008.

[243] J. E. Potter and R. G. Stern. Statistical filtering of space navigation measurements. In *American Institute of Aeronautics and Astronautics Guidance and Control Conference*, volume 13, pages 775–801, August 1963.

[244] W. Press, W. Vettering, S. Teukolsky and B. Flannery. *Numerical Recipes in Fortran*. Cambridge University Press, 1992.

[245] S. J. D. Prince and J. H. Elder. Probabilistic linear discriminant analysis for inferences about identity. In *IEEE 11th International Conference on Computer Vision ICCV*, pages 1–8, 2007.

[246] L. R. Rabiner. A tutorial on hidden Markov models and selected applications in speech recognition. *Proceedings of the IEEE*, **77**(2):257–286, 1989.

[247] C. E. Rasmussen and C. K. I. Williams. *Gaussian Processes for Machine Learning*. MIT Press, 2006.

[248] H. E. Rauch, G. Tung and C. T. Striebel. Maximum likelihood estimates of linear dynamic systems. *American Institute of Aeronautics and Astronautics Journal (AIAAJ)*, **3**(8):1445–1450, 1965.

[249] T. Richardson and P. Spirtes. Ancestral graph Markov models. *Annals of Statistics*, **30**(4):962–1030, 2002.

[250] D. Rose, R. E. Tarjan and E. S. Lueker. Algorithmic aspects of vertex elimination of graphs. *SIAM Journal on Computing*, **5**:266–283, 1976.

[251] F. Rosenblatt. The perceptron: a probabilistic model for information storage and organization in the brain. *Psychological Review*, **65**(6):386–408, 1958.

[252] S. T. Roweis and L. J. Saul. Nonlinear dimensionality reduction by locally linear embedding. *Science*, **290**(5500):2323–2326, 2000.

[253] D. B. Rubin. Using the SIR algorithm to simulate posterior distributions. In M. H. Bernardo, K. M. Degroot, D. V. Lindley and A. F. M. Smith, editors, *Bayesian Statistics 3*. Oxford University Press, 1988.

[254] D. Saad and M. Opper. *Advanced Mean Field Methods Theory and Practice*. MIT Press, 2001.

[255] R. Salakhutdinov, S. Roweis and Z. Ghahramani. Optimization with EM and expectation-conjugate-gradient. In T. Fawcett and N. Mishra, editors, *International Conference on Machine Learning*, number 20, pages 672–679. AAAI Press, 2003.

[256] L. K. Saul and M. I. Jordan. Exploiting tractable substructures in intractable networks. In D. S. Touretzky, M. Mozer and M. E. Hasselmo, editors, *Advances in Neural Information Processing Systems (NIPS)*, number 8, pages 486–492. MIT Press, 1996.

[257] L. Savage. *The Foundations of Statistics*. Wiley, 1954.

[258] R. D. Schachter. Bayes-ball: the rational pastime (for determining irrelevance and requisite information in belief networks and influence diagrams). In G. Cooper and S. Moral, editors, *Uncertainty in Artificial Intelligence*, number 14, pages 480–487. Morgan Kaufmann, 1998.

[259] B. Schölkopf, A. Smola and K. R. Müller. Nonlinear component analysis as a kernel eigenvalue problem. *Neural Computation*, **10**:1299–1319, 1998.

[260] N. N. Schraudolph and D. Kamenetsky. Efficient exact inference in planar Ising models. In D. Koller, D. Schuurmans, Y. Bengio and L. Bottou, editors, *Advances in Neural Information Processing Systems (NIPS)*, number 21, pages 1417–1424. MIT Press, 2009.

[261] E. Schwarz. Estimating the dimension of a model. *Annals of Statistics*, **6**(2):461–464, 1978.

[262] M. Seeger. Gaussian processes for machine learning. *International Journal of Neural Systems*, **14**(2):69–106, 2004.

[263] M. Seeger. Expectation propagation for exponential families. Technical report, Department of EECS, Berkeley, 2005. www.kyb.tuebingen.mpg.de/bs/people/seeger.

[264] J. Shawe-Taylor and N. Cristianini. *Kernel Methods for Pattern Analysis*. Cambridge University Press, 2004.

[265] S. Siddiqi, B. Boots and G. Gordon. A constraint generation approach to learning stable linear dynamical systems. In J. C. Platt, D. Koller, Y. Singer and S. Roweis, editors, *Advances in Neural Information Processing Systems (NIPS)*, number 20, pages 1329–1336. MIT Press, 2008.

[266] T. Silander, P. Kontkanen and P. Myllymäki. On sensitivity of the MAP Bayesian network structure to the equivalent sample size parameter. In R. Parr and L. van der Gaag, editors, *Uncertainty in Artificial Intelligence*, number 23, pages 360–367. AUAI Press, 2007.

[267] S. S. Skiena. *The Algorithm Design Manual*. Springer-Verlag, 1998.

[268] E. Smith and M. S. Lewicki. Efficient auditory coding. *Nature*, **439**(7079):978–982, 2006.

[269] P. Smolensky. *Parallel Distributed Processing: Volume 1: Foundations*, chapter Information processing in dynamical systems: foundations of harmony theory, pages 194–281. MIT Press, 1986.

[270] G. Sneddon. A statistical perspective on data assimilation in numerical Models. In *Studies in the Atmospheric Sciences*, number 144 in Lecture Notes in Statistics. Springer-Verlag, 2000.

[271] P. Sollich. Bayesian methods for support vector machines: evidence and predictive class probabilities. *Machine Learning*, **46**(1-3):21–52, 2002.

[272] D. X. Song, D. Wagner and X. Tian. Timing analysis of keystrokes and timing attacks on SSH. In *Proceedings of the 10th Conference on USENIX Security Symposium*. USENIX Association, 2001.

[273] A. S. Spanias. Speech coding: a tutorial review. *Proceedings of the IEEE*, **82**(10):1541–1582, Oct 1994.

[274] P. Spirtes, C. Glymour and R. Scheines. *Causation, Prediction, and Search*. MIT Press, second edition, 2000.

[275] N. Srebro. Maximum likelihood bounded tree-width Markov networks. In J. Breese and D. Koller, editors, *Uncertainty in Artificial Intelligence*, number 17, pages 504–511. Morgan Kaufmann, 2001.

[276] H. Steck. Constraint-based structural learning in Bayesian networks using finite data sets. PhD thesis, Technical University Munich, 2001.

[277] H. Steck. Learning the Bayesian network structure: Dirichlet prior vs data. In D. A. McAllester and P. Myllymaki, editors, *Uncertainty in Artificial Intelligence*, number 24, pages 511–518. AUAI Press, 2008.

[278] H. Steck and T. Jaakkola. On the Dirichlet prior and Bayesian regularization. In S. Becker, S. Thrun and K. Obermayer, editors, *NIPS*, pages 697–704. MIT Press, 2002.

[279] G. Strang. *Linear Algebra and Its Applications*. Brooks Cole, 1988.

[280] M. Studený. On mathematical description of probabilistic conditional independence structures. PhD thesis, Academy of Sciences of the Czech Republic, 2001.

[281] M. Studený. On non-graphical description of models of conditional independence structure. In *HSSS Workshop on Stochastic Systems for Individual Behaviours*. Louvain la Neueve, Belgium, 22–23 January 2001.

[282] C. Sutton and A. McCallum. An introduction to conditional random fields for relational learning. In L. Getoor and B. Taskar, editors, *Introduction to Statistical Relational Learning*. MIT Press, 2006.

[283] R. S. Sutton and A. G. Barto. *Reinforcement Learning: An Introduction*. MIT Press, 1998.

[284] R. J. Swendsen and J-S. Wang. Nonuniversal critical dynamics in Monte Carlo simulations. *Physical Review Letters*, **58**:86–88, 1987.

[285] B. K. Sy. A recurrence local computation approach towards ordering composite beliefs in Bayesian belief networks. *International Journal of Approximate Reasoning*, **8**:17–50, 1993.

[286] T. Sejnowski. The Book of Hebb. *Neuron*, **24**:773–776, 1999.

[287] R. E. Tarjan and M. Yannakakis. Simple linear-time algorithms to test chordality of graphs, test acyclicity of hypergraphs, and selectively reduce acyclic hypergraphs. *SIAM Journal on Computing*, **13**(3):566–579, 1984.

[288] S. J. Taylor. *Modelling Financial Time Series*. World Scientific, second edition, 2008.

[289] Y. W. Teh, D. Newman and M. Welling. A collapsed variational Bayesian inference algorithm for latent Dirichlet allocation. In J. C. Platt, D. Koller, Y. Singer and S. Roweis, editors, *Advances in Neural Information Processing Systems (NIPS)*, number 20, pages 1481–1488. MIT Press, 2008.

[290] Y. W. Teh and M. Welling. The unified propagation and scaling algorithm. In T. G. Dietterich, S. Becker and Z. Ghahramani, editors, *Advances in Neural Information Processing Systems (NIPS)*, number 14, pages 953–960. MIT Press, 2002.

[291] R. Tibshirani. Regression shrinkage and selection via the lasso. *Journal of the Royal Statistical Society (B)*, 58:267–288, 1996.

[292] H. Tijms. *Understanding Probability*. Cambridge University Press, 2003.

[293] M. Tipping and C. M. Bishop. Mixtures of probabilistic principal component analysers. *Neural Computation*, **11**(2):443–482, 1999.

[294] M. E. Tipping. Sparse Bayesian Learning and the Relevance Vector Machine. *Journal of Machine Learning Research*, (1):211–244, 2001.

[295] M. E. Tipping. Sparse Bayesian learning and the relevance vector machine. *Journal of Machine Learning Research*, **1**:211–244, 2001.

[296] M. E. Tipping and C. M. Bishop. Probabilistic principal component analysis. *Journal of the Royal Statistical Society, Series B*, **61**(3):611–622, 1999.

[297] D. M. Titterington, A. F. M. Smith and U. E. Makov. *Statistical Analysis of Finite Mixture Distributions*. Wiley, 1985.

[298] M. Toussaint, S. Harmeling and A. Storkey. Probabilistic inference for solving (PO)MDPs. Research Report EDI-INF-RR-0934, University of Edinburgh, School of Informatics, 2006.

[299] M. Tsodyks, K. Pawelzik and H. Markram. Neural networks with dynamic synapses. *Neural Computation*, **10**:821–835, 1998.

[300] L. van der Matten and G. Hinton. Visualizing data using t-SNE. *Journal of Machine Learning Research*, **9**:2579–2605, 2008.

[301] P. Van Overschee and B. De Moor. *Subspace Identification for Linear Systems; Theory, Implementations, Applications*. Kluwer, 1996.

[302] V. Vapnik. *The Nature of Statistical Learning Theory*. Springer, 1995.

[303] M. Verhaegen and P. Van Dooren. Numerical aspects of different Kalman filter implementations. *IEEE Transactions of Automatic Control*, **31**(10):907–917, 1986.

[304] T. Verma and J. Pearl. Causal networks: semantics and expressiveness. In R. D. Schacter, T. S. Levitt, L. N. Kanal and J.F. Lemmer, editors, *Uncertainty in Artificial Intelligence*, volume 4, pages 69–76. North-Holland, 1990.

[305] T. O. Virtanen, A. T. Cemgil and S. J. Godsill. Bayesian extensions to nonnegative matrix factorisation for audio signal modelling. In *IEEE International Conference on Acoustics, Speech, and Signal Processing*, pages 1825–1828, 2008.

[306] G. Wahba. *Support Vector Machines, Repreducing Kernel Hilbert Spaces, and Randomized GACV*, pages 69–88. MIT Press, 1999.

[307] M. J. Wainwright and M. I. Jordan. Graphical models, exponential families, and variational inference. *Foundations and Trends in Machine Learning*, **1**(1-2):1–305, 2008.

[308] H. Wallach. Efficient training of conditional random fields. Master's thesis, Division of Informatics, University of Edinburgh, 2002.

[309] Y. Wang, J. Hodges and B. Tang. Classification of web documents using a naive Bayes method. *15th IEEE International Conference on Tools with Artificial Intelligence*, pages 560–564, 2003.

[310] S. Waterhouse, D. Mackay and T. Robinson. Bayesian methods for mixtures of experts. In D. S. Touretzky, M. Mozer and M. E. Hasselmo, editors, *Advances in Neural Information Processing Systems (NIPS)*, number 8, pages 351–357. MIT Press, 1996.

[311] C. Watkins and P. Dayan. Q-learning. *Machine Learning*, **8**:279–292, 1992.

[312] Y. Weiss and W. T. Freeman. Correctness of belief propagation in Gaussian graphical models of arbitrary topology. *Neural Computation*, **13**(10):2173–2200, 2001.

[313] M. Welling, T. P. Minka and Y. W. Teh. Structured region graphs: morphing EP into GBP. In F. Bacchus and T. Jaakkola, editors, *Uncertainty in Artificial Intelligence*, number 21, pages 609–614. AUAI press, 2005.

[314] J. Whittaker. *Graphical Models in Applied Multivariate Statistics*. John Wiley & Sons, 1990.

[315] W. Wiegerinck. Variational approximations between mean field theory and the junction tree algorithm. In C. Boutilier and M. Goldszmidt, editors, *Uncertainty in Artificial Intelligence*, number 16, pages 626–633. Morgan Kaufmann, 2000.

[316] W. Wiegerinck and T. Heskes. Fractional belief propagation. In S. Becker, S. Thrun and K. Obermayer, editors, *Advances in Neural Information Processing Systems (NIPS)*, number 15, pages 438–445. MIT Press, 2003.

[317] C. K. I. Williams. Computing with infinite networks. In M. C. Mozer, M. I. Jordan and T. Petsche, editors, *Advances in Neural Information Processing Systems (NIPS), number 9*, pages 295–301. MIT Press, 1997.

[318] C. K. I. Williams and D. Barber. Bayesian classification with Gaussian processes. *IEEE Transactions on Pattern Analysis and Machine Intelligence*, **20**:1342–1351, 1998.

[319] C. Yanover and Y. Weiss. Finding the M most probable configurations using loopy belief propagation. In S. Thrun, L. Saul and B. Schölkopf, editors, *Advances in Neural Information Processing Systems (NIPS)*, number 16, pages 1457–1464. MIT Press, 2004.

[320] J. S. Yedidia, W. T. Freeman, and Y. Weiss. Constructing free-energy approximations and generalized belief propagation algorithms. *IEEE Transactions on Information Theory*, **51**(7):2282–2312, July 2005.

[321] S. Young, D. Kershaw, J. Odell, *et al. The HTK Book Version 3.0*. Entropic Cambridge Research Laboratory, 2000.

[322] A. L. Yuille and A. Rangarajan. The concave-convex procedure. *Neural Computation*, **15**(4):915–936, 2003.

[323] J.-H. Zhao, P. L. H. Yu and Q. Jiang. ML estimation for factor analysis: EM or non-EM? *Statistics and Computing*, **18**(2):109–123, 2008.

[324] O. Zoeter. Monitoring non-linear and switching dynamical systems. PhD thesis, Radboud University Nijmegen, 2005.

INDEX